W9-BJV-063

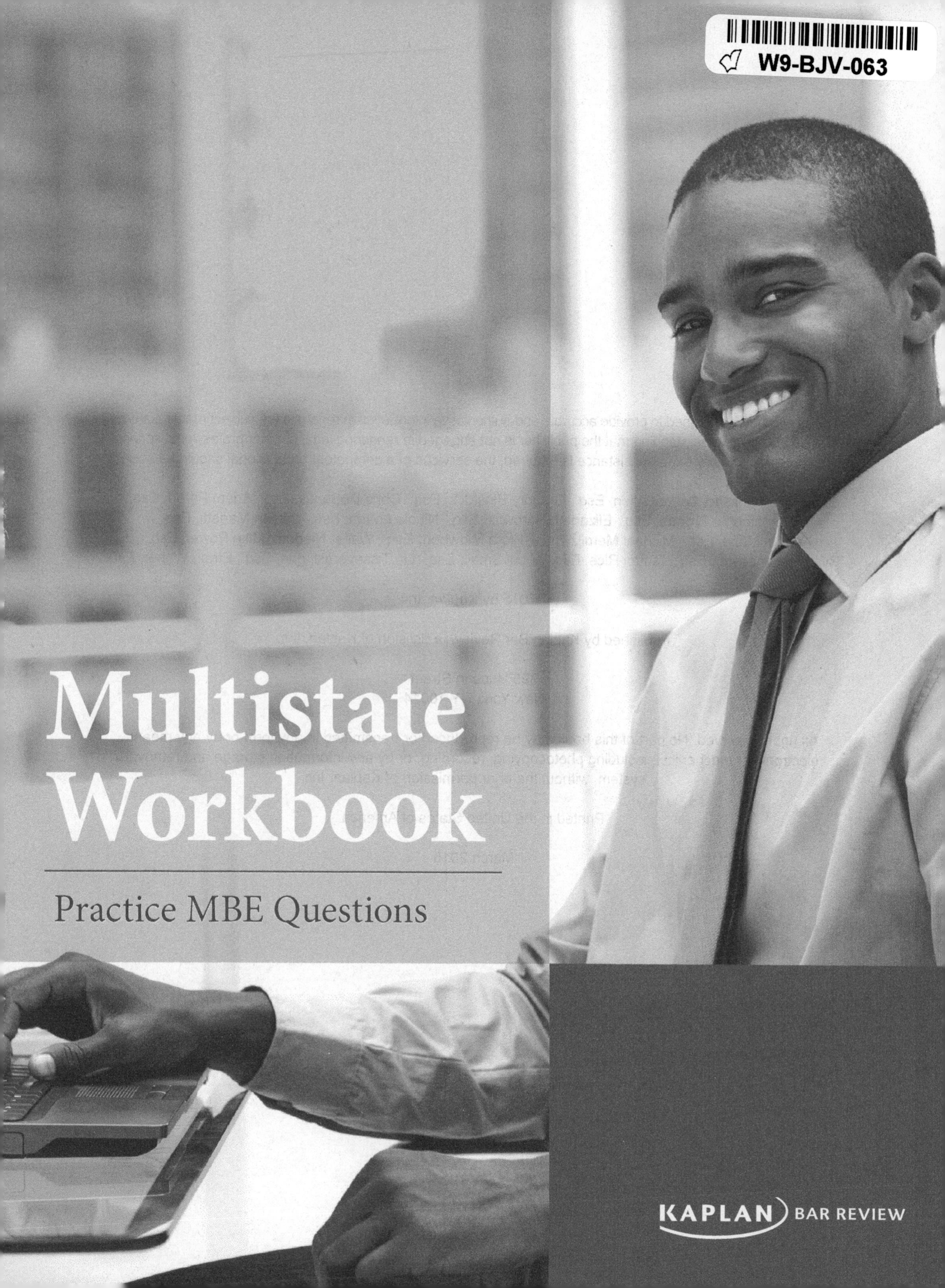

Multistate Workbook

Practice MBE Questions

KAPLAN BAR REVIEW

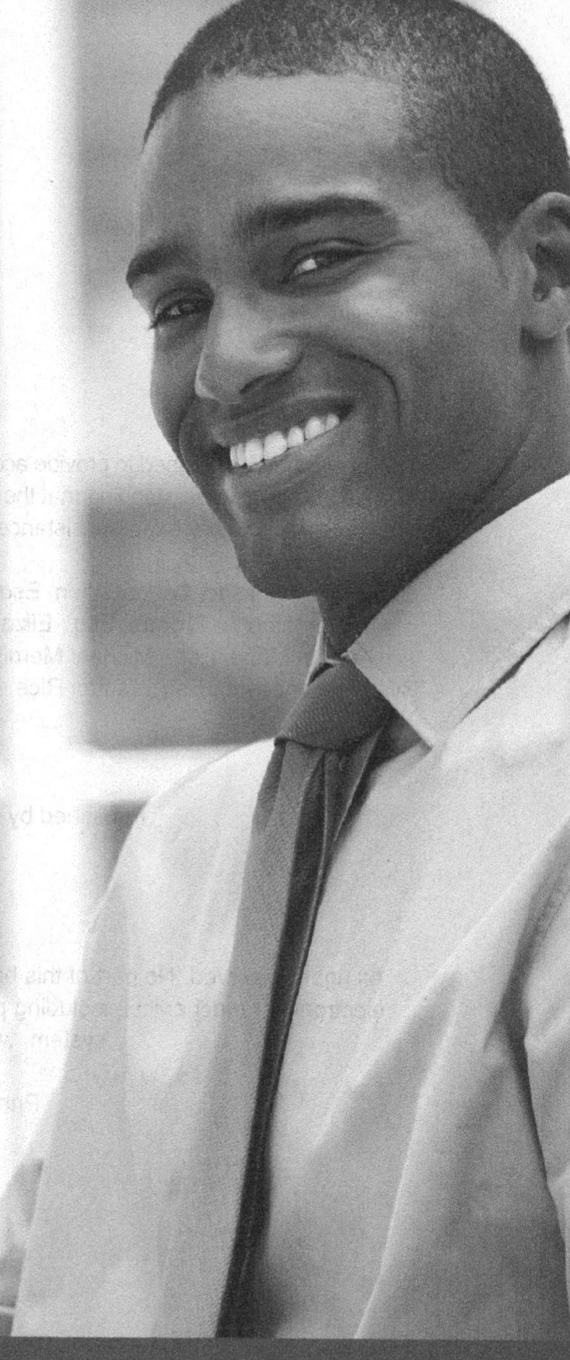

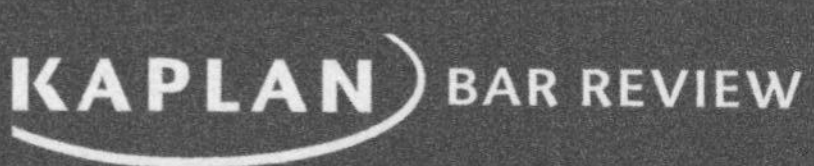

This publication is designed to provide accurate and authoritative information in regard to the subject matter covered. It is sold with the understanding that the publisher is not engaged in rendering legal or other professional service. If legal advice or other expert assistance is required, the services of a competent professional should be sought.

Special thanks to: Lauren Allen, Esq., Gregory Binstock, Esq., Chris DeSantis, Esq., Adam Feren, Esq., Christopher Fromm, Esq., Elizabeth Horowitz, Esq., Nicole Lefton, Esq., Steven Marietti, Esq., Adam Maze, Esq., Michael Merrill, Ph.D., Flora Midwood, Esq., Walter Niedner, Mike Power, Esq., Ryan Rentmeester, Esq., Tammi Rice, Esq., Micol Small, Esq., Lia Tisseverasinghe, Esq., Ethan Weber, Esq.

© 2015 by Kaplan, Inc.

Published by Kaplan Bar Review, a division of Kaplan, Inc.

395 Hudson Street
New York, NY 10014

All rights reserved. No part of this book may be reproduced or transmitted in any form or by any means electronic or mechanical, including photocopying, recording, or by any information storage and retrieval system, without the prior permission of Kaplan, Inc.

Printed in the United States of America

March 2015

TABLE OF CONTENTS

pmbr

Torts

Practice Questions

Answer Grid

1 Ⓐ Ⓑ Ⓒ Ⓓ	21 Ⓐ Ⓑ Ⓒ Ⓓ	41 Ⓐ Ⓑ Ⓒ Ⓓ	61 Ⓐ Ⓑ Ⓒ Ⓓ	81 Ⓐ Ⓑ Ⓒ Ⓓ
2 Ⓐ Ⓑ Ⓒ Ⓓ	22 Ⓐ Ⓑ Ⓒ Ⓓ	42 Ⓐ Ⓑ Ⓒ Ⓓ	62 Ⓐ Ⓑ Ⓒ Ⓓ	82 Ⓐ Ⓑ Ⓒ Ⓓ
3 Ⓐ Ⓑ Ⓒ Ⓓ	23 Ⓐ Ⓑ Ⓒ Ⓓ	43 Ⓐ Ⓑ Ⓒ Ⓓ	63 Ⓐ Ⓑ Ⓒ Ⓓ	83 Ⓐ Ⓑ Ⓒ Ⓓ
4 Ⓐ Ⓑ Ⓒ Ⓓ	24 Ⓐ Ⓑ Ⓒ Ⓓ	44 Ⓐ Ⓑ Ⓒ Ⓓ	64 Ⓐ Ⓑ Ⓒ Ⓓ	84 Ⓐ Ⓑ Ⓒ Ⓓ
5 Ⓐ Ⓑ Ⓒ Ⓓ	25 Ⓐ Ⓑ Ⓒ Ⓓ	45 Ⓐ Ⓑ Ⓒ Ⓓ	65 Ⓐ Ⓑ Ⓒ Ⓓ	85 Ⓐ Ⓑ Ⓒ Ⓓ
6 Ⓐ Ⓑ Ⓒ Ⓓ	26 Ⓐ Ⓑ Ⓒ Ⓓ	46 Ⓐ Ⓑ Ⓒ Ⓓ	66 Ⓐ Ⓑ Ⓒ Ⓓ	86 Ⓐ Ⓑ Ⓒ Ⓓ
7 Ⓐ Ⓑ Ⓒ Ⓓ	27 Ⓐ Ⓑ Ⓒ Ⓓ	47 Ⓐ Ⓑ Ⓒ Ⓓ	67 Ⓐ Ⓑ Ⓒ Ⓓ	87 Ⓐ Ⓑ Ⓒ Ⓓ
8 Ⓐ Ⓑ Ⓒ Ⓓ	28 Ⓐ Ⓑ Ⓒ Ⓓ	48 Ⓐ Ⓑ Ⓒ Ⓓ	68 Ⓐ Ⓑ Ⓒ Ⓓ	88 Ⓐ Ⓑ Ⓒ Ⓓ
9 Ⓐ Ⓑ Ⓒ Ⓓ	29 Ⓐ Ⓑ Ⓒ Ⓓ	49 Ⓐ Ⓑ Ⓒ Ⓓ	69 Ⓐ Ⓑ Ⓒ Ⓓ	89 Ⓐ Ⓑ Ⓒ Ⓓ
10 Ⓐ Ⓑ Ⓒ Ⓓ	30 Ⓐ Ⓑ Ⓒ Ⓓ	50 Ⓐ Ⓑ Ⓒ Ⓓ	70 Ⓐ Ⓑ Ⓒ Ⓓ	90 Ⓐ Ⓑ Ⓒ Ⓓ
11 Ⓐ Ⓑ Ⓒ Ⓓ	31 Ⓐ Ⓑ Ⓒ Ⓓ	51 Ⓐ Ⓑ Ⓒ Ⓓ	71 Ⓐ Ⓑ Ⓒ Ⓓ	91 Ⓐ Ⓑ Ⓒ Ⓓ
12 Ⓐ Ⓑ Ⓒ Ⓓ	32 Ⓐ Ⓑ Ⓒ Ⓓ	52 Ⓐ Ⓑ Ⓒ Ⓓ	72 Ⓐ Ⓑ Ⓒ Ⓓ	92 Ⓐ Ⓑ Ⓒ Ⓓ
13 Ⓐ Ⓑ Ⓒ Ⓓ	33 Ⓐ Ⓑ Ⓒ Ⓓ	53 Ⓐ Ⓑ Ⓒ Ⓓ	73 Ⓐ Ⓑ Ⓒ Ⓓ	93 Ⓐ Ⓑ Ⓒ Ⓓ
14 Ⓐ Ⓑ Ⓒ Ⓓ	34 Ⓐ Ⓑ Ⓒ Ⓓ	54 Ⓐ Ⓑ Ⓒ Ⓓ	74 Ⓐ Ⓑ Ⓒ Ⓓ	94 Ⓐ Ⓑ Ⓒ Ⓓ
15 Ⓐ Ⓑ Ⓒ Ⓓ	35 Ⓐ Ⓑ Ⓒ Ⓓ	55 Ⓐ Ⓑ Ⓒ Ⓓ	75 Ⓐ Ⓑ Ⓒ Ⓓ	95 Ⓐ Ⓑ Ⓒ Ⓓ
16 Ⓐ Ⓑ Ⓒ Ⓓ	36 Ⓐ Ⓑ Ⓒ Ⓓ	56 Ⓐ Ⓑ Ⓒ Ⓓ	76 Ⓐ Ⓑ Ⓒ Ⓓ	96 Ⓐ Ⓑ Ⓒ Ⓓ
17 Ⓐ Ⓑ Ⓒ Ⓓ	37 Ⓐ Ⓑ Ⓒ Ⓓ	57 Ⓐ Ⓑ Ⓒ Ⓓ	77 Ⓐ Ⓑ Ⓒ Ⓓ	97 Ⓐ Ⓑ Ⓒ Ⓓ
18 Ⓐ Ⓑ Ⓒ Ⓓ	38 Ⓐ Ⓑ Ⓒ Ⓓ	58 Ⓐ Ⓑ Ⓒ Ⓓ	78 Ⓐ Ⓑ Ⓒ Ⓓ	98 Ⓐ Ⓑ Ⓒ Ⓓ
19 Ⓐ Ⓑ Ⓒ Ⓓ	39 Ⓐ Ⓑ Ⓒ Ⓓ	59 Ⓐ Ⓑ Ⓒ Ⓓ	79 Ⓐ Ⓑ Ⓒ Ⓓ	99 Ⓐ Ⓑ Ⓒ Ⓓ
20 Ⓐ Ⓑ Ⓒ Ⓓ	40 Ⓐ Ⓑ Ⓒ Ⓓ	60 Ⓐ Ⓑ Ⓒ Ⓓ	80 Ⓐ Ⓑ Ⓒ Ⓓ	100 Ⓐ Ⓑ Ⓒ Ⓓ

1. Intentional Infliction of Emotional Distress
2. Misrepresentation
3. Nuisance
4. Invasion of Privacy
5. Negligence — Causation: Multiple Tortfeasors
6. Negligence — Standard of Care: Statutes and Custom
7. Negligence — Proximate Cause
8. Negligence — Proximate Cause
9. Negligence — "Attractive Nuisance" Doctrine
10. Negligence — Causation: But-for and Substantial Causes
11. Nuisance
12. Negligence — Proof of Fault
13. Negligence — Duty
14. Battery
15. Negligence — *Res Ipsa Loquitur*
16. Negligence — Causation: But-for and Substantial Causes
17. Negligence — Liability: Employees and Agents
18. Negligence — Owners and Occupiers of Land
19. Negligence — Owners and Occupiers of Land
20. Negligence — Owners and Occupiers of Land
21. Products Liability — Defects of Manufacture and Design
22. Negligence — Liability: Employees and Agents
23. Negligence — Liability: Employees and Agents
24. Negligence — Liability: Employees and Agents
25. Products Liability — Express Warranty
26. Products Liability — Defects of Manufacture and Design
27. Assault

28. Intentional Infliction of Emotional Distress — Third-Party Recovery
29. Negligence — Standard of Care: Special Classes
30. Battery
31. Assault
32. Intentional Infliction of Emotional Distress
33. Defamation
34. False Imprisonment
35. Negligence — Standard of Care: Reasonably Prudent Person
36. Negligence — Causation: Multiple Tortfeasors
37. Negligence — Liability: Remote or Unforeseeable Causes
38. False Imprisonment
39. Negligence — Standard of Care: Special Classes
40. False Imprisonment
41. Negligence — Liability: Acts of Others
42. Negligence — Liability: Employees and Agents
43. False Imprisonment
44. Intentional Torts — Defenses: Protection of Property
45. Negligence — Owners and Occupiers of Land
46. Negligence — Acts of Others: Independent Contractors
47. Negligence — Proof of Fault
48. Negligence — Foreseeable Plaintiffs
49. Conversion
50. Conversion
51. Negligence — *Res Ipsa Loquitur*
52. Negligence — Measure of Damages
53. Nuisance
54. Invasion of Privacy

55. Defamation

56. Strict Liability — Wild Animals

57. Nuisance

58. Negligence — Causation: Multiple Tortfeasors

59. Negligence — Causation: Multiple Tortfeasors

60. Nuisance

61. Negligence — Defenses: Comparative Fault

62. Negligence — Standard of Care: Reasonably Prudent Person

63. Negligence — Standard of Care: Reasonably Prudent Person

64. Defamation

65. Negligence — Standard of Care

66. Negligence — Duty

67. Defamation

68. Negligence — Standard of Care: Special Classes

69. Products Liability — Defects of Manufacture and Design

70. Products Liability — Defects of Manufacture and Design

71. Misrepresentation

72. Negligence — Owners and Occupiers of Land

73. Invasion of Privacy

74. Defamation

75. Defamation

76. Negligent Infliction of Emotional Distress

77. Informed Consent

78. Premises Liability

79. Damages

80. Firefighter's Rule

81. Rescuer Liability

82. Defamation
83. Misrepresentation
84. Trespass to Chattels
85. Negligent Misrepresentation
86. Product Liability
87. Product Liability
88. Strict Liability
89. Damages
90. Premises Liability
91. Proximate Cause
92. Trespass to Land
93. Negligent Infliction of Emotional Distress
94. Intrusion Into Seclusion
95. Malicious Prosecution
96. Product Liability
97. Product Liability
98. Product Liability Defendants
99. Strict Liability
100. Battery

1. A circus operates in a rural part of the county. It is the circus's practice to finish each day's entertainment by discharging a so-called aerial bomb into the sky. After exploding, the aerial bomb emits a spectacular rainbow fireworks display that is seen for miles around.

One afternoon, a 10-year-old boy and a few friends went to the fairgrounds to see the circus. After paying their admission, they were about to enter the "big top" when the boy came upon an aerial bomb lying on the ground. Ignorant of what the object really was, but in an exploratory mood, the boy applied a match to the fuse of the fireworks device. It exploded and seriously injured the boy.

After the accident, and before the parents of the boy had retained a lawyer, the adjuster for the circus's insurance carrier contacted the parents several times, trying to negotiate a settlement of their claim against the circus. On each occasion, the adjuster told the parents there was no need for them to hire an attorney because the applicable civil code did not provide for recovery in such a situation. The adjuster was aware that this information was blatantly false. He also warned the parents that unless they accepted his offered settlement of $5,000, they would receive nothing.

For over a month, the adjuster continued to harass the parents. Outraged by the adjuster's actions, the parents sought the advice of a neighbor who recommended that they consult an attorney. The parents went ahead and retained a lawyer who subsequently negotiated a $250,000 settlement with the adjuster's insurance company for the claims relating to the boy's injury from the aerial bomb.

If the parents assert a claim against the adjuster to recover damages for infliction of emotional distress, they will

(A) recover, because the adjuster's actions exceeded the bounds of common decency.
(B) recover, because the adjuster was trying to take unfair advantage of the parents.
(C) not recover, because the parents did not suffer emotional distress that was severe.
(D) not recover, because the parents eventually received a $250,000 settlement from the adjuster's insurance company.

2. A pedestrian was crossing the street when he was hit by a car. The pedestrian suffered a neck injury. The driver of the car that hit the pedestrian had auto insurance. A claims adjuster from that insurance company contacted the pedestrian and discussed the accident with him. The insurance adjuster said, "You're not actually entitled to any compensation for these injuries, under the laws of this state; but I feel bad for you, and I'm a nice guy, so I'm willing to approve a $1,000 payment to you." The insurance adjuster knew that, in fact, the pedestrian would be entitled to compensation under the state's tort law. The pedestrian rejected the offer, retained an attorney, and wound up winning a $550,000 jury verdict on negligence claims against the driver.

If the pedestrian asserts a claim against the insurance adjuster for misrepresentation, will the pedestrian prevail?

(A) Yes, because the insurance adjuster's $1,000 settlement offer was grossly inadequate.
(B) Yes, because the insurance adjuster knew that laws of the state provided for recovery in such a case.
(C) No, because the insurance adjuster's statements did not cause the pedestrian any monetary loss.
(D) No, because the insurance adjuster did not have a fiduciary relationship requiring him to protect the pedestrian's interests.

3. A businessman is the owner of a pet products company, which is engaged in the manufacture and sale of a variety of pet supplies. The businessman's company manufactures such products as pet furniture, toys, beds, collars, leashes, cages, and vitamins. These items are distributed to pet stores throughout the United States and Europe. For many years, the company has conducted its operations from a large factory located in a small town in the southern part of the state. One of the businessman's biggest selling products is specially manufactured high-frequency dog-calling whistles. These whistles are sold to dog-training schools and canine divisions of many police departments. Although these whistles are not audible to people, they are audible to dogs over considerable distances.

Two years ago, a breeder purchased an undeveloped lot in the small town in which the company's factory was located. On her property, the breeder constructed a pet hotel, which was used as a boarding kennel for dogs and cats. This boarding facility was situated about 100 yards from the company's factory. Unknown to the breeder, high-frequency sound waves often emanated from the company's factory when dog-calling whistles were being tested. These sound waves caused the breeder's dogs to howl uncontrollably for many hours during the day and seriously interfered with the operation of her business.

The breeder now brings an action against the businessman and the company to recover damages for the interference with her business caused by the high-frequency sound that reaches her kennel.

The court should rule in favor of

(A) the businessman, because the breeder came to the nuisance after his factory had already been in operation for a number of years.
(B) the businessman, because the breeder's business is abnormally sensitive to harm caused by the high-frequency sound waves.
(C) the breeder, because the high-frequency sound waves constitute a trespass to her premises.
(D) the breeder, because the high-frequency sound waves have seriously interfered with the operation of her business.

4. A well-known Washington newspaper columnist was researching the background of a lawyer who had been nominated to become attorney general of the United States and was awaiting confirmation by the U.S. Senate. One of the columnist's eager young apprentices concocted a plan that he hoped would enable him to gain the columnist's favor.

Late one evening, without telling anyone, the apprentice broke into the lawyer's private office and copied several letters pertaining to "dirty tricks" perpetrated by the lawyer during the most recent presidential campaign. When the apprentice presented the columnist with the fruits of his diligent research, the columnist was quite impressed and immediately printed excerpts from the material.

If the lawyer asserts a claim against the columnist for invasion of right to privacy, the plaintiff will most likely

(A) prevail, because the apprentice's action was an unlawful invasion of private facts.
(B) prevail, because the publication was not newsworthy.
(C) not prevail, because what the columnist printed was true, thus establishing there was no "false light."
(D) not prevail, because the columnist was not involved in the burglary and did not conspire with the apprentice with respect to the burglary.

5. A truck driver negligently changed lanes on the highway without checking to see if it was clear to do so. As a result, a car that was next to the truck was forced off the highway and crashed into a concrete barrier along the roadway. The driver of the car suffered a broken leg. An ambulance arrived and rushed her to the hospital. A doctor there examined the broken leg and ordered X-rays to be taken. The doctor carelessly misread the X-rays and set the broken bone improperly. As a result of the doctor's negligence, the driver's leg never healed completely, and the driver was left with a significant impairment of the use of her leg.

   If the driver of the car brings a negligence action against the driver of the truck, the most likely result is

   (A) the truck driver will not be liable for any damages, because the doctor's negligence constituted a superseding cause that relieved the truck driver of liability.
   (B) the truck driver will be liable for the harm suffered by the plaintiff when her car crashed, but not the additional or enhanced harm resulting from the doctor's careless mistake.
   (C) the truck driver will be liable only if his negligence is regarded by the jury as being more severe than the doctor's negligence.
   (D) the truck driver will be liable for all the harm suffered by the plaintiff, although the doctor may be liable to some extent, as well.

6. A city ordinance forbids washing vehicles parked on city streets. A man washes his car while it is parked on the street in front of his home. The water forms a puddle in the street, which freezes over during the night. Early the next morning, a car driving on the street slides on the ice and crashes into a tree.

   If the driver of the car sues the man and asserts that the man was negligent *per se,* which of the following additional facts would help the man the most?

   (A) The man was not aware of the ordinance.
   (B) The city council enacted the ordinance after someone washing his car was hit by a passing truck.
   (C) The driver lives in the man's neighborhood and saw the man washing his car the day before the accident.
   (D) The driver is not a resident of the city.

7. A patient was admitted to a hospital. He had driven his car despite being intoxicated. As a result, he crashed the car into a tree and suffered a broken nose. After a doctor reset the broken nose, the patient was transferred to a room in the west wing of the hospital. In extreme pain, the patient asked the nurse for a painkiller. Without seeking the doctor's approval, the nurse administered an injection of morphine, which the nurse should have known to be an excessive dosage. The patient died an hour after the injection; the cause of death was a morphine overdose.

   The nurse's injection of morphine to this patient would most likely constitute

   (A) a cause-in-fact, but not a legal cause of the patient's death.
   (B) a legal cause, but not a cause-in-fact of the patient's death.
   (C) a cause-in-fact and a legal cause of the patient's death.
   (D) neither a legal cause nor a cause-in-fact of the patient's death.

8. Late one night, an accountant walked into a bar and ordered a whiskey sour. The bartender served the drink, even though the accountant looked and acted as though he was already very intoxicated. The accountant soon had consumed five more cocktails, which the bartender served, despite the accountant's obviously and unmistakably drunken condition.

   After finishing his sixth drink in the bar, the accountant said good night to the bartender, staggered out of the bar, got into his car, and drove away. After weaving back and forth across the road for several blocks, the accountant crashed his car into a pedestrian who was walking on the sidewalk next to the road. The pedestrian suffered serious injuries to his back and legs.

   The bartender's act of serving drinks to the accountant would most likely be viewed as the

   (A) proximate cause of the pedestrian's injuries.
   (B) superseding cause of the pedestrian's injuries.
   (C) direct cause of the pedestrian's injuries.
   (D) intervening cause of the pedestrian's injuries.

9. A 15-year-old boy was sledding down a pathway through a wooded area of land owned by a woman. The boy had frequently used the pathway for sledding in the previous months. The path, made of concrete, led through the woods from a public highway to a pond in the rear of the woman's property. The pathway was used for sledding and the pond for skating by the residents of the neighboring areas, without the consent of the woman. Furthermore, the woman failed to post any signs forbidding trespassing.

   After the boy had been sledding down the pathway for approximately three hours one morning, he lost control of the sled, and steered it into a tree. The boy suffered serious injuries in the crash.

   If a suit is brought on the boy's behalf against the woman for the boy's personal injuries, the plaintiff will

   (A) recover, under the "attractive nuisance" doctrine.
   (B) recover, because the woman knew or should have known of the frequent trespasses.
   (C) not recover, because the boy was a trespasser.
   (D) not recover, because a 15-year-old boy should have realized the risk.

10. A farmer has a large field where he grows corn. He hires a crop-duster to spray the field, but the crop-duster mistakenly sprays a strong herbicide, rather than a pesticide, and kills all the corn plants in the field. Several days later, a construction company building a house near the farmer's field negligently hits a gas line and starts a fire that burns everything in the area, including the farmer's field.

   If the farmer brings negligence claims against the crop-duster and the construction company in order to recover damages for the destruction of his corn crop, the most likely result is

   (A) only the crop-duster is liable, because its negligence occurred before the construction company's negligence.
   (B) only the construction company is liable, because its negligence would have destroyed the farmer's corn crop no matter what the crop-duster did.
   (C) both the crop-duster and the construction company are liable, because each engaged in a negligent action that was sufficient to destroy the farmer's corn crop.
   (D) neither the crop-duster nor the construction company is liable, because neither is a "but for" cause of the harm.

11. A man and a woman are adjoining landowners in an area of large estates located in the "chateau" region of southeastern Louisiana. In 2000, the man inherited his estate from his father, whose family had owned the property continuously since 1812. The woman purchased her estate in 2008. The man had a stable, which housed many valuable racing horses, on his property. The stable, built in 2002, stood on a portion of the man's land located only 10 feet from the border of the woman's property. Not infrequently, putrid stenches arose from the man's property, caused by large accumulations of horse manure, which were left unattended. The woman had often complained to the man of the noises and odors emanating from the stable.

   The woman brought an appropriate action to enjoin the man's use of the stables.

   Judgment is likely to be for whom?

   (A) The man, because the woman moved onto her property after the stable had been built.
   (B) The man, because a homeowner is entitled to make reasonable use of his property.
   (C) The woman, because the noise, coupled with the odors, substantially interfered with the use and enjoyment of her land.
   (D) The woman, because the man was negligent in permitting the manure to be left unattended.

12. A man and a woman owned adjoining pieces of land. The man moved a giant magnolia tree from another section of his property and had it replanted on his property at a spot just 10 feet from the woman's property. At that time, the woman protested that by locating the tree so close to her land, the man was increasing the risk of injury to the woman's greenhouse, in which the woman cultivated prize-winning flowers.

Hurricanes are quite common in the area. Several years after the replanting of the tree, in the midst of a hurricane, the tree fell on the woman's greenhouse, destroying rare and valuable plants valued at $25,000.

The woman asserted a claim against the man to recover damages for the harm caused by the tree falling on the greenhouse. During trial, the only evidence the woman presented was that the hurricane uprooted the tree, causing it to fall onto her property, and thereby resulting in the damage as claimed.

At the end of the woman's case, the man moved for a directed verdict.

The man's motion will most likely be

(A) granted, because the woman did not produce any evidence to show that the man was negligent.
(B) granted, because the woman's damages resulted from an act of God.
(C) denied, because hurricanes were common in the area.
(D) denied, because the trier of fact may still infer liability for trespass.

13. For many years, a husband and a wife tried to have a child, but the wife was unable to get pregnant. Her family physician had advised her that she was infertile and that it was impossible for her to become pregnant. After missing her period for three months and experiencing other symptoms of pregnancy, the wife consulted the physician. Without administering a pregnancy test, the physician examined the wife and concluded that she had the flu. He prescribed tetracycline, an antibiotic drug, which the wife took for two weeks.

After discontinuing the tetracycline, the wife continued to experience nausea, fatigue, and other symptoms of pregnancy. She then consulted a different doctor, who administered a pregnancy test, which revealed that the wife was, in fact, four months pregnant. Thereafter, she gave birth to a child. When the child developed teeth, they were black and discolored. At the age of 12, the child learned that the black discoloration of his teeth resulted from the tetracycline that the wife took during her pregnancy.

If a claim is brought on the child's behalf against the physician based on malpractice in not administering a pregnancy test to the woman and prescribing tetracycline, judgment is likely to be for whom?

(A) The physician, because an unborn child does not have legal rights stemming from conduct that occurred before birth.
(B) The physician, because no duty of care is owed to an unborn child not in existence at the time medical treatment is rendered.
(C) The child, because a child, if born alive, is permitted to maintain an action for the consequences of prenatal injuries.
(D) The child, because the wife was negligent in failing to seek proper prenatal care.

14. A graduate of law school received notice that she had successfully passed the bar exam. To celebrate passing, the graduate went out with a few friends to a popular campus bar. The graduate's friend ordered a round of Hula Girls for everyone. A Hula Girl is an extremely potent alcoholic drink consisting of 2 ounces of dry gin, 1 ounce of French vermouth, and 1 teaspoon of grenadine. After the drink is mixed, it is then served in a glass with an inverted lemon peel, which is cut at the ends to represent a grass skirt.

Although the graduate had never heard of a Hula Girl, she was in a festive mood and drank it, anyway. A few minutes later, the graduate became very dizzy and attempted to stand up from the barstool. As she tried to walk to the restroom, she became nauseated and vomited over a customer sitting at a nearby table. The customer was embarrassed and greatly humiliated by the incident.

If the customer asserts a claim against the graduate, the plaintiff will most likely

(A) prevail, because the graduate's conduct was extreme and outrageous.
(B) prevail, because an offensive touching resulted.
(C) not prevail, because the graduate's actions were involuntary.
(D) not prevail, because the graduate was unaware what she was drinking.

15. A woman and her 4-year-old son were Christmas shopping at a toy store. The toy store sells a complete array of toys, games, dolls, hobbies, and crafts. The items were displayed on a variety of tables and shelves, which were easily accessible to the customers. While the woman was walking down one of the aisles, her attention became focused on a doll that was prominently exhibited on an overhead display shelf. When the woman approached the doll display, she reached up to grab the doll. As she did so, the woman failed to see a baseball lying on the floor. She tripped over the baseball and fell down, fracturing her hip.

If the woman asserts a claim against the toy store for her injuries, will the doctrine of *res ipsa loquitur* apply on the issue of whether the toy store was negligent and responsible for the baseball being on the floor?

(A) Yes, because the woman was a business invitee on the premises of the toy store.
(B) Yes, because the toy store was in control of the premises at the time of the accident.
(C) No, because another customer may have caused the baseball to be on the floor.
(D) No, because the baseball was an intervening act that cuts off the toy store's liability.

16. A student lent his classmate his car to attend a concert at a theater. Before going to the theater, the classmate drove to a dealer's home to buy some marijuana. The dealer lived approximately two miles from the theater. After picking up the marijuana, the classmate then drove to the concert. As he was driving to the concert, the classmate smoked two marijuana cigarettes so that he could be "high" for the show. While the car was parked outside the theater, through no fault of the classmate, it was struck by another car and damaged. Repairs will cost $750. The driver of the vehicle that struck the student's car fled the scene and cannot be identified.

If the student asserts a claim against the classmate for the damage to the student's car, the plaintiff will recover

(A) the value of the car before it was damaged because the car was damaged while under the classmate's dominion and control.
(B) the value of the car before it was damaged because the classmate used the car for a purpose other than that for which it was lent.
(C) the cost of repairing the car because the car was damaged while under the classmate's dominion and control.
(D) nothing, because the classmate was not negligent in causing the car's damage.

17. A repairman repaired damaged electrical power lines and replaced old, worn-out equipment whenever necessary for the local municipal electrical company. After a violent tornado had ripped through the city, the electrical company was busily trying to restore electrical power to its customers.

The morning after the storm, the repairman was perched on a ladder trying to repair a high-voltage power line. As he was removing the cover of the transformer box, the ladder suddenly slipped on the wet ground, even though it had been properly fixed into position. The repairman struggled to maintain his balance and, luckily, the ladder came to rest against the transformer box. A pedestrian, who was walking on the street below, saw the repairman's predicament and began to climb the ladder to aid him. As the pedestrian was ascending the ladder, his foot slipped, and he fell to the ground. His fall caused the ladder to jar loose the transformer box, which in turn sent the repairman falling to the pavement. The repairman and the pedestrian both suffered serious injuries.

If the pedestrian asserts a claim against the electrical company for his injuries, he will most likely

(A) prevail, because he was attempting to rescue the repairman.
(B) prevail, because a public utility company is strictly liable in tort.
(C) not prevail, because he was negligent in climbing the ladder.
(D) not prevail, because the repairman was not negligent in not affixing the ladder properly.

18. A pedestrian, who was walking along Chestnut Street at 10:20 p.m. on the night of December 3, urgently needed to find a restroom. Just ahead, the pedestrian noticed a private dinner club. As the pedestrian approached the club, he noticed a sign over the front door that read: "ADMITTANCE TO MEMBERS ONLY." Although the pedestrian was not a member of the exclusive club, he entered the dimly lit club, found a door marked "Gentlemen," and entered the restroom.

Which of the following would best describe the pedestrian's legal status when he was in the restroom?

(A) Trespasser.
(B) Guest.
(C) Licensee.
(D) Invitee.

19. A man was out taking a walk one evening when he realized that he needed to use a bathroom. The closest building was a private gymnasium. The man approached the building, and saw a sign on the door that said, "Members only—No restroom facilities available for non-members." The owner of the gym hung up the sign because he knew that people frequently entered the gym just to use the restroom, and he was annoyed by this. However, the owner of the gym knew that the sign was not effective and that people still regularly entered the gym just to use the restroom.

The man needed to use the bathroom very urgently, so he entered the building despite the sign. The restrooms were near the front door of the gymnasium. The man walked directly to the restroom as soon as he entered the building. The clerk working at the front desk in the gymnasium was busy and did not notice the man enter the building or the restroom.

After making use of the restroom facilities, the man washed his hands and proceeded to turn on the electric blow dryer. The dryer, because of a malfunctioning heating coil, emitted intense heat, which caused severe burns to the man's hands.

The man was unaware of the fact that 15 minutes earlier, a gym member had received similar injuries from the malfunctioning dryer and notified the gym's owner. The owner immediately taped a "DO NOT USE" sign to the dryer. However, the sign had fallen to the floor and was lying face down under the bathroom sink when the man was making use of the restroom.

Which of the following would best describe the duty of care that the gym owed to the man?

(A) No duty of care.
(B) A duty to inspect the premises for unknown dangers and to disclose their existence to others.
(C) A duty to warn of any known dangerous conditions on the premises.
(D) An absolute duty of care.

20. A seat in a movie theater collapsed, causing the customer sitting in that seat to fall to the ground and suffer a back injury.

In a personal injury action by the customer against the theater, the customer will most likely

(A) recover, because the theater was under an absolute duty of care to make the premises safe for the protection of its customers.
(B) recover, only if the theater had prior knowledge of the dangerous condition of the seat.
(C) not recover, because the theater was under no obligation to inspect the premises to discover unknown dangers.
(D) not recover, unless the theater failed to make a reasonable inspection of the seats for the safety of its customers.

21. A customer in a restaurant ordered a bowl of the restaurant's famous homemade Manhattan clam chowder. While eating the chowder, the customer broke a tooth on a pebble in the soup, which a reasonable inspection would not have discovered. When the customer complained to the restaurant's owner, the owner admitted that the chowder was not, in fact, homemade, but that it had been poured from a can of chowder purchased from a wholesale distributor of food products.

In a strict liability action by the customer against the restaurant, he will most likely

(A) recover, if a reasonable consumer would not expect the presence of such a pebble in the chowder.
(B) recover, but only if the restaurant had received prior notice of the defective condition of the soup.
(C) not recover, because a reasonable inspection of the soup would not have disclosed the existence of the pebble.
(D) not recover, because the soup would not constitute an unreasonably dangerous product when it was served to the customer.

22. A law clerk normally worked from 9:00 a.m. to 5:00 p.m. each day, or an average of 40 hours per week. One morning, the law clerk came to the office at 9:00 a.m. and started preparing a brief for an upcoming trial. After completing his work at 5:00 p.m. that afternoon, he was about to leave the office when the senior partner of the law firm summoned him. The senior partner told the law clerk that the law firm was representing an important client on an urgent matter that needed immediate research. The law clerk was advised that he would be required to stay at the law office that night and prepare a memorandum. When the law clerk hemmed and hawed, the senior partner handed him the file and said, "I don't care if you stay all night, but you better have this memo on my desk by 8:00 a.m. tomorrow."

Following the senior partner's instructions, the law clerk stayed at the office until 2:00 a.m. preparing the memorandum. By the time he finished, the law clerk was totally exhausted after having worked a total of 17 hours that day. Afterward, the law clerk left the office and started to drive home. Because of his fatigue, he didn't see a pedestrian crossing the street. His car struck the pedestrian, seriously injuring her.

The pedestrian has asserted a tort action against the law firm to recover damages for her injuries.

Which of the following is the most likely result?

(A) The pedestrian prevails, because the law firm was negligent for requiring the law clerk to stay at the law office and finish the memorandum.
(B) The pedestrian prevails, because the law firm is legally responsible for its employees' actions.
(C) The pedestrian loses, because the actions of the law firm were not a cause-in-fact of the pedestrian's injuries.
(D) The pedestrian loses, because the law firm is not responsible for the law clerk's negligence in these circumstances.

23. An employee worked as a delivery person for a drugstore. As part of the employee's duties and responsibilities, he would regularly deliver prescriptions and other items (such as toiletries, cosmetics, vitamins, and gift products) to customers. One afternoon while the employee was on duty, he remembered that it was his girlfriend's birthday. He went ahead and bought her a bottle of perfume from the pharmacy's cosmetics department. The employee paid the full price of $79.95 for the perfume and had the perfume gift wrapped. He then drove to the girlfriend's house in the company van to personally deliver the birthday present. This trip took place during the employee's regular working hours while he was en route to make another delivery from his van. As he was traveling to the girlfriend's house, he was in such a hurry that he drove through a red light and collided with a vehicle owned and operated by a driver. The driver, who had entered the intersection on the green light, tried unsuccessfully to swerve and stop but was unable to avoid the employee's vehicle. The driver was injured in the accident, which caused extensive damage to both vehicles.

If the driver brings suit against the drugstore to recover damages arising from the accident, the driver will probably

(A) prevail, because the employee paid for the perfume.
(B) prevail, because the employee was under the control and direction of the drugstore at the time of the accident.
(C) not prevail, because the employee was acting outside the scope of the employment relationship at the time of the accident.
(D) not prevail, because the drugstore was not negligent in hiring the employee.

24. A furniture store had a truck that an employee of the store used to deliver furniture to the store's customers. One afternoon while the employee was driving the truck to deliver a chair to a customer, the employee negligently ran through a stop sign and hit a car. The driver of the car suffered a leg injury and succeeded in suing the furniture store, recovering $25,000. Assume that all of these events occur in a jurisdiction that has statutes permitting defendants to bring claims for contribution and indemnity.

In the event that the furniture store brings suit against its employee (the truck driver) to recover for its losses, the furniture store will recover

(A) nothing, because the furniture store was primarily liable for the entire amount of damages.
(B) $12,500, because the employer and employee bear equal shares of responsibility for the plaintiff's injuries.
(C) $25,000, because the employee was at fault in causing the accident.
(D) $25,000, unless the furniture store was fully insured against such losses.

25. A 20-year-old student at a state university enrolled in the university's R.O.T.C (Reserve Officers' Training Corps.) program. As part of her R.O.T.C. training, the student was required to spend three weeks at a camp for Marine Corps. summer field exercises. While at the camp, the student was given a new synthetic helmet to wear during her basic training.

An agency purchased the new high-technology helmets for the Army and Marine Corps. to replace the old "steel pot" headgear worn for decades by U.S. soldiers. These new synthetic helmets were manufactured by a corporation and were made of Kevlar, an extremely tough fiber material with high energy-absorbing qualities that made it stronger in some ways than steel.

When the student received her helmet from the Marine Corps., it was packaged in the original carton supplied by the corporation. On the box, there was a picture that depicted an off-duty marine wearing the helmet while riding a bicycle. One afternoon after training, the student decided to take a ride on her bicycle. Believing that it could be used as a bicycle helmet, the student decided to use it for that purpose.

During the ride, the student hit a deep pothole that caused her to be thrown headfirst from the bicycle. As she was flying through the air, the strap from her helmet came loose, and the helmet fell off her head. The student landed on a lawn and was temporarily knocked unconscious. She suffered serious head injuries.

If the student asserts a claim against the corporation to recover damages for her injuries, she will most likely

(A) prevail, because under the doctrine of *res ipsa loquitur,* negligence can be inferred from the fact that the helmet came off the student's head.
(B) prevail, because the original package depicted a picture of a cyclist wearing the helmet.
(C) not prevail, because the student was not using the helmet for its intended purpose.
(D) not prevail, because the helmet had been properly designed by the corporation for its intended use by the Army and Marine Corps.

26. A doctor parked her car in a public parking lot in a downtown area. A construction company was using a large crane to build a new office building next to the parking lot. When the crane was manufactured, some of the welding of its parts was done improperly. No one had ever noticed this manufacturing defect in the crane. The defect caused the crane to break and topple over. Part of the crane fell on the doctor's car.

The doctor's car was completely destroyed. The car was valued at $35,000. The doctor had auto insurance, and the insurance company promptly paid the doctor $35,000 under the insurance policy.

If the doctor brings suit against the manufacturer of the crane, will the doctor prevail?

(A) No, because the doctor had auto insurance, so she suffered no loss.
(B) No, because the manufacturer was unaware of the defect in the crane.
(C) Yes, because the manufacturer sold a product with a dangerous defect.
(D) Yes, because the manufacturer failed to inspect the crane adequately before selling it.

27. An owner ran a sporting goods store that specialized in hunting and camping supplies. His friend had often cautioned him that he should not leave so much of his merchandise out in the open. One day, as the friend entered the store to pay a visit, he decided he'd put his unheeded warnings into action by playing a joke on the owner. The friend took a hatchet that was lying on a display case and swung it over his head as if he were going to strike the owner, who was standing at the register with his back turned. The friend then said, "All right buddy, one false move and it's over." The owner was very frightened at almost being hit with the hatchet but suffered no actual physical or other harm.

If the owner asserts a claim against the friend, the most likely result is that he will

(A) recover, because the friend was negligent.
(B) recover, because he feared the friend would hit him.
(C) not recover, because he suffered no physical harm.
(D) not recover, because the friend was only joking.

28. A security guard had a license to carry a concealed handgun. One day, he was walking past a barber shop when he saw his friend inside getting a haircut. The security guard knew that the barber, an elderly man, had a history of significant heart problems. The security guard decided to play a joke on his friend. The security guard took out his gun, burst through the door of the barber shop, pointed the gun at the friend, and shouted, "Don't move or I'll shoot!" The barber, thinking that an armed intruder was about to shoot the friend, suffered a heart attack and collapsed.

If the barber brings suit against the security guard for infliction of emotional distress and seeks recovery for damages arising from the heart attack, he should

(A) prevail, because the security guard knew the barber was present.
(B) prevail, because the security guard assaulted the friend.
(C) not prevail, because the barber was not a member of the friend's immediate family.
(D) not prevail, because the resulting harm was unforeseeable.

29. A city resident commuted to work each day by subway. After purchasing her subway ticket, the resident entered the subway for her ride downtown to where she was employed. Looking for a seat, the resident was walking toward the rear of the subway car when it came to an abrupt halt. As a result of the sudden stop, the resident fell onto a commuter, injuring him.

If the commuter asserts a claim against the subway company to recover for his personal injuries, the commuter will probably

(A) prevail, because a special duty of care was owed him.
(B) prevail, because the sudden stop caused the resident to fall onto him.
(C) not prevail, if the operator of the subway was not negligent in making the stop.
(D) not prevail, if the resident was negligent in not holding onto the hand rail.

30. A hunter was on his property one day looking for rabbits and other small game, which he shot occasionally for sport. As he rounded a clump of bushes, he spotted a hiker, who, he thought, was a man wanted by the police. The hiker, who had his back to the hunter, was carrying a rifle on his shoulder. The hunter called out to the hiker to stop. The hiker was startled and, as he turned around, his rifle fell forward so that it pointed directly at the hunter. The hunter, thinking the hiker was about to shoot him, fired his rifle at the hiker. The bullet missed the hiker and hit a trespasser on the property. The hunter was aware that people often walked onto his land because there was a pond adjoining the property, which provided boating and fishing activities.

If the trespasser asserts a claim against the hunter for battery, the trespasser will

(A) recover, because the hunter intended to hit the hiker.
(B) recover, because the trespasser suffered a harmful and offensive contact.
(C) not recover, because the hunter accidentally shot the trespasser.
(D) not recover, because the hunter reasonably acted in self-defense.

31. A person was taking a long hike on a trail through a forest in a state park. As the hiker came around a bend in the trail, he suddenly saw a hunter standing next to the trail, looking in the other direction. The hunter was holding a rifle. The hunter turned, causing the rifle to be pointed at the hiker. The hiker felt sure that he was going to get shot, but the gun did not go off.

The hiker asserts a claim for assault against the hunter.

In his action, the most likely result is that the hiker will

(A) recover, because the hunter's rifle was pointed directly at him.
(B) recover, because the hunter's decision to carry the gun was voluntary.
(C) not recover, unless the hunter intended to scare the hiker.
(D) not recover, if the hunter did not intend to shoot the hiker.

32. A certified airline pilot owned a single-engine Cessna plane. One afternoon, the pilot invited his girlfriend, to go flying with him. The girlfriend, who was scared of flying, reluctantly agreed. During the flight, the pilot decided to play a practical joke and shut off the plane's engine. When the plane went into a nosedive, the pilot said, "Oh my God, we're going to crash." The girlfriend became panic-stricken and started screaming hysterically. A few seconds later, the pilot re-started the engine and said, "Don't worry—I was only joking." The plane landed safely and neither person was injured.

If the girlfriend brings suit against the pilot for intentional infliction of emotional distress, she will probably

(A) recover, because a reasonable person would have been distressed by the pilot's actions.
(B) recover, because the pilot's conduct was extreme and outrageous.
(C) not recover, because the pilot intended his actions as a practical joke and, therefore, lacked sufficient intent for an intentional tort.
(D) not recover, because the girlfriend did not suffer any physical injury.

33. A professor was employed by a bar review course as a lecturer. After lecturing for the bar review course for 10 years, the professor was suddenly fired.

Because the professor was such a popular and well-respected individual in the bar review industry, there was much speculation and interest concerning his termination. A reporter for the local law journal telephoned the bar review course's administrative director and inquired why the professor had been fired. The director told the reporter that the professor was fired because the president of the bar review course believed that the professor had embezzled money. The next day, the reporter wrote an article that was published by the law journal, which quoted the director and stated that the professor "was fired because he had embezzled money." It was later learned that the professor was not responsible for any unlawful conduct and had not embezzled funds.

If the professor asserts a defamation action against the law journal, he will most likely

(A) prevail, if the professor proves malice.
(B) prevail, if the newspaper was negligent in not ascertaining whether the professor had actually embezzled any funds.
(C) not prevail, because the director was merely providing an opinion about the reason for the professor's termination.
(D) not prevail, because the law journal was merely repeating what it had been told by a source.

34. A college student was walking home from a party. He had been drinking alcohol at the party and was very intoxicated. Local police officers stopped the student and questioned him. When he refused to answer any of their questions, the police put the student in the back seat of a police car. The police left the student in the back seat of the police car for approximately one hour, and then released him.

If the student asserts a claim against the police for false imprisonment, he will most likely

(A) prevail, unless the police made a valid arrest.
(B) prevail, if he consented to the confinement because he was intoxicated.
(C) not prevail, because police cannot be held liable for false imprisonment.
(D) not prevail, because the student suffered no harm.

35. At 1:00 a.m. one night, two police officers were driving past a tavern when they noticed a man vomiting outside. They stopped their patrol car and walked over to the man, whom they recognized as a troublemaker from the neighboring town. Realizing that the man was extremely intoxicated, they grabbed him and shoved him into their patrol car.

They drove the man around in the police car for a few minutes and told him he had two choices. They would either take him to jail for the night or drive him to the city limits and drop him off there. The man indicated that he didn't want to go to jail. One of the officers then said, "Does that mean you want us to drop you off at the city limits?" The man replied, "Yes." They then drove him to the city limits and left him along a busy highway. Moments later, the man staggered onto the street and was struck by a car driven by a motorist. He suffered multiple injuries.

If the man asserts a claim against the police department based on negligence, he will most likely

(A) recover, because the police should have realized it was dangerous to drop him off where they did.
(B) recover, because the police knew that the man was intoxicated when they dropped him off.
(C) not recover, because the man chose to be driven to the city limits.
(D) not recover, because the motorist's act was a supervening cause of his injury.

36. A 35-year-old man with some experience as a truck driver owned a lumber truck. One day, the man set out driving his truck, heavily loaded with lumber, down a mountain road. Sitting next to the man in the passenger seat was a 19-year-old helper. During the course of the trip, when the truck was going down a long hill, the brakes failed. The man shouted to the helper to jump, but the teenager refused to do so and shouted back to the man that he should try to steer the truck down the hill. The man then opened the door on the passenger's side of the truck and negligently pushed the helper out. The helper, who suffered a broken leg, was rushed to the hospital where he was treated for his injury. As the helper was recuperating, a nurse inadvertently mixed up his chart with that of the female patient in the next room. The nurse gave the helper a fertility pill that made him sterile.

If the helper brings suit against the man to recover damages for his sterility, the man will

(A) recover, because it is foreseeable that a hospital can be negligent in its care of patients.
(B) recover, because the man was negligent in pushing the helper out of the truck.
(C) not recover, because the nurse's act was a supervening superseding cause.
(D) not recover, because it is not foreseeable that a patient would be injured in such a manner.

37. An elevator company installed an elevator in an apartment building. Under the terms of its contract with the owner of the apartment building, the company agreed to carry out regular monthly inspections of the elevator and to make all necessary repairs. The elevator was installed in the apartment complex in January. For the next 10 months, the company made regular inspections. However, starting in November, the company began to have some difficulties with its employees and failed to send inspectors out for three successive months.

On February 20, a woman went to visit her friend, who was a tenant on the 20th floor of the building. The woman used the intercom to call up to the friend, who buzzed to unlock the front door so that the woman could enter the building. The woman headed to the elevator. When the doors opened, several people were already inside the elevator, apparently having entered the elevator from the parking garage below the building. One of the people in the elevator was a man who acted shifty and nervous. By the 12th floor, only four persons were left, including the woman and the man. At that floor, the other two people left, leaving the woman and the man alone on the elevator. Apprehensive at finding herself alone with such an unkempt stranger, the woman pressed the 13th floor button, intending to step out and hoping to find other persons on that floor.

Unfortunately, the elevator stalled, and came to a stop between the 12th and 13th floors. The woman's fears were justified, as the man suddenly grabbed at her purse. When the woman resisted, the man struck her, and she fell unconscious. When the woman recovered consciousness, she found herself in a hospital with a concussion and multiple contusions on her body. She later learned that the elevator had remained stalled for 50 minutes. Thereafter, it moved to the 20th floor, where she was found by her friend, who took her to the hospital. Two weeks later, the police arrested the man and found the woman's purse in his possession. This was the first assault that had occurred in the apartment building. The elevator's stalling was caused by a defective cable that a routine inspection would have discovered.

If the woman brings suit against the owner of the apartment building for negligence, she will most likely

(A) recover, because she was an invitee of a tenant in the building.
(B) recover, because the owner would be vicariously liable for the company's failure to inspect the elevator.
(C) not recover, because the woman was negligent in failing to exit the elevator on the 12th floor when the other occupants exited the elevator.
(D) not recover, because there had been no previous assaults in the apartment building.

38. A young lawyer worked late at her office one night. When she finally decided to go home, she headed to the elevator, got in, and pushed the button for the ground floor. The elevator went all the way to the ground floor, but then just stopped there. The doors did not open. The lawyer tried pushing each of the buttons in the elevator and tried to use the intercom in the elevator to call for help, but nothing on the elevator's control panel seemed to be functioning. The lawyer was afraid that she would be stuck in the elevator all night. She began pounding on the doors and yelling. She started to feel panicked, hyperventilated, lost consciousness, and fell to the floor of the elevator. As she fell, she struck her head on the elevator wall, causing a large bump and bruise on her head. She was unconscious in the elevator for about 30 minutes before a security guard tried to use the elevator and realized it wasn't working. The guard managed to force the doors open and found the lawyer. At that moment, the lawyer regained consciousness. An investigation revealed that the elevator stopped working because it had not been properly maintained. The owner of the building had canceled all service and maintenance work on the elevator in order to save money.

    If the lawyer sues the building owner for false imprisonment, she will most likely

    (A) prevail, because she was confined in the elevator for an unreasonably long period of time.
    (B) prevail, because she was injured during her confinement in the elevator.
    (C) not prevail, because the building owner did not intentionally cause the lawyer to be confined.
    (D) not prevail, because the lawyer was unconscious and unaware of what was happening for most of the confinement period.

39. A 12-year-old boy decided to play a practical joke. Knowing that his parents were giving a dinner party that evening, the boy filled a bucket with ice-cold water and balanced it on the partially open door of the guest bedroom, thinking that his father would take the guests' coats there to put them on the bed. The boy then went off to play at a friend's house. The boy's father decided to keep all the guests' coats in the hall closet instead of putting them in the guest bedroom. Later that evening, one of the guests mistakenly wandered into the guest bedroom while searching for a bathroom. As the guest opened the door, the bucket fell and hit his head, causing a severe cut that required a dozen stitches.

    If the guest sues the boy for negligence, the most likely result is

    (A) the boy wins, because a child's conduct cannot be negligent.
    (B) the boy wins, because the guest unreasonably assumed the risk of entering an unfamiliar room rather than asking for directions to the bathroom.
    (C) the boy loses, because this "practical joke" posed a risk of severe harm and, therefore, the boy had a duty to exercise as much care as a reasonable adult.
    (D) the boy loses, because he did not act with the amount of care that one would expect from a 12-year-old child.

40. A department store had suffered a succession of thefts of merchandise over a period of months. From reports by employees and customers, the department store's manager concluded that the losses were due, wholly or in large part, to the depredations of a female shoplifter, aged 30 to 40 years, about 5 feet 5 inches in height, with red hair and green eyes, who usually wore a suit. This information was passed on to all of the employees of the department store.

One day, a woman entered the store to purchase accessories. The woman was 5 feet 5 inches tall, 37 years old, red-haired and green-eyed, and dressed in a smartly tailored suit. She carried a large shopping bag. The manager noticed her as she picked up, examined, and put down a number of gloves and scarves. After a while, she looked about tentatively, and then started to walk out, swinging her bag. The manager intercepted her and, standing in front of her, politely asked the woman if she would accompany her to the store manager's office. When the woman asked for an explanation, the manager told her of the store's recent experience and the suspicion that the woman might be concealing pilfered merchandise in her bag. Flushing angrily, the woman replied, "Very well," and followed her to the office.

Once there, the manager began to question the woman quite intensively. After the questioning, the manager then asked the woman's permission to inspect the contents of her shopping bag. At first, the woman curtly refused and announced that she had had enough of this nonsense. When she rose to go, the manager told her, "Listen, unless you let me look inside that bag, I'm going to call the police." The woman replied, "Very well," and handed her the bag. The manager inspected the contents of the bag thoroughly but did not find any pilfered merchandise. She then gave the woman permission to leave. The total length of the woman's detention was 30 minutes.

If the woman asserts a claim for false imprisonment against the department store, she will most likely

(A) prevail, because she was detained for an unreasonably long period of time.
(B) prevail, because the manager did not have reasonable grounds to suspect that the woman had committed a theft.
(C) not prevail, because under the circumstances, the manager had reasonable grounds to suspect that the woman had committed a theft.
(D) not prevail, because the manager gave the woman permission to leave after conducting her investigation.

41. A vacationer, on a winter ski holiday, visited a ski lift in a private park. The ski lift company had installed and operated the lift pursuant to a concession agreement with the owner of the private park. Visitors gained entry to the park on payment of a $5 fee, which entitled them to go ice skating, tobogganing, or sledding. A ski lift ticket cost an additional $7 per day. At the top of the ski lift, there was a platform for embarking and disembarking passengers. The ski lift company paid the owner a stipulated rental plus 15 percent of the net proceeds from the lift.

Two employees of the company operated the lift, one from a station at the bottom and the other from a station at the top of the hill. When the vacationer boarded the ski lift, it was late afternoon and most of the skiers had left. He was the sole passenger on the lift. Meanwhile, the employee at the top had left his post to go to the bathroom, asking his friend to keep watch on the lift and to stop it to allow any passengers to disembark. The friend consented, and the employee showed him how to use the control switch.

When the vacationer approached the top, the employee was still away. Instead of stopping the lift to permit the vacationer to get off, the friend allowed the lift to keep moving. The vacationer was carried past the platform, and he was swung violently from side to side as the ski lift started downward. When the employee returned and sized up the situation, he threw the switch, stopping the lift. The vacationer, severely bruised and badly frightened, jumped off the ski lift and completed his descent by foot.

In a personal injury action by the vacationer against the owner of the private park, the vacationer will rely on the concept of

(A) *respondeat superior.*
(B) vicarious liability.
(C) joint venture.
(D) imputed negligence.

42. A man worked as a clerk in a gourmet coffee shop. His friend often stopped by the shop to chat with the man while the man was working. One afternoon, while the friend was visiting the shop, the man needed to use the bathroom. There were no customers in the shop at that moment, so the man asked the friend to watch the store for him while he went in the back to use the bathroom. The friend agreed to do so.

While the man was in the bathroom, a customer came into the store. She wanted to purchase some freshly ground coffee. The shop had a grinding machine that customers could use. The customer selected a bag of coffee beans and then took it to the grinding machine. She was unsure how to start the machine, so she asked the friend for help. The friend tried to show the customer how to use the machine, but he was not familiar with how it worked, and he gave the customer erroneous instructions. The customer tried to follow the friend's instructions, but this led to her getting her finger pinched and cut by the machine.

If the customer asserts a claim against the coffee shop company for her finger injury, the customer will most likely

(A) prevail, because the company would be vicariously liable for the man's unauthorized actions.
(B) prevail, because the friend's negligence would be imputed to the company.
(C) not prevail, because the man acted outside the scope of employment by entrusting the supervision of the shop to his friend.
(D) not prevail, because the company is not liable for the friend's negligence.

43. A ski resort had a lift that carried customers from the bottom to the top of the ski slope. One afternoon, the lift suddenly broke down because of a power failure in the area. A customer was suspended in his lift chair, one-third of the way up the hill and 50 feet above the ground. The customer remained on the lift for five hours until power was restored. He was then returned uninjured to the bottom of the hill.

In a suit against the ski resort, the customer is likely to have action for

(A) false imprisonment.
(B) negligence.
(C) assault.
(D) no cause of action.

44. A neighborhood homeowners' association hired a security company to provide an armed guard to patrol the neighborhood. One evening, the guard saw a young man stealing a rake that a homeowner in the neighborhood had left outside in his yard. The guard ran toward the young man. Seeing the guard, the young man dropped the rake and began to flee. Believing that the young man was about to escape, the guard pulled out his gun and fired a shot at the young man. The bullet struck the young man in the arm.

If the young man asserts a claim against the security company for damages for his injuries, the young man will

(A) prevail, because the guard used unreasonable force to protect the homeowner's property.
(B) prevail, because the guard did not give a warning that he had a gun and was about to shoot.
(C) not prevail, because the young man was trespassing on the homeowner's property.
(D) not prevail, because the young man was engaged in theft when he was shot.

45. A home security protection company provided protection services to property owners in the immediate area. The owner of a summer cottage in the area hired the company to provide 24-hour protection during the winter months when his home was unoccupied. According to the security arrangement, the company's uniformed guards would periodically patrol the property and, if necessary, provide an "armed response" to any unauthorized individuals who were found trespassing on the property.

The company provided security protection to the owner's property for two years. The owner then notified the company that he was planning to sell the cottage. As a result, he requested that the company discontinue its home-protection service, effective immediately. Two weeks later, a burglar broke into the cottage and was ransacking it. As the burglar was exiting from the owner's house carrying a portable television set, he was seen by a security guard working for the company. The security guard, who was driving past the home on security patrol, had not been informed that the owner had discontinued protection services. The security guard suddenly stopped his patrol vehicle and ran toward the burglar shouting, "Stop! Don't move or I'll shoot!" Startled, the burglar dropped the television set and began to flee. Believing that the suspected burglar was about to escape, the security guard pulled out his service revolver and fired a bullet at the burglar. The shot struck the burglar in the leg, seriously wounding him.

If the burglar asserts a claim against the owner for negligently failing to supervise those providing security services for the owner's property, the burglar will probably

(A) prevail, because the burglar was unarmed when he was shot.
(B) prevail, because the owner knew or had reason to know that the company provided an "armed response" to suspected trespassers.
(C) not prevail, because the owner was not present when the shooting occurred.
(D) not prevail, because the owner had discontinued protection services from the company when the shooting occurred.

46. At 10:00 p.m. on November 14, a driver was operating his automobile along Main Street. As the driver was approaching the intersection of Main Street and First Avenue, a motorist, who was driving straight through a red light, suddenly appeared before him. Trying to avoid the motorist, the driver veered his car onto the sidewalk. The car landed in a deep hole in the sidewalk. This hole had been dug by a construction company, which had been repairing a water main break earlier in the day. The construction company had been hired by the local municipal water department. Although the construction company had erected a warning sign advising pedestrians about the hole, there was no fence or barrier surrounding it.

When the driver's car fell into the hole, it ruptured the water main, engulfing the car with water. Within a short time, the driver, unable to escape, drowned in his car, which rapidly filled with water.

In a wrongful death action by the driver's estate against the municipal water department, the estate will most probably

(A) prevail, because sovereign immunity would not attach to non-delegable duties, which are proprietary in nature.
(B) prevail, because the city government would be strictly liable for failing to ensure the water main repair work was done properly.
(C) not prevail, because the municipal water department would not be liable for the negligence of its independent contractor.
(D) not prevail, because sovereign immunity attaches to functions that are governmental in nature.

47. A carpenter was driving home one night after a long day of work. He was driving his car north toward an intersection. There were stoplights at the intersection. The light for the carpenter was green, so the carpenter proceeded to drive through the intersection. A bus entered the intersection from the west and slammed into the carpenter's car. The carpenter was seriously injured in the crash and missed several weeks of work while recovering from the injuries.

Which of the following facts or inferences, if true, would be most helpful in an action by the carpenter against the driver of the bus?

(A) The bus driver had received three speeding tickets in the past.
(B) The carpenter's car was in good condition, and it had passed a safety inspection just a week before the accident.
(C) The traffic signal at the intersection had been inspected the day before the accident and found to be functioning properly.
(D) The bus driver was operating the bus without a driver's license in violation of the State Motor Vehicle Code.

48. A construction company was doing repairs and replacing portions of a sidewalk and railing next to a lake. The construction crew started tearing out the old sidewalk and railing, but stopped work when it started to get dark. The construction crew left without putting up a warning sign or barrier around the work area. A few hours later, a jogger came along the sidewalk. Not realizing the construction work was in progress there, the jogger stumbled and fell at the spot where the construction crew had torn up the sidewalk and railing. The jogger fell into the lake. As the jogger was attempting to stay afloat, he began screaming, "Help! Help! I can't swim. I'm drowning." His screams attracted the attention of a person who was passing on his bicycle. The cyclist immediately hurried to assist the jogger. As the cyclist was leaning over the edge of the lake, trying to help the jogger get out of the water, he lost his balance and fell into the lake. Both the jogger and cyclist suffered serious bodily injuries before they were pulled out of the water by police.

In a negligence action by the cyclist to recover for his personal injuries, the construction company will most probably

(A) be held liable, because the cyclist's attempt to rescue the jogger was foreseeable.
(B) be held liable, because the construction company would be strictly liable to anyone injured by the failure to put adequate warnings or barriers around the site of the sidewalk repairs.
(C) not be held liable, because the cyclist assumed the risk by leaning over the edge of the lake.
(D) not be held liable, because the construction company could not foresee that anyone would be hurt while trying to rescue someone from the lake.

49. An avid baseball fan wanted to purchase tickets for an upcoming baseball game being held at the local stadium. He contacted the stadium's ticket sales office, which advised him that all tickets were to be placed on sale at the stadium at 9:00 a.m. the following day. The fan, who was employed as a bricklayer, realized that he could not leave work to purchase the tickets. Consequently, the fan telephoned his next-door neighbor and asked him if he would be interested in going to the stadium to purchase the baseball tickets. The neighbor told the fan that he would be happy to purchase the tickets for him and that he (the neighbor) also wanted to buy tickets for himself. However, the neighbor said that his car had broken down and that he did not have available transportation to get to the stadium. The fan suggested that he could lend his car to the neighbor. The neighbor agreed, and the following morning the two men met in front of the fan's home.

The fan gave the neighbor the keys to his car and also money with which to buy his baseball tickets. Thereafter, the neighbor drove the fan's car to the stadium where he purchased the tickets for the fan and (using his own money) also bought a set of tickets for himself. The fan had instructed the neighbor to return the car to the fan's home after his trip to the stadium. After the neighbor left the stadium, however, he decided to visit a friend in a town located 120 miles from his home. As the neighbor was driving toward the town, an automobile crashed into him, causing significant damage to the fan's car. The cost of repairing the fan's car was determined to be more than the retail value of the auto.

In an action by the fan against the neighbor to recover damages resulting from the accident, the fan will most likely

(A) recover nothing, because the neighbor was on a joint venture when the accident occurred.
(B) recover the cost of repairing the car.
(C) recover the retail value of the car.
(D) recover, because the neighbor was negligently operating the auto at the time of the accident.

50. The local high school football team won the state championship. After the game the high school held a victory rally at the high school gym. As the team was being honored, the star quarterback of the football team approached one of the cheerleaders and asked her out for a date. The cheerleader, who had a crush on the quarterback, said she'd love to go out with him. The quarterback told her, "Great, I'll pick you up at eight."

Later that evening, the quarterback was getting ready to drive to the cheerleader's home when his car wouldn't start. The quarterback then called his next-door neighbor and asked him if he could borrow his car. The neighbor agreed, but told him, "Okay, but make sure you return it by 2:00 a.m." The quarterback assented and then drove to the cheerleader's house.

After picking her up, they drove to an all-night coffee shop where they spent the night talking and catching up over coffee and waffles. Losing track of time, the quarterback and the cheerleader did not leave the coffee shop until 3:00 a.m. After returning home around 4:00 a.m., the quarterback decided that it was too late to return the car, so he parked it in his driveway. He intended to return the car to the neighbor in the morning.

A short while later, a thief stole the neighbor's car from outside the quarterback's home. The police found the car three months later, undamaged. The neighbor, however, refused to accept the car and brought a claim against the quarterback for conversion.

In his claim, the neighbor will

(A) succeed, because the quarterback could have returned the car and failed to do so.
(B) succeed, because the quarterback left the car in his driveway, and it was stolen.
(C) not succeed, because the quarterback intended to return the identical property he borrowed in an undamaged condition.
(D) not succeed, because the criminal act of the thief was unforeseeable.

51. A pedestrian was walking in front of a hotel in the downtown area when a chair was thrown from an unidentified window. The chair struck the pedestrian on the head, knocking her unconscious. When the pedestrian recovered consciousness, she found herself in a nearby hospital with a doctor in attendance. An examination revealed that the pedestrian had suffered a concussion and severe head lacerations. A subsequent investigation revealed that the chair had, in fact, been thrown from a window at the hotel. None of the hotel's employees or guests, however, admitted culpability for the incident.

If the pedestrian asserts a claim against the hotel for negligence, will the doctrine of *res ipsa loquitur* enable her to recover?

(A) Yes, because the chair was within the control of the hotel.
(B) Yes, because a chair is not usually thrown from a window in the absence of someone's negligence.
(C) No, because the chair was not within the control of the hotel at the time the pedestrian was injured.
(D) No, because the hotel is not vicariously liable for the tortious conduct of its employees.

52. A statute in the state makes it a misdemeanor for any motor vehicle to travel to the left of the center line of any two-way highway, road, or street.

Late for a business appointment, a businesswoman was driving north on a highway when she decided to pass the car in front of her. As she swung across the center line into the southbound lane, her vehicle collided with a fire engine. As a result of the accident, the fire engine was delayed in reaching an owner's house, which was entirely destroyed by fire. The owner's home was located approximately one mile from the accident scene.

If the owner asserts a claim against the businesswoman, he will most likely

(A) recover the fair market value of his house before the fire.
(B) recover that part of his loss that would have been prevented if the businesswoman had not hit the fire truck.
(C) recover nothing, because the businesswoman was not responsible for causing the fire.
(D) recover nothing, because the traffic statute was not designed to protect against the type of harm that the owner suffered.

53. On June 1, a businessman opened a health and massage spa, which was located on First Street in the city. The spa also provided health club facilities, such as saunas, steam rooms, and whirlpool baths.

A 75-year-old spinster resided across the street from the spa. The spinster opposed the opening of the spa because she believed that it was a "cover" for an illegal operation. During the day, the spinster sat in her rocking chair on her front porch and observed a constant stream of businessmen entering the spa.

On the evening of June 29, the spinster, disguising her voice, called the spa and told the businessman, "You pimp, why don't you take your dirty trade elsewhere?" Without paying any attention to the call, the businessman hung up.

The spinster then began making repeated crank telephone calls to the businessman's establishment. Every hour on the hour for the next three weeks, the spinster made her crank calls, harassing the businessman and his employees. As a result of the hourly phone calls, spa business was constantly disrupted, causing the businessman to suffer a decline in the volume of customers. After contacting the police, the businessman discovered that the spinster was the person making the harassing calls.

If the businessman asserts a claim against the spinster, the theory on which he will most likely prevail is

(A) public nuisance.
(B) private nuisance.
(C) intentional infliction of emotional distress.
(D) negligence.

54. A man and a woman had a romantic relationship for one year, but the man ended it. The woman was unable to accept the breakup and continued trying to contact the man. The woman would call the man's home and cellphone many times each day, and also tried to visit the man's home and workplace frequently. The man tried to discourage the woman's behavior, but the woman persisted.

If the man asserts a claim against the woman based on invasion of privacy, the most likely outcome is that the man will

(A) prevail, because the telephone calls intruded upon his seclusion and solitude.
(B) prevail, but only if the man is able to prove malice on the defendant's part.
(C) not prevail, because the telephone calls did not cause the man to suffer any economic loss or hardship.
(D) not prevail, unless the woman's conduct was a crime in some respect.

55. A resident lived in a house across the street from a small office building. One of the offices in that building was that of a criminal defense lawyer. The resident hated the idea of the lawyer's office being close to her home. She felt that it meant dangerous criminals were coming and going in her neighborhood. The resident spent a lot of time looking out her window, trying to figure out which people going in and out of the office building were criminals, and imagining what sorts of crimes they had committed. The resident eventually decided that she needed to drive the lawyer out of the neighborhood. She made a telephone call to the lawyer and said, "You are scum, and so are all of your clients. I know that you're conspiring to commit crimes with all those bad people you represent. The police should arrest you and put you in jail with your clients." The lawyer was very upset by what he heard.

If the lawyer asserts a claim for defamation against the resident based on the telephone call, he will most likely

(A) succeed, because the resident's remarks constituted slander *per se*.
(B) succeed, because the lawyer found the remarks to be upsetting.
(C) not succeed, because the resident's remarks were a matter of personal opinion rather than statements of fact.
(D) not succeed, because the resident's remarks were not published or communicated to anyone but the plaintiff.

56. A resident in an exclusive residential area is a marine biologist. To aid in his study of sharks, he had a large tank built in his backyard in which he placed a great white shark.

Aside from a smell that emanated from the tank, some neighbors were concerned and afraid to let their children outside for fear that they would wander onto the resident's property. In order to convince his neighbors that they had nothing to fear, the resident invited them over to view the shark tank. While a neighbor was standing near the tank, the shark splashed its tail, and the neighbor got very wet. The neighbor, who had a cold, developed bronchitis.

If the neighbor sues the resident for damages incurred from being drenched by the shark and bases her suit on strict liability, she will most likely

(A) recover, because the possessor of wild animals is strictly liable for all injuries caused to others by the animals.
(B) recover, because the smell from the shark tank was a nuisance.
(C) not recover, because she suffered injury only because she had a cold and, therefore, was unusually vulnerable to harm from being splashed with water.
(D) not recover, because she did not suffer the type of harm normally inflicted by a shark.

57. An environmentalist was very interested in environmental issues, particularly protection of wetland areas. He decided to dig out the lawn in his back yard and turn the space into a swampy marsh. Eventually, his back yard was filled with tall grasses, reeds, and other marsh plants. A wide variety of frogs, turtles, snakes, birds, and other animals inhabited the yard. The ground was usually covered by several inches of standing water.

The environmentalist's neighbors were not pleased with the condition of the environmentalist's yard. They complained that it produced foul odors, and they claimed that the standing water was a breeding ground for mosquitoes and other insects.

Several months after the environmentalist converted his yard into a marsh, a real estate investor purchased the house closest to the environmentalist's back yard swamp. The investor lived in a large city several hundred miles away, and he purchased the house next to the environmentalist's for investment purposes. The investor rented the house to a family under a long-term lease. The tenant family complained frequently to the investor about being annoyed by the environmentalist's yard.

If the investor asserts a nuisance claim against the environmentalist, the environmentalist's best defense would be

(A) that he had sound environmental reasons for maintaining the swampy condition of his yard.
(B) that turning his yard into a swampy marsh did not violate any zoning ordinance.
(C) that the investor owns the property but has rented it out, so the investor does not have actual possession or the right to immediate possession of the land.
(D) that when the investor purchased the house, he knew or should have known about the swampy condition of the environmentalist's property.

58. The local jurisdiction has a modified comparative negligence statute in effect that provides:

"Contributory negligence shall not bar recovery in any action by any person or his legal representative to recover damages for negligence resulting in death or injury to person or property, if such negligence was not as great as the negligence of the person against whom recovery is sought, but any damages allowed shall be diminished in proportion to the amount of negligence attributable to the person for whose injury, damage, or death recovery is made."

In addition, this jurisdiction follows joint and several liability for joint tortfeasors.

A buyer recently purchased an undeveloped beachfront lot in the jurisdiction. He hired a building contractor to construct a new house on the property. Thereafter, the contractor employed a subcontractor to provide on-site maintenance. The contractor contracted with a cement company to supply concrete for the foundation of the structure.

After excavation started, an employee of the cement company delivered a load of concrete to the construction site. To facilitate delivery, the contractor and the subcontractor had built an access ramp extending from the street to the lot. As the employee was driving over the ramp, it suddenly collapsed and caused the truck to overturn, seriously injuring the employee.

A subsequent investigation determined that the contractor and the subcontractor negligently used substandard materials in constructing the ramp. In addition, the employee was partially at fault for driving while intoxicated. The employee brought suit against the contractor and the subcontractor to recover damages for his injuries. A special trial was held on the issue of negligence, and it was adjudged that each party was contributorily negligent as follows:

PARTY	DEGREE OF NEGLIGENCE
Plaintiff: (the employee)	40%
Defendant: (the contractor)	35%
Defendant: (the subcontractor)	25%

The employee, who suffered damages in the amount of $100,000, brings a personal injury action against the contractor individually.

He will most likely

(A) recover nothing, because he was more at fault than the contractor.
(B) recover $100,000.
(C) recover $55,000.
(D) recover $35,000.

59. A traffic accident occurred at a road intersection. A motorcycle, a car, and a truck were involved. The motorcyclist was injured and brought suit against the driver of the car and the driver of the truck. The jury returned a verdict finding that the motorcyclist's injuries were caused by negligence on the part of all three of the parties. The jury assigned 55 percent of the fault for the motorcyclist's injuries to the motorcyclist, 25 percent to the driver of the car, and 20 percent to the driver of the truck. The jury found that the amount of the motorcyclist's injuries was $100,000.

The motorcyclist enforces the judgment against the driver of the car and collects $45,000 from the driver of the car.

If the driver of the car then brings an action against the driver of the truck for contribution, the driver of the car should

(A) recover nothing, because he was more at fault than the driver of the truck.
(B) recover $27,000.
(C) recover $20,000.
(D) recover $15,000.

60. A company owns and operates a chemical plant that manufactures paraquat, an herbicide used primarily as a weed killer. The plant is located in a rural area in the southwestern part of the state. In its production of paraquat, the company emits putrid smelling fumes throughout the surrounding countryside. Although the fumes are harmless to health, they are rank and highly offensive. Despite extensive research by the company to alleviate the problem, there is no known way to manufacture paraquat without discharging malodorous fumes into the air. An owner of a large dairy farm that is adjacent to the plant finds the foul-smelling herbicide fumes to be extremely unpleasant and totally objectionable.

The owner brings an action based on private nuisance against the company and seeks to enjoin the manufacture of paraquat at the chemical plant.

Which of the following facts, if proven, will be most helpful to the company's defense?

(A) Federal, state, and local agencies approved the design of the plant and equipment used to produce paraquat.
(B) The company has a contract with the federal government whereby it supplies 80 percent of its paraquat production to the Drug Enforcement Agency, which uses the herbicide as a marijuana eradicator.
(C) The company commenced the manufacture of paraquat at the plant before the owner acquired the land and built his dairy farm.
(D) Paraquat is the only herbicide that can safely and effectively kill marijuana, which, if not controlled, poses a serious drug-enforcement problem.

61. A person owned property next to a highway. After raking leaves on his property into a large pile, the landowner loaded the leaves into several large metal barrels so that he could burn the leaves. Before starting the fire, the landowner telephoned the local weather bureau to determine which direction the wind would be blowing. Because a highway was located on the southern edge of his property, he was aware that it would be unsafe to burn the leaves if the wind was blowing in that direction. The weather bureau, however, indicated that the wind would be gusting in a northerly direction. Shortly after the landowner set the leaves on fire, the wind current unexpectedly shifted and started gusting in a southerly direction. As a consequence, the smoke and ashes blew over the highway, resulting in poor visibility. Moments later, a motorist was driving his automobile on the highway in a westerly direction. The posted speed limit was 45 m.p.h., although the driver was traveling about 55 m.p.h. The driver could not see the highway clearly and crashed his vehicle into a median strip.

If the driver asserts a claim against the landowner, the most likely result is

(A) the landowner will prevail, because the driver was driving in excess of the speed limit.
(B) the landowner will prevail, if his decision to burn the leaves was reasonable under the circumstances.
(C) the driver will prevail, if the smoke from the burning leaves prevented him from clearly seeing the roadway.
(D) the driver will prevail, because the landowner will be strictly liable for causing the accident.

62. A farmer raked up some leaves on his property, put them into a metal barrel, and set the leaves on fire. The farmer then went off to his barn to do some other work. A few minutes later, a wind gust blew some burning leaves onto a neighbor's property, causing a small fire amid some brush.

If the neighbor asserts a claim against the farmer, the neighbor will most likely

(A) recover, because the farmer is strictly liable for the spread of the fire.
(B) recover, because the farmer was negligent in leaving the fire unattended.
(C) recover, because the farmer created a public nuisance in failing to control the fire.
(D) not recover, because the farmer is not liable for an unforeseeable act of God.

63. An auto mechanic was repairing a car in his auto shop when a spark ignited gasoline and oil residue on the floor. The mechanic managed to douse the flames, but not before the fire created giant billows of smoke that floated over onto a neighbor's property and caused the neighbor's home to become discolored.

If the neighbor asserts a claim against the mechanic, the neighbor would most likely be able to recover for

(A) strict liability.
(B) negligence.
(C) nuisance.
(D) trespass.

64. A woman was employed as a legal secretary for a local attorney. After the attorney terminated the woman's employment, she sent a job application and résumé to another attorney. In the résumé she sent to the second attorney, the woman listed her former employment with the first attorney. After receiving the woman's résumé, the second attorney telephoned the first attorney for his opinion of her qualifications. The first attorney replied that he dismissed the woman "because she was unprofessional and incompetent." The first attorney's assessment was based on one malpractice incident for which he blamed the woman, but which, in fact, was attributable to another secretary in his law firm. Although the first attorney reasonably believed that his low rating of the woman was a fair reflection of her performance, he wrongfully held her responsible for the malpractice incident. Based on the first attorney's poor recommendation, the second attorney did not hire the woman.

In a defamation action by the woman against the first attorney, the plaintiff will most likely

(A) prevail, because the first attorney's statement reflected adversely on the woman's professional competence.
(B) prevail, because the first attorney was mistaken in the facts upon which he based his opinion of the woman's performance.
(C) not prevail, because the first attorney had reasonable grounds for his belief that the woman was incompetent.
(D) not prevail, because the woman listed her former employment with the first attorney in her résumé to the second attorney.

65. A husband was about to leave his home for work one morning when his wife ran in from the kitchen explaining that their 4-year-old son had just swallowed some medicine that had been prescribed for use as a skin lotion. Dashing to the car, the husband then drove his wife and ailing son to the nearest hospital. On the way to the hospital, the son had a seizure and stopped breathing. Seconds later, the car went out of control despite the husband's reasonable efforts, swinging across the center line into oncoming traffic, where it collided with a car driven by a driver who was driving in the opposite direction.

In this jurisdiction, a statute makes it a misdemeanor for any motor vehicle to travel to the left of the center line of any two-way highway, road, or street.

If the driver asserts a claim against the husband, the most likely result is that the plaintiff will

(A) prevail, because the husband is strictly liable for violating the statute.
(B) prevail, because the statute was designed to protect motorists such as the driver.
(C) not prevail, because the driver had the last clear chance to avoid the accident.
(D) not prevail, because the husband was acting reasonably in an emergency.

66. A car owner noticed a peculiar "shimmy" in the steering wheel of his automobile, which appeared to him to have been getting worse in the course of the preceding week. A few days after discovering the shimmy in the steering wheel, the car owner lent his automobile to his next-door neighbor. When the neighbor picked up the car, the car owner forgot to tell him about the shimmy. The neighbor was driving the car at a reasonable rate of speed within the posted speed limit when the car began to swerve across the road. The neighbor turned the steering wheel in an attempt to stay on the road. The steering failed, however, and the car veered off the road and onto the sidewalk. The car struck a pedestrian who was injured in the collision.

If the pedestrian initiates suit against the owner of the car, the pedestrian will most likely

(A) prevail, because the car owner knew the steering was faulty and failed to tell his neighbor who borrowed the car.
(B) prevail, because the car owner is strictly liable under the circumstances.
(C) not prevail, because the faulty steering was the cause-in-fact of the pedestrian's harm.
(D) not prevail, because the car owner was a gratuitous lender.

67. On May 19, a telephone operator for the local telephone company received a call in which a male voice said: "I want to report that the downtown sporting arena is going to be blown up tonight." The caller then hung up. The line on which the call was made was a line owned by a woman.

Immediately after receiving the call, the telephone operator reported the threatening conversation to the police. About half an hour later, during which time she had handled a number of other calls, the telephone operator received a call from a police officer who was at the woman's home. He asked her to listen to a voice. After she did, the officer asked the telephone operator if she could identify it. The telephone operator responded that she was positive that it was the voice of the person who had made the threat. As a result of the telephone operator's identification, the woman's boyfriend was arrested and charged with the crime of terrorist threatening.

As a consequence of the arrest, the boyfriend lost his job and suffered embarrassment and ridicule in the community. At trial, however, the telephone operator's identification proved to be erroneous, and the boyfriend was exonerated.

In a defamation action for slander by the boyfriend against the telephone operator and the telephone company, he will most likely

(A) succeed, because the telephone operator's erroneous identification constituted slander *per se.*
(B) succeed, because the telephone operator's erroneous identification resulted in the loss of his good reputation in the community.
(C) not succeed, because the telephone operator's erroneous identification was made without actual malice.
(D) not succeed, because the telephone operator's erroneous identification was protected by a qualified privilege for statements made in the public interest.

68. A homeowner was planning to construct a new pool in her back yard. She hired a well-known pool contractor to design and construct the pool. The contractor, in turn, hired a subcontractor to dig the hole and plaster the pool area. After the subcontractor completed his job, the contractor then hired an electrician to install the heater and wiring for the pool. While the electrician was performing his work, the wiring became disjointed and had to be replaced at a substantial expense to the homeowner.

If the homeowner sues the electrician in tort to recover the damages she suffered because of this occurrence, will the homeowner prevail?

(A) Yes, if the wiring became disjointed because the electrician's plans departed from established standards in the electrical industry.
(B) No, unless the electrical wiring that became disjointed was defective.
(C) No, if the electrician used his best professional judgment in performing the electrical work.
(D) No, unless the homeowner knew that the contractor had hired the electrician to perform the electrical work.

69. A buyer purchased a new convertible from an automobile dealership. A few weeks later, the buyer began smelling a pungent gasoline odor in the vehicle. The buyer immediately took the car to the dealership and told the service manager what was wrong. The service manager indicated that he would take care of the problem and contact the buyer when the car was ready. The next day, the buyer was informed that the problem had been corrected and the car was available for pickup. The buyer then went to the dealership, took possession of his car, and drove off. After traveling about five miles, the buyer again smelled gasoline fumes. Irritated that the problem had not been corrected, the buyer decided to drive back to the dealership. As he was doing so, the car suddenly exploded, and the buyer suffered third-degree burns over 90 percent of his body.

A subsequent investigation revealed that the explosion was caused by a defective gas tank that had ruptured. This produced a gasoline leak that was ignited by sparks from the car's underbody. A reasonable inspection would have disclosed the defective gas tank. The trouble the buyer had described to the service manager was indicative of such a problem.

If the buyer asserts a claim against the manufacturer of the convertible for damages for his injuries, will the buyer prevail?

(A) Yes, if the dealership should have replaced the gas tank.
(B) Yes, because the buyer's injury was caused by the defective gas tank.
(C) No, if the buyer should have realized the gasoline smell presented a hazardous condition and stopped the car before the explosion occurred.
(D) No, unless the gas tank was defective when the car left the manufacturer's plant.

70. A person purchased a new car from a local auto dealership. Over the next month, the purchaser drove the car a little more than 1,000 miles. The purchaser noticed that the car made a squeaking noise when the brakes were applied, so the purchaser took the car back to the dealership to have the mechanic there take a look at it. The mechanic worked on the car and then told the purchaser that the problem had been fixed. A few days later, the brakes failed, causing the purchaser to crash into a tree. The purchaser suffered a serious head injury in the crash.

If the purchaser asserts a claim against the car dealership for damages for his injuries, will the purchaser prevail?

(A) Yes, if the brakes were defective when the dealership sold the car to the purchaser.
(B) Yes, because the dealership is strictly liable for defective repairs on cars it has sold.
(C) No, because the car had been driven more than 1,000 miles.
(D) No, unless the dealership's employee was negligent in repairing the brakes.

71. A woman was employed as a bank teller. One morning, a customer entered the bank to make a deposit. As the customer handed the deposit to the woman, she saw that he had a misprinted $5 bill in his possession. The woman knew that the $5 bill, which had President Lincoln's picture upside down, was worth $500 to bill collectors. The woman then asked the customer if he would like to exchange "that old $5 bill for a new bill." The customer accepted the woman's offer and handed her the misprinted bill for a new one. One week later, the customer learned that the $5 bill that he gave the woman was valued at $500.

If the customer asserts a claim against the woman for deceit, will he prevail?

(A) Yes, because the customer was the true owner of the misprinted bill and, therefore, he was entitled to the benefit of the bargain.
(B) Yes, because the woman did not disclose the true value of the misprinted bill.
(C) No, because the woman made no false representation of fact.
(D) No, because the customer was not justified in relying on the woman's offer.

72. A property owner held title in fee simple to a tract of 20 acres located outside the boundaries of the city. Thereafter, the property owner constructed a shopping center on the property and leased commercial buildings and parking facilities to various tenants. The shopping center, which was located near a public high school, attracted many teenagers who often loitered in the parking lot. The youths frequently harassed shoppers and damaged autos by breaking off windshield wipers and radio antennas.

Customarily, the local police department patrolled the shopping center and drove by three or four times each day. This, however, did not prevent the teenagers from hanging out at the shopping center. One afternoon, a shopper was shopping at the center when an unidentified youth damaged her car by throwing a rock through the back window.

The shopper brings an action against the property owner to recover for the damage to her auto.

She will most likely

(A) prevail, unless the person who was responsible for damaging her car can be identified.
(B) prevail, if the damage to her car could have been prevented had the property owner taken reasonable security measures.
(C) not prevail, because the car was damaged by the malicious acts of an independent third person.
(D) not prevail, because the local police had the primary duty to provide security protection at the shopping area.

73. A legislative assistant to a state senator approached various wealthy lobbyists without the senator's knowledge to solicit illegal campaign contributions for the senator's upcoming re-election campaign. The assistant dictated several letters requesting such contributions, which the senator signed without reading, along with a pile of other correspondence. Before the letters were mailed, however, the senator discovered what had happened and then immediately terminated the assistant's employment.

Later that same evening, after being notified that he was fired, the assistant returned to the senator's office and used his keys, which had not yet been returned, to enter. The assistant made copies of the letters in question. The following day, the assistant turned over the copies of the letters to an investigative reporter from the local newspaper in the area. The reporter had heard about the assistant's dismissal from another staff member and was curious about all the underlying circumstances. After the assistant provided the reporter with all of the pertinent facts, the reporter wrote a news story regarding the senator's solicitation of illegal campaign contributions. Although the reporter's story was printed in the newspaper, he did not reveal the source of his information. As soon as the publication was made, the FBI initiated an investigation of the senator's campaign finances.

If the senator asserts a claim based on invasion of privacy against the newspaper for the publication of the article concerning the solicitation of illegal campaign contributions, the most likely result is that the senator will

(A) prevail, because the newspaper story placed him in a "false light in the public eye."
(B) prevail, because the newspaper disclosed private facts about the plaintiff.
(C) not prevail, unless he is able to prove malice on the defendant's part.
(D) not prevail, because the newspaper was acting in the public interest by printing the news story.

74. A newspaper published a story about a U.S. senator having close ties to people suspected of being involved in organized crime. The senator claimed that the allegations in the newspaper story were false, and he brought a defamation action against the newspaper.

Which of the following is the most accurate statement with regard to the newspaper's liability?

(A) A qualified privilege of fair comment existed because the newspaper was reporting on a matter of public interest.
(B) Because the senator is a public figure, he has the burden of proof to show malice on the part of the newspaper.
(C) The newspaper would not be liable because, under the First Amendment's freedom of the press, the newspaper was privileged to publish the story.
(D) The newspaper would be relieved of any liability for defamation because an absolute privilege existed.

75. A U.S. senator fired one of her staff members for being insubordinate and refusing to follow the senator's instructions about handling several important matters. To get revenge for being fired, the staff member forged some documents that falsely suggested the senator was taking bribes from lobbyists. The staff member anonymously mailed the forged documents to an investigative reporter from a major national newspaper. Based on the forged documents, the newspaper published stories accusing the senator of corruption. The staff member eventually admitted that he had forged and mailed the documents to the reporter.

If the senator brings a defamation suit against the former staff member for forging and mailing the documents to the reporter, the senator will most likely

(A) recover, because the staff member was aware that the documents were false.
(B) recover, because the senator can prove that she suffered actual economic or other harm as a result of the newspaper stories.
(C) not recover, because the senator is a public figure.
(D) not recover, because the First Amendment provides a privilege for speech relating to a legislator and her staff.

76. A historian inherited a necklace from her mother's estate. It originally belonged to her great-great-great-grandmother and had been passed down through the family from mother to daughter since approximately 1840. Although the necklace did not have a particularly high monetary value, it had substantial sentimental value to the historian. When the historian received the necklace, the clasp was broken and one of the stones in the necklace needed to be reset. Although she was reluctant to let the necklace out of her possession even temporarily, she decided to take it to a reputable jewelry store for repairs. She explained to the clerk that she was very nervous about leaving the necklace because it was a family heirloom. When the historian returned to the jewelry store the next day to pick up the repaired necklace, the clerk apologetically explained that it had been misplaced. Several days later, a member of the jewelry store's cleaning service found the necklace in a wastebasket. The historian suffered severe anguish and distress due to the temporary loss of the necklace and the fact that it was nearly disposed of with the garbage. The historian brought suit against the jewelry store for negligent infliction of emotional distress.

What is the most likely result?

(A) The historian will prevail, because it was foreseeable that the historian would be extremely distressed if the jewelry store mishandled the necklace.
(B) The historian will prevail, because the jewelry store breached the duty of care owed to the historian when it misplaced the necklace.
(C) The historian will not prevail, because the jewelry store's negligence did not result in physical harm to the historian.
(D) The historian will not prevail, because the jewelry store did not misplace the necklace with intent to inflict emotional distress.

77. A concert pianist suffered a strained wrist, so he went to visit a doctor. The doctor explained to her that the fastest way to regain complete use of the wrist was to treat it with a series of injections of a drug that blocked pain and reduced inflammation. The concert pianist had discussed with the doctor her need to be ready for an important recital in three weeks. The drug was known to cause calcium buildup in joint tissue in approximately one to two percent of patients treated with it. For most individuals experiencing this side effect, the calcium buildup did not result in noticeable limitation of movement. If it did, the buildup could be surgically removed, and after a brief recovery period (one to two months), complete movement was restored. The doctor did not inform the concert pianist of these facts, and she began a course of treatment consisting of three injections per week for three weeks. At the end of the second week, the concert pianist received in the mail the current edition of a popular health magazine. To her dismay, it contained an article describing the dangers of using the drug that the doctor recommended, pointing out that calcium buildup in the knuckles could be devastating to a pianist.

The concert pianist discontinued treatment immediately and was not able to perform in her upcoming recital due to pain in her wrist, but not because of any calcium buildup in her knuckles. The concert pianist sought treatment from another physician, who recommended a two-month hiatus from piano playing followed by six months of physical therapy. After that time, the concert pianist was able to resume her playing.

Does the concert pianist have a cause of action against the doctor?

(A) Yes, if the concert pianist would not have consented to the use of the drug if she knew about the risks to her mobility.
(B) Yes, if a reasonable person would have considered the information about calcium buildup important.
(C) No, if the doctor had weighed the risks and benefits of using the drug before prescribing it.
(D) No, if the concert pianist suffered no harm from the use of the drug.

78. A woman inherited a 40-lane bowling alley from her father. Having no interest in the business, she closed it for several months while searching for a lessee. The woman knew the carpeting in many places in the building was worn and buckling and the plumbing congested, but she could not muster even enough interest to make repairs.

Finally, she entered into a short-term lease with a businessman, who reopened the alley immediately, planning to make repairs and renovations only in a month if the business became profitable. The businessman shared his plans with the woman and signed the lease. Approximately one week after opening, a league player caught his foot in one of the buckles of the rug, tripped, and broke his leg. His recovery was slow. He could walk only with the aid of crutches for some time.

If the league player sues the woman, who will prevail?

(A) The league player, because bowling alleys are open to the general public.
(B) The league player, because he was a customer of the bowling alley.
(C) The woman, because as the possessor, only the businessman owes any duty to the league player.
(D) The woman, because the businessman had the opportunity to evaluate the condition of the bowling alley prior to signing the lease.

79. While lawfully crossing the street, a pedestrian was hit by a car driven by a driver, who had negligently failed to yield to the pedestrian. A passerby called 911 for help and paramedics quickly arrived to tend to the pedestrian. It was determined that the pedestrian suffered a broken arm and should be transported to a hospital, so an ambulance was summoned. The ambulance was owned and operated by a local ambulance company. While driving the pedestrian to the hospital, the ambulance employee that was driving the ambulance negligently lost control of his vehicle and overturned. The pedestrian suffered a broken leg in the accident.

What is the impact of the ambulance employee's actions on the driver's liability to the pedestrian?

(A) The driver and the ambulance company are jointly and severally liable for the pedestrian's broken leg.
(B) Only the ambulance company is liable for the pedestrian's broken leg because the damages are apportionable.
(C) Only the ambulance company is liable for the pedestrian's broken leg unless the paramedics were negligent in the selection of an ambulance service.
(D) Because the driver caused the accident she is solely liable for the pedestrian's broken leg.

80. One particularly cold night, a homeowner built a fire in his fireplace to heat up the living room as he watched television. When the homeowner decided it was time to go to bed, he looked to the fire and saw that there were no more flames, just glowing embers. He decided it was safe to leave the embers glowing in the fireplace and go to bed.

An hour after the homeowner went to bed an ember rolled out of the fireplace and onto the carpet. The ember ignited the carpet, and the ensuing fire soon spread to the walls of the living room. The homeowner was awakened by his home's smoke detector and escaped unhurt. The local fire department quickly responded to the fire and succeeded in extinguishing fire before any other rooms in the homeowner's house were damaged. However, a firefighter suffered a lung injury due to smoke inhalation while fighting the fire.

If the firefighter files suit against the homeowner for her injuries, will she prevail?

(A) Yes, but only if the homeowner should have known of the possibility that a glowing ember might start a fire.
(B) Yes, if the homeowner was negligent in leaving the fire unattended as he went to bed.
(C) No, because smoke inhalation is one of the risks of working as a firefighter.
(D) No, because the firefighter is not a licensee or invitee.

81. A woman goes fishing in her boat out on the lake at dawn. Few other people are on the lake so early in the morning, and she likes the peace and quiet. A short while later, the woman notices a canoe, with one occupant, heading in her direction. The canoe stops about fifty yards away. The woman is glad that the canoe doesn't come any closer because she doesn't want the movement of the canoe to disturb the fish. The woman then sees the occupant of the canoe stand up and begin to move around, apparently attempting to organize his fishing tackle. Suddenly, the woman's boat overturns. She is not wearing a life preserver and is thrown into the water. At that same moment, the man from the canoe feels a tug on his fishing line. He doesn't want to lose the fish, so he decides to reel it in before going to see if the woman needs any assistance. He determines that at worst, the woman will have to tread water for a few minutes until he gets to her. Unfortunately, the woman does not know how to swim. By the time the man makes her way over to the woman and pulls her out of the water, she is no longer breathing. Although the man promptly administers CPR and the woman is eventually revived by paramedics, she suffers severe brain damage due to being without oxygen for so long.

If the woman's parents sue the man for the woman's injuries, what is the man's best argument in support of a motion to dismiss their claim?

(A) The man's negligence was not the proximate cause of the woman's injuries.
(B) The woman was contributorily negligent.
(C) The man rendered the assistance with care and his assistance did not cause the woman's brain damage.
(D) The man's negligence was not the actual cause of the woman's injuries.

82. A dentist ran a busy solo practice in the city. When not working, the dentist liked to go to car shows with his restored 1965 Ford Mustang. That was the only time he drove the car. It was not a passion his wife shared with him, so he went to the car shows alone. One day, as his 50th birthday approached, the staff at the dentist's office purchased space on a billboard to announce the dentist's big day. The sign wished the dentist happy birthday by name and featured a picture of the dentist in his Ford Mustang, taken while he was passing through a toll booth. The staff thought the picture was funny because the dentist had received a ticket for the trip when his automatic toll paying device had failed. Although her face wasn't clear, there was a woman in the passenger seat of the car that the staff assumed was the dentist's wife. The dentist's wife saw the billboard and confronted her husband, who confessed that he was having an affair. The wife divorced the dentist.

The dentist brings a defamation action against his staff. Will the dentist prevail?

(A) Yes, because the picture of the dentist with another woman could damage his reputation.
(B) Yes, because the dentist can plead additional, extrinsic facts that render the message defamatory.
(C) No, because the picture is factual.
(D) No, because a photograph is not a written communication, and therefore will not qualify as a defamatory message.

83. A girl received a coin collection from her father several years ago for her birthday. After a falling out with her father, she decided to sell the coins and buy designer shoes. She did not know the value of the collection, so she took it to a local appraiser. The girl's friend had taken items to the appraiser for appraisal in the past and told the girl she believed he was fair. The appraiser, an avid coin collector, noticed that several coins in the girl's collection were coins that he had been trying to obtain for years. He knew that the entire collection was worth about $10,000, but he offered her $2,000. The girl was ecstatic that her coin collection was worth so much money, but she was turned off that the appraiser was so pushy about purchasing the coins. Despite his insistence, she took her coin collection to be appraised in the next town over. The second appraiser told her the coin collection was worth about $10,000. The girl sues the first appraiser for misrepresentation.

Should she recover?

(A) No, because she did not suffer any pecuniary loss due to the first appraiser's statements.
(B) No, unless she relied on the first appraiser's statements.
(C) Yes, because the first appraiser acted with intent to induce her to rely on his statements.
(D) Yes, because the first appraiser knowingly made a false statement in his appraisal.

84. A math student and an architecture student attend classes at the local university. The architecture student's calculus final exam is scheduled for Monday, while the math student's exam is scheduled for the following Wednesday. After his final on Monday, the architecture student travels home to visit his family and does not return to the university until the following week. The morning of her final, the math student realizes that her calculator is broken. Without a working calculator, she is certain to fail the exam. The math student enters the architecture student's unlocked dorm room and removes his calculator from his desk drawer. After the exam, the math student returns the calculator in perfect condition to the precise location in which she had found it.

Can the architecture student recover against the math student for trespass to a chattel?

(A) Yes, because the math student knowingly used the calculator without the architecture student's permission.
(B) No, because the architecture student was unaware that the math student had used his calculator.
(C) No, because the math student's use was not a serious interference with the architecture student's rights.
(D) No, because the architecture student cannot prove that he sustained any damages.

85. A realtor showed several homes to an interested family. The family had narrowed their choices to two. One was priced at $250,000 and the other was $400,000. The family had several questions, one being whether the backyard of each house was sufficient to build an in-ground pool. Due to a downturn in the market, the realtor, without first checking, told the family that the cheaper property probably was not suitable but the more expensive one was definitely suitable for a pool. The family successfully bid on the more expensive home and moved in. Two years later, the family contracted to have a pool put in their backyard. The pool constructor conducted some initial tests and told the family that the backyard had insufficient underground support for a swimming pool.

If the family brings a cause of action for negligent misrepresentation against the realtor, will they prevail?

(A) No, because the realtor had no actual knowledge that the backyard was unsuitable for a swimming pool.
(B) No, because the realtor's representations amounted to mere puffery.
(C) Yes, because the realtor was in a fiduciary relationship with the family.
(D) Yes, because it was reasonable for the family to rely on the realtor's representations.

86. A manufacturer sells dandruff shampoo. On the label is a warning advising consumers to apply a small amount of the shampoo to the wrist before applying to the scalp. The label states that this test is necessary because a small percentage of the population may be allergic to the chemicals contained in the product and susceptible to scalp irritation.

A woman recently moved to the United States, and cannot read or speak English. One day, she purchased a bottle of dandruff shampoo from a local drug store. She looked at the warning on the label but did not understand it. She used the shampoo without first applying a small amount to her wrist. Minutes later she began experiencing an allergic reaction and scalp irritation. This was followed by hair loss attributed to the shampoo.

If the woman brings suit against the manufacturer in strict liability, will she prevail?

(A) Yes, because she suffered injury from her use of the product.
(B) Yes, because the manufacturer was aware that a small percentage of the population would suffer an allergic reaction to the shampoo.
(C) No, because she didn't read or speak English.
(D) No, because she assumed the risk by not applying some to her wrist first.

87. As a new car owner was driving home from the dealership, she stopped to cash a check. While she was inside the bank completing her transaction, she forgot that she had left her car keys inside the vehicle. A man was walking through the parking lot and noticed the new automobile with the keys inside. The man immediately hopped inside and drove off, intending to steal the vehicle. Twenty minutes later, the man was driving the vehicle when the steering suddenly malfunctioned. The man was unable to control the vehicle as it swerved across the highway and hit a tree. A subsequent investigation determined that a manufacturing defect caused the steering in the vehicle to malfunction. The investigation further produced evidence that the vehicle was not inspected before it left the dealership.

If the man asserts a strict products liability action against the car dealership, what is the most likely result?

(A) He will prevail, because the dealership failed to inspect the vehicle before selling it.
(B) He will prevail, because the vehicle was sold in a defective condition.
(C) He will lose, because he was not a foreseeable user or consumer of this vehicle.
(D) He will lose, because he was engaged in misuse when the accident occurred.

88. A construction company is a private corporation that has conducted large-scale blasting and excavation projects in the northwestern region of the United States for many years. Several months ago the company's chief financial officer entered into a contract to clear 5,000 acres in a rocky wilderness area for the building of a ski resort. The company began the project by blasting the mountainous terrain to create a level area for the main ski lodge.

The construction company exercised reasonable care in the detonation of all explosives used to conduct the blasting operations. Since the rural area chosen for the ski resort was sparsely populated, the construction company had no reason to anticipate any risks to persons outside the 5,000 acre tract. A rancher lived in the neighboring town and operated a mink farm that was situated on the northwest boundary of the proposed ski resort. The noise and vibrations from the blasting frightened the rancher's mink. The fright, in turn, caused the adult mink to eat their young. Nearly one-third of the rancher's animals have been killed.

In a claim for damages against the construction company, how should the court rule?

(A) For the rancher, because the construction company is strictly liable for the harm caused by the blasting.
(B) For the rancher in trespass, because the fright due to the vibrations caused the mink to eat their young.
(C) Against the rancher, because he assumed the risk that such a business would emerge.
(D) Against the rancher, because the harm to the mink was not a foreseeable result of the risk created by the blasting.

89. The defendant was driving his car along at 40 MPH (the speed limit being 25 MPH). As he approached an intersection, a taxi entered from the right side of the defendant's vehicle. The two cars collided. When the defendant saw the taxi, he was still far enough from the intersection that, considering speed and distance, he might have braked in time, but he failed to do so.

Furthermore, the defendant's brakes were not operating properly. Despite the fact that the defendant was aware that his brakes were malfunctioning, he failed to have the brakes repaired. As the taxi driver approached the intersection, she failed to heed a stop sign, and entered in the path of the defendant's car. The taxi driver was injured in the accident. While not conceding liability on the defendant's part, the defendant's insurance company paid the taxi driver's medical and hospital bills in the amount of $20,000.

Thereafter, the taxi driver brought an action against the defendant to recover damages for her injuries sustained in the accident. The jury returned a verdict and held that: (1) the defendant was responsible for 70 percent of the injuries and the taxi driver was responsible for the other 30 percent of the total negligence in the case; and (2) the taxi driver suffered damages in the amount of $100,000, taking no account of the payment made by the defendant's insurance company. After the verdict was rendered, the court was advised of the $20,000 paid by the defendant's insurance company.

Based upon the given facts, the court should now enter a judgment for the taxi driver in what amount?

(A) $40,000, which represents the proportion of the taxi driver's damages caused by the defendant's negligence, less the proportion caused by the taxi driver's negligence.
(B) $50,000, which represents the proportion of the taxi driver's damages caused by the defendant's negligence, less the medical and hospital payments made by the defendant's insurance company.
(C) $70,000, which represents the proportion of the taxi driver's damages caused by the defendant's negligence, with the medical and hospital payments being disregarded as coming from a collateral source.
(D) $100,000, because the defendant's negligence was greater than that of the taxi driver.

90. A bookstore had just opened for business in a new and larger facility. A contracting company had remodeled the space to suit its specifications, including replastering the walls and ceiling. One morning, shortly after the grand opening, the manager noticed pieces of plaster on the floor near some shelves where some best sellers were on sale.

The manager swept up the plaster on the floor and called the contracting company, demanding that they immediately make necessary repairs. Two hours later, a customer entered the bookstore looking for a recently released murder mystery. As he approached the shelves containing the best sellers and reached for a book, a large piece of plaster fell on the customer's head. The customer had to be hospitalized for a concussion.

If the customer sues the bookstore, will he recover?

(A) Yes, because the book store failed to close the store after the manager noticed the plaster on the floor.
(B) Yes, because the customer is a business invitee.
(C) No, because the contracting company's acts were the actual and legal cause of the injuries.
(D) No, because responsibility for the construction of the building was properly delegated to the contracting company.

91. A man and his friend enjoyed hunting together. One weekend, they went on a quail hunting expedition in a remote wilderness area deep in the mountains. They were hunting in a very desolate area surrounded by mountainous terrain located at least 50 miles from any habitation. With hunting rifles in hand, they were ambling around but no game was visible. After a rather uneventful morning with nothing to shoot at, the man suddenly spotted a large condor. The condor was an endangered species, and to shoot one was a criminal offense. Unable to resist the temptation, the man took a shot at the condor. The bullet missed the vulture, ricocheted off a tree, and struck a state forest ranger who was hiding in a secluded area, watching a trail frequented by drug smugglers. The bullet hit the forest ranger in the eye and permanently blinded him. Neither the man nor his friend was aware of the forest ranger's presence.

If the forest ranger asserts a claim against the man to recover damages for his injury, will he prevail?

(A) Yes, because the man's shooting the gun was the actual cause of the forest ranger's injury.
(B) Yes, because the man intended to shoot the condor.
(C) No, because the man had no reason to anticipate the presence of another person in such a remote area.
(D) No, because the bullet ricocheted off a tree and hit the forest ranger.

92. One morning a 16-year-old boy and his friend were golfing. As the boys approached the 10th hole, which was a par four and 467 yards long, the boy shot first and hit a towering tee shot down the left side of the fairway about 240 yards. The friend then hit his tee shot, which traveled down the middle of the fairway. The ball, however, struck a tree limb that extended over the fairway and deflected onto an adjacent homeowner's property. The homeowner, who was sitting outside on a lounge chair, was struck on the head by the friend's golf ball. She suffered a bump on her head but was not otherwise seriously injured.

If the homeowner brings suit against the friend for trespass, will she prevail?

(A) Yes, because the golf ball intruded onto the homeowner's property.
(B) Yes, because the friend intended the act of hitting the golf ball.
(C) No, because the homeowner did not suffer physical injury.
(D) No, because it was an accidental entry that was unintentional.

93. A patient went to a doctor for treatment of a painful ear condition, which had caused her to experience loss of balance, dizziness, and nausea. While the doctor was examining her inner ear, he noticed a lump of wax. As the doctor was removing the lump, he also noticed what appeared to be the rear legs of an insect. With utmost care, the doctor extracted the foreign object from the patient's ear. The doctor then examined the substance, which proved to be a cockroach. As he held the insect in front of the patient to see, she became hysterical, fainted, and fell to the floor, breaking her collarbone. The incident caused the patient to develop a phobia and she became deathly afraid of insects.

In a suit for damages against the doctor, which of the following torts would provide the patient with her best theory of recovery?

(A) Battery.
(B) Negligence.
(C) Negligent infliction of emotional distress.
(D) Intentional infliction of emotional distress.

94. A young man had strong feelings for a young woman who lived three blocks away from him. They were once classmates in high school, but had since graduated. About two or three times a week, the young man parked his car across the street from the young woman's house and took pictures of the young woman while she was in her backyard. On the last occasion, the young woman saw the young man across the street and immediately filed suit. The young man did not return.

How will the court decide?

(A) The young woman prevails in a cause of action for nuisance.
(B) The young woman prevails in a cause of action for invasion of privacy.
(C) The young woman does not prevail in a cause of action for nuisance, because the young man's conduct did not involve physical intrusion.
(D) The young woman does not prevail in a cause of action for invasion of privacy, because the young man's conduct did not involve physical intrusion.

95. A husband and wife have been married for ten years when the husband decides to divorce the wife. The wife is very angry and thinks of ways she can punish her husband for the divorce. She decides she will convince the prosecutor that the husband is a mass murderer. The wife has no reason to think that the husband is in fact a mass murderer but she tells a compelling story to the prosecutor. The prosecutor brings charges against the husband and during a search of the husband's office the police actually find proof that the husband is a mass murderer. The husband is subsequently convicted. Angry that his wife instituted the proceedings that put him in jail, the husband sues the wife for malicious prosecution because she did not have probable cause to initiate the criminal proceedings in the first place.

Will the husband prevail?

(A) Yes, because at the time the wife convinced the prosecutor to bring charges, she did not know that her husband was a mass murderer.
(B) Yes, because a reasonable person would not have believed that the husband was guilty.
(C) No, because the husband was convicted on criminal charges.
(D) No, because the prosecutor had the last chance to decide whether to bring charges against the husband.

96. A college student purchased a small computer that was designed for both portability and for desktop use. The computer had short legs in the back that pulled out and raised the bottom of the computer up at a slight angle. The student assumed that the legs were there to make the keyboard more ergonomic. When one of the legs would not pull out evenly with the other, the student simply pushed both legs back in and used the computer with its bottom flat to her desk. While she was out of her room, the battery case on the computer dangerously overheated because it could not vent as designed to with the legs in place. It caused a fire that burned all of the contents in two adjoining dorm rooms before it was put out. Luckily, nobody was injured. Later it was determined that the student's particular computer had a defect that caused one of the legs to stick.

Is the manufacturer of the computer liable under strict products liability in a jurisdiction that has not adopted a comparative negligence system for products liability?

(A) Yes, because the computer's defect caused the damage.
(B) Yes, because the computer's defect was not detected by the student.
(C) No, because there no personal injuries.
(D) No, because the student perceived the defect in the computer.

97. A young man lived in a three-bedroom house on top of a large hill with his girlfriend. The couple had just moved in together and so they still needed to buy a lot of furniture and other necessities. The bathtub in the bathroom was very old, so the girlfriend, without telling the young man, went out and bought a brand new bathtub. When the young man came back home he saw the bath tub still sitting outside of the house, because the old bath tub was not yet removed from the bathroom. The young man had always wanted to ride down the hill on which the house was located, so when he saw the bath tub he became very excited. Not knowing that this was a bathtub meant for his house, he attached four wheels and rode down the hill in the bathtub. Mid-way down the hill, however, the bathtub cracked and the man flew out of the bathtub hitting a boulder. The man brings a strict liability action against the manufacturer of the bathtub in a jurisdiction that has not adopted any form of comparative negligence systems.

What is the result?

(A) The young man prevails, because the manufacturer is in the bathtub's distribution chain.
(B) The young man prevails, because the bathtub had a design defect.
(C) The manufacturer prevails, because the young man misused the product.
(D) The manufacturer prevails, because the young man was contributorily negligent.

98. The plaintiff and his friend are roommates. The friend loves retro items from the 1970s and buys a lava lamp which he places on the nightstand in his bedroom. Usually, the roommates do not enter each others' bedrooms. However, one night while the friend is out on date, he calls the plaintiff and asks him to go into the friend's room and get the phone number for his date, who is running late. The friend tells the plaintiff that the phone number is on a piece of paper on his nightstand. The plaintiff turns on the lava lamp while he is looking for the paper. A manufacturing defect in the lava lamp causes it to explode, sending shards of glass into the plaintiff's face. The plaintiff sues the retailer who sold the lamp to his friend under a strict liability theory of products liability.

Can the plaintiff sustain his action against the retailer?

(A) Yes, because the defect in question was a manufacturing defect.
(B) Yes, because the plaintiff was injured while using the product and the retailer is in the chain of distribution of the lamp.
(C) No, because the plaintiff was not a foreseeable plaintiff in this case.
(D) No, because the defect was caused by the manufacturer, not the retailer.

99. The defendant owns a warehouse at the edge of a residential neighborhood. Unfortunately, the warehouse became infested by cockroaches, so the defendant decided to exterminate them. Prior to extermination, the defendant put signs all over the nearby neighborhood warning residents of the upcoming extermination. The defendant took every necessary precaution on the day of the extermination. However, some of the gasses leaked from the warehouse. The wind was especially high that day, and the toxic fumes were carried to the nearby neighborhood. Several of the residents, including two children, became ill from the fumes. The injured residents sued the defendant.

Will the injured residents likely succeed?

(A) Yes, because the defendant breached his duty of care to the residents.
(B) Yes, because the defendant was engaged in an abnormally dangerous activity.
(C) No, because the residents will not be able to prove the defendant's negligence.
(D) No, because the defendant took all possible precautions against injury.

100. A woman wore an expensive new hat to an art gallery opening. While the woman was viewing one of the paintings on display, a man approached and asked what she thought of the painting. The woman responded that the painting was hideous and should not be considered artwork. Unbeknownst to the woman, the man was the artist who had painted the painting. As the woman walked away, the man angrily knocked the hat off the woman's head. The woman did not notice that her hat had been knocked off her head until she walked past a mirror a few minutes later.

Has the man committed battery?

(A) Yes, because he caused an offensive contact with the woman's hat.
(B) Yes, because the hat was expensive and thus the man's actions would offend a reasonable person.
(C) No, because the man did not cause an offensive contact with the woman's person.
(D) No, because the woman did not realize that the man had touched her hat until several minutes later.

KAPLAN BAR REVIEW

Answers and Explanations

1. **(C)** Intentional infliction of emotional distress occurs where the defendant, through extreme and outrageous conduct, intentionally or recklessly causes severe emotional distress to the plaintiff. Emotional distress passes under various names, such as mental suffering, mental anguish, mental or nervous shock, or the like. It includes all highly unpleasant mental reactions, such as fright, horror, grief, shame, humiliation, embarrassment, anger, chagrin, disappointment, worry, and nausea. However, liability for intentional infliction of emotional distress exists only if the plaintiff's distress is truly severe. In the present example, the facts do not indicate that the parents suffered severe emotional distress. The facts simply state that the parents were "outraged by the adjuster's actions." As such, choice (C) is correct because the parents will not recover unless they suffered severe emotional distress. Choice (A) is incorrect because even though the adjuster's conduct was extreme and outrageous, there can be no recovery unless the plaintiffs suffered severe emotional distress. Choice (B) is incorrect because merely trying to take unfair advantage of an individual does not establish infliction of mental distress. Choice (D) is incorrect because it is irrelevant whether the parents received a settlement of the claims for their son's injury from the aerial bomb. The question presented herein relates to the adjuster's liability for infliction of emotional distress, which is a separate cause of action from the tort claim for the son's injuries.

2. **(C)** The tort of misrepresentation requires a false representation of a material fact known by the defendant to be false, which induces actual and justifiable reliance by the plaintiff, resulting in monetary loss. Here, the insurance adjuster may have made false statements, but the pedestrian did not rely on them or suffer any loss as a result of them. Choices (A) and (B) are incorrect because neither addresses the necessary reliance upon a material fact that results in monetary loss. Choice (D) is incorrect because even though the insurance adjuster did not have a fiduciary relationship with the pedestrian, the insurance adjuster could still be liable for misrepresentation if the pedestrian had justifiably relied on the false statements and been harmed by doing so. The liability would be for misrepresentation, not breach of a fiduciary relationship.

3. **(B)** A public nuisance is a substantial, unreasonable interference with a right of the general public. A private nuisance is a substantial, unreasonable interference with a person's right to the use and enjoyment of land. For either type of nuisance, the interference must be unreasonable, meaning that it would adversely affect a reasonable person and not just someone who is abnormally sensitive. Here, the high-frequency sound waves are a problem only for the breeder because her business (a kennel) is abnormally sensitive to them and, therefore, she cannot prevail on a nuisance claim against the businessman. Choice (A) is incorrect because "coming to the nuisance" is not an absolute defense. It is merely one factor the court will consider in weighing the equities. The fact that the sound waves are only a problem because of the breeder's abnormal sensitivity is, therefore, a stronger answer. Choice (C) is incorrect because trespass requires the entry of something tangible (although invisible gases and microscopic particles will suffice) onto the land of another. Sound waves are not sufficiently tangible to produce a trespass claim. Choice (D) is incorrect because in order to be considered a nuisance, the disturbance must *substantially and unreasonably* interfere with the use and enjoyment of one's land. Here, the company's testing of the whistles at the factory was not unreasonable, even though the sound waves substantially interfered with the breeder's business.

4. **(D)** Invasion of privacy occurs where a person intentionally intrudes, physically or otherwise, upon the solitude or seclusion of another person or his affairs. Here, although the burglary was certainly an invasion of the lawyer's privacy, it was the apprentice who did the burglary. Rather than suing the apprentice, the lawyer has asserted a claim against the columnist. The columnist should not be liable for the apprentice's invasion of the lawyer's privacy, unless he was a co-conspirator who had agreed to a plan for the burglary. Choice (A) is incorrect because even though the apprentice invaded the lawyer's privacy, that does not make the columnist liable. Choice (B) is incorrect because if the columnist had been a participant or co-conspirator with respect to the burglary, the fact that the material published was newsworthy would not necessarily save the columnist from liability. Although

there is a constitutional privilege to publish private facts if the matter is one of *legitimate public interest,* it is not an absolute privilege. An action for invasion of privacy may still exist where there is publication of a picture or information that is taken without the plaintiff's consent from a private place or where it is stolen or obtained by bribery or other inducement of breach of trust. Choice (C) is incorrect because "false light" is only one type of invasion of privacy, and it is not the most relevant type here. If the columnist had participated in the burglary or conspired to have it done, he could be liable for invasion of privacy, even if his publication did not portray the lawyer in a false light.

5. **(D)** Where a plaintiff suffers harm caused by a defendant's negligence, and then the plaintiff's injury is worsened by negligent medical treatment of the original injury, courts have long held that the subsequent medical malpractice is foreseeable and ordinarily not a superseding cause that relieves the original defendant of liability. The original defendant, thus, can be held liable for all of the plaintiff's harm, including the enhancement or aggravation of the injury attributable to the medical malpractice. The doctor will be jointly and severally liable along with the original tortfeasor, but the doctor's liability will be limited to the "extra" harm inflicted by the doctor's negligence and will not cover the original injury that the plaintiff suffered before the doctor even became involved in the situation. Under this rule, the truck driver would be liable for all of the plaintiff's harm, although the doctor may be held liable, as well, for the aggravation of the plaintiff's injury. Choice (A) is incorrect because the subsequent medical malpractice will be treated as foreseeable, rather than as a superseding cause. Choice (B) is incorrect because rather than being liable only for the original injury, the truck driver, instead, will be liable for all of the plaintiff's harm, including the part resulting from the subsequent medical malpractice. Choice (C) is incorrect because the truck driver may be held liable regardless of whether his negligence is found to be more or less severe than the doctor's negligence. Remember: On the Multistate Bar Exam, you should assume that joint and several liability applies unless the question states otherwise. Here, the truck driver alone will be liable for the original harm suffered by the plaintiff in the crash, and the truck driver and doctor will be jointly and severally liable for the aggravation of the injury that occurred because of the negligent medical treatment.

6. **(B)** To decide whether the "breach" element of a negligence claim is satisfied, a jury generally must consider all the facts and circumstances to assess whether the defendant exercised reasonable care. However, where the defendant violated a statute (or regulation, ordinance, etc.), the defendant's conduct may be deemed to be negligent *per se,* meaning that the person's conduct is automatically treated as negligent. In order for negligence *per se* to exist, the plaintiff must show that the accident that occurred was the sort of thing the legislature had in mind when it passed the statute. Specifically, the plaintiff must show that (1) the plaintiff is part of the general class of people that the statute was meant to protect; and (2) the plaintiff's injury was within the general type of harm that the statute was meant to prevent. Here, if the city council enacted the ordinance after someone was hit by a passing truck while washing his car, that would be a strong indication that the ordinance was meant to prevent people from being struck by passing vehicles while washing their cars, and was not meant to prevent accidents like the one that occurred because the water froze into a puddle on the street. If the accident was not the sort of thing the city council had in mind when it enacted the ordinance, negligence *per se* would not apply. Choice (A) is incorrect because the man's unawareness of the ordinance would not be a reason for him to avoid liability. Some excuses can be used to avoid negligence *per se,* such as if the defendant was unaware of a crucial fact. For example, if you violate a statute that requires cars to have working taillights, but you are unaware that your taillight has burned out, your unawareness of the fact that your taillight went out will be an excuse that avoids negligence *per se.* Ignorance of the law, however, is a different story and not a valid excuse. Choice (C) is incorrect because the fact that the driver knew the man had washed his car the previous day would not enable the man to avoid liability. At most, implied assumption of risk would reduce the plaintiff's recovery under comparative fault principles, rather than barring it completely. In addition, here, implied assumption of risk probably would not even apply, because the driver was not voluntarily choosing to encounter a known risk, because he did not know about the ice even if he did know the man had washed his car the previous day. Choice (D) is incorrect because the driver may invoke

negligence *per se,* even if he is not a resident of the city. In enacting the ordinance, the city council presumably meant to protect the safety of visitors to the city, as well as city residents.

7. **(C)** It is helpful to understand the difference between proximate, or legal, cause and causation in fact. First, ask yourself, "Has the conduct of the defendant caused the plaintiff's injury?" This is a question of fact. **Note:** Although the defendant's conduct may be the cause-in-fact of the plaintiff's harm, it (the tortious conduct) may or may not be the proximate cause. However, if the defendant's actions constitute the proximate cause, then it must, also, always be the cause-in-fact (of the plaintiff's injury). Here, the nurse's injection of the fatal dosage of morphine would be (1) the cause-in-fact, and (2) the legal, or proximate, cause of the patient's death. Choice (A) is incorrect because the death was a very foreseeable result of the nurse's action and, therefore, the nurse's negligence was the legal, or proximate, cause of the death. Choice (B) is incorrect because if the defendant's actions constitute the proximate cause, then it must, also, always be the cause-in-fact of the plaintiff's injury. Choice (D) is incorrect because the nurse's action was both a cause-in-fact (because the patient would not have died but for the overdose) and a proximate, or legal, cause of the patient's death (because the death was a foreseeable result of administering a fatal dose of morphine).

8. **(A)** The traditional common law rule was that a person who provided alcohol to a minor or a visibly intoxicated person was not liable for resulting harm. The customary explanation was that the drinker was the real cause of the harm, and the alcohol provider was too remote to be treated as a proximate cause of the injuries. A few states enacted "dram shop statutes," which imposed liability on those who serve alcohol to minors or visibly intoxicated people. Even in states without such statutes, however, the majority of courts eventually rejected the traditional rule in favor of holding that alcohol providers can be held liable for foreseeable harm resulting from serving alcohol to minors or visibly intoxicated people. Here, the bartender should have reasonably foreseen that by continuing to serve alcohol to an intoxicated customer, the drinker might endanger himself and others (especially in the operation of his motor vehicle). As a result, the bartender's conduct would be viewed as the proximate cause of the pedestrian's injuries because the automobile accident was a foreseeable intervening force for which the bartender must bear responsibility. Choices (B), (C), and (D) are incorrect because the bartender's actions were the proximate cause, not the superseding, direct, or intervening cause of the pedestrian's injuries.

9. **(D)** A 15-year-old boy who had been sledding on this pathway for a number of previous months should have realized the risk involved in sledding there. In order to recover under the "attractive nuisance" or "infant trespasser" doctrine, it is necessary that the child, because of youth, did not discover the dangerous condition or realize the risk involved. Choice (A) is incorrect because the attractive nuisance doctrine does not apply where the child discovered the dangerous condition or realized the risk involved. Choice (B) is incorrect because even if the woman knew or should have known of the frequent trespasses, she would not be liable if the boy should have realized the risk. Choice (C) is incorrect because the boy's status is not, by itself, enough to bar the claim. He could recover under the attractive nuisance doctrine despite being a trespasser, but not here, because he should have realized the risk here.

10. **(A)** In general, a defendant is liable only if its negligence is a "but for" cause of the plaintiff's injury. That means the plaintiff's injury would not have occurred but for the defendant's negligence. Special rules apply, however, in situations where there are two (or more) things that combine to cause the plaintiff's injury, and any one of them would have been sufficient by itself to cause the injury. In these "duplicative cause" situations, neither thing is actually a but for cause of the plaintiff's injury, but each will be treated as a cause of the plaintiff's injury if it was a substantial factor contributing to the occurrence of the injury. For example, if two defendants negligently start separate fires near your property, both fires then combine to burn down your house, and either one of them

would have been sufficient by itself to cause the damage, each of the two fires will be treated as an actual cause, even though neither was really a but for or essential cause of the harm. In the duplicative cause situations, two or more causes happen at the same time. On the other hand, a "preemptive cause" scenario occurs where one thing causes the plaintiff's injury, and then another potential cause of the same occurs, but it is too late, because it does not take effect until all the harm has already been inflicted. In that situation, only the first thing will be treated as a cause of the plaintiff's injury. This question involves a preemptive cause, rather than a duplicative cause situation. The crop-duster's mistake killed all the corn plants, and the harm was already done before the construction company's negligence and the fire occurred. Therefore, only the crop-duster will be liable because its negligence occurred before the construction company's negligence. Choice (B) is incorrect because the construction company's negligence happened too late to be a cause of the farmer's loss of his corn crop. Choice (C) is incorrect because even though both the crop-duster and construction company were negligent, the crop-duster's negligence occurred first and inflicted all the harm before. The construction company's negligence was too late to cause any of the harm. Choice (D) is incorrect because even though actual cause is generally analyzed through the but for test, special rules apply in duplicative cause and preemptive cause situations. Here, the crop-duster's negligence will be treated as an actual cause of the farmer's loss, even though it was not really a but for cause, because the construction company's negligence would have been sufficient to cause the same damage.

11. **(C)** Offensive odors or loud noises may constitute a private nuisance when they unreasonably and substantially interfere with the use and enjoyment of the plaintiff's land. Choice (A) is incorrect because "coming to the nuisance" (i.e., the fact that the plaintiff moved in after the stable had been built) is not a valid defense to a private nuisance claim and, instead, is merely a factor that a court would consider in deciding whether to grant an injunction. Choice (B) is incorrect because although a property owner is entitled to make reasonable use of property, if that use creates a substantial interference with the use and enjoyment of another's land, it may be enjoined. Choice (D) is incorrect because in order for an injunction to be granted, the crucial consideration is if there was a substantial interference with the plaintiff's use and enjoyment of his property, not whether the defendant was negligent.

12. **(A)** Recently, questions dealing with *directed verdicts and summary judgments* have appeared on the Multistate. Although Civil Procedure is still not a primary Multistate subject, it can be tested in a "crossover" or secondary fashion. A motion for summary judgment is a *pretrial procedure* of "going behind the pleadings" to determine whether a genuine dispute actually exists. To obtain a summary judgment, the moving party must show that *no genuine issue of material fact exists.* A directed verdict, on the other hand, may be requested at the end of a plaintiff's case or after all the evidence is completed. The moving party is basically arguing that the evidence clearly reveals that he must prevail and that there is no reason to send the case to the jury. In deciding whether a directed verdict should be granted, all the evidence is viewed in the light most favorable to the non-moving party. In the present example, the woman is asserting a claim against the man to recover damages caused by the tree falling on her property. In all likelihood, the proper cause of action would be for trespass. In order to prevail, the woman must prove that the man intentionally, negligently, or as a result of an abnormally dangerous activity, caused the tree to enter her land. Obviously, the man did not intentionally cause the tree to fall, because it was uprooted during a storm, nor was the man engaged in an ultrahazardous or abnormally dangerous activity. Therefore, in order for the woman to prevail, she must prove that the man negligently caused the tree to fall. Because the woman did not produce such evidence, choice (A) is correct. Choices (B), (C), and (D) are incorrect because in order for the woman to prevail, she must prove that the man negligently caused the tree to fall.

13. **(C)** As a general rule, a surviving child has a right to recover for tortiously inflicted prenatal injuries. While foreseeability of future injury alone does not establish the existence of a duty owing to an unborn infant by its mother's physicians, it is now beyond dispute that in the case of negligence resulting in prenatal injuries, both the mother and the child *in utero* may be directly injured and are owed a duty. See Albala *v. City of New York,* 54 N.Y.2d 269

(1981). Furthermore, the case of *Highson v. St. Frances Hospital,* 459 N.Y 2d 814 (1983) followed these principles in holding that a cognizable and independent cause of action exists on behalf of the infant *in utero* who is born alive, against a physician for prenatal injuries. Because the discoloration of the child's teeth was proximately caused by the physician's failure to administer a pregnancy test and by his prescription of tetracycline to his pregnant mother, the child may successfully maintain a cause of action for malpractice against the physician. Therefore, choice (C) is correct. Choices (A) and (B) are incorrect because an unborn child does have the right to maintain an action for tortiously inflicted prenatal injuries as a surviving child. Choice (D) presumes that if the wife was negligent in failing to seek proper prenatal care, that would eliminate the action against the physician. However the negligence on the part of the physician would in all probability be the proximate cause of the malpractice action, making (C) a better choice than (D).

14. **(C)** A person is subject to liability for battery if she acts *with the intention of causing* a harmful or offensive contact with the person of the other, and if an offensive or harmful contact directly or indirectly results. If offensive contact occurs unintentionally, then there is no liability for battery. Intent exists if the defendant had the purpose or desire of achieving the harmful or offensive contact or if the defendant acted with actual knowledge that the harmful or offensive contact was substantially certain to occur. Here, the graduate vomited involuntarily. She did not desire to vomit on the customer, nor could she have known with substantial certainty that one drink would make her sick. She thus lacked the requisite intent to be liable for tortious battery. Choice (A) is incorrect because the act was unintentional. Intent is required for the tort of intentional infliction of emotional distress. Choice (B) is incorrect because, even though an offensive touching resulted, there was no intent to cause that offensive touching. Choice (D) is incorrect because the graduate's lack of awareness of what she was drinking may be negligence, but the act was involuntary, thereby lacking the intent necessary for a battery.

15. **(C)** For *res ipsa loquitur* to create an inference of negligence, (1) the event must be of a kind that ordinarily does not occur in the absence of someone's negligence; (2) it must be caused by an agency or instrumentality within the exclusive control of the defendant; and (3) it must not have been due to any voluntary action or contribution on the part of the plaintiff. In applying the doctrine of *res ipsa loquitur* to the issue of the toy store's liability for the woman's fall, the second requirement is crucial, namely, "Was the baseball within the *exclusive control* of the defendant?" Although the toy store had control of the premises in general, that does not mean it had exclusive control of everything in the store. Another customer may have caused the baseball to be on the floor and, thus, *res ipsa loquitur* would not apply here. Choice (A) is incorrect because the fact that the plaintiff was an invitee and the store had a duty to make its premises safe is not sufficient to make *res ipsa loquitur* apply. Choice (B) is incorrect because even though the toy store was in control of its premises, it was not in exclusive control of the particular instrumentality—the baseball on the floor—that caused harm here. Choice (D) is incorrect because the baseball would be an existing condition and, therefore, part of the "set stage," rather than an intervening act.

16. **(D)** The key to Multistate (or other multiple-choice) testing is always to remember that the test maker's main goal is to hide the correct answer! Here, for example, the test maker is trying to mislead students into thinking that this hypothetical situation involves either trespass to chattels or conversion. On the other hand, this is a straightforward negligence question. The student lent the classmate his car to attend a concert. The classmate drove the car to the concert where it was struck. The distracter, or "red herring," intended to confuse you is that the classmate went on a diversion and purchased marijuana. However, the accident did not occur while he was making unauthorized use of the vehicle. As such, there is no liability for either conversion or trespass to chattels. **Exam Tip:** In analyzing Torts questions, remember that an essential element of the plaintiff's cause of action for negligence—or for any other tort, for that matter—is that there must be some reasonable connection (i.e., causation) between the defendant's act and the damage that the plaintiff has suffered. In sum, the classmate's diversion was not the cause of the accident. Choices (A), (B), and (C) are incorrect because there was no conversion or trespass to chat-

tels, and so the classmate would not be liable because he was not negligent in a way that caused the car to be damaged.

17. **(D)** When a city performs a service that might as well be provided by a private corporation, and particularly when it collects revenue from it, the function is considered a "proprietary" one, as to which there may be liability for the torts of municipal agents within the scope of their employment. This is true where the city supplies water, gas, or electricity, or where it operates a ferry, an airport, or a public market. The municipal electrical company, therefore, can be liable if its employee's conduct was negligent. Since the facts indicate that the repairman had properly fixed the ladder in place, Choice (D) is the best answer. Choice (A) is incorrect because the plaintiff will not necessarily be able to recover just because he was attempting a rescue. Under the "rescue doctrine" in tort law, the fact that a person will come to the rescue in an emergency is deemed to be foreseeable. Foreseeability alone, however, is not enough to produce liability. The plaintiff here would need to show that the defendant was negligent, not just that the plaintiff's rescue attempt was foreseeable. Choice (B) is incorrect because there is no basis for strict liability here. The electric company was not selling a defective product. Even if repairing a high-voltage power line might be considered an abnormally dangerous activity, most courts would not impose strict liability for that on a municipally owned company. Choice (C) is incorrect because even if the rescuer were negligent, that would not bar him from recovering if the defendant were also negligent. The plaintiff's negligence would merely reduce the plaintiff's recovery under comparative fault principles. In some states, the plaintiff's recovery would not even be reduced because a rescuer's fault would be ignored unless the rescuer was grossly or wantonly negligent.

18. **(A)** A trespasser is someone who enters land without the owner's express or implied permission. In the present case, the pedestrian would be classified as a trespasser because he entered the premises without the club's permission. Choices (B), (C), and (D) are incorrect because the pedestrian entered the premises without permission and would be classified as a trespasser. Guests, licensees, and invitees enter with some permissive status.

19. **(C)** As a general rule, a possessor of land owes *no duty of care to undiscovered or unanticipated trespassers.* However, once a landowner discovers the presence of a trespasser (or should know of the likelihood of trespassers), then there is a duty *to warn the trespasser of any dangerous conditions known to the occupier or owner of the property.* In the present case, the gym owner knew of the existence of a dangerous condition (namely, the malfunctioning of the electric dryer in the restroom). As a result, the defendant owed a duty to warn trespassers of this dangerous condition. Choice (A) is incorrect because the presence of trespassers in the restrooms was known or foreseeable to the gym owner. Choice (B) is incorrect because the man was a trespasser, so the duty owed to him is to warn of any known dangers, not a duty to inspect. Choice (D) is incorrect because it is the wrong duty owed to a trespasser. The duty is not absolute, but rather the duty owed is to warn of any known dangers.

20. **(D)** A person who enters the premises upon business that concerns the occupier, and upon his invitation (express or implied), is an invitee. The occupant of the property is under an affirmative duty to protect invitees not only against dangers of which the occupant knows, but also against those, which with reasonable care, he might discover. The invitee is sometimes called a business visitor; the typical example is the customer in a store or the patron of a restaurant, bank, theater, fair, or other place of amusement. The occupier is not an insurer of the safety of invitees; he must not only warn of latent dangers that the occupier knows of, but he must also inspect the premises to discover possible dangerous conditions of which he does not know. Choice (A) is incorrect because the duty owed to an invitee is to warn and inspect for dangerous conditions, but it is not an absolute duty. Choice (B) is incorrect because the customer will not recover only if the theater had prior knowledge of the dangerous condition, but also if the theater failed to make a reasonable inspection of the premises. In this respect, the theater has an affirmative duty to inspect the premises and to make them reasonably safe for the protection of its customers.

Choice (C) is incorrect because the theater was under a duty to make a reasonable inspection of the safety of the premises for its customers.

21. **(A)** In cases where a person is injured because something was in food that was not supposed to be there, a "reasonable consumer expectations" test is used in most states. Many years ago, some courts drew a rigid distinction between "foreign" and "natural" items in food. If the item was natural (such as a bone or piece of shell hidden in a dish of food), the defendant who prepared the food would not be liable. If the item was foreign, however, then liability could be imposed. Most courts now have rejected the "foreign/natural" test and, instead, ask whether the presence of the harmful item in the food would have been anticipated by a reasonable consumer. If a reasonable consumer would not have expected a pebble to be in the chowder, then the plaintiff will be able to recover for his injured tooth. Choice (B) is incorrect because there is no requirement that the defendant have prior notice of the defect. Choice (C) is incorrect because strict liability is available in these circumstances. The chowder would be a defective and unreasonably dangerous product, and so the plaintiff would be able to recover under strict liability even though a reasonable inspection by the restaurant would not have led to discovery of the pebble. Choice (D) is incorrect because liability could be imposed on the restaurant if the presence of the pebble in the chowder was something that a reasonable consumer would not expect.

22. **(D)** Under the doctrine of *respondeat superior,* an employer can be held vicariously liable for torts committed by its employees within the scope of their employment. For example, if a furniture company has an employee driving a truck around town to deliver furniture to its customers, the company will be vicariously liable if the truck driver's negligent driving causes harm to someone. On the other hand, when employees are merely commuting to and from work, they are not acting within the scope of their employment, and their employer is not liable if they drive negligently. Here, the law firm will not be liable for the accident that occurred while the law clerk was driving home from work. Choice (A) is incorrect because an auto accident was not a foreseeable risk of the law firm requiring the law clerk to work late for one night. Choice (B) is incorrect because an employer is only liable for torts of its employees committed within the scope of their employment, not for all the employees' actions. Choice (C) is incorrect because causation is just one element of negligence, and is not by itself enough to make the employer liable.

23. **(B)** Under the doctrine of *respondeat superior,* a master is vicariously liable for the torts of a servant committed within the scope of employment. The servant's conduct is within the scope of employment if it is of the kind the servant is employed to perform, occurs substantially within the authorized limit of time and space, and is actuated, at least in part, by a purpose to serve the master. Generally, an employer will be liable even if the injury occurs during an employee's temporary departure from the performance of the work, provided that the deviation from the work was the sort of thing that is foreseeable and expected of employees. Even though the employee was making an unauthorized delivery to his girlfriend at the time he drove through the red light and injured the driver, he was still en route from the drugstore to make another separate, authorized delivery. The drugstore, therefore, can be held liable for the employee's negligence. Choice (A) is incorrect because the fact that the employee paid for the perfume has no bearing on the fact that there was at the time of the accident a master-servant relationship that existed between the employee and the drugstore. Choice (C) is incorrect because the employee was not acting outside the scope of employment, since his deviation from his work was minor and foreseeable. Choice (D) is incorrect because the drugstore can be liable under the doctrine of *respondeat superior,* even if it was not negligent in hiring the employee.

24. **(C)** When one party (such as an employer) is held vicariously liable for harm caused by the negligent conduct of another (such as an employee), the party held vicariously liable is entitled to indemnification from the tortfeasor.

Indemnification means that the full amount of the loss ultimately will be paid by the tortfeasor who was most directly responsible for causing it. The furniture store was held vicariously liable for its employee's negligence and, therefore, it is entitled to be indemnified by the employee for the full $25,000 loss. Choice (A) is incorrect because through indemnification, the furniture store's loss may be shifted to the employee, the party who was primarily at fault. Choice (B) is incorrect because the employer is entitled to full indemnification, not just contribution or partial reimbursement for some of the loss. Choice (D) is incorrect because the furniture store is entitled to indemnification regardless of whether it had insurance covering the amount of the judgment won by the injured plaintiff.

25. **(B)** The student's product liability cause of action will be predicated upon the theory of express warranty due to the fact that the box depicted an off-duty marine wearing the military headgear while riding a bicycle. The student relied upon this pictorial representation as an assertion that the helmet was suitable for this use. As a result, the corporation will be held liable for the student's misuse of the product under this products liability theory. Choice (A) is incorrect because there is no inference of negligence on the part of the corporation. The mere fact that the helmet came off the student's head in a bicycle accident does not necessarily establish an inference of negligence. Choice (C) is incorrect because in the area of products liability, a manufacturer must be held to foresee a certain amount of misuse or carelessness (e.g., standing on a chair) on the part of the user. Choice (D) is not the best answer because, even though the helmet may have been properly designed for its intended use, the fact remains that some misuse is foreseeable, especially here, when the box itself has this depiction on it. Moreover, the student is not necessarily arguing that the helmet was improperly designed; rather, she would be suing under an express warranty theory, so the fact that the helmet was properly designed is a fact that is irrelevant and will not help the corporation.

26. **(C)** The fact that an injured plaintiff has insurance covering a loss does not prevent liability from being imposed on a tortfeasor who caused the plaintiff's injury. The insurance company may wind up receiving the money that the plaintiff wins in the lawsuit, such as through subrogation principles under which the insurance company "stands in the shoes" of the plaintiff and recovers for the loss for which it provided coverage. That is a matter between the insurance company and the insured, however, and it does not affect the tortfeasor's liability. Choice (C) is correct because the manufacturer will be strictly liable if it sold a defective and unreasonably dangerous product. Choice (A) is incorrect because a tortfeasor is liable for damages even though the plaintiff had insurance covering the property damaged. Choice (B) is incorrect because strict liability for selling a defective product applies even if the manufacturer was not aware of the defect. Choice (D) is incorrect because the manufacturer will be strictly liable regardless of whether it failed to inspect the crane adequately or did anything else that was negligent.

27. **(B)** In this situation, the friend would be liable for the intentional tort of assault because the owner feared that he would hit him. Simply defined, assault is an act by the defendant that creates a *reasonable apprehension* in the plaintiff of immediate harmful or offensive contact to the plaintiff's person. Choice (A) is incorrect because the friend is liable for the intentional tort of assault, not for negligence. A negligence claim would require proof of some actual harm. Choice (C) is incorrect because it is *not necessary to prove actual damages* to sustain an action for assault. Choice (D) is incorrect because a defendant can be liable for assault even if he was merely trying to play a joke.

28. **(A)** In a basic "intentional infliction of emotional distress" scenario, the defendant does something extreme and outrageous, and the plaintiff is the target of that act. A trickier situation arises where the plaintiff was not the target of the defendant's extreme and outrageous act, and the plaintiff, instead, suffered severe emotional distress because of something the defendant did to a third person. The plaintiff can recover for intentional infliction

of emotional distress in such a situation if either of the following two requirements is present: (1) the defendant knew the plaintiff was present, and the plaintiff was a close family member of the person who was the target of the defendant's extreme and outrageous conduct, or (2) the defendant knew the plaintiff was present, and what the plaintiff witnessed was so shocking that it caused the plaintiff to suffer actual physical harm, such as a heart attack or stroke. Because the security guard knew the barber was present, and the barber suffered a heart attack from seeing the security guard pretend that he was about to shoot the friend, the barber will be able to hold the security guard liable for intentional infliction of emotional distress. Choice (B) is incorrect because the fact that the security guard could be liable to the friend for assault does not determine whether the security guard could be liable to the barber for intentional infliction of emotional distress. Choice (C) is incorrect because even if the barber is not a member of the friend's family, he can recover for intentional infliction of emotional distress because he suffered a bodily injury when he had a heart attack. Choice (D) is incorrect because foreseeability of the harm is not an element of an intentional infliction of emotional distress claim. Furthermore, in any event, the security guard knew the barber had a bad heart, so the resulting injury here was very foreseeable.

29. **(C)** In order that a negligent actor shall be liable for another's harm, it is necessary not only that the actor's conduct be negligent toward the other, but also that the negligence of the actor be a legal cause of the other's harm. In the present case, if the subway was not negligent, then it cannot be held liable. There are situations in which the actor is under a *special responsibility* to protect the plaintiff from the intentional, or even criminal, misconduct of others. Among such relations are those of (1) carrier and passenger, (2) innkeeper and guest, (3) employer and employee, (4) inviter and business visitor, (5) school district and pupil, and (6) bailee and bailor, among others. However, in such situations, the defendant is under a duty to exercise reasonable care. Choice (A) is incorrect because if the subway was not negligent, then it did not fail to exercise reasonable care. Choice (B) is incorrect because while it is factually correct that the sudden stop caused the resident to fall onto the commuter, the subway company will not be liable unless there was negligence. Choice (D) is incorrect because the commuter could prevail against the subway company if the resident was negligent. That is because of the special relationship that exists between a common carrier and its passengers and its duty to exercise reasonable care in protecting those passengers.

30. **(D)** When a person has reasonable grounds to believe that he is being or is about to be attacked, he may use such force as is reasonably necessary for protection against the potential injury. The actor need only have a reasonable belief as to the other party's actions. In other words, apparent necessity, not actual necessity, is sufficient. As a result, reasonable mistake as to the existence of the danger does not vitiate the defense. Choice (D) is, therefore, correct because the hunter reasonably acted in self-defense when he shot at the hiker. Note that if, in the course of reasonably defending himself, one accidentally injures a bystander, he is nevertheless protected by the defense. Choice (A) is incorrect because it refers to the doctrine of transferred intent, which is not applicable here because the hunter acted reasonably in self-defense. Choice (B) is incorrect because even though the trespasser suffered a harmful and offensive contact, the hunter reasonably acted in self-defense, which would preclude the trespasser from recovering under a battery theory. Choice (C) is incorrect because although the hunter accidentally shot the trespasser, the hunter acted reasonably in self-defense when he shot at the hiker.

31. **(C)** To be liable for assault, the defendant must have intended to put the plaintiff in apprehension of imminent harmful or offensive contact. It is not essential that the defendant intended for the contact actually to occur; it is enough that the defendant intended for the plaintiff to think that the contact would occur. Therefore, the hunter will not be liable for assault unless he intended to frighten the hiker. Choice (A) is incorrect because the fact that the rifle was pointed at the hiker is not enough to create liability without the required intent. Choice (B) is incorrect because even though the hunter decided to carry the gun, he will not be liable for assault unless he intended to put the hiker in apprehension of imminent harmful or offensive contact. Choice (D) is incorrect because the hunter

would be liable for assault if he intended to frighten the hiker, regardless of whether he actually intended to shoot him.

32. **(B)** One who intentionally or recklessly causes severe emotional distress to another by extreme and outrageous conduct is subject to liability for such emotional distress and, if bodily harm results, for such bodily harm as well. In the present case, the pilot's conduct was extreme and outrageous. Furthermore, the girlfriend suffered sufficient emotional distress because the facts indicate that she was panic-stricken. **Exam Tip:** For bar exam purposes, emotional distress includes any of the following types of mental suffering: fright, horror, grief, shame, humiliation, embarrassment, anger, chagrin, disappointment, worry, and nausea. Choice (A) is incorrect because the tort of intentional infliction of emotional distress requires severe and outrageous conduct by the defendant, not just something a reasonable person would find distressing. Choice (C) is incorrect because the pilot should have been substantially certain that the girlfriend would suffer emotional distress, and substantial certainty can establish the intent element for an intentional tort. Choice (D) is incorrect because physical injury is not a required element for intentional infliction of emotional distress.

33. **(B)** For many defamation issues, determining whether the plaintiff is a public or private figure is crucial. A public figure is an individual who has (1) achieved pervasive fame or notoriety (e.g., a movie star or celebrity sports figure), or (2) has voluntarily injected himself/herself into a public controversy. A plaintiff who is a public figure will be required to prove malice in order to recover for defamation. Malice means that the defendant either knew the allegedly defamatory statements were false or acted with reckless disregard for whether they were true or false. Here, the professor is properly viewed as a private figure, even though he may be well known within the bar review industry. Because he is a private figure, the plaintiff merely needs to prove that the newspaper acted negligently, rather than that it acted with malice. Choice (A) is incorrect because it suggests the plaintiff must prove malice here, which is not true because the plaintiff is a private figure. Choices (C) and (D) are incorrect because they suggest the newspaper cannot be held liable, but the plaintiff here can recover if he proves the newspaper was negligent.

34. **(A)** As a general rule, a person detained by the police may recover for false imprisonment unless there was a lawful arrest. Choice (B) is incorrect because consent bars liability for an intentional tort only if the plaintiff was capable of giving valid consent. If the student was highly intoxicated, and the police were aware of that fact, the student's consent would be invalid. Choice (C) is incorrect because the police can be held liable for false imprisonment under some circumstances, such as if they detain someone without a valid reason and without following proper arrest procedures. Choice (D) is incorrect because a defendant may be held liable for false imprisonment even if the plaintiff suffered no specific harm other than being aware of being confined.

35. **(A)** Negligence is failure to exercise the care of a reasonable person under the circumstances. The police were negligent because they should have realized it was dangerous to drop off the man where they did. Choice (B) is incorrect because knowledge of the plaintiff's intoxication is only a factor in determining whether the defendant's actions were negligent. Choice (A) is a better, more complete answer as to why the police were negligent. Choice (C) is incorrect because the plaintiff's choice does not bar liability from being imposed for the negligent actions taken by the police. Choice (D) is incorrect because the motorist's act was a very foreseeable consequence of the police officers' actions, rather than a superseding cause that would bar the officers' liability.

36. **(B)** This is a tricky question dealing with intervening causation. Where a defendant causes injury to a plaintiff, and then subsequent medical malpractice causes the plaintiff's injury to be worsened, courts will treat the subse-

quent medical malpractice as a foreseeable result of the defendant's original negligence. Even if the particular act of medical malpractice in a specific situation may not really be foreseeable, it is generally foreseeable that sometimes medical malpractice will occur, and so courts will treat the subsequent medical malpractice as foreseeable and hold the original tortfeasor responsible for the plaintiff's entire injury. So here, since the man's conduct in pushing the helper out of the truck was negligent, the man will be liable for the helper's injuries, including the sterility resulting from the nurse's error. Choice (A) is a weaker answer because although it contains a correct statement about the foreseeability issue, it does not address whether the man was negligent. If the man was not negligent in pushing the helper, then the man would not be liable for the sterility. Choice (C) is incorrect because if the man was negligent, he can be held liable for the sterility, and the nurse's error will not be a supervening cause that breaks the link between the man's original negligence and the sterility. Choice (D) is incorrect because courts will treat subsequent medical malpractice as being foreseeable.

37. **(D)** In this question, your natural inclination is to find the owner liable for failing to have the elevator inspected. However, in any negligence action, it is necessary that the defendant's negligent conduct be the legal cause of the plaintiff's harm. Here, the woman was injured when she was assaulted by the man. She was not injured by the stalling of the elevator. Therefore, the man's action would be viewed as a superseding cause (or unforeseeable intervening force). The attack did occur when the elevator was stalled, but the connection between the stalling and the attack was basically happenstance. In other words, the attack could just as easily have occurred even if the elevator had not stalled. The owner, therefore, should not be liable on the basis of his failure to ensure that the elevator was properly inspected and maintained. The woman could try to assert a negligence claim based on a theory that the building had inadequate security, but such a claim would be successful only if the woman could prove that the owner was aware of similar crimes occurring in the building in the past. Otherwise, the foreseeability required for liability to be imposed on the owner would be absent. Choice (D) is, therefore, the best answer because it indicates that the owner will not be liable because there had been no previous assaults in the building. Choice (A) is incorrect because, regardless of the woman's status in the building, the owner would not be liable to the woman because of the inadequate connection between the owner's negligence (in not ensuring that the elevator was well inspected and maintained) and the woman's injuries. Choice (B) is incorrect because vicarious liability does not exist here. The contract between the owner and the company does not create an employee-employer relationship, which is necessary to find vicarious liability. Moreover, neither the owner nor the company would be liable for the woman's injuries because of the inadequate connection between the negligence and the injuries. Choice (C) is incorrect because even if the woman's conduct was viewed as negligent, this would only reduce her recovery through comparative negligence, not eliminate any potential recovery.

38. **(C)** Liability for false imprisonment can be imposed where the defendant did an act with the intent of causing the plaintiff to be confined within a limited area, with the result that the plaintiff is confined within a limited area for an appreciable amount of time and is either aware of or harmed by the confinement. As for any intentional tort, intent is a crucial requirement. The required intent can exist where the defendant had the purpose or desire of causing the required result or where the defendant acted with knowledge that the result was substantially certain to occur. Here, the owner of the building might be liable for negligence, but would not be liable for false imprisonment because he or she had no intent for the lawyer (or anyone else) to be confined. Choice (A) is incorrect because the confinement lasted long enough to qualify as false imprisonment, but the intent element is not fulfilled here. Choice (B) is incorrect because the lack of intent bars recovery for false imprisonment here, even though the plaintiff was injured. Choice (D) is incorrect because the lawyer was aware of her confinement for the first few minutes of the confinement, and also because she injured her head as a result of the confinement.

39. **(D)** Liability for negligence generally depends on whether the defendant acted with the care of an ordinary reasonable person under the circumstances. A child, however, is not expected to be able to act as carefully and reasonably as

an adult. Instead, a child is expected to act with as much care as a reasonable child of the same age, intelligence, and experience. This rule enables children to "act their age" and not be held liable for conduct that is below the standard of care that would apply to adults. While that is the general rule for children, an exception applies where a child engages in an activity that is adult in nature, such as operating a car, airplane, or other motor vehicle. Most courts generally seem to agree that a very young child, such as one under the age of 4 or 5 years, is not capable of negligence. A minority of states use a more specific rule known as the "rule of sevens," under which a child under the age of 7 years is treated as being incapable of negligence, and a child from the age of 7 to 14 years is presumptively incapable of negligence. Most states have rejected the rule of sevens and, instead, simply say that very young children are incapable of negligence, without being as specific as the rule of sevens would require. Here, the boy was well above the age of 4 or 5 years, at which age children become capable of negligence; he was not engaged in an adult activity like driving a car, so the general standard of care for children will apply. In other words, the issue will be whether the boy exercised as much care as a reasonable child of the same age, intelligence, and experience would use under the same circumstances. Choice (A) is incorrect because a 12-year-old child's conduct can be negligent. Choice (B) is incorrect because there is nothing unreasonable about trying to find a bathroom to use. The guest could not have expected and did not assume the risk of a bucket falling on his head. Moreover, even if the guest had acted unreasonably, that would merely reduce his damages to some extent under comparative fault principles, rather than barring his claim completely. Choice (C) is incorrect because even though the practical joke was a very dangerous thing to do, it was not an "adult" type of activity, like driving a car and, therefore, the adult standard of care would not apply.

40. **(A)** Traditionally, a merchant could stop a person suspected of shoplifting; but the merchant would be liable for false imprisonment if it turned out that the person was not actually guilty of shoplifting, even if the merchant acted very reasonably and in good faith. In other words, a merchant's privilege to detain shoplifters was very limited and turned on whether the detained person actually had stolen something, not on whether there was a reasonable basis for the merchant's suspicions. Most states have now modified that traditional rule, either by statutes or court decisions, so that the shopkeeper's privilege is broader and allows the merchant to avoid liability if the merchant acts reasonably. The merchant's actions must be reasonable both in the sense that there was a reasonable basis for thinking the person had stolen something and in the sense that the merchant handled the situation reasonably and did not detain the person longer than reasonably necessarily to realize that a mistake had been made and the person was innocent. A 30-minute detention may be an unreasonably long period of time to question a shopper and to discover that a mistake has been made and the shopper is not guilty of any crime. In fact, there are a number of decisions holding department stores liable for false imprisonment involving detentions of 30 minutes or less. Choice (B) is incorrect because the store's employee had reasonable grounds for thinking the woman might be the shoplifter, so the store would not have been liable if it had detained the woman briefly to determine that she was not the thief. It was the length of the detention that was unreasonable here. Choice (C) is incorrect because although the store's employee had reasonable grounds for detaining the woman, the length of the detention was unreasonable. Choice (D) is incorrect because the fact that the store employee eventually permitted the woman to leave does not prevent the store from being liable for false imprisonment if the detention was unreasonable in length.

41. **(C)** In the vacationer's personal injury action against the owner of the park, he will rely principally upon the doctrine of joint venture. The four basic elements of a joint enterprise are as follows: (1) an agreement, express or implied, among the members of the group; (2) a common purpose to be carried out by the group; (3) a community of pecuniary interest in that purpose, among the members; and (4) an equal right to a voice in the direction of the enterprise, which gives an equal right of control. The law then treats each member of the joint enterprise as the agent or servant of the others, and so the act of any one within the scope of the enterprise can be charged vicariously to the rest. Choices (A) and (B) are incorrect because this question involves a joint venture, rather than the type of master-servant or employer-employee relationship that creates vicarious liability through *respondeat superior.*

Choice (D) is incorrect because it is necessary to show liability based upon a joint venture before imputing negligence to the defendant.

42. **(A)** Under the doctrine of *respondeat superior,* an employer is liable for the torts of employees committed within the scope of their employment. Difficult questions often arise about whether an employee's conduct was a total departure from the employer's business or just a roundabout way of doing it. When an employee acts outside the scope of employment, it also can be difficult to determine when the departure from the employer's work is over and the employee has returned to being within the scope of employment. In general, as long as the event occurs during work hours and there is an intent on the part of the employee to serve the employer's purpose, the employer will be liable. Here, the man did not have authorization from his employer to entrust the supervision of the shop to his friend while he was in the bathroom. However, this did occur during the man's work hours, and it was done with the purpose of serving the employer's purposes of operating the shop. The company, therefore, should be vicariously liable for the man's actions here, even though they were unauthorized. Choice (B) is incorrect because the company is vicariously liable for the man's actions, but not for the friend's actions. Choice (C) is incorrect because entrusting the shop to the friend was done within the scope of the man's employment, even if it was not specifically authorized. Choice (D) is incorrect because the company can be held vicariously liable for the man's negligence in entrusting the shop to a friend who did not know how to work the grinding machine.

43. **(D)** The customer would not have any cause of action against the ski resort. The intentional torts of false imprisonment and assault require proof that the defendant acted intentionally, while negligence requires proof that the defendant failed to exercise reasonable care. Here, there is no indication that the ski resort did anything with the intention of trapping the customer on the ski lift, and no indication that the ski lift failed to act with reasonable care. Choices (A), (B), and (C) are incorrect because the customer would not have any cause of action against the ski resort because there was no intentional tort or negligence on the part of the ski resort or its employees.

44. **(A)** The law has always placed a higher value upon human safety than upon mere rights in property, so the majority rule is that *there is no privilege to use any force calculated to cause death or serious bodily injury merely to repel a threat to land or chattels.* A privilege to use such force will exist only if there is a sufficient threat to a person's safety as well as to property interests. The plaintiff here, therefore, will prevail because the guard used unreasonable force. Choice (B) is incorrect because even if the guard had given a warning that he had a gun and was about to shoot and the young man kept running, the guard would not have been entitled to shoot the young man. Choices (C) and (D) are incorrect because the law has always placed a higher value upon human safety than upon mere rights in property. Therefore, the fact that the young man was guilty of trespass and theft would not justify the guard's use of force likely to cause death or serious bodily injury.

45. **(D)** A defendant has no duty of care as to a trespasser whose presence is unknown to him. Further, the owner was under no duty to warn the burglar, a trespasser, of the company's use of deadly force because the owner had duly ordered the company to discontinue its protection service. Consequently, the owner will not bear responsibility for the actions of the protection service. Choice (A) is incorrect because the fact that the burglar was unarmed does not make the owner liable for something that the company's security guard did after the owner terminated the company's services. Choice (B) is incorrect because the owner will not be liable regardless of whether he knew or should have known that the company provided an "armed response." Choice (C) is incorrect because the owner cannot avoid liability on the grounds that he was not present. He will prevail and not be liable because he had already canceled the company's services, not because he was not present at the scene of the shooting.

46. **(A)** Sovereign immunity does not attach to non-delegable duties that are "proprietary" in nature. When the city performs a service that might as well be provided by a private corporation, and particularly when it collects revenue from it, the function is considered a "proprietary" one, as to which there may be liability for the torts of municipal agents within the scope of their employment. On the other hand, immunity from tort liability does attach to functions performed in a "governmental," "political," or "public" capacity. The following are examples of proprietary functions: where a city supplies water, gas, electricity, or where it operates a ferry, wharves, docks, an airport, or public market. Here, the municipal water department should not be protected from liability by sovereign immunity because the water department's agent was negligent with respect to services of a proprietary nature. Choice (B) is incorrect because strict liability would not apply. Choice (C) is incorrect because the municipal water department could be held liable for negligence with respect to a non-delegable duty. Choice (D) is incorrect because sovereign immunity would not apply to this work relating to a proprietary function performed by the city.

47. **(C)** In a negligence case, the plaintiff generally has the burden of proving that the defendant was negligent and that this negligence was a cause of the accident. Proof that the traffic signal was functioning properly would be very helpful proof for the carpenter's case because it would strongly suggest that the bus driver ran through a red light. That would establish that the bus driver was negligent *per se* and that the bus driver's bad driving caused the accident. Choice (A) is incorrect because the fact that the bus driver had some speeding tickets in the past would provide only minimal support for the contention that the bus driver was negligent on this occasion. Choice (B) is incorrect because the fact that the carpenter's car was in good shape and had been recently inspected would shed little light on whether the bus driver was negligent and caused this accident. Choice (D) is incorrect because the fact that the bus driver did not have a driver's license would do little to establish negligence or causation here. While driving without a license is a statutory violation, it probably would not constitute negligence *per se* because it is a technical or administrative requirement, rather than a "rule of the road" that directly relates to how safely or dangerously the vehicle was being operated.

48. **(A)** The "rescue doctrine" recognizes that if a defendant's negligence puts someone in danger, it is foreseeable that another person will come to the rescue of the person who is in danger. If the rescuer is injured, the rescuer can hold liable the defendant whose negligence created the need for the rescue attempt. As Judge Cardozo stated in *Wagner v. International Railway Co.*, 133 N.E. 437 (N.Y. 1921), "Danger invites rescue." Choice (B) is incorrect because strict liability would not apply, and the construction company, instead, would be liable for negligence. Choice (C) is incorrect because someone who attempts to rescue another person from danger will not be treated as having assumed the risk where the alternative is to do nothing and allow the threatened harm to occur. Choice (D) is incorrect because the rescue doctrine provides that the cyclist's rescue attempt will be treated as foreseeable.

49. **(C)** In general, any *major and serious departure will be held to be a conversion*, while minor ones that do no harm will not. Choice (C) is, therefore, correct because the neighbor committed a conversion by his unauthorized use of the motor vehicle (i.e., driving an additional 120 miles to visit a friend). As a result, the neighbor will be liable for the full value of the auto because the accident occurred during the course of this deviation. Choice (A) is incorrect because a joint venture involves parties working together to complete an undertaking in which they have a community of interest and in which they will be operating with equal control over the instrumentalities being used. Here, there was no equal control of the car. Moreover, there was a major departure from the parties' original community of interest when the neighbor drove the car in an unauthorized manner. Choice (B) is incorrect because the proper remedy for conversion is damages equal to the full value of the chattel, not the amount representing costs of repair. Choice (D) is incorrect because the plaintiff can recover for conversion here, without the need to prove negligence.

50. **(B)** Where a person is authorized to use a chattel, but uses it in a manner exceeding that authorization, the person can be held liable for conversion if the unauthorized use of the chattel amounts to a serious violation of another person's rights. To constitute conversion, the unpermitted use must be serious enough to justify requiring the defendant to pay the full value of the chattel. In the present case, the quarterback will be liable for conversion because his failure to return the car on time resulted in its being stolen. Moreover, the fact that the neighbor was deprived of the use of the vehicle for three months was sufficiently serious to constitute a material violation of his ownership rights. Choice (A) is incorrect because the quarterback's failure to return the car right away would not be a sufficiently serious violation of the neighbor's rights to generate liability for conversion. Instead, it was the fact that the quarterback left the car in his driveway and it was stolen that amounted to a serious deprivation of the neighbor's right of control. Choice (C) is incorrect because the quarterback's intent is not the issue in a conversion action. He exceeded the consent that he received from the neighbor, which is the key fact here. Choice (D) is incorrect because conversion is not measured in terms of negligence concepts like foreseeability.

51. **(C)** The doctrine of *res ipsa loquitur* allows a plaintiff to recover when there is strong circumstantial evidence that the defendant was negligent, even though the plaintiff cannot identify exactly what the defendant did that was negligent. The doctrine originated in *Byrne v. Boadle*, 159 Eng. Rep. 299 (1863), a British case involving a person who was walking down the street when he was suddenly struck on the head by a barrel of flour. Figuring that the barrel must have come from the warehouse located next to the spot where he was hit by the barrel, the injured person sued the owner of the warehouse. Although the plaintiff could not show exactly what anyone did that was negligent, the court said that the situation spoke for itself, and that negligence could be inferred because it seemed that a barrel would not fall unless one of the defendant's employees had been negligent in some way. A different situation, with a different result, arose in *Larson v. St. Francis Hotel*, 188 P.2d 513 (Cal. Ct. App. 1948), where a plaintiff was struck by a chair thrown by an unidentified person from an unidentified window of the defendant's hotel. The plaintiff was unable to recover because the building in question was a hotel. It was not clear that the chair was thrown by an employee of the hotel, rather than a guest. The chair, thus, was not under the exclusive control of the hotel and its employees, and there was no sound basis for inferring that the hotel or its employees must have been negligent. This question is like the *Larson* case, rather than the *Byrne* case, so *res ipsa loquitur* does not apply, and the plaintiff will lose. Choice (A) is incorrect because the chair may have been thrown by a hotel guest, so the chair was not under the hotel's exclusive control. Choice (B) is incorrect because even though it may be clear that someone was negligent, that negligent person could have been a hotel guest, rather than a hotel employee. Choice (D) is incorrect because a hotel can be vicariously liable for the tortious conduct of its employees, but it is not clear that it was one of the employees (rather than a hotel guest) who was negligent.

Multistate Nuance Chart:

Torts

Res Ipsa Loquitur	
Byrne v. Boadle (1863)	*Larson v. St. Francis Hotel (1948)*
Facts: Barrel of flour was tossed out of a warehouse window and fell upon a passing pedestrian.	**Facts:** Chair was thrown from an unidentified window in the defendant's hotel.
1.Inference of negligence (i.e., reasonable inference) that the defendant's employee was negligent.	1.No inference of negligence on the part of the defendant's employee because it is just as probable that the chair was thrown by a guest.
2.Instrumentality (i.e., barrel) was within the exclusive control of the defendant.	2.Instrumentality (i.e., chair) was not within the exclusive control of the defendant.
3.Defendant (warehouse owner) is vicariously liable for tortious conduct of employee-servant, which was committed within the scope of the employment relationship.	3.Defendant (hotel owner) is not vicariously liable for the independent torts of the hotel's guests.

52. **(B)** Once it is determined that the defendant's conduct has been a cause of some damage suffered by the plaintiff, a further question may arise as to the portion of the total damage sustained that may properly be assigned to the defendant, as distinguished from other causes. Where a logical basis can be found for some rough practical apportionment, which limits a defendant's liability to that part of the harm that he has, in fact, caused, it may be expected that the division will be made. Upon this basis, the businesswoman will be liable for that part of the damage to the owner's home caused by her negligence in colliding with the fire engine. As a result, choice (B) is the best answer. Choice (A) is incorrect because the owner should not be able to hold the businesswoman responsible for all the damage to his house because it was going to suffer some damage from the fire regardless of what the businesswoman did. Choice (C) is incorrect because the businesswoman can be held liable for the harm that she caused by hitting and delaying the fire truck, even though she did not start the fire at the owner's house. Choice (D) is incorrect because even if the owner cannot prevail on a negligence *per se* theory, he can hold the businesswoman liable for ordinary negligence. Negligence *per se* would not apply here because the fire damage to the owner's house was not the type of harm the legislature meant to prevent when it prohibited people from crossing the center line of roadways. However, even when negligence *per se* is unavailable, a plaintiff can still simply bring an ordinary negligence claim. Here, the owner can argue that the businesswoman failed to exercise reasonable care in her driving and that fire damage to his house was a reasonably foreseeable result of the businesswoman's unsafe driving and collision with a fire truck that was hurrying to the scene of the fire at the owner's house.

53. **(B)** The essence of a private nuisance is a *substantial interference with the use and enjoyment of land.* A private nuisance may consist of an interference with the physical condition of the land itself, such as by vibration or blasting that damages a house, the destruction of crops, flooding, raising the water table, or the pollution of a stream. Also, it may consist of a disturbance of the comfort or convenience of the occupant of the land, such as by repeated telephone calls, by unpleasant odors, by smoke, dust, or gas, and by loud noises, excessive light, or high temperatures. Choice (A) is incorrect because a public nuisance involves substantial interference with rights of the entire community or general public. The defendant's conduct here was a problem only for the businessman and his business, not the entire community. Choice (C) is incorrect because

the conduct here was not sufficiently extreme and outrageous to generate a claim for intentional infliction of emotional distress. It was, however, sufficiently annoying to produce a claim for private nuisance. Choice (D) is incorrect because negligence is not the best theory for the businessman to rely upon when a disturbance amounting to a private nuisance is clearly shown to exist. The spinster's conduct was not careless; it was done deliberately and with the intent of harassing the businessman and his business, so private nuisance is a more fitting cause of action.

54. **(A)** Invasion of privacy is not a single tort but, rather, consists of the four distinct torts of (1) appropriation, for the defendant's benefit or advantage, of the plaintiff's name or likeness; (2) intrusion upon the plaintiff's physical solitude or seclusion; (3) public disclosure of private facts about the plaintiff; or (4) placing the plaintiff in a false light in the public eye. Here, the man could succeed in an invasion of privacy action based on intrusion of his physical solitude and seclusion. The tort has been extended to include persistent and unwanted telephone calls. See *Carey v. Statewide Finance Co.,* 223 A.2d 405 (Conn. Cir. Ct. 1966). Also, the tort has been applied to peering into windows of a home and eavesdropping upon private conversations by means of wiretapping and microphones. Choice (B) is incorrect because malice is not a requirement for an invasion of privacy claim. Choice (C) is incorrect because a plaintiff can recover damages for invasion of privacy even if the plaintiff suffered no economic harm. Choice (D) is incorrect because a defendant's conduct can be tortious even if it is not a crime.

55. **(D)** For a libel or slander claim, it is essential that *the defamatory statements were communicated to someone other than the person defamed.* Where there is no communication to anyone but the plaintiff, a defamation claim simply cannot succeed, although there might be liability on some other theory, such as intentional infliction of emotional distress. Thus, the resident's telephone call to the lawyer would not generate liability for defamation. Choices (A), (B), and (C) are incorrect because liability for defamation can arise only where the allegedly defamatory statement was communicated to someone other than the plaintiff.

56. **(D)** A possessor of wild animals is strictly liable for injuries to others that result from the animals' normally dangerous propensities. For example, if you keep a lion on your property, you will be liable if it attacks someone, even if you exercise as much care as possible in keeping and handling the lion. Likewise, if the shark had bitten someone, the person keeping the shark would have been strictly liable. However, sharks do not normally harm people by splashing them, so the resident would not be strictly liable for the neighbor's illness. Choice (A) is incorrect because although keepers of wild animals are generally strictly liable, that rule does not apply where the harm caused by the animal is not related to the animal's dangerous propensities. Choice (B) is incorrect because although the smell may have been a nuisance, the question asks about the neighbor's ability to recover for the bronchitis she suffered because of being splashed. Choice (C) is incorrect because the fact that the neighbor had a special vulnerability to getting sick, because of her cold, would not bar her recovery. Under the "eggshell skull" or "thin skull" rule, a defendant can be liable even if the plaintiff's harm is unexpectedly severe.

57. **(C)** To recover for the tort of nuisance, the conduct of the defendant must constitute an invasion of one's possessory interest in land. The environmentalist's strongest defense would be that the property was occupied by another family (under a long-term lease) and, therefore, the real estate investor who owned the property was not entitled to actual or immediate possession. Thus, there was not an invasion of the investor's present possessory interest in the land. Choice (A) is incorrect because the environmentalist's property could be a nuisance, even if his motives and environmental objectives were good. Choice (B) is incorrect because the environmentalist's property could be a nuisance, even if it did not violate any zoning ordinances. Choice

(D) is incorrect because the environmentalist's property could be a nuisance, even though he turned it into a swamp before the investor purchased the neighboring property. The fact that the investor "came to the nuisance" (i.e., purchased neighboring property after the nuisance was already in existence) would not necessarily bar the investor's claim and, instead, would be just a factor to be considered in a court's weighing of the equities and its decision about what relief (if any) to grant.

58. **(A)** Under some modified comparative fault statutes, the plaintiff's negligence is compared with that of each individual defendant. For example, if P is 40 percent at fault and is suing D1 who is 10 percent at fault and D2 who is 50 percent at fault, P would be able to recover from D2, but not from D1.On the other hand, the modified comparative fault statutes in other states require the plaintiff's negligence to be compared to the sum of the fault shares of all the defendants. Using the same example, P could recover from either D1 or D2 because her percentage of fault, 40 percent, is less than the aggregate fault (i.e., 60 percent) of D1 and D2.The comparative fault statute in this question refers to the plaintiff's fault being compared to that of "the person" against whom recovery is sought. It does not say that the plaintiff's fault should be compared to the sum or aggregate of all the defendants' shares. The plaintiff employee's share of the fault was 40 percent, which is more than the defendant contractor's 35 percent share. As a result, the plaintiff would be unable to recover. Choices (B), (C), and (D) are incorrect because the comparative fault statute here bars the plaintiff from recovering anything because the plaintiff's share of the fault is greater than the defendant's share.

59. **(C)** On the Multistate Bar Exam, you must assume that pure comparative fault and joint and several liability apply unless the question states otherwise. Under pure comparative fault, the plaintiff can recover damages representing the shares of fault assigned to the defendants, even if the plaintiff's fault exceeded the fault of the defendants. Under joint and several liability, each defendant can be held liable for the full amount of damages owed to the plaintiff, and then the defendant who pays the judgment can use contribution claims to obtain reimbursement from the other defendants for their shares of the judgment. Here, under comparative fault, the plaintiff is able to recover 45 percent of the damages, or $45,000. If the driver of the car is forced to pay the $45,000 under joint and several liability, the driver of the car then can seek reimbursement from the other defendant for its share of the judgment. Choice (A) is incorrect because a contribution claim would be allowed to distribute the liability among the defendants according to their shares of the fault, even if the defendant seeking contribution had the higher share of the fault. Choices (B) and (D) are incorrect because the amount that could be recovered through a contribution claim would be $20,000, which is the truck driver's share of the judgment.

60. **(D)** A private nuisance is defined as a substantial and unreasonable interference with one's use and enjoyment of land. When the plaintiff wishes to have an activity enjoined on the theory of a nuisance, it is necessary to show that the defendant's conduct in carrying on the activity at the place and at the time the injunction is sought is unreasonable. Such conduct is unreasonable *only if the gravity of the harm caused outweighs the utility of the conduct.* This would be so if a reasonable person would conclude that there was a feasible way, economically and scientifically, to avoid a substantial amount of the harm without material impairment of the benefits. In this question, the company's best defense in a private nuisance action would be choice (D). If paraquat was the only herbicide that could safely and effectively kill marijuana, which, if not controlled, would pose a serious drug enforcement problem, then there would be *no* feasible scientific means to avoid the harm without impairing the benefits. In other words, the utility of the conduct would outweigh the harm caused. Choices (A) and (B) are incorrect because neither government approvals nor existence of a government contract address the judicial standard of balancing the utility versus the harm. Choice (C) is incorrect because "coming to the nuisance" is only one factor the courts employ in "balancing the equities."

Multistate Nuance Chart
Torts

Nuisance	
Public Nuisance	**Private Nuisance**
1.Unreasonable interference with a right common to the general public	1.Substantial and unreasonable interference with one's use and enjoyment of the land
2.Interference with public health, public safety, or public peace	2.Private use of land: use that an individual is entitled to make as opposed to a member of the public
3.Damages: One must suffer harm of a different kind from that suffered by others exercising the same public right.	3.Damages: One must suffer significant harm that a normal person in the locality would find annoying or disturbing.

61. **(B)** Liability for negligence can be imposed if the defendant failed to exercise the care of a reasonable person under the circumstances. One of the most common defenses to a negligence claim is that the plaintiff's own negligence was also a cause of the plaintiff's injuries. Under the traditional rule of "contributory negligence," a plaintiff's claim would be barred completely if the plaintiff's negligence was a cause of the plaintiff's injuries. However, in most states, contributory negligence rules have been replaced with comparative fault rules under which the plaintiff's negligence merely reduces the plaintiff's recovery by some percentage set by the jury, rather than barring the plaintiff's claim completely. On the Multistate Bar Exam, you must assume that comparative fault applies unless the question states otherwise. Here, the plaintiff driver will prevail if his conduct was not negligent. Choice (A) is incorrect because even if the driver was negligent by driving in excess of the speed limit, that would merely result in reduction of his recovery to some extent under comparative fault, rather than barring the claim completely. Choice (C) is incorrect because even if the smoke from the burning leaves obscured the driver's vision and caused the accident, that would not make the landowner liable unless the landowner was negligent. Choice (D) is incorrect because there is no reason for strict liability to be imposed on the landowner. Instead, the landowner would be liable only if negligent.

62. **(B)** At early common law, something approaching strict liability for fire was imposed upon landholders. Under the modern view, however, in the absence of legislation, there is no liability for the escape of fire where the defendant was not negligent. There may, as in the present case, be liability for negligence in failing to control the fire or to take adequate precautions with respect to the fire. Choice (A) is incorrect because most courts today do not impose strict liability for handling fire. Choice (C) is incorrect because a public nuisance exists only where there is a significant and unreasonable interference with a right of the entire community or general public. This fire merely caused harm to one person, so it is not a public nuisance. Choice (D) is incorrect because a wind gust is not unforeseeable, and a person can be liable for negligence that causes harm through operation of a natural force, such as wind.

63. **(B)** Liability for negligence can be imposed if the defendant causes harm by failing to exercise the care of a reasonable person under the circumstances. Here, the mechanic could be liable for negligence if he failed to exercise reasonable care. Choice (A) is incorrect because there is no basis for strict liability to be imposed on the mechanic. Although handling flammable substances like gasoline may be an ultrahazardous activity in many circumstances, operating an auto repair shop is not such a dangerous activity that it would be treated as ultrahazardous and subject to strict liability. Choice (C) is incorrect because a nuisance requires a disturbance of a continuing or chronic nature. For example, if a factory emits smoke or dust on a *daily basis,* then an action for nuisance may arise. The smoke here, however, was a one-time occurrence and, therefore, not a nuisance. Choice (D) is incorrect because trespass requires that the defendant intentionally caused someone or something to enter the plaintiff's land. Here, the mechanic did not intentionally create the smoke. In addition, smoke is treated as an intangible item (like noises, odors, lights, etc.) that is incapable of constituting a trespass to another person's land.

Multistate Nuance Chart: Torts

Trespass on Land	Nuisance
1. One who intentionally enters land in the possession of another or causes a thing or a third person to do so is subject to liability 2. Consists of intrusions upon, beneath, and above the surface of the earth 3. Intentional intrusions that cause no harm to the land, as well as intrusions made under a mistaken belief of law or fact, that, nevertheless, subject the actor to liability	1. Substantial and unreasonable interference with one's use and enjoyment of the land 2. Consists (1) of interference with the physical condition of the land (such as by vibrations or blasting that damages a house, the destruction of crops, flooding, or pollution of a stream), or (2) a disturbance to the comfort or convenience of the occupant (such as unpleasant odors, smoke, dust, loud noises, excessive light, or even repeated telephone calls)

64. **(C)** When an employer asks questions and checks references of a job applicant, those who are asked about the applicant have a qualified privilege to answer and give their opinion about the applicant. The statements made about the applicant will be privileged, even if they are false, if they were made in good faith. This qualified privilege serves the purpose of enabling people to speak freely and share information with the employer, who is trying to decide whether to hire the applicant. Choice (C) is, therefore, correct because the statements will be privileged, since the facts state that the first attorney "reasonably believed that his low rating of the woman was a fair reflection of her performance." Choices (A) and (B) are incorrect because they ignore the qualified privilege that will bar the plaintiff's claim here. Choice (D) is incorrect because the fact that the plaintiff listed the defendant as a former employer on her résumé will not bar the plaintiff's claim. It is the fact that the defendant had reasonable grounds for his adverse opinion and statements about the plaintiff that will bar liability from being imposed.

65. **(D)** Under the prevailing view, one who is confronted with an emergency is not to be held to the standard of conduct normally applied to one who is not in such a situation. An emergency has been defined as a sudden or unexpected event or combination of circumstances that calls for immediate action. Under such conditions, the actor cannot reasonably be held to the same conduct as one who has had full opportunity to reflect, even though it later appears that he made the wrong decision. This same concept applies in negligence *per se* situations, because a person who has a valid excuse for violating a statute will not be found negligent *per se*. Valid excuses would include being unable to comply with a statute because of a sudden emergency, like the child's seizure. Choice (D) is, therefore, correct because the plaintiff would not be able to recover because the defendant was acting reasonably in an emergency. Choice (A) is incorrect because strict liability would not apply to violation of a traffic law in an emergency. Choice (B) is incorrect because negligence *per se* would not apply here, even if the statute was designed to protect motorists, like the driver, if the husband has a valid excuse for violating the statute. Choice (C) is incorrect because the "last clear chance" doctrine is obsolete. It was an exception to the doctrine of contributory negligence, allowing a plaintiff to recover, despite being negligent, if the defendant had the last clear chance to avoid the accident. In jurisdictions that have replaced contributory negligence with comparative fault, the doctrine of last clear chance no longer exists. On the Multistate, you must assume pure comparative fault applies unless the question states otherwise. Moreover, even in a contributory negligence jurisdiction, the doctrine of last clear chance would be relevant only where it is the defendant that has the last clear chance to avoid the accident. Here, choice (C) talks about the plaintiff having the last clear chance, so the doctrine would not apply.

66. **(A)** In the case of gratuitous bailments, the majority of courts have treated the guest as a licensee on personal property in essentially the same position as one entering by permission upon the land of another. Application of that analogy has led to decisions in several states holding that while the driver or owner is under a duty to exercise reasonable care for the protection of the guest in his active operation of the car *and is required to disclose to him any defects in the vehicle of which he has knowledge,* he is not required to inspect the automobile to make sure it is safe. Choice (A), therefore, is correct because the car owner will be liable because he knew the steering was faulty and did not tell the neighbor who borrowed the car. Choice (B) is incorrect because the duty upon the car owner to his guest is that of reasonable care, not strict liability. Strict liability for the steering defect would apply only to the manufacturer and other sellers of the car. Choice (C) is incorrect because the pedestrian plaintiff will be able to hold the car owner liable for failing to warn about the known flaw in the car's steering. Choice (D) is incorrect because a gratuitous lender is required to disclose any defects in the vehicle of which he has knowledge.

67. **(D)** A qualified privilege exists for statements made in the "public interest." The privilege is a rather narrow one, protecting communication to those public officers or others who may reasonably be expected to take some effective action on a matter of public, rather than purely private, importance. Thus, anyone has a qualified privilege to give information to proper authorities for the prevention or detection of crime. Choices (A) and (B) are incorrect because the qualified privilege would protect the defendants from liability. Choice (C) is incorrect because the qualified privilege for reporting information of a crime is the key reason the defendants can avoid liability, and the lack of malice alone would not be enough to bar liability from being imposed.

68. **(A)** Skilled workers, such as electricians and carpenters, are obligated to exercise the care of a reasonable person in their profession. Choice (A) is the best answer here because it shows that the electrician's conduct fell below the reasonable standard required by members of his profession. Choice (B) is incorrect because it states that the *only* basis of recovery would be for strict liability. Since the homeowner may recover under a negligence theory, choice (B) is not the best answer. Choices (C) and (D) are incorrect because they state that the homeowner will not prevail. Here, the homeowner will prevail because the electrician, regardless of his using his best professional judgment, can still be liable if his conduct fell below that of a reasonable member of his profession.

69. **(D)** A person, including a manufacturer, who is engaged in the business of selling a product, can be held strictly liable for injuries caused by the product's being defective and unreasonably dangerous. The defect must have existed at the time the product left the defendant's hands. Clearly, if the buyer's car left the manufacturer's plant in a defective condition, then strict liability would be imposed on the manufacturer for all harm proximately caused by the defect. Choice (D) is correct. Choice (A) is incorrect because the manufacturer's liability for selling a defective product does not depend on whether the car dealer was negligent. Choice (B) is incorrect because it addresses only the *present* defective condition of the product. In other words, the manufacturer will be strictly liable only if the defect existed when the car left the manufacturer's hands, and not if the defect arose only later, after the product had been shipped by the manufacturer. Choice (C) is incorrect because even if the plaintiff was negligent for driving the car back to the dealership rather than stopping immediately, that negligence would merely reduce the plaintiff's recovery under comparative fault principles, rather than barring it completely.

70. **(A)** A person who is engaged in the business of selling a product can be held strictly liable for injuries caused by the product's being defective and unreasonably dangerous. The defect must have existed at the time the defendant sold the product. The auto dealer will be strictly liable if the car's brakes were defective at the time the dealer sold the car to the plaintiff. Choice (B) is incorrect because strict liability extends to defects existing at the time of sale, not to defective repairs. Choice (C) is incorrect because no matter how few or how many miles the car was driven, the dealer's liability is based on defects existing at the time of the sale. Choice (D) is incorrect because

a defendant's negligence is irrelevant if he is strictly liable. **Exam Tip:** When the question states that the plaintiff "asserts a claim" against the defendant, look at the status of the defendant to determine if he has potential strict liability for selling a defective product.

71. **(B)** The elements of deceit consist of the following: (1) a false representation made by the defendant; (2) knowledge or belief on the part of the defendant that the representation is false (i.e., "scienter"); (3) an intention to induce the plaintiff to act or to refrain from action in reliance upon the misrepresentation; (4) justifiable reliance upon the representation on the part of the plaintiff; and (5) damage to the plaintiff, resulting from such reliance. As a general rule, an action for deceit will *not* lie for such tacit nondisclosure. To this general rule, however, the courts have developed a number of exceptions. For instance, where the parties stand in some confidential or fiduciary relationship to one another, such as that of principal and agent, executor and beneficiary of an estate, bank and investing depositor, or majority and minority stockholders, there is a duty of full and fair disclosure of all material facts. Therefore, choice (B) is correct because the woman, as a fiduciary, owed the customer a duty of disclosure and was aware that he was acting under a misapprehension as to the true value of the misprinted $5 bill. Choice (A) is incorrect because "benefit of the bargain" is not a tort remedy but, rather, a contract law concept, which means that a part to a contract should be made "whole" if a breach occurs. Choice (C) is incorrect because there was a fiduciary duty between the parties and, therefore, a duty of full and fair disclosure of all material facts. Choice (D) is incorrect because the woman, as a fiduciary, breached the duty she owed to the customer, whether he was justified in relying upon her offer or not.

72. **(B)** This Multistate question is based on section 359 of the Restatement (Second) of Torts, which provides: "A lessor who leases land for a purpose which involves the admission of the public is subject to liability for physical harm caused to persons who enter the land for that purpose by a condition of the land existing when the lessee takes possession, if the lessor (a) knows or by the exercise of reasonable care could discover that the condition involves an unreasonable risk of harm to such persons, and (b) has reason to expect that the lessee will admit them before the land is put in safe condition for their reception, and (c) fails to exercise reasonable care to discover or to remedy the condition, or otherwise to protect such persons against it." The property owner, as lessor, had a duty to exercise reasonable care to remedy the unsafe condition of the parking lot, so choice (B) is correct. Choice (A) is incorrect because the property owner could be held liable even if the youth who threw the rock could be identified. Choice (C) is incorrect because the property owner, as the lessor, had a duty to exercise reasonable care to remedy the unsafe condition and can be held liable for harm resulting from the youth's malicious conduct. Choice (D) is incorrect because the police department's performance of its functions does not relieve the property owner of his duty or liability.

73. **(C)** The senator would be entitled to recover for invasion of privacy only if he were able to prove malice on the part of *the newspaper*. In *Time, Inc. v. Hill*, 385 U.S. 374 (1967), the U.S. Supreme Court applied the *New York Times v. Sullivan* rule to the tort of invasion of privacy. In other words, the Court extended the constitutional privilege (the guarantee of freedom of speech and of the press) to invasion of privacy cases where the published matter in question was in the public interest *unless* the plaintiff established that the defendant acted with "malice." Thus, the misstatements of fact by the newspaper defendant are privileged unless the senator can prove that the misstatements were made with (1) knowledge of falsity, or (2) in reckless disregard of the truth. Students should note that the two branches of invasion of privacy that turn on publicity (placing the plaintiff in a false light and public disclosure of private facts about the plaintiff), are both encompassed within the constitutional privilege. Choice (A) is incorrect because liability for placing the defendant in a false light could not be imposed without proof of malice. Choice (B) is incorrect for the same reason; the newspaper could not be held liable for public disclosure of private facts unless the plaintiff proves malice. Choice (D) is incorrect because if the plaintiff can prove malice, the newspaper will be liable even if it was acting in the public interest by publishing the story.

74. **(B)** In *New York Times v. Sullivan,* 376 U.S. 254 (1946), the U.S. Supreme Court held that the First Amendment's guarantees of freedom of speech and freedom of the press confer a privilege on news media defendants that protects them from liability for false statements about public officials or figures if the statements were made without malice. Malice was further defined by the Court as (1) knowledge of falsity, or (2) reckless disregard of the truth. Therefore, a public official or public figure may not recover for defamatory remarks relating to his official conduct in the absence of proof that the defendant made the statement with malice. Choice (A) is incorrect because the qualified privilege is lost if the newspaper published the statement with malice. Choice (C) is incorrect because the statements must be made without malice in order to have First Amendment protection. Choice v because an absolute privilege did not exist in the facts presented. An absolute privilege exists only for statements made in the following situations: (1) judicial proceedings; (2) legislative proceedings (i.e., matters covered by the Speech and Debate Clause); (3) executive proceedings; and (4) compelled broadcast situations, where the news media is compelled to carry a particular speaker's message (such as a television station required to carry a speaker's message or a newspaper required to print a notice or statement).

75. **(A)** Where a written statement is defamatory on its face (referred to as libel *per se*), the majority of American courts take the position that the injury to the plaintiff's reputation is presumed by law. Libel *per se,* thus, is actionable without pleading or proving special damages. In the present hypothetical situation, the information that the former staff member sent to the reporter would constitute libel *per se* because the documents imputed criminal conduct to the senator. Choice (A) is, therefore, correct because the senator can recover for defamation here without specific proof of harm to her reputation; that harm will be presumed. The fact that the former staff member knew the documents were false satisfies the malice requirement for defamation of a public official or figure. Choice (B) is incorrect because where an action involves libel *per se, proof of actual economic or other harm to the plaintiff's reputation is not required.* Choice (C) is incorrect because the former staff member knew the documents were false and defamatory, so the proof of malice required for a defamation suit by a public official or public figure is present. Choice (D) is incorrect because although legislators have a special privilege under the Constitution's Speech and Debate Clause, that privilege extends only to statements that are part of the legislative process. Statements made by a former staff member about the senator would not be protected by the Speech and Debate Clause.

Explanation: Question 76

The correct answer is: **(C)** The historian will not prevail, because the jewelry store's negligence did not result in physical harm to the historian.

Negligent infliction of emotional distress occurs when a defendant's negligent act causes extreme mental suffering on the part of the plaintiff. Absent physical impact, the majority of courts will not permit recovery on a claim of negligent infliction of emotional distress unless the mental distress caused by the negligence is manifested through physical injury or physical symptoms, such as shock, nightmares, sleeplessness, etc. Therefore, if the historian brings her suit in such a jurisdiction, she will not recover, as mere anguish and distress would be insufficient to recover for negligent infliction of emotional distress without some physical manifestation of distress. If she is in a minority jurisdiction that permits recovery absent a showing of physical harm, she could prevail. Therefore, this is the correct answer.

(A) Incorrect. The historian will prevail, because it was foreseeable that the historian would be extremely distressed if the jewelry store mishandled the necklace.

Even if it was foreseeable that the loss of the necklace would inflict emotional distress, the plaintiff will not be able to recover damages in most jurisdictions absent proof of physical harm. Because no physical harm was suffered here, the historian would not prevail. Therefore, this answer is incorrect.

(B) Incorrect. The historian will prevail, because the jewelry store breached the duty of care owed to the historian when it misplaced the necklace.

Most jurisdictions do not permit recovery for emotional distress merely because the distress was caused by a defendant's negligence, unless the mental distress caused by the negligence is manifested through physical injury or physical symptoms, such as shock, nightmares, sleeplessness, etc. Because there is no evidence of those symptoms here, the historian will likely not prevail. Therefore, this answer is incorrect.

(D) Incorrect. The historian will not prevail, because the jewelry store did not misplace the necklace with intent to inflict emotional distress.

The infliction of emotional distress need not be intentional, or even reckless, in order for the plaintiff to prevail, as long as there is a physical manifestation of the emotional distress. No physical manifestations of emotional distress, such as shock, sleeplessness, etc. are present here. Therefore, this answer is incorrect.

Explanation: Question 77

The correct answer is: **(D)** No, if the concert pianist suffered no harm from the use of the drug.

If the concert pianist had been injured by the drug injections, the doctor could have been held liable for failure to disclose the material risks involved. Physicians owe their patients the duty to inform them of the risks involved in a proposed medical treatment. The disclosure should include the diagnosis, the risks of the proposed treatment, the risks of alternative treatments, and the risk of no treatment. Most jurisdictions now define the duty to disclose in terms of the patient's right to know. These jurisdictions look to whether a reasonable person in the patient's position would attach significance to the information. If that "reasonable patient" would, then the information is material and disclosure is required. In addition to proving that material risks were not disclosed, the plaintiff must show that she was harmed by the treatment and that she would have withheld her consent had she known of the risk of that harm, which in fact occurred. In this case, the concert pianist has no cause of action against the doctor because she has not suffered any harm. Therefore, this is correct.

(A) Incorrect. Yes, if the concert pianist would not have consented to the use of the drug if she knew about the risks to her mobility.

This is incorrect, because it ignores the issue of harm. The concert pianist can show that she would have refused consent and probably also that a reasonable patient in like circumstances, i.e., needing perfect finger mobility, would have withheld consent. However, the concert pianist cannot show that she was harmed.

(B) Incorrect. Yes, if a reasonable person would have considered the information about calcium buildup important.

Again, this is incorrect, because it ignores the issue of harm. The concert pianist can show that she would have refused consent and probably also that a reasonable patient in like circumstances, i.e., needing perfect finger mobility, would have withheld consent. However, the concert pianist cannot show that she was harmed.

(C) Incorrect. No, if the doctor had weighed the risks and benefits of using the drug before prescribing it.

Although the doctor's conduct in choosing the drug injections to treat the concert pianist may have been reasonable, that reasonableness does not affect his liability for failure to disclose the material risks it involved. The concert pianist has no cause of action because she wasn't injured, but this is incorrect because it incompletely states the doctor's duty. Physicians owe their patients the duty to inform them of the risks involved in a proposed medical treatment.

Explanation: Question 78

The correct answer is: **(A)** The league player, because bowling alleys are open to the general public.

Generally, the lessor of real property is not liable for injuries resulting from conditions on the premises. The lease is considered a transfer of all rights and responsibilities with regard to conditions on the premises. There are a number of exceptions to this rule, however. One exception concerns dangerous conditions existing at the time of the lease of property if the lessor knows the lessee will hold the property open to the general public and will not fix the dangerous conditions before he opens the property. The interest in protecting the general public is considered so important that the lessor continues to be liable for those conditions even after the transfer of possession occurs. The woman knew the businessman intended to reopen the property as a bowling alley, open to the general public, and knew that he was not going to fix the dangerous conditions by the time of the opening. The woman therefore remains liable for the condition of the rugs and the injury to the league player.

(B) Incorrect. The league player, because he was a customer of the bowling alley.

The fact that the league player is a customer of the bowling alley indicates that the businessman, as the league player's inviter, owes the league player a duty of reasonable care. The issue in question, however, is the basis for the woman owing the league player a duty of reasonable care. This duty is based upon the woman's knowledge of that her lessee, the businessman, intended to hold the premises open to the public. This is an exception to the rule that the lessor of real property is not liable for injuries resulting from conditions on the premises.

(C) Incorrect. The woman, because as the possessor, only the businessman owes any duty to the league player.

Generally, the lessor of real property is not liable for injuries resulting from conditions on the premises. The lease is considered a transfer of all rights and responsibilities with regard to conditions on the premises. However, one exception concerns dangerous conditions existing at the time of the lease of property if the lessor knows the lessee will hold the property open to the general public without having fixed the dangerous conditions. The interest in protecting the general public is considered so important that the lessor continues to be liable for those conditions even after the transfer of possession.

(D) Incorrect. The woman, because the businessman had the opportunity to evaluate the condition of the bowling alley prior to signing the lease.

The businessman's opportunity to inspect the premises prior to leasing may be relevant to the businessman's knowledge of the conditions and thus his liability, but does not keep the woman from also being liable. Therefore, this is not the best answer.

Explanation: Question 79

The correct answer is: **(A)** The driver and the ambulance company are jointly and severally liable for the pedestrian's broken leg.

The ambulance employee's negligence is an intervening force between the driver's negligent act and the pedestrian's ultimate injury of a broken leg. The driver's conduct forced the pedestrian to be transported via ambulance to a hospital, and it is foreseeable that the ambulance might be involved in an accident, whether by the driver's negligence or otherwise, during the trip. The driver's negligence will not cut off the driver's liability for the broken leg. However, the driver will be solely liable for the broken arm. The driver and the ambulance company will be jointly and severally liable for the broken leg.

(B) Incorrect. Only the ambulance company is liable for the pedestrian's broken leg because the damages are apportionable.

The fact that the damages may be apportion-able would not change the fact that the driver put the sequence of events in motion which foresee-ably led to the pedestrian's broken leg. The damages being apportionable means that the ambulance company will only be liable for the broken leg, not some single indivisible injury of which they were only a partial cause.

(C) Incorrect. Only the ambulance company is liable for the pedestrian's broken leg unless the paramedics were negligent in the selection of an ambulance service.

The driver can be liable for the ambulance employee's negligence if it was a foreseeable, not abnormal, consequence of the driver's negligence, whether or not the paramedics were negligent in the selection of the ambulance service.

(D) Incorrect. Because the driver caused the accident she is solely liable for the pedestrian's broken leg.

The driver is solely liable for the pedestrian's broken arm, but shares liability with the ambulance company for the broken leg.

Explanation: Question 80

The correct answer is: **(C)** No, because smoke inhalation is one of the risks of working as a firefighter.

Under the Firefighter's Rule, a land occupier is not liable for injury to a firefighter or police officer caused by the hazard which brought the firefighter or police officer to the land occupier's premises, whether the hazard was created by the owner's negligence, an accident, or a third party. Such an injury is considered part of the risk of their employment and typically is compensated by the Fire or Police Department's workers' compensation insurance. Injury from smoke inhalation is a very common risk of firefighting. Thus, the homeowner will not be liable for the firefighter's injury.

(A) Incorrect. Yes, but only if the homeowner should have known of the possibility that a glowing ember might start a fire.

Even if the homeowner should have known of the possibility that the embers might start a fire, he would not be liable for his negligent conduct. Under the Firefighter's Rule, a land occupier is not liable for injury to a firefighter or police officer caused by the hazard which brought the firefighter or police officer to the land occupier's premises, whether the hazard was created by the owner's negligence, an accident, or a third party.

(B) Incorrect. Yes, if the homeowner was negligent in leaving the fire unattended as he went to bed.

Even if the homeowner did not behave as a reasonable person with regard to the glowing embers, because the firefighter was injured by the precise risk which is part of her job the homeowner owes her no duty with regard to this type of injury.

(D) Incorrect. No, because the firefighter is not a licensee or invitee.

Whether the firefighter is a licensee or invitee is not important in the context of the type of injury she suffered. Therefore, this is not the best answer.

Explanation: Question 81

The correct answer is: **(C)** The man rendered the assistance with care and his assistance did not cause the woman's brain damage.

Barring certain limited exceptions, one has no duty to help a person in danger, even if one could do so easily and without endangering oneself. Once one does undertake to assist someone, however, he must do so with care. The man here did undertake to assist the woman, and there is no evidence that anything the man did caused the woman's brain damage. The fact that he waited to assist does not make him liable because he had no duty to assist in the first place. Therefore, this is the correct answer.

(A) Incorrect. The man's negligence was not the proximate cause of the woman's injuries.

Except under limited circumstances, one has no duty to assist someone in danger, even if one could do so easily and without endangering himself. The man here had no duty to assist the woman. Once someone does render assistance, he must do so with care. There is no evidence here that once the man began assistance, he did anything wrong. This answer presumes that the man was negligent, so it is incorrect.

(B) Incorrect. The woman was contributorily negligent.

One might be tempted to think that the woman's canoe tipping over might be an issue. However, this answer tests your ability to focus on the real issue, which is whether the man assisted with care. Therefore, this answer is incorrect.

(D) Incorrect. The man's negligence was not the actual cause of the woman's injuries.

Except under limited circumstances, one has no duty to assist someone in danger, even if one could do so easily and without endangering himself. The man here had no duty to assist the woman. Once someone does render assistance, he must do so with care. There is no evidence here that once the man began assistance, he did anything wrong. This answer presumes that the man was negligent, so it is incorrect.

Explanation: Question 82

The correct answer is: **(C)** No, because the picture is factual.

To qualify as a defamatory message, there must be a defamatory statement of or about the dentist that tends to adversely affect his reputation or good name. Further, truth is a defense to defamation. Here, the message at issue is a true representation of an inoffensive situation. The fact that an unidentifiable woman is in the passenger seat of the car of a married man is not likely to insinuate any criminal or amoral behavior on its face, and, in any event, the display is factual. An inoffensive picture which is a truthful representation would generally be considered non-defamatory as a matter of law. Therefore, this answer is correct, and the dentist will not prevail in his defamation action.

(A) Incorrect. Yes, because the picture of the dentist with another woman could damage his reputation.

Perhaps if the image of the woman was clear, and those who knew the dentist could see that the woman was not the dentist's wife, then there might be an arguable case for defamation. Even then, since the image is accurate (not a doctored image), the stronger case might be for invasion of privacy, not defamation. Here, only the wife is aware that the woman in the picture is not the wife. Since defamation requires publication to a substantial minority of reasonable people upon whom the required injurious effect is had, the fact that only the wife appreciates the message will most likely defeat a claim of defamation.

(B) Incorrect. Yes, because the dentist can plead additional, extrinsic facts that render the message defamatory.

If a message is not defamatory per se, the plaintiff may plead additional, extrinsic facts that render the message defamatory. Here, the husband could explain the meaning of the picture and why it appears defamatory to those who know him. However, defamation requires publication of the message to a substantial minority, upon which the required injurious effect is had (such as damage to reputation). Where, as here, only the wife can appreciate the meaning behind the message, a defamation action will likely fail.

(D) Incorrect. No, because a photograph is not a written communication, and therefore will not qualify as a defamatory message.

The form of the communication does not matter where defamation is concerned; a drawing or photograph may be considered libel as easily as a writing. The question is whether the libel designates the plaintiff in such a way as to let those who knew him understand that he was the person meant, and otherwise satisfies the elements of defamation. Therefore, the fact that that the thrust of the message here is embodied in a photograph, and not a written communication, is not an issue that will cause the dentist to lose the defamation suit. This answer is incorrect as a matter of law.

Explanation: Question 83

The correct answer is: **(A)** No, because she did not suffer any pecuniary loss due to the first appraiser's statements.

Luckily for the plaintiff, the first appraiser's manner caused her to seek a second opinion and not take any action in reliance on what he said. To recover for misrepresentation, a plaintiff must establish that: (1) the defendant made a false representation, knowing that it was false or with reckless disregard as to whether it was true or false; (2) the plaintiff materially and justifiably relied on the misrepresentation; and (3) the plaintiff incurred pecuniary damages. Thus, this answer is correct. She cannot recover, because she did not suffer any pecuniary loss.

(B) Incorrect. No, unless she relied on the first appraiser's statements.

To recover for misrepresentation, a plaintiff must establish that (1) the defendant made a false representation, knowing that it was false or with reckless disregard as to whether it was true or false; (2) the plaintiff materially and justifiably relied on the misrepresentation; and (3) the plaintiff incurred pecuniary damages. There is no information in the facts to show that the plaintiff relied on the first appraiser's appraisal in any way or that she had any financial loss. Therefore, this is not the best answer.

(C) Incorrect. Yes, because the first appraiser acted with intent to induce her to rely on his statements.

While the first appraiser may have wanted the plaintiff to rely on his statements, that is not enough to make the plaintiff's suit successful. Besides showing that the defendant made a false representation with knowledge of falsity or reckless disregard for the truth, the plaintiff must also show that she materially and justifiably relied on the representation and incurred pecuniary damages. The facts do not indicate that the plaintiff relied on the representation in any way or that she suffered any financial loss. Thus, this answer is incorrect.

(D) Incorrect. Yes, because the first appraiser knowingly made a false statement in his appraisal.

Although the first appraiser knowingly made a false statement, that is only one element that the plaintiff needs to show to recover for intentional misrepresentation. The plaintiff must also show that she materially and justifiably relied on the representation and incurred pecuniary damages. The facts here do not state any reliance or damages. Thus, this answer is incorrect.

Explanation: Question 84

The correct answer is: **(D)** No, because the architecture student cannot prove that he sustained any damages.

A trespass to a chattel may be committed by intentionally dispossessing another of the chattel, or using or intermeddling with a chattel in the possession of another. Unlike other intentional torts, the plaintiff must prove actual damages from the intermeddling, or in the case of dispossession, by the loss of use. Actual damages is one of the elements of the trespass to chattels cause of action. Because the architecture student will not be able to show any damages on these facts, this answer choice is correct. Here, the math student took the architecture student's calculator to use in her final exam, so her actions were indeed intentional. However, the architecture student cannot prove that he suffered damages as a result of the math student's actions. When the math student was in possession of the architecture student's calculator, the architecture student had completed his final exam and was visiting his family. There is nothing in the facts to suggest that he needed or wanted to use the calculator during the time that the architecture student was in possession of it, or that the value of the calculator was diminished. Therefore, the architecture student unlikely to prevail in a claim for trespass to a chattel.

(A) Incorrect. Yes, because the math student knowingly used the calculator without the architecture student's permission.

A trespass to a chattel may be committed by intentionally dispossessing another of the chattel, or by using or intermeddling with a chattel in the possession of another. Use alone is not sufficient to prove a trespass to a chattel. The plaintiff must prove damages in the actual amount caused by the tortious conduct, or in the case of dispossession, by the loss of use. Here, because there is no indication that the architecture student suffered damages as a result of the math student's use of the calculator, the architecture student is unlikely to prevail. Thus, this answer is incorrect.

(B) Incorrect. No, because the architecture student was unaware that the math student had used his calculator.

In a claim of trespass to a chattel, a plaintiff must prove damages in the actual amount caused by the tortious conduct, or in the case of dispossession, by the loss of use. However, the plaintiff need not be aware of the dispossession. Here, the math student borrowed the architecture student's calculator to use during her final exam, and her act was clearly intentional. However, given that the architecture student had completed his final exam and had no need of the calculator during the time that the math student was in possession of it, and it was returned in good condition, it does not appear that the architecture student suffered any damages as a result of the math student's actions. It is for this reason, not the architecture student's lack of immediate awareness of the dispossession, that the architecture student's claim against the math student is unlikely to succeed. Thus, this answer is incorrect.

(C) Incorrect. No, because the math student's use was not a serious interference with the architecture student's rights.

Unlike the tort of conversion, the tort of trespass to a chattel does not require serious interference with another's use of the chattel. A defendant may be held liable for trespass to a chattel where he intentionally dispossesses another of the chattel or uses or intermeddles with a chattel in the possession of another. This answer is correct in stating that the architecture student's claim against the math student is unlikely to succeed; however, the reason is the architecture student's lack of damages, not that the math student's use was not a serious interference. Thus, this answer is incorrect.

Explanation: Question 85

The correct answer is: **(D)** Yes, because it was reasonable for the family to rely on the realtor's representations.

For a prima facie cause of action in negligent misrepresentation, the following must be proven: 1) a duty of care based on a special relationship between the person making the representation and the person receiving the representation; 2) the representation must be untrue, inaccurate, or misleading; 3) the defendant must have acted negligently in making the representation; 4) the plaintiff must have relied, in a reasonable manner, on the negligent misrepresentation; and 5) the reliance must have been detrimental to the plaintiff in the sense that damages resulted. In this case, there is a special relationship between the family and their realtor. The realtor works on commission and made the representation without knowledge of its truth or falsity to garner a higher commission. While Choice (C) correctly states the majority position that a fiduciary relationship existed between the parties, it is not proof positive that the family will recover. Choice (D) correctly states the requirement that the plaintiff, here the family, reasonably relied upon the realtor's representations to their detriment.

(A) Incorrect. No, because the realtor had no actual knowledge that the backyard was unsuitable for a swimming pool.

(B) Incorrect. No, because the realtor's representations amounted to mere puffery.

(C) Incorrect. Yes, because the realtor was in a fiduciary relationship with the family.

Explanation: Question 86

The correct answer is: **(C)** No, because she didn't read or speak English.

A product may be unreasonably dangerous if there is an inadequate warning regarding its use. The warning on the shampoo bottle was adequate. American manufacturers are not required to place warnings in different languages on products sold within the United States. Choice (D) is incorrect because assumption of the risk applies when the plaintiff subjectively is aware of the risk and consciously disregards it. In the present hypo, the woman was unaware of the risk because she didn't understand English.

(A) Incorrect. Yes, because she suffered injury from her use of the product.

(B) Incorrect. Yes, because the manufacturer was aware that a small percentage of the population would suffer an allergic reaction to the shampoo.

(D) Incorrect. No, because she assumed the risk by not applying some to her wrist first.

Explanation: Question 87

The correct answer is: **(C)** He will lose, because he was not a foreseeable user or consumer of this vehicle.

Under the consumer-contemplation test as stated in Section 402A of the Restatement of Torts 2d, any "foreseeable user" or "ordinary user" of a defectively dangerous product may recover for strict liability. Prosser states that "the user may be a member of the family of the final purchaser, or his employee, or a guest at his table, or a mere donee from the purchaser." In this regard, a thief is not regarded as a reasonably foreseeable user contemplated by the drafters of the Restatement. Note that (D) is incorrect because the man loses due to his status as an unforeseeable user, not because of his misuse of the vehicle.

(A) Incorrect. He will prevail, because the dealership failed to inspect the vehicle before selling it.

(B) Incorrect. He will prevail, because the vehicle was sold in a defective condition.

(D) Incorrect. He will lose, because he was engaged in misuse when the accident occurred.

Explanation: Question 88

The correct answer is: **(D)** Against the rancher, because the harm to the mink was not a foreseeable result of the risk created by the blasting.

Under Restatement of Torts, 2d section 519, (1) One who carries on an abnormally dangerous activity is subject to (strict) liability for harm to the person, land or chattels of another resulting from the activity, although he has exercised the utmost care to prevent the harm. (2) This strict liability is limited to the kind of harm, the possibility of which makes the activity abnormally dangerous." While it is true that blasting is an abnormally dangerous activity, the extent of protection under the rule only applies to harm which is within the scope of the abnormal risk that is the basis of the liability. Thus, one who transports explosives is not liable for every possible harm that may result from carrying on that activity. The owner of a truck carrying dynamite would be strictly liable if an explosion occurs during transport, but not strictly liable if the truck containing explosives simply runs over a pedestrian. Likewise, if the blasting had caused the building that housed plaintiff's mink to collapse, strict liability would apply. However, that due to fright, the rancher's adult mink ate their young is an example of harm which is outside the scope of the abnormal risk created by the blasting operations. Strict liability would not apply. Choice (D) is the correct answer. See Restatement of Torts, 2d section 519, Illustration 1.

(A) Incorrect. For the rancher, because the construction company is strictly liable for the harm caused by the blasting.

(B) Incorrect. For the rancher in trespass, because the fright due to the vibrations caused the mink to eat their young.

(C) Incorrect. Against the rancher, because he assumed the risk that such a business would emerge.

Explanation: Question 89

The correct answer is: **(B)** $50,000, which represents the proportion of the taxi driver's damages caused by the defendant's negligence, less the medical and hospital payments made by the defendant's insurance company.

Once again, you are instructed to assume pure comparative negligence unless told otherwise. In a "pure" comparative negligence jurisdiction, a plaintiff's contributory negligence does not operate to bar her recovery altogether, but does reduce her damages in proportion to her fault. Thus, a plaintiff can recover even if her fault is greater than 50 percent. In this example, the plaintiff's damages award of $100,000 will be reduced by the percentage of fault attributed to her, namely 30 percent or $30,000. The remaining amount, $70,000, will then be reduced by an additional $20,000, representing the payment made by the defendant's insurance company to plaintiff, since this amount comprises part of the $100,000 damage award itself. Therefore, the taxi driver will recover $50,000. Choice (B) is correct. (C) is incorrect because the "collateral sources" rule covers situations where the plaintiff has recovered damages from her own insurance company. Such benefit will not reduce or affect the amount of recovery from the tortfeasor. However, the "collateral sources" rule does not apply here because the defendant's insurance company paid part of plaintiff's damages.

(A) Incorrect. $40,000, which represents the proportion of the taxi driver's damages caused by the defendant's negligence, less the proportion caused by the taxi driver's negligence.

(C) Incorrect. $70,000, which represents the proportion of the taxi driver's damages caused by the defendant's negligence, with the medical and hospital payments being disregarded as coming from a collateral source.

(D) Incorrect. $100,000, because the defendant's negligence was greater than that of the taxi driver.

Explanation: Question 90

The correct answer is: **(B)** Yes, because the customer is a business invitee.

The bookstore hired a contracting company, an independent contractor, to perform renovations to its building. In most jurisdictions, the owner of a commercial enterprise open to business invitees cannot delegate responsibility for the maintenance of the public premises to an independent contractor. If the contractor is negligent in work on the premises, the business will also be liable. The need to protect the customer's safety is deemed more important than the owner being held liable when he is not personally negligent because the owner can obtain insurance or put an indemnity clause in his agreement with the contractor. This is not strict liability as someone--the contractor--must be negligent. It is a form of derivative or vicarious liability. Here, the contracting company was negligent in applying the plaster. The customer has come on the premises to buy a book. He is a business invitee. Both the contracting company and the bookstore will be liable for his injuries and choice (B) is correct. Choice (C) is not correct. The contracting company's acts being the cause of injury does not eliminate the bookstore's liability on a vicarious liability theory. Rather, it is a necessary element. Choice (D) is incorrect. This type of duty cannot be delegated as discussed above.

(A) Incorrect. Yes, because the book store failed to close the store after the manager noticed the plaster on the floor.

(C) Incorrect. No, because the contracting company's acts were the actual and legal cause of the injuries.

(D) Incorrect. No, because responsibility for the construction of the building was properly delegated to the contracting company.

Explanation: Question 91

The correct answer is: **(C)** No, because the man had no reason to anticipate the presence of another person in such a remote area.

A popular Multistate testing area deals with proximate or legal cause. In order to be liable for negligence, defendant's conduct must constitute the legal or proximate cause of plaintiff's harm or injury. According to the rule enunciated in the Palsgraf case, Judge Cardozo stated that a defendant's duty of care is owed only to foreseeable plaintiffs (i.e., those individuals who are within the risk of harm created by defendant's unreasonable conduct). Choice (C) is the best answer because it addresses the fact that the forest ranger was an unforeseeable plaintiff to whom no duty of care was owed. Choice (B) is incorrect because transferred intent does not apply chattel-to-person, only person-to-person.

(A) Incorrect. Yes, because the man's shooting the gun was the actual cause of the forest ranger's injury.

(B) Incorrect. Yes, because the man intended to shoot the condor.

(D) Incorrect. No, because the bullet ricocheted off a tree and hit the forest ranger.

Explanation: Question 92

The correct answer is: **(D)** No, because it was an accidental entry that was unintentional.

According to Restatement of Torts 2d, Section 166, a person is not liable for trespass for an "accidental" entry that is unintentional and non-negligent. Here, for example, the facts state that the friend hit a golf ball down the middle of the fairway. The ball struck a tree limb and then ricocheted onto the homeowner's property. Since this is an "accidental" entry, choice (D) is correct. The distracter is choice (B) because the general outlines advise students that intent to trespass is not required; it is only the intent to do the act that is necessary. MBE Exam Tip: This definition applies to intentional entries that involve mistake (meaning that it is simply the intent to enter that is required). This particular question, however, does not deal with an intentional entry, but an "accidental" entry that was unintentional.

(A) Incorrect. Yes, because the golf ball intruded onto the homeowner's property.

(B) Incorrect. Yes, because the friend intended the act of hitting the golf ball.

(C) Incorrect. No, because the homeowner did not suffer physical injury.

Explanation: Question 93

The correct answer is: **(C)** Negligent infliction of emotional distress.

By process of elimination, choice (C) would be correct. First, choice (A) is incorrect because when the patient consulted the doctor, she impliedly consented to his touching her for the purposes of medical treatment. Alternative (D) is incorrect because the doctor did not manifest any wrongful intent to inflict emotional distress. The tough choice is between (B) and (C). Choice (B) is not the best answer because, to recover for emotional distress inflicted through negligence, the emotional distress must follow some form of physical injury suffered by the plaintiff. Here, the emotional distress occurred before the plaintiff suffered physical injury. Therefore, choice (C) is the preferred answer.

(A) Incorrect. Battery.

(B) Incorrect. Negligence.

(D) Incorrect. Intentional infliction of emotional distress.

Explanation: Question 94

The correct answer is: **(B)** The young woman prevails in a cause of action for invasion of privacy.

Intrusion into seclusion is a form of invasion of privacy that occurs when a defendant unreasonably intrudes into a plaintiff's right to physical solitude or to the plaintiff's privacy of personal affairs or concerns. This type of invasion of privacy includes physical intrusions (placing a web-camera in the plaintiff's house) and non-physical intrusions (photographing the plaintiff in her backyard from off the property). To be actionable, the intrusion must occur where the plaintiff has an expectation of privacy or solitude. Furthermore, the defendant's intrusion must be one that would be highly objectionable to a reasonable person. Here, the young man committed a non-physical intrusion when he took photographs of the young woman while she was in her backyard. Such conduct would be considered highly objectionable to a reasonable person. Therefore, the young woman will prevail in an action for invasion of privacy.

(A) Incorrect. The young woman prevails in a cause of action for nuisance.

A private nuisance is a thing or activity that substantially and unreasonably interferes with the plaintiff's use and enjoyment of her land. The reason that this answer choice is not the best is that during the time the young man was photographing her, the young woman was unaware of his conduct so it did not interfere with the use and enjoyment of her property. The better answer is that the woman will prevail in a cause of action for invasion of privacy.

(C) Incorrect. The young woman does not prevail in a cause of action for nuisance, because the young man's conduct did not involve physical intrusion.

The tort of nuisance, unlike trespass to land, does not require that there be a physical intrusion. Hence, even if there was no physical intrusion, the young man could have still been liable for nuisance. The young man is not liable for nuisance, however, because he did not interfere with the young woman's use and enjoyment of her land so much as he invaded her privacy. She was not aware of his conduct until his last time so his actions never actually interfered with her enjoyment of her property. Invasion of privacy is the better cause of action in this case.

(D) Incorrect. The young woman does not prevail in a cause of action for invasion of privacy, because the young man's conduct did not involve physical intrusion.

The tort of invasion of privacy does not require that there be physical intrusion in order to hold the defendant liable. The type of invasion of privacy in this case, intrusion into seclusion, includes physical intrusions (placing a web-camera in the plaintiff's house) and non-physical intrusions (photographing the plaintiff in her backyard from off the property). To be actionable, the intrusion must occur where the plaintiff has an expectation of privacy or solitude. Furthermore, the defendant's intrusion must be one that would be highly objectionable to a reasonable person. Because any reasonable person would find the young man's conduct highly objectionable, the young woman will most likely prevail in a cause of action for invasion of privacy.

Explanation: Question 95

The correct answer is: **(C)** No, because the husband was convicted on criminal charges.

Malicious prosecution is the institution of criminal proceedings by defendant, done for an improper purpose and without probable cause, that terminate favorably to plaintiff and cause plaintiff damages. Here, the wife did initiate criminal proceedings against the husband for an improper purpose without probable cause. However, the proceedings did not turn out favorably for the husband so as a plaintiff in a malicious prosecution case, the husband has failed to make his case. Note that even if the husband had been found innocent at the criminal trial, which requires proof beyond a reasonable doubt, if the wife could prove in the civil trial by a preponderance of the evidence that the husband was a mass murderer, then the wife has a defense to the charge of malicious prosecution.

(A) Incorrect. Yes, because at the time the wife convinced the prosecutor to bring charges, she did not know that her husband was a mass murderer.

Generally, if the defendant initiating the criminal proceedings does not actually believe the plaintiff to be guilty, then it is established that the defendant lacked probable cause to initiate the proceedings. However, the wife will still escape liability because a plaintiff's conviction on criminal charges is conclusive evidence of probable cause, even if the conviction is subsequently reversed on appeal. Thus the wife is not liable for malicious prosecution.

(B) Incorrect. Yes, because a reasonable person would not have believed that the husband was guilty.

Generally, if a reasonable person possessing the same facts as defendant would not have believed that plaintiff was guilty of the charged offense, then there was no probable cause to initiate criminal proceedings. However, since the husband was actually convicted, the conviction is conclusive evidence of probable cause and the wife will not be found liable.

(D) Incorrect. No, because the prosecutor had the last chance to decide whether to bring charges against the husband.

It does not matter that the prosecutor had the last chance to decide whether to bring charges against the husband. The wrongful conduct is the taking of action that results in commencement of the criminal prosecution of plaintiff. Such actions include persuading a prosecutor to bring charges against plaintiff, signing an affidavit for a warrant, or giving false information to the authorities with knowledge of its falsity. Here, the wife persuaded the prosecutor to bring charges, so she would have been guilty if not for the husband's conviction.

Explanation: Question 96

The correct answer is: **(A)** Yes, because the computer's defect caused the damage.

Unless the plaintiff knew of the defect, comprehended the risks posed by the defect, and voluntarily elected to expose herself to those risks, the manufacturer does not have a defense to strict products liability in a jurisdiction that has not adopted a comparative negligence approach. Here, the computer had a defective leg causing the student to use the computer without the legs extended. As a result, the computer overheated and caused a fire. Although the student comprehended that there was a problem with the leg of the computer, she did not appreciate the risk posed by using the computer in its defective condition.

(B) Incorrect. Yes, because the computer's defect was not detected by the student.

Actually, the student was aware of the defect. She knew that the leg would not pull out correctly. But she did not appreciate the risk of damage that the situation posed. Unless the plaintiff knew of the defect, comprehended the risks posed by the defect, and voluntarily elected to expose herself to those risks, the manufacturer does not have a defense to strict products liability in a jurisdiction that has not adopted a comparative negligence approach.

(C) Incorrect. No, because there were no personal injuries.

Products liability applies to property damage as well as to personal injury. Therefore this answer choice is incorrect.

(D) Incorrect. No, because the student perceived the defect in the computer.

The student did perceive the defect in the computer, but she did not perceive the risk it posed. For the manufacturer to have a defense based on the student knowing about the defect, the student also would have had to appreciate the risk and voluntarily elected to expose herself to it, in a jurisdiction that has not adopted a comparative negligence approach to products liability. As such, this answer choice is incorrect.

Explanation: Question 97

The correct answer is: **(C)** The manufacturer prevails, because the young man misused the product.

In general, if strict liability is otherwise applicable, any plaintiff injured while using a defective product may recover damages from an appropriate defendant. Commercial suppliers at all levels of the distribution chain (i.e., manufacturer, distributor, retailer) may be defendants. In this case, the manufacturer is a proper defendant. However, if a plaintiff uses a product in a manner that is neither intended nor foreseeable, she has misused the product and it cannot be defective. Here, it certainly seems like the young man misused the bathtub by riding it down a hill. Therefore, the product will not be considered defective, and the manufacturer will prevail.

(A) Incorrect. The young man prevails, because the manufacturer is in the bathtub's distribution chain.

Although a manufacturer is a proper defendant for an action for a defective product, because he is in the product's distribution chain, this is not sufficient in this case to establish strict liability. That is because the product will not be considered defective if the plaintiff used the product in a manner that is neither intended nor foreseeable. Here, the young man used the bathtub for an unintended and unforeseeable purpose, so he will not prevail.

(B) Incorrect. The young man prevails, because the bathtub had a design defect.

Although generally a manufacturer will be liable for design defects of a product, the defects will not bring about strict liability if the plaintiff misuses the product. In this case, the young man misused the bathtub, so he will not prevail.

(D) Incorrect. The manufacturer prevails, because the young man was contributorily negligent.

Although this answer is incorrect in stating that the manufacturer will prevail, it offers the wrong reason. Assumption of the risk was the original defense to strict product liability, rather than contributory negligence. Therefore, the plaintiff had to know of the defect, comprehend the risks posed by the defect, and voluntarily elect to expose himself to those risks. In this case, the young man did not know that the bathtub might crack, so he cannot be said to have assumed the risk. Instead, the issue here is his unforeseeable misuse.

Explanation: Question 98

The correct answer is: **(B)** Yes, because the plaintiff was injured while using the product and the retailer is in the chain of distribution of the lamp.

In general, if strict liability is otherwise applicable, any plaintiff injured while using a defective product may recover damages from an appropriate defendant. This includes purchasers and consumers, and their families, friends, guests, and employees. In this case, the plaintiff was injured while using a defective product; therefore, it is appropriate for him to seek damages in a strict products liability action. As for the defendant, in a suit for strict products liability, commercial suppliers at all levels of the distribution chain (i.e., manufacturer, distributor, retailer) are all potential defendants. Therefore, the retailer is an appropriate defendant.

(A) Incorrect. Yes, because the defect in question was a manufacturing defect.

Strict products liability is invoked when a defective product, for which an appropriate defendant is responsible, injures an appropriate plaintiff. There are several types of defects which can lead to strict products liability, including manufacturing defects. However, this is not the only type of defect that can lead to strict products liability. Therefore, it is incorrect to say that the plaintiff can sustain his action because the defect in question was a manufacturing defect.

(C) Incorrect. No, because the plaintiff was not a foreseeable plaintiff in this case.

In general, if strict liability is otherwise applicable, any plaintiff injured while using a defective product may recover damages from an appropriate defendant. This includes purchasers and consumers, and their families, friends, guests, and employees. As such, the plaintiff, being the purchaser's roommate and friend, is indeed an appropriate plaintiff, and this answer choice is incorrect.

(D) Incorrect. No, because the defect was caused by the manufacturer, not the retailer.

Commercial suppliers at all levels of the distribution chain (i.e., manufacturer, distributor, retailer) as well as commercial lessors, new home developers, and sellers of used goods are potential defendants in a strict products liability case. In strict products liability cases, a party in the chain of distribution may be a party even if the party is not at fault. As such, the retailer may still be a defendant even if the defect was a result of the manufacturing process.

Explanation: Question 99

The correct answer is: **(B)** Yes, because the defendant was engaged in an abnormally dangerous activity.

A defendant may be held strictly liable for injuries caused when he is engaged in an abnormally dangerous activity. A judge determines whether an activity is abnormally dangerous by considering whether the activity creates a risk of serious injury as to plaintiff, his land, or his chattels; whether the risk can be eliminated by the exercise of due care; and whether the activity is not usually conducted in that area. Dynamiting, crop-dusting, and exterminating have been found abnormally dangerous. For strict liability to apply, the harm to the plaintiff must have resulted from the type of danger that justified classifying the activity as dangerous. Here, the defendant was engaged in extermination, which is an abnormally dangerous activity. Moreover, the threat of being harmed by toxic fumes is indeed what makes this activity abnormally dangerous. As such, the defendant will be strictly liable for the damages caused to the residents, even though he took precautions.

(A) Incorrect. Yes, because the defendant breached his duty of care to the residents.

Whether or not the defendant breached a duty of care to the residents is irrelevant in this case because a defendant may be held strictly liable for injuries caused by his abnormally dangerous activity. The determinants of whether an activity is abnormally dangerous are whether the activity creates a risk of serious injury as to plaintiff, his land, or his chattels; whether this risk cannot be eliminated by the exercise of due care; and whether the activity is not usually conducted in that area. Here, the defendant was engaged in extermination, an abnormally dangerous activity, and the threat of being harmed by toxic fumes is what makes it abnormally dangerous. As such, the defendant will be strictly liable for the residents' damages, regardless of whether the residents can prove the elements of negligence against the defendant.

(C) Incorrect. No, because the residents will not be able to prove the defendant's negligence.

The residents do not need to prove negligence in this case. Because the defendant was engaged in an abnormally dangerous activity, the residents can sue on a theory of strict liability. As such, this answer choice is incorrect.

(D) Incorrect. No, because the defendant took all possible precautions against injury.

Even if the defendant took all precautions against injury, he may still be liable to the residents under a theory of strict liability. A defendant may be held strictly liable for injuries caused when he is engaged in an abnormally dangerous activity. Here, the defendant was engaged in extermination, which is an abnormally dangerous activity, and the threat of being harmed by toxic fumes is indeed what makes this activity abnormally dangerous. As such, the defendant will be strictly liable for the damages caused to the residents, regardless of the steps he took to protect against injury.

Explanation: Question 100

The correct answer is: **(A)** Yes, because he caused an offensive contact with the woman's hat.

The tort of battery is defined as an intentional act that causes a harmful or offensive contact with the plaintiff or with something closely connected thereto. In this case, the man caused an offensive contact with the woman when he intentionally knocked the hat off her head. Since the hat was closely connected to the woman, the man's action constitutes battery. Note that the fact that the woman did not immediately notice that the man had knocked off her hat is irrelevant. Unlike with the tort of assault, the tort of battery does not require that the plaintiff be aware of the harmful or offensive contact at the time that it occurs. Therefore, this is the correct answer choice.

(B) Incorrect. Yes, because the hat was expensive and thus the man's actions would offend a reasonable person.

The harmful or offensive contact element of a claim for battery is satisfied if the contact would inflict pain or impairment of any body function, or if a reasonable person would regard it as offensive. This answer is tempting in that it refers to the reasonable person standard for an offensive contact. However, this answer incorrectly suggests that the reason that a reasonable person would find the man's contact offensive is that the hat was expensive; in fact, for purposes of determining whether a battery has occurred, the value of the hat is irrelevant. As such, this is not the best answer choice.

(C) Incorrect. No, because the man did not cause an offensive contact with the woman's person.

One of the elements of civil battery is that there must be a harmful or offensive contact with the plaintiff or with something closely connected thereto. In this case, the man touched the woman's hat, which was closely connected to the woman. Therefore, although the man did not cause an offensive contact with the woman's physical person, this element of battery is satisfied under the circumstances, and this answer is incorrect.

(D) Incorrect. No, because the woman did not realize that the man had touched her hat until several minutes later.

The fact that the woman did not immediately notice that the man had removed her hat is irrelevant. With the tort of battery, unlike with the tort of assault, the plaintiff need not be aware of the harmful or offensive contact at the time it occurs. Therefore, this answer is incorrect.

1. INTENTIONAL TORTS: PERSONAL AND EMOTIONAL INJURY

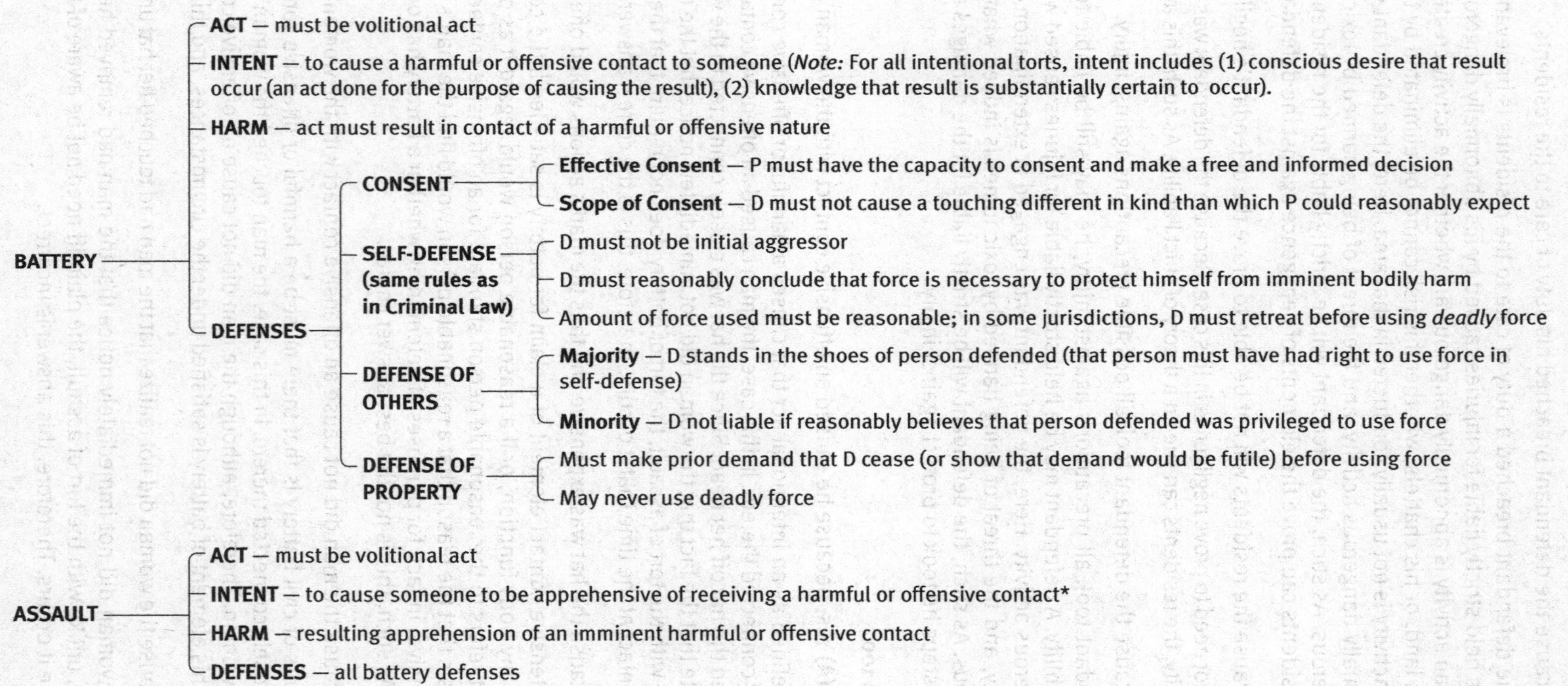

1. INTENTIONAL TORTS: PERSONAL AND EMOTIONAL INJURY (*continued*)

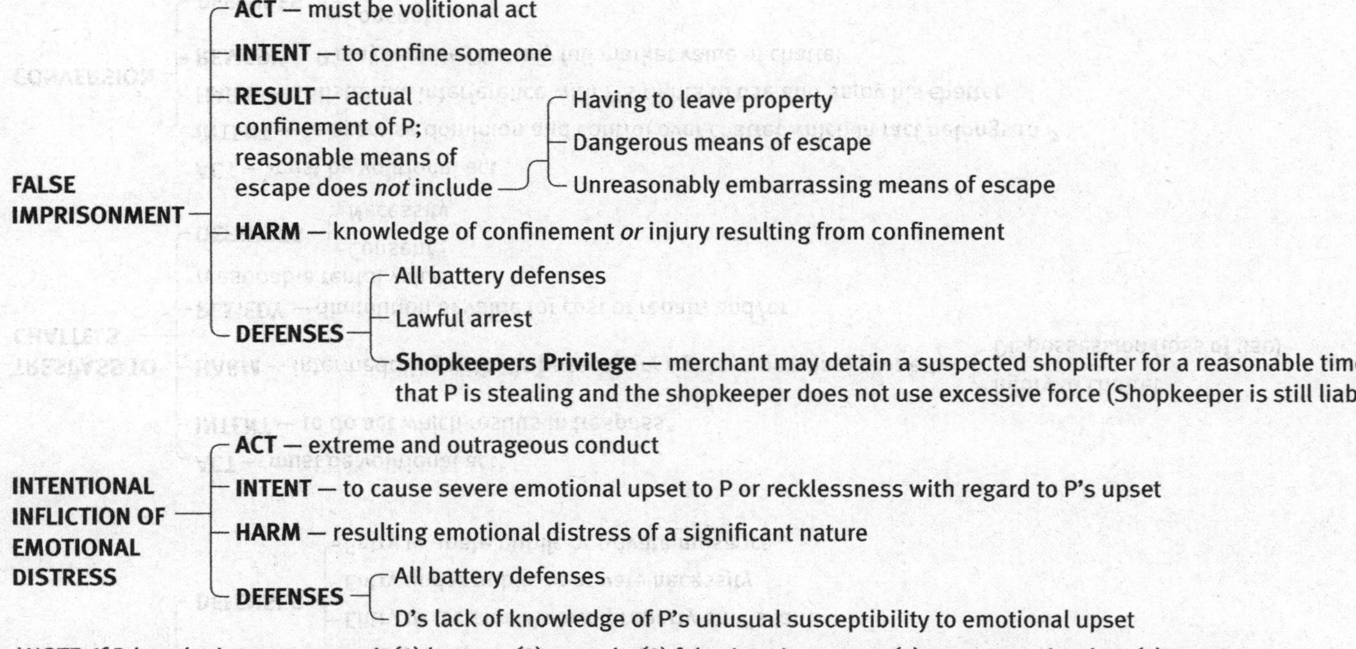

FALSE IMPRISONMENT

- **ACT** — must be volitional act
- **INTENT** — to confine someone
- **RESULT** — actual confinement of P; reasonable means of escape does *not* include
  - Having to leave property
  - Dangerous means of escape
  - Unreasonably embarrassing means of escape
- **HARM** — knowledge of confinement *or* injury resulting from confinement
- **DEFENSES**
  - All battery defenses
  - Lawful arrest
  - **Shopkeepers Privilege** — merchant may detain a suspected shoplifter for a reasonable time if he has probable cause that P is stealing and the shopkeeper does not use excessive force (Shopkeeper is still liable for actual injuries)

INTENTIONAL INFLICTION OF EMOTIONAL DISTRESS

- **ACT** — extreme and outrageous conduct
- **INTENT** — to cause severe emotional upset to P or recklessness with regard to P's upset
- **HARM** — resulting emotional distress of a significant nature
- **DEFENSES**
  - All battery defenses
  - D's lack of knowledge of P's unusual susceptibility to emotional upset

**NOTE: If D has the intent to commit (1) battery, (2) assault, (3) false imprisonment, (4) trespass to land, or (5) trespass to chattels and ends up causing an injury protected by any other of these five torts, the intent requirement is satisfied.*

2. INTENTIONAL TORTS: INJURY TO PROPERTY

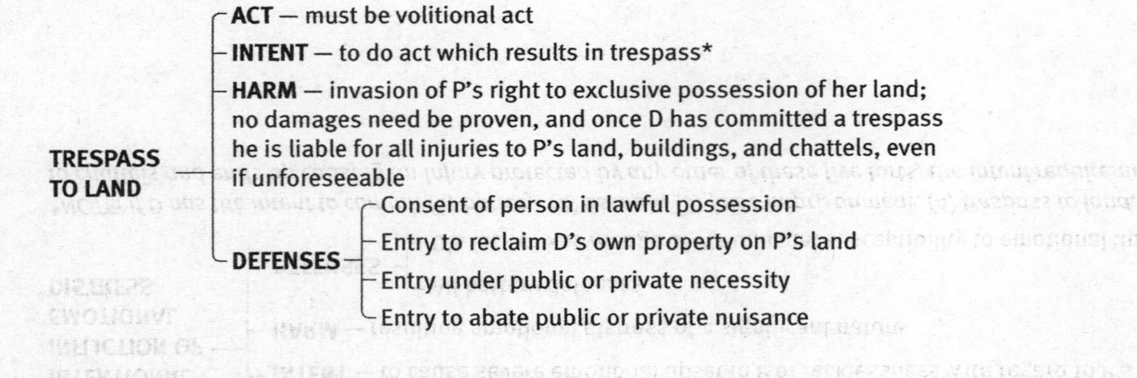

TRESPASS TO LAND
- **ACT** — must be volitional act
- **INTENT** — to do act which results in trespass*
- **HARM** — invasion of P's right to exclusive possession of her land; no damages need be proven, and once D has committed a trespass he is liable for all injuries to P's land, buildings, and chattels, even if unforeseeable
- **DEFENSES**
  - Consent of person in lawful possession
  - Entry to reclaim D's own property on P's land
  - Entry under public or private necessity
  - Entry to abate public or private nuisance

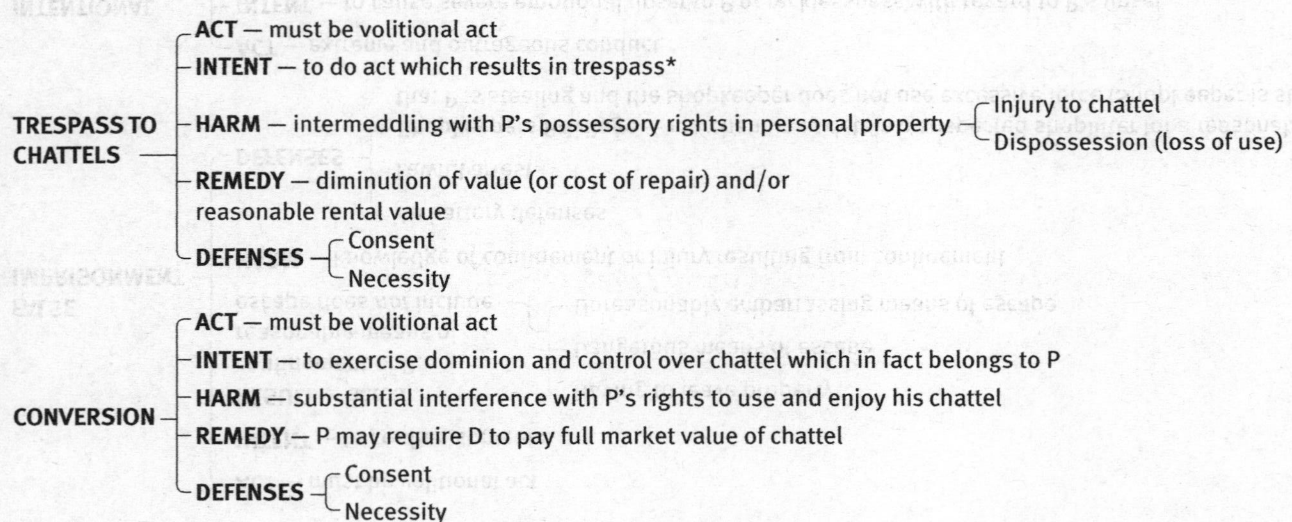

TRESPASS TO CHATTELS
- **ACT** — must be volitional act
- **INTENT** — to do act which results in trespass*
- **HARM** — intermeddling with P's possessory rights in personal property
  - Injury to chattel
  - Dispossession (loss of use)
- **REMEDY** — diminution of value (or cost of repair) and/or reasonable rental value
- **DEFENSES**
  - Consent
  - Necessity

CONVERSION
- **ACT** — must be volitional act
- **INTENT** — to exercise dominion and control over chattel which in fact belongs to P
- **HARM** — substantial interference with P's rights to use and enjoy his chattel
- **REMEDY** — P may require D to pay full market value of chattel
- **DEFENSES**
  - Consent
  - Necessity

**NOTE: If D has the intent to commit (1) battery, (2) assault, (3) false imprisonment, (4) trespass to land, or (5) trespass to chattels and ends up causing an injury protected by any other of these five torts, the intent requirement is satisfied.*

3. DEFAMATION

DEFAMATORY STATEMENT — one which subjects P to hatred, contempt, or ridicule (1st Restatement) or which lowers the esteem in which P is held by third parties (2nd Restatement)

OF OR CONCERNING P — someone must recognize that the statement is about this particular P

- P must be a living human being
- Group defamation
  - **Small group (less than 25)** — all members may have action even if statement is not all-inclusive
  - **Medium group (between 25 and 150)** — may give each member a cause of action if all-inclusive
  - **Large group (over 150)** — no member may sue even if statement is all-inclusive

PUBLICATION — at least one third party must hear the statement and understand its defamatory nature; D must be at least negligent with regard to the publication

PROOF OF SPECIAL DAMAGES OR EXCEPTION (a prima facie case requirement, *not* a rule of damages)

- **Special Damages** — pecuniary loss resulting from a third party's response to the defamatory statement
- **Exceptions**
  - **Slander per se** — oral statements relating to: (1) incompetence in trade or profession, (2) present loathsome disease, (3) commission of serious crime, *or* (4) serious sexual misconduct
  - **Libel (written statements)** — in some states all libel is actionable without proof of special damages, but common law required special damages unless libel is
    - **On its face** — (no innuendo or external knowledge is required to understand the statement's defamatory nature) *or*
    - **Per quod** — (innuendo or external knowledge is required to understand the statement's defamatory nature) *if* defamation relates to a slander per se category

DEFENSES

- **Truth** must go to defamatory sting
- **Absolute Privileges (not defeated by even spite or knowledge of falsity)** — (1) legislative proceeding, (2) judicial proceedings, (3) other official statements of governmental officials, (4) equal time broadcasts, and (5) communications between spouses
- **Common Law Qualified Privileges (defeated by spite or ill will, knowledge of falsity or reckless disregard of truth, and, perhaps, negligence)** — (1) statements in D's own interest, (2) statements in the interest of third persons, (3) statements in the interest of the public, (4) reports of public proceedings, and (5) fair comment opinions
- **First Amendment Qualified Privileges**
  - **Public Officials, Candidates for Public Office, and Well-Known Public Figures** — must prove "malice" as defined by *NY Times v Sullivan* (that D knew statement was false or acted in reckless disregard of truth)
  - **Limited Public Figures** — ordinary persons who *voluntarily* inject themselves into a public controversy are treated as public figures if alleged defamation relates to their position in the controversy but are treated as private persons if defamation concerns other matters
  - **Private Persons** — must prove negligence with regard to truth when defendant is a member of the media; jurisdictions split when D is a private person

DAMAGES (once prima facie case, including existence of some special damages or exceptions, is made)

- All special damages (defined above), including lost customers and lost employment
- Damage to P's reputation
- Damage to P's feelings, including medical bills attributable to P's emotional distress
- Punitive damages (when appropriate)
- *Note:* When First Amendment qualified privilege applies, only actual damages (i.e., those proven with reasonable certainty by P) and not punitive damages may be recovered unless P proves malice

4. NEGLIGENCE

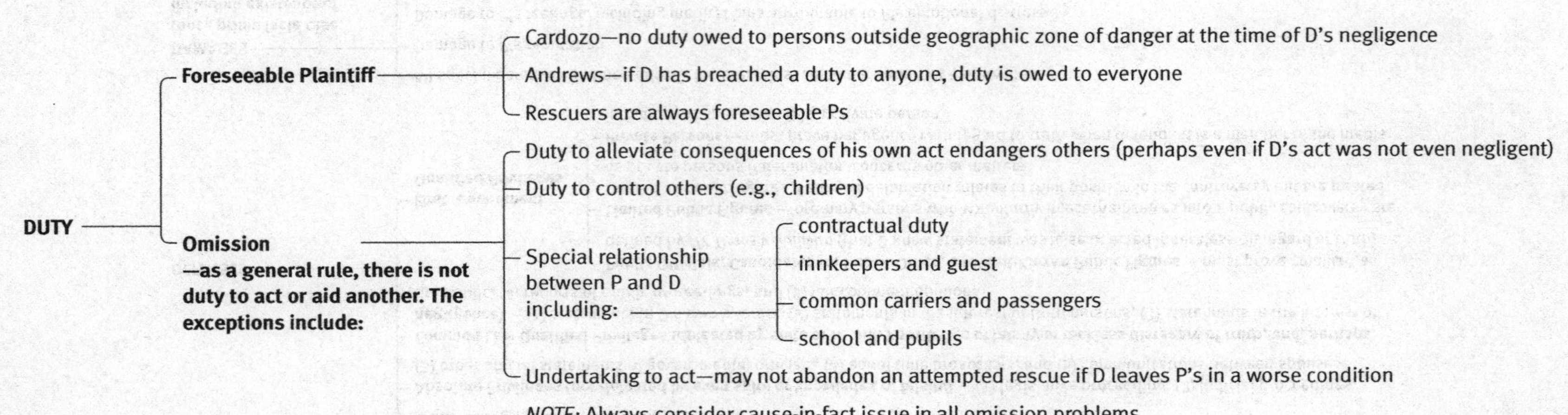

4. NEGLIGENCE *(continued)*

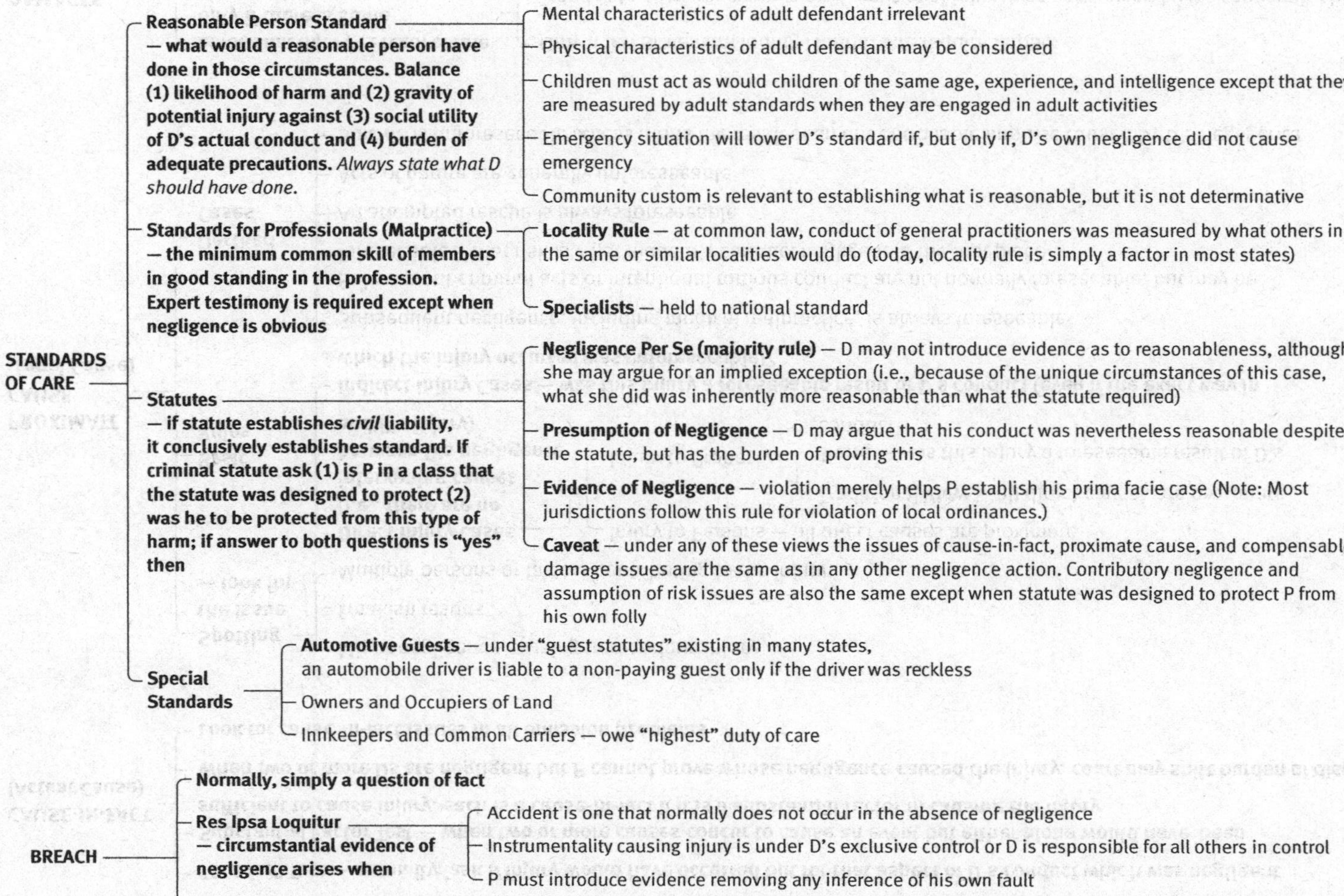

- **STANDARDS OF CARE**
  - **Reasonable Person Standard — what would a reasonable person have done in those circumstances. Balance (1) likelihood of harm and (2) gravity of potential injury against (3) social utility of D's actual conduct and (4) burden of adequate precautions.** *Always state what D should have done.*
    - Mental characteristics of adult defendant irrelevant
    - Physical characteristics of adult defendant may be considered
    - Children must act as would children of the same age, experience, and intelligence except that they are measured by adult standards when they are engaged in adult activities
    - Emergency situation will lower D's standard if, but only if, D's own negligence did not cause emergency
    - Community custom is relevant to establishing what is reasonable, but it is not determinative
  - **Standards for Professionals (Malpractice) — the minimum common skill of members in good standing in the profession. Expert testimony is required except when negligence is obvious**
    - **Locality Rule** — at common law, conduct of general practitioners was measured by what others in the same or similar localities would do (today, locality rule is simply a factor in most states)
    - **Specialists** — held to national standard
  - **Statutes — if statute establishes *civil* liability, it conclusively establishes standard. If criminal statute ask (1) is P in a class that the statute was designed to protect (2) was he to be protected from this type of harm; if answer to both questions is "yes" then**
    - **Negligence Per Se (majority rule)** — D may not introduce evidence as to reasonableness, although she may argue for an implied exception (i.e., because of the unique circumstances of this case, what she did was inherently more reasonable than what the statute required)
    - **Presumption of Negligence** — D may argue that his conduct was nevertheless reasonable despite the statute, but has the burden of proving this
    - **Evidence of Negligence** — violation merely helps P establish his prima facie case (Note: Most jurisdictions follow this rule for violation of local ordinances.)
    - **Caveat** — under any of these views the issues of cause-in-fact, proximate cause, and compensable damage issues are the same as in any other negligence action. Contributory negligence and assumption of risk issues are also the same except when statute was designed to protect P from his own folly
  - **Special Standards**
    - **Automotive Guests** — under "guest statutes" existing in many states, an automobile driver is liable to a non-paying guest only if the driver was reckless
    - Owners and Occupiers of Land
    - Innkeepers and Common Carriers — owe "highest" duty of care
- **BREACH**
  - **Normally, simply a question of fact**
  - **Res Ipsa Loquitur — circumstantial evidence of negligence arises when**
    - Accident is one that normally does not occur in the absence of negligence
    - Instrumentality causing injury is under D's exclusive control or D is responsible for all others in control
    - P must introduce evidence removing any inference of his own fault
  - **Concurrent Conduct — even conduct which is not negligent by itself will be actionable if it combines with similar conduct of others if the other's conduct was foreseeable**

(continued)

4. NEGLIGENCE *(continued)*

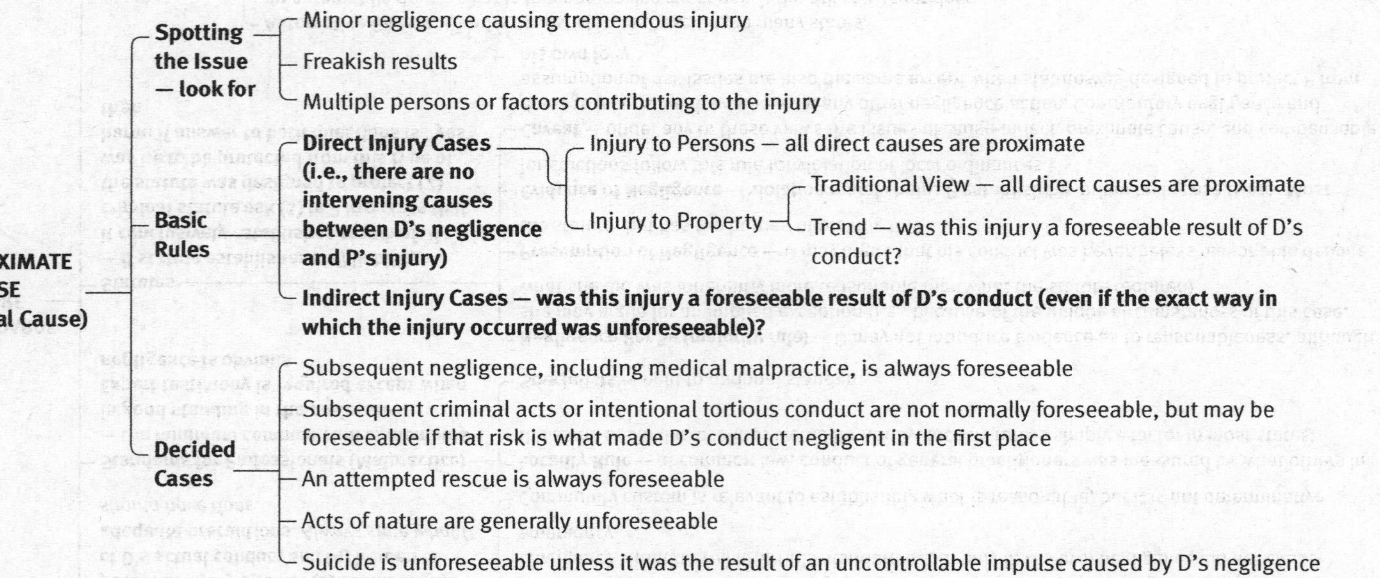

- **CAUSE-IN-FACT (Actual Cause)**
  - **"But for" Test — normally, ask if injury would have occurred but for that aspect of D's conduct which was negligent**
  - **Substantial Factor Test — when two or more causes concur to cause an event but either alone would have been sufficient to cause injury, each is a cause-in-fact if it is a substantial factor in causing the injury**
  - **When two or more Ds are negligent but P cannot prove whose negligence caused the injury, court may shift burden of disproving causation to Ds**
  - **Look for cause-in-fact issues in all omission problems**
- **PROXIMATE CAUSE (Legal Cause)**
  - **Spotting the Issue — look for**
    - Minor negligence causing tremendous injury
    - Freakish results
    - Multiple persons or factors contributing to the injury
  - **Basic Rules**
    - **Direct Injury Cases (i.e., there are no intervening causes between D's negligence and P's injury)**
      - Injury to Persons — all direct causes are proximate
      - Injury to Property
        - Traditional View — all direct causes are proximate
        - Trend — was this injury a foreseeable result of D's conduct?
    - **Indirect Injury Cases — was this injury a foreseeable result of D's conduct (even if the exact way in which the injury occurred was unforeseeable)?**
  - **Decided Cases**
    - Subsequent negligence, including medical malpractice, is always foreseeable
    - Subsequent criminal acts or intentional tortious conduct are not normally foreseeable, but may be foreseeable if that risk is what made D's conduct negligent in the first place
    - An attempted rescue is always foreseeable
    - Acts of nature are generally unforeseeable
    - Suicide is unforeseeable unless it was the result of an uncontrollable impulse caused by D's negligence
- **DAMAGES**
  - **Emotional Injury — recoverable only if there is some accompanying physical injury**
    - Only a few states (including Florida) still require impact
    - Trend is to allow recovery even if emotional injury was not caused by P's concern for her own safety
  - **Pure economic injury not protectable by negligence cause of action**

6. PRODUCTS LIABILITY *(continued)*

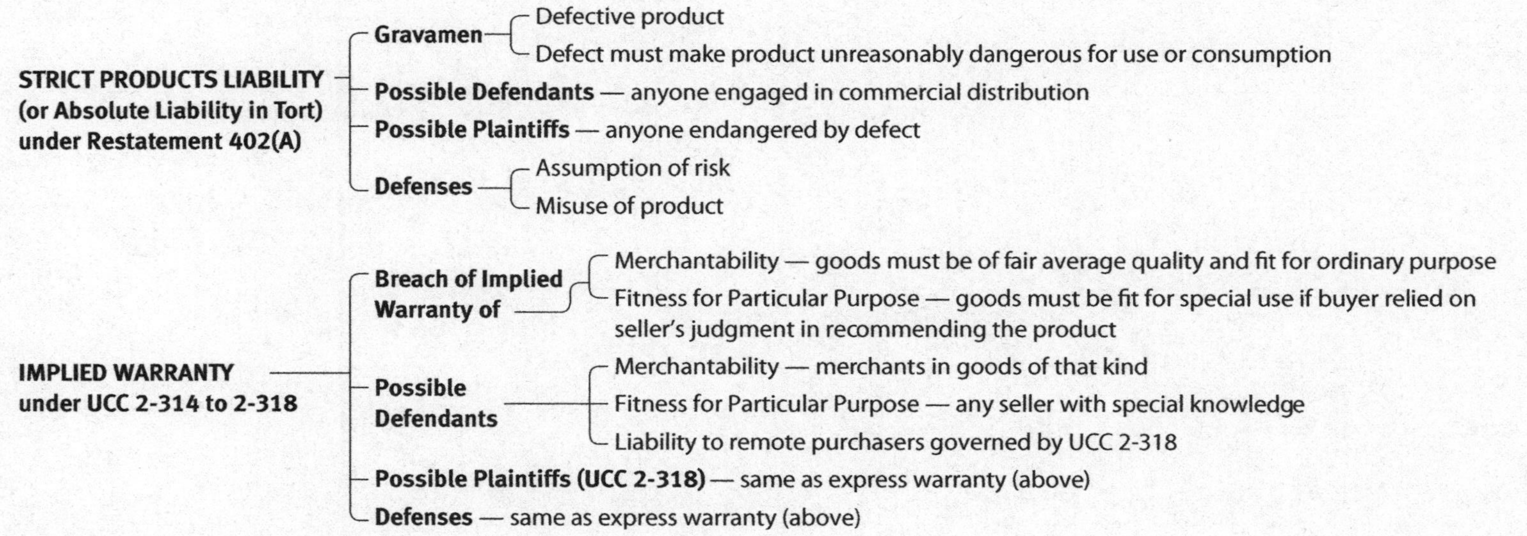

pmbr

Contracts

Practice Questions

Answer Grid

1 Ⓐ Ⓑ Ⓒ Ⓓ	21 Ⓐ Ⓑ Ⓒ Ⓓ	41 Ⓐ Ⓑ Ⓒ Ⓓ	61 Ⓐ Ⓑ Ⓒ Ⓓ	81 Ⓐ Ⓑ Ⓒ Ⓓ
2 Ⓐ Ⓑ Ⓒ Ⓓ	22 Ⓐ Ⓑ Ⓒ Ⓓ	42 Ⓐ Ⓑ Ⓒ Ⓓ	62 Ⓐ Ⓑ Ⓒ Ⓓ	82 Ⓐ Ⓑ Ⓒ Ⓓ
3 Ⓐ Ⓑ Ⓒ Ⓓ	23 Ⓐ Ⓑ Ⓒ Ⓓ	43 Ⓐ Ⓑ Ⓒ Ⓓ	63 Ⓐ Ⓑ Ⓒ Ⓓ	83 Ⓐ Ⓑ Ⓒ Ⓓ
4 Ⓐ Ⓑ Ⓒ Ⓓ	24 Ⓐ Ⓑ Ⓒ Ⓓ	44 Ⓐ Ⓑ Ⓒ Ⓓ	64 Ⓐ Ⓑ Ⓒ Ⓓ	84 Ⓐ Ⓑ Ⓒ Ⓓ
5 Ⓐ Ⓑ Ⓒ Ⓓ	25 Ⓐ Ⓑ Ⓒ Ⓓ	45 Ⓐ Ⓑ Ⓒ Ⓓ	65 Ⓐ Ⓑ Ⓒ Ⓓ	85 Ⓐ Ⓑ Ⓒ Ⓓ
6 Ⓐ Ⓑ Ⓒ Ⓓ	26 Ⓐ Ⓑ Ⓒ Ⓓ	46 Ⓐ Ⓑ Ⓒ Ⓓ	66 Ⓐ Ⓑ Ⓒ Ⓓ	86 Ⓐ Ⓑ Ⓒ Ⓓ
7 Ⓐ Ⓑ Ⓒ Ⓓ	27 Ⓐ Ⓑ Ⓒ Ⓓ	47 Ⓐ Ⓑ Ⓒ Ⓓ	67 Ⓐ Ⓑ Ⓒ Ⓓ	87 Ⓐ Ⓑ Ⓒ Ⓓ
8 Ⓐ Ⓑ Ⓒ Ⓓ	28 Ⓐ Ⓑ Ⓒ Ⓓ	48 Ⓐ Ⓑ Ⓒ Ⓓ	68 Ⓐ Ⓑ Ⓒ Ⓓ	88 Ⓐ Ⓑ Ⓒ Ⓓ
9 Ⓐ Ⓑ Ⓒ Ⓓ	29 Ⓐ Ⓑ Ⓒ Ⓓ	49 Ⓐ Ⓑ Ⓒ Ⓓ	69 Ⓐ Ⓑ Ⓒ Ⓓ	89 Ⓐ Ⓑ Ⓒ Ⓓ
10 Ⓐ Ⓑ Ⓒ Ⓓ	30 Ⓐ Ⓑ Ⓒ Ⓓ	50 Ⓐ Ⓑ Ⓒ Ⓓ	70 Ⓐ Ⓑ Ⓒ Ⓓ	90 Ⓐ Ⓑ Ⓒ Ⓓ
11 Ⓐ Ⓑ Ⓒ Ⓓ	31 Ⓐ Ⓑ Ⓒ Ⓓ	51 Ⓐ Ⓑ Ⓒ Ⓓ	71 Ⓐ Ⓑ Ⓒ Ⓓ	91 Ⓐ Ⓑ Ⓒ Ⓓ
12 Ⓐ Ⓑ Ⓒ Ⓓ	32 Ⓐ Ⓑ Ⓒ Ⓓ	52 Ⓐ Ⓑ Ⓒ Ⓓ	72 Ⓐ Ⓑ Ⓒ Ⓓ	92 Ⓐ Ⓑ Ⓒ Ⓓ
13 Ⓐ Ⓑ Ⓒ Ⓓ	33 Ⓐ Ⓑ Ⓒ Ⓓ	53 Ⓐ Ⓑ Ⓒ Ⓓ	73 Ⓐ Ⓑ Ⓒ Ⓓ	93 Ⓐ Ⓑ Ⓒ Ⓓ
14 Ⓐ Ⓑ Ⓒ Ⓓ	34 Ⓐ Ⓑ Ⓒ Ⓓ	54 Ⓐ Ⓑ Ⓒ Ⓓ	74 Ⓐ Ⓑ Ⓒ Ⓓ	94 Ⓐ Ⓑ Ⓒ Ⓓ
15 Ⓐ Ⓑ Ⓒ Ⓓ	35 Ⓐ Ⓑ Ⓒ Ⓓ	55 Ⓐ Ⓑ Ⓒ Ⓓ	75 Ⓐ Ⓑ Ⓒ Ⓓ	95 Ⓐ Ⓑ Ⓒ Ⓓ
16 Ⓐ Ⓑ Ⓒ Ⓓ	36 Ⓐ Ⓑ Ⓒ Ⓓ	56 Ⓐ Ⓑ Ⓒ Ⓓ	76 Ⓐ Ⓑ Ⓒ Ⓓ	96 Ⓐ Ⓑ Ⓒ Ⓓ
17 Ⓐ Ⓑ Ⓒ Ⓓ	37 Ⓐ Ⓑ Ⓒ Ⓓ	57 Ⓐ Ⓑ Ⓒ Ⓓ	77 Ⓐ Ⓑ Ⓒ Ⓓ	97 Ⓐ Ⓑ Ⓒ Ⓓ
18 Ⓐ Ⓑ Ⓒ Ⓓ	38 Ⓐ Ⓑ Ⓒ Ⓓ	58 Ⓐ Ⓑ Ⓒ Ⓓ	78 Ⓐ Ⓑ Ⓒ Ⓓ	98 Ⓐ Ⓑ Ⓒ Ⓓ
19 Ⓐ Ⓑ Ⓒ Ⓓ	39 Ⓐ Ⓑ Ⓒ Ⓓ	59 Ⓐ Ⓑ Ⓒ Ⓓ	79 Ⓐ Ⓑ Ⓒ Ⓓ	99 Ⓐ Ⓑ Ⓒ Ⓓ
20 Ⓐ Ⓑ Ⓒ Ⓓ	40 Ⓐ Ⓑ Ⓒ Ⓓ	60 Ⓐ Ⓑ Ⓒ Ⓓ	80 Ⓐ Ⓑ Ⓒ Ⓓ	100 Ⓐ Ⓑ Ⓒ Ⓓ

1. Consideration – Modification: Pre-existing Duties
2. Formation – Mutual Assent: Offer and Acceptance
3. Discharge of Contractual Duties
4. Remedies – Restitutionary and Reliance Recoveries
5. Formation – Mutual Assent: Acceptance (UCC)
6. Rights and Obligations of the Parties (UCC)
7. Conditions – Express
8. Conditions – Constructive Conditions of Non-Prevention, Non-Hindrance, and Affirmative Cooperation
9. Conditions – Constructive Conditions of Non-Prevention, Non-Hindrance, and Affirmative Cooperation
10. Consideration – Bargain and Exchange
11. Consideration – Bargain and Exchange
12. Contract Modifications (UCC)
13. Statute of Frauds
14. Statute of Frauds
15. Statute of Frauds
16. Remedies – Measure of Damages (UCC)
17. Remedies – Total and Partial Breach of Contract (UCC)
18. Formation – Mutual Assent: Offer and Acceptance (UCC)
19. Parol Evidence and Interpretation
20. Terms of the Deal (UCC)
21. Contract Modifications (UCC)
22. Impossibility of Performance and Frustration of Purpose
23. Parol Evidence and Interpretation
24. Consideration – Compromise and Settlement of Claims
25. Conditions – Constructive Conditions of Exchange
26. Assignment of Rights and Delegation of Duties

27. Remedies – Total and Partial Breach of Contract
28. Remedies – Specific Performance
29. Impossibility of Performance and Frustration of Purpose
30. Conditions – Express
31. Assignment of Rights and Delegation of Duties
32. Assignment of Rights and Delegation of Duties
33. Assignment of Rights and Delegation of Duties
34. Conditions – Constructive: Independent Covenants
35. Remedies – Liquidated Damages and Penalties
36. Remedies – Liquidated Damages and Penalties
37. Assignment of Rights and Delegation of Duties
38. Conditions – Constructive Conditions of Exchange
39. Remedies – Anticipatory Repudiation
40. Impossibility of Performance and Frustration of Purpose
41. Consideration – Bargain and Exchange
42. Formation – Mutual Assent: Offer and Acceptance (UCC)
43. Rights and Obligations of the Parties (UCC)
44. Rights and Obligations of the Parties (UCC)
45. Impossibility of Performance and Frustration of Purpose
46. Assignment of Rights and Delegation of Duties
47. Impossibility of Performance and Frustration of Purpose
48. Formation – Mutual Assent: Offer and Acceptance
49. Impossibility of Performance and Frustration of Purpose
50. Remedies – Measure of Damages
51. Statute of Frauds
52. Promissory Estoppel
53. Unilateral Contracts

54. Consideration

55. Statute of Frauds

56. Infancy

57. Option Contracts

58. Frustration of Purpose

59. Mutual Mistake

60. Installment Contracts

61. Impossibility

62. Impracticability

63. Personal Services Contracts

64. Damages

65. Requirements Contracts

66. Assignments

67. Delegations

68. Delegations

69. Third-Party Beneficiaries

70. Conditions

71. Unilateral Contracts

72. Statute of Frauds

73. Consideration

74. Requirements Contracts

75. Modifications

76. Modifications

77. Consideration

78. Modifications

79. Consideration

80. Consideration

81. Infancy
82. Modifications
83. Detrimental Reliance
84. Consideration
85. Promissory Estoppel
86. Past Consideration
87. Modifications
88. Consideration
89. Consideration
90. Consideration
91. Illusory Promises
92. Misrepresentation
93. Unilateral Contracts
94. UCC Gap Fillers
95. Acceptance
96. Revocation
97. Infancy
98. The Mailbox Rule
99. Infancy
100. Unilateral Mistake

1. A woman owned an extensive art collection that she displayed in a special room of her home. While the woman was away on a vacation, there was a burglary at her home, and her favorite painting was stolen. Although the painting was insured for $1,000,000 by an insurance company, it had a market value of over $1,500,000.

When the woman returned from vacation, she met with a detective employed by the insurance company to investigate the theft. During their meeting, the woman told the detective that she would pay him an extra $50,000 if he recovered the painting. For the next three weeks, the detective investigated the theft as part of his job responsibilities with the insurance company. Within the course of this investigation, the detective learned who was responsible for the burglary. As a consequence, the culprit was apprehended, and the painting was recovered and returned to the woman.

The detective then requested the $50,000 that the woman had promised to pay him. After the woman refused to make the payment, the detective sued the woman for breach of contract.

Who is most likely to prevail?

(A) The woman, because her promise was gratuitous.
(B) The woman, because the insurance company owed her a pre-existing duty to find the painting.
(C) The detective, because he did the act necessary to constitute an acceptance of the woman's offer.
(D) The detective, because the market value of the painting exceeded its insured value, so there was sufficient consideration to support the woman's promise.

2. A man told his neighbor, "If you will mow my lawn, I will pay you $50." The neighbor then purchased gasoline for the mower so he could mow the lawn. The neighbor wheeled his lawn mower to the man's property and started the engine. At that moment, the man suddenly yelled, "I hereby revoke my offer."

If the neighbor thereafter mows the man's lawn, will he recover the $50?

(A) Yes, because there was an offer for a unilateral contract that became irrevocable prior to the man's attempted revocation.
(B) Yes, under the doctrine of quasi-contract.
(C) No, because the man's revocation was effective, since the neighbor had not completed performance.
(D) No, because the neighbor had done nothing more than prepare to accept the offer prior to the man's revocation.

3. On April 10, the owner of a golf course entered into an oral agreement with a gardener whereby the gardener promised to install all new sprinkler heads on the sprinkler system at the 18-hole golf course. In return, the owner promised to pay the gardener $2,400 upon completion of the job. Since a golf tournament was scheduled for the weekend of April 20–21, the gardener agreed to replace all the sprinkler heads no later than April 19. Before accepting the job, the gardener had inspected the golf course and determined that 240 sprinkler heads had to be replaced.

By April 14, the gardener had installed 80 new sprinkler heads on the first six holes of the 18-hole golf course. That afternoon, however, the owner learned that the gardener had been adjudicated bankrupt on April 12, so he notified the gardener to discontinue the job. The next day, the owner hired a landscaper to complete the installation work at $8 per head. The landscaper installed the remaining 160 sprinkler heads and completed the work on April 19. Despite making reasonable efforts, the gardener was unable to find any gainful employment during the period. Also, the gardener's application for unemployment compensation was rejected at the same time.

Which of the following statements, if found to be true, would provide the owner with legally justifiable grounds for discharging the gardener?

(A) The gardener had been adjudicated bankrupt on April 12.
(B) The gardener had only completed 33 percent of the installation work when he was discharged.
(C) The contract between the owner and the gardener was not in writing.
(D) Half of the sprinkler heads installed by the gardener were determined to be defective, and the gardener refused to replace the sprinkler heads.

4. The owner of a soon-to-open resort complex entered into an agreement with an electrician to install lighting fixtures on the walking paths located on the resort property. The contract stipulated that the work had to be completed by December 1 (the anticipated opening date for the resort), and that the electrician would be paid $5,000 upon completion of the job. Before accepting the job, the electrician had inspected the property and determined that 500 lighting fixtures would be needed to adequately light the pathways.

By November 15, the electrician had installed 150 lighting fixtures. That evening, the owner inspected the property and discovered that the lighting fixtures installed by the electrician did not provide adequate lighting. The next day, the owner immediately discharged the electrician and hired a lighting specialist to complete the installation work at $20 per fixture. The lighting specialist installed the remaining 350 fixtures, completing the work on December 1. The electrician filed suit against the owner.

If it is determined that the owner was legally justified in discharging the electrician, which of the following is the electrician's proper measure of recovery?

(A) $7,000.
(B) $3,500.
(C) Quantum meruit for the reasonable value of his services rendered in installing the 150 fixtures.
(D) Nothing, because the electrician did not complete performance of the entire job.

5. On August 10, a retail stationery store sent the following purchase order to a wholesaler of office supply equipment: "Please ship immediately 24 pairs (two dozen) 3 1/2-inch, right-handed scissors at your current list price of $4 per pair."

The wholesaler received this purchase order on August 12. The next day, the wholesaler ascertained that there were only 18 pairs of 3 1/2-inch, right-handed scissors in stock. The wholesaler, however, found that he had six pairs of 3 1/2-inch, left-handed scissors in stock. Without notifying the stationery store, the wholesaler shipped the 18 pairs of right-handed scissors, along with the six pairs of left-handed scissors, to the stationery store. The stationery store was aware that the wholesale price for the left-handed scissors was $3 per pair, or $1 less than the list price for the right-handed scissors.

Was an enforceable contract formed when the wholesaler shipped the 24 pairs of scissors to the stationery store?

(A) Yes, because the wholesaler's shipment constituted acceptance of the offer, absent a seasonable notification by the wholesaler to the stationery store that the shipment was made for accommodation only.
(B) Yes, because the wholesaler acted in good faith in making the shipment in reliance on the stationery store's offer.
(C) No, because the wholesaler could accept the stationery store's offer only by a prompt promise to ship the goods ordered.
(D) No, because acceptance by performance of an offer for immediate or prompt shipment is legally binding, unless the nonconforming goods are not reasonably resalable.

6. The operator of a hot dog stand sent the following purchase order to a bakery: "We are expecting an increase in business over the upcoming holidays. Please ship immediately 36 dozen 10-inch hot dog buns at your current list price of $6 per dozen."

The day after receiving the purchase order, the bakery shipped 24 dozen 10-inch hot dog buns and 12 dozen 8-inch hot dog buns. The owner of the bakery had instructed his staff to include a message that the bakery did not have enough 10-inch hot dog buns to fill the order, so they were including the 8-inch hot dog buns as an accommodation. However, the shipping department forgot to include the message with the shipment.

Which of the following is the most accurate statement regarding the operator's legal rights following receipt of the hot dog buns?

(A) The operator may either accept or reject all of the hot dog buns upon seasonable notice to the bakery, but it cannot accept only the 10-inch hot dog buns without the bakery's approval.
(B) The operator may either accept or reject all of the hot dog buns, or accept any commercial unit and reject the rest, but must give the bakery seasonable notice of either total or partial rejection.
(C) The operator may either accept or reject all of the hot dog buns, or accept the 10-inch buns and reject the 8-inch buns, but it cannot accept any combination of the hot dog buns.
(D) The operator may either accept or reject all of the hot dog buns, or, provided the bakery gives seasonable notice that the shipment was made for accommodation only, the operator may accept any combination of hot dog buns and reject the rest.

7. An owner of a tract of land in a foothill community hired a general contractor to construct a small summer cottage on the tract of land. The parties entered into a valid, written construction contract that contained a provision that called for an architect's certificate of completion.

After completion of the cottage, the owner hired an architect to inspect the contractor's work and issue the certificate. The architect refused in bad faith to execute the certificate. The contractor then sued the owner for the entire contract amount. The owner argued that the lack of issuance of the certificate excused her from further performance under the contract.

Upon hearing this argument, most courts will

(A) order the architect to execute the certificate.
(B) require the contractor to proceed in equity for reformation to eliminate the clause.
(C) award the contractor damages against the architect.
(D) excuse the condition and require the owner to pay damages to the contractor.

8. The owner of a large unimproved tract of land leased it to a tenant for five years at a monthly rental of $1,500. The rental agreement provided that the land was to be used as farmland. Shortly after the tenant took possession of the tract of land, he built thereon, at his own expense, a barn made of lumber, which was 15 feet wide, 20 feet long, and set on loose bricks. The barn increased the appraised market value of the tract of land from $250,000 to $275,000. The tenant then began farming operations on the land.

Toward the end of the lease period, the owner informed the tenant that he was going to put the tract of land up for sale. The next month, when the lease expired, the parties settled a dispute over the tenant's right, if any, to compensation for the improvements by the following written agreement:

"On the sale of the tract of land, the owner hereby agrees to pay the tenant two-thirds of any sale proceeds in excess of $250,000, provided that tenant may remain on the farm for the next year, rent-free, while the owner tries to sell it. After that time, the tenant may remain on the land until closing of the sale, at a monthly rental of $1,000."

The owner initially set the asking price at $300,000. After receiving scant interest, the owner decided to reduce the price to $260,000. This price reduction so infuriated the tenant that he thereafter made negative comments about the farm to all of the prospective buyers. Finally, 14 months after the agreement between the owner and the tenant was executed, and after rejecting offers for $240,000 and $250,000, the owner sold the tract of land for $256,000 to a buyer who visited the land while the tenant was away on vacation. Thereupon, the tenant, who had failed to pay the last two months' rent as per the agreement, moved out. After closing, the owner refused to pay the tenant any of the sale proceeds, and the tenant brought suit to recover damages for breach of contract.

Which of the following is the owner's most persuasive argument in defense of the tenant's suit?

(A) The tenant committed an uncured material breach of an implied promise to cooperate in the owner's efforts to sell the property, or at least not to hinder the proposed sale.
(B) The tenant's negative comments about the farm to prospective buyers amounted to an anticipatory repudiation of the agreement between the owner and the tenant.
(C) The tenant's failure to pay any rent for the last two months was a material breach of contract that discharged the owner's remaining duties of performance.
(D) The agreement between the owner and the tenant was voidable because it was a restraint on alienation, since it conditioned a promise to pay for a conveyance of land upon an otherwise invalid leasehold contract.

9. A homeowner owned a single-story ranch-style home that was her primary residence. The homeowner received notice that her uncle had passed away and left her a two-story mansion in a neighboring city. The homeowner decided to move her primary residence to the mansion and rent the ranch-style home. She entered into a one-year written lease agreement with a tenant. The agreement set the monthly rent at $1,000. Shortly after the tenant took possession of the home, he built, at his own expense, a room addition onto the home. The room addition increased the appraised market value of the home from $200,000 to $250,000.

At the expiration of the lease, the homeowner informed the tenant that she had decided to sell the home. She offered the tenant the first opportunity to buy the home, but the tenant replied that he could not afford to do so. The tenant did claim that he should be entitled to compensation for the room addition, since it had increased the value of the home, and the homeowner agreed. The tenant and the homeowner then executed the following agreement:

"On the sale of the ranch-style home, the homeowner hereby promises to pay the tenant one-half of any sale proceeds in excess of $200,000, in compensation of the tenant's efforts in constructing the room addition onto the home. In addition, it is hereby agreed that the tenant may remain on the land until the sale is finalized, at a monthly rent of $500."

The homeowner initially set the asking price at $250,000, but received no offers to purchase the home. The homeowner decided to reduce the price to $210,000. This price reduction so infuriated the tenant that he thereafter made negative comments about the home to all of the prospective buyers who visited the home.

Two months later, the homeowner sold the home to a buyer for $206,000. The buyer had visited the home while the tenant was away on a business trip and therefore did not hear the tenant's negative comments. Thereupon, the tenant, who had paid no rent for the final two months, moved out. After the sale was finalized, the homeowner refused to pay the tenant any of the sale proceeds.

Which of the following statements, if true, most persuasively supports the tenant's contention that he is entitled to recover at least $4,000 from the owner (or the equivalent of one-half of the sale proceeds in excess of $200,000, minus two months' unpaid rent at $500 per month)?

(A) The owner breached an implied promise by failing to attempt to sell the property at $250,000, which was the appraised market value of the home.
(B) Since the tenant made no negative comments about the home to the buyer, there is no showing that the tenant's remarks to the other prospective buyers necessarily caused any loss to the owner (i.e., prevented her from selling the home for more than $210,000).
(C) The agreement between the homeowner that the tenant contained only one express condition (i.e., the tenant was permitted to remain in the home during the owner's efforts to sell it), and since that condition has occurred, the tenant is entitled to his share of the proceeds from the sale.
(D) Even if the tenant's failure to pay any rent for the last two months was a material breach of contract, the owner's promise to pay the tenant a share of the proceeds of the sale was an independent covenant.

10. An employee had been employed by a hotel as a window cleaner for eight years when the hotel issued to him and other employees the following certificate:

"In appreciation of the faithful service hitherto rendered by you as an employee of this hotel, there will be paid in the event of your death, if still an employee of this hotel, to the party designated by you below as your beneficiary, the sum of $5,000. The issuance of this certificate is understood to be purely gratuitous."

Upon receipt of the certificate, the employee designated his wife as beneficiary, signed it, and returned the form to the hotel.

One year later, while still employed by the hotel, the employee died.

In an action by the employee's widow against the hotel to recover the sum of $5,000, which of the following, if established, is the strongest argument against enforcement of the certificate agreement?

(A) The widow was unaware of the certificate agreement until after the employee died.
(B) There was no privity of contract between the widow and the hotel.
(C) The widow in no way relied on the hotel's promise to pay the $5,000.
(D) There was insufficient consideration to support the certificate agreement.

11. One morning, an employee arrived at work and found his boss passed out on the floor of his office. The employee determined that his boss was not breathing, immediately rendered CPR to his boss, and succeeded in reviving him. The employee then called the paramedics, who took the boss to the hospital.

Two week later, the boss returned to work. Grateful for the employee's quick action in saving his life, the boss said to the employee, "You'll have a job with me for life."

Which of the following best characterizes the legal relationship between the boss and the employee on that date?

(A) As per the boss's oral promise, the employee had an enforceable lifetime employment contract.
(B) The boss had a duty to pay the employee reasonable compensation for saving his life, based upon a contract implied-in-fact.
(C) The employee's act of saving the boss's life was sufficient past consideration to render enforceable the boss's subsequent promise.
(D) Since the employee gratuitously rendered assistance to the boss, there was insufficient consideration to support the boss's subsequent promise to provide the employee with lifetime employment.

12. A buyer contracted in writing to purchase 1,000 gidgets (which are similar to widgets but are more popular because of their greater durability and resiliency) from a manufacturer for a total contract price of $4,000. After this agreement was executed and before delivery, the buyer and the manufacturer agreed in a telephone conversation to change the quantity term from 1,000 to 800 gidgets.

This modification is probably unenforceable, because

(A) it violates the statute of frauds.
(B) there was no consideration.
(C) the original contract was in writing.
(D) the parol evidence rule bars contradictory terms.

13. A small electronics corporation decided to radically overhaul its manufacturing processes and borrowed $200,000 from the bank for this purpose. The loan was secured by a mortgage on the corporation's plant and building site.

When the debt came due, the corporation was short of ready cash and the bank threatened to foreclose. One of the shareholders of the corporation then intervened on behalf of the corporation and told the bank officials that if they would refrain from any legal action against the company for a year, she would personally see that the debt was paid. The bank orally agreed to the shareholder's arrangement. However, it was never reduced to writing.

The bank's promise to the shareholder to refrain from foreclosing on the mortgage would constitute

(A) a void promise at the time of inception.
(B) a voidable promise as violative of the statute of frauds.
(C) an unenforceable promise, because the corporation had a pre-existing duty to pay the debt at maturity.
(D) an enforceable promise, binding the shareholder as a surety.

14. Upon graduation from high school, a student enrolled in a college close to where he lived. However, since the student did not have a car, he rode the bus to and from the college each day. The student soon discovered that he was spending up to two hours each day to make the round trip to and from college on the bus, whereas the trip could be made in half that time if he had a car. He decided to buy a car and asked his father to accompany him as he looked for a car to purchase.

After visiting a number of car lots, the son finally found a used car to his liking. However, the son only had $2,500 in his bank account, and the price of the car was $10,000. Since the son had not built up a credit history, the car lot was reluctant to sell the car to the son. The father then told the finance manager of the car lot, "If you will sell the car to my son and for any reason he defaults on the payments, I will pay the balance due." The finance manager then approved the deal, which required the son to pay $2,500 down and monthly payments of $500 for 15 months. Six months later, the son defaulted on the payment plan, and the car lot sought recovery from the father without first suing the son.

With regard to the father's obligation under his promise to the finance manager, the court would most likely

(A) relieve the father of liability, because the car lot failed to first sue the son.
(B) relieve the father of liability, because the father was never under a duty as a surety.
(C) not relieve the father of liability, because of the main purpose exception.
(D) not relieve the father of liability, because parents are responsible for the debts of their children.

15. A president of a small computer company decided to expand his operation. On behalf of his company, he borrowed $500,000 from a credit union for this purpose. The company was to repay the loan at the rate of $2,500 per month. The loan was secured by a mortgage on the building that housed the company's operation center.

Eight months later, the company's sales started to drop and the company began experiencing cash flow problems. As a result, the company failed to make its loan payments for three consecutive months, causing the credit union to threaten to foreclose on the mortgage. The president's father, a retired wealthy investor, then intervened on behalf of the company, paid the three missed loan payments, and told the credit union that if they would refrain from any legal action against the company for a year, he would personally see that the debt was paid. The credit union orally agreed to the father's surety arrangement. However, it was never reduced to writing.

Six months later, the company once again missed consecutive payments, and the credit union filed a foreclosure suit against the company. The father did not learn of the suit until a week later, but he raised no objection, since he thought the credit union was violating its agreement with him by foreclosing within the one-year period, thus relieving him of his part of the bargain.

Two weeks later, the credit union's loan officer called the father and said that the credit union would hold off on the foreclosure suit as per their agreement, since the company had just made a new technological development that would place it in a very lucrative and competitive position. Soon after the new technological development took place, the company's business fortunes declined, which resulted in the company's insolvency.

In an action by the credit union against the appointed receiver in bankruptcy and the father, the credit union will most likely recover for the outstanding loan from

(A) the father only.
(B) the receiver only.
(C) either the father or the receiver.
(D) both the father and the receiver.

16. In a written contract, a seller agreed to deliver to a buyer 1,000 widgets at a stipulated price of $10 each, FOB at the seller's place of business. The contract stipulated that "any party who wishes to assign this contract must have the written consent of the other party." On March 1, the seller placed the widgets on board a cargo vessel that was destined to transport the widgets to the buyer. On March 2, the buyer received the following telegram from the seller:

"Please be advised that the widgets are in transit. In addition, I hereby assign all my rights under our contract to our creditor."

The buyer did not consent to the assignment. The next day, the ship carrying the widgets sank in a violent storm, destroying its entire cargo.

If the creditor brings an appropriate action against the buyer, the former will most likely recover

(A) nothing, because the buyer never assented to the assignment.
(B) nothing, because the buyer never received the widgets.
(C) the contract price of $10,000.
(D) the difference between the contract price and the market value of the widgets.

17. A buyer, located on the west coast contacted a seller, located on the east coast, about purchasing flanges that the buyer used in their manufacturing process. The parties entered into a contract whereby the seller agreed to deliver to the buyer 1,000 flanges for $10,000. The contract stipulated that it was FOB at the seller's place of business. The seller then delivered the flanges to a delivery company, which was to transport them to the buyer. While en route, the vehicle that was transporting the flanges was involved in an accident and the flanges were destroyed. When the buyer received notice of the accident, the buyer immediately contacted the seller and demanded that it ship replacement flanges. The seller refused to do so.

In an action by the buyer against the seller for breach of contract, the buyer will

(A) succeed, because the risk of loss was on the seller.
(B) succeed, because the carrier was the seller's agent.
(C) not succeed, because the risk of loss was on the buyer.
(D) not succeed, because of frustration of purpose.

18. A farmer owned a piece of land on which he grew strawberries. Over the years, the farmer had earned a reputation for growing strawberries that were extremely sweet and juicy. For that reason, consumers always looked forward to strawberry season, when the farmer's strawberries would be available.

Hoping to capitalize on the farmer's reputation, a produce retailer who operated three stores in the area contacted the farmer about the possibility of carrying the farmer's strawberries in his stores. After lengthy negotiations, the parties executed the following written agreement:

"The farmer will supply the retailer with all of its needs of strawberries from April through July each year for the next three years. The retailer will pay $5.00 per bushel of strawberries delivered."

On April 1 of the first year of the contract, the retailer submitted an order for 75 bushels of strawberries. Upon receiving the order, the farmer sent the retailer the following fax:

"Your order was way more than I anticipated. If I sent you that many strawberries I would not have enough for my other customers. I can send you 50 bushels, but no more."

The retailer then notified the farmer that if he did not deliver all 75 bushels, the retailer would sue him for breach of contract.

The agreement entered into between the farmer and the retailer would best be described as a(n)

(A) illusory contract.
(B) best efforts contract.
(C) requirements contract.
(D) aleatory contract.

19. A producer of widgets contacted a manufacturer of boxes about the possibility of purchasing specially designed boxes for shipping the widgets to customers. The producer sent the manufacturer a sheet containing the dimensions of the boxes' needs, as well as the logo to be placed on each box. After negotiations, the parties entered into a written contract whereby the manufacturer agreed to supply the producer with as many of the boxes as the producer may require up to a maximum of 10,000 per month. Later that day, the producer telephoned the manufacturer and said that they were running a one-time promotion and expected to sell an unusually large number of widgets. Therefore, for the first month only, they would need 15,000 boxes. The manufacturer agreed to this request.

The manufacturer's oral agreement to supply the producer with the 15,000 boxes for the first month would most likely be held

(A) enforceable.
(B) unenforceable, because their written contract on the same date was the final integration of the terms of their agreement.
(C) unenforceable, because the agreement was violative of the parol evidence rule.
(D) unenforceable, because there was inadequate consideration to support the manufacturer's unilateral promise.

20. A restaurant ran a promotion in a local newspaper, stating the following:

"MOTHER'S DAY SPECIAL

We will be open for brunch on Mother's Day from 10 am to 2 pm offering an extensive selection of dishes to honor mothers of all ages. Call us to reserve your table."

The response to the promotion was more than the restaurant expected, and the restaurant was soon overbooked for the Mother's Day brunch. On the day before Mother's Day, the restaurant owner decided to double-check inventory to make sure the restaurant had enough food and supplies to handle the large Mother's Day crowd. To her horror, she discovered that the restaurant was almost out of eggs. Knowing that a large supply of eggs would be needed for the omelet station, the owner immediately sent the following e-mail to her egg supplier:

"Desperately need 20 flats of Grade AA eggs for tomorrow's brunch. Money is no object. The eggs must be delivered today."

The supplier e-mailed back:

"No problem! I'll load them on the truck and deliver them within the hour."

With respect to the agreement between the owner and the supplier, which of the following statements is most accurate regarding the omission of a fixed contract price?

(A) The contract is unenforceable as violative of the statute of frauds.
(B) The contract is unenforceable, because of indefiniteness.
(C) The contract may be enforceable if it is later modified to include the price term.
(D) The contract is enforceable with reasonable price being fixed at time of delivery.

21. An aluminum can manufacturer entered into negotiations with an aluminum sheeting supplier to supply the manufacturer's requirements of aluminum sheeting. After extensive discussions, the parties signed the following agreement on June 1:

"The supplier agrees to supply all of the manufacturer's requirements of aluminum sheeting for a period of two years beginning on August 1, at a price of $3.00 per unit."

On June 16, the manufacturer notified the supplier that it would need a delivery of 2,000 units by August 1 to accommodate its needs. The supplier informed the manufacturer that it did not contemplate such high requirements, since its plant's capacity was only 2,800 per month. Moreover, the supplier pointed out that in order to meet the manufacturer's order of 2,000 units, it would probably lose two long-time customers, whose outstanding orders would have to be canceled.

After a week of negotiations, on June 23 the supplier orally agreed to deliver 2,000 units of sheeting to the manufacturer by August 1. The parties then signed the following contract:

"The supplier agrees to supply all of the manufacturer's requirements of aluminum sheeting for a period of two years beginning August 1, at a price of $3.50 per unit. The manufacturer agrees that it will require a minimum of 800 units in every month of the agreement."

On June 25 the supplier notified its two long-time customers that it was canceling their August orders (of 800 units) because of other contract commitments.

Which of the following is the most accurate statement regarding the written agreement between the parties on June 23?

(A) The agreement constituted a valid modification of their June 1 contract.
(B) The agreement was unenforceable, since the supplier was under a pre-existing duty to supply the manufacturer with the sheeting under their June 1 contract.
(C) The agreement constituted an enforceable reformation of their June 1 contract.
(D) The agreement was unenforceable, since there was no new consideration.

22. After a week of negotiations, an importer of cigars from a foreign country agreed in writing to supply a smoke shop with all of their needs of cigars for two years at a price of $1 per cigar. The following day, the foreign government was overthrown. One week later, the United States government announced an embargo on the importation of all products from the foreign country. The importer contacted the smoke shop and informed them that as a result of the embargo, the importer would not be able to fill any of the smoke shop's orders for cigars from the foreign country.

What is the probable legal effect of the United States government's embargo on the contract between the importer and the smoke shop?

(A) The smoke shop would be entitled to recover the difference between $1 and the cost of purchasing cigars manufactured in another country.
(B) Both parties' duties of performance would be discharged by frustration of purpose.
(C) Both parties' duties of performance would be suspended through temporary impossibility.
(D) The parties' duties of performance would be excused because of a supervening illegality.

23. A law school advertised in various law journals for a legal ethics and jurisprudence professor. Although a number of lawyers applied for the position, one of the applicants submitted a particularly impressive resume. The dean of faculty for the law school immediately wrote to the applicant to offer him the position. In the letter, the dean offered to employ the applicant for the upcoming academic year, which started on August 15, at a salary of $75,000. The letter also listed the employment terms and conditions, one of which stated that professors are entitled to five paid sick days during the year. The dean included a detailed employment contract containing all these terms, for the applicant's signature.

After the applicant received this letter, he replied by mail, requesting a salary of $85,000 and sick leave of 10 days. Upon receipt of the applicant's letter, the dean telephoned the applicant and told him that the law school followed the American Bar Association guidelines with respect to salary and sick leave for its professors. The applicant acquiesced on the salary question, but insisted that his sick leave be extended to 10 days.

The dean replied, "Let's not permit a minor issue to stand in the way of your coming to teach at our law school. In the event you require more than 5 sick days, I promise that the matter will be taken care of to your benefit." The applicant informed the dean that he would sign the contract and forward it to the dean, which he promptly did.

The applicant began teaching at the law school on August 15. Three months later, the applicant was out sick for five days with laryngitis. The applicant did not miss another school day until Monday, March 8, when he fell ill with food poisoning. This illness kept him home for five additional sick days. The applicant returned to work on March 15. When the applicant received his salary check at the end of the week, his check did not include payment for the previous week (from March 8 to March 12). Accompanying the check was a statement that read:

"Salary payment for period from Monday, March 1 through Friday, March 19 with pro rata deduction to reflect five teaching days missed during said period."

When the applicant received his check, he immediately confronted the dean and requested full payment for the week of March 8 through 12. The dean responded, "I'm sorry, but there is absolutely nothing I can do about it."

The applicant asserted a claim against the law school for breach of contract. The applicant offers to introduce evidence that during his telephone conversation with dean of faculty, the dean promised, if necessary, to provide him with additional sick days.

The most accurate statement concerning the dean's oral promise would be that

(A) parol evidence is admissible to show that the parties assented to their written contract only as a partial integration of their complete contract.
(B) parol evidence is admissible to prove a subsequent oral agreement that varies or contradicts the terms of a prior written contract.
(C) parol evidence is admissible to show that the written contract is not enforceable, because of undue influence or fraud.
(D) parol evidence is inadmissible to prove contemporaneous oral agreements that vary or contradict the terms of a written contract.

24. A law student contacted a tutor about the possibility of hiring the tutor to help the law student prepare for his upcoming finals. The tutor sent the law student a copy of the tutor's standard tutorial agreement. The agreement stated that the tutor's rate was $50 per one-hour session. The law student then telephoned the tutor and said, "This agreement looks fine to me. I'd like you to give me 10 sessions over the next 10 days." The tutor replied, That will be fine. Fill in 10 sessions on the agreement, sign it, and bring it to me tomorrow when we have our first session." The student then said, "I want you to really push me to do my best. In fact, if I get an A in any class I'll pay you an additional $100 for each A."

The next day, the law student brought the signed agreement to the tutorial session. The tutor conducted all 10 sessions. Two weeks later, when the results of the finals were released, the law student excitedly called the tutor and exclaimed, "Thank you so much! I just found out that I received two A's and two B's in my classes!" The tutor then sent the law student a bill for $700. Two days later the tutor received a check from the law student in the amount of $500. Included with the check was a note which read, "You taught me contract law very well. I now know that I am not obligated to pay you the additional $200 for the A's, because that was just a gratuitous promise." On the back of the check the law student typed the following:

"Endorsement of this check by payee constitutes surrender of all claims against me arising out of our tutorial arrangement."

In need of money, the tutor endorsed and cashed the check.

What is the probable legal effect of the tutor's endorsement of the check?

(A) It constituted a discharge of a liquidated claim.
(B) It constituted an accord and satisfaction of an unliquidated claim.
(C) Part payment of a liquidated claim would not constitute a discharge of the entire amount due.
(D) Part payment of an unliquidated claim does not constitute sufficient consideration for the discharge of the entire claim.

25. A businessman was an avid baseball fan who frequently traveled to a casino and placed wagers on baseball games. One October, his beloved baseball team was playing in the playoffs and he wanted to place a large bet on his team. He told one of his employees that he wanted to bet $10,000 on his team to win the championship, but that he did not have the time to travel to the casino to place the bet. He then told his employee that he wanted the employee to travel to the casino and place the bet for him. The businessman and the employee agreed that the employee would travel to the casino, place a $10,000 bet for the businessman and then immediately return. In exchange, the employee would be paid $500. The parties reduced this agreement to writing.

After the agreement was signed, the businessman handed the employee $10,000 and a round-trip airline ticket. The businessman then told the employee that he would be paid $500 after the employee returned.

The employee arrived the next day and immediately went to the casino. There he noticed that the marquis in the parking lot was unlit and covered in a banner that read, "Casino Temporarily Closed Due to Renovations." Unable to reach the businessman by telephone, the employee placed the bet at another gaming establishment located next door to the casino.

The following morning, the employee flew back and gave the betting receipt to the businessman. When the businessman saw that the bet had been made at another gaming establishment, he angrily told the employee, "I purposely directed you to wager that $10,000 at the casino. Since you failed to follow my instructions, the deal's off." As a result, the businessman refused to pay the employee the $500.

If the employee initiates suit for breach of contract, the court will most likely determine that placing the $10,000 wager at the other gaming establishment, rather than at the casino, constituted a

(A) breach of contract.
(B) modification.
(C) constructive condition precedent that was substantially performed.
(D) discharge by impossibility.

26. As part of an externship program conducted by his law school, a law student went to work for a lawyer as a clerk. After six months, the lawyer was very impressed with the law student's work. He called the law student into his office and told him, "I know you were only to work for me for six months in exchange for credit in your law school externship program. However, I'd like you to stay on as a clerk. I'll pay you $25 an hour for any work you do for me between now and the bar exam. In addition, if you put in a minimum of 10 hours per week during that time, I promise to hire you full-time as an associate when you pass the bar exam." The attorney then reduced this agreement to writing, which both he and the law student signed.

The law student continued to work for the lawyer throughout the rest of his law school career and while he was studying for the bar exam. During that time, the law student always worked a minimum of 10 hours per week. While the law student was awaiting the results of the bar exam, his uncle passed away and left him a large apartment building. The law student decided he did not want to practice law but wanted to spend all of his time managing the apartment building. He told his roommate, a fellow law student who was awaiting his bar results, about his plans and told the roommate he would assign to the roommate the right to be hired by the lawyer as an associate, in exchange for $100. The roommate paid the $100 to the law student, who then executed a written assignment of the right to be hired by the lawyer as an associate.

The roommate passed the bar exam, but the lawyer refused to hire him as an associate. Which of the following is the most accurate statement regarding the legal effect of this assignment?

(A) The lawyer would be required to recognize the validity of the assignment so that the roommate would be entitled to be hired as an associate.
(B) The lawyer would be required to recognize the validity of the assignment, but would be entitled to demand adequate assurances of performance from the roommate as to the latter's willingness and professional capacity to perform satisfactory work.
(C) The lawyer would not be required to recognize the validity of the assignment of rights, because a contract to make a future assignment of a right is not an assignment.
(D) The lawyer would not be required to recognize the validity of the assignment, because neither the rights nor the duties under a personal service contract are properly assignable.

27. A gambler learned that a friend of his was planning a vacation to visit some casinos. The gambler, who was an avid college football fan, approached his friend. The gambler explained that he wanted to place a bet with a sports-betting agency that his beloved team would win the college football championship the next year. The gambler further explained that he had read that the odds of his team winning the football championship next year were listed as 100-1, and he wanted to place a $1,000 bet on his team. The gambler told his friend that he would pay him for his efforts. After further discussion, the gambler wrote up the following agreement:

"I hereby promise to pay my friend $100 if he will place a $1,000 bet for me that my favorite team will win the college football championship next year. The bet is to be placed at my lucky casino sports book. I further promise to pay my friend an additional $100 within 30 days after the bet is placed."

Since the gambler knew his wife would be angry if she found out about the bet, the gambler included a clause that the friend promised not to tell anyone about the bet. After both the gambler and his friend signed the agreement, the gambler gave him $1,100, representing $1,000 to place the bet and $100 as the initial payment for the friend's efforts.

The friend then went on vacation. Shortly after arrival, the friend attempted to place the bet for the gambler. However, the friend discovered that the gambler's lucky casino had recently closed its sports book. The friend then entered another casino next door and discovered that they had a sports book, also offering 100-1 odds on the gambler's favorite team winning the college football championship the next year. The friend placed the bet with the other casino's sports book.

After returning from his vacation, the friend gave the betting slip to the gambler. Nothing more was said until 30 days later, when the friend asked the gambler when he was going to receive the final $100. The gambler then refused to pay anything more to the friend.

In a breach of contract action by the friend to collect the $100, which of the following, if true, is the gambler's best defense?

(A) The contract was void *ab initio*, because the contract could not be performed in its entirety within the span of one year.
(B) The friend's placing the $1,000 bet at the other casino instead of at the gambler's lucky casino constituted a material breach of contract, thereby relieving the gambler of any further contractual obligations under the terms of their agreement.
(C) While on vacation, the friend told his girlfriend about the $1,000 that he bet on the gambler's behalf.
(D) Since the gambler's lucky casino no longer had a sports book at which to place the bet, all contractual obligations would be suspended under the doctrine of frustration of purpose.

28. A developer wished to build an apartment house in a local city. He raised $1 million from various sources to fund the project. After searching for a vacant lot that would be sufficient for development, the developer concluded that there was not a suitable vacant lot available. Reluctantly, the developer concluded that he would have to purchase a developed lot, have the existing structures removed, and then build the apartment house. The developer was reluctant to do this, because he had not budgeted for the additional cost of buying a developed property and removing the development.

After a search for an appropriate parcel, the developer purchased a large lot, developed with a single-story residential home, for $200,000. He then spent $50,000 having the residential home removed from the lot. Knowing that it would cost approximately $850,000 to build the apartment house, the developer realized he would need to raise another $100,000. He approached an investor about lending him $100,000. The investor was apprehensive about the project because the developer had not yet lined up a construction firm to build the apartment house. As a result, the parties signed the following written agreement:

"The investor promises to lend to the developer $100,000 at 5 percent interest within 30 days, provided the developer contracts with a construction company to build the apartment house for no more than $850,000. Loan to be repaid at the rate of $1,000 per month, starting one month after the completion of the apartment house. The loan is to be secured by a mortgage on the property."

The developer then contracted with a construction company to build the apartment for $800,000. After the contract was signed and construction had begun, the developer asked the investor when he would be receiving the $100,000 the investor promised to lend him. The investor replied, "I've changed my mind. I think this is too risky an investment. I'm not going to lend you the money."

In an appropriate action to secure specific performance of the investor's promise to lend him the $100,000, the developer will

(A) win, because there is a memorandum that satisfies the Statute of Frauds.
(B) win, because land is unique, making the legal remedy inadequate.
(C) lose, because the developer's only remedy is for damages.
(D) lose, because the developer cannot show detrimental reliance.

29. A woman had spent many years converting her back yard to an authentic Japanese-style garden. Her garden had become a showplace for the neighborhood, and various civic groups and organizations frequently visited the woman's property to enjoy the beauty of the yard. Recently, the woman had read about a particular cymbidium that was native to Japan. Desiring to have one of these cymbidiums planted in her garden, she contacted a number of plant distributors, only to discover that this particular cymbidium had not yet been imported to the United States. She contacted a plant distributor, who she knew had ties to Japan, and asked if it would be possible to acquire one of these cymbidiums from Japan. After checking with local and Japanese authorities, the distributor determined that he could indeed acquire the plant for the woman. The parties then signed a contract that stated the distributor would acquire the cymbidium from a nursery in Japan, have it shipped to the United States and have it planted in the woman's garden for the price of $5,000. The distributor promised that the plant would be in place within six months, and the woman promised to pay $1,000 at the time of the execution of the contract and $4,000 when the cymbidium was planted in her garden. The woman then handed a check for $1,000 to the distributor.

Two weeks later, agricultural officials discovered that a special type of beetle that attacked citrus plants had adapted to using cymbidiums for nesting purposes. The female beetle would lay eggs among the roots of the cymbidiums, and it would sometimes take up to one year for the eggs to hatch. Fearing for the safety of the citrus crops in the United States, the United States government adopted a ban on the importation of all cymbidiums grown in foreign countries. As a result, the distributor was not able to acquire the cymbidium for the woman.

Which of the following best states the legal relationship at this point between the distributor the woman?

(A) The distributor's performance was excused because of impossibility, but the woman can seek restitution.
(B) The distributor's performance was not excused because of the supervening illegality, and the woman can recover damages because of the distributor's prospective inability to perform.
(C) The distributor's performance was not excused because of the supervening illegality, and the woman can recover damages, provided she waits until the date performance was due before filing suit.
(D) Both parties are excused from performance because of the supervening illegality, and neither can recover from the other.

30. After learning that a new housing development was about to be built, a developer began looking for property near the housing development on which he could build a shopping center. After an extensive search, he purchased a three-acre undeveloped tract of land for the purpose of developing a small shopping center. At the time the sale was finalized, the developer told his plans to the seller of the three-acre tract, and also mentioned that he was worried whether he had sufficient funds to complete the project. The seller agreed to lend money to the developer to allow for completion of the project. The seller then wrote out the following contract:

"In order to help the developer with his plans for development of a shopping center on the three-acre tract he has this day purchased from me, I will lend him $50,000 at 10 percent interest provided he signs a contract with a builder for construction of the shopping center on this tract. Repayment to me at the rate of $5,000 per year to be secured by a mortgage on the three-acre tract."

Both parties then signed the contract.

The seller's promise to lend $50,000 to the developer is

(A) a condition precedent in form but subsequent in substance to the developer's duty to enter into a building construction contract.
(B) a condition subsequent in form but precedent in substance to the developer's duty to enter into a building construction contract.
(C) a condition subsequent to the developer's duty to enter into a building construction contract.
(D) not a condition, either precedent or subsequent, to the developer's duty to enter into a building construction contract.

31. A noted author was writing a screenplay that he was adapting from his novel *Quiet Winter*. He assigned in writing 25 percent of any future royalties, when and if the screenplay was made into either a movie or a stage play, to his friend, who had subsidized him during his early years as a struggling writer. Shortly after the screenplay was completed, the author was killed in an auto accident. A movie studio then purchased the screenplay from the executors of the author's estate and filmed the movie *Quiet Winter*, which was a great success.

In an action against the executors of the author's estate to recover her percentage of the movie royalties, the friend will most likely

(A) lose, because under the circumstances an assignment of future rights is unenforceable.
(B) lose, because the attempted gift of royalties failed for non-delivery.
(C) win, because she was an intended beneficiary.
(D) win, because the assignment of future rights is enforceable.

32. An athlete hoped to sign a contract with a professional baseball team to play baseball. He had succeeded in arranging for a tryout at the baseball team's training facilities in a neighboring state. Short on funds and needing a way to get to the training facilities, the athlete approached his friend and said, "If you will drive me to and from the baseball team's training facilities for my tryout and pay for our housing and meal expenses during our stay, I will assign to you 10 percent of my first-year earnings." The friend agreed and drove the athlete to the training facilities. After the tryout, the baseball team offered the athlete a contract to play baseball for the team at $100,000 per year.

When the friend asked when he would be receiving his 10 percent, the athlete replied that $10,000 was much more than the friend deserved and he would pay the friend $1,000 for his efforts. The friend then filed suit to enforce the assignment.

If the court holds the assignment unenforceable, the most applicable legal principle would be

(A) a purported assignment of a right expected to arise under a contract not in existence operates only as a promise to assign the right when it arises and as a power to enforce it.
(B) a contract to make a future assignment of a right is not a validly enforceable assignment.
(C) the friend did not detrimentally rely on the assignment prior to the attempted revocation of the assignment by the athlete.
(D) a gratuitous assignment is revocable, and the right of the assignee is terminated by the assignor's subsequent revocation.

33. An inventor developed a prototype of an automobile engine that she believed was going to revolutionize the automotive industry because of the engine's fuel-efficient properties. As a wedding present to the inventor's brother, the inventor wrote on a wedding card she gave to her brother:

"I hereby assign to you 20 percent of the net profits realized from the production and distribution of my automobile engine within the first year of production."

The inventor then borrowed money from creditors and began to promote her automobile engine. She was contacted by a major automobile manufacturer about the possibility of using the engine in a new line of cars the manufacturer intended to release during the next calendar year. While on her way to meet with the representatives of the manufacturer, the inventor was killed in an automobile collision. The manufacturer then contracted with the executor of the inventor's estate to license the use of the automobile engine design for a 10-year period for $500,000, payable to the estate.

The creditors from whom the inventor borrowed the money to promote her automobile engine have now attached the proceeds from the licensing agreement, which have so far been paid into the estate. The brother also asserts his assigned rights to a share of the proceeds.

In subsequent actions by the creditors and the brother, the court will most probably hold in favor of

(A) the brother, because the rights of an assignee are superior to a lien against the assignor subsequently obtained by legal/equitable proceedings.
(B) the brother, because any proceeds of the assigned right received by the assignor thereafter are held in constructive trust for the assignee.
(C) the creditors, because the inventor's assignment to the brother was unenforceable as a defective assignment.
(D) the creditors, because the rights of creditors/lienors are superior to those of a donee beneficiary.

34. A homeowner entered into a contract with an insurance company to purchase a fire insurance policy for her new home. The policy provided that the insurance company promised to pay up to $500,000 if the said house was destroyed by fire or fire-related explosion, while the homeowner promised to pay a quarterly premium of $400.

The homeowner failed to make the last two quarterly payments before her house burned to the ground. The insurance company refused to pay the homeowner for the loss because of her failure to make the last premium payments.

In an action by the homeowner against the insurance company to recover for the loss of her house, the homeowner's best theory of recovery is that

(A) although she failed to make the last two premium payments, there was a bargained-for exchange.
(B) the insurance company's duty to pay was not expressly conditioned on the homeowner's duty to make the payments.
(C) the insurance company was under an independent duty to pay for the loss.
(D) the homeowner did not receive notice of cancellation.

35. An employee worked for a hardware company in a city under an at-will-employment arrangement that paid the employee a monthly salary of $2,000. After two years, the owner of the hardware store told the employee it was time for them to enter into a more formalized employment agreement. The owner and the employee then both signed a written agreement drafted by the owner, whereby the employee agreed to work for a salary of $3,000 per month. The agreement further specified that either party had a right to terminate the contract by giving 60-days' notice to the other. Moreover, the agreement stipulated that if the employee's employment at the hardware store should be terminated, he would not be able to engage in any aspect of the hardware business for a period of two years within a 50-mile radius of the city. Finally, the agreement stated that should the employee violate this agreement, he would be liable to the hardware company for $1,500.

The written agreement between the owner and the employee would most likely be held

(A) enforceable in all respects.
(B) enforceable only with respect to the salary and termination provisions.
(C) enforceable in all respects, except with regard to the $1,500 penalty clause.
(D) unenforceable in all respects.

36. A school hired a senior citizen to act as a crossing guard at a crosswalk located in front of the school. The contract signed by the parties required the senior citizen to be at the crosswalk every weekday afternoon from 2 pm to 4 pm, and to escort children leaving the school across the street. The senior citizen was to be paid $250 per week for his efforts. The contract also stressed the importance of the safety of the children, and stated that if the senior citizen should fail to show up for work without giving notice in advance so a substitute can be located, the senior citizen would be subject to a $200 per incident penalty.

The contract provision making the senior citizen liable for a $200 per incident penalty may best be described as a(n)

(A) liquidated damage clause.
(B) unliquidated damage clause.
(C) penalty and forfeiture clause.
(D) aleatory clause.

37. A screenwriter had just finished a screenplay for a romantic comedy. After reading the screenplay, a movie studio decided to option the screenplay for production. A lawyer for the movie studio negotiated an agreement with the screenwriter whereby the movie studio would pay the screenwriter $5,000 for the rights to the screenplay, and 10 percent of the gross receipts earned by the distribution of the movie, should the studio decide to film the screenplay. Both sides signed the agreement.

Two weeks later, the screenwriter was at a birthday party for a close friend when she discovered she had forgotten to purchase a gift for her friend. She quickly grabbed a piece of paper and wrote on it:

"I promise that my friend is entitled to 5 percent of the proceeds I will receive for the distribution of the movie to be made from my screenplay."

The screenwriter then signed the paper, placed it in an envelope, and handed it to the friend.

The promise to pay 5 percent of the proceeds to the friend may best be interpreted as a(n)

(A) equitable lien.
(B) conditional assignment.
(C) irrevocable assignment.
(D) gratuitous assignment of future rights.

38. On January 1, as part of a New Year's resolution, a woman signed the following agreement with an exercise facility:

"I hereby enroll in the exercise facility's exercise program. A condition of this contract is that all fees are to be paid in advance. If, however, the total enrollment fees exceed $1,250, then one-third shall be paid upon the signing of said agreement, with one-third payable three months later, and one-third six months later. Under no circumstances shall any fees be refundable."

The woman was informed that the fee for the exercise program in which she wanted to participate was $1,500, and that figure was written into the contract. Upon signing the contract, the woman made her first payment of $500 and started classes the next day.

To most accurately describe the installment payment of $500 due on April 1 as it applies to continued use of the exercise facilities, it should be construed as a(n)

(A) condition precedent.
(B) condition subsequent.
(C) concurrent condition.
(D) express condition.

39. A man who was an avid swimmer moved to a new town and began looking for a facility with a swimming pool that he could use. He signed an agreement with the local swimming club to use their swimming pool four times per week. The agreement, which had a duration of one year, stated that the man could use the pool four times per week for $250 per month, due on the first day of each month. For three months, the man paid the $250 on the first and made use of the swimming pool. Toward the middle of the third month, the man was involved in an automobile accident. Shortly thereafter, the man sent the following letter to the swimming club:

"Please be advised that because of injuries sustained in an automobile accident, my physician has advised me not to engage in any strenuous activities. Since I will not be able to make use of the pool anymore, no further payments will be forthcoming."

Which of the following does not accurately state the immediate legal effect of the man's letter?

(A) The swimming club has the right to bar the man from any further use of the pool.
(B) The swimming club has the right to sue the man immediately for breach of contract.
(C) The man may retract his repudiation if he does so before the swimming club initiates legal action against him.
(D) The swimming club must wait until the date of the next payment in order to sue the man for breach of contract.

40. A woman who was three months pregnant enrolled in a pre-natal and post-natal exercise program at the local gymnasium. The contract signed by the woman was to last for one year and called upon the woman to pay $2,000 in quarterly payments of $500. The contract also specified that all fees were non-refundable.

Upon signing the contract, the woman made her first payment of $500 and started classes the next day. The woman attended classes on a regular basis for the next three months. At the end of the three-month period, the woman was involved in an automobile accident. Although she was not seriously injured, her doctor advised the woman that she needed complete rest. Her doctor told her to avoid strenuous activity and advised her to discontinue her pre-natal exercise classes. One week later, the woman received a billing notice from the gymnasium, indicating that her second installment payment of $500 was past due. She immediately telephoned the manager of the gymnasium and informed him that she would not be attending any further classes because of her accident. Also, the woman said she did not feel obligated to make any additional payments.

Which of the following most accurately describes the woman's duty to pay the gymnasium the second installment fee of $500?

(A) It would be excused, because of impossibility of performance.
(B) It would be excused, because the essential purpose of the contract was frustrated.
(C) It would not be excused, because the contract stipulated that no fees would be refundable.
(D) It would be not excused, because her covenant to make the installment payment is also enforceable as a condition precedent.

41. A man decided to enroll in a creative writing course at a local adult education facility. The man signed an agreement with the facility that he would attend weekly classes at the facility for six months and would pay $500 on the first of each month. Upon signing the contract, the man made his first payment of $500 and attended the weekly class sessions. On the first day of the second month, the man once again made his $500 payment and continued to attend the session. At the start of the third month, the man told the director of the facility's accounting office that he was having financial difficulties, and asked for an extension. The director agreed to permit the man to attend classes while the man tried to get the money to pay the facility. One week later, the man received a letter from the facility informing him that he would be barred from attending any further classes unless the next $500 payment was made.

Is the facility justified in refusing to permit the man to attend classes?

(A) No, because by permitting the man to attend classes without having paid the third monthly installment, the facility waived its right to have that installment fee paid on time.
(B) No, because the facility's allowing the man to attend classes without paying the third monthly installment created an implied contract, thus permitting him to complete the classes without advance payment of the installments.
(C) Yes, because the man's failure to make the third monthly installment payment constituted an anticipatory breach.
(D) Yes, because there was no consideration to extinguish the payment of the third monthly installment fee, which was a material part of the contract.

42. A widget manufacturer and a widget retailer signed the following agreement:

"The manufacturer promises to sell and the retailer promises to buy 10,000 widgets at $50 per 100. One thousand widgets are to be delivered by the manufacturer on the first day of each of the next 10 months. EACH MONTHLY DELIVERY IS A SEPARATE CONTRACT. Payment to be made within 10 days of receipt of each shipment."

The agreement between the manufacturer and the retailer may best be interpreted as

(A) a divisible contract.
(B) an installment contract.
(C) 10 separate contracts.
(D) a requirements-output contract.

43. A lumber supplier and a fence company signed the following agreement on May 1:

"The supplier promises to sell and the fence company promises to buy 7,000 sections of redwood stockade fence at $30 per section. Each section is to be made of good quality split redwood poles and is to be 7 feet long and 6 feet high; 1,000 sections are to be delivered by seller on or before June 1, and 1,000 sections by the first day in each of the following six months. Payment for the sections to be made within 10 days of delivery."

The first shipment of 1,000 sections arrived on May 27, and the fence company sent its payment on June 5. The second shipment arrived on July 1, and the fence company made payment on July 5. The August shipment arrived on the afternoon of August 1. After the initial inspection, the redwood poles were found to be 7 feet long and 6.25 feet high. The manager of the fence company then called the president of the lumber supplier. During their conversation, the president told the manager that the lumber supplier could not replace the August shipment but would allow a price adjustment. The manager refused the president's offer. The next day, the manager sent the president a fax stating that he was hereby canceling all future deliveries and returning the last shipment because of nonconformity.

If the lumber supplier sues the fence company for breach of contract, the court will most likely hold that the lumber company will

(A) succeed, because all deliveries to date have been timely.
(B) succeed, because the president offered to adjust the price for the August shipment.
(C) not succeed, because the president refused to replace the nonconforming poles.
(D) not succeed, because the deviation impaired the value of the entire contract.

44. A supermarket signed a contract with a bakery to provide the supermarket with 100 loaves of whole wheat bread per week for 12 consecutive weeks. The loaves were to be delivered on the first day of each week, with payment to be made within four days of delivery. For the first four weeks, the bakery delivered loaves to the supermarket and the supermarket made the appropriate payments. When the fifth delivery arrived, the supermarket discovered that the shipment contained 80 whole wheat loaves and 20 sourdough loaves. The manager of the supermarket immediately called the bakery to complain about the shipment. The operator of the bakery apologized and offered to send 20 loaves of whole wheat bread within 24 hours.

What is the probable legal effect of the operator's conversation with the manager with regard to the fifth shipment?

(A) The supermarket would have the right to reject the fifth shipment and cancel their contract.
(B) The supermarket would have the right to reject the fifth shipment, but would be held liable for the remaining deliveries.
(C) The supermarket would not be entitled to reject the operator's offer to "cure."
(D) The supermarket would have a right to "cover" by purchasing substitute loaves of bread.

45. A lumber mill contracted to deliver one thousand 8-foot sheets of plywood to a home improvement store on the first of each month for 10 consecutive months starting June 1. The June, July, and August shipments were delivered on time and duly paid for. Then, on August 16, the lumber mill informed the store that the mill would not be able to meet the September 1 delivery date, because its lumber reserve had been destroyed by a forest fire. The mill then asked the store to excuse the mill from further performance. The store refused and demanded that the remaining shipments be delivered on time.

When the September shipment failed to arrive, the store immediately brought suit for breach of contract. How would the court hold?

(A) Judgment for the store, because the mill's duties of performance would not be excused.
(B) Judgment for the store, because the mill should have foreseen such a contingency occurring.
(C) Judgment for the mill, because their performance would be discharged by impossibility.
(D) Judgment for the mill, because their performance would be discharged by frustration of purpose.

46. On May 1, a homeowner and a painter entered into a contract whereby the painter was to paint the homeowner's home in exchange for $10,000. The contract stated:

"The painting is to be done during the month of June, and payment is to be made within one week after the painting is completed. The rights under this contact are not to be assigned."

The painter started the painting on June 1. On June 10, the painter assigned to his nephew the right to receive payment on the painter's contract with the homeowner.

Which of the following statements is most accurate with regard to the painter's assignment to his nephew?

(A) The homeowner would not be obligated to pay the nephew, since the contract was nonassignable.
(B) Since personal service contracts of this nature are nonassignable, the homeowner would be under no duty to pay the nephew.
(C) The assignment would constitute a novation, relieving the homeowner of liability.
(D) The assignment would be irrevocable if it were reduced to writing and signed by the painter.

47. On February 1, an owner of six vacation cottages in a resort area hired a painter to paint all six cottages for $50,000. The contract stipulated that no money would be due until the owner's caretaker approved the work done by the painter.

The painter completed the painting of all six cottages. Two days after the painter had finished the painting, a wildfire destroyed the six cottages. Although the caretaker had inspected four of the cottages to his approval, he had not inspected the other two cottages prior to their destruction.

Which of the following is the LEAST accurate statement with respect to the caretaker's approval of the painting of the cottages?

(A) The owner would only be obligated to pay for the painting of the four cottages that the caretaker approved.
(B) The caretaker's approval of the painting of the two cottages destroyed by the wild fire would be excused.
(C) The owner would be obligated to pay for the painting of all of the cottages.
(D) The impossibility of securing the caretaker's approval would render the owner absolutely liable for all of the painting.

48. On March 1, a homeowner hired a landscaper to landscape his front yard. On March 25, as the landscaper was almost finished with the work on the front yard, the homeowner said to the landscaper, "I'm very pleased with your work to date. If you are willing, I would like you to landscape my backyard, on the same terms and conditions as our existing contract, the work to be completed by May 1. If you can meet that deadline, I'll pay you $10,000 at that time." The landscaper replied, "Agreed. Let's shake hands on it." They shook hands.

What is the probable legal effect of the landscaper's promise on March 25 to landscape the backyard?

(A) The landscaper's promise created an enforceable unilateral contract.
(B) The landscaper's promise created an enforceable bilateral contract.
(C) The landscaper's promise was voidable, since it was not in writing.
(D) The landscaper's promise was illusory, thereby creating an unenforceable contract.

49. A woman owned four beach houses. Each house had star-shaped windows. As the hurricane season was approaching, she hired a carpenter to build storm windows for the star-shaped and deliver them to the four houses. Because of the unique shape of the windows, the carpenter had to do all work by hand. The carpenter and woman signed a contract under which the carpenter promised to build and deliver the storm windows to all four beach houses within 30 days, and the woman promised to pay $8,000 ($2,000 per beach house) within one week of completion of the job.

Two weeks after the contract was signed, a fire destroyed the carpenter's workshop, where he was storing all the completed storm windows before delivery. The carpenter then sent a letter to the woman that read:

"The fire destroyed my equipment and inventory—including the storm windows, which had been completed and which were awaiting delivery. I am dead broke and cannot complete my obligations under the contract." The woman then telephoned the carpenter and told him, "Unless you fulfill your contractual obligations, I will sue you!"

In an action for specific performance to compel the carpenter to build and deliver the storm windows, the woman will most likely

(A) succeed, because the carpenter's loss of the inventory would not excuse his duty of performance.
(B) succeed, because the beach houses would suffer severe damage in the event a hurricane struck without the storm windows having been installed.
(C) not succeed, because the carpenter's performance would be excused by the unforeseeable act of God.
(D) not succeed, because the carpenter's loss of inventory would render his performance impossible.

50. On March 1, a man and a contractor executed a contract that provided that the contractor would construct a two-level redwood deck on each of the eight specified beach houses in a city that the man owned, with all work to be completed by May 1. The contract provided the following:

"The cost is $2,500 per deck, to be paid upon completion of the decks in each of the eight beach houses."

On the morning of March 25, the man went to one of the beach houses as the contractor and his assistants were completing the work on the fourth deck. The man said to the contractor, "I'm very pleased with your progress to date. If you are willing, I would like you to build the same kind of decks on four identical beach houses that I own in a neighboring town, on the same terms and conditions as our existing contract, the work to be completed by May 20. If you can meet that deadline, I'll pay you $10,000 at that time." The contractor replied, "Agreed. Let's shake hands on it." They shook hands.

The contractor completed the work on the beach houses located in the city by April 15 and immediately started the construction of the decks on the four beach houses located in the town. On April 22, a hurricane totally destroyed four of the man's beach houses in the city. In addition, the hurricane demolished a beach house in the town on which the contractor had completed 85 percent of the deck work. Two of the contractor's assistants were seriously injured, and all of his equipment was washed away.

The man then received a letter from the contractor, which stated:

"The hurricane destroyed my equipment, worth $4,000. I am dead broke and cannot complete the work on the three remaining beach houses in the town. Please pay me $20,000 for the work I did in the city, and please send me $2,500 for the deck I built on the beach house in the town."

What is the maximum amount that the contractor may recover from the man for the construction that he completed prior to the hurricane?

(A) $10,000.
(B) $10,000 plus the amount due for 85 percent of the completed work on the town beach house.
(C) $20,000.
(D) $20,000 plus the amount due for 85 percent of the work completed on the town beach house.

51. A homeowner owed a painter $5,000 for services rendered three years ago. The painter had tried for several years to collect the money, but was unsuccessful. Hearing that the homeowner had left the country, the painter had given up on collecting the debt. This jurisdiction has a two-year statute of limitations on contract actions.

Recently, the painter was at a home furnishings expo and saw the homeowner negotiating with a salesperson for some bedroom furniture. The painter approached and said to the salesperson, Make sure you get the money up front. Embarrassed, the homeowner pulled the painter aside and said, I'm sorry, things got bad a few years ago, but I have money now. I will pay you the $5,000 I owe you plus $1,000 interest. Will that cover it? The painter nodded his head. Two weeks later, the homeowner still had not paid the painter, who now brings suit against the homeowner.

For whom should the court rule?

(A) The painter for $5,000, because that is the original amount owed.
(B) The painter for $6000, because the extra $1,000 was reasonable under the circumstances.
(C) The homeowner, because the debt was barred by the statute of limitations.
(D) The homeowner, because the agreement is barred by the statute of frauds.

52. A high school senior had been accepted at both State University and Private University. The tuition at State University was $15,000 per year. The student had planned on going to State University until he discussed his choice of colleges with his wealthy uncle, an alumnus of Private University, who had fond memories of his alma mater and strongly encouraged his nephew to attend Private University. Thereupon, the uncle promised his nephew that he would pay the $35,000 tuition at Private University for the first year if the nephew went there instead of State University. The nephew accepted the uncle's offer and notified Private University that he would be attending college in the fall. The nephew also informed State University that he would not be attending there. Three weeks later, the uncle died in a boating accident. Thereafter, the nephew received a billing notice from Private University informing him that the $35,000 tuition fee was presently due. The nephew contacted the executor of his uncle's estate and requested payment for his Private University tuition. The executor told the nephew that he would not honor the uncle's promise.

In a suit for breach of contract against the uncle's estate, how much will the nephew recover?

(A) $35,000, because there was a bargained-for exchange.
(B) $35,000, because there was justifiable reliance.
(C) $20,000, because the nephew would have been obligated to pay the $15,000 State University tuition notwithstanding the uncle's promise.
(D) Nothing, because the uncle's promise was gratuitous.

53. A wealthy man enjoyed humiliating people for his own amusement. He asked his neighbor who had recently lost his job if he wanted to make some extra cash. The neighbor said yes. The wealthy man told the neighbor he would give him $500 if he went to the local Olympic-size swimming pool on Saturday dressed in a one-piece pink swimsuit and swam two full laps. The neighbor went to the store and bought a pink swimsuit. Once he arrived at the swimming pool, he jumped in and began swimming. As he did, the wealthy man suddenly yelled, "I hereby revoke my offer."

At this juncture, which of the following best states the legal rights and duties of the respective parties?

(A) The neighbor can stop swimming immediately and still recover the $500.
(B) The neighbor can continue swimming the two laps and recover damages for breach of contract.
(C) Regardless of what the neighbor does, the wealthy man is liable to pay him only for the cost of the swimsuit, which the neighbor purchased in reliance on the wealthy man's offer.
(D) Regardless of what the neighbor does, the wealthy man is not liable to pay the neighbor anything because the revocation effectively discharged the wealthy man's obligations under the contract.

54. A dancer borrows money from her friend. The dancer is unable to pay the money back, and years pass. The friend eventually needs the money and contacts the dancer, who consults a lawyer. The lawyer tells the dancer that the statute of limitations on the debt has expired and that she is not legally obligated to repay the loan. The dancer nevertheless promises to do so in writing, but then changes her mind.

May the friend enforce the dancer's recent promise to repay the old loan?

(A) Yes, because the past consideration is sufficient to support a present promise.
(B) Yes, because it was a promise to repay a debt that, but for the statute of limitations, would still be owing.
(C) No, because the recent promise to repay the money was a gratuitous promise.
(D) No, because the recent promise to repay the money was supported only by past consideration.

55. An engineering firm designs and builds automated stamp press machines for industrial manufacturers. All machines are standardly built from stock as ordered, and the engineering firm keeps no completed machines on hand. On April 3, a customer ordered three stamp press machines for making industry-standard automobile replacement parts. The engineering firm offered to sell the machines for $15,000 each, and the customer agreed. They further orally agreed that the engineering firm would ship the first machine on May 15, the second on July 1, and the third on September 1, with payment to be made within 30 days of each delivery. The engineering firm delivered the first machine on May 15, and the customer accepted delivery. On July 2, the second machine was delivered and accepted. The third machine was completed on August 15, but because the customer had made no payment for either of the first two machines, the engineering firm did not notify the customer that the third machine was ready. On August 20, the customer canceled its contract with the engineering firm, and the engineering firm filed a lawsuit to enforce the terms of the contract. The customer defended on the grounds that the Statute of Frauds applied, and no enforceable contract had ever been formed.

What, if anything, will the engineering firm recover?

(A) Damages for a total breach of contract for the sale of two machines, because the goods made for the customer were specialty goods.
(B) Damages for a total breach of contract for the sale of three machines, because the customer accepted the engineering firm's partial performance.
(C) $30,000.
(D) Nothing.

56. A soon-to-be motorist resides in a state that provides that the age of majority is 18 years of age. A month before his 18th birthday, the motorist agreed in writing to purchase a car for $4,500 from a car dealership. The market value of the car is $3,500. When he turned 18, the motorist wrote the car dealership the following letter: I made a bad deal with you guys, and I'm not willing to pay the $4,500, but I will pay $4,000. Before the car dealership could respond, the motorist wrote them another letter telling the car dealership to forget the whole deal.

In an action by the car dealership against the motorist, what can the car dealership recover?

(A) $4,500.
(B) $4,000.
(C) $3,500.
(D) Nothing.

57. A young hairdresser decided to switch careers to interior decorating. To speed the transition, she offered her decorating services to her hairdressing customers. The hairdresser invited one of her regular customers to a preliminary consultation in order for the customer to have an opportunity to hear and evaluate some of the hairdresser's ideas. The hairdresser offered the customer the right to be the hairdresser's first interior decorating client in exchange for a $100 consultation fee, and if the customer was dissatisfied with the ideas, she could refuse the hairdresser's interior decorating services. The customer agrees to this arrangement, and they set up an appointment for the following week. However, the hairdresser gets cold feet and fails to show up for the appointment. Later, the hairdresser tells the regular customer that she has changed her mind about becoming an interior decorator. The customer is forced to hire a decorator at more than triple the hairdresser's proposed fee, and she decides to sue the hairdresser for the extra expenses.

Can the customer recover?

(A) Yes, but only if she relied on the offer to her detriment.
(B) Yes, because the parties formed an option contract when the hairdresser offered the customer the right to be her first client, and the customer promised to hear and evaluate the hairdresser's ideas and paid the $100 consultation fee.
(C) No, because the customer's right to refuse the hairdresser's services if she was dissatisfied with the hairdresser's ideas made her promise illusory.
(D) No, because the hairdresser merely terminated a revocable offer.

58. A bride-to-be contracted with a dive shop to perform an underwater wedding at the engaged couple's favorite southern beach. She paid for the whole event in advance. The wedding was to be held on the first weekend in June, at the very beginning of hurricane season when such storms are a rare occurrence. A week before the wedding, a large tropical storm was predicted for the weekend of the wedding. The bride and groom cancelled their dive plans and got married by a justice of the peace as soon as they heard the forecast. As it turned out, the tropical storm stayed well at sea and did not affect the coastline. When the bride and the dive shop wrote up the contract, the dive shop had not pointed out that a storm was a possibility. Nor had the bride acknowledged it as a risk. The dive shop insisted that the bride should not get a refund for the dive because the shop had been quite willing to carry out or reschedule the dive. The bride insisted that the contract be voided.

If the bride takes the matter to court, will the court find in her favor?

(A) Yes, because of unilateral mistake regarding the potential for a tropical storm.
(B) Yes, because the forecast storm caused the couple to elope, thereby frustrating the purpose of the contract with the dive shop.
(C) No, because both parties to the contract could have performed as contracted.
(D) No, because performance by the dive shop was not rendered impossible.

59. A woman was having a garage sale to clear out some old clothing and to sell off some of her recently deceased mother's items. Included among the items from her mother was an antique silver ring with glass crystals. A neighbor spotted the ring and the woman sold it to the neighbor for $50. The neighbor ran an antique shop and hoped to resell the ring for a profit because antique silver was trendy at the time. The neighbor asked for a written receipt for business purposes and the woman wrote up an invoice for one antique silver ring with glass crystals. A couple of days later, the neighbor informed the woman that the neighbor had discovered that the ring was actually platinum with diamonds and worth considerably more than $50. The woman asked for the ring back but the neighbor refused.

If the woman brings an action to recover the ring, is she likely to prevail?

(A) Yes, because she made a unilateral mistake that the antique's dealer had reason to suspect.
(B) Yes, because of mutual mistake.
(C) No, because the woman assumed the risk that the ring was worth more.
(D) No, because the neighbor was not aware of the woman's mistake.

60. For one week every month, a rancher held cattle from several surrounding ranches in his pens to await shipment by train to the city. The rancher executed a contract with a local feed company to deliver a set amount of feed to his ranch on the first of every month to accommodate his own cows, as well as those who were at his ranch temporarily each month. For several months, the contracted deliveries arrived without incident. One month, the feed company delivered only three quarters of the contractual amount. It was enough to accommodate the rancher while the visiting cattle were on his ranch and would get him through much of the month but would not last the entire month. Frustrated, the rancher told the feed company to take back the short delivery and the rancher secured feed from another company for that month.

Does the original feed company have grounds for an action against the rancher?

(A) Yes, because in installment contracts, the buyer always must let the vendor cure a non-conforming installment before rejecting it.
(B) Yes, because the feed company should have been given a chance to cure the non-conforming delivery before the installment was rejected.
(C) No, because the non-conformity substantially impaired the value of the installment.
(D) No, because the buyer does not have to permit the vendor to cure the non-conforming installment.

61. An art dealer contracted with a patron for an oil portrait of the patron's prize-winning dog. The patron specified that she wanted the same artist who had done a painting for her next door neighbor's dog. The patron paid a 50% down payment on the artwork. After executing the contract, the art dealer discovered that the artist had died of a heart attack. The art dealer secured another artist to complete the portrait, and the results were nearly indistinguishable from the work of the deceased artist. The patron initially loved the piece of art but when the dealer informed her that the work had been done by a different artist than her neighbor's artwork, she refused to pay the balance due for the artwork. The art dealer sued the patron for breach of contract because a provision in the contract specified that commissioned works were non-refundable. The patron claimed that the contract was void and demanded her down payment back.

How is the court likely to decide?

(A) In favor of the art dealer because he produced an acceptable work of art to the patron under the contract.
(B) In favor of the art dealer because the risk had been allocated in the contract with the clause regarding non-refundable commissions.
(C) In favor of the patron because impossibility excused her performance under the contract.
(D) In favor of the patron because of the art dealer's fraud.

62. An oil company has entered into a written contract with a local distributor to provide premium gasoline for his gas stations. The company receives its oil from a country in the Middle East. Shortly after the oil company and the distributor execute the contract, the United States declares war on the Middle Eastern country and, as a result, oil becomes much more limited and the prices skyrocket. Limited oil also means that there is limited fuel to power the ships, planes, and trucks that would deliver the gasoline to the local distributor. The oil company refuses to perform on the contract because doing so would be prohibitively expensive, and is sued by the local distributor after the distributor loses business and is forced to shut down half of its existing gas stations.

Under the Uniform Commercial Code, can the oil company be excused from performing on the contract?

(A) No, because the oil company can only be excused from performing under common law.
(B) No, because increased cost alone does not excuse performance.
(C) Yes, because performance is impracticable.
(D) Yes, because performance is impossible.

63. A coach widely considered to be the best college basketball coach in the country is under contract to be the basketball coach at an eastern college for the next three years. The coach accepts an offer to become the basketball coach at a university, the college's bitter rival. The coach's contract with the college does not contain a non-compete clause.

May the college obtain a negative injunction to prevent the coach from coaching at the rival university during the remaining term of his contract?

(A) Yes, because the coach's talents as a basketball coach are extraordinary.
(B) Yes, because employees may not compete with their employers during the term of their contract of employment.
(C) No, because the contract does not contain a non-compete clause.
(D) No, because equitable relief is not available with respect to contracts for personal services.

64. A teacher owned a home that contained a great deal of woodwork. Because the wood was not in very good condition when he bought the home, he wished to take action to preserve it. He contacted several restoration experts, who described what they could do to preserve the wood in the teacher's home. After considering bids from the various experts, the teacher finally offered a restoration company $2,500 to treat the wood in his home. The restoration company agreed to the terms, but was busy and had a hard time scheduling the treatment of the teacher's home before late autumn. The restoration company finally settled on a week in mid-October. Meanwhile, the teacher had accepted a job in another city and was scheduled to move in August. The teacher offered the house to his brother to live in. In early September, the restoration company contacted the brother and told him of the job they had scheduled at the teacher's home in October. The brother thought that this sounded fine, but he later changed his mind and canceled the project in late September.

Does the restoration company have any legal remedy against the teacher for breach of contract?

(A) Yes, because the restoration company relied on the teacher's offer in scheduling the job for October.
(B) Yes, because the restoration company can recover its lost profits.
(C) No, because there was no mutual assent to the offer.
(D) No, because the brother canceled the job.

65. A hardware supplier and a home builder have a requirements contract. The hardware supplier is supposed to supply the home builder with 10,000 door hinges a month for an entire year. Two months after entering the contract, the home builder decides to go back to school to be a lawyer and wants to abandon the home building business. The homebuilder assigns the contract to his competition. The competition requires the hardware supplier to deliver 20,000 door hinges a month.

Is the contract assignable?

(A) Yes, because requirements contracts can be assigned to a third party.
(B) Yes, because the type of requirement did not change.
(C) No, because the assignment would greatly exceed the homebuilder's rights under the contract.
(D) No, because assigning requirements contracts is against public policy.

66. A florist contracted with a woman to provide flowers for a large garden party at the woman's house. The woman wanted a lot of flower arrangements and the florist stood to make a very good profit from the contract. The florist needed the money to pay off a vendor who had been dropping by her shop every week to try and get payment for an overdue bill. The same week that the florist contracted with the woman for her party, the vendor dropped by again. The florist told the vendor that in exchange for him stopping his frequent visits to her shop to collect, she would have the woman make her check out directly to the vendor, thereby assigning her right to payment under the flower contract. She gave him a copy of her contract with the woman so that he could see that he would be paid in full. The vendor agreed and subsequently stopped dropping by the flower shop. On the day of the party, the florist delivered the flowers and the woman gave the florist a check made out to the florist, because the woman had never been instructed otherwise. When the vendor later contacted the woman and found out that she had paid the florist, he directly went to visit the florist to demand payment.

If the vendor sues the florist for the payment from the woman, will he prevail?

(A) Yes, because the payment had been assigned to him and the woman had not been given notice of the assignment.
(B) Yes, because he gave consideration for the assignment.
(C) No, because the assignment was valid and therefore the only available action is against the woman.
(D) No, because the assignment was gratuitous.

67. A veterinarian developed a busy practice in a small town. As her practice continued to grow, the veterinarian decided to expand her practice and ordered three new examining tables from a dog-supply store. The cost of the tables was $9,000, payable within 60 days of delivery. Before the tables arrived, the veterinarian decided to sell her practice and open a new business in a nearby city. She arranged to sell the small-town practice to her assistant. In the sale agreement, the veterinarian and the assistant included a provision that the purchase of the examining tables from the dog-supply store was assignable. The veterinarian notified the dog-supply store of the assignment. The dog-supply store shipped the three examining tables, and the assistant accepted and used them in the practice but refused to pay for them.

Who is liable for the payment to the dog-supply store?

(A) The assistant is liable but the veterinarian is not, because there was a novation.
(B) The veterinarian is liable but the assistant is not, because the assistant never promised the dog-supply store that he would pay for the tables.
(C) The veterinarian is liable but the assistant is not, because a delegation of duties did not take place.
(D) Both the veterinarian and the assistant are liable.

68. A boater visited a welding business to ask about the business erecting a top on the boater's 30-foot fishing boat in exchange for payment. The welder who met with the boater said that he could do the job on the following weekend and they drew up a contract accordingly. Unfortunately, the welder sprained his shoulder on another job, so he asked his partner to work on the top for the boater, which he did. The boater saw the different welder on his boat and nodded at him, but did not say anything else. Halfway through the job, the second welder got a call asking him to take on a large welding contract immediately for much more money. The second welder abandoned the boater's top job.

Who may the boater sue for breach of contract?

(A) Both the first welder and the second welder.
(B) The first welder only, because the duty was not delegable.
(C) The second welder only, because the duty had been delegated.
(D) The second welder only, because there was a novation when the boater nodded his assent to the second welder.

69. A mechanic restores old cars in his spare time. A race car driver still owes the mechanic $2,200 for an old car that the mechanic restored for the race car driver. The race car driver's friend offers to buy another old car from the race car driver for $2,500. The race car driver accepted the friend's offer and agreed with the friend that the friend would pay the money directly to the mechanic by the end of the current month, March. (The race car driver determined that the $2,500 would pay off the debt to the mechanic, and the remainder might be used by the race car driver as a credit toward future work.) In late April, the mechanic sent the race car driver a past due notice--it turns out that the friend had not paid the mechanic anything, even though the race car driver had already delivered the car to the friend. The mechanic sues the race car driver's friend.

How much can the mechanic recover?

(A) Nothing.
(B) $300.
(C) $2,200.
(D) $2,500.

70. A college dean entered into a contract with a lacrosse coach whereby the coach agreed to coach the college's lacrosse team, and the dean agreed to pay the coach a salary of $3,000 during the season. However, several months later, the lacrosse season was nearly half over, and the coach still had not been paid. Furious, the coach informed the dean that he refused to report to work until he was paid.

Is the coach obligated to continue to coach the remainder of the season?

(A) Yes, because the promise to coach and the promise to pay are independent of one another.
(B) Yes, because the contract did not expressly condition payment for a particular point in the season.
(C) Yes, because parol evidence cannot be used to contradict a writing.
(D) No, if the promise to coach and the promise to pay are dependent on one another.

71. A butcher, a baker, and a dentist were old friends. One day, the baker said to the butcher, I know you have always wanted to buy some of my rare wine. Well, I'll give you one case of the wine, but first you have to give your baseball signed by Babe Ruth to the dentist, because he has been as interested in that baseball as you have been in my wine. The butcher has yet to give the baseball to the dentist.

If the dentist learns of the agreement between the butcher and baker, will he be able to successfully sue to enforce it?

(A) Yes, because the dentist was an intended beneficiary of the agreement between the baker and butcher.
(B) Yes, because the agreement was a valid unilateral agreement.
(C) No, because only the butcher can sue to enforce his agreement with the baker.
(D) No, because the agreement was an unenforceable unilateral agreement.

72. A wealthy financial analyst loaned his best friend/former college roommate $1,500 when the roommate got divorced and moved to the analyst's state. The money was intended to help the roommate move and find a new place to live. At the time, the analyst had a good job and was not worried about the money or his best friend/former roommate's ability to pay the analyst back. He did not press the roommate to repay the loan, even though the roommate had promised to quickly repay him once he had settled in. Several years later, the analyst decided to take a year off and sail around the world. While the analyst was traveling, the statute of limitations ran out on his loan to the roommate. Upon his return, the analyst called his best friend/former roommate and told the roommate that the analyst needed the money back. The roommate had recently taken a new sales job. The roommate told the analyst that the roommate would pay the analyst $250 per month for six months in order to pay off the loan, even though paying this amount would be difficult for him. The following Monday when the roommate went into work, the roommate was informed that he and several other salespeople had been terminated.

What is the roommate's best defense to the analyst's claim for $1,500?

(A) The analyst's phone call was not sufficient to bind the roommate to his promise.
(B) The Statute of Limitations bars the analyst from recovering.
(C) The roommate's duty was discharged by impossibility because the roommate's hardship was more severe than the analyst's hardship.
(D) Past consideration is not enough to support the roommate's new promise.

73. A store owner sent out an employee to make a delivery in the store's van. On the way, the employee got into an accident with a driver, who was injured. The driver sued the store owner and the employee for $50,000 in compensatory damages and $50,000 in punitive damages, arguing that the car accident was caused by the employee's negligence. Pretrial investigation and discovery revealed an uninterested witness to the accident. The witness claimed that the employee had been driving recklessly and ran a red light before slamming into the driver. In a signed writing a month before the trial, the driver offered to settle her claims against the store owner for a cash payment of $40,000. The store owner agreed, saying he would make the payment in two weeks. Based on the store owner's promise, the driver had her negligence action dismissed. Before the store owner paid the $40,000 to the driver, they learned that the witness's testimony was fabricated; the witness had not seen the employee driving recklessly or running a red light. The driver still believed in good faith that the car accident was caused by the employee's negligence. However, based on this new information, the store owner refused to pay the $40,000 to the driver. The driver then brought an action against the store owner for $40,000.

What will be the outcome of this action?

(A) The driver will prevail because the agreement to settle the lawsuit did not require consideration.
(B) The driver will prevail because she believed in good faith that the car accident was caused by the employee's negligence at the time she entered into the settlement agreement.
(C) The store owner will prevail because the revelation of the witness's fabrication demonstrates that there was no consideration to support his promise to pay $40,000.
(D) The store owner will prevail because agreements to settle lawsuits are unenforceable as violating public policy.

74. A prune preserves manufacturer entered into a contract with a fruit grower. The contract provided that the manufacturer would purchase and the fruit grower would supply all of the manufacturer's requirements for prunes for the next five years at a specified price per ton reflecting the most recent market price. The contract stated, in part, that the manufacturer need not order any specified amount of prunes, but would notify the fruit grower of his yearly requirements no later than August 15 of each year. The manufacturer notified the fruit grower that it would need 100 tons of prunes for the year. But before the two parties exchanged any prunes or money under the contract, plum blight struck the major growing areas, including the fruit grower's orchards, causing production to go down and the price of prunes to triple. The fruit grower produced about 120 tons of prunes and decided to sell them on the open market, rather than provide 100 tons at the contract price to the manufacturer.

May the fruit grower rescind the agreement with the manufacturer on the grounds that it was not supported by consideration?

(A) No, because an agreement of that nature does not need any consideration to be enforceable.
(B) No, because the parties' mutual promises to purchase and sell the subject goods are sufficient considerations, even though no specific amount of goods to be sold was stated in the contract.
(C) Yes, because the manufacturer's lack of an obligation to purchase any particular amount of prunes was insufficient consideration to support the fruit grower's return promise.
(D) Yes, because requisite mutuality of obligation between the parties is lacking.

75. A gardener owned and operated a nursery. Although he enjoyed working with plants in general, his special interest was in orchids. Unfortunately, that portion of his business rarely made a profit. The gardener consulted with a horticulturist who specialized in orchids. The horticulturist advised the gardener that the orchids could be a profitable venture if he was willing to make certain changes. The horticulturist stated that she would undertake a program that required the construction of certain raised beds and the use of a special potting material. On March 1, the two parties signed an agreement, which provided that the gardener would pay the horticulturist $10,000 in two equal installments within one month of completion, if the horticulturist succeeded in increasing the gardener's orchid production by 50 percent. The agreement also stated that the horticulturist would complete work by May 1. On April 2, the horticulturist advised the gardener that the work was one-half complete and demanded payment of $5,000. The gardener at first refused to pay but, on further discussion, the parties realized that they had interpreted the within one month of completion language differently. They therefore orally modified their agreement. The gardener agreed to pay the $5,000 immediately, and the horticulturist agreed to create a small additional orchid bed.

Was the modification of the original agreement valid?

(A) Yes, because the Statute of Frauds does not apply to subsequent oral modifications of written agreements.
(B) Yes, because the modification was mutual.
(C) No, because the modification was not supported by consideration.
(D) No, because the modification was oral.

76. A seamstress delivered a bride's wedding dress under a contract calling for a dress to the satisfaction of the bride in exchange for payment of $500. The bride, in good faith, believed that the collar on the dress was not finished properly and that the hem was not the right length. She refused to pay the seamstress anything. On April 1, the seamstress sent the bride a copy of the statement for the dress, with the message written across the bottom, My five year old son was just diagnosed with leukemia, and I need the money for his medical treatment. Please send the $500 before April 15. Although the bride felt sorry for the seamstress, she was displeased with the fit of her dress. On April 10, the bride wrote to the seamstress, I would like to settle this before my wedding. I will pay you $400 if you will rework the collar on my dress. I'll accept the hem as it is. The bride sent the seamstress a check for $400. The seamstress cashed the check and reworked the collar of the dress.

If the seamstress sued the bride for $100 after the seamstress cashed the check without objection, in whose favor should the court rule?

(A) The bride, because the seamstress cashed the check without objection.
(B) The bride, because the seamstress is entitled to recover only the reasonable value of her services.
(C) The seamstress, if she proves that she had sewn the dress according to the agreed-upon design.
(D) The seamstress, because she cashed the check under economic duress.

77. Two friends had little in common. Although hardworking, the fisherman's family was poor and could provide their daughter with only the bare necessities. In contrast, the fisherman's daughter's friend was the offspring of a wealthy industrialist who pampered his daughter and indulged her slightest whim. Still, the girls were best friends throughout school. After high school the fisherman's daughter married a lazy, unemployed womanizer. Two years later, their unhappy marriage ended when the womanizer was shot by a jealous husband. In the interim, the industrialist's daughter had inherited the family fortune. When she heard of the fisherman's daughter's plight, she invited her friend to live with her on the family estate. The fisherman's daughter continued to live there for the next 25 ,years and these were truly the best years of her life. The daughter of the industrialist was concerned, however, that as she grew older, her nephew would attempt to grab control of the family empire. The industrialist's daughter wanted to protect her friend, and she had her lawyer draft the following agreement, which she signed. I hereby agree to purchase for my friend, in her name, the house described in addendum number one. This agreement is made in consideration of my friend's comfort and affection during the past years. The fisherman's daughter also signed the instrument on a line following the word Accepted. Thereafter, the nephew seized control of the family empire, confined his aunt to a sanatorium, and (as his aunt's conservator)disavowed the agreement with the fisherman's daughter. The fisherman's daughter sued her friend's nephew for breach of contract. The nephew asserted the agreement was not enforceable because the promise to purchase the house was not supported by consideration.

In most jurisdictions, would the fisherman's comfort and affection be regarded as sufficient consideration for the industrialist's daughter's promise?

(A) No, because the fisherman's daughter did not give the comfort and affection in exchange for the promise.
(B) No, because the comfort and affection do not have a pecuniary value.
(C) Yes, because it constituted a benefit received by the industrialist's daughter.
(D) Yes, because the industrialist's daughter had a moral obligation to her friend.

78. A city solicited bids for the repair of a crawler tractor used at its city landfill. A mechanic submitted the low bid of $8,500. The next lowest bid was $9,000. The remaining bids were between $10,000 and $11,000. The city awarded the contract to the mechanic. However, before commencing the actual repairs, the mechanic realized that he had made a mistake and underestimated the repair work. If the mechanic completes the job, he will lose money. The mechanic refused to do the work unless the city agreed to pay him $9,000. The city was anxious that the work not be delayed and told the mechanic: "All right. We will pay you $9,000 if you go ahead and perform, even though we think you ought to stick by your bid." The mechanic then went ahead and repaired the crawler tractor. Thereafter, the city paid the mechanic $8,500, saying it had changed its mind about paying the additional amount. The mechanic sued the city for $500, and the city defended on the basis that there was no consideration for its promise to pay the additional amount.

In most jurisdictions, who will prevail?

(A) The mechanic, because the parties mutually rescinded the original contract at the $8,500 price and made a new one at $9,000.
(B) The mechanic, because his forbearance to exercise his right to break the original contract and to pay damages is consideration for the city's promise to pay the additional $500.
(C) The city, because the city's promise to pay the additional amount was obtained by undue influence.
(D) The city, because the mechanic was already duty-bound to do the work for $8,500 when the city promised to pay $9,000.

79. An art dealer was racing to a very important meeting. While crossing the street, he slipped and fell, accidentally throwing a portfolio he was carrying into the air. A pretzel vendor, who was standing nearby, caught the portfolio before it smashed on the ground. "I believe I have a Monet in this portfolio! I'm on my way to an appraiser right now. If I have an original, I'll give you $100,000," the art dealer said to the pretzel vendor. The painting turned out to be a Monet worth $2.8 million. The art dealer wrote the following letter to the pretzel vendor: "Because you saved my Monet from loss or destruction, and inasmuch as you agree to file no claim for ownership of the painting, I will pay you $100,000." The art dealer signed the letter. A week later, the pretzel vendor went to the art dealer's gallery to see about collecting the $100,000. He discovered that art dealer had suffered a massive stroke that had resulted in permanent brain damage, and he had been declared legally incompetent, remembering nothing of the incident with the Monet. The art dealer's legal guardian refused to pay any money to the pretzel vendor.

Under which of the following theories would it be most likely that the pretzel vendor could recover from the art dealer via his guardian?

(A) The art dealer executed a binding unilateral contract.
(B) Promissory estoppel binds the art dealer.
(C) It would be unjust for the art dealer not to give restitution for benefits he retains.
(D) The parties have made a compromise.

80. A bird-watcher was leaving a bird sanctuary resort, where he had just spent a week looking for the rare red-beaked falcon, when he dropped his camera as he was walking past a bluff. The camera plunged down the bluff and before it smashed on the rocks below, a local fisherman who was at the bottom of the bluff, caught the camera. "I have a picture of the rare red-beaked falcon in that camera. If I win the prize for best photo at the upcoming Bird Photos Contest, I'm going to give you $500!" said the bird-watcher to the fisherman. The bird-watcher won first prize. He then wrote the following letter to the fisherman: "Because you saved my camera from destruction and because you agree to file no claim with the Bird Photo Contest against my winning photo, I will pay you $500." The bird-watcher signed the letter. A week later, the fisherman was visiting his sister in the town where the bird-watcher lived and went to his home to see about collecting the $500. The fisherman discovered that the bird-watcher had been hit by a car, was in a coma and had been declared legally incompetent. His legal guardian refused to pay any money to the fisherman.

With respect to the promise to pay $500 to the fisherman because he agreed not to file a claim for the prize money, what additional fact would most strengthen the fisherman's claim?

(A) The fisherman reasonably believed he had a valid claim when the agreement was made.
(B) The fisherman's agreement was made in a writing he signed.
(C) The agreement was witnessed by an objective third party.
(D) The bird-watcher could not have won the contest and the prize without the camera.

81. A boy, one week from reaching the age of majority in his jurisdiction, loved all varieties of music, and enjoyed learning to play various instruments. One afternoon, he walked from school to the town's local guitar shop. He agreed with the shop owner to purchase an electric guitar, payments to be made on a monthly schedule for the following six months. The day after the boy reached the age of majority, he called the shop owner and told him he had been a minor at the time the agreement was struck, and that he wanted to "call the whole deal off. The shop owner told the boy not to worry, and asked that he bring the guitar back to the shop the next day after school.

The next day, as the boy was preparing to pack up the guitar, he received a large check from his grandmother in a belated birthday card. He called the guitar shop owner and told him that "the deal is back on!" The shop owner, feeling that the boy was troublesome, told him "there is no longer any deal, kid."

May the boy enforce the contract?

(A) Yes, because the power to disaffirm a contract is held only by the minor.
(B) Yes, because he ratified the contract.
(C) No, because he disaffirmed the contract.
(D) No, because the shop owner may disaffirm the contract since it does not pertain to necessaries.

82. A restaurant owner ran a tea room and restaurant specializing in English cuisine. The restaurant had a candy counter near the cash register. The candy counter was very popular, because it offered confections not normally available in the region. The Jelly Baby, the restaurant's top-selling candy, was hard to come by, especially during the summer when the only factory in England that produces the candy shut down for maintenance. The restaurant owner purchased her supply of Jelly Baby candies from an importer of British goods. For the past seven years, the importer and restaurant owner had had a written contract whereby the importer promised to supply Jelly Baby candies at $20 a box. As summer approached, the importer realized that the cost of importing goods from Europe was going to increase dramatically. The importer informed the restaurant owner that he would continue to sell her Jelly Baby candies only if she agreed to pay $90 per box. Desperate to meet the demand for the candy, the restaurant owner agreed. In September, when the candy factory was once again open for business, the restaurant owner informed the importer that she would pay only the original purchase price of $20 a box.

Can the importer enforce the new $90-per-box price?

(A) Yes, because the equitable modification doctrine applies.
(B) Yes, if the higher price paid by the restaurant owner was set in good faith.
(C) No, because the factory is once again operating, eliminating any substantial hardship.
(D) No, because it was foreseeable at the time of formation that shortages in the supply of candy would occur.

83. A teenager is fascinated with cars and engines. She is taking auto shop in high school, and she also likes to hang around a garage after school to watch the mechanics work on cars. While she's there, she tries to help out by doing various odd jobs. One day while the teenager is at the garage, the garage owner asks her if she'd like a can of soda pop. The teenager refuses, saying, The cold soda makes one of my teeth hurt. The garage owner knows that the teenager's family can't afford to pay for a dentist, so he says, I'll pay for the dentist. Go get your tooth looked at, and I'll pay for the dental work. The teenager goes to the dentist, and the dentist takes care of her tooth. The dentist charges the teenager $450. The teenager then brings the bill to the garage owner. The garage owner feels that the charge is exorbitant and refuses to pay.

What is the teenager's best argument for requiring the garage owner to pay the $450 dental bill?

(A) Moral obligation.
(B) Past consideration.
(C) Breach of contract.
(D) Detrimental reliance.

84. A patient borrowed $10,000 from a bank to pay off some outstanding medical bills. The bank loaned the patient the money based on her good credit history, but soon after, the patient lost her job and was never again able to attain her previous income level. The patient never repaid the bank and defaulted on the loan. Last year, the Statute of Limitations ran out on the loan, and the bank can no longer compel the patient 's repayment of the loan. In January, the patient wrote a long letter to the bank, explaining that she had recently inherited some money and wished to pay off $7,500 of her loan debt. The patient promised to pay the bank in February, but did not do so. In March, the bank filed a lawsuit against her to recover the promised $7,500.

What, if anything, is the bank entitled to recover?

(A) $10,000.
(B) $7,500.
(C) $7,500, but only if the patient was aware that the statute of limitations on the original debt had run out.
(D) Nothing.

85. An honors student would soon be graduating from college. She wished to take a tour of Europe after graduating. Knowing of the student's desire to travel, the student's great- aunt sent the student a note indicating that she would transfer $2,000 to the student's account after the student returned from her trip. Relying on her great-aunt's promise, the student spent a total of $1,800 on her trip. After the student returned, her great-aunt refused to make the transfer after the great-aunt had seen the drop in the student's final grades in the student's final semester.

Can the student enforce her great-aunt's promise?

(A) No, because the promise was a gift subject to a condition that conferred no benefit on the great-aunt.
(B) No, because the past consideration is insufficient.
(C) Yes, but only to the extent of $1,800, to prevent injustice to the student.
(D) Yes, for the full $2,000, because the promise was a bargained-for exchange.

86. A bodybuilder borrowed a lawnmower from his neighbor. The bodybuilder misused the lawnmower as part of his weight-lifting routine, and it broke down. The bodybuilder took the machine to a repair shop and had it fixed. Later, after paying for the repair, the bodybuilder returned the lawnmower to the neighbor. The neighbor was so impressed with how well the newly repaired machine ran that he told the bodybuilder that the neighbor would repay the bodybuilder for the repair. However, the neighbor never did. The bodybuilder files suit to recover the amount from the neighbor.

Will the bodybuilder prevail?

(A) Yes, because the neighbor's promise was legally enforceable.
(B) Yes, if the bodybuilder relied to his detriment on the neighbor's promise.
(C) No, because there was no consideration for the neighbor's promise.
(D) No, because there was an implied condition precedent that the body builder return the lawnmower to the neighbor in proper working condition.

87. A man owns a small apartment building in town. Several of his tenants have recently moved out, and so the owner hires a painter to paint one of the apartments while it is vacant. The painter agrees to paint the vacant apartment for $400, and she is to complete the work within 30 days. The parties sign a contract stating these terms. Later that day, as the apartment owner is reviewing his calendar, he realizes that new tenants will be moving into the apartment that the painter is going to paint in 15 days, not 30. The owner calls and asks the painter if she can complete the job within 14 days, rather than 30. The painter agrees, but only if the owner promises to pay her an additional $500. The owner reluctantly agrees to the new amount. The painter paints the apartment within seven days, but the owner refuses to pay her the additional $500, and remits payment of $400. The painter files suit against the apartment owner to recover the additional $500.

Who will prevail in this action?

(A) The apartment owner, because the painter had a pre-existing duty to paint the apartment.
(B) The apartment owner, because the painter tried to extort the additional money knowing that the owner was under duress.
(C) The painter, because she made a new promise to the apartment owner in exchange for higher payment.
(D) The painter, because the apartment owner had a pre-existing duty to perform.

88. For years, a linen supply dealer contended that a hotel owner owed him a total of $11,000 for various transactions between the parties. The hotel owner, on the other hand, contended he owed nothing to the linen supply dealer. The hotel owner eventually grew tired of arguing with the linen supply dealer about the money and finally signed a promissory note in which he agreed to pay $6,500 in settlement of their long-running dispute.

If the linen supply dealer files an action against the hotel owner to enforce the promissory note, which of the following is the hotel owner's best defense?

(A) The hotel owner's promise to pay was a gratuitous promise.
(B) The linen supply dealer's initial claim against the hotel owner was barred by the Statute of Frauds because it was not in writing.
(C) Although the linen supply dealer knew that the debt was not actually owed by the hotel owner, the hotel owner was truly in doubt as to whether he owed the debt.
(D) Although the linen supply dealer sincerely believed that the hotel owner owed the debt, the hotel owner believed that he did not owe it.

89. A fisherman was fishing in a stream near his house when he heard someone crying out for help. He moved quickly downstream and found a swimmer who was drowning. The fisherman pulled the swimmer from the river and saved his life. Grateful for the fisherman's heroic efforts, the swimmer included him in his will, devising $10,000 to the fisherman. Five years later, when the swimmer died, the only property he left behind was $25,000, which was in a joint bank account he shared with his wife. After the swimmer died, his wife still felt gratitude toward the fisherman, so she delivered to him a written instrument that said, I hereby agree to pay the sum of $10,000 in consideration for saving my husband's life and in agreement to make no claims against my husband's estate based on my husband's will. Two years later, the swimmer's wife dies, and the fisherman files a claim against her estate for $10,000. The executor of the wife's estate denies his claim, arguing that the instrument was not supported by consideration.

Which additional fact would strengthen the fisherman's claim?

(A) The fisherman reasonably believed he had a valid claim when the swimmer's wife signed the instrument.
(B) The fisherman's agreement was in writing and signed by him.
(C) The fisherman paid the wife the sum of $1.00 when he received her written instrument.
(D) The wife contributed to the accumulation of the bank account's value.

90. A truck driver saved the life of a taxi driver after he was involved in an accident. The taxi driver later rewrote his will to leave $5,000 to the truck driver in gratitude for his actions. However, when the taxi driver died a few years later, he left behind no property apart from an undivided interest in a piece of land held in tenancy by the entirety with his wife, who had purchased the property decades before with money she had inherited from her father. After the taxi driver died, the wife signed and delivered to the truck driver a written instrument that stated, In consideration for having saved my husband's life and in agreement to make no claims against my land based on my husband's will, I promise herewith to pay the sum of $5,000. A short time later, the wife died, and the truck driver filed a claim against her estate for $5,000. The wife's executor contested the truck driver's claim on the ground that the truck driver's instrument was not supported by sufficient consideration.

Is the truck driver likely to prevail?

(A) Yes, because the truck driver did give consideration in exchange for the promise.
(B) Yes, because the wife is morally obligated to the truck driver as a result of his act.
(C) No, because moral obligations are not enforceable.
(D) No, because the wife was not the beneficiary of the truck driver's lifesaving act.

91. A landowner owned one of the few remaining vacant lots in downtown. A buyer offered the landowner $250,000 for the land with a 30-day option to buy for $750. Because the landowner thought that he could find a buyer who would pay more for the property, he rejected the buyer's offer. The buyer said to the landowner, If you make me a written offer to sell your land for $250,000 for 30 days, revocable at your will, I will pay you $750. The landowner agreed and gave the buyer a written document that stated that for the next 30 days he offered his vacant lot to the buyer for $250,000, revocable at his will and pleasure. Later that same day, the landowner learned that a developer would be willing to buy the lot for $300,000. The landowner then called the buyer late in the day to tell her that the written offer was revoked and that he wanted her to pay him the $750. The buyer refused to pay.

If the landowner sues the buyer for the $750, who will prevail at trial?

(A) The buyer, because the Parol Evidence Rule precludes the seller from offering evidence of the buyer's oral offer to pay $750 for the revocable option.
(B) The buyer, because the landowner's 30-day option to sell the property to the buyer was an illusory promise.
(C) The landowner, because the buyer's oral offer to pay for the revocable option was accepted by the landowner when he reduced the agreement to writing.
(D) The landowner, because evidence of the buyer's promise to pay for the revocable option is admissible as a collateral agreement.

92. A porcelain doll collector is 17 years old and has been buying and selling antique and custom-made dolls for the past five years. An older personal shopper, who had never been interested in dolls before, saw the doll collector's showcase at an antique toy convention and decided that she would like to own one. The personal shopper asked the doll collector if she knew where she could get such a doll, and the doll collector showed the personal shopper a very rare and old doll she had in her collection. Although the doll was missing two buttons and a strap on her dress, when the personal shopper asked the doll collector whether the lack of buttons and strap would affect the doll's potential resale value, the doll collector replied that it would have no effect at all. Actually, the doll collector knew that the lack of the buttons and strap probably would interfere substantially with the potential market/resale value of the doll. Unaware of this significance, the personal shopper arranged to come by the doll collector's house the following weekend to bring the doll collector $150 cash and to pick up the doll. The doll collector wrote the terms of their agreement with lipstick on a small receipt she had gotten from buying lunch earlier in the day and both parties signed it. A few days later, the personal shopper found out from one of her clients that the incomplete dress would diminish the resale value of the doll considerably. The personal shopper called the doll collector that night and told her that the deal was off. The doll collector sued the personal shopper for breach of contract.

Will the doll collector prevail?

(A) Yes, because the agreement was a voidable obligation only at the doll collector's election.
(B) Yes, because it was not reasonable for the personal shopper to rely on the doll collector's statement.
(C) No, because the personal shopper relied on a material misrepresentation.
(D) No, because the doll collector cannot enter into an enforceable contract because she is still a minor.

93. On July 15, the following notice was posted on a bulletin board in the employees' lounge of a large commercial bakery: The bakery offers to any employee who wins the annual baking competition an additional prize of $500. All registration forms must be submitted through the personnel department before July 31. The competition, conducted by an outside organization, honors the most creative and competent baker. An employee of the bakery read the notice on July 20 and thereupon decided to intensify her effort to win the competition. She enrolled in two advanced baking classes to improve her skills. She left a note on the personnel director's desk saying, I accept the bakery's offer of the additional prize of $500. The employee submitted her registration form for the competition through the personnel department on July 25, and on September 1 she won the competition. When she sought the additional award, the bakery refused to pay. The employee was subsequently killed during an accidental explosion in the main kitchen facility of the bakery on October 1.

Will the bakery's July 15 promise still be enforceable?

(A) Yes, the promise is still enforceable on principles of promissory estoppel.

(B) Yes, the promise is enforceable by the employee's personal representative, even though the employee had been killed in the bakery explosion on October 1.

(C) No, the promise is not enforceable on policy grounds, because it produced a noncommercial agreement between an employee and her employers.

(D) No, the promise is not enforceable, because the employee, after submitting her application in July, was already under a duty to perform to the best of her ability.

94. After a pastry chef won her fifth consecutive award for one of her classic red velvet wedding cakes at an annual, world-renowned wedding cake creation competition, she was approached by a number of people interested in purchasing one of the wedding cakes. One particularly interested fiancée jotted down the following on a blank piece of paper: I shall be entitled to purchase the highest tiered cake from the next three cakes created by the pastry chef. Price to be determined by conformation at time of selection. Both parties signed the writing, and the fiancée took possession of it. The pastry chef created her next line of wedding cakes five months later. The fiancée selected a seven-tiered cake and presented the pastry chef with a check for $3,000. Cakes from other celebrity/experienced chefs and wedding cake designers ranged in cost at that time from $500 to $2,500 dollars. The pastry chef, who had recently been asked to do a wedding cake for the daughter of the newly elected United States president, refused to sell the cake for less than $10,000. The fiancée immediately brought an action to determine the parties' rights in this matter. The pastry chef asserted that any agreement purportedly formed between him and the fiancée was unenforceable because of the lack of any price term.

Should the court uphold this defense?

(A) No, because an arbitrator will be appointed by the court to settle the dispute between the parties.

(B) No, because the court will set a reasonable price if reference to conformation is inadequate to do so.

(C) Yes, because the parties may not leave an essential contract term to be agreed upon later.

(D) Yes, because both parties are not merchants.

95. A college sought to fill a one-year position for a faculty member who would be taking some time off for a medical operation. It advertised the position and received about 75 applications. The college sent one promising applicant a letter stating that the applicant was being offered the position. The letter included a one-year contract for the applicant to sign. The applicant signed the contract and sent it to the college with a letter indicating that his acceptance would be effective when the college notified the applicant that it had received the applicant's letter and the contract. The applicant dropped the contract and letter in the mailbox on June 28. The next day, the college called him to withdraw its offer, because the faculty member whose position the applicant would be filling had decided to postpone the operation. The college had not yet received his letter and signed contract.

Does the applicant have an enforceable contract with the college?

(A) Yes, because the contract was formed when the applicant sent the contract to the college.
(B) Yes, because the contract was formed when the applicant signed the contract.
(C) No, because the college called the applicant before it received the applicant's letter and contract.
(D) No, because the contract will not be completed within one year of its formation.

96. An actor received a letter from his aunt, stating that she would make her summer home available to him for the summer. The aunt indicated that, while she often rented out the house for $1,000 or more per week, she would allow him to rent it for $700 a week. The letter stated that if he wished to accept her offer, he should send his reply by mail to her Manhattan apartment, and their deal would be effective upon her receipt of his letter. The actor was extremely excited at the prospect of renting his aunt's summer home, and he sent his acceptance of his aunt's offer through a service that promised overnight delivery. That evening, he received a telegram from his aunt indicating that she had changed her mind and that she and her family would be spending the summer on Long Island.

Does the actor have an enforceable contract with his aunt?

(A) Yes, once the aunt receives his reply in Manhattan.
(B) Yes, because his acceptance was effective once he sent his letter by express delivery.
(C) No, because his failure to send his response by mail as directed caused the offer to lapse.
(D) No, because the telegram from the aunt revoked her offer.

97. A 16-year-old student was enjoying her high school ski trip when the weather suddenly turned ugly. It was evident that the students would have to head down the slopes and take the bus home immediately, before the storm left them stranded on the mountain. While everyone waited for the bus, the electrical power in the ski lodge went out. The student was freezing. Many of her classmates purchased jackets and other warm clothes in the lodge gift shop, but the student did not have any money with her. Not wishing to see her get sick, the gift shop manager offered her a coat, saying, Send me the money when you get home. The student agreed and put on the warm jacket. Later, while getting onto the bus, the student caught her right coat sleeve on a protruding screw, causing a minor tear in the jacket.

Upon her return home, the student's parents refused to pay the $200 price for the coat. Therefore, she mailed the coat back to the gift shop manager with a note saying, Thanks for the coat, but I do not want to buy it.

Does the student face liability for the warm jacket?

(A) Yes, because the warm coat kept the student from freezing.
(B) No, because the restitution obligation extends no further than returning the jacket to the gift shop as now.
(C) No, the contract was never binding.
(D) No, she effectively disaffirmed the contract.

98. On May 15, a florist left a note for one of his customers, offering to pay him $2,000 for his truck, with delivery of the truck to be made to the flower shop before 1:00 p.m. on May 20. On May 16, the customer sent a letter to the florist indicating his acceptance of the florist's offer. However, the letter was delayed by a mix-up at the local post office and did not reach the flower shop until May 19. By then, not having not heard back from his customer, the florist had purchased another used truck for $1,800. On May 20, the customer drove his truck to the florist, arriving at about 12:55 p.m. At that time, the florist rejected the customer's truck, stating that he was no longer in need of a delivery truck. The customer filed suit against the florist for breach of contract.

What was the legal effect of the customer's letter of May 16?

(A) Upon the florist's receipt of the customer's letter, a binding unilateral contract was formed between the florist and the customer for the purchase and sale of the customer's truck.
(B) Upon the mailing of the customer's letter, a binding unilateral contract was formed between the florist and the customer for the purchase and sale of the customer's truck.
(C) The customer's letter was a proper acceptance of the florist's offer, effective upon the customer's mailing of the letter.
(D) The customer's letter was not a proper acceptance of the florist's offer, because the letter requested acceptance by delivery of the truck to the flower shop by May 20.

99. A 17-year-old high school student got her hair colored every month at the same salon and always charged it to her mother's account. One month after her 18th birthday, the student was surprised when the management presented her with a bill for services over the previous year, for which her mother had refused to pay. The student also refused to pay, claiming that she never agreed to be charged herself.

Is a court likely to hold the student liable for the costs of the salon's services?

(A) Yes, because the student is no longer a minor and is therefore liable for her own debts.
(B) Yes, because the student contracted for a necessity and is liable, even though she was a minor at the time the services were provided.
(C) No, because the student was a minor at the time that the course of dealing began, and hair coloring is not a necessity.
(D) No, because the student's mother is the primary obligor.

100. The state government advertised for bids from general contractors on construction of a state office. A contractor, who intended to submit a bid on the project, solicited bids from various sub-contractors for framing, electrical work, and plumbing. The contractor received a sub-bid on the plumbing work for the project of $510,000, which was $10,000 lower than any competing sub-bid. After compiling all the acceptable sub-bids, the contractor submitted a bid on the total project for $5 million. It was the lowest bid, and was accepted on that basis. That same day, the contractor notified the plumbing sub-bidder that his sub-bid was accepted. A week later, the plumbing sub-contractor notified the contractor that an accounting error had resulted in his plumbing sub-bid being too low by $50,000; the actual bid should have been $560,000.

If the sub-contractor brings an action to rescind his contract with the contractor for the plumbing work, judgment should be for

(A) the subcontractor, because the error deprives him of the benefit of the bargain of his contract.
(B) the subcontractor, because his unilateral mistake deprives the parties of the meeting of the minds necessary for formation of a contract.
(C) the contractor, because he was unaware of the subcontractor's mistake and had no reason to know of it.
(D) the contractor, because a unilateral mistake can never be the basis for rescission.

Answers and Explanations

1. **(B)** The issue here is the ***pre-existing duty rule***. It does not constitute legal detriment when a party performs an act that he is legally obligated to do. The detective was hired by the insurance company to investigate the theft. Since he had a pre-existing duty to perform this service, his promise to the woman was not supported by consideration and therefore unenforceable. Choice (A) is not the best answer. While it is true that the woman's promise was gratuitous, Choice (B) explains why that was the case. Since Choice (B) is a more complete answer, it wins out over Choice (A). Choice (C) is incorrect, because it does not matter whether the detective had accepted the woman's offer; there is no consideration to support her promise to pay. Choice (D) is wrong for the same reason. The increased market value cannot supply the missing consideration.

2. **(A)** An offer that invites performance of an act as acceptance rather than a return promise ***becomes irrevocable as soon as the offeree has started to perform the act.*** This rule is deemed essential to prevent hardship to the offeree, where his part performance does not benefit the offeror and so would give him no recovery in quasi-contract. Although some of the older decisions have applied the logical view that a unilateral offer may be revoked at any time prior to full completion of the act bargained for, by the ***majority*** rule today such an offer becomes irrevocable as soon as the offeree has started to perform the act requested. Choice (B) is incorrect, because quasi-contract (which is a contract implied at law) is not needed, since there was an enforceable contract between the parties. Choice (C) is wrong, because the fact that the neighbor had started performance made the offer irrevocable, as explained above. Choice (D) is wrong, because the neighbor had gone beyond mere preparation. Buying the gasoline was preparation, starting the lawn mower on the man's property would constitute starting into the requested act.

3. **(D)** The gardener's refusal to replace the sprinkler heads would amount to a material breach. If a defect in the promisor's performance substantially affects the reasonable expectations of the aggrieved promisee, the breach is "material." Here, the owner's reasonable expectations were to have a set of sprinklers that actually functioned properly. Because the gardener's refusal to replace the defective sprinkler heads substantially affected what the owner expected to get from the contract, the owner can treat this as a material breach and a reason to discharge the gardener. Thus, Choice (D) is correct. Choice (A) is incorrect, because insolvency or bankruptcy of the promisee does not of itself constitute such prospective failure of consideration as will discharge the promisor. See Restatement of Contracts 2d, Section Choice (B) is not a strong enough grounds for discharge. The gardener promised to complete the job by April 19. Even though he had only finished 33 percent of the job by April 14, he would still have until April 19 to complete the work. Choice (C) is not a valid reason for discharging the gardener; since the agreement was for the installation of sprinkler heads, it did not cover the sale of goods. Therefore, it did not need to be in writing.

4. **(C)** This is a rather tricky question dealing with Remedies. The electrician was hired to perform the work at a contract price of $5, According to the terms of the agreement, the electrician would be paid ***upon completion of the job.*** As such, the contract does not appear to be divisible. Therefore, Choice (A) is wrong. Although the electrician did not complete performance, he would, nevertheless, be entitled to receive restitution for the part performance that he rendered. A recovery on ***quantum meruit*** usually applies in situations where the plaintiff has performed services for the defendant, but he cannot recover on the contract (either because there was not full performance or because the contract was unenforceable). Choice (B) is wrong, because the measurement of recovery would be based on the reasonable value of the work performed, not on the contract price. The contract price ($5,000 for 500 fixtures) would be a factor in determining the reasonable value, but it would not be conclusive. Choice (D) is incorrect, because the electrician is entitled to some compensation for the work performed to prevent an unjust enrichment to the owner.

5. **(A)** This is a rather tricky unilateral Contracts example. UCC Section 2-206(1)(a), provides that offers generally invite acceptance "in any manner and by any medium reasonable in the circumstances." Generally, an offer may call for acceptance by either ***(1) a return promise or by (2) a specified act.*** Here, the stationery store's offer expressly

called for the wholesaler to ***ship immediately*** the scissors. Thus, this is an example of ***acceptance by performance.*** Under 2-206(1)(b), it is not necessary that the seller's shipment constituting the acceptance be conforming goods. In this situation, if the seller sends nonconforming goods, then the buyer has a cause of action for breach of contract, unless the seller includes a notice of accommodation. Choice (B) is wrong, because, under Section 2-206, the "good faith" of the wholesaler is not a determining factor as to whether a contract was formed. Choice (C) is incorrect, because the offer called for a shipment, not a promise to ship. In addition, 2-206(B) states that an offer to buy goods can be accepted by either a prompt shipment or a prompt promise to ship. Choice (D) is a misstatement of the law. It does not matter whether the goods are reasonably resalable. If they are nonconforming, they will still constitute an acceptance of the offer (absent a notice of accommodation), but the offeror would have a cause of action for breach of contract for the nonconforming shipment.

6. **(B)** Both UCC Sections 2-601 and 2-608 make it clear that the buyer need not revoke or reject the entire amount (of nonconforming goods) but may accept and keep "any commercial unit or units and reject the rest." Therefore, Choices (A) and (C) are incorrect. Likewise, the buyer may ***elect his remedy*** to either reject or revoke acceptance and recover damages for non-delivery under 2-713, or he may cover and collect damages under 2- In any event, a buyer who wishes to reject must "seasonably notify" the seller under Section 2-602; and Section 2-608(2) contains a similar requirement for one revoking acceptance. Choice (D) is wrong. If seasonable notice is given that the nonconforming shipment is meant as an accommodation, the shipment becomes a counteroffer that can either be accepted or rejected.

7. **(D)** In building contracts, the architect's certificate of completion, if made an express condition to the owner's duty of payment, must be produced or excused before the builder will be entitled to the price. The certificate will be excused where its non-production is due to fraud or "bad faith" on the part of the architect. If the architect's refusal to issue the certificate amounts to bad faith, in fact or in law, the courts will excuse the condition. The builder can then recover the contract price on proof of completion of the work without producing the certificate. The recovery will prevent unjust enrichment to the owner. For this reason, choice (D) is the best choice; even though there was an express condition precedent to the owner's duty to pay, that condition will be excused and the owner will be required to pay the contractor. Choice (A) is incorrect, because the majority of courts dispense with the necessity of architects' certificates when withheld in bad faith (excuse their performance as a condition) rather than order their execution. Choice (B) is incorrect, because in most cases the builder does not attack the validity of the contract's provision for an architect's certificate, which would require reformation. Choice (D) is incorrect, because the express condition is excused by the architect's bad faith.

8. **(A)** First, it is important to realize that the owner and the tenant entered into an enforceable bilateral contract that was supported by adequate consideration. The owner is promising to pay the tenant a share of the proceeds from the sale of the tract of land, and in return, the tenant is promising not to sue the owner for the improvements he made on the property. Thereafter, the tenant committed a material breach of an implied promise to cooperate on the owner's efforts to sell the property by making negative comments to prospective buyers. Where a party to a contract for an agreed exchange of performance ***knowingly prevents, hinders, or makes more costly the other's performance, such conduct is a breach of contract*** for which an action will lie. In this situation, the ***breach is of an implied promise against prevention.*** For example, an owner who excludes a contractor from his premises prevents performance of the work to be done. Thus, he is liable in damages for such breach, measured by the contractor's lost profit on the job. In brief, the implied promise against prevention is that neither party will knowingly obstruct or make more expensive the other's performance. Choice (B) is wrong, because anticipatory repudiation is where one party to an executory bilateral contract repudiates the contract in advance of the time set for performance by announcing that he will not perform. Here, the tenant did not anticipatorily repudiate. Choice (C) is incorrect, because failure to pay rent for two months is a partial, non-material breach. Choice (D) is clearly wrong, because the contract between the owner and the tenant does not restrain the alienation of the property.

9. **(B)** The most persuasive argument for the tenant should be one in which the tenant will be deemed not to have breached his contract with the owner. Choice (B) is the correct answer. By showing that the tenant made no negative comments to the buyer, there is no evidence that the tenant breached his implied promise to cooperate by preventing the owner from realizing the maximum possible sales price. Absent such a breach, the tenant would be entitled to recover the proceeds. Choice (C) is incorrect, because the owner's promise to pay the sale proceeds was not conditioned on the tenant's remaining on the premises, but rather in settlement of the tenant's claim for compensation for the room addition. Choice (D) is incorrect, because, while it is true that the owner's promise to pay the tenant a share of the proceeds was an independent covenant from the payment of rent, the owner's duty to pay would still be discharged by the tenant's material breach of an implied promise to cooperate. Choice (A) is incorrect, because the seller is obligated merely to use best efforts to sell at the maximum possible price, not necessarily the appraised market value. The owner did not receive any offers at the appraised value before finally selling.

10. **(D)** The trick to this question is to realize this is really a formation problem. Many students will get distracted by the fact that a third-party beneficiary (the widow) is attempting to sue. However, a third-party beneficiary does not receive any rights unless it is first determined that a valid contract was formed. Here, the hotel made a gratuitous promise to all of its employees. As such, its promise was not enforceable. Since no valid contract involving the payment of the $5,000 was ever formed, the widow never received any right that could be enforced. Choices (A), (B) and (C) are all therefore wrong. Each might have been a concern if the widow had received rights under a validly formed contract, but since that is not the case, they must all be discounted.

11. **(D)** The general rule is that past consideration is not good consideration. Since the boss made his promise in exchange for something the employee had already done, this is past consideration. Some jurisdictions recognize an exception to this rule and will enforce such a promise on the grounds of moral obligation. However, those jurisdictions will do so only when the promise should be enforced to avoid injustice. Here, the employee gratuitously conferred a benefit on the boss; it would not produce an injustice if the boss failed to perform his gratuitous promise. Therefore, even in those jurisdictions that recognize moral obligation, the promise would not be enforced. Choices (A) and (C) are therefore incorrect. Choice (B) is wrong, because there was no implied-in-fact contract formed between the parties. When the employee saved the boss's life, he had no reasonable expectation of compensation for his services.

12. **(A)** According to UCC Section 2-201 (1), "Except as otherwise noted in this section a contract for the sale of goods for the price of $500 or more is not enforceable by way of action or defense unless there is some writing ..." Since this section also applies to (oral) modifications, choice (A) is clearly the best answer. Choice (B) is wrong, because in contrast to the common law rule, modifications under the UCC do not require new consideration to be enforceable. Choice (C) is wrong, because oral modifications of written contracts are permissible under the UCC unless the contract states that it can only be modified in writing. Choice (D) is incorrect, because the parol evidence rule does not apply to subsequent oral agreements.

13. **(B)** The following contracts come within the Statute of Frauds and must be in writing to be enforceable: 1) a contract in consideration of marriage; 2) a contract which, by its terms, cannot be performed within the span of one year; 3) a contract of an executor or administrator; 4) a contract of guarantee or surety; and 5) a contract for the sale of goods of $500 or more. Based on 4), an oral promise to answer for the debt or default of another is unenforceable under the Statute of Frauds. Choice (D) is therefore incorrect. **Exam Tip:** An oral contract that does not comply with the Statute is "unenforceable" rather than "void." As a consequence, Choice (A) is less preferred. Choice (C) is wrong, because there is no reason why the firm's pre-existing duty should also bind its shareholder. The corporate form protects shareholders from liability on corporate debts.

14. **(B)** The father's oral promise to personally guarantee the son's debt is unenforceable under the Statute of Frauds. As a result, Choice (B) is correct, because the father was never under a surety duty to pay the debt. Choice (A) is incorrect, because the contract did not require the car lot to sue the son before liability falls to the father. Choice (C) is incorrect, because under the "main purpose rule," an oral promise by a promisor to pay the debt of another is enforceable where the party making the promise does so to further his own economic advantage. In other words, the consideration for the promise must be beneficial to the promisor either personally or directly. Since the father did not stand to directly benefit himself in guaranteeing the son's loan, the main purpose rule is inapplicable. Choice (D) is an incorrect statement of the law. As a general rule, parents have no such responsibility.

15. **(B)** The father's oral promise to personally guarantee the company's debt was voidable under the Statute of Frauds. Since the father was therefore relieved of liability when his surety promise became voidable, Choice (B) is the only correct answer, since Choices (A), (C), and (D) all provide for recovery from the father.

16. **(C)** If a contract reads ***"F.O.B. seller's place of business,"*** UCC Section 2-319(1)(a) indicates that the seller must then: "ship the goods in the manner provided in Section 2-504 and bear the expense and risk of putting them into the possession of the carrier." Thus, under 2-509(1)(a), ***the risk in such a case passes to the buyer when the goods are "duly delivered to the carrier."*** Since the buyer bore the risk of loss, choice (B) is wrong. Choice (D) is also wrong, because the buyer would have no right to recover damages, since he bore the risk of loss on the widgets. As for the anti-assignment clause, UCC Section 2-210(2) states: "A right to damages for breach of the whole contract or a right arising out of the assignor's due performance of his entire obligation can be assigned despite agreement otherwise." Therefore, the seller was entitled to assign the right to payment without the buyer's consent. Choice (A) is therefore wrong.

17. **(C)** Under UCC Section 2-509(1)(a), where a contract reads "F.O.B. seller's place of business," the risk of loss shifts to the buyer once the seller delivers the goods to the carrier. Therefore, the buyer bore the risk of loss at the time the flanges were destroyed, so the buyer has no right of recovery from the seller. Choices (A) and (B) are therefore wrong. Choice (D) is incorrect, because when a party is charged with assuming the risk of something happening, the occurrence of that event cannot be the basis of a discharge argument, such as frustration of purpose.

18. **(C)** The agreement whereby the farmer agreed to supply all of the retailer's requirements of strawberries for three years would be an example of a requirements contract. With respect to requirements and output contracts, UCC Section 2-306 provides "a term which measures the quantity by the output of the seller or the requirements of the buyer means such actual output or requirements as may occur in good faith, except that no quantity unreasonably disproportionate to any stated estimate or in the absence of a stated estimate to any normal or otherwise comparable prior output or requirements may be tendered or demanded." Moreover, under this Section, a contract for output or requirements is not too indefinite, since it is held to mean the actual good-faith output or requirements of the particular party. Nor does such a contract lack mutuality of obligation, since the party who will determine quantity is required to operate his plant or conduct his business in good faith and according to commercial standards of fair dealing. Therefore, Choices (A) and (D) are incorrect. Choice (B) is not the best answer. While it is true that in a requirements contract the buyer must use best efforts to have requirements, Choice (C) is a more direct label as to the type of contract involved.

19. **(A)** Under the parol evidence rule, evidence of any prior oral or written agreements or contemporaneous oral agreements which alters, varies, or contradicts the terms of a fully integrated writing is barred from admission to contradict that writing. However, the parol evidence rule does not apply to subsequent agreements. Since the agreement in question was formed after the written contract was executed, the parol evidence rule would be inapplicable. Therefore, Choices (B) and (C) are wrong. Choice (D) is wrong because, under the UCC, a modification does not require new consideration to be valid. Thus the agreement is valid, and Choice (A) is the correct answer.

20. **(D)** In compliance with UCC Section 2-305, the parties, if they so intend, can conclude a contract for sale even though the price is not settled. In such a case, the price is a "reasonable price" at the time of delivery if: (a) nothing is said as to price; or (b) the price is left to be agreed by the parties and they fail to agree; or (c) the price is to be fixed in terms of some agreed market or other standard as set or recorded by a third person or agency and it is not so set or recorded. Thus, when there is a gap as to price, UCC Section,2-305 directs the court to determine a "reasonable price." Choices (B) and (C) are therefore wrong. Choice (A) is incorrect, because the e-mails exchanged between the parties would be sufficient to satisfy the Statute of Frauds.

21. **(A)** The June 23 agreement between the manufacturer and the supplier would constitute a validly enforceable modification of their June 1 contractual agreement. In accordance with UCC Section 2-209 (1), an agreement modifying a contract subject to the UCC needs ***no (e.g., new) consideration*** to be binding. Choice (D) is therefore wrong. Choice (B) is incorrect, because the pre-existing duty rule is a consideration concern, and as stated above, consideration is not required for the modification to be valid. Choice (C) is incorrect, because this is not a reformation. A reformation is where a writing is changed to reflect the true agreement of the parties. This goes beyond a reformation, since the entire agreement is being changed, not just the writing.

22. **(D)** The probable legal effect of the United States government's embargo on the foreign country's imports would be to excuse the duties of performance of the parties because of a supervening illegality. Where performance of a contract has become illegal by change in law after the time of contracting, the promisor's duty is discharged unless he has assumed the risk of it or unless his fault has contributed to the prohibition. Therefore, Choice (D) is the best answer. If the embargo had been ***temporary***, then Choice (C) would be correct. Choice (A) is wrong, because the discharge prevents the smoke shop from collecting damages for non-performance. Choice (B) is wrong, because the purpose behind the contract still exists; performance of the contract is not possible, because of the supervening illegality.

23. **(D)** In accordance with the parol evidence rule, when a contract is expressed in a writing which is intended to be the complete and final expression of the rights and duties of the parties, parol evidence of prior oral or written negotiations or agreements of the parties or of their contemporaneous oral agreements, ***which varies or contradicts the written contract, is not admissible.*** The dean's contemporaneous oral promise to extend the applicant's sick leave to 10 days would clearly vary the terms of the written employment contract, and therefore, the applicant would not be permitted to introduce parol evidence of the dean's oral promise. Choice (A) is wrong, because the detailed nature of the employment contract would be strong evidence that it was intended to be a full integration of their agreement. When the face of the writing indicates it is intended to be a complete integration, parol evidence cannot be used to contradict that interpretation. Choice (B) is wrong, because the oral agreement was not subsequent to the forming of the contract; it took place prior to the applicant signing the employment contract. Choice (C) is incorrect, because there is no indication of any fraud or undue influence.

24. **(B)** As a rule, in the case of an unliquidated or disputed obligation, if a tender is made by the debtor of money or other thing as in full satisfaction of his debt, the acceptance by the creditor of that which is tendered constitutes a complete discharge of the debt. Thus, where the debt is unliquidated, meaning the amount is in dispute, a payment of a less amount than the sum claimed on condition that it be accepted in full discharge of the debt constitutes an accord and satisfaction. Here, a dispute existed because the tutor thought she was entitled to $700, but the law student felt she was entitled to only $500. Choices (A) and (C) are therefore wrong, because a liquidated claim is one that is not in dispute. Choice (D) is incorrect, because the consideration to support the accord and satisfaction is deemed to flow from the dispute.

25. **(C)** This is a very tricky question, in which process of elimination is a major factor in determining the correct answer. Choice (A) is incorrect, because it was not possible to place the bet at the casino, since it was temporarily closed. Therefore, the employee was not in breach for failing to do so. Choice (B) is wrong, because a modification is an agreement between the parties to change a contract. The employee tried to contact the businessman when he discovered the casino was closed, but he was unable to do so. There was thus no agreement reached to change the contract. Choice (D) is wrong, because the essence of the agreement was to place a bet on the baseball team to win the championship. In situations where there is an impediment to a matter that, while important, is incidental to the main obligations of the parties, it is permissible to use a commercially reasonable substitute when such is available. Therefore, the contract was not discharged by the closing of the casino, since a commercially reasonable substitute method of performance (placing the bet at the other gaming establishment) was available. That leaves Choice (C). Here, the employee was obligated to travel to the casino and wager $10,000 for the businessman. After the bet was placed, the employee would then receive $500 for his efforts. This meant that the placing of the bet was a constructive condition precedent to the employee's being paid the $500. This condition was substantially performed when the bet was placed at the Keno Palace. As a result, the employee should be entitled to receive that which was promised him, i.e., $500.

26. **(D)** As a general rule, rights and duties that are in their nature limited to exercise by the promisee alone are not transferrable. No right or duty that is limited in its nature to the personality of the promisee alone is capable of transfer without the assent of the promisor. Moreover, an employer's right to an employee's services, where the employee is to work under the personal direction of the employer, is not assignable without the employer's assent, because the duty is impliedly conditioned to render the service to the promisee alone. In this regard, it is often said that personal service contracts are not assignable; in other words, that neither employer nor employee may assign his rights without the other's assent. Therefore, Choices (A) and (B) are wrong, because the lawyer does not have to recognize the validity of the assignment. Choice (C) is wrong, because this is an existing contractual right, not a transfer of a future right that may or may not arise. A transfer of an existing contractual right (provided the transfer is permissible) that is not to arise until a future date is valid.

27. **(C)** The gambler's best defense would be that the friend's telling his girlfriend about the bet constituted a material breach of their agreement. Under the express terms of their written agreement, the friend was forbidden to tell anyone about the bet. Generally, a breach is material wherever the plaintiff's partial failure of performance defeats the purpose of the contract either wholly or in some vital aspect. However blameless the plaintiff may be in failing to perform his promise, if the result of the breach is to deprive the defendant of an essential part of the performance for which he bargained, he is not required to perform his own undertaking. Here, it was important to the gambler that the bet be kept a secret. The friend's telling his girlfriend would thus constitute a material breach, excusing the gambler of further performance under the contract. Choice (A) is wrong for two reasons: First, the agreement was capable of full performance within one year, since the contract would be fully performed when the second payment was made within 30 days. Second, the agreement was in writing, so it would not matter if it was for longer than one year. The writing would satisfy the Statute of Frauds. Choice (B) is incorrect, because the essence of the agreement was to place a bet that his team would win the college football championship the following year. In situations where there is an impediment to a matter that, while important, is incidental to the main obligations of the parties, it is permissible to use a commercially reasonable substitute when such is available. Therefore, the contract was not discharged by the closing of the casino's sports book, since a commercially reasonable substitute method of performance (placing the bet at the other casino at the same odds) was available. Choice (D) is incorrect for the same reason. The purpose of the contract was to place the bet on his team. The closing of the sports book at the casino did not frustrate that purpose.

28. **(C)** It is important to remember that a suit for ***specific performance will not lie if there is an adequate remedy at law.*** It will only lie where the loss cannot be compensated in damages. In the present case, the developer does have an adequate remedy at law, since his measurable damages would be the additional cost to obtain a similar loan from another source. Without a showing that the legal remedy is inadequate, Choice (C) is the preferred alternative. Choice (A) is wrong, because it does not matter whether the Statute of Frauds is satisfied and there is therefore an enforceable contract; the issue here is the remedy the developer is entitled to receive. Choice (B) is not the best answer. While it is true that the uniqueness of land can make the legal remedy inadequate, land is not directly involved in this transaction. This contract is a loan arrangement and nothing more. Choice (D) is incorrect. Detrimental reliance by the developer speaks to whether the contract should be enforced. That is not in issue here, as there clearly is an enforceable contract. The issue is the appropriate remedy.

29. **(A)** Under the modern view, where performance of a contract has become illegal by change of law after the time of contracting, impossibility excuses the promisor's duty unless he has assumed the risk of it or unless his fault has contributed to the prohibition. Since the distributor neither assumed the risk nor contributed to the prohibition, his obligation to provide the cymbidium to the woman would be excused by supervening illegality. Therefore, Choices (B) and (C) are wrong. In such a situation, if the promisee has already rendered performance (as in the present case, when the woman paid the initial $1,000), she may rescind and recover it back, or its value. Consequently, Choice (D) is incorrect.

30. **(A)** The seller's promise to lend the developer $50,000 is a condition precedent in form because this obligation was expressed in the contract ***before*** any reference was made to the developer's obligation to enter into a construction contract on the adjoining lot. However, it should be noted that the seller's promise was subsequent in substance because he would not be obligated to lend the developer the money ***until*** after the latter entered into the construction contract. Choice (B) states this result backwards. Choice (C) is wrong, because true conditions subsequent discharge a duty to perform after it has arisen. That is not the case here, since the seller would not be obligated to perform until after the developer enters into a building contract. That is why it is only subsequent in substance. Choice (D) is incorrect, because the seller's promise is a constructive condition of some sort to the other side's performance.

31. **(A)** In accordance with Section 321 (2) of the Restatement of Contracts 2d, a purported assignment of a right expected to arise under a contract ***not in existence*** operates only as a promise to assign the right when it arises and as a power to enforce it. At the time the author made the purported assignment to the friend, there was no contract in place to turn the screenplay into a movie or a stage play, meaning that the author had no contractual right that he could transfer to the friend. Therefore, Choice (A) is best. Choice (B) is wrong, because immediate delivery is not necessary to make a gift promise enforceable. Choice (C) is wrong, because an intended beneficiary is someone who is designated to receive a benefit under a contract. Since the author had no contract to turn the screenplay into a movie or a stage play, the friend cannot be a beneficiary. Choice (D) is incorrect, because a future right is assignable only when it is an existing contractual right. For example, if the author had signed a contract to have his screenplay produced as a movie, with a promise that he would be paid royalties from that movie, the author would have had an existing future right that could have been assigned.

32. **(A)** An assignment of future rights under a contract not in existence is unenforceable. Since the athlete had not entered into a valid contract with the baseball team at the time, or prior to the time, of his assignment to the friend, there was nothing to assign. Choice (B) is wrong, because some assignments of future rights are enforceable. For example, an assignment of a right to payment expected to arise out of an existing employment or other continuing business relationship is effective in the same way as an assignment of an existing present right. Choice (C) is

wrong, because detrimental reliance cannot change the fact that there is no existing contractual right that can be assigned. In other words, there was nothing on which the friend could have detrimentally relied. Choice (D) is not the best answer. While it is true that gratuitous assignments are revocable, had this been a valid assignment it would not have been gratuitous, since the friend was paying for the purported assignment by driving the athlete to the training facilities and paying the travel expenses.

33. **(C)** An assignment of future rights under a contract not in existence is unenforceable. Since the inventor had not entered into a valid contract for the use of her automobile engine prototype prior to the time of her assignment to her brother, the assignment was unenforceable. Therefore, the creditors acquired a superior possessory interest to the proceeds from the licensing of the automobile engine. Choices (A) and (B) are incorrect, because the brother never acquired enforceable rights from the inventor that would allow him any recovery. Choice (D) is wrong; the brother was not a donee beneficiary. An intended donee beneficiary is someone who is designated to receive a benefit under a contract. Since the inventor had no contract to license the use of his automobile engine at the time of the wedding, the brother cannot be a beneficiary.

34. **(C)** In an aleatory contract, it is uniformly held that the duties of performance are independent and that each party may sue the other for breach even though he himself is in default on his own promise. So even though the homeowner is in default on her promise to pay the premium at the time her house burned, she can, nevertheless, recover for the loss on the uncancelled policy. Note that only when the insurer has expressly conditioned its performance on prompt payment of the premium is its duty a dependent one. Choice (B) is not the best answer. While Choice (B) is a correct statement, Choice (C) better, and more specifically states why the homeowner should prevail. The same is true with Choice (D). While it is technically true, it does not address the key issue as specifically as Choice (C). Choice (A) is wrong, because there is no question that a bargained-for exchange existed. The issue is whether the homeowner's failure to make the two payments discharges the duty of the insurance company. For the reasons stated above, it does not.

35. **(B)** The contract provisions with respect to (a) the covenant not to compete and (b) the penalty and forfeiture clause would be severed from the contract. The restrictive covenant barring the employee from engaging in "any aspect of the hardware business for a period of two years within a 50-mile radius" would be construed as an "unreasonable restraint of trade." The $1,500 payment clause would be a penalty because it is not a reasonable forecast of what the damages should be in the event of a breach by the employee. Therefore, Choices (A) and (C) are incorrect. Choice (D) is wrong, because the provisions regarding salary and termination notice would not be objectionable as against public policy. It is important to note that the termination provision requiring the 60-day notice is valid. However, the stipulation that (upon termination of the employment contract) the employee would be prohibited from engaging "in any aspect of the hardware business for a period of two years, within a 50-mile radius" would be invalidated as a wrongful restraint of trade.

36. **(C)** Choice (C) is correct, because a penalty or forfeiture clause is a sum in excess of the value of the contract and fixed to be paid on breach of it. Students should note that if the parties fix upon a certain sum to be paid on breach of the contract, it may be recovered if it was really fixed upon as liquidated damages for non-performance. However, if it was intended in the nature of a penalty in excess of any loss likely to be sustained, the recovery will be limited to the loss actually sustained. Choice (A) is therefore wrong, because this was not an enforceable liquidated damage clause. Choice (B) is incorrect, because an unliquidated damage claim is one that is in dispute. Here, there is no dispute between the parties. Choice (D) is incorrect, since an aleatory or insurance contract is one in which performance is conditioned upon an event (e.g., house burning down) that may never happen.

37. **(D)** According to Restatement of Contracts 2d, Section 321, the assignment of a future right to payment expected to arise out of an existing employment or other continuing business relation is effective in the same way as an assignment of an existing right. Here, the screenwriter's assignment of a portion of the proceeds she anticipated earning on the distribution of the movie (should it be made) would be effective as a gratuitous assignment, even though the movie did not exist at the time of the assignment. Choice (A) is wrong, because an equitable lien is a court-imposed remedy to prevent unjust enrichment. That would not apply to this situation. Choice (B) is not the best answer. While it is true that there is a condition precedent to the friend's receiving any money (that the movie is made), Choice (D) is a more specific answer, and a more specific answer is always a more preferred answer. Choice (C) is incorrect, because the assignment was gratuitous, and as a general rule, gratuitous assignments are revocable.

38. **(A)** In this situation, the exercise facility will not be obligated to perform its duties under the contract (namely, admit the woman to any further exercise classes) ***until*** she makes the installment payment. Thus, the woman's duty to pay the $500 installment is viewed as a condition precedent to the exercise facility's being obligated to perform its duties under the contract. In other words, the exercise facility may bar the woman from attending any further classes until such time as she makes the installment payment. Choices (B) and (C) are therefore wrong. Choice (D) is incorrect, because an express condition is one that is stated in the contract as making a performance of a promise expressly conditional upon the occurrence of that condition. That was not the case here, because the contract did not specifically state that the exercise facility's performance was conditional upon the woman's making her installment payment.

39. **(D)** Generally, the promisee has the following remedies available after the promisor has repudiated the contract in advance of the time for its performance: (1) sue at once for breach; (2) treat the repudiation as an offer of mutual rescission and accept it in discharge of the contract; (3) treat the repudiation as excusing his own further duty of performance; or (4) ignore the repudiation and urge the promisor to perform. Choice (D) is correct, because it is the only choice that does not accurately reflect one of the immediate legal effects of the man's letter. The swimming club is not required to wait until the date of the next payment, because the man's letter made it clear that he will not pay any more of the money owed under the contract. The man's anticipatory repudiation means that the swimming club does have the right to sue immediately. Since Choice (B) is an accurate legal effect of the man's letter, it is an incorrect choice. Choice (A) is also an accurate legal effect (and therefore an incorrect choice), because the swimming club may now treat the contract as discharged, thereby giving the swimming club the right to prevent the man from making any further use of the pool (if he so chose to return). Students should also be aware that the promisor may retract his repudiation up to the time the promisee has accepted the repudiation or detrimentally relied upon it. Since the man may retract his repudiation so long as the swimming club has not accepted his repudiation (by bringing legal action as in Choice (C), for example), Choice (C) is another accurate legal effect of his letter, making this choice incorrect.

40. **(B)** Choice (B) is correct, because ***frustration of purpose*** will excuse the promisor's duty where (1) the value of the performance bargained for by the promisor is destroyed by the supervening event, and (2) the frustrating event was not foreseeable at the time the parties contracted The woman's accident clearly frustrates the purpose behind the contract, since the woman can no longer take advantage of the exercise classes. Choice (A) is wrong, because subjective impossibility will not excuse the promisor's duty of performance under a contract. The mere personal inability of a promisor to perform is no excuse. This is subjective impossibility. At common law, ***only objective impossibility (i.e., where because of the supervening event the performance cannot be rendered by anyone) will excuse the (promisor's) duty of performance.*** Choice (C) is wrong, because the woman is not seeking a refund of fees paid. Rather, frustration discharges her obligation to make the next payment. Choice (D) is not the best answer. While it is true that her promise to pay is a condition precedent to the gymnasium's allowing her to attend classes, the promise (and the corresponding condition) are discharged by the frustration of purpose.

41. **(D)** Students should be aware that voluntary waiver (of condition) by the promisor is only effective to eliminate a condition that is not a material part of the agreed exchange, one that is only an incident to the promisee's performance. ***A condition, however, that is all or a substantial part of the agreed exchange can only be waived by a substituted contract on sufficient consideration.*** To be sure, the (condition) of the payment of the third monthly installment was a substantial or material part of the agreement between the facility and the man. Consequently, that condition could not be waived or extinguished unless supported by consideration or material change of position by the promisee in reliance, thus amounting to an estoppel. Choice (A) is therefore incorrect. Choice (B) is wrong, because no such implied contract would be created. Choice (C) is wrong, because here, there is a present breach (not an anticipatory breach). An anticipatory repudiation occurs when one party to an executory bilateral contract repudiates the contract ***in advance of the time set for performance by announcing that he will not perform it.*** In the present case, the man did not inform the facility prior to the first day of the third month of his intention to repudiate the contract.

42. **(B)** UCC 2-612(1) defines an installment contract as "one which requires or authorizes the delivery of goods in separate lots to be separately accepted, even though the contract contains a clause that each delivery is a separate contract or its equivalent." Thus, the original agreement would be interpreted as a single installment contract. Choices (A) and (C) are therefore incorrect. Choice (D) is wrong, because a requirements contract is one where the quantity is measured by the requirements of the buyer, and an output contract is one where the quantity is measured by the output of the seller. Since this contract is for a fixed amount (10,000 widgets), it would not be a requirements or an output contract.

43. **(B)** When does the breach of part of an installment contract constitute a breach of the whole? According to UCC 2-612(3), "whenever non-conformity or default with respect to one installment substantially impairs the value of the entire contract there is a breach of the whole." In the official comments, the UCC states that "Cure of non-conformity of an installment...can usually be afforded by an allowance against the price..." Therefore, by offering to make a price adjustment, the non-conformity in the August shipment would not substantially impair the entire contract, so the fence company would have no right to cancel the contract and would be in breach for doing so. Choice (D) is therefore wrong. Choice (A) is incorrect, because the issue is not the timing of the deliveries; it is whether the non-conformity in the August shipment substantially impairs the entire contract. Choice (C) is wrong, because the price adjustment would be a proper attempt to cure the improper delivery; it was not necessary that the poles be replaced.

44. **(C)** The supermarket would not be entitled to reject the operator's offer to cure, since the nonconformity in loaves would not constitute a material breach. When dealing with an installment contract, a specific default or nonconformity with respect to one installment does not constitute a breach of the entire contract unless the non-conformity substantially impairs the value of the entire contract. The problem with the 20 loaves would not substantially impair the entire contract, so Choice (A) is wrong. The UCC also holds that if the seller gives adequate assurances that it will cure any non-conformity, such a cure attempt must be accepted. Therefore, the supermarket would have to accept the operator's promise to cure the problem with the loaves. Choice (B) is therefore wrong, because the supermarket would have no right to reject the fifth shipment. Choice (D) is wrong, because the supermarket would have no right to damages, since the bakery is not in breach, because of the assurance to cure the non-conformity.

45. **(A)** The forest fire would temporarily suspend the mill's duty to deliver the August shipment. Note that temporary impossibility suspends contractual duties; it does not discharge them. When performance once more becomes possible, the duty "springs back" into existence. Therefore, the mill's contractual obligations (with regard to the September, October, November and December shipments) would not be excused by the temporary impossibility (i.e., forest fire). Choices (C) and (D) would therefore be wrong. Choice (B) is not the best answer. The UCC does not state that a party is to be charged with foreseeing a particular contingency; it states that a party cannot use such a contingency as discharging its duty. Therefore, Choice (A) is the more preferred answer.

46. **(D)** In accordance with the Restatement of Contracts 2d, Section 332, unless a contrary intention is manifested, a gratuitous assignment is irrevocable if the assignment is in a writing either signed or under seal that is delivered by the assignor. Choice (D) is therefore an accurate statement. Choice (A) is not an accurate statement, because contractual prohibitions on assignments are generally viewed as just a promise not to assign, meaning any attempted assignment will be effective, but the assignor can be sued for breach for breaking the promise not to assign. Therefore, the assignment to the nephew would be effective. Choice (B) is not an accurate statement, because the payment of money does not involve a personal service and can therefore be assigned. Generally, duties under a personal service contract cannot be delegated. Choice (C) is not an accurate statement. A novation is a three-party agreement that grows out of a delegation. Since there was no delegation of duties, novation is not in issue.

47. **(A)** Under the general rule, impossibility of performance of a condition that is not a material part of the exchange will excuse the condition where otherwise forfeiture would result. Where the promisee (i.e., the painter) has already given the promisor (i.e., the owner) the substantial performance that was bargained for, but because of supervening impossibility has not performed some incidental thing that was made an express condition of the promise, the condition may be excused and the liability of the promisor becomes absolute. Choices (B), (C), and (D) would all therefore be accurate statements. Choice (A) is thus the least accurate and the correct answer.

48. **(B)** On March 25, ***by agreeing to landscape the backyard,*** the man's return promise created an enforceable bilateral contract. ***A bilateral contract is a contract in which mutual promises are given*** as the agreed exchange for each other. On the contrary, a unilateral contract is a contract in which a promise is given in exchange for an actual performance by the other party. Here the parties were exchanging promises (the landscaper promising to landscape the backyard by May 1 and the homeowner promising to pay $10,000), so Choice (A) is wrong. Choice (C) is incorrect, because there is no reason why the contract would have to be in writing. It would not fall within any of the sections of the Statute of Frauds. Choice (D) is incorrect, because the landscaper is obligating himself to landscape the back yard by May 1, so his promise was not illusory.

49. **(A)** The woman and the carpenter had an enforceable bilateral contract whereby the he was obligated to build and deliver the storm windows. The loss of the inventory will not excuse his duty to perform (under the doctrine of subjective impossibility), because the promisor, by entering into the contract, has assumed the risk of his ability to perform. In short, to constitute an excuse through impossibility of performance, the thing promised must be impossible of performance by anyone; it must be physically and objectively impossible. Choice (D) is therefore incorrect. Choice (B) is not a relevant concern. The woman would have assumed the risk of damage to her beach houses by not contracting earlier for the storm windows. Choice (C) is incorrect for the reason stated above; the carpenter would be charged with assuming the risk of the loss of the inventory.

50. **(C)** As per the terms of their agreement, the man was only obligated to pay the contractor $2,500 per deck upon completion. As a result, the contractor will recover $2,500 for each of the eight decks he constructed on the city properties ($20,000). However, the contractor will not be entitled to recover for the ***partial*** work he performed on the one beach house located in the town, since it is generally held that a builder in promising the result has accepted the attendant risks inherently involved. Choices (A), (B), and (D) are all therefore incorrect.

Explanation: Question 51

The correct answer is: **(D)** The homeowner, because the agreement is barred by the statute of frauds.

This question presents an interplay between the statute of limitations and the statute of frauds. Normally, a promise to pay a debt is unenforceable because it lacks consideration. However, a debt that has been discharged due to either bankruptcy or the statute of limitations is enforceable, at least to the extent of the new promise. To be enforceable, the promise to pay the antecedent debt needs to be in writing. Choice (C) has the right conclusion, but for the wrong reason. It is not the statute of limitations that makes the homeowner's promise unenforceable; rather it is the lack of a writing that makes this promise unenforceable, thus choice (D) is correct.

(A) Incorrect. The painter for $5,000, because that is the original amount owed.

(B) Incorrect. The painter for $6000, because the extra $1,000 was reasonable under the circumstances.

(C) Incorrect. The homeowner, because the debt was barred by the statute of limitations.

Explanation: Question 52

The correct answer is: **(B)** $35,000, because there was justifiable reliance.

In the area of contract formation, students are frequently tested on the distinction between bargained-for consideration (choice A) and conditional gift promises made binding by reliance (choice B). Promises are legally enforceable where the promisee has relied on the promise to his injury, even though the reliance was not bargained for. In other words, substantial and detrimental action induced by a gratuitous promise affords a reason for enforcement of the promise without a bargained-for consideration. In this regard, Simpson states, "A promisor who invites his nephew to take a trip to Europe or to undertake a college education by promising reimbursement for expenses incurred should not, after the action in reliance is completed, be permitted to escape fulfillment of his promise on the ground that it was one to make a gift." Contracts, pg. 113. Choice (B) is therefore correct because the nephew attended Private University rather than State University in reliance on his uncle's promise to pay his first year tuition. Clearly, there is justification for enforcement of the promise without bargained-for consideration due to the fact that the nephew would be required to pay $20,000 more in tuition by attending Private University instead of State University the first year. Conversely, it is necessary to distinguish this situation with the well-known case of an uncle who promised to pay his nephew $5,000 if he refrained from "drinking, using tobacco," etc., until he was 21. The nephew fulfilled his uncle's requirements and the court held there was sufficient consideration to support a contract. Although no economic benefit had been received by the uncle, nonetheless there was evidence that he was bargaining for his nephew to conduct himself in accordance with his wishes. In conclusion, this is an important distinction that is frequently tested on the Multistate; ultimately, the question will depend on interpreting whether the promisor intended to make a gift promise or enter into a bargained-for exchange with the promisee.

(A) Incorrect. $35,000, because there was a bargained-for exchange.

(C) Incorrect. $20,000, because the nephew would have been obligated to pay the $15,000 State University tuition notwithstanding the uncle's promise.

(D) Incorrect. Nothing, because the uncle's promise was gratuitous.

Explanation: Question 53

The correct answer is: **(B)** The neighbor can continue swimming the two laps and recover damages for breach of contract.

In this question we have a unilateral contract. While the general rule is that an offeror may revoke an offer prior to acceptance, we have an exception under unilateral contracts. The exception is that once the offeree starts to perform, the offer becomes irrevocable. Therefore, once the neighbor started to perform, the wealthy man's offer became irrevocable. By swimming both laps in the pink swimsuit, the neighbor will have performed the requested act, and thus a contract will be formed. Consequently, the wealthy man is liable for breach of contract if he fails to pay the neighbor $500 as agreed.

(A) Incorrect. The neighbor can stop swimming immediately and still recover the $500.

(C) Incorrect. Regardless of what the neighbor does, the wealthy man is liable to pay him only for the cost of the swimsuit, which the neighbor purchased in reliance on the wealthy man's offer.

(D) Incorrect. Regardless of what the neighbor does, the wealthy man is not liable to pay the neighbor anything because the revocation effectively discharged the wealthy man's obligations under the contract.

Explanation: Question 54

The correct answer is: **(B)** Yes, because it was a promise to repay a debt that, but for the statute of limitations, would still be owing.

This answer is correct because it applies an exception to the general rule that past consideration will not support a contract. A written promise to pay a debt that is barred by the statute of limitations is one of two particular types of promises that are enforceable even if there is no new consideration for them. In this case, the dancer's promise to pay the debt despite the expiration of the statute of limitations is therefore binding.

(A) Incorrect. Yes, because the past consideration is sufficient to support a present promise.

This answer is incorrect because it misstates the general rule. Past consideration generally does not support a contract. This particular promise falls into an exception to that rule because the current promise is to pay a debt that, but for the statute of limitations, would be owing.

(C) Incorrect. No, because the recent promise to repay the money was a gratuitous promise.

This answer is incorrect. It correctly states a general rule, that gratuitous promises are not enforceable, but that rule is not applicable here. Gratuitous promises arise when the promisee has not promised or given anything to the promisor in exchange for the promise. In this case, the dancer's recent promise to repay the money is not gratuitous but instead is supported by the much earlier act of the friend loaning the money in the first place.

(D) Incorrect. No, because the recent promise to repay the money was supported only by past consideration.

This answer is incorrect because it misses the exception to the general rule. Past consideration generally does not suffice to create an enforceable contract. However, when the written promise is to repay a debt that otherwise is not owing because of the statute of limitations, it is binding. Therefore, the dancer's promise to pay the debt is binding.

Explanation: Question 55

The correct answer is: **(C)** $30,000.

This question involves a contract for the sale of goods priced at $500 or more, so it is required under section 2-201 of the UCC to be evidenced in writing. However, the UCC Statute of Frauds has an exception for part performance. Under this exception, no writing is required to enforce a contract for the sale of goods to the extent that the goods have been received and accepted. This exception applies here: Because the customer received and accepted the first two machines from the engineering firm, it will be compelled to pay the engineering firm $30,000 for the two machines delivered and accepted.

(A) Incorrect. Damages for a total breach of contract for the sale of two machines, because the goods made for the customer were specialty goods.

The Statute of Frauds applies to this contract for the sale of goods priced at $500 or more, so it is required under section 2-201 of the UCC to be evidenced in writing unless an exception applies. One such exception is contracts for the sale of specialty goods: If the goods are to be specially manufactured for the buyer and are not suitable for sale to others in the normal course of the seller's business, no writing is required. Here, while the engineering firm made the machines as ordered and did not keep completed machines on hand, the machines were built to normal industry specifications and were not uniquely suited to the customer. As such, the machines do not fall within the definition of specialty goods. Therefore, the specialty goods exception does not apply and this answer is incorrect.

(B) Incorrect. Damages for a total breach of contract for the sale of three machines, because the customer accepted the engineering firm's partial performance.

This question involves a contract for the sale of goods priced at $500 or more, so it is required under UCC section 2-201 to be evidenced in writing unless an exception applies. One such exception is the part performance exception. Under this exception, no writing is required to enforce a contract for the sale of goods to the extent that the goods have been received and accepted. However, while this answer is correct in noting that the engineering firm is entitled to recover damages from the customer, it is incorrect in its assessment of the total amount of damages to which the engineering firm is entitled. Partial performance of a sale-of-goods contract affects only that portion of the contract performed, not the whole contract as this answer states. As such, the parties' oral contract will be enforced for the two machines the customer received and accepted, but the customer will not be liable for the undelivered third machine. Note that this differs from the real property to the extent of performance rule: If either party to an oral agreement conveying an interest in land has partly performed, this is considered clear evidence of a contract and no writing is required and the entire contract is removed from the purview of the Statute of Frauds. Here, however, the parties' contract involved goods, not real property. Therefore, the parties' partial performance makes enforceable only that portion of the contract performed.

(D) Incorrect. Nothing.

The UCC Statute of Frauds requires that certain types of contracts must be written, or else they are voidable by either party prior to full performance. However, no writing is required to enforce a contract for the sale of goods to the extent that the goods have been received and accepted. As such, the parties' oral contract will be enforced with regard to the two machines the customer received and accepted, and this answer is incorrect.

Explanation: Question 56

The correct answer is: **(B)** $4,000.

The motorist's original agreement with the car dealership is voidable because the motorist was a minor at that point. Nevertheless, a minor can affirm his contract after reaching the age of majority for the full amount or for a lesser sum, as he did here for the $4,000. Only the amount affirmed after the age of majority is enforceable.

(A) Incorrect. $4,500.

This answer is incorrect because the motorist did not affirm for the full price. The motorist affirmed the $4,000 price.

(C) Incorrect. $3,500.

This answer choice is a distractor and this incorrect, because it refers to the amount of necessities that the motorist had taken as a minor, but refused to pay for. While shelter, clothing, or food would qualify as necessities, a car does not. Furthermore, that would be an equitable remedy, and here the car dealership and the motorist have a formed contract for $4,000, as affirmed by the motorist.

(D) Incorrect. Nothing.

This answer is incorrect because the motorist did affirm the contract after reaching the age of 18.

Explanation: Question 57

The correct answer is: **(B)** Yes, because the parties formed an option contract when the hairdresser offered the customer the right to be her first client, and the customer promised to hear and evaluate the hairdresser's ideas and paid the $100 consultation fee.

An option contract may be established if the offeree gives consideration in exchange for the offeror's offer. The consideration given by the offeree may be minimal, and it may be given in the form of services. Here, the customer's promise to meet with the hairdresser and hear her ideas, as well as the $100 consultation fee, constitutes valid consideration for the hairdresser's offer. As such, this is the best answer.

(A) Incorrect. Yes, but only if she relied on the offer to her detriment.

Under certain circumstances, detrimental reliance by the offeree may cause an offer to become irrevocable, at least temporarily. However, because this is not the only manner in which an offer may become irrevocable, this answer is incorrect.

(C) Incorrect. No, because the customer's right to refuse the hairdresser's services if she was dissatisfied with the hairdresser's ideas made her promise illusory.

The customer's right to refuse the hairdresser's services if she was dissatisfied with her ideas did not render her promise illusory. The customer must exercise her right to refuse with good faith. In addition, the promise to hear and evaluate the ideas in exchange for the hairdresser's offer, combined with the $100 consultation fee, provided the necessary consideration to establish a contract.

(D) Incorrect. No, because the hairdresser merely terminated a revocable offer.

Because the hairdresser granted her customer an option to enter into the interior-decorating contract, and the customer provided consideration for this option, the hairdresser's offer was not revocable. An option that contains a promise by the offeror that it will be held open for a stated period will be irrevocable for the period if supported by consideration. Here, the hairdresser's offer remained open until the date of the meeting and was supported by the customer's return promise to hear and evaluate the ideas and payment of the consultation fee. Thus, this answer is incorrect.

Explanation: Question 58

The correct answer is: **(C)** No, because both parties to the contract could have performed as contracted.

Impossibility, impracticability, and frustration of purpose are the three defenses that may be raised on facts such as these. Impossibility will not apply because it was not objectively impossible for the bride and groom to get married during the planned underwater dive. The storm stayed away. Impracticability does not apply either because performance had not been made prohibitively expensive or extremely burdensome. The bride's best defense is frustration of purpose. After the threat of the storm caused them to elope, the purpose for the scheduled dive no longer existed. Discharge of contractual obligation for frustration of purpose requires three things: 1) that the principle purpose for entering the contract is frustrated; 2) that the frustration is substantial; and 3) that non-occurrence of the event precipitating the frustration must have been a basic assumption of the contract. Although a close case, in this situation, it is unlikely that the bride will succeed in getting a refund because she scheduled her dive for the first weekend in hurricane season. It could not be reasonably assumed that a tropical storm would not occur during hurricane season. Furthermore, the storm did not strike the coastline, and the wedding could have been performed as scheduled had the couple waited. It was their own haste, rather than the storm or the forecast that frustrated their purpose for the contract.

(A) Incorrect. Yes, because of unilateral mistake regarding the potential for a tropical storm.

Unilateral mistake does not apply to the storm. For unilateral mistake to apply, there must be a faulty assumption about present material facts. In this case, the contingency came after the formation of the contract. Furthermore, even if the mistake on the part of the bride was not knowing when hurricane season began, she is not excused from her performance for unilateral mistake because there was no clerical error and it does not appear on these facts that the dive shop knew of her mistake. As such, this answer choice is incorrect.

(B) Incorrect. Yes, because the forecast storm caused the couple to elope, thereby frustrating the purpose of the contract with the dive shop.

In fact, the forecast storm did not force the couple to elope. They could have waited until their scheduled weekend, in any event, before deciding to get married by a justice of the peace. Had they waited, they could have proceeded with their scheduled underwater ceremony. With that in mind, it is not the storm that caused the frustration of purpose with regard to the dive shop contract, it was their haste. Discharge of contractual obligation for frustration of purpose requires three things: 1) that the principle purpose for entering the contract is frustrated; 2) that the frustration is substantial; and 3) that non-occurrence of the event precipitating the frustration must have been a basic assumption of the contract. Here, as the wedding dive was scheduled during hurricane season, it was not reasonable to assume the non-occurrence of the event, the storm. For these reasons, this answer choice is incorrect.

(D) Incorrect. No, because performance by the dive shop was not rendered impossible.

The performance by the dive shop was not rendered impossible, but that is not the best reason that the bride will not prevail. Impracticability and frustration of purpose, in addition to impossibility, are all defenses for non-performance of a contractual obligation. In this case, frustration of purpose comes the closest to providing a defense to the bride. Discharge of contractual obligation for frustration of purpose requires three things: 1) that the principle purpose for entering the contract is frustrated; 2) that the frustration is substantial; and 3) that non-occurrence of the event precipitating the frustration must have been a basic assumption of the contract. Here, had the couple waited, both parties could have performed under the contract. Furthermore, it was not reasonable to assume the non-occurrence of a tropical storm during hurricane season. Therefore, the bride will not prevail, but not simply because the dive shop was able to perform their obligation under the contract.

Explanation: Question 59

The correct answer is: **(B)** Yes, because of mutual mistake.

When both parties to a contract operate under a shared faulty assumption regarding present facts, the contract is voidable by the disadvantaged party so long as the disadvantaged party did not bear the risk of mistake under the contract. In this case, both parties believed at the time of contract formation that the ring was silver and glass. Nothing was said or written into the sale document that would place the risk of mistake on the woman selling the ring. Therefore, the woman should be able to get the ring back and return the $50.

(A) Incorrect. Yes, because she made a unilateral mistake that the antique's dealer had reason to suspect.

This was not a unilateral mistake case. In this situation, both parties operated under a faulty assumption about present facts as they formed the contract of sale. Because the risk of mistake was not placed on the woman and both parties shared the mistake, the contract is voidable and the woman should get the ring back and return the $50.

(C) Incorrect. No, because the woman assumed the risk that the ring was worth more.

This answer is false. Nothing was said or written into the sale document placing the risk of mutual mistake on the woman. Both parties believed at the time of the sale that the ring was silver and glass. Therefore there was mutual mistake and as the woman did not bear the risk, the contract is voidable by her.

(D) Incorrect. No, because the neighbor was not aware of the woman's mistake.

The statement in this answer choice would be important if this were a unilateral mistake situation. But here, both parties operated under a faulty assumption about the ring and neither bore the risk of mistake. Therefore the disadvantaged party, the woman, may void the contract and get her ring back in exchange for the return of the $50.

Explanation: Question 60

The correct answer is: **(B)** Yes, because the feed company should have been given a chance to cure the non-conforming delivery before the installment was rejected.

In this fact pattern, the short delivery did not substantially impair the value of the installment. There was enough feed to cover the rancher's needs for much of the month. In this case, the rancher should have given the feed company a reasonable amount of time to cure the non-conformity. If the feed company would be unable to cure, then the rancher could cancel the installment.

(A) Incorrect. Yes, because in installment contracts, the buyer always must let the vendor cure a non-conforming installment before rejecting it.

This answer is incorrect because it is too restrictive. The buyer must let the vendor cure its non-conforming installment within a reasonable time when the non-conformity does not substantially impair the value of the installment. Where there is substantial impairment of the installment, the buyer may cancel the installment immediately.

(C) Incorrect. No, because the non-conformity substantially impaired the value of the installment.

This answer is incorrect factually. The delivery of feed would have satisfied the rancher's needs for most of the month. This does not constitute a substantial non-conformity. Therefore, the rancher should have permitted the feed company a reasonable time in which to cure the non-conformity (deliver more feed) before cancelling the installment.

(D) Incorrect. No, because the buyer does not have to permit the vendor to cure the non-conforming installment.

If the non-conformity of the feed company's delivery had been substantial enough to impair the value of the entire installment, then the rancher would not have had to allow the feed company to cure the non-conformity prior to cancelling the installment. Here, the non-conformity did not substantially impair the installment and so the feed company should have been afforded a chance to deliver more feed in a reasonable time before the rancher cancelled the entire installment.

Explanation: Question 61

The correct answer is: **(C)** In favor of the patron because impossibility excused her performance under the contract.

The doctrine of impossibility excuses the performance of both parties under the contract if performance has been rendered impossible by a contingency not in the control of either of the parties that arose or was discovered after the formation of the contract. The impossibility must be objective. In other words, it must be literally impossible for the contract to be carried out. Such is the case here. The contract was not for a portrait of the woman's dog so much as it was a contract for a portrait of the woman's dog to be painted by a specific, identified artist. The death of the artist rendered performance under the contract impossible, and both parties were at that point excused from performance. The fact that commissions are non-refundable does not allocate the risk of impossibility. Had the original artist created a portrait of the dog that the woman didn't like, then the non-refundable commission clause would have come into play. Furthermore, the art patron's decision to secure a different artist was outside of the contract, and the patron is not obligated to pay for the substitute piece.

(A) Incorrect. In favor of the art dealer because he produced an acceptable work of art to the patron under the contract.

The art dealer's obligation under the contract was not to secure an acceptable portrait of the patron's dog. The art dealer was contractually bound to secure a portrait of the patron's dog from a specific artist. Once the art dealer discovered that the artist had died, performance under the contract became objectively impossible and performance by both parties was excused. The fact that the art dealer found a substitute artist was entirely at his own risk, and the patron will not be forced to accept the substitute artwork.

(B) Incorrect. In favor of the art dealer because the risk had been allocated in the contract with the clause regarding non-refundable commissions.

The clause regarding non-refundable commissions would have protected the art dealer if he had been able to get the artwork done by the original artist and then the patron refused to accept the piece. But the non-refundable commission clause does not allocate the risk of impossibility in this case. Perhaps if the contract had included a substitute artist clause, then the risk would have been allocated in the contract. But such is not the case and the impossibility renders the performances by both parties excused. The dealer's decision to find a substitute artist was at his own risk, and the patron will not have to pay for the substitute piece of art.

(D) Incorrect. In favor of the patron because of the art dealer's fraud.

Fraud is not the reason that the patron will not have to pay for or accept the artwork by the substitute artist. The art dealer did not try to pass the work off as that of the original artist. The reason that the patron will succeed in this case is that performance under the contract, as written, became objectively impossible when the artist in the contract died. This excused performance by both parties. The substitute piece of art was commissioned by the art dealer at his own risk in this case.

Explanation: Question 62

The correct answer is: **(C)** Yes, because performance is impracticable.

When the assumptions underlying a contract are faulty, the doctrines of mistake, impossibility, impracticability, and frustration of purposes may be available to excuse a party from performing under the contract. The doctrine of impracticability allows a promisor to be excused from performing on a contract where an unforeseen contingency has made performing prohibitively expensive or otherwise extremely burdensome. In order to show that performing a contract would be impracticable, it must be demonstrated that (1) the impracticability of the performance was caused by some unforeseen contingency; (2) that the risk was not assumed or allocated by the parties; and (3) that the increase in the cost of performance would far exceed what either party anticipated. War or embargo are common examples of contingencies that trigger impracticability. Here, the duty to perform is excused due to impracticability, because (1) there are no facts indicating that declaration of war was foreseen; (2) there are no facts indicating that the risk of war was assumed by or allocated to either party; and (3) the increase in the cost of performance has likely increased substantially.

(A) Incorrect. No, because the oil company can only be excused from performing under common law.

This answer is incorrect because it reaches the wrong conclusion by misunderstanding the rule. The UCC governs the sales of goods and trumps the common law rules. Common law rules apply to contracts for services, real property, or assignment of legal claims. Under this fact pattern, there was a contract for movable goods, gasoline. These goods would be governed by the UCC and the common law would not apply.

(B) Incorrect. No, because increased cost alone does not excuse performance.

While it is true that mere cost increase alone would not excuse performance under the UCC, the doctrine of impracticability allows a promisor to be excused from performance when unforeseen difficulties make performance prohibitively expensive or burdensome. If a shortage caused a marked increase in cost or prevents a seller from securing the supplies necessary for performance, then the impracticability doctrine would be triggered and the promisor would be excused from performing on the contract.

(D) Incorrect. Yes, because performance is impossible.

The doctrine of impossibility is a doctrine which can excuse performance on a contract but it is not the appropriate doctrine for this fact pattern. Impossibility excuses both parties from their obligations under a contract if performance has been rendered impossible by a contingency occurring after the contract was formed. This doctrine requires that performance be objectively impossible and that the occurrence of the contingency was not known to the parties at the time of the contract. Here, the oil company is objectively able to perform on the contract, although the performance will be unduly burdensome. Therefore, the doctrine of impossibility does not apply.

Explanation: Question 63

The correct answer is: **(A)** Yes, because the coach's talents as a basketball coach are extraordinary.

This answer is correct because a negative injunction is available to prevent the coach from competing precisely because his talents are extraordinary. Such relief is not available for all employees, but when an employee has such unusual talents, like a famous opera singer, the courts will enter negative injunctions to protect their employers from competition that would follow a breach of their employment contract.

(B) Incorrect. Yes, because employees may not compete with their employers during the term of their contract of employment.

This answer is incorrect because it overstates the applicable rule. Only those employees whose services are unique, or at least extraordinary, are subject to the equitable relief of a negative injunction to prevent competition. Other employees may have to pay damages, but only the competition of the select few may entitle the employer to injunctive relief.

(C) Incorrect. No, because the contract does not contain a non-compete clause.

This answer is incorrect because a non-compete clause is not necessary for a court to issue the negative injunction. Such a clause would be helpful to the college's case, but the courts have not found such provisions to be essential.

(D) Incorrect. No, because equitable relief is not available with respect to contracts for personal services.

This answer is incorrect because it confuses a negative injunction, which is available with respect to personal services, and specific performance, which is not available for personal services. One requires someone to refrain from rendering service. That order, the negative injunction, is permissible. The other would require a person to affirmatively render service. That order, specific performance, is not available for personal services.

Explanation: Question 64

The correct answer is: **(B)** Yes, because the restoration company can recover its lost profits.

In this case, the teacher offered the restoration company a job, and the restoration company accepted the offer. At that point, the parties had a valid executory contract. The job could be canceled, but if that happened, the restoration company would have a valid claim for monetary damages, in the form of expectation damages, reliance damages, or restitutionary damages. Because the contract was cancelled before the restoration company performed its work, the company could recover its expectation damages, or lost profits from the job. If the restoration company could show other damages, it would be able to recover those damages, as well. However, because none of the other answer choices both reaches the correct conclusion as to whether the restoration company has a legal remedy, and a valid reason why the company has a legal remedy, this is the best answer choice.

(A) Incorrect. Yes, because the restoration company relied on the teacher's offer in scheduling the job for October.

Foreseeable, detrimental reliance can provide consideration for a contract that is otherwise lacking in consideration. However, in this case, there is valid consideration for the contract. The teacher agreed to pay $2,500, and the restoration company agreed to treat the woodwork in the teacher's house. The restoration company will have a legal remedy against the teacher, but not because of any reliance on the part of the restoration company. Thus, this answer is incorrect.

(C) Incorrect. No, because there was no mutual assent to the offer.

This answer choice is contrary to the facts set forth in the question. Even though the parties had trouble finding a mutually convenient date for performance of the restoration work, the parties had reached agreement on the teacher's offer. The teacher offered to pay the restoration company $2,500 to perform the work, and the restoration company accepted that offer. Thus, this answer is incorrect.

(D) Incorrect. No, because the brother canceled the job.

Because the brother was merely living in the teacher's house, and there was no explicit assignment of the contract to the brother, it does not appear that the brother had the authority to cancel the job. Nevertheless, if the teacher permits the job to be canceled and has no excuse for canceling the contract (as appears to be the case here), the teacher can be held liable for breach of contract. Thus, this answer choice is incorrect.

Explanation: Question 65

The correct answer is: **(C)** No, because the assignment would greatly exceed the homebuilder's rights under the contract.

A requirements contract may be assigned to another person. However, a right is not assignable if the monthly requirements would greatly exceed the original contractor's requirements. In this case, the competition required twice the amount of door hinges in comparison to the homebuilder. If the amount were much smaller, it may be conceivable that doubling the amount does not greatly exceed the original rights under the contract. In this case, however, the homebuilder required 10,000 door hinges a month, and the competition doubled that amount to 20,000. Since the monthly requirements greatly exceed those of the original homebuilder under the contract, this contract cannot be assigned to the competition.

(A) Incorrect. Yes, because requirements contracts can be assigned to a third party.

It is true that requirements contracts can be assigned to other people. However, although all rights are assignable, there are certain circumstances in which a contract will not be assignable. In this case, the original contract required the hardware store to supply 10,000 door hinges. The requirement of the competition doubled that number. When an assignment would materially alter the risks or obligations under the contract, the right is not assignable. In this case, since the requirement doubled with the assignment, this requirements contract could not be assigned.

(B) Incorrect. Yes, because the type of requirement did not change.

Although the requirement was still for door hinges, this requirements contract is not assignable. Generally, all requirements contracts are assignable. However, when the risks or obligations would drastically change under the assignment, the requirements contract is not assignable.

(D) Incorrect. No, because assigning requirements contracts is against public policy.

Although the result of this answer choice is correct, the reason is not correct. It is true that this contract is not assignable, but it is not because assigning a requirements contract is against public policy. Generally, all rights are assignable unless the assignment would materially alter the risks or obligations under the contract. In this case, the homebuilder's requirements are 10,000 door hinges a month. If the homebuilder assigns his rights to the competition, the assignment would materially alter the obligations under the contract.

Explanation: Question 66

The correct answer is: **(A)** Yes, because the payment had been assigned to him and the woman had not been given notice of the assignment.

If the woman had been given notice of the assignment, the vendor's proper action would have been against the woman because the assignment was otherwise valid. But since the woman had not received notice of the assignment, she has a valid defense having paid the assignor (the florist). It is against the florist, therefore, that the vendor will have to make his claim. The assignment was valid and not revocable and so the vendor is likely to prevail.

(B) Incorrect. Yes, because he gave consideration for the assignment.

This answer reaches the correct conclusion but for the wrong reason. It is true that the vendor gave consideration for the assignment when he promised to quit trying to collect on the debt that was owed to him. But had the florist notified the woman that the payment had been assigned, then the vendor's action would be correctly made against the woman, not the florist. Therefore the fact that he gave consideration is not what gives him the right to take action against the florist. It is the fact that the woman was never given notice of the assignment and the florist accepted the payment.

(C) Incorrect. No, because the assignment was valid and therefore the only available action is against the woman.

This answer would be correct had the woman been given notice of the assignment. But the woman did not receive notice about the assignment and so her payment to the florist (the assignor) gives the woman a valid defense against the vendor. Now the vendor will have to bring his action against the florist because the assignment was not revocable.

(D) Incorrect. No, because the assignment was gratuitous.

The assignment in this case was not gratuitous because the assignment was made in exchange for the vendor's promise to stop trying to collect from the florist. However, even if that consideration fails for some reason, gratuitous promises are valid where the assignor had donative intent and made delivery. In this case, delivery was the copy of the contract with the woman. Symbolic delivery may suffice in this situation. Therefore, this answer is incorrect.

Explanation: Question 67

The correct answer is: **(D)** Both the veterinarian and the assistant are liable.

If a delegatee fails, refuses, or defectively carries out a delegated duty, the obligor/delegator will be in breach of the contract. Here, the veterinarian is both the obligor and delegator, the assistant is the delegatee, and the dog-supply store is the obligee. As a result of the assignment, the assistant is liable to the store. However, the veterinarian is not released from her obligation: Until it is determined whether the agreement to transfer the practice included the assumption by the assistant of the veterinarian's obligation (the contract said that the obligation was assignable, but did not say that it was actually assigned), the veterinarian is liable to the dog supply store, and the assistant may be liable to the veterinarian. As such, the dog-supply store is entitled to $9,000, which it may recover from either the assistant or the veterinarian, but not both.

(A) Incorrect. The assistant is liable but the veterinarian is not, because there was a novation.

A novation occurs when the original obligee agrees to release the original obligor from performance. The obligor then makes an entirely new agreement with a third party to whom the obligee has delegated obligations. The original obligee has no further responsibilities because of the new agreement. In this case, there is no indication that the dog-supply store has in any way released the veterinarian from her obligation to pay for the examining tables, nor is there any indication that the veterinarian has repudiated her obligation to the dog-supply store.

(B) Incorrect. The veterinarian is liable but the assistant is not, because the assistant never promised the dog-supply store that he would pay for the tables.

If there has been a contract of delegation between an obligor/delegator and delegatee, the obligee is an intended third-party beneficiary of that contract and may sue the delegatee in that capacity. It does not matter that the assistant did not promise the dog-supply store that he would pay the veterinarian's obligation—the assistant can be sued as the veterinarian's delegatee.

(C) Incorrect. The veterinarian is liable but the assistant is not, because a delegation of duties did not take place.

Both the Uniform Commercial Code and the Restatement of Contracts recognize that general language such as I hereby assign my contract creates an assignment of rights and a delegation of duties. If the delegatee accepts this arrangement without protest, he will be deemed to have implicitly promised to assume legal liability for the duties of the assignor/delegator. Here, the transfer of the veterinary practice from the veterinarian to the assistant appears to have assigned the veterinarian's obligation to the dog-supply store to the assistant.

Explanation: Question 68

The correct answer is: **(A)** Both the first welder and the second welder.

In this case, the first welder delegated his performance under the contract to the second welder. There is no indication that the contract forbade delegation and the performance required under the contract is not personal because the boater merely hired the company and agreed to the first welder doing the job. The boater did not set out to specifically hire the first welder. When duties have been effectively delegated, the delegator (the first welder in this case) remains liable to the obligee. Under the theory of third-party beneficiary, the delegatee is liable to the obligee as well. Therefore, the boater may sue both welders for breach, so this answer is correct.

(B) Incorrect. The first welder only, because the duty was not delegable.

The duties under this welding contract were delegable because there is nothing noted in the contract forbidding delegation and the performance obligation is not personal in this case. Sometimes, where the performance requested is personal and the obligee is relying on the reputation, skill, taste, or discretion of a certain party, the duties are not delegable. Here, the boater was interested in the particular welding business, but there is nothing in the facts to indicate that the boater specifically wanted the first welder over the second welder. Therefore, the delegation to the business partner was proper, so this answer is incorrect.

(C) Incorrect. The second welder only, because the duty had been delegated.

When performance under a contract has been delegated, the delegator (in this case the first welder) remains liable to the obligee in the absence of a specific novation. A novation in this situation requires a clear promise by the obligee (the boater) to relieve the delegator of his responsibilities under the contract. Merely nodding his head at the second welder did not create a novation. Hence, the first welder remains liable under the contract. Under the third-party beneficiary theory, the second welder is liable to the boater as well. Therefore, this answer is incorrect.

(D) Incorrect. The second welder only, because there was a novation when the boater nodded his assent to the second welder.

A novation in this delegation of duties situation requires a clear promise by the obligee that the delegator is relieved of his duties under the contract. In return, the obligee accepts the liability of the delegatee. A mere assent to the delegation does not relieve the delegator of responsibility. There must be a clear novation. Because the boater merely nodded his head at the second welder, although the delegation is successful, there is no novation. Therefore, this answer is incorrect.

Explanation: Question 69

The correct answer is: **(D)** $2,500.

This is the correct answer, because as an intended third-party beneficiary, the mechanic may sue to enforce the full amount in the contract. A third party is considered an intended beneficiary of a contract where (1) the contracting parties agree that one of the duties specified must be performed for the intended beneficiary directly, as opposed to being performed for one of the contracting parties; and (2) that was the conscious intention of the contracting party who would otherwise be entitled to the benefit. In this case, the mechanic was named in the contract, and the friend's payment of $2,500 for the race car driver's car was to be paid to the mechanic. Furthermore, the race car driver intended for the mechanic to receive the $2,500 because the race car driver wanted to pay off a debt to the mechanic and give himself a $300 credit. As a result, the mechanic's status as a creditor of the race car driver is not what determines the amount to which he can recover from the friend. Instead, the mechanic's status as an intended third-party beneficiary entitles him to the full amount listed in the contract for $2,500, and his rights become vested when he sues.

(A) Incorrect. Nothing.

This answer is incorrect. Although normally only the parties to a contract may sue to enforce the contract, there is an exception where a third party qualifies as an intended beneficiary of the contract. In addition to the parties to a contract, a third party may sue to enforce a contract if the third party is an intended third-party beneficiary. To qualify as an intended third-party beneficiary, the third party must (1) be designated by name or legal description in the contract, (2) be the direct recipient of performance listed in the contract, and (3) this must be the intended result of the party that would otherwise be entitled to the performance. The motive for designation is not relevant. Here, the mechanic was listed by name in the contract, the friend's payment of $2,500 was to be performed for the mechanic, and the race car driver intended for; the $2,500 that the race car driver was entitled to from the friend to go to the mechanic, so that the race car driver could pay off the debt that the race car driver already owed to the mechanic and obtain a $300 credit. As an intended third-party beneficiary, the mechanic is entitled to enforce the contract for $2,500, making this answer incorrect.

(B) Incorrect. $300.

This answer is incorrect. As an intended third-party beneficiary, the mechanic is entitled to enforce the contract between the race car driver and his friend. The mechanic was listed by name in the contract, the friend's payment of $2,500 was to be performed for the mechanic, and the race car driver intended for the mechanic to receive the money in lieu of the race car driver to pay off the race car driver's outstanding debt to the mechanic. Just as the race car driver is entitled to $2,500, as the third-party intended beneficiary, the mechanic would also be entitled to $2,500.

(C) Incorrect. $2,200.

This answer is incorrect, because the mechanic's right to recover from the friend is a product of the friend's status as an intended third-party beneficiary to the contract between the race car driver and the friend and is not based on the amount the race car driver actually owes the mechanic. We can tell that the mechanic was an intended third-party beneficiary because the mechanic was named in the contract, the friend's $2,500 payment was to be paid to the mechanic, and the race car driver intended that the mechanic receive the $2,500 to pay off a debt to the mechanic and give himself a $300 credit. As a result, the debt of $2,200 is not what determines the amount to which the mechanic can recover from the friend. Instead, the mechanic's status as a third-party beneficiary entitles the mechanic to the full amount listed in the contract for $2,500, and his rights become vested when he sues.

Explanation: Question 70

The correct answer is: **(D)** No, if the promise to coach and the promise to pay are dependent on one another.

Conditions implied-in-law, also known as constructive conditions, function to fix the order of performance when the express terms of the bargain have not. Here, the facts state that the coach agreed to coach the team, and the college agreed to pay him a salary of $3,000 during the season. However, the contract neglected to specify precisely when the coach was to be paid, and it did not expressly condition his salary payment on his continuing to coach for the rest of the season. Given the lack of contractual specificity, a court will resolve this problem through a constructive condition. A court will determine that the promises are independent of one another only where such an intention is clearly expressed or otherwise consistent with the overall purpose of the contract; otherwise, the promises are considered dependent on one another. As noted, here, such an intent is not clearly expressed in the contract. Therefore, without more information, the court is unlikely to find a construction that the promises are independent of one another is consistent with the overall purpose of the contract. It is more likely that the court will find that the coach's obligation to coach is dependent on the university's obligation to pay, and hence, if the coach is not paid, he is not obligated to continue to coach. As such, this is the best answer.

(A) Incorrect. Yes, because the promise to coach and the promise to pay are independent of one another.

Given the lack of contractual specificity, a court will need to resolve this problem through the use of a constructive condition. A court will determine that the promises are independent of one another only where such an intention is clearly expressed or otherwise consistent with the overall purpose of the contract. Otherwise, the promises are considered dependent on one another. As noted, here, such an intent is not clearly expressed in the contract. Therefore, without more information, the court will more likely find that the court will find that the coach's obligation to coach is dependent on the university's obligation to pay, and hence, if he is not paid, he is not obligated to continue to coach. As such, this answer is incorrect.

(B) Incorrect. Yes, because the contract did not expressly condition payment for a particular point in the season.

Because the contract does not specify the payment terms, a court will need to resolve this problem by using a constructive condition. (This is also called a condition implied-in-law.) A court will determine that the promises are independent of one another only where such an intention is clearly expressed or otherwise consistent with the overall purpose of the contract. Otherwise, the promises are considered dependent on one another. As noted, here, such an intent is not clearly expressed in the contract. Therefore, without more information, the court will more likely find that the court will find that the coach's obligation to coach is dependent on the university's obligation to pay, and hence, if he is not paid, he is not obligated to continue to coach. As such, this answer is incorrect.

(C) Incorrect. Yes, because parol evidence cannot be used to contradict a writing.

The Parol Evidence Rule prevents introduction of prior or contemporaneous evidence to contradict a writing. To determine if the parol evidence rule applies, it must first be determined whether the writing is fully integrated. A document is fully integrated if it is a complete and exclusive statement of the agreement. To determine whether a document is fully integrated, it is necessary to examine the four corners of the contract, considering such factors as whether the contract declares itself to be the complete agreement, as well as the complexity and duration of the parties' pre-contract negotiations. If a document is fully integrated, all extrinsic evidence as to its meaning is barred. However, if the agreement is not fully integrated, extrinsic evidence can be admissible to explain or supplement the writing. Here, the facts state that the coach agreed to coach the team, and the college agreed to pay him a salary of $3,000 during the season. However, the contract neglected to specify precisely when the coach was to be paid, and it did not expressly condition his salary payment on his continuing to coach for the rest of the season. Thus, given the contract's failure to include an important specification, it does not appear that the document was fully integrated. As such, it is unlikely that the Parol Evidence Rule will apply to bar the introduction of evidence regarding the terms of payment, and this answer is therefore incorrect.

Explanation: Question 71

The correct answer is: **(D)** No, because the agreement was an unenforceable unilateral agreement.

An offer seeking performance in return is an offer to enter into a unilateral contract. Under a unilateral contract, the offeror is bound only when the offeree completes performance, and the offeree is never bound to perform because she has never promised to do so. However, she will not be entitled to the benefits of the offeror's promise unless and until she performs as required. In this case, the baker made an offer seeking the butcher's performance in return—that is, the giving of the baseball to the dentist. Thus, the unilateral agreement is not enforceable until the butcher gives the dentist the baseball and the dentist cannot compel the butcher to do so.

(A) Incorrect. Yes, because the dentist was an intended beneficiary of the agreement between the baker and butcher.

In a typical contract, the parties promise performances to each other. If one party refuses to perform, the other has standing to bring a claim for breach because the parties are in contractual privity. However, in some contracts, one of the parties promises a performance that will benefit a third-party beneficiary. In that case, an intended third-party beneficiary has standing to sue to enforce the agreement. Here, the dentist is an intended third-party beneficiary of the agreement between the baker and butcher. So, if that agreement was enforceable, the dentist would have legal standing to sue to enforce it. However, in this case, the agreement between the baker and butcher was an unenforceable unilateral contract. Thus, this answer is incorrect.

(B) Incorrect. Yes, because the agreement was a valid unilateral agreement.

An offer seeking performance in return is an offer to enter into a unilateral contract. Under a unilateral contract, the offeror is bound only when the offeree completes performance and the offeree is never bound to perform because she has never promised to do so. However, she will not be entitled to the benefits of the offeror's promise unless and until she performs as required. In this case, the baker made an offer seeking the butcher's performance in return—that is, the giving of the baseball to the dentist. Thus, the unilateral agreement is not enforceable until the butcher gives the dentist the baseball and the dentist cannot compel the butcher to do so. Thus, this answer is incorrect.

(C) Incorrect. No, because only the butcher can sue to enforce his agreement with the baker.

In a typical contract, the parties promise performances to each other. If one party refuses to perform, the other has standing to bring a claim for breach because the parties are in contractual privity. However, in some contracts, one of the parties promises a performance that will benefit a third-party beneficiary. In that case, an intended third-party beneficiary has standing to sue to enforce the agreement. Here, the butcher could sue to enforce his agreement with the baker provided that the butcher had performed as required by giving the dentist the baseball. However, the dentist was an intended third-party beneficiary of the agreement between the baker and butcher. So, the dentist would have legal standing to sue to enforce it as well. However, the agreement between the baker and butcher was an unenforceable unilateral contract. Thus, this answer is incorrect.

Explanation: Question 72

The correct answer is: **(A)** The analyst's phone call was not sufficient to bind the roommate to his promise.

A promise to pay a past debt that is barred by the Statute of Limitations can be enforced even though it is not supported by any new consideration. However, most jurisdictions now require that in order to be enforceable, the new promise must be contained in a signed writing. The creditor's claim will be based on the new promise, and the creditor will be entitled to collect only the amount promised in the signed writing. Thus, the roommate's best defense is that, given that his promise to pay the analyst was an oral promise made over the phone, rather than contained in a signed writing, his promise is not enforceable by the analyst.

(B) Incorrect. The Statute of Limitations bars the analyst from recovering.

In most jurisdictions, a promise to pay a past debt that is barred by the Statute of Limitations can be enforced, even though it is not supported by any new consideration, if the new promise is contained in a signed writing. The creditor's claim will be based on the new promise, and the creditor will be entitled to collect only the amount promised in the signed writing. Thus, the Statute of Limitations does not completely bar the analyst from recovering, and this answer choice is incorrect.

(C) Incorrect. The roommate's duty was discharged by impossibility because the roommate's hardship was more severe than the analyst's hardship.

Under certain circumstances, the doctrine of impossibility will excuse a party from performing under a contract if, due to unforeseen or unforeseeable events, it becomes objectively impossible for him to perform his contractual duties. However, a party's performance is not excused where it is not objectively impossible for him to perform, but merely personally or subjectively impossible. Here, given that the roommate's performance became subjectively, not objectively, impossible for him to perform as a result of his termination, his performance is not excused under the doctrine of impossibility. Thus, this answer is incorrect.

(D) Incorrect. Past consideration is not enough to support the roommate's new promise.

It is true that an agreement to pay a portion of an existing valid debt does not constitute sufficient consideration to support a present contract. However, the roommate modified the agreement when he promised to pay the analyst $250 a month. Given the present modification, the doctrine of past consideration is not the roommate's best defense. Thus, this answer is incorrect.

Explanation: Question 73

The correct answer is: **(B)** The driver will prevail because she believed in good faith that the car accident was caused by the employee's negligence at the time she entered into the settlement agreement.

Compromise of a valid claim is always sufficient consideration to support a promise to pay money made by the person against whom the disputed claim is asserted. Thus, where a disputed claim is settled and it later becomes apparent that the claim was invalid, the claimant's willingness to forgo adjudication is still sufficient consideration to support the other party's promise to pay money if the claimant honestly believed that the claim was valid. On the facts of this question, at the time the settlement was entered into, the driver believed in good faith that the employee had negligently caused the car accident. Thus, the driver's compromise of that potentially valid claim is sufficient consideration to make the store owner's promise to pay $40,000 enforceable, even if the claim is later revealed to be invalid.

(A) Incorrect. The driver will prevail because the agreement to settle the lawsuit did not require consideration. The driver and the store owner may enter into an agreement by which the driver agreed to accept a new performance (payment of a fixed but lesser amount of money) in exchange for an existing duty (payment of a disputed but potentially larger amount of money resulting from the negligence claim). However, such a settlement agreement does require adequate consideration supporting the store owner's promise to pay $40,000. Thus, this answer is incorrect.

(C) Incorrect. The store owner will prevail because the revelation of the witness's fabrication demonstrates that there was no consideration to support his promise to pay $40,000.

It is the apparent validity of the compromisor's claim at the time the settlement agreement is entered into that determines its value as consideration to support the other party's promise to pay money. If the claim is honestly held by the compromisor at the time the agreement is reached, there is sufficient consideration—even if the claim is later revealed to be invalid. Therefore, the fact that the driver's claim may, in fact, be invalid due to the witness's fabricated testimony does not mean that at the time the settlement agreement was entered into the driver's promise to settle the lawsuit was insufficient consideration for the store owner's promise to pay $40,000. Thus, this answer is incorrect.

(D) Incorrect. The store owner will prevail because agreements to settle lawsuits are unenforceable as violating public policy.

Public policy is to encourage the settlement of disputed claims. Thus, settlement agreements, such as the one made by the driver and the store owner, are generally enforceable. Thus, this option is incorrect.

Explanation: Question 74

The correct answer is: **(B)** No, because the parties' mutual promises to purchase and sell the subject goods are sufficient considerations, even though no specific amount of goods to be sold was stated in the contract.

At one time, a requirements contract, such as the agreement involved in this question, would have been regarded as unenforceable because the purchaser had not explicitly agreed to actually purchase any goods from the seller. The purchaser's obligation under the contract was therefore regarded as "illusory"—he might, after all, decide that he required no goods at all—and rendered the entire contract unenforceable because there was no mutuality of obligation. The UCC rendered this analysis of requirements contracts obsolete by providing that every contract involved an obligation of good faith in its performance or enforcement and by expressly permitting the quantity of goods to be purchased or sold to be measured by the requirements of the buyer or the output of the seller as actually occur in good faith, subject to protection from disproportionate demands. Thus, each party to such a contract promises in good faith to buy or sell whatever amount is actually called for by the circumstances, and these mutual promises provide the consideration, making the contract enforceable. Therefore, the requirements contract in this case is enforceable because the mutual promises made by the manufacturer and the fruit grower provided sufficient consideration.

(A) Incorrect. No, because an agreement of that nature does not need any consideration to be enforceable.

A requirements contract, such as the one in this question, needs consideration or a substitute therefore to be enforceable. The UCC converts what was historically regarded as an illusory promise into an actual, meaningful promise by imposing a requirement of good faith and by expressly authorizing the quantity term of the requirements contract to be left open, subject to actual needs. The resulting contracts are enforceable because the mutual promises supply consideration for each other and not, as this choice suggests, because there is no need for consideration.

(C) Incorrect. Yes, because the manufacturer's lack of an obligation to purchase any particular amount of prunes was insufficient consideration to support the fruit grower's return promise.

This option states the historical view of requirements contracts, which has been replaced by the UCC view. Under the UCC, each party to a requirements contract promises in good faith to buy or sell whatever amount is actually called for by the circumstances and these mutual promises provide the consideration, which makes the contract enforceable. Thus, this answer is incorrect.

(D) Incorrect. Yes, because requisite mutuality of obligation between the parties is lacking.

This option is merely a restatement of the historical position—that is, that the lack of a specific quantity term rendered the buyer's or seller's promise illusory and thus made the contract unenforceable. The UCC made such contracts enforceable. Under the UCC, each party to a requirements contract promises in good faith to buy or sell whatever amount is actually called for by the circumstances and these mutual promises provide the consideration, which makes the contract enforceable. Thus, this answer is incorrect.

Explanation: Question 75

The correct answer is: **(B)** Yes, because the modification was mutual.

At common law, courts will not enforce one party's demand for additional performance from the other party due to lack of consideration. This is known as the preexisting duty rule. However, modern courts permit such modification if there is a mutual modification to the contract. Here, the two parties had different interpretations of the time at which payment was to be made. In negotiating the dispute, both parties agreed to modify their performance. The mutual modification constitutes consideration, so a court would enforce the modification. This is therefore the correct answer.

(A) Incorrect. Yes, because the Statute of Frauds does not apply to subsequent oral modifications of written agreements.

This is an overly broad statement which does not apply in this situation. The Statute of Frauds does not apply to this underlying contract, which is primarily a services contract, not a sale of goods for over $500. It is also performable within a year and is not for the sale of land or one of the other categories for which the Statute of Frauds requires a writing. Thus, this is not the best answer.

(C) Incorrect. No, because the modification was not supported by consideration.

This is not the best answer. The common-law pre-existing duty rule holds that a promise to increase one party's performance under an existing contract is not enforceable because it does not involve consideration for the modification. However, that does not apply here, where there was a mutual modification of the parties' performance. The mutual modification constitutes consideration, so the modification here is enforceable.

(D) Incorrect. No, because the modification was oral.

There is no reason why the oral modification in this instance is not valid. The UCC Statute of Frauds does not apply to the underlying contract, which is primarily a services contract, not a sale of goods for over $500. There is no reason to think that a non-UCC Statute of Frauds applies either, as the contract is performable within a year and is not for the sale of land or one of the other categories for which the Statute of Frauds requires a writing. Thus, this is not the best answer.

Explanation: Question 76

The correct answer is: **(A)** The bride, because the seamstress cashed the check without objection.

This contract for the sale of the wedding dress is governed by the UCC. Under the UCC, contracts can be modified in good faith. Here, the contract contained a satisfaction clause, which means that whether or not a party's performance obligation is complete, is up to the discretion of the other party, provided that the determination is made in good faith. The bride in good faith determined that the dress had problems that needed fixing, so the seamstress still had obligations under the original contract. The unhappy bride offered the seamstress a contract modification whereby she would pay less for the dress but would only require the seamstress to fix one of the two alleged problems with the dress. The seamstress, by depositing the check without objection, signaled her acceptance of the modification and therefore would not prevail in a suit for the additional $100.

(B) Incorrect. The bride, because the seamstress is entitled to recover only the reasonable value of her services.

Here, the actions of the seamstress indicate acceptance of a good-faith modification of the contract. If that were not the case, the seamstress might be able pursue remedies under quasi contract for the reasonable value of her services, but she would probably fail. The original contract contained a satisfaction clause that the seamstress did not satisfy. The bride then offered a contract modification that the seamstress accepted by cashing the check without objection. If anything, the seamstress owes the bride a collar repair on the dress.

(C) Incorrect. The seamstress, if she proves that she had sewn the dress according to the agreed-upon design.

The facts state that the bride's belief that the collar and hem were not finished properly was in good faith, which, according to the contract, means that the seamstress had not yet performed satisfactorily. A provision of satisfaction in the contract means that whether or not a party's performance obligation is complete, is up to the discretion of the other party, so long as the determination is made in good faith. The seamstress's only chance to recover the additional $100 was to reject the bride's check and bring an action to recover on the original contract. Instead she cashed the check without objection, thereby signaling her acceptance of the contract modification.

(D) Incorrect. The seamstress, because she cashed the check under economic duress.

The seamstress's economic hardship is not a factor to be taken into account in this situation. The seamstress would be able to recover the additional $100 only if she had rejected the bride's check. Even then, the seamstress would have failed to recover, because the contract contained a satisfaction clause that the bride enforced in good faith.

Explanation: Question 77

The correct answer is: **(A)** No, because the fisherman's daughter did not give the comfort and affection in exchange for the promise.

Where a promise is made for a benefit that has already been received, such as the comfort and affection given by the fisherman's daughter over the years, the conventional wisdom is that the promise is enforceable if the benefit that was received was material and not merely sentimental, and the promisor is the person that received the material benefit. In this case, the benefit already received by the industrialist's daughter was purely sentimental and, therefore, her promise to buy the house for her friend was unenforceable.

(B) Incorrect. No, because the comfort and affection do not have a pecuniary value.

Though it is true that comfort and affection cannot be measured in terms of pecuniary value, pecuniary value is not the only measure of legally sufficient consideration. For example, if the fisherman's daughter had saved the life of the industrialist's daughter, she would have given a benefit to the industrialist's daughter that is materially sufficient to operate as consideration for the industrialist's daughter's promise to buy her a house, even if the lifesaving act itself has no pecuniary value. A promise for a benefit already received is enforceable where the benefit is material (not merely sentimental) and the promisor is the one who received the benefit. Thus, this answer is incorrect.

(C) Incorrect. Yes, because it constituted a benefit received by the industrialist's daughter.

Although the industrialist's daughter did receive a benefit, that benefit was purely sentimental. For a court to enforce a promise for a benefit already received, the benefit needs to have been material and not simply sentimental, and the promisor must have been the one to receive the benefit. The benefit at issue here is not material and, therefore, this answer choice is not correct.

(D) Incorrect. Yes, because the industrialist's daughter had a moral obligation to her friend.

The legal issue in this question is whether or not the benefit received by the industrialist's daughter was material enough to support the later promise for a house. A promise for a benefit already received is enforceable if the benefit was material and not merely sentimental, and if the promisor is the one who received the benefit. Here, the comfort and affection received by the industrialist's daughter was a purely sentimental benefit. Therefore, her promise to purchase the house is unenforceable, and this answer is incorrect.

Explanation: Question 78

The correct answer is: **(D)** The city, because the mechanic was already duty-bound to do the work for $8,500 when the city promised to pay $9,000.

Traditionally, one party's demand for additional performance from the other party to an existing executory contract could not be enforced unless both parties agreed and there was consideration to support the modifications. A modern minority of courts will enforce a modification if both parties assent and there are unanticipated circumstances that have arisen, making some adjustment in performance fair and equitable. Here, no unanticipated circumstances arose, thereby making the attempted modification unenforceable even under the minority rule.

(A) Incorrect. The mechanic, because the parties mutually rescinded the original contract at the $8,500 price and made a new one at $9,000.

In legal rescission, the party wishing to rescind the contract notifies the other party of the rescission, and tenders to the other party any consideration that has been furnished to the rescinding party; the rescinding party then may seek recovery of any benefit conferred on the other party through an action for restitution. Here, the mechanic did not notify the city of the rescission; he merely refused to work until the city agreed to pay him $9,000. It cannot therefore be said that the contract was rescinded. Thus, this answer is incorrect.

(B) Incorrect. The mechanic, because his forbearance to exercise his right to break the original contract and to pay damages is consideration for the city's promise to pay the additional $500.

A few modern courts might recognize this argument, but it is not the majority rule. Thus, this answer is incorrect.

(C) Incorrect. The city, because the city's promise to pay the additional amount was obtained by undue influence.

Where a party's assent was induced by force or threat of force, the contract will not be enforced. There are no facts to indicate that the mechanic induced the city's promise to pay the extra $500 by force or threat thereof; the mechanic merely refused to work until the city agreed to pay $9,000 for the job. If the mechanic failed to perform under the original contract, the city could sue the mechanic for breach. Thus, this answer is incorrect.

Explanation: Question 79

The correct answer is: **(D)** The parties have made a compromise.

Modern courts uphold as legally sufficient consideration the promise not to pursue a claim that is either reasonable or objectively unreasonable but held in good faith. Thus, the pretzel vendor's surrender of what he reasonably or in good faith believed to be a valid claim is consideration, which supports the art dealer's second promise to pay $100,000.

(A) Incorrect. The art dealer executed a binding unilateral contract.

The offer of a unilateral contract seeks a return performance, not a return promise. In this situation, the art dealer bargained for the promise that the pretzel vendor would not file a claim for the painting, not a performance by the vendor. Thus, this answer is incorrect.

(B) Incorrect. Promissory estoppel binds the art dealer.

Promissory estoppel lies only where one party makes a promise to the other under circumstances where, despite the fact that there is no legally sufficient consideration, the second party changes position in reliance upon the promise. In this situation, though there is a question about the sufficiency of the consideration, it does not appear that the vendor changed his position in reliance on the art dealer's promise. Thus, this answer is incorrect.

(C) Incorrect. It would be unjust for the art dealer not to give restitution for benefits he retains.

Restitution arguably applies to any situation where one person has been unjustly enriched by another. Where one party confers a benefit on the other through mistake, the first party may seek return of the benefit through restitution. Here, the vendor was not acting because of a mistake and not under circumstances where a person would expect to be able to compel payment in compensation. Even if restitution might conceivably be a theory under which the vendor could recover some payment from the art dealer, here the vendor already has reached an enforceable compromise with the art dealer. This compromise—not restitution—is a clearer basis for recovery. Thus, this answer is incorrect.

Explanation: Question 80

The correct answer is: **(A)** The fisherman reasonably believed he had a valid claim when the agreement was made.

Traditionally, the rule regarding disputed claims was that a promise to forebear would be regarded as consideration only if the claim was both objectively reasonable and held in good faith. Modern courts uphold as legally sufficient consideration the promise not to pursue a claim that is either reasonable or objectively unreasonable but held in good faith. Therefore, if the fisherman reasonably or in good faith believed that his claim was enforceable, his surrender of that claim is valid as consideration in the new agreement with the bird-watcher.

(B) Incorrect. The fisherman's agreement was made in a writing he signed.

Merely placing a promise in writing does not overcome a lack of consideration. Even though some states presume that a promise in writing is based on adequate consideration, this is only a presumption and can be rebutted by evidence that consideration was lacking. As such, this answer is incorrect.

(C) Incorrect. The agreement was witnessed by an objective third party.

There is no requirement that contracts be witnessed by objective third parties in order to be enforceable. Moreover, having an objective third party witness to the agreement would not supply consideration if consideration were lacking. Therefore, the fisherman's claim would not be any stronger if the agreement had had such a witness. Thus, this answer is incorrect.

(D) Incorrect. The bird-watcher could not have won the contest and the prize without the camera.

Even if the fisherman's act benefited the bird-watcher by preserving his ability to obtain the prize, this fact would not remedy the lack of a bargained-for exchange at the time when the bird-watcher made his initial promise. Thus, this answer is incorrect.

Explanation: Question 81

The correct answer is: **(C)** No, because he disaffirmed the contract.

Minors may form contracts, but their obligations are voidable. Disaffirmance is accomplished by words or deeds that objectively signify the election to avoid liability. The boy's first phone call to the shop owner would constitute a disaffirmance of the contract, since he clearly indicated that he was calling the deal off, and that he had been a minor at the time of the contract's execution. Upon exercising the right to disaffirm a contract, the minor is obligated to return to the other party any goods received under the contract. Note that once a minor disaffirms a contract, a majority of jurisdictions consider the contract void, with title to the property revesting in the other party. Once disaffirmed, therefore, a minor can no longer ratify the contract. Ratification must occur prior to the minor's avoidance of the contract. Therefore, the boy's second phone call, attempting to put the contract back in place, will not serve as a ratification. If the shop owner does not wish to enter into a new contract with the boy, he will not be forced to, and the boy will not be able to enforce the now-void contract. Therefore, because he validly disaffirmed the contract, the boy may not ratify it, and this answer is correct.

(A) Incorrect. Yes, because the power to disaffirm a contract is held only by the minor.

The power of avoidance indeed means that the minor, and no other party to the contract, has the option of voiding the contract on those grounds. However, this does not mean that the boy will be able to enforce the contract here. Disaffirmance is accomplished by words or deeds that objectively signify the election to avoid liability. The boy's first phone call to the shop owner would constitute a disaffirmance of the contract, since he clearly indicated that he was calling the deal off, and that he had been a minor at the time of the contract's execution. Upon exercising the right to disaffirm a contract, the minor is obligated to return to the other party any goods received under the contract. Note that once a minor disaffirms a contract, a majority of jurisdictions consider the contract void, with title to the property revesting in the other party. Once disaffirmed, a minor can no longer ratify the contract. Ratification must occur prior to the minor's avoidance of the contract. Therefore, the boy's second phone call, attempting to put the contract back in place, will not serve as a ratification. Because he validly disaffirmed the contract, the boy may not ratify it, and the contract will not be enforceable by the boy. Therefore, this answer is incorrect.

(B) Incorrect. Yes, because he ratified the contract.

The boy's first phone call to the shop owner would constitute a disaffirmance of the contract; once disaffirmed, a minor can no longer ratify the contract. Ratification must occur prior to the minor's avoidance of the contract. Therefore, the boy's second phone call, attempting to put the contract back in place, will not serve as a ratification. Because he validly disaffirmed the contract, the boy may not ratify it, and the contract will not be enforceable by the boy. Therefore, this answer is incorrect.

(D) Incorrect. No, because the shop owner may disaffirm the contract since it does not pertain to necessaries.

A minor's contract for necessaries is voidable (by the minor). The other party, while having the right in quasi-contract to recover for the reasonable value of the goods or services provided, may not disaffirm. Furthermore, this answer is incorrect because necessaries are items considered necessary for survival, and an electric guitar is not such an item.

Explanation: Question 82

The correct answer is: **(B)** Yes, if the higher price paid by the restaurant owner was set in good faith.

The Uniform Commercial Code applies to contracts for the sale of goods. Here, as the parties' contract is for the sale of candy, the Uniform Commercial Code will govern the contract. Under the UCC, parties to an existing contract are free to modify its terms, and such modifications do not require any further consideration to be binding. However, the modification must have been asserted in good faith. Good faith is defined as the "morality of the marketplace." Unlike under the equity doctrine, the reason prompting the demand need not have been unforeseeable at the time of the formation of the original contract. The other party is not obligated to agree to modify the contract; however, if she does so consent, the modification is binding. Here, if a price of $90 per box does not offend the morality of the market place, the restaurant owner will be bound to the modification, because she previously consented to the increased cost and there are no facts to suggest that the importer intended the higher price to last only for the summer. Thus, it is immaterial that the factory is once again open for business.

(A) Incorrect. Yes, because the equitable modification doctrine applies.

The Uniform Commercial Code applies to contracts for the sale of goods. Here, as the parties' contract is for the sale of candy, the Uniform Commercial Code, not the common law, will govern the contract. Under the UCC, parties to an existing contract are free to modify its terms, and such modifications do not require any further consideration to be binding. Thus, this answer is incorrect.

(C) Incorrect. No, because the factory is once again operating, eliminating any substantial hardship.

The Uniform Commercial Code applies to contracts for the sale of goods. Here, as the parties' contract is for the sale of candy, the Uniform Commercial Code will govern the contract. Under the UCC, parties to an existing contract are free to modify its terms, and such modifications do not require any further consideration to be binding. However, the modification must have been asserted in good faith. Good faith is defined as the "morality of the marketplace." Unlike under the equity doctrine, the reason prompting the demand need not have been unforeseeable at the time of the formation of the original contract. The other party is not obligated to agree to modify the contract; however, if she does so consent, the modification is binding. Here, if a price of $90 per box does not offend the morality of the market place, the restaurant owner will be bound to the modification, because she previously consented to the increased cost and there are no facts to suggest that the importer intended the higher price to last only for the summer. Thus, it is immaterial that the factory is once again open for business. Thus, this answer is incorrect.

(D) Incorrect. No, because it was foreseeable at the time of formation that shortages in the supply of candy would occur.

The Uniform Commercial Code applies to contracts for the sale of goods. This contract is for the sale of candy, so the Uniform Commercial Code will govern. Under the UCC, parties to an existing contract are free to modify its terms, and modifications do not require additional consideration to be binding. However, the modification must have been asserted in good faith. Unlike under the equity doctrine, the reason prompting the demand need not have been unforeseeable at the time of the formation of the original contract. Thus, it is immaterial that seasonal shortages are common, making this answer incorrect.

Explanation: Question 83

The correct answer is: **(D)** Detrimental reliance.

Consideration is required to make an executory bilateral contract legally enforceable. However, in some circumstances, a substitute for consideration will make an agreement enforceable in the absence of consideration. For example, under the theory of promissory estoppel, if a promisee can show that he relied to his detriment on the promisor's promise and his reliance was foreseeable, the promise will be enforced even when there is no consideration. Under the facts presented, the teenager incurred the expense in reliance on the garage owner's promise to pay the dental bill. Thus, detrimental reliance would be the teenager's best argument for enforcement of the garage owner's promise to pay the bill.

(A) Incorrect. Moral obligation.

Moral obligation is a term used by some courts when enforcing a promise to pay a pre-existing debt made in the absence of consideration or a promise to pay for services rendered in the past. Generally, such agreements are unenforceable; however, some courts may enforce such agreements, saying that the promisor's moral obligation to pay the debt furnishes consideration. However, under the facts presented, the moral obligation argument is inapplicable, because the garage owner's promise was neither a promise to pay a pre-existing debt nor a promise to pay for past services. Thus, this answer is incorrect.

(B) Incorrect. Past consideration.

Even if the teenager could be considered to have previously suffered a detriment by doing odd jobs around the garage, this detriment does not provide consideration for the garage owner's promise. Generally, past consideration or, in other words, a detriment suffered in the past (that is, prior to the promisor's promise) does not make a promise enforceable, as the promisor did not bargain for the detriment. Thus, this answer is incorrect.

(C) Incorrect. Breach of contract.

Because the teenager offered no consideration for the garage owner's promise to pay the teenager's dental bill, no enforceable contract was formed between the teenager and the garage owner. As such, a breach of contract argument is destined to fail. In order to prevail, the teenager will have to establish that there was some substitute for consideration. Thus, this answer is incorrect.

Explanation: Question 84

The correct answer is: **(B)** $7,500.

While the doctrine of consideration generally requires a bargained-for exchange, there exists several important exceptions to this requirement, including a written promise to pay a debt that is barred by the statute of limitations. In such a case, a written promise to pay part of an owed debt can be enforced to the extent of the promise, as though it were a bargained-for exchange. However, only the new promise is enforceable. Thus, if the promisor agrees to pay an amount different from that of the original debt, only the new amount can be recovered. In this instance, the patient owed $10,000 to the bank, but the statute of limitations had run out on the enforcement of the debt. However, under this exception to the rule requiring bargained-for consideration, the patient's written promise to pay $7,500 is fully enforceable by the bank. Therefore, this is the correct answer.

(A) Incorrect. $10,000.

This answer assumes that the patient's promise to pay $7,500 revives the enforceability of the entire debt, which is incorrect. The debt's enforceability is only revived to the extent of the new written promise, which in this case is only for $7,500. Thus, this answer is incorrect.

(C) Incorrect. $7,500, but only if the patient was aware that the statute of limitations on the original debt had run out.

This answer assumes that the patient's promise to pay $7,500 hinges on the patient's knowledge of whether the statute of limitations. The debt's enforceability is only revived to the extent of the new written promise, which in this case is only for $7,500. Thus, this answer is incorrect.

(D) Incorrect. Nothing.

If consideration were required here, then this answer would be correct, because the written promise would fail without it. However, an exception to the rule requiring consideration exists for a written promise to pay a debt that is barred by the statute of limitations. In such a case, a promise to pay part of an owed debt can be enforced to the extent of the promise, as though it were a bargained-for exchange. The patient's written promise to pay $7,500 is enforceable by the bank. Therefore, this answer is incorrect.

Explanation: Question 85

The correct answer is: **(C)** Yes, but only to the extent of $1,800, to prevent injustice to the student.

Under the doctrine of promissory estoppel, when there has not occurred a bargained-for exchange, a promise may nevertheless be enforceable if grounds exist to apply a substitute for consideration. A promisor will not be able to assert the defense of lack of consideration if an injustice to the promisee can be avoided only by enforcing the promise. In such case, the promise will be enforced only to the extent necessary to avoid injustice to the promisee. Here, because the student's reliance on her great-aunt's promise caused her to spend $1,800 on her trip to Europe, the great-aunt's promise will be enforceable to the extent necessary to avoid injustice to the student. As such, the great-aunt will be required to pay the student the $1,800 the student spent in reliance on her great-aunt's promise.

(A) Incorrect. No, because the promise was a gift subject to a condition that conferred no benefit on the great-aunt.

It is true that ordinarily, a gift does not constitute consideration, as the element of a bargained-for exchange is missing. However, in some cases, the objective theory of contract formation favors the finding of a bargain if the promisor's promise has induced the promisee to change position in a way that was both foreseeable to the promisor and detrimental to the promisee. Here, it was foreseeable that based on her great-aunt's promise, the student would spend extra money in Europe, because the student expected to receive $2,000 from the great-aunt upon the student's return from Europe. Given the student's detrimental reliance on the great-aunt's promise, the fact that the great-aunt's promise was merely to make a gift will not prevent the student's enforcement of the great aunt's promise. Thus, this answer is incorrect.

(B) Incorrect. No, because the past consideration is insufficient.

It is true that, ordinarily, past consideration cannot support a present agreement. In this case, however, the great-aunt promised to make a gift to the student, not to compensate the student for a past act that benefited the great-aunt. As such, the student's and the great-aunt's agreement did not involve past consideration. Thus, this answer is incorrect.

(D) Incorrect. Yes, for the full $2,000, because the promise was a bargained-for exchange.

The facts indicate that the great-aunt promised to make the student a gift of $2,000. Thus, no bargained-for exchange took place. While the great- aunt's promise to the student may be enforceable under the doctrine of promissory estoppel, despite the lack of a bargained-for exchange, this answer is incorrect.

Explanation: Question 86

The correct answer is: **(C)** No, because there was no consideration for the neighbor's promise.

This answer choice is correct—past consideration will not support a present promise. Here, the bodybuilder had already paid for the repairs to the lawnmower when neighbor made the promise to compensate him. As such, there existed no valid present consideration for the neighbor's promise, and the bodybuilder cannot recover based on that promise. The matter of detrimental reliance does not come into play; furthermore, there is nothing in the fact pattern to indicate that the bodybuilder obtained the repair in expectation of being repaid. As such, the bodybuilder cannot enforce the neighbor's promise. Students should note however, that had the bodybuilder called the neighbor prior to having the repairs done and obtained this same promise, the promise would have been enforceable.

(A) Incorrect. Yes, because the neighbor's promise was legally enforceable.

This answer is incorrect because past consideration will not support a present promise and without such consideration, the neighbor's promise would not be legally enforceable. Here, the bodybuilder had already paid for the repairs to the lawnmower before the neighbor made the promise to compensate the bodybuilder. As such, there existed no valid present consideration for the neighbor's promise, and the bodybuilder cannot recover based on a promise lacking consideration.

(B) Incorrect. Yes, if the bodybuilder relied to his detriment on the neighbor's promise.

This answer choice is incorrect because without valid consideration, it does not matter whether the bodybuilder relied to his detriment on the neighbor's promise. Here, the bodybuilder had already paid for the repairs to the lawnmower when the neighbor made his promise to compensate him. As such, there existed no valid present consideration for the neighbor's promise, and the bodybuilder cannot recover based on that promise.

(D) Incorrect. No, because there was an implied condition precedent that the body builder return the lawnmower to the neighbor in proper working condition.

This answer choice is incorrect because the neighbor's promise is unenforceable for lack of consideration, not as a result of an implied condition precedent. Past consideration will not support a present promise. Here, the bodybuilder had already paid for the repairs to the lawnmower when the neighbor made his promise to compensate him. As such, there existed no valid present consideration for the neighbor's promise, and the bodybuilder cannot recover based on that promise. While this answer correctly notes that the bodybuilder will not prevail, it bases its conclusion on a faulty analysis.

Explanation: Question 87

The correct answer is: **(C)** The painter, because she made a new promise to the apartment owner in exchange for higher payment.

Parties who have entered into a contract may modify the contract. Pursuant to common law, new consideration is required to modify an existing contract. A modification of an existing contract where only one party changes his or her obligations, may fail for lack of consideration. Similarly, where there is only a pretense of a newly formed bargain, the modification will fail. Here, the original bargain was for the painter to paint the apartment in 30 days, not 14 days. When she and the apartment owner modified the agreement, each was required to give new consideration to support the modification. The painter's new consideration was that she would complete the paint job on a much shorter time line than the one set forth in the original contract. The apartment owner's new consideration was his agreement to pay the painter an additional $500. Thus, the parties' modification of the contract is valid, and the owner is obligated to pay the painter the additional $500.

(A) Incorrect. The apartment owner, because the painter had a pre-existing duty to paint the apartment.

This answer choice is incorrect because the painter had a pre-existing duty to paint the apartment in 30 days, not 14 days. The parties subsequently modified the terms of their contract, and this modification was supported by new consideration. Specifically, the painter agreed to complete the paint job within 14 days instead of 30, and the owner agreed to pay the painter an additional $500.

(B) Incorrect. The apartment owner, because the painter tried to extort the additional money knowing that the owner was under duress.

Under modern law, three elements must exist for a successful defense of duress. There must be a threat of harm that is wrongful in nature and the threat leaves the aggrieved party with no reasonable choice but to submit to the threat. On these facts, there was no duress. The apartment owner made a mistake as to timing and had to negotiate a contract modification in order to meet a new deadline. The painter's request for additional compensation was made in good faith to meet this new deadline imposed by the apartment owner.

(D) Incorrect. The painter, because the apartment owner had a pre-existing duty to perform.

The painter will prevail, but not because the owner had a pre-existing duty to pay her. The painter's agreement to perform the paint job on a shorter time line than originally agreed upon and the apartment owner's agreement to pay the painter an additional $500 constituted valid additional consideration for the modification to the original contract. As such, the parties were bound to perform under the contract's new terms. Thus, this answer is incorrect.

Explanation: Question 88

The correct answer is: **(C)** Although the linen supply dealer knew that the debt was not actually owed by the hotel owner, the hotel owner was truly in doubt as to whether he owed the debt.

Valid consideration exists when a claim is surrendered by a party in a good- faith belief that the party is surrendering an enforceable claim. When someone promises to surrender a valid legal claim or to refrain from asserting a legal defense of that claim, that is sufficient consideration for a return promise if it has been bargained for. Where the claim surrendered is not valid, there is insufficient consideration. If the linen supply dealer knew that the hotel owner did not actually owe him the debt, then there would be no good-faith consideration between the hotel owner and the linen supply dealer, because the linen supply dealer would not be surrendering a valid legal claim in exchange for the hotel owner's promise to pay him $6,500. In such a case, the parties' agreement would fail for lack of consideration.

(A) Incorrect. The hotel owner's promise to pay was a gratuitous promise.

This answer is not the best choice because, for one thing, in a business setting, a purely gratuitous promise is rare. On these facts, the hotel owner feels that he does not owe the linen supply dealer the money, but he is either uncertain enough or tired enough of the battle that he's offered to pay a lesser amount to settle things. His best chance to avoid paying on the new promise is if, in fact, the linen supply dealer knew that the money was never owed. In that case, the linen supply dealer has offered no consideration, and the parties' agreement fails.

(B) Incorrect. The linen supply dealer's initial claim against the hotel owner was barred by the Statute of Frauds because it was not in writing.

Given that the parties' promissory note was signed and in writing, it would be enforceable under the Statute of Frauds. It is not required that the transactions on which the parties' dispute is based also be in writing in order for the present agreement to be enforceable. Thus, this answer is incorrect.

(D) Incorrect. Although the linen supply dealer sincerely believed that the hotel owner owed the debt, the hotel owner believed that he did not owe it.

If the linen supply dealer believed that the hotel owner owed him the debt, and the hotel owner believed he did not owe a debt, then a good-faith dispute existed between the parties. As a result, their compromise agreement would be supported by sufficient consideration, because each party would be giving up the right to that which he believed himself to be entitled (the hotel owner to pay nothing, the linen supply dealer to recover the full amount of the alleged debt). As otherwise stated, the hotel owner cannot defend against enforcement of the promissory note by asserting that the parties disputed the debt, because the very purpose of entering into the present agreement was to settle the disputed claim. Thus, this answer is incorrect.

Explanation: Question 89

The correct answer is: **(A)** The fisherman reasonably believed he had a valid claim when the swimmer's wife signed the instrument.

Valid consideration exists when a claim like the fisherman's is surrendered in a good-faith belief that it is an enforceable claim. When someone promises to surrender a valid legal claim or to refrain from asserting a legal defense of that claim, it is sufficient consideration for a return promise if it has been bargained for. If the fisherman believed he had a valid claim against the swimmer and he surrendered it in good faith to the wife, his claim against her estate can be enforced.

(B) Incorrect. The fisherman's agreement was in writing and signed by him.

The mere fact that an agreement is in writing does not make it enforceable absent valid consideration. This answer neglects to consider how and whether consideration was furnished. As such, this answer is incorrect.

(C) Incorrect. The fisherman paid the wife the sum of $1.00 when he received her written instrument.

If the fisherman gave $1.00 in exchange for a promise to receive $10,000 in the future, a new question would arise regarding the adequacy of the consideration. The wife's estate could at least argue that such a one-sided bargain was unconscionable. If valid consideration exists, it is more likely to be found in the fisherman's promise to forgo legal action on his claim than in his payment of $1.00. As such, this answer is incorrect.

(D) Incorrect. The wife contributed to the accumulation of the bank account's value.

The amount the wife may have contributed to the bank account's value is irrelevant. The pertinent issue in this case is whether the fisherman's and the wife's agreement was supported by valid consideration. This answer neglects to consider whether there was valid consideration for the agreement and is therefore incorrect.

Explanation: Question 90

The correct answer is: **(A)** Yes, because the truck driver did give consideration in exchange for the promise.

When the wife promised to pay the truck driver $5,000, she received from the truck driver a promise that he would not pursue a legal action against her based on her husband's will. This return promise by the truck driver constitutes consideration for the wife's promise to pay. The truck driver had a legal claim based on the will of the taxi driver because in modern times, a promise made for a material benefit received can be enforced. The truck driver saved the taxi driver's life, thus conferring a material benefit, and the promisor (the taxi driver) was the one who received the benefit. The taxi driver wrote his promise to pay into his will and by foregoing legal action to enforce the will, the truck driver gave consideration to the wife for her promise to pay him $5,000.

(B) Incorrect. Yes, because the wife is morally obligated to the truck driver as a result of his act.

This answer is incorrect because it arrives at the right result for the wrong reason. Any moral obligation the wife felt to pay the truck driver for having saved the life of her husband is irrelevant to this question. A court may enforce a promise made for a benefit already received when the benefit is material (such as saving a life) and when the promisor is the same person who received the benefit. In this case, when the taxi driver promised through his will to pay the truck driver for having saved his life, the promise was likely enforceable. It was the promise to give up that claim, given by the truck driver to the taxi driver's wife, that counts as consideration for her promise to pay him $5,000.

(C) Incorrect. No, because moral obligations are not enforceable.

Although it is true that purely moral obligations are not enforceable, this answer choice is incorrect because here, the truck driver's promise not to pursue the legal claim constituted valid consideration, which made the promise enforceable. If from the very start, it was the wife of the taxi driver who had promised the truck driver $5,000 for having saved the taxi driver's life, that promise would not be enforceable. To recover on a promise for a benefit already received, the benefit needs to have been a material benefit and the promisor must be the person who received that benefit. In that scenario, there would not have been any material benefit and the wife would not be giving up any legal right to any claim. However, under the facts presented, when the taxi driver left the truck driver $5,000 in his will, the truck driver had a legal claim. Also, when the truck driver promised not to pursue that legal claim in exchange for the wife's promise to pay $5,000, his promise constituted consideration for her promise to pay, which would make the promise enforceable.

(D) Incorrect. No, because the wife was not the beneficiary of the truck driver's lifesaving act.

This answer choice would be correct if not for the promise in the taxi driver's will to pay the truck driver $5,000 for having saved his life. The original promise to pay the truck driver was made by the very person who received the material benefit of the truck driver's lifesaving act. This created a legal claim for the truck driver, which he willingly gave up in exchange for the wife's promise to pay him the money. Because there was consideration, the wife's promise is enforceable.

Explanation: Question 91

The correct answer is: **(B)** The buyer, because the landowner's 30-day option to sell the property to the buyer was an illusory promise.

If, when a contract is being formed, one of the parties does not incur legal detriment because he retains unlimited discretion as to whether or not to perform, his promise is illusory and the contract is unenforceable due to a lack of consideration. Here, the landowner retained an unlimited right to revoke the 30-day option contract. Thus, he did not incur any obligation under the option portion of the contract, and he therefore cannot enforce the landowner's promise to pay $750 for the option to purchase his land. In effect, the landowner created an offer with an automatic lapse date of 30 days hence, for which the buyer owes no consideration, and as with all offers in general, may be revoked prior to acceptance.

(A) Incorrect. The buyer, because the Parol Evidence Rule precludes the seller from offering evidence of the buyer's oral offer to pay $750 for the revocable option.

A key predicate to application of the Parol Evidence Rule is the existence of a valid written agreement. Here, there was no such valid agreement because under the terms of the writing, the 30-day option was an illusory promise. The option contract fails for lack of consideration on the part of the landowner. Thus, this answer is incorrect.

(C) Incorrect. The landowner, because the buyer's oral offer to pay for the revocable option was accepted by the landowner when he reduced the agreement to writing.

Even if the party attempting to enforce a written contract can prove the existence of an offer and an acceptance, he must also prove that there was valid consideration for the contract. The fact that the landowner accepted the buyer's oral offer to pay for a revocable option is not dispositive of the landowner's claim against the buyer. The landowner offered no consideration for the option contract because his promise was illusory, and therefore, the option contract is unenforceable. Thus, this answer is incorrect.

(D) Incorrect. The landowner, because evidence of the buyer's promise to pay for the revocable option is admissible as a collateral agreement.

Evidence of collateral agreements is admissible, but here there was no collateral agreement. A collateral agreement is one that is entirely distinct from the written agreement of the contract at issue. The written agreement here was merely a documentation of the verbal agreement. The contract failed because the promise made by the landowner was illusory. Thus, this answer is incorrect.

Explanation: Question 92

The correct answer is: **(C)** No, because the personal shopper relied on a material misrepresentation.

Although the two parties to a contract ostensibly give the requisite mutual assent, where the assent of one party is arrived at by a misrepresentation as to a material term by the other party, the contract will not be enforced. Here, the assent of the personal shopper was obtained by the personal shopper's misrepresentation that the missing buttons and strap would not affect the doll's resale value. Because of its importance to the personal shopper in entering into the contract, the resale value was indeed a material term of this contract. Thus, the doll collector's misrepresentation as to this term will provide the personal shopper with a successful defense to enforcement of the contract against her.

(A) Incorrect. Yes, because the agreement was a voidable obligation only at the doll collector's election.

While it is true that only the doll collector, and not the personal shopper, may avoid the contractual obligation based on the doll collector's minority status, this answer choice is incorrect because the personal shopper can still get out of the deal based on the doll collector's misrepresentation.

(B) Incorrect. Yes, because it was not reasonable for the personal shopper to rely on the doll collector's statement.

Under the circumstances here (where the doll collector had been in this business for five years), it was arguably reasonable for the personal shopper to have relied on the doll collector's statement regarding the resale value of the doll. Even though the personal shopped was older than the doll collector, it was the doll collector who had superior knowledge and expertise when it came to the buying and selling of dolls based on her years of experience. By contrast, the personal shopper was a total novice who may have justifiably relied on the doll collector's reassurance that the missing buttons and strap would not affect the doll's resale value. Thus, this answer is incorrect.

(D) Incorrect. No, because the doll collector cannot enter into an enforceable contract because she is still a minor.

A contract entered into by a minor is voidable by the minor or his guardian during his minority or within a reasonable time after reaching his majority. However, if the minor or someone on his behalf does not take the appropriate steps to avoid the contract, it is enforceable. Here, the doll collector did not attempt to avoid his contractual obligations; rather, he brought a court action to enforce the contract. Therefore, this choice is wrong both because it misstates the law and because it does not fit the facts set forth in the question.

Explanation: Question 93

The correct answer is: **(B)** Yes, the promise is enforceable by the employee's personal representative, even though the employee had been killed in the bakery explosion on October 1.

The death of the offeree does not terminate the offer where the offer is for a unilateral contract and the offeree has already performed. The contract survives the decedent, and the right to receive performance from the offeror passes to the decedent's estate. Here, since the employee died after winning the competition, her estate would have the right to demand performance from the bakery.

(A) Incorrect. Yes, the promise is still enforceable on principles of promissory estoppel.

Although the bakery's promise would be enforceable here, this answer is incorrect because promissory estoppel would be unnecessary to enforce the bakery's promise. When one party makes a promise without legally sufficient consideration, and the second party changes position in reliance on the promise, the first party is estopped from asserting lack of consideration as a defense. In this situation, the bakery's offer was supported by legally sufficient consideration (the employee's enrollment in the advanced classes and winning the competition). Therefore, promissory estoppel is unnecessary to render the promise enforceable.

(C) Incorrect. No, the promise is not enforceable on policy grounds, because it produced a non-commercial agreement between an employee and her employers.

This answer choice is incorrect, because policy is irrelevant under these circumstances. Policy does not preempt agreements of this type, where actual duties flow from each party and are not based merely on love and affection or social bonds.

(D) Incorrect. No, the promise is not enforceable, because the employee, after submitting her application in July, was already under a duty to perform to the best of her ability.

When a party offers as consideration a promise or an act that she is already required to perform, the consideration is usually found to be inadequate. Here, the employee was under no pre-existing duty to enter the competition, and certainly under no obligation to win. Thus, this answer choice is incorrect.

Explanation: Question 94

The correct answer is: **(B)** No, because the court will set a reasonable price if reference to conformation is inadequate to do so.

UCC section 2-305(1)(a) permits the parties to omit any specification of price, to agree later, or to link price to an objective standard; and if price is omitted or the two options fail, provides that the price shall be a reasonable one at the time of delivery. Thus, since the parties' attempt to link price to the standard of conformation has apparently failed, the court will establish a reasonable price to be paid for the wedding cake.

(A) Incorrect. No, because an arbitrator will be appointed by the court to settle the dispute between the parties.

The mechanism by which a dispute over price is settled, if the parties cannot agree, is for the court to establish a reasonable price. The UCC makes no provision for arbitration of such matters. Thus, this answer choice is incorrect.

(C) Incorrect. Yes, because the parties may not leave an essential contract term to be agreed upon later.

This answer choice is incorrect because the UCC does not consider price an essential term, the absence of which will render a contract unenforceable. The parties have the various options mentioned, the failure of all of which will simply require the court to set a reasonable price.

(D) Incorrect. Yes, because both parties are not merchants.

The UCC occasionally requires merchants to follow special rules of behavior not otherwise applicable to persons selling goods. One way of thinking of this situation is to divide all UCC transactions into three levels of regulation: 1) The basic level applies generally, in the absence of any special circumstances, to all buyers and sellers; 2) Where one of the parties is a merchant, the second level of regulation applies [see, e.g., UCC section 2-205]; 3) When both parties are merchants, the third level is invoked [see, e.g., UCC section 2-207(2)]. This is a distractor intended to make the student think that the rule permitting omission of the price term applies only to the third level of regulation, between merchants. Since this is not the case, this answer choice is inaccurate.

Explanation: Question 95

The correct answer is: **(C)** No, because the college called the applicant before it received the applicant's letter and contract.

Under the mailbox rule, an acceptance is generally effective upon dispatch. Thus, had the applicant merely mailed the contract, the applicant's acceptance of the college's offer would have been effective upon his mailing of the contract on June 28, and a valid contact would have been formed on that date. However, because the applicant expressly stated that his acceptance of the contract would be effective when the college notified him it had received his letter and contract, the mailbox rule does not apply. Given that the college revoked its offer before the applicant effectively accepted it, no enforceable contract was formed.

(A) Incorrect. Yes, because the contract was formed when the applicant sent the contract to the college.

This answer choice is incorrect, because a contract was never formed: the applicant expressly stated that the applicant's acceptance of the contract would not be effective until the college notified the applicant it had received the contract. It is true that under the mailbox rule, an acceptance is generally effective upon dispatch. However, because the applicant expressly stated that his acceptance of the contract would be effective when the college notified him it had received his letter and contract, the mailbox rule does not apply and no enforceable contract was ever formed.

(B) Incorrect. Yes, because the contract was formed when the applicant signed the contract.

While the applicant's signing of the contract indicated his intent to accept the college's offer, it did not create an enforceable contract. In this case, the applicant expressly stated that his acceptance of the contract would be effective when the college notified him it had received his letter and contract. Thus, the college was within its rights to revoke its offer before the applicant accepted the position, and no enforceable contract was ever formed.

(D) Incorrect. No, because the contract will not be completed within one year of its formation.

While contracts that will not be completed within one year of formation fall within the Statute of Frauds, the contract in this question is already in writing. Therefore, this answer is incorrect.

Explanation: Question 96

The correct answer is: **(D)** No, because the telegram from the aunt revoked her offer.

Any offer creates the power of acceptance until the offer is terminated. However, an offer can be revoked any time prior to acceptance. A revocation of an offer is effective when the offeree receives it. Here, the aunt's letter indicated that the actor's acceptance would be effective when she received it. While the actor attempted to accept the offer by sending his letter of acceptance, the aunt had not received this acceptance at the time that she sent the actor the telegram revoking the offer. Therefore, the aunt's telegram validly terminated her offer, and no enforceable contract between the aunt and the actor was ever formed.

(A) Incorrect. Yes, once the aunt receives his reply in Manhattan.

This answer is incorrect, because the aunt had already revoked her offer through her telegram before she received the actor's acceptance and thus no contract was ever formed. An offer can be revoked any time prior to acceptance, and the revocation of an offer is effective when the offeree receives it. While the actor attempted to accept the offer by sending his letter of acceptance, the aunt had not received this acceptance at the time that she sent the actor the telegram revoking the offer. Therefore, the aunt's telegram validly terminated her offer, and no enforceable contract between the aunt and the actor was ever formed.

(B) Incorrect. Yes, because his acceptance was effective once he sent his letter by express delivery.

In the common law era, the only practical means of acceptance were mail or hand-delivery. Therefore, a default rule was created whereby an acceptance was deemed effective as soon as it was dispatched by the offeree (putting the risk of loss or delay on the offeror). Because so many means of communication exist today, the new default rule is that an offeree is impliedly authorized to use any reasonable channel for communicating his or her acceptance, and this acceptance is generally effective upon dispatch. However, this default rule applies only where the offer does not contain clear terms as to what would constitute acceptance. Here, the aunt's letter specified that acceptance would be effective upon receipt of the actor's acceptance, not upon dispatch. Therefore, the default dispatch rule does not apply.

(C) Incorrect. No, because his failure to send his response by mail as directed caused the offer to lapse.

This answer is incorrect, because the offer did not lapse: instead, the aunt properly revoked the offer before receiving the actor's acceptance. While the actor attempted to accept the offer by sending his letter of acceptance, the aunt had not received this acceptance at the time that she sent the actor the telegram revoking the offer. Therefore, the aunt's telegram validly terminated her offer, and no enforceable contract between the aunt and the actor was ever formed.

Explanation: Question 97

The correct answer is: **(A)** Yes, because the warm coat kept the student from freezing.

This is the correct answer option. Minors may form contracts, but their obligations are voidable. Disaffirmance is accomplished by words or deeds that objectively signify the election to avoid liability. Disaffirmance can occur prior to performance or even afterwards. Until the disaffirmance, the contract is binding. Typically, when a minor disaffirms after performance, she must restore any goods or benefits still in her possession. If the goods have been damaged or have depreciated, the restitution obligation extends no further than returning them as now. A minor who receives services is under no obligation to make restitution. However, the only exception is where the minor has received necessities such as food, shelter, clothing, or medical attention. While a minor may disaffirm a contract for necessities, she will remain liable for the reasonable market value of any necessity that cannot be returned in as received condition. Here, when the student mailed the coat back to the gift shop manager with a note saying, Thanks for the coat, but I do not want to buy it, she effectively signified the election to avoid liability, thereby disaffirming the contract. However, given that a storm was approaching, the student was freezing, and she was offered the coat in order to keep her from becoming sick, the coat is most appropriately categorized as a necessity. As such, the student is free to disaffirm her contract to purchase the coat and return it to the gift shop, but she remains liable for the reasonable market value of the warm jacket, since the torn coat is a necessity that cannot be returned in as received condition.

(B) Incorrect. No, because the restitution obligation extends no further than returning the jacket to the gift shop as now.

This is not the correct answer choice. Typically, when a minor disaffirms a contract after performance, she must restore any goods or benefits still in her possession. If the goods have been damaged or have depreciated, the restitution obligation extends no further than returning them as now. The only exception to this rule is for contracts involving goods or services that are necessities such as food, shelter, clothing and medical attention. While a minor may disaffirm a contract for necessities, she will remain liable for the reasonable market value of any necessity that cannot be returned in as received condition. Here, when the student mailed the coat back to the gift shop manager with a note saying, Thanks for the coat, but I do not want to buy it, she effectively signified the election to avoid liability for the cost of the jacket, thereby disaffirming the contract. However, the exception applies to these facts. A bad storm was approaching, the student was freezing, she was offered the coat in order to prevent her from becoming sick, and the coat is most appropriately categorized as a necessity under these circumstances. Thus, while the student is free to disaffirm her contract to purchase the coat, she remains liable for the reasonable market value of the damaged coat, since the necessity cannot be returned in as received condition.

(C) Incorrect. No, the contract was never binding.

This is not correct. At common law, the age of majority was 21 years old; it has been lowered in many states to 18. Minors may form contracts, but their obligations are voidable. In this case, the student was free to form a contract with the gift shop owner to send the money to pay for the warm jacket. At common law, a minor's disaffirmance of a contract is accomplished by words or deeds that objectively signify the election to avoid liability. Disaffirmance can occur prior to performance or even afterwards. Until the disaffirmance, the contract is binding. Thus, the student's contract to buy the jacket was indeed binding, until she sent the note to the gift shop manager effectively disaffirming the contract.

(D) Incorrect. No, she effectively disaffirmed the contract.

This is not the correct answer choice. The minor student would be free to disaffirm the jacket purchase contract. She was able to form the contract to buy the coat, but her obligations are voidable. The student could disaffirm the contract by her words or deeds that would objectively signify the election to avoid liability, such as her note to the gift shop manager that stated, Thanks for the coat, but I do not want to buy it. The student's disaffirmance could occur prior to the performance of receiving the coat, or even afterwards. Until her disaffirmance, the contract to purchase the jacket would be binding upon her. Since the minor student disaffirmed after performance, she was obligated to restore any goods or benefits still in her possession and return the coat to the ski lodge gift shop. The damaged jacket sleeve depreciated the value of the coat, so the minor student's restitution obligation extends further than the common law duty of returning the coat as now. The minor student received the jacket as a necessity, because of the sudden freeze; therefore she would be obliged to pay for the market value of the jacket. Necessities such as food, shelter, clothing, or medical attention are the exception to the rule, and while a minor may disaffirm a contract for necessities, she will remain liable for the reasonable market value of any necessity that cannot be returned in as received condition.

Explanation: Question 98

The correct answer is: **(C)** The customer's letter was a proper acceptance of the florist's offer, effective upon the customer's mailing of the letter.

The common-law mailbox rule is the rule in every American jurisdiction except the federal court of claims. The mailbox rule holds that acceptance of an offer for a bilateral contract by mail is effective upon dispatch, so long as the acceptance is properly posted, with the correct address and postage amount. The mailbox rule applies only to acceptances and not to any other communication between contracting parties. Once the offeree dispatches acceptance, he thereby creates a binding contract. In this case, the florist's letter to the customer constituted an offer for a bilateral contract for the purchase and sale of the customer's truck. The customer properly accepted the offer by mailing his letter of acceptance to the florist, and this acceptance was effective as of the mailing date, May 16, thereby creating a binding bilateral contract between the florist and the customer.

(A) Incorrect. Upon the florist's receipt of the customer's letter, a binding unilateral contract was formed between the florist and the customer for the purchase and sale of the customer's truck.

The florist's letter to the customer constituted an offer for a bilateral contract, not an offer for a unilateral contract. An offer for a unilateral contract requests acceptance by performance of the requested act, rather than by a promise to perform. Given that the florist's letter did not request acceptance by performance, it was not an offer for a unilateral contract. Moreover, because an offer for a unilateral contract requires acceptance by performance, a letter purporting to accept an offer for a unilateral contract would not constitute a proper acceptance of the offer. For these reasons, this answer is incorrect.

(B) Incorrect. Upon the mailing of the customer's letter, a binding unilateral contract was formed between the florist and the customer for the purchase and sale of the customer's truck.

An offer for a unilateral contract requests acceptance by performance of the requested act, rather than by a promise to perform. Here, given that the florist's letter did not request acceptance by performance, it was not an offer for a unilateral contract. Moreover, because an offer for a unilateral contract requires acceptance by performance, a letter purporting to accept an offer for a unilateral contract would not constitute a proper acceptance of the offer. For these reasons, this answer is incorrect.

(D) Incorrect. The customer's letter was not a proper acceptance of the florist's offer, because the letter requested acceptance by delivery of the truck to the flower shop by May 20.

An offer for a unilateral contract requests acceptance by performance of the requested act, rather than by a promise to perform. Thus, if the florist's letter had requested acceptance by delivery of the truck to the flower shop on the specified date, then the customer could have accepted this offer only by performance of the act requested (that is, delivery of the truck to the flower shop on the specified date). However, the florist's letter did not request acceptance by performance. Therefore, acceptance by performance was not required, and the customer's letter of May 16 was sufficient to accept the florist's offer for a bilateral contract. Note also that under the mailbox rule, this acceptance was effective upon the dispatch of the customer's letter on May 16.

Explanation: Question 99

The correct answer is: **(C)** No, because the student was a minor at the time that the course of dealing began, and hair coloring is not a necessity.

While minors may enter into contracts, their contracts are voidable, barring certain exceptions or circumstances, as in contracts for necessities (e.g., food, clothing, medical services). Minors may also, upon their attainment of the age of majority, disaffirm contracts entered into during their minority. Here, it is unclear whether the student entered into any agreement with the hair salon to pay for its services. However, even if she did, hair coloring does not constitute a necessity and, as such, her agreement (if any) with the salon does not fall within the exception to the rule allowing minors to disaffirm contracts.

(A) Incorrect. Yes, because the student is no longer a minor and is therefore liable for her own debts.

Even upon their attainment of the age of majority, parties may, within a reasonable period of time, disaffirm contracts entered into during their minority. In this instance, the teenager's disaffirmance of her contract (if any) with the salon took place within one month of her 18th birthday, which is likely to be considered a "reasonable" period of time. Furthermore, the contract, if any, was for hair coloring, which does not constitute a legal necessity. Thus, this answer is incorrect.

(B) Incorrect. Yes, because the student contracted for a necessity and is liable, even though she was a minor at the time the services were provided.

While minors may enter into contracts, their contracts are voidable upon the minor's disaffirmance, barring certain exceptions, such as contracts for necessities (e.g., food, clothing, and medical services). Hair coloring, however, does not constitute a necessity. Thus, this answer is incorrect.

(D) Incorrect. No, because the student's mother is the primary obligor.

It is unclear from the facts whether the teenager's mother promised the salon to cover these costs. (Of course, without proper authorization, the teenager may not contract on behalf of her mother.) Thus, the likelihood of success of the teen's argument that her mother is the rightful obligor is questionable. Therefore, this answer is incorrect.

Explanation: Question 100

The correct answer is: **(C)** the contractor, because he was unaware of the subcontractor's mistake and had no reason to know of it.

Traditionally, one party's unilateral mistake as to an element of the contract would justify rescission only if the other party knew or reasonably should have known of the mistake and took advantage of the mistaken party's error. This choice identifies this principle in the context of the question. Because the contractor was unaware of and had no reason to know of the subcontractor's accounting error, such a unilateral mistake does not authorize the subcontractor to rescind the contract that was formed when the contractor accepted his sub-bid. (A modern approach to unilateral mistakes permits the mistaken party to rescind if (1) the mistake goes to a basic assumption of the contract; (2) the mistake would impose an unconscionable hardship on the mistaken party; and (3) the hardship to the mistaken party from enforcement of the contract outweighs the detriment to the non-mistaken party caused by rescission. There is nothing in the facts to indicate that the hardship of the $50,000 mistake would be unconscionable or any less detrimental to the contractor than to the subcontractor.)

(A) Incorrect. the subcontractor, because the error deprives him of the benefit of the bargain of his contract.

The fact that the subcontractor's error costs him the benefit of his bargain, which probably means his profit, is not alone enough to justify rescission based on his unilateral mistake. Under the traditional rule for unilateral mistakes, because the contractor did not know, nor have reason to know of the subcontractor's error, the subcontractor may not rescind. Thus, this answer is incorrect.

(B) Incorrect. the subcontractor, because his unilateral mistake deprives the parties of the meeting of the minds necessary for formation of a contract.

A unilateral mistake of the kind made by the subcontractor does not rob the parties of mutual assent, because both agreed to what they thought were the terms of the contract, and neither was mistaken as to what those terms were. The mistake of one party as to the basis for his proposed contract terms has no effect on the mutual assent as to those terms. Thus, this answer is incorrect.

(D) Incorrect. the contractor, because a unilateral mistake can never be the basis for rescission.

This choice goes too far and is an inaccurate statement of law. A unilateral mistake can be the basis for rescission by the mistaken party if the non-mistaken party knows or should have known of the mistake and takes advantage of it, or if the more modern conditions for rescission are present. Thus, this answer is incorrect.

1. OFFER AND ACCEPTANCE

O = Offeror **E = Offeree** **K = Contract**

- **OFFER** — *Statement that (1) reasonably appears to indicate a willingness (2) to be presently bound (3) to a definite commitment (4) upon E's acceptance.*
  - **REASONABLE APPEARANCE** — objective test, applies even to offers made in jest or anger
  - **PRESENTLY BOUND**
    - **NOT EXPRESSION OF FUTURE INTENT OR INTEREST (e.g., request for quotation).**
    - **ADVERTISEMENTS** — generally deemed to be "invitations to an offer" unless quantity is specific, the language of promise is present, and the promise is unlikely to be over-accepted.
  - **DEFINITENESS**
    - **AMBIGUITIES** — construed against O.
    - **ESSENTIAL TERMS**
      - **Parties**
      - **Subject Matter**
      - **Quantity**
      - **Price** — if unstated, UCC implies reasonable price at time of delivery, payment due at time and place buyer receives goods.
      - **Time for Performance** — if unstated, UCC implies reasonable time at seller's place of business.
  - **OFFEREE'S ACCEPTANCE** — formation of the K in the hands of E; no further act by O required.

- **MANNER OF ACCEPTANCE**
  - **MEDIUM** — unless O unambiguously indicates otherwise, offer may accepted by *any medium*.
  - **PERFORMANCE**
    - **BILATERAL CONTRACT** —where offer may be accepted by a return promise, E may also accept by performing, but must inform O that he or she is doing so.
    - **UNILATERAL CONTRACT** — if offer specifically calls for performance (not a mere promise), E must actually complete performance to accept; mere preparation not enough.
  - **SILENCE** — usually an offer cannot be accepted by silence unless previous dealings imply such an acceptance is acceptable.

(continued)

1. OFFER AND ACCEPTANCE *(continued)*

OFFEREE'S RESPONSE

- **UNEQUIVOCAL ACCEPTANCE** — unequivocal acceptance forms a contract upon dispatch ("mailbox rule").
- **EQUIVOCAL ACCEPTANCE: PROPOSING NEW TERMS**
  - **COMMON LAW** — proposal of new terms (not mere inquiries for a better offer) makes acceptance invalid and acts as a *counteroffer* (i.e., a rejection).
  - **UCC** — a "definite and seasonable" acceptance that proposes new but *not inconsistent* terms still forms a K; O may accept or reject new terms.
  - **UCC MERCHANT'S RULE** —*between* merchants, if E proposes new but *not inconsistent* terms, K *includes new terms unless:* (1) O explicitly objects to new terms, (2) new terms materially alter original offer, or (3) offer expressly limited to O's terms
- **REJECTION** — terminates offer when *received* by O.
- **COUNTEROFFER** — operates as a rejection when *received* by O and terminates original offer.
- **INDECISION** — offer remains open until terminated by O or lapse of time.

TERMINATION OF OFFER

- **REVOCATION** — offer terminates when E *receives notice* of O's revocation *in spite of express promise not to revoke unless:*
  - **Paid-for Option** — promise to keep offer open supported by consideration.
  - **UCC Firm Offer** — a merchant's promise to keep offer for the sale of goods open is enforceable without consideration
- **REJECTION** — an express rejection or counteroffer terminates an offer *upon receipt.*
- **INDIRECT REVOCATION** — unaccepted offer terminates when E *learns* of acts by O inconsistent with offer.
- **LAPSE OF TIME** — unaccepted offer expires upon lapse of time stated in offer or after the expiration of a "reasonable time."
- **DEATH OR INSANITY** — unaccepted offer terminates when E *learns* of O's death or insanity.
- **DESTRUCTION OF SUBJECT MATTER** — offer terminates when subject matter of offer is destroyed.
- **INTERVENING ILLEGALITY** — offer legal when made terminates if illegal before acceptance.

2. THIRD-PARTY BENEFICIARIES

DEFINITIONS

Promisee-Benefactor (X) ← **Promisor (Y)**

↓ (from X) ↙ (from Y)

Third-Party Beneficiary (Z)

ISSUE SPOTTING SEQUENCE

THIRD-PARTY BENEFICIARIES: *Contractual rights created in a third person at the time of formation:*

- **STATUS OF BENEFICIARY** *What was the parties' intent with regard to any benefit conferred upon Z?*
  - **INCIDENTAL BENEFICIARY** — if the parties had no specific intent or motive to confer a benefit on Z.
  - **DONEE BENEFICIARY** — if the parties intended to confer a gratuitous gift on Z.
  - **CREDITOR BENEFICIARY** — if the parties intended to confer a benefit on Z to satisfy a pre-existing debt or obligation.
- **RIGHTS OF BENEFICIARY** *If a party fails to perform, what rights does Z have?*
  - **INCIDENTAL BENEFICIARY** — no rights against either Y or X.
  - **DONEE BENEFICIARY** — Z's rights *vest* upon knowledge of X-Y contract (some states require reliance)
    - **Against Y** — Z stands in shoes of X in suit against Y.
    - **Against X** — Z may prevent X from rescinding X-Y contract but may not sue X if Y fails to perform.
  - **CREDITOR BENEFICIARY** — Z's rights vest upon his reliance on X-Y contract.
    - **Against Y** — Z stands in shoes of X in suit against Y.
    - **Against X** — Z may sue X on original obligation, disregarding X-Y contract (unless there was a novation).

3. CONTRACT REMEDIES

- **MONEY DAMAGES** — normal remedy; should place non-breaching party in position he or she would have been in had the contract been performed.
  - **Restitution** — recovery of money already paid to breaching party (less possible *quantum meruit* offset).
  - **Reliance Costs** — recovery of out-of-pocket expenses in preparing to perform.
  - **Incidental Costs** — recovery of costs necessitated by breach directly relating to the contract itself (e.g., shipping, storage, inspection, reselling or repurchasing).
  - **Expected Bargained-For Benefit** — *not* including anticipated profits (see consequential costs).
    - **SALES CONTRACTS** — difference between the market price at the time of breach and the contract price.
    - **SERVICE CONTRACT**
      - **Employee** — full contract price *if* he or she has performed or stands ready to do so (*less* mitigation).
      - **Employer** — recovery limited to costs of replacement.
  - **Consequential Costs and Losses** — money damages resulting from special situation of non-breaching party (*not* including mental anguish or inconvenience).
    - **FORESEEABLE** — reasonably foreseeable costs and losses contemplated by both parties at the time of the contract may be recovered.
    - **MITIGATION** — non-breaching party's recovery must be reduced if he or she fails to take reasonable efforts to reduce costs of breach.
  - **Liquidated Damages** — contractual provision setting the total amount of all money damages in the event of breach
    - **REASONABLE AMOUNT** — amount must be reasonable in light of parties' contemplations at the time of contract.
    - **NECESSARY** — amount of actual damages must be difficult to ascertain.
    - **TAILORED TO CONTRACT** — provision must be tailored to nature of contract (i.e., *not* boilerplate).
  - **Punitive Damages** — only available in extreme cases of malicious or intentional breach (like a separate tort recovery).

3. CONTRACT REMEDIES *(continued)*

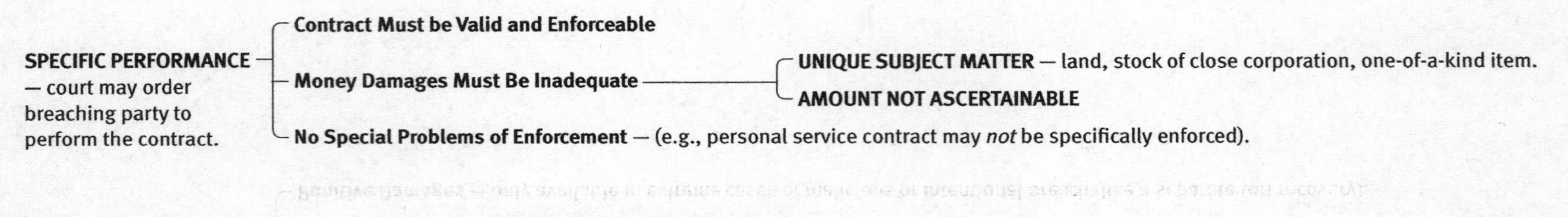

SPECIFIC PERFORMANCE — court may order breaching party to perform the contract.

- **Contract Must be Valid and Enforceable**
- **Money Damages Must Be Inadequate**
  - **UNIQUE SUBJECT MATTER** — land, stock of close corporation, one-of-a-kind item.
  - **AMOUNT NOT ASCERTAINABLE**
- **No Special Problems of Enforcement** — (e.g., personal service contract may *not* be specifically enforced).

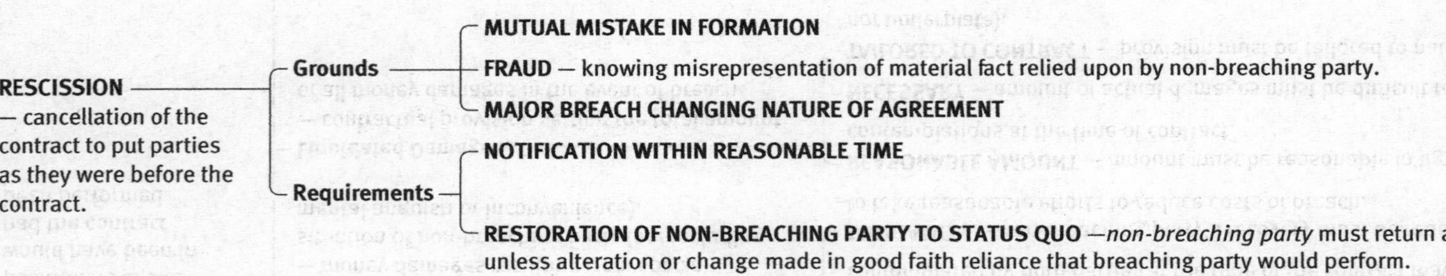

RESCISSION — cancellation of the contract to put parties as they were before the contract.

- **Grounds**
  - **MUTUAL MISTAKE IN FORMATION**
  - **FRAUD** — knowing misrepresentation of material fact relied upon by non-breaching party.
  - **MAJOR BREACH CHANGING NATURE OF AGREEMENT**
- **Requirements**
  - **NOTIFICATION WITHIN REASONABLE TIME**
  - **RESTORATION OF NON-BREACHING PARTY TO STATUS QUO** —*non-breaching party* must return all consideration unless alteration or change made in good faith reliance that breaching party would perform.

REFORMATION — court may reform contract to accurately describe the actual agreement if there was a mutual mistake.

QUASI-CONTRACT — an alternative theory for money damages based on equity rather than contract.

pmbr

Real Property

Practice Questions

Answer Grid

1 Ⓐ Ⓑ Ⓒ Ⓓ	21 Ⓐ Ⓑ Ⓒ Ⓓ	41 Ⓐ Ⓑ Ⓒ Ⓓ	61 Ⓐ Ⓑ Ⓒ Ⓓ	81 Ⓐ Ⓑ Ⓒ Ⓓ
2 Ⓐ Ⓑ Ⓒ Ⓓ	22 Ⓐ Ⓑ Ⓒ Ⓓ	42 Ⓐ Ⓑ Ⓒ Ⓓ	62 Ⓐ Ⓑ Ⓒ Ⓓ	82 Ⓐ Ⓑ Ⓒ Ⓓ
3 Ⓐ Ⓑ Ⓒ Ⓓ	23 Ⓐ Ⓑ Ⓒ Ⓓ	43 Ⓐ Ⓑ Ⓒ Ⓓ	63 Ⓐ Ⓑ Ⓒ Ⓓ	83 Ⓐ Ⓑ Ⓒ Ⓓ
4 Ⓐ Ⓑ Ⓒ Ⓓ	24 Ⓐ Ⓑ Ⓒ Ⓓ	44 Ⓐ Ⓑ Ⓒ Ⓓ	64 Ⓐ Ⓑ Ⓒ Ⓓ	84 Ⓐ Ⓑ Ⓒ Ⓓ
5 Ⓐ Ⓑ Ⓒ Ⓓ	25 Ⓐ Ⓑ Ⓒ Ⓓ	45 Ⓐ Ⓑ Ⓒ Ⓓ	65 Ⓐ Ⓑ Ⓒ Ⓓ	85 Ⓐ Ⓑ Ⓒ Ⓓ
6 Ⓐ Ⓑ Ⓒ Ⓓ	26 Ⓐ Ⓑ Ⓒ Ⓓ	46 Ⓐ Ⓑ Ⓒ Ⓓ	66 Ⓐ Ⓑ Ⓒ Ⓓ	86 Ⓐ Ⓑ Ⓒ Ⓓ
7 Ⓐ Ⓑ Ⓒ Ⓓ	27 Ⓐ Ⓑ Ⓒ Ⓓ	47 Ⓐ Ⓑ Ⓒ Ⓓ	67 Ⓐ Ⓑ Ⓒ Ⓓ	87 Ⓐ Ⓑ Ⓒ Ⓓ
8 Ⓐ Ⓑ Ⓒ Ⓓ	28 Ⓐ Ⓑ Ⓒ Ⓓ	48 Ⓐ Ⓑ Ⓒ Ⓓ	68 Ⓐ Ⓑ Ⓒ Ⓓ	88 Ⓐ Ⓑ Ⓒ Ⓓ
9 Ⓐ Ⓑ Ⓒ Ⓓ	29 Ⓐ Ⓑ Ⓒ Ⓓ	49 Ⓐ Ⓑ Ⓒ Ⓓ	69 Ⓐ Ⓑ Ⓒ Ⓓ	89 Ⓐ Ⓑ Ⓒ Ⓓ
10 Ⓐ Ⓑ Ⓒ Ⓓ	30 Ⓐ Ⓑ Ⓒ Ⓓ	50 Ⓐ Ⓑ Ⓒ Ⓓ	70 Ⓐ Ⓑ Ⓒ Ⓓ	90 Ⓐ Ⓑ Ⓒ Ⓓ
11 Ⓐ Ⓑ Ⓒ Ⓓ	31 Ⓐ Ⓑ Ⓒ Ⓓ	51 Ⓐ Ⓑ Ⓒ Ⓓ	71 Ⓐ Ⓑ Ⓒ Ⓓ	91 Ⓐ Ⓑ Ⓒ Ⓓ
12 Ⓐ Ⓑ Ⓒ Ⓓ	32 Ⓐ Ⓑ Ⓒ Ⓓ	52 Ⓐ Ⓑ Ⓒ Ⓓ	72 Ⓐ Ⓑ Ⓒ Ⓓ	92 Ⓐ Ⓑ Ⓒ Ⓓ
13 Ⓐ Ⓑ Ⓒ Ⓓ	33 Ⓐ Ⓑ Ⓒ Ⓓ	53 Ⓐ Ⓑ Ⓒ Ⓓ	73 Ⓐ Ⓑ Ⓒ Ⓓ	93 Ⓐ Ⓑ Ⓒ Ⓓ
14 Ⓐ Ⓑ Ⓒ Ⓓ	34 Ⓐ Ⓑ Ⓒ Ⓓ	54 Ⓐ Ⓑ Ⓒ Ⓓ	74 Ⓐ Ⓑ Ⓒ Ⓓ	94 Ⓐ Ⓑ Ⓒ Ⓓ
15 Ⓐ Ⓑ Ⓒ Ⓓ	35 Ⓐ Ⓑ Ⓒ Ⓓ	55 Ⓐ Ⓑ Ⓒ Ⓓ	75 Ⓐ Ⓑ Ⓒ Ⓓ	95 Ⓐ Ⓑ Ⓒ Ⓓ
16 Ⓐ Ⓑ Ⓒ Ⓓ	36 Ⓐ Ⓑ Ⓒ Ⓓ	56 Ⓐ Ⓑ Ⓒ Ⓓ	76 Ⓐ Ⓑ Ⓒ Ⓓ	96 Ⓐ Ⓑ Ⓒ Ⓓ
17 Ⓐ Ⓑ Ⓒ Ⓓ	37 Ⓐ Ⓑ Ⓒ Ⓓ	57 Ⓐ Ⓑ Ⓒ Ⓓ	77 Ⓐ Ⓑ Ⓒ Ⓓ	97 Ⓐ Ⓑ Ⓒ Ⓓ
18 Ⓐ Ⓑ Ⓒ Ⓓ	38 Ⓐ Ⓑ Ⓒ Ⓓ	58 Ⓐ Ⓑ Ⓒ Ⓓ	78 Ⓐ Ⓑ Ⓒ Ⓓ	98 Ⓐ Ⓑ Ⓒ Ⓓ
19 Ⓐ Ⓑ Ⓒ Ⓓ	39 Ⓐ Ⓑ Ⓒ Ⓓ	59 Ⓐ Ⓑ Ⓒ Ⓓ	79 Ⓐ Ⓑ Ⓒ Ⓓ	99 Ⓐ Ⓑ Ⓒ Ⓓ
20 Ⓐ Ⓑ Ⓒ Ⓓ	40 Ⓐ Ⓑ Ⓒ Ⓓ	60 Ⓐ Ⓑ Ⓒ Ⓓ	80 Ⓐ Ⓑ Ⓒ Ⓓ	100 Ⓐ Ⓑ Ⓒ Ⓓ

1. Titles – Title Assurance System: Recording Acts: Priorities
2. Rights in Land – Crops
3. Rights in Land – Easements, Profits, and Licenses
4. Rights in Land – Easements, Profits, and Licenses
5. Contracts – Creation and Construction: Statute of Frauds and Exceptions
6. Ownership – Present Estates: Defeasible Fees
7. Rights in Land – Covenants at Law and in Equity: Termination
8. Rights in Land – Covenants at Law and in Equity
9. Public Dedication Offering
10. Rights in Land – Easements, Profits, and Licenses
11. Rights in Land – Covenants at Law and in Equity
12. Rights in Land – Covenants at Law and in Equity
13. Rights in Land – Covenants at Law and in Equity
14. Ownership – Special Problems: Rule Against Perpetuities
15. Ownership – Cotenancy: Severance
16. Rights in Land – Easements, Profits, and Licenses
17. Titles – Transfer by Operation of Law and by Will: Lapse
18. Contracts – Creation and Construction: Remedies for Breach
19. Contracts – Marketability of Title
20. Mortgages – Foreclosure: Deficiency and Surplus
21. Rights in Land – Crops
22. Rights in Land – Easements, Profits, and Licenses
23. Rights in Land – Covenants at Law and in Equity: Creation
24. Mortgages – Transfers by Mortgagor: Distinguishing "Subject to" and "Assuming"
25. Rights in Land – Easements, Profits, and Licenses
26. Rights in Land – Covenants at Law and in Equity
27. Rights in Land – Covenants at Law and in Equity

28. Rights in Land – Easements, Profits, and Licenses
29. Rights in Land – Easements, Profits, and Licenses
30. Rights in Land – Easements, Profits, and Licenses
31. Rights in Land – Easements, Profits, and Licenses
32. Rights in Land – Easements, Profits, and Licenses
33. Rights in Land – Easements, Profits, and Licenses
34. Rights in Land – Lateral and Subjacent Support
35. Ownership – Cotenancy: Alienability, Descendability, Devisability
36. Rights in Land – Easements, Profits, and Licenses
37. Rights in Land – Covenants at Law and in Equity
38. Rights in Land – Covenants at Law and in Equity
39. Rights in Land – Zoning
40. Rights in Land – Zoning
41. Rights in Land – Easements, Profits, and Licenses
42. Ownership – Cotenancy: Relations Among Cotenants
43. Eminent Domain
44. Ownership – Cotenancy: Severance
45. Mortgages – Foreclosure: Deficiency and Surplus
46. Ownership – Cotenancy: Alienability, Descendability, Devisability
47. Ownership – Present Estates: Defeasible Fees
48. Titles – Adverse Possession
49. Titles – Adverse Possession
50. Mortgages – Transfers by Mortgagor: Distinguishing "Subject to" and "Assuming"
51. Mortgages – Types of Security Devices: Purchase Money Mortgages
52. Rights in Land – Easements, Profits, and Licenses
53. Ownership – Cotenancy: Alienability, Descendability, Devisability
54. Rights in Land – Water Rights

55. Ownership – Cotenancy: Severance
56. Ownership – Special Problems: Rule Against Perpetuities
57. Rights in Land – Easements, Profits, and Licenses
58. Titles – Adverse Possession
59. Titles – Adverse Possession
60. Ownership – Present Estates: Defeasible Fees
61. Ownership – Special Problems: Rule Against Perpetuities
62. Rights in Land – Covenants at Law and in Equity: Scope
63. Rights in Land – Covenants at Law and in Equity: Scope
64. Rights in Land – Covenants at Law and in Equity: Scope
65. Rights in Land – Covenants at Law and in Equity: Scope
66. Titles – Transfer by Deed: Need for a Grantee and Other Deed Requirements
67. Titles – Special Problems: Forged Instruments
68. Ownership – Special Problems: Rule Against Perpetuities
69. Ownership – Landlord/Tenant: Termination
70. Ownership – Landlord/Tenant: Types of Holdings: Creation and Termination
71. Ownership – Landlord/Tenant: Termination
72. Ownership – Landlord/Tenant: Termination
73. Ownership – Landlord/Tenant: Habitability and Suitability
74. Ownership – Landlord/Tenant: Types of Holdings: Creation and Termination
75. Rights in Land – Water Rights
76. Forged Deeds
77. Marketable Title
78. Emblements
79. Trade Fixtures
80. Implied Reciprocal Servitudes
81. Easements By Implication

82. Deeds
83. Marketable Title
84. Deeds
85. Duty to Repair
86. Tenant's Duties
87. Assumption of the Mortgage
88. Mortgage Defenses
89. Statute of Frauds
90. Foreclosure Sales
91. Damages
92. Recording
93. Recording
94. Recording Acts
95. The Shelter Rule
96. Mortgages
97. Marketable Title
98. Statute of Frauds
99. Tenancies
100. Statute of Frauds

1. On February 1, a man conveys his orchard to a gardener, and the gardener duly records the conveyance. The following day, the gardener conveys the property to a landscaper; she does not record her deed. Then on February 4, the gardener executes an identical conveyance of the orchard to a friend. The friend gives the gardener a check for $100,000 for the property and records the conveyance, even though he has actual knowledge of the prior conveyance to the landscaper. The landscaper, however, records her deed on February 6. The friend then conveys his interest in the farm to an investor, who gives a purchase price of $115,000 to the friend. On February 5, the investor purchases the farm without notice of the conveyance to the landscaper and duly records the deed.

   Suppose that the jurisdiction in which the property is located has a pure race statute as their deed recordation law.

   Under these circumstances, which of the aforementioned parties would ultimately prevail?

   (A) The investor.
   (B) The landscaper.
   (C) The friend.
   (D) The gardener.

2. A deed executed by a woman in 2001 conveyed a tract of land for a consideration of one dollar, receipt of which was acknowledged, "to my friend for life, but if liquor is ever sold on the tract of land, then to my cousin and his heirs, and if for any reason the interest hereby conveyed to my cousin is not valid, then I reserve the right to re-enter the tract of land and take back my property." In 2004, the friend died intestate before the wheat he had planted could be harvested.

   Who is entitled to the proceeds of the crop?

   (A) The friend's heirs.
   (B) The cousin.
   (C) The woman.
   (D) Divided equally between the friend's heirs and the woman.

3. A widower was the record owner of a lemon grove, a 30-acre parcel of land in a suburb. The widower lived in a farmhouse on the lemon grove and used the property to raise produce. Adjoining the lemon grove directly to the west was a 10-acre farm that was owned in fee simple by a farmer. There was a four-lane highway that adjoined the lemon grove directly to the east.

   The widower, by way of gift, executed a deed naming his daughter as grantee. The deed granted to the daughter and her heirs an antebellum mansion located near the southern edge of the lemon grove. The antebellum mansion was accessible by a little-used road that ran west to east from the farm/grove border to the four-lane highway along the southern boundary of the grove. The daughter recorded her deed and took immediate possession of the property. A short while later, the daughter and the farmer fell in love and began seeing each other quite frequently. In order for the farmer to reach the daughter's house, it was necessary for him to travel over the little-used road across the lemon grove.

   Many years later, the farmer, who was still having an affair with the daughter, met her father at a Rotary Club meeting. They struck up a conversation, and the widower asked the farmer, "Have you been driving your pickup along that little-used back road on my property?" The farmer, who was afraid to tell the widower about his love affair with the daughter, responded with a half-truth, "Yes, I've been using it as a shortcut to the four-lane highway." Unaware that the farmer was also using the path to get to the antebellum mansion to see the daughter, the widower said, "No problem, I just wanted to be sure that it was you who was using the road."

   Thereafter, the widower found out about his daughter's relationship with the farmer. Infuriated, the widower confronted the farmer and told him, "Listen, you lying sneak, if I catch you on my property again, I'm going to have you arrested for trespass." The farmer replied, "Sorry, Pops, but I've acquired an easement over that roadway, and I'll continue to use it anytime I want." Then, the widower institutes an appropriate action to enjoin the farmer from using the roadway across the lemon grove.

   If the widower prevails, it will be because the farmer's use was

   (A) fraudulent.
   (B) permissive.
   (C) not continuous.
   (D) not open and notorious.

4. A landowner was the record owner of a 30-acre orchard outside the city. The landowner lived in a farmhouse on the orchard and used the property to raise produce. Adjoining the orchard directly to the west was a 10-acre vineyard that was owned in fee simple by a farmer. A four-lane highway adjoined the orchard directly to the east.

The farmer discovered that the southern portion of the orchard was rarely used by the landowner for any of the landowner's farming activities and found a convenient gravel road leading from the vineyard across the orchard all the way to the four-lane highway. The farmer used this road adversely and openly for the entire 20-year prescriptive period, and in doing so, the farmer has acquired a prescriptive easement over the roadway across the orchard. Thereafter, the farmer conveys the vineyard to a buyer in fee simple. The deed recited that "the grantor hereby conveys the vineyard, together with an easement for the right of way across the orchard, to the grantee."

After the buyer took possession of the vineyard, the landowner brought an appropriate action to prevent him from using the roadway across the orchard.

The issue that will determine the outcome of this suit is whether

(A) the description in the farmer's deed to the buyer was adequate to identify the portion of the orchard that the farmer used as a roadway.
(B) the buyer will make excessive use of the roadway.
(C) easements can be reserved to third parties.
(D) the easement was appurtenant.

5. A 73-year-old widower owned a 40-acre farm. The widower had two children, a son and a daughter. After the daughter married, she and her husband lived on the farm in a small cottage. From 1985 to 1989, the daughter and the husband helped the widower farm and maintain the property. The widower, whose health was deteriorating, needed the services of the daughter and her husband in order to continue to live on the farm. In December 1989, the daughter told the widower that she and her husband were planning to move out of state. Worried that he could not survive without their help, the widower said to the daughter, "Please don't ever leave. I'm totally dependent on you and your husband. If you stay and continue to care for me and help with the farming, the farm will be yours when I die." The daughter turned down a job offer in a neighboring state and decided to do as the widower requested. For nine years, the daughter cared for her father while her husband handled most of the farming operations. In 1998, the widower died intestate with the daughter and the son as his only surviving heirs. The period required to acquire title by adverse possession in the jurisdiction is seven years.

In an appropriate action to determine the legal and equitable rights of the daughter and the son, respectively, in the farm, the result will depend upon the application of the principles of and exceptions to the

(A) statute of frauds.
(B) parol evidence rule.
(C) law for adverse possession.
(D) doctrine of resulting trusts.

6. A land development company was the owner of a 400-acre tract of land in the Great Lakes region. Over the course of time, the land development company developed two residential subdivisions of the land, an eastern development and a western development, each of which contained 150 acres. These subdivisions were created by separate plats that made no reference to each other. The restrictions in the plats were, however, substantially identical. The plats and each deed provided that "the use of the land herein conveyed is restricted to single-family dwellings only, and this covenant is intended to apply to each and every lot in the subdivision and runs with the land, binding every lot owner, his heirs, and assigns."

After all but four lots in each subdivision had been sold by the land development company, it sold 50 acres of the remaining 100 acres of land to a country club by a deed containing the following provisions:

"This deed is executed and accepted with the understanding that the property above described is hereby restricted so that

(1) said property may be used as a country club, with a golf course, pool, tennis courts, club house, eating facilities, and other improvements appropriate to a country club.
(2) said property may also be subdivided and platted as a residential subdivision similar to the eastern development and the property shall thereafter be used in accordance with and conveyed subject to residential restrictions that shall conform with those restrictions in force against the eastern development.
(3) the restrictions herein contained shall be deemed covenants running with the land, and for breach of any covenant herein, grantor–land development company, its successors and assigns may, at its option, re-enter and terminate the estate conveyed hereby."

At the time of this conveyance, the land development company retained title to the remaining 50 acres in the original 400-acre tract.

Which of the following would best describe the country club's interest in the 50-acre tract that it purchased from the land development company?

(A) Fee simple determinable.
(B) Fee simple subject to condition subsequent.
(C) Determinable fee subject to an executory interest.
(D) Easement appurtenant.

7. A land-development company was the owner of a 400-acre tract of land in the Southwest. Over the course of time, the land-development company developed two residential subdivisions of the land, an eastern tract and a western tract, each of which contained 150 acres. These subdivisions were created by separate plats that made no reference to each other. The restrictions in the plats were, however, substantially identical. The plats and each deed provided that "the use of the land herein conveyed is restricted to single-family dwellings only, and this covenant is intended to apply to each and every lot in the subdivision and runs with the land, binding every lot owner, his heirs, and assigns."

After all but four lots in each subdivision had been sold by the land-development company, it sold 50 acres of the remaining 100 acres of land to a country club by a deed containing the following provisions:

"This deed is executed and accepted with the understanding that the property above described is hereby restricted so that

(1) said property may be used as a country club, with a golf course, pool, tennis courts, club house, eating facilities, and other improvements appropriate to a country club.
(2) said property may also be subdivided and platted as a residential subdivision similar to the eastern tract and the property shall thereafter be used in accordance with and conveyed subject to residential restrictions that shall conform with those restrictions in force against the eastern tract.
(3) the restrictions herein contained shall be deemed covenants running with the land, and for breach of any covenant herein, the land-development company, its successors and assigns may, at its option, re-enter and terminate the estate conveyed hereby."

At the time of this conveyance, the land-development company retained title to the remaining 50 acres in the original 400-acre tract. Thereafter, the land-development company developed an exclusive shopping center on 25 acres of the retained land. In February 2001, the land-development company sold the remaining eight residential lots in the eastern tract and the western tract. The next month, the land-development company executed the following instrument to the country club:

"The land-development company, for itself, its successors, and assigns, does hereby release, surrender and quitclaim all rights, title, or other property interest in that certain acres owned by the country club."

At the time this instrument was executed, the country club had built a club house, golf course, and tennis courts on a portion of its land, and it had 25 acres of vacant land remaining. The country club wishes to commence construction of a new high-rise complex (containing a hotel, shopping mall, apartments, etc.) on the 25 acres of vacant land it possesses.

In an action by one of the homeowners in the western tract to enjoin construction of the complex, plaintiff will most likely

(A) succeed, because the homeowner (or any other landowner in the eastern tract or the western tract) as assignee of the land development company could re-enter the land upon breach of condition subsequent.
(B) succeed, because a common development scheme had been established for the entire 400-acre tract, and the country club's proposed complex would constitute a non-conforming use.
(C) not succeed, because the land development company's instrument of March 2001 effectuated an abrogation of the deed restrictions on the country club's use of its property.
(D) not succeed, because in accordance with deed restriction (b), only a homeowner in the eastern tract would have standing to challenge the country club's proposed construction plan.

8. A land-development company was the owner of a 400-acre tract of land. Over the course of time, the land-development company developed two residential subdivisions of the land, an eastern subdivision and a western subdivision, each of which contained 150 acres. These subdivisions were created by separate plats that made no reference to each other. The restrictions in the plats were, however, substantially identical. The plats and each deed provided that "the use of the land herein conveyed is restricted to single-family dwellings only, and this covenant is intended to apply to each and every lot in the subdivision and runs with the land, binding every lot owner, his heirs, and assigns."

After all but four lots in each subdivision had been sold by the land-development company, it sold 50 acres of the remaining 100 acres of land to a country club by a deed containing the following provisions:

"This deed is executed and accepted with the understanding that the property above described is hereby restricted so that

(1) said property may be used as a country club, with a golf course, pool, tennis courts, club house, eating facilities, and other improvements appropriate to a country club.

(2) said property may also be subdivided and platted as a residential subdivision similar to the eastern subdivision and the property shall thereafter be used in accordance with and conveyed subject to residential restrictions that shall conform with those restrictions in force against the eastern subdivision.

(3) the restrictions herein contained shall be deemed covenants running with the land, and for breach of any covenant herein, the land development company, its successors, and assigns may, at its option, re-enter and terminate the estate conveyed hereby."

At the time of this conveyance, the land-development company retained title to the remaining 50 acres in the original 400-acre tract. Within a few months of the execution of this deed, the country club had built a club house, golf course, and tennis courts on a portion of its land, and it had 25 acres of vacant land upon which it wished to build a complex containing a hotel and shopping mall surrounded by high-rise buildings and luxury apartments.

With respect to the 50-acre tract that the country club purchased from the land-development company, which of the following most accurately describes the deed restrictions (1) and (2)?

(A) Affirmative covenant(s).
(B) Equitable easement(s).
(C) Express easement(s) appurtenant.
(D) Equitable servitude(s).

9. In 1995, an investor purchased a 100-acre tract located in a rural county. Shortly thereafter, the investor prepared a subdivision plan, which created 90 one-acre residential building lots on this tract with the remaining 10-acre lot proposed for a public school building. In the investor's sales brochure promoting the subdivision, he stated that "in addition to the close proximity of the proposed school for subdivision residents, the county school district would not need to expend tax money to acquire this property for school construction." In 1996, the subdivision plan was recorded with the county recorder's office.

During the next few years, the investor sold 50 residential lots to individual purchasers.

In 2002, the investor conveyed the remaining 40 lots and the 10-acre tract to a builder by deed that included language identical to that contained in the first 50 deeds. By 2007, the builder had sold all of the 40 lots. Each of these deeds identified each lot as being a part of the subdivision. On January 9, 2008, the builder sold the 10-acre tract to a buyer. This deed made no mention of the subdivision.

On January 15, 2008, the county school board voted to build a new school on the 10-acre tract. Two weeks later, the buyer began construction of a pizzeria on the 10-acre tract.

In an action by the school board against the buyer to enjoin construction of the pizzeria on the 10-acre tract, the court would grant judgment for

(A) the buyer, because his own deed made no mention of the subdivision.
(B) the buyer, because the dedication was not made to the public in general.
(C) the school district, because the 10-acre tract was designated for public use.
(D) the school district, because the 10-acre tract constituted an equitable servitude.

10. In 2006, an investor purchased a 100-acre tract located in a rural county. Shortly thereafter, the investor prepared a subdivision plan that created 90 one-acre residential building lots on this tract with the remaining 10-acre lot proposed for a public school building. In the investor's sales brochure promoting the subdivision, he stated that "in addition to the close proximity of the proposed school for subdivision residents, the county school district would not need to expend tax money to acquire this property for school construction." In 2007, the subdivision plan was recorded with the county recorder's office.

On January 15, 2009, the county school board voted to build a new school on the 10-acre tract.

The investor's proposed designation of the 10-acre tract for construction of a school building would best be described as a(n)

(A) equitable servitude.
(B) restrictive covenant.
(C) unenforceable restriction.
(D) easement for public use.

11. In 1995, a developer purchased a 100-acre tract located in a northern county of a state. Shortly thereafter, the developer prepared a subdivision plan that created 100 one-acre residential building lots on this tract. In 1996, the subdivision plan was recorded with the county recorder's office.

During the next few years, the developer sold 60 residential lots to individual purchasers. Each deed specified that every lot designated on the subdivision plan was to be recorded in the county recorder's office. Each deed also provided the following: "No house trailer or mobile home shall be built or maintained on any lot within the subdivision."

In 2002, the developer conveyed the remaining 40 lots to a builder by deed that included language identical to that contained in the first 60 deeds. By 2007, the builder had sold all of the 40 lots. Each of these deeds identified each lot as being a part of the subdivision, but did not include the clause relating to mobile homes.

On January 30, 2008, a man who had purchased one of the residential lots from the builder placed a mobile home on his property. A woman who owns a lot in the subdivision initiates suit against the man to force him to remove the mobile home.

Which of the following would be the most accurate statement of law?

(A) There is no enforceable restriction because the mobile-home provision did not "run with the land."
(B) There is no enforceable restriction because the man's deed did not include the mobile-home provision.
(C) The mobile-home restriction would be enforceable because a common development scheme had been established for the entire subdivision.
(D) The outcome turns on whether a common development scheme had been organized for the entire subdivision.

12. In 1996, a developer purchased a 100-acre tract located in a northern county in a state. Shortly thereafter, the developer prepared a subdivision plan that created 100 one-acre residential building lots on this tract. In 1997, the subdivision plan was recorded with the county recorder's office.

During the next few years, the developer sold 60 residential lots to individual purchasers. Each deed specified that every lot designated on the subdivision plan was to be recorded in the county recorder's office. Each deed also provided the following: "No house trailer or mobile home shall be built or maintained on any lot within the subdivision."

In 2003, the developer conveyed the remaining 40 lots to a builder by deed that included language identical to that contained in the first 60 deeds. This deed from the developer to the builder was recorded. By 2008, the builder had sold all of the 40 lots. Each of these deeds identified each lot as being a part of the subdivision, but did not include the clause relating to mobile homes.

On January 30, 2009, a buyer, who had purchased one of the residential lots from the builder, placed a mobile home on his property.

Which of the following statements is LEAST accurate with respect to the buyer's deed?

(A) The covenant prohibiting mobile homes ran with the land as far as the builder, but not as far as the buyer.
(B) The covenant prohibiting mobile homes could be enforced by any subdivision lot owner.
(C) The buyer should have had constructive notice of the restriction against mobile homes.
(D) All subsequent grantees of the builder would be in privity of estate.

13. In 1996, an investor purchased a 100-acre tract located in a northern county of a state. Shortly thereafter, the investor prepared a subdivision plan that created 100 one-acre residential building lots on this tract. In 1997, the subdivision plan was recorded with the county recorder's office.

During the next few years, the investor sold all 100 residential lots to individual purchasers. Each deed specified that every lot designated on the subdivision plan was to be recorded in the county recorder's office. Each deed also provided the following: "No lot shall be used except for residential purposes." By 2009, the area surrounding the subdivision was rezoned for commercial and business uses. One of the lot owners now decides to operate a small beauty parlor in the basement of her home.

In an action by the homeowners in the subdivision to prevent such commercial use, the court will most likely hold that

(A) the residency restriction is no longer enforceable because of the change in the character of the neighborhood surrounding the development.
(B) the residency restriction is no longer enforceable because the area surrounding the development was rezoned for commercial use.
(C) the residency restriction is enforceable, thus preventing any commercial use.
(D) the operation of a beauty parlor would not constitute a violation of the residency restriction.

14. A lawyer owned a 70-acre tract of land. In 1989, the lawyer sold 15 acres of the tract to a friend. The deed of conveyance contained the following clause:

"The parties hereby covenant that if the grantor (the lawyer) proposes to sell any or all of the remaining 55 acres of the tract during (the friend's) lifetime, then the grantee shall have the right of first refusal to purchase said parcel on the same terms and conditions as proposed; and, in the alternative, if grantee (the friend) proposes to sell any or all of the 15 acres of his parcel during (the lawyer's) lifetime, then (the lawyer) shall have the reciprocal right of first refusal."

The friend was approached by a co-worker who offered to purchase his 15-acre parcel for $100,000. The friend did not afford the lawyer an opportunity to exercise his right of first refusal, and he went ahead and sold the property to the co-worker. After the co-worker took possession, the lawyer then learned about the sale. The lawyer immediately brought suit against the friend and the co-worker to enforce the right of first refusal in the deed.

Based on the facts as presented, the lawyer will

(A) win, because the friend has a reciprocal right of first refusal.
(B) win, because the lawyer's right of first refusal does not violate the Rule against Perpetuities because it is limited to his lifetime.
(C) lose, because the rights of first refusal are unreasonable restraints on alienation.
(D) lose, because the rights of first refusal relate only to land that is not conveyed by deed.

15. A retiree was the record title owner in fee simple absolute of a 100-acre farm. In 1998, the retiree devised the property to his daughter and his friend as joint tenants with right of survivorship. The next year, the daughter executed a deed to a co-worker as follows:

"I hereby convey all of my right, title, and interest in the northeast quarter of the farm to the co-worker and his heirs."

Thereafter, the daughter borrowed $100,000 from a lender, and a promissory note was executed as evidence of the debt. In 2008, the daughter defaulted on the loan, and the lender, as judgment creditor, levied upon and sold to his nephew on execution sale all of "(the daughter's) right, title and interest in the south half of the farm." In December 2009, the daughter died intestate, leaving her husband as her sole surviving heir.

Who owns the farm?

(A) The friend and the co-worker are tenants in common of the northeast quarter of the farm; the friend and the husband are tenants in common of the northwest quarter of the farm; and the friend and the nephew are tenants in common of the south half of the farm.
(B) The friend and the co-worker are tenants in common of the northeast quarter of the farm; the friend is the owner in fee of the northwest quarter of the farm; and the friend and the nephew are tenants in common of the south half of the farm.
(C) The friend and the co-worker are tenants in common of the northeast quarter of the farm; the friend and the husband are tenants in common of the northwest quarter of the farm; and the nephew is the owner in fee of the south half of the farm.
(D) The friend and the co-worker are tenants in common of the northeast quarter of the farm; and the friend is the owner in fee of the remaining three-quarters of the farm.

16. A student acquired a 357-acre cattle ranch by inheritance from her father. In 2001, the student conveyed 57 acres of the cattle ranch tract to a buyer. As indicated in the diagram below, the 57-acre tract was not contiguous to any highway or public road. The deed from the student to the buyer conveyed the 57 acres and stated that the parcel would be used "for the purpose of building a home" and also stated that the buyer would receive "access to the land herein conveyed over the main trail across the cattle ranch." The main trail is owned and maintained by the student.

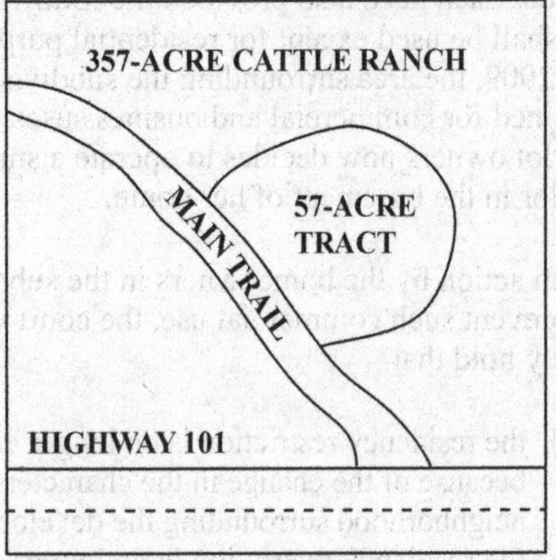

After the buyer took possession of his parcel, he built a home on the premises. Because no electrical power extended to his property, the buyer installed underground electrical wires to obtain electricity. The electrical wires extended beneath the main trail for a distance of approximately three miles.

After the underground lines were installed, the student brought an appropriate action against the buyer demanding payment for the right to make affirmative use of the land beneath the main trail.

If the court rules against the student and holds that the buyer has the right to maintain such electrical wires without any payment to the student, it will most likely be because

(A) use of the main trail for installation of the electrical wires is within the scope of the easement contained in the deed instrument.
(B) the buyer has an easement by implication because the main trail was in existence at the time of the conveyance to the buyer.
(C) an easement in gross is established by necessity for the benefit of the quasi-dominant tenement owner.
(D) there was an apparent and continuous prior use of the main trail by the student before the severance of ownership.

17. A widow was the owner in fee simple of an apartment building. The widow drafted a will by which she devised the apartment building to her granddaughter with residue to her friend and her assistant. One year later, the granddaughter died intestate and was survived by her son who was her sole heir at law.

This jurisdiction has the following statute in effect: "If a devisee of a grandparent or lineal descendant of a grandparent dies at the time of execution of the will or fails to survive the testator, the issue of the deceased person shall take the decedent's share under the will."

The widow then died and her will was admitted to probate. A dispute arose among the friend, the assistant, and the son regarding ownership of the apartment building.

Is the son entitled to any share or interest in the apartment building?

(A) Yes, because under the anti-lapse statute, the granddaughter's interest passes to her son.
(B) Yes, because rules relating to lapse of class gifts do not apply to specific devises.
(C) No, because intestate succession is inapplicable to devolution of title to specific devisees.
(D) No, because the granddaughter predeceased the widow, title to the apartment building passes to the friend and assistant under the residuary clause of the will.

18. A farmer was the record title owner of a 30-acre tract of farmland. The farmer lived out of state and rarely visited the farmland, which remained unoccupied. Adjoining the farmland was a 50-acre ranch, which was owned by a rancher. In 2004, the rancher forged the farmer's signature on a deed and purported to convey the farmland to a grocer. The grocer paid the rancher $100,000 as the purchase price for the farmland.

The following year, the grocer sold the property to a buyer for $125,000. The deed from the grocer to the buyer was properly executed and recorded by the buyer.

This jurisdiction has the following "pure race" recording statute in effect:

"No conveyance or other instrument is valid as against purchasers for a valuable consideration who record first."

After the buyer took possession of the farmland, he renovated the farmhouse that was located on the property and made improvements valued at $50,000. In 2006, the farmer returned to visit his sister. During his visit, the farmer went to the farmland to inspect his farmland. While doing so, he encountered the buyer, who informed the farmer that he was the new owner of the property.

The farmer thereupon instituted suit to quiet title to the farmland. After judgment was rendered in the farmer's favor, the buyer was ejected from the property. The buyer has now filed an appropriate action against the grocer seeking restitution for the loss he incurred with respect to the purchase and improvements made on the farmland.

The buyer will likely recover

(A) nothing, because the grocer was also a fraud victim and suffered a substantial financial loss.
(B) $25,000.
(C) $50,000.
(D) $125,000.

19. A veterinarian was the owner in fee of a 50-acre tract of farmland. The veterinarian contracted to sell her property to an investor for $300,000. The parties signed a written land-sale agreement that provided for 30 monthly installment payments of $10,000 each. According to the terms of the sale agreement, the veterinarian would deliver a warranty deed to the investor upon payment of the last installment. In accordance with state law, the farmland's land-sale agreement was properly recorded.

After making the first 10 installment payments, the investor discovered that there was an unrecorded mortgage on the farmland. The veterinarian, who is the mortgagor, has regularly made her mortgage payments and is not in default. This jurisdiction has the following recording statute in effect:

"No conveyance or instrument is good as against any subsequent purchaser for value and without notice, unless the same be recorded prior to subsequent purchase."

After the investor learned of the outstanding mortgage, he discontinued making further installment payments to the veterinarian. The investor alleged that the veterinarian was in breach of the land-sale agreement due to the existence of the unrecorded mortgage. The investor sues the veterinarian for breach of contract.

If judgment is rendered in favor of the veterinarian, it will be because

(A) the installment land-sale agreement is a security device.
(B) although the land-sale agreement is actually a mortgage, it does not impair the investor's right of redemption.
(C) the prior mortgage has no legal effect on the investor's rights under the installment land-sale agreement.
(D) the time for the veterinarian, as seller, to deliver marketable title has not yet arrived.

20. A landowner was the record title owner of a three-acre tract of land. In order to finance the purchase of the property in 2005, the landowner borrowed $100,000 from the bank, which secured the loan with a mortgage that amortized principal and interest payments over a 15-year period. The bank promptly recorded the mortgage. This jurisdiction has the following recording statute in effect:

"Any unrecorded conveyance or mortgage is invalid as against a subsequent *bona fide* purchaser for value without notice who records first."

In 2006, the landowner subdivided the property into three one-acre lots. He sold lot 1 to his friend for $75,000. The following year, the landowner sold lot 2 to his brother for $60,000. The landowner continued to reside on lot 3. When the landowner sold lots 1 and 2 to the friend and the brother, the deeds did not make any reference to the original mortgage between the landowner and the bank.

In 2009, the landowner was laid off from his job and went into default on his mortgage payments. The bank is now about to institute foreclosure proceedings.

Which of the following most accurately states the rights and obligations of the parties?

(A) The bank can foreclose only on lot 3 because ownership to that parcel is retained by the landowner, the original mortgagor.
(B) The bank has the option of foreclosing on parcels 1, 2, or 3 because the mortgage covered the entire three-acre tract.
(C) The bank must first foreclose on lot 3, and if the proceeds are insufficient, then the mortgagee may foreclose against lots 1 and 2 in the inverse order of their alienation.
(D) The bank can foreclose on lot 3, but not on lots 1 and 2 unless the friend and the brother assumed the mortgage when they purchased their land from the landowner.

21. A retiree owned a 100-acre farm. For many years, the retiree grew tobacco on a 10-acre strip located in the northeast section of the property. In March, the retiree planted his annual tobacco crop, which he usually harvested in early October. In September, the retiree sold his farm to a tobacco grower for $100,000. At the time the retiree conveyed the property to the grower, the tobacco crop was well developed and quite mature. When the retiree and the grower entered into their land-sale agreement, there was no mention of the status or ownership of the tobacco crop.

In early October, after the grower took possession of the property, the retiree contacted him and requested permission to harvest and remove the tobacco crop. The grower refused to allow the retiree to re-enter the property.

The retiree brings suit against the grower seeking to re-enter the property and remove the tobacco crop that he had planted.

Which of the following is correct regarding the respective rights of the parties?

(A) The retiree is entitled to remove the tobacco crop, but he must pay the grower a reasonable value to enter the property, thus gaining access to the crop.
(B) The retiree is entitled to remove the tobacco crop and is not required to pay the grower for entering the property, thus gaining access to the crop.
(C) The retiree is not entitled to remove the tobacco crop and, thus, is not entitled to re-enter the property.
(D) The retiree and the grower each have a colorable title to the tobacco crop, and consequently, there should be an equitable division of the proceeds from the sale of the crop between both parties.

22. An attorney, a botanist, a chemist, and a dentist own adjoining properties. All four are enthusiastic badminton players. They have decided that instead of having each person construct his own badminton court, it would make much more sense if they all could get together to build a set of courts in one place with all parties having equal rights to use them. The parties envision a court layout as appears in the diagram below:

(A)	(B)	(C)	(D)
Attorney	Botanist	Chemist	Dentist
Proposed Access			Proposed Access
	Proposed Badminton Courts		

The parties want the courts physically to occupy part of the botanist's and part of the chemist's land, but they want the attorney and the dentist to have equal right of access to, and use of, the courts with the botanist and the chemist.

Which of the following devices would most likely accomplish the implementation of their proposed badminton court layout and be most readily acceptable to the parties?

(A) A covenant against partition.
(B) An indenture granting cross-easements.
(C) An equitable servitude.
(D) A fee simple upon condition subsequent.

23. Jacqueline, Jessica, Jonathan, and Julianne own adjoining properties. All four are enthusiastic cat lovers. The four neighbors are frustrated at only being able to find "dog parks," without finding a single place for their cats to play. The four neighbors decided to get together to build a fenced-in "cat park" with four fenced sides and a fenced "ceiling" where each person could bring her or his cats to play out in the open with the cats of the other neighbors. The four neighbors decide to place this cat park in the middle of all four properties with all four parties having equal rights to use the park. The parties decided to construct the park in the manner that appears in the diagram below. After the park is constructed, the parties plan to grant each other cross-easements while granting Jacqueline and Julianne (the dominant tenants) the right to enter and use the property of Jessica and Jonathan (the servient tenants).

(A)	(B)	(C)	(D)
Jacqueline	Jessica	Jonathan	Julianne
Proposed Access			Proposed Access
Proposed "Cat Park"			

If the parties want to set up some mechanism to insure that the construction and maintenance costs of the park will be shared fairly among all of the parties, the best way to arrange this is by

(A) an affirmative covenant.
(B) a cooperative organization.
(C) co-ownership in tenancy in common.
(D) implied reciprocal servitudes.

24. A citrus grower was the owner in fee of two adjacent parcels of land in a city: an orange grove and a lemon grove. The grower's title to the lemon grove was subject to an unrecorded 20-year mortgage given to the mortgagee, a bank, in 1990 to secure repayment of a loan for $100,000.

Beginning in November 1993, the following events occurred:

November 1993: The grower died, leaving all of her real property to her husband. The grower's will was admitted to probate. No mention was made of the mortgage given to the bank.

December 1993: Having heard about the grower's death, the bank recorded its mortgage to the lemon grove.

August 1994: The husband executed and delivered to his sister a mortgage deed on the orange grove, which the sister immediately recorded. The mortgage instrument contained the following recitations: "This mortgage is secured by the orange grove and all other real estate that I may own in the city or have an interest in." The husband defaulted on his mortgage obligation to the sister; the amount due on the debt was $100,000.

February 2009: The bank brought suit against the husband to foreclose its mortgage on the lemon grove.

The applicable recording statute provides in part: "No deed or other instrument in writing, not recorded in accordance with this statute, shall affect the title or rights to, in any real estate, of any devisee or purchaser in good faith, without knowledge of the existence of such unrecorded instruments."

Judgment should be for

(A) the husband, if he was unaware of the existence of the mortgage at the time he acquired title to the lemon grove.
(B) the husband, only if the lemon grove was not subject to the mortgage when he acquired title.
(C) the bank, because the husband assumed the mortgage when he acquired title to the lemon grove.
(D) the bank, because property once mortgaged remains mortgaged as against the mortgagor's successors in interest.

25. A developer, owner of several hundred acres in a rural part of the county, drafted a general development plan for the area. The duly recorded plan imposed elaborate limitations and restrictions upon the land in the plan, which was to be developed as a residential district. The restrictions were to extend to all persons acquiring any of the lots and to their heirs, assigns, and lessees. It was further provided that all subsequent owners would be charged with due notice of the restrictions.

Among those restrictions in the general plan were the following:

(22) A franchise right is created in a strip of land 10 feet in width along the rear of each lot for the use of public utility companies with right of ingress and egress.

(23) No house or structure of any kind shall be built on the aforementioned strip of land running through the said blocks.

The franchise right created for public utility companies would most likely be an example of a(n)

(A) license.
(B) equitable servitude.
(C) easement appurtenant.
(D) easement in gross.

26. A developer, owner of several hundred acres in a rural county, drafted a general development plan for the area. The duly recorded plan imposed elaborate limitations and restrictions upon the land in the plan, which was to be developed as a residential district. The restrictions were to extend to all persons acquiring any of the lots and to their heirs, assigns, and lessees. It was further provided that all subsequent owners would be charged with due notice of the restrictions.

Among those restrictions in the general plan were the following:

(22) A franchise right is created in a strip of land 10 feet in width along the rear of each lot for the use of public utility companies with right of ingress and egress.

(23) No house or structure of any kind shall be built on the aforementioned strip of land running through the said blocks.

The court will most likely construe restriction (23) as a(n)

(A) negative easement.
(B) equitable servitude.
(C) affirmative covenant.
(D) fee simple absolute.

27. On October 1, 1980, a developer, owner of several hundred acres in a rural county, drafted a general development plan for the area. The duly recorded plan imposed elaborate limitations and restrictions upon the land in the plan, which was to be developed as a residential district. The restrictions were to extend to all persons acquiring any of the lots and to their heirs, assigns, and lessees. It was further provided that all subsequent owners would be charged with due notice of the restrictions.

Among those restrictions in the general plan were the following:

(22) A franchise right is created in a strip of land 10 feet in width along the rear of each lot for the use of public utility companies with right of ingress and egress.

(23) No house or structure of any kind shall be built on the aforementioned strip of land running through the said blocks.

In 2000, a retiree purchased one of the lots, built a house, and erected a fence in the rear of his property within the restricted area. In 2004, a teacher purchased a lot adjacent to the retiree's property and built a new house. Two years later, a librarian purchased the lot that adjoined the teacher's property. The three deeds to those properties each contained references to the deed book where the general plan was recorded.

In 2008, the librarian began the construction of a seven-foot post-and-rail fence along the line dividing his lot with the teacher's, and along the center of the area subject to the franchise right. Although the teacher objected to its construction, the fence was completed.

If the teacher seeks a mandatory injunction to compel removal of the librarian's fence, the court will most likely

(A) grant relief, because the fence was in violation of the easement restriction.
(B) grant relief, because the encroachment of the fence violated the restriction in the original plan.
(C) deny relief, because the teacher failed to enforce the restriction against the retiree.
(D) deny relief, because the fence would not be construed as "a structure" within the terms of the restriction.

28. An orange grove and a grapefruit grove are two parcels abutting each other. A citrus grower owns the orange grove in fee simple and maintains both his dwelling house and the business he operates on the orange grove. He has a right of way, granted by a written agreement, across the grapefruit grove for crossing the grapefruit grove on foot, by bicycle, or automobile. A farmer is the owner of the grapefruit grove.

The citrus grower's property interest in the use of his right of way across the grapefruit grove may best be described as a(n)

(A) license.
(B) easement in gross.
(C) easement appurtenant.
(D) prescriptive easement.

29. A western parcel, a central parcel, and an eastern parcel are three business lots abutting each other, with the central parcel between the other two lots. A business owner owns the central parcel in fee simple and maintains his dwelling house thereon. He has a right-of-way, granted in a written agreement, across the eastern parcel for crossing the eastern parcel on foot, by bicycle, or automobile. A landscaper is the owner of the eastern parcel. An investor owns the western parcel and conveys it to the business owner in fee simple. The business owner then builds a 15-story office building, covering the western parcel and the central parcel, which houses 6,000 persons during working hours each day. All of these persons use the right-of-way over the eastern parcel, and the business owner uses the way for delivering as many as 30 loads of supplies per day to the office building.

In an action by the landscaper to enjoin the business owner and the office workers from using the right-of-way across the eastern parcel, the court will most likely hold that

(A) the business owner's right-of-way would be extinguished due to excessive use by the office workers.
(B) the business owner's right-of-way would be forfeited due to the unauthorized use by the office workers.
(C) the business owner, by making use of the right-of-way beyond the scope of the original privilege, would permanently be enjoined from using the servient tenement.
(D) Although the business owner may continue to use the right-of-way, the office workers would be enjoined from making such use.

30. A wedding planner owned a summer cottage on the lake. In order to facilitate the access to the cottage, which is located on a knoll above the lake, the wedding planner entered into an agreement with a neighbor, an adjoining land owner, whereby the neighbor, in writing, granted the wedding planner a right-of-way over a strip of land 30 feet in width and a quarter of a mile in length along the eastern margin of the neighbor's property. Without notifying the neighbor, the wedding planner proceeded with his plan to improve the roadbed by having the road asphalted in order to make it more accessible for motor vehicle traffic. Several years later, the neighbor started a sand business, which required him to do heavy hauling that subsequently destroyed the asphalted surface on the road.

Ten years after the neighbor started his sand business, the wedding planner sold his lakefront property to an artist. Shortly after the artist took possession of the cottage and property, the neighbor erected wooden barriers across the roadway, thus obstructing the access to the artist's property.

The interest that the wedding planner acquired in the access road may best be described as

(A) an easement in gross.
(B) an easement implied by prior use.
(C) an easement by necessity.
(D) an express easement.

31. A caterer owned a summer cottage on the lake. In order to facilitate the access to the cottage, which is located on a knoll above the lake, the caterer entered into an agreement with a neighbor, an adjoining land owner, whereby the neighbor, in writing, granted the caterer a right-of-way over a strip of land 30 feet in width and a quarter of a mile in length along the eastern margin of the neighbor's property. Without notifying the neighbor, the caterer proceeded with his plan to improve the roadbed by having the road asphalted in order to make it more accessible for motor vehicle traffic. Several years later, the neighbor started a sand business, which required him to do heavy hauling that subsequently destroyed the asphalted surface on the road.

In an action by the caterer to enjoin the neighbor's use of the road in transporting sand, the court will most likely

(A) issue an injunction against the neighbor to prevent the further use of the road to haul sand.
(B) refuse to grant the caterer's prayer for relief because the servient owner continues to have the right to use his own land.
(C) issue an injunction against the neighbor unless it can be shown that the neighbor's use did not unreasonably interfere with the caterer's right of access.
(D) dismiss the cause of action because the caterer's only remedy would be monetary damages.

32. A chef owned a summer cottage on the lake. In order to facilitate the access to the cottage, the chef entered into an agreement with a neighbor, an adjoining land owner, whereby the neighbor, in writing, granted the chef a right-of-way over a strip of land 30 feet in width and a quarter of a mile in length along the eastern margin of the neighbor's property. Without notifying the neighbor, the chef proceeded to improve the roadbed by having the road asphalted in order to make it more accessible for motor vehicle traffic. Several years later, the neighbor started a sand business, which required him to do heavy hauling that subsequently destroyed the asphalted surface on the road.

Ten years after the neighbor started his sand business, the chef sold his lakefront property to his assistant. Shortly after the assistant took possession of the cottage and property, the neighbor erected wooden barriers across the roadway, thus obstructing the access to the assistant's property.

The assistant's strongest argument in an action against the neighbor for removal of the barriers, which are obstructing his access to the property, would be that

(A) an easement appurtenant is alienable in that any conveyance transferring possession of the dominant tenement also passes the easement privilege.
(B) the assistant, as a *bona fide* purchaser, is protected from the neighbor's obstruction, even though the easement was unrecorded.
(C) because the easement was created by implication, the chef's prior and continuous use gave rise to a prescriptive easement.
(D) the chef and the assistant, being in privity of estate, could "tack on" their successive use periods.

33. A sculptor owned a summer cottage on a small lake. In order to facilitate the access to the cottage, the sculptor entered into an agreement with a neighbor, an adjoining land owner, whereby the neighbor, in writing, granted the sculptor a right-of-way over a strip of land 30 feet in width and a quarter of a mile in length along the eastern margin of the neighbor's property.

After using the roadway for a year, the sculptor and his family moved to Europe for business reasons. The sculptor and his family have not used the cottage for 11 years because of his employment commitment in Europe. During the sculptor's absence, the neighbor constructed an access ramp to his dock, which obstructed the road to the sculptor's cottage. Upon the sculptor's return from Europe, he goes to his lakefront cottage and discovers the obstructing ramp.

The sculptor initiates suit against the neighbor to compel him to remove the ramp. The court would most likely

(A) hold in the neighbor's favor, because the sculptor's absence for 11 years constituted an abandonment of the easement.
(B) hold in the neighbor's favor, because the dominant owner is under an affirmative duty to notify the servient tenement holder of non-use.
(C) hold in the sculptor's favor, because mere non-use, however long continued, will not as a rule effectuate an abandonment.
(D) hold in the sculptor's favor, because of the validity of the agreement for the express grant of the easement.

34. A musician owned a summer cottage on the lake. A neighbor, an adjoining land owner, started a sand business, which required him to do heavy hauling of sand, rocks, dirt, and other materials on his property.

The neighbor's excessive excavating in the course of conducting his sand removal business causes the collapse of a large storage building on the musician's property.

If the musician brings an action to recover damages for the collapse of his storage building, the musician will probably

(A) be successful if he can prove that the neighbor was negligent in his excavations.
(B) be successful, because the neighbor would be strictly liable for his removal of lateral support.
(C) not be successful, because the neighbor could not be held liable for damage to an artificial structure such as a storage building.
(D) not be successful, because an adjacent land owner is under no affirmative duty to laterally support his neighbor's land.

35. On March 1, 1999 a widower, the sole owner and occupant of a piece of property, died and devised the property to both his co-worker and his boss "as their community property." The co-worker and the boss were also siblings, and neither was married. The property consisted of a single-family house with a yard, garage, and driveway.

The boss died intestate on May 1, 2001, leaving her daughter as her sole heir. During her occupancy, the boss paid $3,500 each year in insurance and property taxes. In addition, the premises on the property had a fair market value during this period of $1,500 each year. Following her mother's death, the boss's daughter moved into the house on May 2, 2001. As the administratrix of the boss's estate, the daughter sought to collect from the co-worker one-half of the cost of insurance and property taxes that the boss paid.

Conversely, the co-worker claimed that he was not liable for any of the expenses. Furthermore, the co-worker's attorney advised him that the daughter did not own any interest in the property and that since the boss's death, he (the co-worker) owned the entire property. The attorney also informed the co-worker that the daughter owed him rent for the entire period of her occupancy, and if she continued to occupy the premises, then she would be liable for insurance and property taxes as well.

In an appropriate action to determine the title of the property, what, if any, interest does the daughter have in the said property?

(A) None, because the co-worker acquired title to the whole of the property by right of survivorship.
(B) An undivided one-half interest, because upon the death intestate of a tenant-in-common, the latter's interest descends to his heirs.
(C) An undivided one-half interest, because in a tenancy by the entirety, either sibling can make a testamentary disposition.
(D) An undivided whole interest, because in a joint tenancy, every joint tenant is part and parcel of the unit group that owns the whole.

36.

		Driveway
House	House	
		Garage House
LOT 3	LOT 2	LOT 1
(TEACHER)	(NEIGHBOR)	(CO-WORKER & BOSS)

On March 1, 1999, a landowner, the sole owner and occupant of lot 1, died and devised lot 1 to both his co-worker and his boss "as their community property." The co-worker and boss were siblings, and neither was married. Lot 1 consisted of a single-family house with a yard, garage, and driveway.

On May 1, 1999, the boss moved into the house on lot 1. One year later, the co-worker and the boss executed and delivered the following deed instrument to a neighbor "... hereby grant to (the neighbor) the northerly 30 feet of lot 1, consisting of the paved driveway now existing, to be used for the ingress and egress of motor vehicles, but should (the neighbor) or his heirs and assigns use said property for any other purpose, all the rights, privileges, and immunities herein granted shall cease and determine." In consideration for the said deed, the neighbor paid the co-worker and the boss $2,000 (which they divided equally). The deed was never recorded by the neighbor. Because the boss didn't own a car, she never used the driveway. Similarly, the neighbor never used the driveway because he unexpectedly had his driver's license suspended shortly after executing the above instrument.

The boss died intestate on May 1, 2001, leaving her daughter as her sole heir. Following her mother's death, the daughter moved into the house on May 2, 2001. On June 1, 2001 the neighbor sold lot 2 to a professor by a deed that contained no mention of the driveway located on lot 1. The neighbor and the professor assumed that the latter had the right to use the driveway, so they didn't insert any recitations in their deed instrument regarding the driveway. Immediately upon her taking possession of the premises, the daughter began to use the driveway on lot 1. Consequently, she objected to the professor's use of the driveway.

After the daughter refused to permit the professor to use the driveway, he brought suit to determine his right to continue use of the driveway.

The professor should

(A) win, because he acquired an implied easement to use the driveway as owner of the dominant tenement.
(B) win, because the neighbor's easement to use the driveway was conveyed to the professor.
(C) lose, because the Statute of Frauds was not satisfied.
(D) lose, because the neighbor's non-use of the driveway effectuated an abandonment of the easement.

37. In 1960, a widower, advancing into old age, realizes that he is no longer able to farm his 1,000 acres; therefore, he decides to sell some of the farmland in parcels of 250 acres. The president of a development company is interested in purchasing three of the parcels. The president buys the three parcels from the widower and begins formulating plans for constructing single-family dwelling units on the land, which is located in an upper-middle-class area of the county. The original deed between the widower and the development company contains a provision expressly binding "upon all subsequent grantees, their heirs, and assigns," stipulating that any further subdivisions by any such persons shall be restricted to minimum two-acre lots to be used for single-family dwelling units only.

In the original deed between the widower and the development company, the stipulation that restricted the size and residential character of any subsequent subdivision of the parcels is an example of a(n)

(A) easement.
(B) affirmative covenant.
(C) covenant for quiet enjoyment.
(D) negative covenant.

38. A retiree, advancing in age, realizes that he is no longer able to farm his 1,000 acres and therefore decides to sell some of the farmland in parcels of 250 acres. The president of a development company is interested in purchasing three of the four parcels. The president buys the three parcels from the retiree and begins formulating plans for constructing single-family dwelling units. The original deed between the retiree and the development company contains a provision expressly binding "upon all subsequent grantees, their heirs, and assigns," stipulating that any further subdivisions by any such persons shall be restricted to minimum two-acre lots to be used for single-family dwelling units only.

The development company immediately subdivided two of the parcels into lots of three, four, and five acres, and began construction of homes thereon. The original deed restrictions were enumerated within the special warranty deeds and were given to the purchasers of the homes in the new development, called tract 1.

Two years later, the president sold the remaining 250-acre parcel, which had not been included in the tract 1 subdivision plan, to a contractor. The deed between the president and the contractor included the same restriction as was in the original deed between the retiree and the president. The contractor, in turn, drafted a subdivision plan for the last 250-acre parcel, dividing it into one-acre lots. The contractor then commenced construction of single-family dwelling units in the new development, to be known as tract 2. There was no mention of the restriction for two-acre minimum lots in the deeds to the purchasers of the new homes in tract 2.

In a subsequent action to enjoin the contractor from subdividing the parcel into one-acre lots by any of the present owners of lots in the tract 1 development, the most probable judicial determination would be

(A) that the action should be dismissed because the owners lack standing to sue.
(B) that the action should be dismissed because there is no privity of estate between the owners of the lots in tract 1 and the contractor.
(C) that the action would be successful if tract 2 were considered by the court as part of a common development scheme.
(D) that the action would be successful because the restrictions in the original deed between the retiree and the president will be enforceable.

39. In 1998, a farmer, advancing in age, realizes that he is no longer able to farm his 1,000 acres and therefore decides to sell some of the farmland in parcels of 250 acres. The president of a development company is interested in purchasing three of the four parcels. The president buys the three parcels from the farmer and begins formulating plans for constructing single-family dwelling units on the land. The original deed between the farmer and the development company contains a provision expressly binding "upon all subsequent grantees, their heirs, and assigns," stipulating that any further subdivisions by any such persons shall be restricted to minimum two-acre lots to be used for single-family dwelling units only.

The development company immediately subdivided two of the parcels into lots of three, four, and five acres, and began construction of homes thereon. The original deed restrictions were enumerated within the special warranty deeds and were given to the purchasers of the homes in the new development, called phase 1.

Two years later, the president sold the remaining parcel, which had not been included in the phase 1 subdivision plan, to a contractor. The contractor, in turn, drafted a subdivision plan for the last 250-acre parcel, dividing it into one-acre lots. The contractor then commenced construction of single-family dwelling units in the new development, to be known as phase 2. There was no mention of the restriction for two-acre minimum lots in the deeds to the purchasers of the new homes in phase 2.

Meanwhile, after the farmer's death, his estate is required to sell the remaining 250-acre parcel of his farmland. The buyer is an investor, who proposes to construct a two-level shopping center and parking lot on the property.

The area surrounding phase 1 and phase 2 was rezoned for commercial and industrial uses in 2010. The investor's shopping center has grown to include 150 stores. Now, one of the lot owners in phase 1 contracts to sell his property to two physicians who plan to start a suburban medical practice.

In an action by the homeowners in phase 1 to prevent such commercial use by the physicians, the court will most likely hold that

(A) the restrictions are still enforceable, thus preventing such commercial use.
(B) the restrictions would no longer be enforceable, because the offering of personal services (i.e., medical) would be a conforming use.
(C) the restrictions would no longer be enforceable, because of the change in the character of the neighborhood.
(D) the restrictions would no longer be enforceable, because the opening of a physician's office in a private home would not be construed as a commercial enterprise.

40. A landowner, advancing in age, realizes that he is no longer able to farm his 1,000 acres and therefore decides to sell some of the farmland in parcels of 250 acres. The president of a development company is interested in purchasing three of the four parcels. The president buys the three parcels from the landowner and begins formulating plans for constructing single-family dwelling units on the land. The original deed between the landowner and the development company contains a provision expressly binding "upon all subsequent grantees, their heirs, and assigns," stipulating that any further subdivisions by any such persons shall be restricted to minimum two-acre lots to be used for single family dwelling units only.

The development company immediately subdivided two of the parcels into lots of three, four, and five acres, and began construction of homes thereon. The original deed restrictions were enumerated within the special warranty deeds and were given to the purchasers of the homes in the new development, called phase 1.

Two years later, the president sold the remaining parcel, which had not been included in the phase 1 subdivision plan, to a contractor. The contractor, in turn, drafted a subdivision plan for the last 250-acre parcel dividing it into one-acre lots. The contractor then commenced construction of single-family dwelling units in the new development, to be known as phase 2. There was no mention of the restriction for two-acre minimum lots in the deeds to the purchasers of the new homes in phase 2.

Meanwhile, after the landowner's death, his estate is required to sell the remaining 250-acre parcel of his farmland. The buyer is an investor, who proposes to construct a two-level shopping center and parking lot on the property. The deed for the remaining 250-acre parcel contained the identical restrictions as the deeds to the other three parcels. The investor, ignoring these restrictions, was able to use his political influence to persuade the county zoning board to rezone the said parcel for commercial use The residents of phase 1 seek to enjoin the construction of the shopping center.

The residents will have

(A) little chance of preventing the projected commercial development.
(B) no standing to enjoin the construction of the shopping center.
(C) no chance of succeeding, because the zoning ordinance takes precedence over the covenant running with the land.
(D) success in their cause of action in accordance with the common development scheme.

41. A woman inherited her father's farm when he died testate. Prior to her father's death, the woman had already taken over the operations on the father's farm due to his declining health.

Recently, the woman had granted a coal company rights to strip-mine coal from underneath the farm. Their agreement stipulated that the coal company would pay the woman a per-ton royalty for the coal extracted. In addition, the coal company agreed to fill in the excavated area and replace top soil on the surface of the land.

After the coal company commenced its strip-mining operations, the woman noticed that the company was not filling in the excavated area as previously agreed. However, because the company paid the woman all the coal royalties from the strip mining, she did not voice any objection regarding its failure to replace the top soil. Two years later, the coal company had now completed its strip-mining operation under its arrangement with the woman.

The coal company's right to strip-mine coal from the woman's property would be an example of a(n)

(A) profit a prendre.
(B) license.
(C) easement in gross.
(D) voluntary waste.

42. A man, a teenager, and a woman are siblings who inherited their father's farm when he died testate, leaving his farm to his children as joint tenants. Soon after the father's death, the teenager died and the woman moved to another part of the country. The man has not heard from the woman in many years.

Prior to their father's death, the man and the teenager operated their father's farm. They continued doing so after their father died, sharing all expenses equally and dividing the profits between them. Following the teenager's death, the man has continued to operate the farm for his sole benefit. Recently, the man has granted a coal company rights to strip-mine coal from underneath the farm. Their agreement stipulated that the coal company would pay the man a per-ton royalty for the coal extracted. In addition, the coal company agreed to fill in the excavated area and replace top soil on the surface of the land.

During the coal company's strip-mining operation, the woman returns to the farm and demands a proportionate share of the royalties paid to her brother (the man).

Which of the following is the LEAST accurate statement regarding the woman's right to share in the royalties?

(A) As a joint tenant, the woman would be entitled to contribution for a proportionate share of the royalties.
(B) It would be inequitable for one concurrent owner to receive an disproportionate share of the royalties.
(C) The woman's redomiciling constituted a severance of the joint tenancy, which resulted in a destruction of her interest in the mining royalties.
(D) Because the woman's redomiciling did not effectuate an ouster, she retained her right to contribution as a joint tenant.

43. In 1980, an attorney purchased an 80-acre tract in a rural county. The 80-acre tract included the family home, an exquisite mansion built in 1929 by a wealthy industrialist. For many years, the closest town to the tract had been in the grips of economic decline. However, in 1988 and 1989, several large corporations built plant facilities in the local area.

By the early 1990s, prosperity had burst upon the area. To take advantage of the real estate boom, the attorney divided the 80-acre tract into 160 lots. By 1995, the attorney had sold 90 lots to various individual buyers. Each deed contained the following provisions:

"It is an express covenant and condition that the property hereby conveyed shall not be used for other than single-family residences."

"The grantor hereby covenants for himself, his heirs, successors, and assigns to insert a similar restriction in all deeds to lots now owned by grantor in the 80-acre tract."

In 1996, the county board of supervisors purchased from the attorney 30 lots within the 80-acre tract. The board, which had the power of eminent domain, planned to construct a new county pest-control office on the property. The deed of conveyance from the attorney to the county board of supervisors made no mention of the aforesaid restrictions contained in the deeds to other lot owners in the 80-acre tract. The attorney–county deed, however, did contain a provision, which stated:

"The grantee hereby covenants for itself, its successors, and assigns that this conveyance is made in lieu of the exercise of the power of eminent domain."

Thereafter, the county enacted a zoning ordinance whereby the 30 lots were rezoned to permit the construction of a pest-control office building. When the county started construction, all the other lot owners in the 80-acre tract brought suit to enjoin the building plan or, in the alternative, to recover damages.

If the county board of supervisors, the named defendant, prevails on both counts, it will be because

(A) the power of eminent domain is the equivalent of the power to zone.
(B) the purchase of the 80-acre tract property by a public body with the power of eminent domain is an act of inverse condemnation.
(C) the abrogation of the right to enforce the restrictive covenant is not a compensable taking.
(D) restrictions on the use of land can be enforced only against a buyer whose deed contains the restrictions.

44. A woman owns a tract of land located in a state in the Midwest. On June 1, 2005, the woman sells to a husband and wife an undivided one-half interest in this land for $100,000 (the entire consideration being paid by the husband). The deed to the husband and wife reads as follows: "To (husband) and (wife) and their heirs as tenants by the entirety, and not as joint tenants, and not as tenants in common."

On June 1, 2006, the woman sells her remaining interest in the tract of land to the husband and his brother for $125,000 (the husband pays $80,000 of the purchase price, and the brother pays the balance). The deed to the husband and the brother provides: "To (the husband) and (the brother) and their heirs as joint tenants and not as tenants in common."

The husband conveys to his cousin all his right, title, and interest under the two deeds from the woman. The husband then dies. The brother then dies.

The cousin is thus the owner of

(A) an undivided one-third interest in the land.
(B) an undivided one-quarter interest in the land.
(C) an undivided one-half interest in the land.
(D) an undivided three-quarters interest in the land.

45. A farmer owned an olive grove. The farmer gave a friend a mortgage on the olive grove to secure a loan from the friend to the farmer in the amount of $90,000. The farmer then gave a co-worker a mortgage on the olive grove to secure a loan from the co-worker to the farmer in the amount of $120,000.

The farmer then gave an investor a mortgage on the olive grove to secure a loan from the investor to the farmer in the amount of $110,000. The co-worker then records. The investor then records. Thereafter, the friend records. In a foreclosure proceeding where the friend, the co-worker, and the investor were parties, the olive grove sold for $220,000.

The recording statute in this jurisdiction provided "any written instrument affecting title to land that is not recorded is void against a subsequent purchaser in good faith for valuable consideration, whose conveyance shall be first duly recorded."

If the olive grove sold for $220,000, what dollar amount, if any, should go to the investor?

(A) $0.
(B) $90,000.
(C) $100,000.
(D) $110,000.

46. Ann owns a tract of land. On August 1, 2005, Ann sells to Hunter and Willa, a husband and wife, an undivided one-half interest in this land for $100,000 (the entire consideration being paid by Hunter). The deed to Hunter and Willa reads as follows: "To Hunger and Willa and their heirs as tenants by the entirety, and not as joint tenants, and not as tenants in common."

On August 1, 2006, Ann sells her remaining interest in the tract of land to Hunter and Brandon, his brother, for $125,000 (Hunter pays $80,000 of the purchase price, and Brandon pays the balance). The deed to Hunter and Brandon provides: "To Hunter and Brandon and their heirs as joint tenants and not as tenants in common."

On August 1, 2007, Hunter, Willa, and Brandon die in a common disaster, and as a consequence, the order of their deaths cannot be established by proof. Hunter's will and Willa's will devise whatever interest in the land in question that is subject to disposition by their wills to their son.

Thus, the son owns

(A) an undivided one-third interest in the land.
(B) an undivided one-quarter interest in the land.
(C) an undivided one-half interest in the land.
(D) an undivided three-quarters interest in the land.

47. On May 10, 1955, a rancher, owner of a 300-acre cattle ranch in Texas, conveyed a 20-acre strip across the property as follows:

"To the railroad, its successors and assigns, to have and to hold so long as the same shall be used for railroad purposes."

In 1972, the rancher made the following conveyance:

"To my daughter and her husband and their heirs, as much of the 300-acre cattle ranch as is not described in my deed to the railroad dated May, 10, 1955."

The following year, the rancher, a widower, died intestate, survived by the daughter and a son. In 2000, the railroad decided to discontinue operating its trains over the strip conveyed in 1955.

By 2004, the growth of a nearby town had made the 300-acre cattle ranch valuable as a potential site for homes or for an industrial park. However, as of January 1, 2005, the governing body of the county (in which the ranch sits) took appropriate action, in accordance with Texas statutes, to zone the 300-acre cattle ranch as single-family residential property with a minimum lot size of one acre. The ordinance provided that the exclusion of ranching operations and industrial development was necessary to protect the health of county residents by limiting the extent of waste disposal and preventing pollution of air and the nearby river, the county's major water supply.

The state's power authority has now taken appropriate action to condemn half of the 300-acre cattle ranch, which will be flooded as a result of construction of a dam for a proposed hydroelectric facility. The 150 acres taken includes the 20-acre strip described in the deed to the railroad.

Is the railroad entitled to any compensation from the state's power authority?

(A) Yes, because if all the leased land is condemned for the full balance of the lease term, the lessee is entitled to compensation for the taking of the leasehold estate.
(B) Yes, because the holder of an easement benefit is entitled to compensation for the value lost.
(C) No, because by discontinuing its operation of trains, the railroad's determinable fee terminated.
(D) No, because the holder of an easement is not entitled to compensation when the servient tenement is extinguished by condemnation.

48. A buyer signed a contract to purchase a tract of land from a seller. The contract was signed on May 1, 2006, and the closing is set for June 15, 2006. The land was located in a jurisdiction that has in force the following statute:

Statute of Limitations—"an action to recover the possession of land shall be brought within twenty-one (21) years after the cause thereof accrued, but if a person who is entitled to bring such action at the time the cause accrued is within the age of minority (under 21) or of unsound mind, such action may be brought within ten (10) years after such disability is removed."

This statute was enacted in the jurisdiction in 1930. The land in question had been owned by a rancher in 1960. On September 1, 1960, the rancher died intestate, leaving his nephew as his only heir. The nephew had been born on October 1, 1954. In addition, there is a deed from the rancher's administrator to the seller dated November 1, 1960, which the latter recorded on the same date.

During his title search, the buyer learned that the administrator had never obtained any license to sell the land in question; and also he (the administrator) never formally received the approval of any court with respect to the administration of the rancher's estate. Moreover, the buyer ascertained that the seller entered into possession of the land in question on November 1, 1960.

On the assumption that there are no additional facts, the buyer should be advised that the seller became or will become the owner of the land in question

(A) on November 1, 1960.
(B) on November 12, 1981.
(C) on October 1, 1985.
(D) when the nephew dies.

49. A buyer signed a contract to purchase a tract of land from a developer. The contract was signed on May 1, 2008, and the closing was set for June 15, 2008. The land was located in a jurisdiction that has in force the following statute:

Statute of Limitations—"an action to recover the possession of land shall be brought within twenty (20) years after the cause thereof accrued, but if a person who is entitled to bring such action at the time the cause accrued is within the age of minority (under 21) or of unsound mind, such action may be brought within ten (10) years after such disability is removed."

This statute was enacted in the jurisdiction in 1932. The land in question had been owned by a doctor in 1962. On September 1, 1962, the doctor died intestate. The doctor's administratrix conveyed the tract to the developer on November 1, 1962, which the latter recorded on the same date.

During her title search, the buyer learned that the administratrix had never obtained any license to sell the land in question. The buyer also learned that the administratrix never formally received the approval of any court with respect to the administration of the doctor's estate. Moreover, the buyer ascertained that the developer entered into possession of the land in question on November 1, 1962.

The developer was ousted from the land in question by a woman on October 1, 1982. The developer then recovered possession of the land from the woman in an action of ejectment on December 31, 1982.

The buyer should be advised that the developer became the owner of the land in question on

(A) November 1, 1962.
(B) November l, 1982.
(C) December 31, 1982.
(D) December 31, 2002.

50. Osgood is the record owner of Desertacre, a 100-acre tract of farmland in California's Coachella Valley. Osgood inherited the property from his father and farmed the land until 2006, when he reached the age of 70. He then decided to retire and move to Scottsdale, Arizona. At that time, Osgood conveyed Desertacre to Cutler "for his use during his natural life."

After taking possession of the property, Cutler executed a mortgage on Desertacre in the amount of $100,000. In 2009, Osgood died and in his will, the testator devised Desertacre to his son, Desmond, with remainder to Deirdre. The will provided that Desmond and Deirdre took Desertacre "subject to Cutler's mortgage."

At the time of Osgood's death, Desertacre had a market value of $300,000. When Desmond learned of the devise, he was hesitant about taking title to Desertacre because he did not want to incur any indebtedness. Assume that Cutler is still alive and in possession of the tract.

With respect to the mortgage, Desmond will be

(A) liable for the mortgage, because he is the devisee under the terms of Osgood's will.
(B) liable for the mortgage, because the property was devised subject to the mortgage.
(C) not liable, because there was no assumption of the mortgage.
(D) not liable, because he did not personally grant the mortgage.

51. In 1973, a woman was the actual and record owner of 20 acres of certain undeveloped timberland. In September 1973, the woman mortgaged the 20 acres of timberland to the bank by a mortgage deed (in the traditional form of a conveyance in fee simple subject to a condition subsequent), which was not recorded until January 1974. The mortgage deed contained the following clause immediately after the legal description of the 20 acres of timberland: "Together with all the real property now owned by (the woman) or which shall be owned by (the woman) during the continuance of the indebtedness secured by this mortgage." This mortgage was given, as the recorded instrument revealed, to secure a note for $100,000 repayable over a 40-year term.

In March 2004, the woman, using money loaned by a finance company, purchased a 50-acre mountainous estate situated outside of a major city. This deed was recorded immediately. In April 2004, the woman executed and delivered to the finance company a mortgage to secure its loan. This mortgage was promptly and duly recorded. The finance company had no actual notice of the prior mortgage to the bank.

In February 2007, the woman defaulted on both mortgages. The bank then initiated foreclosure proceedings against the woman and the finance company as joint defendants. In its foreclosure action, the bank averred that its mortgage was a first mortgage on both the 20 acres of timberland and the 50-acre estate. The finance company filed a cross-complaint, alleging that its mortgage was a first mortgage on the 50-acre estate and praying for foreclosure on that parcel of property.

In order to decide this case in favor of the bank, the court does not need to resolve which of the following issues?

(A) Whether the finance company is charged with record notice of the bank's mortgage.
(B) Whether the quoted clause in the mortgage instrument to the 20 acres of timberland covers the 50-acre estate.
(C) Whether the finance company's mortgage is a purchase money mortgage.
(D) Whether the finance company can rely on the doctrine of implied purchase money liens.

52. A seller sold the eastern two-thirds of his land to a buyer, who soon thereafter constructed a house there. One year later, the buyer cleared a path from her home across the seller's retained land to a road that abuts the western boundary of the seller's land. The seller stood by and watched the buyer clear the path, but made no objection. This path is very convenient to the buyer's use of her land, and the buyer used it daily for several months. The path is readily apparent to anyone. Recently, the seller put a barrier across the path. The buyer now has brought an action to have the barrier removed.

The theory giving the buyer her best chance of success would be that

(A) the buyer has an easement by necessity. This would depend on the strength of the court's feeling about the use of the land.
(B) the buyer has an easement by implication. This would depend on whether the convenience was sufficiently strong to amount to "reasonably necessary."
(C) the buyer has an easement by prescription. This would depend on the length of time she used the path prior to the erection of the barrier.
(D) the buyer has an express easement.

53. A landowner, being fee simple owner of an apartment building, devised it "to both my assistant and my friend as tenants in common." Thereafter, the assistant died intestate, leaving his daughter as his only surviving heir. While the assistant's estate was in administration, the friend agreed to convey his interest in the apartment building to the daughter.

A valid conveyance by the friend would be

(A) to the estate of the assistant and its successors and assigns.
(B) to the heirs and assigns of the assistant.
(C) to the daughter and her heirs and assigns.
(D) to the assistant as a former tenant in common with remainder to the daughter.

54. A doctor owned a two-acre tract just outside the city. She subdivided the parcel into 12 lots, numbered 1–12, 11 of which she sold to 11 different buyers. The doctor retained lot 12 to live on. Each deed to the 11 lots sold contained the following restriction:

"It is an express covenant and condition that the property hereby conveyed shall not be used for other than single-family residences."

Two years after the doctor subdivided and sold off the parcels, the purchasers of lots 1–11 had each built residences on their property. In December of that year, the doctor dug a well on her property. From that well, the doctor supplied water to all of the lot owners. One year later, a veterinarian, who lived on the lot adjacent to the doctor's, dug a well in her backyard. Her well caused water to be diverted from the doctor's well, and the doctor is no longer able to get any water.

In an appropriate action by the doctor against the veterinarian, what remedy, if any, is available?

(A) An injunction should be decreed enjoining the veterinarian from using her well.
(B) The doctor should be entitled to recover money damages from the veterinarian.
(C) The veterinarian should be required to supply water to the doctor.
(D) There is no remedy.

55. A professor was the record owner in fee simple absolute of a 30-acre tract of land located in a small town. The professor made a conveyance thereof in these words, "I hereby convey my 30-acre tract to both my friend and my co-worker as joint tenants with right of survivorship."

Two years after making the conveyance to the friend and the co-worker, the friend executed a mortgage on the 30-acre tract of land to a bank to secure a loan. One year after executing the mortgage, the friend died intestate, leaving his uncle as his only heir. At the time of the friend's death, the indebtedness had not been paid to the bank. The jurisdiction in which the 30-acre tract of land is located recognizes a title theory of mortgages.

In an appropriate action, the court should determine that title to the 30-acre tract of land is vested

(A) in the co-worker, with the entire interest subject to the mortgage.
(B) in the co-worker, free and clear of the mortgage.
(C) half in the co-worker and half in the uncle, with both subject to the mortgage.
(D) half in the co-worker, free of the mortgage, and half in the uncle, subject to the mortgage.

56. A shopkeeper is the owner of a vacant lot in fee simple absolute (the record title is also in the shopkeeper). In 1960, the shopkeeper conveyed the property by general warranty deed as follows: "The grantor hereby conveys the vacant lot to my friend, but if the property shall ever be used for church purposes, then to the children of my sister who reach the age of 25." At the time of the conveyance, the sister was single. Thereafter, the sister married and had two sons. Subsequently, one son died in an automobile accident. Three years after that son's death, the sister had a daughter.

In an appropriate action to determine the ownership rights to the vacant lot with all minors represented, title is in

(A) the friend only.
(B) the friend, the son, and the daughter.
(C) the friend, the son, the daughter, and any additional children of the sister born during her lifetime.
(D) the friend, the son, the daughter, and any additional children of the sister born within 21 years after the death of the deceased son.

57. The city installed a sewer line across a residential subdivision. The city acquired a valid easement for construction of the sewer from the development company that owned the subdivision. One year later a buyer purchased a house within the subdivision. Unknown to the buyer, the sewer line ran across his property, approximately 10 feet beneath the foundation of his home. The deed that the buyer received from the grantor, the development company, made no mention of the easement. Ten years after the buyer purchased his house, a crack in the sewer line caused water to leak into the buyer's basement. The flooding resulted in extensive damage to his home. The city has abolished governmental immunity.

In an appropriate action by the buyer against the city to recover damages, the plaintiff will probably

(A) not prevail, because the sewer line was installed before the buyer purchased the property.
(B) not prevail, because the city had acquired a valid easement for the sewer line.
(C) prevail, only if the sewer line was negligently maintained.
(D) prevail, because under the circumstances, the sewer line constituted a public nuisance.

58. In 1985, a landowner, the undisputed owner of an apartment building, leased it to a tenant for a term of seven years. Rent was to be paid in installments due on the first day of each month. One year later, in 1986, the landowner died leaving no heirs. In her will, the landowner left her entire estate to the Girl Scouts of America. The apartment building was not specifically mentioned in the will.

One month after the landowner died, the tenant, having learned of the landowner's death, decided to remain on the property, but stopped paying rent. The Girl Scouts of America organization was unaware of the landowner's gift to the organization until 2009, when attorneys for the organization conducted an inventory of testamentary gifts to the Girl Scouts of America, which revealed that they had a claim to ownership of the apartment building. The statutory period for adverse possession in this jurisdiction is 20 years.

In an ejection action by the Girl Scouts of America against the tenant, the organization will prevail

(A) because the tenant discontinued paying rent following the landowner's death.
(B) if the tenant leased the apartment building to a teacher for three years while he (the tenant) was called into military service.
(C) if the tenant believed that his lease with the landowner was still in effect after the latter died.
(D) because the tenant never paid taxes on the apartment building.

59. In 1985, a widow, the undisputed owner of a cottage, leased it to a tenant for a term of seven years. Rent was to be paid in installments due on the first day of each month. One year later, in 1986, the widow died leaving no heirs. In her will, the widow left her entire estate to the Boy Scouts of America. The cottage was not specifically mentioned in the will.

One month after the widow died, the tenant, having learned of her death, decided to remain on the property, but stopped paying rent. The Boy Scouts of America organization was unaware that the widow made a gift to the organization until 2009, when attorneys for the organization conducted an inventory of testamentary gifts to the Boy Scouts of America, which revealed that they had a claim to ownership of the cottage. The statutory period for adverse possession in this jurisdiction is 20 years.

The tenant's statutory period for adverse possession began to run when

(A) the widow died.
(B) the tenant discontinued paying rent.
(C) the tenant's lease with the widow expired.
(D) the tenant subjectively believed that he no longer had permission to possess the cottage.

60. In his will, a jockey devised his home "to my friend to whom I am everlastingly grateful for the devoted care he has lavished on my horses, but if ever my horses who survive me shall fail to receive proper care, then to my beloved daughter and her heirs, if she be living and own any horses, otherwise to the Equestrian Society."

In an appropriate action to construe the will, the court will determine the friend's interest to be a

(A) fee simple determinable.
(B) fee simple subject to condition subsequent.
(C) fee simple subject to an executory interest.
(D) contingent remainder.

61. In his will, a veterinarian devised his home "to my friend to whom I am everlastingly grateful for the devoted care she has lavished on my prize Pomeranians, but if ever my dogs who survive me shall fail to receive proper care, then to my beloved son and his heirs, if he be living and own any dogs, otherwise to the American Society for the Protection of Animals."

Assuming that the Rule against Perpetuities is in effect in this jurisdiction, which of the following statements is correct regarding the son's interest under his father's will?

(A) It is a contingent remainder.
(B) It is an executory interest of a shifting type.
(C) It is an executory interest of a shifting type that is void under the Rule against Perpetuities.
(D) It is an executory interest of a springing type that is void under the Rule against Perpetuities.

62. A housing corporation owned farmland and prepared a development plan to divide the land into 100 lots and create a residential community on the farmland tract. The Declaration of Covenants created the community association, as an administrative entity, to which the residential community lot owners would pay dues, and which would administer and enforce the regulations and restrictions recited among the covenants. One of the restrictions set forth in the Declaration of Covenants provides that the lots be used only for single-family residences, and that no trade, commerce, or business may be conducted in any single-family residence.

The Declaration of Covenants gives the community association the right to assign all of its rights, powers, titles, easements, and estates granted to it under the Declaration of Covenants. The community association assigned "all the rights, powers, titles, easements, and estates granted to or conferred upon it by the Declaration of Covenants" to a municipal corporation, the city. The community association was then terminated. A chef, the owner of lot 18 in the residential development, proposes to convert his single-family dwelling into a massage parlor. The city asserts an action against the chef to recover money damages.

Which of the following is the best argument for the chef?

(A) The restraint on alienation of his land is invalid.
(B) The city is not in privity of estate with community association.
(C) The benefit is in gross; hence, the burden cannot run.
(D) The burden is in gross; hence, the benefit cannot run.

63. A housing corporation owned a tract of land. The housing corporation prepared a development plan to divide the land into 100 lots and create a residential community on the tract. The Declaration of Covenants created the homeowners' association, an administrative entity that would administer and enforce the regulations and restrictions recited among the covenants. One of the restrictions set forth in the Declaration of Covenants reads:

"There shall never at any time be erected, permitted, or maintained upon any part of the property any structure designed for or used as a saloon or place for the sale or manufacture of malt, vinous, or spirituous liquors."

The Declaration of Covenants was duly recorded and was included in the deed taken by a teacher when he purchased lot 62 in the development. The teacher immediately recorded his deed. The teacher leased his home to a librarian for a term of one year. The lease included the same restrictions as those in the Declaration of Covenants and in the teacher's deed. The librarian immediately began to sell liquor on the premises during weekly "after hours" parties. The homeowners' association sues the librarian in an action for damages.

Which of the following is the best argument for the librarian?

(A) The rule in Spencer's Case prevents the librarian from being liable.
(B) The librarian is not in privity of contract with the homeowners' association.
(C) The librarian is not in privity of estate with the teacher.
(D) Other lots in the immediate vicinity are used for commercial purposes.

64. A housing corporation owned a tract of land and prepared a development plan to divide the land into 100 lots and create a residential community on the tract of land. The Declaration of Covenants created the community association, an administrative entity that would administer and enforce the regulations and restrictions recited among the covenants. One of the regulations set forth in the Declaration of Covenants reads:

"Each purchaser, by the acceptance of a deed therefore, promises to pay the community association an annual assessment or charge to be determined on the basis of the valuation of each individual lot and the improvements thereon. Non-payment of any annual assessment or charge when due shall result in a lien upon the parcel of the property."

A gardener, the owner of lot 29 in the development, sold his land to a landscaper with a deed containing no restrictions. The community association, pursuant the Declaration of Covenants, sues the landscaper to collect the annual assessment for lot 29.

Which of the following is the best argument for the landscaper?

(A) There is not privity of contract between the housing corporation and the community association.
(B) Because the charge constitutes a lien, there is no personal obligation on the landscaper's part.
(C) There is no privity of contract between the gardener and the landscaper.
(D) There is no privity of estate between the gardener and the landscaper.

65. A housing corporation owned a tract of land and prepared a development plan to divide the land into 100 lots and create a residential community on the property. The Declaration of Covenants created the community association, an administrative entity that would administer and enforce the regulations and restrictions recited in the Declaration of Covenants. One of the restrictions reads:

"There shall never at any time be erected, permitted, or maintained upon any part of the property any structure designed for or used as a saloon or place for the sale or manufacture of malt, vinous, or spiritious liquors."

The Declaration of Covenants was duly recorded and was included in the deed taken by a psychologist when he purchased lot 24 in the housing development. The psychologist recorded his deed. The psychologist gave his lot to his son. The deed conveying lot 24 to the son contained no reference to the Declaration of Covenants or any of its provisions. The deed provided that "these premises are conveyed to (the son), his heirs, and assigns, as long as they are used for residential purposes only." The son did not record his deed. The son was unaware of the Declaration of Covenants. The son started a home business selling imported wine from his home. A geologist, the owner of lot 26, which was situated next to the son's lot, brought an action of ejectment against the son.

Which of the following is the best argument for the son?

(A) The deed to the son created a fee simple determinable with a possibility of reverter, giving the psychologist, but not the geologist, the right to sue the son.
(B) Not having been recorded, the condition cannot be enforced against the son.
(C) The geologist is entitled only to an injunction against the son.
(D) The law prohibits a fee simple determinable.

66. A retiree lived in a single-family dwelling in the city. Adjacent to his home was a vacant lot that measured 100 feet by 175 feet. The lot, which the retiree owned, was situated on the corner of Davis Street and University Way. The tract measured 100 feet along Davis Street and 175 feet along University Way.

The retiree executed a deed purporting to convey the vacant lot to his lifelong friend for the consideration of $28,000. After escrow, the deed was delivered to the friend, who immediately filed it with the county recorder's office. The recorded instrument described the property conveyed as "all the tract of land beginning at the northwest corner of Davis Street and University Way; thence west along Davis Street 100 feet; thence north 175 feet; thence west 100 feet; thence south 175 feet along University Way to the place of beginning." Three months after his conveyance to the friend, the retiree died intestate. His heirs have now filed an appropriate action contesting the friend's title to the vacant lot.

Which of the following statements is most accurate concerning the outcome of this suit?

(A) The retiree's heirs will prevail because metes and bounds, rather than streets, are appropriate boundary descriptions.
(B) The friend will prevail because equity will not permit forfeiture for a mere technicality.
(C) The outcome will depend on whether the tract of land was plotted as a lot in a subdivision.
(D) The outcome will depend on whether the last call (175 feet along University Way) prevails over the third call (west 100 feet).

67. A college student and her boyfriend lived together in a one-bedroom apartment in Los Angeles. They were engaged to be married when they purchased an undeveloped parcel of land on a hillside overlooking the Pacific. The deed, which was properly executed and recorded, named the student and the boyfriend as grantees, "not as tenants in common but as joint tenants with right of survivorship."

Thereafter, the boyfriend, who was experiencing financial difficulties, offered to sell the property to his co-worker. Without the student's knowledge, the boyfriend executed a deed that purported to convey the hillside property to the co-worker in fee simple. The boyfriend signed his name and forged the student's name. He then delivered the deed of conveyance to the co-worker, who paid the boyfriend $150,000, which was the fair market value of the property. The co-worker immediately recorded the deed received from the boyfriend. The common law joint tenancy is unmodified by statute.

Title to the property in question is now in

(A) the boyfriend and the student as joint tenants with right of survivorship.
(B) the co-worker and the student as joint tenants with right of survivorship.
(C) the co-worker and the student as tenants in common.
(D) the co-worker as owner in fee simple.

68. Walter, a widower, died in 1997 leaving $1,000,000 to Trend Trust Company in trust to pay the income to his son, Stan, for life. Stan was married to Morgana and had two children, Andrew and Beverly. Walter's will provided in part:

"The net income from this trust shall be paid to my son, Stan, for his life. Upon Stan's death, the net income is to be paid to any widow of Stan. Upon the death of Stan's widow, Trend Trust Company shall then pay the income (from said trust) to the living children of my sister, Harriet, in equal shares."

Harriet's only surviving child, Grace, was born in 2001. Both Stan and Morgana died in an airplane crash in 2009. There is no statute modifying the common law in this jurisdiction.

Harriet, on behalf of Grace, brings an appropriate action against the Trend Trust Company and Walter's estate to allow the distribution of the income from said trust to be paid to Grace.

Is Harriet likely to prevail in this action?

(A) No, because Grace was not a life-in-being at the time of Walter's death.
(B) No, because the provisions under which Grace was intended to take violate the Rule against Perpetuities.
(C) Yes, because that was Walter's intent.
(D) Yes, because all other persons who would have had any claim to the income from the trust corpus are deceased.

69. A landlord, the owner of a large, high-rise apartment building in the city, leased a three-bedroom apartment in the building to a husband and wife. The written lease agreement specified that rent should be paid at a rate of $2,000 per month and provided that the tenants were required to pay two months' rent initially, of which one half, or $2,000, should be held by the landlord as a security deposit. In addition, the lease contained the following provision:

"The duration of this lease shall be month-to-month and either party may have the right to terminate on thirty (30) days' notice."

The lease agreement did not specify whether notice of termination must be in writing, but it did provide that the deposit could be applied, at the landlord's option, to unpaid rent and to reimbursement for damage done by the tenant(s) to the apartment or the fixtures attached thereto.

On January 1, the husband and wife paid the landlord $4,000 and moved in. The tenants then paid the $2,000 rent on the first of each of the months of February, March, and April, and all rents were duly accepted by the landlord.

On February 1, the city enacted a housing code applicable to all multiple dwellings in the city. A provision of that code required that in "any building having a main or central entrance that is open and accessible to the public directly from a public street, a doorkeeper shall be maintained on duty at all times." Although the landlord's building has such an entrance, the landlord failed to comply with the requirement.

On March 15 and again on April 1, the husband and wife lodged complaints with the city's housing authority relating to the landlord's failure to hire a doorkeeper in violation of the code regulation. On April 5, the landlord orally gave notice to the tenants that he was terminating the lease and demanded that they vacate the premises by May 5. No damage was done to the apartment, furnishings, or fixtures. There is no statute applicable to cover any landlord–tenant dispute except those related to housing and building codes.

In the landlord's action to evict, the husband and wife have contested the landlord's right to terminate on May 5.

If the tenants prevail, it will probably be because

(A) there was no damage to the apartment, furnishings, or fixtures.
(B) the statute of frauds requires that the notice of termination be in writing.
(C) the jurisdiction recognizes that retaliatory actions are a defense.
(D) the husband and wife have the option to apply their $2,000 deposit to cover May's rental.

70. A writer owned a building in a city. This was the only piece of real estate that the writer owned. The three-story building had a store on the ground floor and apartments on the other two floors. The writer entered into a leasehold agreement with a shopkeeper, who would lease the first floor, where she planned to open a sporting goods store. After identifying the parties, the operative words of the lease were as follows: "Landlord hereby agrees to lease for the three years the first floor of his building in the city to tenant, reserving unto said landlord annual rental in the sum of $12,000 payable in advance in monthly installments of $1,000."

At the moment of signing, the leasehold agreement entered into between the writer and the shopkeeper

(A) created a periodic tenancy.
(B) could be terminated at will by either party.
(C) did not convey to the shopkeeper a term of years at law.
(D) was void, invalid, and had no legal effect.

71. A widow owned an apartment building. Several years ago, a student, in a signed writing, entered a three-year lease agreement with the widow. The student agreed to pay $800 monthly rent for the third-floor apartment in the widow's building. The original three-year term had long since expired, but the student had continued to pay his rent, and the widow continued to accept it.

If the widow had chosen to evict the student immediately upon the end of the three-year period, and before she had accepted the next rent check, the student's strongest argument to prevent eviction, if true, would have been that

(A) the leasehold contract was void *ab initio*.
(B) the widow had not given the student requisite notice for terminating a periodic tenancy.
(C) the widow had not given the student requisite notice for terminating a term of years.
(D) the terms of the leasehold contract were binding on both parties.

72. A retiree owned a building in a city. Several years ago, an artist, in a signed writing, entered a three-year lease agreement with the retiree. The artist agreed to pay $800 monthly rent for the third-floor apartment in the retiree's building. The original three-year term had long since expired, but the artist has continued to pay his rent, and the retiree continued to accept it. The building became infested with rats after a restaurant was opened in the adjacent building. The artist could not tolerate the rats and served notice on the retiree that he was moving to another city and has not been heard from since.

At common law, what remedy was available to the retiree before she accepted the first rental payment after the end of the initial three-year period?

(A) Eviction of the artist for non-payment of rent.
(B) Recovery of the difference between the lease price and the fair market value of the leasehold for a year.
(C) Recovery of double the rent prorated on a monthly basis for the number of months the artist was on the premises beyond the three-year period.
(D) Require that the artist move out immediately or be held responsible for three years' rent.

73. A professor owned a building in a city. The building had a commercial space on the first floor, with two apartments above it; one on the second, and another on the third floor. Several years ago, a teacher, in a signed writing, entered a three-year lease agreement with the professor. The teacher agreed to pay $800 monthly rent for the third-floor apartment in the professor's building. The original three-year term had long since expired, but the teacher has continued to pay his rent, and the professor continued to accept it.

The professor rented the first floor to a restaurateur, who opened a sushi restaurant there. Within months, there was a citywide hookworm epidemic that was traced to the consumption of raw fish. The city council, in an attempt to protect the public from the parasites, passed an ordinance prohibiting all sushi restaurants from operating in the city. The restaurateur was forced out of business. She locked the doors and left a sign in the window: "Closed until further notice."

Within weeks, rats were attracted to the odor from the fish that was left in the restaurant, and the building became infested with them. The teacher could not tolerate the rats and served notice on the professor that he was moving to another city and has not been heard from since.

The teacher's best defense is that the professor, by permitting the restaurateur to store the fish in the closed restaurant, caused a

(A) partial constructive eviction.
(B) partial actual eviction.
(C) constructive eviction.
(D) breach of implied covenant of habitability.

74. An investor owned a building in a city. This was the only piece of real estate that the investor owned. The three-story building had a store on the ground floor and apartments on the other two floors. The investor entered into a leasehold agreement with a tenant, who would lease the first floor, where she planned to open a sporting goods store. After identifying the parties, the operative words of the lease were as follows: "Landlord hereby agrees to lease for the three years the first floor of his building in the city to tenant, reserving unto said landlord annual rental in the sum of $12,000 payable in advance in monthly installments of $1,000."

After the tenant took possession and the investor accepted her rent payment for the first floor of the building, which of the following most accurately describes the legal relationship between the parties?

(A) A tenancy at will was created.
(B) A periodic tenancy from month-to-month was created.
(C) A periodic tenancy from year-to-year was created.
(D) The tenant's equitable three-year term became a legal three-year term.

75. A rancher is the owner of a ranch situated upon the top of a mountain. Located below the ranch is a 40-acre farm that is owned by a farmer. There is a stream, which is a non-navigable watercourse, that originates at the top of the mountain and runs all the way down into the valley below. Both the ranch and the farm are within the watershed of the stream.

When the farmer purchased the farm in 1974, he began taking water from the stream and used it to irrigate the southern half of his property which he has used as a farm. Prior to 1974, the southern half of the farm had been cleared and placed in cultivation, while the northern half remained wooded and unused except for an occasional hike or gathering of timber for use as domestic fuel. The farmer continued this established pattern of use. Now (January 2010), he is still taking water from the stream and using it to irrigate the southern half of the farm.

In 2008, the rancher built a home on the ranch and began taking water from the stream for domestic purposes. During that year there was heavy rainfall, and this caused the stream to run down the mountain at a high water level. The next year, however, there was a drought. As a result, the stream flowed at a very low level. Consequently, there was only enough water to irrigate the farmer's farmland or, in the alternative, to supply all of the rancher's domestic water needs and one quarter of the farmer's irrigation requirements. The mountain is located in a jurisdiction where the period of prescription is 15 years.

Inasmuch as the stream is still flowing at a very low level and the rancher is continuing to take water for his personal needs, there is insufficient water to irrigate the farm. As a consequence, the farmer brings an appropriate action to declare that his water rights to the stream are superior to those of the rancher. In addition, the farmer moves to have the full flow of the stream passed to him, notwithstanding the effect it might have on the rancher.

If this state follows the doctrine of prior appropriation, judgment should be for whom?

(A) The rancher, because as an upstream landowner, he would have superior rights to the water than a downstream owner.
(B) The rancher, because domestic use is superior to and protected against an agricultural use.
(C) The farmer, because he has obtained an easement by prescription to remove as much water as he may need.
(D) The farmer, because he has put the water to a beneficial use prior to the rancher's use and has continuously used the water.

76. An attorney had a lucrative estate-planning and probate practice, but was in financial difficulty. In order to pay off his debts, the attorney prepared a deed so it appeared that a farmer, one of the attorney's clients, was conveying a property to the attorney. The attorney then forged the signature of the farmer and the acknowledgement of the notary and caused the deed to be recorded in the appropriate county recorder's office. The attorney then offered the property for sale to another client, a young doctor who had come to the attorney for investment advice.

The doctor, who knew nothing of the forgery, agreed to purchase the property for its market value, but insisted that the attorney convey insurable title. The doctor obtained an abstract of title and title insurance from a title company, which had examined the relevant public records and did not detect the forged nature of the farmer-attorney deed. The doctor obtained a warranty deed to the property from the attorney and promptly recorded it.

The farmer executed a warranty deed, conveying the property his niece. He showed her the deed and then placed it in his office safe, telling her, "When you graduate from college, the property will be yours." While visiting the property, the doctor heard a rumor that the farmer had promised to give the property to the farmer's niece. The doctor immediately brought an appropriate action to quiet title. The jurisdiction has a race notice recording statute in effect.

Assuming that all interested parties are joined in the action, to whom should title be granted?

(A) The title company, and they must compensate the doctor an amount equal to the purchase price of the property.
(B) The farmer, because the forged deed by which the attorney purported to take the property is null and void.
(C) The doctor, because he is a subsequent purchaser without notice who first recorded.
(D) The niece, because she is a successor in interest to the farmer.

77. A seller owned a ten-acre tract of undeveloped land, which consisted mostly of swampland and marshes. In March, the seller contracted to sell the property to a buyer for $25,000. Before the date set for closing of escrow, the buyer had the property surveyed and discovered that at least 60 percent of the property was regulated by the wetlands regulatory act.

According to relevant provisions of the wetlands statute, no structure of any kind could be constructed on the swampland portion of the property. Moreover, the state regulatory act restricted development on the adjoining non-swampland section by prohibiting construction of any commercial structures. Before entering into the land sale contract, the buyer had orally made known to the seller that he planned to construct a resort hotel on the property. After being apprised of the situation, the buyer refused to purchase the property.

If the seller brings suit for specific performance, judgment should be for whom?

(A) The buyer, because there was a failure of consideration.
(B) The buyer, because the seller's silence constituted a constructive warranty.
(C) The seller, because the buyer's intended use is immaterial.
(D) The seller, because the buyer's defense is barred by the Statute of Frauds.

78. A farmer owned a 100-acre farm. For many years, the farmer grew tobacco on a ten-acre strip located in the northeast section of the property. In March, the farmer planted his annual tobacco crop, which he usually harvested in early October. In September, the farmer sold his farm to a buyer for $100,000. At the time the farmer conveyed the property to the buyer, the tobacco crop was well developed and quite mature.

When the farmer and the buyer entered into their land-sale agreement, there was no mention of the status or ownership of the tobacco crop. In early October, after the buyer took possession of the property, the farmer contacted him and requested permission to harvest and remove the tobacco crop. The buyer refused to allow the farmer to re-enter the property. The farmer brings suit against the buyer seeking to re-enter the property and remove the tobacco crop which he had planted.

Which of the following is correct regarding the respective rights of the parties?

(A) The farmer is entitled to remove the tobacco crop, but he must pay the buyer a reasonable value to enter the property thus gaining access to the crop.
(B) The farmer is entitled to remove the tobacco crop and is not required to pay the buyer for entering the property, thus gaining access to the crop.
(C) The farmer is not entitled to remove the tobacco crop and, thus, is not entitled to re-enter the property.
(D) The farmer and the buyer each has a colorable title to the tobacco crop, and consequently, there should be an equitable division of the proceeds from the sale of the crop between both parties.

79. A businessman leased a 7,500 square foot store for a period of five years. Planning to open a hardware store, the businessman hired a contractor who installed overhead lighting and built wooden shelves that were nailed into the walls. The contractor also constructed free-standing tables for displaying merchandise. In addition, the businessman hired a builder who constructed a second-floor loft that was structurally attached to the main building. At the expiration of the lease, the businessman decided to vacate the premises and remove the improvements that he made. He began disassembling the loft and started removing the lighting, shelving, and free-standing tables. The landlord immediately filed suit seeking to enjoin the businessman from removing these items.

The court will most likely allow the businessman to remove what items?

(A) Everything.
(B) Everything except the loft.
(C) Everything except the loft and the lighting.
(D) The free-standing tables only.

80. Wishing to promote energy conservation and a renewable resource lifestyle, Muir obtained the appropriate governmental approval to subdivide her 200-acre parcel into 300 half-acre residential lots surrounding a 50-acre wooded "greenbelt." Muir recorded a subdivision plat for this project, which Muir named Greenhome; the plat showed the 300 lots plus an area congruent with the 50-acre greenbelt, labeled on the plat as "City Park." Muir built 200 passive-solar homes in Greenhome and sold them to individual purchasers via warranty deeds, each of which referred to the recorded subdivision plat and contained a restriction that "only single-family residences using passive-solar energy systems as their primary source of heating may be constructed hereon." While there were still 100 unsold lots in Greenhome, Muir sold these remaining properties and the 50-acre greenbelt to Redford.

The Muir-Redford deed referred to the subdivision plat and contained the restriction limiting construction to passive-solar homes. Redford sold the 100 lots as undeveloped properties to individual purchasers. During the same period, Redford conveyed the 50-acre greenbelt to Lukens, in exchange for cancellation of a debt owed by Redford to Lukens. Redford failed to include in the deeds executed by him any mention of the subdivision plat or the restriction limiting construction to passive-solar residences. Each of the deeds involved in the sale of Greenhome properties was promptly and properly recorded.

One of the 100 lots owned by Redford was sold to Wilson. Verde, who purchased a passive-solar home from Muir on a lot adjacent to Wilson's, learned that Wilson intended to heat his home with a coal-burning furnace, which would spew coal dust into the surrounding area. Verde brought an appropriate action against Wilson to enjoin construction of the home heated by the coal-burning furnace.

What will be the probable outcome of this litigation?

(A) Verde will prevail, because he can enforce the implied reciprocal servitude relating to passive-solar heating against Wilson.
(B) Verde will prevail, because Wilson's use of a coal-burning furnace may depress property values in the surrounding area.
(C) Wilson will prevail, because the passive-solar restriction was not mentioned in the deed by which he took his property.
(D) Wilson will prevail, because he was never in privity with Muir.

81. An entrepreneur owned two adjacent ten-story commercial buildings. The buildings were respectively known as Tower One and Tower Two. There was an enclosed walkway, which connected the second floor of each building; shoppers and office workers could walk across the common walkway and gain access to each building. While the buildings were being used in this manner, the entrepreneur sold Tower One to a manufacturer by warranty deed, which made no mention of any rights concerning the walkway. The walkway continued to be used by the occupants of both buildings.

Thereafter, the walkway became unsafe as a consequence of wear and tear. As a result, the manufacturer hired a contractor to repair the walkway. When the entrepreneur saw the contractor removing the carpeting along the walkway, he demanded that the manufacturer discontinue the repair work. After the manufacturer refused, the entrepreneur brought an action to enjoin the manufacturer from continuing the work.

What is the most likely result?

(A) A decision for the entrepreneur, because the manufacturer does not have rights in the walkway.
(B) A decision for the entrepreneur, because the manufacturer's rights in Tower One do not extend to the walkway.
(C) A decision for the manufacturer, because he has an easement in the walkway and an implied right to keep the walkway in repair.
(D) A decision for the manufacturer, because he has a right to take whatever action is necessary to protect himself from possible tort liability from persons using the walkway.

82. A grantor conveyed her only parcel of land to a friend by a duly executed and delivered warranty deed, which provided:

"To have and to hold the described tract of land in fee simple, subject to the understanding that within one year from the date of the instrument said grantee shall construct and thereafter maintain and operate on said premises a public health center." The grantee constructed a public health center on the tract within the time specified and operated it for five years. At the end of this period, the grantee converted the structure into a senior citizens' recreational facility. It is conceded by all parties in interest that a senior citizens' recreational facility is not a public health center. In an appropriate action, the grantor seeks a declaration that the change in the use of the facility has caused the land and structure to revert to her.

In this action, should the grantor win?

(A) Yes, because the language of the deed created a determinable fee, which leaves a possibility of reverter in the grantor.
(B) Yes, because the language of the deed created a fee subject to condition subsequent, which leaves a right of entry or power of termination in the grantor.
(C) No, because the language of the deed created only a contractual obligation and did not provide for the retention of a property interest by the grantor.
(D) No, because an equitable charge is enforceable only in equity.

83. A geologist, owner in fee simple of a quarry, had substantial gambling debts. In an effort to placate her creditors, she gave them mortgages to the quarry. Eventually, the total of the mortgages was greater than the fair market value of the property. When the creditors started sending intimidating representatives to inquire as to the condition of the quarry, the geologist decided that the best course of action was to sell the property. The geologist entered into a purchase and sale agreement with a buyer. The buyer made a significant down payment. The agreement called for the geologist to convey marketable title to the buyer on a specific date. On the closing date, the buyer refused to complete the sale. He said the mortgages made the title unmarketable. The geologist refused to return the down payment. In truth, she had failed to put the money in escrow and had spent it at the casinos. The geologist's only asset was the quarry. Both parties filed suit: the geologist for specific performance, and the buyer for return of his down payment.

Which of the following statements best describes the probable outcome of the suits?

(A) The geologist will obtain specific performance, and the buyer's down payment will not be refunded to him.
(B) The geologist will obtain specific performance, and the buyer's down payment will be refunded to him.
(C) The geologist will not obtain specific performance, and the buyer's down payment will be refunded to him.
(D) The geologist will not obtain specific performance, and the buyer's down payment will not be refunded to him.

84. In order to evade the IRS and his creditors, a landowner transferred title to his property to his good friend. The two men had a verbal agreement that when the landowner's financial problems were settled, the good friend would convey the property back to the landowner. The friend put the deed in his safe. The landowner was sentenced to a prison term for IRS violations. Several years later, he was released from prison. When he arrived at the friend's house, he discovered that the friend had died about a month earlier. The friend had never told his wife about his deal with the landowner. By the time the landowner arrived, the friend's wife had discovered the deed and included it in the inventory of property submitted to the probate court. Because she knew that the landowner and her husband were good friends and that her husband would have wanted the landowner to have the property, she returned the deed and deleted it from the probate inventory. The friend's creditors became suspicious and filed suit to have the property declared part of the estate.

Which of the following statements is most accurate?

(A) The property belongs to the landowner, because the friend did not formally accept title.
(B) The property belongs to the landowner, because the friend was not a bona fide purchaser.
(C) The property is part of the estate, because the friend is presumed to have accepted the deed, and it was not properly conveyed back to the landowner.
(D) The property is part of the estate, but after probate the land will revert back to the original landowner because of their verbal agreement.

85. A tenant resides in an apartment for 15 years. Over the course of the term of the lease, the tenant notices that the seals around the doors and windows have worn down, causing the outside air to leak in, which in turn causes water to come in when it rains. The tenant demands that the landlord fix the problem, but the landlord refuses.

Under common law estate theory, must the landlord repair the premises?

(A) Yes, because the landlord is under a duty to repair the premises while a tenant is living in the building.
(B) Yes, because the landlord is responsible for keeping the building wind and water tight.
(C) No, because the tenant is under a duty to repair the premises, including keeping the building wind and water tight.
(D) No, because the tenant has a duty to repair damage that is the result of ordinary wear and tear.

86. A landlord owned a number of residential rental apartment buildings in the city. The landlord knew his daughter would never be able to work for a living because she was absolutely spoiled. Because the landlord knew that the girl would never be able to afford her own place to live, the landlord gave his daughter one of his large, highly occupied rental apartment buildings. The deed read To my daughter for life, then to my son or his heirs in fee simple.

Which statement below best characterizes the son's and daughter's obligations toward the property?

(A) The son must make all mortgage payments.
(B) The son must pay all property taxes.
(C) The daughter must provide the son with any profits derived from the apartment building.
(D) The daughter must maintain the property in a reasonable state of repair.

87. Owner 1 owes a mortgage obligation to the bank for a loan against her real estate. Owner 1 sells her real estate to Owner 2. Owner 2 and Owner 1 agree that Owner 2 will assume the mortgage. Owner 2 does not enter into an agreement with the bank to assume the mortgage and defaults on the mortgage.

Is Owner 1 responsible to the bank for the balance of the mortgage?

(A) Yes, because Owner 2 did not make the mortgage payments.
(B) Yes, because there was a novation.
(C) No, because there was a novation.
(D) No, because Owner 2 assumed the mortgage.

88. A professional musician is named as mortgagor in a mortgage agreement with Bank No. 1 that he executed on his 17th birthday. The mortgage agreement indicates specifically that its terms are not negotiable. Bank No. 1 was aware of the musician's age when it executed the mortgage agreement. Two weeks after the musician's 18th birthday, Bank No. 1 sells the mortgage to Bank No. 2. The musician subsequently defaults on the mortgage.

Will Bank No. 2 prevail over the musician if the Bank No. 2 files suit to foreclose the mortgage?

(A) Yes, because Bank No. 2 is a holder in due course.
(B) Yes, because Bank No. 1 committed fraud in the transfer.
(C) No, because Bank No. 2 did not commit fraud.
(D) No, because the musician has a real defense to the lawsuit.

89. A landscaper applied for a mortgage with a bank in order to purchase a large plot of land outside of town. He planned to start a private nursery from which he would sell plants to the public. The bank declined his application. Later that week, the landscaper had a conversation with one his wealthy clients about his predicament. The client suggested that the landscaper take out a mortgage from the client. Excited, the landscaper accepted the client's offer and the next day met again with the client to draw up the contract. The note that the two signed read as follows:

Landscaper borrows from Client the sum of $100,000 for the purchase of land on Country Road 11. The land will be used by Landscaper as a plant nursery. Landscaper accepts personal liability for payment of the mortgage that will be secured by the property itself. Landscaper promises to make monthly payments to Client for twenty years. Such payments will include a variable interest rate to be reset yearly, based on the rate offered by XY Bank. The entire balance is due upon sale of the property, should that occur, or if Landscaper defaults.

Is the mortgage note valid?

(A) No, because the description of the property is inadequate.
(B) No, because it does not satisfy the Statute of Frauds.
(C) Yes, because it does satisfy the Statute of Frauds.
(D) Yes, because it is signed by both parties.

90. A homeowner owned a house in a small neighborhood with stable home values. When a brand new elementary school was built nearby, the home values in the neighborhood suddenly skyrocketed. When the homeowner fell behind on her mortgage payments, she elected to put her house on the market, with the hope of taking advantage of the high prices. An appraisal performed in January suggested the home might sell for approximately $200,000. The appraisal did not make any reference to the fact that the property was located at the end of a cul-de-sac, behind which existed a large pig farm. In the summer months, when the wind blew from the direction of the pig farm, the smells at the house could be very strong and unpleasant. Unfortunately, the homeowner was not able to sell her home during the winter months. In June, the bank instituted judicial foreclosure proceedings. The house sold for $98,000, which satisfied the outstanding mortgage but there was nothing left over for the homeowner.

If the homeowner seeks to have the sale set aside, is she likely to prevail?

(A) No, because the sale price does not shock the conscience.
(B) No, because foreclosure sales cannot be set aside for inadequacy of the sale price.
(C) Yes, because foreclosure sales can be set aside for inadequacy of the sale price.
(D) Yes, because the foreclosure sale price was more than fifty percent less than the appraised value.

91. A law student leased an apartment from a landlord near the law school. In accord with the terms of the lease agreement, the student agreed to pay a monthly rental of $1,000 for a term of two years. The landlord was pleased to lease the apartment to the student because he felt she would be a responsible tenant, especially in light of the fact that she was a law student.

After taking possession of the apartment, the landlord began to pester the student by seeking free legal advice. However, the student refused to help the landlord and told him she was only in her first year of law school and wasn't qualified to provide any legal assistance. The landlord continued to harass the student with repeated telephone calls and annoying e-mail messages. Finally, the student refused to talk or communicate with the landlord.

The landlord became infuriated with the student. One afternoon while the student was at the law school, the landlord entered the apartment without her permission using a spare key. He overturned her furniture and removed the linens from the bed. The landlord also took the student's clothing and threw it on the floor. Needless to say, the student became very upset when she returned to the apartment and saw that her belongings had been meddled with. The student later learned that the landlord was responsible for the unauthorized entry and brings suit against the landlord for trespass.

What, if anything, should the student be awarded?

(A) Compensatory damages only.
(B) Compensatory damages, punitive damages, and injunctive relief.
(C) Nothing, because an owner cannot be charged with trespass on his own property.
(D) Nothing, because the rummaging did not amount to a constructive eviction.

92. A cowboy owned a 200-acre ranch in fee simple. After working the land for 40 years, the cowboy conveyed it by quitclaim deed to two lawyers--an associate and a partner--as tenants in common for $1.2 million. Ironically, the lawyers failed to record the deed. They also failed to agree on the use of the land, and the associate conveyed her one-half interest in it to an investor by a properly recorded special warranty deed duly. Soon thereafter, the cowboy approached a real estate corporation and bargained to sell the ranch (again) for $800,000, its current fair market value in a depressed market. In exchange for the purchase price, the cowboy presented the corporation with a general warranty deed, which the corporation duly recorded.

The relevant recording statute states: Every conveyance of real property, other than a lease for a term not to exceed one year, is void as against any subsequent purchaser or mortgagee of the same property or any part thereof in good faith and for valuable consideration, whose conveyance is first duly recorded. The jurisdiction also uses grantor-grantee and grantee-grantor indexes.

In a suit to quiet title, who is likely to prevail?

(A) The partner and the investor, because the corporation can be charged with inquiry notice of the investor's interest in the ranch.
(B) The investor, because the property is located in a race-notice jurisdiction.
(C) The investor and the corporation, as tenants in common.
(D) The corporation, because it cannot be charged with constructive knowledge of the associate-investor deed.

93. A computer programmer purchased a summer home from a retired scientist, but failed to record the deed. A few years later, the scientist joined a religious cult and gave all of his property, including the home, to the cult's high priest, who, although he had knowledge of the previous conveyance, nonetheless recorded the deed. Soon after that, the programmer finally got around to recording her own deed and thus discovered the priest's. The programmer then brought an action to quiet title. The applicable recording act provides, A conveyance of an estate in land shall not be valid as against any subsequent purchaser for value, except such person who has actual notice of it, unless the conveyance is properly recorded.

Who is likely to prevail?

(A) The programmer, because under the common law, the priest, as a donee, is considered to have actual knowledge of the scientist's interest.
(B) The programmer, because the scientist had no interest in the mountain property to pass to the priest.
(C) The priest, because the programmer was a donee-grantee of the property.
(D) The priest, because he recorded his deed first.

94. A young college student was frequently invited by her professor to spend holidays at the remote mountain property owned by the professor's elderly uncle. One day, when the uncle complained of no longer being able to properly care for the property, the student offered to buy it. The uncle agreed, and in exchange for its market value, delivered a warranty deed conveying the property to the student. Alas, the student failed to record her deed. Two months later, the uncle, his mind slipping, purported to convey the property via warranty deed to the professor as a wedding present. The professor immediately recorded her deed. When the student subsequently learned of the professor-uncle deed, she immediately recorded her deed and then brought an action to quiet title to the property.

The applicable recording act provides, A conveyance of an estate in land (other than a lease for less than one year) shall not be valid as against any subsequent purchaser for value, except such person who has actual notice of it, unless the conveyance is properly recorded.

Will the student prevail in her quiet title action?

(A) Yes, because she recorded her deed before commencing the quiet title action.
(B) Yes, because she took the property first in time.
(C) No, because the professor is considered to have actual knowledge of the student's interest via imputation from the donor, her uncle.
(D) No, because she did not record before the uncle conveyed the property to the professor.

95. The owner of a vineyard sold the property to an artist via a warranty deed, which the artist failed to record. The owner subsequently purported to sell the land to a ballerina; the ballerina, who had no actual notice of the owner-artist transaction, promptly recorded her deed. Shortly thereafter, the artist finally recorded his deed.

The ballerina subsequently sold and conveyed the land via warranty deed to a judge. The judge died, devising the land to his grandson. Although he had never communicated with any of the participants, the grandson had nonetheless heard about each of the previous transactions involving the property.

The jurisdiction's recording act provides, A conveyance of an estate in land (other than a lease for less than one year) shall not be valid as against any subsequent purchaser for value, except such persons having actual notice of it, unless the conveyance is properly recorded.

Who owns the property?

(A) The grandson, under the shelter rule.
(B) The grandson, because the first person to record always has paramount interest.
(C) The artist, because he recorded his deed before the ballerina conveyed to the judge.
(D) The artist, because the grandson knew of the artist's interest in the property when the grandson took title.

96. A pianist owned a summer cabin in fee simple absolute. She executed and delivered a quitclaim deed conveying it to her cousin, who accepted the deed but did not record it. A year later, the pianist executed a mortgage on the cabin in favor of a local judge, in order to secure an extension of credit. The judge, who knew nothing of the pianist-cousin conveyance, examined the public records, which showed the pianist as a grantee of the cabin and revealed no subsequent transactions. The judge promptly caused the mortgage instrument to be recorded. The pianist subsequently defaulted on the obligation owed the judge, and the judge instituted judicial foreclosure proceedings as to the cabin. Upon learning of these proceedings, the cousin immediately recorded his deed, and then was permitted by the court to intervene in the foreclosure action and seek a judicial declaration that he was the owner in fee simple of the cabin, free of any encumbrance in favor of the judge. The jurisdiction has a recording act that voids prior interests that are not recorded in favor of subsequent bona fide purchasers.

Who should prevail in this litigation?

(A) The judge, because he was unaware of the cousin's interest in the cabin when he extended credit to the pianist in exchange for the mortgage.
(B) The judge, because the mortgage was recorded before the cousin recorded his deed.
(C) The cousin, because an extension of credit by a mortgagee is not considered value within the operation of the recording act.
(D) The cousin, because a mortgagee is not considered a purchaser within the operation of the recording act.

97. On June 15, a landowner and a purchaser entered into a written agreement which provided, among other things, as follows: The landowner hereby agrees to sell the unimproved property described as (a metes and bounds description appeared here), consisting of 25 acres, to purchaser for the price of $250,000. The landowner to convey good and marketable title. Closing of escrow is to occur no later than September 1. On July 20, the landowner discovered a 20-year-old easement running through the center of the property which a former owner had granted to the city for a possible rail system idea that was later abandoned. The landowner immediately notified the purchaser of the easement and that she had begun negotiations with the city manager and the city-planning department to repurchase the easement and thereby extinguish it. On August 20, the landowner reported that the planning commission was leaning toward revival of the rail line project. When the purchaser asked what was the likelihood of successfully repurchasing the easement, the landowner replied, I'm not sure. The next day, August 21, the purchaser notified the landowner that he was rescinding the contract. The landowner brought an appropriate action for damages for breach of contract, alleging that the market value of the parcel on September 1 was $225,000.

Which of the following is the purchaser's strongest argument that he did not breach the contract of sale?

(A) The landowner did not possess good and marketable title when the contract of sale was formed.
(B) The landowner was unlikely to be able to tender good and marketable title within any reasonable period.
(C) The landowner's entry into the contract relationship without good and marketable title constituted a constructive fraud upon the purchaser.
(D) Since time was of the essence of the contract, the purchaser was entitled to rescind as soon as there was any indication that performance by the landowner might be delayed in any way.

98. The foreperson at a ranch informed the owner that he would be leaving the owner's employ to seek property on which to conduct his own ranching operations. The owner offered to lease the ranch to the foreperson. The foreperson insisted that he wanted his own ranch so the owner offered to add an option clause to the lease that would permit the foreperson to purchase a 200-acre portion of the ranch after expiration of the 10-year lease period. When the foreperson inquired about which 200 acres he could buy, the owner promised to mark off a few different 200-acre parcels and give the foreperson a choice. The foreperson then agreed to the arrangement, and a written lease with option to purchase 200 acres, not specifically described, was drawn up and executed by the parties. No mention was made therein of the owner's promise to mark off 200-acre parcels. The foreperson continued to operate the owner's ranch as a lessee rather than a foreman, and performed all his obligations under the written lease agreement. Although the owner had never marked off any 200-acre parcels as he had promised, the foreperson had (over the course of the lease) selected a particular section of the ranch for purchase and had constructed thereon a corral and paddock. When the lease expired, the foreperson delivered to the owner the purchase price for the 200 acres as provided in the lease-option agreement. The foreperson then demanded a deed to the 200 acres he had selected. The owner refused to convey so the foreperson sought a judgment compelling the owner to specifically perform by conveying the disputed 200 acres.

Which of the following is the strongest argument supporting a judgment in favor of the owner in an action for specific performance?

(A) The owner's obligation to mark off 200-acre parcels for the foreperson's choice was a condition precedent to the duty to convey, such that the failure of the condition precludes the duty to convey from becoming an absolute obligation.
(B) The foreperson will be unable to prove the existence of the option to purchase element of the lease due to operation of the parol evidence rule.
(C) The aspect of the written lease agreement regarding the option to purchase is not enforceable because there was no separate consideration supporting the option to purchase.
(D) The property to be conveyed pursuant to the lease-option agreement is not sufficiently described so as to permit specific enforcement.

99. A zookeeper and a rancher owned several apartments that they leased for profit. Each had been purchased with equal contributions from the two men and the deed to each recited that they had taken title as tenants in common. Although they considered each other as spouses, they knew that the government did not accord their relationship the legal status of a marriage, and thus would not treat their jointly acquired property as marital property in the event of either's death. When a friend told them that property held in joint tenancy passed automatically to the survivor upon the death of one joint tenant, the zookeeper and the rancher made an oral agreement that their real property would thereafter be considered joint tenancy property with right of survivorship. Having made what each considered to be satisfactory arrangements for the disposition of his property after death, neither the zookeeper nor the rancher made a will. Two years later, the zookeeper died intestate, leaving a sister as his sole heir. The sister immediately informed the rancher that she claimed the zookeeper's interest in all real property formerly owned by the zookeeper and the rancher, and that she wished to sell her interest in those properties. The rancher filed an appropriate action to quiet title to the real property.

How should the court rule?

(A) That the rancher is sole owner of the properties, because in reliance on their joint tenancy agreement, the rancher and the zookeeper did not create wills.
(B) That the rancher is sole owner of the properties, because the deeds to the subject properties should be reformed to reflect their joint tenancy status.
(C) That the rancher and the sister own the properties as equal tenants in common, because the zookeeper and the rancher's agreement was ineffective to convert ownership of their properties to joint tenancy.
(D) That the rancher and the sister own the properties as equal tenants in common, because tenants in common may not unilaterally create a joint tenancy out of property already owned by them.

100. A baker owns a patisserie in the city. One day, after 20 years of creating award-winning confections, the baker makes a disastrous coffee creme brulee and is overcome by a desire to dramatically change her life. In her youth, the baker had studied to be a painter, and now she spontaneously decides to pursue a career as an artist. At that moment, a customer enters the patisserie to buy a dozen napoleons. The customer has always cooked as an avocation, but at the sight of the wonders in the baker's store, he bursts out, If only I owned such a place! The baker, already envisioning herself in southern France painting en plein air, responds, If you have the cash, I'll make your dream come true. Each gazes at the other in disbelief for an instant before they launch into a discussion of terms.

The baker and the customer orally agree on a purchase price of $200,000 for the patisserie. As additionally negotiated, the customer gives the baker $20,000 within the hour as a down-payment, and they agree to meet again on the first day of the next month (two weeks hence) to tender performance. During the following week, the baker attempts to paint each night after work, but she soon realizes that she has no gift -- desserts are her true art. She regrets agreeing to sell the patisserie, where she now stays into the wee hours of the night, creating new confections to fight her depression. On the agreed-upon closing date, the customer tenders a check in the amount of $180,000. The baker, however, refuses to convey title to the patisserie to the customer, claiming she cannot bear to part with her life's work.

If the customer files suit for specific performance by the baker, who will prevail?

(A) The baker, under the parol evidence rule.
(B) The baker, under the Statute of Frauds defense.
(C) The customer, under the part performance exception to the Statute of Frauds.
(D) The customer, under the doctrine of equitable conversion.

Answers and Explanations

1. **(A)** In a pure race jurisdiction, the first to record wins; a subsequent purchaser need not be *bona fide* and without notice because he will prevail if he records first. Because the investor recorded before the landscaper, he will prevail under a race statute over the landscaper. Note that the friend will not be part of the competition for title because he has already conveyed the property to the investor. At most, it will be a competition between the investor and the landscaper. Choice (B) is incorrect. The landscaper will not prevail because as between her and the investor, she was last to record. Because of this, she will not be the one to ultimately prevail. Choice (C) is incorrect. The friend will not be part of the competition for title because he has already conveyed the property to the investor. Thus, it will be a competition between the investor and the landscaper. Choice (D) is incorrect. Because the investor will prevail in a race jurisdiction, the gardener will not.

2. **(A)** For Multistate purposes, students are required to know that there are two types of crops: (1) ***fructus naturales,*** those that grow naturally without the aid of man, such as trees, bushes, grasses and the fruits of these, and (2) ***fructus industriales,*** those that come primarily from annual planting, cultivating, and fertilizing, such as wheat, beans, corn, and citrus fruits in orchards. According to the prevailing view, ***fructus naturales are and remain real property for all purposes until they are actually severed from the land.*** On the other hand, ***fructus industriales (also referred to as emblements) are usually annual crops that are, for most purposes, personal property.*** See Smith and Boyer, Law of Property, pp. 244–245. Because wheat is a *fructus industriales* crop (or an *emblement),* it is viewed as being personalty, and so the proceeds from its sale pass to the life tenant's heirs. Consequently, choice (A) is correct. Choice (B) is incorrect. Because the wheat will be considered an emblement and will pass as the personal property of the deceased life tenant, the friend's heirs will be entitled to take the proceeds of the crop. Therefore, the cousin will not be entitled to this personal property. Choice (C) is incorrect. Because the wheat will be considered an emblement and will pass as the personal property of the deceased life tenant, the friend's heirs will be entitled to take the proceeds of the crop. Therefore, the woman will not be entitled to this personal property. Choice (D) is incorrect. Because the wheat will pass as the personal property of the deceased life tenant, the friend's heirs will be entitled to the proceeds of the crop and the heirs do not need to share the proceeds with the woman, the original grantor.

3. **(B)** An easement by prescription arises by adverse use of the servient tenement by the dominant tenant for the period of the statute of limitations. To mature, such an easement against a landowner the user must be (1) adverse as distinct from permissive, (2) open and notorious, (3) continuous and without interruption, and (4) for the period of prescription. In order to acquire title to an easement by adverse user (as well as to gain title to land by adverse possession) ***it must be gained without the consent of the landowner.*** Remember that no one who makes use of the servient tenement with the consent or permission of the owner can claim title to a prescriptive easement. Thus, if the farmer had the widower's permission to use the roadway, then he was given a license. A license simply permits one person to come onto land in the possession of another without being a trespasser. As such, a license arises from consent given by the one in possession of land. Consent being given, no prescriptive right can arise through a license. Choice (A) is incorrect. In order to gain an easement by prescription, the use must be hostile and adverse, meaning not permissive. There is no special requirement that the person using the land intended to do so in such a way as to perpetrate a fraud against the true record owner. While it would be helpful to the widower to argue that his statement to the farmer constituted permission, it would be irrelevant for the widower to argue that the farmer's use was fraudulent. In other words, the farmer's desire to commit a fraud would be irrelevant if the use were truly adverse. Choice (C) is incorrect. There are not enough facts here to know for certain whether or not the farmer used the roadway for the prescriptive period. However, the facts do state for certain that the widower did not mind the farmer's use of the road. It was only after the widower found out about the affair that he considered it trespassing. For this reason, the widower's strongest argument here would be that the use was permissive instead of non-continuous. Choice (D) is incorrect. This element requires that the use of the road cannot be secret or clandestine. The use must be done in a way that a true owner would use the roadway. There are not enough facts here to know for certain whether or not the farmer used the roadway in such a way that the whole world could see. However, the facts do state for certain that the widower did not mind the farmer's use of

the road. It was only after the widower found out about the affair that he considered it trespassing. For this reason, the widower's strongest argument here would be that the use was permissive instead of not open and notorious.

4. **(D)** According to the general rule, when an easement appurtenant is created either by prescription or by conveyance over a servient tenement, the boundaries and extent of such easement become fixed and are binding on both the servient and dominant tenants. Neither such tenant has any more right to change the location of such easement than he has to change the boundaries of the physical servient or dominant tenements. The easement is an incorporeal right, which is real property. So, if this roadway is found to be an easement appurtenant that benefits the dominant tenement, it will be valid and can be conveyed because it would be a real-property interest. Choice (A) is incorrect because the description in the deed instrument is sufficient to identify the land conveyed. Choice (B) is wrong because mere excessive use of an easement (or profit) does not forfeit or ***extinguish*** the easement. In the case of excessive use, the owner of the easement is simply making use of the servient tenement beyond the scope or extent of the use permitted by the easement. So, even if this issue were decided, at most it would tell the parties how much the easement can be used. Because the landowner is trying to stop the buyer completely, the resolution of this issue will still not be helpful. Choice (C) is not correct because according to the language of the deed, the farmer (the grantor) is not reserving an easement to the buyer as a third party. The farmer is simply conveying the vineyard (together with the easement for the right of way across the orchard) to the buyer as the grantee (or second party) to the real estate transaction. It obviously wasn't the farmer's intent to reserve an easement to the buyer as a third party. Moreover, most cases hold that a reservation can be made for no one other than the grantor.

5. **(A)** The statute of frauds requires a writing for enforceability of any contract to create or transfer any interest in land, which includes not only legal estates but also equitable interests and liens, rents, expectant interests and estates, leases, easements, and restrictions upon the use of land. Equity, however, will decree specific performance of an oral land contract, despite the statute of frauds, where there has been substantial reliance on the oral promises. Because this question concerns itself with the daughter and her husband's reliance on the widower's oral promise to convey the farm, the statute of frauds is the applicable legal principle. Choice (B) is wrong because parol evidence requires a complete and integrated writing. Here, no writing was entered into between the parties. Choice (C) is incorrect. Adverse possession, as denoted in choice (C), is inapplicable because the daughter and her husband's possession of the farm was not hostile and adverse. Choice (D) is incorrect. Resulting trusts arise when an express trust fails or when an existing trust fails to exhaust all of the assets of the trust. At this point the court will step in and create a resulting trust based on the settlor's intent. Choice (D) is incorrect because the facts do not indicate the widower intended to establish a trust.

6. **(B)** A fee simple subject to condition subsequent means a fee simple subject to being terminated by exercise of the power of termination or right of re-entry for condition broken. What distinguishes this type of estate from a fee simple determinable is that the estate will continue in the grantee, or his successors, unless and until the power of termination is exercised. The estate in fee simple subject to a condition subsequent does not end automatically upon the happening of the named event. The basic difference, therefore, is that the fee simple determinable automatically expires by force of the special limitation contained in the instrument creating the estate when the stated contingency occurs, whereas the fee simple on condition subsequent continues despite the breach of the specified condition until it is divested or cut short by the exercise by the grantor of his power to terminate. In clause (c), the land development company and its successors had the right to re-enter and terminate the estate and this granted them a right of re-entry. Choice (A) is incorrect. A fee simple determinable is a fee simple estate created to continue ***until some specified event occurs. The estate terminates automatically.*** The principal difference between the two is as follows: In the determinable fee, the estate ***automatically*** comes to an end when the stated event happens, whereas in the fee simple subject to condition subsequent, the termination of the estate is ***not automatic,*** but must be terminated by the entry or exercise of the reserved power by the grantor. Typical words that will create a fee simple determinable include "so long as" and "during." What the country club has here is best described as a fee simple subject to con-

dition subsequent because there were no words of duration used in the grant and because the land development company specifically reserved a right of re-entry. Choice (C) is incorrect. A determinable fee subject to an executory interest is a fee simple estate, whereupon the happening of a named event, ownership is to pass from the grantee to one other than the grantor. If anything, clause (c) reserved a right for the grantor or successors/assigns to re-enter and terminate the present estate. Because the ownership would pass to grantor, this is not a determinable fee subject to an executory interest. Choice (D) is incorrect. An easement is the right of one person to go onto the land in possession of another and make a limited use thereof. An easement is appurtenant when it is attached to a piece of land and benefits the owner of such land in his use and enjoyment thereof. Every easement appurtenant requires two pieces of land that are owned by two different persons. The country club did not receive a right to use the land of another; rather, the country club received a defeasible fee interest in the property.

7. **(C)** Choice (C) is the best alternative because the land-development company's March, 2001 instrument effectively abrogated the deed restrictions on the country club's use of its property. By abrogating the restrictions, the land development company was essentially giving up their future interest in the property because the land-development company could no longer use the violation of the restriction as a means to re-enter and take the property. Clearly, a common developmental scheme was not established for the 400-acre tract. Because the land-development company developed a shopping center on 25 acres of its retained land and also authorized the country club to construct a country club and golf course on its 50 acres, the land-development company intended that the residential developmental scheme should extend only to the 300 acres within the eastern tract and western tract subdivisions. Choice (A) is incorrect. First, the land-development company could no longer re-enter the land upon breach of condition subsequent because the condition had been waived by the land-development company, the grantor. Second, the homeowner is, at most, a grantee of the land-development company and is not a successor or assign of the land-development company. Third, the homeowner is not asking to re-enter the premises and is not asking for an ownership interest in it; rather, the homeowner was seeking to enjoin the construction of the complex. Choice (B) is incorrect. A common developmental scheme was not established for the 400-acre tract. Because the land-development company developed a shopping center on 25 acres of its retained land and also authorized the country club to construct a country club and golf course on its 50 acres, the land-development company intended that the residential developmental scheme should extend only to the 300 acres within the eastern tract and the western tract subdivisions. Choice (D) is incorrect. The deed restriction is there to illustrate the type of restriction that the country club would have been required to abide by and follow. This is not to say that ***only*** the eastern tract residents would have had standing to challenge the construction plan. If there were a common development scheme in place for the entire 400-acre tract, then the homeowner would have had standing to challenge the construction as a resident of the project despite deed restriction (b). The better reason why the homeowner will not succeed is that there are no more restrictions on the country club, and, thus, no residential owner can enjoin the project.

8. **(D)** ***An equitable servitude is a restriction on the use of land enforceable in a court of equity.*** An equitable servitude is more than "a covenant running with the land in equity" because ***it is an interest in land.*** The term "equitable servitude" is broader than "equitable easement" because it applies not only to land, but also to chattel property such as a business. Choice (A) is incorrect because the deed restrictions were negative—or restrictive—covenants rather than affirmative covenants. Choice (B) is incorrect. An equitable easement is an implied easement created by the courts to do equity when one party has been using the land of another and the party being burdened sues to compel removal of the use or encroachment. There is no need to resort to an implied easement because the equitable servitude was created by express language. Choice (C) is incorrect. An easement is the right of one person to go onto the land in possession of another and make a limited use thereof. An easement is appurtenant when it is attached to a piece of land and benefits the owner of such land in his use and enjoyment thereof. Every easement appurtenant requires two pieces of land that are owned by two different persons. The country club did not receive a right use the land of another in these deed restrictions; rather, the country club was being restricted in their use of the property.

9. **(C)** The proposal in the subdivision plan and also in the development brochure to set aside a 10-acre tract for the location of a school building would constitute a public dedication offering. Dedication at common law required no particular form and could be made by any method by which the dedicator expressed his intention: by words, conduct, or writing. When acceptance by public adoption is manifested, there arises a conveyance of an easement for such public use, with the fee remaining in the grantor. In the present case, the school district would be entitled to erect a school on the tract, thereby enjoining the buyer's pizzeria. Choice (A) is incorrect. Even though the buyer's deed made no mention of the subdivision, he will nonetheless be charged with constructive notice of the subdivision and the dedication because the deed that the builder received from the investor mentioned the subdivision and the dedication. Because those restrictions were in the buyer's chain of title, he will be put on constructive notice of them. Choice (B) is incorrect. A dedication can be made from a private land holder to the public generally or to a public body. Here, the school board would be a valid public body. Choice (D) is incorrect. The school district first would need to argue that the land was dedicated to them because this would explain why they can enjoin the construction of the pizzeria. To argue that there is an equitable servitude only explains there is a restriction on the land and still does not explain why the school board has an enforceable interest in the land. Because choice (C) explains how the school acquired its interest (through a dedication), it is the strongest choice.

10. **(D)** The public dedication of the 10-acre tract for the erection of a school would be construed as an easement for public use. Although ordinarily, dedication arises out of the creation of a public use in private land, a municipality or other subdivision may likewise acquire title and then create a public use by dedication. Choice (A) is incorrect. The investor transferred an interest in land from his own ownership to a public body, the school board. He did this through a dedication. An equitable servitude is not a transfer of an interest in land. Therefore, this is an incorrect description of the investor's proposed designation of the tract. Choice (B) is incorrect. Although the investor's dedication does contain a restrictive covenant, this is not the proper description for what is really a transfer of an interest in land. A restrictive covenant is not an interest in land and therefore an incorrect description of the investor's proposed designation of the tract. Choice (C) is incorrect. It is incorrect to call the investor's dedication a restriction because the investor transferred an interest in land to the school board. A restriction is not an interest in land and, therefore, an incorrect description of the investor's proposed designation of the tract.

11. **(C)** When a developer subdivides her land into many parcels and some of the deeds contain a certain restriction and others do not, those restrictions may still be binding upon other purchasers, even though their deeds never contained the restriction. The following two requirements, however, must be met: (1) a common development scheme, and (2) notice. In order for there to be a common scheme, there must be a showing that when the project began, there was a common plan in place that all parcels would adhere to the same restrictive covenant. Here, there would be such a showing because the developer restricted the first 60 parcels and then sold the remaining 40 parcels to the builder by a singular deed that included the same mobile-home restriction. Notice may be met by either actual notice, constructive notice, or inquiry notice, whereby the appearance of the properties would put a prospective buyer (such as the man) on notice that the neighborhood was planned to have certain characteristics. Because there was a common development plan in place for the entire subdivision, the woman will prevail even though the man's deed made no mention of the mobile-home restriction. Choice (A) is incorrect. The original deed provision between the developer and the builder prohibiting "house trailers and mobile homes to be built or maintained on any lot within the subdivision" is an example of a restrictive or negative covenant "running with the land." Therefore, the restriction would be enforceable against the man, even though the prohibition was not contained in his deed. In order for a covenant to "run with the land," the following four requirements must be met: (1) the covenant must be in writing; (2) the covenant must "touch and concern" the land; (3) privity of estate must exist between covenantor and covenantee; and (4) there must be intent that the covenant "run with the land." Because this covenant did run with the land, this choice is incorrect. Choice (B) is incorrect. When a developer subdivides her land into many parcels and some of the deeds contain a certain restriction and others do not, those restrictions may still be binding upon other purchasers, even though their deeds never contained the restriction. The following two requirements, however, must be met: (1) a common development scheme,

and (2) notice. In order for there to be a common scheme, there must be a showing that when the project began, there was a common plan in place that all parcels would adhere to the same restrictive covenant. Here, there would be such a showing because the developer restricted the first 60 parcels and then sold the remaining 40 parcels to the builder by a singular deed that included the same mobile-home restriction. Notice may be met by either actual notice, constructive notice, or inquiry notice, whereby the appearance of the properties would put a prospective buyer (such as the man) on notice that the neighborhood was planned to have certain characteristics. Because there was a common development plan in place for the entire subdivision, the woman will prevail even though the man's deed made no mention of the mobile-home restriction. Because this answer choice states that the woman cannot enforce any restriction because the man's deed was silent, it is incorrect. Choice (D) is incorrect. A common development scheme will be found to exist in the subdivision. In order for there to be a common scheme, there must be a showing that when the project began, there was a common plan in place that all parcels would adhere to the same restrictive covenant. Here, there would be such a showing because the developer restricted the first 60 parcels and then sold the remaining 40 parcels to the builder by a singular deed that included the same mobile-home restriction. Choice (C) is a more complete choice because in presuming that there is a common development scheme, choice (C) states that the restriction would be binding and that the woman would thus prevail.

12. **(A)** Choice (A) is the LEAST accurate because a covenant "running with the land" will be enforceable against successors of the original parties where there is (1) privity of estate; (2) the covenant "touches and concerns" the land; (3) intent that the covenant "run with the land"; and (4) the covenant be in writing. This statement is the least accurate because if the covenant runs with the land, then it can bind grantees beyond the builder. Choice (B) is incorrect. When a developer subdivides her land into many parcels and some of the deeds contain a certain restriction and others do not, those restrictions may still be binding upon other purchasers, even though their deeds never contained the restriction. The following two requirements, however, must be met: (1) a common development scheme, and (2) notice. In order for there to be a common scheme, there must be a showing that when the project began, there was a common plan in place that all parcels would adhere to the same restrictive covenant. Here, there would be such a showing because the developer restricted the first 60 parcels and then sold the remaining 40 parcels to the builder by a singular deed that included the same mobile-home restriction. Notice may be met by either actual notice, constructive notice, or inquiry notice, whereby the appearance of the properties would put a prospective buyer (such as the buyer in this question) on notice that the neighborhood was planned to have certain characteristics. Because there was a common development plan in place for the entire subdivision, any lot owner (in the subdivision) can enforce the covenant against the buyer, even though the buyer's deed made no mention of the mobile-home restriction. Because this answer choice is an accurate statement, it is incorrect. Choice (C) is incorrect. Though the restrictive covenant was not written into the buyer's deed, he would, nevertheless, be held to have constructive knowledge of the prohibition against mobile homes and house trailers. Because the deed from the developer to the builder was in the buyer's chain of title, it will put the buyer on constructive notice of those restrictions because the covenants appeared in the deed. Because the buyer will be held to have constructive notice of these covenants, this answer choice is an accurate statement and thus incorrect. Choice (D) is incorrect. This is an accurate statement because all subsequent grantees of the builder would be in privity of estate and thus would be bound by the covenant. Because the builder is one of the original covenanting parties (the developer being the other), any grantee of the builder's would be in privity of estate and thus be bound.

13. **(C)** The restriction "except for residential purposes" should be interpreted to prohibit the operation of a beauty parlor in defendant's home. Such commercial activity clearly violates the plan and obvious purpose of the covenant and is prohibited by its terms. Choice (A) is incorrect because the change in character of the surrounding neighborhood would not justify failure to enforce the restriction where the original purpose of the restriction could still be realized. Choice (B) is incorrect because the rezoning to commercial use (in the surrounding neighborhood) would not justify failure to enforce the restriction where the original purpose of the restriction could still be realized. Choice (D) is wrong because the operation of a beauty parlor in defendant's home would constitute a violation of the restrictive covenant so as to justify injunctive relief.

14. **(B)** The reciprocal rights of first refusal must "vest," if at all, during the respective lifetimes of the lawyer and the friend. Because the lawyer is a measuring life, we will know within the lawyer's lifetime whether he will exercise his option to purchase the friend's land. Consequently, there is no violation of the rule. Choice (A) is incorrect. The lawyer does not win because the friend also had his own right of first refusal. Even if there were no reciprocal right of first refusal, the lawyer would still prevail because his right of first refusal, standing alone, does not violate the Rule against Perpetuities. Because this answer choice suggests that in order to have a valid right of first refusal, someone else must be given the same courtesy in return, it is incorrect. Choice (C) is incorrect. The inclusion of a ***right of first refusal*** in a deed instrument constitutes a partial restraint on alienation. Such restraints are usually valid, provided they do not violate the Rule against Perpetuities. Choice (D) is incorrect. A deed conveying land can include a right of first refusal. Such a right that is included in a deed can be enforced if necessary. Because rights of first refusal can relate to land that is conveyed by deed, this answer choice is incorrect.

15. **(B)** In a joint tenancy, each joint tenant owns the ***whole of the property, not a share or fractional part thereof.*** In this regard, a joint tenant may convey away his entire interest in jointly owned property or dispose of a fractional part thereof. The daughter's deed to the co-worker carved out and vested in the co-worker an undivided one-half interest in the northeast quarter of the farm, which the co-worker owned as a tenant in common with the friend. Next, because a joint tenant has the right and power voluntarily to dispose of his interest in jointly owned property, his creditors have the right and power to take that interest involuntarily. Therefore, the daughter's judgment creditor, the lender, had the right to levy upon and sell the daughter's interest in the south half of the farm to the nephew. As such, the friend and the nephew are tenants in common of the south half of the farm, each owning an undivided one-half interest therein. Finally, with respect to the northwest quarter of the farm, the daughter and the friend remained joint tenants of that quarter until the daughter's death. The friend's right of survivorship defeats the right of the daughter's surviving heir, the husband. Consequently, the husband can claim no interest in the northwest quarter of the farm. Choice (A) is incorrect. Regarding the northwest quarter of the farm, the daughter and the friend remained joint tenants of that quarter until the daughter's death. The friend's right of survivorship defeats the right of the daughter's surviving heir, the husband. Consequently, the husband can claim no interest in the northwest quarter of the farm. Choice (C) is incorrect. Regarding the northwest quarter of the farm, the daughter and the friend remained joint tenants of that quarter until the daughter's death. The friend's right of survivorship defeats the right of the daughter's surviving heir, the husband. Consequently, the husband can claim no interest in the northwest quarter of the farm. Moreover, the friend and the nephew are tenants in common of the south half of the farm. Choice (D) is incorrect. Because the daughter executed a deed to the co-worker and borrowed from the lender, it is not possible for the friend to be the fee owner outright of the remaining three-quarters under a right of survivorship theory.

16. **(A)** Generally, an easement carries with it certain other rights that allow the easement holder to make those improvements and maintenance requirements that are reasonable in order to allow that easement to carry out its intended purpose. One of the intended purposes was to build a home, and that is what the buyer did. A court will likely allow the buyer the further right to lay wires under the property to connect with an electrical source in order to effectuate the purposes of the easement and to fully enjoy the easement granted to him. Choice (B) is wrong because at the time of the conveyance an ***express easement*** was created in the deed instrument to permit the buyer to have access across the main trail. In order to have an easement by implication, two basic requirements must be met: (1) the benefited parcel and the burdened parcel must at one time have had a common owner, and (2) the circumstances surrounding the severance of the two parcels must indicate an ***intent*** to create such an easement. However, it is not necessary to create an easement in this way because an express easement was granted to the buyer. Choice (C) is wrong because an easement by necessity also arises by implication. However, it is not necessary to discuss the necessity of the easement because there was an express easement granted to the buyer. Choice (D) is incorrect because it simply states two requirements for the creation of an easement by implication. However, this choice fails to explain why the buyer has the right to go beyond the words of the express grant and lay wires under the main trail. This choice is incomplete and incorrect.

17. **(A)** On the MBE, when a statute is given in the facts, the words of that statute become very important to answering the question. In the absence of statute, the exercise of a testamentary power fails if the appointee predeceases the donor. A similar rule applies with respect to testamentary gifts. However, a majority of states have enacted ***anti-lapse statutes that provide if a devisee or legatee predeceases the testator, there is not necessarily a lapsed legacy.*** Designated relatives of the devisee or legatee, such as children, are entitled to take in his stead. Because this jurisdiction has a relevant anti-lapse statute in effect, the granddaughter's interest passes to her son. Choice (B) is incorrect. This choice discusses an issue that is not relevant to these facts. There was no risk of a class gift ever lapsing here because the widow devised the apartment building to the granddaughter and the granddaughter alone. Because the anti-lapse statute will allow the estate to pass to the son (a singular person), there is no issue of a class gift. Choice (C) is incorrect because it falsely suggests that the son cannot take because the granddaughter died intestate and that the statute cannot protect a specific devisee, such as the son. However, the anti-lapse statute does not make such a distinction, and the fact that the granddaughter died intestate will not harm the son's ability to take. Choice (D) is incorrect. Because there is an anti-lapse statute in effect, the apartment building will not pass to the friend and the assistant under the residuary clause of the will. Rather, it will pass to the son as the granddaughter's heir.

18. **(D)** In this question, the buyer is seeking restitution. Although this question appears to involve misrepresentation or deceit, in reality it deals with ***mutual mistake.*** Because the grocer and the buyer were mutually mistaken as to validity of their land sale transaction, the conveyance may be ***rescinded*** and the buyer is entitled to recover the purchase price. When parties enter into an agreement under a misunderstanding (or under mistaken assumptions of fact), courts may rescind the contract and order restitution. In such cases, the mistake must be a serious one or go to the "essence" of the contract. **Exam Tip:** Here, the court is ordering ***rescission of the land-sale contract due to mutual mistake*** and simultaneously granting ***restitution*** to restore the parties to the position they were in before the agreement was entered into. Choice (A) is incorrect. Although this question appears to involve misrepresentation, fraud, or deceit, in reality it deals with ***mutual mistake.*** Because the grocer and the buyer were mutually mistaken as to validity of their land-sale transaction, the conveyance may be ***rescinded*** and the buyer is entitled to recover the purchase price. So, even though the grocer was also a fraud victim, his proper recourse would be against the rancher. As far as the buyer–grocer contract is concerned, mutual mistake will be allowed as a means of allowing rescission and restitution. Choice (B) is incorrect. This amount would be the amount of profit that the grocer gained in selling the property to the buyer. However, to award the buyer only $25,000 would not place him in the position he occupied before the agreement with the grocer was entered into. To allow a true rescission of the deal and give full restitution, the buyer will be awarded the entire $125,000 purchase price. Choice (C) is incorrect. This amount has no significance aside from the fact that it appears to be double the profit that the grocer gained in selling the property to the buyer. However, to award the buyer only this $50,000 would not place him in the position he occupied before the agreement with the grocer was entered into. To allow full restitution, the buyer will be awarded the entire $125,000 purchase price.

19. **(D)** The vendor has an affirmative obligation ***to convey "good" and "marketable" title to the vendee at closing.*** The veterinarian agreed to deliver the warranty deed to the investor upon the final payment of 30 monthly installments. Thus, the veterinarian is not under an obligation to tender "good" and "marketable" title until the date the last $10,000 installment payment is due, so the veterinarian's own mortgage need not be resolved until the date of the last payment. Accordingly, the purchaser may not rescind a land-sale contract before the closing date or when performance is due. Choice (A) is incorrect. Certainly an installment land-sale agreement is a security device. However, this still does not explain why the investor is required to continue paying on that installment land agreement. The investor is required to continue paying because the veterinarian has not breached the land-sale agreement. Because the veterinarian is not required to tender good and marketable title until the time the last payment is due, she has not breached the contract. Choice (D) explains that the reason the veterinarian is not in breach is because the time for performance has not yet arrived. That makes choice (D) a better answer than (A). Choice (B) is incorrect. The right of redemption allows a mortgagor in default to pay off the amount owed to the mortgagee and any interest prior to foreclosure. Because the issue here is when the veterinarian is required to pay

off her own mortgage and when she is required to deliver marketable title, the investor's right of redemption is not in issue. Therefore, this choice is incorrect. Choice (C) is wrong because the mortgage will have the legal effect of rendering title unmarketable if it is not "removed" or "cured" before the date of closing.

20. **(C)** The ***"inverse order of alienation" rule*** applies when a mortgaged tract of land is "sold off" or conveyed in parcels and the various grantees pay full value to the mortgagor without getting a release from the mortgagee. Upon default, if the mortgagee forecloses, the "inverse order" rule will require ***the mortgagee to proceed first against the lands still owned by the mortgagor, and then proceed against the other parcels in the inverse order in which they were sold*** until the mortgage is fully satisfied. The rationale is that the buyer of the first parcel acquired the most equity, and likewise down the line, until the land still held by the mortgagor that has the least equity. As between the mortgagor and the grantees, the mortgagor should pay the debt and his land should be sold first for that purpose. Law of Property, Boyer, pg. 512. If the mortgagee—the bank—forecloses, it must proceed first against lot 3, the land still owned by the landowner, the mortgagor. If the proceeds are insufficient to discharge the mortgage debt, then the mortgagee may foreclose against lots 1 and 2 in the "inverse order of the alienation" (i.e., lot 2 first, then lot 1) until the mortgage is satisfied. Choice (C) states the correct rule of law. Choice (A) is incorrect. Under the "inverse order of alienation" rule, the bank is required proceed first against the lands still owned by the mortgagor, the landowner. Then the bank can proceed against the other parcels in the inverse order in which they were sold. Because this choice states that the bank can foreclose only against lot 3, it is incorrect. Choice (B) is incorrect. Under the "inverse order of alienation" rule, the bank is required to proceed first against the lands still owned by the mortgagor, the landowner. Then the bank can proceed against the other parcels in the inverse order in which they were sold. Because this choice states that the bank has a choice as to which parcel they can foreclose on, it is incorrect. Choice (D) is incorrect. The friend's and the brother's deeds were silent as to the mortgage between the landowner and the bank. These two grantees took their parcels "subject to" the mortgage. Therefore, they are not personally liable. However, the bank can still foreclose on lots 1and 2 to satisfy the mortgage if necessary, even though the friend and the brother took "subject to" the mortgage. The bank, however, cannot sue the friend and the brother personally. Because this choice states that the bank can foreclose on the lots only if the friend and the brother assumed the mortgage, choice (D) is incorrect.

21. **(C)** This question deals with the area of emblements, or ***fructus industriales.*** Growing crops are generally classified as personal property and will pass with a sale or mortgage of the land. Therefore, upon the retiree's sale of his farm to the grower, the growing tobacco crop will pass as personal property, and the retiree will not be entitled to remove it. Choice (A) is incorrect. Growing crops are generally classified as personal property and will pass with a sale or mortgage of the land. Therefore, upon the retiree's sale of his farm to the grower, the growing tobacco crop will pass as personal property, and the retiree will not be entitled to remove it because no longer belongs to him. The retiree is not entitled to enter to remove the tobacco, so his paying the grower to enter is irrelevant. Choice (B) is incorrect. Growing crops are generally classified as personal property and will pass with a sale or mortgage of the land. Therefore, upon the retiree's sale of his farm to the grower, the growing tobacco crop will pass as personal property, and the retiree will not be entitled to remove it because no longer belongs to him. Choice (D) is incorrect. Growing crops are generally classified as personal property and will pass with a sale or mortgage of the land. Therefore, upon the retiree's sale of his farm to the grower, the growing tobacco crop will pass as personal property, and the retiree will not be entitled to remove it because no longer belongs to him. There is no need to engage in an equitable division of the proceeds from the sale of the tobacco crop.

22. **(B)** An indenture granting cross easements would most likely accomplish the plan as well as be most acceptable to all of the parties involved. An indenture is a deed to which two or more persons are parties, in which the parties enter into reciprocal and corresponding grants or obligations to each other. The cross-easements would grant equal rights of access and use to the attorney and the dentist who own the adjoining properties [identified as (A) and (D) on the diagram]. The botanist and the chemist are owners of the servient tenement [lots (B) and (C) on the diagram]. The attorney and the dentist are owners of the dominant tenement [lots (A) and (D)], because they are benefited by the easements.

Thus, easements appurtenant are created by the indenture. Choice (A) is incorrect. A covenant is a restriction on the use of land that is enforceable at law. It is attached to or connected with the estate because it may be enforced against, or by, someone who is not one of the original parties to the covenant. However, this does not explain how the attorney and the dentist will gain access to a badminton court that is on someone else's property. Because a covenant is not an interest in land (but rather a restriction on the use of land), it is not going to give the attorney or the dentist the right to use the property of another. Because an easement is an interest in land, it is a better answer. Choice (C) is incorrect. An equitable servitude is a restriction on the use of land that is enforceable in equity. However, this does not explain how the attorney and the dentist will gain access to a badminton court that is on someone else's property. Because an easement would explain how these two neighbors will gain access to the courts, it is a better answer. Choice (D) is incorrect. A fee interest is not necessary here when the only goal is to give the attorney and the dentist a means to get onto the badminton court on the property of another. This granting of cross-easements will allow the attorney and the dentist to go onto the land of another to access the court, even when the botanist and/or the chemist have granted their properties to another. All that is required here is that the attorney and the dentist be given a right to use the land of another; they do not need to be given a fee interest in the land of another just to be able to use the land. Because this answer choice goes too far in giving actual fee ownership, it is incorrect.

23. **(A)** An affirmative covenant would provide the best legal arrangement under the circumstances. Promises respecting land are referred to as covenants. Here, the covenant would require an affirmative action, thus binding the parties to share in the construction and maintenance costs of the cat park. In effect, the obligation to pay money would be utilized for purposes relating to the land, e.g., it "touches and concerns" the land. Furthermore, the payment relates to the land in which all four of the parties have an interest. Therefore, such a covenant to pay money could be enforceable at law as a ***covenant running with the land.*** *There are four prerequisites for the creation of a covenant at law, as follows:* ***(1) a writing in compliance with Statute of Frauds; (2) an intent that the covenant run with the land; (3) the covenant must "touch and concern" the land; and (4) privity of estate must exist between the covenantor and covenantee.*** Choice (B) is incorrect. ***A cooperative organization (or co-op) is a form of ownership whereby a corporation will hold title to land and/or buildings and will then lease the units to those who own shares in that corporation. No one in this fact pattern desires that there be any ownership interest in the land that the park is built upon. At most, the four neighbors simply desire that the parties promise to pay the costs of construction and maintenance of the cat park. The best way to do this would be through affirmative covenants. Choice*** (C) is incorrect. To create a tenancy in common would create an ownership interest in the land that the park is built upon. ***No one in this fact pattern desires that there be any ownership interest in the land that the park is built upon. At most, the four neighbors simply desire that the parties promise to pay the costs of construction and maintenance of the cat park and then use the cat park. The best way to do this would be through affirmative covenants. Choice*** (D) is incorrect. The issue of implied reciprocal servitudes arises when there is a common development scheme and one of the owners fails to comply with the covenants that the other owners must follow because those covenants do not appear in his specific deed. That is not necessary here because the four parties involved will make affirmative covenants to pay for the construction and maintenance of the cat park. Moreover, this fact pattern does not deal with conformance to a common development scheme, making choice (D) incorrect.

24. **(A)** When the grower died and her will was admitted to probate in November 1993, the bank's mortgage on the lemon grove had not yet been recorded. Therefore, the husband's fee simple title to the lemon grove would be unaffected by the prior unrecorded mortgage (in accordance with the relevant recording statute in effect). So, if the husband was fully unaware of the existence of the mortgage and had no actual notice of it, then he would prevail because there was no constructive notice of this mortgage when he acquired title. Choice (B) is incorrect because it falsely suggests that the only way that the husband can take the lemon grove free of the grower's mortgage is if there were simply no mortgage on the property when he acquired title. Where the language of conveyance is silent, the grantee is considered to take "subject to" the mortgage. This means that the grantee is not personally liable for the mortgage debt. The husband can acquire the lemon grove free of any mortgage because it was not recorded early enough, and this is true even if

there was a mortgage on it when he acquired it. Choice (C) is incorrect. Where the language of conveyance is silent, the grantee is considered to take "subject to" the mortgage. This means that the grantee is not personally liable for the mortgage debt. Because the husband never "assumed" the mortgage, this choice is incorrect. Choice (D) is incorrect. All this choice does is state that the mortgage would continue to bind the property for its duration, and that principle might serve to bind the successors in interest if they "assumed" the mortgage debt. However, the husband never assumed the mortgage, and the mortgage was never recorded anyway, so the husband is not personally liable.

25. **(D)** The franchise right would be construed as an easement in gross. This non-possessory interest is created when the holder of the easement interest acquires his right of special use in the servient tenement independent of his ownership or possession of another tract of land. In an easement in gross, the easement holder is not benefited in his use and enjoyment of a possessory estate (i.e., there is no dominant tenement) by virtue of the acquisition of that privilege. Choice (A) is incorrect because a license is a revocable privilege to enter upon the land of another. The grant from the developer to the utility companies went beyond a mere privilege to enter; rather, this was an intent to grant a strip of land to be used for utility purposes. Choice (B) is incorrect because an equitable servitude is a restriction on the use to which an owner may make of his land. Choice (C) is wrong because the utility company did not possess an adjoining dominant tenement.

26. **(B)** The proviso prohibiting lot owners to construct a house or structure on the strip of land would properly be construed as an equitable servitude. An equitable servitude is a restriction on the use to which an owner may make of his land. It is created (1) by a writing complying with the Statute of Frauds; (2) concerning a promise that "touches and concerns" the land; and (3) by indicating an intention that the servitude exists. The basis for enforcing an equitable servitude is that one who takes land with notice (actual or constructive) of a restriction on the land cannot in equity be allowed to violate that restriction. Choice (A) is incorrect. An easement is the right of one person to go onto the land in possession of another and make a limited use thereof. Restriction 23 is a restriction on the use of land, not the right to use the land of another. Because the restriction, by itself, does not create an easement, choice (A) is incorrect. Choice (C) is wrong because the lot owners are under a negative, not affirmative, obligation to refrain from constructing on the said strip. Choice (D) is incorrect because it is inapplicable inasmuch as Restriction (23) is a restriction on the use of land, not a fee interest in it.

27. **(B)** Because the encroachment of the fence violated the restriction (i.e., equitable servitude), the teacher would be entitled to injunctive relief. Because the plan was recorded and because the librarian is a grantee of the developer, the librarian will have notice of restrictions in the chain of title. Therefore, the teacher can compel the librarian to remove the fence because it violates Restriction (23). Choice (A) is incorrect because the restriction would be construed as an equitable servitude, rather than an easement. Choice (C) is incorrect. Choice (C) falsely suggests that the teacher must also sue the retiree just to be able to seek relief against the librarian. As long as the librarian has violated the covenant, the teacher can enjoin the violation by seeking a mandatory injunction. The fact that the teacher fails to seek an injunction against the retiree (for the retiree's own fence) is irrelevant to his right to seek an injunction against the librarian. Choice (D) is incorrect. Clause (23) uses the language "of any kind" to suggest that there is no set list of things that would trigger the restriction if they were built. A fence would qualify as a structure "of any kind" because the intent was to grant an easement for utilities along that strip and to keep that area free of obstructions regardless of size or substance.

28. **(C)** An easement is deemed appurtenant when the right of special use benefits the holder of the easement in his physical use or enjoyment of another tract of land. ***For an easement appurtenant to exist, there must be two tracts of land; the dominant tenement (which has the benefit of the easement), and the servient tenement (which is subject to the easement right).*** The citrus grower's property interest in the use of his right-of-way across the grapefruit grove would be construed as an easement appurtenant. Choice (A) is incorrect because a license is a revocable privilege to enter upon the lands of the licensor. The call of the question asks what the citrus grower's property interest is; a license

is not a property interest. Choice (B) is incorrect. An easement is in gross when it is intended to benefit the holder of easement personally, rather than in connection with any land the holder owns. In other words, every easement in gross requires only one piece of land (i.e., the servient tenement) that is owned by a person other than the owner of the easement in gross. This easement enhances the enjoyment of the orange grove because it allows for a method of ingress and egress to the orange grove. Thus, the easement is appurtenant, not in gross. Choice (D) is incorrect. An easement may be acquired by prescription in a manner similar to that by which ownership of a possessory estate may be acquired by adverse possession. However, the farmer granted the citrus grower an express easement by written agreement, so it is not necessary to evaluate the elements required for a prescriptive easement.

29. **(D)** ***Mere excessive use of an easement does not forfeit or extinguish the easement.*** In the case of excessive use, the owner of the easement is simply making use of the servient tenement beyond the scope or extent of the use permitted by the easement in its creation. The easement (as it was originally created) still exists and within its scope can be used. However, the user in excess of the scope of the easement can be enjoined and damages may be had for injury caused by the excess user. Thus, although the business owner may continue to use the right of way, the office workers' use of the right of way is not merely excessive, it is wholly unauthorized. Choice (A) is incorrect. The landscaper can obtain an injunction to stop the excessive and unauthorized use of the easement; but excessive use will not be enough to extinguish an easement. At most, the landscaper can stop the usage that is in excess of what he originally granted to the business owner. Choice (B) is incorrect. The landscaper can obtain an injunction to stop the excessive and unauthorized use of the easement; but excessive use will not be enough to create a forfeiture of the easement. At most, the landscaper can stop the usage that is in excess of what he originally granted to the business owner. Choice (C) is incorrect. The landscaper can obtain an injunction to stop the excessive and unauthorized use of the easement; but excessive use will not be enough to cause the business owner from being permanently enjoined from using the easement, because the fact remains that the landscaper gave the business owner an express easement for ingress and egress across the eastern parcel and to make reasonable use of that easement. At most, the landscaper can stop the usage that is in excess of what he originally granted to the business owner.

30. **(D)** Choice (D) is correct because an express easement appurtenant was created by the written agreement between the neighbor (owner of the servient tenement) and the wedding planner (owner of the dominant tenement). This granted the wedding planner the right to use the strip of land across the neighbor's property for ingress and egress. Choice (A) is incorrect because an easement in gross is personal to the owner and the use is not connected in any way with the enjoyment of any other land. Choice (B) is incorrect. Choice (B) is an implied easement viewed by the courts as arising by reason of prior use. It is not necessary to evaluate the requirements for an easement by implication because the easement was given by express grant. Choice (C) is incorrect because it is an implied easement viewed by the courts as arising by reason of necessity. It is not necessary to evaluate the requirements for an easement by necessity since the easement was given by express grant.

31. **(C)** Choice (C) is correct because although the owner of the servient tenement remains the owner of the land subject to the easement he has granted, he may only make such use of the land as long as he does not unduly or unreasonably interfere with the rights created for the dominant owner. Choice (A) is incorrect. This choice goes too far in restricting the neighbor's use of his own land. The neighbor owns the servient tenement and will not be completely enjoined from using the road at all because that would restrict the neighbor too severely. All that is required here is that the neighbor not behave in such a way as to damage or restrict usage of the easement that he granted to the caterer. Because this choice enjoins all use by the neighbor, it is incorrect. Choice (B) is incorrect. Although the owner of the servient tenement remains the owner of the land subject to the easement he has granted, he may only make such use of the land as long as he does not unduly or unreasonably interfere with the rights created for the dominant owner. However, if the use by the servient tenant does unduly interfere with the rights of the dominant owner, then that use can be enjoined. Because this choice falsely suggests that the servient owner can do what s/he wants to the exclusion of the rights of

the dominant tenant, it is incorrect. Choice (D) is incorrect. The caterer, as an easement holder, has rights in this strip of land. One of those rights would be the right to enjoin those uses that interfere with his access to that easement. There is no requirement that the caterer only has a remedy of money damages. The caterer has a right to enjoin those uses that interfere with his use because money damages may not be what the caterer is seeking.

32. **(A)** Choice (A) is the correct choice because today the statutory presumption is in favor of creating easements appurtenant for perpetual duration unless the grant specifically limits the interest. On the other hand, one should note that an easement in gross is generally inalienable. Choice (B) is incorrect because it incorrectly focuses on recording statutes and chain-of-title problems. The concept of *bona fide* purchaser (BFP) comes up when the applicable recording statute will protect a subsequent BFP who takes without notice of prior conveyances. This concept is relevant when competing grantees are vying for the same piece of land. However, there is no such competition taking place here between competing grantees. The assistant has a property interest in the easement because he is a grantee of the chef, the original dominant tenant. This choice provides the assistant with a very weak argument because his status of BFP is irrelevant to helping him explain why he owns an easement across the neighbor's property, even though he was not an original party to the original grant of easement. Choice (A) will explain why the assistant still has a right to cross the neighbor's property and why he has the right to enjoin further use of barriers across the road. Choice (C) is incorrect. The easement was originally created by an express grant. This choice is not accurate on the facts. Choice (D) is incorrect. The concept of tacking arises in adverse possession situations where the current adverse possessor will "tack on" and use a prior adverse possessor's time to meet the statutory period. Not only was no one adversely possessing the property, there was an express grant of easement, so there is no need to consider how long the easement was being used by each party.

33. **(C)** Choice (C) is correct because ***mere non-use, however long continued, will not terminate an express easement.*** In addition, there must be evidence of some affirmative or overt act on the part of the easement holder, i.e., dominant owner manifesting his intent to abandon the easement. Choice (A) is incorrect. Non-use of an easement, no matter how long continued, will ***not*** be sufficient to terminate an easement. However, non-use ***coupled with an intent to abandon*** is sufficient to constitute an abandonment. The sculptor's absence for 11 years will not, alone, be enough to constitute an abandonment of the easement. Choice (B) is incorrect because it falsely suggests that the neighbor will prevail because the sculptor failed to notify the neighbor of his non-use (due to an affirmative duty to notify that the easement will not be used). However, non-use alone will still not be enough to constitute an abandonment anyway. So, even if the sculptor had notified the neighbor that he will not be using the easement due to business reasons in Europe, that will still not be enough to constitute an abandonment, and the neighbor will not prevail. Choice (D) is incorrect because it focuses on the ***creation*** of the easement. Certainly there is a valid agreement for an express easement. There was never any doubt about that. However, this choice does not address why the sculptor still ***retains*** his interest in the easement despite an 11-year absence. The reason the sculptor still has an easement (and the right to compel the neighbor to remove the ramp) is because his non-use was not enough to constitute an abandonment. Because choice (C) addresses this reason, it is a better choice.

34. **(A)** If there is ***negligence*** on the part of the wrongdoer who removes lateral support, then the wrongdoer is liable for all damages that naturally and proximately flow from his negligence, including damages to both land and artificial structures. Choice (B) is incorrect. One who by excavation or otherwise withdraws lateral support from his neighbor's land is ***absolutely and strictly liable*** (regardless of negligence) for land that is in its natural condition. When land has artificial structures on it and those structures are damaged due to a removal of lateral support, the plaintiff must then show negligence on the part of the defendant. Choice (C) is incorrect because it is incomplete. The neighbor could be liable for damage to an artificial structure if there were negligence on his part. The way choice (C) is written forecloses any possibility of there being any liability. Because liability could possibly attach to the neighbor's activities if negligence were found to exist, this choice is incorrect. Choice (D) is incorrect. An adjacent landowner has a duty not to remove lateral support to the extent that strict liability is created if removal

causes damage to land in its natural condition. If there is ***negligence*** on the part of the wrongdoer who removes lateral support, then the wrongdoer is liable for all damages that naturally and proximately flow from his negligence, including damages to both land and artificial structures. Because this choice states that no duty is owed, it is incorrect.

35. **(B)** A tenancy in common was created by the widower's testamentary devise to the co-worker and the boss in spite of the language "as their community property" because they were siblings, not husband and wife. Upon the death intestate of a tenant in common, his interest descends to his heirs. The daughter (as the boss's sole heir) would have an undivided one-half interest in the property. Choice (A) is incorrect. The widower did not convey the property to the co-worker and the boss as joint tenancy with right of survivorship. Joint tenancies are disfavored and require a clear expression of intent to create this estate; otherwise it will not be recognized and there will be tenancy in common. Because this was at most a tenancy in common, there was no right of survivorship and the co-worker will not take the whole of the property under a right of survivorship theory. Choice (C) is incorrect. A tenancy by the entirety requires the unity of husband and wife in order to be effective. Because the co-worker and the boss were siblings, there can be no tenancy by the entirety. Choice (D) is incorrect. The widower did not convey the property to the co-worker and the boss as joint tenancy with right of survivorship. Joint tenancies are disfavored and require a clear expression of intent to create this estate; otherwise it will not be recognized and there will be tenancy in common. It is because this was a tenancy in common that the boss's interest passed to the daughter. This choice is incorrect because it states that the daughter received an undivided whole interest because it was a joint tenancy. If anything, the opposite result would be reached; if the property were truly owned by the co-worker and the boss as joint tenants, the daughter would receive nothing upon the boss's death because of the co-worker's right of survivorship. For these reasons, this choice is incorrect.

36. **(B)** Choice (B) is the best alternative because a conveyance of the dominant tenement (lot 2) carries with it all easements and profits appurtenant thereto as incidents unless it is otherwise expressly provided. When the neighbor conveyed to the professor, the professor received not only the estate of lot 2, but also the easement appurtenant to it that benefits lot 2. Choice (A) is incorrect because an easement by implication arises from the circumstances surrounding the dividing by the owner of a piece of land into two pieces and conveying one of the pieces to another. From such surrounding circumstances, an inference is drawn that the parties intend the creation of an easement. In the present case, the co-worker and the boss created an express easement in the deed instrument permitting the neighbor to use the driveway. Choice (C) is wrong because the written deed instrument does satisfy the Statute of Frauds. Choice (D) is incorrect because mere non-use does not constitute an abandonment of the easement.

37. **(D)** The original deed provision between the widower and the president restricting subdivision of the parcels to minimum two-acre lots for residential use is an example of a restrictive, or negative, covenant running with the land. In order for a covenant to run with the land, the following four requirements must be met: (1) the covenant must be in writing; (2) it must "touch and concern" the land; (3) privity of estate must exist between covenantor and covenantee; and (4) there must be intent that the covenant run with the land. Choice (A) is incorrect. An easement is the right of one person to go onto the land in possession of another and make a limited use thereof. It is an interest in the land itself. The stipulation restricting the size and character is a covenant or a restriction on the use of land and not an interest in the land itself. Choice (B) is incorrect because an affirmative covenant imposes an obligation to perform a duty on the part of the covenantee, i.e., obligation of condominium owner to pay an annual fee for maintenance of common areas. Because this covenant restricts the use of the land, it is more appropriately termed a negative covenant. Choice (C) is incorrect. The covenant of quiet enjoyment is a deed covenant by the grantor that the grantee will not be disturbed in his possession or enjoyment of the property by a third party's lawful claim of title. This issue is inapplicable to these facts.

38. **(D)** Choice (D) is correct because a covenant running with the land will be enforceable against successors of the original parties, where, again, the following four requirements are met: (1) there is privity of estate between the original parties and their successors; (2) the covenant "touches and concerns" the land; (3) the parties intend the covenant to run with the land; and (4) the covenant is in writing. Thus, the subsequent grantees, i.e., owners of tract 1 lots, may enforce the original restrictive covenant between the retiree and the president. Choice (A) is incorrect. A covenant running with the land will be enforceable against successors of the original parties, where, again, the following four requirements are met: (1) there is privity of estate between the original parties and their successors; (2) the covenant "touches and concerns" the land; (3) the parties intend the covenant to run with the land; and (4) the covenant is in writing. Thus, the subsequent grantees, i.e., owners of tract 1 lots, may enforce the original restrictive covenant between the retiree and the president. Because the current owners will have standing to sue, even though they were not the original covenanting parties, this answer choice is incorrect. Choice (B) is incorrect. A covenant running with the land will be enforceable against successors of the original parties. The covenant made by the grantor (the retiree) and grantee (the contractor) will be binding upon successive grantees of the original covenanting parties. The action will be successful and this choice is incorrect. Choice (C) is incorrect. The issue to be resolved in this question is whether or not grantees in the tract 2 development can be bound by the restrictive covenant even though the deeds they received made no mention of it. The restriction can be enforced because the covenant runs with the land and can bind remote grantees of the original covenanting parties. The issue of common development scheme is not the central issue here because it seems clear from the original deed from the retiree to the president that all 750 acres were to have this common feature of minimum lot sizes. This question falsely suggests that the issue of a common development scheme is the only issue that a court would have to decide. However, the enforceability of the restrictions is also in issue, and it is the issue that is most in need of being decided.

39. **(A)** Choice (A) is correct because the change in the character of the neighborhood was not of such a magnitude as to render the restriction unenforceable. As a result, the restrictions must continue to be enforced. Choice (B) is incorrect. The restriction was to single-family dwelling units only. This medical practice will likely not be considered by the court to be a conforming use. Choice (C) is incorrect. While it is true that the area has been rezoned, those zoning ordinances will not serve to invalidate the covenants unless neighborhood conditions have changed sufficiently to make the servitude meaningless. However, the facts only state that the area has been rezoned. The facts do not say that the whole area immediately surrounding phase 2 and phase 1 has changed so much and to such an extent that the restriction renders the property unusable. Moreover, a change in the character of the neighborhood will never be enough to cause the restrictions to be unenforceable. The change in the neighborhood must be so fundamental that the servitude is rendered meaningless because the servitude can no longer survive in this changed neighborhood. Choice (D) is incorrect. This probably would be construed as a commercial enterprise because the doctors are running a for-profit medical clinic.

40. **(D)** A subsequent zoning ordinance will not destroy the restrictive covenant as long as there has not been such a change in the neighborhood as to make the physical use and enjoyment of the restriction meaningless. Quite so, the restrictive covenants in the deeds of the owners of phase 1 will be enforceable in accordance with the common development scheme preserving the residential character of the property. Choice (A) is incorrect. This is the opposite of choice (D), the correct choice. A subsequent zoning ordinance will not destroy the restrictive covenant as long as there has not been such a change in the neighborhood as to make the physical use and enjoyment of the restriction meaningless. Just because the area has been rezoned is not to say the restriction cannot co-exist. Nothing in the facts suggests that the neighborhood has changed so much as to render the covenant now unenforceable; all that has changed is that there has been a rezoning to allow for commercial use. That does not necessarily mean that the neighborhood itself has changed to such an extent as to make the physical use and enjoyment of the restriction meaningless. Choice (B) is incorrect. A covenant running with the land will be enforceable against successors of the original parties, where the following four requirements are met: (1) there is privity of estate between the original parties and their successors; (2) the covenant "touches and concerns" the land; (3) the parties intend the covenant

to run with the land; and (4) the covenant is in writing. Thus, the subsequent grantees, i.e., owners of phase 1 lots, may enforce the original restrictive covenant between the landowner's estate and the investor. Because the current owners will have standing to sue, even though they were not the original covenanting parties, this answer choice is incorrect. Choice (C) is incorrect. A subsequent zoning ordinance will not destroy the restrictive covenant as long as there has not been such a change in the neighborhood as to make the physical use and enjoyment of the restriction meaningless. As long as that does not occur, there is no reason to presume that the zoning ordinance necessarily "trumps" the covenant just because the covenant was arranged through a private agreement.

41. **(A)** ***A profit (sometimes called a "profit a prendre") is a non-possessory interest in land and consists of a right to take the soil or a substance of the soil.*** If the exercise of the right is restricted in the sense that it may be exercised only in connection with the use and enjoyment of a dominant estate, the right is a profit appurtenant. If the right is not so restricted, it is a profit in gross. Choice (B) is incorrect. A license simply ***permits one person to come onto the land in the possession of another without being a trespasser.*** A license is not an interest in land. It is merely a privilege, revocable at the will of the licensor. Because the coal company received the right to take coal from the property of another, their interest is a profit, not a license. Choice (C) is incorrect. An easement is an interest in land that allows the holder of the easement to use the property of another. An easement is in gross when it is intended to benefit the owner or possessor personally, rather than in connection with any land the holder owns. The coal company received more than just the right to use the land of another; it received the right to take substances and things from the property. The company's interest is a profit, not an easement in gross. Choice (D) is incorrect. Voluntary waste consists of injury to the premises or land caused by an intentional or negligent affirmative act of the tenant (either life tenant or tenant for years). However, the term *voluntary waste* refers to the conduct of a tenant, not the right granted. Because the call of the question asks for the name of the interest given, this choice is incorrect.

42. **(C)** Choice (C) is the LEAST accurate statement because the redomiciling (of a joint tenant) does not effectuate a severance. Generally, a severance of the joint tenancy can be made by (1) conveyance *inter vivos*, or (2) by partition only. Be aware that a severance can never be made by will because survivorship is prior to and defeats the effect of the will. Choice (A) is incorrect. A co-tenant out of possession has a right to share in rents and profits received from ***third parties. Because the call of the question asks for the least accurate statement, this choice will be discarded because it is an accurate statement regarding the rights and duties of joint tenants.*** Choice (B) is incorrect. A co-tenant out of possession has a right to share in rents and profits received from ***third parties. While it may be true that the woman should be allowed to receive a proportionate share of the royalties (to do equity), this is not the strongest statement of the four because this is not really expressing a specific rule of law. However, it is still not the least accurate and must therefore be discarded. Choice*** (D) is incorrect. A tenant in possession need not share such profits with a co-tenant out of possession, ***unless there has been an ouster.*** An ouster occurs where one co-tenant manages ***to wrongfully exclude her co-tenants from possession*** of the property. Because the woman's redomiciling alone does not constitute an ouster, the woman still retains the right to share in the proceeds. This choice is an accurate statement and is incorrect.

43. **(C)** The attorney–county deed contained a provision that abrogated the right to enforce the restrictive covenant. If the Board can argue that this is not a compensable taking because the attorney himself abrogated the restriction, the county will not have to pay just compensation because no taking was required. Thus, eminent domain would not be in issue. If the board can successfully argue that there was no taking, then the defendant will prevail. Choice (A) is wrong because the question wants you to presume that the lot owners will ***not*** prevail in their action to recover damages. In eminent domain proceedings, ***just compensation must always be paid to the landowner.*** Thus, if the lot owners fail in their suit to recover damages against the county, then eminent domain was not the means by which the county was able to use the land for an office building because if eminent domain were the controlling issue, the property owners would receive just compensation. Choice (B) is wrong because the question wants you to presume that the lot owners will ***not*** prevail in their action to recover damages. In an inverse

condemnation proceeding, ***just compensation must always be paid to the landowner.*** Thus, if the lot owners fail in their suit to recover damages against the county, then inverse condemnation was not the means by which the county was able to use the land for an office building because if that were the controlling issue, the property owners would receive just compensation. Choice (D) is wrong because an equitable servitude can be enforced against a buyer in a subdivision scheme, even though his/her deed does not necessarily contain the restriction. Whether or not a particular person can enforce an equitable servitude is determined by the intention of the parties.

44. **(B)** At common law, a ***tenancy by the entirety*** was created by a deed or will conveying to a husband and wife. The incident of ***survivorship*** attached such that ***neither spouse acting alone while the marriage existed could sever the tenancy or defeat the right of survivorship.*** See Smith and Boyer, Law of Property, pg. 65–66. Therefore, when the husband conveyed all his interest under the June 1, 2005 deed to the cousin, the tenancy by the entirety remained intact and the cousin received no interest with regard to that one-half interest in the land. A *joint tenancy,* on the other hand, can be *severed by conveyance* of the interest of one of the joint tenants. Such a conveyance destroys the unities of time, title, and interest and results in the creation of a *tenancy in common* (which contains only a unity of possession). Therefore, when the husband conveyed all his interest under the June 1, 2006 deed to the cousin, the joint tenancy was severed with the cousin and the brother each holding an undivided one-half interest as *tenants in common.* Upon the brother's death, no right of survivorship inured to the cousin, so the cousin retains only his one-half interest. Because the two deeds from the woman to the husband each comprised one-half of the entire tract, the cousin's interest is an undivided one-quarter interest in the land. Choice (B) is thus correct. The fact that the husband paid more of the purchase price than the brother under the 2006 deed ($80,000 of the $125,000 purchase price) is irrelevant because ***the husband and the brother took as joint tenants***—the language of the deed so expressed this intent—and therefore, by definition, ***they had to take the same interest (i.e., unity of interest).*** Had they taken as tenants in common, then the husband would have owned a greater interest than the brother, even though both co-tenants would have shared an equal right of possession. Choice (A) is incorrect. The property interests in this fact pattern were never parsed out in thirds. The parcels were conveyed in one-half interests and some interests became quarters (such as when the husband conveyed to the cousin, destroying the joint tenancy). Choice (C) is incorrect. The cousin cannot own a one-half interest in the land because when the husband conveyed to the cousin, that fact severed the joint tenancy that once existed between the husband and the brother. That meant that the brother and the cousin owned as tenants in common, so the most the cousin could have ever owned was an undivided one-quarter interest in the land. Choice (D) is incorrect. The cousin cannot own the one-half interest that the husband held with the wife as tenants by the entirety. Because the husband, acting alone, could not unilaterally convey his interest, that transfer to the cousin had no effect. At most, the cousin could own an undivided one-quarter interest in the land.

45. **(C)** In this race-notice jurisdiction, note that when both the co-worker and the investor took their mortgages, no one else had recorded, so both had taken without notice of any of the other parties. If this were a pure notice jurisdiction, then the investor would prevail here because notice is all that would matter. However. because this is a race-notice jurisdiction, we also require someone to be the first to record. Because both the co-worker and the investor are in the same situation (inasmuch as they both took without notice of any prior mortgagee), we now must see who was the first to record of those two. Because the co-worker recorded before the investor, her security interest will trump the investor's. As a result, the co-worker is able to satisfy her $120,000 claim from the foreclosure proceeds. The investor will be entitled to satisfy as much of her claim as possible and will receive the remaining $100,000. The friend receives nothing from the proceeds of the foreclosure sale because after the investor takes, there is nothing left. Choice (A) is incorrect. Because the investor was the second party to record, she will take some portion from the sale proceeds because the property did at least sell for more than the value of the co-worker's $120,000 claim. Thus, the investor can take the remaining $100,000 from the $220,000 purchase price. Choice (B) is incorrect. This is the amount of the friend's mortgage and is thus an incorrect dollar figure. Moreover, there is nothing to limit the investor's recovery to only $90,000; she is entitled to take the remaining $100,000 from the sale proceeds after the co-worker has been paid. Choice (D) is incorrect. The investor is not entitled to the

full amount of her original mortgage in the olive grove. Because the investor was not the first to record (but rather the second), she must take after the co-worker is paid and runs the risk that what is left over will not be enough to satisfy her debt and that is what occurred here. At most, she will be entitled to the remaining $100,000.

46. **(D)** A tenancy by the entirety is destroyed by the death of both spouses because the entirety interest applies only to a husband and wife during marriage. ***Death, just as divorce, eliminates the unity of person,*** and thus the need for the attribute of survivorship is also eliminated. Disposition of property upon the death of both spouses would then follow just as if the tenancy by the entirety were severed into a tenancy in common. In other words, the heirs would inherit the undivided interest of the deceased cotenant. Similarly, the disposition of a joint tenancy would follow as if a tenancy in common had existed. Therefore, even though neither a tenancy by the entirety nor a joint tenancy can be disposed of by will, a tenancy in common can be so devised. Thus, the son would obtain Hunter and Willa's one-half interest in the land under the 2005 deed as well as Hunter's one-quarter interest under the 2006 deed. Choice (D) is, therefore, the correct answer. See Smith and Boyer, Law of Property, pp. 61–65. Choice (A) is incorrect. The property interests in this fact pattern were never parsed out in thirds. The parcels were conveyed in one-half interests, and some interests became quarters (such as when the death of both Hunter and Brandon severed the joint tenancy passing a one-quarter interest to the son). Choice (B) is incorrect. After the deaths of all the parties, the joint tenancy and the tenancy by the entirety became severed. As a result of all of this, the son would obtain Hunter and Willa's one-half interest in the land under the 2005 deed as well as Hunter's one-quarter interest under the 2006 deed. Because the son now will own an undivided three-quarters interest in the land, this choice is incorrect. Choice (C) is incorrect. After the deaths of all the parties, the joint tenancy and the tenancy by the entirety became severed. As a result of all of this, the son would obtain Hunter and Willa's one-half interest in the land under the 2005 deed as well as Hunter's one-quarter interest under the 2006 deed. Because the son now will own an undivided three-quarters interest in the land, this choice is incorrect.

47. **(C)** First, it is necessary to determine what interest the railroad has across the 300-acre cattle ranch property. The answer is a fee simple determinable, which is a fee simple created to continue until the happening of a stated event. Because the duration of the estate is correlated to the happening of a named event—here, the ceasing to use it for railroad purposes—the estate ***terminates automatically*** by operation of law upon the happening of that event. A very important characteristic of this type of estate is that the instant it is no longer used for railroad purposes, it "reverts" back to the grantor or his heirs. The following words are usually used to create a determinable fee: "until" or "as long as." Choice (A) is wrong because nothing in the deed instrument would indicate the creation of a leasehold interest. The railroad received a fee interest in this strip that could have continued indefinitely as long as the strip was used for railroad purposes. Choice (B) is incorrect because the railroad does not have an easement. The railroad received a fee interest in this strip that could have continued indefinitely as long as the strip was used for railroad purposes. Choice (D) is incorrect because the railroad does not have an easement. The railroad received a fee interest in this strip that could have continued indefinitely as long as the strip was used for railroad purposes.

48. **(C)** Based on the present factual situation, the nephew, as the rancher's only heir, would have until October 1, 1975 (when he reached majority) plus 10 years in which to bring his ejectment action. Therefore, the seller became the owner on October 1, 1985, which, in accordance with the Statute of Limitations, was the last date on which the nephew could initiate an action to recover possession of the land in question. Choice (A) is incorrect. This would have represented the date that the administrator fraudulently gave to the seller to record. This is incorrect because the nephew was a child at the time of this transfer and had until 10 years after reaching the age of 21 (age 31) in which to bring an ejectment action against an adverse possessor. Choice (B) is incorrect. This date does not appear to have any significance to these facts because it is not the date of a significant event nor is this the anniversary of a significant event. Choice (D) is incorrect. The statute allows an ejectment action to be brought, at the very latest, within 10 years of reaching the age of majority or when the disability of unsound mind is removed.

This choice would allow the nephew to bring an ejectment action at any point before his own death, which could be many more than 10 years after reaching the age of majority. Because this statute allows at most 10 years in which to bring the ejectment action, this choice is incorrect.

49. **(D)** Under the doctrine of adverse possession, for one to hold real property adversely, that person's possession must be continuous and unbroken for the entire length of the statutory period. Because the developer was ousted from the land, her possession was disrupted due to the ouster and would not be continuous. Therefore, the developer will not become owner of the property (through adverse possession) until December 31, 2002. Because the administratrix was not in a position to convey legal title (because her administration of the doctor's estate was never formally approved by the court) of the property to the developer, the latter will not acquire legal title to the property until the expiration of the period of adverse possession. Choice (A) is incorrect. Because the manner in which the administratrix disposed of the doctor's property was never approved by the court, the manner in which the developer took title was not proper. The administratrix was not in a position to convey title, so the deed to the developer has no effect. So, even though there was a conveyance on November 1, 1962, that is not the date that the developer took title. Choice (B) is incorrect. The developer was ousted from the land by the woman on October 1, 1982. This date was just one month before the 20-year statutory limitations period would have expired. This act by the woman served to put the developer out of possession and stopped her own possession of the property. Because the developer had been dispossessed of the property, November 1, 1982 will no longer be of any meaning to the developer; she must start all over again. Choice (C) is incorrect. This is the date that the developer, at most, recovered the property from the woman and began to repossess it adversely. If anything this is the beginning of her period of adverse possession.

50. **(C)** A life tenant has the right to use the property during her/his lifetime. This includes the right to mortgage, to create liens, easements, or leases. However, none of these dispositions can extend beyond the period of the life estate. Boyer, Law of Property, pg. 13. Even though Osgood's will provided that Desmond took the property "subject to Cutler's mortgage," this provision would be invalid because the mortgage on Cutler's life estate could never extend past the end of Cutler's life. Because Desmond never assumed the mortgage, he is not personally liable for it. Choice (A) is incorrect. Cutler's mortgage was only as good as the estate attached to it; when Cutler dies, the mortgage will end with the life estate. For this reason, Desmond will not be liable. Moreover, being a devisee does not automatically create liability for Cutler's mortgage. Unless Desmond took the property and expressly assumed the mortgage, Desmond is not personally liable for the mortgage. Choice (B) is incorrect. Cutler's mortgage was only as good as the estate attached to it; when Cutler dies, the mortgage will end with the life estate. For this reason, Desmond will not be liable. So, even though Osgood's will provided that Desmond took the property "subject to Cutler's mortgage," this provision would be invalid because the mortgage on Cutler's life estate could never extend past the end of Cutler's life. Choice (D) is incorrect because it falsely suggests that only the person giving the mortgage can be the liable party. Had Desmond assumed the mortgage when he received the property, he would have been liable even though it was Cutler who initially gave a mortgage on Desertacre. The better reason why Desmond is not liable is because he did not assume the mortgage, as stated in choice (C).

51. **(D)** Questions covering mortgages are frequently tested on the MBE. By definition, ***a mortgage is an interest in land created by a written instrument providing security for the performance of a duty or the payment of a debt.*** Mortgages and assignments thereof should be recorded. Failure to record the mortgage may make it possible for the mortgagor to convey to a *bona fide* purchaser who would take free of the mortgage under the recording act. As such, choice (A) is a correct statement and thus an incorrect choice because the court would have to resolve the issue of whether or not the finance company had record notice of the bank's mortgage. Even though the facts state that the finance company had no actual notice of the mortgage to the bank, if the court finds there is record (or constructive notice), then the finance company will not prevail. Choice (B) is also a correct statement because the deed instrument stated that the mortgage would apply to property "now owned by (the woman)

or which shall be owned" in the future. Consequently, when the woman subsequently purchased the 50-acre estate, the bank would argue that its mortgage interest covers that property as well as the 20 acres of timberland. Note that such "after-acquired" property clauses in mortgage instruments are enforceable as long as the after-acquired property is sufficiently identified to put third parties on notice. Because this issue of whether or not the quoted clause applies to the 50-acre estate is one that the court will, in fact, have to address, choice (B) is incorrect. In addition, choice (C) is also a correct statement because if the finance company's mortgage is viewed as a purchase money mortgage, it would clearly take priority over the "after-acquired" property clause contained in the bank's mortgage instrument. A purchase money mortgage takes priority over other prior mortgages regardless of recording statutes. The purchase money mortgage itself, however, must be recorded. Under these facts, it appears that the finance company's mortgage was a purchase money mortgage, but the court would still have to decide this issue to come to this conclusion, making (C) an incorrect choice. Choice (D) is an issue that the court will not have to resolve, thus making it the correct choice. There is no reason for the finance company to resort to an implied purchase money lien because the court will find that the finance company received a purchase money mortgage.

52. **(B)** An easement by implication generally arises when the owner of two or more adjacent parcels sells one or more of them and it is clear (although no easement was mentioned in the instrument of conveyance) that one was intended. In order to establish an easement by implication, one part of the land must have been used for the benefit of the other part at the time of the conveyance, the use must be apparent and continuous, as well as necessary to the enjoyment of the quasi-dominant tract. In all likelihood, the buyer's best chance of success would be to show that she acquired an easement by implication, rather than an easement by necessity. This is so because a greater degree of necessity is required by the latter easement. For an ***easement by necessity,*** the buyer must prove that the ***easement is "necessary."*** The facts tell us that the buyer used the path regularly, but also that she cleared the path a year after building the house, suggesting that it was convenient—but not ***necessary***. Choice (B) is preferred over choice (A) because an easement by implication does not require as great a burden of proof as an easement by necessity. The question prompt asks for the BEST CHANCE of success. The establishment of an easement by prescription, much like the establishment of ownership by adverse possession requires that the use be (1) adverse as distinct from permissive, (2) open and notorious, (3) continuous and without interruption, and (4) for the statutory period. Because no facts suggest that these elements have been met, answer choice (C) is wrong. Choice (D) is incorrect because no easement was granted expressly through a writing.

53. **(C)** Many students do poorly on the Multistate because they "out-psych" themselves into thinking that every MBE question involves some "trick." This is not true. Sometimes the simple, obvious answer is correct. Here, for example, the facts state that "the friend agreed to convey his interest in the apartment building to the daughter." The question then asked is, "Which of the following would be a valid conveyance by the friend?" The correct answer is "to the daughter and her heirs and assigns," as this language would transfer the friend's interest to the daughter in fee simple. Choices (A) and (B) are wrong because they do not carry out the friend's ***intention, which was to convey his interest in the apartment building to the daughter and not to the estate of the assistant. Furthermore, the language in choice (A) suggests that the assistant's estate can have heirs and assigns. Only a person has heirs and assigns. Choice (D) is incorrect because it is not possible to convey an interest in land to a dead person. Because the assistant is dead she cannot take, so there is no "remainder" for the daughter.***

54. **(D)** Percolating water is water beneath the surface of the earth that is not confined to a known and well-defined channel or bed. ***The common law rule is one of absolute ownership.*** A landowner is not restricted in the withdrawal of percolating water located beneath the surface of her land, ***even if this causes drainage of water from adjoining land to the damage of other landowners.*** An increasing number of states now apply the "reasonable use" rule. Under this rule, all of the landowners have a correlative right with respect to percolating water located beneath

the surface of their land. Even under the reasonable use rule, choice (D) is correct; no facts suggest that the veterinarian's use of the water is unreasonable. Because neither money damages, injunction, nor other equitable relief is available, choices (A), (B), and (C) are wrong. As discussed above, percolating water under the surface is subject to the ***absolute control and ownership*** of the surface owner, and if the withdrawal affects the neighboring landowner, it is ***damnun absque injuria***; that is, an injury without remedy.

55. **(D)** The friend's execution of the mortgage severed the joint tenancy, leaving the co-worker and the friend as tenants in common in the 30-acre tract of land, with the friend's half-interest encumbered by the mortgage. At common law, and still in about 20 states, the mortgage operates as a conveyance of the legal title to the mortgagee. However, such title is subject to defeasance on payment of the mortgage debt. Here, there are no facts that speak to a default. Because the friend severed the joint tenancy in the 30-acre tract of land, by encumbering his interest in it, the uncle may inherit the friend's half-interest in the 30-acre tract of land. If the uncle fails to pay the mortgage, the bank may take ownership of a half-interest in the 30-acre tract of land. Because there has been no default, the bank has no right to do so, and therefore the co-worker owns half and the uncle owns half as tenants in common. Answer choices (A) and (B) are wrong because the mortgage severed the joint tenancy, thus destroying the right of survivorship. Thus, on these facts, title to the 30-acre tract of land cannot vest in the co-worker alone. Choice (C) is incorrect because the friend only had the right to encumber his interest in the 30-acre tract of land. The co-worker's interest cannot be subject to the mortgage.

56. **(A)** In brief, the ***Rule Against Perpetuities*** provides that "no interest (usually meaning, contingent remainders or executory interests) is good unless it must vest, if at all, not later than 21 years after some life in being at the creation for the interest." Remember that the rule is measured from the time the instrument takes effect, and the time for vesting is calculated accordingly. ***In the case of a deed, the period is measured from the date of delivery.*** The contingent remainder in favor of the sister's children who reach the age of 25 violates the Rule against Perpetuities because it might not vest within 21 years of the sister's death. To illustrate, assume that one year after the conveyance the sister gave birth to the son. The sister then dies two years later. Now, 23 years after the sister's death, the son reaches the age of 25. Because this is more than 21 years after the sister's death, it violates the rule (which requires the vesting not later than 21 years after "some life in being"). Hence, no other lives (of the sister's children) can vest; therefore, choice (A) is correct. (B) is incorrect because where a conveyance violates the Rule against Perpetuities, the offending language will be stricken. Here, the language "but if the property shall ever be used for church purposes, then to the children of my sister who reach the age of 25" will be removed, leaving only the language "to my friend." Although the shopkeeper's intent was to give the friend a fee simple subject to an executory interest, the friend will take in fee simple because the second gift violates the Rule Against Perpetuities. Choice (C) is wrong because the son and the daughter will take nothing, because the language that conveyed the vacant lot to them as members of the group "the sister's children who reach the age of 25" will be struck. Choice (D) is incorrect because, as discussed above, the son and the daughter will take nothing. Note that the deceased son need not be the measuring life. Furthermore, artificially closing the class within 21 years of the death of the deceased son—or any other measuring life—cannot bring the conveyance into compliance with the Rule Against Perpetuities, and so, to the extent that it violates the rule, the conveyance will fail.

57. **(C)** A holder of an easement in gross may make reasonable use of the servient tenement as long as her conduct does not unreasonably interfere with the use of the servient tenement owner. Choice (A) is wrong because it falsely suggests that if the city took an easement before the buyer purchased, that circumstance forecloses any chance of recovery. The fact remains that if the city had unreasonably used the servient tenement or negligently maintained the sewer line, then the buyer could still recover, even if the easement for a sewer was granted before the buyer purchased. Similarly, choice (B) is wrong because even though the easement was granted validly, the city could still be liable if they had unreasonably interfered with the buyer's use of the servient tenement or negligently

maintained the sewer line. The city may not make unreasonable use of the sewer and will not necessarily be liable for damage arising from reasonable use. The holder of an easement in gross will be liable for unreasonable interference with the use of the servient tenement, or for damage arising from unreasonable use of the easement. Note that negligent maintenance would constitute unreasonable use. Public nuisance is defined as an unreasonable interference with a right common to the general public. Choice (D) is incorrect. The issue of public nuisance is meant to distract here.

58. **(C)** The tenant's failure to pay rent does not help the Girl Scouts in their action for ejection because it tends to show that the tenant was acting in derogation of the rights of the true owner who would be someone other than himself (the tenant). This would make the tenant's behavior like that of an adverse possessor. For this reason, choice (A) is wrong. Answer choice (B) speaks to the issue of a continuous possession and tacking, but this does not answer the question of whether or not the tenant did so under the belief that he was acting in derogation of the rights of the true owner. In other words, choice (B) does not explain whether or not the tenant was leasing to the teacher to keep the lease alive (so that the tenant would not be in breach of the lease) or whether the tenant did this to keep up a chain of unbroken occupation to meet the elements of adverse possession. As a result, choice (B) is wrong because it does not help the Girl Scouts. The fact that the tenant never paid taxes is immaterial to the Girl Scouts' action because it does not tend to negate the elements of adverse possession. For this reason, choice (D) is incorrect. Answer choice (C) is the best answer because if the tenant's remaining on the land was permissive (due to his belief that the lease was still in effect) then there has been no adverse possession because the tenant would have believed he was only on there as a tenant. This would help the Girl Scouts to prevail.

59. **(D)** Adverse possession must be actual and exclusive, hostile but peaceable, (meaning against the interest of the "true" owner, without physical eviction or eviction by court action), open and notorious, and continuous for the statutory period. The "hostile" element is at issue in this question. There are two views that have interpreted "hostile": the "objective view" and the "subjective view." Under the objective view, the possession must simply be adverse to the owner's rights; the possession must be without the true owner's permission and done in a manner that is inconsistent with true owner's rights. Under the subjective view, "hostility" requires bad faith or intentional trespass, so a mistaken possession in some jurisdictions does not constitute hostility. The former is the default view on the MBE, unless the facts of the question state otherwise. Choice (D) is the best of the lot under either view of what constitutes "hostile." Choice (D) presents an unmistakably hostile possession under either view. The statutory period did not necessarily begin when the widow died. The tenant had a seven-year lease, and arguably had a right to remain on the property even after the widow's death; so, the possession did not necessarily become adverse just because the widow died, and, thus, choice (A) is wrong. This makes choice (C) attractive, but the termination of the lease term is non-determinative of when the adverse possession began. Choice (C) still doesn't tell us whether any further occupation would be without permission (under the objective view) or what the tenant believed when the lease was over (under the subjective view). In other words, the end of the lease does not necessarily mean that the elements of adverse possession necessarily begin. Under that same reasoning, choice (B) is incorrect because stopping rent payments (much like the end of the lease) doesn't tell us whether any further occupation would be without permission (to meet the test under the objective view) or what the tenant believed when he stopped paying rent (under the subjective view). The tenant's presence there may have been permissive for some time after he stopped paying rent. So, choice (D) is a better answer than choice (B).

60. **(C)** A fee simple subject to an executory interest is a fee simple estate, whereupon the happening of a named event, ownership is to pass from the grantee to one other than the grantor. The future interest created in the third party is an executory interest. Here, the daughter has an executory devise. The characteristics of this interest are exactly the same as attach to springing and shifting uses, but the devise, of course, is created by will and not by deed. Choice (A) is incorrect. A fee simple determinable is a fee simple estate created to continue ***until some specified***

event occurs, at which point the estate automatically terminates and reverts to the grantor or his estate. The friend's estate will go to either the daughter or the Equestrian Society, not revert to the jockey. Choice (B) is wrong because in the fee simple subject to condition subsequent, the estate is terminated by the entry or exercise of the reserved power by the grantor (or her heirs) if that power is exercised. However, because the grantor has chosen not to reserve any future interest for himself, but rather devise it to the daughter or the Equestrian Society (should the horses fail to receive proper care), this is not a fee simple subject to condition subsequent. Choice (D) is incorrect. The friend's interest could not be a contingent remainder because a contingent remainder is a future interest. The friend received a present possessory estate (a fee simple subject to an executory interest), which takes effect immediately, as long as he abides by the conditions placed on the estate.

61. **(C)** Executory interests and devises are subject to the Rule against Perpetuities. In the present case, the Rule is violated because it is possible that the son's interest will neither vest nor fail within the lifetime of the friend. This is so because the Pomeranians may fail to receive proper care after the friend's death. Had the son's interest been limited to take effect "if the dogs fail to receive proper care during the friend's lifetime" (instead of "if ever the dogs fail to receive proper care"), then the interest would not have been void under the Rule against Perpetuities. An executory interest of a shifting type is one where the right to possession shifts from one grantee to another grantee. Because the interest would shift from the friend to the son, this is of the shifting type. However, the future interest would fail because the Rule against Perpetuities would void it. Thus, choice (C) is the more complete choice because it addresses both that this is a springing executory interest and that it will be void. Choice (B) is incorrect because it fails to take into account the Rule against Perpetuities. A remainder is a future interest created in a third person that is intended to take after the natural termination of a preceding estate. A contingent remainder is a remainder subject to a condition precedent or created in favor of an unborn person or an existing but unascertained person. The son's future interest is not a remainder because the son would not take upon the natural termination of any preceding estate; rather, the son would take (if at all) when a contingency occurs (the failure of the Pomeranians to receive proper care). The son never received a remainder, so choice (A) is incorrect. A springing executory interest is a future interest that cuts short an estate held by the grantor. Because the veterinarian, the grantor, held no present possessory estate to be divested of (the veterinarian conveyed his home to the friend), the executory interest was not of the springing variety. Thus, choice (D) is incorrect.

62. **(B)** In order for a covenant to run with the land, the following four requirements must be met: (1) there must be a covenant; (2) there must be an intention that the covenant shall run with the land; (3) the covenant must be of a type that "touches and concerns" the land; and (4) there must be privity of estate. With respect to the privity requirements, Smith and Boyer state that "where the running of covenants is allowed the cases seem to agree that if there is (i) privity of estate between the original covenanting parties and (ii) simultaneous ownership by the covenanting parties in the same land and (iii) privity of estate between either of the covenanting parties and his assignee, the covenant will run with the land." In our case, under the terms of the Declaration of Covenants, there is privity of estate between the developer (the housing corporation) and the purchasers of the lots (e.g., the chef). Choice (B) is the best answer because there is no privity of estate between the housing corporation and the community association. The housing corporation simply owns the farmland, and the community association is an administrative entity created by the housing corporation. It has no interest in the farmland, either as a co-owner or as a conveyee of an interest therein. Between the housing corporation and the community association, there is simply the covenant (i.e., Declaration), which constitutes privity of contract. Therefore, there is no successive privity of estate between the community association and the city, because the latter only succeeds to the interest or estate that the association has in the land: none. Answer choice (A) is incorrect because there is no alienation (sale of) land attempted here. The chef doesn't want to sell his lot; he wants to convert it into a massage parlor. Choices (C) and (D) are both incorrect because both misuse language that is used in a discussion of easements, which can be in gross or appurtenant. Indeed an easement appurtenant (but not an easement in gross) will run with the land. However, covenants are being tested here.

Real Property

Covenant Running with the Land	**Equitable Servitude**
1. More than a mere personal contract but less than an easement because technically it is *not* an "interest in land"	1. A restriction on the use of land enforce-able in a court of equity
	2. More than a covenant running with the land because it is an interest in land
2. Requirements: (a) there must be a covenant, (b) an intention that the covenant run with the land, (c) must "touch and concern" the land, and (d) privity of estate	3. Broader than an equitable easement because it applies not only to land but also to chattel property such as a business
3. A covenant "touches and concerns" the land if it makes the land in the hands of the owner either more usable and more valuable or less usable and less valuable.	4. Requirements: (a) may be created by a writing complying with the Statute of Frauds, (b) intention of the parties that there be a restriction, and (c) transferee takes the land with either actual or constructive notice of the existence of the servitude.
4. Legal effect: to make an assignee of the land either benefit by or be burdened by the covenant without being party to the making of the contract	5. Privity of estate is *not* required.
5. Remedies for breach: standard contract remedies (i.e., money damages or specific performance if appropriate)	6. Remedies: equitable remedies
	7. Extinguished: (a) by doing an act that violates the servitude and continuing for the period of the statute of limitations, (b) release by the dominant tenant, or (c) where the purpose and object of the servitude become impossible of achievement (e.g., change in character of neighborhood from residential to commercial)

63. **(B)** In order for the burden to run, we need both horizontal and vertical privity. Vertical privity is lacking, so the burden does NOT run. Absent being bound by a covenant that runs with the land, contract liability would be the only thing to hold the librarian liable to the homeowners' association for damages. Choice (A) is wrong because the **Rule in Spencer's Case** provides that an assignee of either the reversion or of the leasehold estate cannot be held liable for breach of covenant if the covenant is of a type that "does not touch and concern the land." Because the librarian is a tenant, not an assignee, the Rule in Spencer's Case is inapplicable. A tenant is in privity of estate with her landlord. The librarian is the teacher's tenant, and is thus in privity of estate with him. Therefore, lacking privity of estate is simply not the best argument for the librarian. Thus, answer choice (C) is wrong. Answer choice (D) is incorrect because a plaintiff seeking to enforce an equitable servitude may be denied relief on equitable grounds if the purpose of the servitude in a development scheme is impossible to attain because of changed conditions. In this question, the ability to distinguish between legal and equitable remedies makes it easy to eliminate choice (D); the homeowners' association is suing the librarian in an action for money damages (for breach of a covenant), so legal, rather than equitable, remedies are in issue. Because choice (D) presents an argument that is appropriate to refute the enforcement of an equitable servitude, it is misplaced and therefore incorrect. Given that privity of contract is required in order for the burden to run, the librarian's best argument is that he is not in privity of contract with the homeowners' association, and never had a contract with the teacher, or any of the other individuals who purchased lots from the housing corporation. For these reasons, choice (B) is correct.

64. **(B)** The provision, which provides for the annual assessment payable to the community association, is enforceable as a covenant running with the land. The effect of such a covenant is that the benefit, burden, or both pass to succeeding holders of the estate of the original covenanting parties. Here, the landscaper is the gardener's successor in interest and would ordinarily be obligated to perform under the contract. However, choice (B) is the best answer because the Declaration of Covenants stipulates that "nonpayment of any annual assessment or charge when due shall result in a lien upon the parcel of the property." Thus, the landscaper's best argument is that the landscaper is not personally liable for the payment, because failure to pay simply results in a lien on the parcel. Choice (A) is incorrect. Here, privity of contract between the housing corporation and the community association is not necessary. It is sufficient that the community association is the intended recipient of the annual payments. Choices (C) and (D) are incorrect because the conveyance of the property from the gardener to the landscaper created both privity of estate and privity of contract between the parties.

65. **(C)** Under the ***"collateral document rule,"*** where the developer intends a common scheme for the entire parcel of land, including all of the plots, a land owner whose deed does not contain the restriction may be bound by the restriction if the other deeds of the adjacent properties contain the restriction. The purchaser of a plot whose deed does not contain the restriction is deemed to be on constructive notice of the contents of the deeds of adjacent properties. This notice is, of course, constructive notice. However, the purchaser of a plot does not have to be on actual notice of the restriction to be bound by it. Here, the son has constructive notice (record notice) of the common scheme for the housing development. Therefore, choice (C) is the best answer because the geologist may seek to enforce the restriction against the sale of alcohol on the premises as an equitable servitude. The geologist may obtain an injunction to enforce the restriction, but he is limited to injunctive relief and may not eject the son. Choice (A) is incorrect. Although the conveyance did create a fee simple determinable, which would give the grantor (the psychologist) a possibility of reverter, the geologist need not rely on the provision in the psychologist–son deed; he may enforce the restrictions set forth in the Declaration of Covenants. Answer choice (B) is wrong because, despite the fact that the deed was not recorded, the restriction would nevertheless be enforceable because the son would have constructive notice of the restriction. Choice (D) is incorrect. Among the rights attendant to property ownership is the right to freely alienate it. Practically all American states recognize the fee simple determinable.

66. **(D)** As a general rule, no conveyance is valid unless the description of the land sought to be conveyed is sufficient to identify the land. In this question, the deed from the retiree to the friend purports to convey a 100-foot-by-175-foot lot, but the recorded instrument describing the property fails to describe an enclosed area, because the third call goes in the wrong direction. In the heirs' action contesting the friend's title to the vacant lot, the outcome will depend on whether the last call—which establishes an enclosure by stating that the boundary line returns "to the place of beginning"—prevails over the erroneous third call (west 100 feet). Choice (D) is correct. **Note:** When a deed describes the boundaries of the land to be conveyed by reference to monuments, natural or artificial, ***the intention of the parties is the controlling factor*** and all rules of construction are mere aids in determining such intention. Choice (A) is incorrect because street descriptions (i.e., monuments) are appropriate boundary descriptions. Choice (B) is incorrect because an improper boundary description is never considered a "mere" technicality, and if no land is enclosed, the result may be an invalid conveyance. Choice (C) is incorrect because if the tract of land had been platted in a subdivision, it would have been described by a specific parcel number or lot number, not by a boundary description.

67. **(C)** The traditional rule is that a forgery voids the instrument. Placing such a deed on record does not add any legal efficacy to such a forged or undelivered instrument. The recording statutes are not intended for the purpose of assisting wrongdoers, tortfeasors, criminals, and forgers in depriving innocent owners of their real property. It is settled that anything forged is null. However, there is a jurisprudential split as to the issue of "partial validity" under circumstances like these where the boyfriend's signature was real, but the student's was forged. Partial validity of a conveyance has been upheld. More and more states have held that in such situations where the person doing the forging had something to convey, s/he conveys the interest she did have in the property, and ***the***

deed is a nullity to the extent that it is forged. The other party's property, in which the perpetrator of the forgery had no interest, is not conveyed. Therefore, the boyfriend successfully severed the joint tenancy and transferred a half-interest in the property to the co-worker, leaving the co-worker and the student as tenants in common. Choice (A) is attractive under the traditional rule that forgery voids the instrument, but it is incorrect because, as discussed above, modernly, a partial forgery can result in a partial conveyance. Choice (B) is wrong because the joint tenancy is severed by the sale, and the co-worker and the student must hold it as tenants in common. Answer choice (D) is incorrect because the forged instrument cannot transfer the student's interest in the property.

68. **(B)** The Rule against Perpetuities provides: "No interest is good unless it must vest, if at all, not later than 21 years after some life in being at the creation of the interest." Choice (B) is correct because postponing the vesting of an interest until after the death of the "wife" or "widow" of a living person violates the Rule against Perpetuities. This is the classic "unborn widow" scenario. Walter's son may eventually marry someone who has not yet been born when the interest was created, which was when Walter died. Note that this is a testamentary trust, so the interest was created when Walter died. A will speaks at death of the testator, not when s/he wrote the will. Answer choice (A) is incorrect because Grace need not be alive when Walter died. What is required under the Rule against Perpetuities is that the child's interest will definitely vest or fail within 21 years of the death of someone who WAS alive when Walter died. Choice (C) is wrong because the intent of the testator is not determinative here. In fact, the purpose of the Rule against Perpetuities is to prevent the grantor from (accidentally or intentionally) controlling the property indefinitely. The common law tradition of the Rule against Perpetuities assures that the "dead hand cannot reach beyond the grave to control the living." Gray's *Rule against Perpetuities* (1886). Choice (D) is an attractive answer because it is factually true. Stan has died, so he can have no additional widows, and it would seem that Grace, as the only living child of Harriet, would be allowed to take due to the death of the Stan and Morgana. However this is immaterial. Answer choice (D) is wrong because the Rule against Perpetuities requires that it be clear and certain at ***the time of conveyance*** that the interest will vest (or not vest) within 21 years of a life in being. The fact that it might vest, or could vest, during that 21-year period is insufficient to bring the conveyance into compliance with the Rule. Note that some jurisdictions take a wait-and-see approach; the facts say that in this jurisdiction, there is no statute modifying the common law rule.

69. **(C)** The landlord accepted the rental payment of $2,000 on April 1. Four days later he gave them notice to terminate the premises in 30 days, despite the fact that no damage had been done to the premises nor had payment of rent ever been delinquent. When a tenant contests termination of the tenancy based on a landlord's retaliatory actions, the court will place ***the burden of proof on the landlord*** to show that his actions were not retaliatory. Under these facts, the landlord's actions certainly do seem retaliatory based on the husband and wife's complaints to the city housing authority. Furthermore, if the landlord's actions were not motivated by retaliation, he should not have accepted the April 1 rent. Choice (C) is the correct answer. (A) is incorrect because lack of damage to the apartment is not a relevant basis to avoid termination of a periodic tenancy under which either party can terminate. Choice (B) is incorrect because the Statute of Frauds is a defense to contract formation, and therefore would not be the reason a writing might be required to terminate a periodic tenancy. Note that the general rule is that absent a lease term that provides for termination, proper termination of a periodic tenancy requires that written notice be delivered a full period in advance, and that the tenancy terminate at the "natural" end of the period (so the landlord's notice on April 4 would have the effect of terminating the tenancy on May 31). Here, however, the lease defines proper termination as 30 days' notice by either party. No writing is required and the tenancy may terminate on May 5. Although choice (D) presents a true statement, this will not help the tenants defend against the landlord's right to terminate on May 5.

70. **(C)** At the moment of signing, the leasehold agreement did not convey to the shopkeeper a term of years at law. Here, you are being tested on the following (rather obscure) common law rule: At the moment a leasehold contract is entered into (but before the tenant actually takes possession), he is deemed to have an *interesse termini* (or equitable) interest in the leased premises. Once, however, the tenant takes possession and pays part of the rental, then his equitable

interest vests into a term of years at law. Choice (C) is correct because ***at the moment of signing, the leasehold contract entered into between the writer and the shopkeeper did not convey a term of years at law.*** Rather, it created a term of years in equity, or an *interesse termini* interest. Choice (A) is wrong because we know from the facts that a term of years, not a periodic tenancy, was formed. A tenancy for a term of years has a fixed duration that is set forth in the lease, e.g., "for six months" or "for two years." It ends ***automatically*** at the expiration of the term unless the parties agree to renew it. Here, the lease clearly states that the lease tenancy will last for three years. Answer choice (B) is incorrect because a tenancy for a term of years is properly terminated only upon the expiration of the term or upon properly tendered and accepted surrender. The only leasehold estate that can be terminated at will by either party is a tenancy at will. A tenancy at will is an estate in land that is terminable at the will of either the landlord or the tenant. At common law, this estate could be terminated by either party ***without advance notice***. Choice (D) is an attractive answer because the language of the lease is vague with respect to the description of the property. However, choice (D) is incorrect because the description of the property in the lease is adequate to identify it. Here, the facts indicate the building was the only piece of real estate owned by the writer. Thus, the description of the building in the leasehold agreement is sufficient to identify the first floor of that building as the property that the shopkeeper would lease.

71. **(B)** The student's strongest argument is that the widow had not given him notice for terminating a periodic tenancy. Remember a ***periodic tenancy continues indefinitely in the absence of either party's giving notice of termination.*** Answer choice (C) is wrong because the student does not have a tenancy for a term of years. If a tenant continues in possession after his right to possession has ended, the landlord may (1) evict him, or (2) bind him over to a new periodic tenancy. At common law, the new tenancy was usually from year to year when the term of the original lease was one year or more. However, under the modern view, most states today regard the new tenancy as running from month to month. Here, the student stayed in the apartment after his tenancy for a term of years ended. By accepting his continued rent payments, the widow has created a periodic tenancy. Answer choice (D) is incorrect because even though the terms are binding on both parties, a periodic tenancy may be terminated by either party upon proper notice. By process of elimination, we are left with choice (B). The only way the student will successfully avoid the widow's attempt to terminate his periodic tenancy is if she did not provide the requisite notice. Choice (A) is incorrect because it states that the original leasehold contract was void from the beginning. Nowhere in the facts does it state that the lease was void or that there were any circumstances that would render it void. Moreover, the original three-year term had long since expired, so this would be a very weak argument for the student

72. **(D)** When a tenant who is rightfully in possession wrongfully remains in possession (holds over) after termination of the tenancy, he is known as a holdover tenant or a ***tenant at sufferance.*** If a tenant continues in possession after his right to possession has ended, the landlord may (1) evict him, or (2) bind him over to a new periodic tenancy. At common law, the new tenancy was usually from year to year when the term of the original lease was one year or more. However, under the modern view, most states today regard the new tenancy as running from month to month. Choice (D) is therefore correct because the *hold-over doctrine* permitted the landlord to hold the hold-over tenant to another term. Here, because the original lease between the retiree and the artist was for a term of three years, under the *hold-over doctrine* the artist would be liable for another term under the common law rule. Choice (A) is incorrect because the artist had paid rent, so non-payment is an improper ground for eviction. Answer choices (B) and (C) are wrong because the retiree had only two options at the end of the lease—evict the artist or bind him over to a new tenancy. There is no rule at common law that provides such formulas for recovery.

73. **(C)** As a general rule, liability for rent is not affected by the conduct of a lessor (or third person) that merely interferes with the lessee's enjoyment of the leased land. However, if the disturbance is substantial in nature, the lessee may give up possession of the land and thereby avoid further liability under the lease. His defense to a rent action is *constructive eviction.* In this situation, if the lessee sees fit to give up possession of the leased land, he thereby avoids liability for rent that becomes payable after that date. Choice (A) is attractive but incorrect because it addresses the correct theory,

and because the professor did not actually evict the teacher; he had already left. However, constructive eviction, by its definition cannot be "partial". Constructive eviction is a material breach by the landlord that violates the tenant's implied covenant of quiet enjoyment and constitutes a constructive eviction if it renders the premises uninhabitable. Choice (B) is wrong for a similar reason; an eviction, by definition is not partial. Answer choice (D) is not the best answer as the breach of implied warranty of habitability would require that some basic necessity (like running water) is missing, and the landlord, having had the opportunity to cure, did not, and that fact rendered the residence inhabitable. Here, the restaurateur's storage arguably interferes with a property right, but does not make the apartment uninhabitable. Note that in addressing this "best of the lot" type of question, you may be asked to identify the "best of the worst." Here, most of the arguments would likely fail, but choice (C) is the best of the lot.

74. **(D)** An estate for years is an estate the maximum duration of which is measured by a fixed duration that is set forth in the lease, e.g., "for six months" or "for two years." ***At the time of the signing of the lease, the estate for years was not enforceable at law*** because the agreement failed to specify the exact beginning or commencement of leasehold period. Be advised that ***the most important requisite of an estate for years is that it must have a definite beginning and a definite ending*** (however, the ending can be inferred from the beginning). Once the tenant took possession, her estate began a legal three-year tenancy because a commencement date had been established and, therefore, a definite termination date (three years from the commencement date) was established as well. Answer choice (A) is wrong because a tenancy for a term of years, not a tenancy at will, was created because the lease agreement specified the exact term. A tenancy at will is an estate in land that is terminable at the will of either the landlord or the tenant. At common law, this estate could be terminated by either party without advance notice and will continue indefinitely until one of the parties terminates it. Choice (B) is an attractive choice because the agreement does indicate that the rent is to be paid in monthly installments; however, the determinative fact is that the lease agreement specified a term of three years, so it is incorrect. Similarly, Choice (C) is attractive because the agreement does express the amount of rent to be paid in terms of an annual rate, but the key issue is that the tenant agreed to rent the first floor for three years at that rate. Thus, it is also incorrect.

75. **(D)** This question directs us to follow the ***prior appropriation doctrine, under which "first in time is first in right."*** Answer choice (A) is wrong because status as upstream landowner does not allow the rancher to materially affect the farmer's rights under the prior appropriation doctrine, or under the majority rule, which provides that a lower riparian has a right of action against an upper riparian whenever the latter's use of the water materially affects either the quantity or quality of the lake or stream waters, even though such use results in no injury or damage to the lower riparian. Choice (B) is an attractive one because it alludes to the majority rule that applies to non-navigable lakes and streams: water for natural purposes is paramount and takes precedence over the use of water for artificial purposes. Thus, although upper riparians can take all the water they need for natural uses, they cannot take it for artificial purposes unless there is enough water for the domestic needs of the lower riparians. Answer (C) is meant to distract here, as it improperly suggests that the law of easements is applicable here. Because neither land owner enters the land of the other to secure water for his own use, the facts do not trigger easements as an issue.

Explanation: Question 76

The correct answer is: **(B)** The farmer, because the forged deed by which the attorney purported to take the property is null and void.

A forged deed is a nullity and cannot be the foundation for a claim of title by any subsequent purchaser who traces her chain of title to that deed. Although the doctor searched the title records through his agent, the title company, and purchased the property in good faith, he will not be protected under the recording act. Furthermore, the warranty deed from the farmer to his niece was "undelivered" because there was no present intent to pass title until the condition of graduation from college was satisfied. Title remains in the farmer. Choice (B) is correct. MBE Exam Tip: The three ways that conveyances are commonly invalidated on the bar exam are by means of (1) unrecorded deeds, (2) forged deeds, and (3) non-delivery of deeds.

(A) Incorrect. The title company, and they must compensate the doctor an amount equal to the purchase price of the property.

(C) Incorrect. The doctor, because he is a subsequent purchaser without notice who first recorded.

(D) Incorrect. The niece, because she is a successor in interest to the farmer.

Explanation: Question 77

The correct answer is: **(C)** The seller, because the buyer's intended use is immaterial.

The obligation of the seller is to provide "good" and "marketable" title to the buyer at the time set for closing. Existing land-use restrictions do not render title unmarketable (as opposed to zoning restrictions enacted between the time of the sales contract and the time of closing). Because the contract was mutually enforceable and not conditioned on the buyer's intended use, there was no failure of consideration. Therefore, specific performance by the seller will be granted. Choice (D) is incorrect because the buyer's defense is barred by the parol evidence rule, not the Statute of Frauds. By process of elimination, choice (C) is correct.

(A) Incorrect. The buyer, because there was a failure of consideration.

(B) Incorrect. The buyer, because the seller's silence constituted a constructive warranty.

(D) Incorrect. The seller, because the buyer's defense is barred by the Statute of Frauds.

Explanation: Question 78

The correct answer is: **(C)** The farmer is not entitled to remove the tobacco crop and, thus, is not entitled to re-enter the property.

This question deals with the area of emblements, or fructus industriales. Growing crops are generally classified as personal property and will pass with a sale or mortgage of the land. A purported sale of growing crops is considered to be a contract to sell the crops when they come into existence. Maturity of the crop at the time of sale is not a controlling factor (Burby, Real Property, p. 16). Therefore, upon the farmer's sale of his farm to the buyer, the growing tobacco crop will pass as personal property, and the farmer will not be entitled to remove it. Choice (C) is correct.

(A) Incorrect. The farmer is entitled to remove the tobacco crop, but he must pay the buyer a reasonable value to enter the property thus gaining access to the crop.

(B) Incorrect. The farmer is entitled to remove the tobacco crop and is not required to pay the buyer for entering the property, thus gaining access to the crop.

(D) Incorrect. The farmer and the buyer each has a colorable title to the tobacco crop, and consequently, there should be an equitable division of the proceeds from the sale of the crop between both parties.

Explanation: Question 79

The correct answer is: **(B)** Everything except the loft.

Questions involving trade fixtures frequently appear on the bar exam. Trade fixtures are chattels annexed to the land by a tenant for pecuniary gain during his tenancy. As a general rule, trade fixtures are removable by the tenant unless accession occurs. Regarding the doctrine of accession, Smith and Boyer provide an example where a steel "I" beam is built into a structure. The beam thus becomes an accession to the property. As such, it loses its identity as a trade fixture and is not removable (Real Property, p. 226). By analogy, the loft, which is structurally attached to the main building, is viewed as an accession. Choice (B) is therefore correct because all other chattels are trade fixtures and removable.

(A) Incorrect. Everything.

(C) Incorrect. Everything except the loft and the lighting.

(D) Incorrect. The free-standing tables only.

Explanation: Question 80

The correct answer is: **(A)** Verde will prevail, because he can enforce the implied reciprocal servitude relating to passive-solar heating against Wilson.

Implied reciprocal servitudes are a heavily tested area on the MBE. Here, Verde can enforce the passive-solar house restriction as an implied reciprocal servitude that runs with the land to bind Wilson. When a developer divides land into many different lots and sells some of the lots via deeds that contain a restriction such as the passive-solar heat limitation, then sells other lots not expressly subject to the restriction, the courts will enforce the restriction on the subsequently sold lots on the theory that the developer impliedly intended for all such lots to be subject to the restriction. The person seeking to enforce the implied reciprocal servitude must show that there was a common plan or scheme. In this case, evidence of the common plan is shown by the recorded subdivision plat and by the fact that 200 of the 300 lots were sold with the restriction expressly contained in their deeds.

(B) Incorrect. Verde will prevail, because Wilson's use of a coal-burning furnace may depress property values in the surrounding area.

(C) Incorrect. Wilson will prevail, because the passive-solar restriction was not mentioned in the deed by which he took his property.

(D) Incorrect. Wilson will prevail, because he was never in privity with Muir.

Explanation: Question 81

The correct answer is: **(C)** A decision for the manufacturer, because he has an easement in the walkway and an implied right to keep the walkway in repair.

An easement by implication arises from the circumstances surrounding the dividing by the owner of a piece of land into two pieces and conveying one such piece to another. From the surrounding circumstances, an inference is drawn that the parties intend the creation of an easement. Based upon this fact situation, it may be assumed that the entrepreneur intended to grant an implied easement to Tower One to allow the office workers and shoppers access to the walkway connecting the two office buildings. As a consequence, the holder of an easement has the right to do such affirmative acts on the servient tract as are necessary to the enjoyment thereof. According to Smith and Boyer (Law of Property, p. 396), "such right includes the right to repair, maintain, and improve the means by which the easement is made effective."

(A) Incorrect. A decision for the entrepreneur, because the manufacturer does not have rights in the walkway.

(B) Incorrect. A decision for the entrepreneur, because the manufacturer's rights in Tower One do not extend to the walkway.

(D) Incorrect. A decision for the manufacturer, because he has a right to take whatever action is necessary to protect himself from possible tort liability from persons using the walkway.

Explanation: Question 82

The correct answer is: **(C)** No, because the language of the deed created only a contractual obligation and did not provide for the retention of a property interest by the grantor.

The language in the deed created a covenant between the grantor and the grantee. The grantor retained no property interest in the land. The grantee fulfilled his obligation under the contract by constructing a public health center within the prescribed period. Whether the subsequent rededication of the property's use is a breach of the covenant is a matter not contemplated by the question. Because the language of the deed created only a contractual obligation, choice (C) is correct.

(A) Incorrect. Yes, because the language of the deed created a determinable fee, which leaves a possibility of reverter in the grantor.

(B) Incorrect. Yes, because the language of the deed created a fee subject to condition subsequent, which leaves a right of entry or power of termination in the grantor.

(D) Incorrect. No, because an equitable charge is enforceable only in equity.

Explanation: Question 83

The correct answer is: **(C)** The geologist will not obtain specific performance, and the buyer's down payment will be refunded to him.

The contract between the buyer and the geologist called for the geologist to convey marketable title. A marketable title is one that is reasonably free from defects. Mortgages are considered defects of title. While generally a seller would be permitted to use the proceeds of the sale to satisfy the mortgage, in this case, the proceeds of the sale would not cover the mortgages. Because the geologist has no other assets, she will not be able to perfect the title. Given that she cannot perform her part of the contract, the geologist is in breach. As such, she will not be entitled to specific performance. Because the geologist is in breach, the buyer may rescind the contract and recover the down payment.

(A) Incorrect. The geologist will obtain specific performance, and the buyer's down payment will not be refunded to him.

The contract between the buyer and the geologist called for the geologist to convey marketable title. A marketable title is one that is reasonably free from defects. Mortgages are considered defects of title. Usually, a seller is permitted to satisfy mortgages with the proceeds from the sale and is not considered in breach when that occurs. However, the geologist would not be able to satisfy the mortgages with her sale of the property alone and she has no other assets. Therefore, she is in breach and the buyer may rescind the contract and collect his down payment.

(B) Incorrect. The geologist will obtain specific performance, and the buyer's down payment will be refunded to him.

The geologist will not obtain specific performance because the proceeds of the sale would be inadequate to satisfy the outstanding mortgages. Lacking any other assets, the geologist is unable to convey marketable title. As a result, the buyer will be permitted to rescind the contract and recover his down payment.

(D) Incorrect. The geologist will not obtain specific performance, and the buyer's down payment will not be refunded to him.

Mortgages are considered defects of title. While generally a seller would be permitted to use the proceeds of the sale to satisfy the mortgage, in this case, the proceeds of the sale would not cover the mortgages. Because the geologist has no other assets, she will not be able to convey marketable title and is in breach of contract. She will not be able to obtain specific performance. The buyer, however, as a remedy for the geologist's breach of the land sale contract, may rescind the contract and recover his down payment. Therefore, this answer choice is incorrect.

Explanation: Question 84

The correct answer is: **(C)** The property is part of the estate, because the friend is presumed to have accepted the deed, and it was not properly conveyed back to the landowner.

To convey real property by deed, there must be donative intent, delivery and acceptance. The landowner intended to convey the property and delivered the deed to the friend. Most courts presume that a grantee accepts any beneficial conveyance. Therefore, the friend will be presumed to have accepted the deed. To convey title back, all the formalities necessary for any conveyance must be followed. The wife of the friend instead tried to act as though the original conveyance was voided. She will not be able to do that. The original conveyance was proper and now the property must go through probate with the rest of the friend's estate.

(A) Incorrect. The property belongs to the landowner, because the friend did not formally accept title.

While a grantee must accept the deed in order for the conveyance to be complete, most courts presume that a grantee accepts any beneficial conveyance. The fact that the deed was not recorded will not affect the presumption. Since the friend is now dead, and since the agreement between the parties did not conform to the statute of frauds, the landowner's chances of rebutting the presumption are slim.

(B) Incorrect. The property belongs to the landowner, because the friend was not a bona fide purchaser.

A grantee need not be a bona fide purchaser in order to have a valid title. To convey real property by deed, there must be donative intent, delivery and acceptance. The landowner intended to convey the property and delivered the deed to the friend. Most courts presume that a grantee accepts any beneficial conveyance. Therefore, the friend will be presumed to have accepted the deed. In this case, the fact that the friend was not a bona fide purchaser is irrelevant.

(D) Incorrect. The property is part of the estate, but after probate the land will revert back to the original landowner because of their verbal agreement.

To convey real property by deed, there must be donative intent, delivery and acceptance. The landowner intended to convey the property and delivered the deed to the friend. Most courts presume that a grantee accepts any beneficial conveyance. Therefore, the friend will be presumed to have accepted the deed. Once the friend died, the deed became part of the friend's estate and will have to go through probate. The verbal agreement between the landowner and the friend to convey the property back to the landowner is invalid because of the statute of frauds. Therefore this answer is incorrect.

Explanation: Question 85

The correct answer is: **(C)** No, because the tenant is under a duty to repair the premises, including keeping the building wind and water tight.

Under common law estate theory, a landlord had no duty to repair the premises during the duration of the lease. This duty extended to repairs that kept the building wind and water tight. Note that, in contrast, the tenant had a duty not to commit waste, which included within it a duty to repair the premises.

(A) Incorrect. Yes, because the landlord is under a duty to repair the premises while a tenant is living in the building.

Common law estate theory did not require the landlord to repair the premises during the term of the lease. Instead, the tenant had a duty not to commit waste, which included within it a duty to repair the premises. This duty extended to repairs that kept the building wind and water tight.

(B) Incorrect. Yes, because the landlord is responsible for keeping the building wind and water tight.

Under common law estate theory, the landlord did not have a duty to repair the premises during the term of the lease. Rather, the tenant had a duty not to commit waste, which included within it a duty to repair the premises. This duty extended to repairs that kept the building wind and water tight.

(D) Incorrect. No, because the tenant has a duty to repair damage that is the result of ordinary wear and tear.

Under common law estate theory, a landlord was not responsible for repairs of ordinary wear and tear while the tenant was occupying the premises. Although the tenant had corresponding duty not to commit waste on the property, under common law estate theory, this duty usually excepted waste that was the result of ordinary wear and tear.

Explanation: Question 86

The correct answer is: **(D)** The daughter must maintain the property in a reasonable state of repair.

A life tenant has a duty to maintain the property in a reasonable state of repair, with an exception for ordinary wear and tear. Whether the daughter is living in the apartment complex or just collecting profits from rentals within the building, the daughter, as a life tenant, is responsible for the maintenance of the property.

(A) Incorrect. The son must make all mortgage payments.

Because the daughter is a life tenant, she is responsible for paying the interest on a mortgage to the extent profits are derived from the property. In contrast, if the daughter were a tenant for years or a periodic tenant, she would not be responsible for making these mortgage payments.

(B) Incorrect. The son must pay all property taxes.

The daughter will be responsible to pay taxes to the extent that there is a profit derived from the property. If the daughter were a periodic tenant, or a tenant for a term of years, the daughter would be exempted from paying taxes on the property.

(C) Incorrect. The daughter must provide the son with any profits derived from the apartment building.

While the daughter is living, she is the life tenant of the property and is free to do what she wants with the property. If the daughter chooses to rent out all the units, she is permitted to keep the profits, but must also maintain the property in a reasonable state of repair.

Explanation: Question 87

The correct answer is: **(A)** Yes, because Owner 2 did not make the mortgage payments.

The bank has the right to foreclose upon the property because the payments were not made. The issue is whether Owner 2 has liability to the bank. Owner 2, as transferee, did not agree with the bank to assume the mortgage or that Owner 1 would be released from the mortgage. If there had been a novation, then Owner 1 would have been released from payment of the mortgage. Since that did not happen, Owner 1 is still personally liable for the mortgage.

(B) Incorrect. Yes, because there was a novation.

This choice is incorrect because there was no novation. Although Owner 1 is still responsible to the bank it is not because there was a novation. A novation occurs when a transferee of real property and the mortgagee agree that the transferee will assume the mortgage and that the mortgagor will be released from liability. In this case, Owner 2 did not agree with the bank that she would assume the mortgage or that Owner 1 would be released from liability.

(C) Incorrect. No, because there was a novation.

This choice is incorrect because there was no novation. Owner 1 will be responsible for the mortgage but not because there was a novation. A novation occurs when a transferee of real property and the mortgagee agree that the transferee will assume the mortgage and that the mortgagor will be released from the obligation. In this case, Owner 2 and the bank did not enter into a novation and Owner 1 is still responsible for the mortgage.

(D) Incorrect. No, because Owner 2 assumed the mortgage.

Owner 1 is responsible for the mortgage obligation. Owner 1 and Owner 2 had agreed that Owner 2 would assume the mortgage, but Owner 1 is still responsible in the event of default. If there had been a novation between the bank and Owner 2, then Owner 1 would have been released from liability. The facts indicate Owner 2 agreed with Owner 1 to assume the mortgage but did not enter into an agreement with the bank to assume the mortgage. Thus, this choice is incorrect.

Explanation: Question 88

The correct answer is: **(D)** No, because the musician has a real defense to the lawsuit.

A mortgagee may transfer its interest in mortgaged property, however, a transferee takes the mortgage subject to real defenses. One defense to the validity of a contract, including the mortgage agreement here, is infancy. Here, the musician was an infant (minor) at the time he entered into the mortgage agreement with Bank No. 1. Given the musician's ability to assert infancy as a defense to the enforcement of his original mortgage with Bank No. 1, it is unlikely that Bank No. 2 will prevail over the musician in its efforts to foreclose the property.

(A) Incorrect. Yes, because Bank No. 2 is a holder in due course.

In order to be a holder in due course, and thus be able to argue it assumed the mortgage free and clear of any defenses, Bank No. 2 would need to establish that the mortgage note it assumed from Bank No. 1 was negotiable. Here, the facts specifically indicate that mortgage note in question was not negotiable. Thus, Bank No. 2 will have difficulty asserting it is a holder in due course, and this answer choice is incorrect.

(B) Incorrect. Yes, because Bank No. 1 committed fraud in the transfer.

This choice is incorrect because the facts to not indicate the bank committed fraud in the transfer. The facts indicate Bank No. 1 was aware of the musician's age at the time the musician obtained the mortgage. The facts are not sufficient to suggest any fraud occurred when Bank No. 1 transferred its interest in the mortgage to Bank No. 2.

(C) Incorrect. No, because Bank No. 2 did not commit fraud.

This answer choice is incorrect. Although Bank No. 1 may have committed fraud in the transfer to Bank No. 2 by failing to disclose the musician's age at the time the mortgage agreement was originally executed, the fact pattern does not provide enough information to support this conclusion.

Explanation: Question 89

The correct answer is: **(C)** Yes, because it does satisfy the Statute of Frauds.

This mortgage note is subject to the Statute of Frauds because the obligations will not be completed within one year. It easily satisfies the Statute of Frauds, however, because the necessary terms are included and the parties have both signed it. Bear in mind that this note is not for the sale of property. It is for a mortgage loan that will be secured by property. The parties will need to execute the mortgage deed and have it recorded. It is the mortgage deed that requires specificity with regard to the property description, security interest, etc.

(A) Incorrect. No, because the description of the property is inadequate.

The document in question is a mortgage note, not a mortgage deed. The parties will need to execute a mortgage deed and record it. It is the mortgage deed, not the note, that must contain a specific description of the property and, therefore, this answer choice is incorrect.

(B) Incorrect. No, because it does not satisfy the Statute of Frauds.

This answer choice is false. The note would be subject to the Statute of Frauds because it is a contract that is longer than one year in duration. As such, it must contain the subject matter, the terms, and the parties, and it must be signed by the party against whom enforcement is sought. Since both parties signed this otherwise adequate document, it easily satisfies the Statute of Frauds.

(D) Incorrect. Yes, because it is signed by both parties.

This answer is simply not the best choice. The note is valid as a mortgage note, but not because it was signed by both parties. The fact that both parties signed helps the note pass the Statute of Frauds. But the signatures alone are not the only consideration. The writing has to mention the subject matter, the terms and the parties, as well, which it does.

Explanation: Question 90

The correct answer is: **(A)** No, because the sale price does not shock the conscience.

A court will not set aside a foreclosure sale for inadequacy of price unless the sale price is so grossly low that it shocks the conscience. In this case, housing prices had only recently shot up because of the new school. Although the appraiser valued the home at $200,000 during the winter months, this value could have been assessed based on comparable sales in the neighborhood. The actual price that someone might pay for the home could easily have been less than the neighborhood average, especially given the home's proximity to the pig farm and the fact that the house was sold during a month when the pig farm's odors were especially strong. In addition, a foreclosure sale is not obligated to fetch the fair market value for a property. Considering all these factors, the $98,000 foreclosure sale price sounds low, but is unlikely to be found so low as to shock the conscience. Therefore, this is the best answer choice.

(B) Incorrect. No, because foreclosure sales cannot be set aside for inadequacy of the sale price.

This answer choice makes a false assertion. Foreclosure sales may, in fact, be set aside if the price obtained in the foreclosure sale is so grossly low that it shocks the conscience. Undoubtedly, the setting aside of foreclosure sales is a rarity, but it is still available.

(C) Incorrect. Yes, because foreclosure sales can be set aside for inadequacy of the sale price.

This answer choice contains an accurate but incomplete statement. Foreclosure sales can be set aside for inadequacy of the sale price if the price is so grossly low as to shock the conscience. Here, given the undesirable location of the home, thanks to the pig farm, the $98,000 sale price sounds low, but not shockingly low. Therefore, this is not the best answer choice.

(D) Incorrect. Yes, because the foreclosure sale price was more than fifty percent less than the appraised value.

There is no percentage rule involved when a mortgagor seeks to set aside the foreclosure sale of the mortgaged property. The sale will only be set aside for inadequacy of sale price if the price achieved is so grossly low that it shocks the conscience.

Explanation: Question 91

The correct answer is: **(B)** Compensatory damages, punitive damages, and injunctive relief.

Here is a Torts question dealing with the measure of damages for trespass to land. Where the defendant acts willfully or maliciously, he may be liable for punitive damages (in addition to nominal damages for harmless trespass, or compensatory damages for harmful trespass). Clearly, in this trespass example, the landlord would be liable for punitive damages because he acted maliciously in entering the apartment and disrupting the student's furniture and possessions. In addition, the student may also be entitled to compensatory damages and injunctive relief. Choice (B) is therefore correct.

(A) Incorrect. Compensatory damages only.

(C) Incorrect. Nothing, because an owner cannot be charged with trespass on his own property.

(D) Incorrect. Nothing, because the rummaging did not amount to a constructive eviction.

Explanation: Question 92

The correct answer is: **(D)** The corporation, because it cannot be charged with constructive knowledge of the associate-investor deed.

The investor is a purchaser for value, who took without actual, inquiry, or constructive notice of prior claims and was first to record. The jurisdiction uses grantor-grantee and grantee-grantor indexes, requiring the prospective grantee (here, the corporation) to research title to the property by first examining the grantee-grantor index to ascertain the date on which the grantor first obtained title and then examining the grantor-grantee index forward in time from the date the grantor acquired title. The process is repeated for the grantor's grantor by searching under the name of the predecessor in interest of the present grantor in both indexes to determine the chain of title. If the corporation had conducted the appropriate search, it would not have found the deed from the cowboy conveying the property to the two attorneys, because that deed was not recorded. In addition, if the corporation was unaware that the attorneys were grantees of the land, it would not search the grantee index for their names and, therefore, would also fail to discover the deed to the investor. The cowboys-attorneys and associate-investor deeds are not in the corporation's chain of title, and the corporation cannot be charged with constructive notice of their interests. Even though the associate-investor deed was recorded prior to the cowboy-corporation deed, the corporation prevails, because the associate-investor deed was outside the chain of title. As a purchaser for value without knowledge of prior claims, the corporation takes the ranch free of the interests of the partner and the investor.

(A) Incorrect. The partner and the investor, because the corporation can be charged with inquiry notice of the investor's interest in the ranch.

The jurisdiction uses the grantor-grantee, grantee-grantor index method. Even if the corporation had conducted a proper search, it could not have found the cowboy-attorneys deed, because it was never recorded. Without discovering that deed, the corporation would be unable to locate the associate-investor deed. Because the cowboy-attorneys deed was outside the chain of title, the corporation could not acquire knowledge of it or the subsequent conveyance from the associate to the investor. As such, the corporation takes free of the investor's interest because no reasonable investigation would have disclosed the interest. Thus, this answer is incorrect.

(B) Incorrect. The investor, because the property is located in a race-notice jurisdiction.

Even if the investor recorded his deed prior to the corporation's recordation of its deed, the investor has no interest in the ranch, because his deed is outside the chain of title and the corporation, therefore, cannot be charged with constructive notice of his interest. The cowboy-attorneys deed was never recorded, and the corporation, therefore, could not have found it in the indexes, nor would it have searched their names to discover the associate-investor deed, even though it was properly recorded. As a purchaser for value who took the property without knowledge of prior claims, the corporation takes free of the investor's interest despite the fact that the investor recorded first. Thus, this answer is incorrect.

(C) Incorrect. The investor and the corporation, as tenants in common.

Because the cowboy-attorneys deed was never recorded, the associate-investor deed is outside the chain of title. The corporation, therefore, could not have found it in the indexes and thus could not have searched the chain of title leading from the associate to the investor. The corporation cannot be charged with constructive notice of the interest of the partner or the investor, and the corporation takes clear of their claims. Thus, this answer is incorrect.

Explanation: Question 93

The correct answer is: **(B)** The programmer, because the scientist had no interest in the mountain property to pass to the priest.

As a donee, the priest is not protected by the recording act, which operates in favor only of subsequent purchasers. Therefore, in the absence of an applicable recording act, title to the property is determined by the common law, which holds first in time, first in right. Under that rule, when the scientist conveyed the property to the programmer, he lost all interest in it. He, therefore, had nothing to convey to the priest.

(A) Incorrect. The programmer, because under the common law, the priest, as a donee, is considered to have actual knowledge of the scientist's interest.

This answer contains a few errors and misstatements and is thus incorrect. A donee, for one, is not protected by the recording act because, by its terms, it operates in favor only of purchasers. This choice also states an erroneous principle of law: there is no such inference under the common law of actual knowledge.

(C) Incorrect. The priest, because the programmer was a donee-grantee of the property.

This answer is incorrect for any number of reasons. First, the programmer is not a donee—she purchased the property. In any case, the recording act protects subsequent purchasers. The status of the grantee whose interest may be voided (here, the programmer's) is immaterial. Thus, the outcome of this question would be the same whether or not the programmer was a donee.

(D) Incorrect. The priest, because he recorded his deed first.

This answer might be correct if there were no recording act in this jurisdiction. However, under the recording act, the priest does not win title by winning the race to record. Rather, under the recording act, the programmer's interest is protected because the priest had actual knowledge of the earlier conveyance, and was a donee, not a purchaser. Thus, this answer is incorrect.

Explanation: Question 94

The correct answer is: **(B)** Yes, because she took the property first in time.

The critical element of this question is that the professor, as a donee of the mountain property, is not protected by the recording act, which operates in favor only of subsequent purchasers. Because the recording act will not govern this situation, the common-law rule of first-in-time, first-in-right will apply. Because the uncle conveyed to the student first, the student has a superior claim to the property and will prevail in her action to quiet title.

(A) Incorrect. Yes, because she recorded her deed before commencing the quiet title action.

The fact that the student recorded her deed just prior to the quiet title litigation is meaningless. The professor is a donee, not a purchaser and, therefore, the recording act cannot operate in her favor — a donee is not protected by the recording act, which operates in favor only of purchasers. Thus, this answer is incorrect.

(C) Incorrect. No, because the professor is considered to have actual knowledge of the student's interest via imputation from the donor, her uncle.

This choice states an erroneous principle of law: legally, there is no imputation of knowledge between donor and donee. However, such knowledge is immaterial when the recording act, as here, does not benefit donees (such as the professor). Thus, this answer is incorrect.

(D) Incorrect. No, because she did not record before the uncle conveyed the property to the professor.

The fact that the student failed to record the deed prior to the uncle conveying the property to the professor would be an important fact if the professor were a subsequent purchaser. However, because the professor is merely a donee, the recording act will not serve to protect the professor's interest, and the common-law first in time, first in right rule will apply. Because the student is claiming title under an earlier conveyance, she will succeed in her action. This answer choice is therefore incorrect.

Explanation: Question 95

The correct answer is: **(A)** The grandson, under the shelter rule.

This is a complicated one—stick with us. When the owner purported to convey his land to the ballerina, the artist had not recorded his deed, thus (under the recording act) cutting off the artist's interest. The judge's purchase of the property then raises the deed recorded too late issue. If the judge made a title search, he would investigate the index from the time each previous grantor appeared as a grantee until he or she became a grantor. The owner-artist deed would appear after the owner-ballerina deed, and the judge would not have seen it. Thus, the artist's deed is outside the chain of title and does not impart constructive notice.

Because the ballerina's interest is thereby superior to the artist's, so is the interest passed to the judge, another bona fide purchaser for value. The grandson (who is not a bona fide purchaser—not only does he have actual notice of the artist's interest, he is also a donee rather than a purchaser) is nevertheless protected by the shelter rule, which provides that any successor in interest to a person protected by the recording act is similarly protected.

(B) Incorrect. The grandson, because the first person to record always has paramount interest.

The first person to record invariably has paramount interest only in a jurisdiction with a pure race recording act (if then). In this problem, there is a pure notice statute. The ballerina's interest in the property is superior to the artist's because, at the time the ballerina purchased, the artist had not recorded. It made no difference to the ballerina that she subsequently recorded before the artist; even if the artist had subsequently recorded before the ballerina, the ballerina would still be owner of the property. Thus, this answer is incorrect.

(C) Incorrect. The artist, because he recorded his deed before the ballerina conveyed to the judge.

The artist has recorded his deed too late, in that it comes after the ballerina's recording and thus is outside the chain of title. Under the recording act, subsequent bona fide purchasers are not charged with constructive notice of the artist's late deed, and thus his recordation provides him with no protection. Thus, this answer is incorrect.

(D) Incorrect. The artist, because the grandson knew of the artist's interest in the property when the grandson took title.

The shelter rule permits the grandson to succeed to the judge's interest, even though the grandson knew when he took title through inheritance that the artist had once had a previous interest in the property. Because the judge was protected by the recording act from the artist's previously but improperly recorded deed, the grandson succeeds to that protection as the judge's grantee. Thus, this answer is incorrect.

Explanation: Question 96

The correct answer is: **(A)** The judge, because he was unaware of the cousin's interest in the cabin when he extended credit to the pianist in exchange for the mortgage.

A mortgagee who extends credit to the mortgagor is generally considered to have paid value for her interest in the real property within the meaning of the recording act. Thus, as long as the mortgagee had no actual, inquiry, or constructive notice of a prior interest, the recording act will protect the mortgagee's subsequently created interest in the real property. In the present question, that means that the judge's interest as mortgagee is superior to the cousin's, as the judge would be regarded as a subsequent bona fide purchaser as to the pianist-cousin deed. The judge had no constructive notice of the cousin's deed because it was not recorded properly (in fact, it was not recorded at all when the judge made the loan to and received the mortgage from the pianist).

(B) Incorrect. The judge, because the mortgage was recorded before the cousin recorded his deed.

The recording act protects qualifying subsequent purchasers (including mortgagees who extend credit) from the common law first in time, first in right rule. The judge's interest is protected as against the cousin's earlier interest because the cousin failed to timely record. As to these two competing interests, it makes no difference whether the judge recorded or not; he is a subsequent bona fide purchaser, as called for in the pure notice recording act described by the facts. Thus, this answer is incorrect.

(C) Incorrect. The cousin, because an extension of credit by a mortgagee is not considered value within the operation of the recording act.

A mortgagee who concurrently extends credit (e.g., loans money) to the mortgagor is viewed as having paid value as that term is used in the recording act. (However, where the mortgage is executed solely to secure a pre-existing debt, there is no exchange of value that will qualify the mortgagee for protection under the recording statute, and a prior interest such as the cousin's, even though not recorded, would be superior.) Because the judge extended credit in exchange for the mortgage, he is regarded as equivalent to a subsequent bona fide purchaser by the recording act. Thus, this answer is incorrect.

(D) Incorrect. The cousin, because a mortgagee is not considered a purchaser within the operation of the recording act.

A mortgagee is considered a subsequent purchaser as that term is used in the recording act. The mortgagee is granted an interest in the land as security for the concurrent extension of credit; if the landowner defaults on the debt, the mortgagee can convert her mortgage interest into money by a forced sale of the mortgaged property. Thus, if all other conditions are met, the mortgagee is entitled to the protection of the recording act. Thus, this answer is incorrect.

Explanation: Question 97

The correct answer is: **(B)** The landowner was unlikely to be able to tender good and marketable title within any reasonable period.

Generally, the seller in a land sale transaction need not actually possess marketable title until the time for closing, when he is called upon to convey the property to the buyer. Thus, a defect in title existing at the time of formation but which is discovered afterward and which the seller has a reasonable chance of remedying does not give the buyer any cause for rescission prior to the date set for closing. However, there is a modern trend to grant the purchaser a right of immediate rescission if it appears unlikely that the seller will be able to cure her title problems. In this problem, the circumstances demonstrate that the landowner may never be able to repurchase the easement; an easement is an encumbrance that renders title unmarketable. Therefore, the purchaser's strongest argument is to rely on the modern notion that he need not wait for the date set for performance, or a reasonable time after, to discover that the seller will never be able to perform.

(A) Incorrect. The landowner did not possess good and marketable title when the contract of sale was formed.

This is not the correct answer. The normal rule is that failure to possess marketable title is no justification for the purchaser's rescission until the time for tender of performance by the seller, usually the date set for closing, although there is a modern trend to grant the purchaser a right of immediate rescission if it appears unlikely that the seller will be able to cure her title problems. Here, it would not be significant that the landowner did not have marketable title due to the easement when the contract was formed, because the easement is a type of encumbrance that could ordinarily be removed within a reasonable time.

(C) Incorrect. The landowner's entry into the contract relationship without good and marketable title constituted a constructive fraud upon the purchaser.

This is not the correct answer. The facts indicate that the landowner was unaware of the easement when she entered into the contract with the purchaser. Situations like this problem are not unusual, and do not evidence any fraudulent behavior, actual or constructive, on the part of the seller. Title searches are designed with just such difficulties in mind. Where the seller discovers the title defect after formation and attempts to remedy it, there can be no finding of fraud.

(D) Incorrect. Since time was of the essence of the contract, the purchaser was entitled to rescind as soon as there was any indication that performance by the landowner might be delayed in any way.

This answer is not correct. This choice misstates the modern trend by making it too strong, and erroneously applies the principle of time of the essence. Even where time is of the essence, the purchaser must ordinarily give the seller an opportunity to correct any title defects and to tender performance—conveyance of good and marketable title—on the date specified in the contract. Only where there appears to be little likelihood that the title defects will ever be cured may the buyer rescind the contract prior to the time set for performance by the seller.

Explanation: Question 98

The correct answer is: **(D)** The property to be conveyed pursuant to the lease-option agreement is not sufficiently described so as to permit specific enforcement.

The Statute of Frauds requires that a contract for the sale of real property be evidenced by a writing, signed by the party to be charged, and contain all the essential terms of the transaction, such as identification of the parties, a description of the property, the price, and any agreed-to conditions of payment. In this question, the description of the property is too inadequate to permit the court to specifically enforce the purported agreement. There is no way to tell which 200 acres out of the 1,000 acres the owner intended to sell to the foreperson. Since the agreement does not adequately describe the property to be sold, the court cannot enforce it. This is the owner's best defense (of the choices given).

(A) Incorrect. The owner's obligation to mark off 200-acre parcels for the foreperson's choice was a condition precedent to the duty to convey, such that the failure of the condition precludes the duty to convey from becoming an absolute obligation.

Where a condition is attached to the contractual obligations of one party, that condition must be satisfied before the contractual obligations become absolute. This principle operates where the condition is an event or circumstance within the control of the other party, and where the condition is established in the same agreement as the obligation. The owner may not make a promise and then claim that his own promise is a condition precedent to a further performance by him, such that his own failure to perform the second promise excuses him from performing a pre-existing obligation. In addition, even if the owner's own promise regarding the survey could somehow be considered a condition precedent to his own performance of the sales option, a party is not permitted to prevent occurrence of a condition precedent and then claim that the non-occurrence which that party procured excuses performance of the related obligation. Under either analysis, this is not a good defense for the owner.

(B) Incorrect. The foreperson will be unable to prove the existence of the option to purchase element of the lease due to operation of the parol evidence rule.

The parol evidence rule precludes introduction into evidence of an oral agreement made prior to or simultaneously to an integrated written agreement where the purported oral agreement contradicts or varies the terms of the written agreement. The facts of the question clearly indicate that the option agreement was part of the written lease agreement, so there can be no application of the parol evidence rule; no oral agreement is at issue as to the option.

(C) Incorrect. The aspect of the written lease agreement regarding the option to purchase is not enforceable because there was no separate consideration supporting the option to purchase.

The facts indicate that the lease and option were contained in one written agreement. The foreperson's obligations under that agreement (including the duty to pay rent) furnish consideration for any promises made by the owner. An option is an offer that the offeror agrees to hold open for a specified period; by including it in the lease agreement the parties made it part of the bargained-for exchange which constitutes consideration in any bilateral contract. Lack of consideration is thus not a good defense for the owner.

Explanation: Question 99

The correct answer is: **(C)** That the rancher and the sister own the properties as equal tenants in common, because the zookeeper and the rancher's agreement was ineffective to convert ownership of their properties to joint tenancy.

The zookeeper and the rancher owned their real property as tenants in common. In order to hold that same property as joint tenants, a conveyance of some sort would have to occur because joint tenancy traditionally requires unity of time and title (acquired at the same time by the same instrument), equal shares, and unity of possession. If an enforceable agreement existed to make such a conveyance, the rancher could claim ownership in the entirety via court proceedings. However, the Statute of Frauds requires that a contract for the conveyance of real property be in writing. The zookeeper and the rancher's agreement was oral, and the circumstances do not support application of the part performance exception to the Statute of Frauds. The oral joint tenancy agreement is therefore not enforceable, and the sister takes the zookeeper's interest in the properties as his sole heir at law. The result is that the sister and the rancher hold the property as tenants in common.

(A) Incorrect. That the rancher is sole owner of the properties, because in reliance on their joint tenancy agreement, the rancher and the zookeeper did not create wills.

The oral agreement between the rancher and the zookeeper was not valid to establish a joint tenancy because of the Statute of Frauds and in traditional jurisdictions, the lack of a straw man conveyance. Detrimental reliance is not alone a basis for taking a contract for the conveyance of land out of the Statute of Frauds. Detrimental reliance is an alternative ground for enforcing a contract that otherwise lacks consideration. The Statute of Frauds does not address the presence or absence of consideration, and thus the doctrine of promissory estoppel or detrimental reliance does not solve the problems presented by the oral agreement under the Statute of Frauds.

(B) Incorrect. That the rancher is sole owner of the properties, because the deeds to the subject properties should be reformed to reflect their joint tenancy status.

Reformation is a judicial promise by which a written instrument that does not reflect the intentions of the parties is reformed so that it accurately sets forth the agreement as originally intended. Reformation is not available under these circumstances to remedy the lack of a writing.

(D) Incorrect. That the rancher and the sister own the properties as equal tenants in common, because tenants in common may not unilaterally create a joint tenancy out of property already owned by them.

Tenants in common may alter the nature of their ownership by an effective conveyance. The reason the zookeeper and the rancher failed in their intention was because their agreement to do so was oral. Had they used a straw man (not required in all jurisdictions) and conveyed the property in writing to establish unity of time and title, they could have changed their tenancy in common to a joint tenancy. Therefore this answer choice is incorrect.

Explanation: Question 100

The correct answer is: **(B)** The baker, under the Statute of Frauds defense.

The oral agreement between the parties does not satisfy the Statute of Frauds and does not fall under an exception to the statute. A land sale contract must be in writing, be signed by the party to be charged, and contain the essential terms and conditions of the agreement. The parties did not enter into a written agreement, and the baker can successfully raise a Statute of Frauds defense to the customer's action for specific performance where the facts do not show actions taken by the buyer sufficient to satisfy the part performance exception to the Statute of Frauds.

(A) Incorrect. The baker, under the parol evidence rule.

The parol evidence rule protects a written contract between the parties. Here, there is no written contract and so the parol evidence rule does not apply.

(C) Incorrect. The customer, under the part performance exception to the Statute of Frauds.

The customer's down-payment of $20,000 and tender of the purchase price on the appointed day are insufficient acts to satisfy the part performance exception to the Statute of Frauds. The doctrine of part performance requires unequivocal evidence of a contract and a combination of the following: full or partial payment; taking possession; and making substantial improvements. Here, the customer has tendered the purchase price, but he has neither improved the property nor taken possession of it. Thus the buyer's actions are not sufficient to take the agreement out of the Statute of Frauds.

(D) Incorrect. The customer, under the doctrine of equitable conversion.

The doctrine of equitable conversion does not apply where the buyer has entered into a land sale agreement that does not satisfy the Statute of Frauds. Under the doctrine of equitable conversion, the buyer holds equitable title to the property during the pendency of a valid land sale contract while the seller retains legal title. The doctrine of equitable conversion apportions the risk of loss. It is not applicable to this case because the oral contract is invalid.

1. FREEHOLD ESTATES

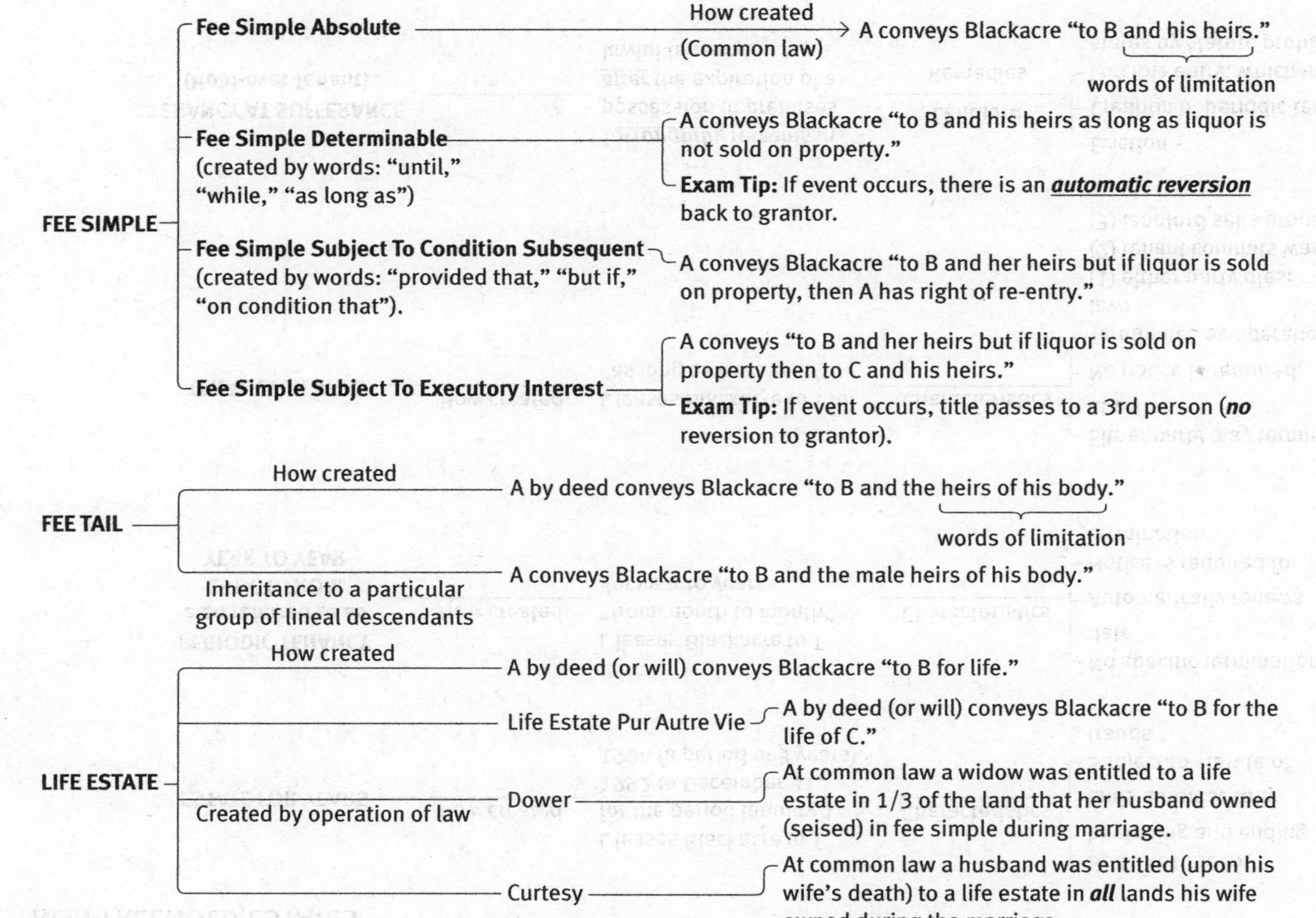

2. NON-FREEHOLD ESTATES

ESTATE FOR YEARS — How created — L leases Blackacre to T for the period January 1, 1992 to December 31, 1994 (a period of 3 years).
- Characteristics
  - Specific time for beginning and ending
  - Ends automatically
  - Subject to statute of frauds

PERIODIC TENANCY also referred to as ESTATE FROM YEAR TO YEAR — How created — L leases Blackacre to T "from month to month" (or year to year).
- Characteristics
  - No specific termination date
  - Automatically renews
  - Notice is required for termination

TENANCY AT WILL — How created — L leases Blackacre to T for "as long as L wishes."
- Characteristics
  - Either party may terminate at will.
  - No notice is required.
  - Terminates by operation of law:
    (1) either party dies;
    (2) tenant commits waste; or
    (3) landlord sells property.

TENANCY AT SUFFERANCE (Hold-over Tenant) — T ***wrongfully*** remains in possession of premises ***after*** the expiration of a lawful tenancy.
- Landlord Remedies
  - Eviction
  - Creation of periodic tenancy
  - Forcible entry, which most states by statute prohibit

3. FUTURE INTERESTS

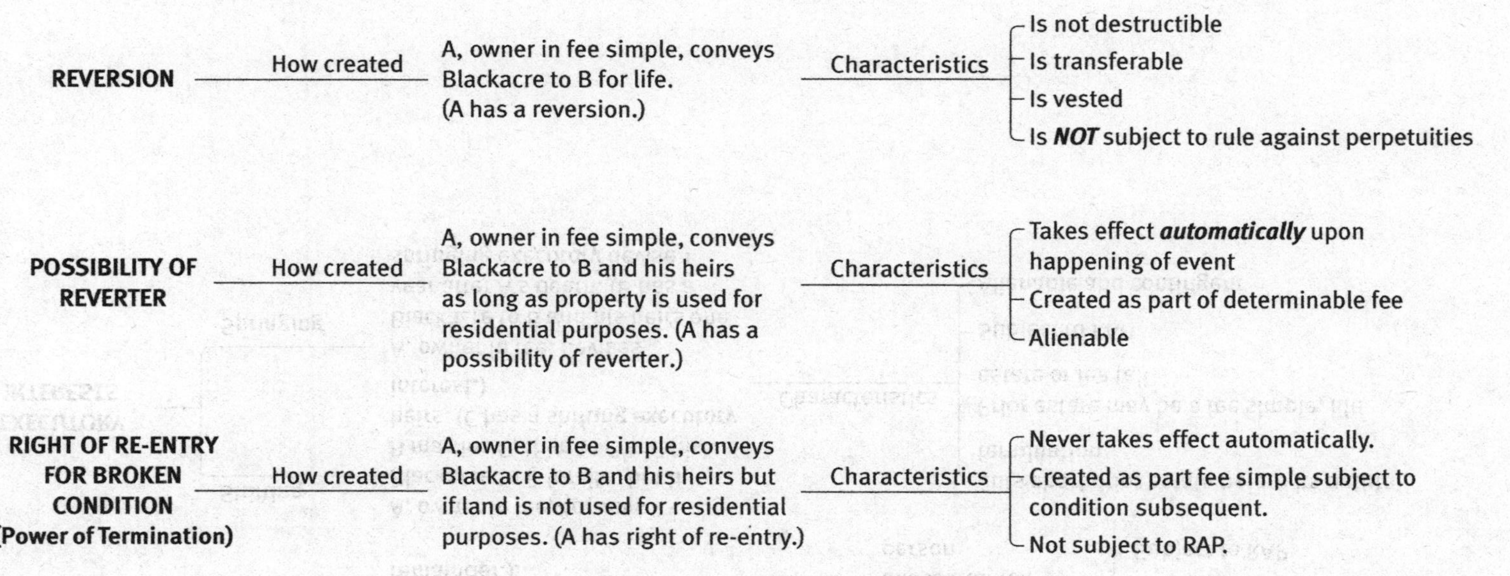

(continued)

3. FUTURE INTERESTS *(continued)*

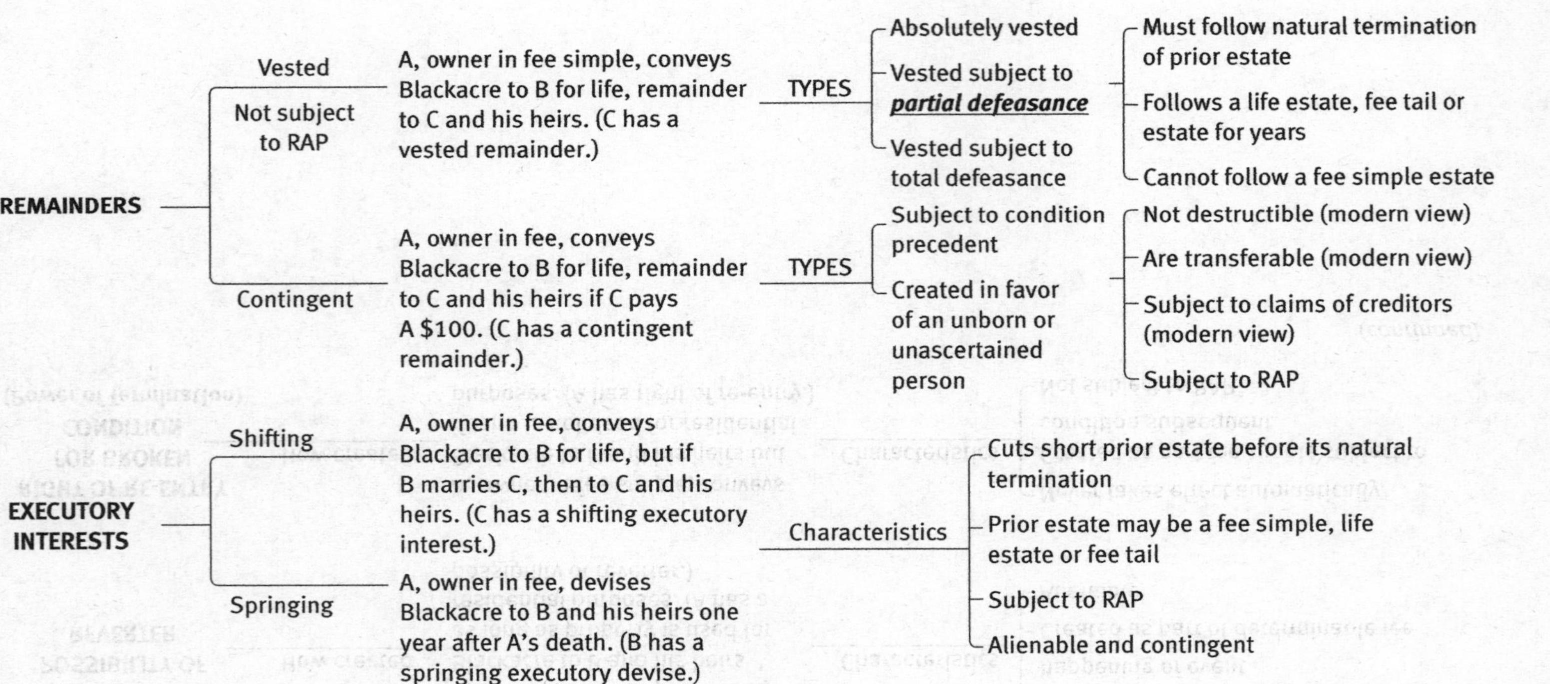

4. NON-POSSESSORY INTERESTS IN LAND

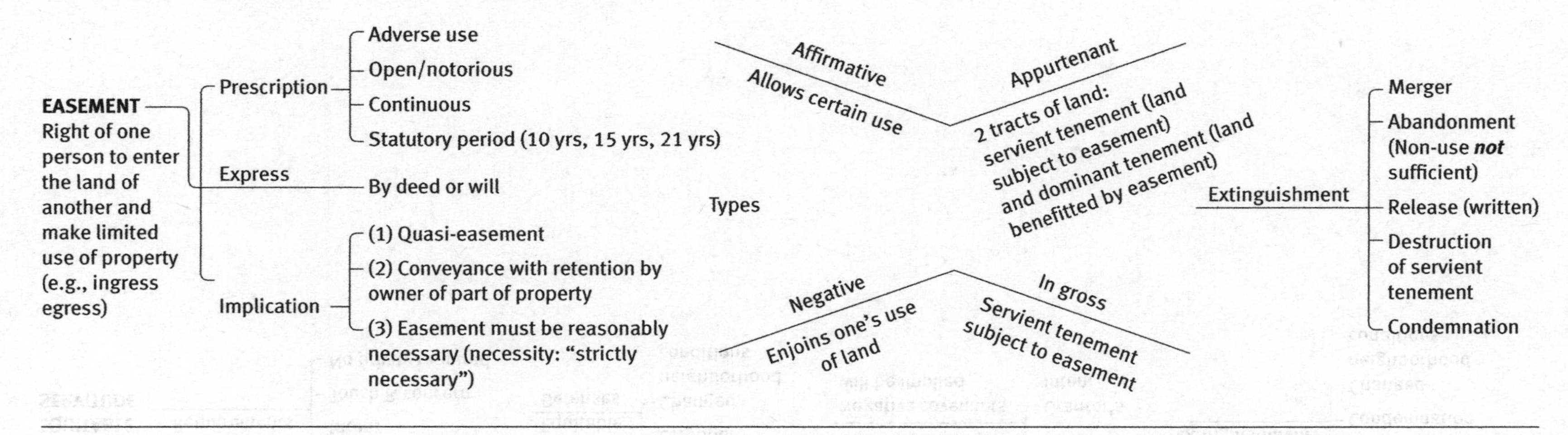

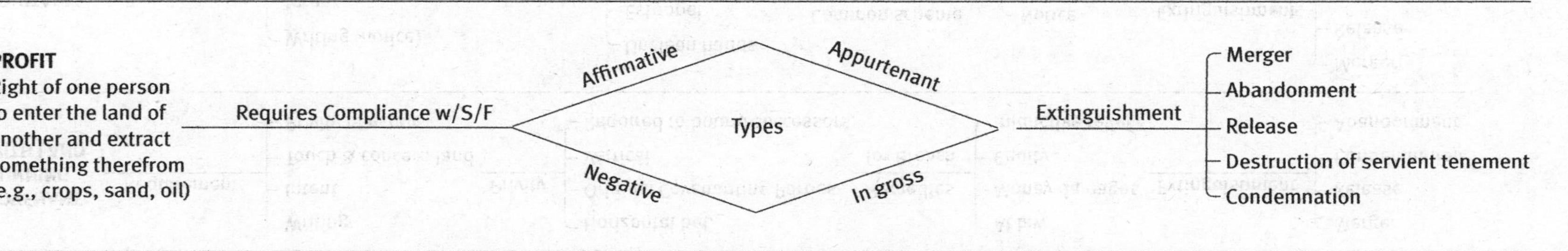

(continued)

4. NON-POSSESSORY INTERESTS IN LAND *(continued)*

LICENSE
Permission to enter another's property without being trespasser

- Revocable
- Irrevocable License Coupled w/Interest

Characteristics
- Personal in nature
- No writing required
- Permissive use
- No prescriptive rights

	LICENSE	EASEMENT	CONTRACT
Consideration:	May be required	Not required	Required
S/F:	No writing required	Writing required	Oral/Written
Revocable:	Yes	No	No

COVENANT RUNNING WITH LAND

Requirements
- Writing
- Intent
- Touch & concern land
- Privity of estate

Privity
- Horizontal bet.
- Original Covenanting Parties
- Vertical
- Required to bound successors

Remedies for Breach
- At law
- Money damages
- Equity
- Injunctive relief

Extinguishment
- Merger
- Release
- Condemnation
- Abandonment

EQUITABLE SERVITUDE

Requirements
- Writing (notice)
- Intent
- Touch & concern
- No privity required

Equitable Defenses
- Unclean hands
- Estoppel
- Changed neighborhood conditions

Common scheme

Negative covenants will be implied
- Notice
- Grantor's intent

Extinguishment
- Merger
- Release
- Condemnation
- Changed neighborhood conditions

5. CONVEYANCING

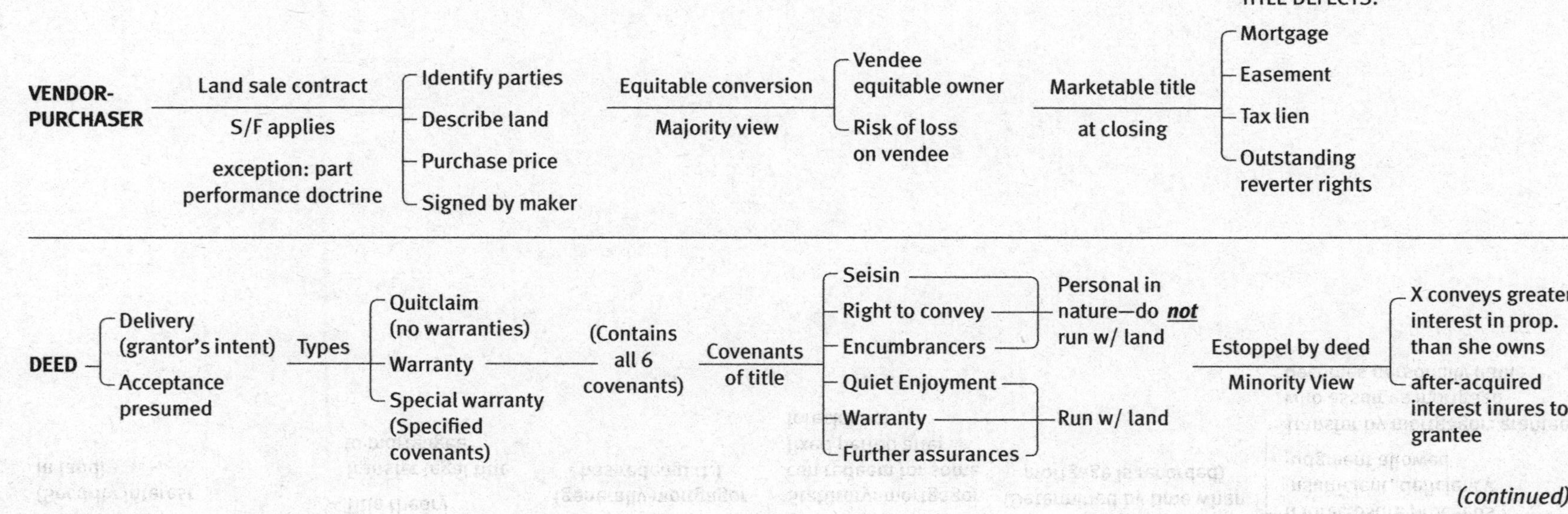

(continued)

5. CONVEYANCING *(continued)*

RECORDING ACTS (protects purchasers not donees, heirs, or devisees)

- **Pure Race**
  - Whoever records first wins
  - Actual notice irrelevant
- **Notice**
  - Subsequent bfp prevails
  - Bfp need not record
- **Race-notice**
  - Subsequent bfp prevails
  - Bfp must also record ***first***

MORTGAGES (Security interest in land)

- **Types**
  - Lien theory
  - Title theory
    - Transfer legal title to mortgagee
- **Redemption** (generally mortgagor has redemp rt.)
  - Equity: mortgagor can pay off mortgage prior to foreclosure
  - Statutory: mortgagor can redeem for some fixed period after foreclosure
- **PRIORITIES** (Determined by time when mortgage is recorded)
  - Prior mortgage prevails over subsequent one
  - Unrecorded mortgage not protected
  - If foreclosure proceeds insufficient, deficiency judgment allowed
  - Transfer by mortgagor: grantee who assumes mortgage becomes personally liable

6. CONCURRENT ESTATES

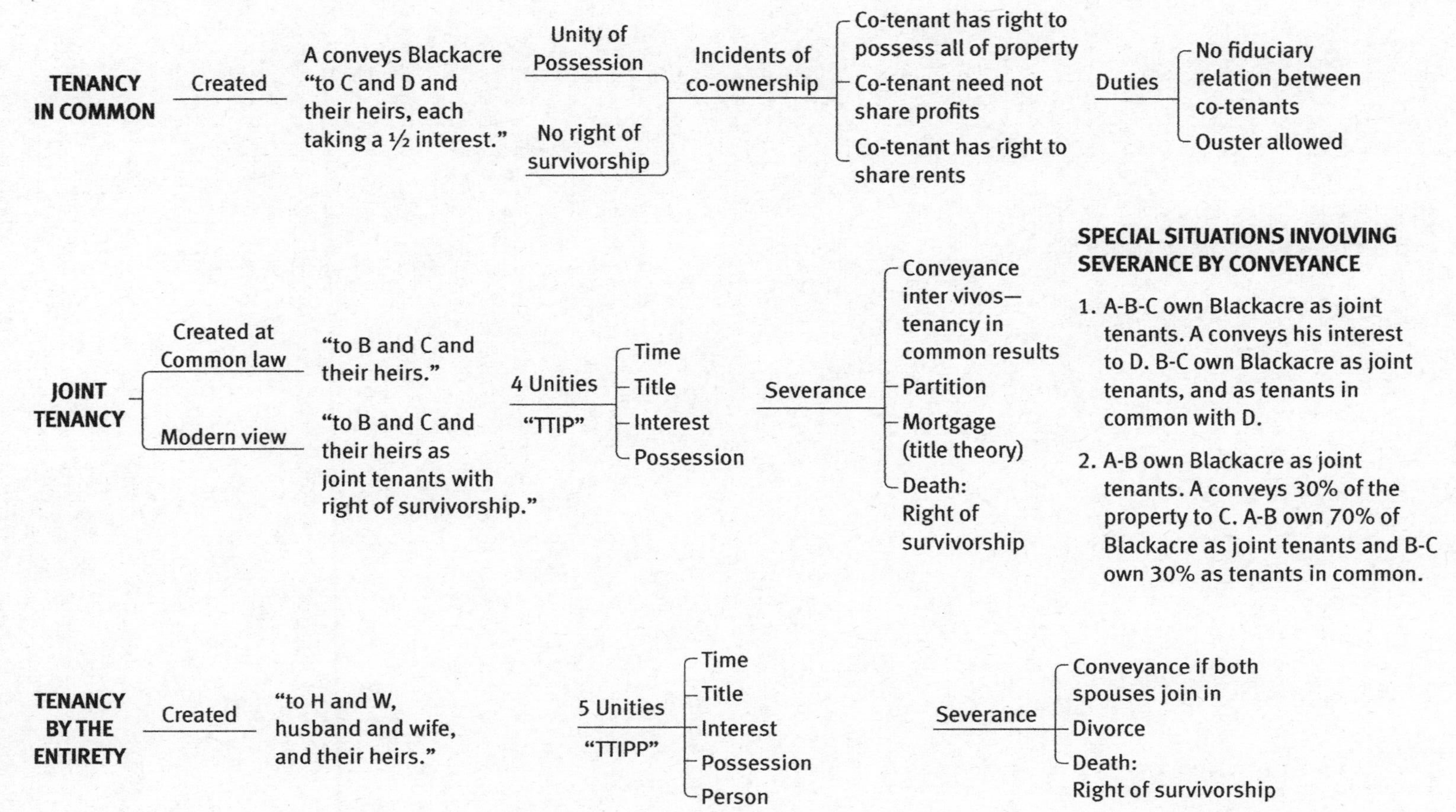

pmbr

Criminal Law

Practice Questions

Answer Grid

1 Ⓐ Ⓑ Ⓒ Ⓓ	21 Ⓐ Ⓑ Ⓒ Ⓓ	41 Ⓐ Ⓑ Ⓒ Ⓓ	61 Ⓐ Ⓑ Ⓒ Ⓓ	81 Ⓐ Ⓑ Ⓒ Ⓓ
2 Ⓐ Ⓑ Ⓒ Ⓓ	22 Ⓐ Ⓑ Ⓒ Ⓓ	42 Ⓐ Ⓑ Ⓒ Ⓓ	62 Ⓐ Ⓑ Ⓒ Ⓓ	82 Ⓐ Ⓑ Ⓒ Ⓓ
3 Ⓐ Ⓑ Ⓒ Ⓓ	23 Ⓐ Ⓑ Ⓒ Ⓓ	43 Ⓐ Ⓑ Ⓒ Ⓓ	63 Ⓐ Ⓑ Ⓒ Ⓓ	83 Ⓐ Ⓑ Ⓒ Ⓓ
4 Ⓐ Ⓑ Ⓒ Ⓓ	24 Ⓐ Ⓑ Ⓒ Ⓓ	44 Ⓐ Ⓑ Ⓒ Ⓓ	64 Ⓐ Ⓑ Ⓒ Ⓓ	84 Ⓐ Ⓑ Ⓒ Ⓓ
5 Ⓐ Ⓑ Ⓒ Ⓓ	25 Ⓐ Ⓑ Ⓒ Ⓓ	45 Ⓐ Ⓑ Ⓒ Ⓓ	65 Ⓐ Ⓑ Ⓒ Ⓓ	85 Ⓐ Ⓑ Ⓒ Ⓓ
6 Ⓐ Ⓑ Ⓒ Ⓓ	26 Ⓐ Ⓑ Ⓒ Ⓓ	46 Ⓐ Ⓑ Ⓒ Ⓓ	66 Ⓐ Ⓑ Ⓒ Ⓓ	86 Ⓐ Ⓑ Ⓒ Ⓓ
7 Ⓐ Ⓑ Ⓒ Ⓓ	27 Ⓐ Ⓑ Ⓒ Ⓓ	47 Ⓐ Ⓑ Ⓒ Ⓓ	67 Ⓐ Ⓑ Ⓒ Ⓓ	87 Ⓐ Ⓑ Ⓒ Ⓓ
8 Ⓐ Ⓑ Ⓒ Ⓓ	28 Ⓐ Ⓑ Ⓒ Ⓓ	48 Ⓐ Ⓑ Ⓒ Ⓓ	68 Ⓐ Ⓑ Ⓒ Ⓓ	88 Ⓐ Ⓑ Ⓒ Ⓓ
9 Ⓐ Ⓑ Ⓒ Ⓓ	29 Ⓐ Ⓑ Ⓒ Ⓓ	49 Ⓐ Ⓑ Ⓒ Ⓓ	69 Ⓐ Ⓑ Ⓒ Ⓓ	89 Ⓐ Ⓑ Ⓒ Ⓓ
10 Ⓐ Ⓑ Ⓒ Ⓓ	30 Ⓐ Ⓑ Ⓒ Ⓓ	50 Ⓐ Ⓑ Ⓒ Ⓓ	70 Ⓐ Ⓑ Ⓒ Ⓓ	90 Ⓐ Ⓑ Ⓒ Ⓓ
11 Ⓐ Ⓑ Ⓒ Ⓓ	31 Ⓐ Ⓑ Ⓒ Ⓓ	51 Ⓐ Ⓑ Ⓒ Ⓓ	71 Ⓐ Ⓑ Ⓒ Ⓓ	91 Ⓐ Ⓑ Ⓒ Ⓓ
12 Ⓐ Ⓑ Ⓒ Ⓓ	32 Ⓐ Ⓑ Ⓒ Ⓓ	52 Ⓐ Ⓑ Ⓒ Ⓓ	72 Ⓐ Ⓑ Ⓒ Ⓓ	92 Ⓐ Ⓑ Ⓒ Ⓓ
13 Ⓐ Ⓑ Ⓒ Ⓓ	33 Ⓐ Ⓑ Ⓒ Ⓓ	53 Ⓐ Ⓑ Ⓒ Ⓓ	73 Ⓐ Ⓑ Ⓒ Ⓓ	93 Ⓐ Ⓑ Ⓒ Ⓓ
14 Ⓐ Ⓑ Ⓒ Ⓓ	34 Ⓐ Ⓑ Ⓒ Ⓓ	54 Ⓐ Ⓑ Ⓒ Ⓓ	74 Ⓐ Ⓑ Ⓒ Ⓓ	94 Ⓐ Ⓑ Ⓒ Ⓓ
15 Ⓐ Ⓑ Ⓒ Ⓓ	35 Ⓐ Ⓑ Ⓒ Ⓓ	55 Ⓐ Ⓑ Ⓒ Ⓓ	75 Ⓐ Ⓑ Ⓒ Ⓓ	95 Ⓐ Ⓑ Ⓒ Ⓓ
16 Ⓐ Ⓑ Ⓒ Ⓓ	36 Ⓐ Ⓑ Ⓒ Ⓓ	56 Ⓐ Ⓑ Ⓒ Ⓓ	76 Ⓐ Ⓑ Ⓒ Ⓓ	96 Ⓐ Ⓑ Ⓒ Ⓓ
17 Ⓐ Ⓑ Ⓒ Ⓓ	37 Ⓐ Ⓑ Ⓒ Ⓓ	57 Ⓐ Ⓑ Ⓒ Ⓓ	77 Ⓐ Ⓑ Ⓒ Ⓓ	97 Ⓐ Ⓑ Ⓒ Ⓓ
18 Ⓐ Ⓑ Ⓒ Ⓓ	38 Ⓐ Ⓑ Ⓒ Ⓓ	58 Ⓐ Ⓑ Ⓒ Ⓓ	78 Ⓐ Ⓑ Ⓒ Ⓓ	98 Ⓐ Ⓑ Ⓒ Ⓓ
19 Ⓐ Ⓑ Ⓒ Ⓓ	39 Ⓐ Ⓑ Ⓒ Ⓓ	59 Ⓐ Ⓑ Ⓒ Ⓓ	79 Ⓐ Ⓑ Ⓒ Ⓓ	99 Ⓐ Ⓑ Ⓒ Ⓓ
20 Ⓐ Ⓑ Ⓒ Ⓓ	40 Ⓐ Ⓑ Ⓒ Ⓓ	60 Ⓐ Ⓑ Ⓒ Ⓓ	80 Ⓐ Ⓑ Ⓒ Ⓓ	100 Ⓐ Ⓑ Ⓒ Ⓓ

1. Perjury
2. Possession of Stolen Property
3. Malicious Destruction of Property — Malice Requirement
4. Criminal Battery
5. Involuntary Manslaughter
6. Self-Defense of Others — "Alter Ego" Rule
7. Criminal Liability — Legal Duty to Act
8. Theft Crimes
9. Bigamy — Absolute Liability
10. *Mens Rea* — Defense of Necessity
11. *Mens Rea* — Intent Required
12. *Mens Rea* — Conspiracy/Attempt
13. Conspiracy — Defense of Withdrawal
14. *Mens Rea* — Requisite Intent
15. Specific and General Intent Crimes (Distinction)
16. Murder — Defense of Intoxication/Defense of Self-Defense
17. Specific Intent Crimes — Intoxication Defense
18. *Mens Rea* — Statutory
19. Intentional Killing — Defense of Duress
20. Manslaughter — False Pretenses
21. Inchoate Offenses — Attempt
22. Attempted Murder
23. Robbery
24. Manslaughter/Murder
25. Defenses — Accomplice Liability
26. Battery — Defense of Intoxication
27. Conspiracy and Attempt

28. Distinction Between Robbery and Assault
29. Federal Conspiracy Statutes
30. Felony Murder Rule
31. Conspiracy — Plurality Requirement
32. Conspiracy
33. Felony Murder Rule
34. Accessory After the Fact
35. Accomplice Liability
36. Accomplice Liability
37. Murder
38. Accomplice Liability
39. Legislative Protected Class Crimes
40. Requisite Mental State
41. Felony Murder — Agency Theory
42. Felony Murder — Agency Theory
43. Felony Murder — Causation
44. Requisite Mental State
45. Robbery/Burglary Distinction
46. Transferred — Intent Doctrine
47. Murder
48. Legal Duty to Act
49. Robbery — *Actus Reus* and *Mens Rea*
50. Vicarious Liability Crimes
51. Attempt — Substantial Step Requirement
52. Attempt — Conspiracy and Co-Conspirator Liability
53. Attempt — Legal Impossibility Defense
54. Reckless Endangerment — Voluntary Intoxication Defense

55. Self-Defense

56. Finders of Lost Property — Larceny

57. Mistake of Fact — Defense for a Specific Intent Crime

58. Larceny

59. Larceny — Fixtures

60. Involuntary Manslaughter

61. Proximate Causation — Element Required for Commission of Crime

62. Depraved-Heart Murder

63. False Pretenses/Forgery

64. Arson

65. Requisite Intent

66. Felony Murder

67. Murder

68. Felony Murder

69. Involuntary Manslaughter — Omission to Act

70. Violation of Federal Criminal Statute

71. Conspiracy — Agreement Requirement

72. Conspiracy — Agreement Requirement

73. Receiving Stolen Property

74. Voluntary Manslaughter

75. Burglary

76. Conspiracy – Intent

77. Conspiracy – Unlawful Purpose

78. Conspiracy – Intent

79. Conspiracy – Unlawful Purpose

80. Attempt

81. Conspiracy – Requirements

82. Conspiracy – Vicarious Liability

83. Imperfect Self-Defense

84. Conspiracy – Withdrawal

85. Privileges and Defenses to Crimes

86. Accomplice Liability

87. Extreme Recklessness Murder

88. Depraved Heart Murder

89. Privileges and Defenses to Crimes

90. Corporate Liability for Crimes

91. Self-Defense

92. Duty-to-Aid

93. Mens Rea

94. Strict Liability

95. Mens Rea

96. Statutory Interpretation

97. Rape

98. Arson/Burglary

99. Burglary

100. Embezzlement

1. The defendant is on trial for rape of the victim. On the night of the offense, the defendant drove the victim home and asked to come inside for a nightcap. The victim refused, saying she had to be up early in the morning. The defendant then forced the victim upstairs at gunpoint and raped her.

   During the trial, the defendant took the witness stand and testified that the victim gave him a ride in her car that evening and forced him to go to her house.

   The defendant's testimony may be used in a subsequent trial as evidence that the defendant committed the crime of

   (A) misprision of felony.
   (B) misprision.
   (C) perjury.
   (D) compounding a felony.

2. Late one evening while the homeowners were away on vacation, Bob entered their home through a broken basement window. Bob knew that the homeowners were collectors of antique weapons. After ransacking the house, he found the prize collection of guns. Bob wrapped the guns in two of the expensive rugs in the home and hurriedly left the house.

   Upon returning from their vacation, the homeowners notified the police of the theft. During the investigation, a detective received a tip that the guns could be found in an old abandoned warehouse on the riverfront. When the police entered the warehouse, they found Sam with the guns. Upon questioning, Sam told the police that he had planned to dispose of the guns through a fence. With the homeowners' consent, the police authorized Sam to deliver the guns to the fence and sell them. As soon as the fence paid Sam and took possession of the guns, the police arrested both Sam and the fence.

   With which of the following crimes should Sam be convicted?

   (A) Larceny.
   (B) Possession of stolen property.
   (C) Burglary and receiving stolen property.
   (D) Burglary and possession of stolen goods.

3. A defendant stole a car and, while he was driving, the brakes suddenly failed, and the car veered out of control. The car jumped the sidewalk and crashed into a home, causing extensive damage to the dwelling.

   The defendant was arrested and charged with larceny and the separate crime of malicious destruction of property. At trial, the prosecution and the defense both stipulated that the malfunctioning of the brakes caused the car to veer out of control and damage the home.

   Assume that the defendant is convicted of larceny for the theft of the car.

   With respect to the second charge of malicious destruction of property, he should be found

   (A) not guilty, because the malice requirement is not satisfied, since the destruction resulted from the car's malfunctioning.
   (B) not guilty, because malicious destruction of property is a lesser included offense of larceny.
   (C) guilty, because malice can be inferred from the defendant's intent to steal.
   (D) guilty, because malicious destruction of property is a general intent crime.

4. The defendant was caught in a thunderstorm while walking down the street. As the defendant was about to open an umbrella that she was carrying, a stranger to the defendant came up to her, snatched the umbrella out of the defendant's hand, and said, "You thief! That's my umbrella." Enraged by being accosted in such a manner, the defendant grabbed for the umbrella with one hand and pushed the stranger with the other. The stranger hung on to the umbrella but fell over backward onto the sidewalk, which was wet and slippery. When the defendant saw the stranger hit the ground, she calmed down, decided the umbrella was not worth all the commotion, and walked off. As it turned out, the umbrella did in fact belong to the stranger, and the defendant had picked it up by mistake when she was left a restaurant earlier that day.

   A few moments later, the stranger got up in a daze and stepped into the gutter, where he was struck by a car that was passing another car on the right, in violation of a state law. The stranger died in the hospital two hours later.

   Which of the following is the most serious crime for which the defendant could be found guilty?

   (A) Battery.
   (B) Larceny.
   (C) Involuntary manslaughter.
   (D) No crime.

5. A victim was leaving his favorite local watering hole and contemplating a late night cheeseburger when he tripped over his own feet and fell on the sidewalk. A few moments later, the victim got up in a daze and stepped into the street, where he was struck by a car driven by the defendant, who was speeding, in violation of a regulation of state law. The victim died in the hospital two hours later.

   Which of the following is the most serious crime for which the defendant should be found guilty?

   (A) Speeding.
   (B) Involuntary manslaughter.
   (C) Voluntary manslaughter.
   (D) Murder.

6. The defendant was walking down the street when he saw a woman struggling with a man over a briefcase. Unbeknownst to the defendant, the woman had just stolen the briefcase from the man on the street. Believing the woman to be the victim of an attack, the defendant intervened and punched the man until the woman was able to get away with the briefcase. Confused as to why he wasn't being hailed as a hero by the woman, the defendant eventually realized that he had been an unwitting accomplice to the woman's theft. The defendant apologized profusely to the man and went home.

   According to the alter ego rule, which of the following statements is correct with respect to the amount of force that the defendant was entitled to use in the woman's defense?

   (A) Since the defendant did not stand in any personal relationship with the woman, he was not justified in using force in her defense.
   (B) Not knowing the true facts, the defendant was not justified in using force to protect the woman because the man was privileged to recapture his briefcase.
   (C) The defendant was justified in using reasonable force in the woman's defense, since he reasonably believed she was in immediate danger of unlawful bodily harm from the man.
   (D) The defendant was justified in using reasonable force in the woman's defense, since his belief that she was in immediate danger of unlawful bodily harm from the man was both objectively and subjectively reasonable.

7. This jurisdiction has the following criminal statute in effect:

"A person is not responsible for criminal conduct if at the time of such conduct, as a result of mental disease or defect, he lacks substantial capacity to appreciate the wrongfulness of his conduct, or to conform his conduct to the requirements of law."

One afternoon, a defendant was babysitting his five-year-old nephew. As they were playing catch outside, the defendant threw the ball over his nephew's head, and it rolled into the street. Instinctively, the nephew ran after the ball but tripped over the gutter and fell in the street. When he tripped, the nephew severely sprained his ankle and couldn't stand up. Moments later, a large garbage truck was backing up and ran over the nephew, killing him. Although the defendant saw his nephew's predicament, he made no effort to rescue him.

Subsequently, the defendant was charged with involuntary manslaughter. At trial, the defendant testified that he was so shocked when he saw his nephew fall near the garbage truck that he froze and was unable to move until it was too late. Following the defendant's testimony, an expert witness testified for the defense that reactions of the sort described by the defendant are not unusual when a truly shocking event occurs.

If the jury believes the testimony of the defendant and his expert witness, the defendant's best defense is which of the following?

(A) The defendant was suffering from temporary insanity.
(B) The defendant lacked the requisite mental state required for the commission of the crime.
(C) The defendant's failure to act was not voluntary.
(D) The defendant's criminal liability was superseded by that of the truck driver.

8. Under which of the following fact situations should the defendant be found NOT guilty of the crime committed?

(A) A defendant was the treasurer of an electronics company. After remodeling his private residence, the defendant owes an outstanding balance of $25,000 to his contractor. Although he had a $100,000 certificate of deposit, the defendant didn't want to cash it because he would incur a penalty for early withdrawal. Consequently, the defendant, without authorization, withdrew $25,000 from the company account to pay his contractor. At the time he made this withdrawal, the defendant honestly intended to repay the money by cashing in his certificate of deposit the following week when it matured. The defendant is charged with embezzlement.
(B) A defendant was a salesman for a cellular phone company. He honestly believed that the company owed him $10,000 in sales commissions that he had earned. The company president disputed owing the defendant any outstanding commissions and refused to pay him anything. After a heated argument with the president, the defendant was fired from his job. Thereafter, still believing that he was entitled to the $10,000, the defendant barged into the president's office and, at gunpoint, demanded the money. Under the threat of being shot, the president handed over $10,000 to the defendant. Subsequently, the defendant is charged with robbery.
(C) A defendant was a new season ticket holder at basketball games. For the first game of the season, the defendant entered the arena to see his team play their rivals. As he was walking to his seat, the defendant saw a vendor selling yearbooks. When the vendor turned his head to make a sale, the defendant took a yearbook without paying. Thinking that he had stolen the yearbook, the defendant hurriedly walked away. After he had taken a few steps, the defendant for the first time saw a sign that read "All Season Ticket Holders Entitled to a Free Yearbook." Unknown to the defendant at the time, if he had presented his season ticket stub to the vendor he would have received a free yearbook. The defendant is charged with larceny.
(D) A defendant, who was unemployed, opened a charge account at a department store by lying on a credit application that she was employed and earning a yearly salary of $20,000. Using her store credit card, the defendant purchased $1,000 in store merchandise. When the bills came due, she failed to make any payments because she was insolvent. At the time the defendant purchased the items, she honestly thought that she would have a job and be in a position to pay for the goods once the bills came due. The defendant is charged with false pretenses.

9. A wife was notified by an airline that her husband's plane had crashed. All passengers aboard were reported lost at sea and presumably drowned. The wife, after making diligent inquiries in good faith, became convinced that her husband was dead. Three years later she re-married. A few months after her re-marriage, the newspaper announced that her husband had been found on a desert island and was rescued. The wife was then prosecuted under the following state bigamy statute.

"Whoever, being married, shall marry any other person during the life of the former spouse shall be guilty of a felony: provided, that nothing in this Act shall extend to any person marrying a second time whose spouse shall have been continually absent from such person for a period of seven years last past, and shall not have been known by such person to be living within that time."

On the charge of bigamy, the wife should be found

(A) guilty.
(B) not guilty, because of the wife's mistake of fact regarding her husband's death.
(C) not guilty, because of the wife's mistake of law regarding her husband's death.
(D) not guilty, because the wife did not have the requisite mens rea to be held criminally liable.

10. In which of the following situations will the defendant's defense of necessity most likely exculpate him of criminal liability?

(A) A defendant was marooned on a desert island, along with a victim and another sailor after their boat capsized during a violent storm at sea. The three sailors had gone without food for two weeks and were on the verge of dying of starvation. Each of the sailors, however, still had a small amount of water left in their canteens with which to subsist. One night, the defendant took the water from the victim's canteen and poured it into his own canteen while the victim slept. The defendant did this in the hope that the extra water would make it possible for him to live a couple of more days so that he would be able to walk across the island to look for help. The next day, the victim died from starvation and dehydration. Two days later, the defendant and the other sailor were rescued. The defendant never walked across the island because he was too weak from body weight loss.
(B) A defendant and a victim were on a hiking expedition together. They were longtime hiking buddies who had climbed many steep and precipitous mountains in the past. As the defendant and the victim were climbing a dangerously steep incline, their ropes suddenly became entangled. As a result of the entanglement, the victim fell 50 feet before he was able to regain his balance and footing. However, the victim's fall caused the defendant to lose his balance, and he was in jeopardy of falling off the mountain. In order to avoid falling, the defendant cut the safety rope that held the victim. This caused the victim to fall 400 feet to his death.
(C) A defendant, who was intoxicated, was driving his car home along a heavily traveled highway. In his inebriated condition, the defendant was swerving his vehicle across the highway. Suddenly, a school bus loaded with children made a wrong turn and headed directly into the path of the defendant's auto. In order to avoid crashing head-on with the school bus, the defendant turned his vehicle onto the sidewalk and struck a victim, a paraplegic, who was confined to a wheelchair. The defendant's auto crushed the victim to death.
(D) A defendant, a bank teller, was on duty when two robbers held up the bank. She was taken hostage and ordered to drive their getaway car. As they were being pursued by the police, the defendant was commanded to drive excessively fast to avoid being captured. While driving at a speed of nearly 100 M.P.H., the defendant approached a busy intersection and saw the victim, a blind person, with a guide dog walking across the street. She slowed down to avoid hitting the pedestrian with the dog. As she did so, one of the robbers stuck a gun against her head and threatened to kill her if she didn't speed through the intersection. Afraid she would be murdered, the defendant accelerated into the path of the victim, killing him and his guide dog.

11. A husband and wife divorced after 17 years of marriage. They had one son, aged 10. As part of the divorce decree, the wife was given custody of the son, while the husband was entitled to weekend visitation.

Thereafter, the husband accepted a new job in a neighboring state. Before relocating, the husband met with an attorney to seek his advice about how he could gain full custody of his son. The attorney told the husband that his new state did not give full faith and credit to divorce proceedings in his former state of residence. As a consequence, the attorney advised the husband that he could take the son to live with him and not be in violation of the law. This was erroneous legal advice, and his new state, in fact, did honor and give full faith and credit to other states' divorce decrees.

When his next scheduled visitation took place, the husband picked up his son at his ex-wife's home. Instead of returning his son, he took him to live with him in his new state. After refusing to return his son to his ex-wife, the husband was subsequently arrested and charged with kidnapping. The applicable statute is defined as "knowingly abducting a person and moving him or her to another location."

Should the husband be found guilty of kidnapping?

(A) Yes, because he unlawfully transported his son to another state, in violation of the divorce decree.
(B) Yes, because mistake of law is no defense.
(C) No, because he lacked the requisite state of mind.
(D) No, because he received erroneous legal advice.

12. Two men agreed to burglarize a home. While they were planning the burglary, the two men learned that the home had a sophisticated alarm system that needed to be disarmed. One of the men told the other that he knew an alarm specialist who could help disarm the security system.

One of the men then approached the alarm specialist and asked if he would assist them in disarming the home's alarm system. The alarm specialist said that he didn't want to participate in the crime but told the man how he could disarm the system himself. The two men thereafter went to the home to commit the burglary.

When they arrived at the home, they saw a vicious guard dog patrolling the fenced-in area of the home. Deciding it would be too risky to confront the dog, the two men abandoned their planned burglary.

Which of the following is the most accurate statement regarding the criminal liability of the two men and the alarm specialist?

(A) The two men are guilty of conspiracy.
(B) The two men and the alarm specialist are guilty of conspiracy.
(C) The two men are guilty of conspiracy and the two men and the alarm specialist are guilty of attempted burglary.
(D) The two men and the alarm specialist are guilty of both conspiracy and attempted burglary.

13. A defendant worked as a short-order cook at a restaurant. After work, the defendant went out drinking with one of the other cooks, and they were commiserating about their lack of money. They decided that the only way out of their rut was to rob a local bank.

They then agreed to carry out a bank heist on the following Friday. In accordance with their plan, the cook on Monday purchased two ski masks to be used in the robbery. On Wednesday, after learning that the cook had bought the masks, the defendant got cold feet and told the cook he was renouncing his involvement in the robbery scheme. On Friday, the cook carried out the robbery without the defendant's participation. This jurisdiction requires an overt act for the crime of conspiracy.

Is the defendant guilty of conspiracy?

(A) Yes, because the cook and the defendant did enter into an agreement to commit the bank robbery.
(B) Yes, because the purchase of the ski masks was a sufficient overt act in the furtherance of the crime.
(C) Yes, because the defendant did not thwart the cook from committing the robbery.
(D) No, because the defendant's withdrawal was effective.

14. A defendant was wearing a black leather jacket when he entered a deli for lunch. He placed his jacket on a coat rack located in the front of the deli. After his meal, the defendant picked up a similar black leather jacket, believing it to be his own. The jacket he took, however, belonged to another customer. The defendant left the deli and walked a short distance before realizing he had taken the wrong jacket by mistake. He then returned to the deli and placed the jacket back on the coat rack. He found his own jacket, which had been partially hidden under a stack of other coats.

If the defendant were arrested and charged with larceny of the other customer's jacket, he will most likely be acquitted because

(A) there was a mistake of fact.
(B) he returned the jacket after discovering his mistake.
(C) he lacked the requisite state of mind.
(D) there was no fraudulent conversion.

15. In which of the following situations would the defendant's intoxication NOT be able to negate his criminal culpability?

(A) A defendant had consumed a fifth of bourbon. Later that same day, he approached a victim and, brandishing a knife, told her to accompany him or he would stab her. He led the victim to his car and then ordered her to disrobe. As the victim was removing her pantyhose, she kicked the defendant in the head, temporarily dazing him. The victim then safely ran from the car. The defendant is arrested and charged with the crime of assault with the intent to commit rape.
(B) A defendant attended a wedding reception at a hotel, where he drank several vodka daiquiris. Following the reception, the defendant engaged in a violent argument with the hotel's parking lot attendant. The defendant took a tire iron from his car and threw it at the attendant. The tire iron missed the attendant and hit a victim as he was entering the hotel. The defendant is arrested and charged with assault with the intent to commit battery.
(C) A defendant had been drinking liquor all evening at a bar with three of his buddies. An undercover detective overheard the defendant and his buddies plot to rob the bar after closing hours. When the defendant attempted to draw a gun from his coat, he was quickly disarmed and placed under arrest by the detective. The defendant is charged with the crime of conspiracy to commit robbery.
(D) At his law school graduation party, a defendant drank two six-packs of beer. Around midnight, the defendant was approached by a girl, who asked him to drive her home. Although the girl was only 15 years old, she had the appearance of a woman in her mid-to-late twenties. The defendant, who had had his eye on the girl all night, quickly agreed, and he showed her the way to his car. Once inside, they engaged in sexual intercourse. The age of consent in this jurisdiction is 17 years old for females. The defendant is subsequently arrested and charged with statutory rape.

16. A defendant had been drinking at a bar for three hours and was visibly intoxicated. A man entered the bar and sat down next to the defendant. After ordering a beer, the man turned to the defendant and said, "Hey buddy, you're sure an ugly looking dude." The defendant ignored the man's insult and turned to walk away. The man then pushed the defendant against the bar and said, "Your face makes me sick to my stomach." The defendant then pulled out a razor and slashed the man's throat, killing him.

If the defendant is prosecuted for the man's murder, he will most likely be found

(A) guilty, because his intoxication was voluntary.
(B) guilty, because he was under a duty to retreat.
(C) not guilty, because of his intoxication.
(D) not guilty, because there is no duty to retreat in a public place.

17. In which case would the defendant's intoxication defense most likely negate his criminal intent?

(A) A defendant is charged with raping a victim. At trial, the defendant testifies that he was so inebriated that he was unable to understand that the victim did not consent to his conduct.
(B) A victim was horseback riding when she was approached by a defendant, who rode up from behind and struck her horse with his riding crop, causing the horse to bolt and throw the victim. On trial for battery, the defendant testified that he was drunk and only fooling around and did not intend to injure the victim.
(C) While intoxicated, a defendant wandered into a victim's barn, lit a match, and began looking for some whiskey that he thought was hidden there. Angered at not finding any liquor, the defendant threw the match into a bale of hay, which quickly ignited, thus causing the destruction of the victim's barn. The defendant is charged with arson.
(D) A defendant is charged with assault with intent to commit rape. While on trial, the defendant testified that he was intoxicated to such an extent that he did not remember striking the victim.

18. A state enacted a statute making it illegal to knowingly sell, purchase, or in any way distribute any form of tobacco to a minor. Violation of the statute was a misdemeanor punishable by a $500 fine and up to 30 days in jail. After the statute's enactment, a defendant sold a pack of cigarettes to a girl who was 17 years of age. Before selling the product to the girl, the defendant carefully examined the girl's driver's license, which indicated that she was, in fact, 17 years old. The defendant nevertheless made the sale because he erroneously believed the age of majority to be 17. The defendant is subsequently charged with violation of the statute, and his mistake is honestly held to have been made.

Such a mistake should

(A) not prevent his conviction, because mistake of the law is no defense.
(B) not prevent his conviction, because the crime imposes absolute criminal liability.
(C) result in his acquittal, because he took reasonable steps to ascertain the girl's age.
(D) result in his acquittal, because he did not possess the requisite mens rea.

19. Two brothers broke into the home of a bank's president and kidnapped the president's wife. The brothers took the wife hostage, pointed a gun at her head, and demanded that she drive them in her car to their hideout. As the wife was driving down the street, a woman pushing her baby in a stroller suddenly stopped in the middle of the intersection. In order to avoid hitting the woman and her child, the wife veered the car to the left, and intentionally struck a bystander, instantly killing him.

If the wife is subsequently prosecuted for the murder of the bystander, she will most likely be found

(A) guilty, because she intentionally veered the car, striking the bystander.
(B) not guilty, by reason of necessity.
(C) not guilty, by reason of duress.
(D) not guilty, by reason of self-defense.

20. Believing she was pregnant, a woman went to see a doctor, a licensed gynecologist, because she wanted an abortion. The doctor examined her and determined that she was not pregnant, but decided that he would tell her she was, in order to earn his $500 fee. After receiving the $500, the doctor proceeded to have the woman admitted to a hospital by falsely informing the hospital authorities that she had a benign tumor on her uterus, which he was going to remove. He performed all the surgical procedures appropriate for an abortion under adequate hygienic conditions, but the woman began hemorrhaging and died.

    The doctor should be found guilty of

    (A) murder and larceny by trick.
    (B) manslaughter and false pretenses.
    (C) battery and larceny by trick.
    (D) murder, battery, and false pretenses.

21. A young boy was one of the players on a little league baseball team. The boy's father hated the coach because he rarely gave his son any playing time. The boy was mostly a benchwarmer who played only an inning or two during the game.

    One night, the father hid behind some shrubbery in front of the coach's home. Armed with a baseball bat, the father intended to break the coach's kneecaps when he came home from work. A man, who resembled the coach, was walking down the street. The father mistakenly believed that this man was the coach. The father jumped out of the bushes and hit the man in the kneecaps with the baseball bat. The man, who was a hemophiliac, died as a result of the injuries suffered in the beating.

    The father is

    (A) guilty of attempted murder of the coach and the murder of the man.
    (B) guilty of attempted murder of both the coach and the man.
    (C) guilty of attempted manslaughter of the coach and murder of the man.
    (D) guilty of attempted battery of the coach and murder of the man.

22. A defendant was driving his car recklessly at a high rate of speed through a residential neighborhood. He was traveling at a speed of over 100 M.P.H. when he lost control of the car and jumped a curb, striking a woman who was walking along the sidewalk. As a result of the collision, the woman suffered severe internal injuries and fractured both legs. She was hospitalized for 11 months and became permanently disabled.

    If the defendant is charged with attempted murder, he should be found

    (A) guilty, because a person is presumed to intend the natural and probable consequences of his acts.
    (B) guilty, because criminal liability is predicated upon the defendant's willful and wanton disregard for the safety of others.
    (C) not guilty, because the defendant did not intend to kill the woman.
    (D) not guilty, because he lost control of the vehicle.

23. A man was at a pub drinking beer and playing darts with a group of friends. Quite intoxicated, the man left the bar around midnight. He was staggering down the street when the defendant approached him from behind. The defendant took out a stick, stuck it against the man's back and told the man to give him his wallet or he was going to shoot him. Frightened, the man fainted and fell to the pavement. The defendant reached into the man's pants pocket and stole his wallet.

    The defendant is guilty of

    (A) attempted robbery.
    (B) robbery.
    (C) larceny.
    (D) assault and larceny.

24. In which of the following situations is the defendant most likely to be found guilty of manslaughter rather than murder?

(A) Not intending to kill, a defendant hits a person over the head with a pipe. As a result, the person dies from head injuries.
(B) Not intending to kill, a defendant throws a large chunk of ice off an overpass onto a busy freeway below. The chunk of ice crashes through a windshield, killing a driver.
(C) Not intending to kill, a defendant kidnaps a victim and takes her to a remote area of the desert. The defendant then drives off, leaving victim alone in the sweltering heat after the ransom is not paid. The next day, the victim dies from exposure because she is unable to reach the nearest town eight miles away.
(D) Not intending to kill, a defendant punches a victim in the face, causing the victim to fall backwards and strike his head on a curb, killing him.

25. A defendant gave a man a gun and instructed him to kill a victim. The man shot and killed the victim with the gun. The man was charged with murder and acquitted. The defendant is now charged with the murder of the victim.

He will be able to assert a valid defense if the man's acquittal was based on which of the following?

(A) Insanity.
(B) Self-defense.
(C) Diminished capacity.
(D) The Wharton Rule.

26. During a drunken quarrel between a husband and a wife, the husband pointed his gun at his wife and said, "If I didn't love you, I'd kill you." The husband thought the gun was unloaded but, in fact, earlier that day his son had loaded it. As a joke, he fired the gun at his wife, wounding her in the shoulder. The husband is later charged with committing a battery upon his wife.

If the husband attempts to prove that he was so inebriated he could not have formed a criminal intent, this would constitute a

(A) good defense, because the charge requires a specific intent.
(B) good defense, because at least a general criminal intent is required for every offense.
(C) poor defense, because voluntary intoxication is not a valid defense to battery.
(D) poor defense, because the husband was not aware that the gun was loaded.

27. An ex-con who had just been released from prison approached two men and asked if they wanted to take part in a bank robbery. The two men both agreed. The ex-con went ahead and planned the robbery. As part of his scheme, the ex-con stole a van, which he intended to use as the getaway vehicle.

According to the ex-con's plan, he would pick up the two men in the van on Friday morning and drive over to the bank where the robbery would occur. The ex-con instructed his cohort that he would be the getaway driver and wait in the van while they entered the bank, armed with shotguns. However, the day before the robbery was to take place, the ex-con was arrested on a parole violation for carrying a concealed weapon and was taken into custody. The two men, nevertheless, decided to carry out the robbery using the van that the ex-con had stolen. On Friday morning, the two men drove to the bank. When they entered, an undercover police detective was waiting and arrested the two men, as the police had received an anonymous tip regarding the robbery earlier that morning.

The ex-con should be found guilty for which of the following crimes?

(A) Automobile theft and solicitation.
(B) Automobile theft and conspiracy.
(C) Automobile theft and attempted robbery.
(D) Automobile theft, conspiracy, and attempted robbery.

28. A wealthy woman often wore expensive jewelry while walking her dog in the park. Her friends warned her against wearing such valuable jewelry because they feared she would be an easy target for muggers. In order to persuade the woman not to wear her expensive jewelry in the park, her friend decided to play a practical joke. One morning, the friend dressed like a man and hid in an area of the park that she knew the woman customarily walked through. As the woman was strolling through the park with her dog that morning, the friend jumped out from behind the bush brandishing a toy pistol and grabbed the woman's diamond necklace from her neck. Startled, the woman became hysterical and began to plead for her life. The friend then removed her male garb, handed the necklace back to the woman and said, "I just wanted to frighten you to teach you a lesson."

If the friend is subsequently prosecuted, she should be found guilty of which, if any, of the following crimes?

(A) Battery.
(B) Assault.
(C) Robbery.
(D) No crime.

29. Shortly after breaking up with the defendant, a woman began dating the victim. The defendant, who still loved the woman, hated the victim. During a holiday weekend, the woman and the victim arranged to go camping in a federal park. The defendant and his friend decided to beat up the victim while he and the woman were on their camping trip. They went to the campsite where the woman and the victim were staying, but they couldn't find the couple, who were hiking in the woods.

Subsequently, the defendant was arrested and charged with conspiracy to commit an assault in a federal park. At trial, the defendant testified that he didn't know he was in a federal park. Moreover, he stated that if he had known, he would never have agreed to the crime.

If the jury believes the defendant, he should be found

(A) guilty, because federal conspiracy laws do not require the mental retainment of jurisdictional requirements.
(B) guilty, because federal conspiracy laws require only an intent to commit a prohibited act, but do not require a knowledge of the surrounding circumstances.
(C) not guilty, because he didn't have the specific intent to commit the crime of assault in a federal park.
(D) not guilty, because he did not agree to commit a crime in a federal park.

30. A defendant decided to rob a bank. She used an unloaded gun in the robbery. The defendant approached the bank teller, pointed her unloaded pistol at him and said, "This is a stick-up . . . give me your money and no one will get hurt."

While the teller was handing the money to the defendant, the victim, a bank patron who was in line, saw the defendant pointing the gun at the teller and fainted. He fell backward and cracked his head on the marble floor. This resulted in a fatal head injury. Moments later, the defendant left the bank with the money. Thereafter, the defendant was arrested.

If the defendant is prosecuted for felony murder and acquitted, the most likely reason will be because

(A) her gun was unloaded.
(B) there was not a sufficient connection between the victim's death and the robbery.
(C) the defendant didn't intend to harm anyone during the robbery.
(D) this jurisdiction has adopted the Redline limitation to the felony murder rule.

31. The defendant and her co-felon decided to rob a bank. They agreed to use unloaded guns in the robbery. As planned, the co-felon entered the bank while the defendant stationed herself outside as a lookout. The co-felon approached the bank teller, pointed her unloaded gun at him, and demanded the money.

While the teller was handing the money to the co-felon, the defendant got scared and fled. The teller, who had a weak heart started to feel faint. He handed over the money to the co-felon, and then clutched his chest and died.

The co-felon was found not guilty by a jury in her trial, which preceded the defendant's trial. The defendant is subsequently prosecuted for conspiracy and acquitted.

Her acquittal most likely resulted because

(A) the defendant abandoned her participation in the crime.
(B) the teller's death was accidental.
(C) the co-felon was acquitted.
(D) the teller was not placed in apprehension of bodily harm.

32. After weeks of deliberation, a boyfriend decided to embark on his plan to rob a bank. As part of his scheme, the boyfriend enlisted his girlfriend, who agreed to drive the getaway car. On the day of the robbery, the girlfriend and the boyfriend drove to the bank. After the girlfriend parked outside and the boyfriend went into the bank, she saw a security guard in the bank and changed her mind and fled on foot, leaving the keys in the car with the motor running. A few minutes later, the boyfriend went into the bank, robbed it, and then ran back to the car. He drove off and was speeding away from the bank when he looked behind to see if he was being followed. As he took his eye off the road, the boyfriend's vehicle struck a pedestrian who was crossing the street, killing her.

For the pedestrian's death, the girlfriend should be found guilty of which, if any, of the following crimes?

(A) Murder.
(B) Involuntary manslaughter.
(C) Voluntary manslaughter.
(D) No crime.

33. After weeks of deliberation, the defendant decided to rob a local liquor store. The defendant purchased a ski mask and then went into the liquor store, put his gun into the face of the clerk, and demanded the money from the register. Terrified, the clerk gave him the money from the register. The defendant pocketed the money, grabbed a bottle of tequila off the shelf for his celebration, and then ran back to the car and drove off. About an hour later, the defendant was slowly approaching his hideout in the outskirts of town when a young child suddenly darted in front of the defendant's car. He applied the brakes but couldn't stop in time. The car struck the child, killing her.

For the child's death, the defendant should be found guilty of which, if any, of the following crimes?

(A) Felony murder.
(B) Involuntary manslaughter.
(C) Voluntary manslaughter.
(D) No crime.

34. Knowing that a homeowner was away on vacation, two men decided to burglarize her home. Since they didn't have a car, the men asked the defendant to drive them to the home. The two men did not tell the defendant what they intended to do there. The defendant drove them to the house. While the defendant waited in the car, the two men entered the home by using a master key to unlock the front door. They then stole several items of expensive jewelry from the bedroom.

Concealing the jewelry in their pockets, they left the house and got back into the defendant's car. Unaware of the theft, the defendant drove the two men back to their apartments. The next day, the two men pawned the jewelry for $5,000. Two weeks later, the two men gave the defendant $500 and told him for the first time about the burglary. The defendant kept the money and did not report the theft to the police.

If the defendant is subsequently prosecuted, he should be found

(A) guilty of receiving stolen property but not guilty of burglary.
(B) guilty of burglary but not guilty of receiving stolen property.
(C) guilty of burglary and of receiving stolen property.
(D) not guilty of either burglary or receiving stolen property.

35. A defendant and his friend were walking down the street when they ran into a victim. The friend turned to the defendant and said that the victim owed him some money. The friend then stopped the victim and demanded the money. The victim refused to pay the money. The friend suddenly said to the defendant, "Give me your gun. I'm going to blow this lowlife away." The defendant gave his friend his gun, and the friend shot the victim to death. As the friend and the defendant were about to leave, the defendant turned to his friend and said, "Let me have my gun back. I think the creep's still alive." The defendant then fired two more shots into the victim's body. Unknown to the defendant, the victim was already dead.

Which of the following is the most serious crime that the defendant can be convicted of?

(A) Attempted murder.
(B) Murder.
(C) Assault with a deadly weapon.
(D) Concealment of a deadly weapon.

36. Co-defendants were dealers at a casino. They had been employed by the casino for four years. One day, they were unexpectedly fired by the casino's new manager. Apparently, the casino hired the new manager to get rid of some of the old-time employees and replace them with new personnel at a lower wage. Angered by their firing, the co-defendants vowed to get back at the casino.

As their revenge, they decided to plant a bomb in the casino and demand $1,000,000. After receiving the money, they would then reveal the location of the bomb and provide details for defusing it. The co-defendants agreed that the casino should be given adequate warning so that nobody would be injured. In accordance with their plan, one of the co-defendants, who was an electronics expert, built the bomb himself. He alone then drove to the casino where he placed the bomb in a hallway closet. Shortly thereafter, the other co-defendant phoned the casino and made a demand for the money. He said a bomb was in the casino and that it would explode in 24 hours unless the money was paid. The casino treated their demand as a crank call and refused to make any payment.

With their plans having gone awry, the co-defendants agreed that one of them should return to the casino and defuse the bomb. As one of the co-defendants was driving back to the casino, the bomb exploded, killing 30 people. A subsequent investigation revealed that a faulty wire caused the bomb to detonate prematurely. A state statute provides that detonating or attempting to detonate a bomb or explosive device in or near a building or dwelling is a felony.

If the co-defendants are charged with violating the aforementioned statute, which of the following statements is correct?

(A) Both are guilty, because each participated in the planning of the crime.
(B) The co-defendant who built the bomb is guilty, because he built and transported the bomb, but the other co-defendant is not guilty, because his phone call was not a substantial step in the furtherance of the crime.
(C) Neither is guilty, because the casino's gross negligence in failing to heed the telephone warning constituted an independent intervening cause of the explosion.
(D) Neither is guilty, because they did not intend for anyone to be killed, but the bomb exploded prematurely.

37. Two co-defendants were investment brokers at a bank. They had been employed by the bank for ten years. One day, they were unexpectedly fired by the bank's new manager. Apparently, the co-defendants' investments had not been performing well in the economic downturn. The co-defendants, upset and humiliated by their firing, vowed to get back at the bank.

As their revenge, they decided to plant a bomb in the bank and demand $2,000,000. After receiving the money, they would then reveal the location of the bomb and provide details for defusing it. The co-defendants agreed that the bank should be given adequate warning so that nobody would be injured.

In accordance with their plan, the co-defendants consulted the Internet, where they found all the information they needed on how to build a bomb. They built the bomb and placed it in a supply closet. Shortly thereafter, they phoned the bank and made a demand for the money. They said a bomb was in the bank and that it would explode in 24 hours unless the money was paid. The bank refused to pay the money.

Realizing that their plan had gone awry, they drove to the bank to attempt to defuse the bomb. As they were driving back to the bank, the bomb exploded, killing 30 people.

If the co-defendants are charged with murder and conspiracy to commit murder, which of the following statements is correct?

(A) Both co-defendants are guilty of felony murder, but neither is guilty of conspiracy to commit murder.
(B) Both co-defendants are guilty of murder and conspiracy to commit murder.
(C) Both co-defendants are guilty of conspiracy to commit murder, but not murder.
(D) Both co-defendants are not guilty of murder and conspiracy to commit murder.

38. A defendant and a classmate were students at a state college. They were spending a leisurely afternoon listening to music in the defendant's dorm room. They had just consumed a six-pack of beer when the classmate asked the defendant if there was anything else to drink. The defendant indicated there wasn't and suggested that his classmate drive to the store and buy another six-pack. The classmate told the defendant that his car wasn't working and asked the defendant if he could borrow his. The defendant assented and gave his classmate the keys to his car. The defendant knew that the classmate was drunk when he lent him his car.

The classmate was driving to the store at an excessive rate of speed. As he approached an intersection, he was traveling at 70 M.P.H. When he came to the intersection, the light turned red. The classmate, who made no effort to stop in time, drove through the red light and collided with another car. The driver of the other car, who had entered the intersection with a green light, was killed in the accident.

In the event that the defendant can be convicted of manslaughter, it will most likely be upon the basis of

(A) responsibility for the accident as an accomplice.
(B) recklessness in lending his car to his classmate.
(C) joint venture in lending his car to his classmate for a common purpose.
(D) vicarious liability for the conduct of his classmate.

39. One afternoon, police officers observed a man and a 14-year-old girl smoking marijuana together. They arrested the man and charged him with the separate offenses of (1) possession of a controlled dangerous substance, and (2) contributing to the delinquency of a minor. The girl was also arrested and charged with being an accomplice to the crime of contributing to the delinquency of a minor.

At trial, the girl's best defense is that

(A) smoking marijuana does not necessarily make her an accomplice to the crime.
(B) the man, the adult principal, must be convicted before any prosecution can be maintained against a minor.
(C) a minor cannot be prosecuted for an adult crime.
(D) since the statute was designed to protect minors, the girl cannot be prosecuted as an accomplice.

40. A defendant and a victim were roommates at college. The defendant was playing the role of a serial killer in the school play and asked the victim if she could leave their apartment for a few hours while she rehearsed. The victim agreed but returned to the apartment shortly thereafter because she was curious and wanted to see the defendant rehearse. The victim quietly came back into the apartment and hid behind some curtains in the dining room in order to watch the defendant rehearse. In her role, the defendant carried a large butcher's knife, with which she stabbed the curtains at her "victim." Unknown to the defendant, the victim, who was hiding behind the curtain, was stabbed in the chest and killed.

If the defendant is prosecuted for the victim's death, she should be found

(A) guilty of murder.
(B) guilty of manslaughter.
(C) guilty of battery.
(D) not guilty.

41. A man and a woman conspired to rob a local bank. After entering the bank, they pulled out guns and ordered everyone to the floor. They demanded money from the tellers but, unknown to them, one of the tellers activated a silent alarm. Within minutes, the bank was surrounded by police officers.

A standoff ensued for several hours with the man and the woman barricaded inside the bank with several hostages. The man decided to try and make a getaway. He took the bank manager and, using her as a human shield, exited the bank. A shooting ensued, and both the man and the bank manager were killed by the police. This jurisdiction follows the agency theory of felony murder.

The woman is charged with felony murder for the deaths of the man and the bank manager. The woman's attorney has filed a motion to dismiss both charges. The court should

(A) grant the motion with respect to the bank manager's death, but deny the motion for the death of the man.
(B) grant the motion regarding the man's death, but deny the motion regarding the death of the bank manager.
(C) grant the motion regarding the deaths of both the man and the bank manager.
(D) deny the motion regarding the deaths of both the man and the bank manager.

42. A boyfriend decided to rob a grocery store after he was let go during a labor dispute. The boyfriend asked his girlfriend to drive the getaway car, to which she agreed, on the condition that no loaded weapons were used during the robbery. On the day of the robbery, the boyfriend and his girlfriend drove to the grocery store. Unknown to the girlfriend, the boyfriend entered the store with a loaded gun. The boyfriend approached one of the cashiers and told him to fill a bag with all the money from the register. When the cashier refused, the boyfriend shot and killed him. He then turned to the next cashier and pointed his gun at her. The cashier suffered a heart attack and died.

The boyfriend then took the money from the registers himself and exited the store. One of the customers had called the police, and they were waiting outside. A shootout ensued, and the boyfriend was killed by the police.

If this jurisdiction follows the agency theory of felony murder, the girlfriend is guilty if how many counts of murder?

(A) One.
(B) Two.
(C) Three.
(D) None.

43. One night, a defendant entered a liquor store, pointed a gun at the cashier, and demanded the money from the register. The cashier was nervous and moving slowly, and when she accidentally spilled all of the money out of the bag and onto the floor, the defendant shot her and left. The bullet lodged close to the cashier's spine, paralyzing her. The defendant was subsequently prosecuted and convicted of robbery and assault with a deadly weapon.

Two months later, the cashier decided she wanted an operation to remove the bullet. The doctors warned the cashier that the procedure was very risky and could result in her death. The cashier decided to go ahead with the surgery and, unfortunately, died as a result.

If the defendant is now prosecuted for felony murder, he should be found

(A) not guilty, because he was not the cause of the cashier's death.
(B) not guilty, because the subsequent prosecution violates double jeopardy.
(C) not guilty, because the cashier decided to have the surgery, aware of the risks.
(D) guilty, because he was the cause of the cashier's death.

44. A defendant was driving his new sports car at a high rate of speed on a busy city street in the middle of the day. A pedestrian was struck by the defendant's car as she was crossing the street and was seriously injured.

A criminal complaint was filed against the defendant and, at trial, he testified that he did not intend to injure anyone, but admitted that he was indifferent as to the consequences of driving recklessly.

Based on the defendant's actions and testimony, he should be found guilty of

(A) attempted murder.
(B) attempted manslaughter.
(C) assault with the intent to cause serious bodily injury.
(D) battery.

45. One night, a victim was in her home when she heard the doorbell ring. When the victim opened the door, she was confronted by three defendants. They pushed the victim inside her house and threatened her with bodily harm if she didn't cooperate. After tying her up with ropes, the trio then proceeded to ransack the victim's home.

They then placed many of the victim's valuables and other possessions into a large sack and hurriedly left her house.

What crimes should the defendants be convicted of?

(A) Assault, battery, and robbery.
(B) Larceny, robbery, and burglary.
(C) Robbery and burglary.
(D) Robbery only.

46. A defendant was angry at his friend for marrying the defendant's former girlfriend. As the friend was painting his house one afternoon, the defendant fired a shot from his gun at him. Although the shot missed the friend, the bullet struck and killed the friend's daughter. The defendant is subsequently charged with the first-degree murder of the daughter. The relevant statutes in effect in this jurisdiction are as follows:

Section 169: Murder in the first degree is the unlawful and intentional killing of a human being with malice aforethought.

Section 170: Malice is expressed when there is manifested a deliberate intention to take away the life of another.

Which of the following, if established, would provide the defendant with his best defense?

(A) He intended to kill the friend and not the daughter.
(B) He intended only to wound the friend.
(C) He was unaware of the elements of malice.
(D) The killing was the result of negligence in missing the friend.

47. An off-duty police officer was standing on a street corner waiting for a bus. A man came up from behind and stole the police officer's wallet from his pants pocket. As the man was running away with the wallet, the police officer pulled out his service revolver. The police officer yelled at the man to stop and then fired several shots in the man's direction. The police officer did not aim directly at the man but shot at the pavement intending to frighten him. One of the bullets ricocheted off the sidewalk and struck the man, killing him.

The police officer is guilty of

(A) assault with a deadly weapon.
(B) involuntary manslaughter.
(C) voluntary manslaughter.
(D) murder.

48. In which of the following situations is the defendant most likely guilty of manslaughter?

(A) A defendant was a guide on a nature walk in a national park. The group was traversing a mountainous path when a mountain lion suddenly appeared. The defendant, who was carrying a loaded gun, knew that mountain lions and coyotes were in the area. The defendant saw that the mountain lion was about to attack one of the hikers. Although the defendant could have easily shot and killed it, he did nothing. The wild animal pounced on the hiker. As she was being savaged, the defendant and the other members of the group ran to safety.
(B) A defendant, a registered nurse, asked her friend out to lunch. While eating, the friend suddenly began choking on a chicken bone. The defendant did nothing to help her friend. The friend choked to death.
(C) A defendant, a physician, was walking home from his office one afternoon when he saw a car hit a man who was trying to cross the street. The victim was knocked to the ground and seriously injured, while the car sped away. The defendant, who could have saved the man's life if he had treated him, continued walking home without rendering assistance. The man died from loss of blood.
(D) A defendant took his four-year-old daughter out in the yard to play. As they were playing catch, the telephone began to ring. The defendant ran into the house to answer the phone. While he was inside, the daughter's ball rolled into the street. As she went to retrieve it, the daughter was struck and killed by a car.

49. In which of the following situations would the defendant most likely be found NOT GUILTY of robbery?

(A) In a dark alley, a defendant approached the victim and said, "Give me the gold ring on your finger or I'll shoot you with this gun." The victim gave him the ring. However, the ring really belonged to someone else, as the victim was just borrowing it for the evening to impress his girlfriend. In addition, the gun that the defendant had in his possession was really a water pistol.
(B) A defendant broke into a house and took a stereo system. After he had placed the system in his car and was about to leave, the homeowner came home and saw him. She raced to the car and started to hit the defendant through the open window in an attempt to get her stereo back. The defendant punched her in the nose and drove away with the system.
(C) A defendant was walking behind a shopper in a mall when he suddenly reached for her gold chain, pulled it from her neck, and ran away into the crowd. The shopper suffered a slight cut on her neck where the chain broke.
(D) A defendant picked the lock on an apartment door. The noise startled the tenant, who had been sleeping. The defendant overpowered the tenant, tied him up, and forced him to disclose where he kept his money. The tenant told the defendant to look in the kitchen cabinet, which he did. The defendant found $120 in cash, took the money, and left the apartment.

50. An owner of a pharmaceutical company manufactures aspirin tablets that it sells in interstate commerce. A woman purchased a bottle of the owner's aspirin from a drugstore. Shortly after taking two of the aspirin tablets, the woman became extremely ill and began having convulsions. She was rushed to the hospital, where it was determined that the aspirin tablets contained strychnine, a poisonous chemical.

The owner of the pharmaceutical company is subsequently charged with violating a federal statute that makes it a misdemeanor to transport impure drugs in interstate commerce.

The owner should be found

(A) guilty, only if he had the authority and responsibility for packaging the aspirin tablets.
(B) guilty, only if he knew or should have known that the aspirin tablets were poisonous.
(C) guilty, only if he personally supervised the packaging of the aspirin tablets.
(D) guilty, only if he knew that other customers had purchased poisonous aspirin tablets in the past.

51. A husband and wife were unhappily married. The husband was an alcoholic who physically abused the wife when he became drunk. After the husband beat up the wife one night, she decided to kill him. The wife, who was experienced in firearms, planned to shoot her husband while he slept. Before carrying out her plan, the wife took out a $1,000,000 life insurance policy on her husband, naming herself as beneficiary.

Shortly thereafter, the husband and wife celebrated their 10th wedding anniversary. They went out to dinner and had a truly enjoyable evening together. After a great night, the wife experienced a change of heart and decided she really loved her husband and didn't want to kill him after all. The wife confessed and told her husband about her plan, begging forgiveness. The husband was outraged. He proceeded to file for divorce and notified the police about his wife's plan.

If the wife is charged with attempted murder, she should be found

(A) guilty, because she purchased the life insurance policy.
(B) guilty, because she intended to kill her husband.
(C) not guilty, because she did not perform a substantial step in carrying out the murder.
(D) not guilty, because she effectively withdrew from the criminal endeavor.

52. A mother hated a girl because she always seemed to outperform her daughter and make her feel inferior. Fearing that the girl would beat out her daughter for the last cheerleading position, the mother decided to kill the girl. One night while the mother and her boyfriend were having dinner, the mother asked him to kill the girl. The mother handed her boyfriend a gun and gave him the home address where the girl lived. Unknown to the boyfriend, the mother gave him the wrong address. By mistake, the boyfriend went to the home of a family who lived across the street from the girl.

The boyfriend rang the doorbell and a woman opened the door. The boyfriend asked the woman if her daughter was home. The woman called for her daughter to come to the front door. When she did so, the boyfriend shot and killed both the woman and her daughter.

The mother should be found guilty for which, if any, of the following crimes?

(A) Conspiracy and voluntary manslaughter.
(B) Conspiracy, attempted murder, and two counts of murder.
(C) Solicitation and two counts of murder.
(D) Solicitation and attempted murder.

53. One evening, a defendant was at a party and offered to sell an ounce of marijuana to a partygoer. The partygoer agreed to purchase the marijuana and gave the defendant $200. In return, the defendant handed the partygoer a bag containing what appeared to be marijuana. At the time of the transaction, the defendant knew that the bag did not contain marijuana but, instead, was oregano.

The defendant is guilty for which, if any, of the following crimes?

(A) Solicitation and attempted sale of narcotics.
(B) Attempted sale of narcotics and false pretenses.
(C) False pretenses.
(D) Solicitation, attempted sale of narcotics, and false pretenses.

54. A man had just won $14,000,000 in the lottery. To celebrate his good fortune, the man took a group of friends to a bar for some drinks. At the bar, the man ordered a round of drinks for everyone. As the man knew, these specific drinks that he ordered were highly intoxicating. A few minutes after finishing his drink, the man stood up to go to the bathroom. As he did so, he became very woozy, lost his balance and fell onto a table. The table flipped over and knocked the customer sitting there backward off his chair. The customer's head struck the floor with such force that he suffered a concussion.

Thereafter, the man was charged with the crime of reckless endangerment, which is defined in this jurisdiction as "reckless conduct causing physical injury to another." At his trial, the man called the bartender who served the drinks on the day in question to testify. The bartender testified that the drinks she served the man and his friends were 95% alcohol. At the close of the bartender's testimony, the state objected and moved to strike her testimony. The trial judge sustained the motion.

Was the trial judge correct in excluding the bartender's testimony?

(A) Yes, because reckless endangerment is a general intent crime.
(B) Yes, because the man's intoxication was voluntary.
(C) No, because the testimony was evidence that the man did not possess the requisite mens rea.
(D) No, because the testimony was evidence that the man's conduct was not voluntary.

55. A boyfriend was unhappy in his relationship with his girlfriend. When the girlfriend got drunk, she would become abusive and beat her boyfriend. During the course of their relationship, the beatings became more violent and more frequent. Unable to endure the physical abuse any longer, the boyfriend hired a hit man to kill his girlfriend. One night while the girlfriend was asleep, the hit man entered the home with a key given to him by the boyfriend and shot the girlfriend to death. Afterward, the boyfriend was prosecuted for murder as an accomplice.

The defense sought to have the judge instruct the jury that the boyfriend acted in self-defense.

Based on the given facts, should the judge give such an instruction to the jury?

(A) No, because the boyfriend's belief in the necessity of deadly force in self-defense was unreasonable.
(B) No, because the boyfriend could have avoided the danger by safely retreating.
(C) Yes, because a reasonable jury could conclude that the boyfriend acted in self-defense by using necessary force to protect himself from the girlfriend's constant violent attacks.
(D) Yes, because a criminal defendant's Sixth Amendment right to a jury trial prohibits a court from refusing to submit affirmative defenses to the jury.

56. A defendant was waiting in line to enter a movie theater when he noticed a free movie pass on the ground. The pass had a space where the owner of the pass needed to write in his name. The defendant waited until he got to the cashier's window and presented the pass, seeking a free admission to the movie, and claiming that he received it as a birthday present from a friend. The cashier told him that the passes were invalid unless the holder's name was entered on the pass. The defendant wrote his name on the pass, gave it to the cashier, and was admitted to the theater.

The defendant is guilty of

(A) larceny.
(B) false pretenses.
(C) forgery.
(D) no crime.

57. A defendant purchased a new car and offered to sell his old car to his neighbor, who always had admired it, for $1,900. The neighbor accepted. As part of their deal, the neighbor took immediate possession of the car and promised to send the defendant a check as soon as possible. One week later, the defendant received a check in the amount of $900. The neighbor had inadvertently sent the check for the incorrect amount. The defendant went ahead and changed the numbers on the check from $900 to $1,900 and changed the words "nine hundred dollars" to "one thousand nine hundred dollars." The defendant then took the check to the neighbor's bank for payment. When he presented it to the teller, she noticed that the check had been altered. The bank immediately contacted the police who arrested the defendant and charged him with forgery. This jurisdiction defines forgery as "making a material alteration in any writing with the purpose to defraud."

At trial, the defendant testified that he honestly believed that the neighbor had made a mistake in drafting the check and that the neighbor meant to make it out for $1,900, the contract price.

If the jury believes the defendant, it should find him

(A) guilty, because his belief was not reasonable.
(B) guilty, because he made no effort to contact the neighbor to determine whether he had made a mistake in sending only $900.
(C) not guilty, because it is irrelevant whether his belief was reasonable or not.
(D) not guilty, because the neighbor did not intend to make a partial payment.

58. A cashier worked part-time at a convenience store. As the cashier was sitting behind the cash register, he noticed a boy enter the store. While the boy walked through the store, the cashier watched him on a hidden camera located behind the cashier's counter. Thereupon, the cashier saw the boy pick up two packs of baseball cards and place them in his coat pocket. The boy then walked to the rear of the store, where he picked up a package of cupcakes.

The boy took the cupcakes to the front counter and paid the cashier for the cupcakes only. The boy started to walk out of the store when the cashier said, "Hey, kid, I'm not charging you for the baseball cards because you paid for the cupcakes. But next time I'm not going to let you get away with it." The baseball cards sold for $5 per pack.

The boy has committed which, if any, crimes?

(A) Larceny.
(B) Larceny by trick.
(C) False pretenses.
(D) No crime.

59. A tenant was cleaning out the bedroom of his apartment as his lease had expired. He carried out his waterbed, dresser, and all of his clothes. As the tenant inspected the room one last time, he noticed a bookcase that he had screwed into the wall when he first moved in. While he pondered whether to remove the bookcase, the tenant concluded that it constituted a fixture and, therefore, was a permanent part of the realty. Nonetheless, the tenant decided that the bookcase would fit nicely in his new apartment, so he removed it from the bedroom wall. When the landlord learned that the tenant had removed the bookcase, he contacted the tenant and demanded that he return it to the apartment. The tenant refused.

If the tenant is subsequently prosecuted for larceny, he will most likely be found

(A) guilty, because the chattel was the personal property of the landlord.
(B) guilty, because severance of the bookcase from the wall was sufficient asportation to constitute larceny.
(C) not guilty, because the tenant cannot be found guilty of theft for removing his own property.
(D) not guilty, because the bookcase was a fixture.

60. A man and a woman were driving eastbound along a steep two-lane winding highway. The woman was driving in front of the man. As the man approached the rear of the woman's car, he became impatient and tried to pass her along a section of the highway designated as a no-passing zone. When the man swerved his car into the westbound lane to pass the woman, he didn't see another driver, who was rounding a curve in the westbound lane. In order to avoid a head-on collision with the man, the other driver swerved his car to the shoulder of the roadway. The other driver, however, was unable to control his car along the narrow strip of the shoulder, and it fell down the steep mountain.

The man and the woman both saw the other driver's car slide down the hillside. They immediately stopped their vehicles and walked over to the edge of the roadway looking for the car. They saw the other driver's car overturned in a gully about 200 feet down the mountain. The man and the woman heard the other driver moaning and calling for help. However, the man and the woman failed to provide any assistance. They walked back to their cars and drove off. Although the man and the woman passed through a business area a short while later, they neither reported the accident nor sought aid for the other driver. Hours later, the other driver died from injuries suffered in the accident.

If the man and the woman are subsequently prosecuted for the other driver's death, the most likely outcome would be that

(A) the man and the woman are both guilty of manslaughter.
(B) the man is guilty of manslaughter only.
(C) the woman is guilty of manslaughter only.
(D) neither the man nor the woman is guilty of manslaughter.

61. A college student who was pledging a fraternity was required to steal a yield sign from a street intersection. At 10:00 P.M. one evening, the student went to the corner and removed the yield sign from the intersection. Motorists driving northbound were required to yield to other vehicles entering the intersection. Two hours later, a man was driving northbound toward the intersection after having just smoked marijuana. Failing to yield, the man crashed into a vehicle, killing the other driver.

If the student and the man are prosecuted for the other driver's death, who shall be held criminally liable?

(A) The student only, because his conduct was the legal cause of the other driver's death.
(B) The man only, because he was high on marijuana when he collided with the other driver's vehicle.
(C) The man and the student, because their acts were concurrent causes of the other driver's death.
(D) Neither the man nor the student, if the other driver had the last clear chance to avoid the accident.

62. A breeder and owner of vicious guard dogs trained his dogs to attack strangers at night. He often sold and leased his guard dogs to various business and factory owners who used the guard dogs to frighten away intruders from entering their premises at night. One evening, the breeder was in the back yard of his home training three of his guard dogs. The back yard was enclosed with a chain link fence and a latched gate that prevented the dogs from running out. After the training session, the breeder opened the gate and permitted the dogs to run loose in his front yard. Minutes later, a man was walking along the sidewalk in front of the breeder's house when he was attacked by one of the dogs. The man suffered severe injuries and died as a result of the attack.

The breeder should be found guilty of

(A) murder.
(B) involuntary manslaughter.
(C) voluntary manslaughter.
(D) reckless endangerment.

63. A collector had an extensive collection of sports memorabilia, which included baseball cards, autographed bats, balls, and old uniforms. The collector would often attend regional shows where he would display his vast collection and meet with other sports enthusiasts.

One day at a sports memorabilia show, the defendant approached the collector with an old baseball glove with what appeared to be an authentic signature of a famous player. Unknown to the collector, the defendant signed the glove himself. The defendant had practiced the distinctive signature of the famous player for several hours before signing the glove with an extremely good likeness of his signature.

The collector examined the glove and asked the defendant if the signature was authentic. The defendant replied that he had purchased the glove at an auction and could not vouch for the authenticity of the signature. The collector paid the defendant for the glove. Later, the collector took the glove to a handwriting expert who informed the collector that the signature on the glove was a very skillful fake, but a fake, nonetheless.

The defendant is guilty of

(A) false pretenses but not forgery, because the glove is not a document with legal significance.
(B) forgery but not false pretenses, because the defendant did not vouch for the authenticity of the glove.
(C) false pretenses and forgery.
(D) neither false pretenses nor forgery.

64. A man was visiting his friend at the friend's cabin. The man decided to surprise the friend with some fireworks, so he purchased some fireworks and hid them under his friend's chair on the friend's porch. That evening, the friend went outside to smoke and dropped his unfinished cigarette next to his chair on the porch. The cigarette ignited the fireworks, and the fireworks immediately exploded, causing extensive damage to the friend and to his cabin. The man was arrested and is being prosecuted for arson.

Will the man be found guilty of arson?

(A) No, because the man never intended to hurt the friend.
(B) No, because the man did not intend to burn down the cabin and was not guilty of wanton and willful misconduct.
(C) Yes, because the man indirectly set fire to the friend's cabin.
(D) Yes, because the injury to the friend and to his cabin was the natural result of the man's actions.

65. There is a state statute making it a misdemeanor "to falsely report a fire either intentionally or recklessly." There were three college roommates who lived together in a small apartment. Two of the roommates decided to play a practical joke on the other roommate, which they liked to do from time to time because he was gullible. The two roommates were seated in the living room of their apartment. The other roommate was in an adjoining room and within earshot of the two roommates.

Knowing that their roommate could hear their conversation, the two roommates falsely stated that a fire had been set at the student center at the college. After overhearing this conversation, the other roommate phoned the fire department and reported this information. Several fire trucks were dispatched to the college and determined the information to be false.

If the two roommates are prosecuted for violating the aforementioned statute, they should be found

(A) guilty, because they caused the false report to be made.
(B) guilty, because they are accomplices to their roommate.
(C) not guilty, because they didn't report the information to the fire department themselves.
(D) not guilty, because they didn't knowingly believe that their roommate would report the information to the fire department.

66. Two defendants were playing poker one night with some friends. Everyone that was playing, including the defendants, was drinking heavily. After losing a large amount of money, the defendants accused the victim of cheating. When the victim tried to leave, the defendants beat him with their fists and, as the victim fell to the ground, they continued by kicking him in the head. The victim suffered a fractured skull in the beating and died as a result of severe head trauma. Thereafter, the defendants reached into the victim's pocket and stole his wallet.

The defendants were arrested and charged with the murder of the victim. Prior to trial, the prosecutor admitted that it was impossible to determine which defendant was responsible for actually fracturing the victim's skull.

If the defendants are prosecuted for felony murder, which of the following would provide their best defense?

(A) The jurisdiction adheres to the inherently dangerous felony requirement.
(B) The jurisdiction follows the independent felony murder rule.
(C) The jurisdiction follows the proximate cause theory.
(D) The jurisdiction follows the agency theory.

67. A defendant hated a victim and decided to kill him. The defendant put a loaded gun in his coat pocket and went outside for a walk, not sure if and when he may see the victim. The defendant passed by a bar and decided to go inside for a drink. While in the bar, he drank several bottles of beer and became intoxicated. While walking home from the bar, the defendant bumped into the victim. As soon as the defendant recognized him, he pulled out his gun and shot and killed the victim.

In this jurisdiction, first-degree murder is defined as a premeditated and deliberate killing. All other forms of murder are second-degree murder.

The defendant is guilty of

(A) first-degree murder.
(B) second-degree murder.
(C) involuntary manslaughter.
(D) voluntary manslaughter.

68. Two women decided to steal some clothing from their favorite store. One of the women carried a large shopping bag containing a gun into the store. The other woman did not know that her partner had a gun in the shopping bag. After the women placed three dresses into the shopping bag, a clerk became suspicious and approached the women. The women tried to leave the store and, as they did, the clerk grabbed the bag, which fell to the floor. When the bag hit the floor, the gun discharged, killing the clerk.

Which of the following would be the women's best defense to the charge of felony murder?

(A) They committed a larceny by placing the three dresses in the shopping bag.
(B) The jurisdiction requires the killing to be independent of the felony.
(C) The jurisdiction follows the agency theory of felony murder.
(D) The killing was accidental and unintended.

69. A girlfriend lived with her boyfriend in a small apartment. The boyfriend was a gun enthusiast who kept a collection of antique pistols and firearms in the apartment. The boyfriend was also an avid baseball fan and had a fanatic devotion to his favorite team. One evening, the boyfriend was watching his beloved team play their archrival on television. His favorite team lost in extra innings. After the game, the boyfriend became despondent and told his girlfriend that he was so disgusted that he was going to kill himself. The boyfriend took one of the pistols from his gun collection and shot himself in the head. As the boyfriend fell to the floor, wounded, his girlfriend couldn't believe her eyes. At first she thought that she should call 911 for an ambulance. But she was afraid that the police might think that she was responsible for the shooting. Consequently, she decided to do nothing. She proceeded to leave the apartment and spent the night at her mother's home.

The boyfriend did not immediately die from the gunshot wound. A subsequent medical examiner's report concluded that the boyfriend died from loss of blood approximately two hours after the shooting. If the girlfriend had sought immediate medical assistance, the boyfriend would have lived.

The girlfriend is subsequently prosecuted for her boyfriend's death. She should be found

(A) guilty of first-degree murder.
(B) guilty of second-degree murder.
(C) guilty of involuntary manslaughter.
(D) not guilty, because she had no legal duty to render assistance.

70. A federal agency has been established for the purpose of stabilizing, supporting, and protecting farm income and prices. The agency is authorized to enter into and carry out such contracts or agreements as are necessary in the conduct of its business.

An export company entered into a contract with the federal agency to transport a variety of goods to foreign countries. Thereafter, the federal agency suspended the export company pending an investigation into possible misuse of official inspection certificates relating to commodities exported to a foreign country. During an investigation relevant to the charge, the president of the export company presented information to the federal agency. Subsequently, the president was charged with violation of a federal statute that states: "It is a felony for any person in a matter within the jurisdiction of a federal agency to knowingly make a false statement."

At the president's trial, the government presented evidence to show that he falsified bills of lading and embezzled over $500,000 of surplus commodities for export. The president testified that he did not know that he was dealing with a federal agency and, hence, the federal government would have jurisdiction over his company's export contract with the federal agency.

As to the significance of the president's ignorance, the court should instruct the jury that it may convict the president

(A) if it finds that the president knew that he was doing business with a federal agency.
(B) if it finds that the president was aware that he might have been doing business with a federal agency.
(C) if a reasonable person would have been aware that he might have been doing business with a federal agency.
(D) even if there was no reason the president should have known that he was doing business with a federal agency.

71. A man and a woman worked in the shipping department at a footwear store. Both of them were disgruntled because they engaged in strenuous work and were paid only minimum wage. One day, they plotted to rob the store after working hours. They knew that the store kept a large amount of cash in a safe located in the manager's office.

Before carrying out their scheme, they approached the defendant, who was a safecracker, to see if he would assist them. The defendant told them that he was not interested in participating in the theft. The next day, the man phoned the defendant and told him they would give him a cut of the money if he would simply advise them on how to break the combination to the lock of the safe. The defendant agreed and provided the man with the information he requested but refused to actually participate in the theft.

Two weeks later, the man and the woman decided to carry out their scheme. Late one night, they drove to the footwear store and parked at the rear entrance. The co-workers planned to hop over a chainlink fence surrounding the store and break in by prying open the window to the manager's office. Unknown to them, the store had a vicious guard dog outside patrolling the property. Seeing the dog, they decided not to commit the robbery.

With regard to the defendant's criminal liability, he is

(A) guilty of conspiracy with the man and the woman.
(B) guilty of conspiracy with the man only.
(C) not guilty of conspiracy because there was no overt act.
(D) not guilty of conspiracy because the man and the woman withdrew and abandoned the criminal endeavor.

72. A mechanic and a janitor were in the cafeteria of the manufacturing plant where they worked, discussing how much they hated their boss. The co-workers both knew that their boss suffered from a serious heart condition that necessitated frequently taking medicine. The mechanic was aware that the boss kept his medicine locked in a desk drawer in his office and suggested that they take his medicine and throw it away. The janitor agreed to be a part of the plan. Unknown to either of the co-workers, their conversation was overheard by the defendant, who also worked at the manufacturing plant.

The defendant, who also hated the boss, decided to join the co-workers and participate in their plan. Although the defendant didn't say anything to the co-workers, he immediately went to the boss's office, broke into his locked desk with a penknife, and found the bottle of medicine. He then left the bottle on top of the desk so it could easily be found by the co-workers. The defendant then hurriedly left the office. A few minutes later, the co-workers went to the boss's office. Just before they entered the office, the janitor got scared and ran away. The mechanic went inside the office, saw the medicine bottle on top of the desk, picked it up and placed it inside her pocketbook. She then walked across the hallway to the bathroom and poured the medicine into the toilet. Later that same afternoon, the boss had a heart attack and went to his office, urgently in need of his medicine. Unable to find his medicine, he collapsed and lost consciousness. A few minutes later, the boss was found dead on his office floor. An autopsy report listed the cause of death as a heart attack and concluded that he would have survived had he taken his medicine. The mechanic was tried and acquitted of conspiracy for the boss's death in a separate trial. Subsequently, the defendant is charged with conspiracy for the boss's death.

He should be found

(A) guilty, because he assisted the mechanic in the commission of the crime, even though he did not enter into the agreement himself.
(B) not guilty, because the mechanic was acquitted of conspiracy.
(C) not guilty, because there was no true agreement.
(D) not guilty, because he did not communicate his intent to participate in the plan to either the mechanic or the janitor.

73. An informer had been arrested many times and had a long police record for theft-related crimes. Recently, the police received information that the informer was involved in the perpetration of a jewelry store heist. In exchange for immunity from prosecution, the informer agreed to act as an undercover police informant. As part of this arrangement, the informer set up a pawnbroker's shop for the purposes of supplying information to the police about trafficking stolen goods.

One day, a man entered the pawnshop and sold the informer a stolen television. Immediately thereafter, the informer contacted the police, who photographed the television and recorded its serial identification number. The informer then displayed it for sale at his pawnshop. A few days later, a defendant entered the store and expressed interest in the television. In confidence, the informer told the defendant that the television was stolen and, consequently, he would sell it to her cheap. Unable to resist the bargain, the defendant bought the television.

The defendant was subsequently arrested and charged with receiving stolen property.

She should be found

(A) not guilty, because the television lost its stolen status when it came into the possession of the informer.
(B) not guilty, because the defendant was entrapped into buying the television.
(C) guilty, because the defendant was aware of the television's stolen status when she purchased it.
(D) guilty, because the police merely maintained surveillance over the television, while the informer took actual possession and control of it.

74. A defendant, a victim, and some of their friends were playing cards at an apartment. One of the friends, who had incurred heavy losses during the evening, became upset after losing a poker hand to the defendant. As the defendant was collecting his winnings, the friend yelled at him, "If I see you cheating again, I'm gonna kick your butt." The defendant immediately stood up, pointed a finger at the friend and said, "Listen, punk, don't blame me because you're a lousy card player." The friend then grabbed the defendant by the shirt and punched him in the face several times.

Visibly angered, the defendant pulled out a gun, aimed it at the friend, and screamed, "That's the last time you'll ever do that to me. You're history." Just as the defendant was about to pull the trigger, the victim jumped in front of the friend and said, "Don't shoot!" The defendant, who had been drinking heavily and was visibly intoxicated, couldn't stop, and fired his gun. The bullet struck the victim in the heart, killing him instantly.

If the defendant is charged with murder, which of the following is the defendant's best argument that the homicide should be manslaughter rather than murder?

(A) The defendant's shooting was in self-defense.
(B) The friend's hitting the defendant was adequate provocation.
(C) The defendant was so intoxicated that he suffered from a diminished capacity.
(D) Since the defendant did not intend to kill the victim, it was an unintentional killing that should be manslaughter.

75. In which of the following situations is the defendant most likely to be found guilty of burglary?

(A) After drinking all night at a bar, a defendant mistakenly entered his neighbor's home and broke a vase while attempting to find the refrigerator.
(B) While walking past an antique store one night, a defendant saw an antique chair that he believed was stolen from him. The defendant broke into the store and took the chair.
(C) Posing as a cable television repairman, a defendant gained access to a victim's home one evening by falsely telling the victim that there was a problem with the cable outlet in her bedroom. Once inside, the defendant stole jewelry from the victim's bedroom dresser.
(D) A defendant broke into his neighbor's garage one evening and took the neighbor's chain saw, intending to use the saw to cut down a tree and then return it. Before the defendant could return the saw, it was stolen from his yard.

76. A florist and his sister decided to play a practical joke on their cousin. The cousin had recently taken a job as a clerk at a 24-hour convenience market and had been assigned to the overnight shift. Knowing that their cousin worked in the market alone for most of the night, the florist and his sister waited outside the market until it was empty of customers and their cousin was alone. They then donned ski masks and entered the market waving realistic looking toy pistols and shouting to the cousin to hand over all the money in the cash register. Their plan was to take the money, keep it until the next morning just before the cousin's shift ended, and then return it. Frightened at the thought of being shot, the cousin complied with their demands and placed all the money from the cash register into a paper bag and handed it to the florist. The florist and his sister then left the market.

The florist and his sister ran around the corner, laughing at the terrified look on their cousin's face when he gave them the money. They decided to go a nearby 24-hour coffee shop, get something to eat, and then return to the market and give back the money. When the two finished their meal, they paid their bill and headed for the market. As they reached the market, the florist realized he had left the bag containing the money in the coffee shop. He ran back to the coffee shop to retrieve it but the bag was gone. The waitress on duty told them she had seen another customer pick up the bag and leave with it. Neither the money nor the customer was ever found.

If the florist and his sister were charged with conspiracy to commit robbery, which of the following is the strongest argument that they are not guilty?

(A) The pistols they used were only toys.
(B) No overt act was committed in furtherance of the conspiracy.
(C) Their intent was to play a joke on the cousin.
(D) The loss of the money was the result of an unforeseeable intervening actor.

77. A baker, a butcher, and a chef loved to play golf. They would spend all day every Saturday and Sunday playing at different courses. On occasion, if their schedules allowed it, they would meet after work and get in a quick nine holes before it got too dark to play. The baker had always wanted to play at the country club, a private golf course in the area that was rumored to have the finest facilities around. The baker had visited the country club before and noticed a sign posted by the entrance citing a local municipal code which stated that it was a criminal trespass for anyone other than members and their guests to enter. One day the baker said to the butcher and the chef that they should go the country club on Sunday afternoon and when no one was looking they should go into the course and start playing. The butcher and chef both laughed and said that sounded like a great plan. As luck would have it, a policeman was standing nearby and immediately arrested the three for conspiracy to commit criminal trespass.

The jurisdiction in which the country club is located follows the common law definition of conspiracy. At trial, the butcher testified that he thought that the baker was a member of the country club and was inviting the butcher and chef to play the course with him. The chef testified that, while he knew the baker was not a member of the country club, he intended to call his uncle, who was a member, to see if he would get them permission to play the course on Sunday. The chef further testified that he figured the three would not attempt to enter the course if permission was not given. The baker did not testify.

Assuming that both the butcher's and the chef's testimony are believed by the jury, the baker should be

(A) convicted, because there was an agreement for an unlawful purpose sufficient to constitute a conspiracy.
(B) convicted, because the baker intended to commit a criminal trespass.
(C) acquitted, because no overt act in furtherance of the conspiracy was performed.
(D) acquitted, because neither the butcher nor the chef agreed to commit an unlawful act.

78. A law student was struggling during her first year of law school. Although she studied the material very hard all semester, she just could not seem to grasp the complex legal concepts covered in class. Her greatest concern was Contracts. Concerned that she would fail the upcoming midterm exam, the student approached her friend, who was also struggling in the same Contracts class, and proposed that they break into the law school administrative offices the night before the exam and steal a copy of the test. The friend agreed. The student then went to the local hardware store and bought some tools to aid in breaking the lock on the door to the administrative offices.

On the night before the Contracts midterm, the student arrived at the law school, but her friend did not show up. After waiting a full hour past the appointed meeting time, the student decided to proceed without her friend. The student broke the lock on the door to the administrative offices and entered, only to be surprised by a school security guard hiding in the darkened office. The security guard turned over the student to the police, who arrested her for burglary, defined in the jurisdiction as the breaking and entering of a structure with the intent to steal.

The friend was arrested and charged with conspiracy to commit burglary. At trial, the friend testified that she only pretended to agree with the student but never intended to go through with the burglary of the administrative offices. In fact, she had told the security guard about the student's plan, and that is why he was waiting inside the office when she entered.

If the jury believes the friend, she should be

(A) convicted, because there was an agreement for an unlawful purpose, and an overt act was performed when the student bought the tools.
(B) convicted, because a private citizen may not assert the privilege of crime prevention available to police officers.
(C) acquitted, because she never intended to burglarize the administrative offices.
(D) acquitted, because she alerted the authorities in time to frustrate the criminal goal of the conspiracy, thereby effectively withdrawing.

79. In a jurisdiction that statutorily defines burglary as the entering of any structure with intent to commit a felony therein (but otherwise follows the common law as to all crimes), a painter, an electrician, and a plumber were prosecuted for conspiracy to commit burglary. Each was tried separately. At each trial, it was established that the three had met at the painter's house, and there and then agreed to go to the local jewelry shop the next evening, break into the closed shop, and take a large uncut diamond from the safe. Each man then left the painter's house to obtain dark clothing and the tools necessary for completing his part of the plan. As prearranged, the three met at the plumber's house a few hours later and secreted their clothing and equipment in his garage. After leaving the plumber's house, the electrician went directly to the police and informed them of the group's activities and intentions. All three were then arrested.

The plumber testified at each trial that the painter had informed him, and he believed, that the large uncut diamond was the property of the painter, which the painter had taken to the jeweler for appraisal, and that the jeweler refused to return the diamond or to acknowledge the painter's ownership. The plumber believed that by assisting the painter, he was merely recovering the painter's diamond.

Assuming that the jury determines that the plumber testified truthfully, he should be

(A) convicted, because there was an agreement for an unlawful purpose, and an overt act in the preparation of the dark clothing and equipment sufficient to constitute a conspiracy.
(B) convicted, because criminal activity undertaken with laudable motives is still criminal.
(C) acquitted, because he lacked the corrupt motive necessary for conviction of conspiracy.
(D) acquitted, because he believed he was agreeing to recover the painter's diamond.

80. An actress was enraged when she learned that her best friend had been carrying on an affair with the actress's husband. The actress went to her father's house and took his shotgun from the gun safe in which it was stored. She then drove to her best friend's house, where she knew her best friend was participating in a regular Wednesday afternoon bridge game. The actress intended to shoot and kill her best friend, but as she drove onto the street where the best friend's house was located, she was stopped and arrested by the police, who had been alerted by her father (to whom she had confided her intentions).

The actress was prosecuted for attempting to violate a statute that made it a felony to enter onto the property of another person for the purpose of committing murder, attempted murder, assault with a deadly weapon, mayhem, rape or kidnapping.

What should be the outcome of this prosecution?

(A) The actress should be found guilty, because the statute is a public safety measure, which she violated by arming herself with the shotgun.
(B) The actress should be found guilty, because she was stopped by the police just short of completing the charged offense.
(C) The actress should be found not guilty, because she cannot be convicted simply of having a guilty mind.
(D) The actress should be found not guilty, because the statute describes an attempt offense, and one cannot be convicted of attempting an attempt offense.

81. Desperately in need of money, a farmer and his wife decided to rob a local bank. They spent several weeks gathering information on the bank and meticulously planning every detail of the robbery. Only after they were satisfied that they had a foolproof plan did they decide to go ahead with the robbery. On the day designated for the robbery, the farmer, as part of the plan, entered the bank posing as a customer seeking to make a deposit. A few moments later, the farmer's wife entered, approached one of the tellers and handed him a note instructing him to place $50,000 in small bills in a bag the wife had handed him. The note also stated that there was another person in the bank wearing a bomb, and that he would detonate it, killing everyone inside, if the teller tried to alert anyone. The teller placed the money in the bag and handed it back to the wife. As she turned to leave the bank, she bumped into another customer, causing the bag to fall to the floor. When the bag hit the floor, it fell open and some of the money tumbled out. Seeing the money fall from the bag, one of the bank's security guards drew his gun and shouted to the wife to freeze. The farmer started to run to his wife's defense, but another of the bank's security guards, who had been standing near the farmer, knocked him to the floor.

The farmer and his wife were arrested and prosecuted in federal court on federal bank robbery charges. They were convicted, and each received a five-year sentence. The farmer and his wife were subsequently prosecuted in state court for conspiracy to commit bank robbery.

What should be the outcome of this trial?

(A) Guilty, because they agreed to rob the bank and performed an overt act in furtherance of the agreement.
(B) Not guilty, because the charge of conspiracy is always a lesser included offense of the target crime, such as bank robbery.
(C) Not guilty, because a prosecution for conspiracy to commit bank robbery after a conviction of bank robbery on the same facts constitutes double jeopardy.
(D) Not guilty, because the federal prosecution bars a subsequent prosecution on the same facts in state court.

82. A college student and his friend manufactured and sold ice, a crystalline form of methamphetamine, to various drug dealers, who in turn used a network of underlings to resell the ice to users. Because purchasers of drugs would occasionally attempt to rob them rather than pay, the student and his friend both kept pistols on their persons at all times during drug transactions.

The friend was at a bar he frequented, when he was approached by the bartender, who was actually an undercover police officer. The friend knew that the bartender had purchased ice from some of the friend's regular customers, and so he believed that the bartender was actually a drug dealer and not a police officer. The bartender arranged to purchase $10,000 worth of ice from the friend and hinted that he would wish to purchase a great deal more in the future. The friend and the bartender agreed to make the exchange of drugs for money an hour later at a nearby parking lot.

The friend and the bartender met at the prearranged time and place. After the bartender had examined the ice and given the friend the money, he identified himself as a police officer and announced that the friend was under arrest. The friend drew his pistol and shot the undercover police officer three times in the chest. Other officers appeared, and the friend surrendered to them. Thirty minutes later, officers with a search warrant raided the building in which the student and the friend kept their ice manufacturing materials. The student was inside and was arrested without resisting. The undercover officer, who was wearing body armor, was not seriously injured by the friend's shots. The friend was convicted of attempted murder of the undercover officer, among other charges.

If the student is charged with attempted murder, he should be found

(A) not guilty, because the conspiracy had terminated upon the friend's arrest, and thus the student could no longer be vicariously liable for the friend's acts.
(B) not guilty, because the friend acted outside the scope of the conspiracy when he shot the undercover officer.
(C) guilty, because he is criminally liable for any crime committed by his co-conspirator, the friend.
(D) guilty, because he knew the friend was armed and might attempt to evade arrest by use of the pistol.

83. A defendant is a firm believer that psychics have the power to see into the future. She consults with a practicing clairvoyant before making any major decisions. The clairvoyant tells the defendant that she senses an evil presence in the defendant's life who plans to murder the defendant in the near future. The clairvoyant describes the evil presence as someone with red hair who is close to the defendant and whom the defendant would never suspect. The only person with red hair the defendant knows is her sister. The following day, the sister visits the defendant on her way home from work. Believing her sister has come to kill her, the defendant strikes her sister in the temple with a fireplace poker, killing her instantly. At her murder trial, in attempts to mitigate the charge, the defendant claims that she killed her sister in self-defense because she believed that her life was threatened.

If the jury finds that the defendant honestly believed that she was acting in self-defense, which of the following is correct?

(A) The defendant will not be convicted of a crime because she had a good faith belief that her life was in danger.
(B) The defendant will be convicted of involuntary manslaughter, because the defendant honestly believed that her life was in danger.
(C) The defendant will be convicted of voluntary manslaughter, because the defendant's belief that her life was threatened was unreasonable.
(D) The defendant will be convicted of murder, because the defendant's life was not actually threatened.

84. Three old school friends, two men and a woman, got together one evening to talk over old times. After each had consumed a few drinks they decided to burglarize a jewelry store the next evening. When the next evening came, the three gathered outside the jewelry store. However, the woman had second thoughts about the burglary. She told the two men that she no longer intended to go through with it and attempted to convince them to give up the plan, but to no avail. The two men entered the jewelry store and looked around. They surprised a night watchman, whom they quickly overcame in a struggle. The two friends tied up and gagged the watchman and left the store without taking any jewelry. Later that evening the watchman died of suffocation as the result of being gagged. The two friends were subsequently arrested and tried for the murder of the night watchman, but were acquitted on a technicality.

The woman was then apprehended and brought to a separate trial for the murder of the night watchman.

Her best defense would be that

(A) she had effectively withdrawn from the conspiracy.
(B) she was not physically involved in the murder.
(C) the result in the trial of her two male friends is res judicata as to her charge.
(D) she lacked the requisite mental state to be guilty of murder.

85. A private citizen was on his way to the firing range when he heard two loud reports that sounded like gunshots and shouts of, Stop, thief! As he pulled his car over to the curb and quickly loaded his revolver, the citizen saw a young man run out the front door of a nearby sporting goods store. The young man appeared to be carrying some kind of pistol in his right hand. The citizen jumped from his car, shouted, Stop or I'll shoot, and fired a warning shot into some soft dirt next to the sidewalk. When the young man kept running, the citizen aimed at the man's right hip and fired. The bullet passed through the young man's heart and killed him. A few minutes later the police arrived and discovered that the young man had shoplifted a $39 replica of a popular firearm from the sporting goods store, a misdemeanor. When the owner saw him leaving the store, he (the owner) had fired at the young man with his own gun and shouted.

If the citizen is prosecuted for a criminal homicide in connection with the young man's death, he should be found

(A) not guilty, because he honestly believed that the young man was an armed, fleeing felon.
(B) not guilty, because he honestly and reasonably believed that the young man was an armed, fleeing felon.
(C) guilty, because the young man had, in fact, committed only a misdemeanor.
(D) guilty, because a private citizen may never use deadly force to prevent the escape of a criminal.

86. A woman in need of cash decided to rob a bank. She needed transportation to the bank and, thus, asked her friend if she would drive her to the bank. The woman did not tell the friend that she planned to rob the bank. The friend agreed and drove the woman to the bank. As the friend waited in the car in the bank parking lot, the woman went inside and took money from a surprised bank teller at gunpoint. As the woman was leaving the bank, a security guard tried to stop her from leaving. In the struggle, the woman shot and killed the guard. The police arrived and arrested the woman and her friend in the bank parking lot.

Which of the following statements most accurately states the criminal liability of the two women?

(A) The woman is guilty of robbery and felony murder, and her friend is guilty of larceny and involuntary manslaughter.
(B) The woman is guilty of robbery and felony murder, and her friend is not guilty of any crime.
(C) Both women are each guilty of robbery and felony murder.
(D) Both women are each guilty of robbery and voluntary manslaughter.

87. Two cousins liked to drive up into the hills and practice shooting with their revolvers. They would usually set up discarded cans and bottles and have contests to see who could be the most accurate or who could shoot the quickest Old West style--drawing from a holster and shooting from the hip, without bringing the pistol to eye level. After one such contest, while the first cousin went to set up some more cans, the second cousin stayed where he was and reloaded his pistol. When the first cousin turned to return to where the second cousin stood, the second cousin said, Hey, look; just like in A Fistful of Dollars! I'm Clint Eastwood! The second cousin then drew his pistol and quickly fired several shots at the first cousin's feet, aiming each time to miss actually striking any part of him. One of the bullets ricocheted off the rocky ground and struck the first cousin in the eye, killing him.

What is the most serious crime with which the second cousin can be charged?

(A) No crime, because the killing was clearly accidental.
(B) Involuntary manslaughter, because the defendant did not intend to kill or injure his cousin.
(C) Voluntary manslaughter, because the defendant did not intend to kill or injure his cousin.
(D) Murder, because the defendant acted with malice.

88. A young man was an avid science fiction fan whose wealthy parents paid little attention to him. For his 18th birthday, his father gave him his own credit card to enable him to indulge most of his fantasies. One day, the young man was watching a television show about extraterrestrials who emigrated to Earth. The episode depicted a cruel game, which the aliens' former masters had compelled them to play, involving a rotating cylinder with several nozzles, one of which sprayed a fatal corrosive liquid on one player, killing him. Each of two players alternatively selected a nozzle and activated it, and the unlucky one who selected the nozzle connected to the deadly liquid lost the game and his life.

The young man was fascinated and determined to duplicate the game for himself. He used his credit card to have a machine built that duplicated the operation of the device on the television show. Since he knew of no corrosive liquid that would be instantly fatal in real life, he decided to have pistols installed instead of nozzles. The two players would sit opposite each other, one would cause the cylinder to spin, and when it stopped with one of the eight pistols pointed at the selecting player, the other player would press a button which fired that pistol. Only one of the pistols was loaded. The players would alternate in an identical fashion, and the game would continue until one player activated the loaded pistol.

When the young man ordered eight pistols from a local gun store, the owner called the young man's father and said that he (the owner) was leery of permitting such an unusual transaction. The father approved the purchase without giving the matter much thought. The young man had the completed machine installed in the guest cottage of their estate and invited his 17-year-old friend, another science fiction freak, to play the deadly game. On the fifth round, the friend spun the cylinder, and, selecting a pistol, the young man pushed the button, and the pistol fired. The barrel was aligned almost exactly with the friend's heart, and he was killed instantly.

If the young man is charged with murder, which of the following is the most likely result?

(A) Conviction of murder.
(B) Conviction of involuntary manslaughter.
(C) Acquittal, because consent is a complete defense.
(D) Acquittal, because the father's contributory negligence is a complete defense.

89. A gun merchant broke into a neighbor's locked home at midnight intending to take a valuable shotgun that he knew was kept in a hall closet. The gun merchant had the shotgun in hand when the neighbor confronted him with a baseball bat. The gun merchant tried to brush past her, but she hit him on the head with the bat. The neighbor tried to hit the gun merchant again, but he shot her with the shotgun, killing her. The gun merchant was prosecuted for felony-murder.

Which of the following, if true, would provide the gun merchant with the strongest defense?

(A) After the neighbor hit him with the baseball bat, the gun merchant became so enraged that he lost control of his actions and shot her.
(B) The gun merchant entered his neighbor's home to retrieve his own shotgun, which he had earlier loaned to her and which she refused to return; he did not realize that he had mistakenly grabbed a different shotgun owned by the neighbor until after he had shot her.
(C) When the neighbor tried to hit the gun merchant for the second time, he pulled the trigger of the shotgun accidentally when he tried to duck to avoid the bat.
(D) The gun merchant had to shoot his neighbor to prevent her from seriously injuring or killing him.

90. A stockbroker was president of a corporation in the business of linking investors with property owners who wished to borrow money. The stockbroker offered to arrange a $25,000 loan for a homeowner, to be secured by the homeowner's residence, in exchange for a fee of $2,500. The stockbroker persuaded a lender to loan the $25,000 to the homeowner at 15 percent interest by falsely representing that the homeowner had $50,000 worth of equity in the home and that the lender would be a second mortgagee. In fact, the homeowner had no equity in his home and the lender became the fourth mortgagee as to that home.

Assuming that the stockbroker is guilty of a felony in connection with the homeowner-lender transaction, is the corporation criminally liable for the same offense?

(A) No, because it is impossible to imprison a corporation.
(B) No, because a corporation cannot have the requisite wrongful mental state to be convicted of a crime.
(C) Yes, but only if the stockbroker is first convicted of the offense in question.
(D) Yes, because the stockbroker was acting within the scope of his duties as president of the corporation.

91. A father was watching his son's little league baseball game when he became incensed at a call by the umpire that he thought was extremely unfair and even mean-spirited. After the game was over, the father went onto the field and confronted the umpire. They had a heated argument. The umpire finally had to call a park security officer to remove the father so that the next little league game could take place. A half-hour later, the father returned to the same baseball diamond with a baseball bat and began arguing with the umpire again, right in the middle of an ongoing game. The father then beat the umpire with the baseball bat, killing him. At the father's trial for the criminal homicide of the umpire, the father testified that during the second argument, the umpire seized him by the throat. The father further stated that he believed that in order to avoid being choked to death, he had to use the baseball bat to kill the umpire.

In the following scenarios, if the jury makes the stated finding, which is the most likely outcome for the father's trial?

(A) The jury disbelieves the father's testimony and convicts him of involuntary manslaughter.
(B) The jury disbelieves the father's testimony and convicts him of voluntary manslaughter.
(C) The jury believes the father's testimony and convicts him of first-degree murder.
(D) The jury believes the father's testimony and finds that the father's beliefs were reasonable, and acquits him of all homicide charges.

92. A hiker and his companion were experienced mountain climbers when using equipment, but neither had much experience in free-climbing. As they were ascending the north side of a mountain, after climbing about 1,000 feet, they came upon a vertical rock face about 30 meters high running horizontally as far as they could see in either sideways direction. The hiker and the companion decided to cache their equipment and free-climb the rock face; their only connection to the equipment was a single line which the hiker would haul up when they reached the top of the rock.

The hiker went first and ascended the vertical surface without incident, although it was a very difficult climb. The companion got three-quarters up the rock face then faltered, calling out to the hiker, I'm too tired; I can't feel the fingers in my left hand. Help me! The hiker could have hauled up their equipment and dropped a safety line to the companion in about five minutes, but he instead spent the next 10 minutes encouraging her to finish the free-climb so that she would not lose her nerve. Twelve minutes after she first called for help, the companion slipped from the rock face and fell to her death.

If the hiker is prosecuted for the criminal homicide of the companion and is found guilty of involuntary manslaughter, which of the following best explains the result?

(A) The companion was a 16-year-old pupil in the hiker's private school, and they were out that day on a school mountain-climbing exercise.
(B) The hiker believed that the free-climb was probably too difficult for both of them but didn't want to appear afraid in front of the companion.
(C) The hiker and the companion were married to each other.
(D) The hiker was a professional mountain climber whom the companion had hired to guide her up the mountain.

93. State X has enacted the following bigamy statute: 1) Every person having a spouse who marries any other person, except in the cases specified in the next section, is guilty of bigamy. 2) Section 1 is inapplicable as to any person a) whose prior spouse is dead, b) whose prior spouse has been absent for seven years without being known to such person to be living, c) whose prior marriage was dissolved by divorce or annulment, or d) who reasonably believes that the prior marriage was terminated by divorce or annulment in another state. 3) Every unmarried person who marries another under circumstances known to the unmarried person that would render the other person guilty of bigamy under the laws of this state is also guilty of bigamy. 4) Bigamy is punishable by a fine of not more than $5,000, imprisonment in state prison not exceeding two years, or both.

A designer and a rancher were legally married in State Y in 1996. The designer's job required her to travel to Metropolis in State X and spend about half of her time there. One day, while in Metropolis, the designer met a psychologist. When he inquired about her marital status, the designer quickly slipped her wedding ring off of her finger and said that she was single. The designer fell in love with the psychologist and they moved into an apartment together in Metropolis. Although she sometimes sleepily referred to him as a rancher at night, and insisted on keeping her income and finances totally secret from him, the psychologist did not suspect that the designer led a double life. When the psychologist asked her to marry him, she agreed. However, when she rejected the first date for the ceremony that he suggested, she said, No, I can't have my anniversaries on the same day. The designer and the psychologist underwent a marriage ceremony in State X. The psychologist is charged with bigamy.

What is his best defense?

(A) He reasonably believed that the designer was unmarried.
(B) He honestly believed that the designer was unmarried.
(C) He made reasonable inquiries as to the designer's marital status.
(D) He asked the designer about her marital status and she claimed to be unmarried.

94. Which of the following is most likely to be a strict liability offense?

(A) A city ordinance making it an infraction, for which a $100 fine is payable, to trespass upon the property of another that is posted as private property.
(B) A state statute providing that the failure to have a current valid inspection sticker on a vehicle is a misdemeanor.
(C) A state statute providing that it is a felony punishable by two, three, or four years in prison to carry a concealed knife whose blade is longer than three and one-half inches.
(D) A federal statute which provides that any person who files an income tax return containing false information has committed a felony punishable by imprisonment for five years and up to $5,000 in fines.

95. A teacher was called as a defense witness on behalf of the defendant in a criminal trial. She provided testimony supporting the defendant's claim of alibi. On cross-examination, the prosecutor asked the teacher if she had previously been convicted of forgery. The teacher replied that she had not.

The teacher was subsequently prosecuted for perjury on the grounds that her testimony regarding her conviction for forgery was false. The jurisdiction defines perjury as knowingly making a false statement while under oath. At trial on the perjury charge, the state proved the teacher's testimony as a witness in the previous trial and that she had been convicted of forgery two years before her appearance as an alibi witness. The teacher testified in her own defense that she had been found guilty of forging her (then) recently deceased husband's signature on a government disability check so that she could buy food for her hungry children and that the governor of the state had immediately commuted the three-year prison sentence she received. The teacher further stated that she believed the commutation of her sentence absolved her of the prior conviction as if it had never occurred. In fact, only a pardon would have had the effect of negating a prior conviction as the teacher believed; commutation merely exempted the teacher from serving the sentence imposed.

If the jury believes the teacher, it should find her

(A) not guilty if the jury also finds that her mistaken interpretation of the effect of commutation was reasonable under the circumstances.
(B) not guilty, because she lacked the necessary mental state.
(C) guilty, because her mistake was one of law.
(D) guilty, because it was unreasonable of the teacher to assume that commutation negated her forgery conviction without consulting an attorney.

96. A driver was prosecuted for violation of a state statute that defines as a felony the taking or accepting of any property, money or services by a state driver's license examiner from or on behalf of an examinee being tested for driving proficiency. Testimony at trial established that the driver was taking his driving test from a state driver's license examiner when he offered the driver's license examiner $1,000 if the examiner would overlook an illegal lane change the driver had just made (which would disqualify him from obtaining a driver's license). The driver's license examiner accepted the $1,000, and was subsequently convicted of violating the same statute for which the driver was being prosecuted as an aider and abettor.

The driver's best argument for a dismissal of the charge against him is that

(A) only a driver's license examiner can commit the crime defined by the subject statute.
(B) he cannot be convicted of committing a crime as to which he is the victim.
(C) the statute is so defined as to indicate that the legislature intended only the recipient of the property, money, or services to be punished.
(D) he did not assist the driver's license examiner in violating the subject statute.

97. The defendant, age 25, met a young woman at the beach. Although the young woman appeared youngish, she was partying and drinking with a number of friends, all of whom appeared to be the defendant's age or older. As the evening progressed and it became dark, the defendant suggested to the young woman that the two of them take a blanket and go off into the scrub and dunes beyond the beach. When they found a secluded spot, the defendant made sexual advances to the young woman, who appeared to consent, permitting him to remove the top of her two-piece bathing suit. When the defendant began to remove the bottom piece of her bathing suit, the young woman protested. The defendant insisted that she permit him to continue. When the young woman held onto her bathing suit bottom with both hands, the defendant grabbed her roughly by the throat and told her to let go otherwise he was going to hurt her. The young woman stopped resisting and the defendant proceeded to have sexual intercourse with her. At the time of the above-described events, the young woman was 16 years old. Statutory rape is defined in this jurisdiction as sexual intercourse with a woman younger than 18 years of age.

The defendant was subsequently prosecuted for rape and statutory rape in a common law jurisdiction.

What should be the outcome of this prosecution?

(A) The defendant should be convicted of statutory rape, but not rape, because she consented.
(B) The defendant should be convicted of rape, but not statutory rape, because he reasonably believed that the young woman was over the age of consent.
(C) The defendant should be convicted of both charges.
(D) The defendant should not be convicted of either charge.

98. A writer was enraged when he learned that his editor was having an affair with his (the writer's) wife. Late one night while the editor was on a business trip out of town, the writer went to the editor's home, kicked in the back door that led to the editor's photography studio and darkroom, and used the volatile chemicals to build an intense fire, intending to burn down the house and destroy several years' accumulation of the editor's irreplaceable negatives and photographs. As the flames leaped to the ceiling and began to burn and char the structure, the writer realized that his marriage had been loveless and empty for some time and that he had unconsciously transferred his feelings of frustration and anger to the editor. The writer grabbed the editor's fire extinguisher and quickly put out the flames before they had destroyed any photographic materials. The writer returned the next night with tools and materials with which he completely repaired the broken back door and replaced all burned portions of the ceiling in the studio. As he was completing this work, police officers who had been summoned by neighbors arrived and arrested the writer.

The writer could properly be convicted of which of the following crimes in connection with the described events?

(A) Arson and burglary.
(B) Attempted arson and burglary.
(C) Burglary only.
(D) Arson only.

99. A welder and his wife lived in a state that defined the crime of forcible rape as sexual intercourse with a woman without her consent, and the welder was aware that the highest state court had interpreted the relevant statute as including within its operation rape where the perpetrator and the victim were married. The welder and his wife had a serious argument, and the wife went to stay at her sister's house in a neighboring state that retained the common law definition of rape, which precludes a conviction of rape where the perpetrator is the husband of the victim. The welder pursued the wife to her sister's house, broke open the locked door at midnight, and entered, intending to compel his wife to have sex against her will. The welder believed that forcing his wife to have sex without her consent constituted rape. The wife's sister, a police officer, arrested the welder as soon as he had crashed through her front door.

Can the welder properly be convicted of common law burglary in State B for breaking and entering the sister's house at night with the stated intention?

(A) No, because he was prevented from accomplishing his intention and was not charged with attempt.
(B) No, because he did not have the requisite intent to commit a felony when he broke and entered the home.
(C) Yes, because he broke and entered the dwelling house of another, at night, with the intent to commit what he believed was a felony.
(D) Yes, because the factual impossibility of the intended felony is not a defense to a charge of burglary.

100. A violinist was planning a vacation to Europe and was making final arrangements for the three weeks she would be out of the country. The last thing she needed to do was to make arrangements for her prize golden retriever dog. The violinist asked her neighbor if he would be willing to keep the dog and care for him until she returned from Europe. The violinist said that she would pay for all the food costs for the dog and give the neighbor an additional $500 for his efforts. The neighbor agreed to care for the dog until the violinist returned from Europe.

Two weeks later the neighbor was walking the dog when he met a breeder, who ran a business breeding dogs and selling their offspring. The breeder saw the dog and recognized that the dog was a purebred, worth at least $5,000. The breeder offered to buy the dog on the spot for $2,500. The neighbor quickly accepted the money and handed over the dog to the breeder.

When the violinist returned from Europe, the neighbor falsely told her that the dog had run away. He then returned the money the violinist had given to him before she left.

In a jurisdiction that recognizes larceny, larceny by trick, embezzlement, and false pretenses as separate crimes, the neighbor is guilty of

(A) larceny.
(B) embezzlement.
(C) obtaining property by false pretenses.
(D) larceny by trick.

Answers and Explanations

1. **(C)** The correct answer is choice (C), as the defendant would be guilty only of perjury in the subsequent trial. This question is essentially testing you on whether you know what a misprision of felony or a general misprision is. A misprision of felony is an old English common law crime. Someone who is guilty of misprision of felony is someone who failed to report a felony. Exceptions were made for family members of the felon and people who could possibly incriminate themselves by reporting the felony. The defendant here is not guilty of those crimes. Therefore, choices (A) and (B) are incorrect. Choice (D) is incorrect. Compounding a felony is essentially an agreement between a victim and defendant that the victim will not prosecute the defendant in exchange for some monetary gain.

2. **(B)** Choice (B) is the only correct choice, since Sam was merely in possession of the stolen guns when the police raided the warehouse. The burglary was committed by someone else. From the given facts, we may not infer that Sam participated in the burglary. Therefore choices (A), (C), and (D) are incorrect.

3. **(A)** Malicious destruction of property is a separate criminal offense, apart from larceny. Therefore, choice (B) is wrong. Choice (C) is incorrect. Certainly, the defendant was guilty of larceny for stealing the vehicle, but the theft by itself will ***not*** satisfy the malice requirement for destruction of property. To be guilty of the crime of malicious destruction of property, there must be evidence presented that the defendant acted maliciously (thus satisfying the *mens rea* requirement). Choice (D) is incorrect because "general intent" crimes still require a *mens rea* whether it be malice, criminal negligence, or recklessness, instead of a "specific" intent (e.g., intent to steal). Here, the defendant did not maliciously destroy the property; the damage to the home resulted from the car's brakes malfunctioning.

4. **(A)** Criminal battery is defined as the unlawful application of force to the person of another, which results in bodily harm, or an offensive touching. Battery is a "general intent" crime where the offensive contact results from the defendant's negligent or reckless conduct. On the other hand, criminal offenses of a "specific intent" nature require that the defendant intends to injure the victim. One of the defenses to criminal battery is defense of property. One whose ***lawful*** possession of property is threatened by the unlawful conduct of another, and who has no time to resort to the law for its protection, may take reasonable steps to protect the property. In the present situation, the defendant obviously was not the rightful owner of the umbrella when she tried to regain possession from the stranger. Nonetheless, the question of whether the defendant was privileged to use reasonable force becomes moot because she actually used ***excessive force*** under the circumstances. The facts state that "the defendant grabbed for the umbrella with one hand and pushed Wesley the stranger with the other." Thus, even if the defendant was privileged to grab the umbrella, she was not privileged to push the stranger. That's why she remains liable for the criminal offense of battery. In this regard, LaFave states that "one may not use more than reasonable force or the amount of force that reasonably appears necessary to prevent the threatened interference with the property." For that reason, choice (A) is a more preferable answer than choice (D). See Criminal Law, pp. 399–400. Choice (B) is incorrect because the defendant did not have the intent to commit larceny when she mistakenly grabbed the wrong umbrella. Choice (C) is incorrect because the defendant's recklessness did not result in the stranger's death. Also, the stranger's death did not stem from the defendant's battery (misdemeanor manslaughter), which would be another theory by which to argue for involuntary manslaughter. Choice (D) is incorrect for the reasons stated above.

5. **(B)** Involuntary manslaughter consists of two types: (1) ***criminal-negligence manslaughter,*** which requires conduct creating an unreasonable and high degree of risk of death or serious bodily injury (i.e., more than ordinary tort negligence); and (2) ***unlawful act manslaughter,*** where the death-causing conduct occurs during the commission or attempted commission of an unlawful act (generally a *malum in se* misdemeanor) involving a danger of death or serious bodily injury. LaFave, Criminal Law, p. 594. *Malum in se* crimes generally include morality offenses and serious traffic offenses, as well as criminal assault or intentional battery. By unlawfully passing another car on the right, the defendant committed a traffic violation (i.e., a misdemeanor) that resulted in the victim's death. The

defendant may be found guilty of involuntary manslaughter based on the fact that his unlawful act directly and proximately caused the victim's death. Therefore, choice (B) is correct. Choice (A) is insufficient, since the motor vehicle violation will merge into misdemeanor manslaughter. Choice (C) is incorrect, since voluntary manslaughter always involves an intentional killing. Choice (D) is incorrect because the defendant's conduct was not of a high enough degree to constitute depraved or wanton recklessness sufficient for depraved-heart murder.

6. **(B)** Generally, with respect to the defense of others, a defendant is justified in defending another person with reasonable force only if he reasonably believes the victim had a right to use such force. That is the majority rule – and that is the rule to apply unless the question instructs otherwise. Here, however, the reader is asked to apply the ***"alter ego"*** rule. Under this modern rule, the defendant is viewed as "standing in the shoes" of the person defended, making the right to defend another extensive with the other's right to defend himself. Thus, the defender who intervenes to protect a perceived victim against a perceived assailant takes the risk that the victim is not, in fact, privileged to defend himself in the manner he employs. Choice (A) is not the best choice. Some jurisdictions limit this defense to situations where a special relationship exists between the defendant and the victim, but application of this minority rule is not prompted by the question. Choices (C) and (D) are incorrect because both choices incorrectly apply the common law reasonable belief standard.

7. **(C)** In Criminal Law, students must distinguish between *actus reus* and *mens rea*. The statute given in the facts is similar to the ***A.L.I. Model Penal Code*** test for insanity. As a defense, it will negate the *mens rea* of the crime committed. The defendant was charged with involuntary manslaughter, a crime requiring criminal negligence. Choices (A) and (B) address the statutory language, in that the defendant could not "conform his conduct (volitionally) to the requirements of law" because he was so shocked that he froze. Although a good argument, both choices use the defense of insanity to negate the *mens rea* of the crime. Choice (C) is even stronger, however, because an *actus reus* must have occurred before a proper defense is even relevant. A person may be criminally liable for his omission to act when (1) there is a legal duty to act under the circumstances, and (2) he can physically perform the act. LaFave, Criminal Law, p. 182. If the defendant's failure to act, where he was babysitting his nephew and had a legal duty to act (based on either relationship or contract), was not deemed to be voluntary, due to the fact that he was so shocked that he was unable to move, then he cannot be criminally responsible for lack of an *actus reus*. This argument is more basic than the other alternatives because it negates an element of the crime itself rather than using a defense to the crime; therefore, choice (C) is the defendant's best defense and the correct answer. Choice (D) is incorrect for the reasons stated above.

8. **(B)** In choice (A), the defendant will be guilty of embezzlement. In *Commonwealth v. Tuckerman*, 76 Mass. 173 (1857), a corporate treasurer took company money to spend for his own purposes. Even though he intended to restore the money later and had sufficient funds to do so, he was convicted of embezzlement. Choice (C) is also incorrect. The defendant will be guilty of larceny because at the time the defendant took the yearbook from the vendor, he intended to steal it. The defendant had no claim of right to the yearbook, since, at the time of misappropriation, he was unaware his season ticket stub entitled him to a copy. Choice (D) is incorrect, as well. Here, the defendant will be guilty of false pretenses. At the time she applied for the credit card, she falsely represented her salary and employment status, thereby inducing the department store to issue a card which that would not otherwise have been given to an insolvent applicant. Her honest belief that employment would come in the future is no defense to the fake representation of her present employment status. Choice (B) is correct. The defendant will not be guilty of robbery. Under the claim of right defense, one may take the property of another honestly, but mistakenly, believing it is his own property. LaFave, Criminal Law, p. 538. There is no larceny because there is no intent to steal.

9. **(A)** The prevailing American view is that ***bigamy is an offense of absolute liability.*** Even in the minority jurisdictions, a defendant remarrying under a *bona fide* mistake of fact may be guilty if the belief in the spouse's death was based on lack of due diligence in determining the facts. Therefore, choices (B), (C), and (D) are incorrect.

10. **(C)** In situations where the pressure of natural physical forces confronts an individual with a choice of two evils, either to violate the criminal law and produce a harmful result, or to comply with the law and produce a potentially greater harm, the defense of necessity is available to justify the former course of action. LaFave, Criminal Law, p. 441. For the defense of necessity to operate, the defendant must have acted with the intention of avoiding the greater harm. In choice (A), the defense of necessity would not be justified, since the defendant still had some water of his own when he took all of the victim's remaining water, causing his death. The possibility of walking across the island would not outweigh taking a human life. Choice (D) is incorrect because it is an example of duress, not necessity. The defendant is being threatened by human forces, not natural forces. Choice (B) is incorrect. Necessity would not be justified under the facts because the victim had regained his balance and footing when the defendant cut the safety rope, killing him. In this case, killing another to save oneself is murder. Choice (C) is the best answer. The defendant's intoxication is irrelevant because he did not cause the dangerous situation; rather, the school bus made a wrong turn and headed directly toward the defendant. ***Killing one person to save many*** would be justified under these facts.

11. **(C)** The kidnapping statute is defined as "***knowingly*** abducting a person." Based upon the advice given him by his lawyer, the husband believed that he could lawfully take his son to the new state and not be in violation of the law. As a consequence, he did not act knowingly, which would negate the mental state or *mens rea* requirement for the commission of this crime. Therefore choices (A) and (B) are incorrect. Choice (C) is better than choice (D) because it eliminates an element of the crime. Remember, anytime you can eliminate an element of a crime, that will be a better explanation as to why the defendant is not guilty than to say a defense exists (e.g., intoxication or mistake).

12. **(B)** Clearly, the two men have entered into an agreement to burglarize the home and are guilty of conspiracy. The more difficult question is whether the alarm specialist can become a party to the crime of conspiracy, even in the absence of any agreement on his part. According to LaFave, it is possible for a person to become a member of a conspiracy ***where he knew of the conspiracy and intentionally gave aid to the conspiratorial objective even though he did not enter into the agreement himself.*** Criminal Law, pg. 534. Consequently, the alarm specialist is guilty of conspiracy because he aided the conspiratorial objective by telling the two men how they could disarm the home's alarm system with the knowledge that they were planning to perpetrate a burglary. Therefore choice (A) is incorrect. The next issue is which, if any, of the defendants are guilty of attempt. At common law, attempt requires an act that constitutes a "substantial step" in the commission or attempted commission of a crime. The two men did not perform a "substantial step" merely by going to the home without any entry. Therefore choices (C) and (D) are incorrect.

13. **(B)** In this jurisdiction, conspiracy requires an overt act. Common law conspiracy did not require an overt act; a conspiracy was punishable even though no act was done beyond the mere making of the agreement. Many states, however, do require an overt act for conspiracy. According to LaFave, the Supreme Court "currently regards the overt act merely as evidence of the offense." Criminal Law, pg. 548. The function of the overt act in a conspiracy prosecution is simply to manifest "that the conspiracy is at work." Consequently, the purchase of the ski masks (to be used in the robbery) would clearly constitute an overt act. Thus, choice (B) is correct. Choice (A) is incorrect because this jurisdiction requires more than just an agreement by two or more individuals with the intent to achieve a criminal objective. Choices (C) and (D) are wrong because the traditional common law rule is that withdrawal is not a defense to conspiracy because the crime is complete with the agreement. Moreover, in jurisdictions which that have added an overt act requirement, ***withdrawal is effective only if it occurs before the overt act has been committed.*** Since the overt act of buying the ski masks occurred before the attempted withdrawal, the defendant would be guilty of conspiracy.

14. **(C)** Larceny at common law may be defined as the (1) trespassory (2) taking and (3) carrying away of the (4) personal property (5) of another (6) with intent to steal it. The crime of larceny requires an intent to steal, (i.e., an intent to deprive the owner of the possession of her property permanently or for an unreasonable length of time). The defen-

dant did not possess an intent to steal (i.e., no *animus furandi*). As a result, choice (C) is correct. Choice (A) is very appealing, as it is a defense which that would apply on these facts. However, an answer choice that cuts off culpability to a defendant by knocking out an element of the crime charged is always a stronger answer than a valid defense. Choice (B) is incorrect because returning the property once a larceny is complete is not a valid defense. Finally, choice (D) is incorrect because a fraudulent conversion is not an element of larceny, but, rather, embezzlement.

15. **(D)** Students should note the distinction between specific and general intent crimes. According to LaFave in his Criminal Law hornbook, it is sometimes stated that intoxication can negate a specific intent which that the crime in question may require (meaning some intent, in addition to the intent to do the physical act which that the crime requires), but it cannot negate a crime's general intent. In this regard, the crimes of (a) assault with intent to commit rape, (b) assault with intent to commit battery, and (c) conspiracy are all specific intent crimes. Therefore, intoxication may serve as a defense to the specific intent crimes enumerated in choices (A), (B), and (C). However, intoxication will not negate the criminal culpability of the defendant in choice (D) because statutory rape is a crime which that imposes "absolute" criminal liability (i.e., no available defense).

16. **(A)** The majority of jurisdictions hold that, while voluntary intoxication may be so great as to negate premeditation and deliberation, this fact serves only to reduce the homicide from first-degree to second-degree murder. Therefore, choice (C) is incorrect. Choice (D) is incorrect. A basic tenet of criminal law is that one may not use more force, in self-defense, than is reasonably necessary. Choice (B) is incorrect, since one who can safely retreat need not do so before using non-deadly force. Thus, the question of retreat is a problem only when deadly force is employed in self-defense. The prevailing view is that the defender who was not the original aggressor need not retreat, even though he can do so safely, before using deadly force upon an assailant whom he reasonably believes will kill him or inflict serious bodily harm.

17. **(D)** Intoxication can negate a "specific intent" crime, but it cannot negate a "general intent" crime. So-called "specific intent" crimes require two elements: (1) an *actus reus* (or the criminal act), and (2) the *mens rea* (or "guilty mind"). Common law larceny, for example, requires the taking and carrying away of the property of another, but it must also be shown that there was an ***intent to steal*** the property. Common law burglary requires a breaking and entry into the dwelling of another, but it must also be established that the defendant acted with the ***intent to commit a felony therein***. On the other hand, so-called "general intent" crimes require only an *actus reus*. In this regard, the crimes of (1) rape, (2) battery, and (3) arson are commonly referred to as "general intent" crimes. These crimes are completed by the criminal act ***without regard to the defendant's intention***. The crime of rape, for example, is committed by the act of non-consensual sexual intercourse, irrespective of the defendant's intention. A key Multistate testing area deals ***with the distinction between crimes of rape and assault with intent to commit rape***. Although rape is a "general intent" crime, assault with intent to commit rape is a "specific intent" crime. Similarly, while battery is a "general intent" crime, assault with intent to commit battery is a "specific intent" crime. Therefore, choices (A), (B), and (C) are incorrect.

18. **(D)** Many statutes defining conduct which that is criminal employ words or phrases indicating some type of *mens rea* (or guilty mind) requirement: (e.g., "intentionally"; "knowingly"; "purposely"; or "fraudulently."). In this regard, LaFave points out that such crimes require "subjective fault" — actually a guilty mind of some sort. For example, the statutory crime of receiving stolen property is generally worded in terms of receiving stolen property "knowing the property to be stolen." Such wording requires that the defendant, to be guilty, ***must know in his own mind*** (i.e., subjectively) that the property he receives is stolen. Similarly, in the present example, since the defendant did not (subjectively) know that he was selling tobacco to a minor, he did not possess the requisite *mens rea*. Therefore, choices (A), (B), and (C) are incorrect.

19. **(B)** Generally, the defense of necessity is limited to those situations where the pressure comes from the physical forces of nature (e.g., storms, hurricanes, earthquakes) rather than from other human beings. Usually, when the pressure is from human beings, the defense, if applicable, is called duress, rather than necessity. However, choice (C) is incorrect because it has been held that duress cannot justify an intentional killing. As a result, choice (B) is preferred in light of the Model Penal Code commentaries, which suggest that the defense (of necessity) should be available in the situation where a person intentionally kills one person in order to save two or more. Therefore, choice (A) is incorrect. Choice (D) is incorrect because the facts do not indicate that the wife was acting in self-defense.

20. **(B)** The doctor is guilty of involuntary manslaughter based on criminal-negligence. For criminal-negligence manslaughter, most jurisdictions require that the defendant's death-causing conduct involve a higher degree of negligence than ordinary (tort) negligence. In addition, most jurisdictions require that the defendant's conduct create an unreasonable and high degree of risk of death or serious bodily injury to another. Clearly, the doctor's conduct (in performing a surgical operation on a woman who wasn't pregnant) was grossly or criminally negligent. He would, therefore, be guilty of manslaughter because the woman's death was causally connected to the unnecessary operation. Also, the doctor would be guilty of false pretenses, since he defrauded the woman of $500. False pretenses, although defined in slightly different ways in the various jurisdictions, consist of these five elements: (1) a false representation of a material fact, (2) which causes the victim (3) to pass title to (4) his property to the wrongdoer, (5) who knows his representation to be false and intends to defraud the victim. Choices (A) and (D) are incorrect because the elements of murder are not met. Choices (C) and (D) are wrong. The battery merges with the greater offense. The doctor may have been guilty of the battery of the woman had she survived the surgery but is criminally liable for homicide, not battery, as the same "harmful or offensive touching" that otherwise would have constituted a battery caused the woman's death.

21. **(D)** In order to be guilty of attempt, the defendant must specifically intend to commit the "target offense." Choices (A) and (B) are, therefore, incorrect ***because the father intended to physically injure the coach, not to kill him.*** Choice (C) is likewise incorrect because attempted manslaughter is a legal anomaly. It is impossible to specifically intend to commit an unintentional killing. Choice (D) is correct because the father did specifically intend to commit a battery on the coach. Furthermore, the father will be guilty of the murder of the man, based on intent to cause serious bodily harm.

22. **(C)** Be aware that the defendant is charged with ***attempted murder***. LaFave and Scott in their Handbook on Criminal Law point out that the crime of attempt consists of: (1) an intent to do an act or to bring about certain consequences, which would, in law, amount to a crime, and (2) an act in furtherance of that intent which, as it is most commonly put, goes beyond mere preparation. As such, attempt is a specific intent crime. Since the defendant in this example did not have the (specific) intent to kill the woman, he would be found not guilty of the inchoate crime of ***attempted*** murder. Therefore, choices (A) and (B) are incorrect. Choice (D) is incorrect because while it is a correct statement of fact, the correct statement of law in choice (C) is a stronger answer.

23. **(B)** ***Robbery, a common law felony, consists of the six elements of larceny: (1) a trespassory (2) taking and (3) carrying away of the (4) personal property (5) of another (6) with intent to steal, plus two additional requirements: that (7) the taking be accomplished by force, violence, or intimidation, and (8) the property be taken from the victim or from his presence.*** To be sure, robbery requires that the taking be done by means of violence or intimidation. The elements of force and fear (or violence or intimidation) are alternatives; if there is force, there need be no fear, and vice versa. As with the crime of assault, the word "fear" in connection with robbery does not so much mean "fright" as it means "apprehension." With regard to the so-called "fear" factor, LaFave states that "if the circumstances are such that a reasonable person would not be scared, a jury might properly infer that the victim, in spite of his testimony to the contrary, was not in fact scared." Criminal Law, pg. 785. ***But if the victim is actually frightened by the defendant into parting with his property, the defendant is guilty of robbery.*** In the present case,

the facts clearly indicate that the man was frightened. As a result, the defendant is guilty of robbery, despite the fact that he threatened the victim with a non-lethal stick. Therefore, choices (A), (C), and (D) are incorrect.

24. **(D)** Choice (A) is an example of intent-to-inflict serious bodily injury murder. Choice (B) is an example of "depraved-heart" murder. Choice (C) is an example of felony murder. Conversely, choice (D) is characteristic of involuntary manslaughter or misdemeanor-manslaughter. Note that the defendant committed a battery (which, at common law, was a misdemeanor) by punching the victim in the face.

25. **(B)** This question deals with the interrelated issues of accomplice liability and defenses. If the man had been convicted of murder, then the defendant would also be criminally liable under an accomplice theory of liability because (1) he had the specific intent that the killing take place, and (2) he aided and abetted in the perpetration of the crime. However, if the acts of the principal in the first degree are found not to be criminal, then the accomplice, or principal in the second degree, cannot not be convicted of the crime. In this regard, there are certain defenses available to the principal in the first degree that are likewise available to the accomplice. One such example is self-defense, which justifies the homicide, therefore making it non–criminal. Thus, choice (B) is correct. Some defenses are personal to the principal and may not be asserted by the accomplice, such as insanity. Insanity serves to excuse – not justify – the otherwise criminal act. Thus, choice (A) is wrong. Choice (C) is incorrect because diminished capacity would merely negate the specific intent to kill, thus mitigating the crime to manslaughter, but does not make the offense non-criminal. This is also a defense that is personal to the principal. If the man lacked the capacity to form the requisite intent, the defendant's intent is not negated. Finally choice (D) is a distracter. Under the Wharton Rule, where two or more people are necessary for the commission of the substantive offense (e.g., adultery, dueling, bribery), there is no crime of conspiracy UNLESS more persons participate in the agreement than are necessary for the crime.

26. **(C)** Voluntary intoxication is a defense only if it disproves the existence of a specific intent required for the crime. Choice (C) is correct, since voluntary intoxication cannot be a defense to battery, a general intent crime. Choices (A) and (B) are incorrect statements of law. Choice (D) is irrelevant because the husband's belief that the gun was unloaded would not affect his intoxication defense.

27. **(D)** Conspiracy may be defined as (1) an ***agreement*** between two or more persons, which constitutes the act, and (2) an ***intent*** to thereby achieve a certain objective which, under the common law definition, is the doing of either an unlawful act or a lawful act by unlawful means. The agreement between the ex-con and the two men to take part in the bank robbery formed the conspiracy. The ex-con is guilty of automobile theft because he stole the van. Furthermore, the ex-con is guilty of attempted robbery because he (1) intended to rob the bank, and (2) performed an act in furtherance of the crime by stealing the car that he intended to use in the bank robbery. Although many students will incorrectly choose choice (C), choice (D) is a better answer because the ***"substantial step"*** requirement was satisfied, thereby making the ex-con guilty of attempt, as well as conspiracy. Therefore, choices (A) and (B) are incorrect, as well.

28. **(A)** Obviously, the friend committed a battery when she grabbed the necklace from the woman's neck. Criminal battery is defined as the unlawful application of force to the person of another. On the other hand, there are two types of criminal assault: (1) the attempted-battery type, and (2) the intent-to-frighten type. The attempted-battery type of assault requires an intent to commit a battery, (i.e., an intent to cause physical injury to the victim). Since the friend did not intend to injure the woman, she would not be guilty of the attempted-battery type of assault (even though she is guilty of the second type). Note that a majority of jurisdictions follow the attempted-battery type of assault, while only a minority of states recognize the intent-to-frighten type. Therefore, choice (B) is incorrect. Furthermore, choice (C) is wrong because robbery requires an intent to steal. Since the friend did not intend to steal the woman's necklace, she cannot be convicted of robbery.

Multistate Nuance Chart

Criminal Law

Inchoate Crimes		
Solicitation	**Conspiracy**	**Attempt**
1. Defendant entices, advises, encourages, orders, or requests another to commit a crime. 2. The crime solicited need ***not*** be committed. 3. The crime requires no agreement or action by the person solicited. 4. Defenses: At common law, no defenses were recognized; under the Model Penal Code, however, renunciation is an affirmative defense. 5. Merges with the target felony.	1. Consists of (a) an agreement between two or more persons to commit a crime, and (b) an intent to achieve the criminal objective. 2. The agreement is the "essence" or "gist" of the crime. 3. Unlike attempt, the crime does not require a "substantial step" in the commission of the crime. 4. Solicitation ***merges*** into conspiracy. 5. If the conspiracy is successful, a conspirator may be subject to conviction for both the conspiracy and the completed crime. 6. Defenses: At common law, withdrawal was not a valid defense; under the Model Penal Code, however, withdrawal is recognized as an affirmative defense if the defendant "thwarted the success of the conspiracy."	1. Consists of (a) an intent to commit a crime, and (b) an act in furtherance or a "substantial step" toward the commission of the offense. 2. The act in furtherance of the crime must go beyond mere preparation. 3. "Specific-intent" crime, i.e., the defendant must have the specific intent to commit the designated crime. 4. Defenses: At common law, legal impossibility but not factual impossibility was a defense to a charge of attempt; under the modern view, however, impossibility is no defense when the defendant's actual intent (not limited by the true facts unknown to him) was to do an act proscribed by law.

29. **(A)** Another extremely popular Multistate testing area deals with ***federal statutory crimes,*** the reason being that this is one of the "gaps" or areas not adequately covered in the "general outline" courses. With respect to federal criminal law, the national government of the United States has very broad "police powers" to create crimes over conduct in federally owned or controlled territory not within the jurisdiction of any state. Thus, the federal government has territorial jurisdiction over (a) conduct on federal land areas not located within the states, such as the District of Columbia and Territories; (b) conduct on federal enclaves (islands of federal territory located within the states), such as army posts, naval bases, post offices, and national parks; (c) conduct on ships and aircraft of American nationality when outside the jurisdiction of the states, as on the high seas or even in foreign waters; and (d) conduct by U.S. citizens which that takes place outside the jurisdiction of any state. For the most part, LaFave points out that federal criminal laws define offenses in terms of substantive misbehavior (e.g., theft) and the matter of

jurisdictional requirements are dealt with separately. In fact, under the Federal Criminal Code, technical issues of jurisdiction are not prominent, "and the government is relieved of any burden of showing that the defendant knew of the special fact which results in federal jurisdiction." LaFave, Criminal Law, pg. 113. By the same token, since federal conspiracy laws do not require the mental retainment of jurisdictional requirements, choice (A) is correct. Choices (B), (C) ,and (D) are all misstatements of law and, therefore, are incorrect.

30. **(B)** At early common law, one whose conduct brought about an unintended death in the commission or attempted commission of a felony was guilty of (felony) murder. American jurisdictions, however, have limited the rule in one or more of the following ways: (1) by permitting its use only as to certain types of felonies; (2) by more strict interpretation of the requirement of proximate or legal cause; and (3) by a narrower construction of the time period during which the felony is in the process of commission. LaFave, Criminal Law, pg. 545. With respect to the proximate or legal cause limitation, it is often said that the death must be a ***foreseeable*** consequence of the felony. That is to say, the death must have been the "natural and probable consequence" of the defendant's conduct. Choice (B) is the best answer because looking at the matter with hindsight, it seems extraordinary that a death would actually come about in such an unforeseeable manner. Choice (A) is incorrect because an unloaded gun is irrelevant for robbery and felony murder. Choice (C) is incorrect because felony murder is based typically on unintended deaths which that result from the commission of certain enumerated felonies. Choice (D) is incorrect because the Redline limitation deals with co-felons, and the defendant acted alone here.

31. **(C)** To constitute a conspiracy, there "must be a combination of two or more persons." LaFave notes that this plurality requirement might be restated in terms of at least two guilty parties, for acquittal of all persons with whom the defendant is alleged to have conspired precludes his (or her) conviction. Criminal Law, pg. 488. Thus, if A and B are jointly charged with a conspiracy not alleged to involve any other parties and the jury returns a verdict of guilty as to A and not guilty as to B, A's conviction may not stand. *Martinez v. People*, 267 P.2d 654 (1954). Choice (A) is incorrect because her withdrawal from the conspiracy was not communicated to her co-felon and, therefore, her liability for crimes committed in furtherance of the conspiracy would not be abrogated. Choice (B) is incorrect because felony murder typically applies to unintended deaths which that result from the commission of certain enumerated felonies. Choice (D) is incorrect because whether the teller was placed in apprehension of bodily harm or not is irrelevant.

32. **(A)** This question is testing students on the scope of liability for conspiracy. First, it is important to realize that a conspiracy existed. According to LaFave, a ***conspiracy*** requires "(1) an agreement between two or more persons which constitutes the act, and (2) an intent thereby to achieve a certain objective which is the doing of either an unlawful act or a lawful act by unlawful means." LaFave, Criminal Law, p. 525. As part of the boyfriend's plan to rob the bank, he enlisted his girlfriend to drive the get-away car, and she agreed. Her subsequent decision not to go through with it is an insufficient basis for ***withdrawal,*** since she did not "thwart the success" of the conspiracy. Choices (B), (C), and (D) are incorrect. The general rule regarding the scope of the conspiracy is that a co-conspirator will be liable for ***all crimes committed in furtherance of the conspiracy.*** Since the killing of the pedestrian occurred during the commission of the robbery, the girlfriend will be liable to the same extent as her boyfriend. She will be guilty of murder. Choice (A) is correct.

33. **(D)** The child's death was unintentional and did not occur as a ***foreseeable result during the commission*** of the robbery. The death of the child occurred an hour later, and the defendant was not speeding at the time. Her act of suddenly darting in front of the defendant's car was not a foreseeable consequence of his get-away from the robbery. Therefore, choice (A) is incorrect. Choice (B) is incorrect because the defendant lacked the requisite mental state for involuntary manslaughter, namely, gross or criminal negligence. He was driving slowly and applied his brakes at the time of the accident. Choice (C) is incorrect, since the killing was not intentional. By process of elimination, choice (D) is correct; the defendant will be guilty of no crime.

34. **(D)** In order to be liable as an ***accomplice*** to the crime of another, one must (a) ***aid, abet, or encourage the perpetrator*** (b) ***with the intent*** thereby to promote or facilitate the commission of the crime. Several terms have been employed by courts and legislatures in describing the kinds of acts which that will suffice for accomplice liability. The most common are "aid," "abet," "advise," "assist," "cause," "command," "counsel," "encourage," "hire," and "induce." The defendant is not subject to accomplice liability because he was unaware that the two men were burglarizing the home. The distracter in this question is the fact that the perpetrators gave the defendant $500 after pawning the jewels. Taking the money (two weeks afterward) does not subject the defendant to accomplice liability because he didn't specifically intend to facilitate the commission of the crime at the moment of its inception. If anything, the defendant would be viewed as an ***accessory after the fact*** for accepting the money. Therefore, choices (A), (B), and (C) are incorrect.

35. **(B)** in this question, a lot of students will incorrectly choose choice (A) because they are aware that under the modern view, impossibility is not a defense (to a charge of attempt) when the defendant's actual intent—not limited by the true facts unknown to him – was to do an act or bring about a result proscribed by law. Although this is true, choice (B) is the preferred answer because the defendant is an accomplice (or principal in the second degree) because he ***aided and abetted*** the friend by supplying him the gun to kill the victim. LaFave notes that to be a principal in the second degree, ***one must be present at the commission of a criminal offense and aid, counsel, command, or encourage the principal in the first degree in the commission of that offense.*** Choice (B) is correct because a principal in the second degree is subject to and accountable for the same crime(s) committed by the principal in the first degree. Choices (C) and (D) are incorrect. While both are crimes the defendant could be convicted of, they are less serious crimes than murder, and, therefore, not the strongest answers.

36. **(A)** Both co-defendants are guilty of violating the statute because although only one built and transported the bombing device, both participated in the planning and carrying out of the crime. The other co-defendant who did not build the bomb is guilty as an accomplice (or accessory before the fact). An individual is criminally liable as an accomplice if he gives assistance or encouragement, or fails to act where he has a legal duty to oppose the crime of another. Certainly, both co-defendants were responsible for the commission of the crime. Choice (B) is incorrect because they are both guilty for the reasons stated above. Choice (C) is incorrect because gross negligence on the part of the casino would not abrogate guilt in a criminal trial. Choice (D) is incorrect because the intentions of the defendants do not matter, as they built a bomb and placed it in the hotel.

37. **(A)** Both co-defendants would both be guilty of felony-murder. By constructing the bomb and placing it in the bank, they would be criminally liable for the explosion, even though it prematurely detonated. At common law, one whose conduct brought about an unintended death in the commission or attempted commission of a felony was guilty of (felony) murder. Today, many jurisdictions limit the rule by requiring that the felony must be dangerous to life (e.g., arson, burglary, robbery, or kidnapping). Certainly, placing a bomb that was activated to detonate would be dangerous to human life. On the contrary, neither co-defendant is guilty of conspiracy to commit murder because they did not intend to kill anyone. Thus, there was no agreement to commit murder. Choice (B) is incorrect because neither defendant is guilty of conspiracy. Choices (C) and (D) are incorrect for the reasons stated above.

38. **(B)** Choice (A) is incorrect because in order to be an accomplice to a crime, one must (1) give assistance, and (2) have the intent to promote or facilitate commission of a crime. The defendant lacked the requisite *mens rea*, since he didn't intend or knowingly encourage the classmate to commit a homicide. Choice (C) is incorrect because joint venture is a torts principle and does not extend to criminal liability. Choice (D) is not the best answer because it is a general principle of criminal law that one is not criminally liable for how someone else acts, unless he directs or encourages or aids the other so to act. Thus, unlike the case of torts, an employer is not generally liable for the criminal acts of his employee, even though the latter does them in furtherance of his employer's business (except in the case of a statutory crime where the legislature has provided otherwise). By process of elimination, choice (B) is the best answer.

39. **(D)** Some crimes are defined in such a way that they may be directly committed only by a person who has a particular characteristic or occupies a particular position, as with ***adultery, which can be committed only by a married person.*** LaFave observes, however, that this has not prevented courts from concluding that others outside the legislative class may be guilty of these crimes (commonly referred to as Wharton rule crimes) on an accomplice theory, or that other persons may likewise be guilty of a conspiracy to commit such crimes. Thus, for example, an unmarried man may be convicted of conspiring with a married man that the latter commit adultery. See LaFave, Criminal Law pp. 491–492. It is important, however, to distinguish the above situation from the present example in which the girl is a member of a ***legislatively protected class.*** In accordance with the rule enunciated in *Gebarbi v. United States*, 287 U.S. 112 (1932), ***one who may not be deemed an accomplice to a crime (because a contrary holding would conflict with the legislative purpose) may likewise not be found to be a member of a conspiracy to commit that crime.*** In *Gebarbi*, the U.S. Supreme Court held that a woman could not be convicted of conspiracy to violate the Mann Act when the man transported the woman from one state to another for immoral purposes, because the Mann Act was designed to protect women. Likewise, in the present example, the girl cannot be prosecuted as an accomplice to the crime of contributing to the delinquency of minors, because the crime statute is designed to protect minors. Choices (A), (B), and (C) are all misstatements of law and, therefore, incorrect.

40. **(D)** The defendant should be found not guilty of any of the crimes in answer choices (A), (B), or (C) because she lacked the requisite mental states. She clearly did not intend to murder, seriously injure, or harm the victim in any way. Therefore, she would not be guilty of murder or battery. The only close call here is involuntary manslaughter, which is an unintentional killing due to criminal negligence. However, in order to show criminal negligence, the defendant must have been aware of an unreasonable or high risk of death or serious bodily injury. Since the defendant was unaware of the risk, her conduct was not criminally negligent. Therefore, choice (D) is correct.

41. **(B)** The majority rule dealing with causation for felony murder is the ***agency theory.*** Under the agency theory, the killing must be caused by one of the felons engaged in the underlying felony. An exception to this rule is the shield theory. If one of the felons, as we have in our question, takes a person hostage or uses them as a shield and they are killed, all of the participating felons are liable for the death. Therefore, the woman will be liable for the death of the bank manager. However, the woman will not be liable for the death of the man under the agency theory because he was killed by the police. Therefore, choices (A), (C), and (D) are incorrect.

42. **(B)** Under the agency theory, the killing must be caused by one of the felons engaged in the underlying felony. Accordingly, the girlfriend is guilty of felony murder for the death of the first cashier because he was shot and killed by her boyfriend, who was her co-felon. The second cashier's death from a heart attack was causally connected to the robbery because she was threatened by the boyfriend after witnessing the murder of her co-worker. Since her co-felon was criminally responsible for causing the second cashier's death, the girlfriend would be guilty of felony murder. Finally, the girlfriend is not guilty of the boyfriend's death because his killing was not caused by her or a co-felon. Therefore choice (B) is correct, and choices (A), (C), and (D) are incorrect.

43. **(D)** One of the elements required for the commission of a crime is causation. As a general rule, the defendant's criminal act must be the proximate or legal cause of the injury suffered by the victim. When dealing with an intervening act, as we are here in our question with the surgery, look to see whether the intervening act was a coincidence or a response to the defendant's prior actions. If the intervening act is a response to the defendant's prior actions, then the defendant will be criminally liable for the consequences. In our question, the surgery was a response to the prior action of the defendant in shooting the cashier, and the defendant will be criminally liable for her death. Therefore, choices (A) and (C) are incorrect. Choice (B) is incorrect. An exception to double jeopardy exists where the defendant was not initially charged with a more serious crime because the additional facts necessary to sustain that charge had not yet occurred or been discovered by the prosecution. This is known as the *Diaz* exception, from the holding of the Supreme Court case of *Diaz v. United States*, 223 US 442 (1912).

44. **(D)** Choices (A) and (B) are incorrect because the defendant did not intend to injure anyone. Remember that attempt, like all inchoate crimes, is a specific intent crime. Choice (C) is incorrect for similar reasons in that the crime is defined as assault with the ***intent*** to cause serious bodily injury. This would also be a specific intent crime for which the defendant does not have the requisite mental state required for conviction. Therefore, by process of elimination, choice (D) is the strongest answer. Battery is a general intent crime for which the defendant's reckless conduct resulting in the injury to the pedestrian will suffice.

45. **(C)** At common law, robbery is a trespassory taking and carrying away of the personal property of another with intent to steal it. Additionally, the property must be taken from the person or his presence and be accomplished by force or intimidation. In addition, robbery may be considered a greater crime than the sum of the two lesser crimes of larceny and assault (or battery). Therefore, since larceny and assault (or battery) merges into robbery, choices (A) and (B) are incorrect. Next, we must consider whether the defendants are guilty of burglary, which, at common law, consisted of the breaking and entering of a dwelling house of another in the nighttime with the intent to commit a felony therein. In order to constitute a breaking at common law, there had to be the creation of a breach or opening. The victim opened the door for the intruders, making choice (D) a tempting answer. However, choice (D) is incorrect because a "constructive breaking" occurred. When entry is gained by fraud, force, threat of force, or through a chimney, then a "constructive breaking" is deemed to have occurred, even though the occupant may have herself provided the opening. Here, the robbers fraudulently got the victim to open the door, and forced their way past her into her home. This constituted a "constructive breaking." As a result, choice (C) is correct because the defendants are guilty of burglary and robbery.

46. **(B)** Choice (A) is wrong because it is well settled in criminal law that under ***the doctrine of transferred intent*** in the unintended-victim (or bad-aim) situation—where A aims at B but misses, hitting C—it is the accepted view that A is just as guilty as if his aim had been accurate. Thus, where A aims at B with a murderous intent to kill, but because of a bad aim he hits and kills C, A is uniformly held guilty of the murder of C. Choice (C) is likewise erroneous because as a general rule, it is frequently said that ignorance of the law is no excuse. Note that ignorance or mistake as to a matter of fact or law is a defense if it is shown that the defendant does not have the mental state required by law for the commission of that particular offense. In the present case, the defendant did have the requisite *mens rea*, because he intended to inflict serious bodily injury on the friend. Choice (D) is incorrect because it is commonly said in civil and in criminal cases that one is presumed to intend the natural and probable consequences of his acts. Thus, LaFave points out, if one carefully aims a gun at his enemy and pulls the trigger; and the bullet strikes the enemy in the heart and kills him, we ought to conclude, in the absence of some other facts, that he intended to kill (though he spoke no words of intent at the time). Similarly, a special application of the presumption that one intends to produce the natural results of his actions is found in the ***deadly weapon doctrine*** applicable to homicide cases: ***one who intentionally uses a deadly weapon on another human being and thereby kills him presumably intends to kill him.*** In this regard, LaFave states that the deadly weapon doctrine is not a category, of murder separate from the intent-to-kill category, but, rather, ***the intentional use of a deadly weapon authorizes the drawing of an inference that the user intends to kill.*** It should be noted that the intentional use of a deadly weapon which that produces death is not necessarily murder, since we still allow the user (defendant) a chance to convince the jury that in spite of his intentional use of a deadly weapon, he did not actually intend to kill. In light of this explanation, choice (D) is wrong because there is a presumption that the defendant intended to kill the friend under the deadly-weapon doctrine. Consequently, by process of elimination, choice (B) is the best answer.

47. **(D)** This is a classic example of ***depraved-heart murder, defined as "extremely negligent conduct which creates not only an unjustifiable but also a very high degree of risk of death or serious bodily injury (though unaccompanied by any intent to kill) and which actually causes the death of another."*** Criminal Law, pg. 541. According to LaFave, shooting a gun at a point near, but not aiming directly at, another person involves a very high degree of unjustifiable homicidal danger, which will do for depraved-heart murder. As a result, the police officer is guilty of murder. Choices (A), (B), and (C) are incorrect, as murder is the most serious crime for which he can be convicted and is, therefore, the strongest answer.

48. **(A)** As with other common law and statutory crimes which that are defined in terms of conduct producing a specified result, a person may be criminally liable when his omission to act produces that result, but only if (1) he has, under the circumstances, a legal duty to act, and (2) he can physically perform the act. For criminal liability to be based upon a failure to act it must first be found that there is a duty to act—a legal duty and not simply a moral duty. According to LaFave, there are seven situations which that do give rise to a duty to act: (1) duty based upon relationship; (2) duty based upon statute; (3) duty based upon contract; (4) duty based upon voluntary assumption of care; (5) duty based upon creation of peril; (6) duty to control conduct of others; and (7) duty of landowner. In this example, choice (A) is correct because the defendant's duty to act to protect the hiker probably would arise out of contract. Since the defendant was a guide at the park, he was employed to take affirmative action to protect hikers from such foreseeable dangers. This situation is analogous to a lifeguard employed to watch over swimmers at a beach. The lifeguard cannot sit idly by while a swimmer at his beach drowns off shore. Omission to do so may make the lifeguard liable for criminal homicide. Note that for a duty to act, by virtue of contract, the victim need not be one of the contracting parties. LaFave, Criminal Law, pp. 182–186. Choices (B) and (C) are incorrect because there would be no legal duty to act under those circumstances. Choice (D) is incorrect because, even though there is a legal duty to act between parent and child, the father wasn't there to prevent the harm and save his daughter.

49. **(B)** Robbery consists of all the six elements of larceny: a (1) trespassory (2) taking and (3) carrying away of the (4) personal property (5) of another (6) with intent to steal it, plus two additional elements: that (7) the property be taken away from the person or presence of another, and (8) the taking be accomplished by means of force or "putting in fear." Choice (B) is correct, since the defendant should be found guilty only of the crime of larceny, not robbery. The defendant took the homeowner's stereo system from her house without any force or intimidation. Since the "taking" and "asportation" elements of robbery did not coincide with the violence or intimidation elements, the defendant would not be guilty of robbery. All eight elements are necessary for a robbery conviction. Choice (A) is incorrect , since the defendant did commit a robbery upon the victim, even though the ring belonged to someone else. To prove robbery, it is not necessary to show that the personal property belonged to the victim at the time of the taking with force or intimidation. Choice (C) is wrong, since the "taking" of the gold chain was directly from the shopper's person. Choice (D) is also incorrect, since the defendant entered the tenant's apartment, overpowered him, and forced him to reveal where he had hidden the money. Thus, the taking was accompanied by violence, and the defendant would be found guilty of robbery.

50. **(A)** There is a great deal of confusion in the substantive criminal law ***between strict liability crimes*** and ***vicarious liability crimes.*** A vicarious liability crime is one wherein one person, though without personal fault, is made liable for the conduct of another (usually his employee). It is common, however, for a vicarious liability statute to also impose strict liability; in such an instance, there is no need to prove an act or omission by the defendant-employer (one by his employee will do), and there is no need to prove mental fault by anyone. Some criminal statutes, for example, specifically impose criminal liability upon the employer for the bad conduct of his employee (e.g., "whoever, by himself or by his agent, sells articles at short weight shall be punished by . . . ," or "whoever sells liquor to a minor is punishable by . . . "). In construing statutes of this type, courts often jump to the unwarranted conclusion that a statute which that imposes strict liability must of necessity also impose vicarious liability. LaFave notes, however, that ***there is no basis for assuming that vicarious liability necessarily follows from strict liability.*** The better view, according to LaFave, is that an employer does not "allow" or "permit" his employee to do an act ***unless he knows of or authorizes it.*** Based on this analysis, the correct answer is choice (A). Choices (B), (C), and (D) are all misstatements of law and, therefore, incorrect.

51. **(C)** In order to be guilty of attempt, the defendant must commit ***an act that constitutes a "substantial step" toward the commission of the crime.*** To be sure, bad thoughts alone cannot constitute a crime. However, precisely the kind of act required is not made very clear by the language which that has traditionally been used by the courts and legislatures. It is commonly said that ***more than an act of preparation must occur.*** The traditional attempt statute requires an "act toward the commission of" some offense; "conduct which tends to effect the commission of" a crime; or an act "in furtherance of" or "tending directly toward" the commission of an offense. LaFave, Crimi-

nal Law, pg. 504. Choice (A) is incorrect. Simply taking out an insurance policy would ***not, by itself, constitute a "substantial step"*** in the commission of attempted murder. Rather, the wife must engage in some action directed toward the actual killing (e.g., placing poison in a glass or pulling the trigger of a gun). Choice (B) is incorrect because, as stated above, the wife has to do more than merely intend to kill her husband; there needs to have been a substantial step. Finally, choice (D) is incorrect, as withdrawal is not a defense to attempt.

52. **(B)** Under an accomplice (or co-conspirator) theory of liability, the mother is guilty of two counts of murder for the killings of the woman and her daughter. To be sure, ***a co-conspirator is criminally liable for all "natural and probable" consequences of the conspiracy.*** With respect to the issue of "foreseeable" crimes, since the mother supplied her boyfriend with a gun (and the wrong address), it was probable that he would kill someone at that location. Many students will be diverted from choosing choice (B) because they know that attempt merges with the completed crime. However, there is no merger, since the mother is guilty of the ***attempted murder of the girl and the murder of the woman and her daughter.*** If the boyfriend had killed the girl, then, of course, there would be a merger. Choices (C) and (D) are not the strongest answer choices because the mother's actions in supplying her boyfriend with the gun raises her culpability to a level beyond the mere solicitation of a crime. Similarly, her actions raise her culpability above manslaughter, and she will be guilty of murder. Therefore, choice (A) is incorrect.

53. **(C)** For the crime of solicitation to be committed, it is only necessary that the defendant (with the requisite intent) have enticed, advised, incited, ordered, or otherwise encouraged another person to commit a crime. Since the defendant was not actually selling narcotics, he cannot be guilty of solicitation. Therefore, choices (A) and (D) are wrong. Choice (B) is incorrect because in *United States v. Oviedo,* 525 F. 2d 881 (1976), the Court held that ***legal impossibility*** precluded a defendant from being guilty of attempted sale of heroin that turned out to be a non-narcotic substance. Therefore, choice (C) is the best answer if the defendant intended to defraud the partygoer by selling oregano instead of marijuana.

54. **(B)** As a general rule, ***voluntary intoxication is no defense for any crime requiring recklessness.*** Although recklessness requires that the defendant be aware of the risk which that his conduct creates, LaFave states that "if the only reason why the defendant does not realize the recklessness of his conduct is that he is too intoxicated, he is guilty of the recklessness which the crime requires." LaFave, Criminal Law, pg. 392. As such, voluntary intoxication cannot be a valid defense. Therefore, the trial court judge was correct in excluding evidence of the man's intoxication. Choice (B) is better than choice (A) because choice (A) merely states a given rule but does not address the intoxication defense. In this question, the key issue is whether the judge will admit or exclude evidence of the man's intoxication as a defense for the crime of reckless endangerment. Choices (C) and (D) are incorrect, as they are not on point to the issue presented in this question.

Multistate Nuance Chart

Larceny

Property Covered	Property *Not* Covered
1. Tangible personal property	1. Nonpayment of services
2. Lost or mislaid property	2. Real property
3. Gas and electricity	3. Abandoned property
4. Contraband	4. Wild animals
	5. Intangible personal property

55. **(A)** A person is privileged to use deadly force in self-defense if (a) ***she reasonably believes that she is in immediate danger of death or serious bodily injury*** and (b) the use of such force is necessary to avoid this danger. The given facts indicate that the boyfriend was not in ***immediate danger*** of unlawful bodily harm. In fact, the girlfriend was asleep when he arranged to have the hit man killed her. The judge should not instruct the jury on self-defense, because the boyfriend has failed to show that he was in immediate danger of serious bodily injury when the murder occurred. Choice (B) is incorrect because there is not a duty to retreat on the Multistate unless the question tells you the jurisdiction has such a duty. Choice (C) is incorrect for the reasons stated above. Choice (D) is incorrect, as it is a misstatement of law.

56. **(D)** In order for the ***finder of lost or mislaid property*** to be guilty of larceny, two requirements must be satisfied. The finder must, at the time of the finding, (1) intend to steal it, and (2) either know who the owner is or have reason to believe (from earmarkings on the property or from the circumstances of the finding) that he can find out the owner's identity. Not only was the defendant unaware of who the owner of the pass was, he also could not determine the owner's identity from the earmarkings of the property. Therefore, the defendant would not be guilty of larceny, and choice (A) is incorrect. Choice (B) is incorrect because false pretenses requires that the ***defendant, by his lies, obtain title to the victim's property.*** The defendant did not obtain title to tangible property but merely free admission to a movie. Choice (C) is wrong because the defendant entered his own name on the pass, rather than forging someone else's name or signature.

57. **(C)** Where the accused has an honest and reasonable belief which, if true, would negate the *mens rea* of a particular offense, such a belief operates as a complete defense by negating a material element of the crime. The general rule is that a reasonable mistake negates a general intent, whereas a specific intent can be negated by a mistaken belief, whether reasonable or unreasonable. Choices (A) and (B) are incorrect. The forgery statute in this question requires the making of a ***"material alteration in any writing with the purpose to defraud"*** — a specific intent. Therefore, if the jury believes the defendant's story that he honestly believed the neighbor meant to draft the check for $1,900, the defendant should be found not guilty, regardless of whether his belief was reasonable or not. Choice (C) is correct. Finally, choice (D) is incorrect because the neighbor's intent is not relevant to determining the defendant's guilt.

58. **(A)** In order to be guilty of common law larceny, the defendant need only carry away the victim's property a slight distance (three inches will suffice) with the intent to steal. In this example, the boy took the baseball card packs, placed them in his coat pocket, and attempted to walk out of the store without paying. Clearly, sufficient asportation occurred. Students should not be distracted by the fact that the storekeeper gave the boy permission to take the cards. Actually, the crime was completed when the boy placed the cards in his pocket (without intending to pay for them), even before reaching the counter area. Choices (B) and (C) are incorrect because there was not a false representation of material fact made by the boy. Choice (D) is incorrect for the reasons stated above.

59. **(D)** At common law, larceny was limited to the taking of tangible personal property. Since larceny was limited to the theft of goods and chattels, ***one cannot be guilty (of larceny) for misappropriations of real property, such as trees, crops, minerals, and fixtures.*** In the present example, the facts clearly state that the bookcase was regarded as a fixture. The tenant cannot be guilty of common law larceny for the removal of the bookcase. Therefore, choices (A) and (B) are incorrect. Choice (C) is incorrect because the book case was no longer the tenant's property.

60. **(B)** For criminal liability to be based upon a failure to act, it must first be found that there is a legal duty to act. Such a legal duty can arise where the defendant either intentionally or negligently creates the victim's peril. By attempting to overtake the woman's car in a "no-passing" zone on a steep, winding highway, the man acted negligently, which created the peril. Since the man created the peril, he had a legal duty to render assistance. His failure to act establishes liability based on criminal negligence, and he will be guilty of manslaughter for the other driver's

death. Choice (B) is correct. The woman will not be guilty of manslaughter; she neither created the victim's peril nor voluntarily undertook to help the victim. No duty to act arose merely by the fact that the woman stopped her vehicle, walked to the edge of the roadway, and heard the victim's call for help. As to the woman, a general rule applies, namely that one has no legal duty to aid another person in peril, even if that aid can be rendered without danger or inconvenience. Therefore, choices (A), (C), and (D) are incorrect.

61. **(A)** Four elements are generally required for the commission of a crime: ***(1) actus reus; (2) mens rea; (3) causal connection;*** and ***(4) harm or injury to the victim.*** In order to be guilty of a crime, the defendant's conduct must be the legal, or proximate, cause of victim's harm. The problem of legal causation arises in both tort and criminal law situations. Here, the man's failure to yield was the actual (or factual) cause of the accident, but the student's removal of the yield sign was the legal cause. Consequently, choice (A) is correct, and the student will be held criminally responsible for the other driver's death. Therefore, choices (B), (C), and (D) are incorrect.

62. **(A)** According to LaFave, "extremely negligent conduct, which creates what a reasonable man would realize to be not only an unjustifiable but also a very high degree of risk of death or serious bodily injury to another though unaccompanied by any intent to kill or do serious bodily injury and which actually causes the death of another" constitutes ***"depraved-heart" murder.*** See Criminal Law, p.541. Since the breeder had trained his guard dogs to attack at night and then opened the gate to let them run loose, he will be criminally responsible for the killing of the man. Such conduct on the breeder's part is more extreme than the gross or criminal negligence standard sufficient for involuntary manslaughter. The breeder will be liable on the theory of depraved-heart murder. While one could argue that the breeder will be liable for the crimes in choices (B), (C), and (D), the most serious crime is in choice (A), which is, therefore, the strongest answer.

63. **(C)** ***Forgery is a crime aimed primarily at safeguarding confidence in the genuineness of documents*** relied upon in commercial and business activity. Though a forgery, like false pretenses, requires a lie, it must be a lie about the document itself: the lie must relate to the genuineness of the document. According to LaFave, if the forger is successful in passing the forged document, receiving property or money for it, he is no doubt guilty of the crime of false pretenses in addition to that of forgery. Therefore choices (A), (B), and (D) are incorrect.

64. **(B)** To be guilty of common-law arson one must burn the dwelling house of another with malice. Malice includes the intent to burn or wanton and willful misconduct that creates a plain and strong likelihood that a protected structure will be burned. To engage in wanton and willful misconduct, the defendant must have recklessly ignored an obvious risk. Because the man was only intending to hide the fireworks under a chair, he could not have been aware of the damage that would likely result. Additionally, hiding fireworks under a chair is not an obviously dangerous act. Thus, the man would not possess the requisite malice to support an arson conviction. Choice (A) is incorrect. The man's intentions toward the friend would be relevant if he were charged with battery or another crime against the person, but arson is a crime against structures, and the man's intent toward the person of the friend is immaterial. Choice (C) is incorrect. Because the man lacked the mental element of malice necessary to support a conviction for arson, the fact that he was the indirect cause of the burning of the cabin is not sufficient to overcome the lack of the requisite mental element. As such, he is not guilty of arson. And Choice (D) is incorrect. No matter how one might argue that this was the natural result of the man's actions, such a result was certainly not obvious. As such, the man cannot be held guilty of wanton and willful misconduct. Additionally, it is arguable that a fire is not the natural result of hiding fireworks under a chair on the porch.

65. **(A)** Choice (B) is wrong because, in order to be subject to accomplice liability, the defendant(s) must intentionally encourage or assist another in the commission of a crime as to which the accomplice has the requisite mental state. The facts don't necessarily indicate that the roommates intended to have their roommate falsely report a fire to the fire depart-

ment, since they were playing a practical joke. Rather, their conduct was reckless. Their roommate is an innocent agent. The roommates would be guilty as the principals for their roommate's false report. Because they are "principals," they cannot be guilty as "accomplices," so choice (B) is incorrect. Choice (C) is wrong because the roommates were responsible for the crime being committed and are, thus, subject to criminal liability as parties to the crime. Choice (D) is incorrect because the language of the statute does not require that the false report be made knowingly.

66. **(B)** In certain situations, like we have here in our question, the homicide will occur first before the underlying felony is committed. In jurisdictions following the independent felony murder rule, the defendant is not guilty of felony murder if the intent to commit the underlying felony is formed after the killing has occurred. Therefore, choice (B) is the best defense, as the defendants only decided to steal the victim's wallet after he lay dead on the ground. Choice (A) is incorrect because robbery would qualify as an inherently dangerous felony. Choices (C) and (D) are incorrect because the defendants would be guilty under both theories, as they were the proximate cause of the victim's death, and a third party did not kill the victim.

67. **(A)** Choice (B) is incorrect. In order for intoxication to negate premeditation and deliberation, it must rob the defendant of his ability to premeditate and deliberate. Here, the defendant had premeditated the killing prior to becoming intoxicated, so it won't be a defense to first-degree murder that at the time of the killing, he could no longer premeditate or deliberate due because to his intoxication. Choices (C) and (D) are incorrect for the reasons stated above.

68. **(A)** One of the elements of felony murder is that the underlying felony must be inherently dangerous. The best defense for the women would be that the underlying crime is larceny, which is not inherently dangerous. Choice (B) is incorrect because the killing was independent of the underlying crime. Choice (C) is incorrect. Under the agency theory, a defendant is guilty of felony murder only when the killing is caused by one of the co-felons. Here, one of the defendants caused the killing by placing the gun in the shopping bag, so this would not be the women's best defense. Finally, choice (D) is incorrect because the killing often is accidental or unintentional. That is the purpose behind the felony murder rule; to hold defendants accountable for killings caused during the commission of inherently dangerous felonies even if they were accidental or unintentional.

69. **(C)** According to LaFave, for criminal liability to be based upon a failure to act, it must first be found that there is a legal duty to act, not simply a moral duty. Generally, one has no legal duty to aid another in peril, even when that aid can be rendered without danger or inconvenience. However, the common law imposes an affirmative duty upon persons standing in certain personal relationships to other persons, as upon (1) parents to aid their small children; (2) husbands to aid their wives; (3) ship's captains to aid their crews; and (4) employers to aid their employees. The novel question presented here is whether a roommate is under a legal duty to render assistance? According to LaFave, ***"if two people, though not closely related, live together under one roof, one may have a duty to act to aid the other who becomes helpless."*** LaFave, Criminal Law, pg. 204. Therefore, choice (D) is incorrect. Since the facts indicate that the girlfriend and boyfriend were living together and carrying on a relationship, the girlfriend would have a duty to render assistance to her boyfriend. In situations where the victim dies on account of an omission to act, the defendant is generally guilty of involuntary manslaughter. Therefore, choices (A) and (B) are incorrect.

70. **(D)** This question deals with violation of a federal criminal statute. According to LaFave, federal criminal statutes define offenses in terms of substantive misbehavior, and the matter of jurisdictional requirements are dealt with separately. The government is relieved of any burden of showing that the defendant knows about the special fact which that results in federal jurisdiction. LaFave, Criminal Law, p. 113. Therefore, the jury should be instructed that it may convict the company's president regardless of his lack of knowledge that he was doing business with a federal agency. The only element of knowledge required by the federal statute is that the defendant ***knowingly*** makes a false statement. Therefore, choices (A), (B), and (C) are incorrect.

71. **(A)** According to the given facts, the defendant agreed to provide the man with information about how to break the combination to the safe. As such, the defendant is guilty of conspiracy because he entered into ***the agreement with the intent that the crime be committed.*** The main problem students have with this question is whether the woman is also a co-conspirator. Surely, the woman did not explicitly take part in the conversation (or agreement) between the defendant and the man. However, according to LaFave, "a mere tacit understanding will suffice and there need not be any written or verbal-statement which expressly communicates an agreement." Criminal Law, pg. 532. In this regard, the agreement need not be shown to have been explicit; it can be inferred from the facts and circumstances of the case. Therefore, choice (B) is incorrect. Undoubtedly, the woman was part of the conspiracy because she approached the defendant the previous day and solicited his aid. Choices (C) and (D) are incorrect for the reasons stated above.

72. **(A)** The issue presented is, is it possible for a person to become a party to the crime of conspiracy even in the absence of any agreement on his part? The answer is yes. According to LaFave, a person with knowledge of the conspiracy "who intentionally gives aid to the conspiratorial objective" is guilty of conspiracy. Criminal Law, pg. 534. Therefore, choices (C) and (D) are incorrect. Choice (B) is incorrect because the conspiratorial agreement involved three persons, namely, the mechanic, the janitor, and the defendant. Even if the mechanic is found innocent of conspiracy, the janitor and the defendant nonetheless could be convicted, which would satisfy the plurality requirement. At common law, there must be two or more guilty parties to a conspiracy. **Exam Tip:** Under the Model Penal Code (modern view), a unilateral agreement will suffice for a conspiracy conviction. For example, if A and B are charged with conspiracy and A is acquitted, B could still be convicted of conspiracy. However, you are advised ***to answer the Criminal Law MBE questions based on the common law*** (rather than the Model Penal Code), unless the question states otherwise.

73. **(A)** Receiving stolen property is defined typically by statute as the ***receiving of stolen property knowing that it is stolen.*** Although most statutes do not specifically mention it, the receiver must, in addition to knowing the property is stolen, intend to deprive the owner of his property. Also, the stolen character of the property and the receiver's receipt of the property must coincide in point of time. In other words, if the property has been ***recovered*** by the owner or by the police, it has lost its status as "stolen" property, and there can be no crime. When the informer agreed to act as an undercover police informant, the police arranged for him to set up a pawnbroker's shop. The stolen television sold from the man to the informer was reported to the police and held for eventual sale to the defendant. At this point, the television was no longer "stolen" property, but "recovered" property. Therefore, the defendant did not receive "stolen" property, and she will be found not guilty. Therefore, choices (C) and (D) are incorrect. Choice (B) is incorrect because the defendant was not entrapped. She ***was already predisposed*** to purchase the television without police inducement.

74. **(B)** Certainly, the defendant's best argument that the homicide should be manslaughter rather than murder is that he acted with adequate provocation in attempting to kill the victim. ***Voluntary manslaughter consists of an intentional homicide committed under extenuating circumstances that mitigate, though they do not justify or excuse, the killing.*** The principal extenuating circumstance is the fact that the defendant (when he killed the victim) was in a state of passion engendered in him by **adequate provocation.** The facts indicate that the victim punched the defendant in the face several times immediately before the shooting. This battery would constitute "reasonable provocation," causing the defendant to lose his normal self-control. Choice (A) is incorrect because the defendant cannot argue that being punched in the face would give rise to the use of deadly force and is, therefore, self-defense. Choice (C) is incorrect because, at common law, voluntary intoxication cannot mitigate murder to manslaughter. Choice (D) is incorrect. Just because a killing is unintentional doesn't necessarily mean that it will be mitigated from murder to manslaughter. There are forms of murder, liked depraved-heart, or intent to cause serious bodily harm, which do not require the intent to kill.

75. **(C)** At common law, burglary is defined as the ***(1) breaking and (2) entering of (3) the dwelling house (4) of another (5) with intent to commit a felony therein.*** Choice (A) is incorrect because the defendant mistakenly entered the home, not intending to commit a larceny or felony therein. Choice (B) is incorrect because, first, an antique store is not viewed as a dwelling house and, second, the defendant did not possess the intent to steal. Choice (D) is wrong because the defendant, again, did not intend to steal or permanently deprive the neighbor of the chain saw. By process of elimination, choice (C) is the best answer. Be advised that gaining entry to the home by fraud would constitute a "constructive breaking," which would satisfy the breaking requirement for burglary.

Explanation: Question 76

The correct answer is: **(C)** Their intent was to play a joke on the cousin.

Conspiracy is an agreement for an unlawful purpose. It requires an agreement and a specific intent to commit the target offense and, in many jurisdictions (by statute), an overt act in furtherance of the conspiracy. If the florist and his sister lacked the specific intent to commit robbery, they could not be guilty of this conspiracy. On these facts, there is support for their argument that they lacked this intent, because their intent was to play a joke on their cousin and return the money taken in the staged robbery. Since they intended to return any money taken in the staged robbery, they lacked the requisite specific intent and are, therefore, not guilty of conspiracy to commit robbery.

(A) Incorrect. The pistols they used were only toys.

The fact that the pistols were toys would not prevent their actions from being a robbery, if they had the requisite intent. The defendants do not have to actually possess force; it is the reasonable belief of the victim that matters. The facts state that the toy pistols were realistic looking. Therefore, it was reasonable for the cousin to think that the pistols were real. The florist and his sister's better argument is to claim they lacked the requisite intent.

(B) Incorrect. No overt act was committed in furtherance of the conspiracy.

If the other elements of conspiracy were present, there were ample acts to satisfy the overt act requirement. An overt act is simply some step forward in furtherance of the criminal goal of the conspiracy. In this problem, the goal of the conspiracy (such as it was) was almost completely accomplished.

(D) Incorrect. The loss of the money was the result of an unforeseeable intervening actor.

The fact that the money taken in the staged robbery was ultimately lost is not relevant to the charged crime. The florist and his sister were charged with conspiracy to commit robbery. Since their intent was to return whatever they received in the staged robbery, they lacked the requisite intent to be guilty of this charge. The subsequent loss of the money cannot change this result.

Explanation: Question 77

The correct answer is: **(D)** acquitted, because neither the butcher nor the chef agreed to commit an unlawful act.

In order for there to be a conspiracy, there must be two guilty minds. This means that if only one person intended to commit a crime (because, for example, the others are feigned accomplices or lack the requisite intent), there can be no conspiracy because there was no real agreement for an unlawful purpose. (Some states modernly abrogate this rule by statute, permitting conviction of one person who agrees with another to commit a crime, even if the other does not really agree. Since the facts state that this is a common law jurisdiction, this modern treatment is inapplicable.) The testimony of the butcher and the chef, if believed, absolves them of guilt because of their lack of criminal intent. As such, the baker cannot be convicted of conspiring with himself.

(A) Incorrect. convicted, because there was an agreement for an unlawful purpose sufficient to constitute a conspiracy.

There was no real agreement for an unlawful purpose, because neither the butcher nor the chef actually agreed to commit criminal trespass. Since there were not two guilty minds, the baker cannot be convicted of conspiracy.

(B) Incorrect. convicted, because the baker intended to commit a criminal trespass.

Even if the baker did intend to commit a criminal trespass by entering the country club without permission, he cannot be found guilty of conspiracy without an agreement with a least one more guilty mind. Since neither the butcher nor the chef possessed a guilty mind, the baker cannot be guilty of conspiracy.

(C) Incorrect. acquitted, because no overt act in furtherance of the conspiracy was performed.

While most jurisdictions require an overt act in furtherance of the agreement as an element of conspiracy, the common law viewed a conspiracy as formed immediately upon the making of the agreement. Since the facts state that the jurisdiction in question follows the common law on conspiracy, an overt act is not needed.

Explanation: Question 78

The correct answer is: **(C)** acquitted, because she never intended to burglarize the administrative offices.

The friend's testimony, if believed, establishes that she was a feigned conspirator--one who merely pretends to go along with the illegal objective but actually alerts the authorities to thwart the conspiracy. As such, she lacks the mens rea for a conspirator; she does not have the specific intent to achieve the target offense (burglary). One who only pretends to agree to the unlawful purpose to prevent the commission of the target offense is not guilty of conspiracy.

(A) Incorrect. convicted, because there was an agreement for an unlawful purpose, and an overt act was performed when the student bought the tools.

The friend lacked the mens rea necessary for a conviction of conspiracy. Thus, as to her, there was no agreement to do an unlawful act, so it does not matter whether an overt act was performed.

(B) Incorrect. convicted, because a private citizen may not assert the privilege of crime prevention available to police officers.

Civilians as well as police officers may claim the privilege of preventing crime. Therefore, this is a misstatement of law. Even more important, this defense is not really applicable here. A privilege is unnecessary, since the friend lacks the specific intent that would be part of the prima facie case of conspiracy.

(D) Incorrect. acquitted, because she alerted the authorities in time to frustrate the criminal goal of the conspiracy, thereby effectively withdrawing.

It is true that the friend's notification to the security guard prevented the crime of burglary from occurring. However, even if her efforts to thwart the crime had been unsuccessful, she would not be guilty of conspiracy, because she lacked the specific intent necessary for that crime. Since it is more accurate to say that the friend never entered into the conspiracy, a discussion of withdrawal as suggested by this choice is not the best answer.

Explanation: Question 79

The correct answer is: **(D)** acquitted, because he believed he was agreeing to recover the painter's diamond.

To be guilty of conspiracy, one must agree to achieve some unlawful purpose. If the goal of the conspiracy is a crime, the conspirators must have the same criminal intent as is necessary for conviction of the target offense. If the plumber's testimony is truthful, he did not intend to steal; he was trying to help the painter retrieve his own diamond, which the jeweler was improperly keeping from the painter. The plumber's mistake would negate the specific intent to steal, which is necessary both for burglary of the jewelry store and for conspiracy to commit that offense.

(A) Incorrect. convicted, because there was an agreement for an unlawful purpose, and an overt act in the preparation of the dark clothing and equipment sufficient to constitute a conspiracy.

A conspirator requires specific intent to commit the target offense. If the jury believes the plumber, it would accept his testimony about mistaken belief of fact as to the true ownership of the uncut diamond, and acquit him because he lacks the specific intent to steal that would support a burglary conviction.

(B) Incorrect. convicted, because criminal activity undertaken with laudable motives is still criminal.

This is an overly general statement. In analyzing criminal responsibility, the focus should be on the specific mental element for each charged offense. Here, the mens rea is lacking, as explained above. Thus, while this choice might technically be an accurate statement of law, it is inapplicable to the plumber because he did not commit a crime.

(C) Incorrect. acquitted, because he lacked the corrupt motive necessary for conviction of conspiracy.

Motive refers to the underlying reasons behind an intended act. To the extent that conspiracy is said to require a corrupt motive, it means that the goal of the conspiracy must be unlawful. Speaking precisely, a corrupt motive is not always required to form mens rea.

Explanation: Question 80

The correct answer is: **(B)** The actress should be found guilty, because she was stopped by the police just short of completing the charged offense.

To be guilty of attempt, the defendant must specifically intend the target offense, plus commit an act that constitutes a substantial step. The facts state that the actress was stopped while driving onto the street where her best friend's home was located, that the actress was armed with a shotgun, and that she intended to kill her best friend. This is sufficient to meet the requirement that she be in the zone of perpetration (beyond mere preparation). Since the actress intended to enter the property in order to shoot her best friend, the mens rea element of specific intent is satisfied.

(A) Incorrect. The actress should be found guilty, because the statute is a public safety measure, which she violated by arming herself with the shotgun.

This is a distractor. The statute does not prohibit merely being armed in public; it requires that the defendant have a specific intent while entering the property of another. Since this choice reaches the correct result based on faulty reasoning, it is not a good answer.

(C) Incorrect. The actress should be found not guilty, because she cannot be convicted simply of having a guilty mind.

The actress is not being convicted merely of having a guilty mind. There is an actus reus; the actress had engaged in an act constituting a substantial step. The actress had embarked upon commission of the proscribed offense and was stopped by the police just short of completion. She has clearly committed an attempt and may therefore be punished.

(D) Incorrect. The actress should be found not guilty, because the statute describes an attempt offense, and one cannot be convicted of attempting an attempt offense.

The statute prohibits physical entry for the purpose of committing the specified offenses. As noted above, the actress attempted to effectuate that entry, with the requisite mens rea. There is no rule of law that a defendant cannot be convicted of attempt as to an offense which itself describes an attempt offense. For example, it is possible to commit attempted burglary, even though burglary is itself defined in terms of having an intent to commit a future offense.

Explanation: Question 81

The correct answer is: **(A)** Guilty, because they agreed to rob the bank and performed an overt act in furtherance of the agreement.

Conspiracy is an agreement for an unlawful purpose. It requires a specific intent to accomplish the target offense, an agreement between two guilty minds, and in many jurisdictions, an overt act in furtherance of the conspiracy. All elements were met here. Both defendants in this question agreed to rob the bank, and this agreement was carried out. The fact that they were convicted in federal court of violating the federal bank robbery statute does not prevent a conspiracy charge. These are separate offenses for double jeopardy purposes.

(B) Incorrect. Not guilty, because the charge of conspiracy is always a lesser included offense of the target crime, such as bank robbery.

This choice is a misstatement of law. In order to be a lesser included offense, every material element of the lesser offense must be contained within the elements of the greater offense. Conspiracy is not a lesser included offense of the target crime, since conspiracy requires an agreement and most target crimes do not.

(C) Incorrect. Not guilty, because a prosecution for conspiracy to commit bank robbery after a conviction of bank robbery on the same facts constitutes double jeopardy.

The Fifth Amendment's prohibition against double jeopardy does not apply when separate sovereigns are involved, as here. A conviction in federal court will not trigger double jeopardy as to a conviction in state court, even if it involves exactly the same offense, because the federal government and each state government are separate sovereigns.

(D) Incorrect. Not guilty, because the federal prosecution bars a subsequent prosecution on the same facts in state court.

Because separate sovereigns are involved, double jeopardy is not violated. A federal prosecution does not bar one in state court, and vice versa, even if the same offense is involved.

Explanation: Question 82

The correct answer is: **(D)** guilty, because he knew the friend was armed and might attempt to evade arrest by use of the pistol.

The student is vicariously liable for the attempted murder committed by the friend, because both are co-conspirators. Since the two had been conspiring to violate drug laws, each is liable for crimes committed by the other in furtherance of the conspiracy. The attempted murder by the friend is imputed to the student because it was committed in furtherance of the conspiracy and was a reasonably foreseeable consequence of that conspiracy. Since both men were armed in order to resist any attacks by other drug deal participants, it was reasonably foreseeable to the student that the friend would use his pistol to resist arrest.

(A) Incorrect. not guilty, because the conspiracy had terminated upon the friend's arrest, and thus the student could no longer be vicariously liable for the friend's acts.

A conspiracy continues in effect until abandonment or success. An arrest of one co-conspirator does not automatically terminate the conspiracy, since other co-conspirators may continue to commit acts in furtherance of the conspiracy. That appears to be the case here, where the student was at the ice manufacturing site while the friend was being arrested.

(B) Incorrect. not guilty, because the friend acted outside the scope of the conspiracy when he shot the undercover officer.

The friend's violent resisting of arrest by shooting the undercover officer was within the scope of the conspiracy to violate the drug laws. The presence of the pistol was the result of the conspirators' anticipation of potential violence, and it is reasonable and logical to attribute to the conspirators a willingness to also violently resist capture by the police. Therefore, the use of weapons to shoot a police officer was a reasonably foreseeable consequence of the conspiracy.

(C) Incorrect. guilty, because he is criminally liable for any crime committed by his co-conspirator, the friend.

This choice goes too far in attributing vicarious liability to a co-conspirator. The student is liable only for crimes committed in furtherance of the conspiracy and that were a reasonably foreseeable consequence of the conspiracy. Thus, if the friend had attempted to rape the bartender, the student would probably not be vicariously liable, since such an act would not further any drug deals or prevent arrest, nor would it be a reasonably foreseeable consequence of a conspiracy to manufacture and sell drugs.

Explanation: Question 83

The correct answer is: **(C)** The defendant will be convicted of voluntary manslaughter, because the defendant's belief that her life was threatened was unreasonable.

This fact pattern presents an example of imperfect self-defense. Imperfect self-defense may mitigate murder to voluntary manslaughter where a defendant was either at fault in starting an altercation, or unreasonably, but honestly, believed that harm was imminent or that deadly force was necessary. In this case, the defendant honestly believed that her sister was going to kill her. However, her belief was unreasonable and thus, her crime will likely be mitigated to voluntary manslaughter.

(A) Incorrect. The defendant will not be convicted of a crime because she had a good faith belief that her life was in danger.

The defendant's good faith belief alone is not enough to relieve her of any kind of guilt in relation to the death of her sister. This situation presents an example of imperfect self-defense - imperfect self-defense may mitigate murder to voluntary manslaughter where a defendant was either at fault in starting an altercation, or unreasonably, but honestly, believed that harm was imminent or that deadly force was necessary. Therefore, since the woman had a good faith, but unreasonable, belief that her sister would kill her, she will most likely be deemed to have committed voluntary manslaughter.

(B) Incorrect. The defendant will be convicted of involuntary manslaughter, because the defendant honestly believed that her life was in danger.

Where a defendant kills a victim under the honest but unreasonable belief that the defendant's life was in danger (and therefore, the defendant was justified to use deadly force in self-defense), this may mitigate the defendant's crime from murder to voluntary manslaughter, not involuntary manslaughter. As such, this is not the correct answer choice.

(D) Incorrect. The defendant will be convicted of murder, because the defendant's life was not actually threatened.

Even if the defendant's life was not actually threatened, she would have been justified in using deadly force if she had had a reasonable belief of an imminent threat. It is only because her belief was unreasonable that it does not operate as a defense in this case. Moreover, note that where a defendant kills a victim under the honest but unreasonable belief that the defendant's life was in danger (and therefore, the defendant was justified to use deadly force in self-defense), this may mitigate the defendant's crime from murder to voluntary manslaughter. As such, the defendant in this case will most likely not be found guilty of murder, and this is not the correct answer choice.

Explanation: Question 84

The correct answer is: **(A)** she had effectively withdrawn from the conspiracy.

To withdraw from a conspiracy for vicarious liability purposes (note that the crime of conspiracy is complete upon agreement, but the woman is being prosecuted for murder, not for conspiracy to burglarize), the defendant must perform an affirmative act that would inform a reasonable person of the withdrawal and that, in fact, communicates the withdrawal to all co-conspirators in time for them to effectively abandon the conspiracy. The woman has met these elements since she indicated her refusal to proceed with the burglary before her two male friends had entered the store. Since she withdrew from the conspiracy, she is not vicariously liable for the murder subsequently committed by her two friends during the course of the burglary.

(B) Incorrect. she was not physically involved in the murder.

Under the traditional rule, all members of a conspiracy are liable for any crimes committed by any one or more members of the conspiracy if the crime was committed in furtherance of the conspiracy and was a reasonably foreseeable consequence of the conspiracy. Here, if the woman had not withdrawn, she would have been vicariously liable for the murder of the watchman because silencing him furthered the conspiracy (prevented its participants from being caught) and the death was reasonably foreseeable, since violence may have been needed to prevent capture, and suffocation is a foreseeable consequence of gagging.

(C) Incorrect. the result in the trial of her two male friends is res judicata as to her charge.

The doctrine of res judicata applies in civil, not criminal, trials. Therefore, the doctrine of res judicata would be inapplicable to the trial of the woman.

(D) Incorrect. she lacked the requisite mental state to be guilty of murder.

Where a conspirator is vicariously liable for the crimes committed by her co-conspirators, she need not meet the other elements of the involved crimes. The fact that the woman was not present, took no part in, and had no malice toward the watchman has nothing to do with her vicarious liability for his murder. Only by withdrawing from the conspiracy can she insulate herself from liability for the crimes of her former co-conspirators.

Explanation: Question 85

The correct answer is: **(C)** guilty, because the young man had, in fact, committed only a misdemeanor.

Deadly force may not properly be used to apprehend a fleeing misdemeanant, whether by a police officer or by a private citizen. If a police officer makes a reasonable mistake about whether a dangerous felony has been committed, or whether a particular person is a dangerous felon, the officer's mistaken use of deadly force is often excused. A private citizen does not enjoy the same protection; even a reasonable mistake about the basis for using deadly force robs the citizen of the privilege to use such force, and he is liable for a resulting homicide. Here, the young man was a shoplifter/misdemeanant who was not actually armed. The citizen was, therefore, not privileged to use deadly force to prevent his escape, even though the young man reasonably appeared to be an armed felon, and the citizen is criminally liable for the young man's homicide.

(A) Incorrect. not guilty, because he honestly believed that the young man was an armed, fleeing felon.

Any mistake about the actuality of a dangerous felony, the armed or dangerous nature of the felon, or the identity of the dangerous felon negates a citizen's privilege to use deadly force to prevent the escape of a dangerous felon. This choice suggests the opposite--that a good faith belief on the part of the citizen as to the requisites for use of deadly force is sufficient to insulate him from criminal liability for a resulting homicide. Since this is not true, this choice is incorrect.

(B) Incorrect. not guilty, because he honestly and reasonably believed that the young man was an armed, fleeing felon.

Any mistake, including a reasonable one, takes away the citizen's privilege to use deadly force against a dangerous felon. (This differs from a police officer's ability to use deadly force if she reasonably believes it necessary to apprehend a felon.) This choice suggests otherwise and is, therefore, inaccurate.

(D) Incorrect. guilty, because a private citizen may never use deadly force to prevent the escape of a criminal.

This choice goes too far in its statement of legal principle. If a dangerous felony has been committed and the use of deadly force is necessary to prevent the escape of the felon, a private citizen may use the same amount of deadly force as a police officer. The difference between the private citizen and the police officer is that the citizen is essentially strictly liable. If the private citizen is wrong and uses deadly force against someone who is not a fleeing felon, he will be criminally liable. A police officer, on the other hand, is privileged if he has a reasonable but incorrect belief that the person is a fleeing felon.

Explanation: Question 86

The correct answer is: **(B)** The woman is guilty of robbery and felony murder, and her friend is not guilty of any crime.

This choice is the correct answer because the woman killed the security guard while in the perpetration of an inherently dangerous felony--robbery. However, her friend would have no liability. The friend would only be liable for the two crimes if she acted as an accomplice. Here, the friend did assist in the commission of the crime because she did drive the old woman to the scene of the crime and probably would have helped her escape. However, to be considered an accomplice, the individual must provide assistance or encouragement with the intent that the crime be committed. Thus, in this case, the friend would not be considered the woman's accomplice because the friend did not intend to assist or encourage the commission of a robbery.

(A) Incorrect. The woman is guilty of robbery and felony murder, and her friend is guilty of larceny and involuntary manslaughter.

This choice tries to impose criminal liability on the friend, but she bears no criminal liability for robbery or the security guard's death. The friend could only bear responsibility as an accomplice. However, an accomplice must provide assistance or encouragement with the intent that the crime be committed. That is not the case here because the friend did not intend to assist or encourage the commission of a robbery.

(C) Incorrect. Both women are each guilty of robbery and felony murder.

This choice is incorrect because the friend does not have any liability. She did not directly take part, and she is also not an accomplice because she did not assist or encourage the woman with intent that the woman commit the crime.

(D) Incorrect. Both women are each guilty of robbery and voluntary manslaughter.

The woman is guilty of robbery and felony murder, but her friend has committed no crime. She did not assist or encourage the woman, intending that the woman commit a crime, so she is not an accomplice.

Explanation: Question 87

The correct answer is: **(D)** Murder, because the defendant acted with malice.

Murder is a homicide as to which the defendant acted with malice. Malice can consist of intent to kill, intent to seriously injure, wanton and willful misconduct, or felony-murder. Willful and wanton misconduct is behavior which creates a very high risk of death or serious bodily injury and is often described synonymously as recklessness. On these facts, the defendant manifestly created a very high risk when he fired his pistol aiming near, but not at, his cousin, since the possibility of a mis-aimed shot or a ricochet (as actually happened) was great and the consequences would be very serious. The defendant could be convicted of murdering his cousin even though he did not intend to kill or injure him.

(A) Incorrect. No crime, because the killing was clearly accidental.

A defendant may be exercising all due care and may kill through no fault of his own, in which case there is no crime. However, a defendant may act with negligence, with gross or criminal negligence, or with recklessness, and each level of risk-creation has different criminal penalties. If reckless, the defendant may be found to have acted with malice and be guilty of murder. If a defendant acts with gross negligence (also called criminal negligence), a resulting homicide is classified as involuntary manslaughter. Since the defendant was extremely reckless toward his cousin, the accidental killing is a murder, and this choice is incorrect.

(B) Incorrect. Involuntary manslaughter, because the defendant did not intend to kill or injure his cousin.

A defendant who kills without intending to do harm must have the wrongfulness of his conduct assessed on a continuum from reasonableness, to gross or criminal negligence, to extreme recklessness (wanton and willful misconduct). If the defendant acted reasonably, there is no crime. If the defendant acted with gross negligence, the homicide is classified as involuntary manslaughter. If the defendant engaged in wanton and willful misconduct, the homicide is murder. In this problem, the defendant's firing at his cousin was clearly more wrong than gross negligence, since the risk created was very high. Consequently, the homicide should be charged as murder rather than involuntary manslaughter.

(C) Incorrect. Voluntary manslaughter, because the defendant did not intend to kill or injure his cousin.

Voluntary manslaughter is an intentional killing where mitigation negates the presence of malice and reduces the classification of the homicide from what would otherwise be murder. Although the defendant intended to miss his cousin and, thus, cannot be said to have intended to kill or injure him, he engaged in wanton and willful misconduct without mitigation. Therefore, he should be charged with murder.

Explanation: Question 88

The correct answer is: **(A)** Conviction of murder.

The young man's actions would constitute murder under the laws of any state. Under the facts presented, the man's act at the very least constituted depraved heart murder, and may even have constituted first-degree, intent-to kill murder. Depraved heart murder is an illegal action that demonstrates a callous disregard for human life and results in death. Here, the man's act of designing the machine and orchestrating the fatal game certainly demonstrated a callous disregard for human life, and it did result in the death of one of the participants. Depraved heart murder is classified under the common law as second-degree murder. It is even arguable, however, that the man's act constituted first-degree murder, which is an intent to kill murder plus premeditation. The young man's act was certainly premeditated, in that he ordered parts for the machine from different places, in advance. Moreover, the young man intentionally planned that the game would continue until one of the participants activated the loaded pistol and was killed (or seriously injured), arguably demonstrating an intent to kill. Therefore, it is possible that the young man will be convicted of first-degree murder, rather than merely of depraved heart murder. In either case, however, the young man is almost certainly guilty of murder, in either the first or second degree. Therefore, this answer is correct.

(B) Incorrect. Conviction of involuntary manslaughter.

Involuntary manslaughter is the unlawful but unintentional killing of a human being without malice aforethought. There are two primary types of involuntary manslaughter: misdemeanor manslaughter, and criminally negligent manslaughter. In this case, however, the death did not result from the young man's commission of a non-felony act, nor was the death the result of mere negligence. Instead, the game involved deadly weapons and the almost certain death of one of the participants. Therefore, the young man's act will not be mitigated from murder to involuntary manslaughter, making this answer incorrect.

(C) Incorrect. Acquittal, because consent is a complete defense.

Consent by a victim is a valid defense only when it directly negates a specific element of the crime, as with rape. One cannot give legally valid consent to death or serious bodily injury. Therefore, this answer is incorrect.

(D) Incorrect. Acquittal, because the father's contributory negligence is a complete defense.

The father's conduct, no matter how negligent, would not be a superseding cause sufficient to excuse the young man's illegal act. Moreover, the negligence of others does not affect the young man's callous disregard for human life or his intent to kill. Therefore, this answer is incorrect.

Explanation: Question 89

The correct answer is: **(B)** The gun merchant entered his neighbor's home to retrieve his own shotgun, which he had earlier loaned to her and which she refused to return; he did not realize that he had mistakenly grabbed a different shotgun owned by the neighbor until after he had shot her.

The theory of the prosecution would be felony-murder because the killing occurred during a burglary. If the gun merchant intended to retrieve his own shotgun when he broke into and entered his neighbor's home, then he is not guilty of burglary (no felonious intent), so felony-murder cannot apply. This is a stronger argument than the other choices.

(A) Incorrect. After the neighbor hit him with the baseball bat, the gun merchant became so enraged that he lost control of his actions and shot her.

A homicide that occurs during the commission of a burglary is murder. Thus, the gun merchant cannot argue that the killing was done in the heat of passion after the neighbor hit him in the head with the bat. A felony murder can never be mitigated since the context of the killing (occurring during a specified felony), and not the mental state of the killer, determines the classification of the homicide as murder.

(C) Incorrect. When the neighbor tried to hit the gun merchant for the second time, he pulled the trigger of the shotgun accidentally when he tried to duck to avoid the bat.

The fact that the gun merchant pulled the trigger accidentally means he did not intend to kill anyone, but he is still liable for first-degree murder because he was committing a burglary, so the felony-murder rule applies. Therefore, these facts offer no defense.

(D) Incorrect. The gun merchant had to shoot his neighbor to prevent her from seriously injuring or killing him.

Under this fact pattern, the gun merchant still is guilty of felony-murder because the killing of the neighbor occurred during a burglary. The fact that the neighbor attacked the gun merchant with deadly force would not excuse or justify the merchant's use of force when the theory is felony-murder.

Explanation: Question 90

The correct answer is: **(D)** Yes, because the stockbroker was acting within the scope of his duties as president of the corporation.

Here, the stockbroker committed a felony while conducting what is clearly corporate business--arranging loans between investors and property owners. The corporation is therefore liable for the same offense.

(A) Incorrect. No, because it is impossible to imprison a corporation.

This is not the correct answer. At early common law, one justification for not holding a corporation liable for crimes committed by its agents was that it had no body which could be imprisoned. In modern times, the possibility of fines or other non-imprisonment sanctions has obviated the old common law rule. Corporations can be liable for criminal offenses, even though it is not possible to incarcerate a corporation.

(B) Incorrect. No, because a corporation cannot have the requisite wrongful mental state to be convicted of a crime.

This answer is incorrect. Although old common law doctrine held that a corporation had no mind, and thus could not possess a criminal mental state, the modern rule is that the wrongful mental state of the corporate agent is imputed to the corporation. Thus, corporations may be convicted of crimes if their agents have the requisite mens rea.

(C) Incorrect. Yes, but only if the stockbroker is first convicted of the offense in question.

This is not the best answer. It is true that a corporation can only act through its human agents, and so is criminally liable solely because of the acts of its agent. Therefore, it is necessary to prove that the acts of the agent constituted a crime in order to hold a corporation liable for the crime. However, it is not necessary that the agent be convicted of that crime first.

Explanation: Question 91

The correct answer is: **(D)** The jury believes the father's testimony and finds that the father's beliefs were reasonable, and acquits him of all homicide charges.

Even where there is no actual threat of deadly force against a defendant, if there reasonably appears to be such a threat, and the defendant honestly believes that he must defend himself with deadly force, a resulting homicide is justified. If the jury believed the father's testimony about his subjective beliefs, and further found that those beliefs were reasonable, the father would be guilty of no crime in the homicide of the umpire.

(A) Incorrect. The jury disbelieves the father's testimony and convicts him of involuntary manslaughter.

This choice is not correct on the facts. Involuntary manslaughter is an unintentional killing without malice aforethought. Conviction on involuntary manslaughter charges is not a plausible outcome on these facts. The facts state that the father left the area and returned, armed with a weapon, the baseball bat. He then deliberately resumed his argument with the umpire, which ended in the umpire's death by beating. A jury could not plausibly conclude that the father had no malice aforethought when the father left the vicinity, returned with a weapon, and--without provocation--behaved aggressively to the victim.

(B) Incorrect. The jury disbelieves the father's testimony and convicts him of voluntary manslaughter.

This answer is not the best choice. Voluntary manslaughter is an intentional homicide with extenuating circumstances that mitigate criminal liability to some degree. Voluntary manslaughter is a killing that is intentional but occurs in the heat of passion. Here, the father left the vicinity for about half an hour before returning to resume his argument with the umpire. The father had an adequate period to cool off, and, therefore, the heat of passion cannot mitigate his liability for his actions.

Note that if the jury believed that the father thought his life was in danger, voluntary manslaughter is a likely verdict. However, the choice states that the jury did not believe the father's testimony, so this is an incorrect answer choice.

(C) Incorrect. The jury believes the father's testimony and convicts him of first-degree murder.

This choice is not correct, although the jury may believe the father's testimony and still convict him of a crime if it finds that the father's belief that his life was in danger was not reasonable. If the defendant honestly believes that a deadly attack requires the use of deadly force in self-defense, but is unreasonable in so believing (i.e., a reasonable person in the same circumstances would not think deadly force was necessary in self-defense), a resulting homicide is no longer justified, but may be mitigated from murder to voluntary manslaughter.

In contrast, a conviction on first degree murder charges requires the jury to find that the defendant acted with malice and deliberation. If the jury believed the father's testimony regarding his fear for his life, then it would be a contradiction for the jury to also find that the father acted with malice and deliberation. Thus, this is an incorrect answer.

Explanation: Question 92

The correct answer is: **(B)** The hiker believed that the free-climb was probably too difficult for both of them but didn't want to appear afraid in front of the companion.

Although there is no general duty requiring one person to come to the aid of another in peril, there are circumstances in which such a duty does exist. Where the defendant places the victim in peril, where a special relationship exists between defendant and victim, or where the defendant gratuitously begins to render aid, and then discontinues aid, leaving the victim in greater peril, the defendant will be held criminally liable if his failure to give or continue aid results in the death of the victim. This question illustrates the second of the three categories, the special relationship basis. This choice is the only alternative in which no special relationship is suggested between the hiker and the companion; thus, the hiker had no duty to come to her aid and cannot be criminally liable for that omission. However, if the hiker realized beforehand that the free-climb was probably beyond the companion's abilities and proceeded anyway, he has engaged in gross negligence which, since it resulted in the companion's death, is also a criminal homicide. In each of the other choices, a special relationship created a duty to aid the companion that increased the hiker's criminal liability.

(A) Incorrect. The companion was a 16-year-old pupil in the hiker's private school, and they were out that day on a school mountain-climbing exercise.

Schools have a special relationship with their pupils such that if the pupils are in peril, aid must be given, even if the school did not create the danger. Criminal liability for failure to act when a duty to rescue exists is based, as in more ordinary circumstances, on the mental state of the defendant. If the situation is such that the defendant knows his failure to act is sure to result in the death of the victim, or is substantially certain to lead to such a result, the defendant is liable for murder, since his mental state is equivalent to an intent to kill. If there is no substantial certainty of death, but a very high risk of death or serious injury, the defendant who fails to rescue has acted with wanton and willful misconduct and is again liable for murder. If the circumstances create a high degree of risk, greater than ordinary negligence, the defendant will be liable for involuntary manslaughter. On the facts of this question, a free-climb on a vertical rock face 1,000 feet up a mountainside would present a danger of almost certain death, or at least a very high risk of death, to a climber with no safety equipment who lost her grip due to exhaustion. Where the hiker has a duty to rescue and ignores it, he is guilty of murder.

(C) Incorrect. The hiker and the companion were married to each other.

This answer choice is incorrect. Criminal liability can be imposed on a defendant for an omission to act where there is a legal duty to act and the defendant can physically perform the act. Such a legal duty may arise based on a relationship, such as spouses who are married to each other. Failure to rescue when that omission means almost certain death for the victim is equivalent to intent to kill with malice, and classifies the resulting death a murder, not involuntary manslaughter. Here, the hiker was watching his companion slip off the rock, although he refused to throw the safety line to her. His failure to act was almost certain to result in death, and it did. As such, his conduct rose above criminal negligence (which would have resulted in involuntary manslaughter, rather than murder).

(D) Incorrect. The hiker was a professional mountain climber whom the companion had hired to guide her up the mountain.

This answer is not correct because under the circumstances it describes, the defendant would be guilty of murder, not involuntary manslaughter. The proprietor-customer relationship, at least where the businessperson assumes a responsibility for more than merely selling goods to the customer, is sufficient to create a duty to rescue the customer from peril. Failure to fulfill that duty under circumstances which present a substantial certainty of death to the victim is the equivalent of a homicide committed with malice, and is, therefore, a murder.

Explanation: Question 93

The correct answer is: **(B)** He honestly believed that the designer was unmarried.

The psychologist could only be guilty of bigamy if he actually knew circumstances that would render the other person (the designer) guilty of bigamy (see section 3 of the statute). This choice indicates that the psychologist honestly believed that the designer was unmarried, regardless of how preposterous that belief appears. Therefore, he lacked the mental element of knowledge, whether his belief was reasonable or not. He is not guilty of bigamy.

(A) Incorrect. He reasonably believed that the designer was unmarried.

This is not the correct answer. Whenever a criminal statute requires knowledge as the mental state, the fact that a reasonable person would have discovered the requisite knowledge is immaterial if the defendant actually did not do so. (While it may be possible for a defendant to be intentionally ignorant under circumstances where the court will consider such ignorance equivalent to guilty knowledge, these facts do not describe such a situation.)

(C) Incorrect. He made reasonable inquiries as to the designer's marital status.

This answer is not correct because it implies that the psychologist had a duty to gain actual knowledge of the designer's marital status or be guilty of bigamy, and that is not the case. The statute says the psychologist is guilty of bigamy if he knew that the designer was married. He had no such knowledge, and he had no duty to investigate. Thus, an assertion that the psychologist made reasonable attempts to ascertain the designer's marital status is not a defense to a bigamy charge. Whenever a criminal statute requires knowledge as the mental state, the fact that a reasonable person would have discovered the requisite knowledge is immaterial if the defendant actually did not do so. The psychologist's guilt or innocence hinges on his knowledge, not the diligence of his investigation.

(D) Incorrect. He asked the designer about her marital status and she claimed to be unmarried.

This is not the correct answer. If the psychologist learned that the designer was a married woman, the psychologist would be guilty of bigamy, regardless of the designer's misrepresentations. The fact that the designer lied about her marital status is irrelevant if the psychologist knew, or discovered, that she lied and was already married.

Explanation: Question 94

The correct answer is: **(B)** A state statute providing that the failure to have a current valid inspection sticker on a vehicle is a misdemeanor.

Four categories of crime are likely to be strict liability offenses: regulatory offenses, public welfare offenses, morality crimes, and selling liquor to a minor. A requirement that a vehicle have a valid inspection sticker is a public welfare statute. Two major factors which indicate that a defined crime is a public welfare offense (and, therefore, treated as imposing strict liability) are: 1) that the penalty is not severe; and 2) that the harm to the public from the prohibited behavior is serious. The crime described in this choice--operating a vehicle on public roads without a valid inspection sticker--is only a misdemeanor, and the harm to the public that could result from violation is very serious. It is most likely that a violator would be subject to strict liability--that is, liable without fault or a showing of bad intent.

(A) Incorrect. A city ordinance making it an infraction, for which a $100 fine is payable, to trespass upon the property of another that is posted as private property.

This is not the correct answer. There are four categories of crime that are likely to be strict liability offenses: regulatory offenses, public welfare offenses, morality crimes, and selling liquor to a minor. An ordinance requiring citizens to respect posted property rights does not fit into any of these categories. Therefore, a trespasser would not necessarily be liable just because she set foot on posted property. Instead, a prosecutor enforcing this ordinance against a trespasser would need to show that the trespasser had intended to enter the posted property with knowledge that she was trespassing.

(C) Incorrect. A state statute providing that it is a felony punishable by two, three, or four years in prison to carry a concealed knife whose blade is longer than three and one-half inches.

This answer is incorrect. In general, proof of requisite intent must be established for crimes, with only a few exceptions that carry strict liability. The strict liability crimes are: regulatory offenses, public welfare offenses, morality crimes, and selling liquor to a minor. The only strict liability category into which this crime arguably fits is public welfare offense. However, a crime is a public welfare offense only if: 1) the penalty is not severe; and 2) the harm to the public from the prohibited behavior is serious.

In this case, the severity of the punishment probably disqualifies the offense from the category of public welfare offenses, and therefore strict liability would not apply. Instead, a prosecutor would need to show that the defendant had the requisite intent to violate the statute.

(D) Incorrect. A federal statute which provides that any person who files an income tax return containing false information has committed a felony punishable by imprisonment for five years and up to $5,000 in fines.

This is not the best answer. Of the four categories of crime that carry strict liability--regulatory offenses, public welfare offenses, morality crimes, and selling liquor to a minor--only public welfare offense is arguably applicable to making false statements on a federal tax return. However, two major factors indicate that a defined crime is a public welfare offense: the penalty is not severe and the harm to the public from the prohibited behavior is serious.

Here, the severe punishment associated with the defined crime of filing a false income tax return renders it unlikely that this would be considered a public welfare offense. Where the consequences of violation are serious, some wrongful intent or fault is necessary to support a conviction. Thus, conviction under this statute requires a showing that the defendant knew the statements were false when he made them.

Explanation: Question 95

The correct answer is: **(B)** not guilty, because she lacked the necessary mental state.

The teacher has been charged with knowingly making a false statement while under oath. If the teacher's current testimony is believed, then she lacked the criminal intent required by the perjury statute. When a defendant lacks the mens rea for the charged offense, it is irrelevant whether the mistake that negates mens rea is one of fact or law, and the mistake need not even be reasonable. Therefore, this is a better answer than the other choices, which improperly limit the kind of mistake that can negate the mens rea.

(A) Incorrect. not guilty if the jury also finds that her mistaken interpretation of the effect of commutation was reasonable under the circumstances.

This is not the correct answer. The teacher's belief that the commutation of her sentence wiped out the conviction for forgery, even though unreasonable, prevents her from having the mental state necessary for conviction of perjury--knowing falsehood. Because she believed what she was saying was true (in the cross-examination following her alibi testimony in the first trial), she cannot be guilty of perjury as defined.

(C) Incorrect. guilty, because her mistake was one of law.

This answer is incorrect. The teacher's mistake of law does result in a finding of not guilty of perjury; since the teacher believed what she was saying was true, then she lacked the mens rea for perjury. She is not relying on the affirmative defense of mistake of law, which would not help her. Rather she is arguing that, because of her mistake, the prima facie elements of perjury are not met.

(D) Incorrect. guilty, because it was unreasonable of the teacher to assume that commutation negated her forgery conviction without consulting an attorney.

This answer is incorrect. The teacher has been charged with knowingly making a false statement while under oath. Any kind of mistake, reasonable or unreasonable, can negate the mens rea for the offense of perjury as defined in this problem. The teacher's belief that the commutation of her sentence wiped out the conviction for forgery, even though unreasonable, prevents her from having the mental state necessary for conviction of perjury--knowing falsehood.

Explanation: Question 96

The correct answer is: **(C)** the statute is so defined as to indicate that the legislature intended only the recipient of the property, money, or services to be punished.

Based on the given wording from the statute, only the recipient and not the giver appears to be within the intended scope of that statute. Where a crime is based upon a transaction necessarily involving at least two people, and the legislature includes only one of them within the operation of the statute, this is an indication that the legislature intended that the other person (or class of persons) not be punished by the statute. The statute at issue mentions only the recipient of the property, money, or services—the driver's license examiner. The driver's best argument is that he is outside the statute's scope.

(A) Incorrect. only a driver's license examiner can commit the crime defined by the subject statute.

This is not the best answer. Even though a crime may only be committed by a particular class of persons, accessories not within that class may be convicted of aiding and abetting. For example, common law rape may be committed only by a man against a woman, yet if a second woman holds the victim or threatens the victim with force to overcome the victim's objections, the second woman may be convicted of committing rape as an aider and abettor.

(B) Incorrect. he cannot be convicted of committing a crime as to which he is the victim.

This is not the correct answer. It is generally true that the victim of a crime may not be convicted of aiding and abetting the principal in the first degree. For instance, a minor female may not be convicted of aiding and abetting a statutory rape even though she consented to the act of sexual intercourse. It is not clear that the statute in this problem was intended to protect the examinee. It can be argued with equal justification that the statute was intended to protect all citizens from driver's license examiners who corruptly permit incompetent drivers to obtain driver's licenses.

(D) Incorrect. he did not assist the driver's license examiner in violating the subject statute.

This answer choice is incorrect on the facts. The driver offered the examiner the $1,000 in exchange for a good driving test result. The examiner accepted the bribe, in violation of the statute. The examiner would not have taken or accepted the money if the driver had not offered it. Clearly the driver assisted the examiner in violating the subject statute, therefore, this is a poor argument in favor of dismissal of the charges against the driver.

Explanation: Question 97

The correct answer is: **(C)** The defendant should be convicted of both charges.

At common law, rape is unlawful sexual intercourse with a woman without her consent. If the defendant establishes that he reasonably believed that the woman had given consent, he is not guilty of rape. In this question, the circumstances clearly indicate that any consent by the young woman was obtained by threat of force. Therefore, she did not provide consent and the defendant is guilty of rape. As to the statutory rape charge (defined as sexual intercourse with a female who has not attained a certain age, younger than 18 in this case), as implicitly recognized by this choice, the defendant should be convicted because, in a majority of jurisdictions, even a reasonable mistake as to the age of a minor is no defense to a charge of statutory rape.

(A) Incorrect. The defendant should be convicted of statutory rape, but not rape, because she consented.

There is no reason why the defendant cannot be convicted of both rape and statutory rape. The defendant had sexual intercourse with the young woman without her consent, and, thus, he is guilty of rape. The fact that she submitted to the sexual act is not proof of her consent, because that submission was a result of the defendant's threat.

(B) Incorrect. The defendant should be convicted of rape, but not statutory rape, because he reasonably believed that the young woman was over the age of consent.

Most jurisdictions do not consider it a defense to statutory rape that the defendant reasonably believed that the victim was over the age of consent. Thus, the fact that the defendant might reasonably have believed that the young woman was 18 or older would not preclude his being convicted of statutory rape.

(D) Incorrect. The defendant should not be convicted of either charge.

In this case the defendant committed both rape and statutory rape. He had sexual intercourse with the young woman without her consent, which means he is guilty of rape. Additionally, the fact that the young woman was younger than the age of consent means he is guilty of statutory rape.

Explanation: Question 98

The correct answer is: **(A)** Arson and burglary.

The writer is guilty of both arson and burglary. Burglary is the entry of a protected structure (at common law a dwelling at night) with the intent to commit a felony therein. The burglary was completed when the writer first entered the house of the editor with the intent to burn it down. Arson is the burning of the dwelling house of another with malice. (Malice is either the intent to burn the dwelling house of another or wanton and willful misconduct that creates a plain and strong likelihood that such a structure will be burned.) The arson was completed when the structure of the house was burned by the fire. The subsequent change of heart does not absolve the defendant of guilt for either crime, once the necessary elements have been met. This is a favorite MBE trick. The arsonist (or burglar) who later repents is still an arsonist (or burglar) on the MBE.

(B) Incorrect. Attempted arson and burglary.

The writer completed the crime of arson when he burned the ceiling of the editor's home. The fact that he later repaired the damage had no relevance to his guilt for arson and does not alter the completed crime to one of attempt (but might affect his punishment).

(C) Incorrect. Burglary only.

The defendant committed both burglary and arson, because he burned and charred the structure. When a person burns the dwelling of another with malice, he is deemed to have committed arson. In this case, the defendant completed the crime when he burned the structure of the house.

(D) Incorrect. Arson only.

The answer is correct in that it states that the defendant committed arson, but he also committed burglary. He broke and entered the dwelling house of another with the intent to commit a felony, which in this case was arson. He is, therefore, guilty of burglary as well, and this answer is incorrect.

Explanation: Question 99

The correct answer is: **(B)** No, because he did not have the requisite intent to commit a felony when he broke and entered the home.

The welder is not guilty of burglary, because the crime of burglary requires an intent to commit a felony in the structure that the defendant enters. Here the defendant intended acts that do not amount to a felony in the jurisdiction in which the structure is located. Therefore, he lacked the mens rea for burglary. When evaluating intent for burglary purposes, remember that a defendant intends acts--not legal labels. Look at the intended acts--not what defendant thinks about the felonious quality of those acts.

(A) Incorrect. No, because he was prevented from accomplishing his intention and was not charged with attempt.

The crime of burglary is complete when the defendant breaks and enters while intending to perform an act inside a dwelling house of another which constitutes a felony. It is immaterial whether the target felony is actually completed. Thus, if the act the welder intended--compelling his wife to have sexual intercourse against her will--had been a felony in State B, the welder would have been guilty of burglary as soon as he broke and entered the sister's house. Since this choice reaches the correct result based on faulty reasoning, it is not the correct answer.

(C) Incorrect. Yes, because he broke and entered the dwelling house of another, at night, with the intent to commit what he believed was a felony.

In order to be guilty of burglary, the defendant must intend acts that constitute a felony when he breaks and enters the protected structure. The act that the welder intended to commit inside the house was not a felony in State B, and, thus, he cannot be convicted of burglary, even though he mistakenly believed that what he intended to do was a crime.

(D) Incorrect. Yes, because the factual impossibility of the intended felony is not a defense to a charge of burglary.

Factual impossibility refers to the situation where the objective sought to be achieved by the defendant is proscribed by the criminal law, but because of facts unknown to the defendant when he attempts to commit the target offense, he is unable to complete that offense. This problem presents an example of legal impossibility, where the act intended to be committed by the defendant is not a crime. Legal impossibility is a defense to a criminal charge based on the defendant's intent to commit an act that he mistakenly believes is a crime. Thus, although this choice states an accurate principle of general law, it is inapplicable to this question, and, thus, is incorrect.

Explanation: Question 100

The correct answer is: **(B)** embezzlement.

Embezzlement is the fraudulent conversion of property by one in rightful possession of the property. Under these circumstances, the neighbor would be guilty of embezzlement because the violinist entrusted the dog to the neighbor and then the neighbor caused the violinist to be permanently deprived of the dog as a result of his sale to the breeder.

(A) Incorrect. larceny.

Larceny is a trespassory taking and carrying away of tangible personal property of another with the intent to permanently deprive the owner thereof. In this case, the neighbor is not guilty of larceny because, originally, he obtained possession of the dog with the violinist's consent. There was no trespassory taking in this case. Therefore, he did not commit larceny.

(C) Incorrect. obtaining property by false pretenses.

Obtaining property by false pretenses is a crime where a false representation of a present or material fact by the defendant causes the victim to pass title to the property to the defendant who knows the representation to be false and intends to thereby defraud the victim. The neighbor is not guilty of obtaining property by false pretenses because, among other reasons, he never obtained title to the dog. The violinist only transferred possession of the dog to the neighbor until she returned from Europe. Thus, the neighbor did not commit this crime.

(D) Incorrect. larceny by trick.

Larceny by trick is a form of larceny whereby the defendant obtains possession of the personal property of another by means of a representation or promise that he knows is false at the time he takes possession. In this case, the neighbor did not make any representations or promises that he knew to be false at the time he took possession. Therefore, he did not commit larceny by trick.

1. ELEMENTS OF CRIMES

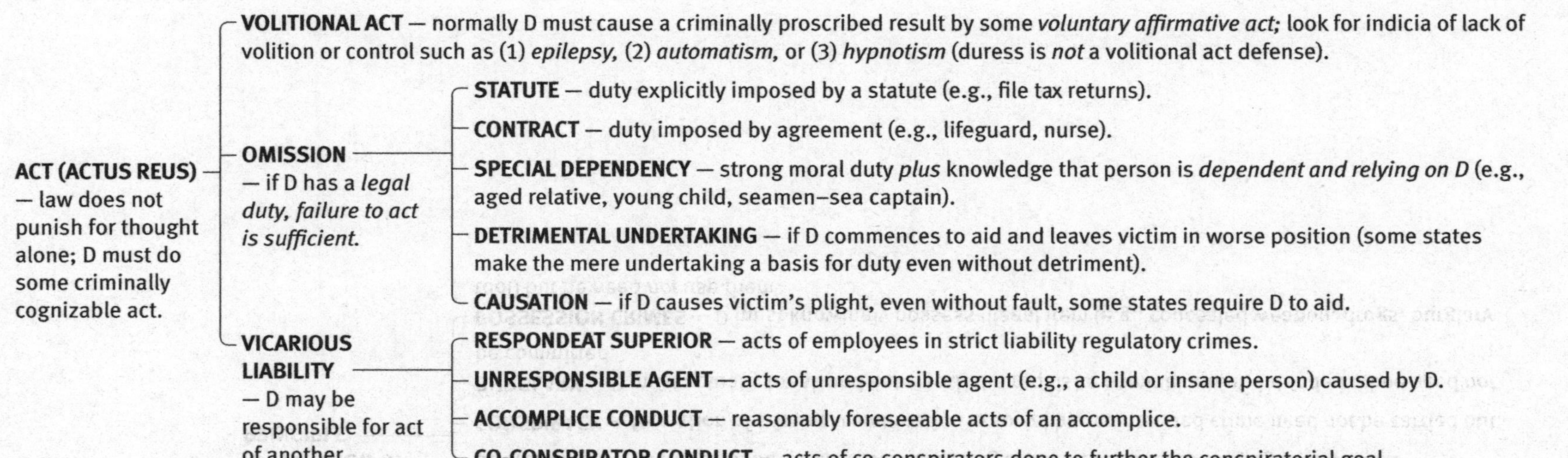

- **ACT (ACTUS REUS)** — law does not punish for thought alone; D must do some criminally cognizable act.
  - **VOLITIONAL ACT** — normally D must cause a criminally proscribed result by some *voluntary affirmative act;* look for indicia of lack of volition or control such as (1) *epilepsy,* (2) *automatism,* or (3) *hypnotism* (duress is *not* a volitional act defense).
  - **OMISSION** — if D has a *legal duty, failure to act is sufficient.*
    - **STATUTE** — duty explicitly imposed by a statute (e.g., file tax returns).
    - **CONTRACT** — duty imposed by agreement (e.g., lifeguard, nurse).
    - **SPECIAL DEPENDENCY** — strong moral duty *plus* knowledge that person is *dependent and relying on D* (e.g., aged relative, young child, seamen–sea captain).
    - **DETRIMENTAL UNDERTAKING** — if D commences to aid and leaves victim in worse position (some states make the mere undertaking a basis for duty even without detriment).
    - **CAUSATION** — if D causes victim's plight, even without fault, some states require D to aid.
  - **VICARIOUS LIABILITY** — D may be responsible for act of another.
    - **RESPONDEAT SUPERIOR** — acts of employees in strict liability regulatory crimes.
    - **UNRESPONSIBLE AGENT** — acts of unresponsible agent (e.g., a child or insane person) caused by D.
    - **ACCOMPLICE CONDUCT** — reasonably foreseeable acts of an accomplice.
    - **CO-CONSPIRATOR CONDUCT** — acts of co-conspirators done to further the conspiratorial goal.
- **INTENT (MENS REA)** — criminal law focuses on the *culpability* (e.g., blameworthiness) of D by examining his *state of mind with regard to the criminal consequence* (see Mens Rea JIG).
  - **PURPOSEFUL** — if D does an act with the *conscious object of causing the criminal result.*
  - **KNOWING** — if D does an act *consciously aware of the fact that a criminal result is practically certain.*
  - **RECKLESS** — if D is *consciously aware of the fact that his act creates a substantial and unjustifiable risk that a criminal result will occur.*
  - **NEGLIGENT** — if D *creates an unreasonable risk that a criminal result will occur.*
  - **VOLUNTARY** — if D does a *volitional act which causes a criminal result* (i.e., strict liability).

(continued)

1. ELEMENTS OF CRIMES *(continued)*

- **CAUSATION** — D's act must cause the particular result proscribed by the definition of the crime.
  - **PROXIMATE CAUSE** — must be the *cause-in-fact* with *no unforeseeable intervening causes.*
    - **CAUSE-IN-FACT**
      - **"But For"** — but for D's act the result would not have occurred when it occurred.
      - **Substantial Factor** — even if not "but for," D's act was a *substantial factor* or an *independently sufficient cause* of the result.
    - **INTERVENING CAUSES** — D normally acts on a "set stage" including unforeseeable abnormalities of victim, but if an *unforeseeable independent act intervenes* between D's act and the criminal result, *D is not responsible.*
  - **APPLICATION OF PRINCIPLE**
    - **HOMICIDE** — D must cause the death of another human being within one year of act.
    - **FALSE PRETENSES** — D's misrepresentation must cause V to give up title to property (i.e., V must *rely* on misrepresentation).
    - **ATTEMPT** — D need *not* cause intended result, manifested culpability is sufficient.
    - **SOLICITATION** — D need *not* be successful in inducing another, act of encouraging is sufficient.
    - **CONSPIRACY** — formation of criminal combination is social harm, intended crime need *not* be carried out.
    - **BURGLARY** — D must actually break and enter with the requisite criminal intent, intended crime need *not* be committed.
    - **POSSESSION CRIMES** — D must knowingly possess illegal item (e.g., concealed weapon, drugs, burglary tool) but he need *not* use them.

2. MENS REA

ISSUE SPOTTING SEQUENCE

(1) ***What state of mind is required by the crime charged?***

(2) ***What was D's state of mind with regard to the criminally proscribed consequence at the time he did the act causing that consequence?***

(3) ***Are there any special facts negating D's culpability (i.e., any mens rea defenses)?***

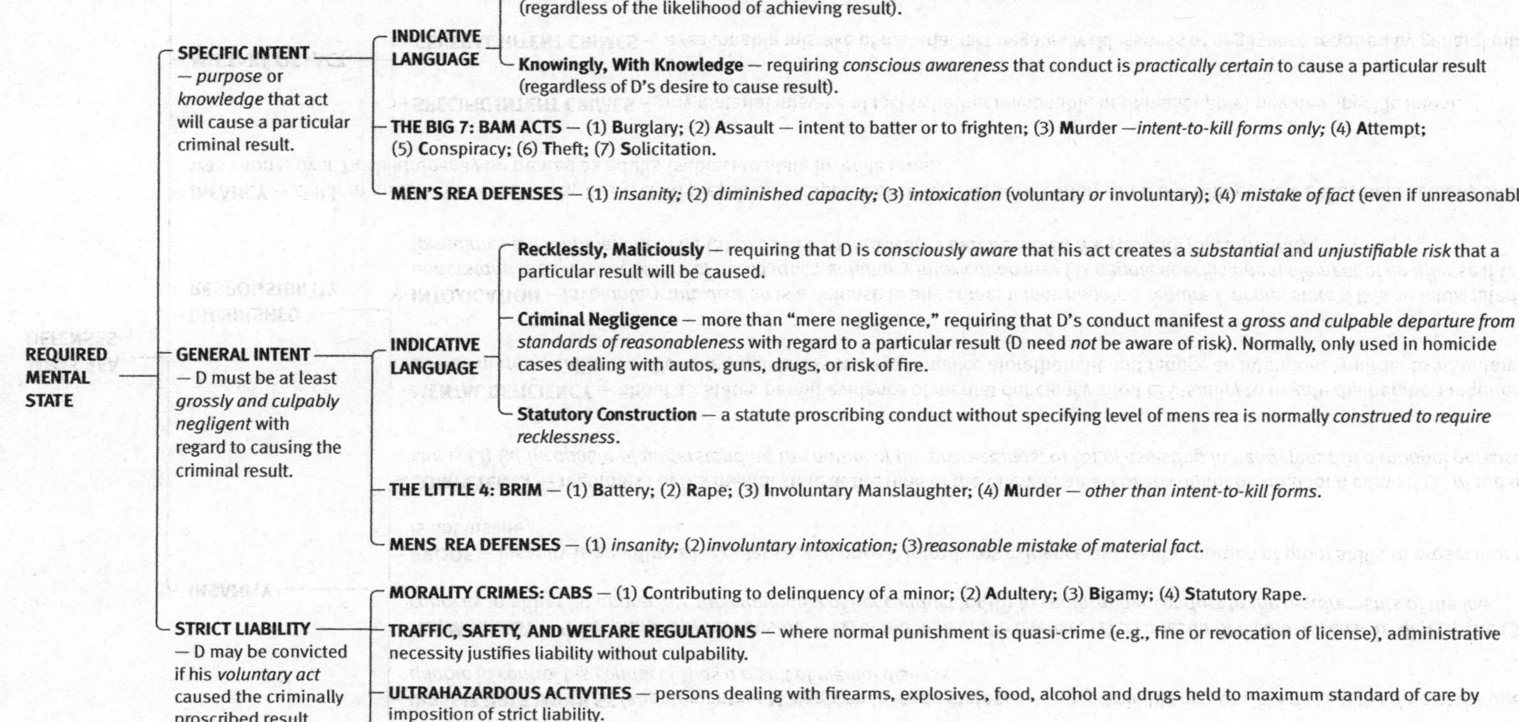

- **REQUIRED MENTAL STATE**
  - **SPECIFIC INTENT** — *purpose* or *knowledge* that act will cause a particular criminal result.
    - **INDICATIVE LANGUAGE**
      - **Intentional, Deliberate, Willful (Purposeful)** — words requiring an act with the *conscious object* to cause a particular result (regardless of the likelihood of achieving result).
      - **Knowingly, With Knowledge** — requiring *conscious awareness* that conduct is *practically certain* to cause a particular result (regardless of D's desire to cause result).
    - **THE BIG 7: BAM ACTS** — (1) **B**urglary; (2) **A**ssault — intent to batter or to frighten; (3) **M**urder —*intent-to-kill forms only;* (4) **A**ttempt; (5) **C**onspiracy; (6) **T**heft; (7) **S**olicitation.
    - **MEN'S REA DEFENSES** — (1) *insanity;* (2) *diminished capacity;* (3) *intoxication* (voluntary *or* involuntary); (4) *mistake of fact* (even if unreasonable).
  - **GENERAL INTENT** — D must be at least *grossly and culpably negligent* with regard to causing the criminal result.
    - **INDICATIVE LANGUAGE**
      - **Recklessly, Maliciously** — requiring that D is *consciously aware* that his act creates a *substantial* and *unjustifiable risk* that a particular result will be caused.
      - **Criminal Negligence** — more than "mere negligence," requiring that D's conduct manifest a *gross and culpable departure from standards of reasonableness* with regard to a particular result (D need *not* be aware of risk). Normally, only used in homicide cases dealing with autos, guns, drugs, or risk of fire.
      - **Statutory Construction** — a statute proscribing conduct without specifying level of mens rea is normally *construed to require recklessness.*
    - **THE LITTLE 4: BRIM** — (1) **B**attery; (2) **R**ape; (3) **I**nvoluntary Manslaughter; (4) **M**urder — *other than intent-to-kill forms.*
    - **MENS REA DEFENSES** — (1) *insanity;* (2)*involuntary intoxication;* (3)*reasonable mistake of material fact.*
  - **STRICT LIABILITY** — D may be convicted if his *voluntary act* caused the criminally proscribed result.
    - **MORALITY CRIMES: CABS** — (1) **C**ontributing to delinquency of a minor; (2) **A**dultery; (3) **B**igamy; (4) **S**tatutory Rape.
    - **TRAFFIC, SAFETY, AND WELFARE REGULATIONS** — where normal punishment is quasi-crime (e.g., fine or revocation of license), administrative necessity justifies liability without culpability.
    - **ULTRAHAZARDOUS ACTIVITIES** — persons dealing with firearms, explosives, food, alcohol and drugs held to maximum standard of care by imposition of strict liability.
    - **MENS REA DEFENSES** — none, strict liability requires only a voluntay act.
- **DETERMINING MENTAL STATE**
  - **PRESUMPTION** — D is *presumed* to intend to cause the *natural and probable consequences* of his conduct.
  - **EVIDENCE OF INTENT** — look for direct statements by D or circumstantial evidence (such as motive) which tend to indicate D's state of mind with respect to the criminally proscribed consequences.

(continued)

2. MENS REA *(continued)*

MENS REA DEFENSES

- **INSANITY**
  - **M'NAGHTEN TEST (majority rule)** — D not criminally responsible if (1) *at the time of the offense* D was (2) *laboring under such a defect of reason from a disease of the mind* as (3) *not to know* (a)*the nature and quality of his act* or, if he did know it, (b) *he did not know that the act was wrong.*
  - **IRRESISTIBLE IMPULSE (supplementary M'Naghten in many states)** — D not criminally responsible if (1) *at the time of the offense*, D (2) *was unable to control his conduct* (3) *as a result of mental disease.*
  - **ALI/MPC TEST** — D not criminally responsible if (1) *at the time of the offense*, (2) *as a result of mental disease or defect*, she (3) *lacks substantial capacity* to either (a) *appreciate the criminality of her conduct*, or (b) *to conform her conduct to the requirements of the law.*
  - **PROOF** — insanity is an affirmative defense, but once D introduces evidence of insanity, burden of proof shifts to prosecutor to show D is not insane.
  - **COMPETENCY** — regardless of D's mental state at the time of the offense, an accused *cannot be tried* for a crime if (1) *at the time of trial*, she is (2) (a) *incapable of understanding the nature of the proceedings*, or (b) *of assisting in her defense in a rational or reasonable manner*.
- **DIMINISHED RESPONSIBILITY**
  - **MENTAL DEFICIENCY** — about 12 states permit evidence of mental deficiency short of insanity to negate deliberation requirements of first degree murder; California allows mental illness to negate malice aforethought and reduce an intentional murder to voluntary manslaughter.
  - **INTOXICATION** —*involuntary intoxication* is a defense to any crime; it *may negate a required mental state* if D is so intoxicated that *he did not understand the criminal nature of his conduct; voluntary intoxication* may (1) *negate specific intent element of an offense* if (2) *before he formulates the criminal intent* he (3) *becomes so intoxicated that he lacked the capacity for culpability.*
- **INFANCY** — children under 7 cannot crimes; 7–14, child presumed incapable of crime, but prosecution can rebut with evidence that child actually understood his conduct was wrong; over 14 children may be treated as adults (subject to state juvenile laws).
- **MISTAKE OF FACT**
  - **SPECIFIC INTENT CRIMES** — any material mistake of fact (whether reasonable or unreasonable) negates specific intent.
  - **GENERAL INTENT CRIMES** — a reasonable mistake of material fact negates recklessness or negligence required by general intent crime.
- **MISTAKE OF LAW** — generally no defense, but MPC allows defense if (1) D *reasonably* relied upon *official interpretation* of a law which was *later declared invalid*; (2) *without fault, D was not apprised of administrative rule;* (3) *if knowledge of legal status is an element of the offense;* or (4) where statute *requires an affirmative act*.

3. ATTEMPTS

D is guilty of an attempt to commit a crime if: (1) with the *specific intent to cause a criminal result,* he (2) *does some legally sufficient act toward the commission of* the intended crime.

SPECIFIC INTENT — D must be either purposeful or knowing with regard to causing the result proscribed by the underlying crime; always look for specific intent defenses, especially intoxication and exculpating mistake. Remember, specific intent is required for all attempts, even if substantive crime is strict liability (e.g., attempted bigamy).

SUFFICIENT ACT — must be beyond mere preparation; a question of law for the judge.

- **LAST ACT** — the *last act* required of D is always sufficient, even if subsequent acts of another are necessary (e.g., P puts poison in V's pills on nightstand).
- **UNEQUIVOCAL ACT** — if D's act *unequivocally manifests criminal intent* it is sufficient (very often even the last act does not do this, however).
- **CORROBORATING ACT** — best view focuses upon the significance of D's act in *demonstrating that D had the firm and present intent to commit the crime* (under this view the act must corroborate the existence of firm intent).

IMPOSSIBILITY

- **FACTUAL IMPOSSIBILITY** — *if crime would have resulted had the facts been as D thought they were, impossibility is no defense*: (1) *inherently inadequate instrumentality* (D mistakes sugar for poison); (2) *error in time or place* (D attempts to "pick" an empty pocket, or kill a person already dead). Factual impossibility is based upon a mistake which does *not* negate culpability (i.e., D is worse than he appears).
- **LEGAL IMPOSSIBILITY**
  - **STATUS OF GOODS** — some courts hold that D cannot be guilty of an attempt to possess stolen property if property possessed is not in fact "stolen" (i.e., true owner consented to use of property to apprehend D). Under this view, a mistake as to the legal status of a thing provides a valid defense. Most courts and MPC treat this as factual impossibility (rather than legal impossibility) and deny the defense.
  - **INTENDED RESULT IS NOT ILLEGAL** — if D believes an act is illegal but it is not, he cannot be guilty of an attempt simply by doing that act since the conduct actually intended is not regarded as socially harmful, thus, D must manifest a willingness to do an act actually proscribed by law.
  - **DEFINITION OF CRIME EXCLUDES D** — if, according to the definition of a crime, it is impossible for D to commit the substantive offense, there can be no attempt by D.

ABANDONMENT — crime of attempt is complete once a legally sufficient act has been committed, but some courts and MPC allow a defense if D (1) *voluntarily abandons the criminal act* (2) *prior to completion of the substantive crime* (3) *under circumstances manifesting a complete renunciation of criminal intent*. Look for extrinsic causes of withdrawal which are *not defenses* (e.g., fear of apprehension, selection of a different victim, etc.)

4. CONSPIRACY

(1) Agreement* between (2) *two or more persons* (3) who have the *specific intent* (4) to either (a) *commit a crime* or (b) to *engage in dishonest, fraudulent or immoral conduct injurious to public health or morals.

AGREEMENT — there must be a *true agreement* to promote or facilitate a particular objective

- **AGREEMENT SUFFICIENT** — at common law, the agreement itself is the only act required to complete the crime; federal and about half of states now require some *additional overt act* in furtherance of the conspiracy (although the act need not be illegal in itself and only one conspirator need do an act).
- **PROOF** — agreement may be inferred from concert of action (look for mutual adoption of a common purpose).
- **FALSE AGREEMENT** — secret police agent or other "false agreement" situations are not conspiracies — there must be true actual intent to carry out unlawful objective by at least two parties. (MPC is contra; party with true intent is still liable).
- **UNKNOWN CONSPIRATORS** — D must agree with at least one other person but need *not* agree with (or even know identity of) all other members of the conspiracy.
- **SINGLE OR MULTIPLE CONSPIRACY** — the agreement is the essence of conspiracy; thus, there is only one conspiracy even if agreement encompasses separate diverse criminal acts and even if agreement entails a continuous course of criminal conduct.

TWO OR MORE PERSONS

- **STATUS DEFENSE TO SUBSTANTIVE CRIME** — if D conspires with B, it is no defense to either party that D may not be capable under the legal definition to commit underlying crime himself (e.g., a man cannot rape his own wife).
- **DIPLOMATIC IMMUNITY** — that one party is immune from prosecution is no defense to other party.
- **DIMINISHED CAPACITY DEFENSES** — if B, the only other conspirator, possesses a diminished capacity defense negating specific intent (e.g., intoxication, infancy, insanity), a few courts preclude conviction of D as well as B; better view including MPC permits convictions of D regardless of B's *personal mens rea defenses*.
- **ACQUITTAL ON MERITS** — if B, the *only* other conspirator, is acquitted *on the merits* (i.e., not because of procedural or personal mens rea defenses), D may not be convicted.
- **HUSBAND-WIFE** — today, D may conspire with a spouse (not so at old common law).
- **WHARTON'S RULE**
  - **Consent Crimes** — if crime logically requires the voluntary participation of another (e.g., bribery, incest, adultery, gambling), there is no conspiracy unless agreement involves *an additional person not logically essential.*
  - **Plurality Required by Substantive Crime** — if substantive crime requires a number of participants (e.g., 5 or more conducting gambling operations), there can be no separate charge of conspiracy *unless* agreement involves persons who are not guilty of the substantive crime itself.
  - **Model Penal Code** — abandons Wharton's Rule.

4. CONSPIRACY *(continued)*

SPECIFIC INTENT — D must have the specific intent with regard to a criminal objective.

- **MENS REA DEFENSES APPLY** — D may assert any mens rea defenses which negate specific intent.
- **PURPOSEFUL AGREEMENT** — it is always sufficient that D enters the agreement with the conscious object of causing, promoting or facilitating a result which he knows to be criminal.
- **CORRUPT MOTIVE DOCTRINE** — many states require that D actually had a *corrupt motive* (that he knew that intended conduct was illegal) except where the act is inherently wrong.
  - **Mere Knowledge** — normally not sufficient, but conviction is possible if: (1) goods supplied are *highly dangerous* (e.g., explosives), or *highly regulated* (e.g., drugs); (2) the crime is *very serious* (e.g., homicide, kidnapping); (3) there is *continuous involvement*, or (4) if D *affirmatively encouraged* use more of his goods when he had reason to know that the use was illegal.
  - **Knowledge Plus Stake** — D may be convicted if he *knows* that his goods or services are used for a criminal purpose *and* he has a *"stake" in the success of the criminal objective* (e.g., D charges an inflated price).

CONSPIRATORIAL OBJECTIVE

- **CRIME** — it is a conspiracy to agree to commit any crime, including a misdemeanor.
- **PUBLICLY INJURIOUS ACT** — it is a conspiracy to agree with another to do any act (even if lawful) which is injurious to public health or morals and is accomplished by dishonest, fraudulent, corrupt or immoral means (MPC and some states are *contra* limiting conspiracies to "crimes").

DEFENSES

- **ABANDONMENT** — once a conspiracy has been formed, it is no defense that D subsequently withdrew, even if done prior to the completion of the underlying crime. (MPC and some states *contra*, but only if D: (1) completely renounces criminal purpose, *and* (2) makes substantial efforts to prevent the commission of the underlying crime.)
- **IMPOSSIBILITY** — factual impossibility is not a defense though D may prevail if the conspiratorial objective is simply not illegal, regardless of D's contrary belief.

(continued)

4. CONSPIRACY *(continued)*

SPECIAL CONSEQUENCES

- **SEPARATE OFFENSE** — conspiracy is a separate offense, distinct from the underlying crime (i.e., there is no merger).
- **VENUE** — a criminal charge may be brought in any county where some act in furtherance was committed by any party, *or* where the agreement was made.
- **HEARSAY EVIDENCE** — in a trial for conspiracy, otherwise inadmissible hear say statements of co-conspirators are admissible against D if *made in furtherance of the conspiracy*.
- **VICARIOUS LIABILITY**
  - **General Rule** — in addition to conspiracy and the substantive crime intended, D may be convicted of other crimes committed by members of conspiracy *in furtherance of conspiratorial goal* (it is no defense that D did not intend nor know of the acts.)
  - **Chain Conspiracy** — if D is part of a "chain" of known illegal acts (e.g., smuggling–wholesaling–retailing of drugs), he is liable for all crimes committed to further the conspiratorial goal (look for *"community of interest"*).
  - **Wheel Conspiracy** — if D conspires with B and B enters into similar separate and unrelated agreements for similar crimes with X and Y, B is the "hub" of a "wheel conspiracy;" if there is a *community of interest* so that D, X, and Y are interested in the success of each other's agreements with B, there is a "rim" connecting all the "spokes" in *one conspiracy* and all parties are liable for the criminal acts of the others. If there is no community of interest, there are 3 separate conspiracies and only B is liable for the acts of all others (as well as for 3 conspiracies).

ATTEMPTED CONSPIRACY (SOLICITATION) — one who attempts to induce, encourage or command another to commit a crime is guilty of solicitation; if the other person agrees there is conspiracy.

DURATION — vicarious liability lasts until the goal of the conspiracy is achieved (including *immediate escape*) or D withdraws by informing all co-conspirators. (In many states, D must make some substantial effort to prevent the crime.)

5a. CRIMINAL HOMICIDE ISSUES

Issue Spotting Sequence: (1) Is D responsible for an *act* causing the death? (2)Was D's act the *cause* of the death? (3) Was the act directed at *another* person? (4) Was the person *living* at the time of the act? (5) Did D possess a *criminal intent* with respect to the death? (6) Was there any *legal justification*?

ACT

- **Voluntary Affirmative Act** — act is sufficient even if it is itself lawful and/or inherently non dangerous. If immediate killing act was involuntary due to epileptic seizure or sudden unconsciousness, look to see whether the last voluntary act done by D was done with awareness of possibility of loss of control .
- **Omission** — death caused by D's failure to do an act he had a *legal duty* to do as the result of: (1) special statute, (2) contractual delegation, (3) special relationship of dependency, (4) voluntary undertaking (if abandonment puts victim in worse position) or (5) D's innocent act imperils victim.
- **Vicarious Liability** — D is responsible for homicidal acts of: (1) unresponsible agents put into motion by D, (2) accomplices—if act was reasonably foreseeable, and (3) co-conspirators—if act was done in furtherance of the conspiratorial goal (whether it was foreseeable or not).

CAUSE

- **Cause-in-fact**
  - **But For** — D's act was a necessary condition of result; "but for" the act, the victim would have lived longe r.
  - **Independently Sufficient** — even if not the "but for" cause, D's act was sufficient in itself to produce result.
  - **Substantial Factor** — even if not either the "but for" cause or an independently sufficient cause, D's act was at least a substantial factor in producing result.
- **Proximate Cause**
  - **Outside Time Limit** — at common law, the victim must die within a year and a day of the injury inflicted by D. Modern states extend time up to 3 years.
  - **Pre-existing Conditions** — D "takes his victim as he finds him" and acts on a "set stage," therefore, even unknown and unforeseeable pre-existing conditions which contribute to V's death do *not* intervene to break the chain of causations. Though D is criminally responsible for the direct results of his c onduct from a causation stand point, unusually unforeseeable conditions may create a mens rea defense.
  - **Intervening Causes** — a separate event or act which occurs between D's cause-in-fact conduct and the death will *supersede* D's act and break the chain of causation if the intervening act or event was: (1) *Independently sufficient* to cause the death, (2) *unforeseeable*, and (3) an *independent* act of god or another person not directly and logically flowing from D's act. (Some courts will also relieve D of responsibility if the intervening force was *dependent*). Failure of intervening rescue does *not* break the chain of causation.

(continued)

5a. CRIMINAL HOMICIDE ISSUES *(continued)*

DEATH OF ANOTHER — suicidal acts and attempts are not sufficient for homicide though many states separately punish attempted suicides especially if they endanger or injure innocent persons.

LIVING PERSON

- **Unborn Infants** — a victim has to be "born alive" and separated from its mother before homicide responsibility can arise. Some courts hold that a "viable" unborn fetus is a person for homicide purposes if it was sufficiently developed to be capable of living independently from its mother. State has right to declare a fetus "alive" after the first trimester of pregnancy. *Roe v Wade.*
- **Comatose Victims** — death occurs at the moment all bodily functions permanently cease, and not before. Because of life sustaining equipment that can support biological life and minimal body functions long after irreparable deterioration of the brain, the notion of "brain death" is a possible alternative.

CRIMINAL INTENT — homicide crimes are "graded" in terms of the culpability of D with respect to the death (See Flowchart 5A) but the following mental states are sufficient for some form of criminal homicide.

- **Specific Intent to Kill** — D has the specific intent to kill if he is either *knowing* or *purposeful* with regard to the death. This includes willful, deliberate, premeditated and deliberate killings. Unless justified, all intentional killings are either murder or voluntary manslaughter. Intent to kill is an express form of malice aforethought.
- **Unintentional Killings** — D can be guilty of criminal homicide even if there was no intent to kill at the time of the death-causing act. Unintentional killings may either be murder or manslaughter but intent is criminal if D: (1) *intends to cause great bodily harm, a forcible felony or resist a known lawful arrest*, (sufficient states for implied malice aforethought and, therefore, murder), (2) was *reckless* with regard to the death (wanton reckless disregard for human life is an extreme form sufficient for murder), (3) was *criminally negligent* with regard to the death, *or* (4) *intends to commit a malum in se unlawful act* (or inherently dangerous crime) not amounting to a forcible felony.

5a. CRIMINAL HOMICIDE ISSUES *(continued)*

LEGAL JUSTIFICATION (See Flowchart 7)

- **Self Defense** — at the time of the act D (1) *reasonably believed* (2) that the *amount of force used was necessary* to protect himself from (3) *imminent* (4) *great bodily harm or death*. D may not be aggressor and, in minority of states, he must retreat before using deadly force if he knows he can do so with complete safety (except in his own home).
- **Defense of Other** — D's act was (1) done *in defense of another person* and (2) the *person defended had a legal right to use the same amount of force used by D*. D "stands in the shoes" of the person defended and his conduct is judged in terms of actual facts. MPC, N.Y., and modern view permit defense if D reasonably believed that person defended would have been legally justified in using the force employed by D. Some states require person defended to be a close relative.
- **Prevention of Crime** — D's act was intended to (1) *prevent commission of a forcible felony* (e.g., burglary, arson, robbery, rape, kidnapping, felonious assault) which (2) was *actually being committed* and (3) the *force used was reasonably believed necessary*. MPC, N.Y., and modern view judge D in terms of his reasonable belief about the commission of the felony, not the actual facts.
- **Apprehension of Dangerous Felon** — D's act was (1) *done to effectuate an arrest or prevent escape* of a person who (2) *actually* (3) had *committed a forcible felony*, (4) the *force used reasonably appeared to be necessary*, and (5) the *act did not unreasonably endanger innocent bystanders*. If D is a peace officer his conduct will be judged in terms of his reasonable belief as to the commission of the underlying felony, not by the actual facts.
- **Necessity** — D's act was (1) *done to prevent imminent loss of life* (2) under circumstances where *according to ordinary standards of intelligence and morality* (3) the *harm sought to be avoided outweighed the harm caused by the act.*
- **Defenses not available** — deadly force is *not* justified on a theory of *duress, entrapment, defense of property* (though if victim was committing a burglary or robbery prevention of a forcible felony justifies a killing); or *consent* ("mercy killing" or euthanasia is not a recognized defense but it can mitigate sentencing).

5b. HOMICIDE CRIMES

MURDER — Unlawful killing with malice aforethought, no degrees of murder at common law.

- **Intent to Kill** — Includes both *purposeful* (conscious object) and *knowing* (practically certain) killings. Specific intent defenses available to negate mens rea. Under modern statutes, if intent to kill is supplemented by *deliberation* and *premeditation* (mental states revealing a relatively calm, "cold-blooded," reflective killing as opposed to a sudden, impulsive or spontaneous killing). If victim does not die, D is guilty of attempted murder.
- **Unintentional Killing — Wanton Reckless Disregard for Life** — Unintended killing resulting from an act done with a *conscious and knowing* disregard of a *plain and strong likelihood* that an *unjustified death or serious injury will result*. Any facts which negate conscious awareness of the risk may prevent mens rea (but voluntary intoxication may not negate recklessness). More than "mere recklessness;" act must reveal a wanton depraved indifference to human life. If victim does not die, no attempted murder since no specific intent to kill.
- **Unintentional Killing — Intent to Cause Great Bodily Harm (GBH)** — Unintended killing resulting from an act done with the purpose or knowledge that it cause *serious protracted injury* or create a *substantial risk of death* (very similar to recklessness). Includes any intentional wounding with a gun or knife, breaking of bones, clubbing, poisoning or an act designed to produce unconsciousness by drugs or violence. Intent to do GBH may be negated by mistake, extreme intoxication, and in minority, by diminished mental capacity. If victim does not die, no attempted murder. Under modern statutes unintended death resulting from *intentional use of poison or explosives, torture*, or *ambush* (lying in wait) is first degree.
- **Unintentional Killing — Intent to Resist Known Lawful Arrest** — Unintended killing resulting from act done in resistance of a *known lawful arrest*. D must actually know that the arrest is under lawful authority and mens rea defenses may negate that knowledge. If victim does not die, no attempted murder.
- **Unintentional Killing — Intent to Commit a Felony** — Unintended killing proximately caused by and during the commission of a felony or an attempted felony. Wide state variations as to the *nature of the underlying felony* (most limit to forcible felonies — burglary, arson, robbery, rape, kidnapping), the *degree of offense* (usually first degree), and *special limitations* (usually as to the status of the killer or victim). *No* attempted murder if victim does not die.
  - **Special Limitations** — modern view permits felony murder (FM) only if D or a criminal accomplice directly kills the victim and where victim is an innocent person (not an accomplice)
  - **Underlying Felony Must be Proved** — any defense to the underlying felony (e.g., claim of right to a burglary or robbery) absolves D of FM responsibility.
  - **Perpetration** — felony includes period from attempt (i.e., act beyond preparation) through immediate flight until final rest.

5b. HOMICIDE CRIMES *(continued)*

VOLUNTARY MANSLAUGHTER
An intentional murder "mitigated" by facts negating malice aforethought.

- **Intentional Killing — Provocation** — Intentional killing done in the *heat of passion caused by legally sufficient provocation* (actual or threatened battery or perceived infidelity — *not mere words*). Provocation must be such that it might render a reasonable ordinary person to lose self-control and act rashly. "Cooling off" period between provocation and killing act destroys defense. Normal range of physical and temperamental defects are *not* taken into account but extreme disabilities of a permanent nature *may* be considered by a liberal court. Modern trend is to liberalize types of legally sufficient provocation and focus on culpability; MPC allows any "extreme emotional disturbance" regardless of cause. If victim does not die, some courts hold D for *attempted voluntary manslaughter;* others only for felonious assault.
- **Intentional Killing — Mistaken Justification** — Intentional killing done with an *actual* but *unreasonable or erroneous* belief that the act was legally justified. Includes use of excessive force, unreasonable belief that harm was imminent, error as to the rights of a person being defended, etc. — called *imperfect self-defense*. If victim does not die, some convict of attempted voluntary manslaughter; others felonious assault.
- **Intentional Killing — Diminished Capacity** — While most states allow evidence of mental defect short of insanity and extreme intoxication to negate the "premeditation" aspect (reducing a charge to second degree murder), a small minority go further and permit a showing of diminished mental capacity to *negate malice aforethought* and reduce the charge to voluntary manslaughter. Diminished capacity applies only to homicide charges.

(continued)

5b. HOMICIDE CRIMES *(continued)*

INVOLUNTARY MANSLAUGHTER
An unintentional unlawful killing without malice aforethought.

- **Unintentional Killing — Ordinary Recklessness** — Unintended killing resulting from an act done with a *conscious disregard* for a *substantial* and *unjustifiable* risk of *death or serious injury* but one that does *not* demonstrate a wanton depraved indifference to human life. The distinction between ordinary recklessness resulting in involuntary manslaughter and depraved recklessness resulting in murder is merely a question of degree to be determined as an issue of fact.
- **Unintentional Killing — Gross and Culpable Negligence** — Unintended killing resulting from a negligent act which reveals a wanton disregard of the risk of death or serious injury. More than ordinary negligence, it must be *gross* and *culpable* but it is *not* required that the prosecutor prove that D was consciously aware of the risk (compare to recklessness). Normally deals with mishandling of an *inherently dangerous instrumentality* (e.g., guns, explosives, automobiles), *product* (e.g., food and drugs) or *situation* (e.g., risk of fire in a public place).
- **Unintentional Killing — Unlawful Act Rule** — Unintended killing proximately caused by and during the commission or attempted commission of a *malum in se* (i.e., wrong in itself) misdemeanor or felony (*if* jurisdiction limits FM rule to forcible felonies). Sometimes called the misdemeanor-manslaughter rule. Many states apply rule only to *inherently dangerous crimes* or *non-dangerous crimes committed in an unusual and inherently dangerous manner*. Look for this possibility whenever FM fails.
- **Unintentional Killing — Provocation and Mistaken Justification** — Unintended killing resulting from an *act only intended to wound or frighten* done in the heat of passion with *legally sufficient provocation* or in *an honest but erroneous belief that the force used was legally justified*, (compare to voluntary manslaughter where the intent was to kill).

6. COMMON LAW BURGLARY

(1) Trespassory (2) breaking and (3) entering (4) a dwelling (5) in the nighttime (6) with specific intent to: (a) commit a larceny or (b) any felony (7) therein.

TRESPASSORY — entry must be without consent, but entry gained by misrepresentation of identity or other trick is trespassory.

BREAKING — D must use force to create an opening for his entry. In many states, unlawful "remaining in a store after closing is a constructive breaking, through common law requires that the breaking must be done to gain entry, not exit. Some states abandon the breaking requirement entirely.

ENTERING — D must physically intrude victim's property.
- **D'S BODY** — any portion of D's body is sufficient.
- **INSTRUMENT** — any tool or hook invading the property is sufficient if it is used to achieve the criminal purpose (as opposed to using it to merely gain entry).

DWELLING — structure must be a place where one *normally* sleeps (though it need not be occupied at the time of entry).
- **INCLUDES CURTILAGE** — structures immediately surrounding the dwelling (e.g., enclosed in the area of the "yard") and physically connected buildings.
- **INCLUDES BOATS AND TRAILERS WHERE PEOPLE SLEEP**
- **MODERN STATUTES EXTEND TO ALL "ENCLOSED STRUCTURES" ABANDONING THE DWELLING REQUIREMENT**

NIGHTTIME — entry must occur 30 minutes before sunset or after sunrise. This requirement is *abandoned under modern "breaking and entering" statutes*.

SPECIFIC INTENT
- **LARCENY**
  - **Intent to Commit Any Larceny is Sufficient (even if petty larceny)**
  - **Be Sure all Elements of Larceny are Specifically Intended:** (1) trespassory taking, (2) carrying away, (3) personal property, (4) known to be owned by another, (5) intent to permanently deprive. The claim of right defense is particularly likely to arise, if it does, there is no burglary.
- **ANY FELONY** — intent to commit *any* felony is sufficient, but look for defenses to the underlying felony.

THEREIN — D must intend to commit the crime *in the dwelling* (or enclosed structure); it is not sufficient that D broke and entered only to get to another place.

7. JUSTIFICATION FOR THE USE OF FORCE

SELF-DEFENSE — if D has a (1) *reasonable fear* of (2) *imminent* (3) *bodily harm* he may use (4) that amount of force which is *reasonably necessary* to prevent the harm (5) unless D is an *aggressor*.

- **REASONABLE FEAR** — D must *actually* and *reasonably* believe that V is threatening imminent bodily harm (belief need not be correct).
- **IMMINENT HARM** — *D must believe harm is imminent* although D may seize last reasonable opportunity to defend himself if V attempts to deprive him of the capacity for self-defense (as where V attempts to tie D up and torture him later). Note: If threat of harm is past, D has no right of self-defense.
- **BODILY HARM** — "self-defense" is not available to prevent or respond to insults regardless of how offensive or vile, *use of force justified only to prevent a reasonably anticipated battery.*
- **NECESSARY FORCE** — *short of deadly force*, D may use that amount of force that is *reasonably necessary to prevent the threatened harm;* if D uses *excessive force*, he becomes an aggressor and loses the right of self-defense.
  - **DEADLY FORCE** — (1) *force intended to cause death* or (2) *force creating a substantial likelihood of causing great bodily harm* (including death).
  - **RECIPROCITY** — D may only use deadly force to respond to deadly force.
  - **RETREAT RULE (minority)** — D may not use deadly force if he *actually knew he could have prevented the harm by retreating.*
    - **D must subjectively believe that he could retreat in complete safety.**
    - **D need not retreat from his own home (many states include any place of nightly repose and some include offices and automobile).**

AGGRESSOR LIMITATION

- **AGGRESSOR** — D is an aggressor if (1) *he strikes* the first blow or (2) *commits a crime against V.*
- **REGAINING RIGHTS OF SELF-DEFENSE** — aggressor regains the right to use forc e in self-defense if (1) *he abandons aggression completely and V actually perceives the abandonment*, or (2) *V uses excessive force.*

DEFENSE AGAINST UNLAWFUL ARREST — D may use reasonable, non-deadly force to prevent an unlawful arrest or unlawful attac hment of her property, but she acts at her own risk; the arrest or attac hment must, in fact, be unlawful or the defense is denied. (Modern view prevents all use of force to resist any arrest, even if unlawful.)

7. JUSTIFICATION FOR THE USE OF FORCE *(continued)*

DEFENSE OF OTHERS — in defending another person (V) from imminent injury, D is justified in using only the amount of force which V could use in his own defense; D stands in the shoes of V and if V was, in fact, the aggressor, the force used by D is not privileged. (MPC and modern trend allow D's conduct to be measured by the reasonable person standard — if D reasonably believed the force used was justified, the defense is valid.)

DEFENSE OF PROPERTY — modern day *non-deadly* force may be used to prevent theft, destruction or trespass of property. If deadly force was used, look to see whether it could be justified as *self-defense* (e.g., as where D shot an armed robber) or *to prevent a dangerous forcible felony* (e.g., as where D shot a burglar intruding into his home).

LAW ENFORCEMENT DEFENSES — police officers and private citizens may use force in preventing crimes and effectuating an arrest. Normally, courts are more liberal in allowing force to *prevent* a crime (especially a felony) than in an after-the-crime arrest.

- **POLICE** — may use amount of force, *including deadly force*, which *reasonably appears necessary* as long as force is *not disproportionate* to the offense involved or the resistance offered (Some states limit use of deadly force to prevent commission of a dangerous forcible felony or apprehension of a dangerous fleeing felon.)
- **CITIZEN** — may use the same amount of force as police officer except *D acts at his own risk;* defense is denied if D is mistaken about the commission of the crime. (MPC and modern trend test D's conduct by reasonable person standard.)

NECESSITY — force, including deadly force, is justified to avoid an (1) imminent public or private injury, (2) resulting from natural physical forces, (3) which injury is about to occur through no fault of the actor and which is (4) of such gravity that (5) according to ordinary standards of intelligence and morality (6) the desirability of avoiding the injury clearly outweighs the state's interest in preventing the proscribed conduct.

8. CRIMINAL LAW

ACQUISITION BY STEALTH, FORCE, OR THREAT

LARCENY — (1) trespassory (2) taking and (3) carrying away of (4) personal property (5) known to be another's with (6) the intent to permanently deprive.

- **TRESPASSORY** — taking by stealth or force.
- **TAKING OF POSSESSION (caption)** — D must take possession and acquire dominion and control; there can be no larceny if D already has lawful possession.
- **CARRYING AWAY (asportation)** — larceny complete when D carries the property away from the point of taking; slight movement is sufficient.
- **PERSONAL PROPERTY** — D must take tangible personal property at common law, but most states have special statutes for theft of services and other intangibles.
- **OF ANOTHER** — D must specifically know the property is owned by another; any bona fide claim of right is a complete defense. Also look for mens rea defenses of mistake or intoxication.
- **INTENT TO PERMANENTLY DEPRIVE** — D must intend to *permanently* deprive the owner of the property *at the time of the taking;* no larceny if D intends to restore the identical property taken, but intent is sufficient if D: (1) intends to pay a cash equivalent at a later time, (2) intends to return only if a reward is paid, or (3) recklessly exposes property to loss.

ROBBERY — (1) larceny (be sure all elements are present) (2) from a person (3) accomplished by force or putting in fear (i.e., threat). Includes threat to person, his family, or his property.

- **FROM A PERSON** — taking from the "presence" of a person is sufficient if force or threat was needed to sever the property from the person's control.
- **FORCE OR THREAT** — must precede or accompany the taking. *Armed robbery* is an aggravated form where D uses a weapon or an article designed to look like a weapon.

EXTORTION — statutory extension of common law robbery consisting of (1) the use of malicious threats with the (2) specific intent to (3) compel a person to either (a) pay money, or (b) do or refrain from doing any act against his will (commonly referred to as "blackmail").

- **INJURY** — includes threats to injure V or his family or to injure V's property.
- **ACCUSATION** — includes threats to charge or prosecute V with a crime (whether or not V actually committed the crime) if used to cause V to do an act or pay money; claim of right is no defense.
- **DISGRACE** — includes threats to expose V to disgrace or extreme humiliation.
- **NEED NOT BE IMMEDIATE** — unlike robbery, the threat need not relate to an immediate harm.

8. CRIMINAL LAW *(continued)*

ACQUISITION BY FRAUD OR TRICK

OBTAINING PROPERTY BY FALSE PRETENSES — (1) *acquisition of title* (not mere possession) of (2) personal property (3) by means of a representation of fact (*not* a promise of future performance) (4) known by D to be false (5) at the time of acquisition.

- **TITLE** — the owner must intend to convey permanent unfettered possession (i.e., title) to D in a *sale* or *trade* transaction.
- **REPRESENTATION** — unlike larceny by trick, it is *not* sufficient that D makes a false promise; there must be misrepresentation of a present or past *fact* or there is no crime.
- **SCIENTER** — D must know of the falsity of the representation at the time of acquisition.
- **RELIANCE** — owner must actually rely on D's misrepresentation.

LARCENY BY TRICK — (1) taking of possession (not title) of (2) personal property (3) known to be owned by another (4) with the intent to permanently deprive (5) where such taking is accomplished by means of a representation or promise (6) known by D to be false (7) at the time of the taking.

- **POSSESSION** — the owner must intend to convey only temporary possession to D in a *rental, loan,* or *bailment* transaction.
- **REPRESENTATION** — includes misrepresentation of past or present facts *and* a false promise to return the property.
- **SCIENTER** — D must actually know the representation or promise was false at the time of the taking.
- **RELIANCE** — owner must actually rely on D's misrepresentation or D is only liable for attempt.

CONVERSION

LARCENY BY CONVERSION — same as larceny by trick except that there is *no false representation;* the intent to permanently convert the property for D's own exclusive use must be formed *after* the lawful acquisition of possession in a rental, loan, or bailment situation.

EMBEZZLEMENT — a variation of larceny by conversion developed to deal with (1) the improper use (i.e., conversion) of (2) property (3) entrusted to D's custody; there is no need for the intent to permanently deprive and no need for a misrepresentation.

- **CONVERSION** — D need only apply the property to a *personal use* to be guilty, regardless of the intent to restore or even the actual restoration of the property.
- **PROPERTY** — by some statutes includes title to real property.
- **ENTRUSTMENT** — D must have acquired custody of the property as a result of a special fiduciary relationship (e.g., trustee, agent, employee).

Criminal Procedure

Practice Questions

Answer Grid

1 Ⓐ Ⓑ Ⓒ Ⓓ	11 Ⓐ Ⓑ Ⓒ Ⓓ	21 Ⓐ Ⓑ Ⓒ Ⓓ	31 Ⓐ Ⓑ Ⓒ Ⓓ	41 Ⓐ Ⓑ Ⓒ Ⓓ
2 Ⓐ Ⓑ Ⓒ Ⓓ	12 Ⓐ Ⓑ Ⓒ Ⓓ	22 Ⓐ Ⓑ Ⓒ Ⓓ	32 Ⓐ Ⓑ Ⓒ Ⓓ	42 Ⓐ Ⓑ Ⓒ Ⓓ
3 Ⓐ Ⓑ Ⓒ Ⓓ	13 Ⓐ Ⓑ Ⓒ Ⓓ	23 Ⓐ Ⓑ Ⓒ Ⓓ	33 Ⓐ Ⓑ Ⓒ Ⓓ	43 Ⓐ Ⓑ Ⓒ Ⓓ
4 Ⓐ Ⓑ Ⓒ Ⓓ	14 Ⓐ Ⓑ Ⓒ Ⓓ	24 Ⓐ Ⓑ Ⓒ Ⓓ	34 Ⓐ Ⓑ Ⓒ Ⓓ	44 Ⓐ Ⓑ Ⓒ Ⓓ
5 Ⓐ Ⓑ Ⓒ Ⓓ	15 Ⓐ Ⓑ Ⓒ Ⓓ	25 Ⓐ Ⓑ Ⓒ Ⓓ	35 Ⓐ Ⓑ Ⓒ Ⓓ	45 Ⓐ Ⓑ Ⓒ Ⓓ
6 Ⓐ Ⓑ Ⓒ Ⓓ	16 Ⓐ Ⓑ Ⓒ Ⓓ	26 Ⓐ Ⓑ Ⓒ Ⓓ	36 Ⓐ Ⓑ Ⓒ Ⓓ	46 Ⓐ Ⓑ Ⓒ Ⓓ
7 Ⓐ Ⓑ Ⓒ Ⓓ	17 Ⓐ Ⓑ Ⓒ Ⓓ	27 Ⓐ Ⓑ Ⓒ Ⓓ	37 Ⓐ Ⓑ Ⓒ Ⓓ	47 Ⓐ Ⓑ Ⓒ Ⓓ
8 Ⓐ Ⓑ Ⓒ Ⓓ	18 Ⓐ Ⓑ Ⓒ Ⓓ	28 Ⓐ Ⓑ Ⓒ Ⓓ	38 Ⓐ Ⓑ Ⓒ Ⓓ	48 Ⓐ Ⓑ Ⓒ Ⓓ
9 Ⓐ Ⓑ Ⓒ Ⓓ	19 Ⓐ Ⓑ Ⓒ Ⓓ	29 Ⓐ Ⓑ Ⓒ Ⓓ	39 Ⓐ Ⓑ Ⓒ Ⓓ	49 Ⓐ Ⓑ Ⓒ Ⓓ
10 Ⓐ Ⓑ Ⓒ Ⓓ	20 Ⓐ Ⓑ Ⓒ Ⓓ	30 Ⓐ Ⓑ Ⓒ Ⓓ	40 Ⓐ Ⓑ Ⓒ Ⓓ	50 Ⓐ Ⓑ Ⓒ Ⓓ

1. Involuntary Confessions
2. Consent Searches
3. Burdens of Proof and Persuasion
4. Miranda Rights
5. Right to Counsel/Right to a Jury Trial
6. Fourth Amendment Standing
7. Miranda Rights
8. Fourth Amendment – State Action
9. Massiah Rights
10. Sixth Amendment Right of Confrontation
11. Terry Stop-and-Frisk
12. Probable Cause
13. Reasonable Suspicion
14. Fourth Amendment Standing
15. Terry Stop-and-Frisk
16. Search Warrants
17. Lineups
18. Excessive Bail
19. Pinkerton Liability
20. Right to a Speedy Trial
21. Identifications
22. Double Jeopardy
23. Fruit of the Poisonous Tree Doctrine
24. Consent Searches
25. Massiah Rights
26. Fourth Amendment Standing
27. Sixth Amendment Right to Counsel

28. Open Fields Doctrine
29. Burdens of Proof and Persuasion
30. Sixth Amendment Right to a Public Trial
31. Burdens of Proof and Persuasion
32. Sixth Amendment Right of Confrontation
33. Sixth Amendment Right to Counsel
34. Miranda Rights
35. Eighth Amendment Protections
36. Sixth Amendment Right to a Speedy Trial
37. Sixth Amendment Right to Counsel
38. Constitutional Protections in Jury Trials
39. Ineffective Assistance of Counsel
40. Lineups
41. Fourth Amendment Search and Seizure
42. Due Process Protections
43. Miranda Rights
44. The Exclusionary Rule
45. School Searches
46. Applicability of the Fifth Amendment
47. The "Knock and Announce" Rule
48. Miranda Rights
49. Voluntariness of Pleas
50. Ineffective Assistance of Counsel

1. A defendant is suspected of a carjacking and kidnapping. Following a 15-minute car chase, the defendant is shot by the police and swerves off the road. When the police arrive at the car, the victim is not in the car. The defendant, however, is severely injured and in need of immediate medical treatment. The police call an ambulance and accompany the defendant to the hospital, where he is seen by a doctor. At the hospital, a detective pulls the doctor aside and tells her that the police must find out what the defendant did with the missing victim, and the detective urgently presses the doctor to help the police obtain the information. The doctor agrees. The doctor returns to the defendant's room and tells the defendant that unless the defendant discloses the whereabouts of the victim, the doctor will let him die. The doctor glances out the window of the hospital room and sees the detective nod his head in support. The doctor repeats her statement to the defendant and pretends to leave. The defendant calls the doctor back and tells her that the victim can be found in an alley downtown. The doctor passes this information on to the detective. In the defendant's ensuing trial, the defendant's attorney moves to suppress the defendant's statement to the doctor.

The court should find that the statement is

(A) admissible, because the doctor was not a law enforcement officer.
(B) admissible, because the detective did not put the doctor in the position to obtain the statement from the defendant.
(C) inadmissible, because the defendant's statement was coerced.
(D) inadmissible, because the defendant was seriously ill at the time he consented to giving the statement.

2. A teacher was driving home one night when he was stopped by a police officer for having a malfunctioning rear taillight. Acting on a hunch and based on many years of police experience, the officer asked the teacher if he could search the vehicle. When the teacher agreed, the officer founded a loaded pistol under the driver's seat. The teacher was then arrested. The teacher was unaware that the pistol was under the seat, because it had been placed there by his roommate when he borrowed the vehicle the day before. The teacher had previously been convicted of robbery and had served a term in state prison as a consequence. The district attorney charges the teacher with being an ex-convict in possession of a firearm, a statutory felony, and the teacher moves to suppress the pistol on Fourth Amendment grounds.

Which of the following is the state's strongest argument in favor of permitting admission of the pistol?

(A) The search was reasonable under the circumstances, because it was based upon the experience and knowledge of a veteran police officer.
(B) The search was incident to a valid arrest.
(C) The teacher consented to the search.
(D) The search was reasonable due to the inherent mobility of a motor vehicle.

3. A man was found guilty of robbery. Subsequently, there was a sentencing hearing. Based on statutory sentencing guidelines, the judge was given discretion to sentence the defendant to an incarceration term of between 5 and 15 years in prison. According to the statutory guidelines, the judge could impose an enhanced sentence if he or she determined by a preponderance of the evidence that the defendant was motivated by a biased purpose. The judge sentenced the man to an enhanced term of 17 years after determining that his motivation for committing the robbery was due to the race of the victim. This issue of racial motivation was presented to the judge for the first time at sentencing. The judge, however, indicated that she would not have been able to impose the enhanced sentence if the reasonable doubt standard had been applied. The defendant's attorney has filed an appeal claiming a constitutional violation.

   Should the defendant's sentence be overturned?

   (A) Yes, because any fact that increases the penalty beyond the maximum set by statutory guidelines must be proved to the finder of fact beyond a reasonable doubt.
   (B) Yes, because the enhanced sentence was based upon factors unrelated to the robbery charge.
   (C) No, because the preponderance of evidence standard in sentencing hearings is constitutionally permissible.
   (D) No, because the judge indicated that she would not have been able to impose the enhanced sentence if the reasonable doubt standard applied.

4. Under which of the following fact situations would the defendant's Miranda waiver most likely be ineffective?

   (A) A defendant recently graduated from law school. At her graduation party, the defendant became highly intoxicated. Following the party, the defendant drove home in her automobile. She fell asleep at the wheel and crashed into another vehicle, injuring the driver. Shortly after the accident, a police officer came on the scene and arrested the defendant, charging her with D.U.I. The defendant was then given her Miranda warnings and transported to the police station. Upon questioning, the defendant, who was still highly intoxicated, waived her Miranda rights and made an incriminating statement.
   (B) A defendant stabbed a victim after a violent argument. Following the victim's death, the police arrested the defendant and charged him with murder. He was transported to the station house where Miranda warnings were given. Afterwards, the defendant was interrogated and proceeded to waive his Miranda rights. He then confessed to committing the crime. At trial, a psychiatrist testified that the defendant was mentally ill and his confession was not the result of a knowing and intelligent waiver.
   (C) A defendant was a 15-year-old high school sophomore. He possessed normal intelligence and experience for a youth of his age. One night, he and two friends attended a concert. After the concert, the defendant and his friends went on a spree assaulting and robbing victims in the park. The next day the defendant was arrested. After being subjected to persistent questioning for two hours, the defendant was first given his Miranda warnings. The defendant then waived his Miranda rights and offered a confession. At trial, the defendant claims he did not make a knowing and intelligent waiver.
   (D) A defendant was a 16-year-old juvenile in police custody on suspicion of murder. After he was given his Miranda warnings, he requested to have his probation officer present. He was on probation for a series of juvenile offenses. His request was denied. During a brief interrogation, the defendant proceeded to waive his Miranda rights and made incriminating statements that linked him with the crime. At trial, the defendant's lawyer claims that his waiver was ineffective because his request to see the probation officer was the equivalent of asking for a lawyer.

5. A defendant was arrested and subsequently charged with possession of marijuana, a misdemeanor. The maximum punishment for this misdemeanor offense was seven months imprisonment and a $500 fine.

Following his arrest, the defendant, who was found to be indigent, requested that an attorney be appointed to represent him and a jury trial. At his arraignment, the judge denied both his requests. The defendant was subsequently found guilty and received a six-month suspended sentence. The defendant appeals the judge's ruling in denying him an attorney and the right to a jury trial.

Will the appellate court likely hold that the trial judge's ruling was correct?

(A) Yes, with respect to the right to counsel.
(B) Yes, with respect to the right to a jury trial.
(C) Yes, with respect to the right to counsel and the right to a jury trial.
(D) No, with respect to the right to counsel and the right to a jury trial.

6. A woman has a lease for a one bedroom apartment. Her boyfriend, who is not on the lease, frequently visits but never spends the night at the apartment with her. One evening, the police are called because the boyfriend is engaged in aggravated assault involving an unrelated third party in the parking lot of the apartment complex. The boyfriend flees and witnesses see the boyfriend enter the woman's apartment. When police arrive at the woman's apartment, they knock and the woman answers the door. Police ask if they can enter and search the apartment and the woman gives officers permission to enter and search. Officers locate a pile of items containing numerous stolen and counterfeit checks made payable to the boyfriend, a stolen handgun, drugs, and the boyfriend's government identification card on the bed in the bedroom. The boyfriend is arrested for the illegal items located. At trial, the boyfriend's attorney argues that the exclusionary rule should apply and the evidence should be excluded.

Does this rule apply?

(A) No, this rule is only available in deportation and parole revocation hearings.
(B) No, the boyfriend does not have standing to raise a Fourth Amendment violation claim.
(C) Yes, it is a mandatory remedy for a violation of the defendant's Fourth Amendment rights.
(D) Yes, the police did not have a warrant to search and seize.

7. A security guard was covering a local parade when a car accident occurred on a nearby side street. The police were unable to respond immediately because of the parade, and the security guard was the first person on the scene. The security guard called in the details to a police detective, who informed him that the driver of one of the cars was wanted for the murder of her husband. The guard quickly handcuffed the woman, who turned to him and asked, "Is this because I killed my husband?" A police officer arrived shortly thereafter and escorted the woman to the police station.

At the station, another detective, assuming that the arresting officer must have properly advised the driver of her Miranda rights, began questioning her without issuing Miranda warnings. The driver began telling the detective about the car accident and her "jerk" of a husband. After about 30 minutes, the detective redirected her to the subject of the murder. The driver told him, "So what if I did kill him, don't you think he deserved it?" The detective said, "So did you kill him?" At that, the driver looked stunned and requested a lawyer. At trial, the driver's attorney moves to suppress her statement to the detective.

The court is likely to rule that the driver's statement is

(A) admissible, because of her previous voluntary statement.
(B) admissible, because the detective believed that the arresting officer had administered the Miranda warnings.
(C) inadmissible, because the statement was not clearly inculpatory.
(D) inadmissible because it was not preceded by a Miranda warning.

8. A man is a suspect in the disappearances and suspected murders of three female students at the local college. A police detective is convinced that the man is the culprit and that he continues to stalk young women, but he has been unable to gather sufficient evidence to obtain a search warrant. He has requested permission to search the man's home and been refused. In desperation, he takes to parking down the street from the man's house, hoping to see something that will tip the scales and allow him to obtain a warrant. One afternoon while the detective is staking out the man's house, a furnace repair truck pulls up. The detective approaches the truck and explains the situation, suggesting that if the repairman has the opportunity to look around a bit, he might be able to help crack the case. The repairman, alone in the basement, opens some boxes and finds four college IDs and a woman's blouse with blood on it. He stuffs the items into his toolbox and takes them to the detective. The names on three of the IDs match the missing girls.

If the state attempts to introduce the IDs at trial, the court should rule them:

(A) inadmissible.
(B) admissible, because the repairman is a private citizen.
(C) admissible, because of the inevitable discovery doctrine.
(D) admissible, because the repairman was invited onto the property by the man.

9. Harvey was arrested and charged with a robbery. His bail was lowered at his initial bail hearing, but not enough for him to get out of jail. The State's case was somewhat thin, but they had suspicions that Harvey was the mastermind behind more than 25 high-end robberies. In an attempt to bolster their case they put Alex in the cell next to him. They offered Alex a probationary term with no state prison time on his eighth burglary charge if he helped them out. He was instructed not to ask any questions of Harvey but just to listen, and let prosecutors know if Harvey incriminated himself. After returning from his preliminary hearing, Harvey made a statement in his cell that, "money buys 'justice,' my lawyer will have me walking out the door in no time. Those dumb ass prosecutors better realize they need more than a guilty defendant, they need evidence."

What is the likely result of Harvey's motion to disallow the statement at trial?

(A) It will be denied, because Alex did not elicit the statement from Harvey.
(B) It will be denied, because Alex was not a police officer.
(C) It will be granted, because Alex was an agent of the police and did not Mirandize Harvey.
(D) It will be granted, because Alex's actions violated the Massiah Rule.

10. A gardener was charged with assaulting a landscaper. A friend of the gardener saw the alleged assault of the landscaper. The gardener planned to call his friend as a defense witness at trial, but the friend moved to another state before the trial.

Regarding the absence of the friend as a witness, the prosecutor

(A) can argue in closing that the friend's failure to testify suggests that his testimony would have been adverse to the gardener.
(B) can use the friend's failure to testify as impeachment evidence.
(C) cannot cite the friend's absence unless the gardener has the opportunity to rebut.
(D) cannot comment on or argue regarding the friend's failure to testify.

11. In a smash-and-grab theft, numerous gold necklaces were stolen from a jewelry store. The store manager quickly called in the theft to the police. When the details of the theft were broadcast over the police radio, a newly inducted patrolman happened to be on patrol near the store. After hearing the radio call, the patrolman saw a jogger running down the street.

The patrolman stopped the jogger and asked, "What are you up to?" The jogger replied that he was on his lunch break, during which he likes to go for a jog. The patrolman, skeptical of the lunchtime-jog story, searched the jogger for the stolen jewelry. He did not find any jewelry, but he did uncover an illegal 9-millimeter handgun and arrested the jogger on the spot. The jogger later moved to suppress evidence of the handgun.

The most likely result is that the motion will be

(A) granted, because there was no reasonable suspicion for the search.
(B) granted, because the officer had no right to stop the jogger.
(C) denied, because the patrolman made a valid Terry stop and frisk.
(D) denied, because the jogger's possession of the gun indicated that the jogger was in fact armed and dangerous.

12. A man has been bullied all of his life and decides it's time to take revenge on the world. He buys a shotgun and plans to rob the local library. Even though he knows there is usually not a lot of money in the library's cash registers, the local librarian used to call the man "Chubby," and the man never got over it. The man bursts through the door of the library, waving his gun in the air, yelling for the librarian to come out, because "Chubby" has something for him. A frightened young woman is working at the library that day and quietly informs the man that the librarian quit his job six months ago and that she is the new librarian. Angered by this bit of news, the man fires at the woman. She ducks, but the bullet grazes her arm, injuring her. The man runs from the library and gets into his car, a green car of a certain well-known make and model. From the window of the library, the woman sees the man get into his car and calls police with a description of the man and the car. She is unable to get the man's license plate number, but the chief of police, who happens to be the woman's uncle, orders that police should search every green car of the same make and model in the city. About six hours later, a police officer spots the man driving around in his green car on the other side of town. The officer calls for backup, pulls the man over, and demands he exit the vehicle. The officer's backup arrives, and he searches the man's vehicle, including the glove compartment, back seat, and trunk. He finds the man's shotgun in the trunk, along with a bag full of heroin, and takes them as evidence. His backup handcuffs the man and places him in the back of the squad car. The state moves to admit the evidence seized from the man's car over objection by the man's attorney.

What is the likely outcome?

(A) The evidence is inadmissible, because there was no probable cause.
(B) The evidence is inadmissible, because the police had no basis to stop the man's vehicle.
(C) The evidence is admissible, because the automobile exception applies.
(D) The evidence is admissible, because the search was incident to arrest.

13. Defendant was wandering down the street in a drunken stupor, weaving in and out between other pedestrians, sometimes on the sidewalk and sometimes stepping out into the street. On several occasions, he was almost hit by cars. Officer noted Defendant's several near-misses and decided he should step in to help. He approached and asked Defendant his name, and Defendant told him. Officer then asked Defendant if he was all right. Defendant responded by mumbling something about how he loved her and shouldn't have done it. Figuring that Defendant was just a bum on a binge, Officer didn't take Defendant's comments seriously. Hoping simply to remove the remaining alcohol from Defendant's person so that Defendant could sober up, Officer reached into Defendant's coat pockets and, to his surprise, found a small zip gun. Officer asked, "What are you doing with this, man? These things are dangerous." When Defendant did not respond, Officer grew angry and pressed him, saying, "I asked you a question, and you're going to answer it." Defendant then told Officer that he killed his girlfriend and dumped her body in a drainage ditch down the road. Officer then placed Defendant under arrest and read him his rights.

At Defendant's trial, Defendant's attorney moves to have all evidence suppressed on the grounds that Officer's stop of Defendant was improper.

What is the likely result?

(A) Defendant's motion to suppress will be granted, because Officer did not have probable cause.
(B) Defendant's motion to suppress will be granted, because Officer's detention of Defendant exceeded the allowable time frame for a Terry stop.
(C) Defendant's motion to suppress will be denied, because there was reasonable suspicion that criminal activity was afoot.
(D) Defendant's motion to suppress will be denied, because Officer was only trying to protect Defendant.

14. A college student was arrested after a high-profile drug raid on his apartment. The next day, a concerned citizen called the police. He told the police that he had seen the student's picture on the news, and that he rented an apartment to the student, although the student rarely visited the apartment and used a different name when he signed the lease. The citizen said he suspected something funny was going on. The detective who took the call went to the apartment, which he entered with the landlord's key, and discovered an extremely large quantity of narcotics, packaging material, scales, and other paraphernalia.

An analysis of fingerprints obtained from the search revealed that the student was indeed the person renting the apartment. At the student's subsequent trial, the landlord testified that he would have entered the apartment the following day to change the air filters and would have discovered and reported the illegal activity. The student challenged the search of the apartment, and the prosecutor challenged the student's standing to object to the search.

The court will likely rule that

(A) the college student has standing to challenge the search, because incriminating items were found.
(B) the college student has standing to challenge the search, because he had a possessory interest in the premises searched.
(C) the college student does not have standing to challenge the search, because he did not use the apartment as a home.
(D) the college student does not have standing to challenge the search, because by renting the apartment in a false name, he waived his right to privacy.

15. The police received a call that there had just been an armed robbery at a local grocery store. When the police arrived at the store, the clerk gave a description of the robber and said that he had pulled a sawed-off shotgun out of his long coat and pointed it directly at her face. The police then broadcasted the clerk's summary over the radio. A few minutes later, two officers in a marked unit saw a man walking quickly and nervously, glancing back and forth. His clothing and build fit the basic description that had been reported over the radio. The patrol officers pulled up to the man and jumped out of the car with their guns drawn, ordering, "Put your hands on your head and get on the ground." The man quickly complied. One of the officers immediately frisked the suspect, and then reached into the man's long coat and pulled out the shotgun. They then arrested him. The man was subsequently charged with robbery.

If the man challenges the constitutionality of his initial encounter with the police, the trial court is likely to find that

(A) the stop was proper under Terry, but the frisk was not.
(B) both the stop and the frisk were proper under Terry.
(C) neither the stop nor the frisk were constitutional under the Fourth Amendment.
(D) the entire encounter was constitutional under the inevitable discovery doctrine.

16. A member of the police department's drug task force submitted a request for a search warrant on February 2. The officer requested to search the premises at 321 1st Street for methamphetamine, as well as the ingredients and equipment required to manufacture it. In his affidavit supporting the request, the officer had been told that a methamphetamine lab was being operated there. He stated that on February 1, he had been alerted to the lab's existence by an informant who had provided accurate and reliable information previously in similar cases. The informant had told the officer that he knew the homeowner of the house and that he (the informant) had been present at the house when the homeowner moved equipment for manufacturing methamphetamine into the house on the morning of January 31, according to the affidavit.

Based on that affidavit, the magistrate issued the search warrant on February 2, and 321 1st Street was duly searched. There was no sign of methamphetamine or a methamphetamine lab on the premises. However, the officers who searched the house did find some items in plain view that had been recently stolen from a jewelry store. The homeowner, who was present when the house was searched, was arrested and charged with receiving stolen property. At a pretrial hearing, the homeowner moved to have the evidence that was seized during the search suppressed on the grounds that the search warrant was invalid. The homeowner claimed that she did not know the informant and that the informant never been to her house at 321 1st Street. Based on evidence presented during the hearing, the judge found that the informant had provided the officer with false information.

Which of the following is correct?

(A) The judge should grant the motion to suppress the evidence only if the informant knowingly provided false information to the officer.
(B) The judge should grant the motion to suppress the evidence only if he determines that the officer knew that the informant's statements were false.
(C) The judge should grant the motion to suppress the evidence, because neither methamphetamine nor the ingredients and equipment to manufacture methamphetamine were found in the house.
(D) The judge should grant the motion to suppress the evidence, because the officer's affidavit was based entirely on hearsay.

17. Dennis has decided that he has no future and wants to "go out in a blaze of glory." He heads for the local bank, where he holds a .357 Magnum up to the clerk's face and orders her to fill a bag with cash. The clerk complies, and Dennis leaves with the bag of cash. However, a police officer is waiting outside. Before the officer spots him, Dennis shoots the officer in the head, killing him. The officer's partner, hearing the shot, comes out of the nearby deli where he and his partner had stopped to pick up lunch. The partner sees Dennis driving away in a blue, late-model Honda Accord. He is unable to get even a partial view of the license plate. The police chief instructs all the officers to come in, and he issues an order that all blue, late-model Honda Accords are to be stopped and searched until they find the person who killed the officer. Eight hours later, an officer pulls over Dennis in his blue Honda Accord and calls for backup. The police immediately order Dennis to exit the car, and then they handcuff him and order him to lie down on the ground. While one officer stands over Dennis, the others search his entire vehicle. When they open the trunk, they find the gun and the bag of money from the bank, which contained marked bills. Simultaneous to the trunk search, Dennis tells the officer hovering over him, "Get out of my face or I'll do you the same as I did your brother in blue." With that, the officer starts to beat Dennis. He demands, "Give up what you did or I'll kill you myself!" Dennis, pummeled into submission, gives the officer his detailed account of what he did that day. The officers use their police radio to put out a general request for the dead officer's partner and the bank clerk to show up to identify Dennis. In their radio call, the police state that they have captured the suspect, that they have his gun and the money from the bank, and that he has confessed. The dead officer's partner hears the radio transmission and comes to the scene. Upon his arrival, he immediately identifies Dennis. The clerk comes to the scene and also identifies Dennis. Dennis is then transported to the police station. On the way there, he repeatedly states that he wants his lawyer. Once Dennis arrives at the station house, he is booked and read his rights, following which he is moved into an interrogation room, where the Chief tells him that things will go easier for him if he tells them what occurred. Dennis initially says nothing. Finally, after 10 hours of silence in the interrogation room, he tells them the whole story again.

Which of the show-up identification procedures is likely to be admissible at Dennis's trial?

(A) The bank clerk's only.
(B) The officer's only.
(C) Both the bank clerk's and the officer's.
(D) Neither the bank clerk's nor the officer's.

18. The police receive a report of an armed robbery at a local convenience store. The first officers at the scene get a description of the suspect from the store clerk and immediately send it out over the radio. Among the details given by the clerk is that the robber pulled a handgun out of his back pocket and pointed it directly at her face. A few minutes after the call goes out on the radio, a patrol unit sees a teenager a few blocks from the store, who is walking quickly and nervously looking around. His clothing, build, and features fit the basic description given by the clerk. The officers follow the teenager in their car for a block, then jump out with guns drawn. They frisk the teenager and immediately find a gun. The officers then take the teenager to the police station where he is held overnight.

The next morning the teenager goes before a judge without a lawyer, and the judge sets bail at $20 million, telling the teenager, "You are a danger to society, and I am going to make sure that while you are awaiting trial you cannot hurt anyone else." A week later the grand jury indicts the teenager for armed robbery. The teenager's new, court-appointed attorney challenges the constitutionality of his client's first appearance in front of the judge.

How is the court likely to rule?

(A) The teenager's right to counsel has been violated.
(B) The bail set by the court violates the Eighth Amendment prohibition against excessive bail.
(C) The bail hearing must be held after the indictment.
(D) The objections to the teenager's bail, if any, had to be raised at his bail hearing.

19. A boyfriend calls his girlfriend and tells her that he wants to commit a burglary with one of his friends at the girlfriend's neighbor's house. The boyfriend asks the girlfriend to call him the next time that the neighbors leave their home for the day. Three days later, the girlfriend calls the boyfriend to tell him that the neighbors are gone. In that conversation, the girlfriend asks for a share of whatever is stolen from the house and the boyfriend agrees. The girlfriend also agrees to call the boyfriend if the neighbors return to the home so that the boyfriend can run out of the back door without being seen or caught. The boyfriend then calls his best friend who shows up at the house with a gun for himself and a second gun for the boyfriend. The boyfriend refuses to carry the second handgun. The boyfriend and best friend enter the home by kicking in the front door only to find that the neighbors are actually home. The best friend begins shooting and the homeowner is able to retrieve a handgun and return fire. The homeowner and the best friend are both killed in the exchange.

Can the girlfriend be charged with the death of the homeowner?

(A) Yes, the girlfriend can be charged under the Pinkerton doctrine.
(B) Yes, the girlfriend can be charged under the theory of accomplice liability as either a principal in the first degree or in the second degree.
(C) No, the girlfriend did not know that the best friend was going to bring a gun.
(D) No, this falls within the Redline limitation.

20. A defendant committed a string of violent armed robberies at fast food restaurants which resulted in injuries to several victims. Police immediately arrested the defendant for the first armed robbery but continued to investigate the subsequent incidences. The prosecution did not indict the case until after the police had secured warrants with respect to the subsequent armed robberies. It was determined that the case did not meet the criteria for federal prosecution. It took 40 days from the time of the first arrest to secure all of the applicable warrants and have the case indicted by the grand jury. Due to the judge's backlog of cases, this case was not scheduled for trial for one year. Once on the trial calendar, the defense attorney filed one motion every month for four months. The defendant remained in custody the entire time, unable to make the high bond. On the day of trial, the defense attorney made a pretrial motion requesting a complete dismissal of all charges and argued that the defendant's Sixth Amendment Right to a Speedy Trial was violated.

Which of the following should the judge not consider in determining the outcome of the dismissal motion?

(A) The defendant never asserted his right to a speedy trial.
(B) The defendant filed a series of pretrial motions and suppression hearings.
(C) The prejudice to the defendant.
(D) That the trial did not occur within 70 days of the indictment.

21. A plumber and an electrician have been friends for many years. The plumber tells the electrician that he has an easy burglary for them to pull off. He tells the electrician that a local jewelry store always leaves jewelry lying around on the counters after showing it to customers. The plumber tells the electrician that all he has to do is drive the getaway car, and that he (the plumber) will handle the inside part all by himself.

The next afternoon, the electrician drops the plumber off in front of the store. The plumber goes into the store, looks around, and spies a large pile of gold jewelry on the counter. He walks up to the counter, scoops up the jewelry, pockets it, and runs for the door. No one follows, and the plumber makes it out of the store without anyone even noticing. As the plumber nears the corner where he is to meet the electrician, he turns to see if he is being followed. In the process, he accidentally slams into a pedestrian. The plumber recovers his footing and runs to the car in which the electrician is waiting. The pedestrian takes note of the license plate number and calls the police on his cell phone.

A few blocks away, a patrol vehicle sees the car and executes a stop. The police officers order the plumber and the electrician to exit the vehicle. As they step out of the car, the electrician starts babbling that the jewelry store heist was all the plumber's idea and that he didn't want to go along, but that he thought he could help to keep something really bad from happening. The officers order them both to the ground and frisk them, at which time the police find the stolen jewelry in the plumber's pocket.

Meanwhile, another patrol vehicle pulls up with the pedestrian for a show-up. The pedestrian tells the police that the plumber is the one who knocked him over. A third patrol car brings the jewelry store owner, who also identifies the plumber as the perpetrator of the theft of the jewelry. At the plumber's ensuing criminal trial, the plumber's lawyer moves to exclude the on-the-scene identifications of the plumber from use at his trial.

What is the likely outcome of the plumber's motion?

(A) The identification by the pedestrian will be excluded, because the procedure violated the plumber's due process rights.
(B) The identification by the jewelry store owner will be excluded, because it was unnecessarily suggestive.
(C) Both identifications will be excluded.
(D) Both identifications will be admitted.

22. A gang member went into a convenience store and held up the clerk at gunpoint. The clerk resisted and the gang member shot him during the struggle. The gang member was charged with armed robbery, felony murder, and first-degree murder. Felony murder requires the commission or attempt of a separate felony; first-degree murder requires the intent to kill.

A state statute provides that the sentence for armed robbery can be up to 15 years, the sentence for felony murder and murder up to 40 years each, and that a defendant convicted may be sentenced to consecutive sentences. The gang member was convicted of all three crimes and sentenced to serve consecutive sentences of five, 25, and 25 years. On appeal, the gang member argued that such consecutive sentencing placed him in double jeopardy for the same crime. The state argued that this sentence was proper because the state statute expressly authorized consecutive sentencing.

Which of the following crimes may the gang member be convicted of without violating his double jeopardy rights?

(A) Armed robbery and either felony murder or murder.
(B) Felony murder and either armed robbery or murder.
(C) Murder and either armed robbery or felony murder.
(D) All three crimes.

23. One afternoon, a driver was driving his old beat-up truck along the highway when a police officer pulled him over. When the officer came up to the driver's side window of the car, the driver asked him, "What did I do wrong?" The officer replied, "Nothing, I just picked your car at random so that I could check your license and registration. May I see them?" The driver handed the officer his license and reached over to the glove compartment to get his registration. As the officer watched the driver do this, he noticed what appeared to be a handle of a gun protruding from under the passenger side of front seat. The gun turned out to be an illegal sawed-off shotgun. The officer arrested the driver on weapons charges. At trial, the driver's attorney moved to suppress the gun seized by the officer.

The motion to suppress will most likely be

(A) denied, because the handle of the shotgun was in plain view.
(B) denied, because the seizure of the gun resulted from a lawful investigatory stop.
(C) granted, because, as the fruit of an illegal search, the gun should be excluded.
(D) granted, because the officer did not have probable cause to believe that the driver had or was engaged in criminal activity.

24. An avid gardener likes to tend to her herb garden. She also raises a few marijuana plants in her basement under special growing lights. From time to time, she sells her crop to friends and acquaintances. The gardener decides to go skiing for a few days. Her plants are on an automatic drip-watering system. However, the gardener asks her elderly next-door neighbor if she would not mind feeding her cat and taking care of her mail for a few days. The neighbor agrees. The gardener has told the neighbor on a prior occasion that the plants in her basement are catnip plants for her cat. While the gardener is gone, two police officers come to the door while the neighbor is in the gardener's house feeding the cat. The officers ask if they can search the gardener's house. The neighbor gives permission saying, "Yes, I don't think the gardener would mind. She's such a nice young lady." The police find the marijuana plants in the basement and arrest the gardener when she returns from her trip.

If the gardener's attorney files a motion to suppress the finding of the marijuana plants, which of the following facts, if true, would be least supportive of her motion?

(A) The gardener told the neighbor not to answer the door or the telephone when she was in the gardener's house.
(B) The gardener had given the neighbor a set of keys to her house.
(C) The police officers told the neighbor that she would have to go to the police station with them if she did not allow them to search.
(D) The police did not have a warrant to search the gardener's house.

25. A grand jury indicted a man for the armed robbery of a wine shop. Several days later, a detective meets with a customer of the wine shop who was present at the time of the robbery. The customer asks the detective whether a diamond engagement ring has been recovered. She adds that her 27-year-old husband had died less than a year ago from cancer, and the ring is very important to her. The detective promises that he will look into the matter. The detective then goes down to the county jail, advises the man of his Miranda rights, and describes to him the story of the engagement ring and how desperately the customer wishes to recover this token of her love for her dearly departed husband. The man tells the detective that he dumped the ring in the sewer because he was interested only in cash, not in the various personal items customers had given him.

Is the man's statement admissible?

(A) No, because the detective used coercive practices to obtain the statement.
(B) No, because the defendant has already been indicted for armed robbery of the wine shop.
(C) Yes, because the defendant was read his Miranda rights.
(D) Yes, because the statement was given to help the victim retrieve her property.

26. A police officer believed that a woman was a drug dealer. Determined to catch her, the officer snuck into the woman's apartment while she was at work and while he was off duty. Under her bed, the officer found a suitcase in which he discovered a substantial amount of cocaine.

Based on the suitcase and its contents, the officer then obtained a warrant to search the apartment of the woman's neighbor. The neighbor lived in the adjacent apartment and the police officer had reliable sources who indicated that the neighbor and the woman were co-conspirators. The warrant was executed by two other officers, who found large quantities of cocaine, packaging materials, and other indicia of the drug trade.

What is the likely outcome of the neighbor's motion to suppress the items found at her apartment?

(A) The evidence will be suppressed, because the warrant was issued based on illegally obtained evidence.
(B) The evidence will be suppressed, because of the Good-Faith Clause of the Exclusionary Rule.
(C) The evidence will be admitted, because the neighbor lacked standing to challenge the illegal search of the woman's apartment.
(D) The evidence will be admitted, because the officer had probable cause to search the woman's apartment.

27. Defendant is a drug dealer who police believe may be involved in the contract killing of a rival drug dealer. The defendant has previously been arrested on a charge for driving while intoxicated and is currently under indictment. The defendant has a private attorney on that case and is out on bail. An undercover police officer knows that the defendant is out on bail on the driving while intoxicated charges and begins to casually engage the defendant in conversation about the murder of the rival drug dealer. In this conversation, the defendant asks the officer, "You're not police, are you?" and the officer never reveals that he is a police officer. The defendant brags to the police officer that the defendant is the one who ordered the killing of the rival drug dealer. The next day, based on the statements made by the defendant, an officer obtains a warrant for the defendant and the defendant is arrested for charges stemming from the contract killing. In a motion to suppress the defendant's statements to the undercover police officer, the defendant's attorney argues that the defendant's Sixth Amendment right to counsel was violated.

What argument, if any, would support the suppression of the defendant's statements regarding the killing?

(A) The statement will not be suppressed because the Sixth Amendment right to counsel is offense-specific.
(B) The defendant had an attorney at the time he was questioned by the undercover officer.
(C) The defendant did not effectively waive his right to an attorney.
(D) The officer deceived the defendant.

28. A defendant owned a 40-acre tract of farmland located in a rural community. He conducted a small farming operation on the property and grew corn which he sold to local produce companies. One day, the county police received an anonymous tip that the defendant was growing marijuana on his farm. Acting on this information, the police flew over his farm in a surveillance plane and took pictures of the landscape using a camera that one of the officers bought at a local electronics store. After the pictures were developed, they revealed what appeared to be marijuana plants growing alongside a section of the corn crop. In an unmarked vehicle, two undercover police officers then drove to the defendant's farm. They climbed over a chain-link fence and walked around the farm. While surveying the terrain, they came upon a small marijuana patch. The officers then noticed fresh footprints that led from the marijuana patch to a nearby cabin. Believing that marijuana was being stored in the cabin, the police officers decided to immediately secure a search warrant. After obtaining the warrant, they returned to the defendant's farm and entered the cabin. Inside the cabin, the police found a large cache of marijuana that had been recently harvested. The defendant was then arrested and charged with unlawful possession of marijuana. The defendant files a pretrial motion to suppress the marijuana as evidence on grounds of an illegal search and seizure.

Will the evidence be suppressed?

(A) No, because the officers secured a warrant before entering the cabin, despite the fact that their earlier actions may have been unlawful.
(B) No, because the warrant was validly issued and based upon information lawfully obtained.
(C) Yes, because the marijuana was the fruit of an illegal search and seizure, as the police did not have probable cause to conduct overflight surveillance.
(D) Yes, because the police were unlawfully on the defendant's property when the marijuana patch was initially discovered.

29. Defendant is convicted of murdering his neighbor. At the sentencing phase, the prosecution introduces as aggravating evidence a letter obtained from Defendant's house that indicates that Defendant murdered the neighbor because of the neighbor's race. The letter had been obtained by police detectives in violation of the Fourth Amendment but had not been introduced or mentioned at the guilt phase of the proceeding. The jury finds by a preponderance of the evidence that racial animus was Defendant's motive in carrying out the murder, which under the statute increases the sentence beyond the normal statutory maximum. On appeal, Defendant argues that the imposition of the sentence was unconstitutional and that the sentence be vacated and the case remanded for re-sentencing.

Should the appellate court vacate defendant's sentence and remand the case for re-sentencing?

(A) Yes, because the exclusionary rule bars the introduction of evidence seized in violation of the Fourth Amendment.
(B) Yes, because the jury applied the wrong standard in evaluating the racial animus sentence enhancement.
(C) No, because the exclusionary rule does not apply at sentencing.
(D) No, because the jury's sentencing procedures were constitutionally adequate.

30. A secretary is charged with a series of murders that have attracted widespread press attention. Concerned that the press attention would compromise the impartiality of the jury, the secretary moves to have the press and public excluded from the courtroom. In support of her motion, the secretary presents expert evidence that the impartiality of juries can be affected by excessive trial publicity.

Should the trial court grant the motion?

(A) Yes, because criminal defendants have an absolute right to waive their right to a public trial.
(B) Yes, because the secretary has shown that his right to a public trial would be compromised if the press were not excluded.
(C) No, because the press has a Sixth Amendment right to be present at all criminal proceedings absent an overriding interest.
(D) No, because the press because the press has a Sixth Amendment right to be present at all criminal proceedings.

31. Defendant is tried for the murder of three of his neighbors. While conceding that he killed the neighbors, Defendant's lawyer contends that Defendant was legally insane because he had not taken his antipsychotic medication for several years, which constitutes both a defense to the crime and a violation of due process to try Defendant in that state. Defendant's counsel concedes that when Defendant is taking the medication, he is sane. In response, the Court orders Defendant to take the medication and for the trial to proceed. Defendant is convicted of the crimes by the jury, which finds that the government has proven by a preponderance of the evidence that defendant was sane. On appeal, Defendant argues that the trial court's treatment of his allegations of insanity violated his constitutional rights.

Should the appellate court reverse the conviction?

(A) Yes, because a court may not require the Defendant to take antipsychotic drugs against his will so as to have the Defendant competent to stand trial.
(B) Yes, because the government failed to prove sanity beyond a reasonable doubt.
(C) No, because a court may require the Defendant to take antipsychotic drugs against his will to make the Defendant competent to stand trial.
(D) No, because the government's proof of sanity was constitutionally sufficient.

32. Defendant was charged with the physical abuse of a 12-year-old child. At trial, the child was unwilling to testify against Defendant, so the court ordered that a screen be placed between Defendant and the child. The child testified about Defendant's abuse from behind the screen, and Defendant's attorney was given an opportunity to cross-examine the child. During the cross-examination, Defendant made strange noises that seemed disruptive to the witness. The trial court ordered that the Defendant be gagged until the child left the witness stand. Based largely upon the child's testimony, Defendant was convicted of child abuse. On appeal, Defendant asked the appellate court for a new trial on the ground that the trial court's handling of the child witness was a violation of his constitutional rights.

Should the appellate court grant a new trial?

(A) Yes, because the use of a screen to shield child witnesses violates the Confrontation Clause.
(B) Yes, because the Confrontation Clause was violated when the court required Defendant to be gagged during the testimony.
(C) No, because the use of a screen to shield child witnesses does not necessarily violate the Confrontation Clause.
(D) No, because Defendant's lawyer had an ample opportunity to cross-examine the child witness.

33. A court appointed counsel for an indigent man being tried for criminal trespass and arson. At the start of trial, the man argued that he was not competent to stand trial. After a competency hearing before the jury, the jury determined that the man was competent to stand trial. At this point, the man attempted to fire his lawyer and represent himself. The judge determined that the man was incompetent to represent himself and denied his request. At trial, the man cooperated with his counsel in directing his defense, but was convicted. On appeal, the man argues for a new trial on the ground that his right to counsel has been violated.

Should the appellate court grant a new trial?

(A) Yes, because the competency of a criminal defendant must be decided by a judge and not the jury.
(B) Yes, because a person who is competent to stand trial necessarily has the right to proceed pro se.
(C) No, because the man's right to counsel has not been violated.
(D) No, because a defendant who is incompetent to represent himself in court must be civilly committed rather than tried.

34. Early in the morning, Internal Revenue Service agents visit the home of Taxpayer, who is being investigated for criminal tax evasion. The agents identify themselves and their purposes and ask Taxpayer if they might enter the home to speak with him, to which Taxpayer agrees. The agents then proceeded to ask Taxpayer about his finances and tax payments for two hours, during which time Taxpayer made several incriminating statements. Taxpayer was arrested and charged with tax fraud. At trial, the prosecution introduced evidence of Taxpayer's statements to the agents, over his objection. Taxpayer was convicted and on appeal argues that the conviction should be reversed due to the unconstitutional admission of the statements.

Should the court of appeals reverse the conviction?

(A) Yes, because Taxpayer was not sufficiently apprised of his constitutional rights.
(B) Yes, because the agents entered the home without a search warrant.
(C) No, because Taxpayer consented to the warrantless entry into his home.
(D) No, because the agents did not need to apprise Taxpayer of his constitutional rights.

35. After a long trial, a jury convicts Defendant, an African-American man, of capital murder. The same jury then proceeded to the sentencing phase of the trial, to consider whether to impose the only two sentences available under state law in a capital murder case: a death sentence or life imprisonment without parole. At the sentencing phase, Defendant seeks to introduce statistical evidence that in the jurisdiction, African-American men are 10 times more likely to receive the death penalty than are other men. After hearing the statistical evidence, along with that dealing with mitigating and aggravating circumstances, the jury sentences Defendant to death. On appeal, Defendant argues that the procedures at the sentencing phase were constitutionally insufficient and that the case should be remanded for re-sentencing.

Should the appellate court grant the motion?

(A) Yes, because the statistical evidence renders the death penalty in the state cruel and unusual punishment.
(B) Yes, because the same jury decided both guilt and sentencing.
(C) No, because the statistical evidence is insufficient to render the death penalty cruel and unusual punishment in this case.
(D) No, because the death penalty is not cruel and unusual punishment.

36. Defendant and Accomplice are arrested for murder. Five days later, they are indicted in state court. Without objection from Defendant, the state decides to try Defendant and Accomplice one after the other, starting with Accomplice. Accomplice's trial is plagued by procedural issues, including a series of continuances sought by Accomplice's lawyer. Defendant is released on bail pending the outcome of Accomplice's trial. After three years, Accomplice is convicted, and the state begins preparations for Defendant's trial. Defendant moves to have all charges dropped on the ground that Defendant's right to a speedy trial has been violated.

Should the court grant the motion?

(A) No, because Defendant's right to a speedy trial has not been violated.
(B) No, because Defendant waived the right to speedy trial by failing to object to the state's decision to try Accomplice first.
(C) Yes, because Defendant's right to a speedy trial has been violated.
(D) Yes, because the Speedy Trial Act of 1974 has been violated.

37. After a series of armed robberies of pedestrians in and around the city's downtown entertainment district by a masked man, Defendant is indicted and charged with armed robbery. Witness works as a bouncer at one of the bars in the entertainment district and had seen one of the robberies. The police arrange for a lineup in the hope that Witness could identify Defendant. Defendant is a male of average height. The police line up seven men and three women of varying heights within the normal range for men. Witness identifies Defendant as the robber from the lineup. Defendant is represented by a lawyer, but the lawyer was not permitted to be present at the lineup. At trial, the key piece of prosecution evidence is the identification and testimony of Witness. Defendant is convicted and on appeal moves to have the conviction set aside based on the improper admission of the lineup.

Should the appellate court reverse the conviction?

(A) Yes, because Defendant's right to counsel was violated.
(B) Yes, because the lineup was unnecessarily suggestive and violated due process.
(C) No, because Defendant's right to counsel was not violated.
(D) No, because the lineup did not violate due process.

38. Defendant is an African-American woman charged with criminal state income tax evasion. The state income tax statute provides that criminal income tax evasion must be tried before a jury of between six and 12 persons. During jury selection, the jury pool was selected from Defendant's community, and was 55% white and 45% Asian, which was roughly proportionate to the population of the larger community in which Defendant resides, which is 52% white, 46% Asian, and 2% African-American. The jury pool of 50 prospective jurors was 50% women and 50% men. The prosecution used all of its three peremptory strikes on women, all three of whom were tax lawyers for large law firms. At the end of jury selection, the judge empanelled a jury of six, four of whom were white and two of whom were Asian. Defendant objects to the jury on the ground that her Sixth Amendment rights to a jury trial have been violated, and requests a new jury.

Should the trial court grant the motion?

(A) Yes, because the racial composition of the jury is insufficient.
(B) Yes, because all of the peremptory strikes were exercised against women.
(C) No, because a jury of six persons in a criminal case is constitutionally insufficient.
(D) No, because the selection of the jury does not violate Defendant's right to a fair trial.

39. A woman is arrested and charged with the arson of a fire station. At trial, forensic evidence links her to the materials used to start the fire and an eyewitness testifies that she saw the woman entering the building shortly before the fire began. Defendant's court-appointed lawyer is trying his first case and received the case with only a short time to prepare for trial. Moreover, the woman's lawyer cross-examines the prosecution's witnesses in a way that most lawyers in the community would consider to be below a reasonable standard and does not present a defense at the conclusion of the prosecution's case in chief. The woman is convicted of arson. On appeal, she asserts that she is entitled to a new trial on the grounds that she was denied her Sixth Amendment right to counsel at trial.

Should the appellate court grant a new trial?

(A) Yes, because her lawyer was unconstitutionally ineffective.
(B) Yes, because her lawyer failed to present a defense.
(C) No, because the lawyer was not unconstitutionally ineffective.
(D) No, because the appointment of a court-appointed attorney satisfied the requirements of the Sixth Amendment right to counsel.

40. A suspect was arrested and charged with rape. The suspect's attorney arrived at the police station to observe the identification lineup of his client by the victim. The attorney was directed to wait in the hallway outside the identification room. The attorney remained seated in the hallway while inside the identification room, the six members of the lineup, including the suspect, stood on one side of the one-way mirror in full view of the victim who was standing on the other side in the viewing area. The lineup members stepped forward one by one for a closer inspection. After the first two lineup members had been presented to the victim, the officer realized that the suspect's attorney was not present and immediately brought him into the identification room. The remaining members of the lineup stepped forward after which the victim identified the suspect as the man who raped her. At trial, the defense objected to the introduction of the lineup evidence.

Should the lineup identification of the defendant be excluded?

(A) No, because the attorney's absence from the lineup procedure was based on a good faith mistake by the police.
(B) No, because the attorney was present for most of the time that the suspect was presented in the lineup for identification by the victim and there were no other legal improprieties in the lineup procedure.
(C) Yes, because the right to have counsel present at a post-charge lineup includes the right to have counsel present for the entire lineup.
(D) Yes, unless the victim fails to make an independent identification at trial.

41. A known drug dealer living in a basement apartment stored drugs in a locked front closet near his front door. As he was about to leave his house, a police officer was standing in the stairwell with a trained drug-sniffing dog and asked the drug dealer if he could come in and ask him some questions. The drug dealer refused to speak to the police officer and ordered him to leave the stairwell unless the officer could produce a warrant. The officer stepped closer to the doorway, and the dog pulled the officer toward the front closet signaling the presence of drugs. Based on probable cause supplied by the dog's behavior, the officer broke open the front closet door and found a large stash of cocaine. The drug dealer was then arrested and the cocaine was seized.

Should the court grant the drug dealer's motion to suppress evidence of the cocaine seized from the closet?

(A) Yes, because a warrantless search and seizure of items within the defendant's home is not permissible absent exigent circumstances.
(B) Yes, because the search and seizure required a warrant to justify the initial intrusion into the house.
(C) No, because the cocaine was seized as a search incident to a lawful arrest.
(D) No, because the drug sniffing dog's signal provided probable cause to search the locked closet.

42. A foreign student lawfully residing in the United States was detained and questioned by police after the police received information that the student was a bomb maker. The student refused to answer police questions and asserted the Fifth Amendment Privilege against self-incrimination. Later, the court entered an order against the student requiring him to answer questions on the ground that aliens did not have the right to assert the protections of the Fifth Amendment. The student later admitted his bomb making activities and was convicted at trial. On appeal, the student argued that his conviction should be reversed because his Fifth Amendment rights were violated.

Should the student's conviction be reversed on appeal?

(A) Yes, because there was insufficient probable cause to detain the student for questioning.
(B) Yes, because resident aliens are entitled to all due process protections under the Fifth Amendment.
(C) No, because the student's bomb making activities created a threat to national security authorizing the suspension of due process rights.
(D) No, because aliens may not avail themselves of constitutional privileges.

43. The Coast Guard arrested three men while out sailing in a stolen yacht. They were arrested and placed in an interrogation room. As the police officer started to give them their Miranda warnings, one of the men said, "As soon as you check my record, you'll find out that I am on parole for transporting drugs. I will admit that we stole the boat to do a drug deal if you guarantee federal instead of state custody." The other two men remained silent while the first man gave a full confession.

The two men who remained silent pled not guilty to the charge of stealing the yacht. At their trial, the prosecutor introduced evidence that both men remained silent when the other admitted that all three of them had committed the crime and signed a full confession. Defense counsel objected to the admission of the evidence.

How should the court rule on the objection?

(A) Overruled, because silence in this situation is indicative of guilt and is an implied admission.
(B) Overruled, because the man who confessed had voluntarily waived his right to remain silent.
(C) Sustained, because an accomplice's evidence is inherently unreliable and unduly prejudicial.
(D) Sustained, because under this circumstance, the men who remained silent had no duty to deny the accomplice's confession of guilt.

44. A wife killed her husband's secretary believing the secretary was having an affair with her husband. Detectives believed the wife had committed the murder and later persuaded the wife's maid to remove a wine glass from the house so that it could be used for fingerprint comparisons with a gun found near the body. The fingerprints matched. The prosecutor introduced evidence of the fingerprint comparisons to the grand jury. The wife's lawyer later filed a motion to suppress the evidence of the fingerprint comparisons so as to prevent consideration by the grand jury, contending that the evidence was illegally acquired.

Should the court grant the motion to suppress?

(A) Yes, because the detectives only had reasonable suspicion and not probable cause.
(B) Yes, because the maid was acting as a law enforcement agent and the seizure required a warrant.
(C) No, because the exclusionary rule does not apply to grand jury proceedings.
(D) No, because the glass was removed by a private citizen and not a police officer.

45. Several students at a public high school told the principal that a junior was selling illegal drugs at his locker to other students at the school. The junior was called into the principal's office and he immediately denied the accusations. The principal grabbed the junior by the arm and took him to the locker and demanded that the junior unlock the locker. The junior opened it and the principal observed bags of marijuana on the top shelf. The principal called the police and the junior was later arrested when the drugs field tested positive. The junior was charged with possession of a controlled substance with intent to sell. At trial, the prosecution planned to introduce the marijuana seized from the junior's locker into evidence.

Should the court grant junior's motion to suppress the introduction of the evidence?

(A) Yes, because there was adequate time to obtain a warrant.
(B) Yes, because the police lacked probable cause to field test the drugs.
(C) No, because the principal had a reasonable suspicion that the junior was had illegal drugs in his locker.
(D) No, because the principal was not acting as an agent of law enforcement at the time of the illegal search.

46. A foreign businessman, during his visit to the United States, was detained by the FBI after the Chinese embassy requested the FBI to question the business man about certain money laundering activities in China. The businessman refused to answer the FBI's questions and asserted the Fifth Amendment Privilege against self-incrimination. Later, the businessman was granted immunity from prosecution in the United States. The businessman still refused to answer questions when he was questioned before the grand jury claiming that the grant of immunity did not protect him from prosecution in China. The court entered an order against the businessman requiring him to answer questions on the ground that the constitutional protections of the Fifth Amendment did not apply to threatened foreign prosecutions.

Can the businessman be held in contempt of the court order requiring him to testify?

(A) Yes, because the constitutional protections of the Fifth Amendment do not apply to threatened foreign prosecutions.
(B) Yes, because the businessman was not a lawful resident alien and therefore, had no constitutional protections.
(C) No, because the businessman was lawfully in the United States and had constitutional rights.
(D) No, because the grand jury is a secret proceeding and the Chinese government has no legal right to access secret grand jury testimony.

47. A police officer has received a tip that, when a man in a specific vehicle enters a house on a nearby street, the people in the basement will be helping the man process, weigh, and package the heroin he will be bringing. The officer has been told that, while the group is doing this, they will have one person patrolling the house and guarding the front door. The officer has verified the information with independent investigation and received search and arrest warrants from a magistrate. When he goes to the house at the specified time, he sees that the front door is slightly ajar and walks in with his gun drawn and without announcing himself. The situation is as the informant said it would be and, with the help of several other police officers, the officer carries out his arrest and search warrants.

Will the evidence gathered be admissible?

(A) Yes, because the officer had proper search and arrest warrants.
(B) Yes, because the officer did not damage the house upon entry.
(C) No, because the officer did not knock and announce himself before entering.
(D) No, because there were no exigent circumstances at the time he entered the house.

48. A small-town police officer sees a hitchhiker who she believes may know something about a recent burglary at a fast food restaurant. She pulls over and asks the hitchhiker whether he has a moment to talk. It turns out that the hitchhiker is trying to go in the direction of the police station, about 5 miles away, so she offers him a ride and says they can talk on the way. When she mentions the burglary, the hitchhiker says "Some of the guys will tell you I was there, but that's just because they're mad at me." The officer pulls into the police station parking lot and lets the hitchhiker out. After she does some additional investigation, she gets a warrant to arrest the hitchhiker for the burglary a week later.

Can the hitchhiker's statement to the officer be used at trial?

(A) Yes, because the hitchhiker was not arrested immediately after the statement.
(B) Yes, because his statement was voluntary.
(C) No, because the hitchhiker was not given a Miranda warning before he spoke.
(D) No, because the hitchhiker was in a police car when he made the statement.

49. A lawyer is arrested for the voluntary manslaughter of her best friend. There is a substantial amount of evidence against her, including the fact that two witnesses saw her with a bloody knife, crying and screaming, "I can't believe I killed him. Things just got out of hand." She is so overcome by remorse with what she has done that she appears at her arraignment a day later without counsel and says, "I'm guilty. Let's not waste any time hashing this out. Just enter my guilty plea, your honor." The judge does so without further comment, and then dismisses the court. The lawyer later changes her mind and decides she wants a trial.

Can the lawyer withdraw her plea?

(A) Yes, because there was not enough time for her to obtain counsel before the arraignment.
(B) Yes, because the judge did not personally discuss the voluntariness of the plea on the record.
(C) No, because she had the legal background to be aware of the consequences of what she was doing.
(D) No, because guilty pleas cannot be withdrawn.

50. A woman was arrested for shoplifting a $7,000 bracelet from a couture boutique. There was video of her putting the bracelet on her wrist and looking around to see whether anyone noticed. The bracelet had not been paid for, and the woman was wearing it, with tags attached, at the time of her arrest. She was found to be indigent and appointed a lawyer. The lawyer, who was struggling with personal problems, left most of the investigation of the case to his paralegal, who had only been out of paralegal school for two months. At trial, the lawyer dozed off several times and neglected to make any objections. The woman was convicted

Can the woman successfully argue ineffective assistance of counsel on appeal?

(A) Yes, because the lawyer did not do the necessary investigation of her case.
(B) Yes, because the lawyer was not awake for the entire trial.
(C) No, because she cannot show that she would have prevailed with effective counsel.
(D) No, because she cannot show that she was likely to prevail with effective counsel.

Answers and Explanations

Explanation: Question 1

The correct answer is: **(C)** inadmissible, because the defendant's statement was coerced.

The defendant's statement is inadmissible for a few reasons. The doctor obtained the defendant's statement by threatening to withhold medical treatment, an act which would result in the defendant's almost certain death. A statement obtained by threat of death cannot be considered voluntary under Miranda v. Arizona [384 U.S. 436 (1966)]. Furthermore, while the doctor herself was not a law enforcement agent, the defendant's statement was nevertheless obtained at the direction of the police and without the proper Miranda warnings.

(A) Incorrect. admissible, because the doctor was not a law enforcement officer.

While it is true that the doctor was not a law enforcement agent, the defendant's statement was obtained at the direction of the police, through the detective's request to the doctor. Under the Federal Rules of Criminal Procedure, a non-member of law enforcement who acts at the direction of the police must nevertheless comply with the rules of criminal procedure regarding statements obtained from defendants. Here, the detective directed the doctor to obtain the statement, and the doctor failed to issue the defendant the proper Miranda warnings and used the threat of withholding essential medical treatment in order to obtain the defendant's statement. The fact that the doctor was not a member of law enforcement is insufficient to make this statement admissible when it was coerced and improperly solicited from the defendant. As such, this choice is incorrect.

(B) Incorrect. admissible, because the detective did not put the doctor in the position to obtain the statement from the defendant.

It is true that if the detective had installed a non-member of law enforcement in the doctor's position for the express purpose of obtaining an incriminating statement from the defendant, this fact would serve as additional evidence that that person was acting at the direction of the police. However, even if, as in this case, the police themselves did not install the doctor in this position, the fact that the detective approached the doctor and demanded the doctor's help in obtaining information from the defendant nevertheless makes the doctor an agent of the police. And, where a party acts as an agent of law enforcement, he or she is required to comply with the federal rules in soliciting information from the accused. As such, this response is incorrect.

(D) Incorrect. inadmissible, because the defendant was seriously ill at the time he consented to giving the statement.

A statement by a seriously ill party can still be admissible so long as it is voluntary. Here, the doctor obtained the defendant's statement by threatening to withhold medical treatment, an act which would result in the defendant's almost certain death. A statement obtained by threat of death cannot be considered voluntary [Miranda v. Arizona, 384 U.S. 436 (1966)]. Thus, the manner in which the defendant's statement was obtained, not the defendant's medical condition, makes his statement inadmissible. As such, this response is incorrect.

Explanation: Question 2

The correct answer is: **(C)** The teacher consented to the search.

If consent is validly given, there is no invasion of any reasonable expectation of privacy, and the officer does not need a warrant nor any exception to the warrant requirement to justify a search. Here, because the teacher agreed to allow the officer to search the vehicle, the seizure of the pistol was proper.

(A) Incorrect. The search was reasonable under the circumstances, because it was based upon the experience and knowledge of a veteran police officer.

Even under the moving-vehicle exception, there must be probable cause for the search. Here, there are no facts indicating probable cause, only the hunch of an experienced police officer. A warrantless search of a movable vehicle is permitted where the police have probable cause to believe that the vehicle contains contraband or the fruits, instrumentalities, or evidence of crime. The hunch of an experienced officer would not be sufficient on its own to constitute probable cause. Thus, this answer is incorrect.

(B) Incorrect. The search was incident to a valid arrest.
A stop of a vehicle for a traffic-type violation is not a custodial arrest sufficient to allow an officer to search a driver or a car without a warrant. Here, there the officer had no reason to arrest the teacher, and thus no probable cause for arrest, prior to the search. Lacking probable cause for an arrest, the officer cannot assert that the search was incident to arrest. Thus, this answer is incorrect.

(D) Incorrect. The search was reasonable due to the inherent mobility of a motor vehicle.
The mobility of a car may dispense with the search warrant requirement when a police officer has probable cause to search. This means the officer must be aware of facts and circumstances such that a reasonable person would conclude that seizable objects are located on the person or at the place to be searched. Here, the officer had no probable cause to justify the warrantless search of the vehicle. Lacking probable cause, the officer had no basis for the warrantless search under the moving-vehicle exception. Thus, this answer is incorrect.

Explanation: Question 3

The correct answer is: **(A)** Yes, because any fact that increases the penalty beyond the maximum set by statutory guidelines must be proved to the finder of fact beyond a reasonable doubt.

The Constitution requires that any fact that increases the penalty for a crime beyond the prescribed statutory maximum, other than the fact of a prior conviction, must be charged in an indictment and proved beyond a reasonable doubt [Apprendi v. New Jersey, 530 U.S. 466 (2000)]. The constitutional basis for this holding lies in both the Due Process Clause of the Fifth Amendment and the jury trial guarantee of the Sixth Amendment. In accordance with the Apprendi decision, the defendant's sentence should be overturned. Choice (A) is correct. Note: Both state and federal sentencing guidelines are subject to the Apprendi rule.

(B) Incorrect. Yes, because the enhanced sentence was based upon factors unrelated to the robbery charge.

(C) Incorrect. No, because the preponderance of evidence standard in sentencing hearings is constitutionally permissible.

(D) Incorrect. No, because the judge indicated that she would not have been able to impose the enhanced sentence if the reasonable doubt standard applied.

Explanation: Question 4

The correct answer is: **(C)** A defendant was a 15-year-old high school sophomore. He possessed normal intelligence and experience for a youth of his age. One night, he and two friends attended a concert. After the concert, the defendant and his friends went on a spree assaulting and robbing victims in the park. The next day the defendant was arrested. After being subjected to persistent questioning for two hours, the defendant was first given his Miranda warnings. The defendant then waived his Miranda rights and offered a confession. At trial, the defendant claims he did not make a knowing and intelligent waiver.

The Miranda right to silence can be waived either expressly or impliedly. A Miranda waiver is based on voluntariness as determined by the "totality of circumstances." To determine if a knowing and intelligent waiver has occurred, the court views both the (1) competence of the defendant, i.e., age, experience, intelligence, and ability to fully understand the warnings; and (2) the conduct of the police, namely as to whether there has been overreaching. In the present example, choice (A) is incorrect because defendants have generally been unsuccessful in claiming that their Miranda waivers should be held invalid because they were either intoxicated or under the influence of drugs or medication at that time. Likewise, choice (B) is incorrect inasmuch as the "personal characteristics of the defendant existing at the time of the purported waiver are relevant only as they relate to police overreaching." See Colorado v. Connelly [479 U.S. 157 (1986)], where the court rejected a state court ruling that a defendant's Miranda waiver was not voluntary because he suffered from a psychosis that interfered with his ability to make free and rational choices. The court concluded that "Miranda protects defendants against government coercion but goes no further than that." As a result, choice (C) is the best answer because the defendant was subjected to persistent questioning for two hours before receiving his Miranda warnings. Courts have held waivers invalid where the defendant had been held in custody for an extended period of time before being given the warnings, or where the defendant had first been subjected to persistent questioning. Choice (D) is incorrect because in Fare v. Michael C. [439 U.S. 1310 (1978)], the court held that a juvenile's request to have his probation officer present was not a per se invocation of Miranda rights.

(A) Incorrect. A defendant recently graduated from law school. At her graduation party, the defendant became highly intoxicated. Following the party, the defendant drove home in her automobile. She fell asleep at the wheel and crashed into another vehicle, injuring the driver. Shortly after the accident, a police officer came on the scene and arrested the defendant, charging her with D.U.I. The defendant was then given her Miranda warnings and transported to the police station. Upon questioning, the defendant, who was still highly intoxicated, waived her Miranda rights and made an incriminating statement.

(B) Incorrect. A defendant stabbed a victim after a violent argument. Following the victim's death, the police arrested the defendant and charged him with murder. He was transported to the station house where Miranda warnings were given. Afterwards, the defendant was interrogated and proceeded to waive his Miranda rights. He then confessed to committing the crime. At trial, a psychiatrist testified that the defendant was mentally ill and his confession was not the result of a knowing and intelligent waiver.

(D) Incorrect. A defendant was a 16-year-old juvenile in police custody on suspicion of murder. After he was given his Miranda warnings, he requested to have his probation officer present. He was on probation for a series of juvenile offenses. His request was denied. During a brief interrogation, the defendant proceeded to waive his Miranda rights and made incriminating statements that linked him with the crime. At trial, the defendant's lawyer claims that his waiver was ineffective because his request to see the probation officer was the equivalent of asking for a lawyer.

Explanation: Question 5

The correct answer is: **(D)** No, with respect to the right to counsel and the right to a jury trial.

There is no constitutional right to a jury trial for petty offenses—only for serious offenses, e.g., felonies. For purposes of the right to a jury trial, an offense is serious if imprisonment for more than six months is authorized. Because the maximum imprisonment was seven months, the defendant would be entitled to a jury trial. By the same token, a defendant has a right to counsel for misdemeanor offenses if there is the possibility of imprisonment. According to the holding in Alabama v. Shelton [535 U.S. 654 (2002)], a suspended sentence that may end up in the actual deprivation of a person's liberty (i.e., imprisonment) may not be imposed under the Sixth Amendment unless the indigent defendant was provided the assistance of counsel in the prosecution of the crime charged. Choice (D) is the best answer because the judge's instruction was incorrect with respect to both the right to a jury trial and the right to counsel.

(A) Incorrect. Yes, with respect to the right to counsel.

(B) Incorrect. Yes, with respect to the right to a jury trial.

(C) Incorrect. Yes, with respect to the right to counsel and the right to a jury trial.

Explanation: Question 6

The correct answer is: **(B)** No, the boyfriend does not have standing to raise a Fourth Amendment violation claim.

The exclusionary rule is used to deter unlawful police conduct by making inadmissible any evidence or statements that were obtained in violation of the Fourth Amendment. However, before a defendant can assert a Fourth Amendment violation claim, that defendant must have standing and must personally be the victim of the police's unreasonable conduct. A court is tasked with determining if the defendant has a legitimate expectation of privacy in the invaded place. This apartment belonged to the woman and not the boyfriend. The boyfriend was not listed on the lease and was never more than an overnight guest. The woman, the lawful occupant of the property, gave police permission to search the location and they located the illegal items in plain view. The boyfriend does not have standing the challenge the search and seizure and has no legitimate expectation of privacy in this space. Additionally, there was nothing improper about the police entry into the apartment since they were given permission to enter by the woman.

(A) Incorrect. No, this rule is only available in deportation and parole revocation hearings.

This answer choice is incorrect because it states the opposite of an appropriate limitation to the exclusionary rule: the exclusionary rule is unavailable in deportation and parole revocation hearings. Furthermore, this hearing is neither for the deportation of the defendant nor revocation of the defendant's parole.

(C) Incorrect. Yes, it is a mandatory remedy for a violation of the defendant's Fourth Amendment rights.

The exclusionary rule is specifically not meant as a remedy for a violation of the defendant's Fourth Amendment Rights. It is meant as a deterrence for police misconduct by making physical and testimonial evidence inadmissible in court when police do not comport with Fourth Amendment requirements. This rule is not to be used as a mandatory remedy by the courts.

(D) Incorrect. Yes, the police did not have a warrant to search and seize.

The exclusionary rule is not automatically triggered in any situation in which police fail to obtain a warrant. It is important to note that police do not always need a warrant in order to obtain physical evidence. There are many exceptions to the warrant requirements. Two such exceptions to the warrant requirements are consent and plain view. Here, the lawful occupant, who had authority to provide consent to search, gave consent for officers to enter the location and conduct a search. Once inside of the location, the illegal items were located in plain view. This satisfies both the consent and plain view requirements for a warrantless search.

Explanation: Question 7

The correct answer is: **(D)** inadmissible because it was not preceded by a Miranda warning.

All statements obtained pursuant to custodial interrogation must be preceded by Miranda warnings. Here, the driver had been taken into custody and transported to another location for questioning. As such, without being advised of her Miranda rights, statements made during her custodial interrogation include the statements she made to the detective.

(A) Incorrect. admissible, because of her previous voluntary statement.

This answer suggests an irrelevant issue. The fact that a previous statement was given in some other place or in a non-custodial context does not affect the admissibility of a statement. The driver's previous voluntary statement to the security guard did not negate the requirement that her custodial interrogation by the detective be accompanied by proper Miranda warnings. Thus, this answer is incorrect.

(B) Incorrect. admissible, because the detective believed that the arresting officer had administered the Miranda warnings.

The detective's good-faith belief that an arresting officer had issued the driver her Miranda warnings does not mitigate the requirement that all statements obtained pursuant to custodial interrogation be preceded by proper Miranda warnings. The good-faith exception applies only in cases where a warrant is being executed and is inapplicable under the facts presented. Thus, this answer is incorrect.

(C) Incorrect. inadmissible, because the statement was not clearly inculpatory.

Culpability is irrelevant. Any statement obtained pursuant to custodial interrogation must be preceded by proper Miranda warnings, regardless of whether the statement is inculpatory or exculpatory. Thus, this answer is incorrect.

Explanation: Question 8

The correct answer is: **(A)** inadmissible.

The State may not circumvent the warrant requirement by employing a private citizen to act on its behalf. Although the repairman acted voluntarily and was not a member of law enforcement, he acted at the behest of the detective and is, therefore, an agent of the state for purposes of the search he conducted and the seizure of the IDs and the blouse. Since the search was conducted without a warrant, the evidence is inadmissible.

(B) Incorrect. admissible, because the repairman is a private citizen.

In these circumstances, the repairman acted as an agent of the state because he was performing a search at the behest of the detective. Although he was invited on the premises by the man, his actions were outside the scope of his permission to be on the premises and were not undertaken at his own initiative but under the direction of law enforcement. Hence the evidence is inadmissible.

(C) Incorrect. admissible, because of the inevitable discovery doctrine.

The inevitable discovery rule applies where evidence would have been discovered independent of the bad search. There is no information to suggest that the IDs would ultimately have been discovered through legitimate means.

(D) Incorrect. admissible, because the repairman was invited onto the property by the man.

Although the repairman was on the premises with the permission of the man, his actions exceeded the scope of his authorization by the man and were undertaken at the behest of law enforcement. As such, he acted as an agent of the state although he is not a member of law enforcement.

Explanation: Question 9

The correct answer is: **(A)** It will be denied, because Alex did not elicit the statement from Harvey.

Absent an effective waiver, the deliberate eliciting of any incriminating statements made by a defendant without the assistance of an attorney violates the Sixth Amendment right to counsel, once formal charges have been filed [Massiah v. United States, 377 U.S. 201 (1964)]. Where a paid government informant deliberately elicited statements from a defendant in his jail cell, a violation of the right to counsel occurred and such statements were held inadmissible [United States v. Henry, 447 U.S. 264 (1980)]. However, passive listening by a cell mate informant does not violate the right to counsel [Kuhlmann v. Wilson, 106 S. Ct. 2616 (1986)]. Alex, the State's informer, did not in any way elicit the statement from Harvey. Therefore, Harvey's statement is admissible.

(B) Incorrect. It will be denied, because Alex was not a police officer.

Alex was acting as an agent of the State and is therefore bound by the same restrictions as police officers. The State cannot use private citizens to circumvent Constitutional requirements. However, Harvey's motion to dismiss will be denied on other grounds.

(C) Incorrect. It will be granted, because Alex was an agent of the police and did not Mirandize Harvey.

The Miranda rule applies only to statements made during custodial interrogation. Although Alex is an agent of the police, no interrogation took place.

(D) Incorrect. It will be granted, because Alex's actions violated the Massiah Rule.

Under Massiah, once formal charges have been filed, the deliberate eliciting of any incriminating statements made by a defendant without the assistance of an attorney violates the Sixth Amendment right to counsel, unless the defendant has effectively waived the right [Massiah v. United States, 377 U.S. 201 (1964)]. Here, Alex, the State's informer, did not in any way elicit the statement from Harvey. Therefore, Harvey's statement is admissible.

Explanation: Question 10

The correct answer is: **(D)** cannot comment on or argue regarding the friend's failure to testify.

All parties have the right to call, examine, and cross-examine witnesses in a criminal trial. Under the Sixth Amendment, a defendant has the constitutional right to confront all witnesses called against him or her, and no inference springs from the failure of either party to call a witness. Allowing the prosecutor to comment on the failure of the friend to testify would violate the gardener's right to cross-examine the friend. If the prosecutor suggests or implies that the friend's testimony would be adverse to the gardener, then the prosecution is effectively using the friend as a witness against the gardener without giving the gardener the chance to cross-examine the witness.

(A) Incorrect. can argue in closing that the friend's failure to testify suggests that his testimony would have been adverse to the gardener.

A prosecutor cannot argue at any time that an absent witness's testimony would have been adverse to a defendant, no matter the stage of the trial. Allowing the prosecutor to comment on the failure of the friend to testify would effectively violate the gardener's Sixth Amendment right to cross-examine the friend. Thus, this answer is incorrect.

(B) Incorrect. can use the friend's failure to testify as impeachment evidence.

Allowing the friend's absence to be used to impeach a witness would violate the gardener's Sixth Amendment right to cross-examine witnesses used against him. The argument that the friend's absence is somehow adverse to the defendant effectively uses the friend as a witness. The defendant has a Sixth Amendment right to confront that witness, which would be violated by his absence. Thus, this answer is incorrect.

(C) Incorrect. cannot cite the friend's absence unless the gardener has the opportunity to rebut.

A prosecutor cannot argue at any time that an absent witness's testimony would have been adverse to a defendant, even if a defendant's attorney has the opportunity to rebut such a statement. Thus, this answer is incorrect.

Explanation: Question 11

The correct answer is: **(A)** granted, because there was no reasonable suspicion for the search.

In Terry v. Ohio [392 U.S. 1 (1968)], the Supreme Court held that police have the ability to do a limited search for weapons of areas within a suspect's control based on a reasonable and articulable suspicion that the person stopped was armed and dangerous and had been, is, or was about to engage in a criminal act. A Terry stop and frisk has two parts: the stop and the frisk. When Terry-stopping someone, the officer must have a reasonable suspicion that criminal activity has, is, or is about to be, committed. During the course of the stop, if the officer feels that the suspect is in possession of a weapon that is of danger to him or others, he may conduct a pat-down of the suspect's outer clothing garments to search for weapons. For the frisk to be constitutional, the officer must have conducted a pat-down for his personal safety or the safety of others in the area.

Here, given the news of the nearby theft and that the jogger was running, the patrolman was most likely justified in Terry-stopping the jogger. However, although a Terry stop may be valid, the cause for the stop does not automatically give rise to cause to frisk. In this case, the jogger offered the patrolman a reasonable explanation of his activity; furthermore, the facts indicate that the patrolman's search of the jogger was not conducted for the safety of the patrolman or any of the others nearby and that the search was not for weapons, but for evidence of the jewelry theft. As such, the patrolman's stop and frisk of the jogger was not a valid Terry stop and frisk.

(B) Incorrect. granted, because the officer had no right to stop the jogger.

An officer always has the right to stop someone for a brief period of time for questioning if there is a reasonable belief that criminal activity may be afoot. Seeing the jogger running near the store soon after the jewelry theft was almost certainly legitimate cause for the patrolman to briefly detain the jogger for questioning. Thus, this answer is incorrect.

(C) Incorrect. denied, because the patrolman made a valid Terry stop and frisk.

A Terry stop and frisk has two parts: the stop and the frisk. Here, the frisk was not valid. For the frisk to be constitutional, the officer must testify that he or she conducted the pat-down for his personal safety, or the safety of others in the area. Here, the pat-down was simply a search for evidence of the jewelry theft. Thus, this answer is incorrect.

(D) Incorrect. denied, because the jogger's possession of the gun indicated that the jogger was in fact armed and dangerous.

The fruits of an illegal search or arrest cannot be used to justify the search or the arrest. As such, this answer is incorrect.

Explanation: Question 12

The correct answer is: **(A)** The evidence is inadmissible, because there was no probable cause.

While the police chief ordered that all green cars of the same make and model be stopped, the fact remains that the car was not at all a unique or a conspicuous vehicle, it was more than six hours after the library incident that the officer spotted the man's car and pulled him over, and the man's car was spotted on the other side of town. With no information beyond the color, make, and model of the suspect's car, the basis for the officer's stop of the man's vehicle was highly questionable. However, even more than the stop itself, for which there existed some grounds, however tenuous, the search of the man's vehicle clearly does not meet the probable cause requirement, and the evidence seized during this improper, warrant-less search is therefore inadmissible.

(B) Incorrect. The evidence is inadmissible, because the police had no basis to stop the man's vehicle.

While the police chief ordered that all green cars of the same make and model be stopped, the fact remains that the car was not at all a unique or a conspicuous vehicle, it was stopped on the other side of town and it had been six hours since the library incident. Therefore the officer's stop of the man's vehicle was highly questionable. However, the permissibility of the officer's stop of the man's vehicle is independent and not determinative of the legality of the officers' search of the vehicle. Even more than the stop itself, for which there existed some grounds, the search of the man's vehicle clearly does not meet the probable cause requirement. As such, the evidence is inadmissible.

(C) Incorrect. The evidence is admissible, because the automobile exception applies.

The automobile exception does not eliminate the need for probable cause. According to the automobile exception, once the police have probable cause to search the moving or temporarily stopped vehicle, they may seize the vehicle and search it later, even if there is sufficient time to obtain a warrant between seizure of the vehicle and search. Additionally, the police may inspect a container within an automobile if they have probable cause to believe the container has contraband or evidence, even where the police do not have probable cause to search the entire car. In this case, the officer did not have probable cause to search the car, so the automobile exception will not help.

(D) Incorrect. The evidence is admissible, because the search was incident to arrest.

The officer's search of the man's vehicle occurred before the man was arrested and, in fact, before there existed probable cause for his arrest. As such, the search cannot constitute a search incident to arrest.

Explanation: Question 13

The correct answer is: **(A)** Defendant's motion to suppress will be granted, because Officer did not have probable cause.

Defendant's action of wandering in and out of oncoming traffic was bizarre enough to create a public danger. As such, Officer clearly had a reasonable suspicion that Defendant was publicly drunk or using drugs and was creating a hazard. While this reasonable suspicion was sufficient grounds for the officer to stop and question the man, the officer did not have sufficient grounds to frisk the man. To perform a Terry stop and frisk the drunken man, the officer must have had a reasonable and articulated suspicion that the man was armed and dangerous. As there are no facts indicating such a suspicion, the officer's action of going into the man's coat was improper, and the evidence will be suppressed.

(B) Incorrect. Defendant's motion to suppress will be granted, because Officer's detention of Defendant exceeded the allowable time frame for a Terry stop.

The permissible time frame for a Terry stop is the length of time that it takes for the officer to reasonably ascertain whether criminal activity is afoot. Here, the facts do not indicate any unnecessary lingering on the part of the Officer; rather, the facts imply that Officer's stop of Defendant proceeded efficiently and was fairly brief in duration. There is nothing to suggest that the stop was improperly long or dragged out. Thus, this answer is incorrect.

(C) Incorrect. Defendant's motion to suppress will be denied, because there was reasonable suspicion that criminal activity was afoot.

This answer choice states the standard by which Officer could stop and question the man. However, for Officer to go further and actually frisk or pat Defendant down, he must have had a reasonable and articulated suspicion that Defendant was armed and dangerous. As this was absent, Officer's search of Defendant was improper and the evidence should be suppressed.

(D) Incorrect. Defendant's motion to suppress will be denied, because Officer was only trying to protect Defendant.

Although an officer may always approach and ask a citizen anything, he may not detain him without a reasonable suspicion that criminal activity is afoot. As such, Officer's intent to protect Defendant is irrelevant to the analysis of whether Officer's stop and detention of Defendant was legal. Thus, this answer is incorrect.

Explanation: Question 14

The correct answer is: **(B)** the college student has standing to challenge the search, because he had a possessory interest in the premises searched.

The college student clearly had an expectation of privacy in the apartment searched. When a defendant has a possessory interest in the premises searched and the search violates the defendant's Fourth Amendment rights, the defendant has standing to challenge the validity of the search.

(A) Incorrect. the college student has standing to challenge the search, because incriminating items were found.

In determining whether a person's Fourth Amendment rights against unlawful search and seizure have been violated, the test is whether the individual has a reasonable expectation of privacy in the area searched, not whether incriminating evidence is found. Certainly, a person who rents an apartment and pays rent has a reasonable expectation of privacy in the apartment. Thus, this answer is incorrect.

(C) Incorrect. the college student does not have standing to challenge the search, because he did not use the apartment as a home.

Any place in which a person has a reasonable expectation of privacy is protected from illegal search and seizure, not just a place of residence. Thus, this answer is incorrect.

(D) Incorrect. the college student does not have standing to challenge the search, because by renting the apartment in a false name, he waived his right to privacy.

The false name is irrelevant. In determining whether a person's Fourth Amendment rights have been violated, the test is whether the individual has a reasonable expectation of privacy in the area searched. Certainly, a person who rents an apartment and pays rent has a reasonable expectation of privacy in the apartment, regardless of whether that individual uses a false name. Thus, this answer is incorrect.

Explanation: Question 15

The correct answer is: **(B)** both the stop and the frisk were proper under Terry.

Under Terry v. Ohio [392 U.S. 1 1968)], a police officer must have reasonable suspicion of a crime in order to stop a suspect. If the police officer has a reasonable and articulable suspicion that a suspect is armed and dangerous, the officer may also, without probable cause, perform a pat-down search—i.e., a frisk—for concealed weapons. Here, the fact that the man met the description of the perpetrator, was spotted close to the scene of the robbery, and was acting suspiciously and walking quickly all support a reasonable suspicion by the officers that he might be the suspect. The use of the gun in the crime also supports the reasonable and articulable suspicion that the suspect may be armed and dangerous.

(A) Incorrect. the stop was proper under Terry, but the frisk was not.

Actually, both the stop and the frisk were proper under the Terry standard. Here, the fact that the man met the description of the perpetrator, was spotted close to the scene of the robbery, and was acting suspicious and walking fast all support a reasonable belief by the officers that he might have committed a crime. In addition, the facts easily constitute a reasonable and articulable suspicion that the man might be armed and dangerous, thus permitting the officers to frisk him, under Terry. Thus, this answer is incorrect.

(C) Incorrect. neither the stop nor the frisk were constitutional under the Fourth Amendment.

To the contrary. Under Terry v. Ohio [392 U.S.1 [1968)], both the stop and the frisk were constitutional. The stop requires the reasonable suspicion of a crime (either in the past, under away, or about to be committed), and the frisk requires a reasonable and articulable suspicion that the suspect is armed and dangerous —both of which are satisfied here by the facts. Thus, this answer is incorrect.

(D) Incorrect. the entire encounter was constitutional under the inevitable discovery doctrine.

The conclusion is correct, but the analysis is not. The inevitable discovery rule applies where police unlawfully seize evidence that they would have eventually discovered by legal means. Thus, the doctrine is applicable only where the initial search was illegal. In this case, the officers' search of the man was legal.

Explanation: Question 16

The correct answer is: **(B)** The judge should grant the motion to suppress the evidence only if he determines that the officer knew that the informant's statements were false.

Evidence seized pursuant to a defective search warrant (a warrant not based on probable cause) will not automatically be excluded. The evidence is still admissible as long as the police officer obtaining the warrant did not lie to the magistrate, and the police officers executing the warrant reasonably were acting on good faith reliance. Even though the informant provided the officer with false information, the judge should deny the motion to suppress only if the officer's reliance was not reasonable.

(A) Incorrect. The judge should grant the motion to suppress the evidence only if the informant knowingly provided false information to the officer.

The informant's intent is irrelevant. A defective search warrant does not necessarily trigger the exclusionary rule. The evidence will be admissible as long as the officer obtaining the warrant did not lie to the magistrate and the officers executing the warrant acted in good faith. Even if the informant had knowingly provided false information, the evidence should not necessarily have been excluded. Thus, this answer is incorrect.

(C) Incorrect. The judge should grant the motion to suppress the evidence, because neither methamphetamine nor the ingredients and equipment to manufacture methamphetamine were found in the house.

The fact that the police did not find what they were looking for does not automatically invalidate the search and the seizure of the stolen jewelry. The officers' warrant will likely be deemed valid as long as they acted in good faith. The jewelry would then be subject to the plain-view doctrine—with the valid warrant, the police would be lawfully positioned (and, under the second element of the doctrine, it would be immediately apparent that the jewelry is incriminating). Thus, this answer is incorrect.

(D) Incorrect. The judge should grant the motion to suppress the evidence, because the officer's affidavit was based entirely on hearsay.

A warrant may be supported by an affidavit based entirely on hearsay as long as the affidavit indicates by a totality of the circumstances (including the reliability of the informant and the basis of the informant's knowledge) that there is a fair probability the items sought will be located at the place to be searched. Thus, this answer is incorrect.

Explanation: Question 17

The correct answer is: **(A)** The bank clerk's only.

Only the identification process conducted with regard to the bank clerk was proper. An unnecessarily suggestive identification is inadmissible as a violation of due process. Dennis, the defendant, had not yet been formally charged, so no right to have counsel present at his identification had yet attached. Neither is there any indication in the facts that there was anything improperly suggestive about the clerk's show-up. Therefore, her identification of Dennis is admissible. However, the officer's show-up identification of Dennis was flawed, in that he knew of the evidence seizure and of Dennis's confession. The officer's knowledge of these facts would be highly likely to have an improper influence on the officer's identification, thereby violating Dennis's due process rights. As such, the officer's show-up identification of Dennis is not admissible.

(B) Incorrect. The officer's only.

The officer's show-up identification of Dennis was flawed, so only the clerk's identification would be admissible. An unnecessarily suggestive identification violates due process and is inadmissible. At the time of his identification, the officer had heard of Dennis's capture, the evidence seizure, and Dennis's confession. The officer's knowledge of these facts would be highly likely to exert an improper influence on the officer's identification, thereby violating Dennis's due process rights. Thus, the officer's show-up identification of Dennis is not admissible.

(C) Incorrect. Both the bank clerk's and the officer's.

The police officer had different information than the clerk did when identifying Dennis, and only the identification process used for the bank clerk was proper. Dennis had not yet been formally charged, so his right to have counsel present at an identification had not yet attached. In addition, the facts do not indicate that there was anything improperly suggestive about the clerk's show-up, so her identification likely did not violate Dennis's due process rights. Therefore, her identification of Dennis is admissible. In contrast, the officer's show-up identification of Dennis was flawed because he already knew of the evidence seizure and of Dennis's confession. The officer's knowledge of these facts would be highly likely to have an improper influence on the officer's identification, which would violate Dennis's due process rights. As such, the officer's show-up identification of Dennis is not admissible.

(D) Incorrect. Neither the bank clerk's nor the officer's.

Although it is correct that the officer's identification would not be admissible, the bank clerk's identification was properly conducted and would be admissible. The defendant, Dennis, had not yet been formally charged, so the right to have counsel present at his identification had not yet attached. There is also no indication in the facts that there was anything improperly suggestive about the clerk's show-up which would violate Dennis's due process rights. Therefore, the clerk's identification of Dennis is admissible. The officer's show-up identification of Dennis, however, was flawed, in that he knew other officers had seized evidence and obtained Dennis's confession. The officer's knowledge of these facts would be highly likely to have an improper influence on the officer's identification, resulting in a violation of Dennis's due process rights. Therefore, while the officer's show-up identification of Dennis is not admissible, the clerk's identification is admissible.

Explanation: Question 18

The correct answer is: **(B)** The bail set by the court violates the Eighth Amendment prohibition against excessive bail.

While there is no constitutional right to bail, the Eighth Amendment prohibits excessive bail. Under the circumstances of this case, $20 million is almost certainly likely to be deemed excessive.

(A) Incorrect. The teenager's right to counsel has been violated.

The right to counsel does not attach until formal charges have been filed. Because the teenager was not indicted until a week after this appearance, his right to counsel has not been violated. Thus, this answer is incorrect.

(C) Incorrect. The bail hearing must be held after the indictment.

While the indictment typically precedes the bail hearing, there is no such requirement. Rather, a bail hearing must be set and conducted during or soon after arraignment. Thus, this answer is incorrect.

(D) Incorrect. The objections to the teenager's bail, if any, had to be raised at his bail hearing.

Just as courts have specifically held that a denial of bail may be raised at any time during criminal proceedings, the court would likely hold that an excessive-bail objection may also be raised at any time. Thus, this answer is incorrect.

Explanation: Question 19

The correct answer is: **(A)** Yes, the girlfriend can be charged under the Pinkerton doctrine.

Felony murder is a killing proximately caused during the commission of an inherently dangerous felony. Felony murder charges may be brought for intentional killings, accidental killings, and for killings by the accused's accomplices. Here, the girlfriend is liable for all of the natural consequences of the criminal acts under vicarious liability because she is an accomplice to the crime and a conspirator. Therefore the girlfriend may be charged with felony murder because the deaths were proximately caused during the commission of a serious and inherently dangerous felony by her accomplices.

(B) Incorrect. Yes, the girlfriend can be charged under the theory of accomplice liability as either a principal in the first degree or in the second degree.

This answer is incorrect because, although it reaches the right conclusion, it relies on an inapplicable rule. A defendant can be convicted of a crime under Accomplice Liability in one of four ways - as the principal in the first degree, as the principal in the second degree, as an accessory before the fact, or as an accessory after the fact. In order to be a principal in the first degree, the defendant would have to have the requisite mens rea as well as be present to physically perform the criminal act. To be a principal in the second degree, the defendant would have to have the same requisite mens rea and only needs to aid, abet or encourage the commission of the crime while being present at the scene of the crime. Here, although the girlfriend aided and encouraged the boyfriend to commit the burglary, the girlfriend was not present at the time that the crime was committed and therefore, cannot be charged under this theory of a crime relating to the death of the homeowner.

(C) Incorrect. No, the girlfriend did not know that the best friend was going to bring a gun.

The girlfriend agreed to participate in the burglary of her neighbor's home by providing the boyfriend with information about the homeowners and requesting proceeds of the crime. She also took a substantial, overt step towards to the commission of the crime by calling her boyfriend back and telling the boyfriend that the homeowners were away from the home. By doing each of these things, she made herself a conspirator, and the Pinkerton doctrine provides that each conspirator is liable for the crimes of co-conspirators where the crimes are a foreseeable outgrowth of the conspiracy and committed in furtherance of goal of the conspiracy. Thus, under Pinkerton, she would be liable for the death of the homeowner because such violence would be a foreseeable outgrowth of a burglary and because the shooting was committed in furtherance of the burglary.

(D) Incorrect. No, this falls within the Redline limitation.

Under this majority rule relating to felony murder, a defendant cannot be held criminally liable for the death of a co-conspirator or co-perpetrator which occurs during the commission or attempted commission of a serious or inherently dangerous felony. However, the call of the question here asks whether the girlfriend can be charged in the death of the homeowner, not the death of the best friend. This answer would be correct if the question asked whether the girlfriend could be charged in the death of the best friend.

Explanation: Question 20

The correct answer is: **(D)** That the trial did not occur within 70 days of the indictment.

The Right to a Speedy Trial is a right which is guaranteed by the Sixth Amendment in both the federal and state courts. There are a few distinctions between cases which are heard in the state court and those which are heard in the federal courts. Here, the facts indicate that it was determined that this case was not suited for federal prosecution. Therefore, any rules which apply specifically to the federal courts would not be applicable here. The Speedy Trial Act of 1974 requires that a prosecutor seek a federal indictment within thirty days of the arrest of a defendant and that the trial be held within seventy days of that indictment. If this was a federal case and this type of defense motion was made, the judge would have to determine whether or not the requirements of the Speedy Trial Act were satisfied. However, because this case is not being handled federally, the requirement that the trial begin within seventy days of indictment is irrelevant to the issue of whether the defendant's Right to a Speedy Trial was violated.

(A) Incorrect. The defendant never asserted his right to a speedy trial.

One of the factors that a judge must balance in determining whether a defendant's Sixth Amendment speedy trial rights have been violated is whether or not the defendant ever asserted his right to a speedy trial. It would have been proper for that right to have been asserted before the day of trial.

(B) Incorrect. The defendant filed a series of pretrial motions and suppression hearings.

A defendant's right to a speedy trial is waived when a defendant willfully delays the trial by filing pretrial motions or seeking suppression hearings. Here, rather than filing one set of pretrial motions, the defense attorney delayed the trial by multiple months by filing one motion every month for four months. Based on this behavior, the defendant may have waived his right to a speedy trial. This is an appropriate circumstance for the judge to consider.

(C) Incorrect. The prejudice to the defendant.

In addition to balancing the length and reasons for a delay of trial and the defendant's assertion of his right to a speedy trial, the judge must balance the prejudice to the defendant which occurs as a result of the delay. Such a prejudice may include incarceration which is determined to be oppressive, memory loss by witnesses, loss of evidence, and anxiety to the defendant. All of these would be appropriate considerations.

Explanation: Question 21

The correct answer is: **(D)** Both identifications will be admitted.

A show-up, like any other identification procedure, will be considered valid unless it is unnecessarily suggestive and likely to produce an irreparable, mistaken identification [Stovall v. Denno, 388 U.S. 293 (1967)]. Here, there is no indication that either of the two show-ups was unduly suggestive—the defendant wasn't, for example, handcuffed or forced to pose in an incriminating position. As such, the identifications are admissible as evidence.

(A) Incorrect. The identification by the pedestrian will be excluded, because the procedure violated the plumber's due process rights.

The show-up of the pedestrian will be admitted (as will the show-up of the store owner). A show-up will be considered constitutional—i.e., not violative of a defendant's due process rights—as long as it is not unnecessarily suggestive and not likely to produce an irreparable, mistaken identification. Nothing in the facts suggests that this show-up was unnecessarily suggestive. Thus, this answer is incorrect.

(B) Incorrect. The identification by the jewelry store owner will be excluded, because it was unnecessarily suggestive.

The court would likely hold both show-ups constitutional. A show-up will be deemed constitutional as long as it is not unnecessarily suggestive and not likely to produce an irreparable, mistaken identification. Nothing in the facts suggests that the show-up of the jewelry store owner (or the show-up of the pedestrian) was unduly suggestive. Thus, this answer is incorrect.

(C) Incorrect. Both identifications will be excluded.

To the contrary—both identifications will likely be admitted. A show-up is considered a valid identification procedure as long as it is not (1) unnecessarily suggestive; and (2) likely to produce an irreparable, mistaken identification. Nothing in the facts suggests that either of the two show-ups was unduly suggestive. Indeed, the show-ups might be considered even more fair than the typical show-up in that there was another person present (the electrician) besides only the police officers and the accused. Thus, this answer is incorrect.

Explanation: Question 22

The correct answer is: **(D)** All three crimes.

The gang member could be legally convicted of, and consecutively sentenced for, all three crimes. This question poses two potential double jeopardy issues, neither of which proves fatal. The first issue is whether consecutive punishments for a single criminal act constitute double jeopardy. The answer is no. The Supreme Court has specifically held that when a legislature expressly authorizes multiple punishments for the violation of separate criminal statutes, such punishments do not violate the double jeopardy clause. The second potential issue is whether the conviction on two separate murder counts for the same act constitutes double jeopardy. Under the present facts, the answer is again no. Two crimes occurring out of the same transaction are considered the same offense unless one of them requires proof of an additional element not contained in the other. Here, the first-degree and felony murder counts respectively require a separate felony and the intent to kill.

(A) Incorrect. Armed robbery and either felony murder or murder.

This answer suggests a non-existent double jeopardy issue. Neither the consecutive sentences, nor the fact that a single criminal act led to two separate murder convictions, violates the bar against double jeopardy. The Supreme Court has explicitly allowed such consecutive sentencing and has also held that two crimes occurring out of the same act are considered the same offense unless one of them (as here) requires proof of an additional element. Thus, this answer is incorrect.

(B) Incorrect. Felony murder and either armed robbery or murder.

The conviction on appeal does not violate the double jeopardy clause. The Supreme Court has ruled that consecutive sentencing for crimes stemming from a single criminal act is constitutional. It has also held that two crimes occurring out of the same act are to be considered the same offense unless one, as here, requires proof of an additional element. Thus, this answer is incorrect.

(C) Incorrect. Murder and either armed robbery or felony murder.

The gang member may, in fact, be charged with all the crimes. Neither the consecutive sentencing nor the multiple charges stemming from the same criminal act constitute double jeopardy. Thus, this answer is incorrect.

Explanation: Question 23

The correct answer is: **(C)** granted, because, as the fruit of an illegal search, the gun should be excluded.

The Fourth Amendment of the Constitution does not permit police officers to stop individual cars at random merely to check the driver's license and registration. To justify the stop, a police officer must have a reasonable belief of criminal activity, such as the reasonable belief that the driver has violated a traffic law. Furthermore, the Fourth Amendment prevents the fruits of illegal searches and seizures from being used as evidence at trial. Thus, this is the best answer.

(A) Incorrect. denied, because the handle of the shotgun was in plain view.
Under the Fourth Amendment, a police officer must have a reasonable suspicion of criminal activity to justify a stop. Here, while the handle of the gun was in the plain view of the officer, it was only in view after the officer illegally stopped the driver's vehicle. Thus, the plain-view doctrine does not apply. Thus, this answer is incorrect.

(B) Incorrect. denied, because the seizure of the gun resulted from a lawful investigatory stop.
A lawful investigatory stop requires a reasonable suspicion of criminal activity supported by articulable facts. Here, the officer had no such reasonable suspicion when he stopped the driver. The stop, therefore, violated the Fourth Amendment. Thus, this answer is incorrect.

(D) Incorrect. granted, because the officer did not have probable cause to believe that the driver had or was engaged in criminal activity.
Probable cause is not required for a lawful stop by a police officer. To make a lawful stop, the officer needs only a reasonable belief that the suspect is involved in criminal activity. A lack of probable cause is, therefore, an inappropriate standard for judging the motion to suppress. Thus, this answer is incorrect.

Explanation: Question 24

The correct answer is: **(B)** The gardener had given the neighbor a set of keys to her house.

The motion filed by the gardener's attorney would rest on the assertion that the marijuana was the fruit of an illegal search of the gardener's house. The Fourth Amendment guarantees that people will not be subjected to unreasonable searches and seizures of their property. Generally, for a search to be considered reasonable, the police officers must have a warrant to conduct the search. However, a warrant is not required in certain circumstances, including where the police officers obtain consent to conduct the search. However, the consent must be voluntary and intelligent, and the person granting consent must have the apparent authority to consent. Giving the neighbor a set of keys to her house would tend to show that the neighbor had control or use of the premises, and thus the authority to consent to the search—the exact opposite of what the gardener hopes to establish.

(A) Incorrect. The gardener told the neighbor not to answer the door or the telephone when she was in the gardener's house.

This argument could be a little helpful for the gardener, but wouldn't win the motion on its own. If the gardener expressly told the neighbor not to answer the door or the telephone, then the neighbor did not have authority to consent to the search. However, any person who has joint control or use of the premises may consent to a valid search, and the police need only have a reasonable belief that the third party has actual authority for the search to be valid. If the gardener can prove that she instructed the neighbor not to answer the door or the telephone, that piece of evidence might help establish that the police had no reasonable belief that the neighbor had authority to consent to the search. Thus, this answer is incorrect.

(C) Incorrect. The police officers told the neighbor that she would have to go to the police station with them if she did not allow them to search.
A warrant is not required where the police officers obtain consent to conduct the search. However, the consent must be voluntary and intelligent, and the person granting consent must have the apparent authority

to consent. Here, if the officers coerced the neighbor into consenting, then the consent was not voluntary. This fact could defeat the validity of the search, even if the neighbor were found to have apparent authority to consent to the search. Thus, this answer is incorrect.

(D) Incorrect. The police did not have a warrant to search the gardener's house.

This is an important part of any argument the gardener might make, but insufficient to win the motion on its own. Searches conducted without a warrant are unconstitutional unless one of the exceptions applies. Therefore, while this argument would support her motion, the gardener would still have to establish that none of the exceptions (most significantly here, consent) applied. Thus, this answer is incorrect.

Explanation: Question 25

The correct answer is: **(B)** No, because the defendant has already been indicted for armed robbery of the wine shop.

Once formal charges have been filed, the deliberate eliciting of any incriminating statements made by a defendant without the assistance of an attorney, and absent an effective waiver, violates the Sixth Amendment right to counsel. Here, the defendant had been formally charged by indictment. Therefore, he had the right to have counsel present while the detective questioned him.

(A) Incorrect. No, because the detective used coercive practices to obtain the statement.

Coercion includes threats, physical abuse, or promises of leniency. To determine whether a statement has been coerced, the totality of the circumstances must be considered. However, merely telling the defendant that a victim unknown to him greatly desired her ring back does not constitute coercion. As such, it is not true that the detective used coercive practices to obtain the statement. Thus, this answer is incorrect.

(C) Incorrect. Yes, because the defendant was read his Miranda rights.

The Miranda rule applies during any custodial interrogation. However, once formal charges have been filed, other requirements, beyond Miranda, apply. Here, the detective obtained the statement after the man had been indicted. Therefore, the right to a Miranda warning is not the sole issue. The man's right to counsel was also implicated. Thus, this answer is incorrect.

(D) Incorrect. Yes, because the statement was given to help the victim retrieve her property.

All statements made by a defendant are admissible as long as they are obtained in compliance with constitutional requirements, regardless of the defendant's intent. Thus, if the man's statement was obtained in compliance with Miranda and Massiah, it would have been admissible. Alas, it wasn't. Thus, this answer is incorrect.

Explanation: Question 26

The correct answer is: **(C)** The evidence will be admitted, because the neighbor lacked standing to challenge the illegal search of the woman's apartment.

While the initial search of the woman's apartment was illegal, the neighbor lacks standing to challenge that search. The warrant, though based on illegally obtained evidence, was based upon adequate probable cause, and there is no indication that material false statements were made or relied upon.

(A) Incorrect. The evidence will be suppressed, because the warrant was issued based on illegally obtained evidence.

Although the warrant was in fact based on illegally obtained evidence, the neighbor lacks standing to challenge the search that uncovered that evidence. More significantly, the warrant was based upon adequate probable cause, and there is no suggestion that the officers made or relied upon material false statements in securing the warrant. Thus, this answer is incorrect.

(B) Incorrect. The evidence will be suppressed, because of the Good-Faith Clause of the Exclusionary Rule.

This is a red herring. There is no Good-Faith Clause of the Exclusionary Rule, but rather a good-faith exception. It does not apply to this search, which was conducted pursuant to a validly issued warrant. Thus, this answer is incorrect.

(D) Incorrect. The evidence will be admitted, because the officer had probable cause to search the woman's apartment.

The officer did not have probable cause to search the apartment and, in any case, did not obtain a warrant to do so. However, the neighbor has no standing to challenge that search, and the warrant for her apartment was properly issued regardless of the validity of the prior search.

Explanation: Question 27

The correct answer is: **(A)** The statement will not be suppressed because the Sixth Amendment right to counsel is offense-specific.

The Sixth Amendment right to counsel is offense-specific and therefore, police can question a suspect about other offenses even if those offenses are similar factually to the offense for which the suspect is actually charged. The fact that the defendant has an attorney on the driving while intoxicated charge does not preclude the police from discussing a homicide for which the defendant has not been charged. Under this fact pattern, the undercover officer was not interrogating or questioning the defendant about the contract killing. Instead, the officer was having a casual conversation and the defendant was bragging.

(B) Incorrect. The defendant had an attorney at the time he was questioned by the undercover officer.

Unlike the Sixth Amendment right to counsel, the right to counsel under the Fifth Amendment is not offense-specific. The Fifth Amendment right, however, only applies to custodial interrogations. Since there was neither custody nor interrogation, only the Sixth Amendment right to counsel is implicated here and the Sixth Amendment right to counsel is offense-specific.

(C) Incorrect. The defendant did not effectively waive his right to an attorney.

Any incriminating statements made by the defendant without the benefit of counsel would be inadmissible without an effective waiver of the right to have an attorney present once formal charges have been filed against the defendant. However, the defendant in this case had not been taken into custody or arrested on any charges relating to the contract killing. No formal charges had been filed. Therefore, the defendant's Sixth Amendment rights had not been triggered.

(D) Incorrect. The officer deceived the defendant.

Statements can be deemed to be inadmissible if they violate the Due Process Clauses of the Fifth and Fourteenth Amendments, if they violate the Sixth Amendment right to counsel, if they violate the Fifth Amendment right against self-incrimination, or if they are fruits of an illegal arrest or search under the Fourth Amendment. Here, the defense attorney made a challenge to the admissibility of the defendant's statements based on the Sixth Amendment right to counsel. However, this answer relies on the violation of the Due Process Clause. Due Process Clause violations show that a statement is involuntary and therefore inadmissible. One of the ways that such a violation can occur is when the police offer false promises of dropping charges in an effort to elicit confessions. It is important to note that police do have broad reign to trick and deceive a defendant during an interrogation so long as they do not make false promises. This answer fails for multiple reasons. First, it does not fall within the scope of the Sixth Amendment. Second, the officer did not deceive by making any false promises of dropping charges in order to elicit the defendant's statements. And lastly, the defendant was not being interrogated at the time that the statements were made.

Explanation: Question 28

The correct answer is: **(B)** No, because the warrant was validly issued and based upon information lawfully obtained. According to the open fields doctrine, any unoccupied or undeveloped area outside of the curtilage (even if fenced or posted with no trespassing signs, such as wooded areas, desert, vacant lots in urban areas, open beaches, reservoirs, and open waters) is not afforded Fourth Amendment protection. Specifically, it was held to be no search to engage in aerial photography of the outdoor areas of a large fenced-in industrial complex [Dow Chemical Co. v. United States, 476 U.S. 227 (1986)]. Furthermore, use of police aircraft flying over the defendant's home and observing marijuana plants growing within the fenced curtilage was held to be no search because the plants were readily discernible to the naked eye within a public navigable airspace [California v. Ciraolo, 476 U.S. 207 (1986)].

(A) Incorrect. No, because the officers secured a warrant before entering the cabin, despite the fact that their earlier actions may have been unlawful.

Choice (A) is incorrect because based upon the Dow Chemical and Ciraolo decisions, the conduct of the police was not unlawful.

(C) Incorrect. Yes, because the marijuana was the fruit of an illegal search and seizure because the police did not have probable cause to conduct overflight surveillance.

Choice (C) is likewise incorrect because the marijuana was not the fruit of an illegal search and seizure.

(D) Incorrect. Yes, because the police were unlawfully on the defendant's property when the marijuana patch was initially discovered.

Choice (D) is incorrect because the police could enter the defendant's farm without a warrant because it was an open field.

Explanation: Question 29

The correct answer is: **(B)** Yes, because the jury applied the wrong standard in evaluating the racial animus sentence enhancement.

With the exception of the fact of a prior conviction, any fact that increases the sentence of a crime beyond the normal statutory maximum requires a jury to prove it beyond a reasonable doubt. In this case, the jury found the aggravating factor of racial animus, but only by a preponderance of the evidence. Because the preponderance of the evidence standard is a less demanding standard, the application of the sentence enhancement is unconstitutional. The case should therefore be remanded for re-sentencing.

(A) Incorrect. Yes, because the exclusionary rule bars the introduction of evidence seized in violation of the Fourth Amendment.

This is a correct statement of the law, but it is inapplicable to sentencing. Evidence seized in violation of the Fourth Amendment cannot be introduced at trial due to the exclusionary rule, there is no such bar to its introduction at sentencing to set the level of the sentence. In this case, the letter is admissible at sentencing, even though it is the product of an unlawful search.

(C) Incorrect. No, because the exclusionary rule does not apply at sentencing.

This is a correct statement of the law. The exclusionary rule applies only to keep evidence seized in violation of the Fourth Amendment out of the guilt phase of a trial, and not the sentencing phase. However, this is merely a necessary and not a sufficient rule in this case.

(D) Incorrect. No, because the jury's sentencing procedures were constitutionally adequate.

This is an incorrect conclusion. Any fact that increases the sentence of a crime beyond the normal statutory maximum (other than a prior conviction) requires a jury to find it beyond a reasonable doubt. In this case, the jury found the aggravating factor of racial animus, but only by a preponderance of the evidence.

Because the preponderance of the evidence standard is a less demanding standard than the reasonable doubt standard, the jury's sentencing procedures were not constitutionally adequate.

Explanation: Question 30

The correct answer is: **(C)** No, because the press has a Sixth Amendment right to be present at all criminal proceedings absent an overriding interest.

Although the Sixth Amendment right to a public trial belongs to the criminal defendant and not to the press, members of the press and public also have a Sixth Amendment right to be present at all criminal trials. The interest of the press and public to attend trials can only be eliminated if the trial court finds an overriding interest that requires a closed trial. In this case, the secretary has produced only generalized evidence that some juries can be prejudiced by excessive trial publicity, which does not meet the high standard of an overriding interest. Because the standard has not been met, the press has a right to attend the trial and the motion should be denied.

(A) Incorrect. Yes, because criminal defendants have an absolute right to waive their right to a public trial.

Although the Sixth Amendment right to a public trial does belong to the criminal defendant and not to the press, the right is not absolute. Members of the press and public also have a Sixth Amendment right to be present at all criminal trials, unless the trial court finds an overriding interest that requires a closed trial. Therefore, this is not the best answer.

(B) Incorrect. Yes, because the secretary has shown that his right to a public trial would be compromised if the press were not excluded.

The facts do not support this conclusion. To close a trial to the press, the court must find an overriding interest that requires a closed trial. In this case, the secretary has produced only generalized evidence that some juries can be made impartial by excessive trial publicity, which does not meet the high standard of an overriding interest. Because the standard has not been met, the press have a right to attend the trial and the motion should be denied.

(D) Incorrect. No, because the press because the press has a Sixth Amendment right to be present at all criminal proceedings.

The press does have a Sixth Amendment right to be present at all criminal proceedings. However, this right can be superseded if the trial court finds an overriding interest that requires a closed trial. In this case, the secretary has produced only generalized evidence that some juries can be made impartial by excessive trial publicity, which does not meet the high standard of an overriding interest. But because this answer choice does not consider the possibility that the secretary's evidence constitutes an overriding interest, it is not the best answer.

Explanation: Question 31

The correct answer is: **(B)** Yes, because the government failed to prove sanity beyond a reasonable doubt.

Once allegations of serious mental illness or insanity going to the Defendant's ability to appreciate criminality are made in a criminal case, the Constitution requires that the government prove the sanity of the defendant beyond a reasonable doubt. In this case, the jury only found that there was a preponderance of the evidence of sanity, which is a lower evidentiary standard. Because the proof of sanity in this case was insufficient, the conviction is invalid.

(A) Incorrect. Yes, because a court may not require the Defendant to take antipsychotic drugs against his will so as to have the Defendant competent to stand trial.

This is an incorrect statement. It is constitutional for the government to give anti-psychotic drugs to a mentally ill defendant against the defendant's will in order to make the defendant competent for a trial on serious criminal charges. Because this is exactly what the court did in this case, its actions in administering the drugs were constitutional.

(C) Incorrect. No, because a court may require the Defendant to take antipsychotic drugs against his will to make the Defendant competent to stand trial.

While a court is permitted to give anti-psychotic drugs to a mentally ill defendant against the defendant's will in order to make the defendant competent for a trial on serious criminal charges, this alone is insufficient to convict a mentally ill defendant. Once allegations of serious mental illness or insanity going to the Defendant's ability to appreciate criminality, the Constitution requires that the government prove the sanity of the defendant beyond a reasonable doubt. Because the jury only found that Defendant was sane by a preponderance of the evidence, the conviction is invalid.

(D) Incorrect. No, because the government's proof of sanity was constitutionally sufficient.

Once allegations of serious mental illness or insanity going to the Defendant's ability to appreciate criminality arise in a criminal prosecution, the Constitution requires that the government prove the sanity of the defendant beyond a reasonable doubt. In this case, the jury only found that Defendant was sane at the time of the crime by a preponderance of the evidence, which is a less-demanding standard. Because the government's proof of sanity was thus constitutionally insufficient, this answer is incorrect and the conviction should be overturned.

Explanation: Question 32

The correct answer is: **(A)** Yes, because the use of a screen to shield child witnesses violates the Confrontation Clause.

Criminal defendants have a fundamental Sixth Amendment right to confront their accusers in court, which gives the defendant the general right to observe and cross-examine accusing witnesses and to be physically present during the testimony. However, the Supreme Court has held that this right is violated when the court interposes a screen between the defendant and a child witness in a child abuse case. In this case, because the use of the screen violated the confrontation clause, Defendant is entitled to a new trial.

(B) Incorrect. Yes, because the Confrontation Clause was violated when the court required Defendant to be gagged during the testimony.

Although the confrontation clause gives the right to be present, observe, and cross-examine witnesses, it is not absolute. In particular, a court may gag a disruptive defendant, or even exclude him or her from the courtroom if necessary. Because the court in this case exercised this power under what appear to be reasonable circumstances, there is no violation of the confrontation clause as a result of the gag.

(C) Incorrect. No, because the use of a screen to shield child witnesses does not necessarily violate the Confrontation Clause.

The Supreme Court has held that the use of a screen to shield child witnesses is a violation of the Confrontation Clause. This answer is therefore incorrect.

(D) Incorrect. No, because Defendant's lawyer had an ample opportunity to cross-examine the child witness.

Although the essence of the right protected by the confrontation clause is the ability to cross-examine the witnesses, the right also includes the right to be present and confront adverse witnesses. In particular, the Supreme Court has held that the use of a screen to shield child witnesses is a violation of the confrontation clause. In this case, the ability of Defendant's lawyer to engage in cross-examination does not cure the violation of the confrontation clause produced by the use of the screen by the court.

Explanation: Question 33

The correct answer is: **(C)** No, because the man's right to counsel has not been violated.

A criminal defendant who is competent to stand trial may nevertheless be declared incompetent to represent himself and thus receive a mandatory court-appointed counsel, as long as the defendant is able to meaningfully participate in his defense with counsel. Because these factors were satisfied in this case, Defendant's right to counsel has not been violated.

(A) Incorrect. Yes, because the competency of a criminal defendant must be decided by a judge and not the jury.

Although a criminal defendant may request a determination of his or her competency to stand trial by a judge as a matter of constitutional right, determinations of competency by a jury do not violate the constitution unless the defendant insists on a judicial determination. In this case, because the man did not insist on a judge, the competency determination by the jury was proper.

(B) Incorrect. Yes, because a person who is competent to stand trial necessarily has the right to proceed pro se.

This is an incorrect statement of the law. The standard for competency to stand trial is a lower threshold than the competency to represent one's self pro se. However, the defendant must retain the ability to participate in his case. In this case, the determination that the man was competent to stand trial thus does not preclude a separate determination that the man was not competent to proceed pro se. Because the man was able to participate in the case, the right to jury trial was not violated here.

(D) Incorrect. No, because a defendant who is incompetent to represent himself in court must be civilly committed rather than tried.

This is an incorrect statement of the law. A criminal defendant who is incompetent to stand trial must be civilly committed. However, a criminal defendant (like the one in this case) who is competent to stand trial but incompetent to represent himself without counsel must defend stand trial with counsel.

Explanation: Question 34

The correct answer is: **(D)** No, because the agents did not need to apprise Taxpayer of his constitutional rights.

Miranda v. Arizona [384 U.S. 436 (1966)] requires that, to protect the privilege against self-incrimination, the police must apprise a suspect of his constitutional rights before a custodial interrogation. A custodial interrogation is one in which the defendant is not free to leave or terminate questioning. Here, the interrogation was not custodial because it occurred in Taxpayer's home after he consented to a warrantless entry by the agents. Because the agents entered the home without a warrant, Taxpayer could have required that they leave at any time. Therefore, this is the correct answer.

(A) Incorrect. Yes, because Taxpayer was not sufficiently apprised of his constitutional rights.

Miranda v. Arizona [384 U.S. 436 (1966)] only requires that the police must apprise a suspect of their constitutional rights before a custodial interrogation - one in which a defendant is not free to leave. In this case, because the agents were in Taxpayer's home without a search warrant, they were only lawfully present in the home with his consent, which he could have revoked at any time. The interrogation was thus not custodial, and he therefore had no right to be apprised of his constitutional rights prior to any incriminating statements he made.

(B) Incorrect. Yes, because the agents entered the home without a search warrant.

This answer emphasizes an incorrect issue. While a warrant is normally required before police or other government agents enter a home, the warrant requirement can be waived by the consent of the homeowner, which was validly given in this case.

(C) Incorrect. No, because Taxpayer consented to the warrantless entry into his home.

This is a necessary but not sufficient condition to uphold the admissibility of the confession. Taxpayer's consent to the warrantless entry into the home is relevant in this case because it establishes that the I.R.S. agents were in the home with Taxpayer's consent. Because of the consent, they could be required to leave at any time. The interrogation was thus non-custodial. However, this is not the best answer available because the question of whether the agents were required to read Taxpayer his Miranda rights is the main issue and is unaffected by the consented-to search.

Explanation: Question 35

The correct answer is: **(B)** Yes, because the same jury decided both guilt and sentencing.

The Supreme Court has held that, to be constitutional, capital trials must contain a number of procedural safeguards to prevent violations of the Eighth Amendment. The procedural safeguard most relevant here is that a different jury must decide the Defendant's sentence than decided the Defendant's guilt. In this case, because the same jury is ruling on guilt and sentencing, the procedures violate the Eighth Amendment, and the Defendant's motion should be granted.

(A) Incorrect. Yes, because the statistical evidence renders the death penalty in the state cruel and unusual punishment.

The Supreme Court has held that unless the defendant can show actual discrimination in his or her case, the disproportionate use of capital punishment on one race does not violate the Eighth Amendment. Because this answer rests on an incorrect legal conclusion, it is not a basis for granting Defendant's motion.

(C) Incorrect. No, because the statistical evidence is insufficient to render the death penalty cruel and unusual punishment in this case.

The Supreme Court has held that unless the defendant can show actual discrimination in his or her case, the disproportionate use of capital punishment on one race does not violate the Eighth Amendment. However, just because the statistical evidence is not sufficient to vacate the sentence, it does not follow that there are no other defects in the state's capital punishment regime. Therefore, this answer is insufficient to justify the conclusion that Defendant's motion should be granted.

(D) Incorrect. No, because the death penalty is not cruel and unusual punishment.

Although the death penalty is constitutional if applied in accordance with the procedural safeguards mandated by the Supreme Court, it is incorrect to say that it is not cruel and unusual punishment. If the procedural safeguards are not present, a state's capital punishment rules can constitute cruel and unusual punishment.

Explanation: Question 36

The correct answer is: **(A)** No, because Defendant's right to a speedy trial has not been violated.

The Sixth Amendment includes the constitutional right to a speedy trial. Whether the right has been violated requires a balancing test, involving four factors: (1) the length of the delay; (2) the reason for the delay; (3) the defendant's assertion of his or her right to speedy trial; and (4) prejudice to the defendant, including evidence loss and oppressive incarceration. In this case, a court is unlikely to find a violation of the right to a speedy trial because (1) the delay in this case is largely due to the actions of Accomplice and not the state; (2) there is no evidence that Defendant objected to the trial delay; and (3) there is no apparent loss of evidence loss, and Defendant was not incarcerated pending trial. Thus, Defendant's right to a speedy trial has not been violated.

(B) Incorrect. No, because Defendant waived the right to speedy trial by failing to object to the state's decision to try Accomplice first.

A Defendant can waive his right to a speedy trial, for example, by willful acts to delay the trial. However, failure to object is not alone sufficient to waive the right to a speedy trial. In fact, it is only one of the four factors that courts use to determine whether the right to a speedy trial has been violated. Therefore, this is not the correct answer.

(C) Incorrect. Yes, because Defendant's right to a speedy trial has been violated.

In this case, the Defendant's speedy trial right has not been violated. Applying the four-part test for a violation of the speedy trial right, we can see that in this case, a court is unlikely to find a violation of the right to a speedy trial because (1) the delay in this case is largely due to the actions of Accomplice and not the state; (2) there is no evidence that Defendant objected to the trial delay; and (3) there is no apparent loss of evidence loss, and Defendant was not incarcerated pending trial. Thus, Defendant's right to a speedy trial has not been violated.

(D) Incorrect. Yes, because the Speedy Trial Act of 1974 has been violated.

The Speedy Trial Act of 1974 is a federal statute requiring a federal indictment to issue within 30 days of arrest and trial to start within 70 days of indictment. However, this statute is inapplicable here because it applies only to federal courts, and this case involves a state prosecution.

Explanation: Question 37

The correct answer is: **(A)** Yes, because Defendant's right to counsel was violated.

The Sixth Amendment guarantees an accused the right to counsel not only at his trial but at any critical confrontation by the prosecution at pretrial proceedings where the results might well determine his fate and where the absence of counsel might affect the right to a fair trial. The Supreme Court has held that defendants have a right to have counsel present at post-indictment lineups. In this case, because there was a post-indictment lineup at which counsel was not permitted to be present, the lineup violated the right to counsel and its admission at trial would be unconstitutional.

(B) Incorrect. Yes, because the lineup was unnecessarily suggestive and violated due process.

Any lineup will violate due process and be inadmissible if it is unnecessarily suggestive and is likely to produce a mistaken or misleading identification. This requires a fact-intensive inquiry, but in this case it is unlikely that a court would find the identification suggestive. The facts do not show any aspect of the lineup that would suggest to Witness that he should select Defendant.

(C) Incorrect. No, because Defendant's right to counsel was not violated.

The Sixth Amendment guarantees an accused the right to counsel not only at his trial but at any critical confrontation by the prosecution at pretrial proceedings where the results might well determine his fate and where the absence of counsel might affect the right to a fair trial. The Supreme Court has held that defendants have a right to have counsel present at post-indictment lineups. It is unclear whether this right attaches to a post-arrest, pre-indictment lineup, but the law is clear that there is a right to have counsel present at post-indictment lineups. Because counsel was not permitted to be present at the post-indictment lineup, the lineup violated the right to counsel and its admission at trial would be unconstitutional.

(D) Incorrect. No, because the lineup did not violate due process.

Although the lineup did not violate due process, that is not the only issue implicated here. The Sixth Amendment right to counsel applies to post-indictment lineups. In this case, the lineup did not violate due process because it was not unnecessarily suggestive or rigged against Defendant, but it was still unconstitutionally applied because it denied Defendant his Sixth Amendment right to counsel.

Explanation: Question 38

The correct answer is: **(D)** No, because the selection of the jury does not violate Defendant's right to a fair trial.

The jury selection procedures here are constitutionally sufficient for three reasons. First, a jury of six persons in a non-capital criminal case is constitutional. Second, the racial composition of the jury is sufficient because it was selected from a representative cross-section of the community. Third, although all three prosecution's peremptory strikes were exercised against women, because the strikes had a rational basis (tax lawyers might prejudge a tax evasion case), they do not appear to rise to the level of unconstitutional purposeful gender discrimination.

(A) Incorrect. Yes, because the racial composition of the jury is insufficient.

The Sixth Amendment guarantee of a right to a jury trial includes the guarantee of a jury of one's peers. However, in practice this means merely that the jury must be selected from a representative cross-section of the community, and no distinct and significant racial group can be excluded from the pool. In this case, the jury pool is a representative cross-section of the community. Although there are no African-Americans in the jury, in this community the small proportion of African-Americans means that they do not constitute a significant minority, and thus there is no evidence of racial discrimination in the selection of the jury.

(B) Incorrect. Yes, because all of the peremptory strikes were exercised against women.

When exercising peremptory challenges, a lawyer need not identify a cause, but may strike for any rational reason other than race or gender. In this case, although the use of the challenges against women might raise an inference of gender discrimination, the fact that all three of the women struck were corporate tax lawyers (who might prejudge a tax evasion case) is a sufficiently rational reason to exercise peremptory challenges against them.

(C) Incorrect. No, because a jury of six persons in a criminal case is constitutionally insufficient.

This is an incorrect statement of the law. The Supreme Court has held that in a non-capital criminal case, a six-person jury is the minimum number that is constitutionally sufficient. Provided that the jury is unanimous, six jurors are sufficient to convict in a criminal case without violating the fair trial guarantee.

Explanation: Question 39

The correct answer is: **(C)** No, because the lawyer was not unconstitutionally ineffective.

The Sixth Amendment requires not just that a defendant have access to a lawyer, but also includes the right to the effective assistance of counsel. However, proving ineffective assistance of counsel is difficult. To prevail on an ineffective assistance of counsel claim, a defendant must show that counsel was ineffective (for instance, by deviating from the norms that are professionally acceptable) and that there was a reasonable likelihood that the outcome of the case would have been different but for the ineffectiveness of counsel. In this case, counsel appears to have been ineffective on the first element as a result of inexperience and inability. However, the case against Defendant is so strong that it is hard to imagine any substantial likelihood that the case would have come out differently if counsel had not been ineffective. Thus, as a matter of Sixth Amendment law, Defendant is not entitled to a new trial because her lawyer was not unconstitutionally ineffective.

(A) Incorrect. Yes, because her lawyer was unconstitutionally ineffective.

To prevail on an ineffective assistance of counsel claim, a defendant must show both that counsel was ineffective (for instance, by deviating from the norms that are professionally acceptable) and that there was a reasonable likelihood that the outcome of the case would have been different but for the ineffectiveness of counsel. Here, the woman is unlikely to make this second showing, because it is hard to see how the outcome of the case would have been different if the lawyer had been more effective. This answer is therefore incorrect.

(B) Incorrect. Yes, because her lawyer failed to present a defense.

The failure to prevent a defense is not necessarily ineffective assistance of counsel. While the failure to present a defense may be enough to show that counsel was inadequate, a party challenging effective assistance must also show that the case would probably have turned out differently with better representation. On these facts, the woman probably cannot make the second showing, because the evidence against her is so overwhelming.

(D) Incorrect. No, because the appointment of a court-appointed attorney satisfied the requirements of the Sixth Amendment right to counsel.

The Sixth Amendment right to counsel includes the right to have a court-appointed lawyer if the defendant cannot afford one. However, it also includes the guarantee that counsel will not be unconstitutionally ineffective. Because the answer choice does not contemplate this possibility (which is the most important issue in this example), this is not the best answer choice.

Explanation: Question 40

The correct answer is: **(C)** Yes, because the right to have counsel present at a post-charge lineup includes the right to have counsel present for the entire lineup.

The evidence of the lineup should be excluded from the trial. A post-charge lineup is a critical stage of the prosecution at which a defendant has the absolute right to counsel. Once the government has initiated adversary judicial criminal proceedings, the presence of counsel is a prerequisite to the conduct of a lineup. This right attaches as soon as the accused is within sight of a potential identification witness. Here, the attorney was not present in the room until after the lineup had commenced. Good faith mistake and correct lineup procedures do not change the result.

(A) Incorrect. No, because the attorney's absence from the lineup procedure was based on a good faith mistake by the police.

(B) Incorrect. No, because the attorney was present for most of the time that the suspect was presented in the lineup for identification by the victim and there were no other legal improprieties in the lineup procedure.

(D) Incorrect. Yes, unless the victim fails to make an independent identification at trial.

Explanation: Question 41

The correct answer is: **(B)** Yes, because the search and seizure required a warrant to justify the initial intrusion into the house.

The motion should be granted because the search and seizure required a warrant to justify the initial intrusion across the threshold into the defendant's home. To have a Fourth Amendment right, a person must have a legitimate expectation of privacy with respect to the place searched or the item seized. In the instant case, the place searched was the defendant's home, which is a place in which a person has a legitimate expectation of privacy. Consent to enter was not granted and no other exceptions to the warrant requirement apply. The fact that the dog later supplied probable cause did not justify the initial intrusion into the house. Answer choice (A) is too narrow. Other warrant exceptions such as consent or plain view might apply to justify a warrantless search.

(A) Incorrect. Yes, because a warrantless search and seizure of items within the defendant's home is not permissible absent exigent circumstances.

(C) Incorrect. No, because the cocaine was seized as a search incident to a lawful arrest.

(D) Incorrect. No, because the drug sniffing dog's signal provided probable cause to search the locked closet.

Explanation: Question 42

The correct answer is: **(B)** Yes, because resident aliens are entitled to all due process protections under the Fifth Amendment.

A resident alien enjoys the rights guaranteed by the Fifth Amendment that would be afforded any citizen and a resident alien may invoke these rights in any proceeding, civil or criminal, administrative or judicial, investigatory or adjudicatory. Among the rights bestowed under the Fifth Amendment is the right to refuse to give any disclosures which the witness reasonably believes could be used in a criminal prosecution or could lead to other evidence that might be so used. [United States v. Balsys, 524 U.S. 666 (1998); Kastigar v. United States, 406 U.S. 441, 444-45 (1972) Kwong Hat Chew v. Colding 344 U.S. 590 (1953)].

(A) Incorrect. Yes, because there was insufficient probable cause to detain the student for questioning.

(C) Incorrect. No, because the student's bomb making activities created a threat to national security authorizing the suspension of due process rights.

(D) Incorrect. No, because aliens may not avail themselves of constitutional privileges.

Explanation: Question 43

The correct answer is: **(D)** Sustained, because under this circumstance, the men who remained silent had no duty to deny the accomplice's confession of guilt.

Once "Mirandized," a defendant in custody has no duty to speak at all, and the exercise of this constitutional right cannot be used against a defendant to show guilt. The Miranda warnings provide an express assurance that silence cannot be used against the defendant at a subsequent trial.

(A) Incorrect. Overruled, because silence in this situation is indicative of guilt and is an implied admission.

(B) Incorrect. Overruled, because the man who confessed had voluntarily waived his right to remain silent.

(C) Incorrect. Sustained, because an accomplice's evidence is inherently unreliable and unduly prejudicial.

Explanation: Question 44

The correct answer is: **(C)** No, because the exclusionary rule does not apply to grand jury proceedings.

The motion should be denied. The exclusionary rule does not apply in grand jury proceedings. As found in United States v. Calandra, 414 U.S. 338 (1974), illegally seized evidence is admissible in grand jury proceedings.

(A) Incorrect. Yes, because the detectives only had reasonable suspicion and not probable cause.

(B) Incorrect. Yes, because the maid was acting as a law enforcement agent and the seizure required a warrant.

(D) Incorrect. No, because the glass was removed by a private citizen and not a police officer.

Explanation: Question 45

The correct answer is: **(C)** No, because the principal had a reasonable suspicion that the junior was had illegal drugs in his locker.

The motion should be denied. Only reasonable grounds for a search are needed to justify searches by public school officials. Neither a warrant nor probable cause is required. A school search will be held reasonable if: (i) it offers a moderate chance of finding evidence of wrongdoing; (ii) the measures adopted to carry out the search are reasonably related to the objectives of the search; and (iii) the search is not excessively intrusive in light of the age and sex of the student and the nature of the possible crime.

(A) Incorrect. Yes, because there was adequate time to obtain a warrant.

(B) Incorrect. Yes, because the police lacked probable cause to field test the drugs.

(D) Incorrect. No, because the principal was not acting as an agent of law enforcement at the time of the illegal search.

Explanation: Question 46

The correct answer is: **(A)** Yes, because the constitutional protections of the Fifth Amendment do not apply to threatened foreign prosecutions.

In United States v. Balsys, 524 U.S. 666 (1998) the Supreme Court held that the Fifth Amendment's protections for aliens cannot be invoked where the fear is of foreign prosecution.

(B) Incorrect. Yes, because the businessman was not a lawful resident alien and therefore, had no constitutional protections.

(C) Incorrect. No, because the businessman was lawfully in the United States and had constitutional rights.

(D) Incorrect. No, because the grand jury is a secret proceeding and the Chinese government has no legal right to access secret grand jury testimony.

Explanation: Question 47

The correct answer is: **(A)** Yes, because the officer had proper search and arrest warrants.

The Supreme Court has stated that arresting officers are supposed to "knock and announce" before entering a house to make an arrest. However, they are not required to if doing so would be dangerous or futile or would make it impossible for them to carry out their duties. Because the officer knew that someone would be armed and poised to react, he decided that the safer course would be to try to surprise the person guarding the door. The fact that the officer has proper search and arrest warrants also makes it unlikely that the evidence, gathered properly, will be excluded.

(B) Incorrect. Yes, because the officer did not damage the house upon entry.

A police officer can break windows or other property if it is necessary to carry out a warrant. In this instance, it was not necessary because the door was slightly open. This is not the correct answer, though, because the fact that the police did not damage the house does not automatically make evidence they gathered admissible.

(C) Incorrect. No, because the officer did not knock and announce himself before entering.

Officers are supposed to "knock and announce" before entering a house to make an arrest if doing so would not be dangerous, futile, or make it impossible to carry out the arrest. Because the officer in this situation knew that someone would be armed and on guard, it is not unreasonable that he thought he would be safer if he surprised the residents. Note that a failure to knock and announce when it is appropriate does not lead to automatic exclusion of the evidence gathered.

(D) Incorrect. No, because there were no exigent circumstances at the time he entered the house.

One of the exigent circumstances that can justify not doing a "knock and announce" is that the officer has a reasonable suspicion that doing so would be dangerous, futile, or make it impossible to carry out the arrest. That appears to have been the case here because the officer in this situation knew that someone would be armed and on guard. It is therefore not correct to say that there were no exigent circumstances.

Explanation: Question 48

The correct answer is: **(B)** Yes, because his statement was voluntary.

Under the Miranda decision, the Supreme Court established that a defendant's statement must be excluded at trial unless the defendant was given a proper warning before custodial interrogation. On these facts, there is a small possibility that a court would hold that the hitchhiker was in custody, since a reasonable person would not feel that he was free to leave while he was a passenger in a moving car. However, there is no chance that a court would find an interrogation on these facts. An interrogation requires that police know (or reasonably should know) that their actions or questions are likely to elicit an incriminating response. Asking someone who is not under arrest whether he knows something about a particular crime is not likely to elicit an incriminating response, although it did in this situation.

(A) Incorrect. Yes, because the hitchhiker was not arrested immediately after the statement.

This question focuses on whether there was a custodial interrogation such that the police officer was obligated to give the hitchhiker a Miranda warning. The custodial aspect is a variety of factors to determine whether a suspect felt that he was free to leave the presence of the police. Whether there is an interrogation is determined by whether the police know (or reasonably should know) that their actions or questions are likely to elicit an incriminating response. Whether the suspect is arrested immediately after the statement is not decisive.

(C) Incorrect. No, because the hitchhiker was not given a Miranda warning before he spoke.

A Miranda warning is necessary whenever police employ custodial interrogation. It is slightly possible, though unlikely, that a court would find that the hitchhiker was in custody - a reasonable person would not feel that he was free to leave while he was a passenger in a moving car. However, there is just no interrogation on these facts. An interrogation requires that police know (or reasonably should know) that their actions or questions are likely to elicit an incriminating response. Simply asking someone who is not under arrest whether he knows something about a particular crime is not likely to elicit an incriminating response. Because this was not a custodial interrogation, a Miranda warning was unnecessary.

(D) Incorrect. No, because the hitchhiker was in a police car when he made the statement.

If the officer needed to give the hitchhiker a Miranda warning and did not, the court cannot admit the statement at trial. Therefore, it's important to determine whether there was a custodial interrogation. There is a small possibility that a court would find that the hitchhiker was in custody because a reasonable person would not feel that he was free to leave while he was a passenger in a moving car. However, that does not resolve the question in favor of exclusion because there was no interrogation. Police are interrogating when they know (or reasonably should know) that their actions or questions are likely to elicit an incriminating response. Such was not the case here.

Explanation: Question 49

The correct answer is: **(B)** Yes, because the judge did not personally discuss the voluntariness of the plea on the record.

The Supreme Court has determined that, when there is an error in taking a plea, the plea can be withdrawn and reentered. For a plea to be voluntary and intelligent, the judge must verify on the record that the defendant understands the nature of the charge against her, the maximum possible sentence and any mandatory minimums that apply, the fact that she need not plead guilty, and the fact that she is entitled to a jury trial which is waived if she pleads guilty. Here, the judge did not make the requisite findings of voluntariness and knowingness on the record, so it is likely that the lawyer can withdraw her plea.

(A) Incorrect. Yes, because there was not enough time for her to obtain counsel before the arraignment.

Defendants do have a right to counsel at arraignments. However, it is unclear from the facts here whether the lawyer sought counsel or whether she waived the right to counsel. As a result, this does not seem to be the best answer.

(C) Incorrect. No, because she had the legal background to be aware of the consequences of what she was doing.

To show that a plea is voluntary and intelligent, the judge must verify on the record that the defendant understands the nature of the charge against her, the maximum possible sentence and any mandatory minimums that apply, the fact that she need not plead guilty, and the fact that she is entitled to a jury trial which is waived if she pleads guilty. There is no specific exemption from this requirement for lawyers or other people with more legal knowledge than the general public, so this is not a correct answer choice.

(D) Incorrect. No, because guilty pleas cannot be withdrawn.

In accepting a guilty plea, the judge must verify on the record that the defendant understands the nature of the charge against her, the maximum possible sentence and any mandatory minimums that apply, the fact that she need not plead guilty, and the fact that she is entitled to a jury trial which is waived if she pleads guilty. If the judge does not do so, the plea is not considered to be knowing and voluntary, and it can therefore be withdrawn.

Explanation: Question 50

The correct answer is: **(D)** No, because she cannot show that she was likely to prevail with effective counsel.

To appeal a criminal conviction successfully on the basis of ineffective assistance of counsel, it is not enough to show that counsel was incompetent. A defendant must show both that counsel was ineffective (e.g., the lawyer deviated from appropriate norms) and that the defendant was reasonably likely not to have been convicted if she had had effective counsel. This is therefore the correct answer choice.

(A) Incorrect. Yes, because the lawyer did not do the necessary investigation of her case.

This is a factor in showing that there was ineffective assistance of counsel. However, for it to rise to the level of deprivation of the right to counsel, one must show both that counsel was ineffective (e.g., the lawyer deviated from appropriate norms) and that the defendant was reasonably likely not to have been convicted if she had had effective counsel. Here, it is unlikely that the defendant could prevail because of the overwhelming evidence of her guilt.

(B) Incorrect. Yes, because the lawyer was not awake for the entire trial.

This answer choice gives one of the facts on which the defendant would base her claim of ineffective assistance of counsel. Note, however, that it is not enough to show that the lawyer was incompetent. To show deprivation of the right to counsel, one must show both that counsel was ineffective (e.g., the lawyer deviated from appropriate norms) and that the defendant was reasonably likely not to have been convicted if she had had effective counsel.

(C) Incorrect. No, because she cannot show that she would have prevailed with effective counsel.

This is close to the correct answer but is not quite right. While courts will presume that counsel is effective, a defendant can show that she was deprived of her right to counsel by showing both that counsel was ineffective (e.g., the lawyer deviated from appropriate norms) and that the defendant was reasonably likely not to have been convicted if she had had effective counsel. She does not have to go so far as to prove that she would have prevailed with effective counsel.

MIG 1 OVERVIEW

EXCLUSIONARY RULE — to deter unconstitutional police conduct, evidence will be excluded from D's trial

- **SEARCH AND SEIZURE** — evidence resulting from an ***unreasonable invasion*** of D's ***reasonable expectations*** of privacy (including arrests and detentions) in the absence of a properly issued or executed warrant or conditions justifying the invasion without a warrant.
- **INTERROGATIONS** — statements as well as confessions which were (1) ***coerced***, (2) elicited during a ***custodial interrogation*** in the absence of warnings or waiver, (3) made ***after arraignment*** in the absence of D's lawyer, or (4) made during an ***unreasonable delay*** between arrest and arraignment.
- **IDENTIFICATIONS** — evidence of a pretrial identification (or courtroom identification derived directly therefrom) made under circumstances where there was unnecessary suggestion which created a substantial likelihood of irreparable misidentification.

RELIABILITY AND FAIRNESS SAFEGUARDS — to assure a fair and accurate disposition of D

- **RIGHT TO COUNSEL** — D has right to the assistance of ***effective counsel*** at all ***critical stages*** of a ***criminal proceeding*** including (1) custodial interrogations, and (2) arraignments if plea made, (3) preliminary hearings, (4) post indictment line-ups, (5) trials where ***imprisonment is actually imposed***, (6) sentencing and probation proceedings and (7) appeals as a matter of right. Counsel must at least be "reasonably competent" under modern trend, but D is not entitled to appointed counsel of choice (i.e., no meaningful relationship required).
- **DUE PROCESS (FAIR TRIAL)** — D is entitled to a trial free of error, influences or pressures which unjustifiably tend to affect the outcome (such as, (1) prejudicial pretrial ***publicity***, (2) judicial or juror ***bias***, (3) ***intimidation***, (4) ***improper comment***, (5) ***failure of prosecutor to correct false testimony or disclose exculpatory evidence***). Statute requiring loiterers to provide "credible and reliable" identification violates due process. Where D exercises a statutory right to appeal misdemeanor convictions, a subsequent prosecution for a felony arising from the same facts violates due process because of an unrebutted presumption of prosecutorial vindictiveness.
- **BURDEN OF PROOF** — prosecutor must prove all elements of the offense "beyond a reasonable doubt." Any presumption operating in a criminal case must be based upon reasonable inference and may not shift burden on each element to D. State may impose burden of proof on D with respect to certain ***affirmative defenses*** or ***mitigating facts*** (e.g., provocation) but may not instruct jury to presume intent from the facts.
- **CONFRONTATION AND PROCESS** — D must have opportunity to compel attendance of witnesses in his defense and to cross-examine prosecution witnesses (although hearsay is permitted if qualified under reasonable rules of evidence).

INDIVIDUAL RIGHTS AND DIGNITY SAFEGUARDS — to protect D from arbitrary and unreasonable government conduct

- **JURY TRIAL** — (1) D has right to an impartial (though not an ethnically balanced) jury ***in all trials where imprisonment of more than 6 months is possible***; (2) a jury of 6 is sufficient, (3) a unanimous verdict is ***not*** constitutionally required; (4) peremptory challenges may not be made if racially motivated.
- **DOUBLE JEOPARDY** — D may not be tried twice for the ***same offense*** unless the first trial ended in a ***legally necessary mistrial*** or the result was ***reversed on D's appeal based on an error of law*** (not sufficiency of evidence). Acquittal of criminal charges does not preclude a civil forfeiture of firearms. Collateral estoppel is a separate doctrine which precludes trial if D already acquitted of crime based on same facts.
- **RIGHT AGAINST SELF-INCRIMINATION** — D may not be (1) required to testify in his own trial, or (2) if testifying in any case (civil or criminal), he may not be compelled to answer a question unless D has waived the right or has been granted proper "use immunity"; statutes which impose unreasonable requirements of disclosure violate this right; right applies only to ***testimonial communications***; D entitled to a "no inference of guilt" instruction if D refuses to testify. D must produce business records under subpoena.
- **EQUAL PROTECTION** — indigent D must be provided with: (1) ***counsel*** at all critical stages and on appeals permitted as a matter of right, (2) ***free transcripts*** (if required to perfect appeal), and (3) ***possibly experts or investigators*** necessary to an effective defense.
- **SPEEDY TRIAL** — once D has been ***formally charged***, he must be given a speedy trial; no absolute standard but courts consider (1) length of delay, (2) reason for delay, (3) whether D demanded early trial or caused delay, and (4) whether delay was prejudicial to a fair trial.
- **NOTICE OF CHARGES** — D must be apprised of all elements of the offense in an indictment or information.
- **CRUEL AND UNUSUAL PUNISHMENT** — D may not be punished for illness or status and penalty must be proportionate to crime (e.g., life sentence for writing a bad check is improper); death penalty not *per se* invalid but must be administered so as to consider the individual circumstances of D's crime; an accomplice who did not kill, attempt to kill, intend to kill or intend to use deadly force cannot be sentenced to death.
- **SENTENCING** — D entitled to counsel but not to an adversary proceeding with cross-examination.
- **GUILTY PLEAS** — valid if judge informs D of all rights and consequences (even without counsel) and determines that plea was voluntary and intelligently made (even if D asserts his innocence to the charge at the time of the plea).
- **JUVENILE PROCEEDINGS** — D has right to (1) counsel, (2) confrontation, (3) notice of charges, (4) silence, and (5) proof beyond reasonable doubt; he has ***no right*** to (1) bail, (2) public trial, (3) jury trial, (4) indictment (applicability of exclusionary rule undecided).
- **RIGHT TO BAIL** — a suspect awaiting trial has a constitutional right to be released on reasonable bail unless charged with a capital offense ***and*** the proof of guilt is evident.

MIG 2 EXCLUSIONARY RULE

PROCEDURAL ASPECTS — a (1) ***timely motion to suppress*** must be made by one with (2) ***standing*** (i.e., a ***reasonable expectation of privacy*** was invaded) and all (3) ***fruits derived from the illegal conduct*** (unless taint is dissipated by ***independent source, inevitable discovery*** or ***attenuation***) where (4) ***conduct was by a government agent*** (i.e., ***state action***) and (5) the evidence is ***offered to prove guilt*** of D (***not*** for grand jury, impeachment, sentencing, etc.)

SEARCHES AND SEIZURES (S&S)

- **THRESHOLD QUESTION** — Fourth Amendment requirements only apply if government invades a ***reasonable expectation of privacy***; limitations do ***not*** apply to (1) ***voluntary disclosures to indiscreet confidants***, (2) ***bank records***, (3) ***abandoned property***, (4) ***pen registers***, (5) ***voice exemplars***, (6) ***"plain view" observations*** (from a lawful vantage point), or (7) searches conducted with *consent*
- **WARRANT** — S&S authorized by a warrant is valid if: (1) issued by ***neutral magistrate***, (2) from facts under ***oath***, (3) sufficient to allow ***independent judgment*** of the existence of (4) ***probable cause*** and the warrant (5) ***specifically limits the intrusion*** and is (6) ***reasonably executed***. Searches made pursuant to reasonable ***good faith*** reliance on a defective warrant are valid
- **NO WARRANT** — warrantless S&S is reasonable if: (1) officer has ***probable cause*** and (a) evidence could be ***lost or destroyed by delay***, (b) police are in ***"hot pursuit"*** of a felon or (c) suspected evidence is in an ***automobile on the open highway*** or an easily accessible public parking lot; (2) the search is made ***incident to a lawful inventory, stop or arrest***, or (3) occurs at or near an ***international border***

ARRESTS — proper if authorized by ***valid warrant*** (see above) or without a warrant if it is a mere "stop" (i.e., temporary detention) based on ***reasonable suspicion of criminality*** or a "full blown arrest" based on ***probable cause that suspect committed a felony***. An arrest takes place where a person detained reasonably believes he is not free to leave.

STATEMENTS AND CONFESSIONS — inadmissible if it was: (1) ***involuntary***, (2) taken in violation of *Miranda* rule, (3) was taken after ***formal charge in counsel's absence*** (*Massiah*) or (4) was the ***fruit of other illegal conduct***

COURTROOM IDENTIFICATIONS — an in-court ID is inadmissible if it is the fruit of an ***unnecessarily suggestive*** pretrial ID procedure conducive to ***irreparable mistaken identification***

MIG 3 APPLICABILITY OF FOURTH AMENDMENT

NO REASONABLE EXPECTATION OF PRIVACY

- **INDISCREET CONFIDANTS** — D "assumes the risk" that any person he talks to will (1) elicit and report "private" conversations or (2) transmit or tape record the conversation. Thus, no probable cause or warrant is required. *Hoffa v US* (1966); *US v White* (1971).
- **BANK RECORDS** — no reasonable expectation of privacy with regard to checks, deposit slips and other bank records as depositor takes "the risk" in revealing his private affairs to another that the information will be conveyed to the gov't. Thus, gov't may subpoena records without probable cause or warrant. *US v Miller* (1976) — California Supreme Court contra.
- **VOICE EXEMPLARS** — no reasonable expectation that others will not know the sound of D's voice; thus, grand jury may subpoena voice exemplars without probable cause or warrant. *US v Dionisio* (1973).
- **DISCARDED OR ABANDONED PROPERTY** — one has no privacy interest in property he discards or premises he abandons. Some courts forbid inspection of garbage until it is commingled in a common trash receptacle. ***Note:*** police cannot trespass to obtain evidence if it is discarded.
- **ELECTRONIC DEVICES** — one has no reasonable expectation of privacy in the telephone numbers dialed, thus, police may install a "pen register" to record numbers called without probable cause or warrant. *Smith v Maryland* (1979); police may also place an electronic transmitting device for tracking on packages or cars without probable cause. *US v Knotts* (1983).
- **DOG SNIFFS** — the use of dogs to sniff for drugs is permissible without probable cause or warrant of luggage in police custody. *US v Place* (1983).

PLAIN VIEW (FROM LAWFUL VANTAGE POINT). Plurality in *Coolidge v N.H.* (1971); evidence must be discovered *"inadvertently."* Plurality in *Texas v Brown* (1983); evidentiary nature need not be "immediately apparent."

- **PUBLIC PLACE** — observations made from a public place do not entail any invasion of privacy unless police use a very sophisticated mechanical device (e.g., long range parabolic microphone) which goes beyond reasonable expectations; use of flashlights, binoculars and other ordinary sense-enhancement devices are permitted.
- **PRIVATE OPEN AREAS** — trespassory entry onto a private open area (e.g., a field) involves no significant intrusion of privacy and observations made therefrom are proper without probable cause or warrant.
- **CONSENT TO PRIVATE PLACE** — if police obtain access to the "vantage point" by voluntary consent, D waives constitutional expectations of privacy to matters observed.
- **POLICE INVENTORIES** — if police have a lawful right to inventory property in their possession, observations made during the reasonable exercise of that right are proper without additional cause or justification.
- **JUSTIFIABLE INTRUSIONS** — if police or others have a legal right to enter a premise for any lawful purpose (e.g., pursuant to a warrant, "hot pursuit" of felon, response to call for help, inspection for damage or dangerous conditions), observations made during the reasonable exercise of this right are lawful without additional cause.
- **FRISK INCIDENT TO LAWFUL STOP** — where there is a lawful right for a limited search (e.g., a surface "pat down"), police may enter inner clothing if they "feel" items which are "probably" weapons.

CONSENT TO A SEARCH OR ENTRY

- **SCOPE OF CONSENT** — consenting party controls scope of the intrusion and conduct exceeding the reasonable scope of the consent is unlawful.
- **MUST BE VOLUNTARY** — under "totality of circumstances" the consent must be ***voluntary***; actual or implied coercion is forbidden but deceit does not vitiate consent unless it is extreme (e.g., consent to search based on false representation that officer possesses a warrant). *Bumper v North Carolina* (1968); police not required to inform a suspect that he need not consent, *Schneckloth v Bustamonte* (1973), even if suspect is in custody, *US v Watson* (1976) — N.Y. is contra in certain cases.
- **IMPLIED CONSENT** — statutes which ***require*** a person to consent to search "at any time" as a condition of a license to engage in certain regulated activities (e.g., dealing in drugs, firearms, cigarettes) are ***valid unless unreasonable***; consent to a baggage search may also be implied as a condition to travel by air or to cross U.S. borders.
- **ADVANCE CONSENT** — ***explicit prior consent*** (e.g., contract provision) to permit searches of rented lockers or premises is valid if not made under duress and if D knew he was consenting; a probationer or parolee may be required to give advance consent for police search as a condition of probation or parole.
- **THIRD PARTY CONSENT** — a search is reasonable if consent was given by any person who has ***joint use or access*** to the property or premises searched; D assumes the risk that a person who has the right to have or use property will permit others to do so. *US v Matlock* (1974). Reasonable good faith belief that the person consenting had authority (i.e., "apparent authority") will probably be sufficient.

MIG 4 VALID WARRANT

NEUTRAL MAGISTRATE — warrant must be issued by a ***neutral judicial officer***, *Shadwick v Tampa* (1972).

SUPPORTED BY OATH — facts supporting warrant must be given under oath whether by oral testimony or affidavit. If D makes substantial showing that affiant lied or was reckless re: truth, hearing must be held to determine validity of probable cause and warrant, *Franks v Delaware* (1975).

INDEPENDENT JUDGMENT — facts stated must be in sufficient detail to permit magistrate to make an ***independent judgment*** that the search will yield the specified evidence, for ***"mere conclusions" are improper***, *Riggin v Virginia* (1966).

SPECIFICITY — warrant must specifically limit intrusion by specifically describing items or persons to be seized and/or place to be searched; technical mistakes (e.g., wrong street number) normally ***not*** fatal ***if*** officer cannot mistake the place to be searched; place searched may be owned by non-suspect (including a newspaper) *Zurcher v Stanford Daily* (1978); warrant to search for contraband implicitly carries authority to detain occupants, *Michigan v Summers* (1981); vague warrant cannot be saved by personal supervision of magistrate, *Lo-Ji Sales v New York* (1979).

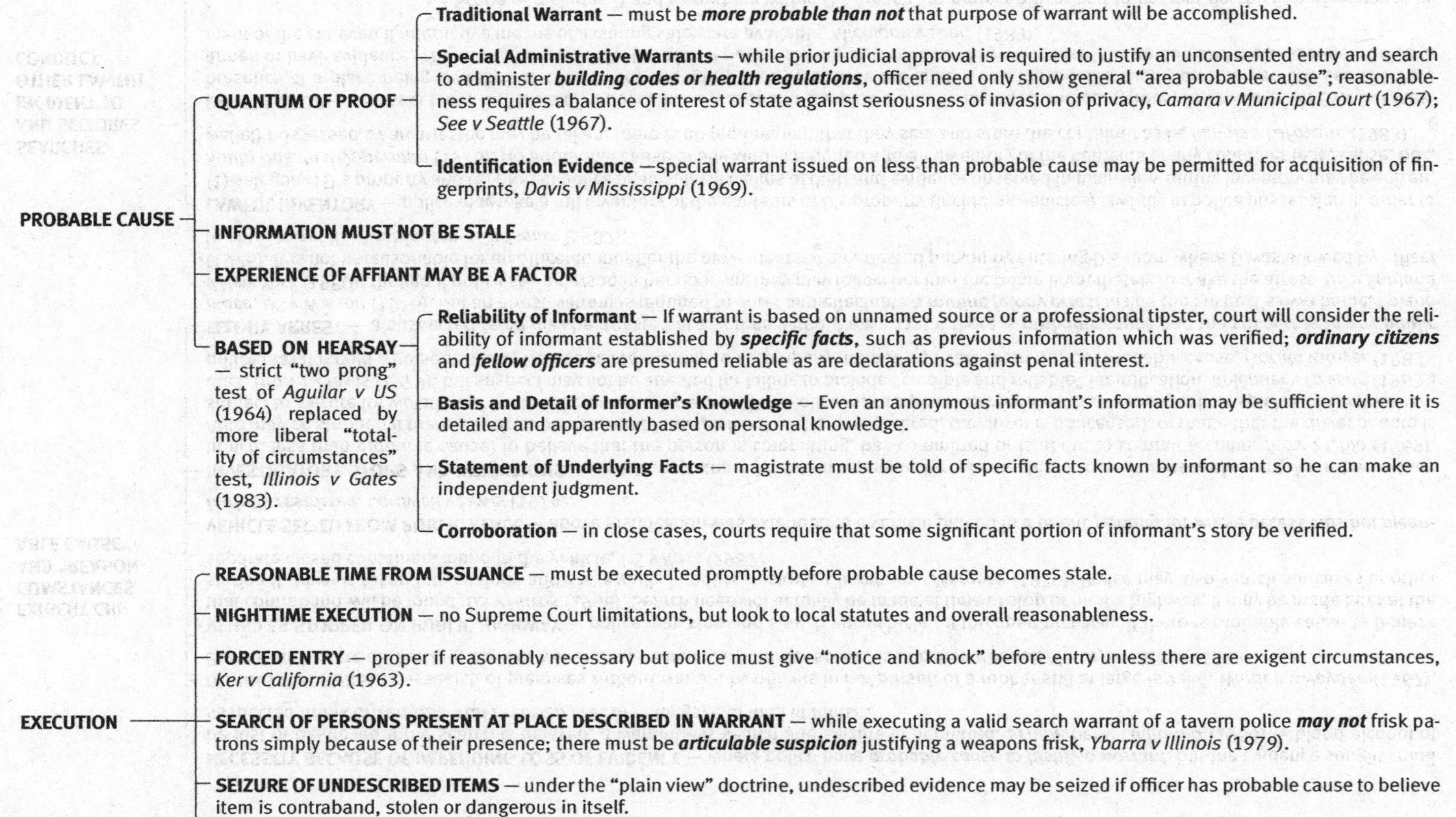

PROBABLE CAUSE

- **QUANTUM OF PROOF**
  - **Traditional Warrant** — must be ***more probable than not*** that purpose of warrant will be accomplished.
  - **Special Administrative Warrants** — while prior judicial approval is required to justify an unconsented entry and search to administer ***building codes or health regulations***, officer need only show general "area probable cause"; reasonableness requires a balance of interest of state against seriousness of invasion of privacy, *Camara v Municipal Court* (1967); *See v Seattle* (1967).
  - **Identification Evidence** —special warrant issued on less than probable cause may be permitted for acquisition of fingerprints, *Davis v Mississippi* (1969).
- **INFORMATION MUST NOT BE STALE**
- **EXPERIENCE OF AFFIANT MAY BE A FACTOR**
- **BASED ON HEARSAY** — strict "two prong" test of *Aguilar v US* (1964) replaced by more liberal "totality of circumstances" test, *Illinois v Gates* (1983).
  - **Reliability of Informant** — If warrant is based on unnamed source or a professional tipster, court will consider the reliability of informant established by ***specific facts***, such as previous information which was verified; ***ordinary citizens*** and ***fellow officers*** are presumed reliable as are declarations against penal interest.
  - **Basis and Detail of Informer's Knowledge** — Even an anonymous informant's information may be sufficient where it is detailed and apparently based on personal knowledge.
  - **Statement of Underlying Facts** — magistrate must be told of specific facts known by informant so he can make an independent judgment.
  - **Corroboration** — in close cases, courts require that some significant portion of informant's story be verified.

EXECUTION

- **REASONABLE TIME FROM ISSUANCE** — must be executed promptly before probable cause becomes stale.
- **NIGHTTIME EXECUTION** — no Supreme Court limitations, but look to local statutes and overall reasonableness.
- **FORCED ENTRY** — proper if reasonably necessary but police must give "notice and knock" before entry unless there are exigent circumstances, *Ker v California* (1963).
- **SEARCH OF PERSONS PRESENT AT PLACE DESCRIBED IN WARRANT** — while executing a valid search warrant of a tavern police ***may not*** frisk patrons simply because of their presence; there must be ***articulable suspicion*** justifying a weapons frisk, *Ybarra v Illinois* (1979).
- **SEIZURE OF UNDESCRIBED ITEMS** — under the "plain view" doctrine, undescribed evidence may be seized if officer has probable cause to believe item is contraband, stolen or dangerous in itself.
- **DETENTION INCIDENTAL TO WARRANT** — a valid search warrant for contraband implicitly carries with it the limited authority to detain occupants of the premises while a proper search is conducted, *Michigan v Summers* (1981).

MIG 5 WARRANTLESS SEARCHES

EXIGENT CIRCUMSTANCES AND "REASONABLE CAUSE"

- **NECESSITY BECAUSE OF IMPENDING LOSS OF EVIDENCE** — where police ***have probable cause to justify a warrant***, but the evidence sought could be lost or destroyed if the search is delayed, a warrantless search and seizure is permitted, *Schmerber v California* (1966) — blood alcohol of suspected drunk driver; *US v Van Leeowen* (1970) — luggage or mail in transit.
- **DURING HOT PURSUIT** — search of premises without warrant by officers in ***hot pursuit*** of a robber still at large is valid, *Warden v Hayden* (1967). But a state statute authorizing blanket warrantless search of a "murder scene" is unconstitutional, *Mincey v Arizona* (1978).
- **VEHICLES STOPPED ON PUBLIC HIGHWAY** — police may stop and search any vehicle on the open highway; if there is probable cause to believe that contraband will be found, *US v Harris* (1968). Search need not actually be made at time of stop or on the highway, it may be made later at the station if driver is taken into custody and car lawfully in police custody, *Chambers v Maroney* (1970). Police may also search suitcases or other separate closed containers found in the vehicle, *US v Ross* (1982).
- **VEHICLE SEIZED FROM PUBLIC PLACE** — above justification was extended to a vehicle parked in ***a public parking lot where access was not meaningfully restricted***, *Cardwell v Lewis* (1974).
- **INVESTIGATORY STOPS AND DETENTIONS** — police may stop and detain a person for questioning if there is ***reasonable suspicion*** (more than hunch, less than probable cause) to believe that the person is committing, has committed or is about to commit a crime, *Terry v Ohio* (1969). Auto may be stopped if there is ***articulable reasonable suspicion*** that it is unregistered, the driver is unlicensed, or that either the driver or auto is subject to seizure for violation of the law, *Delaware v Prouse* (1979). Police may ***stop*** and ***ask for*** ID without reasonable suspicion of criminal conduct, *Brown v Texas* (1979); but suspect may not be arrested for failing to provide "credible and reliable" identification, *Kolender v Lawson* (1983); police may not hold a person's plane ticket and ***require*** him to accompany them to a private room without probable cause, *Florida v Royer* (1983).
- **FELONY ARREST** — a suspected ***felon*** may be arrested at any time without a warrant if there is ***probable cause*** and the suspect is in any ***public place***, *US v Watson* (1976). But an arrest warrant is required to enter and effectuate a ***routine felony arrest*** inside the suspect's own home, *Payton v New York* (1980); though if police see a person in her doorway they may follow her into the home immediately to make the arrest, *US v Santana* (1976). It is not unreasonable for an officer to monitor the movements of an arrested person by entering D's room where D was allowed by officer to enter to get ID, *Washington v Chrisman* (1982).

SEARCHES AND SEIZURES INCIDENT TO OTHER LAWFUL CONDUCT

- **LAWFUL INVENTORY** — police may take a full inventory of the contents of D's property (including vehicles) lawfully in police possession in order to (1) safeguard D's property and (2) protect police against false claims of theft and evidence observed in plain view during inventory may be seized, *South Dakota v Opperman* (1976). No additional cause of any kind is required and an inventory of the contents of any container (e.g., valise, box, wallet) possessed by an arrestee may be taken; there is no requirement that they seal and store the container as is, *Illinois v LaFayette* (1983).
- **LAWFUL STOP** — a suspect may be "frisked" if police have reasonable suspicion that he is armed and dangerous, *Terry v Ohio* (1969). But mere presence at a place being lawfully searched is not enough; police must have articulable and reasonable suspicion that persons searched are armed or have evidence, *Ybarra v Illinois* (1979). However, if police lawfully stop a driver they may "frisk" his person ***and*** the passenger compartment of the car even if alternative means of assuring safety are available, *Michigan v Long* (1983).
- **LAWFUL ARREST** — D and his "immediate presence" may be searched incident to a lawful arrest
  - **Scope** — includes D and everything within D's "reach" to protect officer and to prevent destruction of evidence by D, *Chinel v California* (1969). Recent case law suggest that police may search passenger area of vehicle only if it is reasonable to suspect that D might access vehicle or that vehicle contains evidence *Arizona v Gant* (2009).
  - **Timing** — must be substantially contemporaneous to arrest but may precede arrest slightly, *US v Chadwick* (1977).
  - **Crime** — full search of arrested person is justified regardless of the crime giving rise to the arrest; even traffic arrests (though some states contra), *US v Robinson* (1973).

BORDER SEARCHES

- **AT BORDER** — merely crossing a US border (or its functional equivalent) justifies a search and/or seizure of person, luggage or mail without cause.
- **FIXED CHECKPOINTS** — vehicles may be "stopped" without cause at a fixed checkpoint in the vicinity of the border, but police must have probable cause to fully search the vehicle, *US v Martinez-Fuerte* (1976).
- **ROVING PATROLS** — vehicles may be "stopped" if police have reasonable suspicion, but search requires probable cause, *US v Almeida-Sanchez* (1973); *US v Brigmono-Ponce* (1975).

MIG 6 STATEMENTS AND CONFESSIONS

INVOLUNTARY STATEMENTS — compelled statements violate the Fifth Amendment right against self-incrimination; ***involuntariness*** is viewed in the ***totality of circumstances***.

- **PHYSICAL FORCE** — virtually any use of force to extract a statement will disqualify a statement.
- **PROMISES AND TRICKS** — police are given broad leeway to trick and deceive during interrogation but extreme cases of falsely playing on suspect's sympathies and promises of leniency in return for a confession can justify treating statement as involuntary, *Spano v New York* (1959).
- **UNCONSCIOUSNESS** — statements taken from a semiconscious D are improper, *Mincey v Arizona* (1978).
- **LOSS OF JOB** — statements elicited from a public employee under threats of discharge are involuntary.

MIRANDA RULE — a suspect who is in ***custody*** may not be ***interrogated*** unless he is first told that: (1) he has a ***right to remain silent***, (2) that ***statements made will be used against him***, (3) that he has a ***right to the presence of an attorney***, and (4) that ***if he can't afford an attorney one will be appointed***.

- **CUSTODY** — occurs when suspect is deprived of freedom of action *in any significant way* (more than "stop" or brief detention but not necessarily an arrest; examine from police point of view: was there a ***manifestation of intended control*** (statement by D to his probation officer without warnings was O.K. since D was not in custody when questions were asked, *Minnesota v Murphy* (1984).
- **INTERROGATION** warnings need only be given if police interrogate (i.e., attempt to elicit an incriminating response).
  - **Spontaneous Statements** — ***Miranda*** does not apply to unsolicited spontaneous confessions or "blurted out" statements.
  - **Conduct** — interrogation includes conduct which police know is reasonably likely to elicit an incriminating response especially if police play on known weaknesses of D, *Rhode Island v Innis* (1980).
- **ASSERTION OR WAIVER** — suspect may either assert any of the rights encompassed in warning or waive them.
  - **Assertion** — once asserted all interrogation must cease immediately and a subsequent waiver from subsequent but proximately close interrogation is improper, *Edwards v Arizona* (1981), unless clearly done in good faith by different officers, *Michigan v Mosley* (1976). Request for a person other than an attorney such as a mother or probation officer is ***not*** an assertion of the right to silence, *Fare v Michael C* (1979).
  - **Waiver** — state must prove *knowing and intelligent* waiver; prosecution carries "heavy burden" but waiver need not be explicit or written, *North Carolina v Butler* (1979).
- **FORM OF WARNINGS** — no ritualistic form is required as long as substance is clear but warnings must be given to every suspect — even police and hardened criminals, *North Carolina v Butler* (1974).
- **USE** — an actual statement taken in violation of Miranda may be used to impeach direct testimony, *Harris v New York* (1971); but the fact that D asserted his right to silence and failed to explain may ***not*** be used to impeach credibility of court testimony, *US v Hale* (1975) unless D's pre-arrest silence is ***clearly inconsistent*** with defense asserted at trial, *Jenkins v Anderson* (1980).

RIGHT TO COUNSEL: MASSIAH — once ***formal charges have been filed*** and D has a lawyer, incriminating statements may not be elicited from D without a clear waiver of the right to counsel; this is so whether D is in custody or not.

- **On Bail** — surreptitiously recorded conversation by secret police agent while D was out on bail violated right to counsel, *Massiah v US* (1964).
- **If Asserted** — once right to counsel is asserted, all attempts to elicit statements must cease, *Brewer v Williams* (1977).

FRUIT OF ILLEGAL CONDUCT — a statement or confession may be suppressed if it was fruit of any prior unconstitutional conduct such as an illegal search and seizure or identification procedure even if statement itself was voluntary and given after valid waiver of *Miranda* and *Massiah* rights. ***NOTE:*** D must have standing to object to the source illegality.

MIG 7 IDENTIFICATION PROCEDURES

SELF-INCRIMINATION — Fifth Amendment privilege against self-incrimination only applies to ***testimonial communicative evidence*** not physical evidence. Thus, a suspect may be compelled to participate in a fair line-up, provide hair, blood or voice samples and to put on or remove clothes, toupees, etc., *Schmerber v California* (1966); *Wade v US* (1967).

RIGHT TO COUNSEL — once formal charges have been brought, a suspect has a right to the presence of counsel at any line-up, *Kirby v Illinois* (1972); but not at photographic displays, *US v Ash* (1973). The right to counsel at this stage may be waived, *Wade v US* (1967). [Omnibus Crime Control Act seeking to override cases holding a right to counsel at a line-up is probably unconstitutional. In N.Y., suspect has a ***non-waivable*** right to counsel at a post-charge line-up, *P v Settles* (1978).]

DUE PROCESS — an I.D. procedure is violative of Due Process when it is "(1) *unnecessarily* (2) *suggestive* and (3) *conducive to irreparable mistaken identification*;" any in-court I.D. tainted thereby is inadmissible, *Stovall v Denno* (1967).

- **TOTALITY OF CIRCUMSTANCES** — in determining whether in-court I.D. is the "fruit" of the pretrial I.D. consider (1) witness's opportunity to observe criminal at time of the act; (2) witness's degree of attention; (3) accuracy and specificity of witness's prior description, and (4) the level of certainty of witness, *Neil v Briggers* (1972).
- **HEARING** — hearing must be held as to propriety of pretrial I.D. but need not be outside the presence of the jury, *Watkins v Sowders* (1981).
- **PHOTOGRAPHIC DISPLAYS** — only factors which are unnecessarily suggestive will taint a photo I.D. (e.g., repetitive display of same photo, circle or marks on photo, etc.).
- **LINE-UP** — persons must be of similar but not identical physical characteristics; particular suspect must not unduly stand out or otherwise be pointed to by prosecution or police, *Foster v California* (1969) — D only person to be in two separate line-ups and to wear jacket similar to one worn by robbers.
- **ONE PERSON SHOW-UPS** — not violative ***per se*** if justified by special circumstances.

MIG 8 RIGHT TO COUNSEL

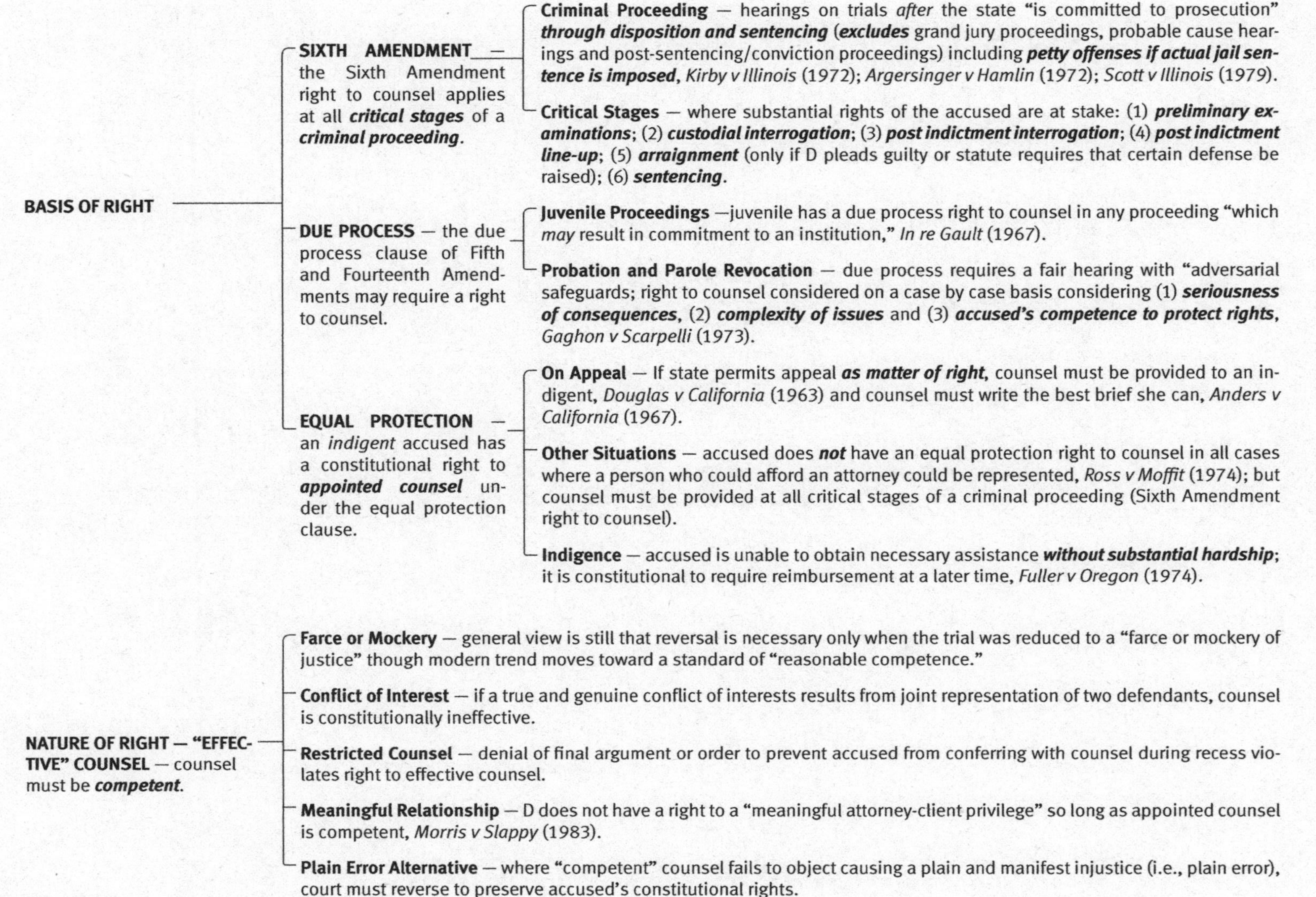

- **BASIS OF RIGHT**
  - **SIXTH AMENDMENT** — the Sixth Amendment right to counsel applies at all ***critical stages*** of a ***criminal proceeding***.
    - **Criminal Proceeding** — hearings on trials *after* the state "is committed to prosecution" ***through disposition and sentencing*** (***excludes*** grand jury proceedings, probable cause hearings and post-sentencing/conviction proceedings) including ***petty offenses if actual jail sentence is imposed***, *Kirby v Illinois* (1972); *Argersinger v Hamlin* (1972); *Scott v Illinois* (1979).
    - **Critical Stages** — where substantial rights of the accused are at stake: (1) ***preliminary examinations***; (2) ***custodial interrogation***; (3) ***post indictment interrogation***; (4) ***post indictment line-up***; (5) ***arraignment*** (only if D pleads guilty or statute requires that certain defense be raised); (6) ***sentencing***.
  - **DUE PROCESS** — the due process clause of Fifth and Fourteenth Amendments may require a right to counsel.
    - **Juvenile Proceedings** —juvenile has a due process right to counsel in any proceeding "which *may* result in commitment to an institution," *In re Gault* (1967).
    - **Probation and Parole Revocation** — due process requires a fair hearing with "adversarial safeguards; right to counsel considered on a case by case basis considering (1) ***seriousness of consequences***, (2) ***complexity of issues*** and (3) ***accused's competence to protect rights***, *Gaghon v Scarpelli* (1973).
  - **EQUAL PROTECTION** — an *indigent* accused has a constitutional right to ***appointed counsel*** under the equal protection clause.
    - **On Appeal** — If state permits appeal ***as matter of right***, counsel must be provided to an indigent, *Douglas v California* (1963) and counsel must write the best brief she can, *Anders v California* (1967).
    - **Other Situations** — accused does ***not*** have an equal protection right to counsel in all cases where a person who could afford an attorney could be represented, *Ross v Moffit* (1974); but counsel must be provided at all critical stages of a criminal proceeding (Sixth Amendment right to counsel).
    - **Indigence** — accused is unable to obtain necessary assistance ***without substantial hardship***; it is constitutional to require reimbursement at a later time, *Fuller v Oregon* (1974).
- **NATURE OF RIGHT — "EFFECTIVE" COUNSEL** — counsel must be ***competent***.
  - **Farce or Mockery** — general view is still that reversal is necessary only when the trial was reduced to a "farce or mockery of justice" though modern trend moves toward a standard of "reasonable competence."
  - **Conflict of Interest** — if a true and genuine conflict of interests results from joint representation of two defendants, counsel is constitutionally ineffective.
  - **Restricted Counsel** — denial of final argument or order to prevent accused from conferring with counsel during recess violates right to effective counsel.
  - **Meaningful Relationship** — D does not have a right to a "meaningful attorney-client privilege" so long as appointed counsel is competent, *Morris v Slappy* (1983).
  - **Plain Error Alternative** — where "competent" counsel fails to object causing a plain and manifest injustice (i.e., plain error), court must reverse to preserve accused's constitutional rights.
- **WAIVER** — the right to counsel may be waived "knowingly and intelligently."
  - ***Accused Must Be Clearly Competent to Waive.***
  - **Proceeding Pro Se** — accused has right to represent self, *Faretta v California* (1975).

pmbr

Evidence

Practice Questions

Answer Grid

1 Ⓐ Ⓑ Ⓒ Ⓓ	21 Ⓐ Ⓑ Ⓒ Ⓓ	41 Ⓐ Ⓑ Ⓒ Ⓓ	61 Ⓐ Ⓑ Ⓒ Ⓓ	81 Ⓐ Ⓑ Ⓒ Ⓓ
2 Ⓐ Ⓑ Ⓒ Ⓓ	22 Ⓐ Ⓑ Ⓒ Ⓓ	42 Ⓐ Ⓑ Ⓒ Ⓓ	62 Ⓐ Ⓑ Ⓒ Ⓓ	82 Ⓐ Ⓑ Ⓒ Ⓓ
3 Ⓐ Ⓑ Ⓒ Ⓓ	23 Ⓐ Ⓑ Ⓒ Ⓓ	43 Ⓐ Ⓑ Ⓒ Ⓓ	63 Ⓐ Ⓑ Ⓒ Ⓓ	83 Ⓐ Ⓑ Ⓒ Ⓓ
4 Ⓐ Ⓑ Ⓒ Ⓓ	24 Ⓐ Ⓑ Ⓒ Ⓓ	44 Ⓐ Ⓑ Ⓒ Ⓓ	64 Ⓐ Ⓑ Ⓒ Ⓓ	84 Ⓐ Ⓑ Ⓒ Ⓓ
5 Ⓐ Ⓑ Ⓒ Ⓓ	25 Ⓐ Ⓑ Ⓒ Ⓓ	45 Ⓐ Ⓑ Ⓒ Ⓓ	65 Ⓐ Ⓑ Ⓒ Ⓓ	85 Ⓐ Ⓑ Ⓒ Ⓓ
6 Ⓐ Ⓑ Ⓒ Ⓓ	26 Ⓐ Ⓑ Ⓒ Ⓓ	46 Ⓐ Ⓑ Ⓒ Ⓓ	66 Ⓐ Ⓑ Ⓒ Ⓓ	86 Ⓐ Ⓑ Ⓒ Ⓓ
7 Ⓐ Ⓑ Ⓒ Ⓓ	27 Ⓐ Ⓑ Ⓒ Ⓓ	47 Ⓐ Ⓑ Ⓒ Ⓓ	67 Ⓐ Ⓑ Ⓒ Ⓓ	87 Ⓐ Ⓑ Ⓒ Ⓓ
8 Ⓐ Ⓑ Ⓒ Ⓓ	28 Ⓐ Ⓑ Ⓒ Ⓓ	48 Ⓐ Ⓑ Ⓒ Ⓓ	68 Ⓐ Ⓑ Ⓒ Ⓓ	88 Ⓐ Ⓑ Ⓒ Ⓓ
9 Ⓐ Ⓑ Ⓒ Ⓓ	29 Ⓐ Ⓑ Ⓒ Ⓓ	49 Ⓐ Ⓑ Ⓒ Ⓓ	69 Ⓐ Ⓑ Ⓒ Ⓓ	89 Ⓐ Ⓑ Ⓒ Ⓓ
10 Ⓐ Ⓑ Ⓒ Ⓓ	30 Ⓐ Ⓑ Ⓒ Ⓓ	50 Ⓐ Ⓑ Ⓒ Ⓓ	70 Ⓐ Ⓑ Ⓒ Ⓓ	90 Ⓐ Ⓑ Ⓒ Ⓓ
11 Ⓐ Ⓑ Ⓒ Ⓓ	31 Ⓐ Ⓑ Ⓒ Ⓓ	51 Ⓐ Ⓑ Ⓒ Ⓓ	71 Ⓐ Ⓑ Ⓒ Ⓓ	91 Ⓐ Ⓑ Ⓒ Ⓓ
12 Ⓐ Ⓑ Ⓒ Ⓓ	32 Ⓐ Ⓑ Ⓒ Ⓓ	52 Ⓐ Ⓑ Ⓒ Ⓓ	72 Ⓐ Ⓑ Ⓒ Ⓓ	92 Ⓐ Ⓑ Ⓒ Ⓓ
13 Ⓐ Ⓑ Ⓒ Ⓓ	33 Ⓐ Ⓑ Ⓒ Ⓓ	53 Ⓐ Ⓑ Ⓒ Ⓓ	73 Ⓐ Ⓑ Ⓒ Ⓓ	93 Ⓐ Ⓑ Ⓒ Ⓓ
14 Ⓐ Ⓑ Ⓒ Ⓓ	34 Ⓐ Ⓑ Ⓒ Ⓓ	54 Ⓐ Ⓑ Ⓒ Ⓓ	74 Ⓐ Ⓑ Ⓒ Ⓓ	94 Ⓐ Ⓑ Ⓒ Ⓓ
15 Ⓐ Ⓑ Ⓒ Ⓓ	35 Ⓐ Ⓑ Ⓒ Ⓓ	55 Ⓐ Ⓑ Ⓒ Ⓓ	75 Ⓐ Ⓑ Ⓒ Ⓓ	95 Ⓐ Ⓑ Ⓒ Ⓓ
16 Ⓐ Ⓑ Ⓒ Ⓓ	36 Ⓐ Ⓑ Ⓒ Ⓓ	56 Ⓐ Ⓑ Ⓒ Ⓓ	76 Ⓐ Ⓑ Ⓒ Ⓓ	96 Ⓐ Ⓑ Ⓒ Ⓓ
17 Ⓐ Ⓑ Ⓒ Ⓓ	37 Ⓐ Ⓑ Ⓒ Ⓓ	57 Ⓐ Ⓑ Ⓒ Ⓓ	77 Ⓐ Ⓑ Ⓒ Ⓓ	97 Ⓐ Ⓑ Ⓒ Ⓓ
18 Ⓐ Ⓑ Ⓒ Ⓓ	38 Ⓐ Ⓑ Ⓒ Ⓓ	58 Ⓐ Ⓑ Ⓒ Ⓓ	78 Ⓐ Ⓑ Ⓒ Ⓓ	98 Ⓐ Ⓑ Ⓒ Ⓓ
19 Ⓐ Ⓑ Ⓒ Ⓓ	39 Ⓐ Ⓑ Ⓒ Ⓓ	59 Ⓐ Ⓑ Ⓒ Ⓓ	79 Ⓐ Ⓑ Ⓒ Ⓓ	99 Ⓐ Ⓑ Ⓒ Ⓓ
20 Ⓐ Ⓑ Ⓒ Ⓓ	40 Ⓐ Ⓑ Ⓒ Ⓓ	60 Ⓐ Ⓑ Ⓒ Ⓓ	80 Ⓐ Ⓑ Ⓒ Ⓓ	100 Ⓐ Ⓑ Ⓒ Ⓓ

1. Vicarious Admissions
2. Judicial Notice
3. Subsequent Remedial Measures
4. Character Evidence — Admissibility in Civil Case
5. Prior Tort Claims
6. Similar Acts or Injuries
7. Hearsay
8. Judicial Notice — Blood Tests
9. Expert Testimony — Use of Treatises
10. Demonstrative Evidence — Paternity (Exhibition of Child)
11. Admissions Not Admissible in Settlement or Compromise Negotiations
12. Prior Inconsistent Statement Admissible for Impeachment Purposes
13. Hearsay
14. Hearsay
15. Best Evidence Rule
16. Non-hearsay — Knowledge or Awareness of Defect
17. Re-direct Examination — Refute Inference of Bias
18. Evidence of Habit
19. Marital Privilege
20. Attorney-Client Privilege — Lawyer's Representatives
21. Termination of Marital Privilege
22. Hearsay
23. Hearsay
24. Evidentiary Admissions — Pleadings
25. Hearsay
26. Hearsay
27. Hearsay

28. Bias — Testimony of Police Informer in Criminal Prosecution
29. Lay Witness — Personal Knowledge Requirement
30. Authentication of Handwriting — Lay Witness
31. Hearsay
32. MIMIC Rule — FRE 404 (b)
33. Probative Value/Impeachment
34. Hearsay
35. Grand Juries
36. Firsthand Knowledge/Best Evidence Rule
37. Hearsay
38. Cross-Examination
39. Hearsay
40. Hearsay
41. Impeachment
42. Spousal Privilege — Confidential Communications
43. Impeachment
44. Surprise Witness
45. Psychiatrist-Patient Privilege
46. Character Evidence — Negligent Entrustment Cases
47. Opinion Testimony
48. Settlement Negotiations
49. Evidence of Absence of Similar Accidents
50. Hearsay
51. Non-hearsay — Utterance Offered to Show Its Effect on Hearer
52. Demonstrative Evidence
53. Subsequent Remedial Measures (FRE 407)
54. Prior Identification

55. Impeachment — Prior Inconsistent Statement
56. Attorney-Client Privilege
57. Attorney-Client Privilege
58. Attorney-Client Privilege
59. Attorney-Client Privilege
60. Failure to Call a Witness at Trial
61. Failure of Defendant to Testify at Trial
62. Admission Made in Connection With Offer to Pay Medical Expenses
63. Offer to Pay Medical Expenses
64. Admissibility of X-Rays
65. Former Testimony/Hearsay Exception
66. Opinion Testimony
67. Expert Testimony
68. Attorney-Client Privilege
69. Character Evidence
70. Admissibility of Photographs
71. Failure of Defendant to Take the Stand
72. Federal Privilege Law (FRE 501)
73. Character Evidence — Inadmissibility of Extrinsic Evidence
74. Character Evidence — Negligent Entrustment Case
75. Habit Evidence
76. Foundational Requirements
77. Objections
78. Learned Treatise Hearsay Exception
79. Vicarious Admissions
80. Hearsay
81. Prior Inconsistent Statements

82. Statement for Purposes of Medical Diagnosis/Treatment

83. Declarations of Present Bodily Condition

84. Vicarious Admissions

85. Excited Utterance

86. Foundational Requirements

87. Attorney-Client Privilege

88. Fifth Amendment Privilege against Self-Incrimination

89. Applicability of Privileges in Federal Court

90. Attorney-Client Privilege

91. Offers or Promises to Pay Medical, Hospital, or Other Expenses

92. Subsequent Remedial Measures

93. Evidence of Liability Insurance

94. Habit Evidence

95. Character Evidence

96. Personal Knowledge Requirement

97. Witness Credibility

98. Preliminary Considerations of Admissibility

99. Judicial Notice

100. Authentication

1. A salesman, who had worked 20 years for the same company, was suddenly terminated for no apparent reason. Thereafter, the salesman sued the company, alleging age discrimination. At trial, he wants to call an employee of the company as an adverse witness. The salesman seeks to have the employee testify that she was present at a company board meeting when the company's president allegedly said, "Now, I'm sure that everyone agrees that the salesman is too old, and he really doesn't typify the image we want our employees to project." It is the common practice of the company to tape record all such board meetings. Moreover, it is customary for the company's secretary to transcribe the tapes following the board meetings.

Upon objection by the company's attorney, the employee's proposed testimony will be held

(A) admissible, because the employee was present during the board meeting.
(B) admissible, because the president's statement was an admission by a company representative.
(C) inadmissible, because the tape of the meeting is the best evidence.
(D) inadmissible, because the secretary's transcribed notes are the best evidence.

2. A customer sued a printing company for negligence, claiming that the holiday cards he specially ordered were of poor quality and had his name misspelled. At trial, the customer shows the court a printed statement from a printer's association defining the minimum standard of skill for the printing industry in the community. The customer asks the court to take judicial notice that the printed statement constitutes the applicable standard of care for printing companies in the area.

The court should

(A) grant the request, because it promotes expeditious and economical disposition of the proceedings.
(B) grant the request, because the standard of care is amply supported by information supplied to the court.
(C) deny the request, because judicial notice cannot be taken of matters that are ultimate issues in the case.
(D) deny the request if the judge determines that the statement is subject to reasonable dispute.

3. A grocery store is sued by a customer for damages for injuries allegedly suffered to the face and forearms, which resulted from his collision with the store's automatic doors. The customer contended that at the time of the mishap, the doors were programmed to swing outward, taking would-be customers entering the store, by surprise. At trial, the customer testified to both the nature of his injuries and the events leading up to their occurrence. The grocery store denied that the doors to its store were in any way unsafe or that the customer's injuries were caused by his encounter with the doors. The customer's sister testified at trial that she accompanied her brother to the store the day of the accident and witnessed the outward swinging doors, which struck him. She further alleged that when she returned to the store the following week, the doors had been re-programmed to swing inward.

The trial judge should rule the sister's testimony

(A) admissible as a commonsense impression for which a lay opinion is entirely proper.
(B) admissible as a tacit admission of a party opponent.
(C) inadmissible, on the grounds of irrelevancy.
(D) inadmissible, on the grounds of public policy considerations.

4. A man is suing a store for damages for injuries allegedly suffered when a can of soup fell on his toe while he was shopping. At trial, the store calls a member of the local community to testify that the man's reputation for honesty is poor, and that he is known far and wide as the biggest storyteller in town.

This testimony is

(A) admissible, but only to show the likely exaggeration of the man's alleged injuries.
(B) admissible, but only to discredit the man's testimony that the accident happened in the manner in which he claims it did.
(C) inadmissible character evidence.
(D) inadmissible, because the man's testimony has not yet been rebutted by the store, and his credibility is, therefore, not yet susceptible to attack.

5. A plaintiff alleges in a lawsuit against a store that he purchased a hot dog with chili that gave him food poisoning and caused him excruciating pain. The store offers into evidence certified copies of court proceedings revealing that the plaintiff has filed three similar lawsuits in the last 18 months against other convenience stores, claiming food poisoning resulting from the purchase of food from those stores.

   These copies should be ruled

   (A) inadmissible, because of the best evidence rule.
   (B) inadmissible, because they are irrelevant to the present claim.
   (C) inadmissible, because there is the danger of undue prejudice to the plaintiff, which outweighs the probative value of the evidence.
   (D) admissible, because they establish a pattern of similar actions.

6. While shopping at a mall, a woman suffered injuries when an escalator malfunctioned, crushing her foot. The woman brings suit against the mall. At trial, she calls another shopper to testify that he rode the same escalator just moments before the woman's accident and had to jump in the air at the last minute to avoid getting his foot crushed in the escalator.

   This testimony is

   (A) inadmissible, because it is irrelevant.
   (B) inadmissible, because it is not known whether the other shopper the woman was exercising reasonable care in riding the escalator.
   (C) admissible, because it tends to prove that a dangerous condition was present at the time the woman's foot was crushed in the escalator.
   (D) admissible, because of its probative value in establishing that the woman's injury was caused by the malfunctioning escalator.

7. A witness is scheduled to testify in a criminal case. To prove that he was a juvenile on a given date, evidence is offered that on that date he was confined in a juvenile detention facility.

   If a party wished to argue that this evidence is hearsay, whom would he point to as the hearsay declarant?

   (A) The witness on the stand.
   (B) The party offering the evidence.
   (C) The juvenile authorities.
   (D) The witness.

8. During a custody dispute, a court granted the request of the defendant and appointed a clinical pathologist to conduct the blood grouping tests of the child, the complainant, and the defendant. After first stating all of his qualifications at the non-jury trial, the pathologist testified that he and his associates made five separate blood grouping tests and that all proper safeguards were taken to protect the integrity and accuracy of the tests. The pathologist also offered more detailed testimony about the testing procedures and stated that no discrepancies were found in the testing methods. Finally, the pathologist made the statement that the blood grouping tests were conclusive in proving that the defendant could not be the father of the child.

   If the complainant's attorney makes an objection to the introduction of the blood tests into evidence, the court will most likely

   (A) sustain the objection, because the blood tests are not conclusive evidence of paternity.
   (B) sustain the objection, because blood tests have not been generally recognized by the scientific community.
   (C) overrule the objection, because the court will take judicial notice of the accuracy of such tests.
   (D) overrule the objection, because the blood tests are an admission.

9. An accounting professor has been called as a defense expert witness in a white-collar criminal case. He testified that accounting records conclusively demonstrated that the defendant had not committed any type of fraud. On cross-examination of the professor, the prosecuting attorney asked him if he was familiar with a particular treatise. The professor responded affirmatively. The attorney then asked him if the treatise was accepted as authoritative and if he was aware of the conclusions regarding the ability of accountants to detect fraud. The professor responded in the affirmative. The prosecutor now attempts to read the following section of the treatise into evidence: "It is virtually impossible to state with conclusive certainty the existence, or lack thereof, of fraud in the majority of white-collar crime cases, given the sophistication of defendants and the variety of accounting methods available."

On objection by the defendant's attorney, the trial judge will

(A) overrule the objection and permit the entire treatise to be introduced into evidence.
(B) overrule the objection and permit only the contradictory statements to be read into evidence.
(C) sustain the objection, because the statements in the treatise are hearsay not within any recognized exception.
(D) sustain the objection, because the professor did not rely on the treatise in making his conclusions.

10. During a paternity trial, the mother's attorney asks to have the baby girl, now 36 months old, exhibited for the purpose of calling attention to certain facial resemblances between the child and the reputed father. The defendant's attorney objects to the offering of the baby into evidence for comparison.

The trial judge should

(A) permit the child to be exhibited as a non-objectionable form of demonstrative evidence.
(B) not permit the child to be exhibited, because such an exhibition would be highly prejudicial to the defendant.
(C) permit the child to be exhibited as within the hearsay exception of pedigree.
(D) not permit the child to be exhibited, because such an exhibition would be self-serving to the complainant.

11. A man was driving his car when he suddenly hit a pedestrian as she was crossing the street. Following the accident, an ambulance was summoned and the pedestrian was taken to a nearby hospital. The man, who also drove to the hospital, approached the pedestrian in the emergency room while she was being treated for her injuries. When the pedestrian saw the man, she told him, "You went through that red light. You could have killed me." She then asked the man for $5,000 to cover her anticipated medical expenses. The man replied that he would have to think about it. Shortly thereafter, the man sent a letter to the pedestrian in which he wrote, "I realize I drove through the red light. Naturally, I would like to settle this without any litigation. I'm willing to pay all your medical expenses and give you $2,000 if you don't sue me." The pedestrian did not accept the man's offer and brought suit against him.

At trial, the pedestrian's attorney offers the first sentence of the letter into evidence, and the man objects. The trial judge should rule the evidence

(A) admissible as an admission.
(B) inadmissible as an admission made in connection with an offer to pay medical expenses.
(C) inadmissible as an admission made in connection with settlement negotiations.
(D) inadmissible, because documents must be offered in their entirety.

12. In a suit between a plaintiff and a defendant arising out of an automobile accident, a bystander was called to the stand to testify that the defendant had driven through a red traffic light immediately before the collision. On cross-examination by the defense, the bystander admitted to having made a prior statement to a friend that he was not sure if the traffic signal was yellow or red when the defendant drove through the intersection.

The trial judge should

(A) permit the jury to consider the prior statement as substantive evidence.
(B) permit the defendant to call other witnesses to confirm the fact that the prior statement had been made.
(C) on request by the defendant, instruct the jury that the bystander's testimony that the defendant had driven through the red light be disregarded.
(D) on request by the plaintiff, instruct the jury that the prior statement may be used only to impeach the bystander's credibility, and not as substantive evidence.

13. A defendant is charged with murder and relies upon a claim of self-defense. At trial, the defendant attempts to show that prior to the killing, he was told by a drinking buddy that "The victim has killed five men and would as soon kill a man as look at him."

If the statement by the drinking buddy is offered into evidence to prove that the victim, in fact, killed the five men, the statement should be ruled

(A) admissible, because the statement is offered to demonstrate its effect on the defendant.
(B) admissible, because it qualifies under the state of mind exception to the hearsay rule.
(C) inadmissible, because it is hearsay not within any recognized exception.
(D) inadmissible, because it is self-serving.

14. A fan attended a minor league hockey game in his hometown. Unfortunately, he was only able to obtain tickets in the visitor's section. While at the game, he became involved in an altercation with a fan of the visiting team. When the fan cheered for a home team goal, the visiting fan turned around and threatened to kill the home fan if he didn't shut up. The home fan pulled a knife out of his pocket and stabbed the visiting fan in the arm. At his trial for aggravated assault, the home fan wants to introduce a statement from a witness who was standing next to the visiting fan at the game. The statement, which the witness had made earlier in the game when the home fan cheered for the home team, was, "You'd better watch out. At a hockey game last week, the visiting fan put two guys in the hospital when they wouldn't shut up. One of them had 33 stitches after the visiting fan bashed his head against the steps."

Assume that the witness's statement is offered as proof of the effect it produced in the home fan's mind. In this regard, the statement would most likely be

(A) admissible as non-hearsay.
(B) admissible as a present sense impression.
(C) inadmissible as hearsay not within any recognized exception.
(D) inadmissible, because the statement is self-serving.

15. A customer purchased a mattress from a furniture store. The mattress had a defective spring, which one of the manufacturer's workers had not properly tied down. When the customer slept on the mattress, she was wounded in the back by the sharp point of the spring. The customer sued the furniture store for negligence and breach of warranty.

At trial, the customer testified that the salesman assured her that the furniture store inspected each mattress before delivery. Furthermore, the customer testified that she remembered the salesman telling her that "The furniture store stands behind all of its mattresses with a lifetime guarantee." She is then asked if the salesman made any other representations about the mattress. The customer stated, "Yes, in fact the day before the mattress was delivered, I received a letter from him thanking me for my patronage at the furniture store. As I recall, he also made some assurances about the manufacturer's mattresses." The customer's attorney then asked, "What assurances were made in the letter?"

The customer's answer is

(A) admissible as an admission.
(B) admissible as a declaration against interest.
(C) inadmissible, under the best evidence rule.
(D) inadmissible as hearsay not within any recognized exception.

16. A man suffered frostbite when he spilled a soft drink on his lap that he had purchased from a restaurant. The man sued the restaurant for negligence and damages. At trial, the man's attorney calls a witness to testify that the witness also suffered frostbite when she spilled a soft drink in her lap that she had purchased at the restaurant two weeks earlier. The witness also states that she told the restaurant about her injury immediately after suffering it.

Upon objection by the restaurant's attorney, the trial judge should rule the witness's testimony

(A) admissible to prove the restaurant's negligence, provided that the court gives a cautionary instruction that the testimony should not be considered as bearing on the issue of damages.
(B) admissible to prove that the restaurant should have been aware of the danger of frostbite posed by its soft drinks.
(C) inadmissible, because it is not probative of a fact in issue.
(D) inadmissible, because it seeks to put into evidence separate, unrelated transactions with a third party.

17. In a breach of contract action brought by a supplier against a grocery store for refusing to buy his artisanal bread and goat cheese, the supplier calls his ex-wife to testify about the business the supplier operated and the financial effect of the breach on his business and personal finances. On cross-examination she admits that she is the supplier's former spouse. Thereafter, on re-direct, the supplier's attorney seeks to have the ex-wife testify that she and the supplier have not spoken to each other since their bitter divorce proceeding three years ago.

    The ex-wife's testimony is

    (A) admissible under the family history exception to the hearsay rule.
    (B) admissible, because the ex-wife's answer might rebut the inference of bias.
    (C) inadmissible, because it relates to a collateral matter.
    (D) inadmissible, because it is irrelevant to any substantive issue in the case.

18. A plaintiff sued a defendant for injuries that the plaintiff suffered when he was struck by the defendant's car. At trial, the plaintiff testified that he was walking across the street inside a crosswalk at the time the defendant's car hit him. This action takes place in a jurisdiction that has a statute in effect requiring all motorists to stop and permit pedestrians to cross streets at designated crosswalks.

    The defendant contended that the plaintiff ran into the street outside the crosswalk. Furthermore, the defendant testified that he immediately applied his brakes when he saw the plaintiff dart into the street, but couldn't stop his car in time to avoid hitting him. In support of the defendant's testimony, the defendant calls a neighbor to testify that she has observed the plaintiff frequently during the years that she has lived on that street, and that the plaintiff "always crosses the street outside the crosswalk."

    The neighbor's testimony is likely to be

    (A) admitted, because it tends to show that the plaintiff was careless.
    (B) admitted, because it is probative of the plaintiff's habit of crossing the street outside the crosswalk.
    (C) excluded, because the neighbor was not an eyewitness to the accident.
    (D) excluded, because her testimony is impermissible evidence of character to show defendant's plaintiff's conduct on a particular occasion.

19. A husband and wife had a stormy relationship. The husband, who was an alcoholic, frequently beat his wife when he became drunk. One day, the husband had been drinking beer while watching football on television. After his favorite team lost a close game, the husband went into a violent rage. As he was storming around the apartment, he suddenly grabbed his wife and led her outside to their car. He then ordered her to get inside the vehicle.

    The husband was driving around aimlessly when he negligently collided with another car. The other driver, who was injured in the accident, brought suit against the husband to recover damages. Thereafter, the husband retained an attorney to represent him. At his first consultation with the attorney, the husband was accompanied by his wife. During the conference, the attorney's secretary took notes of the meeting. Two weeks later, the wife separated from the husband. She then hired a lawyer to represent her in a suit against the husband for battery and false imprisonment. At the trial between the husband and the other driver, the other driver's attorney calls the wife to testify. She proposes to testify that her husband was intoxicated at the time of the accident.

    Upon objection by the husband's attorney, the wife's proposed testimony will most likely be

    (A) admissible as a proper lay opinion.
    (B) inadmissible, under the attorney-client privilege.
    (C) inadmissible, under the marital privilege.
    (D) inadmissible, because the wife is biased.

20. A husband visits an attorney seeking a divorce because of his wife's infidelity. At the client consultation, the attorney's secretary took notes. With the permission of the husband, the attorney's law clerk also sat in on the consultation to see how the attorney conducted these meetings. Shortly after this initial consultation with the attorney, the secretary quit. During the divorce trial, the wife's attorney seeks to call the secretary to testify about what the husband told the attorney during the initial client consultation.

    Upon objection, the secretary's proposed testimony will most likely be

    (A) admissible, because her presence during the meeting destroyed the attorney-client privilege.
    (B) admissible, because the law clerk's presence during the meeting destroyed the attorney-client privilege.
    (C) inadmissible, because the attorney-client privilege disqualifies the secretary from testifying to such confidential communications.
    (D) inadmissible, because it is hearsay not within any recognized exception.

21. A husband and his wife are involved in a contested divorce and child custody battle. Ignorant of the adversarial system, they both visited a family law attorney together for an initial consultation. The attorney advised them that he could not represent them both. The wife found another attorney. During the trial, the wife's attorney calls the wife to testify. She states that during the initial consultation she and her husband had with his attorney, she privately told the attorney, when her husband was taking a bathroom break, that her husband had a bad drinking problem, which was one of her major reasons for seeking a divorce and custody of the children.

    Upon objection by the husband's attorney, the wife's testimony should be

    (A) admitted, because the spousal privilege is inapplicable, since the parties are living in separation.
    (B) admitted, because the marital communication privilege is inapplicable in a lawsuit involving the parties.
    (C) excluded, because the wife is incompetent to testify to marital communications because she is not the holder of the privilege.
    (D) excluded, because confidential statements made during a joint consultation are privileged communications between clients and their attorneys.

22. A plaintiff brought an action against a defendant for personal injuries resulting from a car accident in which the defendant's car, negligently driven by his cousin, struck the telephone booth in which the plaintiff was resting. Liability is based on a statute making owners of automobiles liable for the negligent actions of those driving with the consent of the owner of the vehicle. The plaintiff offered into evidence the testimony of his doctor that the plaintiff had said to the doctor, when consulting the doctor for treatment, that he felt pain in his back immediately after the accident, and that pain persisted.

    The trial court should rule this testimony

    (A) admissible as a spontaneous declaration.
    (B) admissible under the hearsay exception of declaration of present bodily condition.
    (C) inadmissible as hearsay not within any recognized exception.
    (D) inadmissible as conclusions.

23. During his lunch break one day, an employee took a company vehicle to a fast-food restaurant and got into an accident on the way back. The driver of the other car sued the company. The company, in its defense, claimed that the employee's use of the vehicle was unauthorized. At trial, the company calls the employee's boss. The boss offers to testify that the employee called him five minutes after the accident and stated, "I hope you won't be sore, because I took the company car without permission."

    The court should rule that this evidence is

    (A) admissible as a declaration against interest.
    (B) admissible as an admission.
    (C) inadmissible, because the employee was not unavailable.
    (D) inadmissible, because it violates the employee's Fifth Amendment rights.

24. Following their law school graduation party, a graduate and his roommate were driving home in an automobile that was owned and operated by the graduate. As they were approaching an intersection, their vehicle collided with a motorcycle whose rider was seriously injured in the accident. The rider sued the graduate for operating his motor vehicle in excess of the speed limit. In addition, the roommate brought suit against the rider for operating his motorcycle negligently and driving through a red light. The roommate subsequently reached an out-of-court settlement with the graduate and dismissed the lawsuit against him.

At trial against the rider, the roommate testified that he observed the rider drive his motorcycle through a red light and then swerve into the path of the graduate's automobile. In rebuttal, the rider offered into evidence the roommate's complaint against the graduate alleging that the latter was driving "at an excessively high rate of speed at the time the accident occurred."

The complaint is

(A) admissible as an admission.
(B) admissible as a declaration against interest.
(C) admissible under the former testimony exception to the hearsay rule.
(D) inadmissible, because the suit was dismissed as part of a compromise.

25. A driver was severely injured when his car burst into flames after he was rear-ended in a minor auto accident. The driver filed suit against the manufacturer. To prove negligent design by the manufacturer, the driver offers the portion of the transcript from a prior trial in which an expert witness testified that in his opinion the car was unsafe as designed.

The testimony could qualify under the hearsay exception for former testimony

(A) only if the manufacturer had been a party to the former proceeding.
(B) whether or not the manufacturer had been a party to the former proceeding.
(C) if this exception has been held incompatible with the confrontation clause of the Sixth Amendment.
(D) if the manufacturer had an opportunity to cross-examine the expert at the former preceding.

26. In order to establish the unavailability of a witness at trial

(A) it is sufficient to show that the witness is not presently in court.
(B) it is necessary to show that he has died.
(C) it is necessary to show that every reasonable effort has been made to procure his attendance.
(D) if living, it is necessary to show that he is insane.

27. While riding her bicycle along the street, a woman was struck by a vehicle that she didn't see. Subsequently, the woman sued the driver of the vehicle to recover damages for her injuries.

At trial, the woman calls a police officer to testify that a few minutes after the accident, a driver stopped him and said, "Hey, officer, I just saw an accident involving a red truck that hit this girl who was riding a bicycle. The truck left the scene of the accident and I followed it to a warehouse." The police officer then testified that he immediately drove to the warehouse and saw the defendant sitting in a red truck that was parked in the lot. The driver is available to testify at trial.

Upon objection by the defendant's attorney, the police officer's testimony regarding the driver's statement should be

(A) admissible as a statement of recent perception.
(B) admissible as a present sense impression.
(C) inadmissible, because the driver was available to testify at trial.
(D) inadmissible as hearsay not within any recognized exception.

28. In a prosecution of a defendant for receiving stolen property, an informer testified that the defendant sold him a stolen stereo, which the defendant knew had been stolen. During direct examination, the informer testified that he was unemployed but sometimes worked part-time as a substitute teacher.

On cross-examination, the defendant's attorney asked the informer if he had recently filed an application to become a police officer. The informer responded affirmatively. The defendant's attorney then asked the informer the following question: "Isn't it true that you hope that by acting as an undercover agent, the police department will overlook the fact that you had two misdemeanor convictions for possession of marijuana?" The prosecuting attorney immediately objected.

The trial judge should rule that the defendant's attorney's inquiry concerning the informer's hopes and misdemeanor convictions is

(A) improper, as evidence of conduct not related to truthfulness.
(B) improper, as relating to convictions of crimes not punishable by imprisonment in excess of one year.
(C) proper, as tending to show the informer's bad character for truthfulness.
(D) proper, as relevant to the informer's possible bias.

29. A wife is the beneficiary of a policy issued by an insurance company, insuring the life of her husband, now deceased. The policy contained a clause providing that double indemnity is payable in the event that death of the insured "results directly, and independently of all other causes, from bodily injury effected solely through external violent and unexpected means."

The husband was found dead in the chicken shed of his farm. His death resulted from wounds caused by a shotgun blast. The wife filed the necessary papers with the insurance company concerning proof of her husband's death. The insurance company admitted liability for the face amount of the policy but rejected the wife's claim for double indemnity.

The wife then instituted suit against the insurance company demanding judgment according to the double indemnity provisions of the husband's insurance policy.

At trial, the wife was called to testify about the events on the day of her husband's death. The wife said that she was in the kitchen when she heard a gunshot in the shed. As she rushed out of the house, she saw their neighbor running from the shed. The neighbor is present in court.

As a witness, the wife was

(A) competent, because she had personal knowledge of the matter.
(B) competent, because the neighbor is available to testify.
(C) incompetent, because she had a personal interest in the outcome of the lawsuit.
(D) incompetent, because she was testifying to facts occurring after her husband's death.

30. At a defendant's trial for the murder of his former employer, the prosecutor offers into evidence a note that was found during a lawful search of the defendant's apartment. The note states: "The demon compels me to kill my former employer. I thirst for his bloody spirit." At trial, the defendant's former girlfriend is called by the prosecution to testify that the handwriting was, in fact, the defendant's. The defendant's attorney objects.

The trial judge should

(A) sustain the objection on the grounds that the former girlfriend's testimony would be inadmissible opinion evidence.
(B) sustain the objection on the grounds that identification of handwriting requires expert testimony.
(C) overrule the objection on the grounds that the former girlfriend qualifies as an authenticating witness.
(D) overrule the objection on the grounds that the letter qualifies as a past recollection recorded exception to the hearsay rule.

31. A customer is suing a car dealer for selling him a salvaged vehicle that the car dealer had represented as being brand new. A few weeks before trial, the car dealer approached his sister and said, "Sis, I need some sympathy. I sold a salvaged vehicle to a customer, and now he's suing me. I didn't mean any harm by it. I inspected the vehicle and everything." Unknown to either the car dealer or his sister, the sister's boyfriend was at the front door and overheard this conversation. When the time for trial came around, the car dealer left the country and refused to attend the trial, telling his attorney to handle it. The customer's attorney attempted several times to secure the car dealer's attendance at trial, but was unsuccessful. At trial, the sister's boyfriend is called to testify about the conversation he overheard.

On objection by the car dealer's attorney, the court will most likely rule the testimony

(A) admissible as a statement of then-existing mental or emotional condition.
(B) admissible as a declaration against interest.
(C) admissible as a statement of present sense impression.
(D) inadmissible as hearsay not within any recognized exception.

32. A defendant is on trial for false pretenses. He is charged with selling worthless stock in a dummy corporation to unwitting investors. The defendant is alleged to have masterminded a scheme wherein he set up a nonexistent corporation that never conducted business. The victims were sent prospectuses containing false financial data, which induced them to purchase stock in the phony corporation.

At trial, the prosecution seeks to introduce into evidence proof that the defendant had set up 10 other so-called dummy corporations that never existed.

This evidence is

(A) admissible, to show defendant's character trait for dishonesty.
(B) admissible, to show his intent to defraud.
(C) inadmissible, because character cannot be proved by specific instances of misconduct.
(D) inadmissible, because the evidence is not relevant.

33. A husband and his passenger were killed in an auto collision involving a defendant. The husband's wife now brings an action to recover damages for loss of society and companionship. The wife testified that she and her husband had a close relationship and that they were happily married for over 15 years. Then on cross-examination, defendant's counsel asked her if she "was aware of the affair that her husband was having with his passenger?"

The wife's attorney immediately objected to this question. The judge should rule that the question is

(A) objectionable, because the question is beyond the scope of direct examination.
(B) objectionable, because it was highly prejudicial.
(C) unobjectionable, because plaintiff's knowledge of such an affair was probative of the value to be placed on her loss.
(D) unobjectionable, because it was relevant on the issue of negligence.

34. A defendant in an automobile accident case is being sued by the estate of the driver of the other car. At trial, the defendant calls an eyewitness to the collision. The eyewitness testifies that after the crash, he immediately ran to the other driver's car to try to render assistance. The eyewitness observed the other driver covered with blood from the top of his head down to his toes. He was moaning, gasping, and crying out, "I did not see the other car coming!" The other driver died 10 minutes later. The estate's attorney objects to the eyewitness's testimony.

The trial judge should rule that his testimony is

(A) admissible as a declaration against interest.
(B) admissible as a dying declaration.
(C) inadmissible as hearsay not within any recognized exception.
(D) inadmissible, because this testimony cannot be admitted in civil cases.

35. A defendant was arrested and charged with involuntary manslaughter for causing a vehicular homicide. A grand jury was convened, and various witnesses were subpoenaed. At the grand jury, a witness was asked the following question by the prosecuting attorney: "Is it not true that 20 minutes after the accident you told the police that the defendant's car went through the red light?" He answered, "Yes."

The defendant was also subpoenaed to appear before the grand jury. The defendant was represented by counsel at the grand jury hearing. During questioning he was shown the witness's statement from his testimony. No objection was made to the introduction of the witness's statement.

At the defendant's trial, the prosecuting attorney seeks to introduce into evidence the witness's statement from the deposition taken at the grand jury hearing. The defendant's attorney objects to this proffer of evidence.

The objection at trial will be

(A) granted, because the statement is hearsay not within any recognized exception.
(B) granted, because the questioning of the witness was leading.
(C) denied, because the defendant's attorney did not object at the grand jury hearing that the witness's testimony was hearsay.
(D) denied, because the defendant's attorney did not object at the grand jury hearing that the questioning of the witness was leading.

36. A man was arrested and charged with robbery. Upon being taken into custody, he was given his Miranda rights and then taken to the police station for booking. At the stationhouse, the man told a police officer that he was prepared to make a confession. The police officer then turned on a video recorder and videotaped the man's confession.

At trial, the prosecution called the police officer to testify to the incriminating statements that the man made in his confession.

Upon objection by the man's attorney, the police officer's proposed testimony is

(A) inadmissible, because the videotape is the best evidence of the man's confession.
(B) inadmissible, because it is hearsay not within any recognized exception.
(C) admissible, because the police officer had first-hand knowledge of the confession.
(D) admissible, because the man was given his Miranda rights before the confession was elicited.

37. A heavyset man with long red hair robbed a liquor store. Thereafter, a man was arrested and charged with the armed robbery. At the man's trial, the owner of the liquor store was called to testify. He admitted that he was unable to identify the man, who now had a shaven head, as the robber. The prosecuting attorney then handed the owner six photographs. He proposed to testify, over defense objections, that he had previously told the prosecuting attorney that picture #4, admittedly a picture of the man before he shaved his head, was a picture of the person who robbed his store.

The owner's proffered testimony should be adjudged

(A) admissible as a prior identification by the witness.
(B) admissible as past recollection recorded.
(C) inadmissible, because it is hearsay not within any recognized exception.
(D) inadmissible, because it is a violation of the man's right of confrontation.

38. A supermarket had just reopened after a two-week closing for renovations. On the morning of the reopening, a woman was shopping when she suddenly fell and suffered a broken leg. Thereafter, the woman sued the supermarket for personal injuries. In her suit, the woman claimed that she tripped over a paint bucket that had been lying in one of the aisles.

At trial, the woman called another customer to testify that while he was shopping he heard a thud, turned around and saw the woman fall on the floor. He also testified that he saw an empty paint bucket lying a few feet from the woman's leg. On cross-examination, the customer got into an argumentative exchange with the supermarket's attorney. When asked his opinion of what caused the woman's fall, the customer testified, "She fell because she tripped on the bucket." He admitted on cross-examination, however, that he didn't actually see the woman trip on the bucket. The supermarket's attorney then asked the customer the following question: "If you didn't see the woman trip on the bucket, how do you know that she fell because of it?" The customer answered, "Because my girlfriend who was shopping with me told me later that she saw the woman trip over the bucket."

The supermarket's attorney moves to strike the customer's last answer. If the trial judge overrules the defendant's motion and permits the customer's answer to stand, it will most likely be because

(A) the customer's answer was invited by the supermarket's attorney's question.
(B) the customer's answer was based on firsthand knowledge.
(C) the customer's answer was a statement of recent perception.
(D) the customer's answer was a present sense impression.

39. Four men entered into a lease as tenants of a five-bedroom house. They each had a separate bedroom and used the fifth bedroom as a laboratory to manufacture the illegal drug methamphetamine.

One of the men was the so-called money man; he provided the funds to make the rental payments and to purchase the laboratory equipment. One of the other men was the chemist; he had both an undergraduate and graduate degree in chemistry and knew the formula and procedure for producing methamphetamine. Another of the men had sold drugs in the past and knew potential buyers of the methamphetamine. Finally, the fourth man was the enforcer; his role in the scheme was to make sure that no unauthorized persons entered onto the premises of the house.

The four men had been involved in this drug venture for seven months when they were finally arrested and charged with conspiracy to manufacture and distribute methamphetamine, and distribution and manufacture of methamphetamine. During the trial, the prosecution wishes to introduce as evidence against the money man, a statement made by the enforcer to the landlord at the time of the signing of the lease, in which the enforcer said, "No matter what you charge us for rent, you better O.K. it with the money man, because he's the one who will really be paying it." The money man's attorney objects.

The judge's ruling on admissibility will depend on

(A) whether the enforcer actually paid all of the rent.
(B) whether the enforcer had a legal obligation to pay the rent under the terms of the lease.
(C) whether the landlord may be considered a party opponent.
(D) whether the statement was made during the course of and in furtherance of the conspiracy.

40. A defendant has been charged with manufacturing illegal firearms in violation of federal firearms laws. In its case-in-chief, the government wants to introduce a copy of the defendant's transcript from a technical college to show his certificate as gunsmith. The college is no longer in existence, though, and the whereabouts of the previous officials and employees are unknown. However, the transcript bears a seal above the registrar's signature, and the court has taken judicial notice of the existence of the college and has found that it is normal for a college to compile a transcript. Finally, the information about the defendant on the transcript has been corroborated by a government witness. Assume the prosecution provided the defendants with a copy of the transcript before trial and informed them of its intent to introduce it as evidence.

The transcript will be admitted

(A) as a business record, because the custodian can testify as to how the records of the college were kept.
(B) under the general hearsay exception, as the transcript in these circumstances has sufficient circumstantial guarantees of trustworthiness.
(C) only if the registrar's signature can be authenticated by an expert witness.
(D) only if the defendant waives his right to object to its admission.

41. A victim was killed by a gunshot in the presence of three men. The fatal wound was inflicted by a single shot, and there was no suggestion of a conspiracy among those present. One of the three men was charged with the killing.

The prosecution called one of the other men as its first witness. His testimony, if true, established that the defendant fired the shot that killed the victim. The defendant's attorney then called the man's longtime neighbor to impeach him.

Which of the following offers of evidence is most likely to be admitted for the impeachment of the man?

(A) Testimony that the witness is a cocaine addict.
(B) Testimony that the witness embezzled money from his employer last year.
(C) Testimony that the witness is not, in the neighbor's opinion, worthy of belief.
(D) Testimony that the witness is an atheist.

42. A man and a woman were passengers on a plane. They were seated next to one another in the first-class section of the plane. Midway through the flight, the woman excused herself and went to the restroom. While she was gone, the man rummaged through the woman's purse and stole $100 in cash. Unknown to the man, a flight attendant saw him steal the money. As is customary in such situations, the flight attendant radioed ahead, and police officers arrested the man when the plane landed.

The man was subsequently charged with violating an applicable federal larceny statute. During the trial, the prosecuting attorney called the man's wife as a willing witness against her husband. She proposed to testify that the man confided to her that he did steal the woman's money during the flight. The man's attorney objected on the grounds of hearsay and privilege.

The wife's proposed testimony is

(A) admissible, because it is neither hearsay nor privileged.
(B) inadmissible, because it is hearsay not within any recognized exception, though it is not privileged.
(C) inadmissible, because it discloses a privileged communication, though it is not hearsay.
(D) inadmissible, both because it discloses a privileged communication and because it is hearsay not within any recognized exception.

43. A defendant was prosecuted for assault and battery after he admitted striking the victim with a pool cue during a barroom argument. The defendant claimed that he acted in self-defense after he was attacked by the victim, who was drunk and belligerent. At trial, the defendant called a witness who testified that the victim was the aggressor in the altercation. On cross-examination of the witness, the prosecuting attorney asked the witness the following question: "Isn't it true that when you filed your federal income tax return last year, you failed to report the interest income from your savings accounts?" The prosecuting attorney was informed of this fact by the witness's accountant.

Upon objection by the defendant's attorney, the prosecutor's question is

(A) improper, because it is not relevant to the issues in the case.
(B) improper, because the defendant has not been convicted of any crime in connection with the tax return.
(C) within the court's discretion to allow, because filing a false income tax return is an act that bears on the witness's truthfulness.
(D) within the court's discretion to allow, because federal income tax evasion is a crime punishable by imprisonment in excess of one year.

44. A plaintiff sued a trucking company for injuries allegedly suffered when a speeding truck jackknifed and struck her car.

Which of the following pieces of evidence, if offered by the plaintiff, is most likely to be admitted by the court?

(A) Testimony concerning subsequent repairs to the truck paid for by the trucking company where they have stipulated to ownership.
(B) Color pictures of a plastic surgeon operating on the plaintiff showing the incision and bloody surgical tools.
(C) Testimony from the plaintiff's boss concerning the amount of time she has missed work, when payroll records had already been admitted as evidence of the plaintiff's lost wages.
(D) Testimony of a surprise witness to the accident when the court is willing to grant the trucking company a continuance to prepare for cross-examination.

45. One night, a defendant went to play bingo. After losing at bingo, the defendant went on a violent rampage. He stole a car and then picked up a woman at a local bar. After she rejected his advances, the defendant stabbed her to death. The defendant was subsequently arrested and charged with felony-murder under an appropriate federal criminal statute.

The defendant admitted committing the crime but pleaded not guilty by reason of insanity. At trial in federal court, the prosecuting attorney calls the defendant's psychiatrist to testify as to the defendant's mental state at the time of the killing. The defendant's attorney objects, claiming that the testimony would violate the psychiatrist-patient privilege.

The objection should be

(A) sustained, provided the state law recognizes the psychiatrist-patient privilege.
(B) sustained, provided the court concludes that the privilege should be recognized as part of modern common law.
(C) overruled, because no such privilege is specifically provided in the Federal Rules of Evidence.
(D) overruled, because the right to a fair trial overrides the use of a privilege to prevent full exploration of the facts in federal court.

46. A man and a defendant were college roommates. With the defendant's permission, his roommate borrowed the defendant's baseball bat to use in an intramural baseball game. During the course of the game, the roommate struck out with the bases loaded. Angry at himself, the roommate took his bat and flung it into the stands. The bat struck a fan in the face and fractured his nose.

The fan sued the defendant for his injury, alleging that the defendant was negligent in lending his baseball bat to his roommate when he knew that his roommate was irresponsible with bats. At trial, the fan offers evidence that on four separate occasions during the past year the roommate had negligently thrown bats during other baseball games.

The fan's proffered evidence is

(A) admissible to show that the roommate was negligent on the occasion when the fan was injured.
(B) admissible to show that the roommate was irresponsible in the use of bats.
(C) inadmissible, because it is evidence of character.
(D) inadmissible, because character must be proved by evidence in the form of reputation or opinion.

47. A husband and a wife are filing for divorce. At issue is the market value of the house they own. During the divorce proceedings, the husband's lawyer calls a neighbor to testify that the market value of the home exceeds $100,000. She states that her testimony is based on an estimate contained in an appraisal report that she saw. The appraisal had been prepared at the husband's request by a well-known real estate company in the area.

Upon objection by the wife's attorney, the neighbor's testimony will be held

(A) admissible as proper lay opinion.
(B) admissible, because she had firsthand knowledge of the estimate contained in the appraisal report.
(C) inadmissible, because it involves a privileged communication between husband and wife.
(D) inadmissible, because the neighbor has not been shown to be an expert on real estate market values.

48. A woman was driving to work when her car was struck by another car. At the time of the accident, the other driver had momentarily taken his eyes off the road while he placed a CD in his dashboard player. Following the collision, which resulted in the woman's car being extensively damaged, the woman demanded that the other driver pay for the repair work. Whereupon, the other driver said to the woman, "If you will take $2,000, I'm certain my insurance company will pay for it." The woman refused the other driver's offer and sued him for damages.

If, at trial, the woman seeks to testify to the other driver's statement, this proffered evidence should be ruled

(A) admissible as an admission by a party-opponent.
(B) admissible as a statement against interest.
(C) inadmissible as a statement made in conjunction with settlement negotiations.
(D) inadmissible as a self-serving declaration.

49. Two cars were driving within the legal speed limit as they approached an intersection. There are no traffic lights, stop signs, or warnings posted at this intersection. Both vehicles entered the intersection simultaneously and collided. In the accident, one of the drivers suffered a broken pelvis and internal injuries. Although the other driver's truck was slightly damaged, he did not suffer any physical injuries.

Thereafter, the injured driver sued the city for negligence, claiming that the city failed to provide adequate warning at the intersection, which she contended was particularly dangerous and heavily traveled. At trial, the city attorney offers evidence that the intersection has been the same for 14 years, and no other accidents have occurred during that time.

Upon objection by the injured driver's attorney, this evidence should be

(A) admitted as relevant evidence of a fact of consequence to the action.
(B) admitted, provided that the jury is instructed about the danger of inferential negative evidence.
(C) excluded, because it is improper negative evidence.
(D) excluded, because the dangers of unfair prejudice and confusion of the issues may tend to mislead the jury.

50. A relevant fact in a plaintiff's suit is the magnitude of an explosion at an oil refinery one evening. At trial, the plaintiff was asked on direct examination if he remembered the explosion. He replied, "I recall my son running into the home and screaming that the car windows just shattered." The son was available to testify at trial.

The defendant's attorney makes a motion to strike the plaintiff's answer. The trial judge should rule the plaintiff's testimony

(A) admissible, because the son is available as a witness.
(B) admissible, whether or not the son is available as a witness.
(C) inadmissible as hearsay not within any recognized exception.
(D) inadmissible under the excited utterance exception, because it can be a product of reflection and deliberation.

51. A commissioner of a sports league was charged with embezzling funds by increasing the amount of his allocated travel expenses without the approval of a majority of the team owners. In accordance with the bylaws of the league's charter, the commissioner was required to obtain the approval of at least half the owners before raising his expense allocation.

At trial, the commissioner seeks to testify that his predecessor told him that he had authority under the league's charter to raise his expense allocation.

The commissioner's testimony is

(A) admissible, to show that the commissioner lacked criminal intent.
(B) admissible as evidence of the routine practice of an organization.
(C) inadmissible as hearsay not within any recognized exception.
(D) inadmissible, because the league's charter is the best evidence.

52. A defendant was arrested at an airport when the small suitcase he was carrying was found to contain heroin. The defendant, who did not challenge the legality of the airport search, was subsequently prosecuted for possession of heroin.

At trial, the defendant testified on his own behalf and said that the suitcase belonged to his girlfriend who was accompanying the defendant when he was arrested. The girlfriend died in a skydiving accident two weeks before the defendant's trial. Moreover, the defendant testified that although he was a former heroin addict, he had not used any heroin in the past three years. On cross-examination, the prosecuting attorney asked the defendant to roll up the sleeves of his shirt and exhibit his arms to see if there were any needle marks.

This request is

(A) objectionable, because the defendant has a privilege against self-incrimination.
(B) objectionable, because the probative value is substantially outweighed by the danger of unfair prejudice.
(C) permissible, because such evidence is relevant to the defendant's credibility.
(D) permissible, because the defendant waived his privilege against self-incrimination by taking the stand.

53. A professional football player was seriously injured when the football helmet he was wearing shattered as he was being tackled during a game. The player subsequently asserted a claim against the manufacturer of the helmet to recover damages for his injury.

At trial, the player's attorney calls a former employee of the manufacturer to testify that three weeks after the player suffered his injury, the manufacturer devised a new design for its football helmets.

The former employee's testimony is

(A) admissible as an admission.
(B) admissible as circumstantial evidence that the player's injury was traceable to the defective design of the football helmet.
(C) inadmissible, because of the public policy behind taking safety precautions.
(D) inadmissible, because the former employee is no longer authorized to speak on behalf of the manufacturer.

54. A large man with red hair robbed a liquor store. Thereafter, a defendant was arrested and charged with the armed robbery. At the defendant's trial, several eyewitnesses testified that they had seen a large redheaded man pull out a gun and rob the owner of the liquor store. The defendant appeared at trial with a shaven head. The prosecution calls a corrections officer to testify that the defendant had red hair when he was first brought to jail. The defendant's counsel objects.

The trial judge should rule the correction officer's testimony

(A) admissible as a prior identification.
(B) admissible, for the limited purpose of clarifying the discrepancy in the witnesses' testimony.
(C) inadmissible as hearsay not within any recognized exception.
(D) inadmissible, because it is opinion testimony.

55. In a false imprisonment action by a plaintiff against a defendant, the plaintiff calls a witness to testify that the incident occurred on particular date. The witness was not questioned about an affidavit he made for trial in which he stated that the incident occurred on a different date. After the witness left the stand, but before he was excused, the defendant's attorney offers into evidence the affidavit.

Assuming that the affidavit is properly authenticated, the trial judge should rule it

(A) admissible as substantive evidence.
(B) admissible for impeachment purposes only.
(C) inadmissible, because the defendant's attorney failed to question the witness about the affidavit while on the stand.
(D) inadmissible as hearsay not within any recognized exception.

56. In which of these situations are the communications set forth privileged?

(A) An attorney was a member of a seven-attorney law firm. On a busy day, three of his partners had clients waiting to see them, and all of the chairs in the office waiting room were filled. A woman had an appointment with the attorney, and the attorney came out to greet her in the crowded waiting room. As the woman saw the attorney she said, "Am I glad to see you! I need a will made up right away, because I don't want my rotten son to get any of my money. He will just throw it away at the race track." The attorney replied, "Let's go back to my office to discuss this matter." The attorney prepared a will for the woman.
(B) A woman arrived at a law office for an appointment and was escorted to her attorney's office. She sat down and said to the attorney, "You know, I pay you a large retainer every year for your valued counsel. I need some advice now. There was a fire in my house yesterday. It was minor, but I'm covered for $15,000 under my fire insurance policy. I didn't have any furniture in the room where the fire took place, but I want to put in a claim for a sofa and love seat. How should I go about it?" The attorney refused to give her any advice.
(C) A woman engaged an attorney to represent her in adoption proceedings. During the course of his representation, she told the attorney some very personal facts about her lifestyle that the attorney needed in order to prepare a petition for adoption. The adoption took place, but the woman never paid her agreed fee to the attorney. The attorney sued the woman to collect his fee.
(D) A woman consulted an attorney regarding a sale of 70% of the stock of a closely held corporation in which the woman was the majority shareholder. She explained the reason for the sale and divulged the financial condition of the corporation and its prospects for the future. The attorney determined that the transaction would be complicated. Since he felt he was inexperienced in handling such a transaction, the attorney decided to decline to represent the woman. The woman nevertheless sold her stock with the assistance of another attorney.

57. One afternoon, a pilot was flying a small airplane when it suddenly ran out of gas. As he was coming in for an emergency landing, the plane crossed into a neighboring state at a very low altitude. At this time, a 9-year-old boy was walking to school when he was struck and injured by an object, which may have fallen from the plane.

In federal court, a negligence suit was brought against the pilot by the father of the boy for his son. Accompanied by his father, the boy had visited an attorney for preliminary discussions regarding the case. However, the father did not retain the attorney to represent his son in the lawsuit. Instead, the father hired another lawyer to handle the case.

At trial, the pilot's attorney calls the consulting attorney to testify what the boy had said to him regarding his physical condition during the consultation that the attorney had had with the boy and his father.

The attorney's testimony is

(A) admissible, because the attorney-client privilege was waived by the filing of the lawsuit.
(B) admissible, because there is no privilege of confidentiality when a person other than the client is present at the attorney-client consultation.
(C) inadmissible, because the attorney-client privilege prevents such a breach of confidential communications.
(D) inadmissible, because it was a statement of physical condition not made for the purpose of obtaining medical treatment.

58. A taxpayer was notified by the government that her individual income tax was underpaid by $1,012.69. The taxpayer retained an attorney to represent her in contesting the assessment. During the preparation of his client's case, the attorney suggested that it might be a good idea if the taxpayer hired an accountant to organize her records and prepare a financial statement for the year in question. Following the attorney's advice, the taxpayer consulted an accountant, an old family friend, who prepared a financial statement, which the attorney referred to at trial.

During the trial, the attorney representing the government called the accountant to testify about statements that the taxpayer made to him.

The accountant's proposed testimony is

(A) inadmissible, because it would violate the attorney-client privilege.
(B) inadmissible, because it would violate the taxpayer's privilege against self-incrimination.
(C) inadmissible as violative of the work-product rule.
(D) admissible as an admission.

59. Late one afternoon, a woman was hitchhiking when she was picked up by a man. Shortly thereafter, the man stopped and parked his car in a roadside rest area. They were smoking marijuana when another car skidded and crashed into the man's car. The collision damaged the man's car and inflicted personal injuries upon him. The woman was likewise injured. In fact, the impact produced a state of unconsciousness in her that lasted several minutes.

The woman sued the other driver seeking to recover for his alleged negligence. At trial, the woman testified to her injuries and to the other driver's negligence. In defense, the other driver called an attorney who lived next door to the woman. The attorney proposed to testify that after the accident, the woman consulted him about her claim and asked the attorney in confidence how she could falsely testify that she wasn't smoking marijuana at the time of the accident.

Upon objection by the woman's attorney, the attorney's testimony is

(A) admissible as an admission.
(B) admissible as a statement against interest.
(C) inadmissible, because it violates the woman's privilege against self-incrimination.
(D) inadmissible, because it violates the attorney-client privilege for confidential communications.

60. A shopper sued a supermarket for injuries allegedly suffered from a collision with the store's automatic doors. The shopper contended that the doors, which were programmed to swing inward, swung outward and injured him as he attempted to enter the store one afternoon. The shopper's brother-in-law, who was an eyewitness to the accident, was not called to testify at trial. Moreover, the shopper's attorney failed to depose the brother-in-law, who redomiciled out of state shortly after the accident.

With respect to the shopper's failure to offer the brother-in-law's testimony at trial, on request by the supermarket's attorney, the court should

(A) instruct the jury that it raises the presumption that the brother-in-law's testimony would have been unfavorable to the shopper.
(B) instruct the jury that it constitutes an adoptive admission that the brother-in-law's testimony would have been unfavorable to the shopper.
(C) permit the supermarket's attorney to argue that it raises a presumption that the brother-in-law's testimony would have been unfavorable to the shopper.
(D) neither instruct the jury on the matter nor permit the supermarket's attorney to argue the matter.

61. During the murder trial of a defendant, the prosecution presented four witnesses to the brutal slaying of the victim. The evidence pointed to the fact that the defendant beat her about the head and neck with a baseball bat, causing severe injuries to her brain and her ultimate death.

The prosecution rested, and the defendant presented two witnesses, his brother and his girlfriend, who testified that the defendant was dining at an elegant restaurant on the other side of town at the time of the alleged murder. The defendant presented no other witnesses.

During his closing argument to the jury, the assistant district attorney called attention to the fact that the prosecution witnesses had no apparent reason to have any bias toward the prosecution or against the defendant. He then noted that the defendant's witnesses had clear motives to falsify their testimony and favor the defendant. The assistant district attorney added, "If the defendant was on the other side of town, why didn't he tell us himself? Why didn't he get on the stand? What was he hiding? Those are questions for you, the jury, to answer."

The defendant was convicted of first-degree murder and sentenced to life imprisonment.

On appeal, his conviction should be

(A) reversed, because the prosecutor improperly referred to the possible motives or interests of the defense witness.
(B) reversed, because the defendant's constitutional rights were violated during the closing argument.
(C) reversed, because the assistant district attorney referred to the defendant's failure to testify.
(D) reversed, because the assistant district attorney's argument violated the defendant's rights under the Fifth and Fourteenth Amendments.

62. A woman sued a man for personal injuries that she suffered when she was struck by the man's car. The man's car hit the woman as she was walking across the street. Immediately after the accident, the man ran over to the woman and said, "I know I was driving fast, but you weren't paying attention where you were walking. Anyhow, I'm willing to pay all your medical expenses."

At trial, the woman calls an eyewitness to the accident. The eyewitness proposes to testify that he heard the man tell the woman, "I know I was driving fast." The man's attorney objects.

If the eyewitness's testimony is admitted, it will most likely be because the proffered evidence is

(A) admissible as an opinion.
(B) admissible as an admission.
(C) admissible as a present sense impression.
(D) admissible as a declaration against interest.

63. One day, while visiting a plastic surgery clinic for a routine Botox treatment, a patient received an excessive dose of Botox from a new medical assistant on the staff. Her face frozen in a grotesque grimace, she demanded to speak to the doctor. The doctor said, "Listen, why don't you go over to the emergency room and send the bills to me? I'll take care of your medical expenses." The patient subsequently sued the doctor for negligent hiring of the medical assistant and for damages. At trial, she proposes to call the doctor's administrative assistant, who was present during her conversation with the doctor. The patient wants the administrative assistant to testify to the doctor's offer to pay her medical bills.

The doctor's attorney objects. The trial judge should

(A) sustain the objection, because the patient's medical records are the best evidence of the doctor's negligence.
(B) sustain the objection as an offer to pay the medical bills.
(C) overrule the objection, because the evidence is relevant as to the question of the doctor's negligent hiring.
(D) overrule the objection, because an offer to pay medical bills is an inferential admission.

64. A surgeon performed an appendectomy on a patient in an operating room at the local hospital. The surgeon was assisted by a nurse who was assigned to the operation by the hospital. During the patient's early convalescence, he complained of pain not explicable as an ordinary post-operative symptom. On investigation, it turned out that the surgeon, who had bandaged him following the operation, had done so in such a manner as to constrict certain blood vessels. The faulty bandaging had caused acute pain and retarded the patient's recovery.

After the patient's eventual recovery, he sued the surgeon for malpractice, claiming $25,000 in damages. In his case-in-chief, the patient called the nurse to testify that shortly after the surgery, she saw the surgeon destroy the postoperative x-rays of the patient's abdomen.

Upon objection by the surgeon's attorney, the trial judge should rule the nurse's testimony

(A) admissible, provided that the judge determines that the surgeon destroyed the x-rays as a cover-up.
(B) admissible, but leave the weight of the nurse's testimony to be determined by the jury.
(C) inadmissible, because the probative value is substantially outweighed by the danger of unfair prejudice.
(D) inadmissible, because it is extrinsic evidence of a collateral matter.

65. A plaintiff is the beneficiary of a policy issued by an insurance company insuring the life of his wife, now deceased. The policy contains a clause providing that double indemnity is payable in the event that death of the insured "results directly, and independently of all other causes, from bodily injury effected solely through external violent and accidental means."

The plaintiff's wife met her death in the silage shed of her farm. The death resulted from wounds caused by the discharge of a double-barreled shotgun. The plaintiff was arrested and prosecuted for the murder of his wife. After a lengthy trial, the plaintiff was acquitted of the charge.

After the insurance company refused to pay the plaintiff's insurance claim, the plaintiff instituted this civil action. The complaint sets forth the policy, alleges the facts surrounding the death of the insured, avers that the death was within the policy provisions for double indemnity payment, and demands judgment accordingly.

At trial, the insurance company's attorney proposes to introduce excerpts from the plaintiff's murder trial. The plaintiff's attorney objects to the introduction of such evidence.

The trial judge should rule the proffered evidence

(A) admissible as a declaration against interest.
(B) admissible as former testimony.
(C) inadmissible, because of collateral estoppel.
(D) inadmissible, because of double jeopardy.

66. A rescuer was driving on an isolated portion of a country road. His headlights caught a figure lying at the side of the road. The rescuer stopped to investigate and found a victim, who was bleeding from head wounds and appeared to have been severely beaten.

The rescuer then lifted the victim into his car and drove her to the hospital, a half-hour trip. When they arrived at the hospital, the rescuer carried the victim into the emergency room. He left her with a nurse and then returned home. Although the victim recovered from her injuries, she sued the hospital for malpractice, claiming that she was not promptly given medical attention.

At trial, the nurse proposes to testify that when the victim was first brought to the hospital, she was unconscious. The victim's attorney objects and moves to strike the nurse's testimony.

The trial judge should

(A) sustain the objection, because it goes to an ultimate issue in the case.
(B) sustain the objection, because the nurse is not qualified to render an expert opinion.
(C) overrule the objection, because it is a shorthand rendition of what she observed.
(D) overrule the objection, because there are independent grounds to show a present sense impression.

67. A doctor is charged with the murder of his wife. The prosecution alleges that he murdered his wife by giving her a massive injection of succinylcholine while she was asleep. Succinylcholine is a drug used in small quantities by anesthesiologists as a muscle relaxant. The prosecution claims that the fatal dose given to the wife so totally relaxed her lung muscles that she suffocated.

During the trial, a toxicologist, who had no previous knowledge of the case, sat in court and heard all of the evidence about the wife's death and autopsy.

As part of the doctor's defense, his attorney calls the toxicologist to give his opinion on the cause of the wife's death.

May the toxicologist so testify?

(A) Yes, because he can identify the data upon which his opinion is based.
(B) Yes, because an expert may base his opinion on facts made known to him at the trial.
(C) No, because he has no personal knowledge of the wife's death.
(D) No, because the cause of death is an issue to be decided by the jury.

68. For nearly three months, a supermarket underwent extensive renovations. The store was temporarily closed during the renovation period. The day the supermarket reopened, the store manager noticed that small fragments of plaster had fallen from a section of the ceiling. He promptly posted signs warning shoppers of the hazardous condition. The signs, which were printed in bold letters, read: "ATTENTION SHOPPERS – BE ON THE LOOKOUT FOR FALLING PLASTER."

That same afternoon, a shopper was shopping in the supermarket and noticed the signs. She looked at the ceiling but didn't see any plaster falling. Moments later, she was placing some squash in a bag when a section of the ceiling suddenly fell on her head. She suffered a concussion and head lacerations.

Thereafter, the shopper brought a tort action against the supermarket to recover for the injuries she suffered. Her attorney hired a physician to examine the shopper in order to assist the attorney in preparing the case.

At trial, the supermarket's attorney calls the physician that the shopper's attorney hired as a witness and seeks to ask the physician about statements concerning the injuries that the shopper had made to the physician in confidence and that the physician had in turn communicated to her attorney.

The physician's testimony should be

(A) admitted, because the shopper waived the physician-patient privilege by placing her physical condition in issue.
(B) admitted, because the shopper's statements are deemed admissions of a party-opponent.
(C) excluded, because the shopper's statements are protected by the physician-patient privilege.
(D) excluded, because the shopper's statements are protected by the attorney-client privilege.

69. A defendant was charged with killing a victim during a barroom fight. The defendant claimed that he acted in self-defense when he was attacked by the victim. At trial, the defendant called a witness who testified that he witnessed the altercation and that the victim was the aggressor. The witness further testified that he has known the defendant for 10 years and that the defendant is a peaceable man who was acting reasonably in self-defense. The prosecution then offered the testimony of the victim's brother-in-law, who proposed to testify that the victim was a peaceable and law-abiding person.

Upon objection by the defendant's attorney, the brother-in-law's proposed testimony is

(A) admissible, for the purpose of rebutting the contention that the defendant was a peaceable person.
(B) admissible, for the purpose of repudiating the defendant's claim of self-defense.
(C) inadmissible, because the victim's character cannot be proved by the brother-in-law's testimony.
(D) inadmissible, because the defendant did not directly attack the victim's character.

70. A man claims to have inherited property from a wealthy businessman. The man's birth certificate shows that he was born out of wedlock. The record of a proceeding for a support order shows that the businessman was adjudged to be father of the man. However, the man can establish his status as heir of the businessman only if he was legitimated by the marriage of his mother and the businessman subsequent to his birth. Thus, the man must prove that this marriage occurred.

The man's attorney has not been able to discover any marriage license or certificate. However, the attorney does have a photograph that shows a couple dressed in wedding clothes. The scene is the front of a church. Bystanders are seen to be throwing rice at the couple and they seem to be responding by smiling and bowing down. The attorney was given the photograph by the man. He found it in his mother's effects following her death. The man believes that the bride in the picture is his mother. He cannot identify the groom. The attorney was informed by a former acquaintance of the businessman who has seen the snapshot that he thinks the groom is the businessman.

If the attorney seeks to introduce the photograph as proof that the mother and the businessman were married, the trial judge should rule the photograph

(A) admissible, only if the photographer is available to testify concerning the circumstances under which the photograph was taken.
(B) admissible, only if a witness verifies that it is a correct and accurate representation of the relevant facts.
(C) inadmissible as non-verbal hearsay not within any recognized exception.
(D) inadmissible as not the best evidence.

71. A defendant was charged with attempting to possess and distribute narcotics. The defendant was arrested after allegedly trying to purchase several kilos of heroin from an undercover government agent. At trial, the undercover agent testified about the defendant's efforts to arrange the drug transaction. The defendant's defense, on the other hand, consisted entirely in attacking the undercover agent's credibility.

During his summation, the prosecuting attorney, over defendant's objections, stated that he had produced the only witness who was willing to take the stand and testify to what occurred at the meeting when the undercover agent arrested the defendant. Based on the undercover agent's uncontradicted testimony, the prosecuting attorney urged the jury to convict the defendant. The defendant was convicted and, on appeal, argued that the judge erred in permitting the prosecutor's statement.

The defendant's conviction should be

(A) reversed, because the prosecutor's remarks constituted improper comment about the defendant's right to testify.
(B) reversed, because the prosecutor's remarks were not proper rebuttal to defense attacks on the undercover agent's credibility.
(C) affirmed, because it is immaterial; the probative value of the defendant's failure to testify is outweighed by the danger of unfair prejudice.
(D) affirmed, because the prosecutor had the right to express the strength of the evidence he had pursued.

72. A national association brought suit in federal court against a city. The suit charged the city with violating several federal statutes. During the trial, the association's attorney called the city attorney as an adverse witness. The city attorney asserted the attorney-client privilege and objected that the matters communicated to him were intended to be confidential.

The issues raised by the objections of the city attorney should be resolved under

(A) federal privilege law.
(B) the privilege law of the forum state.
(C) either federal privilege law or the privilege law of the forum state as determined by the court.
(D) either federal privilege law or the privilege law of the forum state, whichever the court determines is more likely to admit the evidence.

73. Two defendants were prosecuted for conspiracy to rob a bank. An undercover officer of the local police department was the most important government witness. The defendants' principal defense was entrapment.

The undercover officer testified for the government that he was present at a meeting with the defendants during which they plotted to rob the bank. He further testified that the idea of robbing the bank had first been suggested by one of the defendants, and that afterward, the undercover officer stated that he thought it was a good idea.

Thereafter, the defendants' counsel called a witness who testified that the undercover officer had a bad reputation for truthfulness. The defense then called a second witness who proposed to testify that the undercover officer once perpetrated a hoax on the police department and was reprimanded.

The second witness's proposed testimony is

(A) admissible, because the hoax resulted in a reprimand of the undercover officer.
(B) admissible, because a hoax is probative of the undercover officer's untruthfulness.
(C) inadmissible, because it is essentially cumulative impeachment.
(D) inadmissible, because it is extrinsic evidence of a specific instance of misconduct.

74. One morning, a woman telephoned her next-door neighbor and asked if she could borrow her car. The woman explained that her car was being serviced and would not be ready for a couple of days. The woman told her neighbor that she had a doctor's appointment that afternoon and would return the car immediately afterwards. The neighbor agreed and gave the woman permission to use her car. As the woman was driving to her doctor's office, she collided with another car.

As a result of the accident, the other driver brought suit against the woman and the neighbor to recover for her personal injuries. The other driver asserted a claim against the neighbor for negligent entrustment of an automobile and charged the woman with negligent operation of a motor vehicle.

In her case-in-chief, the other driver called a witness to testify to three incidents of careless driving on the woman's part during the past six months.

The trial judge should rule the testimony

(A) admissible as circumstantial evidence that the woman was negligent on this occasion.
(B) admissible, because the witness had personal knowledge of the woman's poor driving record.
(C) admissible against the neighbor as evidence of the woman's lack of fitness.
(D) inadmissible, because specific acts are not admissible except to rebut evidence of good character.

75. A college student owns an expensive sports car. His friend called him up one afternoon and asked to borrow his car for a date he had that night. The college student generously lent the car to his friend. On his way home from the date, basking in the memories of a beautiful evening, the friend lost control of the car and hit a pedestrian.

As a result of the accident, and after learning that the friend had no money and no insurance, the pedestrian brought suit against the college student to recover for his injuries. He asserted a claim against the college student for negligent entrustment of a vehicle. During his case, the pedestrian introduced evidence that the friend had been in several previous accidents. In his defense, the college student offered the testimony of his girlfriend that the college student frequently lent his car to his friend. The girlfriend further testified that the college student gave his friend permission to use his car only after determining that the friend was a careful and attentive driver.

The girlfriend's testimony is

(A) admissible as evidence of habit.
(B) admissible as a present sense impression.
(C) inadmissible, because it goes to the college student's character.
(D) inadmissible, because she is biased.

76. A wind surfer brought an action against a boater when the wind surfer was seriously injured on the water. During the course of the lawsuit, an important question of consequence was the wind speed on the afternoon of the accident. At trial, the wind surfer calls an orthopedic surgeon to testify. The surgeon, who is an amateur boating enthusiast, testified that he was navigating his sailboat when the boater hit the wind surfer. Furthermore, the surgeon testified that in the cockpit of his boat he maintains a sophisticated electronic weathering device that measures wind speed, temperature, and barometric pressure at periodic intervals. The wind surfer's attorney then offers into evidence the computer printout from the surgeon's weathering device measuring the wind speed at the time of the accident.

Upon objection by the boater's attorney, is the printout admissible?

(A) Yes, as past recollection recorded.
(B) Yes, as the record of regularly conducted activity.
(C) Yes, as long as there is foundation testimony as to the accuracy and good working condition of the surgeon's electronic weathering device on the afternoon in question.
(D) No, because it is hearsay not within any recognized exception.

77. A mushroom farmer sued a supermarket owner for breach of contract. The farmer called a witness to testify that the farmer produced and shipped the mushrooms to the supermarket as requested. On cross-examination, the supermarket's attorney asked the witness the following question: "Would you please tell the court the date that the farmer shipped the mushrooms to the supermarket?" The witness responded, "I have known the farmer since we both began volunteering at a local homeless shelter, and he has always produced the finest mushrooms in the area." The supermarket's attorney objects and moves to strike the witness's answer.

How should the court rule on the objection?

(A) Sustain the objection, because a party's credibility cannot be bolstered until it has been impeached.
(B) Sustain the objection, because the witness's answer is non-responsive.
(C) Sustain the objection, because character evidence is generally inadmissible in a breach of contract action.
(D) Overrule the objection, because a witness on cross-examination must be given latitude to answer questions.

78. A husband was arrested and charged with murdering his wife. During the husband's trial, the prosecution called a forensic scientist to testify that the husband's DNA was present at the crime scene and on the murder weapon. The forensic scientist testified that the statistical probability based on DNA and linking the husband to the crime scene was one out of 12,300,000,000 people. The forensic scientist concluded that it was statistically improbable that another individual would have the same genetic match as the husband's. The forensic scientist further stated that he has based his research on information contained in the treatise titled "The Science of DNA."

The husband's attorney seeks to cross-examine the forensic scientist regarding his testimony related to DNA. During cross-examination, the husband's attorney shows the forensic scientist a photocopy of page 232 from The Science of DNA. Defense counsel then seeks to question the expert about the information contained on that page and to admit that page as an exhibit into evidence.

Upon objection by the prosecution, how should the trial judge rule?

(A) The photocopy may be admitted as an exhibit and the witness may be questioned about the document.
(B) The photocopy may not be admitted as an exhibit but the witness may be questioned about the document.
(C) The photocopy may be admitted as an exhibit but the witness may not be questioned about the document.
(D) The photocopy may neither be admitted as an exhibit nor may the witness be questioned about it since the original book must be produced.

79. A taxi driver took his car to a local shop to have the transmission repaired. A mechanic was working on the transmission when the hydraulic lift broke. This caused the car to fall on top of the employee, injuring him. The taxi driver, who happened to be standing nearby, saw the incident and rushed over to help the mechanic. As the taxi driver tried to free the mechanic from the metal entanglement, the hydraulic pump (an apparatus connected to the lift) suddenly burst, propelling a sharp metal fragment into the taxi driver's stomach. The taxi driver received a deep laceration.

The taxi driver then initiated suit against the transmission shop based on negligent maintenance of the hydraulic lift. At trial, the taxi driver called the chief inspector for the state's Department of Occupation Safety and Health Administration (OSHA), who testified about an official report of the accident as prepared by an OSHA investigator. The taxi driver proposes to introduce a segment of the report that quotes the employee's statement, made to the OSHA investigator in an interview at the transmission shop, as to the cause of the accident.

Upon objection by the shop's attorney, how should the trial judge rule on the objection as to the report?

(A) It is admissible as past recollection recorded.
(B) It is admissible as an admission incorporated in a public record.
(C) It is inadmissible, because such documents must be offered in their entirety.
(D) It is inadmissible, because it is hearsay not within any exception.

80. A woman sued a man for injuries suffered when her car was sideswiped by a speeding red sports car that had driven through a red light at the intersection of Broad Street and Grand Avenue. The rate of speed of the sports car and its color are in issue. A witness to the incident proposes to testify that just before the accident she was at home listening to a broadcast on her police-band radio when the dispatcher said: "Attention all cars; be on the lookout for a red sports car heading south on Broad Street at an excessive rate of speed." The witness then said she looked out her window in time to see a red sports car leaving the scene of a collision with the woman's car.

Upon objection by the man's attorney, is the witness's testimony relating to what she heard over the police-band radio admissible?

(A) Yes, because she had firsthand knowledge of the broadcast.
(B) Yes, as a statement of present sense impression.
(C) No, under the best evidence rule.
(D) No, as hearsay not within any recognized exception.

81. After being found not guilty of felony murder, a man is being sued for wrongful death. The plaintiff called the medical examiner to testify that the defendant's DNA was found on the victim's shirt. The medical examiner surprised the plaintiff and testified that he did not find any evidence of the defendant's DNA on the victim's shirt. The plaintiff then questioned the medical examiner with the medical report that he prepared, which stated he did find the defendant's DNA on the victim's shirt. The medical examiner testified that while his signature did appear at the bottom of the report, he did not prepare it. The plaintiff then sought to introduce the medical report into evidence.

Assuming a proper foundation has been laid, is the report admissible?

(A) Yes, for purposes of impeachment only.
(B) Yes, for impeachment and as substantive evidence.
(C) No, because it is hearsay not within any recognized exception.
(D) No, because the plaintiff cannot impeach its own witness.

82. A widow sued a neighbor for the sudden death of her husband. When he died, the husband had been hospitalized for injuries he suffered when he allegedly fell over a hose spread across the sidewalk in front of the neighbor's house. On cross-examination of the emergency room physician who treated the husband in the hospital, the neighbor's lawyer asked, Don't your records show that the deceased told you he had been a bit tipsy before he fell and landed on his head on the neighbor's sidewalk? The widow's lawyer objected.

How should the court rule?

(A) The husband's statement should be admissible only for impeachment purposes.
(B) The husband's statement is admissible hearsay because it is a statement of cause reasonably pertinent to diagnosis or treatment.
(C) The husband's statement is inadmissible hearsay.
(D) The deceased's statement is inadmissible because the declarant is dead.

83. A restaurant patron sued a fast-food restaurant, alleging that she slipped and fell on a grease puddle on the floor that the restaurant had negligently failed to clean up within a reasonable time. As part of her case, to show the extent of damages, the restaurant patron offered the following testimony of her boyfriend: When he asked the restaurant patron to go sailing with him the day after the accident, she replied, Sailing, no way! It will be a wonder if I can even stand up; my backside is killing me! Opposing counsel objects to this testimony.

Should the trial court rule that the evidence is admissible or inadmissible?

(A) Inadmissible, because the declarant must be unavailable for a declaration of present bodily condition to be admitted.
(B) Inadmissible, because a recorded recollection must be in writing.
(C) Admissible, as an excited utterance.
(D) Admissible, as a declaration of present bodily condition.

84. A driver was involved in a high-speed car accident. A truck owned by a trucking company ran the driver's compact car off the road into a ditch. The driver was not hurt, but the side and front of his car were crushed. In a suit against the trucking company, the driver offers the testimony of a witness that after the truck driver ran into the driver's car, the truck driver said, I should have been watching the road. The trucking company is the only defendant, and the truck driver is available to testify.

How should the trial judge rule on the testimony?

(A) Admissible, as a declaration against interest.
(B) Admissible, as a non-hearsay vicarious admission.
(C) Inadmissible, because it is not a present sense impression.
(D) Inadmissible, as hearsay not within an exception.

85. A plaintiff was involved in a high-speed collision on the San Diego freeway. A sideswipe occurred between the plaintiff's pickup truck and a trailer truck. The sideswipe caused the plaintiff's truck to careen down the road and into an embankment. The plaintiff was not hurt badly, but her pickup and the load of furniture she was hauling was totally destroyed. At trial, the plaintiff called a witness to the collision to testify that she heard an unidentified high-pitched voice scream, Oh, my God, that trailer truck sideswiped that poor little pickup.

How should the trial judge rule on this testimony?

(A) Inadmissible, because it contains inadmissible opinion evidence.
(B) Inadmissible, as hearsay not within any of the exceptions.
(C) Admissible, as a declaration of existing state of mind.
(D) Admissible, as an excited utterance.

86. In an employee's wrongful discharge action against her employer, the employer alleges that the employee falsified her employment history before joining the employer's staff. Her resume, admitted into evidence without objection, shows that she worked for the federal Department of the Interior as a purchasing agent for three years. The employer sought to introduce payroll records from the Department of the Interior for that entire period, showing there had never been a paycheck issued to someone with the employee's name.

Is this evidence admissible?

(A) No, because the prejudice outweighs the probative value of the records because she may have had another name during that time period.
(B) No, unless the person who prepared the records will testify.
(C) Yes, although they can only be admitted in summary form to prevent wasting the court's time.
(D) Yes, provided an appropriate person lays a foundation for the records.

87. A plaintiff brought an action for fraud against the defendant who was an attorney. The plaintiff's complaint alleged, among other things, that the defendant had advised a client, a brokerage firm, to misrepresent certain transactions made on its own behalf as having been made for fictitious undisclosed principals in order to fraudulently induce the plaintiff and other actual customers of the brokerage firm to invest in securities that the defendant and the brokerage firm knew were worthless, all to generate brokerage fees. The defendant filed an answer denying every allegation in the complaint. The plaintiff then filed a request for discovery demanding that the defendant produce all brokerage firm transaction records in her possession, so that the plaintiff could demonstrate that the defendant had been aware of the misrepresented transactions. The defendant refused to comply on the grounds that, although they were otherwise discoverable, she had obtained any such records from the brokerage firm in the course of her attorney-client relationship, and that any such records were protected by the attorney-client privilege. The plaintiff sought a court order compelling the defendant to produce the subject records.

How should the court rule on this discovery motion?

(A) For the plaintiff, because the defendant has made no showing that the brokerage firm has asserted the attorney-client privilege as to the records.
(B) For the plaintiff, because the records are not the type of material protected by the privilege.
(C) For the defendant, if the brokerage firm intended that its records be confidential when it turned them over to the defendant.
(D) For the defendant, because the records fall within the work product doctrine.

88. A husband was charged with embezzling from the company at which both he and his ex-wife worked. The embezzlement occurred before the couple was married. The couple recently married during a wild weekend on a company retreat in Las Vegas. They divorced a few days later, and everyone assumed the marriage was an alcohol-induced mishap. The ex-wife was not charged with any crime as there was no evidence she was involved in the embezzlement and no one knew the couple was romantically involved prior to their sudden marriage. However, the husband and ex-wife both know that the wife helped the husband cover up his embezzlement. The husband has remained silent about his ex-wife's involvement to protect her. The prosecutor calls the ex-wife as a witness but she does not want to testify, fearing her involvement will be discovered.

Can the ex-wife assert a privilege?

(A) Yes, she can assert the Fifth Amendment privilege against self-incrimination to avoid testifying as a witness at all.
(B) Yes, she can assert the Fifth Amendment privilege to avoid answering questions that would expose her to liability for the crime.
(C) Yes, she can assert the spousal privilege to avoid testifying as a witness at all.
(D) Yes, she can assert the marital communication privilege to avoid answering questions about confidential communications between the spouses occurring prior to or during the marriage.

89. A mechanic files suit against a 17-year-old high school student in state court for injuries arising out of an automobile accident. The student removes the case to federal court based on diversity jurisdiction. The law of the state in which the federal district court sits provides for a testimonial privilege for parent-child communications. For the privilege to apply, the child must be minor. The mechanic wishes to call the student's mother, who was not involved in the accident, as a witness to question her about any admissions the student may have made to her about the accident. The student asserts the parent-child privilege.

Is the state law privilege applicable in this case?

(A) Yes, because the federal court must apply the privilege rules of the state in which it sits.
(B) Yes, unless the parties choose at trial to have federal common law apply.
(C) No, because the federal court must apply the federal common law related to privileges.
(D) No, because the student waived the state law privilege by removing the case to federal court.

90. A photographer sued a manufacturer for personal injuries based on product liability when a firecracker that the photographer purchased spontaneously combusted. At the request of the manufacturer's insurance company, the manufacturer prepared a report of the accident, and that report was delivered to the attorney who represented the manufacturer. The photographer requested a copy of this report, but the manufacturer's attorney refused to permit the photographer to see it.

Will the photographer succeed in a motion to compel production of this report?

(A) Yes, because the insurance company requested the report.
(B) Yes, because the report may contain discoverable evidence even though the report itself may be inadmissible.
(C) No, because the report is privileged pursuant to the attorney-client privilege.
(D) No, because the report may contain subsequent remedial measures that the manufacturer underwent to produce a safer product.

91. A dentist and a banker were skiing down some advanced slopes at a local ski hill. As the two skiers approached the giant jump in the middle of the mountain, the banker cut off the dentist, sending the dentist stumbling down the hill. The dentist yelled out, I think my knee just popped out. The banker responded, I'm so sorry. I know I cut you off. So, don't worry, I'll pay your medical bills. It just so happened that the dentist did not suffer any physical injuries requiring medical treatment, but his very expensive skis were severely damaged to the extent that he had to replace them. The dentist brought an action against the banker to recover the cost of the skis. At trial, the dentist attempted to testify regarding the banker's statements.

Can the trial court permit the dentist to testify about the banker's statements, to prove liability?

(A) Yes, the banker's statement that he cut off the dentist is admissible to prove liability.
(B) Yes, the entire statement is admissible to prove liability.
(C) No, because offers to pay medical bills and any accompanying comments are inadmissible to prove liability.
(D) No, because the banker's statements are likely to be more prejudicial than probative.

92. A therapist suffered a severe bout of bronchitis last year. His doctor prescribed a three-week supply of antibiotics. The antibiotics are manufactured by a pharmaceutical company. A warning on the medicine's package informed consumers that the drug could cause a loss of balance or dizziness. After a few days off, the therapist went back to work and continued taking the antibiotics as instructed. On his way to work one day, shortly after taking his antibiotic, he was walking down the stairs of his apartment building when he lost his balance and tumbled forward, injuring his head and breaking his wrist. His attorney filed an action against the pharmaceutical company in federal court, claiming that the pharmaceutical company was negligent in its warning for the drug and responsible for the therapist's injuries. At the trial, the therapist's attorney sought to offer into evidence the fact that the pharmaceutical company had expanded its warning label on the antibiotics this year and that the new warning advised consumers not to walk around for at least two hours after taking the medicine, because the medication could cause a loss of balance or dizziness.

Is this evidence admissible to prove negligence?

(A) No, because evidence of a new warning cannot be used to prove negligence concerning the old warning.
(B) No, because the evidence of this year's warning is not relevant to the therapist's accident, which occurred last year.
(C) Yes, because the evidence is a declaration against interests and an exception to the hearsay rule.
(D) Yes, the evidence can be used to show the need for a more extensive warning.

93. A 12-year-old girl was crossing the street in a school crosswalk when she was struck by a car. The girl's mother, who was waiting across the street to pick up her daughter, immediately drove the girl to the hospital. The driver of the car, concerned for the young girl, followed them to the hospital. While in the waiting room with the distraught mother, the passenger of the car told the mother: Don't worry; I have great auto insurance on this car that will cover all the medical bills. As a result of the accident, the girl suffered a near total loss of vision in her left eye. The girl's father is duly appointed the girl's guardian ad litem. He files an action against the driver and passenger on the girl's behalf. At trial, the father's attorney seeks to call the mother to testify to the statement made by the passenger at the hospital. The driver's attorney objects.

Under the Federal Rules of Evidence, may the court admit the testimony?

(A) No, because the passenger's insurance is not relevant.
(B) No, because it is prejudicial and therefore must be excluded.
(C) Yes, because it can be offered as an admission of the driver's negligence or liability.
(D) Yes, because it can show the ownership or control of the vehicle that struck the girl.

94. A plaintiff sues a pizzeria for an injury that the plaintiff sustained when he tripped and fell on the pizzeria's allegedly defective stairway. There was no eyewitness to the fall. At trial, the pizzeria's attorney calls a witness who lived next door to the pizzeria in the same building as the plaintiff. She said that on nice evenings she sipped drinks on the porch and on such evenings she had seen the plaintiff exit the building and visit the pizzeria many times. Her testimony was that the plaintiff always cavorts down the stairs two at a time whenever he goes down a set of stairs, whether those to the apartment building or the pizzeria.

Is the witness's testimony admissible?

(A) Yes, because the testimony tends to show that the plaintiff is a careless person.
(B) Yes, because the testimony is probative of habit and, therefore, of conduct in conformity with the habit.
(C) No, because there was no eyewitness to corroborate the testimony.
(D) No, because the testimony is impermissible evidence of character to show conduct.

95. A defendant was charged with the armed robbery of a gas station. The defendant denied all the allegations and pleaded not guilty. At trial, the defendant called his brother as a witness. The brother was to testify that the defendant's had a reputation as a gentle person who wouldn't hurt a flea.

Should the court allow the brother's testimony to be admitted as evidence at trial?

(A) Yes, because it tends to prove that the defendant is not the type of man who would commit armed robbery.
(B) Yes, because it is relevant to the question of whether the defendant's denial of guilt can be believed.
(C) No, because the defendant has not yet testified.
(D) No, because a sibling's testimony in these circumstances is unreliable.

96. Because of an oil company's questionable safety record, the board of directors bought a life insurance policy from an insurance company on the life of the president of the company. The life insurance policy provided for payment of the face amount if death occurred as a result of an accident. The president's wife took out a policy from the same company that paid triple the face amount if death resulted from a violent, intentional act. The president died as a result of a fall from an offshore oil rig he was inspecting. The cause of death was drowning. The company claimed it was just another accident, and the insurance company agreed.

The wife claimed it was intentional and filed suit against the insurance company, demanding payment of triple the face amount of the policy. She testified that she was on the rig at the time of the accident, and that she saw a worker running away from the spot where the president had been standing just seconds before his fall. The insurance company's lawyer objected to the wife's competency to testify.

Should the president's wife be ruled competent to testify?

(A) No, because she has a financial stake in the outcome of the trial.
(B) No, because she would be testifying about matters relating to the estate of the deceased.
(C) Yes, because she has personal knowledge of the matter.
(D) Yes, because the hearsay exception for present sense impression applies.

97. During a hairdresser's personal injury suit, a co-worker testified against the hairdresser. The hairdresser then called the salon owner, who testified that, in his opinion, the co-worker was a chronic liar. The hairdresser then called an accountant, who testified that the co-worker cheated on his tax return two years ago.

Is the accountant's testimony admissible?

(A) Yes, because it is evidence of a prior crime.
(B) Yes, because cheating on a tax return involves dishonesty.
(C) No, because it is extrinsic evidence of a specific instance of misconduct.
(D) No, because it is cumulative evidence.

98. A plaintiff files a breach of contract claim. A supplier had earlier sued the defendant on a similar issue. Since the previous trial involving the supplier's claim, the supplier's health and memory have deteriorated severely due to Alzheimer's disease. At the trial of the plaintiff's claim against the defendant, the plaintiff wishes to introduce the supplier's trial testimony from the previous trial, claiming that the supplier is unavailable to testify. The plaintiff offers evidence of supplier's incomprehensible recent statements and confused memories to demonstrate the severity of his Alzheimer's and thus his unavailability as a witness. The defendant objects.

Who should review the supplier's prior testimony to determine its admissibility?

(A) Neither the judge nor the jury, because the evidence regarding the supplier's recent statements showing the extent of his Alzheimer's is hearsay not within any exception.
(B) Both the judge and the jury, because the evidence regarding supplier's recent statements showing the extent of his Alzheimer's falls within an exception to the hearsay rule.
(C) The judge, regardless of whether the evidence regarding supplier's recent statements showing the extent of his Alzheimer's constitutes hearsay.
(D) The jury, regardless of whether the evidence regarding supplier's recent statements showing the extent of his Alzheimer's constitutes hearsay.

99. The distance between a pizza parlor and a plaintiff's home is an issue in the plaintiff's negligence suit against the pizza parlor. The plaintiff asks the court to take judicial notice of the distance.

Which of the following statements most accurately describes the proper response for the court?

(A) The court must take judicial notice of the distance if the plaintiff makes a proper request and furnishes the court with a reputable map or a printout from a reputable computer program.
(B) The court may take judicial notice of the distance if the plaintiff makes a proper request, gives timely notice, and furnishes the court with a reputable map or a printout from a reputable computer program.
(C) The court may not take judicial notice unless both parties agree.
(D) The court may not take judicial notice, because the distance is not capable of ready and accurate determination if there are different routes that a driver could take between the pizza parlor and the plaintiff's house.

100. In a civil trial, the plaintiff seeks to introduce a large number of documents against the defendant. In order to prove that the defendant had signed the documents being offered, the plaintiff presented a certified copy of an unrelated legal document which contains the defendant's signature and which was filed with the local town hall before the trial. This offering was challenged by the defense attorney who objected and claimed that this was an improper way to authenticate or identify the other documents.

Is this unrelated legal document admissible or inadmissible for this purpose?

(A) Inadmissible, because the plaintiff did not show the chain of custody of the legal document.
(B) Inadmissible, because only the defendant can identify the defendant's signature.
(C) Admissible, because the document sought to be introduced is unrelated to the matter before the court.
(D) Admissible, because the trier of fact can make the comparison.

Answers and Explanations

1. **(B)** FRE 801(d)(2)(D) allows a statement by a party's agent or servant concerning a matter ***within the scope of the agency or employment, made during the existence of the relationship,*** to be admissible against the party as ***a vicarious admission.*** In *O'Donnell v. Georgia Osteopathic Hospital,* 748 F.2d 1543 (1984), the plaintiff's claim based upon age discrimination was upheld where the Court admitted (as a vicarious admission) the testimony of the person who replaced the plaintiff describing discussions he had had with the hospital's executive director concerning the plaintiff's treatment. The statements made by the company's president concerning the salesman's age not typifying the company's image were made within the scope of his employment and during the existence of the relationship. As such, his testimony will be admissible as a vicarious admission. Choice (B) is correct. Choice (A) is incorrect because the mere fact that the employee was *present* at the board meeting and had personal knowledge is insufficient in itself to admit an out-of-court statement which that otherwise be hearsay. Allowing the statement as an admission however, under choice (B), addresses this issue, ***since admissions, by definition, are non-hearsay.*** Choices (C) and (D) are incorrect. The best evidence rule is not relevant under these facts. The employee's testimony of what the president said is based on ***personal*** knowledge and is not reliant on any tape recording or transcribed notes.

2. **(D)** A ***judicially noticed fact must be one not subject to reasonable dispute in that it is either (1) generally known within the territorial jurisdiction of the trial court or (2) capable of accurate and ready determination*** by resort to sources whose accuracy cannot reasonably be questioned. FRE 201. Choice (D) is the best choice because, according to the rule, a judge will not take judicial notice of a fact over which there is a reasonable dispute. Choice (C) is incorrect because it is too conclusory. While courts are hesitant to take judicial notice over matters that are the ultimate issues in a case, that is not to say that courts will always refrain from doing so. Choice (A) is wrong. If the statement in (A) were correct, a judge could take judicial notice of nearly every disputed issue at trial in order to save time and promote efficiency. Choice (B) is also incorrect. There simply isn't enough information about this document to determine whether it amply supports or defines the standard of care for printers.

3. **(D)** Evidence of ***subsequent remedial measures is generally excluded*** on grounds that the possible relevancy of the evidence is outweighed by public policy considerations (e.g., encouraging repairs after accidents). Therefore, choices (A), (B), and (C) are incorrect.

4. **(B)** Note that the witness's testimony (regarding the man's reputation) is inadmissible character evidence. As a general rule, character evidence is ***not*** admissible in a civil case unless defendant's character is "in issue" (e.g., in defamation or negligent entrustment cases). Thus, choice (C) does state a correct rule of law. However, choice (B) is a better answer because even though the witness's testimony is not admissible as character evidence, it is admissible for purposes of impeachment. According to FRE 608, for impeachment purposes ***opinion and reputation evidence of character*** (subject to the limitation that such evidence may refer only to character for truthfulness or untruthfulness) are admissible. In this case, testimony about the man's character for truthfulness is properly admissible to impeach him. Choice (A) is wrong because it lists an incorrect purpose for the admission of the evidence. Choice (D) is also wrong. Once a witness in a case testifies, his or her credibility is at issue. There is no requirement to first rebut the witness's testimony in order to attack his credibility.

5. **(C)** Since evidence of prior tort claims is generally inadmissible because of the chance for prejudice and conclusion, choice (C) is correct. Choice (A) is incorrect because certified copies may be admitted in lieu of original documents. Choice (B) is wrong because the evidence may have some probative value. Choice (D) is incorrect because the probative value is outweighed by the prejudicial effect of the evidence.

6. **(C)** The testimony is admissible to prove the ***existence of the condition that the woman claimed caused her injuries.*** When there appears to be sufficient proof of similarity in conditions and proximity in time to the accident, such evidence is admissible. Choice (A) is wrong, since the information is, indeed, relevant. Choice (D) is an incorrect statement, since the evidence is only admissible to prove the existence of the condition, but not that the accident happened. Choice (B) is incorrect because it establishes an unnecessary condition precedent for the use of this evidence.

7. **(C)** In this question, the facts tell you that someone will argue that this evidence is hearsay. In every hearsay statement, the out-of-court statement is made by the declarant. Here, the statement would be that the witness was confined in a juvenile detention facility. That statement would have been made originally by the juvenile authorities. So choice (C) is the best choice. Choice (A) is not as good because it is not necessarily true. The witness on the stand might have had nothing to do with the witness's juvenile records. Choice (B) is wrong. The party offering hearsay evidence is rarely the declarant. Choice (D) is incorrect because the witness would not have been responsible for the creation and maintenance of his juvenile records.

8. **(C)** The court is warranted in taking judicial notice of the correctness of such blood tests excluding paternity where it is shown that the person making the tests is qualified and that no discrepancies were found in the testing method. See FRE 201. Choice (A) states an incorrect standard. Evidence does not have to provide conclusive proof of the matter at issue to be admissible. Choice (B) is wrong because blood tests are, in fact, generally recognized as accurate by the scientific community. Choice (D) is incorrect because a blood test is not an admission within the meaning of FRE 801(d).

9. **(B)** Under FRE 803 (18), the following are not excluded by the hearsay rule "... to the extent called to the attention of an expert witness upon cross-examination or relied upon by him in direct examination statements contained in published treatises, periodicals, or pamphlets on a subject of history, medicine, or other science or art, established as a reliable authority by the testimony or admission of the witness or by other expert testimony or by judicial notice. ***If admitted, the statements may be read into evidence but may not be received as exhibits."*** Choice (A) is wrong because ***only the entire treatise itself cannot be placed into evidence.*** Choice (C) is incorrect. ***The statements in the treatise are hearsay, but fall within a recognized hearsay exception.*** Choice (D) is also wrong. ***One purpose of this hearsay exception is to test the knowledge of expert witnesses on cross-examination and provide contradictory testimony to the fact-finder.***

10. **(A)** The majority of states hold that a trial court may, in its discretion, permit a child to be exhibited (e.g. demonstrative evidence) in a proceeding for the purpose of showing a resemblance to the putative father. *Judway v. Kovacs*, 239 A.2d 556 (1967). Accordingly, choice (A) is correct, and choice (B) is incorrect. Choice (C) is incorrect. The hearsay exception for pedigree requires an out-of-court statement. The live exhibition of a child at trial cannot constitute an out-of-court statement by any stretch of the imagination. Choice (D) is wrong. Much of the evidence admitted in an adversarial trial is self-serving to the offering party.

11. **(C)** In accordance with FRE 408, evidence of (1) furnishing or offering or promising to furnish, or (2) accepting or offering or promising to accept, a valuable consideration in compromising or attempting to compromise a claim that was disputed as to either validity or amount, it is not admissible to prove liability for the claim or the amount. Two grounds for the rule of inadmissibility may be advanced: (1) lack of relevancy, and (2) the public policy aspect is to promote the settling of disputes, which would be discouraged if offers of compromise were admitted in evidence. Choices (A) and (B) are incorrect because of the public policy considerations of FRE 408. Choice (D) is incorrect. There is no requirement for a proponent to offer documents in their entirety. The Rule of Completeness in FRE 106 does, however, permit an adverse party to demand the contemporaneous admission of any part of a recording or writing that ought to, in fairness, be considered, along with the portion offered by the proponent of the evidence.

12. **(D)** This is an example of another key Multistate testing area, namely, whether a prior inconsistent statement should be admissible as substantive evidence or for the limited purpose of impeaching the witness. Under the Multistate viewpoint, these prior statements will often be inadmissible as evidence of what they state because they constitute hearsay and are not within any exceptions to the hearsay rule. Even though inadmissible hearsay as evidence of the facts stated, they are nevertheless admissible for the limited purpose of impeaching the witness. See McCormick on Evidence, pp. 66–67, 601–602. Consequently, choice (D) is correct. Choice (A) is incorrect. The evidence can be considered for its impeaching value, but not substantively. Choice (B) is incorrect. If a witness denies making an inconsistent statement, the opposing party can offer extrinsic evidence of it under FRE 613. Since this witness admitted the inconsistency, there is no need for extrinsic evidence of it. Choice (C) is wrong because it is inconsistent with the purposes of impeachment by prior inconsistent statements. Impeaching statements are not admitted to prove their truth, but rather to demonstrate that the witness is inconsistent.

13. **(C)** Choice (C) is correct since, under FRE 801, hearsay is any extra-judicial statement offered in evidence to prove the truth of the matter stated. Choice (A) is incorrect because the fact pattern tells us that the statement is being offered to prove that the victim killed five men. It is not being offered to prove its effect on the defendant. Choice (B) is wrong because the statement does not satisfy the foundational elements of FRE 803(3): it is not a statement of the declarant's then-existing physical or mental condition. Finally, choice (D) is incorrect. "Self-serving" is not a valid evidentiary objection.

14. **(A)** Choice (A) is correct, since the witness's statement that the visiting fan had put two men in the hospital at a hockey game the week before is being offered to show its effect on the defendant's state of mind and not offered to prove the truth of the assertion. Thus, the witness's statement bears upon the reasonableness of the home fan's fear to justify his self-defense plea. Choice (B) is wrong. The statement does not satisfy the foundational elements of FRE 803(3): it is not a statement of the declarant's then-existing physical or mental condition. Choice (C) is incorrect because the statement is not being offered as hearsay. Finally, choice (D) is incorrect. "Self-serving" is not a valid evidentiary objection.

15. **(C)** This is a classic Multistate example where the ***"best evidence" rule*** is the correct answer. The best evidence (or, commonly, the original document) rule provides that ***in proving the terms of a writing, where the terms are material, the original writing must be produced*** unless it is shown to be unavailable for some reason other than the serious fault of the proponent. Here, since the customer is attempting to testify as to ***the assurances (or representations) made in the salesman's letter to support her breach of warranty action,*** the writing itself would be the "best evidence" for proving the terms contained therein. Choice (A) is incorrect because there is no admission involved in the contents of the letter. Choice (B) is also wrong. Even if the salesman is unavailable to testify, this is not a statement against interest, but rather a thank-you letter and, possibly, a warranty declaration. Choice (D) is also incorrect. The answer to the question would not be offered for the truth of the matter asserted, but rather to establish what was said.

16. **(B)** One of the most commonly tested areas in Evidence comes under relevancy, where evidence is offered to prove the existence of a particular physical condition, situation, or defect. In a suit alleging fraud or breach of warranty, for example, the plaintiff must prove that the defendant knew of the defective product, or ought, in the exercise of reasonable care, to have learned of it. Here, the plaintiff will want to prove directly that the ***defendant had knowledge of other accidents, injuries, or complaints*** as circumstantial evidence that the defendant was aware of the defect. Choice (A) is incorrect because the evidence cannot prove negligence by itself. Choice (C) is incorrect; as explained above, the evidence is probative. Choice (D) is an incorrect statement of the law of evidence.

17. **(B)** Certainly, the law recognizes the slanting effect upon human testimony of the emotions or feelings of the witness toward the parties or the self-interest of the witness in the outcome of the case. Partiality, or any acts, relationships, or motives reasonably likely to produce it, may be proved to impeach credibility. In most states the impeacher may

inquire as to the facts of ***bias*** on cross-examination as the first step in impeachment. By the same token, ***the reply to bias (or any new matter) drawn out on cross-examination is the normal function of the re-direct,*** and examination for this purpose is a matter of right, though its extent is subject to the control of the judge's discretion. Choice (A) is incorrect. The purpose of the re-direct is to attack the charge that the ex-wife's testimony is biased, not to establish the fact of her former marriage. Choice (C) is wrong because witness motive and bias are never a collateral matter at trial. For similar reasons, choice (D) is also incorrect; bias and motive are always relevant.

18. **(B)** According to FRE 406, "Evidence of the ***habit of a person or of the routine practice of an organization,*** whether corroborated or not and regardless of the presence of eyewitnesses, is relevant to prove that the conduct of the person or organization on a particular occasion was in conformity with the habit or routine practice." Words such as "always" or "invariably" are necessary to prove habit. Choice (A) is true, but it is a weaker answer than choice (B) because habit under FRE 406 is more specific to the fact pattern. Choice (C) is wrong because the neighbor is not testifying about the accident itself, but rather to the plaintiff's habits. Choice (D) is incorrect. Although one can argue that habit evidence is a form of character evidence, its use is permissible under FRE 406 if the foundational elements are met.

19. **(C)** At common law, under the ***marital privilege,*** a husband or wife shall not be required or, without consent of the other, if living, allowed to disclose a confidential communication made by one to the other during marriage. A majority of courts have construed "communications" to extend to facts, conditions, and transactions, as well. McCormick even points out that the marital privilege has been said to apply to "any information secured by the wife (or husband) as a result of the marital relation and which would not have been known in the absence of such relation." Accordingly, ***"information secured by one spouse through observation during the marriage as to the health, or intoxication, habitual or at a particular time, or the mental condition of the other spouse would be protected by the privilege."*** Evidence, pp. 163–164. **Note:** at the time of trial, even though they are separated, the husband and wife are still married, so the privilege still applies. Choice (A) is wrong. Although the wife's observation about the husband's intoxication is likely lay opinion testimony, the marital privilege will prohibit her from sharing her observation and opinion at trial. Choice (B) is incorrect. There is no indication that the information the wife wants to share occurred during an attorney-client consultation. Finally, choice (D) is incorrect. Biased witnesses frequently testify at trial, and it is the job of the advocate in the adversarial system to bring the bias to the attention of the fact-finder.

20. **(C)** It is the essence of the ***attorney-client privilege*** that it is limited to those communications that the client either expressly made confidential or which she could reasonably assume, under the circumstances, would be understood by the attorney as so intended. In cases where the client has one of his agents attend the conference, or the lawyer calls in his clerk or confidential secretary, the presence of these intermediaries will be assumed not to militate against the confidential nature of the consultation. McCormick, pg. 189. Thus, choices (A) and (B) are incorrect answers. Choice (D) is a wrong answer because the fact pattern tells us nothing about the nature of the statements made during the consultation.

21. **(B)** When two or more persons, each having an interest in some problem or situation, jointly consult an attorney, their confidential communications with the attorney will be privileged in a controversy of either or both of the clients with the outside world. But McCormick notes that it will often happen that the two original clients will fall out between themselves and become engaged in a controversy in which the communications at their joint consultation with the attorney may be vitally material. In such a situation, it is clear "that the privilege is inapplicable." Evidence, pg. 189. Furthermore, the marital privilege does not apply to either, (1) prosecutions for crimes committed by one spouse against the other, or (2) actions by one spouse against the other. Consequently, choice (B) is correct, and choice (D) is incorrect. Choice (A) is wrong because the spousal privilege applies, regardless of the current marital status of the parties (and separation is not divorce). Choice (C) is incorrect. Either party can claim the marital privilege.

22. **(B)** Due to the fact that the statement ***was not made immediately following the occurrence,*** choice (A) is incorrect. Choice (C) is incorrect because, although hearsay, it falls within a recognized exception. Choice (D) is not accurate, since the plaintiff did not state a legal conclusion (e.g., the ailment was caused by the accident). But rather, he stated that "he felt" pain in his back following the accident. Choice (B) is correct, and the evidence would be admissible as a declaration of present bodily condition, a recognized exception to the hearsay rule.

23. **(C)** Choice (A) is incorrect because there is no showing that the declarant is unavailable. Choice (B) is incorrect because the employee is not a party opponent and there is no showing of agency. Choice (D) is an incorrect statement of law. Choice (C) is the correct answer, since unavailability would be a requirement to bring the statement in as a declaration against interest.

24. **(A)** ***A party's pleading in one case,*** whether a final one or one later withdrawn, amended, or superseded, ***is freely usable against him as an evidentiary admission in any other litigation.*** Choice (B) is incorrect because ***there is no showing of unavailability. Choice (C) is incorrect because a pleading is not "former testimony."*** Choice (D) is an incorrect statement of the law.

25. **(B)** Although the FRE make former (reported) testimony admissible when proffered against a party, such testimony is also admissible against a predecessor in interest to the former proceeding. Choice (A) is too limited an answer, while choices (C) and (D) are simply incorrect. Thus, choice (B) is the best answer.

26. **(C)** Absence from the courtroom is not enough; thus, choice (A) is not the best answer. Choice (B) is incorrect, since death is not the only circumstance for unavailability. Choice (D) is incorrect, as insanity is only one of the conditions that make a person unavailable. Therefore, the best alternative is choice (C).

27. **(D)** A favorite Multistate testing area deals with ***distinguishing between the hearsay rule and the rule requiring firsthand knowledge.*** The distinction is whether the witness purports to give the facts directly upon his own credit or whether he purports to give an account of what another has told him and this is offered to evidence the truth of the other's report. Here, you must read the question carefully. You're being asked to determine the admissibility of ***the police officer's testimony regarding the driver's statement.*** Although the police officer can properly testify to his own observations, he cannot testify to what the driver told him because it is being offered to prove the truth of the driver's statement and, thus, inadmissible hearsay. Choices (A) and (B) are, therefore, incorrect because both of them discuss hearsay exceptions. Choice (C) is also incorrect. It suggests that the hearsay would be admissible if only one could establish the unavailability of the driver. The driver's statement, however, doesn't fit into any hearsay exceptions under FRE 803, 804, or 807.

28. **(D)** Partiality, or any acts, relationships, or motives reasonably likely to produce it, may be proved to impeach credibility. McCormick notes that ***self-interest*** may be shown in a criminal case when the witness testifies for the state and it is shown that an indictment is pending against him. By analogy, in this case, the defense attorney may show the informer's self-interest, or bias, because he filed an application to become a police officer and had two misdemeanor convictions on his record. Choice (A) is incorrect because the issue here is bias and not necessarily truthfulness. Choice (B) is a wrong answer, and somewhat deceptive. The rule it states is true if one is trying to accomplish an impeachment by proof of prior conviction under FRE 609. That is not the purpose of the impeachment by evidence of bias in this case. Choice (C) is incorrect. Evidence of motive or bias does not necessarily prove character for untruthfulness; it merely provides a vehicle for suggesting that the witness's testimony on this occasion is less worthy of belief.

29. **(A)** Under FRE 602, a witness must have personal knowledge of the matter he is to testify about. The requirement of ***"personal knowledge" means that the witness must have observed the matter*** and must have a present recollection of his observation. Choice (B) is incorrect, since the neighbor's availability is irrelevant with respect to the wife's competency to testify. Choice (C) is incorrect, since one having a personal interest is competent to testify. Choice (D) is wrong because, under the circumstances, the Dead Man's Statute is inapplicable.

30. **(C)** In accordance with FRE 901 (a)(2), a lay person with sufficient familiarity with the handwriting of another person may be called upon to prove or disprove the genuineness of such handwriting. Here, one may properly infer that a former girlfriend would have sufficient familiarity with the handwriting of her boyfriend. Thus, the former girlfriend would be afforded a basis for identifying the defendant's handwriting specimen. Given the authentication rules of FRE 901, choices (A) and (B) are both incorrect. Choice (D) is incorrect because none of the foundational elements for past recollection recorded apply to this fact pattern.

31. **(B)** In accordance with FRE 804(b)(3), the car dealer's statement, "...I sold a salvaged vehicle to the customer," may properly be admissible as a declaration against interest. Whenever you are dealing with a declaration against interest, there are two things to remember. First, it must be a declaration against one's (i.e., the declarant's) (1) penal, (2) pecuniary, or (3) proprietary interest(s). Second, the declarant must be unavailable to testify at trial. In the present case, the car dealer's out-of-court statement subjected him to pecuniary liability. As a result, it would qualify as a declaration against interest. According to FRE 804, a person can be considered unavailable if he "is absent from the hearing and the proponent of a statement has been unable to procure [his] [attendance or testimony]." Choice (A) is wrong because the car dealer's statement does not relate to his mental or emotional condition. Choice (C) is incorrect because the statement describes a past act and not a current impression. And finally, choice (D) is wrong because, even though the statement is hearsay, it fits within a recognized exception.

32. **(B)** In accordance with FRE 404(b), evidence of other crimes, wrongs, or acts is not admissible to prove the character of a person in order to show that he acted in conformity therewith. It may, however, be admissible for other purposes, such as proof of motive, opportunity, intent, preparation, plan, knowledge, identity, or absence of mistake or accident. It may be helpful to remember this exception by the acronym ***MIMIC: M-motive, I-intent, M-mistake (absence of which), I-identity, and C-common scheme or plan.*** Choice (A) is wrong because the evidence is being offered for intent and not to show character. Choice (C) is a true statement, but the wrong answer here because the evidence is being offered for a non-character purpose. Choice (D) is incorrect. The evidence is relevant to show intent.

33. **(C)** Choice (C) is correct since, in plaintiff's action for loss of society and companionship, the existence of her husband's infidelity and plaintiff's knowledge of it would be probative of the value to be placed upon husband's loss. Moreover, the question would be directly related to, and in impeachment of, her testimony on direct examination. Choice (A) is wrong; the statement is squarely within the scope of direct. Choice (B) is incorrect. Some of the most effective evidence at trial is highly prejudicial. FRE 403 only excludes prejudicial evidence if its prejudicial impact substantially outweighs its probative value. Choice (D) is wrong. The evidence is relevant for loss, but has nothing to do with negligence.

34. **(B)** In accordance with FRE 804 (b), in a prosecution for homicide or in a civil action or proceeding, a statement made by a declarant, while believing that his death was imminent, concerning the cause or circumstances of what he believed to be his impending death is not excluded by the hearsay rule. While the common law required that the "dying declaration" be that of the homicide victim, ***the Federal Rules of Evidence have expanded the theory of admissibility to apply equally in civil cases.*** Thus, choice (B) is correct, and choice (D) is incorrect. Choice (A) is incorrect because there is nothing to indicate that the statement was against a penal, pecuniary, or proprietary interest. Choice (C) is wrong because the statement does satisfy a recognized hearsay exception.

35. **(A)** Grand jury proceedings have traditionally been shrouded in secrecy. Substantial controversy has surrounded the issue of disclosure of testimony given by grand jury witnesses. Clearly, the defense has a right of access to such testimony under Fed. Rule Crim. Pro. Section 26.2(a) once a government witness has testified on direct. Here, the question presented is whether a defendant is required to make objections at the grand jury proceeding in order to preserve the issue at trial. As a general rule, ***objections that are "substantive" in nature (e.g., relevancy and hearsay) may be raised for the first time when the deposition is offered in evidence at trial.*** McCormick, pg. 127. Therefore, choice (A) is correct and, for the same reasons, choice (C) is incorrect. However, ***objections that go to the "manner and form" of questions/answers (e.g., nonresponsive or leading) must be made at the time the deposition is taken.*** Choice (B) is, therefore, incorrect because no objection was lodged at the proceeding to the form of the question. Although it is a true statement, choice (D) is not the best answer here. Choice (A) is a stronger answer because it provides a contingency (if the defendant's attorney objects on hearsay grounds) that, if true, would ensure the objection was sustained.

36. **(C)** The ***best evidence rule applies only when the proponent is attempting to prove the contents or terms of a writing.*** Sometimes, a writing recites or records a perceivable event or condition, such as a marriage (marriage certificate), payment of money (receipt), or the utterance of certain words (transcript). Here, the proponent wishing to prove the underlying event may offer testimony as an observer. This does not involve the best evidence rule because ***the proponent is not attempting to prove the terms of a writing, but merely is presenting evidence of an event perceived by a witness with firsthand knowledge.*** Therefore, choice (A) is a wrong answer. In this question, the police officer's testimony is not reliant on the writing or the videotape. He had firsthand knowledge of the man's confession because he was present and overheard it. Choice (B) is wrong because the police officer is testifying based on personal knowledge and not introducing a hearsay statement. Choice (D) is incorrect because the issue of proper Miranda warnings is not relevant to admissibility under these facts.

Exam Tip: This distinction between the best evidence rule and firsthand knowledge is frequently tested on the MBE. Remember, the best evidence rule applies only ***when the proponent is attempting to prove the contents or terms of a writing.***

37. **(A)** FRE 801(d)(1)(C) defines as non-hearsay a prior statement by a witness of identification of a person made after perceiving him, if the person making the identification is ***available*** to testify at the trial or hearing and ***subject to cross-examination*** concerning the statement. There is no requirement that the witness first be impeached. Nor does a prior identification require that the identifying witness make a positive in-court identification. Choice (A) is correct, since the owner had previously identified the man in picture #4. Choice (C) is incorrect, since prior identifications are defined as non-hearsay. Choice (D) is incorrect because the man's right to confrontation is not violated, since the owner is available in court and subject to cross-examination. Choice (B) is incorrect because the past recollection recorded hearsay exception involves first, an attempted refreshing of the witness's recollection that fails, followed by the witness ***reading the words*** of a memorandum or record into evidence. In this case, the only writing is a photograph.

38. **(A)** Choice (B) is wrong because the customer's answer was not based upon firsthand knowledge. In order to have firsthand knowledge, a witness ***must have actually observed the fact*** (to which he is testifying). The facts clearly indicate that the customer did not see the woman fall. Choice (C) is incorrect because the customer did not perceive the woman falling. Choice (D) is wrong because declarations concerning a present sense impression require that the declarant observe the event at the time the statement is made. In other words, the ***declaration must be made contemporaneously with the observation.*** By process of elimination, choice (A) is the best answer.

39. **(D)** If the enforcer's statement was made during the course of and in furtherance of the conspiracy, the statement would be admissible as an admission. Under FRE 801(d)(2), "A statement is not hearsay if the statement is offered against a party and is (subsection E) ***a statement by a co-conspirator of a party during the course and in furtherance of the conspiracy."*** The enforcer's statement concerning the fact that the money man would be paying the rent for the premises where the methamphetamine was being manufactured would certainly fall within the "course of and furtherance of" the conspiracy to manufacture and distribute methamphetamine. All other statements would be incorrect as to prove the admissibility of the enforcer's statement against co-conspirator, the money man.

40. **(B)** The transcript would be admitted under FRE 807, which is the residual "catch-all" exception since, under the circumstances, the circumstantial guarantees of trustworthiness would be met. The court here took (1) judicial notice of the existence of the college and of the fact that colleges normally compile such records, (2) found that the copy of the transcript was an authentic copy because of the registrar's seal, and (3) received corroborating testimony concerning the contents of the transcript. Therefore, the transcript was properly authenticated and reliable under the circumstances. Choice (A) is incorrect, since the custodian of the record was not available to testify as required by FRE 806 (6). Choice (C) is wrong, since an expert witness is not required under the FRE for authenticating a document. Choice (D) is incorrect, since it implies that the transcript is not admissible. Refer to *United States v. Hitsman et al.*, 604 F.2d 443 (5th Cir. 1979), concerning one of the first instances wherein a federal court has invoked the residual "catch-all" hearsay exception.

41. **(C)** Without question, Evidence is one of the toughest areas on the Multistate exam. Although the Evidence fact patterns are rather short and simple, the questions themselves are very tricky. Here, for example, is an extremely difficult question dealing with impeachment. Most students will be tempted to choose choice (B). With regard to impeachment, FRE 609 provides, "For the purpose of attacking the credibility of a witness, evidence that he has been convicted of a crime shall be admitted but only if the crime (1) was punishable by death or imprisonment in excess of one year, or (2) involved dishonesty or false statement." Choice (B) is wrong, then, because the neighbor testified that the witness "embezzled money," not that he was ***convicted*** of embezzlement; FRE 609 does not apply. Choice (C) is the best answer because FRE 608 states, "The credibility of a witness may be attacked or supported by evidence in the form of opinion or reputation, but subject to these limitations: (1) the evidence may refer only to character for truthfulness or untruthfulness." You are being tested here on the distinction between impeachment by opinion and by conviction of a crime.

42. **(C)** This is an extremely tricky question because, in light of the holding in *Trammel v. California*, 445 U.S. 40 (1980), you might be tempted into choosing choice (A). This is incorrect, however, because although in federal courts one spouse ***may*** testify against the other in criminal cases, with or without the consent of the party spouse, there is one very important limitation. According to footnote 42 in *Trammel*, ***confidential communications*** between the spouses are nevertheless privileged. Since the facts indicated that ***"the man confided" to his wife, his communication is deemed to be confidential and, therefore, remains privileged.*** The statement is not hearsay because it is an admission under FRE 801(d). Choice (A) is wrong because the statement is privileged. Choice (B) is wrong because the statement is not hearsay within the meaning of FRE 801(d), but it is privileged. Choice (D) is incorrect because the statement is privileged, but is not hearsay.

43. **(C)** This question deals with the highly tested area of ***"bad act"*** impeachment. FRE 608(b) states that "Specific instances of the conduct of a witness, for the purpose of attacking or supporting his credibility, other than conviction of crime as provided in Rule 609, may not be proved by extrinsic evidence. They may, however, in the discretion of the court, if probative of truthfulness or untruthfulness, be inquired into on cross-examination of the witness (1) concerning his character for truthfulness or untruthfulness, or (2) concerning the character for truthfulness or untruthfulness of another witness as to which character the witness being cross-examined has testified." The prosecuting attorney's impeachment of the witness, the defense witness, is proper in this case, since the questioning inquires into ***unconvicted acts bearing on untruthfulness*** — i.e., failure to report income interest on

the witness's tax return. Since admissions of such specific instances of conduct are ***discretionary,*** choice (C) is the correct answer. Choice (A) is incorrect because, as discussed above, the evidence could be admissible on the issue of credibility. Choice (B) is incorrect. For the proposed use of this evidence, a prior conviction is not necessary. Choice (D) is wrong. Allegations of serious offenses that have not yet resulted in a conviction cannot be used for impeachment unless they can be tied into an issue, such as truthfulness, as in this example.

44. **(D)** Choice (D) is the best choice. This has high probative value, and the prejudice that could result from a surprise witness can be overcome by the continuance. The easiest way to answer this question is by process of elimination. Choice (A) is wrong. Even though evidence of subsequent remedial measures is sometimes admissible to show ownership and control (though not for an inference of negligence), it is unnecessary here to prove that the defendant owned the truck, since that issue was stipulated. Choice (B) is incorrect. A court would most probably sustain an objection under FRE 403 on the grounds that the evidence is too inflammatory and would encourage the jury to decide the issue on an emotional basis. In other words, the pictures are unduly prejudicial, even though they may have some limited probative value as to the extent of injury. **Note:** The examiners often use gross, disgusting evidence to test you on FRE 403. Choice (C) is wrong. This evidence is cumulative, and a judge could exclude it under Rule 403 on the grounds that it is time-consuming and adds little to the case.

45. **(B)** The FRE do not contain a specific physician-patient (or any other) privilege. However, FRE 501, the only federal rule on privilege, is often tested on the MBE. It provides as follows: "Except as otherwise required by the Constitution of the United States or provided by Act of Congress or in rules prescribed by the Supreme Court pursuant to statutory authority, the privilege of a witness, person, government, State, or political subdivision thereof shall be governed by the principles of the common law as they may be interpreted by the courts of the United States in the light of reason and experience. However, in civil actions and proceedings with respect to an element of a claim or defense as to which State law supplies the rule of decision, the privilege of a witness, person, government, State, or political subdivision thereof shall be determined in accordance with State law." The defense attorney's objection to the testimony of the defendant's psychiatrist may not be sustained under choice (A) because the defendant's trial is a ***criminal case***, and in accordance with FRE 501, the principles of ***common law*** (not state law) will govern. Choice (B) is correct because, under FRE 501, common law "as interpreted . . . in the light of reason and experience," will determine the privileges applicable in federal question and criminal cases. See McCormick, Evidence, pg. 182. Choice (C) is wrong for the reasons discussed above. Choice (D) is also incorrect. Frequently, privilege law operates to exclude relevant and valuable evidence, thereby interfering with the full exploration of the facts in court. For sound policy reasons, however, we have decided, as a society, that this is an acceptable price to pay.

46. **(B)** FRE 404(a) states the general rule for character evidence in a civil case: "Evidence of a person's character or a trait of his character is not admissible for the purpose of proving that he acted in conformity therewith on a particular occasion." However, under FRE 405(b), "In cases in which the character or a trait of character of a person is an essential element of a charge, claim, or defense, proof may also be made of specific instances of his conduct." In the fan's suit against the defendant, he is alleging that the defendant was ***negligent in lending*** his bat to his roommate, knowing that he was irresponsible with bats. Since the cause of action here is ***negligent entrustment,*** character is in issue. Therefore, FRE 405(b) applies, allowing evidence of the roommate's ***specific acts*** to be admissible to show the character trait that is in issue, specifically, the roommate's irresponsible use of bats. Evidence of this trait will then be relevant to the defendant's negligent entrustment. Choice (B) is, thus, correct. Choice (A) is incorrect; the fan's testimony is not being used to show the roommate's negligence on this occasion, but rather to show the defendant's negligence in lending his roommate his bat. Choice (D) is incorrect, since character evidence need not be limited to reputation or opinion evidence when character is in issue.

47. **(D)** FRE 701 states that "if the witness is not testifying as an expert, his testimony in the form of opinion or inference is limited to those opinions or inferences which are (a) rationally based on the perception of the witness and (b) helpful to a clear understanding of his testimony or the determination of a fact in issue." Lay opinion under FRE 701 must be based on ***personal knowledge.*** Generally, a property owner is qualified to give an opinion as to the value of his property. However, the facts here state that the witness is a neighbor, not the property owner. Moreover, she has no personal knowledge of the fact on which the appraisal report based the market value. Therefore, the neighbor's testimony will be inadmissible. Choices (A) and (B) are incorrect, since FRE 602 requires evidence "sufficient to support a finding that the witness has personal knowledge of the matter." The neighbor's testimony as to real estate market value would require an expert opinion (since experts need not have personal knowledge of the subject matter of their testimony). Choice (D) thus provides the correct rationale.

48. **(C)** Under FRE 408, "Evidence of (1) furnishing, offering, or promising to furnish, or (2) accepting, offering, or promising to accept, a valuable consideration in compromising or attempting to compromise a claim which is disputed as to either validity or amount, is not admissible to prove liability . . ." Since the other driver's statement to the woman offering $2,000 to pay for the damage to her car was an attempt to settle, it would be inadmissible for public policy reasons. Therefore, choice (C) is correct. **Note:** Be aware that ***any statement made in connection with a settlement offer will be inadmissible to prove fault or value of the claim.*** For example, where the defendant says, "I know I drove through the red light. Anyway, I'm willing to settle and pay for the damage to your car," the ***entire statement*** is inadmissible to prove fault. Choice (A) is incorrect because the other driver's offer to settle is not an admission. Choice (B) is incorrect. First, FRE 408 would preclude the statement and, second, declarations against interest require a showing of unavailability of trial, which is not present in this fact pattern. Choice (D) contains a rule that is nowhere to be found in evidence law and is, therefore, incorrect as a distracter answer choice.

49. **(A)** A commonly tested area on both the MBE and state essays deals with ***absence of similar accidents.*** FRE 403 states that "although relevant, evidence may be excluded if its probative value is substantially outweighed by the danger of unfair prejudice, confusion of the issues, or misleading the jury, or by considerations of undue delay, waste of time, or needless presentation of cumulative evidence." Application of this rule poses considerable difficulty for a defendant wishing to establish the nonexistence of an unduly dangerous condition through the lack of previous accidents. The key determination required to establish ***relevancy*** in this case is a showing of ***substantial identity of material circumstances.*** By showing fixed or stable conditions, safe use, and an extensive number of experiences, the similarity requirement may be satisfied and, on balance with the probative value, will justify admission. Lilly, Introduction to the Law of Evidence, p. 149. In the classic case of *Erickson v. Walgreen Drug Co.*, 120 Utah 31 (1951), evidence that over 4,000 people a day, for 15 years, in all weather conditions, had used a terrazzo entranceway without anyone slipping, was held admissible negative evidence. Similarly, where a ***heavily traveled intersection has remained the same for 14 years without any accidents during that time,*** such evidence should be found relevant and admissible to show nonexistence of a dangerous condition. Choices (B) and (C) are, therefore, incorrect. Choice (A) is correct and a better answer than choice (B), since a jury instruction would not necessarily be required under these facts, but would be subject to the discretion of the court.

50. **(B)** FRE 803(1) provides that a ***present sense impression*** is admissible as a recognized hearsay exception. Thus, a statement describing or explaining an event or condition made while ***the declarant was perceiving the event or condition or immediately*** thereafter is not excluded by the hearsay rule. Hearsay exceptions under FRE 803 apply regardless of the declarant's availability at trial. Thus, choice (B) is correct, and choice (A) is incorrect. Choice (C) is incorrect because the statement of the son is, in fact, admissible as a present sense impression. Choice (D) misstates the excited utterance exception, which does not apply if the statement is the result of reflection and deliberation. Choice (D) is, therefore, incorrect.

51. **(A)** This is a Multistate example of non-hearsay because the predecessor's statement or utterance is being offered to show its effect on the commissioner, the listener. That is to say, the commissioner is attempting to prove that he acted honestly (without criminal intent) in increasing his expense allocation based upon the information provided him by the predecessor. Consequently, the commissioner's testimony is ***not*** hearsay because its value does not rest upon the truth of the predecessor's statement. Therefore, choice (C) is incorrect. On the contrary, the predecessor's utterance is being offered only to show the effect it had on the commissioner's subsequent conduct (i.e., he reasonably believed that he had the power as commissioner to raise his expense allocation). Choice (B) is incorrect because the foundational elements of FRE 406 on habit and routine practice are not met here: there is no evidence of what the organization "always" or "invariably" did. Choice (D) is wrong because the contents of a writing are not at issue here.

52. **(C)** Choices (A) and (D) are wrong because the ***privilege against self-incrimination applies only to evidence that is testimonial in nature.*** Choice (C) is correct because the prosecuting attorney is attempting to attack the defendant's credibility. According to FRE 806, "When a hearsay statement, or a statement defined in Rule 801(d)(2) has been admitted in evidence, the credibility of the declarant may be attacked, and if attacked may be supported, by any evidence which would be admissible for those purposes if declarant had testified as a witness." In our case, the defendant testified that he "had not used any heroin for the past three years." Consequently, it is proper for the prosecution to attack his credibility by seeing if there are any needle marks on his arms. Choice (B) is wrong. For most criminal defendants, the unfortunate reality of trial includes the introduction in evidence against them of highly prejudicial evidence. This fact pattern contains insufficient information to balance probative value and prejudicial impact.

53. **(C)** In accordance with FRE 407, "When, after an event, measures are taken which, if taken previously, would have made the event less likely to occur, evidence of the subsequent measures is not admissible to prove negligence or culpable conduct in connection with the event." Choice (B) is wrong because, although some courts permit evidence of subsequent repairs in strict liability cases, this is not the majority rule. Furthermore, you should not assume that this is a strict liability action, since the facts simply state that the player is asserting a claim against the manufacturer. Quite conceivably, the player may be bringing suit for negligent manufacture or breach of warranty, in which case evidence of subsequent repairs is clearly inadmissible. Choice (A) is wrong because the former employee is no longer an employee of the company and cannot make vicarious admissions on its behalf under FRE 801(d)(2)(D). Choice (D) is incorrect because the former employee is testifying as a fact witness and is not speaking on behalf of the manufacturer.

54. **(B)** Choice (B) is a better answer than choice (A) because the corrections officer's testimony does not qualify as a prior identification. ***A prior identification requires that on a prior occasion, a statement of identification be made.*** For example, if A testifies that on a prior occasion B pointed to the accused and said, "That's the man who robbed me," the testimony, even though it is hearsay, would be admissible as a prior identification if B is present in court and available for cross- examination. Similarly, if B has himself testified to the prior identification. In either case, a prior statement of identification was made before trial. Here, on the other hand, no prior statement was made. Rather, the corrections officer is being called to testify at trial (for the first time) regarding the defendant's appearance when he was arrested. Choice (C) is incorrect because no out-of-court statements are involved in the corrections officer's testimony. Choice (D) is wrong. The corrections officer is testifying about a factual observation and not an opinion.

55. **(B)** In accordance with FRE 607, the credibility of a witness may be attacked by any party calling him (to testify). According to McCormick, there are five main lines of attacking the credibility of a witness. The first, and probably the most effective and most frequently employed, is an attack by proof that the witness, on a previous occasion, has made statements inconsistent with his present testimony. Therefore, choice (B) is the best answer. The second is an attack by a showing that the witness is ***biased.*** The third is an attack upon the character of the witness. The fourth is an attack by showing a defect of capacity in the witness to observe, remember, or recount the matters testified about.

The fifth is proof by other witnesses that material facts are otherwise than as testified to by the witness. Choices (A) and (D) are wrong because, under the traditional view of hearsay, previous statements are inadmissible as substantive evidence (i.e., as evidence of what they state) because they constitute hearsay and are not within any exceptions to the hearsay rule. Choice (C) is incorrect because, under these facts, the witness has not been excused. Therefore, the witness can be afforded an opportunity to explain or deny the inconsistence under FRE 613.

56. **(D)** Under the FRE, there are no specific privilege provisions. FRE 501 provides that the privilege of a witness shall be governed by the principles of common law as they may be interpreted by the courts of the United States in light of reason and experience. However, in civil actions and proceedings, with respect to an element of a claim or defense as to which state law applies the rule of decision, the privilege of a witness shall be determined in accordance with state law. Thus, the common law attorney-client privilege is applicable in our factual situations. The client has a privilege to refuse to disclose and to prevent other persons from disclosing any confidential communications between himself and his attorney. Choice (D) is the best answer, since the woman intended that her disclosures to the attorney about the corporation were confidential and in furtherance of the rendition of legal services that she sought from the attorney. McCormick, in The Handbook on Evidence, p. 179, states that "Communications in the course of preliminary discussion with a view to employing the lawyer are privileged though the employment is in the 'upshot' not accepted by the attorney.... Payment, or agreement to pay a fee, however, is not essential." In choices (A), (B), and (C), the communications between the attorney and his client are not confidential and, therefore, not protected by the attorney-client privilege. In choice (A), the communication is made publicly and, therefore, there is no expectation of confidentiality. In choice (B), the communication was made in connection with the woman's attempt to get the attorney to assist her in a fraud. Such statements are not confidential. In choice (C), the statements are not confidential because they were integrated into the pleadings of the case.

57. **(C)** The privilege for communications of a client with his attorney hinges upon the client's belief that he is consulting a lawyer in that capacity and has manifested intention to seek professional legal advice. According to the holding in the case of *In re Dupont's Estate*, 140 P.2d 866 (1943), ***communications in the course of preliminary discussion with a view of employing the attorney are privileged*** even though the attorney is never hired. Choice (A) is wrong; the privilege cannot be defeated by the filing of a lawsuit. Choice (B) is incorrect. The father's position as father and guardian *ad litem* of his minor child puts him on the same footing as the child for purposes of determining the existence of the privilege. Choice (D) is incorrect. Choice (D) misstates the medical hearsay exception, which permits the admissibility of information provided for the purpose of obtaining medical treatment.

58. **(D)** In *Fisher v. United States*, 425 U.S. 391(1976), the court held that compliance with a subpoena for an accountant's records (that defendant had given his attorney in preparation for trial) did not violate the defendant's 5th Amendment privilege against self-incrimination. For this same reason, choice (B) is incorrect. Choices (A) and (C) are incorrect because the accountant was *not* a representative of the attorney. The facts do not state that the attorney hired the accountant. Rather, the accountant was employed by the taxpayer. A "representative of the lawyer" is one employed by the attorney to assist the attorney in the rendition of professional legal services.

59. **(A)** Under the attorney-client privilege, a client has a privilege to refuse to disclose and to prevent any other person from disclosing confidential communications made for the purpose of facilitating the rendition of professional legal services to the client between himself (or his representative) and his attorney (or his attorney's representative). However, there are exceptions when there is not privilege. For example, the ***privilege is lost if the services of the attorney were sought or obtained to enable or aid anyone to commit or plan to commit what the client knew or reasonably should have known to be a crime or fraud.*** Thus, choice (A) is correct, and choice (D) is incorrect because the woman sought the attorney's advice about committing perjury or falsely testifying about the incident. Choice (B) is incorrect

because there has been no showing of unavailability in this case. Choice (C) is incorrect. Voluntary statements made to others outside the courtroom are not covered by the privilege against self-incrimination.

60. **(D)** A popular Multistate testing area deals with whether the ***failure of a party to call a particular witness*** (or the failure to take the stand himself as a witness) allows his adversary to use this failure as a basis for invoking an adverse inference. Although there are a large number of cases supporting the inference, under the prevailing view, if the witness is "equally available" to both parties, no inference springs from the failure of either to call him. McCormick, Law of Evidence, pg. 657. McCormick points out that "the possibility that the inference may be drawn invites waste of time in calling unnecessary witnesses or in presenting evidence to explain why they were not called." Most important, McCormick notes that "the availability of modern discovery procedures serves to diminish both the justification and the need for the inference." Law of Evidence, pg. 657. For this reason, answers (A), (B), and (C) are all incorrect.

61. **(D)** In *Griffin v. California*, 380 U.S. 609 (1965), the U.S. Supreme Court held that the self-incrimination guarantee of the 5th Amendment, as applicable to the states under the 14th Amendment, forbids either comment by the prosecution of an accused's silence or instructions by the court that such silence is evidence of guilt. The comments by the prosecutor during his closing argument that the defendant failed to take the stand would be violative of the defendant's right against self-incrimination. Choices (B) and (C) are also correct, but choice (D) is a better answer because it is more specific and on point to the facts of the question. Choice (A) is incorrect. The motives and bias of a party's witnesses are fair game in closing argument.

62. **(B)** If the eyewitness's testimony is admitted, it will most likely qualify as an admission. According to FRE 409, "Evidence of furnishing or offering or promising to pay medical, hospital, or similar expenses occasioned by an injury is not admissible to prove liability for the injury." As is so often the case on the MBE, an admission may be made in connection with an offer or promise to pay medical or hospital expenses. In this instance, the admission of liability is admissible, but evidence of offering or promising to pay medical (or similar) expenses is inadmissible, in accordance with public policy considerations. Choice (A) is incorrect. The statement, even if it is in the form of an opinion, is an admission by a party opponent. Choice (C) is wrong because the statement does not "describe or explain an event or condition made while the declarant was perceiving the event or condition, or immediately thereafter." Choice (D) is wrong because there is no indication of the man's unavailability at trial.

63. **(B)** As noted previously, evidence of payment (or offering or promising to pay) of medical, hospital, or similar expenses of an injured party by the opposing party, is *not* admissible. The reason often given is that such payment or offer is usually made from human impulses and not from an admission of liability, and that to hold otherwise would tend to discourage assistance to the injured person. Choice (B) is correct because the aforesaid rule is often phrased in terms of "humanitarian motives." See FRE 409 Advisory Committee's Note. For the same reasons, choice (D) is incorrect. Choice (A) is wrong because it incorrectly states the best evidence rule. Choice (C) is incorrect. The doctor's offer to pay medical bills might be relevant to the issue of negligent hiring, but this tenuous connection will be trumped by the policy considerations of FRE 409.

64. **(B)** The nurse's testimony as to seeing the doctor destroy the postoperative x-rays of the patient's abdomen should be admissible. Since the patient's suit for malpractice is based on the faulty bandaging ***following*** the operation, the ***postoperative*** x-rays would be relevant, not collateral, to show the effects of the constricted blood vessels on the patient's retarded recovery. Under FRE 401, relevant evidence is that which tends to make the existence of a fact of consequence more (or less) probable than it would otherwise be. ***Relevant evidence is generally admissible under*** FRE 402. Once admitted, the jury then determines the weight of the evidence. Choice (B) is the correct

answer, since the relevance of the postoperative x-rays goes to the malpractice issue being litigated, namely the patient's postoperative pain and slow recovery. Proof of a cover-up is not a foundational prerequisite to admissibility. Choice (C) is incorrect, since the probative value of the nurse's testimony far outweighs the danger of unfair prejudice; testimony regarding destruction of the x-rays will not confuse the issues, mislead the jury, or cause undue delay. FRE 403. Choice (D) is incorrect because the destruction of the x-rays is not a collateral matter.

65. **(B)** This is an extremely tricky Evidence example. Many students will recognize that unavailability (as a witness) is a requirement for the former testimony exception to the hearsay rule. Although this is true, former testimony may often be given in evidence without meeting the requirements of unavailability and confrontation. McCormick states that these requirements are applicable only when admission of the evidence is sought under the hearsay exception. However, when the former testimony is offered for some non-hearsay purpose, as to show the commission of the act of perjury, to refresh recollection, or impeach a witness at the present trial by proving that he testified differently on a former occasion, the restrictions of the hearsay exception do not apply. See McCormick, pg. 615. Since all other choices are clearly inapplicable, choice (B) is the only conceivably correct answer.

66. **(C)** According to FRE 701, "If the witness is not testifying as an expert, his testimony in the form of opinions or inferences is limited to those opinions or inferences which are (a) rationally based on the perception of the witness and (b) helpful to a clear understanding of his testimony or the determination of a fact in issue." Choice (C) is correct because the federal rules have adopted the so-called shorthand rendition rule, which incorporates the more liberal notion of sanctioning the admission of opinions on grounds of "expediency" and "convenience," rather than "necessity." Choice (A) is incorrect because an opinion witness can testify to the ultimate issue in a case under FRE 704. Choice (B) is incorrect. The nurse is not offering an expert opinion but, rather, an opinion within the province of lay witnesses. Choice (D) is incorrect. The nurse is not testifying to an out-of-court statement by a hearsay declarant, but rather to her own observations and conclusions.

67. **(B)** FRE 703 provides that the ***"facts or data in the particular case upon which an expert bases an opinion or inference may be those perceived by or made known to him at or before the hearing."*** Since an expert may base his opinion on facts made known to him at the trial, choice (B) is correct. Choice (A) is incorrect because FRE 705 states that an expert can testify to her opinion or inferences without having to first testify to the underlying facts or data. Choice (C) is incorrect. Under FRE 703, an expert is not required to have firsthand knowledge of the case. Finally, FRE 704 permits expert opinion on the ultimate issue in a case. Therefore, choice (D) is an incorrect answer.

68. **(D)** Choices (A) and (C) are both incorrect, as the physician is an attorney representative and not the shopper's physician. Choice (D) is the best answer because the physician is a "representative" of the shopper's attorney and, therefore, the communications between the shopper and the physician will be privileged under the attorney-client privilege. Choice (B) is wrong because the shopper's statements describe her injuries and are not admissions.

69. **(B)** When the accused has produced evidence that the deceased attacked him, thus grounding a claim of self-defense, this, when met by counter-evidence, raises an issue of conduct: Was the deceased or the accused the first aggressor? It is universally held that when such evidence has been produced, the accused may introduce testimony of the reputation of the deceased for turbulence and violence. Moreover, McCormick points out that "it is equally well settled of course that the prosecution may meet this by rebutting testimony of his (the victim's) good reputation for peacefulness." Evidence, pp. 460–461. Thus, choice (B) is correct. Choice (A) is incorrect because evidence of the victim's peaceful character does not rebut the testimony that the defendant is a peaceful person. Choice (C) is incorrect. According to FRE 405, relevant character evidence can be established by reputation or opinion testimony,

as was done in this case. Choice (D) is incorrect. In order for the prosecution to introduce evidence of the victim's peaceful character in a homicide case, there is no requirement that the defense directly attack the victim's character. Instead, it is enough for the defense to introduce evidence that the victim was the first aggressor.

70. **(B)** McCormick instructs that the principle upon which photographs are most commonly admitted into evidence is the same as that underlying the admission of illustrative drawings, maps, and diagrams. Under this theory, a photograph is viewed merely as a graphic portrayal of oral testimony, ***and becomes admissible only when a witness has testified that it is a correct and accurate representation of relevant facts personally observed by the witness.*** Under this theory, the witness need not be the photographer; therefore, choice (A) is incorrect. Choice (C) is an incorrect statement of law and is, therefore, a wrong answer. Choice (D) is the wrong answer because the photograph itself is being introduced into evidence. Therefore, the best evidence rule is not implicated.

71. **(A)** Under the prevailing view, ***the failure of a defendant to take the stand himself as a witness does not allow his adversary to use this failure as a basis for invoking an adverse inference.*** See McCormick, Law of Evidence, pg. 656. Choice (B) is the wrong answer because the issue here concerns improper comment on the defendant's failure to testify and not the proper scope of rebuttal evidence. Choice (C) is incorrect as a matter of law. Choice (D) is incorrect. Prosecutors may strike hard blows, but they must be fair ones.

72. **(A)** FRE 501 states that "except as otherwise required by the Constitution of the United States or provided by Act of Congress or in rules prescribed by the Supreme Court pursuant to statutory authority, the privilege of a witness, person, government, State or political subdivision thereof shall be governed by the ***principles of the common law*** as interpreted by the courts of the United States in the light of reason and experience." In other words, on matters governed by federal substantive law—and this will generally be true in criminal cases, civil actions brought by the United States, and private federal question cases—federal courts are to apply and develop a ***federal common law of privilege.*** Since this question deals with a federal question, the issues should be resolved under federal privilege law. Choice (A) is, therefore, correct. Choices (B) and (C) are wrong because they state the wrong rule about the choice of privilege law. Choice (D) is incorrect in its suggestion that a court should select evidentiary law based on its greater likelihood to ensure the admission of evidence at trial.

73. **(D)** FRE 608(b) provides that "specific instances of the conduct of a witness, for the purpose of attacking or supporting his credibility, other than conviction of crime as provided in FRE 609, ***may not be proved by extrinsic evidence."*** Choice (A) is incorrect. The fact pattern tells us nothing about the maximum penalty for a hoax. Furthermore, according to FRE 609(a)(1), evidence of an accused's convictions for serious offenses must be more probative than prejudicial to be admitted. The exception for crimes involving deception and false statement is narrowly interpreted, and it is not at all clear whether perpetrating a hoax would qualify. Choice (B) is also incorrect because it is not necessarily true that a hoax is probative of untruthfulness. Finally, choice (C) is the wrong answer because it is not likely that two witnesses would be considered cumulative. Under FRE 403, a judge can exclude the needless presentation of cumulative evidence.

74. **(C)** According to FRE 405(b), "In cases in which character or a trait of character of a person is an essential element of a charge, claim, or defense, proof may also be made of specific instances of his conduct." Therefore, choice (D) is incorrect. In connection with FRE 405 are situations where the owner of a motor vehicle or any dangerous object is charged with liability for the acts of a person using it on grounds of ***negligent entrustment*** of the vehicle or object to an incompetent or unfit person. In such cases, ***the character of the custodian is in issue and his acts come in to show it.*** Thus, the witness's testimony is admissible to show the neighbor's negligence (namely, that she was aware or should have been aware that the woman was a careless driver) in entrusting her vehicle to the woman. Therefore, choice (C) is the correct answer. Choice (A) is incorrect. Character evidence is propensity evidence, not circumstantial evidence. Choice (B) is incorrect. Personal knowledge alone is insufficient to admit character evidence at trial.

Evidence Nuance Chart

Admissibility of Character Evidence

Civil Cases	Criminal Cases
Character evidence is generally ***not admissible*** unless character is "in issue." There are certain civil actions where character is in issue and, thus, character evidence is admissible. They include: **(1) Defamation** **(2) Child Custody** **(3) Negligent Entrustment** **(4) Negligent Hiring**	Character evidence in ***not admissible*** unless defendant "opens the door" and places his character in issue by either (1) calling a character witness on his behalf, or (2) taking the stand to testify to his good character. Thereupon, the prosecution, in rebuttal, may present evidence refuting the accused's asserted good character.

75. **(C)** This is a highly tested Multistate area dealing with negligent entrustment. Where the owner of a motor vehicle or any dangerous object is charged with liability for the acts of a person using it on grounds of negligent entrustment, ***the character of the custodian is in*** issue, and his acts come in to show it. Such character evidence is probative on the issue of whether the entrustor was negligent in lending the instrumentality to the custodian or entrustee. Note, however, that ***the entrustor's character is not in issue.*** Therefore, the college student's character is not in issue, since he is the person making the entrustment. That's why character evidence is not admissible in this question. Choice (A) is wrong because ***habit evidence applies to a person's regular response to a repeated specific situation. The words "always," "invariably," "automatically," or "without fail" will tip off a habit issue.*** Conversely, "frequently" or "generally" will not. Choice (B) is wrong because the testimony describes past acts directly observed by the witness and is not a hearsay statement. Finally, choice (D) is incorrect. Biased evidence is not *per se* inadmissible. In an adversarial system, it is up to the advocate to convince the fact-finder that a biased witness is less worthy of belief.

Explanation: Question 76

The correct answer is: **(C)** Yes, as long as there is foundation testimony as to the accuracy and good working condition of the surgeon's electronic weathering device on the afternoon in question.

In her personal injury action, the wind surfer is offering a computer printout from the surgeon's sophisticated electronic weathering. Regarding this computer printout, students should begin by understanding that under F.R.E. 1001(3), "If data are stored in a computer or similar device, any printout or other output readable by sight, is an 'original.'" There is no "best evidence" problem as to the admissibility of the computer printout. Finally, as long as a foundation for the authenticity of the scientific wind device is laid, it will be admissible. Therefore, choice (C) is correct.

(A) Incorrect. Yes, as past recollection recorded.

(B) Incorrect. Yes, as the record of regularly conducted activity.

(D) Incorrect. No, because it is hearsay not within any recognized exception.

Explanation: Question 77

The correct answer is: **(B)** Sustain the objection, because the witness's answer is non-responsive.

With respect to rulings on evidence, F.R.E. 103 provides that a timely objection or motion to strike should state the specific ground(s) for the objection. Usually, objections will either go to the "manner and form" of a question or answer or to the "substance," such as relevancy and hearsay. Here, Choice (B) is better than (A) because the witness's answer is non-responsive in form to the question being asked of the witness. The supermarket's attorney is asking the witness the date the mushrooms were shipped and the witness is responding that the farmer "volunteered at a homeless shelter." On the other hand, answer (A) goes more to a "substantive" objection.

(A) Incorrect. Sustain the objection, because a party's credibility cannot be bolstered until it has been impeached.

(C) Incorrect. Sustain the objection, because character evidence is generally inadmissible in a breach of contract action.

(D) Incorrect. Overrule the objection, because a witness on cross-examination must be given latitude to answer questions.

Explanation: Question 78

The correct answer is: **(B)** The photocopy may not be admitted as an exhibit but the witness may be questioned about the document.

According to the "learned treatise" exception to the hearsay rule, virtually all courts have permitted the use of learned materials in the cross-examination of an expert witness. F.R.E. 803 (18) provides that "if admitted, the statements may be read into evidence but may not be received as exhibits." Consequently, choice (B) is correct.

(A) Incorrect. The photocopy may be admitted as an exhibit and the witness may be questioned about the document.

(C) Incorrect. The photocopy may be admitted as an exhibit but the witness may not be questioned about the document.

(D) Incorrect. The photocopy may neither be admitted as an exhibit nor may the witness be questioned about it since the original book must be produced.

Explanation: Question 79

The correct answer is: **(B)** It is admissible as an admission incorporated in a public record.

A vicarious admission is a statement by an employee or agent, made within the scope of the employment relationship, that is being offered against the employer. The facts state that the shop's employee made a statement to the chief inspector for OSHA. That statement was contained within an OSHA accident report. Because the OSHA accident report was a public record, and the employee's statement was an admission, the correct answer is (B).

(A) Incorrect. It is admissible as past recollection recorded.

(C) Incorrect. It is inadmissible, because such documents must be offered in their entirety.

(D) Incorrect. It is inadmissible, because it is hearsay not within any exception.

Explanation: Question 80

The correct answer is: **(D)** No, as hearsay not within any recognized exception.

It is imperative that students focus their attention on the interrogatory or "call of the question." This question deals with the admissibility of the witness's testimony relating to what she heard over the police-band radio. Consequently, choice (A) is incorrect because in order to have firsthand knowledge, the witness must have actually observed the event to which she is testifying. The witness is not testifying to what she saw, but rather to what she heard. Choice (B) is incorrect because a present sense impression is a statement that describes or explains an event made while the declarant is observing the event or made immediately thereafter. Again, the witness is not testifying to what she observed, but rather to what she heard. As a result, the witness's testimony relating to the dispatcher's statement is inadmissible hearsay because it is being offered to prove the truth of the matter asserted, namely, that the "red sports car was speeding."

(A) Incorrect. Yes, because she had firsthand knowledge of the broadcast.

(B) Incorrect. Yes, as a statement of present sense impression.

(C) Incorrect. No, under the best evidence rule.

Explanation: Question 81

The correct answer is: **(B)** Yes, for impeachment and as substantive evidence.

This is an evidence question addressing impeachment by a prior inconsistent statement. According to F.R.E. 613(b) "extrinsic evidence of a prior inconsistent statement by a witness is not admissible unless the witness is afforded an opportunity to explain or deny the inconsistency." Now, with regard to choice (A), the Federal Rules do not allow the substantive use of a prior inconsistent statement unless it is made "under oath" subject to the penalty of perjury at a trial, hearing, or in a deposition (F.R.E. 801(d)(1)(A)). Accordingly, many students will be tempted to go with the choice (A) answer. However, a careful reading of the facts will show that the prosecution is introducing the medical report into evidence. As such, the medical report will qualify as a business record, as it is made in the course of a regularly conducted business. In this regard, the medical report may properly be admitted both as substantive evidence and for purposes of impeachment. Therefore, choice (B) is the best answer.

(A) Incorrect. Yes, for purposes of impeachment only.

(C) Incorrect. No, because it is hearsay not within any recognized exception.

(D) Incorrect. No, because the plaintiff cannot impeach its own witness.

Explanation: Question 82

The correct answer is: **(B)** The husband's statement is admissible hearsay because it is a statement of cause reasonably pertinent to diagnosis or treatment.

Though it is hearsay, this statement is admissible under Federal Rule of Evidence 803(4) as a statement for the purpose of medical diagnosis or treatment. This exception allows not only a description of past symptoms and medical history, but also comments regarding the cause of the medical condition insofar as reasonably pertinent to treatment. Alcohol use would be pertinent to the cause of his medical condition and would therefore be admissible under this exception.

(A) Incorrect. The husband's statement should be admissible only for impeachment purposes.

If a declaration is admissible only for impeachment purposes, that means that it is hearsay not within a recognized exception. That is not true here—the husband's statement is admissible under a recognized exception of the Federal Rule of Evidence. Thus, this answer is incorrect.

(C) Incorrect. The husband's statement is inadmissible hearsay.

The husband's statement is admissible under Federal Rule of Evidence 803(4) as a statement for purpose of medical diagnosis or treatment. Therefore, this is not the best answer.

(D) Incorrect. The deceased's statement is inadmissible because the declarant is dead.

The Federal Rules of Evidence contain hearsay exceptions that apply only if the declarant is unavailable and ones for which it does not matter whether the declarant is unavailable. They do not contain any that do not apply because the declarant is unavailable. Therefore, the fact that the declarant is dead is immaterial to whether his statement to the physician is admissible, so this is not a good choice.

Explanation: Question 83

The correct answer is: **(D)** Admissible, as a declaration of present bodily condition.

This statement about the restaurant patron's pain is within the hearsay exception for statements of present bodily condition. The present bodily condition exception is separate from the Federal Rule of Evidence exception for statements for the purpose of medical treatment, so it need not be to a medical provider or her agent to be admissible. The declarant's availability is immaterial for both exceptions.

(A) Incorrect. Inadmissible, because the declarant must be unavailable for a declaration of present bodily condition to be admitted.

The declarant need not be unavailable for a declaration of present bodily condition to be admitted. Thus, this answer is incorrect.

(B) Incorrect. Inadmissible, because a recorded recollection must be in writing.

It is true that a recorded recollection must be in writing, but that is not the applicable exception here. This statement is not being offered to refresh a witness's memory but to establish her pain level shortly after the accident. Thus, this answer is incorrect.

(C) Incorrect. Admissible, as an excited utterance.

The hearsay exception for excited utterances allows in statements made while the declarant is under the influence of a startling event or condition. Under the circumstances, it is unlikely that the restaurant patron was still in such an excited condition. Therefore, this is not the best choice.

Explanation: Question 84

The correct answer is: **(B)** Admissible, as a non-hearsay vicarious admission.

Under Federal Rule of Evidence 801(d)(2), a statement is not hearsay if the statement is offered against a party and is a statement by his employee or agent (i.e., vicarious admission) concerning a matter within the scope of his agency or employment and made during the existence of the relationship. The federal rules are liberal in allowing these vicarious admissions, and there is a trend among state courts to allow them as well, even when the employee is not in the type of position generally recognized as an authorized spokesperson for the company.

(A) Incorrect. Admissible, as a declaration against interest.

A declaration against interest is a statement that is so far against the declarant's interests or so likely to subject him to criminal or civil liability when it was made that a reasonable person would not have said it unless he thought it was true. However, this exception is only available if the declarant is unavailable, so it does not fit this situation. Also, according to Federal Rule of Evidence 801, the statement is not hearsay. Thus, this answer is incorrect.

(C) Incorrect. Inadmissible, because it is not a present sense impression.

This choice is incorrect because the statement is, in fact, admissible. The hearsay exception for a present sense impression is a close choice, because it does not require the declarant's unavailability. It applies when the declarant is describing or explaining an event while he was perceiving it or immediately afterward. However, note that, according to Federal Rule of Evidence 801, the statement is not hearsay. Thus, this answer is incorrect.

(D) Incorrect. Inadmissible, as hearsay not within an exception.

Under Federal Rule of Evidence 801, the statement is not hearsay because it is a vicarious admission made by the trucking company's agent that is being offered against the trucking company. Therefore, this is not the best choice.

Explanation: Question 85

The correct answer is: **(D)** Admissible, as an excited utterance.

Under Federal Rule of Evidence 803(2), the statement of the unidentified bystander, made in the presence of the witness, should qualify as an excited utterance within the meaning of that exception to the hearsay rule. The theory of this exception is simply that there has been some startling occurrence that has temporarily stilled the capacity of reflection and produces utterances free of conscious fabrication. This event was sufficiently startling, the statement was made while the declarant was under the stress of the startling event, and the statement related to the startling event. Therefore, the elements for this hearsay exception are present.

(A) Incorrect. Inadmissible, because it contains inadmissible opinion evidence.

This is not a good answer because the witness would be testifying as to matters personally heard rather than an opinion.

(B) Incorrect. Inadmissible, as hearsay not within any of the exceptions.

Actually, one of the Federal Rules of Evidence hearsay exceptions applies. This event was sufficiently startling, the statement was made while the declarant was under the stress of the startling event, and the statement related to the startling event. Therefore, the statement is admissible as an excited utterance. Thus, this answer is incorrect.

(C) Incorrect. Admissible, as a declaration of existing state of mind.

The existing mental condition exception to the hearsay rule doesn't quite fit here because the types of things it would be used to prove, such as plan, motive, or intent, would not be reasons for this witness to testify. Another hearsay exception would be more appropriate. Thus, this answer is incorrect.

Explanation: Question 86

The correct answer is: **(D)** Yes, provided an appropriate person lays a foundation for the records.

Federal Rule of Evidence Rule 803(7) allows the use of records to prove absence of an entry in the records as long as the documents satisfy the requirements for records of a regularly conducted activity: there must be a regular business practice to make such records; they must be made at or near the time of the event and be made by a person with knowledge of the matters therein. This foundation may be established by the testimony of the custodian of the records or other qualified person.

(A) Incorrect. No, because the prejudice outweighs the probative value of the records because she may have had another name during that time period.

The employee can counter the prejudicial effect of this evidence by showing what her name was during the period. The judge should let the jury resolve any conflicts in the evidence on this point. This would not be a strong case for keeping relevant evidence from the jury under Federal Rule of Evidence 403. Thus, this answer is incorrect.

(B) Incorrect. No, unless the person who prepared the records will testify.

The person who prepared the records need not testify as long as the records' custodian or other qualified person lays a foundation. Thus, this answer is incorrect.

(C) Incorrect. Yes, although they can only be admitted in summary form to prevent wasting the court's time.

Although it is true that voluminous records may waste the court's time, the Federal Rules of Evidence hearsay exception for the absence of an entry in business records do not require that the offering party summarize them. Whether to summarize and the type of summary appropriate would be in the court's discretion. Thus, this answer is incorrect.

Explanation: Question 87

The correct answer is: **(B)** For the plaintiff, because the records are not the type of material protected by the privilege.

The attorney-client privilege permits a client to prevent anyone from testifying about confidential communications made to an attorney for the purposes of obtaining legal services. Written communications are protected, but an otherwise admissible document is not brought within the purview of the privilege simply because the client gives it to the attorney. Thus, records of the brokerage firm that was the defendant's client cannot be within the privilege, because by definition they cannot be a confidential communication; they had an existence wholly independent of the attorney-client relationship and came into the defendant's hands only because they (or copies) were transferred to her by the client brokerage firm. Because the defendant admits that the records are otherwise subject to discovery, and they are not protected by the attorney-client privilege, the defendant must produce them.

(A) Incorrect. For the plaintiff, because the defendant has made no showing that the brokerage firm has asserted the attorney-client privilege as to the records.

Although the client is the holder of the attorney-client privilege, an attorney is bound to assert the privilege on her client's behalf until authorized to waive it. Thus, the fact that the brokerage firm client has not asserted the privilege does not affect the defendant's actions, unless the firm affirmatively authorized her to waive the privilege. The materials sought are not protected by the privilege, however, so a better answer will state that it is not a confidential communication within the attorney-client privilege. Thus, this answer is incorrect.

(C) Incorrect. For the defendant, if the brokerage firm intended that its records be confidential when it turned them over to the defendant.

The fact that a pre-existing document is given to an attorney by a client, even if the client desires that the document remain confidential, does not convert the document into a confidential communication within the attorney-client privilege. The records as originally maintained by the brokerage firm would not be subject to the privilege, and they do not become so because the firm gave them to the defendant, its attorney. Thus, this answer is incorrect.

(D) Incorrect. For the defendant, because the records fall within the work product doctrine.

The work product doctrine prevents discovery or disclosure of work prepared by an attorney in anticipation of litigation or trial (with certain exceptions). The records sought by the plaintiff cannot be such work product because they were not prepared by the defendant at all; as brokerage firm records they were given to her by her client and existed independently of any work that she did for that firm. Thus, this answer is incorrect.

Explanation: Question 88

The correct answer is: **(B)** Yes, she can assert the Fifth Amendment privilege to avoid answering questions that would expose her to liability for the crime.

The Fifth Amendment privilege against self-incrimination allows a witness to refuse to answer questions if the answers would expose the witness to criminal liability. The privilege does not allow a witness, who is not the accused, to avoid testifying at all. Therefore, the ex-wife will have to testify as a witness but will not have to answer questions that will implicate her in a crime. Therefore, this answer is correct.

(A) Incorrect. Yes, she can assert the Fifth Amendment privilege against self-incrimination to avoid testifying as a witness at all.

The Fifth Amendment privilege against self-incrimination protects an individual from having to answer questions at trial that will expose him to criminal liability. However, only the accused can invoke the privilege to refuse to take the witness stand at all. A witness can invoke the privilege but must still take the stand. The privilege will allow that witness only to avoid answering questions if the answers would expose that individual to criminal liability. Therefore, the ex-wife, who has not been accused and is not on trial, cannot assert the Fifth Amendment privilege to avoid testifying as a witness at all but merely to avoid answering questions that would implicate her. Therefore, this answer is not correct.

(C) Incorrect. Yes, she can assert the spousal privilege to avoid testifying as a witness at all.

The spousal privilege allows a spouse to refuse to testify as a witness against her spouse in a criminal trial. However, the spousal privilege does not survive a divorce. The couple in this case divorced prior to trial. So the ex-wife can no longer assert the spousal privilege to avoid testifying as a witness.

(D) Incorrect. Yes, she can assert the marital communication privilege to avoid answering questions about confidential communications between the spouses occurring prior to or during the marriage.

The marital communication privilege protects confidential communications between spouses from disclosure and can be asserted by either spouse. The privilege also survives a divorce, but it only applies to communications occurring during the marriage. While the ex-wife can assert this privilege even though she is now divorced from the husband, she cannot assert the privilege to avoid answering questions about communications that occurred prior to their marriage while the embezzlement was allegedly committed. The marital communication privilege will only allow the ex-wife to avoid revealing any confidential discussions that occurred during their very brief marriage. Therefore, this answer is incorrect.

Explanation: Question 89

The correct answer is: **(A)** Yes, because the federal court must apply the privilege rules of the state in which it sits.

In a diversity action, the federal court must apply the substantive law of the state in which it sits and federal procedural law. Because evidence law is procedural, the Federal Rules of Evidence generally apply in federal court. However, under some circumstances, rules of evidence may have a substantive effect on a case and affect its outcome. For example, the existence of a particular testimonial privilege may have a substantive effect on a case. Because of the significance of testimonial privileges, Federal Rule of Evidence 501 provides that, in civil actions, where an element of a claim or defense is not based on a federal question, testimonial privileges are determined by state law. Therefore, under the facts presented, the federal court must apply the privilege rules of the state in which it sits.

(B) Incorrect. Yes, unless the parties choose at trial to have federal common law apply.

The parties can't choose at trial whether state law or federal law will apply. If the Federal Rules of Evidence require the court to apply state law to a particular ruling, the court has no option but to apply state law. Thus, this answer is incorrect.

(C) Incorrect. No, because the federal court must apply the federal common law related to privileges.

The federal court must apply the federal common law of privileges in criminal cases and federal question cases, but not in civil actions and proceedings in diversity. Federal Rule of Evidence 501 provides that, in civil actions, privilege with respect to an element of a claim or defense governed by state law shall be determined in accordance with state law. Thus, this answer is incorrect.

(D) Incorrect. No, because the student waived the state law privilege by removing the case to federal court.

Privileges can be waived under certain circumstances, for example, by the disclosure of the privileged information by the holder of the privilege to a person not encompassed by the privilege. However, the student has not waived her state law privilege by removing the case to federal court. The federal court will follow the Federal Rules of Evidence, and Federal Rule of Evidence 501 provides that in civil actions and proceedings, with respect to an element of a claim or defense governed by state law, privilege shall be determined in accordance with state law. Thus, this answer is incorrect.

Explanation: Question 90

The correct answer is: **(C)** No, because the report is privileged pursuant to the attorney-client privilege.

Any person (i.e., a client) who engages in a confidential communication with an attorney or someone who the person reasonably believes is an attorney for the purpose of seeking legal advice or representation has a privilege that allows that person to prevent anyone from testifying about the confidential communication. A routine report prepared by an employee of the manufacturer, pursuant to company policy or at the request of a corporate executive, would not become privileged simply because the company subsequently turned the report over to its counsel for use in litigation. However, here, the report was requested by the insurance company for the purpose of reporting the information to the attorney hired to represent the manufacturer in the lawsuit. Given the circumstances, the report is within the attorney-client privilege and is inadmissible at trial, as well as being protected from discovery.

(A) Incorrect. Yes, because the insurance company requested the report.

The insurance company is obligated to provide a defense for its insured. It does so by employing an attorney to represent the manufacturer. When a client (such as the manufacturer) makes a confidential communication to the attorney, it is immaterial that the communication was prompted by a request from the insurer. Thus, this answer is incorrect.

(B) Incorrect. Yes, because the report may contain discoverable evidence even though the report itself may be inadmissible.

Discovery is not limited to admissible evidence. Information that might lead to admissible evidence but is itself inadmissible is generally subject to disclosure via discovery. However, the attorney-client privilege for confidential communications extends beyond trial; matters within the privilege are also protected from disclosure via discovery. Thus, this answer is incorrect.

(D) Incorrect. No, because the report may contain subsequent remedial measures that the manufacturer underwent to produce a safer product.

If the only objection to revealing information via a discovery device is that the information would not be admissible if offered into evidence at trial, the objection is not valid and the discovery request must be complied with, because information available in discovery includes that which might lead to admissible evidence. Thus, the fact that the information sought might be inadmissible at trial as a subsequent remedial measure is not a basis upon which the manufacturer could refuse to produce the document to the photographer. Thus, this answer is incorrect.

Explanation: Question 91

The correct answer is: **(A)** Yes, the banker's statement that he cut off the dentist is admissible to prove liability.

Under Federal Rule of Evidence 409, evidence of payment or offering or promising to pay medical, hospital, or similar expenses caused by an injury is not admissible to prove liability on the part of the person who has paid (or offered/promised to pay) for the injury. However, unlike statements made in connection with an offer to settle or compromise (which are not admissible), statements made in conjunction with an offer or promise to pay medical expenses are admissible and can be severed from the inadmissible statements concerning the offer. In this case, the banker's statement that he will pay the dentist's medical bills is not admissible to prove liability. However, his statement that he cut off the dentist could be admissible to prove liability for the accident and resulting damage to the dentist's skis. Therefore, this answer is correct.

(B) Incorrect. Yes, the entire statement is admissible to prove liability.

Federal evidence rules render inadmissible evidence of an offer or promise to pay medical expenses as proof of liability. However, that rule does not prohibit the admission of any other statements made in conjunction with or at the same time as the offer to pay medical expenses. This rule is in contrast to the rule concerning admissibility of evidence concerning an offer to compromise, which also prohibits admission of any statements made in connection with that offer to compromise. Therefore, the banker's offer to pay the dentist's medical expenses will not be admissible to prove the banker's liability for the accident. His statement acknowledging that he cut off the dentist would, however, be admissible. Therefore, this answer is incorrect.

(C) Incorrect. No, because offers to pay medical bills and any accompanying comments are inadmissible to prove liability.

Federal rules of evidence state that offers to pay medical bills are inadmissible to prove liability. However, the rules do not bar admission of any other statements made in conjunction with that offer to pay medical bills. This is not to be confused with the rule concerning evidence of offers to compromise. That rule excludes not just evidence of the offer to compromise but any statements made in connection with the offer as well. In this case, the banker made an offer to pay the dentist's medical expenses, not an offer to compromise. Therefore, any other statements, such as the statement acknowledging that he cut off the dentist, will be severed from the offer to pay medical expenses and would be admissible. Therefore, this answer is incorrect.

(D) Incorrect. No, because the banker's statements are likely to be more prejudicial than probative.

Federal rules of evidence state that even relevant evidence can be ruled inadmissible if it is likely to be more unfairly prejudicial than probative. Note that the rule focuses on the unfairness of the prejudice. Any evidence presented against the defendant could be considered prejudicial to the defendant. The rules will exclude only that evidence that is unfairly prejudicial. In this case, the banker's statement is probative of his actions—he states that he cut off the dentist—which could be found to be the cause of the accident and thus a source of liability. Therefore, his statement about cutting off the dentist is not likely to be unfairly prejudicial or more prejudicial than probative, and this answer is incorrect.

Explanation: Question 92

The correct answer is: **(A)** No, because evidence of a new warning cannot be used to prove negligence concerning the old warning.

Federal Rules of Evidence provide that evidence of remedial measures taken by a defendant after a plaintiff has been injured is inadmissible to prove the defendant's negligence or the need for a warning. Such evidence may be admitted only to prove, where appropriate, that the defendant owned or controlled the item that injured the plaintiff, for impeachment purposes, or to show that precautionary measures were feasible (if controverted). Therefore, evidence of these remedial measures would not be admissible, and this answer is correct.

(B) Incorrect. No, because the evidence of this year's warning is not relevant to the therapist's accident, which occurred last year.

Federal Rules of Evidence provide that relevant evidence is evidence having any tendency to make the existence of any fact that is of consequence to the determination of the action more probable or less probable than it would be without the evidence. Here, a change in the warnings would likely be relevant to the therapist's action and whether the warning the therapist was given was adequate. However, relevant evidence is not always admissible. While this evidence is relevant, it is not admissible to prove negligence for other reasons. Therefore, this answer is incorrect.

(C) Incorrect. Yes, because the evidence is a declaration against interests and an exception to the hearsay rule.

Generally, under the Federal Rules of Evidence, out-of-court statements offered to prove the truth of the matter asserted are inadmissible as hearsay. A declaration against interests is among the exceptions to the hearsay rule and, therefore, could be admissible. However, to be a declaration of interest the statement would need to be so contrary to declarant's proprietary or pecuniary interests or likely to subject the maker to civil or criminal liability, that a reasonable person wouldn't have made the statement. Merely changing a warning does not necessarily subject the company to liability. Additionally, this evidence is inadmissible to prove negligence pursuant to another rule of evidence. Therefore, this answer is incorrect.

(D) Incorrect. Yes, the evidence can be used to show the need for a more extensive warning.

The evidence concerning the change in the warning would be evidence of remedial measures. Federal Rules of Evidence provide that evidence of remedial measures taken by a defendant after a plaintiff has been injured is inadmissible to prove the defendant's guilt or fault for the accident. Such evidence may be admitted only to prove, where appropriate, that the defendant owned or controlled the item that injured the plaintiff, for impeachment purposes, or to show that the precautionary measures were feasible (if controverted). Therefore, this evidence would not be admissible to show negligence and that a more extensive warning was needed, and this answer is incorrect.

Explanation: Question 93

The correct answer is: **(D)** Yes, because it can show the ownership or control of the vehicle that struck the girl.

Federal Rule of Evidence 411 allows the admission of evidence of liability insurance to prove ownership, control or agency, or to prove bias or prejudice of a witness. Such evidence is not admissible, however, to prove wrongful conduct or negligence. Thus, the passenger's statement is admissible because it can be used to prove the passenger owned or controlled the automobile involved in the accident. However, it cannot be used to prove the passenger was negligent or liable for the girl's injuries.

(A) Incorrect. No, because the passenger's insurance is not relevant.

Federal Rule of Evidence 411 allows the admission of evidence of liability insurance to prove ownership, control or agency, or to show bias or prejudice of a witness. Thus, the evidence does have some relevance, and this answer is incorrect.

(B) Incorrect. No, because it is prejudicial and therefore must be excluded.

Evidence that is relevant may still be inadmissible if its probative value is outweighed by the danger of unfair prejudice created by the evidence. Federal Rule of Evidence 403 requires a balancing of probative value and potential prejudice. Evidence that may be prejudicial is, therefore, not automatically excluded. The court here may find that the passenger's statement that he had insurance that would cover the injuries had probative value to prove the passenger owned the vehicle and that with proper instructions to the jury the evidence of insurance would not be unduly prejudicial. Therefore, it is possible the court could admit the evidence, and this answer is incorrect.

(C) Incorrect. Yes, because it can be offered as an admission of the driver's negligence or liability.

While it is true that the passenger's statement in some respects resembles an admission, Federal Rule of Evidence 411 specifically addresses the admissibility of evidence of liability insurance. Such evidence is admissible only to prove agency, ownership or control, or to show bias or prejudice of a witness. It cannot be offered to prove liability. Therefore, this answer is incorrect.

Explanation: Question 94

The correct answer is: **(B)** Yes, because the testimony is probative of habit and, therefore, of conduct in conformity with the habit.

The witness's testimony is admissible under Federal Rules of Evidence as evidence of habit—i.e., a regular response to a repeated specific situation that is committed without a high degree of forethought. The key word to establish habit is always. Even though the witness only sees the plaintiff on nice evenings, the plaintiff apparently always does the same thing on his way down the pizzeria's steps and his apartment building's steps. The evidence shows it is plaintiff's habit to take the steps two at a time. This evidence of habit can be used to show the plaintiff's conformity with that habit—i.e., that he went down the steps of the pizzeria two at a time—at the time of the accident. Therefore, this answer is correct.

(A) Incorrect. Yes, because the testimony tends to show that the plaintiff is a careless person.
This answer may be tempting but it is incorrect. Testimony aimed at demonstrating the character—in this case, carelessness—of the plaintiff would be inadmissible. Character evidence is inadmissible under Federal Rules of Evidence to prove conduct. Therefore, evidence that plaintiff was careless would not be admissible to prove his conduct on the night of the accident. Therefore, this answer is incorrect.

(C) Incorrect. No, because there was no eyewitness to corroborate the testimony.
This testimony could be admissible as evidence of habit to show the plaintiff's regular response to a given situation, done without a high degree of forethought—i.e., that the plaintiff always took the stairs two at a time. Evidence of habit need not be corroborated. Therefore, the lack of an eyewitness would not render this testimony inadmissible and this answer is incorrect.

(D) Incorrect. No, because the testimony is impermissible evidence of character to show conduct.
While it is true that evidence of character is not admissible to show conduct, under the Federal Rules of Evidence, this testimony may be introduced as evidence of habit, which is admissible. Evidence of habit shows a person's regular response to a particular situation, performed without a high degree of forethought—i.e., that the person always acts the same way in a situation. In this case, the testimony could be offered to show the plaintiff always takes stairs two at a time. Thus, this testimony would be admissible habit evidence for purposes of showing plaintiff's conduct on the night of the accident. Therefore, this answer is not correct.

Explanation: Question 95

The correct answer is: **(A)** Yes, because it tends to prove that the defendant is not the type of man who would commit armed robbery.

A criminal defendant may introduce evidence of his character that is inconsistent with the charged offense. Thus, in this case, the brother's testimony is admissible to show that a gentle non-violent man like the defendant would not commit the violent crime of armed robbery. Note, however, that the introduction of this evidence will place the defendant's character in issue, so that the prosecution may impeach the brother with questions about specific instances of the defendant's behavior that are contrary to the witness's testimony.

(B) Incorrect. Yes, because it is relevant to the question of whether the defendant's denial of guilt can be believed.
Under the facts presented, the brother's testimony is admissible not merely to bolster the defendant's credibility, but to show that it was unlikely that such a gentle, non-violent man as the defendant would commit the violent crime of armed robbery. As such, this is not the best answer choice.

(C) Incorrect. No, because the defendant has not yet testified.

The witness testimony offered here need not be offered after the defendant's testimony. Therefore, this is not a correct answer.

(D) Incorrect. No, because a sibling's testimony in these circumstances is unreliable.

Whether a sibling may be prejudiced in the defendant's favor is a question for the finder of fact to consider. However, this consideration affects only the weight, not the admissibility, of the proffered testimony. As such, this answer is incorrect.

Explanation: Question 96

The correct answer is: **(C)** Yes, because she has personal knowledge of the matter.

This is a matter about which the wife has personal knowledge, and she is competent to testify under Federal Rule of Evidence 602. Having a financial stake in the outcome does not affect competency. Under the Federal Rules of Evidence, a witness is competent if (s)he has the capacity to perceive and recollect and understands the duty to tell the truth. Note that the jury can assess her potential bias and weigh her testimony accordingly.

(A) Incorrect. No, because she has a financial stake in the outcome of the trial.

Under a common law dead man's statute, the wife would be barred from testifying about conversations or transactions with her deceased husband. However, the Federal Rules of Evidence (FRE) do not contain such a rule. Also, she is not testifying as to a conversation or transaction with the decedent, so a dead man's statute would not apply to this testimony even if the FRE had one. Note that the jury can certainly consider the wife's bias, which affects the weight the jury will accord her testimony.

(B) Incorrect. No, because she would be testifying about matters relating to the estate of the deceased.

Common law dead man's statutes disqualify financially interested witnesses from testifying in civil trials about conversations or transactions with the decedent. However, the Federal Rules of Evidence do not contain a dead man's statute, so this is not a correct answer.

(D) Incorrect. Yes, because the hearsay exception for present sense impression applies.

This is not the best choice because there is no hearsay issue in this problem. The wife is going to testify about what she saw on the occasion of her husband's death. The facts do not discuss any out-of-court statement.

Explanation: Question 97

The correct answer is: **(C)** No, because it is extrinsic evidence of a specific instance of misconduct.

Specific instances of conduct cannot be introduced to attack the credibility of a witness under the Federal Rules of Evidence. A witness can be questioned about specific instances on cross-examination, but extrinsic evidence of specific instances of conduct, such as testimony of third parties, cannot be introduced to impeach the witness. Therefore, the accountant's testimony is not admissible and this answer is correct.

(A) Incorrect. Yes, because it is evidence of a prior crime.

While prior crimes can be admissible to impeach a witness under the Federal Rules of Evidence, particularly when an element of the crime involves dishonesty or false statements, there must be a conviction for that rule to apply. In this case, there is no evidence that the co-worker was convicted for cheating on his tax return. The accountant has merely stated that the co-worker cheated on a tax return. Thus, this would be evidence of specific instances of conduct. Therefore, this answer is incorrect.

(B) Incorrect. Yes, because cheating on a tax return involves dishonesty.

Cheating does involve dishonesty. However, the accountant's statement that the co-worker cheated does not mean the co-worker was convicted of a crime. Past criminal convictions could be used to impeach a witness, particularly when the crime involves dishonesty or false statements. But since there is no evidence the co-worker has been convicted, this rule would not apply to admit the evidence. This is really extrinsic evidence of specific instances of conduct, which is not admissible to impeach a witness but merely may be inquired into on cross-examination of the witness at issue. In this case, the co-worker is not being cross-examined, but rather third-party testimony is offered to show specific instances of conduct to impeach the co-worker. This evidence would not be admissible, and, therefore, this answer is not correct.

(D) Incorrect. No, because it is cumulative evidence.

Relevant evidence can be excluded if it is cumulative evidence that will merely waste the court's time and is unnecessary. It is unlikely that this evidence would be found cumulative, as there is only one other piece of evidence regarding the co-worker's credibility—the salon owner's opinion that the co-worker is a chronic liar. Thus, the court would not be likely to exclude the evidence on the basis that it is cumulative. Additionally, the evidence is inadmissible for other reasons. Therefore, this answer is incorrect.

Explanation: Question 98

The correct answer is: **(C)** The judge, regardless of whether the evidence regarding supplier's recent statements showing the extent of his Alzheimer's constitutes hearsay.

The Federal Rules of Evidence require that the judge determine preliminary questions of witness competency, privileges and the admissibility of evidence. The judge is not bound by the rules of evidence, except the rules of privilege, in making such a determination. Therefore the judge can consider evidence that is otherwise inadmissible hearsay to determine the admissibility of another piece of evidence. In this case, the recent out-of-court statements of the supplier that show that Alzheimer's has affected his ability to testify could be subject to the hearsay rule. But that would not prevent the judge from considering those statements in deciding whether the supplier's testimony at the prior trial was admissible in this trial. Whether the evidence of unavailability is hearsay does not affect who makes the determination as to admissibility. Therefore this answer is correct.

(A) Incorrect. Neither the judge nor the jury, because the evidence regarding the supplier's recent statements showing the extent of his Alzheimer's is hearsay not within any exception.

Former testimony given as a witness at another hearing of the same or a different proceeding, where the party against whom the evidence is offered (or a predecessor in interest to the party) had an opportunity and similar motive to develop the testimony by direct, cross or redirect examination is admissible under the hearsay rule if the witness is unavailable. The Federal Rules of Evidence require the judge to make the preliminary determination regarding admissibility. The judge is not bound by the rules of evidence in making that determination (except the rules of privilege). Therefore the judge can consider the evidence of the supplier's recent statements to determine if Alzheimer's has rendered the supplier unavailable to testify in this trial, even if that evidence is hearsay. Thus, this answer is incorrect.

(B) Incorrect. Both the judge and the jury, because the evidence regarding supplier's recent statements showing the extent of his Alzheimer's falls within an exception to the hearsay rule.

The offered testimony may, in fact, be admissible. Former testimony given as a witness at another hearing of the same or a different proceeding, where the party against whom the evidence is offered (or a predecessor in interest to the party) had an opportunity and similar motive to develop the testimony by direct, cross, or redirect examination is admissible under the hearsay rule if the witness is unavailable. However, the Federal Rules of Evidence dictate that the judge, not the jury, makes the preliminary determination of admissibility. The jury would not be reviewing the supplier's testimony, so this answer is incorrect.

(D) Incorrect. The jury, regardless of whether the evidence regarding supplier's recent statements showing the extent of his Alzheimer's constitutes hearsay.

The Federal Rules of Evidence dictate that the court, and not the jury, decides whether evidence is admissible. The jury is not permitted to decide whether the supplier's former testimony is admissible, or, for that matter, even to be exposed to the evidence until the judge decides that the evidence is admissible. Therefore this answer is incorrect.

Explanation: Question 99

The correct answer is: **(A)** The court must take judicial notice of the distance if the plaintiff makes a proper request and furnishes the court with a reputable map or a printout from a reputable computer program.

In a trial, most facts must be established by the introduction of evidence as proof of those facts. Under Federal Rules of Evidence 201, evidence of certain facts is not required, because the judge must take judicial notice of such facts. To require the court to take judicial notice, the fact must be one which is not subject to reasonable dispute, either because it is: 1) generally known within the territorial jurisdiction of the court; or 2) capable of accurate and ready determination by resort to sources whose accuracy cannot reasonably be questioned. If a party requests judicial notice and provides the court with the necessary information to substantiate the fact, the court must take judicial notice. Here, the requirements were met, so judicial notice is mandatory.

(B) Incorrect. The court may take judicial notice of the distance if the plaintiff makes a proper request, gives timely notice, and furnishes the court with a reputable map or a printout from a reputable computer program.

If the fact is one not reasonably subject to dispute, a party has made a proper request, and the party provides the court with necessary information to substantiate the fact that is the subject of the request, the court is required to take judicial notice of the fact at issue and does not have discretion to deny the request. Therefore, this answer is not correct.

(C) Incorrect. The court may not take judicial notice unless both parties agree.

An agreement is not required, because judicial notice is mandatory if the fact is one not reasonably subject to dispute, a party has made a proper request, and the party provides the court with necessary information to substantiate the fact that is the subject of the request. Therefore, this is not the best answer.

(D) Incorrect. The court may not take judicial notice, because the distance is not capable of ready and accurate determination if there are different routes that a driver could take between the pizza parlor and the plaintiff's house.

The court can readily and accurately determine the shortest distance between these two points by resorting to sources whose accuracy cannot reasonably be questioned, such as a reliable map or atlas. If the defendant has reason to dispute the distance calculated by the plaintiff, the defendant can object to the court taking judicial notice of the distance between the two locations. If there is no such objection, however, then the court is required to take judicial notice of facts, such as the distance between two locations that can be readily ascertained by reference to sources whose accuracy cannot reasonably be questioned.

Explanation: Question 100

The correct answer is: **(D)** Admissible, because the trier of fact can make the comparison.

Documents may be authenticated or identified in court by a number of methods. One such method is by comparison by the trier of fact or by an expert witness with specimens that have been authenticated. This question is multi-layered because it requires knowing whether the legal document is admissible as well as whether the prior filed unrelated legal document was authenticated. Certain documents are self-authenticating, i.e., extrinsic evidence as to their authenticity is not required. The copy of a document authorized by law to be recorded or filed and actually recorded or filed in a public office, certified as correct by the custodian or other person authorized to make such certification, is one type of self-authenticating document. The document sought to be introduced here is a certified copy of a document filed in a public office, and therefore is self-authenticating. As such, it would be admissible and the trier of fact would be able to make the comparison between the signature on this document and the ones on the other documents.

(A) Incorrect. Inadmissible, because the plaintiff did not show the chain of custody of the legal document.

This answer is incorrect because it reaches the wrong conclusion by citing to the wrong rule. This answer references the authentication of physical objects. A physical object may be authenticated by testimony of personal knowledge by someone who is familiar with the object, by distinctive markings or characteristics, or by showing a chain of custody. Documents may be authenticated by a number of methods. It is not required that the party seeking to introduce the document show chain of custody. Therefore, this answer is incorrect.

(B) Incorrect. Inadmissible, because only the defendant can identify the defendant's signature.

It is not necessary for a defendant to identify his or her own signature on a document. While this is one way for a document to be identified, documents may be authenticated in many other ways and many are self-authenticating (i.e., extrinsic evidence is not required for their authentication). One such way for a document to be authenticated is for the trier of fact to compare the document with one that has been authenticated.

(C) Incorrect. Admissible, because the document sought to be introduced is unrelated to the matter before the court.

A document sought to be introduced as evidence in court must be authenticated (i.e., a foundation must be laid to show that the document is what its proponent claims it is). A number of methods exist for such authentication, one of which is for the trier of fact to compare the document with a document that has already been authenticated. There is no requirement that the already authenticated document be unrelated to the matter before the court in order for such comparison to be made. Therefore, this response is incorrect. Note that the certified copy of the filing with the town hall would be self-authenticating because certified copies of documents filed with a public office are self-authenticating.

1. OVERVIEW: PROPHES

P – Probative Sufficiency **R** – Reliability **O** – Opinion **P** – Privilege **H** – Hearsay **E** – Examination **S** – Substitutes for Evidence

PROBATIVE SUFFICIENCY – must be sufficiently probative to warrant admission.

- **LOGICAL RELEVANCY** – *must have some tendency to prove or disprove a fact of consequence.*
  - **Similar Happenings and Transactions** – proponent must show a *substantial identity of material circumstances.*
  - **Absence of Similar Happenings (Negative Evidence)** – proponent must show (1) a *substantial identity of material circumstances* and that (2) *happening would have been known by witness if it occurred.*
  - **Foundation (Authentication and Identification)** – proponent must offer *sufficient evidence to sustain a finding that the evidence* (e.g., a writing, physical object, or voice) is *what its proponent purports it to be.* FRE allows self-authentication in some cases.
- **LEGAL RELEVANCY** – *may not be substantially more prejudicial than probative.*
  - **Liability Insurance** – inadmissible to prove negligence, but may prove disputed ownership or control and bias of witness or potential juror.
  - **Settlements and Compromises (Including Offers)** – to encourage out-of-court settlements, inadmissible as an admission of fault or to establish value of claim, but may explain delay or show bias.
  - **Subsequent Remedial Measures** – to encourage safety measures, inadmissible to prove negligence, but may prove disputed ownership or control and, under modern trend, that there was a *defect* for strict liability.
  - **Character Evidence** – *reputation, specific instances of conduct, or personal opinion* bearing on character or propensity is inadmissible to prove conduct consistent therewith except if *habit* or, in criminal cases only, if *mercy rule* or *prosecutor's rule* applies. May be used to prove (1) *character, if an essential element* of the case; (2) relevant *knowledge of another's character*, or (3) to *impeach a testifying witness* (subject to limitations on extrinsic evidence).
  - **Impeachment** – witness may be asked questions which tend to discredit (intrinsic impeachment), but *extrinsic evidence of bad character may be used to impeach only if in the form of conviction* or *it is relevant to a material matter beyond witness credibility.*

(continued)

1. OVERVIEW: PROPHES *(continued)*

RELIABILITY – must meet a minimal threshold of trustworthiness.

- **WITNESS COMPETENCY** – FRE abandons mental and moral prerequisites, defects go to weight, common law disqualifies a witness if court finds witness cannot (1) *accurately recount the facts and give meaningful testimony*, or (2) *understand the significance of the obligation to tell the truth.*
- **SCIENTIFIC DEVICES AND TESTS** – proponent must establish that (1) device or theory is *recognized and accepted in the relevant scientific community;* (2) the *device used was in proper working order;* and (3) *device was operated and interpreted by a qualified person.*
- **BEST EVIDENCE RULE (ORIGINAL WRITING RULE)** – when the *contents of a writing are in issue*, the *original* (includes reliable photocopy under FRE) must be *produced* or shown to be *unavailable*. Contents are in issue if (1) writing has independent legal significance, (2) proponent offers a writing, or (3) witness testimony is dependent on the contents of writing.
- **DEADMAN'S ACT** – *abandoned under FRE* and many states; where it applies, it prevents testimony as to a transaction with a now deceased or incompetent party unless the testimony is corroborated by independent evidence.

OPINION

- **LAY OPINION** – non-experts may give *sensory opinions* within common experience so long as there is a sufficient opportunity to perceive; quasi-experts may give moderate expert-type opinions if sufficient foundation is laid.
- **EXPERT OPINION** – expert opinion may be given if (1) it *assists the fact finder* (many states require that the opinion be *necessary*, i.e., relate to matters beyond common understanding), (2) the witness is *qualified as an expert*, and (3) the opinion is *within the state of the art of the field of expertise*. May be based on matters not in evidence and inadmissible matter if of the type relied on by reasonable experts: expert may be cross-examined regarding contents of authoritative treatise (common law requires reliance).

PRIVILEGE

- **RELATIONSHIP** – communication must be made as part of a statutorily designated relationship, no requirement of fee or acceptance of case if communicator was seeking professional advice or treatment. Minority view – reasonable belief that relationship exists is sufficient.
- **COMMUNICATION** – except in special circumstances, only verbal communications are protected, not observations or impressions (but separate *spousal privilege* prevents testimony as to any matter, not just revelation of a confidential communication).
- **CONFIDENTIALITY** – presence of inessential person not otherwise privileged precludes privilege (persons who advance the purpose of the privilege such as doctors or investigators employed to aid a lawyer are protected by privilege).
- **HOLDER** – only holder may waive privilege, privilege may be asserted by another *on holder's behalf*, but holder controls.
- **WAIVER** – holder permanently loses privilege as to communications voluntarily revealed by him or by another if holder fails to object when he had an opportunity to do so.
- **EXCEPTIONS** – privilege not available in suits between persons in the protected relationship; joint clients or where communication was made to advance a crime or fraud.

1. OVERVIEW: PROPHES *(continued)*

HEARSAY

- **EXCLUSIONS** – out-of-court assertion *admissible for a relevant purpose not dependent on its truth:* (1) state of mind of the declarant or listener (2) prior statement to impeach, or (3) rehabilitate verbal event.
- **EXEMPTIONS** – under the FRE, certain out-of-court statements are not hearsay even when used to prove their truth: (1) *admissions*, (2) *prior I.D. of a testifying witness*, (3) *prior sworn statements inconsistent with courtroom testimony;* (4) *prior consistent statements used to rebut inference of recent fabrication or undue influence.*
- **EXCEPTIONS** – Admissions, Declaration against interest, Dying declaration, Excited utterance, Mental state exception. Physical sensation. Business record, Official written statement, Past recollection recorded, Prior recorded testimony. Sense impressions, Expert exception, Equivalency exception.

EXAMINATION

- **DIRECT EXAMINATION** – look out for: (1) leading, (2) narrative, (3) assuming facts, (4) compound, and (5) argumentative.
- **CROSS-EXAMINATION** – must generally be within scope of direct exam; leading questions proper.

SUBSTITUTES FOR EVIDENCE

- **JUDICIAL NOTICE** – no formal proof required for: (1) state and federal laws and regulations; (2) universally known facts, or (3) facts subject to undisputed verification.
- **PRESUMPTIONS** – directs the jury's fact finding process by a special instruction; *FRE and majority – presumption only shifts burden of producing evidence to party opposing presumed fact;* in some states, certain presumptions based on a strong public policy shift burden of persuasion to opponent of presumed fact.

2. LOGICAL RELEVANCY

CIRCUMSTANTIAL EVIDENCE – fact to be proved must be inferred from other facts; admissible if it has *some tendency to prove or disprove a fact of consequence*. Is fact to be proved more likely with the evidence than it was without it?

- **SIMILAR ACCIDENTS OR INJURIES** – may prove dangerousness of a particular condition or knowledge of that condition by prior or subsequent similar happenings if a *substantial identity of all material circumstances* is shown – burden is on proponent to lay foundation.
- **SIMILAR CONTRACTS OR TRANSACTIONS** – to prove or clarify the terms of a transaction or agreement, proponent may offer evidence of similar but unrelated transactions with opposing party, but not with third parties (some cases have allowed third party evidence as court has broad discretion).
- **NEGATIVE EVIDENCE** – proponent may prove that other similar happenings did *not* occur to prove safety of a particular condition or no notice if proponent shows (1) *a substantial identity of material circumstances* with respect to evidence, and (2) that *happening would have been observed by witness if it had occurred.*
- **OTHER INFERENCES MAY BE EQUALLY OR MORE PLAUSIBLE** – evidence need only have *some tendency* to prove fact sought; close questions tend to be resolved in favor of admission.

CONNECTING EVIDENCE (AUTHENTICATION OR IDENTIFICATION) – evidence must be authenticated or identified as a condition precedent to admissibility by the offer of preliminary facts sufficient to support a finding that the matter in question is what its proponent claims. FRE 901(a).

WRITINGS

- **Personal Knowledge** – testimony from any witness with personal knowledge that the writing was prepared by the person claimed. FRE 901(b)(1).
- **Identification of Handwriting** – non-expert opinion as to genuineness based on familiarity not acquired for purposes of litigation, FRE 901(b)(2), or comparison with an authenticated exemplar by a qualified expert or the trier of fact. FRE 901(b)(3).
- **Circumstantial Evidence** – evidence indicating that information revealed or matters stated in the writing tend to identify the source as a particular person or firm (sometimes called the "reply message" doctrine), based on notion that the contents, *other* than direct statements of self-identification such as signatures or letterheads, if unique, can create a sufficient inference as to who prepared the writing. Do not confuse with forms of self-authentication. FRE 901(b)(4).
- **Public Records or Reports** – evidence that a purported public record was in the custody of the proper public office. FRE 901(b)(7). Includes electronic data.
- **Ancient Writing** – evidence that a writing (1) is in such a condition as to create no suspicion regarding its authenticity, (2) was in a place where, if authentic, it should likely be, *and* (3) it is at least 20 years old. FRE 901(8). Common law required 30 years. Note, there is also a hearsay exception for properly authenticated ancient writings. FRE 803(16).
- **Self-Authentication** – extrinsic evidence of authenticity is not required with respect to a number of special writings including (1) *public documents* if sealed or certified, (2) *official publications* purportedly issued by public authority, (3) *newspapers and periodicals* indicating publisher, (4) *trade inscriptions* such as tags, labels, or signs purporting to indicate origin, ownership, or control, and which were affixed in the course of business, (5) *acknowledged documents*, (6) *commercial paper*, and (7) *documents identified by statutory presumption*. FRE 902.

VOICES

- **Personal Knowledge** – testimony from any witness who heard the statement, saw the speaker, and has personal knowledge of the identity of the speaker. FRE 901(b)(1).
- **Identification of Voice** – where speaker is unseen or unknown, an opinion identifying a voice based upon hearing the voice under circumstances connecting it with the alleged speaker (whether heard first-hand, by recording, or telephone), or by comparison by an expert or the trier of fact with an authenticated exemplar of the voice. FRE 901(b)(3), (4).
- **Distinctive Characteristics** – evidence of unique contents, internal patterns, or other distinctive characteristics (e.g., accent) taken in conjunction with the circumstances. FRE 901(b)(4).
- **Special Rule for Telephone Conversations** – in addition to the above methods, a *person* can be identified by evidence that (1) a telephone call *was made to a number assigned to that person by the telephone company*, and (2) circumstances *including self-identification*, show the person answering to be the one called. FRE 901(b)(6)(A). In the case of a *business*, (1) evidence that a *call was made to a number assigned to the business by the telephone company*, and (2) the *conversation related to business reasonably transacted over the telephone*. FRE 901(b)(6)(B).

PHYSICAL OBJECTS – physical objects such as guns, heroin, etc., may be identified as above including: (1) *personal knowledge* – testimony recognizing the object to be what it purports to be; (2) *distinctive characteristics or markings;* and (3) *chain of possession* – testimony accounting for objects' whereabouts from point of incident at issue until trial (must also show no likelihood of tampering).

3. LEGAL RELEVANCY

Otherwise relevant evidence is inadmissible if, taken as a whole, its probative value is substantially outweighed by the danger of (1) unfair prejudice, (2) confusion of the issues, (3) misleading the jury, or by (4) considerations of undue delay, waste of time, or needless presentation of cumulative evidence. FRE 403.

DISCRETIONARY EXCLUSION

TYPICAL PROBLEMS – *gruesome evidence* (e.g., gory color photos, blood-stained objects), *statistical probabilities, prior bad acts used to impeach a criminal defendant-witness* (even if permitted under character and impeachment rules).

FACTORS

- **LIMITING INSTRUCTION** – is it likely that cautionary instruction will protect against improper inference?
- **ALTERNATIVES** – are there less offensive ways of proving the same facts available to proponent?
- **MATERIALITY** – is the evidence directed toward a critical central issue or merely toward background or corroborative facts? (The more important the evidence, the more likely it is to be admitted since probative value is higher.)
- **NATURE OF RISK** – will admission of the evidence create a risk of convicting an innocent person? (Exclusion is most likely upon objection of a criminal defendant.)

(continued)

3. LEGAL RELEVANCY *(continued)*

MANDATORY EXCLUSION

Special statutory or common law rules specifically prohibiting certain forms of evidence to be used to prove certain facts.

LIABILITY INSURANCE – *evidence that a person was or was not insured for liability at the time of an injury is inadmissible for the purpose of proving that such person acted negligently or wrongfully.* Admissible to prove other relevant facts: (1) *agency*, (2) *ownership or control* (if disputed), (3) *bias or prejudice of a witness* (e.g., witness employed by insurance company liable for judgment rendered). FRE 411. **Rationale:** evidence tempts fact finder to improperly consider ability-to-pay and possibly "deep pocket" of insurance company.

SUBSEQUENT REMEDIAL MEASURES – *evidence of a remedial measure, taken or authorized by a civil defendant after the occurrence of an injury, is inadmissible for the purpose of proving negligence or culpable conduct of the defendant.* Admissible to prove other relevant facts: (1) *ownership or control* (if disputed), (2) *feasibility of precautionary measures* (if disputed), and (3) *impeachment* of defendant's testimony. FRE 407. **Rationale:** to encourage persons to make products and premises as safe as they can be made by removing chance that remedial act will be used as an admission.

- **REMEDIAL MEASURE** – includes repairs, changes in procedure, termination or additional training of employee, adoption of rule or other improvement tending to make a product or condition safer.
- **PRODUCTS LIABILITY ACTION** – recent state cases hold that rule does *not* bar use of evidence of subsequent design changes as evidence of "defect' in a products liability case since cause of action does not require showing of negligence or culpable conduct.

ACTUAL OR ATTEMPTED COMPROMISE – *evidence respecting an actual settlement of a disputed claim or an attempt to compromise such claim (including any statement made during compromise negotiations) is inadmissible to prove the validity or value of the claim.* Admissible to prove other relevant facts: (1) *bias* of a witness, (2) *explain delay* (if undue delay is claimed), and (3) *obstruction of justice.* FRE 408. **Rationale:** to encourage out-of-court settlement of disputes.

- **FINAL SETTLEMENT** – rule only excludes statements or acts directed at a final resolution of a dispute; it does *not* exclude payments of or offers to pay for damages unless meant as a mutually binding settlement (see below re: medical expenses).
- **EXCLUDES EXPLICIT ADMISSIONS** – *contra to common law*, the FRE bars all statements made during good faith compromise discussions.

PAYMENT OR OFFER TO PAY MEDICAL BILLS – *evidence of the payment or offer to pay medical, hospital, or similar expenses resulting from an injury at issue is inadmissible to prove liability for the injury.* FRE 409. Common law has no analog. **Note:** specific admissions not necessary to the offer to pay *are* admissible. **Rationale:** to encourage Good Samaritan payments.

PLEAS AND OFFERS TO PLEA — *evidence of an offer to plead guilty, nolo contendere or actual pleas later withdrawn (as well as any statements made in connection therewith) are inadmissible in any civil or criminal case.* Such evidence is admissible to impeach testimony or prove perjury, or if in the form of a *voluntary and reliable statement made on the record in court.* FRE 410. **Rationale:** to advance the policies of nolo contendere, plea bargaining, and to make meaningful the judicial decision to allow a plea to be withdrawn.

3. LEGAL RELEVANCY *(continued)*

CHARACTER EVIDENCE (See Flowchart 4) – *evidence of a person's character is inadmissible to prove conduct on a particular occasion except when it is: (1) in the form of habit (invariable repeated behavior), (2) used to impeach a witness (subject to limitations imposed by impeachment rules), or (3) reputation or personal opinion offered by a criminal defendant to show innocence, or by the prosecutor to rebutsuch evidence* (i.e., the "Mercy Rule") and *(4) specific implicating facts not derived from disposition alone* (e.g., motive, opportunity, intent, knowledge, identity, or plan). Admissible (subject to discretionary exclusion discussed above) for relevant purposes other than proving conduct: (1) *character or reputation as a primary issue*, and (2) *knowledge of character or disposition*. FRE 404. **Rationale:** to prevent undue prejudice caused by a focus on the character of a person rather than the particular facts of the litigation.

EXTRINSIC IMPEACHMENT: COLLATERAL MATTER RULE – *evidence not elicited on cross-examination from a witness himself is inadmissible to impeach that witness unless the impeachment goes to a material matter and, in certain cases, the witness has been, or will be afforded, an opportunity to explain or deny the evidence.* **Rationale:** credibility with respect to a nonmaterial fact is collateral; extrinsic evidence only tending discredit on a collateral matter may confuse the issues, mislead the jury, and consume an undue amount of time.

- **MATERIALITY** – evidence must either tend to discredit (1) the testimony as a whole by showing *bias, defects in perception or memory, or untrustworthy character* (manifested by a conviction), or (2) testimony about an outcome-affecting fact as by showing a material *inconsistent statement.*
- **CONFRONTATION** – in order to make extrinsic impeachment a last resort, proponent normally required to confront the witness with the evidence *prior* to the offer, however, under FRE 613(b), it is sufficient to permit confrontation after the evidence is admitted. No confrontation is required for the use of convictions.
- **CONTRADICTION** – evidence admissible on a substantive issue (i.e., other than impeachment) may be offered extrinsically regardless of its tendency to discredit a previous witness (this is so even at common law where a party may not impeach his own witness).
- **MINORITY RULE** – some states (e.g., California) reject Collateral Matter Rule and permit extrinsic evidence on any substantive or credibility issue.

4. CHARACTER EVIDENCE

GENERAL RULE: Evidence of a Person's Character or Disposition is Inadmissible Proof of the Conduct of that Person on a Particular Occasion Except as Otherwise Permitted by Law.

ISSUE SPOTTING SEQUENCE: (1) Is the evidence a form of character evidence? (2) Is the evidence admissible to prove factors other than conduct? (3) If used to prove conduct, is the evidence admissible under a specific exception to the general rule?

(1) FORMS.

- **REPUTATION** – Evidence purporting to state the community reputation of a person (P); witness need not actually know P.
- **PERSONAL OPINION** – Evidence which includes a personal opinion (as opposed to community opinion) of P's character or disposition; witness must actually know P.
- **OTHER ACTS** – Evidence of acts done by P either prior or subsequent to the conduct at issue in the case.

(2) NON-CONDUCT USES – Character evidence is not excluded by the general rule if its relevancy is not dependent on proving specific conduct of the person characterized.

- **CHARACTER AS AN ULTIMATE ISSUE** – All appropriate forms admissible to prove P's character where it is an essential element of: (1) a *cause of action or claim* (e.g., character of parent in child custody action; mental condition of testator in probate dispute); (2) a *defense* (e.g., truth in defamation action; insanity in criminal case); or (3) *the existence or amount of damages* (e.g., reputation before and after alleged injury). FRE 405.
- **KNOWLEDGE OF CHARACTER** – If the use of character evidence is limited to proving that one person knew or should have known of the character of another (P), e.g., *negligent entrustment, self-defense*), all appropriate forms are admissible. If used to test the knowledge and qualifications of a reputation witness regarding P, questions may be asked of witness on cross-examination as to whether he "had heard" of specific acts of P which would bear on reputation – questions must be asked in good faith; acts may not be too remote to affect P's present reputation; court may exclude if P is a party and the question is more prejudicial than probative.

4. CHARACTER EVIDENCE *(continued)*

(3) EXCEPTIONS – In the following specific situations character evidence may be used to prove conduct because of special considerations which make the evidence more probative than prejudicial.

- **CHARACTER OF ACCUSED (MERCY RULE)** – An accused may offer either good reputation or personal opinion (but *not* specific acts) which tends to prove her innocence in a criminal case. If accused does offer good character evidence, prosecutor may rebut by evidence of bad character (but only in the form of reputation or opinion). FRE 404(a)(1). Common law only permits reputation.
- **VICTIM'S CHARACTER OFFERED BY ACCUSED** – Except in rape cases, an accused may offer evidence of the character of an alleged victim in a criminal case in the form of reputation, opinion or by specific relevant instances of conduct elicited on cross-examination. If accused does offer, prosecutor may rebut. FRE 404(a)(2). In rape cases, reputation or opinion evidence of the victim's past sexual behavior is *not* admissible but evidence of past sexual behavior (i.e., specific acts) may be offered if: (1) acts with person other than accused tend to prove that accused was not the source of semen or injury, *or* (2) past acts with accused tend to show consent. In both cases, accused must make a written motion and offer of proof and court shall conduct an in-chambers hearing to decide whether and to what extent the past sexual behavior will be admitted. FRE 412.
- **STRONG CIRCUMSTANTIAL EVIDENCE: OTHER ACTS** – In a criminal or civil action, any party may prove that a person did a specific act of a particular occasion by character evidence in the form of specific acts if such evidence establishes: (1) *motive*, (2) *opportunity*, (3) *knowledge or intent* (including absence of mistake or accident), (4) *preparation or plan*, or (5) *identity* (as with *modus operandi*). FRE 404(b). Evidence is *not* dependent on "mere disposition" as it closely and specifically links the person to the act in question.
- **HABIT** – Evidence of a person's habit (i.e., invariable automatic pattern of behavior) may be used to prove conduct in conformity to the habit. FRE 406. No need for corroboration. Considered highly probative of conduct (also applies to routine practice of an organization). FRE 406.
- **WITNESS' CHARACTER RE: CREDIBILITY** – Character evidence may be used to impeach or rehabilitate the testimony of a witness. Admissibility depends on form and whether evidence conforms with impeachment rules (e.g., collateral matter rule).
  - **REPUTATION FOR TRUTH AND VERACITY** – Proper to impeach or rehabilitate if witness qualified? no special foundation required.
  - **PERSONAL OPINION** – Permitted if witness qualified; no special foundation. FRE 608(a). Common law does *not* permit.
  - **OTHER ACTS**
    - **FELONY CONVICTIONS** – Name and fact of conviction of any felony permitted even if underlying crime does *not* involve dishonesty or false statement. May be elicited on cross-exam *or* proved extrinsically, no special foundation. FRE 609.
    - **MISDEMEANOR CONVICTIONS** – Name and fact of conviction permitted but only if underlying crime involves dishonesty or false statement. May be elicited on cross-exam *or* proved extrinsically, no special foundation. FRE 609. Minority (e.g., California) do not permit at all.
    - **UNCONVICTED CONDUCT** – Witness may be impeached by direct evidence of specific acts by the witness (*not* arrests, indictments, etc.) which bear on truthfulness or honesty, *may be elicited on cross-exam asking if the witness actually did the act, no extrinsic evidence permitted if witness denies act.* FRE 609. Minority (e.g., California) do not permit use of unconvicted conduct.
    - **REVERSED AND UNCONSTITUTIONAL CONVICTIONS** – May not be used but if appeal is still pending, use permitted.
    - **JUVENILE CONVICTIONS** – May only be used to impeach a prosecution witness in a criminal case, not the defendant or a defense witness.
    - **DISCRETION** – Court may always exclude impeaching evidence if it is deemed more prejudicial than probative. If a party is the witness (especially a criminal accused), court will carefully examine the probative value of convictions and other acts to determine relevancy (i.e., does act relate closely enough to truthfulness or honesty, is it too remote?). Convictions over 10 years old must be specifically examined for probative value. FRE 609(b).

5. MINIMAL RELIABILITY

TESTIMONIAL COMPETENCE

OATH OF AFFIRMATION – Witness must declare that he will testify truthfully, by oath or affirmation administered in a form calculated to awaken his conscience and impress his mind with the obligation to do so. FRE 603. At common law, witness must also demonstrate that he understands the obligation to tell the truth.

PERSONAL KNOWLEDGE – A witness may not testify to a matter unless evidence is introduced sufficient to support a finding that he has personal knowledge of the matter. FRE 602.

MENTAL CAPACITY – FRE 601 abandons all common law requirements relating to capacity to perceive and tell the truth. Thus, no witness is incompetent to testify by virtue of age, mental illness (including illness directly related to knowing and telling the truth), use of drugs or alcohol (even if shortly before testifying) or any other fact – all such facts may be used to impeach the witness and go to weight rather than admissibility. Common law is contra requiring, on objection, a special judicial finding that the witness has the capacity to accurately observe, remember, and recount the facts.

FINANCIAL INTEREST IN OUTCOME: DEAD MAN'S RULE – The FRE abandons the common law dead man's rule which disqualifies witnesses who have a financial interest in the outcome of a civil suit (applicable where the opposing party is incapable of testifying because of death or mental incompetency). Many major states (e.g., New York, Florida) still retain such statutes, which differ substantially in specific provisions.

SPECIAL STATUS

- **JUDGE AS A WITNESS** – A judge may not testify in any trial in which he is presiding. FRE 605.
- **JUROR AS A WITNESS** – A member of the jury may not testify as a witness in a case in which she is sitting as a juror. FRE 606(a). A juror is also incompetent to testify as to any matter or statement occurring during the course of the jury's deliberations, nor may she testify as to any matter which influences her vote or any other juror's vote even upon an inquiry into the validity of an indictment or verdict. **Exception:** May testify re: *extraneous prejudicial information* brought to jury's attention or whether there was an *improper outside influence.* FRE 606(b).
- **ATTORNEY AS A WITNESS** – Although there are major ethical restrictions regarding the testimony of an attorney, her partner or associate in any case in which she is representing a client, an attorney is *not* incompetent under the evidence rules.

BEST EVIDENCE RULE (BER): EXCLUSION OF SECONDARY EVIDENCE

In **(1)** *proving the contents of a writing*, **(2)** the *original* writing itself **(3)** must be *produced* **(4)** or shown to be *unavailable* **(5)** *by the proponent* of the secondary evidence **(6)** unless the writing refers to a *collateral issue*.

(continued)

5. MINIMAL RELIABILITY *(continued)*

(1) PROVING CONTENTS OF WRITING – BER only applies when the evidence offered is intended to prove what the writing says; not applicable if evidence merely seeks to establish there was a writing or if the actual precise content of the writing is irrelevant to its evidentiary value.

CONTENTS IN ISSUE

- **Category 1: Writing Has Independent Legal Significance** – Rights or obligations at issue arise from, and are directly affected by, the precise content of the writing. **Examples:** Actions based on a *will, written contract, lease;* liability affected by specific *written notice or disclaimer; defamatory writing, manuscripts and books* in copyright actions; recordings of *defamatory statements or extortionate threats* where action is based on precise words; *photos or motion pictures* in pornography action.
- **Category 2: Writing Offered as Evidence** – Party puts contents of writing in issue by offering it in evidence even if writing is not of independent legal significance. **Examples:** *Receipt* to prove payment; *transcripts* or *minutes* to prove what was said at prior hearing or meeting; *letters, memos, notes* to prove knowledge, intent, motive or attitude of author or recipient; *x-ray* to prove injury. (**Note:** Writing must also be authenticated and avoid hearsay rule).
- **Category 3: Testimony Reliant on Writing** – Witness puts contents of writing in issue if his testimony is derived from what he saw in a writing, rather than from personal knowledge of the facts evidenced by the writing (i.e., witness is merely a conduit for the writing itself). **Examples:** testimony based upon a letter, x-ray, tape recording, transcript, receipt, bank or business records. (**Note:** Underlying writing is usually hearsay.)

WRITING DEFINED – Includes all forms of tangible writings, sound and electronic recordings of all forms, and photographs of all sorts including pictures, prints, x-rays, video tapes, and motion pictures. FRE 1001(1)(2).

(2) ORIGINAL – Includes (1) the writing, recording, or photograph itself; (2) any "counterpart" of the original intended to have the same effect as the original (e.g., multiple copies of a contract); (3) any "duplicate original" produced by the same impression as the original (e.g., carbon copies), or from the same plate or matrix (e.g., printed or mimeographed copies), or by photographic process (includes photocopies, enlargements and miniatures). FRE 1001(3)(4). Duplicates are treated as original unless there is a *genuine question of authenticity*, or under the circumstances, the court believes it would be *unfair* not to require the original itself. FRE 1003. Common law does *not* treat photocopies as originals unless they were made in the ordinary course of business as a business record.

(continued)

5. MINIMAL RELIABILITY *(continued)*

(3) PRODUCED – Original need not be actually offered in evidence so long as it is produced for examination and inspection. **Example:** memo qualifying for past recollection recorded may be read into evidence, but writing itself cannot be introduced; same for portions of learned treatises used to cross-examine an expert.

(4) UNAVAILABILITY – The BER is only a rule of preference; if the original is not available, secondary evidence may be used.

- **LOST OR DESTROYED** – Sufficient if all originals are lost or destroyed, so long as unavailability does not result from bad faith conduct of proponent. FRE (1004(1).
- **UNOBTAINABLE** – Cannot be obtained by any available judicial process or procedure. FRE 1004(2).
- **POSSESSION OF OPPONENT** – Party now objecting was put on notice that the contents of a writing would be in issue at the time he had possession of the original of the writing and said party does not produce the original. FRE 1004(3).
- **IMPRACTICALITY** – If contents of *voluminous writings* cannot conveniently be examined in court, a chart, summary, or calculation may be presented so long as originals were reasonably made available for inspection and copying. FRE 1006. Also, certified copies of *public records* are admissible because original is "unavailable." FRE 1005.

(5) BURDEN ON PROPONENT – Foundational facts relating to admissibility of secondary evidence (e.g., unavailability) are to be decided by the judge. However, if there is a dispute as to (1) whether the asserted writing ever existed at all; (2) which of several writings is in fact the original; or (3) whether the secondary evidence correctly reflects the contents of the original; the issue is for the jury to decide. FRE 1008. If original is unavailable, any form of secondary evidence is admissible; there is no hierarchy of secondary evidence. Some states prefer written copies to oral testimony.

(6) COLLATERAL ISSUE EXCEPTION – BER does not apply where the writing is not closely related to a controlling issue (i.e., *de minimus* exception). FRE 1004(4).

6. OPINIONS

NON-EXPERT

- **PERSONAL PERCEPTION** – knowledge required by opinion must be *rationally derived* from *personal perception*.
  - **Adequate Opportunity to Perceive** – perception must be *sufficient in time and scope* to justify conclusion (look out for split second judgments and perception – impeding facts).
  - **Exceptions** – personal knowledge *not* required for (1) opinions of sanity by a *subscribing witness* or (2) opinions about oneself including property, condition mental state, etc. (see below).
  - **Opinions About Oneself** – relating to one's own *mental state* (including intent, motive, emotion), *physical or mental condition* (including nature and cause of condition, disease or illness), *personal history* (including name, age, parentage), *property* (including ownership and value), and *value of services*.
- **SPECIAL NEED** – opinion must be *necessary to effective communication* of the perception or especially *helpful to a clear understanding of the facts*.
  - **Sensory Descriptions** – *odors and sounds* and their sources, *colors, temperature, taste*.
  - **Measurements** – *speed, weight, height, distances* in general (e.g., "fast," "heavy," "tall," "far,") or specific terms (e.g., mph, pounds, feet and inches).
  - **Identifications** – of *property* or *persons* including distinguishing characteristics such as voice, footsteps, age.
  - **Physical Condition of Others** – general perceptions of *injury, fatigue, intoxication*.
  - **Mental Condition of Others** – rationality, normality, competency and sanity, but stronger foundation of knowledge is required and opinion must avoid legal conclusion.
  - **Meaning of Conduct** – "nodding" affirmatively, "indicating" agreement, who "started" or "provoked" a fight. Broad discretion to *exclude* opinions of this type.
- **RANGE OF COMMON EXPERIENCE** – opinion must be about a *matter* within common experience and within the *scope and range* of common experience. Look out for conclusions re: extreme or refined observations (e.g., 100 mph, 500 yards, 10 tons, explicit diagnoses). If opinion is beyond scope of common experience, must qualify as an expert opinion.

(continued)

6. OPINIONS *(continued)*

EXPERT

- **BEYOND COMMON EXPERIENCE** – opinion must relate to matter that is *sufficiently beyond common experience* so that the opinion of an expert would *assist the trier of fact*. This is especially important when the expert does not have personal knowledge.
- **QUALIFIED AS AN EXPERT** – proponent of expert must persuade the judge that person has special knowledge, skill, experience, training, *or* education to qualify him/her as an expert on the subject to which the opinion relates. Court has broad discretion in this area and each opinion must be measured against the particular qualifications of the witness and the state of the art of the field to which the opinion relates.
- **BASIS OF OPINION** – expert opinion may be based on any proper matter including materials not in evidence, and assumed facts.
  - **Proper Matter** – may be based on matters which are not in evidence and which are themselves inadmissible *if* of a type reasonably relied on by experts in the field involved.
    - **If Based on Statement of Another** – declarant of statement or opinion providing basis of expert opinion may be called by adverse party and examined as if on cross-X.
    - **If Based on Improper Matter** – court must exclude opinion.
  - **Assumed Facts** – may be hypothetical in nature and based on explicitly designated "assumed facts" which have been or will be supported by sufficient admissible evidence to sustain a finding of their existence.
  - **Basis of Opinion** – expert may but, unless otherwise required by the court, need not state the reasons for the opinion on direct exam. Such reasons may be elicited on cross exam.
- **CROSS EXAMINATION OF EXPERT** – expert may be examined as to (1) qualifications as an expert, (2) subject to which opinion relates, (3) matter and reasons upon which opinion is based, and (4) compensation and any other facts bearing on possible bias.
  - **Federal Rule** – FRE 803(18) provides that expert may be examined re: statements contained in *published* treatises, periodicals, or pamphlets if shown to be *reliable authority* by admission of the witness, other expert testimony or judicial notice. Statements so used are also admissible substantively as an exception to the hearsay rule.
  - **Common Law Rule** – expert may *not* be examined in regard to the content or tenor of a published work *unless* (1) the witness referred to, considered or relied upon such publication in arriving at or forming his opinion, (2) the witness wrote the publication, or (3) the publication, has been separately admitted in evidence. If use of statements in a publication are permitted under (1), such statements are *not* admissible as substantive evidence.

7. COMMUNICATIONS PRIVILEGES

ISSUE SPOTTING SEQUENCE: (1) *Is there a protected relationship:?* (2) *Was there a communication?* (3) *Was it confidential?* (4) *Has the holder asserted the privilege?* (5) *Was there a waiver?* (6) *Do any exceptions apply?*

(1) RELATIONSHIP — privileges are designed to foster socially important relationships which require mutual trust and confidence; must normally be specified by statute, though FRE applies "common law" to federal cases and state law where state law controls controversy.

- **INTENT OF COMMUNICATION** – existence of "relationship" determined by the subjective intent of the communicator to derive benefits of protected relationship.
  - **Client** – must seek professional advice or consultation; no prior relationship, actual or anticipated compensation, or actual acceptance of case is required. Corporation is a client if communication is made by an officer or director (i.e., "control group"), *or* by an employee at the direction of a superior.
  - **Patient** – must seek diagnosis or treatment; no prior relationship, compensation, or actual treatment required.
  - **Penitent** – one who communicates to a clergyperson in accordance with the rules or practice of a religious denomination.
- **ACTUAL STATUS OF CONFIDANT** – parties must actually be capable of entering privileged relationship; if there is a mistake as to the capacity of a confidant, no privilege (modern view is contra if belief was reasonable).
  - **Attorney** – must be *licensed to practice law in any state or nation; not* disbarred lawyers and unlicensed law graduates.
  - **Physician** – must be *licensed medical practitioner* (M.D. or equivalent) *in any state or nation*.
  - **Psychotherapist** – if not an M.D. (*psychiatrists* are M.D.'s) must be licensed under authority of state; some states include marriage counselors, clinical social workers, and psychologists.
  - **Spouse** – must be legally married.
  - **Clergy** – person must be authorized under rules of the religion to hear confessions.

(2) COMMUNICATION – under common law, only *verbal* communications may be privileged; observations and impressions resulting from confidential protected relationships are *not* protected.

- **BOTH WAYS** – all confidential communications are protected regardless of which party makes them (e.g., attorney's to client/client's to attorney).
- **GENERATED DURING AND FOR THE RELATIONSHIP** – statements, records, and other documents *preexisting* the relationship as well as communications made *incidental* to the relationship are *not* protected even if later transmitted to privileged person, though the "information" may not be elicited from the privileged professional.
- **MODERN TREND** – observations made by a spouse (especially in context of the "marital home") and observations of a medical doctor during physical examination may be protected *if the holder appeared to rely on the sanctity of relationship to permit the observation*.

(continued)

7. COMMUNICATION PRIVILEGES *(continued)*

(3) CONFIDENTIALITY – communication must be the unique product of the confidential relationship made under circumstances safeguarding the confidentiality; presence of an *inessential* or a *non-privileged third person* prevents privilege. Confidentiality is presumed; proponent must show no confidentiality.

- **INESSENTIAL THIRD PERSONS** – person is "inessential" unless presence advances the purposes of the relationship (stenographers, researchers, investigators, interpreters, and experts needed by a lawyer are essential.)
- **NON-PRIVILEGED PERSON** – disclosure in the presence of an inessential person does not defeat the privilege if that person is separately privileged (e.g., a spouse).
- **PROTECTS COMMUNICATION, NOT INFORMATION** – even if holder has disclosed the same information in non-privileged contexts, the specific "communication" of that information made in a privileged relationship *is* protected (e.g., lawyer may not be required to testify even if any other person could be).
- **EAVESDROPPERS** – at common law, eavesdroppers may testify (modern view is *contra*) but the communication is still privileged with respect to those in the protected relationship.

(4) HOLDER – the "holder" controls the privilege; it must be asserted (or waived) by him or on his behalf.

- **ATTORNEY-CLIENT** – client is holder; after death, passes to personal representative.
- **PHYSICIAN OR PSYCHOTHERAPIST-PATIENT** – patient is holder; after death, passes to personal representative.
- **HUSBAND-WIFE** – both parties are holders (even after marriage is dissolved).
- **CLERGY-PENITENT** – usually both are holders.
- **JUDGE MAY ASSERT** – in the absence of a holder or authorized representative, the court may, on its own motion, assert privilege.

(5) WAIVER – privilege is waived if holder (1) *voluntarily reveals a significant part of the communication*, or (2) *fails to object to disclosure when he had an opportunity and right to do so.*

(6) EXCEPTIONS – for public policy reasons, privileges may not be asserted in certain situations, especially where the lawsuit is between the parties to the privileged relationship or to joint holders of the same privilege.

- **ATTORNEY-CLIENT** – privilege not applicable (1) in suit between attorney and client, (2) in suit between joint clients, (3) where communication was designed to advance a crime or fraud, or (4) if the communication relates to the intent of a now deceased client with respect to the disposition of property.
- **PHYSICIAN OR PSYCHOTHERAPIST-PATIENT** – privilege not applicable (1) in suit between doctor and patient, (2) patient has put his mental or physical condition in issue, (3) doctor appointed by court, or (4) in criminal cases (minority view – e.g., California).
- **HUSBAND-WIFE** – not applicable (1) in suit between holders, or (2) in criminal case based on assault of spouse or child.
- **CLERGY-PENITENT** – no exceptions; applicable in all actions.

8. APPROACH TO HEARSAY

ISSUE SPOTTING SEQUENCE: *(1) Is there an assertion? (2) Was it made out of court? (3) Who is the declarant? (4) What is asserted?*

(1) ASSERTION

- **VERBAL COMMUNICATION** – includes all written and oral assertions, including tape recordings.
- **NON-VERBAL COMMUNICATION**
  - **ASSERTIVE CONDUCT** – gesture or act done with the *primary intent* to assert or communicate information or opinion (e.g., lineup I.D., "o.k." sign); usually in response to a question.
  - **NON-ASSERTIVE CONDUCT** – under some theories of hearsay (*not* the FRE), conduct is treated as an assertion if the act is used as *circumstantial evidence of the belief of the actor* in order to *prove the truth of the belief* – the conduct is used as an implied assertion of belief (e.g., the fact that a ship captain took his family aboard a ship used to prove the ship was seaworthy).

(2) OUT-OF-COURT – any assertion not made at the present hearing, *including* assertions made in other courts, assertions made under oath, and all writings.

(3) DECLARANT – person who made the out-of-court assertion; the source of the information (identification of the declarant is critical to analysis of the "assertion" and the substantive assertion contained therein).

(4) ASSERTION – isolate the statement made by the declarant (as opposed to the "testimony" of the witness reporting the statement) to determine precisely what is being asserted. **Note:** If there are two or more out-of-court statements (e.g., a written report of an oral statement), analyze each assertion separately.

8. APPROACH TO HEARSAY *(continued)*

ISSUE SPOTTING SEQUENCE: *(5) Is the assertion relevant for a non-hearsay use (i.e., a use not dependent on the statement's truth)? (6) If used to prove its truth, is the assertion specifically exempted from the hearsay rule? (7) If neither an exclusion nor an exemption apply, does the assertion qualify for a hearsay exception?*

(5) RELEVANT NON-HEARSAY USE (HEARSAY EXCLUSIONS) – under the definition of hearsay, an out-of-court assertion is hearsay only if it is offered to prove its truth. If the evidentiary value of a statement is not dependent on the accuracy of the assertion contained therein, the reliability of the declarant is not critical, and the need for cross-examination is removed. Out-of-court assertions relevant irrespective of their truth are non-hearsay (i.e., they are *excluded* from the hearsay rule).

- **STATE OF MIND** – fact that statement was made tends to prove a *relevant state of mind of the declarant or listener irrespective of the truth of the assertion (normally, used to prove knowledge, intent, attitude, or belief of a party).*
- **IMPEACHMENT OR REHABILITATION** – prior statement of a witness used to impeach or rehabilitate (prior statement need not be true to show inconsistency nor to rebut charge of recent fabrication). **Note:** FRE permits sworn statements made at a hearing or deposition to be used as substantive evidence.
- **VERBAL EVENT** – statement which has probative significance totally independent of any communicative content: (1) *transactional words* (e.g., contract or a will, operative words of a legal notice, demand, or donative intent, (2) *tortious words* of defamation, and (3) *questions or commands*, etc.

(6) STATUTORY EXEMPTIONS – FRE 801(d) specifically *exempts* from the hearsay definition certain kinds of out-of-court statements *even though they are offered to prove their truth* and otherwise meet the hearsay definition.

- **ADMISSIONS (see Hearsay Exception Flowchart 10)** – though treated as non-hearsay under the FRE, the nature and scope of "admissions" are analyzed in the more traditional context of hearsay *exceptions*. FRE 801(d)(2).
- **PRIOR IDENTIFICATIONS** – *if declarant testifies in court* with respect to identification of a person, any prior statement identifying the person made after perceiving him is non-hearsay. FRE 801(d)(1)(c).
- **PRIOR CONSISTENT STATEMENTS** – *if declarant testifies* and has been *impeached by a claim of recent fabrication or undue influence*, any statement made prior to the alleged time of fabrication or undue influence is non-hearsay. FRE 801(d)(1)(B).
- **PRIOR SWORN INCONSISTENT STATEMENTS** – *if declarant testifies*, any prior *sworn* statement (subject to penalty of perjury) is non-hearsay if given at trial, hearing, or deposition. FRE 801(d)(1)(A).

(7) ADMISSIBLE HEARSAY (EXCEPTIONS) – if an out-of-court assertion *is* offered to prove its truth and it is not exempted by the FRE, it is hearsay. Much hearsay, however, is admitted because of considerations of trustworthiness, necessity, and fairness. The scope and form of admissible hearsay is embodied in the 30 or so *hearsay exceptions* enumerated in FRE 803 and 804. The most important exceptions are analyzed in Flowchart 10.

9. HEARSAY EXCEPTIONS AND EXEMPTIONS

Admissions

DIRECT ADMISSION – (1) statement of a party (2) offered against that party.

ADOPTIVE – (1) statement made in party's presence (2) party's conduct or silence manifests adoption of truth (3) offered against that party.

AUTHORIZED – (1) declarant authorized by party (2) to speak concerning the subject (3) offered against the authorizing party.

EMPLOYEE/AGENT (FRE, not Common Law) – (1) statement by a party's employee or agent (2) made during the relationship (3) concerning a matter within the scope of employment (4) offered against the party.

CO-CONSPIRATOR – (1) statement by a co-conspirator of party (2) made in furtherance of the conspiratorial goal (3) offered against the party (4) if independent evidence of conspiracy (5) sufficient to persuade judge (common law contra-prima facie case sufficient).

Declaration Against Interest
- (1) unavailable declarant (includes death, incompetency, beyond jurisdiction, assertion of privilege)
- (2) against financial or penal interest (common law – financial only)
- (3) against interest when made
- (4) reasonable person would not make it unless true

Dying Declaration
- (1) unavailable declarant (common law – declarant must be dead)
- (2) belief that death was imminent
- (3) relates to cause or circumstances of threatened death
- (4) personal knowledge, not opinion or speculation
- (5) offered in civil or criminal homicide case (common law – homicide only)

Official Written Statement
- (1) written statement (including electronic data)
- (2) by public official
- (3) setting forth (a) activities of public office, or (b) observations made or recorded in course of legal duties (*not* police report in criminal case), or (c) factual findings of official investigation (*not* against D in criminal case) unless circumstances indicate lack of trustworthiness.

Past Recollection Recorded
- (1) memo or record of facts
- (2) personal knowledge of declarant or reliable source
- (3) made when facts were fresh
- (4) memory exhausted
- (5) declarant testifies it accurately reflects former knowledge
- (6) may be read into evidence only (unless adverse party offers)

Prior Testimony
- (1) testimony given under oath
- (2) previously given in former hearing or deposition
- (3) party (or predecessor in interest) *against* whom offered
- (4) had *opportunity* and *similar incentive* examine testimony (common law – parties and issues must be identical)
- (5) unavailable declarant (prosecutor has special heavy burden)

Sense Impression (FRE, not Common Law)
- (1) statement describing or explaining an event or condition
- (2) made while or immediately after declarant was perceiving it

(continued)

9. HEARSAY EXCEPTIONS AND EXEMPTIONS *(continued)*

EXCITED UTTERANCE
- (1) startling event
- (2) made under stress of excitement (common law – statement must be spontaneous, and made during or immediately after event)
- (3) relating to event

MENTAL STATE

PRESENT MENTAL STATE – explicit statement of mental state may prove existence of the mental state or conduct of declarant consistent with intent (some courts allow to prove conduct of a third person)

FORMER MENTAL STATE – explicit statement of past belief or remembrance may prove facts re declarant's will, but not otherwise.

PHYSICAL STATE

PRESENT PHYSICAL STATE – description of present sensation or condition may prove existence of condition (need not be made to a doctor).

FORMER PHYSICAL STATE (FRE, not Common Law) – (1) statement or description of (a) medical history, or (b) past symptom or sensation, or (c) character or nature of external cause (2) *if made for* diagnosis or treatment (3) and *if pertinent* to diagnosis or treatment.

BUSINESS RECORD
- (1) written statement (including electronic data)
- (2) made in regular course of business
- (3) near time of receipt of information
- (4) declarant has personal knowledge or source reliable
- (5) unless circumstances indicate lack of trustworthiness

EXPERT CROSS-EXAMINATION (FRE, not Common Law)
- (1) during examination of expert
- (2) statements in treatises, periodicals or pamphlets
- (3) established as reliable authority by (a) testimony, (b) admission of witness, or (c) judicial notice
- (4) may be read into evidence (not admissible as exhibit)

EQUIVALENCY (FRE, not Common Law)
- (1) circumstantial guarantees of trustworthiness equivalent to other exceptions
- (2) evidence of a material fact
- (3) more probative than other reasonably available evidence
- (4) interests of justice will be served
- (5) timely notice to adverse party providing fair opportunity to response (including particulars of statement, name and address of declarant)

IDENTIFICATION (FRE, not Common Law)
- (1) prior statement of a witness-declarant
- (2) identifying a person
- (3) made after perceiving that person

CONSISTENT STATEMENT (FRE, not Common Law)
- (1) prior statement of a witness-declarant
- (2) consistent with testimony
- (3) offered to rebut charge of recent fabrication or improper influence or motive

INCONSISTENT STATEMENT (FRE, not Common Law)
- (1) prior statement of a witness
- (2) inconsistent with testimony
- (3) given subject to penalty of perjury
- (4) at a deposition, trial, or other proceeding

ADDEM P. BOPP, SEE ICI

10. THE BIG 10 EXCEPTIONS

A-Admission **D**-Declaration v. Interest **D**-Dying Declaration **E**-Excited Utterance **M**-Mental State **P**-Physical State **B**-Business Record
O-Official Records **P**-Past Recollection Recorded **P**-Prior Recorded Testimony

A-ADMISSION – Rationale: gamesmanship and fairness – a party should not be permitted to exclude his own statements because of inability to cross-examine. Treated as non-hearsay *exemption* under FRE; a hearsay *exception* under common law.

- **STATEMENTS OF PARTY-OPPONENT** – (1) statement *made by a party* to a lawsuit (2) *offered against him* by his opponent. Personal knowledge of declarant *not* required; need *not* be against interest when made; includes pleas of guilty (unless withdrawn); but not convictions. FRE 801(d)(2)(A).
- **STATEMENT ADOPTED BY PARTY-OPPONENT (TACIT ADMISSION)** – (1) statement *of another* (2) *made to or in the presence of a party* (3) who by *conduct or silence manifests an unequivocal adoption or belief in* the truth of the statement, and (4) *offered against the party* by his opponent. FRE 801(d)(2)()B).
  - **Must Hear and Be Able To Deny** – party must have heard or read statement, and he must have been reasonably capable of denying truth of assertion.
  - **Reasonable To Expect Denial** – circumstances must have been such that a reasonable person would have denied the assertion if it were not true; remember right to silence in custodial situations.
- **STATEMENT OF ANOTHER ATTRIBUTED TO PARTY-OPPONENT (VICARIOUS ADMISSION)** – (1) statement made *by another* (2) *attributed to a party* and (3) *offered against the party* by his opponent.
  - **Authorized Statements** – (1) a statement made by a person explicitly or implicitly *authorized by a party* (2) to *speak on the party's behalf* (3) *offered against the party* by his opponent. Authority to *speak* is *not* necessarily co-extensive with authority to act. FRE 801(d)(2)(C).
  - **Employee Statements** – (1) a statement *made by a party's employee or agent* (2) *concerning a matter within the scope of his agency or employment* (3) *made during the course of the relationship* (4) *offered against the party* by his opponent. No authority to speak is required; common law has no similar provision. FRE 801(d)(2)(D).
  - **Statement of Co-Conspirator** – (1) a statement *made by a party's co-conspirator* (2) *during the conspiracy* and (3) *in furtherance of the conspiratorial goal* (4) *offered against the party* by the prosecutor (5) if the *underlying conspiracy can be established by independent evidence sufficient to persuade the judge* (by preponderance) that conspiracy exists. FRE 801(d)(2)(E). Common law only requires *prima facie case* prior to admission, not preponderance.
  - **Statement of Predecessor in Interest** – (1) statement made *by a previous owner of property* (2) *during ownership* (3) *offered against the owner-party* by his opponent. Common law, *not* FRE.
  - **Statement of Decedent in a Wrongful Death Action** – (1) statements made by *the decedent in a wrongful death action* (2) *offered against the party who brings the action.* Common law, *not* FRE.

(continued)

10. THE BIG 10 EXCEPTIONS *(continued)*

D-DECLARATION AGAINST INTEREST – (1) statement by an *unavailable declarant* (2) so far *against financial or penal interests* (3) *when made* (4) that a *reasonable person would not have made it unless he believed it to be true.* FRE 804(b)(3). **Rationale:** unavailability indicates necessity, against interest assures trustworthiness. If statement is against penal interest and is offered to exculpate D, "corroborating circumstances must clearly indicate trustworthiness." Common law limits statements to those against financial interest; a small minority admit statements against social interest as well.

D-DYING DECLARATION – (1) statement by an *unavailable declarant* (2) made while the *declarant believed his death was imminent* (3) concerning the *cause or circumstances* of what he believed to be his impending death which is (4) offered in a *homicide prosecution or any civil case.* FRE 804 (b)(2). **Rationale:** declarant would not want to die with a lie on his lips.

- **INADMISSIBLE IN CRIMINAL CASES OTHER THAN HOMICIDE** – common law *only* admits in criminal homicide cases; FRE extends to civil cases, but not other types of criminal cases.
- **DECLARANT NEED NOT BE DEAD** – (common law is contra).
- **PERSONAL KNOWLEDGE** – statement must relate personal observations not opinion or speculation.

E-EXCITED UTTERANCE – (1) statement *relating to* a (2) *startling event* or condition (3) made while the declarant was *under the stress.* FRE 803(2). **Rationale:** excitement and stress preclude fabrication.

- **SPONTANEITY NOT REQUIRED** – under strict common law rule, statement must be "spontaneous" (the intervention of a question such as "What happened?" can defeat exception, and creates opportunity for fabrication), not so in FRE.
- **TIMING OF STATEMENT** – under common law, statement must be made "during or immediately after the exciting event." Under FRE, substantial time may pass so long as declarant is still under original stress of the event.
- **DECLARANT** – need not be known or identified; availability is of no consequence.

M-MENTAL STATE – statements which purport to *directly and explicitly* state or describe declarant's mental or emotional condition. FRE 803(3). Distinguish from statements which are merely *circumstantial evidence* of the declarant's state of mind (i.e., hearsay exclusions).

- **PRESENT MENTAL STATE** – *statement purporting to reveal any presently held intent, belief, attitude, emotion, or feeling is admissible to prove the true existence of that mental state.* Some states allow statement to prove conduct of person other than declarant, but FRE comment urges contrary construction. **Rationale:** no memory or perception problems.
- **FORMER MENTAL STATE** – *statement of memory or belief is not admissible to prove the fact remembered or believed unless it relates to relevant facts concerning the declarant's will.* **Rationale:** expediency and necessity.

P-PHYSICAL STATE – statements which purport to state or describe declarant's physical sensations or condition.

- **PRESENT PHYSICAL STATE** – *statement purporting to describe any present physical sensation or condition is admissible to prove the existence of that physical state.* Includes statements of present pain made to any person. FRE 803(3). **Rationale:** no memory or perception problems: tends to be necessary.
- **FORMER PHYSICAL STATE** – (1) statement purporting to describe a medical history including *past pain, symptom or sensation, or the inception or general character of the external source* of the physical condition is admissible if: (2)*it was made for purposes of medical diagnosis or treatment,* and (3) it is *reasonably pertinent to the diagnosis or treatment.* FRE 803(4). **Rationale:** no perception problems, desire for effective diagnosis or treatment tends to guarantee sincerity and trustworthiness.

10. THE BIG 10 EXCEPTIONS *(continued)*

B-BUSINESS RECORD – (1) *written statement* (2) made in *the regular course of business* (3) *at or near the time of receipt of the information* (4) by a *person with knowledge* (5) unless the source of the information or circumstances of preparation indicate *lack of trustworthiness.* FRE 803(6). **Rationale:** memory problems are avoided by requirement of timely recording and trustworthiness is assured by systematic checking, continuity and business reliance on the statements.

- **FOUNDATION** – foundation may be established by the custodian of the record or any person who can identify the record and testify as to mode of preparation; the declarant need not testify.
- **DATA COMPILATION** – business records may be in the form of electric data storage tapes and the like.
- **OPINIONS OR DIAGNOSIS** – statement may contain an *opinion or diagnosis.* Common law is generally contra.
- **KNOWLEDGE** – declarant must have personal knowledge or information recorded *or* the record must be made from information transmitted by one with knowledge.
- **BUSINESS** – "business" includes any institution (including the government), association, profession or occupation.
- **REGULAR COURSE OF BUSINESS** – many cases exclude records made for purposes of litigation (even if made by an investigator in the regular course of his duties); FRE has no absolute rule, but authorizes the court to exclude records where there is a manifest lack of trustworthiness.
- **ABSENCE OF ENTRY** – (1) evidence that a matter is *not* included in a business record is (2) *admissible to prove the non-occurrence or non-existence of the matter if the matter was of a kind that was regularly reported* unless the sources of information or other circumstances indicate a *lack of trustworthiness.* FRE 803(7).
- **COMMERCIAL PUBLICATIONS** – (1) statement contained in *market quotations, tabulations, lists, directories, or other published compilations* (2) generally used and relied upon (3) by the public or persons in particular occupations. FRE 803(17).

(continued)

10. THE BIG 10 EXCEPTIONS *(continued)*

O-OFFICIAL WRITTEN STATEMENTS (Public Records) – Rationale: special trustworthiness is derived from fact that statement was made by or to a public employee with duty to accurately record and no apparent motive to falsify: necessity results from likelihood that declarant will have no independent memory of contents. "Record" includes reports, statements, or data compilations (including electronic data) in any form.

- **RECORD OF PUBLIC ACTIVITY** – (1) *written statement* (2) of a *public employee or agency* (3) *concerning the activities of the public office or agency*. FRE 803(8)(A).
- **RECORD OF OBSERVATION** – (1) *written statement* (2) of a *public employee or agency* (3) concerning observations made (4) while carrying out a *duty imposed by law* (5) *as to matters which there was a duty to report* (6) except that in criminal cases, records of observations made by law officers are not admissible. FRE 803(8)(B).
- **REPORT OF FINDINGS** – (1) *written statement* (2) of a *public officer or agency of factual findings or conclusions* (3) resulting from an *investigation or inquiry within the employee's or agency's legal duties* (4) unless the sources of information or other circumstances indicate a *lack of trustworthiness* (5) except that such reports are *not admissible against a criminal defendant.* FRE 803(8)(C).
- **ABSENCE OF RECORD OR ENTRY** – (1) *evidence that a matter is not included in a public record is* (2) *admissible to prove the non-occurrence or non-existence of a matter of which record is regularly made and preserved* (3) *if a certification is offered, or if testimony is produced to show that a diligent search failed to disclose the record or entry.* FRE 803(10).
- **RECORDS OF VITAL STATISTICS** – (1) *written statements* (2) *of births, fetal deaths, deaths or marriages* if (3) the *report* was made to a *public official* (4) *pursuant to requirements of law.* FRE 803(9).
- **CERTIFICATE OF MARRIAGE, BAPTISM AND SIMILAR** – (1) *written certificate* (2) issued by a *clergyman, public official or other person* (3) *authorized by law or the practices of a religion to perform a marriage or religious ceremony* (4) *indicating that such ceremony was performed* (5) *if the certificate was issued at the time of the act or within a reasonable time thereafter.* FRE 803(12).
- **RECORDS OF DOCUMENTS AFFECTING PROPERTY** – (1) *record of public office* (2) *relating to the existence, content, execution or delivery of a document* (3) which *affects an interest in property* (*not* just land) if (4) such record is *kept pursuant to statutory authority.* FRE 803(14). May prove content of document as well as fact of execution or delivery.

(continued)

10. THE BIG 10 EXCEPTIONS *(continued)*

P-PAST RECOLLECTION RECORDED – (1) statement contained in a *memorandum or record* (2) made by one with *personal knowledge* (3) recording facts perceived by him while the *matter was still fresh in the declarant's mind* provided that (4) the *declarant has first exhausted his present recollection*, (5) testified that he knows the *statement truly reflected his knowledge at the time* and (6) the statement *is read into evidence* only. FRE 803(5). **Rationale:** memory problems avoided by requirement of timely record, necessity results from exhausted memory and trustworthiness somewhat safeguarded by opportunity to cross-examine declarant.

- **DECLARANT MUST TESTIFY** – person who wrote memo must testify as a witness to lay necessary foundation re: exhausted present memory and accuracy of memo.
- **PRESENT MEMORY EXHAUSTED** – court must find that declarant-witness has insufficient recollection to enable full and accurate testimony on the fact(s) recorded.
- **NOT ADMISSIBLE AS EXHIBIT** – writing itself not admissible unless offered by the adverse party.
- **RELATED ISSUES** – distinguish from (1) present memory refreshed where memo actually jogs recollection and is not used as substantive evidence; (2) business record where memo made in ordinary course of business; (3) look out for multiple hearsay – look to reliability of the ultimate source of information.

P-PRIOR TESTIMONY – (1) statement made in the form of *testimony* (2) by an *unavailable person* (3) *given at another hearing or in a deposition* (4) if the *party against whom the testimony is now offered* (or his predecessor in interest) (5) had an *opportunity* and (6) *similar motive to develop the testimony* on direct or cross-examination. FRE 804(b)(1). **Rationale:** necessity is a result of unavailability and trustworthiness is supported by prior opportunity to develop and examine testimony.

- **TESTIMONY** – must be under oath or affirmation, but need not be recorded in verbatim transcript (even if it is, the transcript is not required).
- **UNAVAILABILITY** – in criminal cases, prosecutor must show every reasonable and diligent effort to produce declarant.
- **SIMILAR ISSUES** – issues need not be identical (common law was contra) and testimony may be given in unrelated proceeding if the *present opponent* was involved in suit and had opportunity and incentive to develop testimony.
- **SIMILAR PARTIES** – parties need not be identical (common law contra); person offering testimony need not have been involved in prior proceeding; in civil cases, party must accept testimony previously offered by or against predecessor in interest.

11. EXAMINATION OF WITNESSES

OBJECTIONS TO FORM

- **NARRATIVE** – Question too broad and general; testimony will be less rapid, distinct or effective than is reasonably possible and tends to include irrelevant and other inadmissible responses.
- **LEADING** – Question on *direct exam* suggests the desired response by its form, substance or tone. Leading questions *are allowed:* (1) on *cross-exam;* (2) as to *undisputed preliminary facts;* (3) in examining witnesses with *comprehensive problems;* (4) in examining *hostile witnesses on direct;* (5) in examining *experts;* (6) when used to *refresh recollection*.
- **ARGUMENTATIVE** – Question not asked for purpose of eliciting new information but for rhetorical or argumentative effect.
- **ASSUMING FACTS NOT IN EVIDENCE** – Question contains an assumption of a fact that is not supported by any evidence in the record (e.g., "Are you still beating your dog?").
- **COMPOUND** – Question embodies at least two separate aspects which make the answer unclear or ambiguous. Look for questions containing "or" as well as separate questions attached by "and" (e.g., "Did you see *or* hear him come home?" "Did you see *and* hear come home?").
- **AMBIGUOUS OR UNINTELLIGIBLE** – Question that is unclear as to meaning or that may not be easily understood by the witness or invites an answer that may not be easily understood in light of the question.
- **SPECULATION** – Question asks witness to speculate or conjecture (aspect of opinion testimony). Look out for "Is it possible" questions. Witness need not be certain but must be able to answer with a reasonable degree of conviction.
- **ASKED AND ANSWERED** – Question previously answered adequately resulting in unconstructive repetition and cumulative evidence – broad leeway allowed on cross-exam.
- **MISSTATES EVIDENCE** – Question contains preface which misstates, characterizes or misconstrues evidence or testimony.
- **OPPRESSIVE AND HARASSING** – Question or conduct which will cause witness undue embarrassment or emotional stress.
- **NON-RESPONSIVE** – Answer is not responsive to Question; either party may have answer stricken. Court has discretion to not strike unresponsive answers and volunteered testimony if it is otherwise relevant and admissible, and if elicited by a proper question.

pmbr

Constitutional Law

Practice Questions

Answer Grid

1 Ⓐ Ⓑ Ⓒ Ⓓ	21 Ⓐ Ⓑ Ⓒ Ⓓ	41 Ⓐ Ⓑ Ⓒ Ⓓ	61 Ⓐ Ⓑ Ⓒ Ⓓ	81 Ⓐ Ⓑ Ⓒ Ⓓ
2 Ⓐ Ⓑ Ⓒ Ⓓ	22 Ⓐ Ⓑ Ⓒ Ⓓ	42 Ⓐ Ⓑ Ⓒ Ⓓ	62 Ⓐ Ⓑ Ⓒ Ⓓ	82 Ⓐ Ⓑ Ⓒ Ⓓ
3 Ⓐ Ⓑ Ⓒ Ⓓ	23 Ⓐ Ⓑ Ⓒ Ⓓ	43 Ⓐ Ⓑ Ⓒ Ⓓ	63 Ⓐ Ⓑ Ⓒ Ⓓ	83 Ⓐ Ⓑ Ⓒ Ⓓ
4 Ⓐ Ⓑ Ⓒ Ⓓ	24 Ⓐ Ⓑ Ⓒ Ⓓ	44 Ⓐ Ⓑ Ⓒ Ⓓ	64 Ⓐ Ⓑ Ⓒ Ⓓ	84 Ⓐ Ⓑ Ⓒ Ⓓ
5 Ⓐ Ⓑ Ⓒ Ⓓ	25 Ⓐ Ⓑ Ⓒ Ⓓ	45 Ⓐ Ⓑ Ⓒ Ⓓ	65 Ⓐ Ⓑ Ⓒ Ⓓ	85 Ⓐ Ⓑ Ⓒ Ⓓ
6 Ⓐ Ⓑ Ⓒ Ⓓ	26 Ⓐ Ⓑ Ⓒ Ⓓ	46 Ⓐ Ⓑ Ⓒ Ⓓ	66 Ⓐ Ⓑ Ⓒ Ⓓ	86 Ⓐ Ⓑ Ⓒ Ⓓ
7 Ⓐ Ⓑ Ⓒ Ⓓ	27 Ⓐ Ⓑ Ⓒ Ⓓ	47 Ⓐ Ⓑ Ⓒ Ⓓ	67 Ⓐ Ⓑ Ⓒ Ⓓ	87 Ⓐ Ⓑ Ⓒ Ⓓ
8 Ⓐ Ⓑ Ⓒ Ⓓ	28 Ⓐ Ⓑ Ⓒ Ⓓ	48 Ⓐ Ⓑ Ⓒ Ⓓ	68 Ⓐ Ⓑ Ⓒ Ⓓ	88 Ⓐ Ⓑ Ⓒ Ⓓ
9 Ⓐ Ⓑ Ⓒ Ⓓ	29 Ⓐ Ⓑ Ⓒ Ⓓ	49 Ⓐ Ⓑ Ⓒ Ⓓ	69 Ⓐ Ⓑ Ⓒ Ⓓ	89 Ⓐ Ⓑ Ⓒ Ⓓ
10 Ⓐ Ⓑ Ⓒ Ⓓ	30 Ⓐ Ⓑ Ⓒ Ⓓ	50 Ⓐ Ⓑ Ⓒ Ⓓ	70 Ⓐ Ⓑ Ⓒ Ⓓ	90 Ⓐ Ⓑ Ⓒ Ⓓ
11 Ⓐ Ⓑ Ⓒ Ⓓ	31 Ⓐ Ⓑ Ⓒ Ⓓ	51 Ⓐ Ⓑ Ⓒ Ⓓ	71 Ⓐ Ⓑ Ⓒ Ⓓ	91 Ⓐ Ⓑ Ⓒ Ⓓ
12 Ⓐ Ⓑ Ⓒ Ⓓ	32 Ⓐ Ⓑ Ⓒ Ⓓ	52 Ⓐ Ⓑ Ⓒ Ⓓ	72 Ⓐ Ⓑ Ⓒ Ⓓ	92 Ⓐ Ⓑ Ⓒ Ⓓ
13 Ⓐ Ⓑ Ⓒ Ⓓ	33 Ⓐ Ⓑ Ⓒ Ⓓ	53 Ⓐ Ⓑ Ⓒ Ⓓ	73 Ⓐ Ⓑ Ⓒ Ⓓ	93 Ⓐ Ⓑ Ⓒ Ⓓ
14 Ⓐ Ⓑ Ⓒ Ⓓ	34 Ⓐ Ⓑ Ⓒ Ⓓ	54 Ⓐ Ⓑ Ⓒ Ⓓ	74 Ⓐ Ⓑ Ⓒ Ⓓ	94 Ⓐ Ⓑ Ⓒ Ⓓ
15 Ⓐ Ⓑ Ⓒ Ⓓ	35 Ⓐ Ⓑ Ⓒ Ⓓ	55 Ⓐ Ⓑ Ⓒ Ⓓ	75 Ⓐ Ⓑ Ⓒ Ⓓ	95 Ⓐ Ⓑ Ⓒ Ⓓ
16 Ⓐ Ⓑ Ⓒ Ⓓ	36 Ⓐ Ⓑ Ⓒ Ⓓ	56 Ⓐ Ⓑ Ⓒ Ⓓ	76 Ⓐ Ⓑ Ⓒ Ⓓ	96 Ⓐ Ⓑ Ⓒ Ⓓ
17 Ⓐ Ⓑ Ⓒ Ⓓ	37 Ⓐ Ⓑ Ⓒ Ⓓ	57 Ⓐ Ⓑ Ⓒ Ⓓ	77 Ⓐ Ⓑ Ⓒ Ⓓ	97 Ⓐ Ⓑ Ⓒ Ⓓ
18 Ⓐ Ⓑ Ⓒ Ⓓ	38 Ⓐ Ⓑ Ⓒ Ⓓ	58 Ⓐ Ⓑ Ⓒ Ⓓ	78 Ⓐ Ⓑ Ⓒ Ⓓ	98 Ⓐ Ⓑ Ⓒ Ⓓ
19 Ⓐ Ⓑ Ⓒ Ⓓ	39 Ⓐ Ⓑ Ⓒ Ⓓ	59 Ⓐ Ⓑ Ⓒ Ⓓ	79 Ⓐ Ⓑ Ⓒ Ⓓ	99 Ⓐ Ⓑ Ⓒ Ⓓ
20 Ⓐ Ⓑ Ⓒ Ⓓ	40 Ⓐ Ⓑ Ⓒ Ⓓ	60 Ⓐ Ⓑ Ⓒ Ⓓ	80 Ⓐ Ⓑ Ⓒ Ⓓ	100 Ⓐ Ⓑ Ⓒ Ⓓ

1. Individual Rights – Equal Protection
2. Individual Rights – State Action
3. Individual Rights – Equal Protection
4. Individual Rights – Equal Protection
5. First Amendment – Freedom of Expression: Time, Place, and Manner
6. Individual Rights – Equal Protection
7. Judicial Review – Case or Controversy
8. Powers of Congress – Other Powers
9. Individual Rights – Equal Protection
10. Individual Rights – Equal Protection
11. Individual Rights – Equal Protection
12. Powers of Congress – Commerce, Taxing, and Spending
13. Judicial Review – Case or Controversy
14. Individual Rights – Privileges and Immunities Clause
15. First Amendment – Establishment Clause
16. First Amendment – Freedom of Expression: Content
17. First Amendment – Freedom of Expression: Unprotected Expression
18. Judicial Review – Case or Controversy
19. First Amendment – Freedom of Assembly
20. First Amendment – Freedom of Expression: Invasion of Privacy
21. Powers of Congress – Commerce, Taxing, and Spending
22. First Amendment – Freedom of Expression: Content
23. Individual Rights – Equal Protection
24. Individual Rights – Equal Protection
25. Individual Rights – State Action
26. First Amendment – Freedom of Expression: Content
27. First Amendment – Freedom of Expression: Content

28. Individual Rights – Procedural Due Process
29. Individual Rights – Procedural Due Process
30. Speech and Debate Clause
31. Individual Rights – Fundamental Rights
32. Judicial Review – Case or Controversy
33. Individual Rights – State Action
34. First Amendment – Free Exercise Clause
35. Powers of Congress – Commerce, Taxing, and Spending
36. First Amendment – Freedom of Expression: Unprotected Expression
37. Individual Rights – Equal Protection
38. Federal-State Relationship – Powers Reserved to the States
39. Constitutional Provisions Applicable to Corporations
40. Federal-State Relationship – Powers Reserved to the States
41. Powers of Congress – Commerce, Taxing, and Spending
42. Individual Rights – Obligation of Contracts
43. Federal-State Relationship – Powers Reserved to the States
44. Federal-State Relationship – Powers Reserved to the States
45. Individual Rights – Procedural Due Process
46. Individual Rights – Procedural Due Process
47. Individual Rights – Equal Protection
48. Powers of Congress – Commerce, Taxing, and Spending
49. Individual Rights – Equal Protection
50. First Amendment – Freedom of Expression: Content
51. Individual Rights – Equal Protection
52. First Amendment – Freedom of the Press
53. Powers of the President – Treaty and Foreign Affairs
54. Judicial Review

55. First Amendment – Freedom of Expression: Unprotected Expression
56. First Amendment – Free Exercise Clause
57. First Amendment – Free Exercise Clause
58. Individual Rights – Equal Protection
59. Powers of Congress – Commerce, Taxing, and Spending
60. Judicial Review – Case or Controversy
61. Individual Rights – Privileges and Immunities Clause
62. Individual Rights – Privileges and Immunities Clause
63. Powers of Congress – Commerce, Taxing, and Spending
64. Judicial Review – Jurisdiction
65. Judicial Review – Case or Controversy
66. Individual Rights – Voting
67. Powers of Congress – Other Powers of Congress
68. Powers of the President – Chief Executive
69. Powers of the President – Commander-In-Chief
70. Judicial Review – Case or Controversy
71. First Amendment – Establishment Clause
72. Individual Rights – Procedural Due Process
73. Individual Rights – State Action
74. Individual Rights – Equal Protection
75. First Amendment – Free Exercise Clause
76. Establishment Clause
77. Establishment Clause
78. Equal Protection
79. Affectation Doctrine
80. War and Defense Powers
81. State Regulation of Commerce

82. Commerce Clause
83. Levels of Speech Protection
84. Time, Place, and Manner Restrictions
85. Intimidation
86. Appointment of Federal Officers
87. Freedom of Religion
88. Commerce Clause
89. Treaties
90. Constitutional Standing
91. Equal Protection
92. Executive Agreements
93. Freedom of the Press
94. Regulation of Speech
95. Incitement
96. Freedom of Religion
97. Federal Preemption
98. Federal Immunity
99. Procedural Due Process
100. Federal Preemption

1. In a secluded county, where prejudice festers and discrimination flourishes, there is a lovely lake, which the county has developed and maintained for recreational purposes. Although it is not the only lake in the county, it is the largest and most scenic, and it attracts visitors from miles around. One of its biggest assets is the excellent fishing and boating, which is available to the public at large.

Three years ago, in order to enhance the recreational aspects of the lake, the county leased a sizable portion of the lake and surrounding parkland to a company owned by the most prominent family in the county. The lease required the company to construct and operate a first-rate yacht house and club, complete with bar, restaurant, and private marina, and to pay the county 10% of its net profits as rent. The company set up bylaws, which were reviewed and approved by the county at the time the lease was negotiated. According to the bylaws, the yacht club, complete with its restaurant and bar, would be open to members only, and the membership committee was empowered to set up strict membership "standards," as well as the cost of membership fees and dues.

Upon completion of the facilities, the state granted the company a license to sell alcoholic beverages in its restaurant and bar. The membership committee announced that the membership fee was $5,000 and the monthly dues $75. Furthermore, the membership committee had a policy of approving only membership applications from men, while disapproving and denying all applications from women. There were other similar facilities within the county available to women.

A woman resident of the county brings suit against the company, claiming that her membership application was denied only because she is a woman, and that its policy of excluding women as a group denies her equal protection rights. Which of the following is the most accurate statement?

(A) The plaintiff will lose, because classifications based on sex have not yet been held to violate the equal protection clause.
(B) The plaintiff will prevail unless denial of membership to women can be justified by some "compelling interest," since such discrimination is "suspect" and requires the strictest equal protection test.
(C) The plaintiff will lose, because other similar facilities are available to women.
(D) The plaintiff will prevail unless the company can prove some important basis for the exclusion of women.

2. A county owns a large expanse of land next to the ocean. Four years ago, in order to enhance the recreational aspects of the land, the county leased most of it to a private company. The lease required the company to construct and operate a first-rate golf course and country club—complete with bar, restaurant, and private marina—and to pay the county 15% of its net profits as rent. The company set up bylaws, which were reviewed and approved by the county at the time the lease was negotiated. According to the bylaws, the golf course and country club, complete with its restaurant and bar, would be open to members only, and the membership committee is empowered to set up strict membership "standards," as well as the cost of membership fees and dues.

Upon completion of the facilities, the state granted the company a license to sell alcoholic beverages in its restaurant and bar. The membership committee announced that the membership fee is $5,000 and the monthly dues $75 per month. Furthermore, the membership committee had a policy of approving only membership applications for Latino Men, while disapproving and denying all applications of women, African Americans, white Americans, and other minorities.

A white resident of the county, upon denial of membership, brings an action against the company seeking injunctive relief to compel his admission claiming that denial of membership to white residents violates his right to equal protection. Which of the following statements is most accurate?

(A) The company will prevail because its denial of membership lacks the requisite state action.
(B) The plaintiff will win because even though the company is a privately owned corporation, the state has affirmatively encouraged or facilitated its discriminating acts.
(C) The company will win, because the plaintiff lacks standing to assert the rights of discrimination against white Americans as a group.
(D) The plaintiff will win, because denial of membership to white residents cannot be justified by a rational basis.

3. A county owns a large expanse of land next to the ocean. Four years ago, in order to enhance the recreational aspects of this land, the county leased most of it to a company. The lease required the company to construct and operate a first-rate luxury hotel—complete with bar, restaurant, and private marina—and to pay the county 15% of its net profits as rent. The company set up management and operations bylaws for its new hotel, which were reviewed and approved by the county at the time the lease was negotiated.

Upon completion of the facilities, the state granted the company a license to sell alcoholic beverages in its restaurant and bar. The hotel announced that the least expensive room was $1,000 per night.

Much of the population in the county cannot afford to stay at the new hotel. One resident who cannot afford to pay the hotel fees brings an action against the company, claiming that the high fees operate to discriminate against the poor, in violation of the constitutional right to equal protection. What is the most likely result of this action?

(A) The company will lose because social class constitutes a suspect classification under the equal protection clause.
(B) The company will win, because hotel privileges are not an important or basic enough deprivation, for those unable to pay for them, to be held to violate equal protection.
(C) The resident will win because all public rights cannot be limited to those who can afford them.
(D) The resident will win because discrimination against poor people violates the equal protection clause of the Fourteenth Amendment.

4. An indigent man was suffering from a chronic asthmatic and bronchial illness. The man redomiciled to a new state and shortly thereafter suffered a severe respiratory attack and was sent by his attending physician to a nonprofit private community hospital. Pursuant to a state statute governing medical care for indigents, the hospital notified county officials that it had in its hospital an indigent who might qualify for county care and requested that the man be transferred to the county's public hospital facility. In accordance with the approved procedures, the private hospital claimed reimbursement from the county in the amount of $1,069 for the care and services it had provided.

Under the relevant state statute:

"Individual county governments are charged with the mandatory duty of providing necessary hospital and medical care for their indigent sick. In order to qualify for such hospital and medical care, an indigent shall be resident of the county for the preceding 12 months in order to be eligible for free non-emergency medical care."

As a consequence, the county refused to admit the man to its public hospital or to reimburse the private hospital because the man had not been a resident of the county for the preceding year. In an action in federal court against the county challenging the constitutionality of the residency requirement for providing free medical care for indigents, the court will most likely declare the statute

(A) constitutional, because the statute promotes a compelling state interest.
(B) constitutional, because the statute is a proper exercise of state action.
(C) constitutional, because the statute is within the state's police power to regulate the health, safety, and welfare of its citizens.
(D) unconstitutional, because it violates the equal protection clause of the Fourteenth Amendment.

5. A state fair is held annually in a county on a large tract of state-owned property. In recent years, many outside organizations have entered the fairgrounds and distributed literature and paraphernalia to the many thousands of patrons visiting the fair. State fair officials did not endorse any of these organizations but permitted them to disseminate their materials throughout the fairgrounds without charge. Lately, however, many families attending the fair have complained about being harassed by canvassers from these various organizations.

In an effort to protect the safety and welfare of the persons visiting the fair, the state legislature enacted a law prohibiting anyone from selling or distributing materials at the state fair. This new statute provided, however, that groups could pay a $50 license fee and distribute their literature from enclosed booths. These booths would be set up along the entrance to the fairgrounds and rented to anyone wishing to sell or distribute materials or soliciting money during the fair.

The first year that the statute went into effect, approximately 40 groups rented booth space. There were various organizations paying the $50 license fee. A group of scientists opposed to the use of aerosol spray cans, requested permission to distribute literature at the fairgrounds. The scientists claimed that they simply wanted to warn people of the perils created by the disintegration of the ozone layer from the dispersion of fluorocarbons into the atmosphere. State fair officials offered to lease the scientists a booth at the $50 fee, but refused to permit solicitation activities outside the booth enclosures. The scientists were unwilling to pay the $50 license fee and instituted suit in state court seeking a court order permitting them to distribute literature anywhere in the fairgrounds area.

Which of the following is the strongest argument in support of the constitutionality of the statute?

(A) The statute applies to the limited area of the state-owned fairgrounds, and does not discriminate among the various organizations by way of their political, religious, or commercial viewpoints.
(B) The statute applies to representatives of popular organizations, as well as to representatives of unpopular organizations, and is a democratic expression of the will of the people because it was adopted by the state legislature.
(C) The statute is necessary to protect the safety and welfare of persons using a state facility, and does not discriminate among diverse viewpoints since there is an alternative means by which these organizations can reach their audience.
(D) The statute protects the patrons of a public facility against unwanted invasions of their privacy by restricting the solicitation activities of those organizations that the patrons do not support.

6. A permanent resident alien applied for a position as a state trooper. A state trooper is a member of the state police force, a law enforcement body that exercises broad police authority throughout the state. The position of state trooper is filled on the basis of competitive examinations taken by all of the applicants. After the resident alien applied for the position, the state authorities refused him permission to take the qualifying examination. The state authorities based their refusal on state statute, which provided:

"No person shall become a member of the state police unless he/she shall be a citizen of the United States."

Thus, under this provision, as a prerequisite to becoming a member of the state police, an alien must relinquish his foreign citizenship and become a citizen. In an opinion upholding the validity of the statute, the State Attorney General noted that since police officers fall within the category of important non-elective officials who participate directly in the execution of broad public policy, only citizens of the United States should be qualified to apply for such positions."

At the time the resident alien applied for a position as a state trooper, he was a citizen of a foreign country and not currently eligible for citizenship. As a result of a federal statute, Congress has imposed a five-year residency requirement for the attainment of citizenship. Under this federal law, an alien must reside in this country for a period of five years as a prerequisite before applying for citizenship. At this time, the resident alien had only lawfully been residing in the United States for two years, and thus would not be eligible to apply for naturalization until three years later.

If the resident alien brings suit in federal court challenging the constitutionality of the state statute limiting the membership of its state police force to citizens of the United States, the court will most likely declare the statute

(A) constitutional, because the statute is within the state's plenary power to regulate the health, safety, and welfare of its citizens.
(B) constitutional, because citizenship bears a rational relationship to the special demands of the police function.
(C) unconstitutional, because it constitutes a violation of the equal protection clause of the Fourteenth Amendment.
(D) unconstitutional, because it constitutes a violation of the due process clause of the Fourteenth Amendment.

7. Congress has recently enacted a statute legalizing marijuana. The law, signed by the President, imposes a tax of $1 on each pack of marijuana cigarettes sold in the United States. In an inseverable portion of that same law, the entire proceeds of the tax are appropriated on a continuing basis for direct payments to an art museum. The public museum is dedicated to the collection of pictures, artifacts, weapons, and other historical memorabilia of past wars.

Which of the following most clearly has standing to attack the constitutionality of this appropriation of the tax monies to the art museum?

(A) A state, other than the one in which the museum is located, in which several other public museums are located that are not subsidized by this law.
(B) A nonprofit organization of war veterans that claims it can demonstrate a greater need for the funds than can the museum.
(C) A purchaser of marijuana cigarettes who is required to pay the tax.
(D) An association of medical doctors that alleges that the legalization of marijuana will result in a public health hazard.

8. Congress enacted a statute taxing the sale of automobiles. In an inseverable portion of that same law, the entire proceeds of the tax are appropriated on a continuing basis for direct payments to an education fund. The education fund is dedicated to educating people about the importance of mass transportation as an alternative to automobiles, which the fund considers a major source of pollution.

As a matter of constitutional law, which of the following statements concerning the continuing federal appropriation to the education fund is most accurate?

(A) It is constitutional because Congress could reasonably believe that such a subsidy to this particular museum will benefit the cultural life of the nation as a whole.
(B) It is constitutional because Congress can demonstrate that such a subsidy is rationally related to a legitimate public interest.
(C) It is unconstitutional because it is not apportioned among the several states on an equitable basis.
(D) It is unconstitutional because it advances the welfare only of those persons who are interested in clean air.

9. A state has recently enacted a statute wherein aliens are forbidden from owning more than 10 acres of land within the state. Subsequent to the statute a resident alien enters into a contract to buy 50 acres of land located in the state.

Assume that the statute empowers the state to bring an ejectment action against any alien who owns more than 10 acres of land. If the resident alien brings an action in federal court to enjoin the state from enforcing the statute against him, his best argument is

(A) the statute violates the privileges or immunities clause of the Fourteenth Amendment.
(B) the statute violates the contract clause.
(C) the statute violates the commerce clause in that it interferes with land ownership.
(D) the statute violates the equal protection clause of the Fourteenth Amendment.

10. A state has recently enacted a statute wherein aliens are prohibited from owning any commercial real estate within the state. Subsequent to the statute, a lawful resident alien enters into a contract with another lawful resident alien to purchase the latter's office building.

Assume that both resident aliens join in a declaratory judgment action to test the validity of the state statute in federal court. The court should rule that

(A) the state has the burden of proof to show that there is a compelling state interest to support the statute.
(B) the burden of proof is on the resident aliens to show that there is no compelling state interest to support the statute.
(C) the resident aliens do not have standing.
(D) either resident alien has standing, but not both.

11. A state has had a tremendous influx of retired people in recent years. There has been considerable concern among state health officials who foresee that many of the senior citizens will become victims of price gouging on certain medical supplies and services. In an attempt to curb such fraudulent sales practices, the state legislature has enacted a law prohibiting the sale of hearing aids by non-physicians. The measure provides, however, that all non-physician sellers who are presently engaged in the business of selling hearing aids will not be affected.

Assume that after the statute goes into effect, a non-physician moves to the state and wants to open a business selling hearing aids. After being advised that the state law prohibits him from doing so, he brings suit challenging the constitutionality of the statute. The most likely result is that the state law will be declared

(A) constitutional, because there is a rational basis for distinguishing between non-physicians are not so engaged.
(B) constitutional, because a state has the power to regulate any phase of local business, even though such regulations may have some effect on interstate commerce, provided that Congress has not enacted legislation regarding the subject matter.
(C) unconstitutional, because it denies non-physicians who are not presently engaged in the business of selling hearing aids the equal protection of the law, in violation of the Fourteenth Amendment.
(D) unconstitutional, because it violates the commerce clause, since Congress has plenary power to regulate any activity that has any appreciable effect on interstate commerce.

12. Over the last several years, the economy of a state has substantially changed. The state's economy used to be based solely on heavy industry. However, the state legislature approved legalized gambling within the state. As a consequence, many casinos and new hotels were built and the state's economy boomed. These moves were often induced by the granting by the state of special tax benefits for the construction of new casinos and hotels under state statutes.

Recently, however, neighboring states have legalized gambling and offered greater tax incentives to the gaming industry. As a result, many of the casino and hotel owners have begun to leave the state. The unemployment and social welfare benefits the state has had to pay have substantially increased, burdening the remaining casinos, and also making it difficult for the state to lower its taxes to remain competitive with other states.

On account of this predicament, the state legislature passed, and the governor duly signed, an emergency bill into law. According to the statute, the state imposed a one cent tax on the playing of any slot machine in any gambling casino. Since virtually all the slot machines required a payment of either a dime, quarter, or dollar, the imposition of this tax required a major costly adaptation on each slot machine to allow for the deposit of the additional one cent tax. Although many casino owners have complained about the tax, their only alternative is to absorb the tax themselves and lose one cent per game. As a consequence of the tax, fewer slot machines are purchased in the state by the casino owners. No manufacturer of slot machines is located in the state.

Which of the following constitutional provisions provide the strongest ground to attack the validity of the state tax bill?

(A) The commerce clause.
(B) The equal protection clause of the Fourteenth Amendment.
(C) The due process clause of the Fourteenth Amendment.
(D) The privileges and immunities clause of Article IV, Section 2.

13. A state recently imposed a one cent tax on the playing of any coin-operated video game in any restaurant. Since virtually all of the video games required a payment of either a dime, quarter, or dollar, the imposition of this tax required a major costly adaptation on each video game to allow for the deposit of the additional one cent tax. Although many video game owners have complained about the video game tax, their only alternative is to absorb the tax themselves and lose one cent per game. As a consequence of the tax, fewer video games are purchased by the restaurant owners. No manufacturer of video games is located in the state.

Which of the following is most likely to have standing to bring suit challenging the constitutionality of the video game tax bill in an appropriate federal court?

(A) A manufacturer of video games who is attempting to sell them to a restaurant owner in the state.
(B) A state resident who frequently plays video games at restaurants.
(C) A national video game association whose members travel to the state to play video games at restaurants.
(D) The director of the state's youth organization who wants to provide video games that only play for free at recreation centers within the state.

14. The board of a state university has adopted the following rule concerning residency requirements: "A student will be considered a legal resident of the state for the purpose of registering at the university if such person is over the age of 21 and has established a legal residence in the state for at least one year next preceding the last day of registration for credit."

A student moved to the state and immediately enrolled at the state university. Since he did not fulfill the university residency requirement, the student was required to pay $1,800 tuition each semester, which was $400 more than the tuition of state resident-students.

In an action by the student challenging the constitutionality of the provision governing the determination of residency for the purpose of fixing a fee differential for out-of-state students in public college, the court will most likely declare the provision

(A) unconstitutional, because it constitutes a violation of the equal protection clause of the Fourteenth Amendment.
(B) unconstitutional, because it constitutes a violation of the privileges and immunities clause of Article IV, Section 2.
(C) constitutional, because the fee differential promotes a compelling state interest.
(D) constitutional, because the provision does not trigger strict scrutiny.

15. During a violent electrical storm one night, a bolt of lightning struck a public high school building and set it ablaze. The high school was severely damaged and needed to be rebuilt. As a consequence, the city council held an emergency meeting to determine what measures should be taken to locate an appropriate alternative facility in which to conduct classes. Thereupon, the city council passed the following resolution: "During restoration of the high school building, classes shall be conducted at the most suitable facility which submits the lowest bid. In determining a 'suitable' facility, the city council shall consider such factors as location and available classroom space."

Several bids were submitted. The lowest bid was submitted by a church. The church was located on the same block as the high school and contained sufficient seating capacity for all students. In addition, there were a sufficient number of separate rooms to allow different classes to meet at the same time. The city council voted unanimously to accept the church's offer. Furthermore, the church agreed to remove all religious symbols and paraphernalia from the classrooms utilized by the students. Only the main chapel was exempt, so that it could remain open for prayer. No high school classes or activities were to be held in the main chapel.

A parent of one of the high school students is upset at this arrangement. On his son's behalf, the parent has filed suit in federal district court to challenge the constitutionality of permitting public school classes to be held in a church. Judgment for whom?

(A) The city, because the classroom arrangement does not inhibit or advance religion.
(B) The city, because the church was the lowest bidder in accordance with the emergency ordinance.
(C) The plaintiff, because the present arrangement for conducting classes in a church-owned facility constitutes excessive entanglement with religion.
(D) The plaintiff, because the emergency measure was not necessary to further a compelling state interest.

16. An owner had a record store in the downtown business area of a city. A famous rock group was scheduled to perform at the local civic center and the owner featured the band's records in a special sale for the two weeks prior to the concert. In order to promote his sale, the owner installed loudspeakers on the outside of his store window so that he could play the band's records for people walking by to hear. It was the owner's hope that when they heard the records, the passersby would turn into customers and buy the band's records.

    Subsequently, the owner was cited for violating a city ordinance which provides that:

    "An owner of property located within the city limits shall not permit to be used on his property any device which causes sounds, other than clock chimes, to be heard upon the street or sidewalk. Violation of this ordinance shall subject the property owner to a fine of $50.00 for each occurrence."

    If the owner is successful in challenging this ordinance in court, the court would most likely reason that

    (A) the ordinance violates equal protection because some sounds are permitted, while others are not.
    (B) the ordinance violates the owner's rights of freedom of speech, because there is not valid interest to support the ordinance.
    (C) the ordinance violates the owner's rights of freedom of speech, because a municipality may not regulate the use of sound amplification equipment.
    (D) the ordinance violates the owner's rights under the First and Fourteenth Amendments, because it is vague in defining unpermitted sounds.

17. A man outraged by the recent church decision to clear a famous philosopher of charges of heresy, decided to present a lecture, open to the public, disproving the philosopher's theories. A state statute provides that: "state universities can permit the use of their lecture halls to the public for worthwhile programs of public benefit, upon approval of the school board."

    The appropriate school board refused to make a university lecture hall available to the man on the grounds that the proposed lecture was not of worthwhile benefit to the public.

    As a result, the man brought suit in a state court against the school board and requested injunctive relief requiring the board to allow him the use of the lecture hall. The trial court denied relief and dismissed the suit. The judgment was affirmed by the state appellate court, and is now before the U.S. Supreme Court.

    In analyzing the state statute, which of the following statements is least accurate?

    (A) The statute is unconstitutionally overbroad, because it may result in the exclusion of protected speech as well as unprotected speech.
    (B) The statute, as applied to the man, does not violate his First Amendment rights because his proposed speech is not political and, therefore, not among the classes of speech that are protected.
    (C) Indirect speech, regulations are only permissible if necessary to serve compelling state interests.
    (D) The statute is a prior restraint on speech, which unconstitutionally vests unfettered discretion in the school board to decide who may use university lecture halls.

18. For the past 20 years a city by the beach has been a popular location for surfboarding. City residents have recently complained that the surfers are creating a public nuisance by littering the beaches, harassing sunbathers, and injuring swimmers with their surfboards. As a consequence, the city adopted an ordinance prohibiting all surfing on its beaches. The newly enacted ordinance further prohibited the sale of surfboards within the city's limits. An out of state surfboard manufacturer had planned to sell a new line of fiberglass surfboards in the city in the upcoming year. This is now precluded by the recently adopted measure.

    If the manufacturer seeks to enjoin application of the city ordinance, which of the following is the WEAKEST defense for the city?

    (A) There is no case or controversy.
    (B) The manufacturer's case is moot.
    (C) The manufacturer lacks standing.
    (D) The case is not ripe.

19. A group advocating the resumption of U.S. diplomatic relations with certain foreign countries planned to hold a rally at a park in the downtown section of a city. The group secured a rally permit in accordance with a local ordinance. Several members of the group, including a political science professor at a state university and one of the group's leaders, were scheduled to give speeches. Other members of the group were assigned to walk among the crowd to solicit signatures for a petition, which the group planned to present to the President.

    A large crowd gathered in the park at the appointed date and time, anxiously waiting for the speeches to begin. As the professor, the first speaker, began addressing the gathering, a television news team started filming her presentation, which was to be shown on the local news that evening.

    After the professor finished her speech, a few members of the crowd began hissing and booing and shouting. The police soon arrived and attempted to break up the rally. Several members of the group, including the professor, were arrested for inciting a riot.

    Which of the following would be the most accurate statement with regard to the police halting the rally?

    (A) The police were justified, since the rally threatened imminent violence and serious disorder.
    (B) The police were justified in order to protect the group's leaders.
    (C) The police violated the group's First Amendment rights of assembly.
    (D) Since the group obtained the rally permit, the police were not permitted to interfere with the staging of the rally.

20. A professor employed by a state university is a well-known critic of foreign policy and has sometimes publicly stated that he wished for the United States to suffer some collective political tragedy in retribution for all the harms it does to the world. The professor was recently involved in a highly visible political protest against the government. The police eventually shut down the protest because they felt that it was becoming unruly. A television crew covered the entire rally.

On the six o'clock news that evening, the film of the protest rally was shown during the broadcast. A news anchorman then made the following commentary: "It's a shame that public funds are spent to pay the salaries of such university professors, who are not grateful for what this country has done for them. In my opinion, these people like the professor should be deported."

If the professor asserts a claim based on invasion of privacy against the television station and the anchorman for his television commentary, the most likely result is that the professor will

(A) not prevail, because the criticism was not directed at the professor personally.
(B) not prevail, because the broadcast was privileged as being in the public interest.
(C) prevail, because the professor, as a private individual, was placed in a false light.
(D) prevail, because the comments were made with actual malice.

21. As a legislative aide to a U.S. Senator you are called upon to provide an analysis of the constitutionality of a bill pending congressional approval. The bill imposes a 15% tax upon the gross annual receipts from the sales of all birth control devices. The bill has the strong support of conservative and pro-life organizations. The stated purpose of the proposed measure is to raise revenue and spur population growth across the country.

In your learned opinion, the proposed tax is probably

(A) constitutional, because the fact that the tax applies to all sales of every type of birth control device invalidates any possible objection to the tax on the grounds that it violates the equal protection clause of the Fourteenth Amendment.
(B) constitutional, because the fact that controversial policy motives may have induced the enactment of an otherwise reasonable measure calculated to raise revenue does not *ipso facto* invalidate the tax.
(C) unconstitutional, because in inseverable aggregates, the domestic purchases and sales of birth control devices affect interstate and foreign commerce.
(D) unconstitutional, because the tax burdens the fundamental right to privacy of users of birth control devices without establishing a compelling national interest for doing so.

22. A state university was the scene of campus protests against nuclear weapons. A group of students painted purple a statue of the university's founder in protest to the university's federally subsidized nuclear weapon experimental studies. The leader of this group of students was a first-year student from a neighboring state who established residency in the state after beginning classes.

The group leader had been the recipient of a $5,000 annual grant from the state to finance his education. However, the aid was withdrawn because of a state statute, which provided: "Any student attending a state university who engages in disruptive campus activities will not be eligible for state aid."

The group leader was married to a fellow student. However, in light of his involvement in defacing the statue and the loss of his state aid, his wife left him. At that time, the group leader received a tax bill for $150. This tax was imposed uniformly by the city on all individuals over 19 years of age, with the exception that full-time female college students were exempted. The tax notice stated that his wife, 22 years of age, qualified for the exemption, and there was no bill enclosed for her.

Subsequently, the group leader moved in with his new girlfriend and began making arrangements to secure a divorce. However, the group leader was not able to obtain a divorce, since he had not fulfilled the 12-month residency requirement as imposed by state law.

In an action by the group leader against the state challenging the constitutionality of the state statute regarding disruptive campus activities in order to regain his $5,000 annual grant, the court will most likely declare the statute

(A) constitutional, because it promotes a compelling state interest.
(B) constitutional, because it is a proper exercise of state action designed to regulate the activities of state university students.
(C) unconstitutional, because it is vague and overbroad.
(D) unconstitutional, because it is discriminatory on its face.

23. In order to encourage college enrollment, a state provides a tax exemption of $200 for state taxes for those who are full-time students at colleges within the state. Female students who attend half-time are still permitted a $100 tax exemption, whereas male students who attend half-time are no longer permitted any tax exemption.

Which of the following most accurately summarizes the correct rule of constitutional law regarding the state tax exemption for students who enroll half-time?

(A) The tax exemption would be invalidated as a denial of due process.
(B) The tax exemption would be invalidated as violative of the equal protection clause.
(C) The tax measure would be upheld as within the area of substantive due process.
(D) The tax measure would be upheld as within the power of a municipality to tax different classes of persons unequally.

24. A couple were married, and four months later, they wished to obtain a divorce. However, the state in which they were married prohibits a couple from obtaining a divorce until they have resided in the state for at least 12 months.

In an action by the couple challenging the constitutionality of the residency requirement of the state divorce law, the court will most likely declare the provision

(A) constitutional, because the requirement promotes a compelling state interest.
(B) constitutional, because it is within the area of state action.
(C) unconstitutional, because it constitutes a violation of the equal protection clause.
(D) unconstitutional, because it constitutes a violation of the privileges and immunities clause of Article IV, Section 2.

25. A privately owned shopping center leases retail store space to private retailers. A group of students from a local high school were distributing pamphlets commemorating a national holiday in the enclosed mall area of a privately owned shopping complex. The management of the shopping complex requested that the students cease distributing the pamphlets or leave the premises. When they refused, the police were summoned to disperse the students. Upon the arrival of the police, the students were removed from the premises.

Subsequently, the students brought suit in federal court seeking an injunction that would order the shopping complex management to allow them to distribute the pamphlets within the mall. The students will

(A) prevail, because pamphleteering is a speech-related activity, which is protected by the First and Fourteenth Amendments.
(B) prevail, because there is not an anti-pamphleteering statute.
(C) not prevail, because pamphleteering on private property is not a constitutionally protected activity.
(D) not prevail, because pamphleteering may be prohibited as a public nuisance that invades the privacy interest of persons not wishing such communicative contact.

26. A state legislature has recently enacted a statute making it a misdemeanor to curse or revile or use obscene or opprobrious language toward or in reference to a police officer performing his duties. A student at a state university organized a demonstration on campus to protest the war. The rally was attended by a group of 50 students who shouted anti-war messages at cars passing by.

To show his contempt for the United States, the student sewed the American flag to the rear of his jeans. When a police officer saw the flag sown on the student's jeans, he approached and told him to remove the flag or he would be placed under arrest. The student became angered and shouted at the police officer, "Listen, you bastard, I'll wear this rag anywhere I please." The student was subsequently placed under arrest and charged with violating the state statute.

The student subsequently brings suit in state court challenging the constitutionality of the statute. The strongest constitutional argument for the student is that

(A) the statute is void for vagueness under the Fourteenth Amendment's due process clause.
(B) the statute is invalid because it violates the petitioner's freedom of speech under the First Amendment.
(C) the statute is an abridgment of freedom of speech under the First Amendment because less restrictive means are available for achieving the same purpose.
(D) the statute is overbroad and consequently invalid under the First and Fourteenth Amendments.

27. A state legislature has recently enacted the following statute:

"Statute 1221. It shall be unlawful for an individual to publicly mutilate, trample upon, deface, or treat contemptuously the flag of the United States. Whoever shall violate this statute shall be guilty of a misdemeanor."

To show his contempt for the United States, an antigovernment protestor sewed the American flag on the rear of his jeans. He was subsequently placed under arrest and charged with violating Statute 1221.

If the protestor is subsequently prosecuted under Statute 1221 for his flag misuse, he

(A) should be convicted.
(B) should not be convicted, because the lack of ascertainable standards for defining "treat contemptuously" violates the equal protection clause of the Fourteenth Amendment.
(C) should not be convicted, since the statutory language is void for vagueness under the First and Fourteenth Amendments.
(D) should not be convicted, because the statute has a chilling effect on nonverbal forms of speech and, therefore, is invalid under the First and Fourteenth Amendments.

28. A state legislature recently enacted a statute legalizing harness racing. The statute authorized pari-mutuel betting at certain track locations within the state. A seven-member commission was established and empowered to supervise and regulate the sport's activities. Under an inseparable provision of the statute, the commission was authorized to suspend the racing license of any trainer whose horse tested positive for illegal drugs. The statute permitted the commission to make the suspension without any prior hearing. However, suspended trainers were entitled to a prompt post-suspension hearing and decision on any issues in dispute.

The racing season was inaugurated at the largest racetrack in the state. The featured race was a $1,000,000 harness race for 2-year-old trotters. After the awards presentation, the winning horse underwent a standard drug test and traces of cocaine were found in his urine sample. Immediately thereafter, the horse was disqualified and the commission suspended the horse's trainer, without a prior hearing.

Without seeking a post-suspension hearing as provided by statute, the trainer brings suit in federal district court challenging the constitutionality of the state harness racing law. The statute is probably

(A) constitutional, because being granted a racing license is a privilege, not a right.
(B) constitutional, because the state's interest in suspending the license of horse trainers suspected of illegal drugging is sufficiently important to permit the suspension of any prior hearing.
(C) unconstitutional, because the suspension provision unreasonably interferes with a trainer's right to contract with horse owners and seek gainful employment.
(D) unconstitutional, because the suspension provision violates due process by not affording a prior hearing.

29. Proposed legislation was offered to a state legislature that would reorganize the state police. The bill created a great deal of controversy, both in and outside the state government. Several leaders of the minority party in the legislature decided to oppose the legislation. One member of the minority party disagreed with his party's opposition to the bill and publicly announced his support for the legislation.

The minority party leaders called a caucus to discuss and determine their legislative strategy for floor debate on the bill. When the disagreeing member appeared at the door of the caucus room, he was denied admission because of his anti-party stance. He was also informed that he would be removed from all of his committee assignments.

During the caucus, the party members discussed other means of disciplining the member for his party insubordination. It was suggested that they issue a press release in which the party would publicly castigate him for his actions. The leader of the party said that "the member is a cutthroat politician who is only looking out for where his next buck will come from."

Which of the following constitutional provisions would give the ousted member his best grounds for challenging his exclusion from the party caucus?

(A) The equal protection clause of the Fourteenth Amendment.
(B) The right of assembly as guaranteed by the First Amendment.
(C) The speech and debate clause.
(D) The due process clause of the Fourteenth Amendment.

30. During a Senate debate, members discussed how to punish a particular senator for having publicly rebuked the head of his party. One of the members suggested that the party inform television reporters that the senator in question is "an opportunist who has very little loyalty to his own party and will switch sides at the earliest convenience."

In determining whether the senator has a valid cause of action against the member for his remarks, which of the following most accurately reflects the applicable rule of law?

(A) The senator must prove actual malice in order to recover for defamation.
(B) Any remarks made during the debate were privileged.
(C) The remarks violated the senator's First Amendment right of privacy by placing him in a "false light."
(D) The remarks constitute a "fair and substantial" relation to "important governmental objectives."

31. Congress, under intense lobbying pressure has enacted a statute prohibiting the sale of contraceptive devices to married persons. The act further prohibits the use of contraceptive devices by married persons. Congress claimed that the statute was passed because it might help deter illicit sexual relationships.

The law is most likely

(A) constitutional, because it is a regulation of interstate commerce.
(B) constitutional, because it is a measure promoting the general welfare.
(C) unconstitutional, because the law deprives the manufacturers of contraceptives of their property interest without just compensation.
(D) unconstitutional, because it violates the right of privacy of contraceptive users.

32. A state legislature enacts a statute prohibiting the sale of contraceptive devices to married persons. This state statute prohibits the use of contraceptive devices by married persons. A physician who practices in the state brings suit in federal court challenging the constitutionality of the state contraceptive statute. The physician attacks the validity of the statute on the grounds that it prevents him from giving professional advice concerning the use of contraceptives to three patients, all of whom are married, whose condition of health might be endangered by child bearing.

The plaintiff is likely

(A) to have standing.
(B) to have standing *jus tertii.*
(C) not to have standing.
(D) not to have standing *jus tertii.*

33. The owner of a test prep company sent an advertisement regarding the company's review courses to a local newspaper. In an accompanying letter, the owner instructed the newspaper to publish the ad in an upcoming edition. The ad was received by the newspaper's advertising editor.

The next day the editor phoned the owner and told her that he would not permit the newspaper to run the ad. When the owner asked for an explanation, the editor replied, "My daughter took your review course and scored low on her entrance exams to college and didn't get into the college of her choice. Because of your instructors, she's now working at the mall. That's why I'm prohibiting the newspaper from publishing your ad." The editor then forwarded a letter to the owner reiterating his newspaper's refusal to have the ad published.

In an appropriate action, the owner brings suit against the editor and the newspaper seeking an order that would require the newspaper to publish the advertisement. In such action, who will prevail?

(A) The owner, because such advertising is protected by the First Amendment under the commercial speech doctrine.
(B) The owner, because there is a constitutional right of advertising under the First and Fourteenth Amendments.
(C) The editor and newspaper, because Congress is empowered to prohibit untruthful advertising, even where it urges the purchase of a legal, validly offered item.
(D) The editor and newspaper, because there is no constitutional right of advertising under the First and Fourteenth Amendments.

34. A prisoner was serving a life sentence in a state prison as a result of his conviction for the murder of a child who had trespassed onto his farmland. The prisoner came from a family of farmers, dating back to at least 1750. His family believed that all nourishment comes from the ground and that one's soul will be saved only if his diet consists totally of natural, farm-grown food. The prisoner followed that belief and ate only fresh fruits and vegetables. He further believes that a higher power has commanded him to eat only vegetarian foods.

When the prisoner entered the prison state prison officials agreed to grant his wishes and served him only fresh fruits and vegetables for his meals. After six months, deciding that catering to his special diet was overly burdensome and administratively unworkable, the officials decided to stop giving the prisoner special treatment and began to serve him the same food as served to the rest of the prison population. Although nothing physically prohibited the prisoner from eating and surviving on the general prison population's diet, he refused to eat the food that was not in conformity with his special diet.

The prisoner's best constitutional argument to support his claim of the right to a fresh fruit and vegetable diet is based on

(A) the First Amendment.
(B) the Eighth Amendment's prohibition against cruel and unusual punishment, as applied to the states.
(C) the Fourteenth Amendment's substantive due process clause.
(D) the Fourteenth Amendment.

35. Several states have enacted laws shielding reporters from being compelled to release the names of confidential sources. Now, Congress, under intense lobbying pressure from the press, proposes to enact legislation forbidding any state from requiring journalists to reveal the sources of their news articles in civil suits.

Which of the following is the strongest constitutional argument in support of this proposed law?

(A) Congress has the authority under the commerce clause to regulate the flow of news.
(B) Acts of Congress are the supreme law of the land and take precedence over any conflicting state laws.
(C) Congress is essentially reaffirming the free speech guarantees of the First and Fourteenth Amendments.
(D) Under Article I, Section 8, Congress has the authority to secure to authors and inventors the exclusive right to their respective writings and discoveries.

36. A motel advertises the showing of pornographic, or adult movies in the privacy of each room. The motel has a strict policy permitting adults only to occupy the rooms. The state has recently enacted a statute that prohibits the showing of any obscene film in an area open to the public.

The owner of the motel is prosecuted for violating the statute by showing pornographic movies in the motel rooms. On appeal, the owner's conviction will probably be

(A) sustained, because a state can use its police power to prohibit the showing of pornography in public areas.
(B) sustained, because a state may use local standards in determining whether a movie has redeeming literary, artistic, political, or scientific merit.
(C) overturned, because his prosecution violates the right of consenting adults to view such films in private.
(D) overturned, because the First and Fourteenth Amendments prohibit the suppression of sexually oriented materials on the basis of their allegedly obscene contents.

37. Each year the state provides a number of non-interest-bearing loans and/or scholarships to candidates for the degree of L.L.B or J.D. at the state's law school. The applicable state statute limits eligibility to citizens of the United States and aliens seeking U.S. citizenship. A candidate for a J.D. degree at the state law school applied for one of the non-interest-bearing loans. Since he did not intend to seek U.S. citizenship, he was refused the loan for ineligibility under the state statute.

In a suit by the candidate challenging the constitutionality of the state statute, he will

(A) win, because the statute is violative of the privileges or immunities clause of the Fourteenth Amendment.
(B) win, because classifications by a state that are based on alienage are inherently suspect and subject to close judicial scrutiny.
(C) lose, because the statute promotes a compelling state interest.
(D) lose, because alienage classifications are not, *per se,* unconstitutional under the Fourteenth Amendment's equal protection clause.

38. A state has a statute generally prohibiting the installation and use of radar detection devices in any motor vehicle operating on the roadways within the state. This prohibition was enacted to prevent motorists from evading radar or speed checkpoints on county and state highways. A neighboring state has no such regulation in effect. By the same token, Congress has taken no action on the matter.

A resident of the neighboring state has installed a radar detection device in his automobile. While driving to visit his mother he is arrested and charged with violating the aforementioned state statute. The resident files a complaint challenging the constitutionality of the state statute.

As applied to the resident, the state prohibition against the use of radar detection devices is likely to be held

(A) constitutional, because it protects a legitimate state interest.
(B) constitutional, because the commerce clause does not invalidate a state regulation relating to interstate commerce unless Congress takes express action to do so.
(C) unconstitutional, because the state statute fails to give credit to the law of a neighboring state.
(D) unconstitutional, because it unduly burdens interstate commerce.

39. Which of the following constitutional provisions is applicable to corporations?

(A) The privileges and immunities clause of the Fourteenth Amendment.
(B) The comity clause of Article IV.
(C) The Fifth Amendment's prohibition against compulsory self-incrimination.
(D) The equal protection clause of the Fourteenth Amendment.

40. A state has recently enacted a statute that provides no person or company may be awarded any state construction contract unless the person or company agrees to hire only citizens of the state. The primary purpose of the statute is to help alleviate the state's high rate of unemployment.

Which of the following, if established, is the strongest argument in support of the statute if it is attacked as violating the commerce clause?

(A) The statute will help racial minorities living in the state obtain gainful employment.
(B) The state has the highest unemployment rate in the country.
(C) If the state uses its own taxpayer funds to purchase construction materials, it is responsible for creating demand for the required labor.
(D) The statute was overwhelmingly adopted by the voters of the state.

41. In light of the current oil glut, many oil producing states have experienced extreme economic hardship. Due to the precipitous drop in oil prices, many oil companies have been forced to cut back on oil production and lay off many workers. As a result, unemployment has reached all-time high levels in several states. In order to alleviate this potentially catastrophic situation, the one of those state's legislatures recently enacted a statute requiring that 10% of all oil produced within the state be purchased by the state and reserved for use by state residents. The purpose of the statute was twofold: (1) it was intended to stimulate the oil industry within the state by encouraging more production and exploration, and (2) it was designed to create an oil reserve so that state residents and industries would not suffer unduly from future oil shortages. Subsequently, Congress enacted a statute forbidding states to reserve local resources for local use in this manner.

Is this state statute constitutional?

(A) Yes, because Congress has not expressly forbidden states to reserve local resources for local use.
(B) Yes, because the state statute requires that the oil be used for the general welfare of the people in emergency situations.
(C) No, because a state may not protect its residents from out-of-state competition for its natural resources without the express permission of Congress.
(D) No, because application of the statute denies non-oil producing companies to equal protection of the law, in violation of the Fourteenth Amendment.

42. A state built a racetrack that was specially designed and constructed for thoroughbred horseracing. State bonds were issued to finance the construction of the racetrack. The bond agreement provided that for the first five years the racetrack was in operation, at least $2 from each admission charge would be used to repay the bond debt. The bond agreement further stipulated that if the proceeds from the admission charges during the first five years were not sufficient to repay the bondholders, then at least $1 from each admission charge for the next five years would be applied to make the necessary bond payments.

After the racetrack was built and in operation for two years, the state legislature passed a bill requiring the racetrack to admit all senior citizens over the age of 65 for the discounted admission fee of 50 cents. This law is probably

(A) constitutional, because it is a justifiable exercise of the state's police power.
(B) unconstitutional, because it denies citizens under the age of 65 the equal protection of the law.
(C) unconstitutional, because it impairs the obligation of the bondholders' contract.
(D) unconstitutional, because it is an *ex post facto* law.

43. A state built a baseball stadium and issued bonds to finance its construction. The bond agreement provided that for the first five years the stadium was in operation, at least $2 from each admission charge would be used to repay the bond debt. The bond agreement further stipulated that if the proceeds from the admission charges during the first five years were not sufficient to repay the bondholders, then at least $1 from each admission charge for the next five years would be applied to make the necessary bond payments.

Assume that three years after the stadium had been in operation, a subsequent session of the state legislature passed a bill entirely prohibiting baseball because four players were killed in playing mishaps. This statute is probably

(A) constitutional, because it is a justifiable exercise of the state's police power.
(B) constitutional, because of the clear and present danger of baseball playing in the state.
(C) unconstitutional, because it impairs the obligation of the bondholders' contract.
(D) unconstitutional, because it violates the due process rights of the baseball team owners.

44. A state built a casino and issued bonds to finance its construction. On five occasions, there were episodes of violence in various casinos in the state. The state police attributed the violence to greed and fear at the casinos.

To prevent such violence, the state legislature passes a statute prohibiting all gambling at privately owned casinos in the state. Is this law likely to be held constitutional if most casinos in the state were owned by those from out-of-state?

(A) Yes, because the act was expressly authorized by the state legislature.
(B) Yes, but only if the local interest in safety outweighs the burden of interstate commerce.
(C) No, because out-of-state casinos are part of interstate commerce.
(D) No, because the statute violates the due process rights of the owners of the casinos.

45. A high school student was suspended for five days by school officials after he came to school wearing a beard. The school had a rule prohibiting any student from growing a beard or mustache while attending classes. The rule required an automatic five-day suspension in such cases. The student, who was aware of the rule prohibiting beards and mustaches, requested a trial-type hearing before the suspension was imposed.

If the school board denies the student's request for a trial-type hearing, which of the following statements is most accurate?

(A) The suspension violated the student's due process rights because it deprived him of his entitlement to an education.
(B) The denial of a trial-type hearing violated the student's due process rights because the suspension was arbitrarily imposed.
(C) The denial of a trial-type hearing did not violate the student's due process rights because under the circumstances, he had no right to a hearing.
(D) There was no violation of the student's due process rights because his conduct could be deemed so injurious to school discipline that it warranted suspension prior to a hearing.

46. A high school junior was charged by the school administration with violating certain sections of the disciplinary code, specifically, he was charged with being disrespectful to a teacher by using profanity and with using abusive language to a fellow student.

The principal, sent the student's parents a letter notifying them of the three-day suspension for the above-mentioned charges. The suspension was to take effect on February 1. The principal also included a copy of the disciplinary code in the letter. On January 19, the student and his mother met with the principal in his office to discuss the matter, and the student admitted that he used abusive language to a fellow student.

On January 22, the student's parents received a letter informing them that his teacher had upheld the school administration's decision to suspend their son. They were then notified of a hearing on the recommended suspension to be held at the school. The parents did not attend this hearing, but were advised that the school board upheld the suspension, effective February 1.

Which of the following most accurately summarizes the applicable rule of constitutional law with respect to the student's suspension?

(A) The student's suspension deprived him of liberty and property without due process, as guaranteed by the Fourteenth Amendment.
(B) The student's conduct was protected under the First Amendment's guarantee of freedom of speech.
(C) The student's suspension did not constitute a denial of due process.
(D) The disciplinary code violated the student's right to a compulsory school education.

47. A state legislature passed a law requiring state universities to have male and female students live in separate dormitory facilities. The law was passed in order to curtail the increasing number of co-ed pregnancies on college campuses.

Two students at a state university are engaged to be married and wish to share a dormitory room together. Citing the law, university housing officials refuse to allow them to live together in a campus dormitory facility.

The students bring an appropriate action to challenge the constitutionality of the law. Which of the following correctly states the applicable burden of persuasion?

(A) Since the law deals with the fundamental right of privacy, the state must show that it furthers a compelling state interest.
(B) Since the law deals with the freedom of association, the state must show that it furthers a compelling state interest.
(C) Since the law involves gender discrimination, the state must prove that the law is substantially related to an important state interest.
(D) Since the law does not affect a fundamental right or involve gender discrimination, the burden is on the plaintiffs to show that it is not rationally related to a legitimate governmental interest.

48. The prime minister of a foreign country was assassinated by a group of right wing extremists. The prime minister's death triggered a civil war between rival factions within the country. To prevent U.S. involvement in this country's political crisis, Congress passed an appropriations bill prohibiting any funding for U.S. military operations in this foreign country.

The appropriations bill was passed over a presidential veto. Thereafter, the President issued an executive order directing U.S. Navy and Army troops to the foreign country to restore order.

Is this executive order constitutional?

(A) Yes, because the President, as commander-in-chief of the armed forces, has the power to authorize such military expeditions.
(B) Yes, because the President has inherent power to regulate foreign affairs as long as there is no formal declaration of war.
(C) No, because the President cannot usurp Congress's spending power by taking action that supersedes a congressional appropriations bill.
(D) No, because the executive order was neither authorized by federal statute nor ratified by the Senate.

49. A recent law school graduate took and passed the bar examination. Before the swearing-in ceremony, however, the graduate received a letter from the bar examiners indicating that his admission would be delayed until a character fitness investigation had been completed. The examiners also requested information as to whether the graduate had ever been arrested, convicted, or placed on probation for a criminal offense. The graduate had been arrested as a juvenile for possession of marijuana. He was placed in a special drug education program for first-time juvenile offenders and was told that the arrest would be expunged. Since the graduate believed that he had been totally exonerated of criminal liability, he didn't report the arrest on his bar application form.

The bar examiners had, in fact, received an anonymous letter making reference to the graduate's juvenile arrest and suggesting that he was not morally fit to be admitted as an attorney. In addition, the letter provided detailed information about the facts related to the offense. As a result, the examiners hired a special investigator, to look into the matter. As part of the investigator's inquiry, he went to the clerk of the juvenile court where the offense occurred and demanded access to the records concerning the graduate. The clerk refused, citing a state statute that required all court and police records relating to juveniles be sealed. After all other attempts to gain access to the records proved futile, the bar examiners filed suit in federal district court demanding access to the relevant documents.

The court should rule that, as applied to this case, the state statute regarding the sealing of juvenile records is

(A) constitutional, because juveniles are entitled to the equal protection of the laws.
(B) constitutional, because the state has a strong and legitimate interest in rehabilitating juvenile offenders, and this is furthered by protecting them from embarrassment in later life through revelation of juvenile offenses.
(C) unconstitutional, because the bar examiners, as a quasi-judicial agency, is entitled to have access to all relevant public documents.
(D) unconstitutional, because it hinders the interests of justice by preventing the bar examiners from determining the fitness of candidates to practice law.

50. A city enacted an ordinance prohibiting the singing and chanting of songs from 1:00 P.M. to 1:00 A.M. by two or more persons if such noise is audible off the premises where the singing takes place. The ordinance expressly exempted from its purview the singing or chanting of religious songs.

After the ordinance was enacted and went into effect, several college students were walking down the street on their way to a victory celebration following a big college football game. They began loudly chanting, "We're number 1...we're number 1." One of the residents who lived on the street was greatly disturbed by the noise and reported the incident to the police, who were immediately summoned to the scene. The students who engaged in the chanting were arrested and charged with violating the ordinance.

The students who were prosecuted now bring suit challenging the constitutionality of the city ordinance. Which of the following would constitute their WEAKEST argument against enforcement of the city ordinance?

(A) The ordinance deprives persons of their freedom of expression, in violation of the First and Fourteenth Amendments.
(B) The ordinance deprives persons of their liberty without due process of law because the ordinance is not related to any legitimate community interest.
(C) The statutory language of the ordinance is vague and overbroad since it attempts to encompass all forms of singing.
(D) The ordinance deprives the persons of the equal protection of the laws by impermissibly distinguishing between religiously inspired singing and all forms of singing.

51. A citizen of a state was arrested and charged under a state statute making it a felony for "a male to sell or give alcoholic beverages to a female under the age of 14." At his trial, the citizen attacked the validity of the state statute on federal constitutional grounds.

The court will likely hold the statute to be

(A) constitutional, because under the Twenty First Amendment, a state has exclusive authority to regulate the use and sale of intoxicating liquors.
(B) constitutional, because the state could reasonably believe that young females need more protection than young males under these circumstances.
(C) unconstitutional, because it lacks a legitimate purpose and, therefore, is violative of the Fourteenth Amendment.
(D) unconstitutional, because the law treats males and females differently without adequate justification and, therefore, is violative of the Fourteenth Amendment.

52. During a hotly contested gubernatorial election, a local newspaper endorsed the candidacy of a corporate official of a chemical company. Inspired by a progressive revolt against the chemical company's domination of the state government, the corporate official's opponent, won by an extremely close margin.

After the new governor took office, he vowed to get back at the company that owned the local newspaper for its newspaper's endorsement of the corporate official. Using his influence, the new governor was instrumental in getting the state legislature to pass a bill that imposed a special tax on the sale of ink and paper used in the publication of newspapers and periodicals of general circulation. The tax bill was signed into law by the governor.

The strongest constitutional basis upon which to challenge the validity of the tax would be the

(A) equal protection clause of the Fourteenth Amendment.
(B) bill of attainder provision under Article I, Section 10.
(C) privileges or immunities clause of the Fourteenth Amendment.
(D) First Amendment, as incorporated in the Fourteenth Amendment.

53. After months of negotiations, the United States and Canada entered into a tax treaty that provided that neither country would impose income taxes on citizens of the other nation. The treaty, which was ratified by the Senate, was supported by professional baseball and hockey players. Many Canadian hockey players, who were employed by American teams and lived in the United States during the hockey season, lobbied for passage of the treaty, since they were subject to the payment of both U.S. and Canadian income taxes. In like manner, many American baseball players, who lived in Canada during the baseball season, objected to the same dual taxation.

In violation of the treaty, a Canadian court convicted a U.S. citizen who resided in Canada, of illegally evading the payment of Canadian income taxes. The U.S. citizen, who was a member of a Canadian baseball team, resided in Canada during the baseball season. Following his conviction, the President announced that the previously effective tax treaty would no longer be abided by the United States. The President proclaimed that Canada's refusal to honor the treaty rendered it invalid. As a result, the President ordered the Internal Revenue Service to begin collecting income taxes from Canadian citizens residing in the United States in the same manner that it collects taxes from other residents of this country.

A Canadian citizen and resident of the United States, sues in an appropriate federal court, seeking a declaratory judgment that the treaty with Canada remains valid and effective. Therefore, he contends that the Internal Revenue Service may not collect U.S. income taxes from him.

Which of the following is the strongest constitutional basis that may be urged in support of this claim?

(A) The President's unilateral termination of a treaty benefiting residents of the United States cannot be effective until a hearing is afforded to persons who would be affected by such action.
(B) The courts have exclusive authority to determine whether a particular treaty has, in fact, been breached by another nation.
(C) A ratified treaty is the supreme law of the land and, therefore, remains effective until superseded by another treaty or statute.
(D) The treaty created a property right in Canadian citizens residing in the United States that cannot be taken away without just compensation.

54. The United States and Mexico entered into a tax treaty that provided that neither country would impose income taxes on citizens of the other nation. The treaty was ratified by the Senate. Recently, the President, angry over Mexico's perceived failure to abide by the terms of the treaty, has decided that the United States would not honor any of the terms of the treaty. The President then ordered the Internal Revenue Service to begin collecting income taxes from Mexican citizens residing in the United States in the same manner that it collects taxes from other residents of this country.

A Mexican citizen and resident of the United States sues in an appropriate federal court, seeking a declaratory judgment that the treaty with Mexico remains valid and effective. Therefore, he contends that the Internal Revenue Service may not collect U.S. income taxes from him.

Which of the following is the strongest constitutional grounds for the federal court to refuse to decide the suit on its merits?

(A) The citizen has no standing to bring his suit.
(B) The case presents a nonjusticiable political question.
(C) The case is moot because the President has already taken definitive action with respect to the effectiveness of this treaty.
(D) The citizen is not entitled to a federal adjudication of this case because as a resident alien, he is not protected by the privileges or immunities clause of the Fourteenth Amendment.

55. A state has enacted a criminal statute prohibiting the mailing of obscene materials to any person. The owner of a publication company was prosecuted and convicted of violating the state obscenity law by mailing adults sexual literature that appealed to their prurient interests.

During the owner's trial, the judge instructed the jury that determining if the mailed materials were obscene depended in part on whether they were offensive to the average or normal person under contemporary community standards, and that the community standards test must be considered in light of the fact that many children reside in the community. Furthermore, the judge instructed the jury that in determining whether the materials were obscene, it could also consider evidence of pandering, or whether the materials were marketed purposely to appeal to the recipients' prurient interest in sex.

The owner appealed her conviction, alleging a denial of her First Amendment rights. Which of the following is the strongest argument why the appellate court should reverse the owner's conviction?

(A) The method by which materials are marketed or advertised is not probative of whether they are obscene.
(B) It is an unconstitutional invasion of privacy for the government to interfere with the content of closed mailings intended for the private use by consenting adults.
(C) Under the First Amendment, the community's standards for children may not be applied in determining what constitutes obscenity for adults.
(D) Obscenity is to be determined by applying national standards, not contemporary community standards.

56. A 2-week-old baby had developed a severe case of jaundice. A pediatrician informed the infant's father that unless his daughter received immediate medical treatment, she would die. The father, who was very religious, refused to permit the pediatrician to administer the necessary treatment. He explained that his faith in his religion would restore his daughter to good health. As a consequence, the pediatrician sought an order from the state court, where the father was present, permitting the pediatrician to provide the necessary medical treatment to the infant.

Which of the following is the father's strongest constitutional argument against the court order?

(A) The order violates the due process clause of the Fourteenth Amendment.
(B) The order violates the equal protection clause of the Fourteenth Amendment.
(C) The order violates the free exercise clause of the First Amendment, as incorporated by the Fourteenth Amendment.
(D) The order violates the privileges or immunities clause of the Fourteenth Amendment.

57. A 3-week-old baby, came down with a very high fever. The baby's pediatrician informed the mother that unless her son received immediate medical treatment, he would die. The mother objected on religious grounds. She claimed that it would be better for her son to die if that was his fate. The pediatrician sought an order from the state court. The mother was present with her lawyer at the court.

In deciding whether it may issue such an order in face of all relevant constitutional defenses by the mother, which of the following must the state court consider?

(A) Whether medical treatment is necessary to save the baby's life.
(B) Whether the mother's refusal to authorize medical treatment is justified on the basis of current knowledge.
(C) Whether the hospital is owned and operated by the state.
(D) Whether the mother is a taxpayer of the state in which the court is located.

58. A state statute provides that an illegitimate child may not inherit from his father's property. The state law, however, does permit illegitimate children to inherit from and through their mothers. A man died intestate, leaving neither spouse nor any children other than an illegitimate son. The man's wife and his daughter died one year later in a motor vehicle accident. The illegitimate son filed suit in an appropriate court alleging that the state statute, which bars an illegitimate child from sharing in his father's estate is invalid, and that he should be declared the lawful heir of the man's estate.

In challenging the validity of the state statute, will the illegitimate son prevail?

(A) Yes, because most state laws that discriminate against illegitimate children have been invalidated to ensure that a state's concern over illicit relationships is not the basis for punitive measures against the product of such a relationship.
(B) Yes, because he has been deprived of property without due process, since his fundamental right to inherit has been compromised without a compelling state need.
(C) No, because a state may promote the just and expeditious disposition of property at death by denying intestate succession to all illegitimate children.
(D) No, because discrimination against illegitimate children is not suspect and, therefore, the law does not violate the equal protection clause if it is substantially related to a legitimate state interest.

59. A state has recently enacted a statute prohibiting the disposal of any nuclear wastes within the state. This law does not contravene or conflict with any federal statutes. A man operates a company in the state that is engaged in the disposal of nuclear wastes. Subsequent to the passage of the state statute, the man, not yet aware of the new law, entered into contracts with many out-of-state firms to dispose of their nuclear wastes in the state. On account of this new law, however, the man will be unable to perform these contracts.

Assume that the man has standing to challenge this state law. Which of the following presents his strongest constitutional grounds to challenge the state law prohibiting the disposal of nuclear wastes within the state?

(A) The commerce clause.
(B) The equal protection clause of the Fourteenth Amendment.
(C) The privileges and immunities clause of Article IV, Section 2.
(D) The contract clause.

60. A shrimp fishery is located in the coastal waters of a state. A large part of the catch is either frozen or canned, and distributed nationwide. The state legislature passed a statute requiring payment of a license fee of $25 for each shrimp boat owned by a resident and $2,500 for each boat owned by a nonresident.

A resident of a neighboring state was a commercial shrimp fisherman who was denied a license after refusing to pay the $2,500 fee. The resident brought suit in federal court challenging the constitutionality of the state shrimp boat licensing statute. The federal court should

(A) hear the case on its merits.
(B) dismiss the suit because the resident lacks standing.
(C) dismiss the suit because it involves a question of state law.
(D) abstain from jurisdiction because the constitutional issue should be litigated first in a state court.

61. There is a thriving source of crawfish that live in a state. The state owns a fleet of boats that trawl for crawfish. The state is willing to sell the crawfish to in-staters for $1 per pound and to out-of-staters who come to the state for $5 per pound. The state felt that the increased fee for out-of-staters was a reasonable contribution toward the protection they received from the state.

Assume that the federal court decided to hear the case. The statute is likely to be found

(A) constitutional, because it is a valid exercise of the state's police power.
(B) constitutional, because the fee was a reasonable contribution toward the protection that the state government gave nonresidents.
(C) unconstitutional, because it places a discriminatory burden on interstate commerce.
(D) unconstitutional, because it constitutes a violation of the privileges and immunities clause under Article IV.

62. A state has passed a law that provides that only residents of the state who are citizens of the United States can own agricultural land in the state. A out-of-state farmer who is a U.S. citizen has contracted, subsequent to the aforementioned law, to purchase a farm from a landowner, which is located in the state. The landowner, who is a resident of the state, has been informed by his attorney that his sales agreement with the farmer is null and void under state law.

Which of the following is the best constitutional argument to contest the validity of the state statute?

(A) The contract clause prohibition against a state from enacting any law that will impair the obligation of contracts.
(B) The privileges and immunities clause of the Fourteenth Amendment.
(C) The privileges and immunities clause under Article IV, Section 2.
(D) The national property power provision under Article IV, Section 3.

63. Recently, Congress enacted a statute requiring all boat owners to register their boats with a newly created federal boat registry. Among the purposes of the statute are the prevention of theft of boats in coastal waters and the protection of the rights of individual boat owners throughout the United States.

Congress enacted the statute despite the fact that all states require boat owners to register their craft with the state department of motor vehicles. In addition, there is uncontradicted evidence that most stolen boats are kept or resold in the state in which the theft occurred. Nonetheless, an increasing number of boats are transported to other states and other countries for resale.

Is the statute likely to be held constitutional?

(A) No, because most stolen boats remain within the state in which they were stolen.
(B) No, because the registration of boats is a matter reserved to the states by the Tenth Amendment.
(C) Yes, because Congress could determine that the transportation of stolen boats affects interstate commerce.
(D) Yes, because Congress has the power to regulate property for the general welfare.

64. A state legislature has recently enacted a statute requiring all prospective voters in state elections who wish to write-in a candidate to print the candidate's full name, and designate the office for which the candidate is running. The statute provides that such information must be written on the ballot in ink in an appropriate space.

A write-in candidate for the office of Attorney General is a Chinese-American. The candidate is of the opinion that he needs a large turnout of Chinese voters in order to win the election. As a result, his campaign manager decides to mail to every registered Chinese voter a tear-off sticker, which bears the candidates name along with the office of Attorney General. Since many native Chinese people are not proficient in reading and writing English, the campaign manager believes that many of the voters will have difficulty writing the candidate's name and office on the ballot. As a result, the campaign manager has mounted an extensive media campaign to inform voters on how to apply the stickers to the ballot.

Five months prior to the election an election official notifies the candidate's campaign committee that the tear-off stickers do not comply with the state statute. In her letter, the official explains that state election officials are of the opinion that it is necessary for potential voters to write the candidate's name in ink. Therefore, she concludes that the stickers do not comply with statutory requirements.

Three weeks later, the candidate filed suit in federal district court against the election officials, claiming that their interpretation of the state statute violates the U.S. Constitution. Thereafter, one of the candidate's opponents filed suit in state court seeking to prevent state election officials from counting any write-in ballots with stickers. The state court has now scheduled a prompt hearing on this matter. In addition, the state court has indicated that it hopes to render a decision on the merits within the next three weeks.

Which of the following statements is correct concerning the federal court's adjudication of the candidate's suit?

(A) The federal court should hear the case on the merits.
(B) The federal court should refuse to hear the case because it presents a nonjusticiable political question.
(C) The federal court should refuse to hear the case because of the abstention doctrine.
(D) The federal court should remand the case to the state court to decide the constitutional issue presented.

65. A state has recently enacted a statute requiring all prospective voters in state elections who wish to write-in a candidate to print the candidate's full name, and designate the office for which the candidate is running. The statute provides that such information must be written on the ballot in ink in an appropriate space.

A write-in candidate is a German-American and is of the opinion that he needs a large turnout of German voters in order to win the election. As a result, his campaign manager decides to mail to every registered German voter a tear-off sticker, which bears the candidate's name and office for which he is running. Since many native German people are not proficient in reading and writing English, the campaign manager believes that many of the voters will have difficulty writing the candidate's name and office on the ballot. As a result, the campaign manager has mounted an extensive media campaign to inform voters on how to apply the stickers to the ballot.

Five months prior to the election an election official notifies the candidate's campaign committee that the tear-off stickers do not comply with the state statute. In her letter, the official explains that state election officials are of the opinion that it is necessary for potential voters to write the candidate's name in ink. Therefore, she concludes that the stickers do not comply with statutory requirements.

Three weeks later, the candidate filed suit in federal district court against state election officials, claiming that their interpretation of the state statute violates the U.S. Constitution.

Which of the following sets forth the strongest constitutional argument the candidate could make against the interpretation of the statute by the state officials?

(A) It unreasonably discriminates against German voters who lack a proficiency in the English language.
(B) It unreasonably discriminates against write-in candidates for public office.
(C) It unreasonably interferes with the exclusive federal election power as embodied in the Fifteenth Amendment.
(D) It unreasonably interferes with the 1965 Voting Rights Act outlawing literacy tests.

66. A write-in candidate is a Mexican-American and is of the opinion that he needs a large turnout of Mexican voters in order to win the election. As a result, his campaign manager, decides to mail to every registered Mexican voter a tear-off sticker, which bears the candidate's name and office for which he is running. Since many native Mexican people are not proficient in reading and writing English, the campaign manager believes that many of the voters will have difficulty writing the candidate's name and office on the ballot. As a result, the campaign manager has mounted an extensive media campaign to inform voters on how to apply the stickers to the ballot.

Five months prior to the election an election official notifies the candidate's campaign committee that the tear-off stickers do not comply with the state statute. In her letter, the official explains that state election officials are of the opinion that it is necessary for potential voters to write the candidate's name in ink. Therefore, she concludes that the stickers do not comply with statutory requirements.

Three weeks later, the candidate filed suit in federal district court against state election officials claiming that their interpretation of the state statute violates the U.S. Constitution.

Which of the following, if established, sets forth the strongest constitutional argument supporting the election official's interpretation of the statute?

(A) Voter turnout among registered Mexican American voters who lack proficiency in English has been less than 1% of the entire state total in recent elections.
(B) A state statute requires that each voting booth be equipped with an ink pen to facilitate the writing in of votes.
(C) Since large numbers of write-in votes generally increase the time needed to count all votes, it is necessary to cast such votes in a uniform manner.
(D) The potential for voting fraud is substantially greater with preprinted stickers.

67. A state assemblyman made a visit to a foreign country. To protest U.S. foreign policy, the assemblyman and the foreign country's leader issued a joint statement criticizing the United States' involvement in the political affairs of neighboring countries.

Following the assemblyman's return to the United States, he was prosecuted under a federal criminal statute making it unlawful for any citizen not specifically authorized by the President to negotiate with a foreign government for the purpose of influencing the foreign government in relation to a dispute with the United States. The law further provides that "any citizen who knowingly counsels, aids, or abets a foreign government in a dispute with the United States...shall, upon conviction... be punished by imprisonment for not more than five years or a fine of not more than $10,000, or by both fine and imprisonment...."

Which of the following is the strongest constitutional basis for upholding the validity of the aforementioned federal statute?

(A) Federal criminal laws dealing with international affairs need not be as specific as those dealing with domestic affairs.
(B) Under its enumerated powers, Congress may legislate to preserve the monopoly of the national government over the conduct of U.S. foreign affairs.
(C) The President's inherent power to negotiate for the U.S. with foreign countries authorizes him to punish citizens who engage in such negotiations without permission, even in the absence of statutory authorization.
(D) Article I, Section 8 of the Constitution grants Congress concurrent power with the President to regulate external affairs with foreign countries.

68. Which of the following executive orders will most likely be found unconstitutional?

(A) The President issued an executive order requiring all executive branch employees to use exclusively one brand of ballpoint pens and pencils as their writing utensils. According to a study, the federal government could save in excess of $250,000 a year in office supply costs if all executive agencies were to use standardized pens and pencils.

(B) The President issued an executive order requiring all executive branch employees to wear only white shirts and blouses during regular working hours. According to the President's directive, executive employees are prohibited from wearing colored (e.g., blue or yellow) or striped shirts and blouses while on duty. The President issued the order in an effort to establish a uniform dress code for all executive employees.

(C) In 1887, Congress passed a law establishing a federal Commission of Birdwatchers. The Commission, which is still in effect, consists of seven members who are appointed by the President. The Commission's main function is to go on periodic retreats to photograph and study North American birds and their migratory habits. Believing that the Commission is archaic, the President decides that any future funding will simply be a waste of money. He thus executes an executive decree abrogating the Commission of Birdwatchers.

(D) A devastating hurricane damages an island which is part of a foreign country. The storm destroys many homes, resulting in death and injury to thousands. In response to a request from the foreign government for emergency aid, the President, without seeking the advice and consent of the Senate, issues an executive decree authorizing U.S. Army troops to the island to provide medical and humanitarian assistance.

69. The President announced that a newly created military rapid deployment force would be engaging in joint training exercises with the military forces in a foreign country. Following the President's announcement, Congress enacted a statute that unequivocally prohibited "the U.S. Armed Forces from conducting military exercises with foreign military forces unless Congress has received notice of such intention to take such action at least three months before the joint military exercises become effective."

This statute is most likely

(A) constitutional, because the President, in this instance, has not been called by Congress into actual service as Commander-in-Chief.

(B) constitutional, because of Congressional power under the War Powers Act.

(C) unconstitutional, because of the President's authority to execute the laws of the United States.

(D) unconstitutional, because of the President's authority as Commander-in-Chief of the Armed Forces.

70. Congress recently enacted a statute permitting a governmental agency to make a gift of federal property to private individuals or organizations, provided that it be used "to further good relations and better understanding with foreign governments."

The Secretary of Defense planned to give an old military cargo plane to a national organization who supports future pilots. Before making the gift, the Secretary was approached by the head of a church. The church leader indicated that he would be sponsoring a worldwide crusade and suggested to the Secretary that such an undertaking would serve to strengthen relations with foreign governments. The Secretary donated the plane to the church instead of the organization.

Who would have the best standing to challenge the Secretary's action?

(A) A citizen of the United States.

(B) A taxpayer of the United States.

(C) The national organization.

(D) A state within the United States.

71. Congress recently passed a law that would grant, for free, federally owned buses to a religious organization. The congressional statute stipulates that the religious organization must use the buses to travel across America to spread the moral message of sexual abstinence to teenagers at school assemblies.

Which of the following is the strongest constitutional grounds for invalidating the gift of the buses to the religious organization?

(A) The gift violates the equal protection rights of secular organizations.
(B) The gift violates the establishment clause.
(C) The gift is a taking of federal property without just compensation.
(D) The gift violates the commerce clause.

72. A city has granted a license to a private utility company to provide electrical service to the residents in the city. After approving the license to the utility company, the city council then passed a measure by which the utility company was required to insert in its monthly billing statements a letter from a private consumer group criticizing the high cost of electrical service. The cost of printing and mailing the monthly letter was paid entirely by the consumer group. Nonetheless, the utility company vehemently objected to having such a critical letter enclosed in their monthly billing statements. However, the city council warned the utility company that unless it complied with the directive, the city would revoke its license for electrical service. The utility company filed suit in federal court seeking a hearing prior to its license being revoked by the city council.

Which of the following constitutional provisions would provide the utility company with the strongest grounds with which to challenge the city council measure?

(A) The due process clause.
(B) The equal protection clause.
(C) The privileges and immunities clause of Article IV.
(D) The commerce clause.

73. A student at a private university was receiving financial aid from the university based on a financial aid application he completed at the time of his enrollment. During finals at the end of the fall semester, the student was caught cheating. His chemistry professor saw him looking at a fellow student's exam paper and copying the answers to three multiple choice questions. The professor notified the honor committee, which immediately found an honor code violation and ordered that the student receive a failing grade in the course. In addition, in accordance with the rules of the university, the student's financial aid was terminated.

The student filed a lawsuit seeking reinstatement of his financial aid. The student's only argument was that his due process rights were violated in that he did not receive a notice of, or a hearing on, the alleged honor code violation.

Which of the following facts, if true, would be most helpful to the student?

(A) The university was in financial difficulties and could not meet its payroll expenses.
(B) The university did not re-allocate the student's financial aid to another deserving student.
(C) The university received support from the state.
(D) The honor committee sent the student a letter to advise him of the hearing date.

74. A woman was employed as a state trooper. Although the state provides both sexes with equal pay and benefits, the state has adopted a policy that prohibits the assignment of female officers to its special undercover narcotics division. This is a moderate risk position that sometimes involves violent encounters with drug dealers. Since the special narcotics division was first established, five undercover agents have been killed in the line of duty. It is because of the state's concern with the safety and well-being of its female officers that it has adopted such a policy.

The woman, who desired to be a member of the narcotics division, filed an application for assignment as a special drug agent. After she was rejected for the position, the woman sued the state in federal court to enjoin enforcement of its stated policy on the grounds that it is unconstitutional.

As a matter of constitutional law, which of the following results in this suit is most appropriate?

(A) Judgment for the woman, because the facts asserted do not demonstrate that the particular classification contained in this policy is substantially related to the advancement of an important state interest.
(B) Judgment for the woman, because the terms and conditions of state government employment are privileges or immunities of state citizenship that may not be abridged by the state on the basis of gender.
(C) Judgment for the state, because it is within a state's police power to insulate the terms and conditions of governmental employment.
(D) Judgment for the state, because the state has articulated a rational basis for this classification and, therefore, a court may not substitute its judgment for that of responsible state officials.

75. An employee is an orthodox member of his faith. He has recently been hired as a forest ranger by the state. In accordance with the orthodox tradition of his religion, the employee wears a covering on his head throughout the day. The director of the state forestry department has notified the employee that he will not be permitted to wear his head covering while on duty. A state forestry regulation provides that all forest rangers are required to wear only standard headgear in the interests of maintaining a uniform dress code conducive to the furtherance of the department's morale, efficiency, and professional standard of conduct. Although the employee wants to pursue a career as a forest ranger, he feels that his religious beliefs should not be compromised by a governmental agency.

In trying to resolve his dilemma, the employee seeks your legal advice. You should advise him that in light of relevant U.S. Supreme Court decisions, the state regulation is probably

(A) constitutional, because although the employee has a constitutional right to the free exercise of his religion, a state may impose reasonable regulations that are rationally related to the furtherance of a state interest.
(B) constitutional, because the interest of the state in vindicating a carefully considered professional judgment by the forestry director that wearing such religious apparel would interfere with the department's morale and efficiency is sufficient to contravene the wishes of its members to wear headgear required by their religious beliefs.
(C) unconstitutional, because in accordance with the free exercise clause of the First Amendment, a state has no power to regulate religious beliefs.
(D) unconstitutional, because an individual has a fundamental right to seek gainful employment, and a state cannot arbitrarily and unreasonably regulate against such economic activity.

76. The state legislature enacted a statute requiring that every high school English class use the Psalms of the Bible as the sole basis for teaching poetry. The preamble to this legislation recited: We find and declare that the Psalms of the Holy Bible are great poetry independent of their religious significance, and that the academic interests of the students of this state will be best served by using the Psalms as models of outstanding verse. An atheist objects to the use of religious materials in his high school age daughter's classroom, so he brings an action in federal court to enjoin enforcement of the statute.

How should the district court rule?

(A) For the father, because the statute violates the First Amendment establishment clause.
(B) For the father, because the statute interferes with his right to free exercise of his religion.
(C) For the state, because the challenged legislation has a clearly stated secular purpose.
(D) For the state, because the court may not infringe upon the legislature exercise of discretion about the artistic merit of the Psalms.

77. New scientific research suggests there is a good chance that life exists in other solar systems. Consequently, the Federal Government has decided to use satellite technology to transmit messages to extraterrestrials concerning the importance of preparing for the Judgment Day. Representatives of each of Earth's major religions are allowed to prepare a ten-minute message which would be broadcast into space 24 hours per day.

What is the most likely result if a proper challenge is made to the expenditure of $50 million on this program?

(A) This action by the Federal Government will be upheld as a valid exercise of the spending power.
(B) This expenditure will be upheld as a proper extension of Congress's power to regulate commerce with foreign nations.
(C) This expenditure will be invalid under the First Amendment.
(D) This expenditure will be struck down because there is no rational relationship to any federal power.

78. The Sons of the Mayflower is a fraternal organization with several thousand members in a state. Founded in 1923, the bylaws of the Sons of the Mayflower originally required that in order to be a member, one must have been able to trace one's ancestry to the Pilgrims who came to North America on the ship for which the organization was named. In 1953, during a period of severely declining membership, the bylaws were altered to permit membership by any male American citizen. The organization works closely with state and local governments on many of its projects. For example, the organization runs all the extracurricular athletic programs for public schools in the state. In return, the state and local governments provide financial support for the organization's operations, including providing free use of a government building used as the organization's headquarters and meeting place. A female descendant of the Mayflower Pilgrims applied for membership in the Sons of the Mayflower. She received a letter from the chapter president informing her that women were not eligible for membership in the Sons of the Mayflower.

If the woman sues in federal court to compel the Sons of the Mayflower to permit her to join, what will be the probable outcome?

(A) The woman will prevail, because the organization's extensive ties to state and local government mean its exclusion of women constitutes state action for purposes of the Fourteenth Amendment.
(B) The woman will prevail, because excluding women is not substantially related to an important government interest.
(C) The Sons will prevail, because they need only show that their exclusion of women is rationally related to a legitimate government interest.
(D) The Sons will prevail, because they can show that a compelling state interest justifies exclusion of women from their membership.

79. Several states have enacted "state shield" laws that provide a varying range of protection for news persons compelled to release the names of confidential sources. Now, Congress, under intense lobbying pressure from the press, proposes to enact legislation forbidding any state from requiring journalists to reveal the sources of their news articles in civil suits.

Which of the following is the strongest constitutional argument in support of this proposed law?

(A) Congress has the authority under the commerce clause to regulate the flow of news.
(B) Acts of Congress are the supreme law of the land and take precedence over any conflicting state laws.
(C) Congress is essentially reaffirming the free speech guarantees of the First and Fourteenth Amendments.
(D) Congress has the authority to secure to authors and inventors the exclusive right to their respective writings and discoveries.

80. Due to troubled economic times, Congress passed a bill which increased taxes on citizens in order to replenish the country's war chest. One of the reasons for the current financial difficulties is that the United States has just ended an expensive ten-year war with a small African country. However, the United States is now in peace. Many citizens are complaining about paying into the war fund when there is absolutely no wartime in sight in the upcoming years. Many challenge the constitutionality of the taxation.

Can Congress tax the citizens in this manner?

(A) Yes, pursuant to the Constitution's Civil War Amendments.
(B) Yes, because Congress has war and defense powers.
(C) No, because the taxation exceeds Congress' narrow authority under the circumstances.
(D) No, because the government cannot increase taxes to fund war during peacetime.

81. State Blue is known for its coal production. Fearful of an impending glut on the market and the consequent effect on the local coal industry, the State Blue legislature enacts a law that prohibits the sale of coal within the state boundaries at less than $25/ton, which is the current market price.

This law is most likely to be held constitutional as applied to which of the following coal vendors?

(A) A neighboring state vendor offering coal for sale to the general public in State Blue at $20/ton.
(B) A State Blue vendor offering coal for sale to the U.S. Veteran's Hospital in the state at $20/ton.
(C) A State Blue vendor offering coal for sale to a manufacturing plant in State Blue at $20/ton.
(D) A foreign vendor offering coal for sale to the general public in State Blue for $20/ton.

82. Congress was concerned about the privacy of Internet communication and banking transactions conducted at automated teller machines. In order to increase the protections afforded these electronic transactions and communications, Congress enacted a statute. Under the statute, all encryption technology used to secure Internet and automated teller machine transactions was subject to federal regulation. The statute strictly regulated the development, use, and sale of all encryption software.

One provision of the statute expressly empowered a federal agency to regulate the import and export of all encryption technology with foreign countries. Accordingly, the federal agency was given authority to prohibit the export of any encryption system of software if, in the judgment of the federal agency, the export would threaten national security or other foreign policy interests.

A recognized expert on management information systems has developed an encryption software program that he was negotiating to sell to a company in a foreign country. The federal agency has refused to issue an authorization approving the sale of the expert's encryption software to the foreign company. Subsequently, the expert filed suit in federal district court challenging the constitutionality of the federal statute.

Is the federal statute constitutional?

(A) Yes, under the commerce clause.
(B) Yes, because Congress has the power to regulate for the general welfare.
(C) No, because it deprives the expert of a property right without just compensation.
(D) No, because it usurps the power of the executive branch to conduct foreign affairs.

83. In a small college town, every third Thursday in April for the past twenty five years, college students and local citizens gather together downtown and run for a mile in the nude to celebrate the end of the school year and beginning of spring. In the past few years, there has been an increase in the number of reports made to the police regarding adults who have brought very young children to witness this event. Other reports include more serious allegations of unwanted touching, sexual misconduct, and even the rape of two of the runners. Despite police efforts to monitor the longstanding and traditional event, there has been a fair steady trend of increasingly violent and aggressive behavior. In response, the local government banned the running of the naked mile. In the subsequent two years, the number of complaints to police on the third Thursday in April has markedly declined. Many of the yearly runners came together to challenge the constitutionality of the ban.

Is the ban an unconstitutional regulation of First Amendment rights?

(A) Yes, because it does not pass strict scrutiny.
(B) Yes, because its restriction on speech is greater than that necessary to protect the government interest.
(C) No, because the speech it regulates receives a lower level of protection.
(D) No, because the speech it regulates is child pornography.

84. In the past two years, a community has experienced a series of violent incidents that resulted in serious bodily injuries when mourners attacked picketers outside of military funerals. Concerned about disruptive behavior outside of funeral homes and cemeteries, the local government passed a law regulating all picketing, demonstrating, or the posting of signs between the hours of 11 a.m. and 3 p.m. on public land within fifty feet of the gates of a funeral home or cemetery. After the law was enacted, an eight-year-old was killed by a stray bullet during a shooting targeting a government official. At the child's midday funeral, mourners from all around the country peacefully lined the sidewalks around the cemetery with signs showing support for the child's family and requesting an end to unnecessary gun violence. All mourners outside of the cemetery gates were asked to take down their signs and disperse. The mourners challenged the regulation as unconstitutional.

Should the mourners have been allowed to remain outside of the cemetery?

(A) No, because their speech defamed gun manufacturers.
(B) No, because the law is a reasonable regulation of time, place, and manner of speech.
(C) Yes, because the law does not serve a significant government interest.
(D) Yes, because the mourners were peaceful.

85. One year ago, a local group burned a cross on the front lawn of the home of a member of the community. That group intended to intimidate the homeowner so that he would leave the community. As a result of this action, the state prohibited cross-burning that is done with the intent to intimidate. The local group sued the state for violating its First Amendment rights.

Will the regulation of the cross burning be held constitutional or unconstitutional?

(A) Constitutional, because it bans conduct.
(B) Constitutional, because the government is the speaker.
(C) Unconstitutional, because it bans expression.
(D) Unconstitutional, because the government may not regulate speech.

86. The Federal Aircraft Safety Act establishes safety and performance standards for aircraft manufactured in the United States. The Act creates a five-member aircraft commission to investigate air traffic safety, make recommendations to Congress for new laws, make further rules establishing safety and performance standards, and prosecute violations of the Act. The chairman is appointed by the president, two members are selected by the Senate, and two by the House of Representatives. A United States aircraft manufacturer seeks to enjoin enforcement of the commission's rules.

Which of the following is the best argument that the aircraft manufacturer can make?

(A) Legislative power may not be delegated by Congress to an agency in the absence of clear guidelines.
(B) The commerce power does not extend to the manufacture of aircraft not used in interstate commerce.
(C) The aircraft manufacturer is denied due process of law because it is not represented on the commission.
(D) The commission lacks authority to enforce its standards because not all of its members were appointed by the president.

87. A small cult of Satan worshippers had a religious ritual in which they would sacrifice a cat to the glory of Satan after a live dissection of the animal in which it endured frightful pain. During one such sacrifice, the cult leader was arrested on the complaint of the state humane officer and charged under a statute punishing cruelty to animals.

Should the cult leader be found guilty under the anti-cruelty statute?

(A) Yes, because belief in Satan does not enjoy constitutional protection.
(B) Yes, because sincere religious belief is not an adequate defense on these facts.
(C) No, because the enforcement of the law against the cult leader violated his constitutionally guaranteed freedom of religion and religious expression.
(D) No, because the beliefs of the cult members in the need for the sacrifice might be reasonable, and their act was religious.

88. After a series of fatal collisions on crowded state highways involving cars and long-haul eighteen wheel trucks, a state enacted a law which banned trucks with eighteen wheels from traveling through the center of cities without specific routing documents indicating that the trucks were making deliveries inside of the city limits. This forced many such trucks to take a longer route around major cities within the state and use access roads. Many of the access roads are poorly maintained and the truckers found that they needed a special set of tires to drive across this type of road. The state, understanding the condition of the roads, requires trucking companies within the state to fit their trucks with these special tires in order to receive permits to haul. Trucks driving for companies based within the state were all automatically fitted with these tires but trucks from out of the state were not. There is no national standard pertaining to tires and no other state has required this type of special tire. This type of tire only costs slightly more than the generally accepted tire.

Is the law constitutional?

(A) Yes, because the law merely incidentally burdens interstate commerce.
(B) Yes, because the law is a public health measure.
(C) No, because only the federal government may enact legislation affecting interstate commerce.
(D) No, because the law furthers no ostensible benefit.

89. The President of the United States entered into a treaty with a foreign country. According to the terms of the treaty, the treaty was to take effect immediately upon the parties' signing of the treaty. The President and the representative of the foreign country signed the treaty. Congress neither ratified nor consented to the treaty.

Is the treaty in effect in the United States?

(A) Yes, because Congress has delegated treaty-making power to the President.
(B) Yes, because the treaty is self-executing by its terms.
(C) No, because Congress neither ratified nor consented to the treaty.
(D) No, because of the separation of powers doctrine.

90. In recent years, the governmental standards for manufacturing and distributing a certain anti-depression medication were relaxed. As a result, there was less monitoring of the side effects of this medication. It was later determined that the anti-depressants cause certain types of cancer. One woman who had been taking these anti-depressants developed a non-fatal cancer which can be directly attributed to the medication. The woman is pregnant. This medication has not been shown to cause any birth defects. The woman later found out that she is terminally ill with a completely unrelated illness which cannot be caused by the anti-depressants. The woman challenges the constitutionality of the governmental standards and files suit in federal court on behalf of her unborn child against the agency that enforces these standards, for damages based on the future loss of the child's parent.

Can the woman file suit on behalf of her unborn child?

(A) No, because the court lacks jurisdiction.
(B) No, because there is no causation.
(C) Yes, because the unborn child is unable to bring the suit on his or her own behalf.
(D) Yes, because the anti-depressants will cause the death of the woman.

91. A state legislature enacts a statute providing that any person engaging in the business of electrolysis in the state is required to first obtain a license. The statute further states that the license applicant must offer proof of having graduated successfully from a state-approved electrolysis program consisting of at least two semesters of course and lab work, proof of residency within the state for a period of not less than 12 months, and proof of U.S. citizenship. Electrolysis is a method of removing body hair permanently by use of an electric current.

Is the statutory requirement of U.S. citizenship constitutional?

(A) No, because it constitutes a bill of attainder.
(B) No, because it violates the Fourteenth Amendment's equal protection clause.
(C) Yes, because it is reasonably related to ensuring the health and safety of clients.
(D) Yes, because it is within the police power reserved to the state under the Tenth Amendment.

92. The American and Canadian governments decide to create a joint commission to address the problem of declining populations of coastal wildlife. The commission is charged with determining whether particular shores should be closed and whether the two governments should impose bans or moratoriums on certain threatened animals. The U.S. president signs an executive agreement authorizing the commission to promulgate appropriate hunting regulations and to enforce and adjudicate the regulations against U.S. and Canadian hunting, fishing, and touring companies.

One of the commission's first acts is to institute a hunting limit on Canadian elk and an outright ban on hunting moose. A U.S. border state, which has one of the nation's richest coastal hunting reserves, passes legislation requiring all hunting operations using state coastal land to register for a fee and to meet or fall below state hunting limits, which are more restrictive than those set by the joint commission.

If the joint commission brings an action in federal court to enjoin the state from enforcing its hunting regulations, will the commission prevail?

(A) Yes, because the state law discriminates against hunting companies that are based outside of the state.
(B) Yes, because the executive agreement supersedes inconsistent state law.
(C) No, because state law should prevail when the issue involved is regulation of state industry.
(D) No, because state conservation issues should be dealt with by each state.

93. The President signs into law a bill imposing a special tax on all ink and paper used by publishers of newspapers and other periodicals. A newspaper publisher has decided to challenge this new federal tax because it does not apply to other consumers of ink and paper.

Which of the following constitutional provisions will best support the publisher's challenge?

(A) The Equal Protection Clause of the Fourteenth Amendment.
(B) The Privileges and Immunities Clause.
(C) The Due Process Clause.
(D) The First Amendment.

94. A newly-enacted state criminal statute provides, in its entirety, No person, without provocation, shall employ opprobrious words or abusive language, when such is used to or of another and tends to cause a breach of the peace. A 40-year-old man followed a small child home from school, yelling offensive four-letter words. The child repeatedly asked the man to leave him alone, but the man refused.

In a subsequent prosecution of the man, the first under this statute, the man

(A) can be convicted.
(B) cannot be convicted, because the First and Fourteenth Amendments bar punishing speech of the sort described here.
(C) cannot be convicted, because, though his speech here may be punished by the state, the state may not do so under this statute.
(D) cannot be convicted, because the average user of a public street would think his speech/action here was amusing and ridiculous rather than opprobrious.

95. Which of the following defendants could constitutionally be punished under a state statute which made criminal the incitement of others to perform any criminal act?

(A) A college student who tells a noontime rally of several hundred students at the university that the corporate structure of the United States reeks from its own corruption and will, when the time is right, be cleansed by the purifying fire of violent revolution, brothers and sisters; I will lead you in that glorious purifying bloodbath.
(B) A white supremacist who tells a clandestine meeting of seventeen followers that I believe that the nonwhite races are vermin created by Satan and should be eradicated on sight by right-thinking white Americans.
(C) A war protester who tells several thousand members of a protest march that the war that's going on is illegal and immoral, and you should all go to the draft board offices right now and burn their records as a symbol of our contempt for their illegal war.
(D) A member of the radical People's Revolutionary Army, whose manifesto states that each soldier of the People's Revolutionary Army will take constant and immediate action to destroy the government of the fascist United States and to execute the officials of that government. She joined the PRA two years ago and has attended one weekly meeting and one PRA bake sale.

96. A small agrarian religious community of about 150 people is sincere and pious in its religious belief that modern mankind has turned away from God's purpose and the only way that they can hope to do God's work is to completely turn away from modern life. One of their firmly held beliefs is that any form of education other than the knowledge that is found in their holy book is useless and the work of the devil. Consequently, they refuse to teach their children how to read or write. Instead they require their children to learn elaborate oral stories of their particular religious beliefs and ethics. The state superintendent of education informed the elders of the community that it was illegal for parents to refuse to send children under the age of 14 to either public or private schools which meet the minimum requirements of an educational institution in the state. When, after a period of 6 months, the elders still refused to send their children to any approved schools, the state began legal proceedings to have the court order them to send their children to state public schools. The elders' main defense is that to require their children to attend public school violates their First Amendment rights to freedom of religion.

Will the elders prevail in court?

(A) Yes, because their religious practices are guaranteed freedom from interference by the state by the First Amendment.
(B) Yes, because their method of educating their children is a fundamental tenet of their faith, so the First Amendment bars the state from requiring them to send their children to public school.
(C) No, because the state has an important state interest in educating the children located within its jurisdiction.
(D) No, because the sincerity of the elders' religious beliefs does not entitle them to a special exception from the state's compulsory education law.

97. State A, State B, and State C are adjacent to each other. States A and State C permit the use of automobile radar-detection devices, but State B strictly forbids them in order to discourage speeding and reduce auto accidents. A resident of State C is interested in purchasing an auto radar device. He drove to State A to purchase a new improved automobile radar-detection device from a manufacturer there. While driving back across State B to return to his home, the State C resident stopped to purchase gas in State B. A State B police officer who happened to be at the gas station saw the radar device visible on the front seat of the State C resident's car. The officer charged the State C resident, pursuant to the State B statute, with illegal possession of a prohibited radar device.

A valid federal administrative rule, adopted under a federal consumer product safety act, regulates the design of radar devices. The rule was issued to prevent the devices from causing injury to human beings by electrical shock while persons were installing the devices. No other federal law applies.

Which of the following best states the effect of the federal rule on the State B statute?

(A) The federal rule preempts the State B statute, because the federal rule regulates the same subject matter, radar devices.
(B) The federal rule preempts the State B statute, because the federal rule does not contain affirmative authorization for continued state regulation.
(C) The federal rule does not preempt the State B statute, because the State B statute regulates traffic safety, a field of exclusive state power.
(D) The federal rule does not preempt the State B statute, because the purposes of the federal rule and the State B statute are different.

98. A corporation is privately owned and incorporated in State A. The corporation contracted with the United States to construct and operate a general store in a federal park in State B. State B imposed a gross receipt tax on all business conducted within the state. State B then sued the corporation to collect that tax on the receipts the corporation received under this federal contract. No federal statutes or administrative rules are applicable, and the contract between the United States and the corporation does not mention state taxation.

The court should hold the state tax, as applied here, to be

(A) constitutional because a state has exclusive jurisdiction over all commercial transactions executed wholly within its borders.
(B) constitutional because private contractors performing work under a federal contract are not immune in these circumstances from nondiscriminatory state taxation.
(C) unconstitutional because it violates the Supremacy Clause.
(D) unconstitutional because it imposes an undue burden on interstate commerce.

99. A boat company provides ferry rides from the mainland to several islands off the coast of State Blue, as well a commuter boat service to the capital city. The company's contract with the state brings in nearly $4 million per year. Even with the boat service, travel into the capital city remains difficult, and the state legislature has begun to consider revitalizing an old rail line that connects the suburbs to the capital city.

The boat company operator opposes the revitalization and speaks out against it on local television, thus stoking the ire of a state senator, for whom the rail line is a pet project. The senator calls for a hearing on the awarding of the commuter boat service contract and introduces a resolution in the Senate chambers stating that the boat company won the contract illegally and resolving to revoke the operator's license and renegotiate the contract for the state. The state licensing board then examines the boat company's operations and finds serious safety problems. The board revokes the operator's license after he is unable to address the board's concerns adequately.

If the boat company operator challenges the revocation of his license, the operator should

(A) not prevail, because the impairment of the public contract was reasonable.
(B) not prevail, because the operator's boats endangered public safety.
(C) prevail, because the legislature's act constituted a bill of attainder.
(D) prevail, because the operator was denied due process.

100. A study funded by the National Violence Prevention Network found a strong correlation between the use of violent video games and juvenile crime. Congress enacted legislation providing that all video games must be rated on the packaging so that parents can determine before purchase whether and to what degree a video game contains violent content. The rating system had five categories, ranging from suitable for all ages to violent content unsuitable for anyone under 18. The federal legislation was silent on state regulatory authority, but expressly stated that a uniform regulatory scheme was needed to avoid confusion and difficulty in administration.

After finding the rating system inadequate to prevent excessively violent video games from entering their homes, the citizens of one state prevailed upon their lawmakers to impose a stronger rating system on video games sold in the state. The state legislature duly enacted a law providing that all video games sold in the state must be packaged with clearly marked information indicating each type of violent scenario or act depicted, as well as the federally mandated rating. A major national manufacturer of video games challenged the state rating statute in federal court.

The most likely outcome of the suit is that the state statute will be found

(A) constitutional, because regulatory authority over video games does not rest exclusively in the federal arena.
(B) constitutional, because the state statute does not directly conflict with the federal rating system.
(C) unconstitutional, because of the undue burden the state statute imposes on interstate commerce.
(D) unconstitutional, if Congress intended the federal rating system to occupy the field.

Answers and Explanations

1. **(D)** Choice (A) is incorrect because classifications based on sex have been held to violate equal protection. Choice (B) is wrong because such discrimination has not yet been held "suspect" and, therefore, need not be justified by a compelling interest. Choice (C) is incorrect because the existence of similar facilities would not preclude a finding of "state action." Choice (D) is the correct answer, since discrimination based on sex is subject to a "quasi-suspect" standard of review.

2. **(B)** Although the company is a privately owned corporation, the state has affirmatively encouraged and facilitated its discriminating acts, thus choice (A) is incorrect because "state action" exists. Choice (C) is an incorrect statement and not applicable to the fact situation. Choice (D) is wrong, since racial discrimination is "suspect" and, therefore, cannot be justified by some "rational basis." This is true, even if white Americans, a majority race, are the subjects of discrimination. Choice (B) is the strongest answer available.

3. **(B)** The equal protection clause provides heightened protection for groups whose legal classifications are suspect (e.g., classifications based on race, ethnicity, nationality, and religion) and for groups whose legal classifications are quasi suspect (e.g., gender, illegitimacy). The poor may have been the subject of discrimination by the legislature, but they are not members of a suspect or quasi-suspect class. Only rational review will be applied, which the county probably will pass with ease. Sometimes, the court may reject a law for violating the equal protection clause if the law denies a very important (albeit not fundamental) right like education. *See Plyler v. Doe,* 457 U.S. 202 (1982). The right to stay in a luxury hotel is not equivalent to such a right. Choice (A) is incorrect. The equal protection clause provides heightened protection for groups whose legal classifications are suspect (e.g., classifications based on race, ethnicity, nationality, and religion) and for groups whose legal classifications are quasi suspect (e.g., gender, illegitimacy). The poor may have been the subject of discrimination by the legislature, but they are not members of a suspect or quasi-suspect class. Only rational review will be applied, which the county probably will pass with ease. Choice (C) is too general a statement, because not all public rights are protected. Choice (D) is too broad, because not all discrimination against the poor violates equal protection.

4. **(D)** In *Memorial Hospital v. Maricopa County,* 415 U.S. 250 (1974), the U.S. Supreme Court held that an Arizona statute requiring one year's residence in a county as a precondition to receiving nonemergency hospitalization or medical care at public expense was unconstitutional as "an invidious discrimination against the poor," thus violative of the equal protection clause of the 14th Amendment. The Court found that this classification infringed upon interstate travel and in so doing, found that it was irrelevant that the classification also burdened travel by persons within their own state. Under the circumstances, the State of Arizona burdened the right to travel by denying benefits that were essential to the daily life of the new indigent in the state. The Court, in reviewing the state's justification for this residency requirement, utilized the strict scrutiny test. Therefore, choice (D) is correct, and choice (A) is incorrect. Choice (B) is incorrect. Idiomatically, there is no proper exercise of "state action." The state action doctrine refers to the idea that the government has acted and is thus theoretically subject to the U.S. Constitution. Choice (C) is incorrect. The state certainly has police powers under the 10th Amendment to regulate issues related to the health, safety, and welfare of its citizens. However, there are limits to what the state may do. The 14th Amendment's Equal Protection Clause would prohibit the state from denying to the poor essential medical services as described in our example. *See Memorial Hospital v. Maricopa County,* 415 U.S. 250 (1974).

5. **(C)** This Constitutional Law question presents some very close answer choices in the area of regulation of 1st Amendment freedom of speech. Regarding noncommunicative aspects of free speech, such as time, place, and manner regulations in public forums, courts will generally uphold ***reasonable*** restrictions. Choice (A) is persuasive on this issue. Where speech ***content*** is restricted, however, the courts apply a more rigid test whereby a compelling state interest must be justified before government regulation is permitted. Choice (B) addresses this issue, since the restrictions of the Fairgrounds Bill are content-neutral. Choice (D) seeks to balance the rights of free speech against

the patrons' right of privacy. Choice (C), however, presents the strongest argument to support the Fairgrounds Bill. In the area of ***solicitation,*** the court uses a ***balancing test*** to determine, upon weighing the individual's rights of free speech against the state's police powers interest in protecting the safety, welfare, and privacy interests of its citizens, that the challenged measure is reasonable and nondiscriminatory, and that ***there is no less-drastic alternative means available*** [*Beard v. Alexandria,* 341 U.S. 622 (1951)—requirement of homeowner's consent held a valid restriction on ***commercial*** solicitation, whereas a ban on ***all*** door-to-door solicitation was found to be too restrictive].

6. **(B)** In accordance with *Foley v. Connellie,* 98 S.Ct. 1067 (1978), the U.S. Supreme Court upheld the validity of a New York statute that limited the membership of the New York State Police Force to U.S. citizens. The Court stated that "in the enforcement and execution of the laws, the police function is one where citizenship bears a rational relationship to the special demands of the particular position." Thus, in applying the rational basis test, the Supreme Court held that the performance of the police function is an important public responsibility, which can be limited to a particular class (here, U.S. citizens only). Students should note that ***although aliens are extended the right to education and public welfare, along with the ability to earn a livelihood and engage in licensed professions, the right to govern and carry on a governmental function is reserved to citizens only.*** Therefore, the state police force statutory provision would not be violative of the Equal Protection Clause of the 14th Amendment. Though choice (A) is also correct, choice (B) is the preferred alternative, as it specifies the underlying rationale for upholding the constitutionality of the statute. Choice (C) is incorrect. Generally, classifications by the state that discriminate against lawful aliens are subject to strict scrutiny. Not so here, however. In *Foley v. Connellie*, 98 S.Ct. 1067 (1978), the U.S. Supreme Court upheld the validity of a New York statute that limited the membership of the New York State Police Force to U.S. citizens. The Court stated that "in the enforcement and execution of the laws, the police function is one where citizenship bears a rational relationship to the special demands of the particular position." Thus, in applying the rational basis test, the Supreme Court held that the performance of the police function is an important public responsibility, which can be limited to a particular class (here, U.S. citizens only). Finally, choice (D) is incorrect because there is no fundamental right to be a police officer.

7. **(C)** This Multistate question deals with the issue of ***standing.*** To satisfy the minimum constitutional requirements imposed by the "case and controversy" limitation of Article III, a plaintiff must demonstrate a definite and concrete personal stake in the outcome. First, the plaintiff must show ***actual injury in fact.*** Second, she must show causation (namely, that resolution of the grievance in her favor will eliminate the harm alleged). Under these facts, choice (C) is correct because the purchaser of marijuana cigarettes can demonstrate actual injury. Choices (A) and (B) are too remote. Also, the association of doctors would lack standing, since the general rule is against assertion of third-party rights except in limited situations. Choice (D) is incorrect because the doctors lack standing. To satisfy the minimum constitutional requirements imposed by the "case and controversy" limitation of Article III, a plaintiff must demonstrate a definite and concrete personal stake in the outcome. First, the plaintiff must show ***actual injury in fact.*** The medical doctors cannot show such injury.

8. **(A)** Choice (A) is correct because Congress can tax an activity, even if such a tax has a regulatory effect, provided that the ***dominant intent of the tax is fiscal (i.e., revenue-raising).*** Certainly, Congress has constitutionally taxed bookmakers, guns, and narcotics despite its substantial regulatory effect. In addition, under its ***spending powers,*** Congress can spend money (it collects from taxes) to "provide for the common Defense and general welfare of the United States." In this regard, a reasonable belief by Congress that payment of the tax fund proceeds to the education fund would benefit the cultural life of the nation as a whole would certainly fall within the proper scope of its federal taxing and spending powers. Choice (B) is incorrect. In a sense, the proposition contained in this answer is true. However, choice (A) is better because it references the specific constitutional power that authorizes Congress's action. Choices (C) and (D) are incorrect because, even if they were factually true, under the Tax and Spend Clause of Article I, Section 8, Congress is not required to apportion its subsidy among the states on an equitable basis. Rather, Congress is given broad discretion in taxing and spending under Article I, Section 8 for the "general welfare" [*United States v. Butler*, 297 U.S. 1 (1936)].

9. **(D)** The resident alien's best argument is the fact that the statute violated his rights under the Equal Protection Clause of the 14th Amendment. Congress has plenary power over the admission of aliens, but once admitted, most state discrimination against them is "suspect" and can only be upheld if necessary to protect a "state's special interest." Although there are earlier decisions upholding state statutes limiting or barring aliens from owning land (within the state), it is highly unlikely that such a statute would be upheld in light of recent decisions. Since the resident alien is not a citizen, choice (A) is wrong because the Privileges and Immunities Clause is only applicable to citizens of the United States. Choice (B) is wrong because the contract did not take place prior to the enactment of the statute. Choice (C) is a weak argument because the limitation of land ownership is within the state and does not affect interstate commerce.

10. **(A)** The federal government has power over aliens, but classifications by a state that are based on alienage are inherently suspect and subject to heightened judicial scrutiny. Since the statute makes a suspect classification, the burden of proving a compelling state interest rests with the state. Choice (B) is wrong because it incorrectly places the burden on the resident aliens. Choices (C) and (D) are incorrect because both resident aliens can establish standing based on the rationale [as expressed by the Supreme Court in *Shelley v. Kraemer*, 334 U.S. 1 (1948)] that "the civil rights intended to be protected from discriminatory state action by the Fourteenth Amendment are the rights to acquire, enjoy, own ***and dispose of*** property." Both have standing because the statute abrogates both the right to acquire and alienate property.

11. **(A)** The U.S. Supreme Court has long recognized that almost all statutes and other forms of government regulation classify (or discriminate) people. As a result, the Court has established several different tests for determining their permissibility under the equal protection clause. The two major tests are the "traditional," or rational basis test, and the "strict scrutiny," or compelling interest test. For virtually all economic and social regulations, the Court employs the traditional equal protection test, usually defined as follows: "The classification (or discrimination) is valid if it is rationally related to a proper (or constitutionally permissible) state interest." Under this rational basis test, a classification is presumed valid and will be upheld unless the person challenging it proves that it is "invidious" or "wholly arbitrary." Thus, the challenger has the burden to prove that ***the regulation is not rationally related to a legitimate state interest***. [*McGowan v. Maryland,* 366 U.S. 420 (1961)]. Conversely, government action that intentionally discriminates against racial or ethnic minorities is "suspect" and, thus, subject to "strict scrutiny." Since this question deals with a matter of "economic and social welfare," it will be reviewed under the basic rationality test. Therefore, choice (A) is the best answer. Choice (B) is incorrect because the commerce clause alone can limit state regulation. Choice (C) is incorrect. The equal protection clause provides heightened protection for groups whose legal classifications are suspect (e.g., classifications based on race, ethnicity, nationality, and religion) and for groups whose legal classifications are quasi suspect (e.g., gender, illegitimacy). Non-physicians may have been the subject of discrimination by the legislature, but they are not members of a suspect or quasi-suspect class. Only rational review will be applied, which the state probably will pass with ease. Finally, choice (D) is incorrect because the mere recitation that Congress has plenary powers to regulate interstate commerce is insufficient to invalidate the statute.

12. **(A)** Pursuant to the Commerce Clause, Congress has complete power to authorize or forbid state taxation that affects interstate commerce. Undoubtedly, the state tax adversely affects interstate commerce because the facts indicate that all manufacturers of slot machines are out-of-state. As such, the Commerce Clause affords the strongest constitutional grounds to attack the state tax. Choice (B) is incorrect. The manufacturers may have been the subject of discrimination by the legislature, but they are not members of a suspect or quasi-suspect class. Only rational review will be applied, which the state probably will pass with ease. Choice (C) is incorrect. There is no fundamental right under the due process clause to purchase affordable slot machines. Also, property has not been taken without due process of law because the owners still legally possess all of their slot machines. Choice (D) is incorrect. The privileges and immunities clause of Article IV, Section 2 only protects a U.S. citizen from discrimination by a state if that state's discrimination against out-of-staters is likely to discourage them from

traveling to the state [*Saenz v. Roe*, 526 U.S. 489 (1999)]. *Saenz* involved a California law that would have made moving to California financially prohibitive for many people receiving welfare from other states and who would continue to need welfare in California. No such facts are present in our example.

13. **(A)** With respect to standing, a person asserting the violation of a constitutional or statutory right must show a ***direct and immediate personal injury*** due to the challenged action. The facts clearly indicate that fewer slot machines are being purchased by casino owners on account of the tax. As a result, choice (A) is correct because a manufacturer of slot machines can show a "direct injury" from application of the tax. Note that associations of individuals may have standing to assert the rights of its members, at least so long as the challenged infractions adversely affect its members' associational ties. However, choice (C) is wrong because the associational members have not suffered a "direct" and "immediate" harm, since their tax liability is optional (namely, they are not required to play the video games). Choice (B) is not the strongest answer because a state resident is not required to play the slot machine. Hence, it is hard for him to show a direct and immediate injury. Choice (D) is incorrect. The youth organization is not required to play the video games. Hence, it is hard for it to show a direct and immediate injury.

14. **(D)** In *Arizona Board of Regents v. Harper*, 495 P.2d 453 (1972), the Arizona Supreme Court held that a board of regents has the authority to adopt a rule requiring residence of one year before a student may be classified as a resident of the state to qualify for lesser charges. Thus, the one-year residency requirement, in order for a student to qualify for lesser tuition charges, did not violate the Due Process, Equal Protection, or Privileges and Immunities Clauses of the U.S. Constitution. In this regard, lower tuition rates at state universities are valid and do not trigger strict scrutiny [*Starns v. Malkerson*, 326 F. Supp. 234 (1971)]. Choice (A) is incorrect. The student may have been the subject of discrimination by the legislature, but he is not a member of a suspect or quasi-suspect class. Only rational review will be applied, which state university probably will pass with ease. Choice (B) is incorrect. The Supreme Court has never recognized a right under the privileges and immunities clause for in-state college tuition. Choice (C) is not the best answer. The reference to "compelling state interest" implies that strict scrutiny will be used, but that in turn implies that the student has a fundamental right under the Privileges and Immunities Clause to the same tuition as the in-staters. But, as elaborated in choice (B), he doesn't. Accordingly, rational review will be used, which state university will easily pass.

15. **(A)** Under the *Lemon* test, as a general rule, a government program will be valid under the establishment clause ***if it (1) has a secular purpose; (2) has a primary effect that neither advances nor inhibits religion; and (3) does not produce excessive government entanglement with religion***. Many of the cases involving the establishment clause involve religious activities in public schools (e.g., prayer and Bible reading). This question has an interesting twist: namely, whether public school classes can be held in a church building. Under the circumstances, there does not appear to be an establishment clause violation because the city's action neither advances nor inhibits religion. Therefore, choice (A) is correct. Choice (B) is incorrect, as it ignores the religious establishment clause issue discussion, above. Choice (C) is incorrect. Excessive government entanglement with religion does not appear to be the case given that: (1) the church agreed to remove all religious symbols and paraphernalia from the "classrooms" utilized by the students; (2) only the main chapel was exempt so that it could remain open for prayer; and (3) no high school classes or activities were to be held in the main chapel. Finally, choice (D) is incorrect. The plaintiff will not win, and the city does not have to prove that there was a "compelling state interest." Under the circumstances, there does not appear to be an establishment clause violation, because the city's action neither advances nor inhibits religion.

16. **(D)** Choice (D) provides the best legal reasoning if the owner is successful in challenging the city's sound amplification ordinance. In accordance with the 1st Amendment's guarantee of freedom of speech, a state or municipality may regulate the use of sound amplification equipment, depending on the interests involved [*Kovacs v. Cooper*, 336 U.S. 77 (1949)]. The test applied by the courts in this 1st Amendment area (regarding the constitu-

tionality of such an ordinance) is that "the government action must further an important governmental interest unrelated to the message being communicated." According to the facts presented here, the municipality would not have an overriding interest in prohibiting the use of any sound device, except clock chimes, by a property owner in the city of Wilton. Choice (A) is incorrect, as the equal protection clause protects people, not sounds. Choice (B) is an incorrect statement of law. Choice (C) is incorrect because a state may regulate the use of sound amplification devices (e.g., sound trucks) in the interests of privacy and public tranquility.

17. **(B)** Choice (B) incorrectly suggests that only certain classes of speech are protected. Speech is GENERALLY protected; however, there are certain classes of speech that are unprotected (e.g., obscenity, fighting words, and slander). Choice (A) is an accurate statement because the statute is likely to be over-inclusive; it is vulnerable to a facial attack as unconstitutionally overbroad. Choices (C) and (D) are also accurate statements and, therefore, incorrect. Indirect speech regulations are permissible only if necessary to serve compelling state interests. Prior restraints on speech are not, *per se,* unconstitutional, but where the power to decide which speech will be affected is vested in an individual or entity who may decide, at their own discretion, and where there are no specific guidelines or oversight for such a decision, the discretion is considered ***unfettered***, and the restraint on speech will not withstand constitutional muster.

18. **(B)** As a general rule, a case is "moot" when there is no case or controversy once the matter has been resolved. In our example, the city's WEAKEST defense is that the manufacturer's case is moot because the matter (whether the manufacturer is precluded from selling his surfboards in the city) has not been resolved. Choice (A) is incorrect. Article III, Section 2 requires the existence of a "case or controversy" before a federal court may hear the case. In other words, there must be an actual dispute. This is not the weakest defense by the city, because the manufacturer has not tried to violate the law and, therefore, does not yet know whether he would be prosecuted under it. Furthermore, since the manufacturer had not meant to sell the boards until a year later, we do not know if the city would have changed its mind and repealed the ordinance. Choice (C) is incorrect, as the manufacturer would not appear to lack standing. One of the requirements for standing is the causation requirement. The manufacturer cannot be certain that he would actually be prosecuted under the law. Furthermore, since the manufacturer had not meant to sell the boards until a year later, we do not know if the city would have changed its mind and repealed the ordinance. Choice (D) is incorrect. The ripeness doctrine holds that "a claim is not ripe for adjudication if it rests upon contingent future events that may not occur as anticipated or, indeed, may not occur at all" [*Texas v. United States*, 523 U.S. 296 (1998)]. Here, since the manufacturer had not meant to sell the boards until a year later, we do not know if the city would have changed its mind and repealed the ordinance.

19. **(C)** Under the circumstances, the police clearly violated the group's 1st Amendment right of peaceful assembly. It is well established that ***assemblies or speeches that threaten imminent violence or serious disorder can be halted by the police to prevent physical injury,*** but unless the risk of disruption is clearly demonstrated, the gathering is protected. In the case at bar, the police would not be justified to break up the rally merely because of the jeering of a few members of the crowd. Moreover, if the risk of disruption is caused by a hostile crowd, the first duty of the police is to protect the speaker from the crowd, not to stop the speech and arrest the speaker. Therefore choice (C) is correct, and choice (A) is incorrect. Choice (B) is not the strongest answer because there is insufficient evidence to suggest that the leaders were in imminent danger. Choice (D) is incorrect. The mere possession of a permit does not confer absolute rights of free speech and assembly. If there is an imminent danger of violence or disorder, the police have a duty to protect the speakers and, if that is not possible, to halt the speech to avoid the imminent harm.

20. **(B)** In *Time Inc. v. Hill,* 385 U.S. 374 (1967), a case involving this particular invasion of privacy branch, the Supreme Court held that the 1st Amendment prohibited recovery for invasion of privacy in cases where the published matter was in the public interest, unless the plaintiff established that the defendant acted with malice. Malice here, as in *New York Times v. Sullivan*, goes to knowledge of falsity or reckless disregard for the truth. Moreover, choice (B) is the best answer because the 1st Amendment constitutional privileges likely encompass all pure ***opinions***, whether false or not. As such, ***only statements of fact can be actionable as defamatory.*** In this example, the facts clearly state that the TV commentator, said, "In my opinion...these people like the professor should be deported." Since the anchorman was merely voicing his opinion, choice (B) is a better answer than choice (D). Choice (A) is incorrect because it is irrelevant, whether or not the criticism was directed at the professor "personally." What matters is whether the statement is a factual representation—a statement capable of being proved either true or false—because that is the only way to prove liability. Choice (C) is incorrect. A false light tort involves a defendant publishing factual information about the plaintiff; which tends to place the plaintiff in a false light; and which would be very offensive to a reasonable person were the latter in the plaintiff's situation. In our example, there are no factual representations being made by the TV commentator, only opinions.

21. **(B)** Congress is granted broad powers of taxation by express constitutional provisions, namely, Article I, Section 8 (taxing and spending power) and the 16th Amendment (federal income tax without apportionment). The taxing power is virtually plenary. The standard used to analyze the validity of a federal tax is whether or not the ***dominant intent is fiscal.*** In other words, even if a federal tax does have some incidental regulatory effect, it will nevertheless be upheld if it does, in fact, ***raise revenue.*** The stated purpose of the proposed Senate bill for a 15% gross receipts tax is to raise revenue and spur population growth. Applying the aforementioned standard, the proposed federal tax will be constitutional. Choice (B) is correct, since it states the proper rationale. Choices (A), (C), and (D) are incorrect because validity of a federal tax is not analyzed under the principles of equal protection, the commerce clause, or the right to privacy.

22. **(C)** The state statute providing that "any student... who engages in disruptive campus activities will not be eligible for state aid" would be declared unconstitutional for vagueness and overbreadth. Clearly, the court will invalidate such a statute because "disruptive campus activities" is too general and overbroad and can be read as prohibiting constitutionally protected activity. Therefore, for these reasons, choice (C) is correct, and choice (A) is incorrect. Choice (B) is incorrect. Idiomatically, there is no proper exercise of "state action." The state action doctrine refers to the idea that the government has acted and is thus, theoretically, subject to the U.S. Constitution. Choice (D) is incorrect. The problem with the statute is not that it discriminates on the basis of viewpoint or content. The problem lies in that the statute suffers from substantial vagueness and overbreadth in its reference to "disruptive campus activities."

23. **(B)** Such laws explicitly distinguishing between males and females have been invalidated as violative of the Equal Protection Clause of the 14th Amendment unless they serve the objective of offsetting unequal opportunities for women (or men, as the case may be). In the present case, ***there is no important governmental interest*** available to support a tax exemption for only full-time female college students and not ***male*** students. Choice (A) is incorrect. Generally, a property interest is not protected under the 14th Amendment's Due Process Clause unless there is a reasonable expectation of continued receipt of the benefit. [*Board of Regents v. Roth*, 408 U.S. 564 (1972)]. In our example, no such reasonable expectation of continued receipt of the benefit exists for the college men because the law had already informed them that failure to enroll fulltime will erase the tax exemption. Choice (C) is incorrect. There is no substantive fundamental right protected by the due process clause that has been denied by the tax exemption. Most substantive rights protected by the due process clause concern the rights of bodily and familial autonomy. Choice (D) is incorrect. States may have the power to tax different people in different ways, but it may not do so in a way that violates the Constitution. Here, the tax exemption—having a gender classification—will be subject to intermediate review and will likely fail such review.

24. **(A)** Limited residency requirements (of one year or less) for obtaining divorces have been upheld as promoting a compelling state interest in the exercise of the state's police powers to legislate to protect the health, safety, welfare, and morals of its citizens. Choice (B) is incorrect, since the concept of state action pertains to nullifying state legislation that impairs the privileges and immunities of citizens of the United States, or which injures them in life, liberty, or property without due process of law, or which denies to any of them the equal protection of the laws. Choice (C) is incorrect. While they may have been the subject of discrimination by the legislature, they are not members of a suspect or quasi-suspect class. Only rational review will be applied, which the state probably will pass with ease. Choice (D) is incorrect. In order to show a violation of the privileges and immunities clause, there must be an initial showing of discrimination by the state against out-of-staters. In our example, there is no such discrimination.

25. **(C)** In accordance with *Hudgens v. NLRB*, 424 U.S. 507 (1971), the owner of a private shopping center may exclude persons who want to distribute pamphlets, since no "state action" is present. The Supreme Court held that, so long as the state does not aid, command, or encourage the suppression of free speech, the 1st Amendment would not be violated by the shopping center owners. The operation of the shopping complex was not part of a privately owned town and, therefore, did not involve the assumption of a public function by private persons. Since pamphleteering on private property is not a constitutionally protected activity, injunctive relief would not be granted to the students. Choices (A) and (B) are incorrect because there is no state action in this example; thus, the Constitution does not apply. Choice (D) is incorrect. The nuisance action is unnecessary, and it is superfluous to discuss the privacy interests of persons not wishing to be accosted by pamphleteers.

26. **(D)** The state statute would be construed as overbroad and, thus, invalid under the 1st and 14th Amendments. The Supreme Court, in *Lewis v. City of New Orleans*, 415 U.S. 130 (1974), applied the overbreadth doctrine to a similar New Orleans ordinance, which was invalidated under the 1st and 14th Amendments. In that case, as well as in the factual situation here, the ordinance effectively punished all obscene and offensive speech, even though some of the speech may have been protected by the 1st Amendment. Since Section 1220 may have included constitutionally protected speech, the statute should have been more narrowly drawn to protect such 1st Amendment activities. Choice (A) is not the best answer. If a statute is unduly vague, it will be voided on its face. The rationale is that the audience will suffer a chilling effect by being afraid to speak at all. Here, the statute is vague in at least two respects: in the reference to "opprobrious language" and in the reference to "treat contemptuously." Both references, however, are more objectionable because they suffer from overbreadth by prohibiting speech that is protected by the 1st Amendment. Choice (B) is not the strongest choice. This answer presumes that the statute is invalid only because it violates the 1st Amendment. The statute is actually invalid on its face, without having to determine whether it violates the speaker's rights in this instance. Choice (C) is incorrect. This answer presumes that the statute, on its face, is valid and that the constitutional problem resides in its application to the instant facts. But the statute is void on its face.

27. **(C)** or **(D)** In accordance with *Smith v. Gognen*, 415 U.S. 566 (1974), where the petitioner had been convicted of violating a similar flag-misuse statute for sewing a U.S. flag to the seat of his pants, the Supreme Court held that the ***statutory language was void for vagueness*** under the 1st and 14th Amendments. The flag-misuse statute was declared vague because no clear distinction had been made between what type of treatment of the flag was or was not criminal. Furthermore, the statutory terminology, "treat the flag contemptuously," is lacking of any ascertainable standards and is, therefore, violative of the Due Process Clause of the 14th Amendment. Students should note that the police and courts should not be given such broad discretion in determining what constitutes flag contempt as to be violative of the 1st and 14th Amendments' constitutional safeguards. Choice (B) is incorrect because this question presents a due process violation, not an equal protection issue. Choice (A) is incorrect because the statute here suffers from undue vagueness and, thus, will be voided on its face.

28. **(B)** The 14th Amendment's procedural due process clause operates as a limitation on state action by providing an individual the guarantees of both notice of the charges brought against him, as well as an opportunity to be heard, whenever the deprivation of any life, liberty, or property interest has occurred. The individual whose interests are affected must be granted a fair procedure to determine the factual basis and legality for such action. If the government terminates an individual's ability to engage in a profession, a procedure must be afforded to determine the individual's fitness to engage in that profession. Specifically, in *Barry v. Barchi,* 443 U.S. 555 (1979), the court held that the New York licensing system for horse training created a "property" interest in licensed trainers protected by the Due Process Clause and ***a post-suspension hearing was required.*** In this question, the state statute affording a post-suspension hearing will be upheld. Therefore, choice (B) is correct. Choice (A) is incorrect. The rights-privilege distinction has been abandoned by the Supreme Court. Instead, the Court looks to whether there is a reasonable expectation of the continuance of the government benefit. Here, the trainer will be able to show such expectation. Choice (C) is incorrect because there is no fundamental right to contract; nor is there a fundamental right to "seek gainful employment." Finally, choice (D) is incorrect. Under a licensing scheme, a right to a hearing prior to revocation of the license is not required, although a right to a hearing is required after the revocation of the license.

29. **(D)** The due process clause of the 14th Amendment would furnish the plaintiff's best grounds for challenging his exclusion from his party's caucus. Whenever a governmental instrumentality acts so as to deprive someone of any interest, the first question to ask is whether the interest qualifies as "life," "liberty," or "property." If so, the due process safeguards of notice and some form of hearing are required. In the present hypo, the plaintiff's exclusion from the caucus would be a deprivation of his property interest (i.e., stripping a duly elected public official of his right to participate in his party's meeting). Choice (A) is incorrect, while the plaintiff may have been the subject of discrimination by the legislature, he is not a member of a suspect or quasi-suspect class, and only rational basis review will be applied. Choice (B) is not the strongest answer. The right to assemble would not be the best argument, since the party members do not wish to associate with the plaintiff. To force them to do otherwise probably would violate their right to assemble. Choice (C) is incorrect. There is no violation of the right of speech if there is a valid time, place, and manner regulation for the speech. Such a law regulates the secondary effects of the speech (not the speech) and provides reasonable alternatives for the speech. Here, one can argue that the minority party is not punishing Turner, *per se.*

30. **(B)** "The Senators and Representatives... for any Speech or Debate in either House... shall not be questioned in any other Place" [U.S. Const. art. I, sec. 6, cl. 1]. It is important to note that virtually every state has adopted similar speech and debate clauses in their respective state constitutions. Choice (A) is incorrect. The senator did not offer any factual representations. The actual malice test requires that the speaker offer some factual representation (later proved inaccurate) either deliberately knowing of its inaccuracy or in reckless disregard. Choice (C) is incorrect. A false light tort involves a defendant publishing factual information about the plaintiff, which tends to place plaintiff in a false light, and which would be offensive to a reasonable person were the latter in plaintiff's situation. In this question, there are no factual representations being made, only opinions. Choice (D) is incorrect because, even if this were factually true, it does not matter for legal purposes. Therefore, choice (B) is correct, because the statement would be privileged, since the Speech and Debate Clause protects legislators and their aides against criminal or civil proceedings for "legislative acts."

31. **(D)** In *Griswold v. Connecticut,* 381 U.S. 479 (1965), the U.S. Supreme Court invalidated a similar statute restricting the ***use of contraceptive devices by married couples as violating the right of privacy of married persons.*** The Court held that the statute violated the due process clause because it deprived these married persons the liberty protected by the 5th Amendment. Choice (A) is incorrect. Even if Congress is empowered under the Commerce Clause to enact this law, Congress would still run afoul of the fundamental right to contraceptives in the 5th Amendment's due process clause. Choice (B) is incorrect. Article I, Section 8, reads: "The Congress shall have Power to lay and collect Taxes, Duties, Imposts and Excises, to pay the Debts and provide for the common defence and general welfare of the United States." The Supreme Court has taken the reference to "general welfare" to mean that Congress enjoys great discretion in how

it chooses to allocate money for the public [*United States v. Butler*, 297 U.S. 1 (1936)]. There is no such allocation of money in our example; just a regulation. Choice (C) is incorrect. In *Lucas v. South Carolina Coastal Council*, 505 U.S. 1003 (1992), the Court stated that a taking occurs where "regulation denies all economically beneficial or productive use of the land." Here, the congressional law does not deprive the manufacturers all property interest in contraceptives, because the manufacturers may still sell the contraceptives to people who are not married.

32. **(D)** In *Tileston v. Ullman*, 318 U.S. 44 (1943), the U.S. Supreme Court ruled that a medical doctor does not have third-party standing to attack a state anti-contraceptive statute on the grounds that it prevents him from giving his professional advice concerning the use of contraceptives to three patients whose condition of health might be endangered by child bearing. On the contrary, if the person is convicted of prescribing, selling, or giving away contraceptives, in the defense of that action, he may then raise the third-party rights of the recipients. [*Eisenstadt v. Baird*, 405 U.S. 438 (1972)]. Under this reasoning, choice (D) is correct and, therefore, choices (A) and (B) are incorrect. Choice (C) is incorrect. The physician would seem to have standing. First, if he tried to violate the state law, he would be convicted and, thus, would suffer harm. Second, there's causation, because the state is directly responsible for the potential prosecution and the physician is able to show that the state can remedy its harm by repealing its law.

33. **(D)** There is no constitutional right of advertising under the 1st and 14th Amendments. Certainly, a private newspaper is not required under the Constitution to accept and publish all forms of advertising. Choice (A) is incorrect. There is a lack of state action because the newspaper is a private entity. Accordingly, the newspaper cannot violate a person's constitutional rights, although other legal remedies might be available. Choice (B) is not the best answer. There is a constitutional right to commercial speech, meaning that the government may not infringe on such a right. However, there is no constitutional right to "advertise" in a private newspaper. Choice (C) is incorrect. Congress's powers are not legally relevant for this example. There is no constitutional right of advertising under the 1st and 14th Amendments. Certainly, a private newspaper is not required under the Constitution to accept and publish all forms of advertising.

34. **(D)** The prisoner's best constitutional argument will be based on the 1st Amendment's free exercise clause, which is applicable to the states through the 14th Amendment. Even though it is not known whether his belief is properly classified as a religion for 1st Amendment purposes, choice (D) still provides the prisoner's best argument. Although choice (A) seems correct, choice (D) is the better answer, since state action is involved. When there are apparently two correct answers to a question, you should select the alternative more on-point to the facts in the question. As illustrated in this question, in the area of Constitutional Law, when a particular question relates to one's rights under any of the first eight Amendments to the U.S. Constitution, such rights are only afforded through the due process clause of the 14th Amendment. Therefore, in our hypo, choice (D) is the preferred answer, as it refers to both the 1st and 14th Amendments. Choice (B) is incorrect. The 8th Amendment guarantees that inmates shall be served adequate food, not food to their tastes. Choice (C) is incorrect. There is no fundamental right to religious expression or to vegetarianism under the 14th Amendment's Substantive Due Process Clause.

35. **(A)** Under the "affectation doctrine," the U.S. Supreme Court has recognized that Congress has ***the power to regulate any activity, whether carried on in one state or many, which has any appreciable effect—directly or indirectly—upon interstate commerce.*** Choice (B) is incorrect. The Supremacy Clause cannot serve as a basis for a congressional statute, although once passed, the congressional statute, under the logic of the supremacy clause, can take precedence over a state statute. Choice (C) is incorrect because Congress has no legislative power under the 1st Amendment. Congress has legislative powers under Section 5 of the 14th Amendment but, in our example, it is not clear how the congressional statute would further some

14th Amendment right. Choice (D) is not the best answer. Article I, Section 8 states that Congress has the authority "To promote the Progress of Science and useful Arts, by securing for limited Times to Authors and Inventors the exclusive Right to their respective Writings and Discoveries." This clause refers to Congress's authority to bestow patents and copyright, not freedom of the press.

36. **(C)** The Multistate examination tests not only your ***knowledge of the substantive rules of law; it also tests your reading comprehension ability.*** The state statute prohibits the showing of any obscene film "in an area open to the public." Since the films were being shown in the privacy of the motel rooms (and occupancy was limited to consenting adults), the owner's conviction would be overturned because the statute would be inapplicable. Also, for Multistate purposes, students should be familiar with *Stanley v. Georgia,* 394 U.S. 557 (1969), in which the U.S. Supreme Court held that mere private possession of obscene matter is not a crime. Although the states retain broad power to regulate obscenity, that power simply does not extend to mere possession by the individual in the privacy of his home. Choice (A) is incorrect for the reasons stated above. Choice (B) is incorrect. The reference to literary, artistic, and the like refers to the *Miller* obscenity test. Obscenity as a legal category receives no constitutional protection. However, in this example, it's not certain that we're dealing with obscenity, but with pornography. Obscenity is defined as material that is (1) patently offensive; (2) appeals to prurient interests; and (3) the work, taken as a whole, lacks any serious literary, artistic, political, or scientific value [*Miller v. California,* 413 U.S. 15 (1973)]. Even if the material in the hotel is deemed obscene, students should be familiar with *Stanley v. Georgia,* 394 U.S. 557 (1969), in which the U.S. Supreme Court held that mere private possession of obscene matter is not a crime. Although the states retain broad power to regulate obscenity, that power simply does not extend to mere possession by the individual in the privacy of his home. Choice (D) is incorrect. As a general matter, materials deemed obscene do not enjoy hardly any constitutional protection. However, students should be familiar with *Stanley v. Georgia,* 394 U.S. 557 (1969), in which the U.S. Supreme Court held that mere private possession of obscene matter is not a crime. Although the states retain broad power to regulate obscenity, that power simply does not extend to mere possession by the individual in the privacy of his home. Moreover, in this example, it's not certain that we're dealing with obscenity, but with pornography. Obscenity is defined as material that is (1) patently offensive; (2) appeals to prurient interests; and (3) the work, taken as a whole, lacks any serious literary, artistic, political, or scientific value [*Miller v. California,* 413 U.S. 15 (1973)].

37. **(B)** In accordance with *Nyquist v. Mauclet,* 432 U.S. 1 (1977), the U.S. Supreme Court invalidated, under the equal protection clause of the 14th Amendment, a state law that granted aid for higher education to citizens and resident aliens who were or would be applying for citizenship. The Court found no "compelling state interest" in encouraging citizenship or limiting general programs to those who determine its policy. Therefore, choice (B) is correct, and choice (C) would be incorrect under our facts. Choice (A) is incorrect because the privileges or immunities clause of the 14th Amendment does not protect those who are non-U.S. Citizens. Choice (D) is incorrect. Technically, it is true that alienage classifications are not, *per se,* unconstitutional under the 14th Amendment's equal protection clause. However, such classifications will still be subject to strict scrutiny, and the state must show that its law contains compelling governmental interests [*Graham v. Richardson,* 403 U.S. 365 (1971)].

38. **(A)** As a general rule, state laws regulating roadways and highways are usually upheld as constitutional unless they unduly burden interstate commerce. Since the facts do not indicate that the state statute unduly burdens interstate commerce, choice (A) is preferred over choice (D). Another variation of how this rule can be tested involves the enactment of a state law prohibiting the use of metal studs or cleats on vehicular tires. Even though the facts may indicate that the cleats and studs give better traction in ice and snow, the statute may still be upheld as constitutional if it serves a legitimate state interest by reducing damage to state highways. Choice (B) is incorrect.

The commerce clause of Article I, Section 8 ***can*** invalidate state regulation if such regulation presents an undue burden on interstate commerce. But that does not appear to be the case in this example, given that both in-staters and out-of-staters must comply with the same prohibition. Choice (C) is incorrect. Article IV, Section 1 contains the Full Faith and Credit Clause: "Full Faith and Credit shall be given in each State to the public Acts, Records, and judicial Proceedings of every other State. And the Congress may by general Laws prescribe the Manner in which such Acts, Records and Proceedings shall be proved, and the Effect thereof." But the law in our example would not be covered under the Full Faith and Credit Clause.

39. **(D)** The equal protection clause of the 14th Amendment is applicable to corporations. Choices (A) and (B) are incorrect because neither the privileges and immunities clause nor the comity clause applies to corporations, because the term "citizen" does not include corporations. Choice (C) is incorrect because, under the 5th Amendment (the prohibition of compulsory self-incrimination), the word "person" fails to include corporations or other business entities [*Bellis v. United States,* 409 U.S. 322 (1973)].

40. **(C)** As a general rule, ***the Commerce Clause prohibits a state from enacting regulations that discriminate or burden interstate commerce.*** In accordance with *Dean Milk Co. v. City of Madison,* 340 U.S. 349 (1951), a state may not create economic barriers to out-of-state products or impose on them costs that are more burdensome than those imposed on comparable local commerce in order to protect local interests. However, the Commerce Clause does not prevent the state, when acting itself as a purchaser or seller of goods, from buying only from or selling only to local business or from giving subsidies only to its residents. See *Reeves v. Stake,* 447 U.S. 429 (1980), where discrimination merely affects a market created by a state's own purchases, and the state is, thus, a market participant, rather than a market regulator. Choices (A) and (B) are incorrect. A state has police powers under its 10th Amendment to create "gainful employment" for racial minorities. But there are constitutional limits to this aim, including the dormant Commerce Clause. As a general rule, ***the Commerce Clause prohibits a state from enacting regulations that discriminate or burden interstate commerce.*** In accordance with *Dean Milk Co. v. City of Madison,* 340 U.S. 349 (1951), a state may not create economic barriers to out-of-state products or impose on them costs that are more burdensome than those imposed on comparable local commerce in order to protect local interests. Choice (D) is incorrect. Even if this were factually true, it would not be legally relevant in overcoming the legal obstacles presented by the Commerce Clause.

41. **(C)** In Constitutional Law, students must be familiar with the area of ***state regulation of interstate commerce.*** As a general rule, where Congress has not acted, and where no uniform national scheme of regulation exists, states are free to act in the regulation of interstate commerce, provided that the purpose or the effect of such regulation does not discriminate against interstate commerce. In this regard, states may not favor local interests by protecting them against out-of-state competition [*Dean Milk Co. v. City of Madison,* 340 U.S. 349 (1951)]. In addition, the Court has struck down state laws regulating the ***conservation of local natural resources.*** Since state laws enacted to protect local, publicly owned natural resources (e.g., minerals, wild animals) will generally be invalidated if they discriminate against interstate commerce, choice (C) is correct. Choice (A) is incorrect. Even in the absence of congressional prohibition, the commerce clause has a silently negative effect in its "dormant" condition. No state is permitted to pass laws that unduly burden interstate commerce and, hence, violate the commerce clause of Article I, Section 8. In our example, the state appears to burden interstate commerce by hoarding local resources for itself, instead of permitting out-of-staters to buy them. Choice (B) is incorrect. A state enjoys the right under its 10th Amendment police powers to regulate welfare (as well as health, safety, and morals). However, the state may not invoke its police powers to violate the dormant commerce clause. In our example, the state appears to burden interstate commerce by hoarding local resources for itself, instead of permitting out-of-staters to buy them. Choice (D) is not the best answer. Non-oil-producing companies may have been the subject of discrimination by the legislature, but they are not members of a suspect or quasi-suspect class. Only rational review will be applied, which the state probably will pass with ease.

Multistate Nuance Chart

Constitutional Law

State Regulation of Interstate Commerce

Permissible	**Not Permissible**
1. Where state is acting as a market participant (i.e., purchaser or seller of goods;	1. Supersession where state law is *in conflict* with act of Congress;
2. Regulations for protection of public health or welfare;	2. When state regulation discriminates or unduly burdens interstate commerce;
3. Quarantine and inspection laws;	3. Regulations for conservation of local resources.
4. Regulations concerning the use of local highways;	
5. Regulations regarding the transportation or importation of intoxicating liquors as provided under the 21st Amendment.	

Basic Test

As a general rule, state regulation of interstate commerce is ***permissible*** if:

(1) the state regulation does not discriminate against interstate commerce;

(2) the subject matter is not one that the Court concludes inherently requires uniform, national regulation; and

(3) the state interest underlying the regulation is not outweighed by the burden on interstate commerce (i.e., the "balance of interests" favors state, as opposed to national, interests).

42. **(C)** Article I, Section 10 (Contract Clause) provides: "No State shall pass any Law impairing the Obligation of Contracts." In this example, the state was obligated under the terms of the bond agreement to apply at least $2 from each admission charge (to the racetrack) for the repayment of the bond debt. Consequently, it is an impairment of the Contract Clause for the state to pass a subsequent statute reducing the admission charge for senior citizens to 50 cents. By analogy, in *United States Trust Co. v. New Jersey*, 431 U.S. 1 (1977), the U.S. Supreme Court declared a New Jersey statute unconstitutional because the law impaired the state's contractual obligation to the bondholders of the Port Authority of New York and New Jersey. Choice (D) is incorrect because the *ex post facto* clause applies to retroactive laws that are criminal in nature. Choice (A) is incorrect because it is an impairment of the Contract Clause for the state to pass a subsequent statute reducing the admission charge for senior citizens to 50 cents. Choice (B) is incorrect; while those under 65 years may have been the subject of discrimination by the legislature, they are not members of a suspect or quasi-suspect class. Only rational review will be applied, which the state probably will pass with ease.

43. **(A)** It is within the state's ***police powers to enact legislation for the protection of the health, safety, and welfare of its citizens.*** Clearly, most state regulations place some burden on interstate commerce. In such situations, the Court balances the nature and extent of the burden (which the state regulation would impose on interstate commerce) against the merits and purposes of the regulation. Choice (B) is incorrect because the clear and present danger test applies to the abridgement or restraint of freedom of speech where there is a substantial threat of violence. This doctrine is not applicable in our case because the question does not relate to freedom of speech. Choice (C) is incorrect. Technically, the bondholders may still enforce the contract against the stadium because the prohibition against baseball does not necessarily impair the contractual obligations accrued by the state. Bondholders can still sue the state for payment, and the state is still liable to honor those obligations. Choice (D) is incorrect. Generally, a property interest is not protected under the 14th Amendment's Due Process Clause unless there is a reasonable expectation to continued receipt of the benefit [*Board of Regents v. Roth*, 408 U.S. 564 (1972)]. In our example, no such reasonable expectation to continued receipt of the benefit exists for the owners because there was nothing to guarantee that the stadium would be a success or that people would attend games.

44. **(B)** As noted in the previous question, the Court generally attempts to ***balance the nature and extent of the burden*** (which the state regulation imposes on interstate commerce) ***against the merits and purposes of the regulation.*** Accordingly, choice (B) is the preferred answer. Choice (A) is incorrect because, even if this were factually true, it would not overcome the legal obstacles presented by the dormant commerce clause of Article I, Section 8. Under the dormant commerce clause, a state is not permitted to place undue burdens on interstate commerce. Choice (C) is incorrect. This fact, in itself, would not necessarily prohibit the state from regulating out-of-state casinos as long as it was done in a way that did not unduly burden interstate commerce. Choice (D) is incorrect. Generally, a property interest is not protected under the 14th Amendment's Due Process Clause unless there is a reasonable expectation to continued receipt of the benefit [*Board of Regents v. Roth*, 408 U.S. 564 (1972)]. In our example, no such reasonable expectation to continued operation appears to exist.

45. **(C)** Another key Multistate testing area deals with educational rights of students. In *Goss v. Lopez*, 419 U.S. 565 (1975), the U.S. Supreme Court held that fair procedures had to be established for determining the basis of the suspension of students from public school systems. As a general rule, a student is not entitled to a trial-type hearing when his dismissal or suspension is ***with just cause***. Certainly, a rule prohibiting students from growing beards or mustaches would seem to be compatible with the orderly operation of the school. On the other hand, the Court in *Goss v. Lopez* did note that when the suspension or termination of a student's educational benefits may affect his employment or associational opportunities in the future, there may be a due process violation involved. Choice (D) is incorrect because the student was ***not entitled to a hearing*** under the circumstances. Choice (A) is incorrect. There is no fundamental right to an education under the 14th Amendment's due process clause [*Plyler v. Doe*, 457 U.S. 202 (1982)] if harm to the student inheres not in his right to an education but in harm to his reputation, which is protected by the 14th Amendment's due process clause. *See Goss v. Lopez*, 419 U.S. 565 (1975). Choice (B) is incorrect. It's not clear that the student's right was denied arbitrarily. Even if the right were arbitrarily denied, the Supreme Court has not recognized that a student would be entitled to a trial, although at least a hearing by the school would be required [*Goss v. Lopez*, 419 U.S. 565 (1975)].

46. **(C)** In *Hillman v. Elliott* (1977), the U.S. Supreme Court held that due process with respect to a three-day suspension of a student from public high school required that the student be given notice of charges, an explanation of evidence against him if he denied the charges, and an opportunity to present his version of the incident. In the instant case, the student was afforded such due process safeguards. Choice (A) is incorrect for the reasons stated above. Choice (B) is incorrect. A high school is not a public forum where speakers enjoy broad rights of free

speech. Further, the school code that prohibited the student's speech would not be subject to strict scrutiny, but only an easy rational review if it were deemed to be a proper time, place, and manner regulation. A proper time, place, and manner regulation does not prohibit the speech, but only its secondary effects, and such a regulation leaves reasonable alternatives for the speech. Here, the school code can be interpreted as prohibiting not the student's criticism of both the teacher and his fellow student, but prohibiting the potential for distraction and disorder that his speech may cause. Plus, the student can probably air the same sort of message outside the school. Choice (D) is incorrect because there is no fundamental right to an education under the 14th Amendment's due process clause (or anywhere else). [*Plyler v. Doe*, 457 U.S. 202 (1982)].

47. **(D)** Gender classifications will merit intermediate review. The court will ask whether there are important governmental interests and whether the means are substantially related. Paramount in gender cases is whether the statute is advancing some debilitating stereotype regarding females. Here, there is an important government interest (preventing pregnancies), but it's not clear that such debilitating stereotypes are being advanced. Therefore, choice (D) is correct and choice (C) is incorrect. Choice (A) is incorrect because, since the students are ***not married,*** the privacy issue of related individuals living together is unripe. Choice (B) is incorrect. There is no fundamental right to associate in this example. It is similar to *Village of Belle Terre v. Boraas*, 416 U.S. 1 (1974). There, the Court subjected to an easy rational review a city code that prohibited the cohabitation by groups of three or more persons unrelated by blood or marriage. The Court stressed that the unrelated person—unlike married persons—do not enjoy a fundamental right to associate with each other. Similarly, in our example, the students are not yet married and, thus, have no fundamental rights to exercise.

48. **(C)** Another frequently tested Constitutional Law area is, to what extent does an executive agreement (or order) override an earlier enacted federal statute? According to Nowak, ***an executive agreement does not supersede inconsistent provisions of earlier acts of Congress***. To be sure, the appropriations bill passed by Congress prohibiting funding for military operations in the foreign country will be controlling. The President does not have the power to override this congressional act by issuing a subsequent executive order. Choice (A) is incorrect. The President does enjoy Article II powers to act as a commander-in-chief. But he or she must first be summoned into action by Congress and, second, the President does not have the constitutional power to override a congressional statute in his or her capacity as commander-in-chief. Similarly, choice (B) is incorrect because, while the President does enjoy Article II powers to engage in various aspects of foreign policy, the President does not have the constitutional power to override a congressional statute in his or her role as a participant in foreign affairs. Choice (D) is incorrect. The chief problem is not that the executive order was not authorized by the Senate or Congress. The chief problem is that the President is not authorized by the Constitution to override an otherwise valid law; which would be a violation of the principle of the separation of powers.

49. **(B)** Juveniles are neither a suspect nor a quasi-suspect class of persons. Therefore, state laws dealing with juveniles will be scrutinized by the court under neither the compelling state interest nor the middle tier standard of review. ***The mere rationality test applies.*** Specifically, if the statute in question is rationally related to the furtherance of a legitimate state interest, the court will uphold it as constitutional. Choice (B) is correct because the sealing of court and police records of juveniles clearly serves the legitimate state interest in rehabilitation of juvenile offenders so as to be free from embarrassment in later life. Choice (C) is incorrect because by satisfying the requisite scrutiny of the rational basis test, the state law supersedes the right of the Committee of Bar Examiners to have access to otherwise public documents. Choice (A) is incorrect. Juveniles may have been the subject of discrimination by the legislature, but they are not members of a suspect or quasi-suspect class. Only rational review will be applied, which the government probably will pass with ease. Choice (D) is incorrect because "hindering the interests of justice," as used in this answer, is not a legally relevant claim for purposes of constitutional analysis.

50. **(B)** The city ordinance may be attacked as a violation of protected 1st Amendment freedom of expression, since it prohibits ***all*** singing and chanting for 12 hours every day in areas that are traditionally viewed as ***public forums.*** Time, place, manner limitations on speech-related conduct are permitted when achieved by ***reasonable content-neutral*** regulations that further a significant governmental purpose. Such an ordinance must be narrowly drawn so as not to establish a total ban on protected rights of free speech. Since the city ordinance does not appear to satisfy this standard, a 1st Amendment free speech attack by the students will be a strong challenge. Therefore, choice (A) is incorrect. Choice (C) is also incorrect because it presents a strong challenge in the form of the vagueness and overbreadth doctrines. By proscribing protected as well as prohibited speech for half of each day everywhere in the city, the ordinance is clearly overbroad on its face. Similarly, due to the uncertainty-producing effect as to what conduct is restricted by the words "singing and chanting of songs" and "audible off the premises," a vagueness challenge should be successful. Choice (D), another strong argument, is incorrect since nonreligious songs—which are certainly areas of protected speech—are being treated differently from religious songs, thereby raising an equal protection challenge to be reviewed using the strict scrutiny standard. By process of elimination, choice (B) is correct because the due process argument it presents is the weakest basis to attack the ordinance.

51. **(D)** Classifications based on gender are not "suspect," but neither are they judged by the traditional (or rational basis) test. On the contrary, intentional discrimination against members of one sex are ***"quasi suspect" and violate equal protection unless they are substantially related to important government objectives.*** In *Craig v. Boren*, 429 U.S. 190 (1976), the U.S. Supreme Court invalidated an Oklahoma law permitting the sale of beer to women at age 18 but required males to be 21. The Court held that ***classification by gender must serve important governmental objectives and must be substantially related to the achievement of those objectives.*** Choice (A) is incorrect. The 21st Amendment does not maintain that a "state has exclusive authority to regulate the use and sale of intoxicating liquors." Even if this were legally true, the state law should not violate other parts of the Constitution. Choice (B) is incorrect because this is not the standard under which we determine whether a state should be allowed to discriminate based on gender. Choice (C) is incorrect. When considering gender classifications, the Supreme Court takes particular offense at those governmental means that perpetuate a debilitating gender stereotype for girls and women. Such regulations are not likely to pass intermediate review, the review to which all gender classifications are subject.

52. **(D)** In *Minneapolis Star & Tribune Co. v. Minnesota Commission of Revenue*, 460 U.S. 575 (1983), the Court found that a state tax statute imposing a "use tax" on paper and ink products consumed in the production of certain publications violated the 1st Amendment. Justice O'Connor found that the tax was not the result of an impermissible or censorial motive but that the tax violated the 1st Amendment because it singled out the press for special taxation and had the effect of targeting a small group of newspapers for a special tax. The majority did not employ equal protection analysis. In light of the *Minneapolis Star & Tribune* decision, the special Print Tax imposed on the publication of newspapers would best be challenged as a violation of the 1st Amendment. Choice (D) is, therefore, preferred over choice (A). Choice (B) is incorrect. Article I, Section 10 prohibits a bill of attainder, a law passed by Congress to sentence someone for a crime in the absence of a trial. No such laws were passed in the example. Choice (C) is incorrect. The privileges or immunities clause of the 14th Amendment protects only U.S. citizens. A newspaper company is not a U.S. citizen.

53. **(C)** Since a treaty is viewed on an equal footing with the Constitution and Acts of Congress, it is considered to be "the supreme law of the land" (Article VI, Section 2). When a treaty is approved by two-thirds of the Senate, the President then ratifies it and the treaty becomes an agreement binding as an international obligation. Nowak, Constitutional Law, pg. 183. A treaty can be ***superseded*** by another treaty, properly ratified, or by subsequent Act of Congress. This result stems from the rule that where there is a conflict between a treaty

and an Act of Congress, they are of equal weight, and the last one in time will control [*Chae Chan Ping v. United States,* 130 U.S. 581 (1889)]. Therefore, the strongest argument that the treaty between the United States and Canada is valid and effective is choice (C). The due process arguments presented in choices (A) and (D) are weaker choices, since nonpayment of income tax has never been regarded as an ***entitlement*** (i.e., welfare or disability benefit) for which a hearing or payment of just compensation must be afforded. Choice (B) is incorrect, since ***exclusive*** authority is not vested in the courts to determine whether another nation has breached a treaty. A nation might remain accountable to other parties to the treaty under the "law of nations" or even under the President's broad authority to represent the United States in foreign relations [*Clark v. Allen,* 331 U.S. 503 (1947)].

54. **(B)** Under Article III, Section 2, the Court possesses substantial power in the areas of international affairs and foreign policy. However, historically the Court often defers to the judgment of Congress and the President when a conflict involving foreign affairs arises. Nowak, Constitutional Law, pg. 179. The political question doctrine has been used as a means of evading judicial review when issues in the area of foreign relations are presented. In *Baker v. Carr,* 369 U.S. 186 (1962), Justice Brennan cited the following passage that "The conduct of the foreign relations of our Government is committed by the Constitution to the Executive and Legislative—the 'political'—Departments of the Government, and the propriety of what may be done in the exercise of this political power is not subject to judicial inquiry or decision" [*Oetjen v. Central Leather Co.,* 246 U.S. 297 (1918)]. Because the validity and enforcement of the treaty is an issue of international affairs, the political doctrine appears to be the strongest basis for the Court to refuse to decide the claim. The *Baker* case noted, however, that in the absence of any conclusive congressional or executive action, the Supreme Court will allow review of issues of foreign affairs, while still retaining its character of judicial independence and integrity. Choice (A) is incorrect. The requirements for standing would seem to be present: The citizen can show ***injury,*** since he will have to pay income tax to the United States; he can show ***causation*** because the President caused him to be taxed in the United States; and he can show redressability by showing that the President can prevent his injury by honoring the treaty. Choice (C) is incorrect. The case is not moot because the issues have not been resolved. The citizen will continue to be taxed in the United States. Choice (D) is incorrect because while it is true that only U.S. citizens are protected under the privileges or immunities clause of the 14th Amendment, aliens, even illegal aliens, are entitled other forms of constitutional protection.

55. **(C)** Choice (A) is incorrect because evidence of "pandering" on the part of the defendant (commercial exploitation for the sake of prurient appeal) may be probative on whether the material is obscene [*Ginzburg v. United States,* 383 U.S. 643 (1966)]. Choice (B) is incorrect because although private possession of obscenity at home is not a crime [*Stanley v. Georgia,* 394 U.S. 557 (1969)], transportation and importation of obscene materials for either public or private use may be prohibited [*United States v. Orito,* 413 U.S. 139 (1973); *United States v. Twelve 200-Ft. Reels,* 413 U.S. 123 (1973)]. Choice (D) is, likewise, not our best answer because under the first two prongs of the Roth–Miller test, obscenity should be determined in accordance with "community standards," not necessarily a "national standard." *In Jenkins v. Georgia,* 418 U.S. 153 (1974), it was held that a juror may draw on knowledge of the vicinity from which he comes, and the court may either direct the jury to apply "community standards" without specifying what "community" or defining the standard in more precise geographic terms.

56. **(C)** American courts have upheld the right of the state to protect the health and safety of minor children over the religiously based objections of the children or their parents. Thus, the courts have uniformly appointed guardians to consent to necessary medical treatment (such as blood transfusions) for children even though the treatment violates the child's or parent's religion. It should be noted that ***when objection to medical treatment is based on religious principles, a serious free exercise clause problem is presented.*** However, if the individual's preference is not religious in nature (and there is only a conflict between personal choice relat-

ing to health and state medical regulations), the decision would be resolved under the due process clause. Choice (A) is incorrect because the father was afforded due process because a judge reviewed the facts and issued an order. Choice (B) is incorrect. The equal protection clause provides heightened protection for groups whose legal classifications are suspect. One of those categories is religion. However, the court order would not seem to be directed at religionists while leaving non-religionists alone. That is, the court would probably have issued the same order for an atheist parent who objected to the doctor's treatment on secular philosophical grounds. Choice (D) is incorrect. The privileges or immunities clause protects people against discrimination by states against out-of-staters. That does not appear to be the case in our example.

57. **(B)** This is an example of a very tricky Multistate question because the test maker knows that many students will incorrectly choose choice (A). Clearly, choice (A) is arguably correct. Choice (B), however, is the best answer because, in deciding whether to order medical treatment for a minor, the courts will balance the objections of the parent against the health and safety of the minor. See *Jehovah's Witnesses v. King County Hospital*, 278 F. Supp. 598 (1968) for a more detailed analysis of the modern balancing test. Choice (C) is not the best answer. This would not be a relevant legal consideration for purposes of analysis under the free exercise clause; a publicly owned hospital would not be permitted to violate free exercise clause rights. Choice (D) is incorrect because even if Janet had never paid her taxes, she would still be entitled to her free exercise clause rights.

58. **(A)** ***Illegitimacy is a "quasi-suspect" classification*** (as in gender) and, thus, subject to an intermediate level of scrutiny. Therefore, whenever a state (or other non-federal government entity) passes a law discriminating against illegitimates, the burden of persuasion is on the state. In such cases, the state must demonstrate that the law furthers "an important state interest," otherwise it is deemed unconstitutional. According to the holding in *Trimble v. Gordon*, 430 U.S. 762 (1977), a state cannot absolutely exclude illegitimate children from inheriting from their intestate fathers. Therefore, (A) is correct, and choice (C) is incorrect. Choice (D) is partly correct inasmuch as illegitimacy is not a "suspect" classification, though choice (D) is wrong because in *Trimble*, a similar Illinois statute excluding illegitimate children inheriting from their father was deemed unconstitutional as not being substantially related to a legitimate state interest. Choice (B) is incorrect. There is no fundamental right to inherit under the due process clause.

59. **(A)** The strongest constitutional basis to challenge the state law is the Commerce Clause. The disposal of nuclear waste is an item of interstate commerce, as is the disposal of garbage. In *City of Philadelphia v. New Jersey*, 437 U.S. 617 (1978), the Court held a New Jersey statute prohibiting out-of-state waste disposal in New Jersey dump sites to be invalid under the Commerce Clause since the disposal of garbage was an item in interstate commerce. By analogy, the state statute is discriminatory because it creates an undue burden on out-of-state nuclear firms by prohibiting them from entering the state to dispose of their waste. Contract Clause is a much weaker argument for the man since private contracts can be validly modified by state legislation, which is necessary to achieve a legitimate public interest. Choice (A) is the best answer. Choice (B) is incorrect. The man may have been the subject of discrimination by the legislature, but the man is not a member of a suspect or quasi-suspect class. Only rational review will be applied, which the state probably will pass with ease. Choice (C) is incorrect. The privileges and immunities clause of Article IV, Section 2 prohibits states from discriminating against nonresidents. The statute here, however, does not; it prohibits the disposal of any nuclear wastes within the state, which does not discriminate against nonresidents. Choice (D) is incorrect. The contract clause of Article I, Section 10 prohibits states from impairing the obligation of contracts. However, the contracts clause applies only to contracts that were made prior to the state statute that ostensibly impairs fulfillment of their obligations.

60. **(A)** Choice (B) is incorrect because the resident can show that enforcement of the patently unconstitutional statute causes him injury in fact, economic and otherwise. Choice (C) is incorrect because in the leading case of *Toomer v. Witsell,* 334 U.S. 385 (1948), the U.S. Supreme Court ruled a similar South Carolina law unconstitutional of violating the privileges and immunities clause of Article IV. The test is whether there are ***valid reasons for a state to make distinctions based on one's state citizenship and whether the degree of discrimination bears a "close relation" to these reasons***. Choice (D) is incorrect because the suit does not in large part turn on an unsettled question of state law. Moreover, the ***abstention*** doctrine is inappropriate where a state court ruling would not be helpful in a determination of the constitutional issue.

61. **(D)** Choice (D) is the best answer in light of the *Toomer* decision. In the leading case of *Toomer v. Witsell,* 334 U.S. 385 (1948), the U.S. Supreme Court ruled a similar South Carolina law unconstitutional of violating the privileges and immunities clause of Article IV. The test is whether there are ***valid reasons for a state to make distinctions based on one's state citizenship and whether the degree of discrimination bears a "close relation" to these reasons***. Choice (A) is incorrect. The state does have police powers under the 10th Amendment to regulate welfare, including environmental and economic welfare. However, in exercising these police powers, the state may not violate the Constitution. Here, State will violate the privileges and immunities clause of Article IV. Choice (B) is incorrect because it is not a legally relevant consideration. Choice (C) is not the best answer. The state is acting like another market participant who is selling crawfish and, thus, immune from analysis under the dormant commerce clause.

62. **(C)** There are two privileges and immunities clauses contained in the U.S. Constitution. First, Article IV, Section 2 provides: "The citizens of each state shall be entitled to all Privileges and Immunities of citizens in the several states." This clause prohibits ***state discrimination against nonresidents*** (of the state) in respect to "essential activities" or "basic rights" unless the discrimination is closely related to a substantial purpose. Since ownership of property involves a "basic right," this constitutional provision is most applicable. The second Privileges or Immunities provision is contained in the 14th Amendment and provides in part: "No state shall make or enforce any law which shall abridge the privileges or immunities of citizens of the United States." These privileges and immunities have been limited to those rights that arise out of the relationship of the individual and the national government (e.g., the right to travel freely from state to state; the right to petition Congress for redress of grievances; the right to vote for national officers; and the right to assemble peaceably). Therefore, choice (C) is stronger than choice (B). Choice (A) is incorrect because the contracts clause applies only to those contracts made prior to the enactment of the state statute that ostensibly impairs the obligation of contracts. Choice (D) is incorrect. The national property clause in Article IV, Section 3 mentions nothing about the right of local governments to enact the sort of legislation referenced in our example.

63. **(C)** Under the "affectation doctrine," Congress has the power to regulate any activity—whether carried on in one state or many—that has an appreciable effect upon interstate commerce. Although federal power over interstate commerce is potentially "all-persuasive," it is not necessarily exclusive. Thus, Congress has absolute authority to define the distribution of federal and state regulatory power over interstate commerce. Just as Congress may permit state regulation of interstate commerce, it may also prohibit state regulation of any part of interstate commerce. Choice (A) is incorrect because even if this were factually true, Congress's regulation would still be valid under the Commerce Clause of Article I, Section 8. Choice (B) is incorrect. The 10th Amendment permits the states to exercise police powers for purposes of regulating health, safety, welfare, and morals. However, Congress may also regulate in these areas if it can find authorization in the Constitution. In this example, Congress can find such power in the Commerce Clause. Finally, choice (D) is incorrect. Article I, Section 8, reads: "The Congress shall have Power to lay and collect Taxes, Duties, Imposts and

Excises, to pay the Debts and provide for the common Defence and general Welfare of the United States." The Supreme Court has taken the reference to "general Welfare" to mean that Congress enjoys great discretion in how it chooses to allocate money for the public [*United States v. Butler*, 297 U.S. 1 (1936)]. There is no such allocation of money in our example; just a regulation.

64. **(C)** Here's a really difficult choice between abstention and justiciability. Generally speaking, a federal court will ***"abstain" or temporarily "stay its hand" whenever presented with an unsettled question of state law.*** Thus, federal courts will permit the state courts to resolve such issues before exercising jurisdiction. Choice (B) is less preferred because questions involving ***political rights*** (such as deprivation of the right to vote or legislative apportionment) are not necessarily "political questions." They may involve claims under the Equal Protection Clause of the 14th Amendment or even the 15th Amendment, which have well-developed judicial standards. Refer to *Baker v. Carr*, 369 U.S. 186 (1962), for a more detailed analysis of justiciability and factors regarding political questions. Finally, choices (A) and (D) are not the best answers because, as is stated above, the court will abstain from hearing this matter.

65. **(B)** From a standpoint of standing, choice (B) is a better answer than choice (A). This is because a person asserting the violation of a constitutional or statutory right must show a "direct and immediate personal injury" due to the challenged action. Choice (B) is correct because the candidate will argue that he is adversely affected by the election official's interpretation of the statute. On the other hand, it is more difficult for a claimant to have standing to assert the rights of third persons. That's why the candidate will be in a better position to bring suit for himself rather than on behalf of the German voters in choice (A). Choices (C) and (D) are wrong because federal election laws do not prevent a state from regulating absentee ballots. In fact, in *McDonald v. Board of Elections*, a state law granting the right to vote by absentee ballot to only certain classes of people was upheld. The Court ruled that the right to vote was ***not involved*** because the state did not preclude the appellants from voting by other means.

66. **(D)** Sometimes on the Multistate ***it is necessary to simply use common sense.*** Here, for example, choice (D) states that the decision should be upheld because it minimizes the potential for election fraud. Clearly, under a "strict scrutiny" standard of review, this will serve a compelling state interest and best justify the election official's action. Choice (A) is incorrect because even were this factually true, the right to vote is a fundamental right, and the state must try to protect it. Choice (B) is incorrect because this would not necessarily resolve the problem about lack of English proficiency. Choice (C) is not the best answer. Even if this were factually true, the right to vote is a fundamental right, and the state must try to protect it. Trying to save time in this manner would hardly seem a compelling state interest.

67. **(B)** The power of the federal government in regard to foreign affairs is exclusive. Powers, such as those to make treaties, to declare war, to conclude peace, and to maintain diplomatic relations with other nations are deemed "necessary concomitants of nationality," which has been interpreted to mean that they would have vested in the federal government even if they had never been mentioned in the Constitution, and are as broad as similar powers held by other sovereign nations [*United States v. Laws*, 163 U.S. 258 (1896)]. Choice (A) is incorrect. Federal criminal laws dealing with international affairs, like those dealing with domestic affairs, must meet the same requirements for specificity insofar as both must adhere to constitutional norms of due process. Choice (C) is incorrect. The President does not enjoy constitutional authority to punish citizens in the absence of congressional authorization. If the President possessed such powers, he would violate the principle of the separation of powers by exercising rights that belong to the legislature as well as those that belong to the judiciary. Choice (D) is not the best answer. Congress and the President may enjoy concurrent powers to regulate external affairs with foreign countries, but the powers are not the same, and Congress may invoke its own constitutional powers under Article I to regulate foreign affairs.

68. **(C)** The President may properly issue ***an executive order to ensure efficient operation of all executive agencies.*** The President's executive order to require all executive branch employees to use exclusively one brand of ballpoint pens and pencils could be upheld as a cost-efficient measure falling within the permissible scope of the President's power as Chief Executive. President Ford issued an executive order requiring all executive agencies to use only letter-size 8-1/2" X 11" paper. This cost-saving measure was held constitutional. Choice (A) is, therefore, incorrect. Choice (B) is also incorrect because it invites a similar type of regulation, namely that all executive branch employees wear only white shirts and blouses during regular working hours. Such an executive order could further efficient operation of executive departments based on the notions of teamwork and single-mindedness, which a uniform dress code inspires. Choice (D) is incorrect because, under the President's broad emergency powers as Commander-in-Chief, he may summon U.S. Army troops (or the National Guard) by executive decree for medical and humanitarian purposes without advice or consent of the Congress. Choice (C) is correct because an executive order may not be issued to supersede an earlier act of Congress. Nowak, Constitutional Law, 3rd Ed., p. 211. Since the Commission of Birdwatchers was established by federal law, the President's executive order to abolish the Commission would be unconstitutional.

69. **(A)** Article II, Section 2 states: "The president shall be Commander in Chief of the Army and Navy of the United States, and of the Militia of the several States, ***when called into the actual service of the United States***. . . ." Congress has not called the President into actual service in our example. Therefore, choice (A) is correct, and choice (D) is incorrect. Choice (B) is incorrect because the war powers resolution applies to situations when the armed forces are engaged in hostilities or where there is imminent involvement in hostilities. The facts in our case do not indicate that the armed forces were involved in hostilities. Choice (C) is incorrect. The President has the authority under Article II to execute laws passed by Congress, not to create his or her own.

70. **(C)** Here, you must be familiar with the decision in *Valley Forge Christian College v. Americans United,* 102 S.Ct. 752 (1982), in which a federal taxpayer was ***denied*** standing to challenge a gift of federal surplus property to a church college as violating the establishment clause. The Court held that the challenge was not to a federal expenditure under Congress's taxing and spending power, but to an exercise of Congress's power "to dispose of property belonging to the United States" under Article IV, Section 3, Clause 2. Many students will incorrectly choose choice (B) based on the holding in *Flast v. Cohen,* 392 U.S. 83 (1968). According to *Flast,* a federal taxpayer has standing to challenge a federal appropriation and spending measure if she can establish the challenged measures as (1) enacted under Congress' taxing and spending powers, and (2) it exceeds some specific limitation on the taxing and spending powers. **Note:** Be advised, however, ***that taxpayers have not been successful where the appropriation measure is challenged on grounds other than the 1st Amendment's establishment clause.*** Choice (A) is, likewise, incorrect because persons have ***no standing*** as citizens to claim that federal statutes violate the Constitution. Similarly, choice (D) is incorrect because absent congressional authorization of such a suit, a state has ***no standing*** to attack a federal statute on the grounds that Congress has exceeded its delegated powers. Under such circumstances, the state has not suffered any injury, and the matter is purely a "political question" [*Massachusetts v. Mellon,* 262 U.S. 447 (1923)]. Once again, by process of elimination, choice (C) is the strongest answer.

71. **(B)** In order not to violate the establishment clause, a statute (or other government action) must (1) have a secular purpose; (2) have a principal or primary effect that neither advances nor inhibits religion; and (3) not foster excessive government entanglement with religion [*Lemon v. Kurtzman,* 403 U.S. 602 (1971)]. As a practical matter, the Establishment Clause bars government sponsorship of religion, government financial support of religion, and active involvement in religious activities. Choice (A) is incorrect. Legal classifications that discriminate against religious groups would trigger strict scrutiny. But the classification in our example discriminates against secularists. Thus, the classification will be subject to rational review, which the federal

government should be able to pass with ease. Choice (C) is incorrect. The 5th Amendment's takings clause prohibits the government from taking ***private*** property without just compensation. In our example, the property belongs to the federal government. Choice (D) is incorrect. Idiomatically, Congress cannot violate the Commerce Clause; rather, Congress either has authority under the Commerce Clause or it does not. In our example, Congress may pass this legislation under the Commerce Clause because its stipulation regarding the terms of the devise are related to interstate commerce.

72. **(A)** The 14th Amendment's Due Process Clause provides procedural safeguards against arbitrary deprivation whenever a governmental agency acts ***to deprive a person of her "life, liberty, or property" interests.*** Since a corporation or company is considered a "person," due process protection would extend to General Electric in this problem. Choice (A) is clearly correct because the Parkview City Council is threatening to revoke its license for electrical service unless General Electric agrees to enclose the consumer letter in its monthly billing statements. Thus, if General Electric failed to comply with the city directive, it would face losing its electrical contract which, in turn, would effectively constitute a property deprivation. Choice (B) is incorrect. General Electric may have been the subject of discrimination by the legislature, but General Electric is not a member of a suspect or quasi-suspect class. Only rational review will be applied, which city probably will pass with ease. Choice (C) is incorrect because the privileges and immunities clause of Article IV applies only to U.S. citizens. General Electric is not a U.S. citizen. Choice (D) is incorrect. In order to find a violation of the dormant commerce clause, there must be a showing that the local government has placed undue burdens on interstate commerce. In our example, there is no evidence to suggest that the city's law protects utility companies like GE that reside in the city while burdening those outside the city.

73. **(C)** Choice (C) is most accurate because it is the only alternative that is helpful to the student. The fact that the university received support from the state is evidence of the "joint contract" between the university and the government. Under the concept of state action, where the private actor and government can be said to be in a "symbiotic relationship," the private actor will be subject to constitutional restraints. As a consequence, since the student did not receive notice or a hearing before his financial aid was terminated, the actions of the university (which would be treated as a government agent) were violative of the due process clause of the 14th Amendment. Choices (A) and (B) are incorrect because these facts would not carry legal relevance for our purposes. Choice (D) is incorrect because this would tend to hurt the student's argument insofar as it demonstrates that the university is trying to afford the student due process.

74. **(A)** As noted in the following chart, gender classifications are subject to a "middle-tier" standard of review. The burden of persuasion is on the government to demonstrate that the classification (or discrimination) is substantially related to an ***important governmental interest.*** Choice (A) correctly states the applicable standard of review for gender classifications. Choice (C) is incorrect to the extent that it relies on the decision in *Foley v. Connellie*, which allowed a state to exclude "aliens" from its police force. In *Foley*, the Supreme Court held that New York can prevent aliens from becoming state troopers. According to the *Foley* doctrine, a state could prevent aliens from holding certain state positions that involve a ***governmental function*** (e.g., public school teachers, police officers, and probation officers). Because this decision was specific to "aliens," it would be inapplicable to this question, which pertains to discrimination on the basis of gender classification, not alienage. Choice (B) is incorrect because the privileges or immunities clause of the 14th Amendment protects U.S. citizens from discrimination against out-of-staters, not discrimination based on gender. Choice (D) is incorrect. The reference to "rational basis" suggests that rational review is in order. But we have a gender classification, which will trigger intermediate review [*Craig v. Boren,* 429 U.S. 190 (1976)].

Multistate Nuance Chart

Equal Protection

STRICT SCRUTINY	INTERMEDIATE SCRUTINY	RATIONAL BASIS
BURDEN on STATE	BURDEN on STATE	BURDEN on PLAINTIFF
to show that the challenged measure is necessary to further a ***compelling state interest***	to show that the statute is ***substantially related to an important governmental objective***	to show that the statute is not ***rationally related to a legitimate state interest***
Covers three areas: **(1) Suspect Classifications:** Race Alienage National origin **(2) Fundamental Rights:** Right to vote Right to travel Right to privacy (includes): (a) Contraception (b) Abortion (c) Marriage (d) Procreation (e) Private Education (f) Family Relations **(3) Protected 1st Amendment Rights**	Covers: (1) Gender (2) Illegitimacy (3) Children of illegal aliens	Covers: (1) Social or economic welfare measures (e.g., welfare benefits) (2) Education – public (3) Housing (4) Unrelated people living together (5) Bankruptcy (6) Age (7) Poverty (8) Wealth (9) Mental retardation (10) Necessities of life (e.g., food, shelter, clothing, and medical care)

75. **(B)** In *Goldman v. Weinberger*, 106 S.Ct. 1310 (1986), the Court ruled against the free exercise claim of an Orthodox Jewish Air Force captain to wear a yarmulke while on duty. Giving broad deference to the professional judgment of the military authorities in determining the need to place restrictions on certain aspects of religiously motivated conduct, the Court stated that the use of standardized uniforms "encourages the subordination of personal preferences and identifies in favor of the overall group mission." Choice (B) is the best answer, since it closely approximates the specific language used by the Court in the *Goldman* case. While refusal by the ***military*** to accommodate an individual's free exercise claim is subject only to rational basis standard review, based on the Court's broad deference, the strict scrutiny standard applies to ***state*** regulation of free exercise claims. Therefore, choice (A) is incorrect. Choice (C), a true statement, is incorrect because the wearing of a head covering is a form of religious ***conduct***, not a religious belief. The procedural due process argument in choice (D) is incorrect because the state regulation in question directly affects the employee's free exercise of religion and is not depriving him of his right to seek gainful employment.

Explanation: Question 76

The correct answer is: **(A)** For the father, because the statute violates the First Amendment establishment clause.

The state statute advances religion. When a government action has no secular purpose, a primarily religious effect, or excessively entangles the government with religion, the government action violates the establishment clause [Lemon v. Kurtzman, 403 U.S. 602 (1971)]. Here, requiring that all high school English classes use the Psalms as the sole basis for teaching poetry appears to have a religious purpose and primarily a religious effect. Moreover, the state would probably have to supervise the teachers to insure that use of the Bible was limited to its literary and poetic value, not its religious meaning. While the public schools may study the Bible as a literary work, most legislative efforts to require that the Bible be used in the schools have been struck down.

(B) Incorrect. For the father, because the statute interferes with his right to free exercise of his religion.

The statute does not burden the father's free exercise rights. A government regulation that burdens a claimant's right to exercise religion will be upheld if it is neutral and generally applicable, but will be struck down if it discriminates against religion. Here, there is no burden on the father's free exercise rights. He is not prohibited from practicing atheism in any way. The challenge here is based upon the government assisting religion in a manner which is prohibited by the establishment clause, not burdening religion. Thus, this is not the best answer because it fails to address the proper religion clause which this statute violates.

(C) Incorrect. For the state, because the challenged legislation has a clearly stated secular purpose.

The court is not bound by the stated legislative purpose behind the statute. The law here appears to have been intended to benefit religion because it mandated that all poetry education in high school English classes must rely solely on the Bible. The Supreme Court will look behind the stated purposes of a statute to determine the actual legislative intent. In addition, regardless of what the intent was, the statute will have a primary effect of advancing religion if the Bible is used to the exclusion of secular poetry. Monitoring the religious content of the Bible poems and instruction will require excessive government entanglement with religion. If a government regulation has no secular purpose, has a primarily religious effect, or promotes excessive entanglement of the government with religion, the regulation must fall. Since this fails to address these three requirements, it is not the best answer.

(D) Incorrect. For the state, because the court may not infringe upon the legislature exercise of discretion about the artistic merit of the Psalms.

When a government action has no secular purpose, a primarily religious effect, or excessively entangles the government with religion, the government action violates the establishment clause [Lemon v. Kurtzman, 403 U.S. 602 (1971)]. This choice wrongly characterizes the inquiry of the court. A court will determine whether the statute violates any of the three prongs of the Lemon test. It is not interested in the legislature's determination of the artistic merit of the Psalms. Here, the statute violates the establishment clause. Since this choice fails to recognize this, it is not the best answer.

Explanation: Question 77

The correct answer is: **(C)** This expenditure will be invalid under the First Amendment.

This federal expenditure violates the First Amendment establishment clause. Government action that has no secular purpose, a primary effect which either advances or inhibits religion, or would require excessive government entanglement with religion will be struck down as violating the First Amendment establishment clause [Lemon v. Kurtzman, 403 U.S. 602 (1970)]. Here, the purpose of the law seems to be to advance religion (preparing for Judgment Day), the effect of allowing religious messages on a government sponsored satellite transmission also appears to be primarily religious, and there may be too much entanglement between religion and the government as the government may have to monitor the content of the religious messages.

(A) Incorrect. This action by the Federal Government will be upheld as a valid exercise of the spending power.
A Federal Government expenditure will only be valid if it is both for the general welfare and not in violation of any portion of the Constitution limiting the power of the federal government. The spending power is broadly interpreted such that just about any expenditure will be found to be for the general welfare. However, the First Amendment's establishment clause expressly limits the Federal Government's spending power, and this expenditure violates that clause.

(B) Incorrect. This expenditure will be upheld as a proper extension of Congress's power to regulate commerce with foreign nations.
The power to regulate commerce with foreign nations would not authorize this expenditure. Article I does provide that Congress is authorized to regulate both interstate and international commerce. Thus far, there is no indication that this power extends to interplanetary commerce. Even if it did, the commerce power is limited by the establishment clause of the First Amendment. Since this choice fails to recognize this limitation on the commerce clause power, it is not the best answer.

(D) Incorrect. This expenditure will be struck down because there is no rational relationship to any federal power.
There is a rational relationship between the expenditure and the spending power. Congress may spend for the general welfare. The existence of life in other solar systems, and the efforts to communicate with them, would be considered within the general welfare. The courts will not question Congress's determination that an expenditure is within the general welfare. However, the courts will examine whether an expenditure violates some other constitutional provision, like the establishment clause. Since this fails to recognize this limitation on government power, it is not the best answer.

Explanation: Question 78

The correct answer is: **(B)** The woman will prevail, because excluding women is not substantially related to an important government interest.

Equal protection under the Fourteenth Amendment applies to state action. The organization's close ties to state and local governments (such as receiving substantial government financial support and performing the public function of running the extracurricular athletic programs for public schools) should be sufficient to justify a finding of state action. Because the Fourteenth Amendment equal protection clause requires that government discrimination on the basis of gender be justified as substantially related to an important government interest (intermediate scrutiny), this choice gives the correct standard. Nothing in the facts indicates that the organization's exclusion of the woman will withstand intermediate scrutiny.

(A) Incorrect. The woman will prevail, because the organization's extensive ties to state and local government mean its exclusion of women constitutes state action for purposes of the Fourteenth Amendment.

Although state action is present, because of the organization's extensive entanglement with state and local governments, that by itself is not enough to establish that a constitutional violation has occurred. Instead, the validity of the state action that occurs through the organization's discriminatory membership policy will depend on application of intermediate scrutiny. If the Sons of the Mayflower can show that their exclusion of women is substantially related to an important government interest, it will be upheld even though it constitutes state action subject to Fourteenth Amendment equal protection.

(C) Incorrect. The Sons will prevail, because they need only show that their exclusion of women is rationally related to a legitimate government interest.

The Fourteenth Amendment equal protection clause requires that government discrimination on the basis of gender be justified as substantially related to an important government interest. The organization's close ties to state and local governments (such as receiving substantial government financial support and performing the public function of running the extracurricular athletic programs for public schools) should be sufficient to justify a finding of the requisite state action to impose equal protection clause standards.

(D) Incorrect. The Sons will prevail, because they can show that a compelling state interest justifies exclusion of women from their membership.

The compelling government interest test is reserved for government discrimination against suspect categories or fundamental rights. Here, the discrimination against the female descendant is based solely upon her gender. Gender is only entitled to the intermediate scrutiny test which requires the government to show that the regulation is substantially related to an important government interest. Thus, this is not the best choice for two reasons: 1) it applies the wrong standard' and 2) the information given is not enough to say that the organization meets the standard.

Explanation: Question 79

The correct answer is: **(A)** Congress has the authority under the commerce clause to regulate the flow of news.

Under the so-called "affectation doctrine," the U.S. Supreme Court has recognized that Congress has the power to regulate any activity, whether carried on in one state or many, which has any appreciable effect--directly or indirectly--upon interstate commerce [Wickard v. Filburn, 317 U. S. 111 (1942)].

(B) Incorrect. Acts of Congress are the supreme law of the land and take precedence over any conflicting state laws.

(C) Incorrect. Congress is essentially reaffirming the free speech guarantees of the First and Fourteenth Amendments.

(D) Incorrect. Congress has the authority to secure to authors and inventors the exclusive right to their respective writings and discoveries.

Explanation: Question 80

The correct answer is: **(B)** Yes, because Congress has war and defense powers.

Congress has enumerated powers to collect taxes and spend money for the general welfare, to borrow money on the credit of the United States, to regulate commerce with foreign nations and among the several states, to declare war, and to raise and support the armed services. The war power confers upon Congress very broad authority to initiate whatever measures it deems necessary to provide for the national defense in peacetime as well as in wartime. Furthermore, the modern trend is to uphold any tax as valid if it is a revenue-raising measure (rather than a regulatory measure).

(A) Incorrect. Yes, pursuant to the Constitution's Civil War Amendments.

The Civil War Amendments are the Thirteenth, Fourteenth, and Fifteenth Amendments. The Thirteenth Amendment bans slavery, the Fourteenth Amendment prohibits the states from violating due process, equal protection, and privileges and immunities, and the Fifteenth Amendment prohibits the states from discriminating in voting rights. As such, they are not applicable to Congress' taxation of citizens.

(C) Incorrect. No, because the taxation exceeds Congress' narrow authority under the circumstances.

This answer is incorrect because it reaches the wrong conclusion by misunderstanding the rule. The applicable rule in this pattern is the War and Defense Powers Clause. As it pertains to the war and defense powers, Congress has very broad authority to initiate whatever measures it deems necessary to provide for national defense. This answer misstates the scope of the authority granted to Congress.

(D) Incorrect. No, because the government cannot increase taxes to fund war during peacetime.

The War Powers Clause allows great breadth in Congress' authority to take necessary measures to provide for national defense in both peacetime and during periods of warfare. Therefore, this answer is incorrect.

Explanation: Question 81

The correct answer is: **(C)** A State Blue vendor offering coal for sale to a manufacturing plant in State Blue at $20/ton.

States have the power (concurrent with the federal government) to regulate commerce within their own borders. Such regulation will generally be upheld if it is purely local (intrastate), and neither produces a lack of uniformity that is of federal concern nor is already preempted by federal legislation in the area. Because choice (C) presents a case of purely intrastate commerce, the regulation will likely be upheld. Choice (A) is not the best choice. Although this is precisely the situation the legislation was probably intended to prohibit, the state's regulation of an out-of-state vendor with respect to in-state sales would unduly burden interstate commerce. Choices (B) and (D) are not the best choices. Both situations involve state action in an area preempted by the federal government. In choice (B), the state statute purports to regulate a sale to the U.S. government, an area of intergovernmental immunity. In choice (D), the state statute purports to affect commerce with foreign powers, an area reserved to the federal government.

(A) Incorrect. A neighboring state vendor offering coal for sale to the general public in State Blue at $20/ton.

(B) Incorrect. A State Blue vendor offering coal for sale to the U.S. Veteran's Hospital in the state at $20/ton.

(D) Incorrect. A foreign vendor offering coal for sale to the general public in State Blue for $20/ton.

Explanation: Question 82

The correct answer is: **(A)** Yes, under the commerce clause.

Article I, Section 8 of the U.S. Constitution grants Congress plenary power to regulate interstate commerce and commerce with foreign nations. Because Congress does have the power to regulate commerce with foreign nations, the legislation is constitutional. As such, the federal agency would have the authority to regulate the sale of the expert's encryption software program to a foreign company.

(B) Incorrect. Yes, because Congress has the power to regulate for the general welfare.

(C) Incorrect. No, because it deprives the expert of a property right without just compensation.

(D) Incorrect. No, because it usurps the power of the executive branch to conduct foreign affairs.

Explanation: Question 83

The correct answer is: **(C)** No, because the speech it regulates receives a lower level of protection.

Certain categories of speech receive lower levels of protection than general speech. Generally, a law regulating speech must pass a strict scrutiny analysis, i.e., the regulation must be necessary to further a compelling government interest. However, this speech is sexual speech, which is a special category of speech that receives a lower level of protection than general speech. Sexual speech may be regulated so long as the regulation serves a substantial government interest and leaves open reasonable alternative channels of communication. For example, the Supreme Court has held that a ban on public nudity was constitutional [Barnes v. Glen Theatres, Inc., 501 U.S. 1030 (1991)]. Here, there is a substantial government interest in maintaining morality, protecting children, and ensuring the safety of the members of the community. This can be accomplished by prohibiting nude running through the streets of the town. This ban does achieve its purpose as evidenced by the sharp decline in complaints to the local police. The ban is proper and constitutional.

(A) Incorrect. Yes, because it does not pass strict scrutiny.
This answer is incorrect because it reaches the wrong conclusion by misunderstanding the applicable rule. Generally, government may regulate speech if the regulation passes strict scrutiny, i.e., the regulation is necessary to further a compelling government interest. However, certain forms of speech are unprotected by the First Amendment: restrictions on such speech are permissible even if they would fail a strict scrutiny analysis. Furthermore, certain forms of speech, specifically commercial speech and sexual speech, receive lower levels of protection than general speech. Regulations of sexual speech must serve a substantial government interest, and leave open reasonable alternative channels of communication. The naked mile would constitute sexual speech and, as such, would be subject to a lower level of protection. Because it is not required that sexual speech passes strict scrutiny in order to be regulated, this answer is incorrect.

(B) Incorrect. Yes, because its restriction on speech is greater than that necessary to protect the government interest.
This answer is incorrect because it reaches the wrong conclusion by making a false assumption. A regulation of sexual speech must serve a substantial government interest and leave open a reasonable alternative channel of communication. It is not required that the regulation be necessary to protect the government interest. The speech being regulated in this example is sexual speech. Therefore, even if the regulation is not necessary to further a government interest, it is permissible because it serves a substantial government interest and leaves open reasonable alternative channels of communication.

(D) Incorrect. No, because the speech it regulates is child pornography.
This answer is incorrect because it reaches the right conclusion but does so by utilizing the wrong rule. Child pornography is a type of unprotected speech which may be regulated. However, it relates to the manufacturing, possession, sale, and distribution of visual depictions of sexual conduct involving children. Although this fact pattern involves conduct of a sexual nature and children who are witnesses to the conduct, there is nothing in the fact pattern to suggest that the children were involved in a manner which would arise to the level of child pornography. The appropriate category which would allow for the regulation of this type of speech is sexual speech.

Explanation: Question 84

The correct answer is: **(B)** No, because the law is a reasonable regulation of time, place, and manner of speech.

The government may reasonably regulate the time, place, or manner of speech in public areas like streets, sidewalks, and parks. These regulations focus on the conduct and method but not the content or message of the speech. In order to be constitutional, the regulation must be content neutral as to both the subject matter and the viewpoint, it must be narrowly tailored to serve a significant and important government interest, and it must leave alternative channels of communication open. Here, it is very apparent that the regulation is content-neutral given that it prohibits all picketing, demonstrating, or the posting of signs during a four-hour window. This regulation is narrowly tailored, restricting certain types of conduct during only a four-hour window in the middle of the day. It serves the government interest by reducing violence which stems from confrontations between mourners and people surrounding those mourners during funerals. And it allows for alternative communication by allowing demonstrations and protesting during the remaining twenty hours of the day in the exact same location. However, with this restriction, mourners who do not wish to be disturbed are able to grieve in peace without being confronted by the messages of others.

(A) Incorrect. No, because their speech defamed gun manufacturers.

This answer is incorrect because, although it reaches the correct conclusion, it does so by citing to a rule which is inapplicable or irrelevant. This answer choice refers to defamation. Constitutional restrictions apply to defamatory speech where the plaintiff is either a public official or public figure or where the defamatory statement involves a manner of public concern. This rule does not apply to the facts in this pattern. There are no facts which indicate that the mourners made any defamatory statements, only that the signs called for an end to unnecessary gun violence. This does not defame the any gun manufacturers. Therefore, this is an improper basis for the mourners not being allowed to remain outside of the cemetery.

(C) Incorrect. Yes, because the law does not serve a significant government interest.

This answer is incorrect because it is the second-best answer. In order for the government to restrict the time, place, and manner of speech in public areas, the regulation must be narrowly tailored to serve a significant and important government interest. This leaves the definition of "significant and important" up for interpretation to a certain extent. For our purposes, we will assume that reducing violence which leads to serious injuries over a period of years if a legitimate, significant, and important government interest. Here, the government is not seeking to specifically restrict the speech of the picketers of military funerals. The regulation is seeking to restrict all speech and conduct which could potentially erupt in violence between mourners and those surrounding the mourners. Maintaining the peace does serve a significant interest.

(D) Incorrect. Yes, because the mourners were peaceful.

This answer is incorrect based on a factual mistake. It cites to facts which are irrelevant to our inquiry. The three-part test used to determine the constitutionality of time, place, or manner regulations of speech and assembly in public places contemplates content, narrow tailoring, and alternative communication. It does not contemplate the characteristics of those being regulated. The regulation in this fact pattern restricts all picketing, demonstrating, or the posting of signs between the hours of 11 a.m. and 3 p.m. on public land within fifty feet of the gates of a funeral home or cemetery. It does not make a distinction between peaceful versus non-peaceful picketers or demonstrators.

Explanation: Question 85

The correct answer is: **(A)** Constitutional, because it bans conduct.

The government cannot censor all categories of speech or engage in content-based discrimination among different categories of speech, even in circumstances where the speech is offensive. However, the government does have the ability to regulate certain types of speech. For example, the government can regulate conduct which has an incidental burden on speech if: (1) the regulation furthers an important or substantial state interest that is unrelated to the suppression of free speech; and (2) the restriction on speech is no greater than necessary to the furtherance of the state interest. The government may also regulate the time, place, and manner of speech. In Virginia v. Black [538 U.S. 343 (2003)], the Supreme Court ruled that a state may ban cross burning carried out with the intent to intimidate. The statute here prohibits cross burning carried out with the intent to intimidate. Therefore, it is constitutional.

(B) Incorrect. Constitutional, because the government is the speaker.

This answer is incorrect because of a factual mistake. The conclusion is unsupported by the facts. There is no information in this fact pattern that would suggest that the group burning the cross is a group affiliated with or working behalf of the government. If the cross burners were a part of the government, there would be no question that this conduct could be regulated. Where the speaker is the government and not a private actor, the government may discriminate based on the content of the speech. However, it is not so much the speech which is being regulated here but the conduct. Conduct can be regulated whether or not the speaker is the government, if: (1) the regulation furthers an important or substantial state interest that is unrelated to the suppression of free expression; and (2) the restriction on expression is no greater than necessary to the furtherance of the state interest.

(C) Incorrect. Unconstitutional, because it bans expression.

This answer is incorrect because it reaches the wrong conclusion by misunderstanding the law. The government has the ability to regulate certain types of speech. After applying a strict scrutiny analysis, the government can regulate conduct that has an incidental burden on speech, speech where the government is a speaker, and unprotected speech. The government may also regulate the time, place, and manner of speech. Regulations of conduct that have an incidental burden on speech are allowable if: (1) the regulation furthers an important or substantial state interest that is unrelated to the suppression of free expression; and (2) the restriction on expression is no greater than necessary to the furtherance of the state interest. The Supreme Court ruled in Virginia v. Black [538 U.S. 343 (2003)] held that a state may ban cross burning carried out with the intent to intimidate.

(D) Incorrect. Unconstitutional, because the government may not regulate speech.

This answer is incorrect because it is extreme. While it is true that the government may neither censor all categories of speech nor engage in content-based discrimination among different categories of speech, it is not true that the government may not regulate any speech. Regulation of speech is allowable when it passes strict scrutiny.

Explanation: Question 86

The correct answer is: **(D)** The commission lacks authority to enforce its standards because not all of its members were appointed by the president.

Congress may not, by itself, appoint executive officers. Under Article III, the president appoints ambassadors, Supreme Court judges, and all other officers of the United States. Congress may vest the appointment of inferior officers in the president, the federal courts, or department heads, but Congress has no power to appoint officers or inferior officers itself. Thus, the commission lacks authority to enforce its orders because this commission is an executive agency, due to its prosecutorial functions, and four of its members are appointed by Congress.

(A) Incorrect. Legislative power may not be delegated by Congress to an agency in the absence of clear guidelines.

Congress may delegate legislative power to executive agencies under very general guidelines. In the 1930s, the Supreme Court struck down a few federal statutes on the ground that they attempted to make excessive delegations of legislative authority to executive agencies without sufficient standards. Since then, however, the Supreme Court has never struck down any other federal laws under this non-delegation doctrine, even though many federal statutes delegate enormous amounts of authority to executive agencies with only very minimal directions. Here, the aircraft commission would enjoy the same investigative and rulemaking power that Congress has under its power to regulate interstate commerce. The delegation of these powers would be valid, making this answer incorrect.

(B) Incorrect. The commerce power does not extend to the manufacture of aircraft not used in interstate commerce.

The Commerce Clause power extends to the manufacture of all aircraft, regardless of where they are operated. Congress can regulate the manufacture of all aircraft because the production would have a substantial effect on interstate commerce. Thus, Congress could delegate investigatory and rule-making power over aircraft production to the aircraft commission.

(C) Incorrect. The aircraft manufacturer is denied due process of law because it is not represented on the commission.

There is no constitutional right to be represented on a regulatory commission. As long as the delegation of authority is constitutional, the commission may properly regulate the aircraft manufacturer.

Explanation: Question 87

The correct answer is: **(B)** Yes, because sincere religious belief is not an adequate defense on these facts.

Although the cult leader may have had a sincere religious belief in animal sacrifice, that does not shield him from criminal liability in this situation. The Supreme Court has ruled that a religiously neutral law of general applicability can be applied even to sincere religious conduct without violating the free exercise clause of the Constitution [Employment Division v. Smith, 494 U.S. 872 (1990)]. There is no indication here that the animal cruelty statute was in any way targeted at religious observance, so this is the best answer.

(A) Incorrect. Yes, because belief in Satan does not enjoy constitutional protection.

This is an incorrect answer because it implies that the religious belief is the issue, which is not true. In essence, all beliefs are protected by the Constitution. However, some conduct may rightfully be prohibited, even if it is motivated by sincere religious belief. The Supreme Court has held that a religiously neutral law of general applicability can be applied even to sincere religious conduct without violating the Constitution's free exercise clause [Employment Division v. Smith, 494 U.S. 872 (1990)]. Therefore, this is not a correct answer.

(C) Incorrect. No, because the enforcement of the law against the cult leader violated his constitutionally guaranteed freedom of religion and religious expression.

This is not the best answer because even religious conduct is not protected if it violates a religiously neutral law of general applicability. In this case, the anti-cruelty statute was not aimed at religion, so its application to the ritual sacrifice does not violate the cult leader's constitutional rights. Thus, this answer is incorrect.

(D) Incorrect. No, because the beliefs of the cult members in the need for the sacrifice might be reasonable, and their act was religious.

The reasonableness of the cult's beliefs is not the important issue here. Rather, the fact that their conduct violated a religiously neutral law of general applicability is the reason why the cult leader can be found guilty of animal cruelty. Thus, this answer is incorrect.

Explanation: Question 88

The correct answer is: **(A)** Yes, because the law merely incidentally burdens interstate commerce.

The Tenth Amendment provides that the powers not delegated to the United States by the Constitution, nor prohibited by it, are reserved to the states respectively, or to the people. The Commerce Clause gives Congress the power to regulate interstate commerce. Where Congress has not enacted legislation, the states are free to regulate local transactions affecting interstate commerce, subject to certain limitations. These limitations are generally known as the Dormant Commerce Clause, or the negative implications doctrine. One such limitation applies to state laws that merely incidentally burden interstate commerce (as opposed to discriminating on their face between in-state and out-of-state economic actors). When a law does incidentally burden interstate commerce, the state must show that the law serves an important state interest and that the burden on interstate commerce is not excessive in relation to the interest served. Here, the law does not discriminate on its face between in-state and out-of-state actors, but it incidentally burdens interstate commerce. The important state interest the law serves is to reduce the number of traffic fatalities. That is an important interest. The measure is not excessive because the cost of these special tires is only slightly higher than the cost of the generally accepted tires. Therefore, this is the best answer.

(B) Incorrect. Yes, because the law is a public health measure.

This answer is incorrect because it reaches the right conclusion but does so by relying on an irrelevant or inapplicable rule. Generally, public health measures are upheld against constitutional challenges as long as they do not discriminate against or unduly burden interstate commerce. This rule generally applies to matters such as quarantine and inspection. Public health would not extend to matters involving traffic safety.

(C) Incorrect. No, because only the federal government may enact legislation affecting interstate commerce.

It is not correct that only the federal government may pass legislation affecting interstate commerce. States may enact legislation that incidentally burdens interstate commerce, if the legislation serves an important state interest and the burden on interstate commerce is not excessive in relation to the interest served.

(D) Incorrect. No, because the law furthers no ostensible benefit.

This answer is incorrect because it reaches the wrong conclusion by factual mistake. If a state regulation furthers no ostensible benefit and imposes a substantial burden on interstate commerce, it will likely be held unconstitutional. Here, the benefit is the lives of citizens who will be protected by rerouting the trucks and reducing the risk of collisions. This regulation does not impose a substantial burden on interstate commerce because the special tires that would be necessary for safe travel are only slightly more expensive then the generally used tires.

Explanation: Question 89

The correct answer is: **(C)** No, because Congress neither ratified nor consented to the treaty.

For the treaty to be in effect in the United States, Congress must still consent to the treaty or ratify the treaty. Self-execution deals with treaties that will go into effect without any subsequent legislative provision by Congress beyond consent or ratification. In other words, a self-executing treaty is a treaty which has automatic domestic effect as federal law upon ratification. Therefore, with no Congressional ratification or consent, the treaty is not in effect, regardless of the proposed terms discussed in the fact pattern. Therefore, this answer is correct.

(A) Incorrect. Yes, because Congress has delegated treaty-making power to the President.

Congress has not delegated treaty-making power to the President. Rather, the President's treaty power is one of the President's enumerated powers under the Constitution. Therefore, this answer is incorrect.

(B) Incorrect. Yes, because the treaty is self-executing by its terms.

Under the President's treaty power, the President has the power to enter into treaties with foreign countries. Treaties have the force of law, and may be either self-executing or non-self-executing. A self-executing treaty takes effect without the necessity of any further action by Congress, once there has been Congressional ratification or consent. Note that non-self-executing treaties additionally require Congress to pass legislation implementing the provisions of the treaty.

(D) Incorrect. No, because of the separation of powers doctrine.

The treaty is not in effect because of the lack of Congressional ratification or consent. The President's treaty power is one of the President's enumerated powers under the Constitution, and therefore, there has been no violation of the separation of powers doctrine. Indeed, it is the separation of powers which has made this treaty ineffectual without Congressional ratification or consent. Therefore, this answer is incorrect.

Explanation: Question 90

The correct answer is: **(B)** No, because there is no causation.

Article III of the U.S. Constitution requires a person litigating a constitutional question to show three things - injury in fact, causation, and redressability. Here, the injury in fact would be the imminent death of the mother of the unborn child. The redressability would be monetary damages. It is the issue of causation that keeps the woman from filing suit on behalf of her unborn child. For causation, injury must be caused by the violation of a duty affecting the plaintiff's rights arising under the constitution or federal law. This means that the injury must be caused by the challenged action. Here, causation cannot be established. The mother is seeking to sue the manufacturers of the anti-depressants on behalf of the unborn child for the loss of the child's mother. The loss of the mother will not be caused by the anti-depressants. Therefore, there is no causation.

(A) Incorrect. No, because the court lacks jurisdiction.

Federal courts have jurisdiction over cases arising under the U.S. Constitution, federal laws, and treaties. The woman in this example is challenging the constitutionality of federal regulations. Therefore, a federal court would have jurisdiction to hear the case. As such, this answer is incorrect.

(C) Incorrect. Yes, because the unborn child is unable to bring the suit on his or her own behalf.

The fact that the unborn child is unable to bring a lawsuit does not make the mother's lawsuit permissible. In order to challenge a law on constitutional grounds, a litigant must show injury in fact, causation, and redressability. The standards being challenged in this lawsuit did not cause the mother's terminal illness, or the child's future loss of his mother. Therefore, the mother cannot show causation. As such, this answer is incorrect.

(D) Incorrect. Yes, because the anti-depressants will cause the death of the woman.

This answer is incorrect because of a reading comprehension error. While it is true that the anti-depressants caused cancer in the woman, the cancer is non-fatal. The woman will ultimately die from an unrelated terminal illness. This answer fails because the anti-depressants will not cause the death of the woman.

Explanation: Question 91

The correct answer is: **(B)** No, because it violates the Fourteenth Amendment's equal protection clause.

State alienage classifications are examined under the strict scrutiny test, under which the state must show a compelling government interest in the classification to withstand a constitutional challenge. If the state cannot show a compelling interest in excluding all aliens from operating electrolysis businesses, the citizenship requirement will be struck down. Here, it will be difficult, if not impossible, for the state to meet the standards of the strict scrutiny test. As such, it is likely that the citizenship requirement will be held to violate the constitutional guarantee of equal protection of the laws as applied to aliens.

(A) Incorrect. No, because it constitutes a bill of attainder.

A bill of attainder is a legislative act that inflicts punishment on named individuals or upon easily ascertainable members of a group without a judicial trial. The citizenship requirement is not a bill of attainder. Thus, this answer is incorrect.

(C) Incorrect. Yes, because it is reasonably related to ensuring the health and safety of clients.

Even though the state has the authority to regulate electrolysis businesses for the health and safety of its citizens, it may not regulate in a manner that violates individual constitutional rights. The citizenship requirement discriminates on the basis of alienage and, therefore, the equal protection clause is implicated. State alienage classifications are examined under the strict scrutiny test, under which the state must show a compelling government interest in the classification. This answer wrongly applies the rational basis test to the statute in question and, as such, is incorrect.

(D) Incorrect. Yes, because it is within the police power reserved to the state under the Tenth Amendment.

Even though the police power reserved to the states under the Tenth Amendment authorizes the state to regulate the electrolysis business for the health and safety of state citizens, the regulation may not withstand constitutional scrutiny if it infringes upon individual constitutional rights. The citizenship requirement classifies license applicants on the basis of alienage, and thereby implicates the equal protection clause. State alienage classifications are examined under the strict scrutiny test, under which the state must show a compelling government interest in the classification. This is a very difficult test for a state to meet, and few statutes are upheld under this test. Thus, this answer is incorrect.

Explanation: Question 92

The correct answer is: **(B)** Yes, because the executive agreement supersedes inconsistent state law.

Under the Supremacy Clause of Article II, the Constitution and laws of the United States are the supreme law of the land. Any state law in direct conflict with a valid federal law is preempted by it if the federal law is intended to occupy the field. The state legislation includes a regulation that imposes hunting limits in direct conflict with the federal limits set by the joint commission. The president was authorized under Article II powers to enter into the executive agreement concerning international hunting regulations; therefore, the executive agreement supersedes inconsistent state law.

(A) Incorrect. Yes, because the state law discriminates against hunting companies that are based outside of the state.

There is no fundamental right to pursue a living free of government regulation. Moreover, it is unlikely that the commission could raise the discrimination claims of the hunting companies regulated by the state law. Because the question presents the issue of a conflict between state and federal law, the answer should address the source of power of state and federal governments to regulate. Thus, this answer is incorrect.

(C) Incorrect. No, because state law should prevail when the issue involved is regulation of state industry.

The Supremacy Clause of Article II provides that the Constitution and laws of the United States are the supreme law of the land. Any state law in direct conflict with a valid federal law is preempted by it if the federal law is intended to occupy the field. Here, the state legislation includes a regulation that imposes hunting limits in direct conflict with the federal limits set by the joint commission. Thus, this answer is incorrect.

(D) Incorrect. No, because state conservation issues should be dealt with by each state.

A valid executive agreement preempts state regulation of resources within state boundaries. Under the police power reserved to the states under the Tenth Amendment, the states may regulate for the general health, safety, and welfare of state citizens. However, even a valid exercise of state regulatory power is preempted by a superseding federal law. The executive agreement creating the joint U.S. and Canada commission was a valid exercise of the president's power over international relations. The state regulations are preempted by the federal law. Thus, this answer is incorrect.

Explanation: Question 93

The correct answer is: **(D)** The First Amendment.

The tax violates the First Amendment freedom of the press. The U.S. Supreme Court has held that a tax imposed solely on newspapers and news periodicals is violative of freedom of the press.

(A) Incorrect. The Equal Protection Clause of the Fourteenth Amendment.

Both the Fourteenth Amendment's Equal Protection Clause and the Article IV, Section 2 Privileges and Immunities Clause only apply to the state and local governments. This federal tax on the press violates freedom of the press, as stated in the correct choice.

(B) Incorrect. The Privileges and Immunities Clause.

Both the Fourteenth Amendment's Equal Protection Clause and the Article IV, Section 2 Privileges and Immunities Clause only apply to the state and local governments. This federal tax on the press violates freedom of the press, as stated in the correct choice.

(C) Incorrect. The Due Process Clause.

The tax does not appear to burden any substantive or procedural due process rights. Rather, the tax directly burdens freedom of the press, which is protected by the First Amendment, as stated in the correct choice.

Explanation: Question 94

The correct answer is: **(C)** cannot be convicted, because, though his speech here may be punished by the state, the state may not do so under this statute.

This statute is void on its face and cannot serve as the basis for convicting the man. A regulation of speech is void for vagueness when persons of common intelligence would have to guess at its meaning. In so doing the statute may also be struck down as being substantially over-broad because the statute would prohibit persons from engaging in a substantial amount of constitutionally protected speech because they are unsure of the scope of the statute. Here, there is no way of knowing what is opprobrious or abusive language. People would have to guess what kinds of language the statute prohibited. When a statute is struck down on vagueness or over-breadth grounds, it cannot operate to punish anyone. Thus, the man cannot be convicted under this statute even though his speech might be punishable under a more narrowly drafted statute.

(A) Incorrect. can be convicted.

The man cannot be convicted under this statute because the statute is void on its face for vagueness and over-breadth. Even though it might be possible to prosecute the man under a more narrowly drawn statute, this one will not do.

(B) Incorrect. cannot be convicted, because the First and Fourteenth Amendments bar punishing speech of the sort described here.

Speech of this sort can be prohibited without interfering with the First and Fourteenth Amendments. The right to freedom of speech as guaranteed by the First Amendment (and made applicable to the states and local governments by the Fourteenth Amendment) does not protect violent or obscene speech. The man's utterance of four-letter words at the child may well have been unprotected because it was obscene. The problem here is that the statute is vague and over-broad, which makes it facially invalid. Thus, this is not the best answer because the man's speech may have been punishable under the First and Fourteenth Amendments.

(D) Incorrect. cannot be convicted, because the average user of a public street would think his speech/action here was amusing and ridiculous rather than opprobrious.

This choice assumes that the language the man used might not be prohibited by the statute. There is no way to make this determination without knowing exactly what the man said. Regardless of the words used, the statute is vague and over-broad. The fact that the statute is void on its face, as suggested by the correct choice, is a much better reason to dismiss the action.

Explanation: Question 95

The correct answer is: **(C)** A war protester who tells several thousand members of a protest march that the war that's going on is illegal and immoral, and you should all go to the draft board offices right now and burn their records as a symbol of our contempt for their illegal war.

This situation seems to be the one where imminent lawless action is most likely to occur. The First Amendment freedom of speech generally prohibits the government from regulating the content of speech unless the government action is necessary to advance a compelling government interest. However, certain types of speech receive no protection, such as speech that is intended and likely to cause imminent lawless action [Brandenburg v. Ohio, 395 U.S. 444 (1969)]. The student requested his followers to all go to the draft board offices right now and burn their records. This is speech which may be prohibited because at least some of the thousands of followers are likely to follow their leader's command to perform the illegal act. Moreover, the conduct fits within the statute because it is speech which incites others to perform a criminal act. When the speech is constitutionally unprotected and falls within a narrowly drafted speech statute, such as this, it can be punished.

(A) Incorrect. A college student who tells a noontime rally of several hundred students at the university that the corporate structure of the United States reeks from its own corruption and will, when the time is right, be cleansed by the purifying fire of violent revolution, brothers and sisters; I will lead you in that glorious purifying bloodbath.

This student did not attempt to incite the other students to perform imminent lawless action. He told the assemblage that the revolution would occur when the time is right. Speech that proposes lawless action in the indefinite future cannot be punished.

(B) Incorrect. A white supremacist who tells a clandestine meeting of seventeen followers that I believe that the nonwhite races are vermin created by Satan and should be eradicated on sight by right-thinking white Americans.

The fact that the white supremacist stated an intolerant and violent point of view is not the same as inciting imminent lawless action. Speech that proposes lawless action in the indefinite future cannot be punished.

(D) Incorrect. A member of the radical People's Revolutionary Army, whose manifesto states that each soldier of the People's Revolutionary Army will take constant and immediate action to destroy the government of the fascist United States and to execute the officials of that government. She joined the PRA two years ago and has attended one weekly meeting and one PRA bake sale.

Membership in a group that advocates violence cannot be punished unless the member knows of the illegal purpose of the group and has the specific intent to further that illegal purpose. This member's involvement with the PRA is too limited to suggest that she had the specific intent to engage in violence.

Explanation: Question 96

The correct answer is: **(D)** No, because the sincerity of the elders' religious beliefs does not entitle them to a special exception from the state's compulsory education law.

The elders' freedom of religion claim will fail because the statute requiring children to be educated is a neutral and generally applicable law, not a measure with the intent or effect of discriminating against anyone's exercise of their religion. Although one case allowed Amish children to be exempt from a state law requiring children to attend high school [Wisconsin v. Yoder, 406 U.S. 205 (1972)], the Supreme Court more recently held that a neutral, generally applicable law does not violate the free exercise clause even if it punishes conduct engaged in as a religious practice [Employment Division v. Smith, 494 U.S. 872 (1990)]. Also, note that, in the Yoder case, children went to public school until the eighth grade and then received further practical training, as contrasted with the case here in which children were not allowed to attend school or become literate at all.

(A) Incorrect. Yes, because their religious practices are guaranteed freedom from interference by the state by the First Amendment.

Freedom of religious practice is not absolutely protected. Only religious beliefs are absolutely protected. Here, the elders have refused to enroll their children in state-approved private or public school. They are not entitled to a special exemption from the obligation to comply with a neutral and generally applicable law [Employment Division v. Smith, 494 U.S. 872 (1990)].

(B) Incorrect. Yes, because their method of educating their children is a fundamental tenet of their faith, so the First Amendment bars the state from requiring them to send their children to public school.

The state regulation requires that the children attend public or private schools approved by the state, not that they must go to public school. The Court has upheld the right of the Amish to refuse to send their children to high school because of their religious beliefs [Wisconsin v. Yoder, 406 U.S. 205 (1972)]. In the Yoder case, the Amish children did learn basic educational skills and were part of a longstanding, large and well-established community in which most of the children would continue to live after reaching adulthood. Here, however, the elders are refusing to give their children any formal education. Thus, this is not the best answer because they do not have the constitutional right to keep their children completely illiterate.

(C) Incorrect. No, because the state has an important state interest in educating the children located within its jurisdiction.

This choice misapplies the test for measuring free exercise violations. Once it is established that the law interfering with religious exercise is neutral and generally applicable, rather than discriminatory, the law cannot violate the free exercise clause. The fact that the government regulation advances an important state interest is not material. Since this choice fails to address the applicable rule, it is not the best answer.

Explanation: Question 97

The correct answer is: **(D)** The federal rule does not preempt the State B statute, because the purposes of the federal rule and the State B statute are different.

State or local regulations of interstate commerce that directly or indirectly conflict with a valid federal law will be struck down as a violation of the Supremacy Clause. Here, there is no direct conflict because the federal law does not expressly preclude state or local regulation of radar devices. That is, there is no indication that federal regulation is so pervasive that all state or local regulations of the subject are preempted, there are no facts to suggest that the automobile radar device is a subject calling for uniform national regulation, and the existence of the State B statute prohibiting the possession of radar-detection devices does not interfere with the full accomplishment of the federal purpose. The federal purpose is to protect radar devices from injuring installers. The purpose of the State B statute is to prevent the devices from injuring persons in speeding accidents.

(A) Incorrect. The federal rule preempts the State B statute, because the federal rule regulates the same subject matter, radar devices.

A state or local regulation is not preempted simply because it regulates the same subject area as a valid federal law. The state or local regulation must directly or indirectly conflict with the federal law. There is no direct or indirect conflict here because the federal law did not expressly prohibit state or local regulation of the same subject, and the purposes of these two laws are different. Thus, this answer is incorrect.

(B) Incorrect. The federal rule preempts the State B statute, because the federal rule does not contain affirmative authorization for continued state regulation.

Affirmative authorization by Congress is not generally required to insulate state or local regulations of interstate commerce from a preemption challenge. Rather, it may be necessary under the negative implications of the Commerce Clause. Thus, this answer is incorrect.

(C) Incorrect. The federal rule does not preempt the State B statute, because the State B statute regulates traffic safety, a field of exclusive state power.

Regulation of traffic safety is not exclusive to the states. Pursuant to its interstate commerce power, Congress can regulate all activities that may have a substantial impact on the national economy. The state statute is not preempted because this is an area where non-conflicting state and federal regulations may co-exist, not because the subject of highway safety is exclusive to the states. Thus, this answer is incorrect.

Explanation: Question 98

The correct answer is: **(B)** constitutional because private contractors performing work under a federal contract are not immune in these circumstances from non-discriminatory state taxation.

A state tax levied against an independent contractor hired by the federal government is valid as long as the tax does not discriminate against the federal government or its agents. While state and local governments are forbidden by the Supremacy Clause from directly taxing or regulating the federal government, they are allowed to impose indirect, non-discriminatory taxes on the federal government. In this regard, state taxes imposed upon federal employees, federal contractors and federal lessees have been upheld because the legal incidence of the taxes did not fall upon the federal government and the taxes were applied to all employees, contractors or lessees, not just the federal ones. Because the State B tax was imposed on all businesses in the state, the corporation must pay the tax.

(A) Incorrect. constitutional because a state has exclusive jurisdiction over all commercial transactions executed wholly within its borders.

This is not the best choice because it overstates the ability of the state and local governments to tax or regulate within their borders. A state cannot exercise exclusive jurisdiction over federal government activities, regardless of where the activity takes place. The police power of the states does not extend to regulation or taxation imposed directly on the federal government, even if the federal government is engaged in commercial activities inside the state.

(C) Incorrect. unconstitutional because it violates the Supremacy Clause.

State governments may indirectly tax or regulate the federal government by imposing taxes on federal employees, contractors, or lessees as long as the tax does not discriminate against the federal agents. Therefore, this is not the best choice, because the tax was payable by the federal contractor (not directly by the federal government) and was imposed on all businesses (non-discriminatory). Moreover, there were no applicable federal statutes, administrative rules or contractual language which might directly preempt the tax.

(D) Incorrect. unconstitutional because it imposes an undue burden on interstate commerce.

State or local regulations or taxes imposed on interstate commerce will be struck down as violative of the Commerce Clause if the laws discriminate against interstate commerce or impose an undue burden on interstate commerce. A state tax on the gross receipts of all business conducted within the state as applied to an out-of-state corporation does not, without additional facts, impose an undue burden on interstate commerce. This choice states that a gross receipts tax imposed on all business conducted within the state is, by definition, an undue burden on interstate commerce. However, there are no facts to suggest that the tax is exceedingly high or excessively interferes with the interstate flow of goods and services. Thus, this is not the best choice because it erroneously suggests that any gross receipts tax applied to out-of-state businesses doing business in the state amounts to an undue burden on interstate commerce.

Explanation: Question 99

The correct answer is: **(B)** not prevail, because the operator's boats endangered public safety.

A license is a protected property interest that cannot be taken away without procedural due process. The operator was given notice and an opportunity to be heard: the facts state that he was unable to address the board's concerns adequately, indicating that he did appear before the board to counter the charges. Pursuant to the state's police power, the state licensing board had authority to revoke the operator's commercial boating license if operation of the vessels endangered the public.

(A) Incorrect. not prevail, because the impairment of the public contract was reasonable.

A state government is prohibited from impairing the obligation of public contracts other than to a reasonable degree when the government seeks to modify its own contracts. The licensing board's revocation of the operator's license is separate from any action the state government may take to renegotiate the contract for the state, a renegotiation that has not yet taken place. Thus, this answer is incorrect.

(C) Incorrect. prevail, because the legislature's act constituted a bill of attainder.

A bill of attainder is a legislative act that inflicts punishment on a named individual, such as the operator. If the legislature had taken action to revoke the operator's license, then the revocation would have been an unconstitutional bill of attainder. However, according to the facts, the legislature did not act on the senator's resolution. Thus, this answer is incorrect.

(D) Incorrect. prevail, because the operator was denied due process.

A license to operate commercial vessels is a protected property interest that cannot be taken away without procedural due process. The operator was given notice and an opportunity to be heard. The facts state that he was unable to address the licensing board's safety concerns adequately, indicating that he was given an opportunity to address them. Therefore, the operator was not denied due process prior to revocation of his license. Thus, this answer is incorrect.

Explanation: Question 100

The correct answer is: **(D)** unconstitutional, if Congress intended the federal rating system to occupy the field.

Even if a state statute is not expressly preempted, the statute may be impliedly preempted if Congress intended the federal law to occupy the field. On the issue of regulating the content of video games, Congress has not expressly prohibited state regulation. However, the state law would still be struck down if the court finds Congress intended the federal law to occupy the field. A court will consider (1) whether the federal scheme is so comprehensive that Congress left no room for the states to enact supplemental laws, and (2) whether there is a need for a uniform regulatory scheme to avoid confusion and difficulty in administration. Here, the court is likely to find that the federal video game rating system legislation is so pervasive as to preempt supplemental state law and will therefore strike down the state statute, even though such state legislation is not expressly prohibited.

(A) Incorrect. constitutional, because regulatory authority over video games does not rest exclusively in the federal arena.

This is an incorrect answer, because even if the federal legislation is not exclusive, the state statute can be preempted pursuant to the Supremacy Clause. The Constitution makes specific federal powers exclusive, such as the power to coin money. Congress can also make federal legislation exclusive by specifically prohibiting state regulation in a particular field. Under the facts presented, the federal video game rating legislation is silent on state regulatory authority. Because neither the Constitution nor Congress has prohibited state regulation in the field of video game rating systems, the state statute is not expressly preempted. However, there may be implied preemption, which the answer fails to consider. Thus, this answer is incorrect.

(B) Incorrect. constitutional, because the state statute does not directly conflict with the federal rating system.

Where there is a direct conflict between a federal and a state law, the state law is void. The state statute does not conflict with the federal video game ratings scheme; it merely supplements it. However, even if there is no direct conflict, there may be express preemption (where the Constitution or Congress limits regulation to federal authority) or implied preemption (where Congress intends federal law to occupy the field). This answer fails to consider the possibility that the state statute may be preempted despite the lack of direct conflict with federal law. Thus, this answer is incorrect.

(C) Incorrect. unconstitutional, because of the undue burden the state statute imposes on interstate commerce.

The issue of state burdens on interstate commerce arises where no federal regulatory scheme preempts the state regulation. However, in this question there is both a federal and a state video game rating system, so the question is whether the federal scheme preempts the state scheme, either expressly or impliedly. Thus, this answer is incorrect.

1. FEDERAL JUDICIAL AUTHORITY

Organization of the Federal Court System

- **ARTICLE III** — vests the judicial power in the Supreme Court and such inferior courts as Congress may establish; jurisdiction limited to "cases and controversies." Compare: Article I Courts (tax courts, courts in the District of Columbia) are vested with administrative, as well as judicial functions; no lifetime tenure for Article I judges. Role of Congress: plenary power both to establish lower federal courts and to confer and remove jurisdiction over Article III courts.
  Note that Article III courts may not give advisory opinions, although state courts may do so

- **POWER OF JUDICIAL REVIEW** — *Marbury v Madison* — held that the Supreme Court may determine the constitutionality of acts of other branches of government; federal courts may also review state court decisions

- **JURISDICTION OF THE SUPREME COURT** — Original (trial level) — extends to "all cases affecting Ambassadors, other public Ministers and Consuls, and those in which a State shall be a Party"; Congress may neither enlarge nor restrict, but may give concurrent jurisdiction to lower federal courts (except in cases between 2 or more states where the Supreme Court has exclusive jurisdiction) Appellate—extends to all other Article III cases and controversies; Congress may broadly regulate, but may not preclude review of an entire class of cases

- **TWO STATUTORY MEANS** — Provided by Congress to Invoke the Supreme Court's Appellate Jurisdiction: 1. Appeal (mandatory review)—applies to decisions of 3-judge federal district courts
  2. Certiorari (discretionary; 4 or more justices vote to hear a case) — applies to decisions of the highest state courts regarding federal law issues, and decisions of US Courts of Appeal

(continued)

1. FEDERAL JUDICIAL AUTHORITY *(continued)*

Judicial Review (doctrine empowering federal courts to refuse to hear a case, despite subject matter jurisdiction)

- **STANDING** — concrete personal stake in the outcome is required by Article III — Injury in Fact — specific, not theoretical, injury must arise from the government conduct being complained of; usually economic injury, but need not be — Redressability (Causation) — the relief sought must eliminate the harm alleged; plaintiff's injury must be within the "zone of interests" Congress meant to protect — Prudential Limitations — self-imposed by the Court; no "citizen" standing for abstract, generalized grievances; a corporation has standing to challenge a federal statute where the injury is to the organization itself; no third party standing, unless plaintiff herself has suffered injury which adversely affects her relationship with third parties, who have difficulty asserting their own rights; no taxpayer standing because the interest is too remote, except a federal taxpayer has standing to make an establishment clause challenge to an expenditure which exceeds some specific limitation on the taxing and spending power *(Flast v Cohen)*
- **MOOTNESS** — a case brought too late; an actual controversy must exist at all stages of review, unless the issue is capable of repetition, yet evading review (pregnancy, elections)
- **RIPENESS** — a case brought too early; a genuine, immediate threat of harm must exist (no declaratory judgment allowed before a law is enforced)
- **POLITICAL QUESTIONS** — nonjusticiable issues committed to other branches of government (e.g., foreign affairs, Guaranty Clause issues, congressional membership requirements; but not apportionment of legislative districts)
- **11TH AMENDMENT** — provides a state cannot be sued in federal court without consent; however, state officials may be sued for federal law violations; local governments can be sued; the United States or another state may sue a state; Congress can remove a state's immunity (e.g., for civil rights violations)
- **ABSTENTION**
  - Pullman doctrine applies where a federal claim is based on an unsettled issue of state law; procedurally, the federal court retains jurisdiction of the federal claim
  - Younger doctrine prohibits review/enjoining of pending state criminal proceedings, criminally related civil proceedings, and civil contempt proceedings; procedurally the party is sent back to state court for all purposes
- **ADEQUATE AND INDEPENDENT STATE GROUNDS** — The Supreme Court will not review a state decision based on a clear, adequate, independent and fully dispositive nonfederal ground

2. SEPARATION OF POWERS

Doctrine of Enumerated Powers

- **FEDERAL GOVERNMENT (FG)** — has only that authority which the Constitution confers on it, either express or implied
- **10th AMENDMENT** — powers not delegated to the FG are retained by the States under the 10th Amendment; under their police power, the States can legislate to protect any health, safety, welfare, morals, or aesthetics interest
- **NECESSARY AND PROPER CLAUSE** — grants Congress the authority to carry into execution any enumerated power; not an independent source of power

Federal Legislative Power (Article 1, §8 Enumerated Powers)

- **COMMERCE POWER** — plenary power which regulates both interstate and foreign commerce
  - Affectation Doctrine — regulates any activity which has a substantial economic effect on the stream of interstate commerce
  - Cumulative Impact Doctrine — even an entirely intrastate commercial or economic activity which has a cumulative impact on interstate commerce may be regulated
- **TAXING AND SPENDING POWER** — plenary power to tax and spend for the general welfare; general welfare clause is not an independent source of power
  - Spending Power — Congress can attach strings to federal appropriations, thereby regulating indirectly where it cannot legislate directly
  - Taxing Power — a federal tax is valid if the dominant intent is fiscal; direct taxes (income tax) must be apportioned; indirect taxes (sales, use and excise taxes) must be geographically uniform
- **WAR POWER** — to declare war, raise and support an army and navy, and make rules to regulate the armed forces; pervasive economic regulatory power during war; regulation may continue even after cessation of hostilities
- **OTHER ENUMERATED POWERS** — postal power; power over District of Columbia; power to coin money; power to propose Constitutional amendments; immigration and naturalization; copyright, patent, bankruptcy powers; impeachment power
- **IMPLIED POWERS** — broad investigatory power enforceable by contempt sanction; plenary admiralty power

Delegation of Legislative Power

- **LEGISLATIVE VETO** — Congress can delegate its legislative power to executive and administrative agencies, but cannot subsequently retract it — such a "legislative veto" is unconstitutional *(INS v Chadha)*

(continued)

2. SEPARATION OF POWERS *(continued)*

Federal Executive Power (Article II)

- **DOMESTIC POLICY** — Power and obligation to faithfully execute the laws
  - Appointment Powers — President can appoint purely executive officers (such as Cabinet members), ambassadors, public ministers, consuls and Supreme Court judges "with the advice and consent of the Senate"; Congress may not appoint members of bodies having administrative or enforcement powers, and may only appoint its legislative staff members; Congress can delegate appointment of "inferior officers" (such as a special prosecutor) to either the President, department heads, or the judiciary.
  - Removal Powers — the Constitution is silent; the President may remove purely executive officers (Cabinet members) without cause, but good cause is required to remove administrative officials with fixed terms of special need for independence from President; Congress has no power of summary removal
  - Veto Power — President has 10 days to exercise his veto, which may then be overridden by 2/3 vote of each house; President has no legislative power nor any power to impound funds
  - Pardon Power — extends only to federal crimes, not state crimes
  - Executive Privilege — to refuse to disclose information (military and diplomatic secrets); privilege must yield to important government interests
  - Absolute immunity in civil suits for damages based on actions taken while in office
- **FOREIGN POLICY** — Commander in Chief of the Armed Forces — may establish military governments in occupied territories; broad emergency powers
  - Treaty Power — requires consent of 2/3 of the Senate.
  - Executive agreement — informal means by which the President can conduct day-to-day economic and business transactions between foreign countries without Senate consent
  - Foreign Affairs — President's power is not plenary, but is shared with Congress; sources of such power include: 1) Commander-in-chief; 2) Treaty Power; 3) Congressional Authorization (delegation by Congress of its commerce power to the President)

3. FEDERALISM (Federal limitations on state power)

Intergovernmental Immunities

- **STATE REGULATION OF THE FEDERAL GOVERNMENT** — FG and its agencies are immune from state taxation and regulation; however, nondiscriminatory state taxes on federal contractors and employees are valid.
- **FEDERAL PROPERTY POWER (Art. IV, §3)** — Congress may dispose of and make all needful rules and regulations respecting the territory or other property of the United States; generally applies to wild animals, federal buildings and enclaves, military ships and planes, Indian reservations
- **FEDERAL GOVERNMENT REGULATION OF THE STATES** — states are not immune under 10th or 11th amendments (FG may sue a state; one state may sue another state); FG may tax proprietary state businesses
- **10TH AMENDMENT** — powers not delegated to the FG, nor constitutionally prohibited to the states, are reserved to the states; a weak limitation on the federal commerce power; FG may not compel states (rather than private entities) to enact a particular regulatory program [e.g. regulate radioactive waste or take title to it — *N.Y. v U.S.*]

Dormant Commerce Clause

- **NEGATIVE IMPLICATIONS DOCTRINE** — where Congress has not otherwise regulated, the states are free to regulate interstate commerce; regulation must be 1) non-discriminatory — may not favor or protect local interests, and 2) not unduly burdensome — state interest is balanced against the burden on interstate commerce such that no less restrictive alternative means is available
- **EXCEPTION** — Market Participant Doctrine — where the state uses its own taxpayer funds to create the market, it may favor its own residents with subsidies and hiring preferences
- **COMPARE:** Article IV Privileges and Immunities Clause — prevents discrimination by one state against citizens of another state regarding basic economic rights and liberties; N/A to corporations or aliens

State Taxation of Interstate Commerce

- **REQUIREMENTS:** state tax must be reasonable and nondiscriminatory to satisfy the Commerce Clause, and a substantial nexus (more than "minimum contacts") must exist between the state interest and the activity being taxed to satisfy the Due Process Clause
- **GENERAL PRINCIPLES** — goods or commodities "in the stream" of interstate commerce are exempt from state taxation, but may be taxed at the beginning and end of transit, as well as if there is a break in transit, Instrumentalities (cars, planes, trains, etc.) may be taxed provided the tax is fairly apportioned to the extent of taxpayer use (taxable situs requirement)

Supremacy Clause Article VI, §2

- **FIELD PREEMPTION** — any state law in an area where Congress intends to occupy the field is unconstitutional (e.g., FAA, NLRB)
- **CONFLICT PREEMPTION** — any state law in actual conflict with a federal law will be unconstitutional. Note: where federal law only establishes minimum standards, states may afford greater protection by enacting stricter laws than required by federal standards

4. PROTECTION OF INDIVIDUAL RIGHTS

Bill of Rights (the 1st 10 Amendments restrict the FG)

SELECTIVE INCORPORATION — under the 14th Amendment Due Process Clause, most Bill of Rights limitations are applicable to the states, except for a few provisions such as:

- 5th Amendment right to a grand jury in criminal cases
- 7th Amendment right to jury trial for civil cases

Retroactive Legislation

- **CONTRACTS CLAUSE** — prevents the states (not the FG) from enacting legislation which retroactively impairs the obligation of either public or private contracts; usually, the state's police power "modification" argument prevails over the plaintiff's "impairment" argument
- **EX POST FACTO LAWS** — make criminal conduct that was not a crime when committed, or increase the punishment for a crime after its commission, or decrease the amount of evidence needed to convict; such legislation which retroactively alters the criminal law is unconstitutional as applied to both the state and federal governments
- **BILL OF ATTAINDER** — legislative punishment of a named group or individual without judicial trial; applies to both state and federal governments

4. PROTECTION OF INDIVIDUAL RIGHTS *(continued)*

State Action

DEFINITION: a threshold requirement of government conduct which must be satisfied before discrimination can be restricted under the 14th or 15th Amendments; 13th Amendment can punish purely private acts of discrimination without showing state action

EXAMPLES OF STATE ACTION

PUBLIC FUNCTION — where a private entity is performing activities traditionally and exclusively carried on by the state (e.g., a company town)

SIGNIFICANT STATE INVOLVEMENT — public school system; use of state-owned textbooks by a private school; "symbiotic relationship" or situation where the state facilities, encourages, or authorizes discrimination in areas such as housing, employment, or providing essential services

COMPARE: NO PUBLIC FUNCTION — a privately owned utility company under heavy state regulation; operation of a nursing home

COMPARE: NO STATE ACTION — granting of a liquor license; private school discharging teachers; private school licensed by the state

Procedural Due Process

the procedural safeguards of NOTICE and a HEARING are available whenever there is a serious deprivation of any life, liberty or property interest

- **PROCEDURE** — the court balances the severity of harm to the individual against the administrative costs of the government to determine what, if any, safeguards are required
- **PROTECTED LIBERTY INTERESTS** — commitment to a mental institution; right to contract; right to engage in gainful employment; right to refuse unwanted medical care; right of natural parents in the care and custody of their children; not injury to reputation
- **PROPERTY INTERESTS (entitlements)** — right to public education; welfare benefits; liability benefits; continued public employment where termination can only be "for cause"; revocation of a driver's license

(continued)

4. PROTECTION OF INDIVIDUAL RIGHTS *(continued)*

Takings

- private property may not be taken for public use without just compensation; eminent domain and inverse condemnation require compensation, but exercise of state police power "regulation" does not
- a per se taking consists of a confiscation (public easement granted across owner's beachfront property) or a physical occupation (cable TV wire installed in all the hallways of city rental units) or a regulation which denies the owner all reasonable economically viable use (post-purchase zoning ordinance which prohibits the owner from erecting any permanent structures on his land); "balancing" test determines whether taking has occurred when there is no per se taking

Substantive Due Process

- **ECONOMIC REGULATION** — regulation must meet rational basis scrutiny
- **FUNDAMENTAL RIGHTS** — regulation must meet strict scrutiny standard
  - **RIGHT TO VOTE OR BE CANDIDATE** — other than for minimum age or residency requirements or payment of reasonable filing fees, regulation must meet the strict scrutiny standard. Generally voting districts for federal, state, and local elections are required to adhere very closely to the one person-one vote principle *(Reynolds v. Sims)*; exception for special limited-purpose districts (water storage district). Apportionment and districting schemes which distort voting districts for racial or political purposes is unconstitutional gerrymandering
  - **RIGHT TO TRAVEL** — durational residency requirements are invalid for receiving state medical care or welfare benefits, but valid for reduced tuition at state universities, obtaining a divorce, or registering to vote in a state primary election; foreign travel is subject only to rational basis scrutiny
  - **RIGHT TO PRIVACY (mnemonic CAMPER)** — **C**ontraception — applies to the sale and use of contraceptives by both married and unmarried persons
    Abortion — states may not prohibit abortions before viability, but may regulate as long as they create no "undue burden" on the right to obtain an abortion *(Planned Parenthood v. Casey)*; there is no right to abortion funding, even for indigents; consent of one or both parents or a judge, may be required for a minor to obtain an abortion
    Marriage — any restriction on the right to marry (interracial marriage) is prohibited
    Procreation — closely related to contraception
    Education — right of parents to educate their children outside of public schools
    Relations — right of related persons to live together; "anti-group" ordinances generally prohibited

5. EQUAL PROTECTION

an equal protection challenge arises where persons similarly situated are treated differently

3 Standards of Review

STRICT SCRUTINY — (regulation unlikely to succeed) — burden on the state to show the law is necessary (i.e. no less restrictive alternative means exists) to a compelling interest; applies to 3 areas:

1. Protected 1st Amendment Rights
2. Suspect Classes (mnemonic RAN)
   - **R**ace — purposeful discrimination required; race-based affirmative action plans are subject to strict scrutiny whether passed by the state *(Richmond v Croson)* or by the federal government *(Adarand Construction v Pena)*
   - **A**lienage — federal regulation is subject only to rational basis scrutiny, whereas state regulation is subject to strict scrutiny, except where participation in government (policemen, teachers, serving on a jury list) is involved; illegal aliens are not suspect
   - **N**ational Origin
3. Fundamental Rights — Right to Vote
   - Right to Travel
   - Right to Privacy

Middle-tier (Intermediate) Scrutiny — burden on the state to show the law is substantially related to an important interest, applies to 2 areas:

1. Gender
2. Illegitimacy

(1. and 2.) — purposeful discrimination required; affirmative action permitted subject to middle-tier test

Rational Basis Scrutiny — (regulation likely to succeed) — burden is on plaintiff to show the law is not rationally related to any legitimate interest; applies to all other classifications including 1. Poverty 2. Age 3. Mental Retardation 4. Necessities of life (food, shelter, clothing, medical care) 5. Economic and social welfare measures

6. FIRST AMENDMENT GUARANTEES

Freedom of Religion

FREE EXERCISE CLAUSE — an individual's religious beliefs are absolutely protected; conduct in furtherance of those beliefs may be regulated; a law that discriminates against a person's religious conduct is subject to a strict scrutiny, but no special accommodations for religious conduct are required where a law is neutral and generally applicable; e.g., use of peyote during religious ceremonies is conduct which may be prohibited despite the individual's religious beliefs which required this practice (*Oregon v Smith*); a Jewish soldier may be compelled by the Air Force not to wear his yarmulke as part of his military uniform (*Goldman v Weinberger*)

ESTABLISHMENT CLAUSE — Main Principle: the government may not aid or prefer one religion or sect over another, subject to strict scrutiny review;

—Test: to be constitutional, a sect-neutral government aid/program must satisfy 3 requirements under the *Lemon* test — the law must 1) have a secular purpose; 2) have a primary effect that neither advances nor inhibits religion, and 3) not foster excessive government entanglement with religion

— General Principles: government sponsored religious activities in public schools are unconstitutional (daily Bible readings; a moment of silent, voluntary prayer; prohibition of the teaching of evolution); government aid to parochial schools may not be used for religious purposes (use of textbooks, busing, health tests), but such aid is constitutional if made available to all students at public and private schools

—Tax Deduction – reimbursing parents for tuition paid only to *religious* schools is invalid; similarly, tax exemptions available only for religious organizations (no sales tax for religious publications) is an invalid endorsement of religion, but property tax exemptions for religious property have been upheld; religious displays (nativity scenes; menorahs) are permissible in public places provided no one religion is being favored over another

6. FIRST AMENDMENT GUARANTEES *(continued)*

Freedom of Speech Approach

4 TYPES OF FACIAL ATTACKS — Overbreadth — statute punishes both protected as well as unprotected speech
Vagueness — statute is so unclearly defined that persons of ordinary intelligence must guess at its meaning
Prior Restraint — government action restricting free speech in advance of publication is generally invalid (licensing permits, injunctions; 'gag' order barring the media from pretrial publicity); valid where national security interests are compelling, or for the regulation of obscene books and films where procedural safeguards are afforded
Unfettered Discretion — where a licensing official has unfettered discretion as to whether to confer or deny a permit

ESSAY APPROACH

Track One — or — **Track Two**

Track One

Ask: Is the Government's Action **Content Specific** (regulates the message)

If content specific, then ask: Is the speech being regulated **Protected** or **Unprotected**

Protected: If "protected" then apply strict scrutiny i.e. — the statute is unconstitutional unless the government can show the law is necessary to a compelling interest

Unprotected: Unprotected includes clear and present danger; defamation; obscenity; child pornography; fighting words; fraudulent commercial speech

Track Two

Content Neutral —Time, Place, or Manner Regulation (regulation does not depend on the speaker's identity, message, or viewpoint)

If content neutral regulation of time, place, manner, then apply a 3-part test: the regulation must

1) further a significant government interest (e.g., noise, crowd, or litter control; traffic safety)
2) be narrowly tailored (no more restrictive than necessary), and
3) leave open alternative channels of communication (e.g., commercial door-to-door solicitation without invitation of the homeowner may be restricted because other avenues of communication exist such as the mail, newspaper advertisements, radio and television)

(continued)

6. FIRST AMENDMENT GUARANTEES *(continued)*

Freedom of Association — unmentioned First Amendment right encompassing activities such as accepting government benefits, public employment or seeking membership in various organizations

- **Public Employment and Bar Membership** — may not be denied based upon an individual's group affiliation unless the government can show the person 1) is a knowing (scienter) and active (dues-paying) member of a subversive group and 2) has the specific intent to further the group's unlawful objectives *(Keyishian v Bd. of Rights)*
- **Loyalty Oaths** — generally *invalid* as a condition to public employment, however, an oath to support the Constitution and oppose overthrow of the government has been upheld *(Cole v Richardson)*
- **Disclosure Requirements** — to avoid a chilling effect on First Amendment activities disclosure is generally not required, unless the government could make such membership illegal

Freedom of the Press — read together with the "free speech" clause as a single guarantee; generally the press has no greater privilege than the ordinary citizen

- **Right of Access** — both the public and the press have a right to attend a criminal trial, which may be outweighed by an overriding government interest
- **Newsperson's Privilege** — no privilege exists to refuse to disclose confidential sources to a grand jury *(Branzburg v Hayes)*, but states may enact "shield" laws to afford such protection
- **Broadcasting** — may be regulated more closely than the press due to the limited number of frequencies available — "equal time" broadcasts may be required *(Red Lion)*, yet on the other hand a newspaper need not provide equal space for political rebuttal *(Miami Herald)*

6. FIRST AMENDMENT GUARANTEES *(continued)*

Freedom of Speech Content — most forms of speech are protected subject to the strict scrutiny standard; 6 forms of unprotected speech may be regulated

- **CLEAR AND PRESENT DANGER** — speech 1) directed at producing imminent unlawful action and 2) likely to produce such action *(Brandenburg v Ohio)*
- **DEFAMATION** — public officials, public figures, and limited public figures (those who voluntarily inject themselves in the limelight) must prove malice: knowing falsity or reckless disregard for the truth *(Times v Sullivan)*
  - — private person plaintiffs — constitutional limitations apply only where the defamatory statement involves a matter of public concern, in which case negligence must be proven (no liability without fault); punitive damages are not awarded absent proof of malice *(Gertz v Welch)*
- **OBSCENITY** — to be obscene, the speech must 1) appeal to the prurient interest in sex applying contemporary community standards, 2) depict sexual conduct in a patently offensive way, and 3) lack serious literary, artistic, political, or scientific value *(Miller v California)*
  - — merely offensive language is not obscene; however, profane language on the airways may be restricted *(Pacifica Foundation)*; private possession of obscene materials in one's home is protected (except for child pornography), although viewing, sale and distribution of such obscene material may be vigorously regulated (movie ratings, zoning ordinances)
- **CHILD PORNOGRAPHY** — outside the protection of the First Amendment; visual depictions of sexual conduct including children may be punished even if not "obscene" under *Miller (N.Y. v Ferber)*
- **FIGHTING WORDS** — restricted speech includes personally abrasive language likely to incite the average person to commit acts of physical violence *(Chaplinsky v N.H.)*; however, statutes designed to punish only particular viewpoints are invalid — e.g. fighting words that provoke violence on the basis of race, religion, or gender *(R.A.V. v St. Paul)*
- **FRAUDULENT COMMERCIAL SPEECH** — generally commercial speech is protected but may be restricted as to false or deceptive advertising or illegal products; a lawful, narrowly tailored regulation will be valid if it directly advances a substantial government interest and there is a reasonable "fit" between the means used and the legislation's end *(Central Hudson; SUNY v Fox)*; attorneys may advertise, provided it is not misleading; in-person solicitation for profit is not protected.
- **OTHER AREAS** — symbolic speech (where the medium itself is the message) may be restricted where the regulation furthers an important government interest unrelated to the suppression of speech and the incidental burden on speech is no greater than necessary; e.g., unconstitutional to ban flag burning *(U.S. v Eichman)*
  - — freedom not to speak — allows children not to be compelled to salute or pledge allegiance to the American flag, and allows a motorist to cover the motto ("Live Free or Die") portion of her license plate

(continued)

6. FIRST AMENDMENT GUARANTEES *(continued)*

Time, Place, Manner Restrictions — reasonable restriction of speech conduct is permitted by means of content-neutral time, place, manner regulations

- **PUBLIC FORUMS** — (streets, parks, sidewalks) — regulations must satisfy 3-part test (See Track Two test on previous page)
- **NONPUBLIC FORUMS** — (jails, military bases, mailboxes, billboards, public buses, government buildings, airport terminals)
  - — to be valid the regulations must be 1) viewpoint neutral (i.e., content may be regulated, but limiting the presentation to only one view is impermissible) and 2) reasonably related to a legitimate government interest

Licensing Statutes

- **REQUIREMENTS** — to be valid, a licensing scheme must relate to an important government objective, be clearly written, narrowly drawn, and reasonably regulate time, place and manner of speech
- **IF STATUTE IS VALID ON ITS FACE** — the speaker may not ignore the statute and must seek a permit. If the request is denied, even wrongfully, the speaker must nonetheless seek prompt judicial relief before speaking; otherwise a subsequent claim of violation of 1st Amendment rights will fail
- **IF STATUTE IS VOID ON ITS FACE** — due to overbreadth, vagueness, prior restraint, or unfettered discretion — the speaker may ignore the statute and speak, as well as successfully defend against any subsequent prosecution (*Shuttlesworth v Birmingham*)
- **IF AN INJUNCTION IS ISSUED** — where the speaker is enjoined from speaking, she must obey the injunction (even if it is facially invalid) or appeal from it. Invalidity of the injunction must be established on appeal and is no defense to a subsequent charge of contempt (*Walker v Birmingham*)

pmbr

Federal Civil Procedure

Practice Questions

Answer Grid

1 Ⓐ Ⓑ Ⓒ Ⓓ	21 Ⓐ Ⓑ Ⓒ Ⓓ	41 Ⓐ Ⓑ Ⓒ Ⓓ	61 Ⓐ Ⓑ Ⓒ Ⓓ	81 Ⓐ Ⓑ Ⓒ Ⓓ
2 Ⓐ Ⓑ Ⓒ Ⓓ	22 Ⓐ Ⓑ Ⓒ Ⓓ	42 Ⓐ Ⓑ Ⓒ Ⓓ	62 Ⓐ Ⓑ Ⓒ Ⓓ	82 Ⓐ Ⓑ Ⓒ Ⓓ
3 Ⓐ Ⓑ Ⓒ Ⓓ	23 Ⓐ Ⓑ Ⓒ Ⓓ	43 Ⓐ Ⓑ Ⓒ Ⓓ	63 Ⓐ Ⓑ Ⓒ Ⓓ	83 Ⓐ Ⓑ Ⓒ Ⓓ
4 Ⓐ Ⓑ Ⓒ Ⓓ	24 Ⓐ Ⓑ Ⓒ Ⓓ	44 Ⓐ Ⓑ Ⓒ Ⓓ	64 Ⓐ Ⓑ Ⓒ Ⓓ	84 Ⓐ Ⓑ Ⓒ Ⓓ
5 Ⓐ Ⓑ Ⓒ Ⓓ	25 Ⓐ Ⓑ Ⓒ Ⓓ	45 Ⓐ Ⓑ Ⓒ Ⓓ	65 Ⓐ Ⓑ Ⓒ Ⓓ	85 Ⓐ Ⓑ Ⓒ Ⓓ
6 Ⓐ Ⓑ Ⓒ Ⓓ	26 Ⓐ Ⓑ Ⓒ Ⓓ	46 Ⓐ Ⓑ Ⓒ Ⓓ	66 Ⓐ Ⓑ Ⓒ Ⓓ	86 Ⓐ Ⓑ Ⓒ Ⓓ
7 Ⓐ Ⓑ Ⓒ Ⓓ	27 Ⓐ Ⓑ Ⓒ Ⓓ	47 Ⓐ Ⓑ Ⓒ Ⓓ	67 Ⓐ Ⓑ Ⓒ Ⓓ	87 Ⓐ Ⓑ Ⓒ Ⓓ
8 Ⓐ Ⓑ Ⓒ Ⓓ	28 Ⓐ Ⓑ Ⓒ Ⓓ	48 Ⓐ Ⓑ Ⓒ Ⓓ	68 Ⓐ Ⓑ Ⓒ Ⓓ	88 Ⓐ Ⓑ Ⓒ Ⓓ
9 Ⓐ Ⓑ Ⓒ Ⓓ	29 Ⓐ Ⓑ Ⓒ Ⓓ	49 Ⓐ Ⓑ Ⓒ Ⓓ	69 Ⓐ Ⓑ Ⓒ Ⓓ	89 Ⓐ Ⓑ Ⓒ Ⓓ
10 Ⓐ Ⓑ Ⓒ Ⓓ	30 Ⓐ Ⓑ Ⓒ Ⓓ	50 Ⓐ Ⓑ Ⓒ Ⓓ	70 Ⓐ Ⓑ Ⓒ Ⓓ	90 Ⓐ Ⓑ Ⓒ Ⓓ
11 Ⓐ Ⓑ Ⓒ Ⓓ	31 Ⓐ Ⓑ Ⓒ Ⓓ	51 Ⓐ Ⓑ Ⓒ Ⓓ	71 Ⓐ Ⓑ Ⓒ Ⓓ	91 Ⓐ Ⓑ Ⓒ Ⓓ
12 Ⓐ Ⓑ Ⓒ Ⓓ	32 Ⓐ Ⓑ Ⓒ Ⓓ	52 Ⓐ Ⓑ Ⓒ Ⓓ	72 Ⓐ Ⓑ Ⓒ Ⓓ	92 Ⓐ Ⓑ Ⓒ Ⓓ
13 Ⓐ Ⓑ Ⓒ Ⓓ	33 Ⓐ Ⓑ Ⓒ Ⓓ	53 Ⓐ Ⓑ Ⓒ Ⓓ	73 Ⓐ Ⓑ Ⓒ Ⓓ	93 Ⓐ Ⓑ Ⓒ Ⓓ
14 Ⓐ Ⓑ Ⓒ Ⓓ	34 Ⓐ Ⓑ Ⓒ Ⓓ	54 Ⓐ Ⓑ Ⓒ Ⓓ	74 Ⓐ Ⓑ Ⓒ Ⓓ	94 Ⓐ Ⓑ Ⓒ Ⓓ
15 Ⓐ Ⓑ Ⓒ Ⓓ	35 Ⓐ Ⓑ Ⓒ Ⓓ	55 Ⓐ Ⓑ Ⓒ Ⓓ	75 Ⓐ Ⓑ Ⓒ Ⓓ	95 Ⓐ Ⓑ Ⓒ Ⓓ
16 Ⓐ Ⓑ Ⓒ Ⓓ	36 Ⓐ Ⓑ Ⓒ Ⓓ	56 Ⓐ Ⓑ Ⓒ Ⓓ	76 Ⓐ Ⓑ Ⓒ Ⓓ	96 Ⓐ Ⓑ Ⓒ Ⓓ
17 Ⓐ Ⓑ Ⓒ Ⓓ	37 Ⓐ Ⓑ Ⓒ Ⓓ	57 Ⓐ Ⓑ Ⓒ Ⓓ	77 Ⓐ Ⓑ Ⓒ Ⓓ	97 Ⓐ Ⓑ Ⓒ Ⓓ
18 Ⓐ Ⓑ Ⓒ Ⓓ	38 Ⓐ Ⓑ Ⓒ Ⓓ	58 Ⓐ Ⓑ Ⓒ Ⓓ	78 Ⓐ Ⓑ Ⓒ Ⓓ	98 Ⓐ Ⓑ Ⓒ Ⓓ
19 Ⓐ Ⓑ Ⓒ Ⓓ	39 Ⓐ Ⓑ Ⓒ Ⓓ	59 Ⓐ Ⓑ Ⓒ Ⓓ	79 Ⓐ Ⓑ Ⓒ Ⓓ	99 Ⓐ Ⓑ Ⓒ Ⓓ
20 Ⓐ Ⓑ Ⓒ Ⓓ	40 Ⓐ Ⓑ Ⓒ Ⓓ	60 Ⓐ Ⓑ Ⓒ Ⓓ	80 Ⓐ Ⓑ Ⓒ Ⓓ	100 Ⓐ Ⓑ Ⓒ Ⓓ

1. Jury Trials
2. Jurisdiction and Venue
3. Jurisdiction and Venue
4. Motions
5. Pretrial Procedures
6. Motions
7. Jurisdiction and Venue
8. Jurisdiction and Venue
9. Jurisdiction and Venue
10. Jurisdiction and Venue
11. Verdicts and Judgments
12. Verdicts and Judgments
13. Verdicts and Judgments
14. Jurisdiction and Venue
15. Jury Trials
16. Motions
17. Pretrial Procedures
18. Jurisdiction and Venue
19. Appealability and Review
20. Jurisdiction and Venue
21. Jurisdiction and Venue
22. Jurisdiction and Venue
23. Pretrial Procedures
24. Pretrial Procedures
25. Verdicts and Judgments
26. Jury Trials
27. Jurisdiction and Venue
28. Verdicts and Judgments

29. Pretrial Procedures
30. Jurisdiction and Venue
31. Jury Trials
32. Motions
33. Verdicts and Judgments
34. Appealability and Review
35. Pretrial Procedures
36. Jurisdiction and Venue
37. Pretrial Procedures
38. Jurisdiction and Venue
39. Jurisdiction and Venue
40. Verdicts and Judgments
41. Law Applied by Federal Courts
42. Pretrial Procedures
43. Pretrial Procedures
44. Jurisdiction and Venue
45. Law Applied by Federal Courts
46. Verdicts and Judgments
47. Pretrial Procedures
48. Jury Trials
49. Law Applied by Federal Courts
50. Verdicts and Judgments
51. Jurisdiction and Venue
52. Jurisdiction and Venue
53. Pretrial Procedures
54. Motions
55. Law Applied by Federal Courts
56. Verdicts and Judgments

57. Pretrial Procedures
58. Pretrial Procedures
59. Pretrial Procedures
60. Verdicts and Judgments
61. Appealability and Review
62. Pretrial Procedures
63. Pretrial Procedures
64. Verdicts and Judgments
65. Pretrial Procedures
66. Verdicts and Judgments
67. Motions
68. Jurisdiction and Venue
69. Motions
70. Jury Trials
71. Jurisdiction and Venue
72. Pretrial Procedures
73. Pretrial Procedures
74. Jury Trials
75. Pretrial Procedures
76. Jury Trials
77. Motions
78. Jurisdiction and Venue
79. Jurisdiction and Venue
80. Pretrial Procedures
81. Pretrial Procedures
82. Pretrial Procedures
83. Motions
84. Law Applied by Federal Courts

85. Jurisdiction and Venue
86. Pretrial Procedures
87. Jurisdiction and Venue
88. Jurisdiction and Venue
89. Jurisdiction and Venue
90. Appealability and Review
91. Jurisdiction and Venue
92. Jurisdiction and Venue
93. Jurisdiction and Venue
94. Jurisdiction and Venue
95. Pretrial Procedures
96. Jury Trials
97. Appealability and Review
98. Pretrial Procedures
99. Jurisdiction and Venue
100. Jurisdiction and Venue

Question 1

A plaintiff sued a defendant in federal court for declaratory judgment that the plaintiff was not liable to the defendant for breach of a contract. Diversity jurisdiction existed. The defendant filed a counterclaim against the plaintiff and sought damages for breach of their contract. The defendant made a timely jury demand. The plaintiff made a motion to strike the jury demand. The court granted the motion.

Was the court correct to strike the jury demand?

(A) Yes, because the plaintiff did not seek a legal remedy.

(B) Yes, because the constitutional right to a jury only extends to forms of action that, unlike declaratory judgments, existed at the time of the adoption of the Seventh Amendment.

(C) No, because the defendant sought a legal remedy.

(D) No, because parties have a constitutional right to a jury in civil cases in federal court.

Question 2

A State A man sued a car rental service in a State A state court for state-law violations resulting in damages in excess of $100,000. The car rental service sought removal to federal court, claiming that it was actually a citizen of State B. The man argued that the rental service had offices in 48 states, including State A. In fact, the rental service had its management training center, telesales center, and all of its service garages in State A, along with the majority of its rental fleet (2,000,000 cars were in State A; the next closest state was State C with 1,000,000). The corporation argued that its board of directors and all of its top management were based in State B, and that the corporation was directed and controlled from there.

What state is the corporation a citizen of?

(A) State B, because the corporation is controlled from there.

(B) State B, because the board of directors and all of the top management are there.

(C) Any of the states in which it operates, as it likely has sufficient minimum contacts to face suit there.

(D) State A, because the majority of its business is located in State A.

Question 3

A State Y corporation filed a suit against a beer brewers' union. The suit claimed over $200,000 in damages for alleged defamation that occurred during the union's attempt to unionize the corporation's employees. The union was an unincorporated labor union with its principal place of business in State Z. The union asked the court to remove the case to federal court based on diversity jurisdiction. The union claimed it was a citizen of State Z, although some of its members were citizens of State Y. Importantly, it noted that its principal place of business was in State Z, and over 90 percent of its members and 100 percent of its board of directors were State Z citizens. The court ruled in its favor and removed the case to federal court. The company appealed, seeking to have the case returned to state court.

Should the action be heard in federal court?

(A) Yes, because the union's principal place of business is in State Z.

(B) Yes, because the citizenships of the board of directors made State Z its "nerve center."

(C) No, because some of the union members were from State Y.

(D) No, because defamation is not a federal claim recognized by Congress.

Question 4

A woman opened up a new coffee shop right across the street from a man's coffee shop, which had been in business for over 50 years. Soon after the opening of the new shop, the man started losing a significant amount of business. Enraged by the fact that she had encroached on his business, the man filed a complaint in federal court arguing the "woman's coffee shop illegally encroached on his historically recognized business territory." He then started placing advertisements for his coffee shop on her coffee shop's windows, and got his 12-year-old son to prank call her shop at all hours of the day and night.

Assuming the federal court has jurisdiction to hear the lawsuit, what should the woman do in response to the complaint?

(A) File a motion for summary judgment.

(B) File a counterclaim regarding the man's signs and prank calls.

(C) File a motion for dismissal.

(D) File a motion for judgment as a matter of law.

Question 5

For several years, a corporation received complaints regarding one of its medical devices. Ultimately, a man sued in federal court after he was injured when one of the devices failed during a medical procedure. The man sent a discovery request to the company asking for "all documents regarding the device." The corporation produced a few paper files, and admitted that although there had likely been "thousands" of emails regarding the device over the years, all emails were automatically deleted every three months to free up storage space in employee inboxes. The last such deletion occurred three days before the man filed suit. Corporation technicians said that it might be possible to recover some of the emails, but it would likely require the hiring of expensive data recovery experts who might not be able to recover anything. The corporation stated that the man would have to pay for any experts needed to recover the data. The man argued he should not be required to pay to recover the documents, since the corporation was the one who deleted them.

Should the court order the corporation to pay to recover the lost emails?

(A) Yes, because sanctions for the email deletion are appropriate.

(B) Yes, because the corporation controls the relevant storage devices.

(C) No, because the deletions appeared to be routine.

(D) No, because the emails are not reasonably accessible.

Question 6

A plaintiff sued a defendant in federal court. The jury returned a verdict for the defendant, and the court entered final judgment for the defendant. Eighteen months later, the plaintiff discovered that the defendant had intentionally withheld highly relevant and admissible evidence from the plaintiff despite proper discovery requests. The plaintiff immediately moved for relief from the judgment.

Should the trial court grant the motion for relief from the judgment?

(A) Yes, because the plaintiff has discovered new evidence.

(B) Yes, because the defendant perpetrated a fraud.

(C) No, because more than one year has passed since entry of judgment.

(D) No, because more than 28 days has passed since entry of judgment.

Question 7

A doctor living in State A traveled weekly to State B to perform surgeries in an understaffed, rural hospital there. The hospital changed its policies on outside doctors using its facilities and demanded that each visiting doctor pay the hospital a one-time $50,000 fee to continue to use the facilities. The doctor believed this was a breach of the contract he and others had with the hospital and filed suit in State B federal district court based on diversity jurisdiction, seeking an injunction preventing the hospital from demanding that any of the 12 visiting doctors who used the hospital pay the $50,000 fee. None of the other 11 visiting doctors joined in the suit, but the injunction sought by the plaintiff would have benefited all of them.

If the hospital argues that the court does not have subject-matter jurisdiction, will it prevail?

(A) Yes, because the doctor can be considered a citizen of State B.

(B) Yes, because the cost of the injunction to the doctor is not sufficient to meet the amount-in-controversy requirement.

(C) No, because the cost of the injunction to the hospital is sufficient to meet the amount-in-controversy requirement.

(D) No, because the amount-in-controversy requirement may be met by aggregating the claims of all plaintiffs.

Question 8

A man files a defamation claim for $80,000 against a former employee. The man is a citizen of State A and the former employee is a citizen of State A. The action was filed in State A state court. The employee filed a counterclaim for age discrimination based upon federal law.

Can the man have the cased removed to federal court?

(A) Yes, because the counterclaim is a federal question.

(B) Yes, because the amount in controversy exceeds $75,000.

(C) No, because there is not diversity of citizenship between the parties.

(D) No, because only defendants can remove to federal court.

Question 9

A tourist living in State A travelled to an amusement park in State B. While there, a tour guide working for the amusement park asked the tourist if he wanted to be a test subject for a new ride. The tourist agreed and the tour guide locked the tourist inside a ride that he had been developing on his own and which worked poorly. The tourist demanded to be let out, but the tour guide refused to do so. The tourist later filed a state law false imprisonment tort claim seeking $100,000 in damages in State B federal district court. The action was based on diversity jurisdiction, and named both the amusement park and the tour guide, who was a foreign national living temporarily in State B and who planned to move back to his home country to start his own amusement park. After filing the suit, the tourist moved to State B to start an organization devoted to exposing problems with the amusement park.

If the amusement park and tour guide move to dismiss the case for lack of subject-matter jurisdiction, will it prevail?

(A) Yes, because there is no longer complete diversity among the parties.

(B) Yes, because an alien may not be a defendant in a diversity jurisdiction action.

(C) No, because diversity is determined at the time the action is filed.

(D) No, because the amusement park is a citizen of the state in which the district court is located.

Question 10

A State A man was abandoned by his wife who left their home to move to State B. She filed for divorce against the man in State B, but she did not serve process on him. The man had never been to State B and had no contacts with the state. Meanwhile, the man's father received a letter that led him to believe he had won a million dollar lottery and that he needed to go to State B to claim his winnings. The man accompanied his father to State B to claim the winnings, although the man did not believe the father had actually won anything. After they arrived in State B, the father found out that he had not won the lottery, and the company that had sent him the letter was later shut down for sending letters fraudulently enticing people to come to State B. While in State B, however, the man was served by his wife with a summons related to the State B divorce proceedings.

If the man argues that he is not subject to personal jurisdiction in State B, will he prevail?

(A) No, because he was served while physically present in State B.

(B) No, because he consented to personal jurisdiction in State B.

(C) Yes, because his presence in State B was procured by fraud.

(D) Yes, because he did not have minimum contacts with State B.

Question 11

Plaintiff sued Defendant for violation of federal securities laws. The court granted a motion to dismiss after the Plaintiff failed numerous times to abide by the court's orders in discovery. Plaintiff did not appeal. Instead, Plaintiff filed a second action against the same defendant, alleged the same wrongful acts, and sought damages under the same federal securities laws. Defendant timely raised a defense of *res judicata*.

Should the defense of *res judicata* prevail?

(A) Yes, because Plaintiff alleged the same facts in the two suits.

(B) Yes, because the first dismissal acts as an adjudication upon the merits.

(C) No, because the allegations in the first case were not actually litigated or actually decided in the first action.

(D) No, because the court in the first action never reached the merits of Plaintiff's claims.

Question 12

The parties to a federal civil case waived their rights to a jury trial. The parties tried the case to the court. At the close of the plaintiff's case, the trial court ruled that the plaintiff had not sustained her burden of proof and that accordingly the defendant was entitled to judgment as a matter of law. The court entered judgment for the defendant without requiring the defendant to present his case and without the entry of findings of fact and conclusions of law.

Did the trial court err in directing entry of judgment at the close of the plaintiff's case without the entry of findings of fact and conclusions of law?

(A) Yes, because the trial court must enter findings of fact and conclusions of law when it directs entry of a judgment other than a judgment on a jury verdict.

(B) Yes, because the court is entering judgment on partial findings.

(C) No, because findings of fact and conclusions of law are not required when a court dismisses a plaintiff's claim.

(D) No, because findings of fact and conclusions of law are not required when a court determines that one party is entitled to judgment as a matter of law.

Question 13

A federal agency pursued civil charges against a stockbroker suspected of violating federal security laws by selling unregistered securities to ineligible customers. The agency agreed to a lesser number of depositions and interrogatories than it was entitled to in return for an agreement that the stockbroker would submit to a verdict assented to by at least 10 jurors. Twelve jurors were impaneled but one became ill and left the proceedings. The other 11 jurors returned a verdict that the stockbroker was liable on all of the agency's claims. When polled, only eight of the jurors indicated that they assented to the verdict.

Which of the following actions may the court now take?

(A) Order a new trial.

(B) Direct the jury to deliberate further until unanimity is reached.

(C) Dismiss the action with prejudice.

(D) Approve the jury's verdict.

Question 14

A State A CFO worked for a State A corporation for five years, and in the final three months of her work there, she came to find out that the corporation had been engaged in illegal environmental practices and had falsified its records regarding those practices. She attempted to remedy the situation by reporting to the CEO but was told to mind her own business. She reported the corporation's practices to the EPA and was promptly fired as a result of her doing so. She filed suit against the company in the state court of State A, arguing that she was owed damages based on a federal law providing protection to whistleblowers like herself. She also asserted a state law contract action against the corporation, arguing that the corporation owed her $80,000 in childcare and private school expenses that she was promised during the first three years of her employment contract, but for which she was never reimbursed. The corporation removed the case to federal district court.

If the CFO requests that the court remand the case back to state court, how will the court likely rule?

(A) Grant the motion to remand both claims to state court.

(B) Deny the motion to remand both claims to state court.

(C) Deny the motion to remand the whistleblower claim but grant the motion to remand the contract claim.

(D) Deny the motion to remand the contract claim but grant the motion to remand the whistleblower claim.

Question 15

A plaintiff filed a civil case for damages and made a timely jury demand. The case proceeded to trial. The court submitted the case to the jury in the form of a general verdict together with written questions about three of the crucial issues of fact in the case. The jury's answers to the written questions were consistent with each other but two of those answers were inconsistent with the general verdict. The court approved entry of a judgment that was consistent with the general verdict.

Did the trial court err in approving entry of a judgment that was consistent with the general verdict but inconsistent with two of the answers to written questions?

(A) Yes, because the only judgment a court could direct to be entered would be one consistent with the answers to written questions.

(B) Yes, because the trial court may only order a new trial under these circumstances.

(C) No, because the trial court may order entry of a judgment that is consistent with either the answers to the written questions or the general verdict.

(D) No, because the only judgment a court could direct to be entered would be one consistent with the general verdict.

Question 16

A plaintiff sued a defendant in federal court and alleged that the defendant's product caused the plaintiff injury when the product was used in the plaintiff's workplace. The defendant filed a motion for summary judgment and, without citing the court to anything in particular in the discovery record, argued that the plaintiff would not be able to prove causation. When the plaintiff did not come forward affirmatively with evidence that defendant's product caused the plaintiff's injuries, the court granted summary judgment.

Did the court err when it granted summary judgment?

(A) Yes, because the defendant was required to support the assertion that there was no genuine issue of material fact as to causation by citing to particular parts of materials in the record.

(B) Yes, because the defendant had the burden at summary judgment to prove that it did not cause the injury.

(C) No, because the plaintiff had the burden to demonstrate that there was a genuine issue of material fact as to causation by citing to particular parts of materials in the record.

(D) No, because the plaintiff would have had the burden of proof at trial.

Question 17

A man was injured while using a hot plate he had purchased at a discount retailer in State A during a car trip from State B to State C where he ultimately resided. The man alleged the hot plate spontaneously combusted and burned his belongings and injured him. He brought suit in federal district court in State C against the retailer, based on diversity jurisdiction, and alleged total damages of $100,000, including punitive damages. The retailer filed an answer with several affirmative defenses. At trial, the retailer learned that the man had delayed filing suit because he did not think he could win, and only filed suit two years after the alleged incident because he had lost his job and needed money. The retailer sought to present evidence showing that the man unreasonably delayed his claim, but the man argued that such evidence was outside the scope of the pleadings because the retailer did not assert the affirmative defense of laches in its answer.

If the retailer now seeks to amend its pleadings to include the affirmative defense of laches, may the court grant the retailer leave to amend its pleading?

(A) No, unless the amended answer can be filed within 21 days of the original answer.

(B) No, because trial has commenced.

(C) Yes, because the man has objected to evidence not being within the scope of the pleadings.

(D) Yes, if the court grants a continuation.

Question 18

After being fired from her job, a woman sued her former employer in federal court for failing to pay her the minimum hourly wage as required under the Fair Labor Standards Act. Her claim was for over $75,000 in damages. The employer was incorporated in State A and had its corporate offices in State B, although all of its stores and manufacturing plants were located State C. It had a small sales office in State B, but that office only sold t-shirts and other small items. However, all corporate decisions came out of the State B office. The woman was a citizen of State B. The employer moved to dismiss, claiming that federal jurisdiction did not exist because the woman and the company were citizens of the same state, and because there was no federal question because the woman had entered her employment through a college internship program, and the Fair Labor Standards Act did not apply to "interns."

Does the federal court have jurisdiction over the matter?

(A) Yes, because the woman's claim is based on federal law.

(B) Yes, because the employer's primary place of business is in State C.

(C) No, because the Act does not apply to the woman since she is an intern.

(D) No, because the employer's nerve center is in State B.

Question 19

A federal district court granted summary judgment for the defendant after reviewing the pleadings, affidavits, depositions and other summary judgment evidence. The plaintiff appealed that judgment to the United States Circuit Court of Appeals. The Court of Appeals reversed the trial court's judgment after applying a *de novo* standard of review.

Was the Court of Appeals correct to apply a *de novo* standard of review?

(A) Yes, because a summary judgment is a judgment rendered as a matter of law.

(B) Yes, because this was an appeal from a decision rendered without a trial.

(C) No, because the trial court reviewed affidavits, depositions and other summary judgment evidence, and therefore the Court of Appeals should have applied a "clearly erroneous" standard.

(D) No, because the trial court reviewed affidavits, depositions and other summary judgment evidence, and therefore the Court of Appeals should have applied an "abuse of discretion" standard.

Question 20

A man travelled from his home in State A to a boat race in State B. While at the boat race, he got into a fight with a woman from State C. The man suffered severe injuries, and spent over a month in a State B hospital before returning home to State A. The hospital stay cost $120,000. After a month at home, he had to move in with his daughter in State C for a few weeks so she could take care of him. While there, the man decided to sue the woman in State C state court for battery and violation of his federal civil rights.

May the man's claim be heard in State C state court?

(A) Yes, because the woman is from State C.

(B) No, because federal courts have exclusive jurisdiction over federal civil rights cases.

(C) No, because the man is not domiciled in State C.

(D) No, because a federal court would have jurisdiction through diversity.

Question 21

A man was driving home one night from his security guard job, where he had been drinking from a flask all evening, when he saw a police checkpoint. Knowing that he would be arrested and then lose custody of his daughter, the man turned down a side street to flee from the checkpoint and sped to get away from officers chasing him. In the process he struck a young woman from his church and killed her. He was convicted of involuntary manslaughter and sentenced to 20 years in prison. The judge, who lost his own daughter in a drunk driving accident, also required that the man's cell be covered with picture of the young woman, and that home videos of her life would constantly play in his cell for the entire 20 years. Such a sentence had never been imposed before. The man, who had pled guilty to the crime, appealed the sentence, but the state's highest court upheld the sentence. Ten months after that court upheld the sentence, the man became suicidal over the day-to-day conditions of his punishment, and filed a *habeas corpus* petition to a federal district court, arguing that his sentence violates the Eighth Amendment.

May the court review his *habeas corpus* petition?

(A) No, because he is not contesting his innocence.

(B) No, because he failed to file his appeal within 90 days of his final judgment of custody.

(C) No, because a *habeas corpus* petition may only be based on alleged violations of the Fifth or Fourteenth Amendments.

(D) Yes, the court may review his petition.

Question 22

A Swiss corporation sued a State A man in United States federal court over an oil lease. The corporation claimed damages in excess of $75,000. During discovery, several experts noted that since it was impossible to know how much the oil lease would actually be worth until drilling started, the amount of damages could be as low as $5,000 and as high as $5 million. The man asked the federal court to dismiss the case based on lack of subject-matter jurisdiction.

Does the federal court have jurisdiction?

(A) Yes, because the man is a State A citizen.

(B) Yes, because the corporation is a Swiss citizen.

(C) No, because the claim may be worth less than $75,000.

(D) No, because the corporation is a Swiss citizen.

Question 23

A corporation sued a man in federal court. The man considered answering the complaint instead of filing a motion to dismiss.

If the man answers the complaint, which defense will he not be able to include in his answer?

(A) More definite statement.

(B) Improper service.

(C) Improper venue.

(D) Failure to state a claim.

Question 24

A movie producer believed his partner was embezzling funds from their production company, which was based in State A. Specifically, when his accountant looked at the company's finances, it appeared that there were several purchases related to a home the partner owned in State B. The producer sought a temporary restraining order against his partner, but was unable to notify his partner of the order because his partner was on a movie set in the Amazon Rain Forest that was completely cut off from civilization. The producer's attorney had tried to contact the set several times, but a large tropical storm had moved into the area, and she couldn't reach anyone there. Even so, it appeared the partner still had access to the company account, as money continued to flow out of it.

What would be the most appropriate action for the producer's attorney to take?

(A) Certify in writing the efforts made to give notice.

(B) Request a hearing in order to explain the efforts made to give notice.

(C) Immediately move for a preliminary injunction.

(D) File a motion for a temporary restraining order with the State A attorney general.

Question 25

An author sued a publisher in federal court for violation of federal copyright laws and won. The author then sued the publisher in federal court under diversity jurisdiction for violation of a state fraud law. The facts alleged in the second case were the same as in the first case, although the statutory source of the claim was different.

The publisher makes a timely plea of the affirmative defense of *res judicata*. Should that defense succeed?

(A) Yes, because the two claims arise from the same events and they both could have been brought in the first case.

(B) Yes, because the two claims arise from the same events.

(C) No, because the Federal Rules of Civil Procedure permit but do not require a plaintiff to join all claims he has against the defendant.

(D) No, because the two cases contain different causes of action.

Question 26

A plaintiff and a defendant stipulated to trial by a jury of five members. All five members of the jury participated in the verdict, and the jury returned a unanimous verdict in favor of the defendant. The court concluded that the evidence supported the jury's verdict. The court entered judgment on the verdict.

Did the court err in entering judgment on the verdict?

(A) Yes, because the jury began with five members.

(B) Yes, because the jury began with fewer than 12 members.

(C) No, because the parties stipulated to accept a verdict by a jury of five.

(D) No, because the verdict was supported by the evidence.

Question 27

A man sued a trucker for negligence. The man took a summons and a copy of the complaint and walked into a bar where he knew the trucker was drinking. The man handed the summons and a copy of the complaint directly to the trucker as soon as he saw him in the bar.

Assuming the case was properly filed in federal court, was service of process proper?

(A) Yes, because the man gave the trucker a summons and copy of the complaint by hand.

(B) Yes, because the plaintiff may serve process by any means reasonably calculated to apprize interested parties of the pendency of the action.

(C) No, because the man is a party to the lawsuit.

(D) No, because there is no indication the summons was presented to the clerk for signature and seal.

Question 28

A visiting professor from State A took his students from State B on a trip to a cave to observe ancient art that had been painted on the cave walls. While there, a student was killed when she drowned in a pool of water inside the cave. Other students alleged that the professor had caused the student's death by pushing her into the pool, and the professor was arrested for manslaughter and put on trial in State B state court. The state court jury acquitted the professor of manslaughter on the grounds that the state failed to prove that the professor caused the student's death. The parents of the student then brought a wrongful death action against the professor in State B federal district court for causing the daughter's death.

If the professor argues that the wrongful death action is barred, will he likely prevail?

(A) Yes, because the wrongful death action is barred by claim preclusion.

(B) Yes, because the wrongful death action is barred by issue preclusion.

(C) No, because the standard of proof is generally more modest in a civil case.

(D) No, because the parents were not parties to the criminal case.

Question 29

A State A lawyer represented an actor from State B who had been arrested on obscenity charges in State A after performing his graphic one-man show detailing the ups and downs of his love life. The actor was convicted and served 90 days in jail. The actor sued the lawyer in State A federal district court, arguing that the lawyer committed malpractice under State A law and requesting $300,000 in damages. The actor still owed the lawyer $30,000 in unpaid legal fees related to the representation.

Which of the following statements regarding the lawyer's potential claim for the unpaid legal fees is true?

(A) The lawyer cannot file a counterclaim for the fees in federal court.

(B) The lawyer may file a counterclaim for the fees in federal court, and if he does not he will waive the claim.

(C) The lawyer may file a counterclaim for the fees in federal court, but, if he does not, he will not waive the claim.

(D) The lawyer must file a counterclaim for the fees in federal court.

Question 30

In which of the following situations is the defendant least likely to be found to have a duty to waive service?

(A) A State A university fired an associate professor who then moved to State B permanently, but traveled to Africa to volunteer for a year in a refugee camp, where he is presently. The university believed the associate professor made defamatory remarks regarding the university and filed a defamation suit against the associate professor in State A federal court. The university requested that the associate professor waive service.

(B) A State A paralegal worked for a State A attorney, but was fired by the attorney after failing to complete a filing on time. The paralegal believed she was fired in violation of federal employment laws and filed suit against the attorney in federal court. The attorney told the paralegal he would waive service if and when she made a request. Several months later, she requested that he waive service.

(C) Two State A men formed a general partnership to provide landscaping services to corporate clients. A large State B corporation believed that the men improperly used one of its trademarks in their landscaping company logo and filed suit in State B federal court against the partnership and requested that the partnership waive service.

(D) A husband moved from State A to State B, leaving his wife in State A. The wife filed suit for divorce against the husband in the only federal district court in State B. Although the wife was originally from State B and her entire family lived in State B, she requested that the husband waive service.

Question 31

A plaintiff filed a case against a defendant and alleged that the defendant discriminated against the plaintiff on the basis of race, in violation of federal law. During jury selection, the defendant's counsel used her three peremptory challenges to strike all the jurors who were of the same race as the plaintiff. When the plaintiff's counsel objected, the defendant's counsel argued that she was permitted to use her client's peremptory challenges to strike the jurors on the basis of race.

Was the defense counsel correct that she was permitted to use her client's peremptory challenges to strike potential jurors on the basis of race?

(A) Yes, because the case involved alleged race discrimination.

(B) Yes, because peremptory challenges may be exercised for any reason.

(C) No, because peremptory challenges are not permitted without an objectively reasonable basis.

(D) No, because peremptory challenges may not be exercised on the basis of race.

Question 32

A plaintiff won a jury verdict in federal court. Twenty-two days after the court entered judgment on the verdict, the defendant filed a motion for new trial because the court made a small error when the court read the charge to the jury. The defendant immediately objected. The court sustained the objection, corrected itself and made sure that the jury understood the charge. All parties and the court agreed that the court made the error.

Should the court grant the motion for new trial?

(A) Yes, because the court committed a procedural error.

(B) Yes, because the defendant preserved a procedural error by a timely objection.

(C) No, because the motion for new trial was filed too late.

(D) No, because the procedural error was harmless.

Question 33

An engineer sued a car manufacturer for violation of federal patent laws. The court granted a motion to dismiss after the engineer failed numerous times to abide by the court's orders in discovery. The engineer did not appeal. Instead, the engineer filed a second action against the car manufacturer, alleged the same wrongful acts, and sought damages under the same federal patent laws. The car manufacturer timely raised a defense of *res judicata*.

Should the defense of *res judicata* prevail?

(A) Yes, because the engineer alleged the same facts in the two suits.

(B) Yes, because the first dismissal acts as an adjudication upon the merits.

(C) No, because the allegations in the first case were not actually litigated or actually decided in the first action.

(D) No, because the court in the first action never reached the merits of the engineer's claims.

Question 34

A plaintiff sued a defendant and sought a preliminary injunction. After a hearing, the court denied the request for the preliminary injunction. The plaintiff's lawyer advised the plaintiff that the court's decision was not immediately appealable. The plaintiff sought a second opinion from another lawyer, who advised that the denial of the request for a preliminary injunction was immediately appealable.

Was the denial of the preliminary injunction immediately appealable?

(A) Yes, because all decisions on preliminary injunctions are immediately appealable.

(B) Yes, because the decision conclusively determined an important question that was completely separate from the merits and was effectively unreviewable on appeal.

(C) No, because it was not a final judgment.

(D) No, because the injunction was denied.

Question 35

A woman sued a corporation in federal court after she spilled hot soup in her lap. The woman sent the corporation a discovery request seeking "all documents concerning its soup." The corporation produced an enormous amount of electronic records. After the corporation turned over the records, it discovered that it had inadvertently produced privileged documents. When it notified the woman's attorney of the inadvertent disclosure, the attorney told the corporation that the production defeated any claim of privilege and she could now use the document as part of the woman's main case.

Is the attorney correct in her analysis?

(A) Yes, because the production took away any claim of privilege.

(B) Yes, because the production was made to a party opponent.

(C) No, because the corporation notified the other party.

(D) No, because the discovery request produced an enormous amount of documents.

Question 36

A man filed a class action on behalf of all purchasers of a company's cellphone. According to the complaint, the cellphone would explode if it was left charging for too long. The class was made up of all purchasers of the cellphone. The cellphone was sold in State A, State B, State C, and State D. The man is a citizen of State B, and the company was incorporated in State C and had its primary place of business in State D. At trial, the company argued that there was no diversity of citizenship between the parties. According to company records, 75 percent of purchasers were from State B, 20 percent were from State A, three percent were from State C, and two percent were from State D.

Can the man's claim be heard in federal court?

(A) Yes, because the majority of purchasers are from State B.

(B) Yes, because the man is a citizen of State B.

(C) No, because some of the class members are from State D.

(D) No, because some of the class members are from State C.

Question 37

A man sued a delivery driver and his employer in federal court after the delivery driver hit the man with his truck. The employer filed a claim against the driver, claiming the driver should indemnify the employer because his negligence caused the accident.

Can the employer file its claim against the delivery driver in the same action?

(A) Yes, because it is a valid counterclaim.

(B) Yes, because it is a valid cross-claim.

(C) No, because the employer and delivery driver are co-defendants.

(D) No, because the plaintiff is the master of his claim.

Question 38

During a storm, an oil tanker travelling in the Mississippi River ran into a large underwater pipe. The pipe burst, sending millions of gallons of sewage into the water. A town sued the ship in federal court, claiming severe damage to its riverfront.

Does the federal court have jurisdiction over the matter?

(A) Yes, because the case has a maritime nexus.

(B) Yes, because the case involves interstate commerce.

(C) No, because the town is claiming damage to the riverbank.

(D) No, because the accident did not occur at sea.

Question 39

A woman who is a citizen of State A was dating a man who was a citizen of State B for two years. They broke up and she sued the man when he would not return some jewelry that she claimed was hers. The woman mailed the service and complaint to the man at his residence in State B, along with a request for waiver of the service. The man chose not to agree to the woman's request for waiver of service.

Assuming the federal court has jurisdiction over the matter, may the man choose not to agree to the waiver of service?

(A) Yes, but he may be liable for expenses and attorneys' fees.

(B) Yes, because the Federal Rules of Civil Procedure guarantee his right to service in accordance with federal law.

(C) No, because mail is a reasonable means of apprizing the man of the pending action.

(D) No, because the man is an individual and not a corporation, partnership, or association.

Question 40

Pepper brings an action against Dick in a state court of general jurisdiction in State A. Pepper is a citizen of State A, and Dick is a citizen of State B. Pepper alleges that Dick has infringed upon a patent recently granted to Pepper by the U.S. Patent and Trademark Office. Pepper seeks $75,000 in damages and an injunction barring Dick from further acts of infringement.

Patent infringement matters are within the exclusive jurisdiction of the federal courts. Dick is personally served with a copy of the summons and complaint when his airplane lands at a State A airport on a short stop while on his way to State C. Dick fails to answer the complaint, and Pepper obtains a default judgment. Pepper then seeks to enforce the judgment in a State D state court.

Which of the following is correct?

(A) The court in State A did not have subject-matter jurisdiction over the action, so Pepper's judgment is not entitled to Full Faith and Credit from a State D court.

(B) The State A state court never obtained personal jurisdiction over Dick, so the judgment is not entitled to Full Faith and Credit from a State D court.

(C) By failing to appear, Dick waived his right to object to subject matter and personal jurisdiction.

(D) By failing to appear, Dick waived his right to object, but only as to the State A court having personal jurisdiction over Dick.

Question 41

A plaintiff brought a civil action in the United States District Court for the District of State A under diversity jurisdiction. The plaintiff amended her complaint against the defendant to add a claim that arose from the same events for which the plaintiff sought relief in the original claim. Between the filing of the original complaint and the amended complaint, the statute of limitations expired on the claim that was added by amendment. State law in State A did not permit "relation back" of claims added by amendment after limitations expired. The defendant sought summary judgment on the added claim on the basis of limitations.

Should the court grant summary judgment on the basis of the limitations defense?

(A) Yes, because the federal court sitting in diversity must defer to state law as part of the Erie Doctrine.

(B) Yes, because otherwise plaintiffs would have an incentive to forum shop and choose federal court over state court.

(C) No, because the Federal Rules of Civil Procedure allow for "relation back" in these circumstances.

(D) No, because the difference between state and federal law is merely a matter of procedure.

Question 42

A woman filed a class action in federal district court on behalf of a nationwide class of over 2,000 users of a corporation's insect spray after her young son developed asthma. According to the claim, the insect spray violated health and safety laws and raised the likelihood of asthma and other respiratory diseases in the families of spray users. Along with federal rules governing health and safety, several states have their own health and safety laws regarding insect spray, and state law experts will be required in each of the class members' states to adequately investigate individual claims. Because of the scope of the action, the woman hired a nationally recognized law firm to handle the matter.

Should the federal court grant class certification?

(A) Yes, because the woman will fairly and adequately protect the interests of the class.

(B) Yes, because the woman's claim is representative of the claims of the class.

(C) No, because multiple state laws regarding health and safety are involved.

(D) No, because the class is so numerous that joinder of all members is impracticable.

Question 43

An online music listening service called Melodia charged listeners a subscription fee to access its music files. Users of the service became upset when it learned that Melodia had been selling information about their listening habits to marketers without their consent, and lawyers filed a class action lawsuit in federal district court on behalf of the users, alleging violations of federal privacy laws. The lawsuit named Melodia, headquartered in Texas, and Sassy Consulting, a consulting firm based in Russia, who had advised Melodia and which had no jurisdictional contacts with the U.S. allowing for personal jurisdiction in any U.S. court. The lawyers provided proper notice to each of the plaintiffs in the proposed class, including, among others, 100 users in Vietnam with no contacts with the U.S., and who did not respond to the notice, and 1,000 users in the U.S. who did not respond to the notice. The defense now argues that the court may not include the 100 Vietnamese users, the 1,000 U.S. users who did not respond, and Sassy Consulting in the case.

Which of those parties may the court include in the class action proceedings?

(A) None of the parties.

(B) The 1,000 U.S. users.

(C) The 1,000 U.S. users and the 100 Vietnamese users.

(D) The 1,000 U.S. users, the 100 Vietnamese users, and Sassy Consulting.

Question 44

A woman was hit by a car while walking her dog. The woman was a citizen of State A. The driver was a citizen of State B. The woman sued the driver in a State A state court, claiming $40,000 in damages based on her personal injuries. After a visit to a doctor revealed the need for more surgeries, the woman amended her complaint to add another $50,000 in damages. The driver filed a motion to remove the case to federal court.

Can the case be removed to federal court?

(A) Yes, after the woman amended her complaint to add $50,000 in damages.

(B) Yes, because the defendant made the request for removal.

(C) No, because the original claim was for $40,000 in damages.

(D) No, because the woman's claim is for personal injuries.

Question 45

While visiting friends at a party in another state, a bodybuilder picks up the host and swings him around by his ankles in an attempt to demonstrate her strength. In so doing, she hits the host's head on a ceiling fan, causing him a brain injury and some facial scarring. The local prosecutor prosecutes the bodybuilder for battery, but she is acquitted. The host then brings a civil suit against the bodybuilder in federal court for battery. The bodybuilder's attorney claims that, because the bodybuilder was acquitted of battery in the earlier suit, the host is precluded from bringing a civil battery suit.

Is the bodybuilder's attorney correct?

(A) Yes, because the prosecution and the civil suit arose from the same incident.

(B) Yes, because the Constitutional prohibition on double jeopardy forbids a civil trial.

(C) No, because issue preclusion (collateral estoppel) does not apply between criminal and civil cases.

(D) No, because a criminal conviction has a higher standard of proof than a finding of civil liability.

Question 46

Pauly sued Dominic in a State A court of general jurisdiction for injuries suffered in an auto accident in State A. Pauly is a citizen of State A, and Dominic is a citizen of State B. State A is a comparative negligence state.

The jury finds Dominic 80% at fault and Pauly 20% at fault and rules that Dominic must pay Pauly $16,000 for the latter's injuries. Since all of Dominic's assets are in State B, Pauly sued Dominic on the State A judgment in a State B court. State B is a contributory negligence state.

Assuming the State A decision is final, which of the following statements is correct?

(A) State B must grant Full Faith and Credit to the State A judgment if Dominic had a full and fair opportunity to litigate on the merits.

(B) *Res judicata* precludes Pauly from suing on the State A judgment in State B, because the two actions involve the same parties and the same occurrence.

(C) Full Faith and Credit need not be granted to the State A judgment.

(D) The State B court may hold a trial *de novo*, because that jurisdiction does not recognize comparative negligence.

Question 47

Plaintiff filed her complaint in federal court on June 13 and alleged that Defendant Megacorp Holdings, Inc. ("MHI") engaged in sex discrimination through the acts of her supervisor. Plaintiff served the registered agent for MHI on June 20. The statute of limitations on her claim expired on June 21. Plaintiff learns on June 23 that she and the supervisor actually were employed by Megacorp Industries, Inc. ("MII"), a subsidiary of MHI. Plaintiff filed a first amended complaint on June 25 to add MII as a defendant and to seek damages for the sex discrimination perpetrated by her supervisor. Also on June 25, Plaintiff served the registered agent for MII, the same person who had been served with the original complaint as the registered agent for MHI. MII asserted a timely statute of limitations defense.

Should the statute of limitations defense prevail?

(A) Yes, because Plaintiff did not obtain leave of court to file the amended complaint.

(B) Yes, because the amended complaint against MII was filed after the limitations period expired.

(C) No, because MII and MHI had the same registered agent.

(D) No, because the filing of the amended complaint will relate back in time to the filing of the original complaint.

Question 48

During jury selection for a trademark trial, a federal court had a smaller pool than usual due to a winter storm that made getting to the courthouse quite treacherous. The court was able to seat 12 jurors, but did not have a big enough pool to provide for alternates. The judge decided not to delay because the extended weather forecast did not show marked improvement for at least a week. Three days into the trial, two jurors developed bronchitis and could not attend the trial both because of their own discomfort and the distraction they caused to others.

Should the judge declare a mistrial?

(A) Yes, because there are now fewer than 12 jurors and there are no alternates.

(B) Yes, because the federal rules require that each jury have 12 jurors and three alternates.

(C) No, because the court does not know whether the jurors who are sick can return soon.

(D) No, because federal courts only require a unanimous jury of six.

Question 49

A gardener suffers the sudden onset of irregular heartbeat, for which he has needed extensive hospitalization and the insertion of a cardiac pacemaker. This is apparently due to a medication he was taking for ulcers. He sues the manufacturer, which is based in another state, in federal court. A previous user of the ulcer drug had sued the manufacturer in a state court for the same problem and won. The gardener files a summary judgment motion establishing in the manufacturer's responsibility for his injuries based on *res judicata*.

Should the court find the manufacturer liable to the gardener based on *res judicata*?

(A) Yes, because the gardener suffered the same type of injury as the plaintiff in the prior action.

(B) Yes, because it does not appear that the gardener could have joined the prior action.

(C) No, because the gardener's injury did not arise from the same transaction or occurrence as the previous case.

(D) No, because the previous case was not heard in the same court.

Question 50

An author obtained copyright protection on a poem she had published. The author sued a man in federal court for copyright infringement. After a bench trial, the trial court entered findings of fact and conclusions of law. The finding of fact that disposed of the case was that the author's copyright was invalid because she plagiarized the poem from another's work. From this finding of fact, the Court reached the dispositive conclusion of law, that the author could not recover for copyright infringement. The author then sued a woman for infringing the same copyright. The woman raised the defense of collateral estoppel in a timely answer.

Should the defense of collateral estoppel prevail?

(A) Yes, because the validity of the copyright was an issue in both cases and the author lost that issue in the first case.

(B) Yes, because the author lost the issue of the validity of the copyright in a forum of her own choosing.

(C) No, because the parties in the two cases were not the same.

(D) No, because the author did not have a full and fair opportunity to litigate the validity of her copyright in the first case.

Question 51

Two professors from a university in State A visited a farm in State B to conduct research. While there, the professors realized the owner of the farm had developed an extremely valuable plant strain. The professors, acting on behalf of the university, offered the owner a contract to purchase certain rights to the strain for $500,000 on the condition that the owner would share in 20% of all future profits earned by the university from its work with the plant strain and the university would not enter into any further contracts regarding the strain that did not mention and/or provide for payment to the owner. The owner and the professors signed the contract in State B. Representatives from the university then traveled to State C to meet with a developer who offered the university $5 million for a 50% ownership in the plant strain. The representatives accepted and they and the developer signed a contract in State C, which did not provide for payment to the owner and did not mention him. The owner filed suit against the university for breach of contract in a federal district court in State D, which was known for its hostility to State A and especially the university, but the defendant successfully transferred the action to State A on the grounds that State D was an improper venue. State D's choice of law rules require that, in breach of contract actions, the substantive law of the state where the contract was originally signed should apply, while State A's choice of law rules require that the substantive law of the state in which the actual breach took place should apply.

What is the source of the substantive law that the court will apply?

(A) State A law.

(B) State B law.

(C) State C law.

(D) State D law.

Question 52

A man and a woman decided to get married in Las Vegas, Nevada. The man was domiciled in Vermont, and the woman was domiciled in Colorado. When they arrived in Las Vegas, the couple had a huge fight and called off the wedding. They returned to their home states. However, a few months later, the man quit his job, drove to Colorado, and rented a house. He told his friends, "I'm staying in Colorado for as long as it takes to get her back." The man got a job and started dating the woman again. Three months later, the couple went to Las Vegas to get married again, and again had another fight. This time, the man suffered a broken nose, which required over $75,000 worth of reconstructive surgery. They both returned to Colorado. At that point, the man decided to sue the woman in Colorado federal court for battery, claiming the amount of his surgery as damages.

May the man bring his suit in federal court?

(A) Yes, because the man was a citizen of Vermont when the injury occurred.

(B) Yes, because the man was a citizen of Colorado when the injury occurred.

(C) No, because the man was a citizen of Vermont when the suit was filed.

(D) No, because the man was a citizen of Colorado when the suit was filed.

Question 53

A State A energy company engaged a State B exploration company to explore potential natural gas resources in State A. The energy company oversaw the work while the exploration company operated the machinery to conduct the exploration. During the exploration, an underground explosion occurred, killing three of the exploration company's workers. The exploration company sued the energy company for negligently overseeing the work. The energy company employed a geology expert to investigate the facts and help the energy company prepare for trial, but the geology expert will not testify at trial.

If the exploration company seeks to depose the geology expert in order to learn about the expert's opinions, will the court allow it do so?

(A) No, because experts may not be deposed before trial.

(B) No, because experts may only be deposed with regard to facts, not opinions.

(C) Yes, because experts may be deposed as to both facts and opinions.

(D) Yes, but only if the plaintiffs show exceptional circumstances under which it is impracticable for them to obtain the information by other means.

Question 54

A federal prisoner filed a *pro se* claim in federal district court against the prison where he was housed, alleging only that he had told prison officials numerous times in one week that he did not feel well and wanted to see a doctor and that their failure to help him get medical attention was a violation of the Eighth Amendment ban on cruel and unusual punishment. The prison, in its answer, raised a 12(b)(6) defense, stating that the prisoner had failed to state a claim on which relief could be granted. The federal court dismissed the claim without further comment 90 days later.

Is the prisoner entitled to revise and resubmit his claim?

(A) Yes, because a *pro se* litigant is entitled to amend his claim one time as of right.

(B) Yes, because all litigants are entitled to amend a claim one time as of right.

(C) No, because 12(b)(6) dismissals are with prejudice unless the court states otherwise.

(D) No, because he did not state any damages that resulted from the alleged constitutional violation.

Question 55

A pipefitter in an oil refinery is suffering from throat cancer. His lawyer files a workers' compensation suit based on the opinion of a medical expert that the pipefitter's cancer was caused by one of the industrial solvents the pipefitter often used in his job. Both sides present information on the issue, and the workers' compensation judge finds for the defendant on the basis that there is not a sufficient causal link between the solvent and the pipefitter's cancer. The pipefitter later sues the manufacturer of the solvent in federal court for damages caused by his cancer.

If the manufacturer moves for summary judgment based on the lack of causality that the workers' compensation court found, what will be the pipefitter's best argument to defeat summary judgment?

(A) That the manufacturer was not a party to the prior case.

(B) That issue preclusion (collateral estoppel) cannot be used offensively.

(C) That the two cases were filed in different forums.

(D) That the issue was not fully and fairly litigated in the previous case.

Question 56

Delasandro is a stock broker in State A. He handles the accounts of Annie and Betty. Delasandro decided to invest some of Annie's and Betty's money in a new super venture company he had just started. Unfortunately, things did not go well.

In a period of four months, all of Annie's and Betty's money was gone. Betty sued Delasandro for breach of a fiduciary duty. She recovered a default judgment for the full amount of her claim.

Which of the following statements is correct?

(A) Betty's judgment should have no effect upon a subsequent lawsuit by Annie against Delasandro.

(B) Betty's judgment is *res judicata* with respect to a subsequent lawsuit by Annie against Delasandro.

(C) Assuming the mutuality doctrine is inapplicable, a court may permit Annie to assert collateral estoppel in a subsequent lawsuit by Annie against Delasandro.

(D) Because Annie and Betty are in privity, Annie cannot recover because of the *res judicata* effects of the initial judgment for Betty.

Question 57

State A passed a law providing a cause of action for citizens who discovered evidence of a business entity using bribery or other illegal business practices to secure contracts with the state government to sue the offending entity and recover a percentage of the revenues received by the entity for the contract. A woman found evidence that a State B corporation used illegal business practices to secure a contract to build a State A parking garage. She also found evidence that the same corporation used similar business practices to secure a contract to provide security services at State A courthouses. The woman sued the corporation in federal district court in diversity jurisdiction, alleging two separate claims against the corporation based on the two different incidents. The corporation was concerned that a jury that heard evidence of multiple incidents of illegal business practices would bias the jury against it, and wanted the court to separate the claims into two different trials.

Which of the following facts, if true, will be most helpful to the corporation in making this argument?

(A) Hearing evidence related to the security service issue would unnecessarily confuse the jury with regard to the parking garage issue.

(B) The cause of action provided by the state law does not require that a plaintiff bring all known claims against another party at one time.

(C) There is no factual connection between the parking garage issue and the security service claims, and the claims would require completely distinct evidentiary showings.

(D) The woman has indicated to the corporation that she has evidence supporting a third claim against the corporation that she intends to bring should the first two claims be successful.

Question 58

Based on the available facts, in which of the following scenarios is a federal court most likely to allow a party's request for discovery?

(A) In a construction litigation case, a party seeks discovery of emails between the general counsel of a corporation and its CFO regarding potential litigation risks to the corporation, but which copied all of the officers of the corporation and their support staff.

(B) In a class action federal securities fraud litigation related to a corporation's undisclosed risk of insider trading liability, a party seeks discovery of all of the corporation's non-privileged emails related to insider trading. Reviewing and producing said emails will require 500 man-hours to complete.

(C) In an employment discrimination case, the plaintiff seeks all of the defendant's non-privileged emails related to the payment of bribes to foreign entities.

(D) In a copyright action in which a writer alleges damages of $5,000 from a publisher, the writer seeks production of all non-privileged emails relating to the publisher's work with a book that the writer claims was plagiarized from him. Reviewing and producing said emails will require 500 man-hours to complete.

Question 59

A man sued a publishing company, claiming that the company's book about a child who goes to wizarding school infringed his copyright in his own book about a child who goes to wizarding school. During a meeting, the company showed the man that its book came out six years before the man claimed to have written his own book. The company's book had been a huge success, and was available in almost every bookstore in the world. The book also contained a notice of copyright on its front cover. The man told the company he was not giving up his lawsuit, as he had never read the company's book.

The company served a motion for sanctions upon the man. Twenty days later, the man responded by saying he was standing by his complaint.

Would sanctions be appropriate in this case?

(A) Yes, because the man could have easily discovered the company's earlier copyright.

(B) Yes, because the man waited 20 days to answer.

(C) No, because the complaint was valid on its face.

(D) No, because discovery had not yet been completed.

Question 60

A student sued a corporation that owned a fast food chain for selling a veggie taco that in fact did contain some meat in it. The student sought $1,000 in damages. A jury in state court returned a special verdict for the student and found that the corporation's veggie taco did contain some meat in it. The corporation was then sued in federal court by a class of 3900 plaintiffs. The class action complaint alleged the veggie taco that was sold by the corporation had meat in it and sought damages of over $5,000,000. Class counsel filed a motion for partial summary judgment and argued that the corporation should be estopped from contesting whether the veggie taco that was sold by the corporation had meat in it.

Should the court grant the motion for partial summary judgment?

(A) Yes, because the issue of whether the veggie taco that was sold by the corporation had meat in it was actually litigated and decided in the first case and was essential to the judgment.

(B) Yes, because the corporation had a full and fair opportunity to litigate the issue in the first case.

(C) No, because the stakes in the second case are much greater than the stakes were in the first case.

(D) No, because the members of the class were not parties to the first case.

Question 61

A plaintiff brought claims in federal court against three defendants. The plaintiff obtained summary judgment against one defendant, but the plaintiff's summary judgment motions as to the other two defendants were denied. The trial court determined that there was no just reason for delay and entered final judgment as to the claim against the first defendant. The first defendant immediately appealed the grant of summary judgment by the trial court, and the plaintiff made a motion to dismiss the appeal.

Should the Court of Appeals grant the motion to dismiss the appeal?

(A) Yes, because not all of the claims in the case have been fully adjudicated.

(B) Yes, because the grant or denial of a summary judgment is not appealable immediately.

(C) No, because a grant of summary judgment is a final judgment.

(D) No, because the trial court entered final judgment on the claim against the first defendant after finding that there was no just reason for delay.

Question 62

A woman sued a landscaper and a plumber in federal court for damages done to her home. The landscaper and plumber often did work together as part of a "total home makeover package." Over 70 homes had purchased the package in the past three years. When the landscaper received notice of the woman's suit, he filed cross-claims against the plumber for breach of contract for the work on the woman's house and for breach of contract for a package sold to a neighboring home.

Can the landscaper file his claims against the plumber in the same action?

(A) Yes, because the claims are part of the same transaction or occurrence.

(B) Yes, because the claims are being filed against his co-defendant.

(C) No, because efficiency interests would not be served by joinder.

(D) No, because the claims are completely unrelated.

Question 63

An investor sued the directors of a corporation after the corporation's stock fell, alleging that the directors had violated federal securities laws by fraudulently withholding information that should have been made available to the corporation's investors. The directors filed an answer denying the allegations and raising the affirmative defenses of unclean hands and laches. The case went to trial, and after hearing the testimony offered by the investor's witnesses, the directors' lawyers filed a motion to dismiss, arguing that the investor had failed to state a claim upon which relief may be granted.

If the investor argues that this motion is not timely, will the investor prevail?

(A) Yes, because a motion on these grounds must be filed prior to an answer.

(B) Yes, because the case has proceeded to trial.

(C) No, because the investor is required to plead fraud with particularity.

(D) No, because such a motion may be filed at trial.

Question 64

A plaintiff sued a defendant in federal court for damages in connection with an automobile accident, including damages for pain and suffering. Federal jurisdiction existed. The defendant was not a minor or an incompetent. The plaintiff had the defendant properly served with the summons and the complaint. The defendant did not appear or otherwise respond to the complaint, and the clerk entered a default against the defendant when the plaintiff demonstrated by affidavit that the defendant had failed to plead or otherwise defend. The plaintiff requested the clerk to enter default judgment against the defendant and submitted an affidavit that specified the damages that the plaintiff believed himself to be entitled to recover.

Must the clerk enter the default judgment?

(A) Yes, because the defendant did not appear in the action.

(B) Yes, because the plaintiff submitted an affidavit that set forth his damages.

(C) No, because the court must enter all default judgments.

(D) No, because the suit was not for a sum certain or a sum that can be made certain by computation.

Question 65

Which of the following actions by a court is least likely to be valid?

(A) A plaintiff requests that a corporation submit to a Rule 30(b)(6) deposition. The corporation designates an individual to attend the deposition, but the individual fails to do so. The court orders a default judgment in favor of the plaintiff.

(B) The attorney for a defendant does not act in good faith in working with the plaintiff's attorney to create a discovery plan. The plaintiff's attorney complains to the judge, who immediately sanctions the defense attorney by requiring her to pay the reasonable costs caused by her lack of good faith.

(C) A plaintiff fails to return interrogatories within the 30 days specified by the court. The court immediately stays the proceedings until the interrogatories are completed.

(D) The court orders the minor son of a plaintiff to submit to a Rule 35(a) physical examination. The plaintiff fails to produce the son for the examination. The court orders a default judgment in favor of the defendant.

Question 66

Plaintiff sued Defendant in federal court because Defendant did not pay for a shipment of goods. Diversity jurisdiction exists. Defendant consulted with Lawyer, who investigated whether Defendant had a defense to the claim. While Lawyer continued to investigate, Lawyer filed a Notice of Appearance in the case but did not file an answer. By affidavit, Plaintiff showed the clerk that Defendant was in default and showed the amount due for the sale of the goods. The clerk entered a default judgment against the defendant for that amount and for costs. Lawyer immediately moved to set aside the default judgment.

Should the court grant the motion to set aside the default judgment?

(A) Yes, because Lawyer filed an appearance in the case.

(B) Yes, because a judgment must be entered by the court rather than the clerk.

(C) No, because the claim was for a sum certain.

(D) No, because the Plaintiff showed the amount due by affidavit.

Question 67

A plaintiff filed a civil case in federal court against a defendant. The defendant responded with a motion to dismiss for failure to state a claim upon which relief can be granted. After the court denied that motion, the defendant filed an answer in which the defendant asserted that the court lacked personal jurisdiction. Two days later, the defendant filed an amended answer and asserted the defense of lack of venue.

Did the defendant waive the defense of lack of venue?

(A) Yes, because the defendant did not include it in the answer.

(B) Yes, because the defendant did not include the defense in the motion to dismiss.

(C) No, because the defense appeared in an amended answer filed as a matter of course.

(D) No, because lack of venue may not be waived.

Question 68

A man and a woman were driving when they were struck from behind by a delivery truck. The man and woman were State A citizens, while the truck was owned by a corporation incorporated in State B with its principal place of business in State C. The man suffered over $100,000 in damages, while the woman only suffered $5,000. The man sued the corporation in a State C federal court based on diversity. The woman soon joined the man's suit. The corporation then requested the suit be removed to state court, since the woman's claim failed to meet the amount-in-controversy requirement.

Does a federal court have jurisdiction over the matter?

(A) Yes, because federal jurisdiction is determined on the date the suit is filed.

(B) Yes, because the man has over $100,000 in damages.

(C) No, because the woman only suffered $5,000 in damages.

(D) No, because auto accidents are matters left to the states.

Question 69

At the close of the plaintiff's case in a federal civil trial, a defendant moved for judgment as a matter of law. The court denied the motion. The defendant did not make a motion for judgment as a matter of law at the close of all the evidence. The jury returned a verdict for the plaintiff. Twenty-nine days after the court entered judgment on the verdict, the defendant filed a renewed motion for judgment as a matter of law. The plaintiff argued that the court could not entertain the renewed motion for judgment as a matter of law, and the court agreed.

Was the court correct to conclude that it could not entertain the renewed motion for judgment as a matter of law?

(A) Yes, because the defendant did not make a motion for judgment as a matter of law at the close of all the evidence.

(B) Yes, because the renewed motion for judgment as a matter of law was filed too late.

(C) No, because a renewed motion for judgment as a matter of law may be made within one year of the entry of judgment on a jury verdict.

(D) No, because the defendant made a motion for judgment as a matter of law at the close of the plaintiff's case.

Question 70

A jury of 12 members returned a unanimous verdict in federal court. On its own, without a motion from a party, the trial judge polled the members of the jury and discovered that two members of the jury did not assent to the verdict. The parties had not stipulated to accept a verdict from a particular number of jurors. The judge ordered a new trial.

Did the judge err when he ordered a new trial?

(A) Yes, because a verdict of 10 of 12 jurors was sufficient in federal court to support a judgment.

(B) Yes, because the court was required to order the jurors to resume deliberations under these circumstances.

(C) No, because the court had the option to order further deliberations or a new trial under these circumstances.

(D) No, because the court was required to order a new trial once the polling revealed that a juror did not assent to the verdict announced to the court.

Question 71

A man filed a stockholder's derivative suit in State A federal district court against two corporations. The man was from State B, and both corporations were based and incorporated in State A. Initially, the man and the corporations were clearly antagonistic to each other, but, during trial, there was a merger between one of the corporations and a subsidiary. The court decided that the subsidiary's merger changed the interests of that corporation, placing its interests and the man's interests on the same side. Consequently, it realigned that corporation as a plaintiff and dismissed the case because of lack of diversity. The man appealed, arguing the federal court still had jurisdiction.

Should the court rule in the man's favor?

(A) Yes, because jurisdiction is determined at the time the suit is filed.

(B) Yes, because the action was originally brought in federal court.

(C) No, because the realignment caused both sides of the conflict to be citizens of State A.

(D) No, because federal courts are masters of their own jurisdiction.

Question 72

A corporation sued a man in federal court for slander. The man, a State A citizen, met with his attorney and told him that the federal court did not have jurisdiction over the matter because the corporation had all of its factories in State A and was thus a State A citizen. The man further stated that the corporation was incorporated in State B, and had an office in State C where the corporation's directors were based. Based on the man's statements, the attorney filed a motion to dismiss.

Should the court grant the motion?

(A) Yes, because the corporation's primary place of business is in State A.

(B) Yes, because the corporation is incorporated in State B.

(C) No, because the corporation's primary place of business is in State C.

(D) No, because the attorney based the motion on the man's statements.

Question 73

A man in State A rode his motorcycle to a hotel in State B. When he arrived at the hotel in State B, he drove his motorcycle into the hotel's parking structure, but the motorcycle's brakes failed and the accelerator became stuck, causing him to hurtle uncontrollably through the structure. He looked for a wall he could maneuver into in order to stop the motorcycle, but the structure simply ended with no wall or railing, just a steep drop-off, and he and the motorcycle flew straight off the tall structure and through a hotel skylight into the lobby, causing significant damage to the hotel and injury to the man. The man sued the hotel in federal district court based on State B tort law claims, arguing that the parking structure was negligently designed and maintained. The hotel filed a counterclaim against the man for the damage to the hotel.

If the man believes the manufacturer of the motorcycle was negligent and will be liable to the hotel for any damages assessed to him based on the counterclaim, what is the best procedural tool for the man to bring the manufacturer into the action?

(A) Intervention.

(B) Third-party complaint.

(C) Rule interpleader.

(D) Statutory interpleader.

Question 74

In a civil case in federal court, the trial judge conducted the voir dire. When the judge completed her questioning, the attorneys for the parties suggested that additional follow-up questions should be asked and requested the court's permission to ask the follow-up questions themselves. The particular questions they sought to ask were directed to possible bases of challenges for cause. The trial judge recognized that the suggestions were proper. The court refused, however, to allow the attorneys to ask the questions and instead asked the questions herself.

Did the trial judge err when she refused to allow the attorneys for the parties to ask proper follow-up questions during jury selection?

(A) Yes, because attorneys for the parties have the right to ask proper questions directly of prospective jurors during jury selection in federal court.

(B) Yes, because the questions were directed to possible bases for challenges for cause.

(C) No, because the judge chose to ask the questions herself.

(D) No, because attorneys are not allowed to ask questions directly of prospective jurors during jury selection in federal court.

Question 75

A homeowner in State A had strange and disturbing experiences in his house and decided to sell the house and move far away. Two newlyweds in State A bought the house from the homeowner, who took the money and moved to State B. The newlyweds had similar experiences to those of the homeowner and they believed the experiences were attributable to paranormal activity in the house. The newlyweds sued the homeowner in federal district court for $100,000 for failing to disclose the alleged paranormal activity when they purchased the house. Before selling the house, the homeowner had taken out an insurance policy to indemnify himself from any liability relating to allegations of paranormal activity on any property he has owned or previously owned.

Is the homeowner required to make the newlyweds aware of this policy?

(A) No, because evidence of an insurance policy cannot be used to show that the homeowner acted wrongfully.

(B) No, because insurance coverage is not relevant to the newlyweds' claims or the homeowner's defenses.

(C) Yes, because the homeowner is required to provide disclosure of the policy without awaiting a discovery request.

(D) Yes, but only if the newlyweds specifically requested disclosure of any insurance policies.

Question 76

A plaintiff and a defendant tried a civil case in federal court to a jury. The trial court had set, as a deadline for the submission of proposed jury instructions, the date of the final pretrial conference, which occurred three days before trial commenced. At the close of the evidence, the plaintiff sought to file new requests for jury instructions on issues that could have reasonably been anticipated as of the date of the final pretrial conference.

Did the plaintiff have the right to file the new requests for jury instructions?

(A) Yes, because closing arguments had not yet occurred.

(B) Yes, because the jury had not yet been instructed.

(C) No, because the requests concerned issues that could have been reasonably anticipated as of the date of the final pretrial conference.

(D) No, because the date set by the court for submission of proposed jury instructions had passed.

Question 77

Irene made an appointment with Dr. Pupil because she was suffering from an irritating sensation in her eyes. Dr. Pupil treated Irene with eye drops in his office. Over the next three weeks, the irritation increased to the point that opening her eyes was excruciating. Soon, the eye pain became so severe that she had to stay in the hospital for two weeks. Irene sued Dr. Pupil in U.S. District Court and requested a trial by jury. At trial, Irene testified to the foregoing and then called Dr. Converse to the stand. Dr. Converse testified that he had examined Irene and performed an eye cleaning procedure. He further testified that his examination had revealed extensive damage to the surface of her eyes consistent with having been burned by an acidic substance. Irene offered no other witnesses or evidence.

Dr. Pupil took the stand and testified that Irene had been suffering from extreme eye irritation caused by some kind of allergy and that he had treated her eyes with a saline solution. On cross-examination he stated that he did store an acidic substance normally used in a different procedure in the same cabinet with the eye drops he claimed to have used on Irene. He then rested his case. In rebuttal, Irene called Dr. Converse, who testified that in his professional opinion, the injury to her eyes was not consistent with any allergy. No further evidence was presented. Dr. Pupil moved for a directed verdict, and the motion was granted.

If Irene appeals, how should the Court of Appeals decide?

(A) Reverse the judgment and order a new trial.

(B) Reverse the judgment and direct that judgment be entered for Irene.

(C) Affirm the judgment.

(D) Affirm the judgment, because Irene did not prove beyond a reasonable doubt that Dr. Pupil inadvertently applied an acidic substance to her eyes.

Question 78

An employee residing in State A worked for an employer whose principal place of business was located in State B. After many years of loyal service, the employer fired the employee without cause. Believing that her termination was unlawful and was the result of discrimination on the basis of sex, the employee filed a lawsuit against the employer in federal district court in State B asserting violations of various state laws as well as state common law claims. The total amount of damages sought by the employee, inclusive of attorney's fees and costs, in her complaint was $75,000. One week after the employee filed her lawsuit, she permanently moved her residence to State B. After being properly served with the complaint, the employer filed a motion to dismiss the complaint for lack of subject-matter jurisdiction. State B follows the majority view.

If the court grants the employer's motion to dismiss, it most likely relied on which of the following grounds?

(A) The complete diversity requirement between the parties was not satisfied.

(B) The amount-in-controversy requirement was not satisfied.

(C) The federal question requirement was not satisfied because the employee did not make a claim under the federal anti-discrimination laws.

(D) The court did not have supplemental jurisdiction over the employee's claims.

Question 79

A State A man traveled to State B to visit the main showroom of Remnant Cycles, a luxury motorcycle manufacturer, to see an extremely limited edition of a new motorcycle called "Infinitus." The man bought an Infinitus to ride back to State A, but, while he was riding it through State C, he noticed that it was leaking gas and stopped at a State C Remnant dealership to have it serviced. Back in State A, the man observed that it was still leaking gas and took it to his State A mechanic, who was an authorized reseller of Remnant Cycles. The mechanic did some work, but the next week the gas tank exploded while the man was riding it, and he suffered injuries. He brought a state product liability case in State A state court against Remnant Cycles, the Remnant dealership, and the mechanic, alleging $500,000 in damages.

If the defendants now seek to remove the case to federal court, will they be able to do so?

(A) No, unless the defendants can show that the mechanic was fraudulently joined.

(B) No, because the case does not present a federal question.

(C) Yes, unless the plaintiff can show that the mechanic was not fraudulently joined.

(D) Yes, because two of the defendants are diverse from the plaintiff.

Question 80

A State A developer created a text-messaging service so that users could send encrypted, password-protected texts to one another. A number of users, including those in State A, paid a subscription fee to use the service for their business activities that required confidentiality. The service began sending numerous unsolicited texts to its users at all hours, in violation of State A consumer protection laws, and a class action attorney filed a lawsuit in State A state court asserting a private cause of action under those laws.

Under which of the following scenarios may the developer successfully remove the case to federal court based on diversity jurisdiction?

(A) The class is made up entirely of 100,000 users from State A and the amount in controversy is $1 million.

(B) The class is made up entirely of 750 users from State A and 250 users from State B and the amount in controversy is $12 million.

(C) The class is made up entirely of 60 users from State A and 60 users from State B and the amount in controversy is $6 million.

(D) None of the above.

Question 81

The Department of Homeland Security, concerned about foreign nationals entering federal courthouses to harm employees, promulgated a regulation requiring everyone passing through security at courthouses to present either an courthouse employee identification or, in the case of non-employees, a government-issued form of identification, such as a driver's license. An immigration lawyer responded by filing a petition for a temporary restraining order against enforcement of the regulation on behalf of one of his immigrant clients.

Which of the following would be the best support for the petition for a temporary restraining order?

(A) A report showing that there have been no previous incidents of terrorism in federal courthouses.

(B) An affidavit alleging that, if the client did not attend her hearing next week, she would be subject to a deportation order.

(C) An investigative report demonstrating that other federal security regulations have not been uniformly administered.

(D) Affidavits of several clients stating that it was a hardship for them to obtain a government-issued form of identification.

Question 82

A general contractor believed that his partner was embezzling funds from the company. In the company's records, the general contractor had discovered strange purchases including decorative tile and brick that seemed to be going into a backyard garden area at his partner's home.

What is the best way the contractor should proceed in this matter?

(A) Ask the court to enter a temporary restraining order.

(B) Ask the court for a preliminary injunction.

(C) Ask the court for summary judgment.

(D) Ask the court for depositions.

Question 83

In a federal civil case: (1) the plaintiff presented evidence and rested; (2) the defendant presented evidence and rested; (3) the court gave the jury charge; (4) the lawyers presented closing arguments; and (5) the case was submitted to the jury. While the jury was deliberating, the defendant made a motion for judgment as a matter of law. The plaintiff argued in response that the motion was untimely.

Was the motion for judgment as a matter of law untimely?

(A) Yes, because it was filed after the case had been submitted to the jury.

(B) Yes, because it was filed after the defendant presented evidence.

(C) No, because the plaintiff had been fully heard.

(D) No, because the jury had not reached a verdict.

Question 84

A plaintiff filed a case against a defendant in state court. The defendant properly removed the case to federal court because of diversity of citizenship and amount in controversy. In the state court, jury verdicts were required to be in the form of special verdicts by which the jury answered specific questions of fact. The federal judge in the diversity case submitted the case to the jury through a general verdict with written questions. The plaintiff objected and argued that the federal court was required to follow the state court procedure of submitting the case to the jury by special verdict.

Was the federal court sitting in diversity required to follow the state procedure of submitting the case to the jury by special verdict?

(A) Yes, because the case was originally filed in state court.

(B) Yes, because federal courts must follow state law in diversity cases.

(C) No, because the Federal Rules of Civil Procedure authorize what the federal judge did.

(D) No, because the method of submitting a case to a jury is not outcome-determinative.

Question 85

A man died and was survived by his ex-wife. The man's will left all of his assets to his housekeeper. The man was a citizen of State A, while his ex-wife was a citizen of State B. The housekeeper was a Canadian citizen in the United States on a work visa. The man's estate consisted of two apartment buildings, each of which was worth $1 million dollars. The man's ex-wife sued the man's estate in federal court, arguing that the will should be invalidated.

Does the federal court have jurisdiction over the suit?

(A) Yes, because the ex-wife is a citizen of State B.

(B) Yes, because the housekeeper is a foreign citizen.

(C) No, because the ex-wife is trying to invalidate a will.

(D) No, because the man's assets are only real property.

Question 86

A man was fired from his job as the Chief Marketing Officer for a private security corporation, and he filed a federal employment discrimination suit against the corporation and its CEO individually, arguing that he had been improperly fired due to his religious views. The man served 25 interrogatories on the corporation and the CEO, all to be completed and returned within 30 days. The defendants have raised a number of objections to the interrogatories.

Which of the following objections to the interrogatories is a court most likely to find valid?

(A) The man has exceeded the number of interrogatories allowed as a matter of right.

(B) Interrogatories cannot be directed to corporate entities, and instead must be directed to a specific representative of that entity.

(C) One of the interrogatories directed towards the CEO has asked him to disclose whether he has ever used illegal recreational drugs, and is thus irrelevant.

(D) The man has not given the defendants sufficient time to complete the interrogatories.

Question 87

A State A man filed suit in federal court against a corporation incorporated and based in State B. While the action was pending, the man died. A special administrator was substituted for the man in the action. The special administrator was a citizen of State B. Because of this change, the federal court dismissed the suit for lack of diversity.

Was the federal court's ruling correct?

(A) Yes, because the citizenship of the named plaintiff has changed.

(B) Yes, because there would have been no diversity had the special administrator initially filed the suit.

(C) No, because the deceased was a citizen of State A.

(D) No, because the deceased initially filed the suit.

Question 88

After losing her suit in federal court against a company for violation of her patent, a woman sued her attorney for legal malpractice. She claimed that the attorney had failed to raise several valid patent infringement claims on her behalf.

May the woman's claim be heard in federal court?

(A) Yes, because the original claim was in federal court.

(B) Yes, because it will be necessary to determine federal law in regard to the infringement claims.

(C) No, because a malpractice claim is not a federal claim.

(D) No, because the court will only be looking at the possible effect of raising the claims in the first suit.

Question 89

A wife and her husband in State A were both writers. The husband fell in love with another woman in State B, and divorced the wife and moved to State B. A year later, the husband learned that the wife had just sold a novel to a publishing company which he believed was based on his writing ideas that she had improperly used. He filed suit against her in State B federal district court. The husband delivered the proper papers to a process server, but the process server failed to serve the wife. Months later, the husband called the wife only to find out that she had never heard of his lawsuit. The husband then sent her a written request for waiver of service of process, which met the requirements for such a waiver, and the wife immediately responded by waiving service. The wife then filed a motion to dismiss, arguing that she had no contacts with State B and thus the court did not have personal jurisdiction over her.

If the husband now argues that the wife may not assert the argument that the court does not have personal jurisdiction over her, will he prevail?

(A) No, because the husband was responsible for any insufficiency in the service of process.

(B) No, because the wife did not waive her objections to the court's jurisdiction.

(C) Yes, because the wife waived her objections to the court's jurisdiction.

(D) Yes, because waiver of service automatically subjects a party to a court's jurisdiction.

Question 90

A plaintiff filed a civil case in federal court and sought discovery of certain attorney-client communications on the basis of the crime-fraud exception to the privilege. The trial court entered an order denying the discovery but issued a written certification that the order involved a controlling issue of law about which a substantial ground for difference of opinion existed and that an immediate appeal might materially advance the termination of the litigation. The Court of Appeals declined to hear the appeal.

Did the Court of Appeals err when it declined to hear the appeal?

(A) Yes, because the trial court certified that its order involved a controlling issue of law about which a substantial ground for difference of opinion existed and that an immediate appeal might materially advance the termination of the litigation.

(B) Yes, because the order denying the discovery was immediately appealable as of right.

(C) No, because the order was not a final judgment.

(D) No, because the Court of Appeals had discretion to decline to hear the appeal.

Question 91

A man from State A took a one-day vacation to State B where he visited a casino. There, he placed several bets on sporting events. He quickly lost all his money, and then asked for, and received, a loan from the casino to place further bets. He lost all that money as well and immediately drove back to State A. He had never been in State B before that day and pledged never to return. Several months later the casino filed suit against him in State B court to recover payment on the loan paid to the man. The man argued, however, that the court did not have jurisdiction over him. State B has no long-arm statute.

What is the casino's best argument that the State B court has jurisdiction over the action?

(A) The court has *in personam* jurisdiction because it may exercise specific jurisdiction over the man.

(B) The court has *in personam* jurisdiction because the man has systematic and continuous contacts with State B.

(C) The court has *in personam* jurisdiction because the state has a substantial interest in regulating gambling.

(D) The court has *in rem* jurisdiction.

Question 92

A State A woman purchased a skin-care product over the internet from a distributor headquartered and incorporated in State B. She used the product in State A and developed a rare skin disease that she believed was attributable to a perceived defect in the product. She brought a state law tort claim against the company in a federal district court in State C, under the belief that the State C court would be more amenable to her claim and based on the fact that the company was subject to personal jurisdiction in State C.

If the company now brings a motion to have the case dismissed based on improper venue, how should the court rule?

(A) Allow the case to proceed in State C.

(B) Dismiss the case.

(C) Transfer the case to State A or State B.

(D) Either dismiss the case or transfer the case to State A or State B.

Question 93

A State A songwriter submitted several of her compositions to a website service that offered to host the material to television and film producers who were looking to purchase material for their programming. The songwriter was never contacted through the service, so she was surprised to see three of her songs on two different TV shows: the show "Cactus Dogs" had used two of her songs, and the show "Biltmore Days" had used one of her songs. She assessed her damages to be $30,000 per song, and sued the producers of Cactus Dogs as well as the producers of Biltmore Days as co-defendants in federal district based on her federal copyright claims against all of them.

If the co-defendant producers argue that the court does not have subject-matter jurisdiction, will they prevail?

(A) Yes, because the plaintiff must have at least one claim that meets the amount-in-controversy requirement.

(B) Yes, because the plaintiff's claims against the co-defendants are not common and undivided.

(C) No, because the plaintiff may aggregate her claims to meet the amount in controversy.

(D) No, because the plaintiff's claims arise under federal law.

Question 94

An athlete from State A was drafted out of high school to play for a professional sports team in his hometown and signed to a five-year contract. During that time he became both a local hero and a national celebrity. At the end of his contract, the athlete negotiated with another team in State B to play for them at triple the salary he was earning in State A. In a press conference, the athlete announced he was going to go play in State B and that he was very happy to be leaving State A. The citizens of State B were overjoyed, while the citizens of State A were heartbroken and angry. Soon, however, the owner of the State B team realized he did not have enough money to pay the athlete the agreed upon salary and sought to have the contract rescinded by filing suit in federal court against the athlete on the grounds that the athlete had violated the terms of the contract. The owner filed the action in State A federal district court, believing the court and jury would be more receptive to his arguments. Soon after the complaint was filed, the athlete moved to State B, partially on account of the fact that the vast majority of people in State A had come to despise him, and sought to transfer the case to federal district court in State B.

Can the athlete successfully transfer the case to State B federal district court?

(A) Yes, if he can show that the State B court is an adequate forum, and that the State A court was significantly inappropriate.

(B) Yes, because he is now a resident of State B.

(C) No, because he was a resident of State A at the time the action was filed.

(D) No, because the case was brought in a proper venue.

Question 95

A woman sued a man in federal court for negligent infliction of emotional distress. The man's attorney believed there were several problems with the complaint. However, he was unsure regarding what defenses would be lost if not raised in the initial response.

Which potential defense does not have to be raised in the initial response?

(A) Failure to state a claim.

(B) Lack of personal jurisdiction.

(C) Improper venue.

(D) Improper service of process.

Question 96

A plaintiff filed a case in federal court and sought a permanent injunction. Federal subject-matter jurisdiction existed. There was no statutory right to a jury trial. No party demanded a jury. At trial, the court ordered on its own motion that a jury would decide all issues. The defendant objected, but the court overruled the objection.

Did the court err when it ordered trial by jury over the objection of a party?

(A) Yes, because the jury was not merely advisory.

(B) Yes, because the plaintiff did not demand a jury.

(C) No, because the plaintiff had a constitutional right to trial by jury of the case.

(D) No, because the court had discretion to order a jury trial of all issues.

Question 97

A highly successful professional dancer lost her career when a manufacturing defect in her car caused an accident that left her unable to use her legs. She presented evidence that showed that her loss over a lifetime due to the accident would be approximately $2.7 million. A federal jury found in her favor, but awarded only $500,000 to compensate for the loss of income.

Which of the following motions would be the best option for the dancer to obtain the amount of damages she requested?

(A) A motion for a new trial on the damages issue.

(B) A motion for additur.

(C) A motion for remittitur.

(D) A motion for relief from a judgment or order.

Question 98

A waitress filed an employment discrimination suit against her employer in federal court. Her suit claimed that the employer had sexually harassed her and then fired her when she spurned his advances. The employer responded that he was justified in firing the waitress because she was trying to meet and pick up male customers. During discovery, the employer sought to discover detailed information about the waitress's sexual history, including the names of every person she had sex with in the past 10 years. The waitress refused to answer deposition questions related to this subject, and the employer brought a motion to compel. The court denied the motion to compel and granted the waitress's cross-motion for a protective order.

Was the court correct in granting the protective order?

(A) Yes, because of the unreasonable intrusion on the waitress's privacy.

(B) Yes, because information of this nature is never appropriate for discovery.

(C) No, because the information is evidence of habit.

(D) No, because the information is evidence of motive.

Question 99

A State A tourist met with a representative from a State C travel agency in State A to plan a trip to a resort in State B and signed a contract reserving her stay at the resort. The tourist was injured while on a ropes course at the resort. The tourist sued both the resort and the travel agency. The tourist filed the suit in federal district court in State C, asserting state law contract claims in diversity jurisdiction. The defendants successfully transferred the action to a federal district court in State B, where most of the witnesses and evidence were located. The State C choice of law rules required that the substantive law of the place where the incident giving rise to a plaintiff's injuries be applied, while the State B choice of law rules required that the substantive law of the state in which the contract was signed be applied.

What is the source of the substantive law that the court will apply?

(A) State A law.

(B) State B law.

(C) State C law.

(D) Federal common law.

Question 100

A State A toymaker developed a robot that responded to children's thoughts and took it from his home in the Eastern District of State A to a toy convention taking place in the Northern District of State A. There he showed it to two manufacturers, one from the Eastern District of State A, and one from the Western District of State B, the latter of which was headquartered and incorporated in State B, although it had a retail store in the Western District of State A. The two manufacturers colluded to steal the toymaker's designs and repurpose them for their own benefit.

If the toymaker now seeks to file a federal trademark claim against both manufacturers in federal court, in what venues can he file his claim?

(A) The Northern District of State A.

(B) The Eastern District of State A.

(C) The Northern and Eastern Districts of State A, and the Western District of State B.

(D) The Northern, Eastern, and Western Districts of State A, and the Western District of State B.

Answers and Explanations

Explanation: Question 1

The correct answer is: **(C)** No, because the defendant sought a legal remedy.

The constitutional right to a jury trial in federal court attaches to civil claims for damages, even when the claim is a counterclaim. This plaintiff may not eliminate the defendant's right to a jury for the damage claim merely by using the declaratory judgment statute to align himself as the plaintiff.

(A) Incorrect. Yes, because the plaintiff did not seek a legal remedy.

Even when plaintiffs do not seek legal remedies but instead seek merely declaratory judgments or even injunctions, a defendant will have a right to a jury on all issues that would be essential to a counterclaim for damages. The alignment of the parties does not determine whether the constitutional right to a jury attaches.

(B) Incorrect. Yes, because the constitutional right to a jury only extends to forms of action that, unlike declaratory judgments, existed at the time of the adoption of the Seventh Amendment.

The Seventh Amendment to the United States Constitution "preserves" the right to a jury trial, and that might lead some to conclude that it applies only to forms of action that existed at the time of its adoption. The Supreme Court of the United States, however, has taken a different view and has applied the right to a jury to damage claims that are counterclaims in cases where the plaintiff seeks declaratory and even injunctive relief. A court sitting in equity in 1791 would have decided all the issues without a jury, but now that law and equity are combined in federal court the defendant's right to a jury trial on the damage claim attaches even though it is brought as a counterclaim.

(D) Incorrect. No, because parties have a constitutional right to a jury in civil cases in federal court.

This answer is incorrect because it is overbroad. If the only claim in a federal civil case is a claim for equitable relief, then the constitutional right to a jury trial does not apply.

Explanation: Question 2

The correct answer is: **(A)** State B, because the corporation is controlled from there.

For federal diversity jurisdiction, courts look at the corporation's place of incorporation and principal place of business in determining a corporation's citizenship. The question does not include any information on incorporation, so it is only testing the concept of principal place of business. To determine a corporation's principal place of business, courts will look at its "nerve center." Importantly, courts will determine where the corporation's nerve center is by looking at where decisions concerning the control and direction of the corporation are made [Hertz Corp. v. Friend, 130 S.Ct. 1181 (2010)]. Here, the question states that those decisions are all made in State B.

(B) Incorrect. State B, because the board of directors and all of the top management are there.

For federal diversity jurisdiction, courts look at the corporation's place of incorporation and principal place of business in determining a corporation's citizenship. To determine a corporation's principal place of business, courts will look at its "nerve center." Importantly, courts will determine where the corporation's nerve center is by looking at where decisions concerning the control and direction of the corporation are made [Hertz Corp. v. Friend, 130 S.Ct. 1181 (2010)]. While one could perhaps correctly assume that corporate decisions are made where the board of directors and all of the top management are, the correct answer choice explicitly states that the corporation is controlled from there. Since this statement makes an assumption about the corporation unnecessary, it is a better answer choice.

(C) Incorrect. Any of the states in which it operates, as it likely has sufficient minimum contacts to face suit there.

Corporate citizenship is determined by principal place of business and place of incorporation. Importantly, determining whether there is diversity jurisdiction relates to the question of whether a court has subject-matter jurisdiction over a case. "Minimum contacts" relates to questions regarding personal jurisdiction.

(D) Incorrect. State A, because the majority of its business is located in State A.

While the majority of its business activities may be in State A, a corporation's principal place of business is determined by looking at a corporation's "nerve center," specifically the place where decisions concerning the corporation are made.

Explanation: Question 3

The correct answer is: **(C)** No, because some of the union members were from State Y.

In determining the citizenship of an unincorporated association, courts look at the citizenship of all of the association's members. Here, since some of the members are State Y citizens, there is no diversity of citizenship here to confer jurisdiction on the federal court.

(A) Incorrect. Yes, because the union's principal place of business is in State Z.

Although the union's principal place of business is in State Z, the citizenship of an unincorporated association is the citizenship of all of its members. This answer choice is presenting one of the possible places of citizenship for an incorporated association, like a corporation.

(B) Incorrect. Yes, because the citizenships of the board of directors made State Z its "nerve center."

Although all of the board members are State Z citizens, the citizenship of an unincorporated association is the citizenship of all of its members. This answer choice is presenting one of the possible places of citizenship for an incorporated association, like a corporation. Importantly, courts will often use the "nerve center" test in determining where a corporation's principal place of business is.

(D) Incorrect. No, because defamation is not a federal claim recognized by Congress.

Through diversity jurisdiction, courts can hear claims other than those specifically provided for in federal law.

Explanation: Question 4

The correct answer is: **(C)** File a motion for dismissal.

A court will dismiss a complaint under Rule 12(b)(6) in the following circumstances: (1) the complaint fails to state a cognizable claim; (2) the complaint provides insufficient facts; or (3) the complaint contains an allegation that negates one or more elements of the cause of action. Here, the man is suing the woman for "encroaching on his historically recognized business territory," which is not a legal claim.

(A) Incorrect. File a motion for summary judgment.

For summary judgment, the court looks beyond the pleadings to the actual facts of the case. Here, the main problem is that the man's complaint does not actually state a legal claim, so looking at the facts beyond the complaint is unnecessary.

(B) Incorrect. File a counterclaim regarding the man's signs and prank calls.

While the woman may have claims regarding the signs and prank calls, this is not the most effective way to deal with the man's complaint.

(D) Incorrect. File a motion for judgment as a matter of law.

After the plaintiff closes his or her case, the defendant may move for judgment as a matter of law. If granted, the motion results in judgment for the defendant. Here, it would be much better for the woman to end the case at the pleading stage, rather than go through an entire trial.

Explanation: Question 5

The correct answer is: **(C)** No, because the deletions appeared to be routine.

When electronic information is destroyed or deleted, sanctions may not be imposed if the destruction or deletion is a "routine, good faith operation of an electronic information system" [Fed. R. Civ. P. 37]. Here, although the last deletion took place three days before the man filed his claim, and although there were many complaints regarding the device, there was no indication that this was anything more than a routine, "automatic" deletion or that this was somehow done in expectation of litigation. Consequently, sanctions such as requiring the corporation to pay the data recovery experts are likely inappropriate.

(A) Incorrect. Yes, because sanctions for the email deletion are appropriate.

When electronic information is destroyed or deleted, sanctions may not be imposed if the destruction or deletion is a "routine, good faith operation of an electronic information system" [Fed. R. Civ. P. 37]. Here, although the last deletion took place three days before the man filed his claim, and although there were many complaints regarding the device, there was no indication that this was anything more than a routine, "automatic" deletion or that this was somehow done in expectation of litigation. Consequently, sanctions such as requiring the corporation to pay the data recovery experts are likely inappropriate.

(B) Incorrect. Yes, because the corporation controls the relevant storage devices.

Although the corporation controls the relevant storage devices, forcing it to pay the data recovery experts would clearly be a sanction. Importantly, when electronic information is destroyed or deleted, sanctions may not be imposed if the destruction or deletion is a "routine, good faith operation of an electronic information system" [Fed. R. Civ. P. 37]. Here, it appeared that the deletion met this requirement as there is no indication of a lack of routine or good faith.

(D) Incorrect. No, because the emails are not reasonably accessible.

While the emails accessibility may or may not be reasonable, the important question is whether it is appropriate to sanction the corporation by making it pay for the data recovery experts. When electronic information is destroyed or deleted, sanctions may not be imposed if the destruction or deletion is a "routine, good faith operation of an electronic information system" [Fed. R. Civ. P. 37]. Here, although the last deletion took place three days before the man filed his claim, and although there were many complaints regarding the device, there was no indication that this was anything more than a routine, "automatic" deletion or that this was somehow done in expectation of litigation.

Explanation: Question 6

The correct answer is: **(C)** No, because more than one year has passed since entry of judgment.

Federal Rule of Civil Procedure 60(b) permits the trial court to grant relief from a final judgment under certain circumstances. Those circumstances include what happened here, because the defendant perpetrated a fraud and committed misconduct. However, a plaintiff who seeks relief on that basis, which appears in Rule 60(b)(3), must make the motion within one year of the entry of judgment. Here, eighteen months have passed.

(A) Incorrect. Yes, because the plaintiff has discovered new evidence.

The discovery of new evidence is not sufficient to obtain relief from a judgment. New evidence is a basis for relief from judgment only if the plaintiff shows that he could not have discovered the evidence through the exercise of reasonable diligence in time to make a motion for new trial and seeks relief from the judgment within one year.

(B) Incorrect. Yes, because the defendant perpetrated a fraud.

This defendant did perpetrate a fraud, and fraud is a basis under Federal Rule of Civil Procedure 60(b) for a motion for relief from judgment. However, such a motion must be made within one year of the entry of judgment, and here more than a year has passed.

(D) Incorrect. No, because more than 28 days has passed since entry of judgment.

The motion for relief from judgment is late, but not because the plaintiff only had 28 days from the entry of judgment to file it. A motion like this one, which concerns fraud and misconduct by the defendant, must be filed within one year of the entry of judgment. The time limit for a motion for new trial, on any basis, is 28 days, but the motion for relief from judgment on this basis has the more lenient, one-year deadline.

Explanation: Question 7

The correct answer is: **(C)** No, because the cost of the injunction to the hospital is sufficient to meet the amount-in-controversy requirement.

If a suit seeks an injunction, the amount in controversy can be met by either the injunction's worth to the plaintiff, or the cost of the injunction to the defendant. Here, although the cost of the injunction is worth only $50,000 to the doctor, it will cost the hospital $600,000 as it is seeking to impose the fee on 12 different doctors. Therefore, the cost to the defendant will meet the amount-in-controversy requirement.

(A) Incorrect. Yes, because the doctor can be considered a citizen of State B.

Citizenship for purposes of diversity jurisdiction is based on where a party resides and intends to remain permanently. Here, the doctor lives in State A, and the fact that he sometimes travels to State B does not make him a citizen of State B.

(B) Incorrect. Yes, because the cost of the injunction to the doctor is not sufficient to meet the amount-in-controversy requirement.

As stated above, where a suit seeks an injunction, the amount in controversy can be met by either the injunction's worth to the plaintiff, or the cost of the injunction to the defendant. Here, the cost of the injunction to the hospital is $600,000.

(D) Incorrect. No, because the amount-in-controversy requirement may be met by aggregating the claims of all plaintiffs.

This is an incorrect statement of law. The amount-in-controversy requirement may not be met by aggregating the claims of multiple plaintiffs. Furthermore, there is only one plaintiff in this action.

Explanation: Question 8

The correct answer is: **(D)** No, because only defendants can remove to federal court.

An action brought in state court may be removed by the defendant to federal court if the case originally could have been brought by the plaintiff in federal court [28 U.S.C. § 1441]. Here, the issue is that the plaintiff is trying to remove the case to federal court, and plaintiffs cannot do so.

(A) Incorrect. Yes, because the counterclaim is a federal question.

While the counterclaim is a federal question, the issue is that a plaintiff cannot ask for removal to federal court.

(B) Incorrect. Yes, because the amount in controversy exceeds $75,000.

While the amount in controversy is over the threshold for diversity jurisdiction, the major issue is that the plaintiff is making the motion for removal.

(C) Incorrect. No, because there is not diversity of citizenship between the parties.

While there is not diversity of citizenship between the parties, the bigger issue is that the man, the plaintiff, is trying to have the action removed to federal court. As plaintiff, he cannot do so.

Explanation: Question 9

The correct answer is: **(C)** No, because diversity is determined at the time the action is filed.

For a federal court to exercise subject-matter jurisdiction, there must be complete diversity between the plaintiffs and the defendants, and the amount in controversy must be over $75,000. Diversity is determined at the time the action is filed. When this action was filed, the tourist was a citizen of State A, the amusement park was considered a citizen of State B, and the tour guide was a citizen of his home country. The fact that the tourist later moved to State B does not destroy diversity.

(A) Incorrect. Yes, because there is no longer complete diversity among the parties.

While the tourist did move to State B and so would be considered to be a citizen of State B going forward, diversity is determined at the time the action is filed. Because the tourist was still residing in State A when the action was filed, there will be complete diversity among the parties.

(B) Incorrect. Yes, because an alien may not be a defendant in a diversity jurisdiction action.
This is an incorrect statement of law. An alien may be a defendant in a diversity jurisdiction. In this situation, the tour guide will be considered a citizen of his home country, because he plans to move back.

(D) Incorrect. No, because the amusement park is a citizen of the state in which the district court is located.
The fact that a defendant is a citizen of the state in which the federal district court is located is irrelevant to determining whether the court has subject-matter jurisdiction.

Explanation: Question 10

The correct answer is: **(A)** No, because he was served while physically present in State B.

A state has personal jurisdiction over a party when that person is served while physically present in the state, even if the person is only there temporarily. This does not apply when the plaintiff has fraudulently enticed the party to enter the state. While the lottery company may have committed fraud which caused the man to come to State B, the wife played no part in this fraud and therefore there is personal jurisdiction over the man.

(B) Incorrect. No, because he consented to personal jurisdiction in State B.
While it could be said that physical presence in a state is indirectly a consent to jurisdiction, consent in this context generally refers to an express consent by a defendant to submit to personal jurisdiction, and here the above answer choice more accurately states why State B has personal jurisdiction over the man.

(C) Incorrect. Yes, because his presence in State B was procured by fraud.
As stated above, while the lottery company may have committed fraud which caused the man to come to State B, the wife played no part in this fraud and therefore there is personal jurisdiction over the man.

(D) Incorrect. Yes, because he did not have minimum contacts with State B.
Minimum contacts with a state comes into play when personal jurisdiction over a party is based on a long-arm statute, but here personal jurisdiction was based on the man being physically present in the state.

Explanation: Question 11

The correct answer is: **(B)** Yes, because the first dismissal acts as an adjudication upon the merits.

A dismissal for discovery misconduct is an involuntary dismissal. Under Federal Rule of Civil Procedure 41(b), all involuntary dismissals except dismissals for lack of jurisdiction, improper venue, or failure to join a party under Rule 19 act as adjudications upon the merits unless the court says otherwise. An "adjudication upon the merits" does not mean that the court has actually considered the merits. Instead, it simply means that *res judicata* will bar the case from being brought again. Therefore, this answer is correct.

(A) Incorrect. Yes, because Plaintiff alleged the same facts in the two suits.

Some dismissals are without prejudice, which means that the Plaintiff could bring them again even if they alleged the same facts. For example, dismissals for lack of jurisdiction, lack of venue, or failure to join a party under Rule 19 are without prejudice unless the court directs otherwise. Therefore, this answer is incorrect.

(C) Incorrect. No, because the allegations in the first case were not actually litigated or actually decided in the first action.

These are the requirements for collateral estoppel rather than for *res judicata*. The questions for purposes of *res judicata* are whether the plaintiff is trying to bring the same claim (clearly so) against the same defendant (also true) and if so whether that claim has been disposed of "on the merits" in a final judgment. Whether any issue has been "actually litigated" and "actually decided" are not relevant. Therefore, this answer is incorrect.

(D) Incorrect. No, because the court in the first action never reached the merits of Plaintiff's claims.

Under Federal Rule of Civil Procedure 41(b), this claim has been dismissed in a way that acts as an adjudication upon the merits, regardless of whether the court ever considered the underlying merits of the claims. "Adjudication upon the merits" does not require that anyone actually consider the merits. It simply means that *res judicata* will bar the claims in the future. Therefore, this answer is incorrect.

Explanation: Question 12

The correct answer is: **(B)** Yes, because the court is entering judgment on partial findings.

The court allowed the plaintiff to be fully heard and then decided that the plaintiff had not sustained her burden on an issue that the plaintiff had to prove in order to win. The court is empowered at that point, under Federal Rule of Civil Procedure 52(c), to enter judgment for the defendant on partial findings. However, the court is required to enter findings of fact and conclusions of law when it enters judgment on partial findings, just as it is required to do at the close of a complete bench trial.

(A) Incorrect. Yes, because the trial court must enter findings of fact and conclusions of law when it directs entry of a judgment other than a judgment on a jury verdict.

This answer is incorrect because it is overbroad. The court may enter judgments other than judgments on a jury verdict in more than one way. If the judgment is based upon partial findings in a bench trial, the court must enter findings of fact and conclusions of law under Federal Rule of Civil Procedure 52(c). If, however the court is entering judgment as a matter of law after a jury trial, under Rule 50, the court is not required to enter findings of fact and conclusions of law.

(C) Incorrect. No, because findings of fact and conclusions of law are not required when a court dismisses a plaintiff's claim.

This statement is true, but the court is not "dismissing" the plaintiff's claim. Under Rule 52(a)(3), the court need not enter findings of fact and conclusions of law when it dismisses a case under Rule 12, such as when the plaintiff has failed to state a claim upon which relief can be granted. Here, however, the court is not granting a motion to dismiss but instead is entering a judgment on partial findings. In that circumstance, Rule 52(c) requires the court to enter findings of fact and conclusions of law.

(D) Incorrect. No, because findings of fact and conclusions of law are not required when a court determines that one party is entitled to judgment as a matter of law.

Judgments as a matter of law can be rendered in more than one way. A summary judgment, for example, is a judgment as a matter of law, and under Rule 52(a)(3) no findings of fact and conclusions of law are necessary when the court grants summary judgment. Similarly, no such findings or conclusions are required when the court renders judgment as a matter of law during or after a jury trial. However, when one party's entitlement to win emerges as a result of partial findings during a bench trial, Rule 52(c) requires findings of fact and conclusions of law. A judgment on partial findings is, in effect, a judgment as a matter of law.

Explanation: Question 13

The correct answer is: **(A)** Order a new trial.

Pursuant to Fed. R. Civ. P. 48(c), where a poll of the jury reveals a lack of unanimity or lack of assent by the number of jurors that the parties stipulated to, the court may direct the jury to deliberate further or order a new trial. Here, the parties stipulated to a verdict assented to by 10 jurors, but only eight have assented thus far. Therefore, the court may order a new trial.

(B) Incorrect. Direct the jury to deliberate further until unanimity is reached.

While the court may direct the jury to deliberate further, it would not be appropriate to require the jury to do so until it reaches unanimity, as the parties have stipulated to a verdict assented to by only 10 jurors, and the court will honor that stipulation.

(C) Incorrect. Dismiss the action with prejudice.

As stated above, the court's options here are to either direct the jury to deliberate further or order a new trial. Dismissing the action with prejudice is not an option available to the court.

(D) Incorrect. Approve the jury's verdict.

As stated above, the court's options here are to either direct the jury to deliberate further or order a new trial. Approving the jury's verdict when only eight members of the jury have assented to the verdict is not an option available to the court.

Explanation: Question 14

The correct answer is: **(C)** Deny the motion to remand the whistleblower claim but grant the motion to remand the contract claim.

The whistleblower claim presents a federal question so the federal court will have jurisdiction over it, but the contract claim is a state law question and there is no diversity among the parties. The court cannot exercise supplemental jurisdiction over the contract claim, because childcare and school expenses promised in her contract do not arise out of the same transaction or occurrence as the whistleblower claim.

(A) Incorrect. Grant the motion to remand both claims to state court.

While the contract claim will be remanded to state court, the whistleblower claim arises under federal law, and thus the court will have jurisdiction based on a federal question.

(B) Incorrect. Deny the motion to remand both claims to state court.

While the federal court cannot exercise subject-matter jurisdiction over the state contract claim, it can sever the claim from the whistleblower claim, which presents a federal question, and hear the whistleblower claim while remanding the contract claim to state court.

(D) Incorrect. Deny the motion to remand the contract claim but grant the motion to remand the whistleblower claim.

This answer choice reverses the actions the court will take. As stated above, the federal court cannot exercise subject-matter jurisdiction over the state contract claim, but it can sever the claim from the whistleblower claim, which presents a federal question, and hear the whistleblower claim while remanding the contract claim to state court.

Explanation: Question 15

The correct answer is: **(A)** Yes, because the only judgment a court could direct to be entered would be one consistent with the answers to written questions.

Federal Rule of Civil Procedure 49(b)(3) governs this situation. The court has three options. The court may direct entry of a judgment that is consistent with the answers to the written questions, notwithstanding the general verdict. The court may order the jury to give further consideration to its answers and its verdict. The court may order a new trial. The court does not have the option to direct entry of a judgment that is consistent with the general verdict but inconsistent with the answers to the written questions.

(B) Incorrect. Yes, because the trial court may only order a new trial under these circumstances.

Ordering a new trial is one of three options that the court may take under these circumstances. The others are to direct entry of a judgment that is consistent with the answers to the written questions or to direct the jury to give further consideration to its answers and its verdict.

(C) Incorrect. No, because the trial court may order entry of a judgment that is consistent with either the answers to the written questions or the general verdict.

The court does have the option to direct entry of a judgment that is consistent with the answers to the written questions but does not have the option to do what it did here, direct entry of a judgment that is consistent with the general verdict.

(D) Incorrect. No, because the only judgment a court could direct to be entered would be one consistent with the general verdict.

The court may not direct entry of a judgment that is consistent with the general verdict. If the court chooses to direct entry of judgment, it must be a judgment that is consistent with the answers to the written questions.

Explanation: Question 16

The correct answer is: **(A)** Yes, because the defendant was required to support the assertion that there was no genuine issue of material fact as to causation by citing to particular parts of materials in the record.

Federal Rule of Civil Procedure 56 sets forth the procedures for summary judgment. A defendant who does not have the burden of proof on an issue at trial may not simply "call" and place upon the opposing party the burden to come forward with evidence on the issue. Rather, under Rule 56(c)(1), the party cites the court to particular parts of the materials in the record to demonstrate that there is an absence of evidence to support the proposition.

(B) Incorrect. Yes, because the defendant had the burden at summary judgment to prove that it did not cause the injury.

A defendant in this situation could prevail at summary judgment by proving that one of the facts the plaintiff must prove is untrue, but the rules do not require defendants to meet such a high burden. Instead, a defendant may demonstrate that the plaintiff who will have the burden of proof at trial will not be able to prove a particular crucial fact. The defendant does that by citing the court to particular parts of materials in the record as if to say to the court that this is where the evidence the plaintiff will need should be, and yet it is not there. The defendant may win, in other words, without proving the negative but instead by demonstrating in the record that the plaintiff will not be able to prove the positive.

(C) Incorrect. No, because the plaintiff had the burden to demonstrate that there was a genuine issue of material fact as to causation by citing to particular parts of materials in the record.

The movant here the defendant had a burden to discharge before this burden would be placed on the defendant. The defendant may not simply "call" and require the plaintiff to come forward with evidence that shows the existence of a genuine issue of material fact. The plaintiff only would have had the burden if the defendant had first made a showing from particular parts of materials in the record that there was an absence of such evidence. The defendant in this case did not do so.

(D) Incorrect. No, because the plaintiff would have had the burden of proof at trial.

This question is about the burden at summary judgment rather than the burden at trial. The plaintiff at trial will have the burden to prove causation, but at summary judgment the defendant had the burden at least to come forward and show an absence of evidence to prove the proposition that the plaintiff must prove at trial. The defendant did not discharge that burden in this case.

Explanation: Question 17

The correct answer is: **(C)** Yes, because the man has objected to evidence not being within the scope of the pleadings.

Pursuant to Fed. R. Civ. P. 15(b), a court may allow a party to amend its pleadings when the other party objects to evidence as not having been within the scope of the pleadings. Therefore, because the man made the objection, the court is free to allow the retailer to amend its pleadings.

(A) Incorrect. No, unless the amended answer can be filed within 21 days of the original answer.

A pleading may be amended as a matter of right within 21 days of the filing of the original pleading, but this is not the only scenario in which a party may amend its pleadings. Here, the court may allow the retailer to do so because the man has objected to evidence as not being within the scope of the pleadings.

(B) Incorrect. No, because trial has commenced.

As stated above, a court may allow a party to amend its pleadings when the other party objects to evidence as not having been within the scope of the pleadings.

(D) Incorrect. Yes, if the court grants a continuation.

The court may grant a continuation so that the other party may meet the evidence, but the court is not required to do so as a condition of permitting a party to amend its pleadings.

Explanation: Question 18

The correct answer is: **(A)** Yes, because the woman's claim is based on federal law.

Federal district courts have original jurisdiction over all civil actions "arising under the Constitution, laws, and treaties of the United States" [28 U.S.C. § 1331]. For a case to arise under federal question jurisdiction, the federal question must appear on a fair reading of a well-pleaded complaint. Here, the woman's claim is clearly based on federal law. The fact that the employer is defending itself by claiming the federal law does not apply to her because she is an intern does not affect the analysis.

(B) Incorrect. Yes, because the employer's primary place of business is in State C.

For citizenship purposes in determining a diversity jurisdiction, corporations are citizens of the place they are incorporated and their "nerve center" specifically where corporate decision-making takes place. Although all of its other operations are in State C, its nerve center is in State B, making the employer a citizen of State A and State B.

(C) Incorrect. No, because the Act does not apply to the woman since she is an intern.

Federal district courts have original jurisdiction over all civil actions "arising under the Constitution, laws, and treaties of the United States" [28 U.S.C. § 1331]. For a case to arise under federal question jurisdiction, the federal question must appear on a fair reading of a well-pleaded complaint. Here, the woman's complaint is clearly based on federal law. There may ultimately be a question regarding the federal law's application, but this does not defeat the federal court's jurisdiction over this federal question.

(D) Incorrect. No, because the employer's nerve center is in State B.

For citizenship purposes in determining a diversity jurisdiction, corporations are citizens of the place they are incorporated and their "nerve center"—specifically, where corporate decision-making takes place. While it is true the corporation is a citizen of State B based on its nerve center, and that the woman is a citizen of State B, these facts are ultimately irrelevant because a federal court would have jurisdiction over the matter based on a federal question.

Explanation: Question 19

The correct answer is: **(A)** Yes, because a summary judgment is a judgment rendered as a matter of law.

Under Federal Rule of Civil Procedure 56(a), the trial court may grant summary judgment only if the movant demonstrates that there are no genuine disputes as to any material fact and that the movant is entitled to judgment as a matter of law. The trial court engages in no assessments of credibility. The Court of Appeals does not defer to the trial court on questions of law, and thus the Court of Appeals must apply a *de novo* standard to the appeal of a summary judgment.

(B) Incorrect. Yes, because this was an appeal from a decision rendered without a trial.

Not all decisions a trial court makes before a trial are reviewed *de novo.* For example, a party may appeal a pretrial decision about a discovery issue. Perhaps the trial court terminated a deposition because it was being conducted in such a manner as to oppress the deponent. The Court of Appeals will apply an "abuse of discretion" standard to such decisions and will be much more deferential to the trial court, whose immersion in the context of the case makes it much easier to rule correctly on such matters.

(C) Incorrect. No, because the trial court reviewed affidavits, depositions and other summary judgment evidence, and therefore the Court of Appeals should have applied a "clearly erroneous" standard.

The trial court's review of the summary judgment evidence was not to make any credibility determinations to which the Court of Appeals should defer. Rather, the review of that evidence was to determine whether the movant was entitled to judgment as a matter of law on that record. Given that the Court of Appeals can review that record and make the decision whether the movant is entitled to judgment as a matter of law just as easily as the trial court can, the Court of Appeals will apply a *de novo* standard rather than the more deferential "clearly erroneous" standard.

(D) Incorrect. No, because the trial court reviewed affidavits, depositions and other summary judgment evidence, and therefore the Court of Appeals should have applied an "abuse of discretion" standard.

"Abuse of discretion" is a highly deferential standard of review, and there is no need for such deference under these circumstances. The trial court has granted summary judgment, which must mean that the trial judge believes that no reasonable jury will be able to find for the plaintiff that the defendant was entitled and at trial would have been entitled to judgment as a matter of law. That is a question of law, not fact, and the Court of Appeals will not defer to the trial court on questions of law. The proper standard is "*de novo*" review.

Explanation: Question 20

The correct answer is: **(A)** Yes, because the woman is from State C.

To hear a claim, a court must have both personal and subject-matter jurisdiction. A state court has personal jurisdiction over its citizens. Assuming the State C state court has broad subject-matter jurisdiction over battery cases, it would not make a difference that the battery took place in State B as opposed to State C. As explained below, the other three answers clearly make misstatements of the law, making this assumption reasonable and the best answer.

(B) Incorrect. No, because federal courts have exclusive jurisdiction over federal civil rights cases.

Federal courts do not have exclusive jurisdiction over civil rights cases. Importantly, Congress has allowed state courts to hear federal civil rights cases, and the mere presence of a federal issue in a state claim is generally not sufficient to impose federal jurisdiction.

(C) Incorrect. No, because the man is not domiciled in State C.

Although the man is not domiciled in State C, the primary question is where the woman is domiciled since she is the defendant of this suit. Consequently, the fact the man is not domiciled in State C is irrelevant.

(D) Incorrect. No, because a federal court would have jurisdiction through diversity.

The fact that a federal court would have diversity jurisdiction does not affect the ability of the plaintiff to have the claim heard in state court, if he chooses to file the claim there.

Explanation: Question 21

The correct answer is: **(D)** Yes, the court may review his petition.

The man has met all the requirements for a valid petition. A prisoner may submit a petition based on alleged violations of the Eighth Amendment where there is not clearly established law contrary to his petition. Furthermore, he exhausted his state remedies and filed the petition in a timely manner.

(A) Incorrect. No, because he is not contesting his innocence.

A *habeas corpus* petition may not be submitted to show actual innocence, but rather to argue that a prisoner's imprisonment is in violation of his constitutional rights, which is what the man's petition validly does here.

(B) Incorrect. No, because he failed to file his appeal within 90 days of his final judgment of custody.

This implies an incorrect statement of law. A prisoner has a year from his final judgment of custody to file a petition.

(C) Incorrect. No, because a *habeas corpus* petition may only be based on alleged violations of the Fifth or Fourteenth Amendments.

This is an incorrect statement of law. A prisoner may also submit a *habeas corpus* petition arguing that his punishment is cruel and unusual in violation of the Eighth Amendment.

Explanation: Question 22

The correct answer is: **(A)** Yes, because the man is a State A citizen.

Under Section 1332(a)(2), district courts have subject-matter jurisdiction over disputes between citizens of a State and citizens or subjects of a foreign state, so long as the amount-in-controversy requirement is satisfied. Importantly, the amount stated by the pleader will ordinarily be accepted, unless there is a legal certainty that the claim is really for less than $75,000. Here, the amount in controversy could meet the requirement, and the corporation has pleaded the required amount. Importantly, the man's State A citizenship is what gives a United States federal court jurisdiction over this matter (i.e., two foreign nationals could not sue each other in a United States court).

(B) Incorrect. Yes, because the corporation is a Swiss citizen.

Under Section 1332(a)(2), district courts have subject-matter jurisdiction over disputes between citizens of a State and citizens or subjects of a foreign state, so long as the amount-in-controversy requirement is satisfied. The important thing to note about this answer choice is that it provides no actual connection to a United States court. Without a U.S. citizen involved, a federal court would not have jurisdiction.

(C) Incorrect. No, because the claim may be worth less than $75,000.

Under Section 1332(a)(2), district courts have subject-matter jurisdiction over disputes between citizens of a State and citizens or subjects of a foreign state, so long as the amount-in-controversy requirement is satisfied. Importantly, the amount stated by the pleader will ordinarily be accepted, unless there is a legal certainty that the claim is really for less than $75,000. Here, the amount in controversy could meet the requirement, and the corporation has pleaded the required amount.

(D) Incorrect. No, because the corporation is a Swiss citizen.

Under Section 1332(a)(2), district courts have subject-matter jurisdiction over disputes between citizens of a State and citizens or subjects of a foreign state, so long as the amount-in-controversy requirement is satisfied. Here, the fact that the corporation is a Swiss citizen would not defeat federal jurisdiction.

Explanation: Question 23

The correct answer is: **(A)** More definite statement.

A motion for a more definite statement is meant to give the defendant a clear statement of the claim so the defendant can adequately respond. Importantly, the defendant must make this motion before filing a responsive pleading [Fed. R. Civ. P. 12]. This makes sense, because if an opposing party could understand the claim enough to file a responsive pleading, there would be no reason to request a more definite statement.

(B) Incorrect. Improper service.

A defendant may object to service of process in a motion to dismiss [Fed. R. Civ. P. 12(b)]. If a plaintiff fails to properly effect service according to the federal rules, the case should be dismissed. If this defense is not raised in the initial response, it is lost. Since the man's answer will be his initial response, he can raise it now.

(C) Incorrect. Improper venue.

Venue is the federal court in which an action is filed. Venue in federal cases is primarily based on the type of subject-matter jurisdiction. If this defense is not raised in the initial response, it is lost. Since the man's answer will be his initial response, he can raise it now.

(D) Incorrect. Failure to state a claim.

A court will dismiss a claim under Rule 12(b)(6) if the complaint fails to state a cognizable claim. This defense is not lost if not made in the initial response. Important to this question, however, is that there is no rule stating it cannot be included in the initial response or answer.

Explanation: Question 24

The correct answer is: **(A)** Certify in writing the efforts made to give notice.

A court may issue a temporary restraining order without written or oral notice to the adverse party [Fed. R. Civ. P. 65(b)(1)]. However, temporary restraining orders will issue without notice only if: (1) specific facts in an affidavit or verified complaint clearly show that immediate and irreparable injury, loss, or damage will result to the movant before the adverse party can be heard in opposition; and (2) the movant's attorney certifies in writing any efforts made to give notice and the reasons why notice should not be required. Here, since money is still leaving the account, it seems the producer can show immediate and irreparable injury. Thus, out of the four answer choices, the best move is to go for the temporary restraining order, and it seems the attorney will be able to get the order she is seeking as long as she certifies in writing her attempts to give notice and the reasons why notice should not be required.

(B) Incorrect. Request a hearing in order to explain the efforts made to give notice.

A court may issue a temporary restraining order without written or oral notice to the adverse party [Fed. R. Civ. P. 65(b)(1)]. However, temporary restraining orders will issue without notice only if: (1) specific facts in an affidavit or verified complaint clearly show that immediate and irreparable injury, loss, or damage will result to the movant before the adverse party can be heard in opposition; and (2) the movant's attorney certifies in writing any efforts made to give notice and the reasons why notice should not be required. This answer choice incorrectly implies that the attorney's explanation may be done orally.

(C) Incorrect. Immediately move for a preliminary injunction.

A preliminary injunction may only be issued by a court on notice to the adverse party [Fed. R. Civ. P. 65(a)(1)]. Here, the facts of the situation seem to make such notice impossible.

(D) Incorrect. File a motion for a temporary restraining order with the State A attorney general.

A court may issue a temporary restraining order without written or oral notice to the adverse party [Fed. R. Civ. P. 65(b)(1)]. However, temporary restraining orders will issue without notice only if: (1) specific facts in an affidavit or verified complaint clearly show that immediate and irreparable injury, loss, or damage will result to the movant before the adverse party can be heard in opposition; and (2) the movant's attorney certifies in writing any efforts made to give notice and the reasons why notice should not be required. Filing a notice with a state attorney general would not be a way to avoid these requirements.

Explanation: Question 25

The correct answer is: **(A)** Yes, because the two claims arise from the same events and they both could have been brought in the first case.

Res judicata will bar any claims that arise from the events alleged in the first case if those claims were brought or could have been brought in the first case. Here, the state law claims could have been joined in the first case. By not including the state law claims, the plaintiff in effect "split" his claim and is subject to a *res judicata* defense in the second action.

(B) Incorrect. Yes, because the two claims arise from the same events.

This answer is incorrect because it is possible for claims to arise from the same events but for it not to be possible for the plaintiff to join them in the first case. For example, if the author had filed the state law claim first in state court, he would not have been able to join federal claims that were within the exclusive jurisdiction of the federal court. A second action raising those claims, in federal court, would not be barred by *res judicata* merely because the underlying facts are the same. The author would have never had the chance to litigate the federal claim.

(C) Incorrect. No, because the Federal Rules of Civil Procedure permit but do not require a plaintiff to join all claims he has against the defendant.

It is important to be careful about the permissive rules of joinder and other doctrines that affect the ability or necessity of joining claims. Here, it is true that Federal Rule of Civil Procedure 18 allows but does not require the plaintiff to join these claims in the first case. However, the entirely separate doctrine of *res judicata* in effect requires joinder of the claims on pain of losing the omitted one forever if the second claim could be brought in the federal case. Here, the state law claim could have been brought in the first case, and therefore joinder was required rather than permitted, if the author wished to have those state law claims adjudicated at all.

(D) Incorrect. No, because the two cases contain different causes of action.

The key is not the legal source of the claim or the theory of recovery. The key is that the two claims are arising from the same facts. The doctrine of *res judicata* forces plaintiffs to bring all theories of recovery about a particular set of facts in one case (when it is possible to do so), so that the parties and the system will have to deal with only one case rather than multiple cases. Parties may not "split" claims by bringing successive suits about the same facts, even if the theories of recovery or the sources of the remedies are different.

Explanation: Question 26

The correct answer is: **(A)** Yes, because the jury began with five members.

Under Federal Rule of Civil Procedure 48(a), a jury trial must begin with a minimum of six members. Under Rule 48(b), it is possible for the parties to stipulate that they will accept a verdict of fewer than six jurors, but the case cannot begin with fewer than six.

(B) Incorrect. Yes, because the jury began with fewer than 12 members.

Historically, juries consisted of 12 members. However, Rule 48(a) now provides that jury trials can begin with no more than 12 members and no fewer than six.

(C) Incorrect. No, because the parties stipulated to accept a verdict by a jury of five.

The parties' stipulation to accept a verdict from five jurors would have been effective under Rule 48(b), as long as the case had begun with at least six jurors, as required by Rule 48(a). Here, the trial began with just five jurors.

(D) Incorrect. No, because the verdict was supported by the evidence.

The fact that the evidence supported the verdict was enough to preclude the court from taking the case away from the jury and entering judgment for the plaintiff as a matter of law, notwithstanding the verdict. However, the problem was that the case should not have begun with fewer than six jurors. That was the minimum required by Rule 48(a).

Explanation: Question 27

The correct answer is: **(C)** No, because the man is a party to the lawsuit.

Service may be properly made by any person who is: (1) not a party to the suit and (2) over the age of 18 years old. Here, since the man is a party to the suit, he may not personally deliver the summons and complaint to the trucker.

(A) Incorrect. Yes, because the man gave the trucker a summons and copy of the complaint by hand.

Service may be properly made by any person who is: (1) not a party to the suit and (2) over the age of 18 years old. Here, since the man is a party to the suit, he may not personally deliver the summons and complaint to the trucker.

(B) Incorrect. Yes, because the plaintiff may serve process by any means reasonably calculated to apprize interested parties of the pendency of the action.

While hand delivery would certainly apprize an interested party of the pendency of the action, parties to the suit may not deliver service themselves.

(D) Incorrect. No, because there is no indication the summons was presented to the clerk for signature and seal.

After the plaintiff has filed a complaint, he or she may present a summons to the clerk for signature and seal. If the summons meets the format requirements, then the clerk will certify the summons and issue it to the plaintiff so that the plaintiff can serve the defendant. Here, the problem is that the man is serving the summons and complaint himself.

Explanation: Question 28

The correct answer is: **(C)** No, because the standard of proof is generally more modest in a civil case.

An acquittal is generally not likely to have preclusive effect in a civil case, as the standard of proof is generally more modest in a civil case. Therefore, the fact that the jury decided that the state was not able to prove beyond a reasonable doubt that the professor caused the student's death will not prevent her parents from bringing a civil case.

(A) Incorrect. Yes, because the wrongful death action is barred by claim preclusion.

Claim preclusion is not the relevant legal concept here, as the issue of whether the professor caused the student's death, and not a particular claim, is the topic in dispute.

(B) Incorrect. Yes, because the wrongful death action is barred by issue preclusion.

As stated above, an acquittal is generally not likely to have preclusive effect in a civil case, as the standard of proof is generally more modest in a civil case. Thus the parents may bring a wrongful death case despite the fact that the professor was acquitted of manslaughter.

(D) Incorrect. No, because the parents were not parties to the criminal case.

While a party who was not a party to the previous action may not be able to offensively use issue preclusion in many situations, the better answer here is that issue preclusion will not be allowed where the burden of proof in the previous action, which was a criminal case, was higher than in the present action, which is a civil case.

Explanation: Question 29

The correct answer is: **(B)** The lawyer may file a counterclaim for the fees in federal court, and if he does not he will waive the claim.

The lawyer's claim regarding fees arises out of the same transaction as the actor's claim of malpractice, which means it is a compulsory counterclaim. A compulsory counterclaim must be raised at trial or else it is waived in both the original action or in any other action.

(A) Incorrect. The lawyer cannot file a counterclaim for the fees in federal court.

Although the lawyer's claim for $30,000 in unpaid fees would not by itself meet the amount-in-controversy requirement for diversity jurisdiction, the court will have supplemental jurisdiction because it arises out of the same transaction or occurrence as the actor's claim alleging malpractice.

(C) Incorrect. The lawyer may file a counterclaim for the fees in federal court, but, if he does not, he will not waive the claim.

This is an incorrect answer because, as stated above, the lawyer's claim is a compulsory counterclaim and a compulsory counterclaim must be raised at trial or else it is waived in both the original action or in any other action.

(D) Incorrect. The lawyer must file a counterclaim for the fees in federal court.

This answer choice in not quite accurate because, while the lawyer will waive his claim by not raising it as a counterclaim, there is no requirement that he must raise the counterclaim.

Explanation: Question 30

The correct answer is: **(B)** A State A paralegal worked for a State A attorney, but was fired by the attorney after failing to complete a filing on time. The paralegal believed she was fired in violation of federal employment laws and filed suit against the attorney in federal court. The attorney told the paralegal he would waive service if and when she made a request. Several months later, she requested that he waive service.

A defendant has a duty to waive service if the defendant is: (a) located within the judicial district that is litigating the case; (b) located in a foreign country at the time of service; or (c) a corporation, partnership, or an association. This factual scenario does not fit within any of those categories. The fact that the attorney said he would waive service does not create a duty to waive service.

(A) Incorrect. A State A university fired an associate professor who then moved to State B permanently, but traveled to Africa to volunteer for a year in a refugee camp, where he is presently. The university believed the associate professor made defamatory remarks regarding the university and filed a defamation suit against the associate professor in State A federal court. The university requested that the associate professor waive service.

A defendant has a duty to waive service if the defendant is located in a foreign country at the time of service. Thus, because the associate professor was in Africa at the time of service, he has a duty to waive service.

(C) Incorrect. Two State A men formed a general partnership to provide landscaping services to corporate clients. A large State B corporation believed that the men improperly used one of its trademarks in their landscaping company logo and filed suit in State B federal court against the partnership and requested that the partnership waive service.

A defendant has a duty to waive service if the defendant is a partnership. Because the defendant here is a partnership, it has a duty to waive service.

(D) Incorrect. A husband moved from State A to State B, leaving his wife in State A. The wife filed suit for divorce against the husband in the only federal district court in State B. Although the wife was originally from State B and her entire family lived in State B, she requested that the husband waive service.

A defendant has a duty to waive service if the defendant is located within the judicial district that is litigating the case. Here, the action was in State B and the husband lives in the only district in State B, therefore he has a duty to waive service.

Explanation: Question 31

The correct answer is: **(D)** No, because peremptory challenges may not be exercised on the basis of race.

The Supreme Court of the United States has held that peremptory challenges may not be exercised on the basis of race or sex. Here, defense counsel apparently admitted that he used his peremptory challenges deliberately to remove potential jurors of a certain race from the jury. That was improper.

(A) Incorrect. Yes, because the case involved alleged race discrimination.

The fact that the case was about race discrimination is irrelevant to the question of whether the lawyer could exercise peremptory challenges on the basis of race. The rule against the use of race or sex in jury selection is about protection of the jurors' constitutional rights and has nothing to do with the particular subject matter of the litigation.

(B) Incorrect. Yes, because peremptory challenges may be exercised for any reason.

It was true historically that peremptory challenges could be exercised for any reason. The word "peremptory" means, "admitting of no contradiction." Nevertheless, the Supreme Court of the United States has held that there are limits on the exercise of peremptory challenges.

(C) Incorrect. No, because peremptory challenges are not permitted without an objectively reasonable basis.

The Supreme Court has placed only two limits on the exercise of peremptory challenges. They may not be exercised on the basis of race or sex. The Court has not, however, imposed a general rule that all peremptory challenges must have an objectively reasonable basis. If a lawyer can convince a court that there is a reason other than race or sex for the strikes that the lawyer has made even if those reasons are not objectively reasonable then the lawyer has done nothing wrong.

Explanation: Question 32

The correct answer is: **(D)** No, because the procedural error was harmless.

Motions for new trial may be based on weight of the evidence, excessiveness or inadequacy of the verdict or, as here, procedural error. However, not every procedural error gives rise to a right to a new trial. Federal Rule of Civil Procedure 61 provides that such errors are not grounds for a new trial unless justice requires it, when a party's substantial rights are affected. Here, the court made an error but quickly fixed the problem. Because the error made the trial merely imperfect, but not unfair, the error is not a basis for a new trial.

(A) Incorrect. Yes, because the court committed a procedural error.

The court did commit a procedural error, and sometimes procedural errors will lead to new trials. The error, however, must be one that affected the substantial rights of the parties and made the trial unfair. Here, the court quickly corrected itself and made sure that the jury properly understood the charge. The procedural error was harmless and therefore cannot be a basis for a new trial.

(B) Incorrect. Yes, because the defendant preserved a procedural error by a timely objection.

Most errors must be preserved or they are deemed to be waived. The purpose of that rule is to give the trial court the chance to correct any errors during the trial. Here, that rule operated as it was intended to operate. The defendant objected and the court immediately fixed the problem. By fixing the problem, the court rendered the error harmless and not a basis for a new trial.

(C) Incorrect. No, because the motion for new trial was filed too late.

Under Federal Rule of Civil Procedure 59(b), the defendant had 28 days from entry of judgment to file the motion for new trial. Here, the motion was filed after 22 days. The motion was therefore timely. The court must deny it because the error was harmless, not because the motion was filed too late.

Explanation: Question 33

The correct answer is: **(B)** Yes, because the first dismissal acts as an adjudication upon the merits.

A dismissal for discovery misconduct is an involuntary dismissal. Under Federal Rule of Civil Procedure 41(b), all involuntary dismissals except dismissals for lack of jurisdiction, improper venue, or failure to join a party under Rule 19 act as adjudications upon the merits unless the court says otherwise. An "adjudication upon the merits" does not mean that the court has actually considered the merits. Instead, it simply means that *res judicata* will bar the case from being brought again.

(A) Incorrect. Yes, because the engineer alleged the same facts in the two suits.

Some dismissals are without prejudice, which means that the engineer could bring them again even if they alleged the same facts. For example, dismissals for lack of jurisdiction, lack of venue, or failure to join a party under Rule 19 are without prejudice unless the court directs otherwise.

(C) Incorrect. No, because the allegations in the first case were not actually litigated or actually decided in the first action.

These are the requirements for collateral estoppel rather than for *res judicata*. The questions for purposes of *res judicata* are whether the plaintiff is trying to bring the same claim (clearly so) against the same defendant (also true) and if so whether that claim has been disposed of "on the merits" in a final judgment. Whether any issue has been "actually litigated" and "actually decided" are not relevant.

(D) Incorrect. No, because the court in the first action never reached the merits of the engineer's claims.

Under Federal Rule of Civil Procedure 41(b), this claim has been dismissed in a way that acts as an adjudication upon the merits, regardless of whether the court ever considered the underlying merits of the claims. "Adjudication upon the merits" does not require that anyone actually consider the merits. It simply means that *res judicata* will bar the claims in the future.

Explanation: Question 34

The correct answer is: **(A)** Yes, because all decisions on preliminary injunctions are immediately appealable.

The general rule is that only final judgments of the district courts are appealable, but 28 U.S.C. Section 1292(a) provides that certain interlocutory orders are immediately appealable. One set of such orders includes ones that grant, continue, modify, refuse or dissolve injunctions, and ones that refuse to dissolve or modify injunctions. Here, because the court has refused to grant a preliminary injunction, the order is immediately appealable.

(B) Incorrect. Yes, because the decision conclusively determined an important question that was completely separate from the merits and was effectively unreviewable on appeal.

This answer describes another set of circumstances under which an interlocutory order may be appealed immediately. This doctrine is the "collateral order" doctrine. That doctrine is unnecessary in this circumstance because the denial of the preliminary injunction is appealable under the statute, and furthermore a decision on a preliminary injunction is not "separate from the merits" as an order must be to qualify for the collateral order doctrine. One of the criteria for evaluating a request for a preliminary injunction is likelihood of success on the merits.

(C) Incorrect. No, because it was not a final judgment.

This situation is one of the exceptions to the general rule that only final judgments may be appealed. Here, because the court refused to issue a preliminary injunction, the order may be appealed even in the absence of a final judgment.

(D) Incorrect. No, because the injunction was denied.

Any order that grants, continues, modifies, refuses or dissolves an injunction, and ones that refuse to dissolve or modify injunctions, are immediately appealable. It is not just those that grant preliminary injunctions that are immediately appealable.

Explanation: Question 35

The correct answer is: **(C)** No, because the corporation notified the other party.

Because of the huge amount of documents that can be produced during electronic discovery, if a party inadvertently discloses privileged information, it can notify the party opponent, who must then destroy, return, or hold such inadvertently disclosed documents until a determination regarding privilege is made by the court [Fed. R. Civ. P. 26]. Consequently, since the corporation has informed the woman and her attorney, the attorney cannot go ahead and use the documents without a court ruling allowing her to do so.

(A) Incorrect. Yes, because the production took away any claim of privilege.

Because of the huge amount of documents that can be produced during electronic discovery, if a party inadvertently discloses privileged information, it can notify the party opponent, who must then destroy, return, or hold such inadvertently disclosed documents until a determination regarding privilege is made by the court [Fed. R. Civ. P. 26]. Consequently, the document's privilege was not automatically stripped by its inadvertent production.

(B) Incorrect. Yes, because the production was made to a party opponent.

Because of the huge amount of documents that can be produced during electronic discovery, if a party inadvertently discloses privileged information, it can notify the party opponent, who must then destroy, return, or hold such inadvertently disclosed documents until a determination regarding privilege is made by the court [Fed. R. Civ. P. 26]. Consequently, the documents cannot automatically be used simply because the production was made to a party opponent.

(D) Incorrect. No, because the discovery request produced an enormous amount of documents.

Because of the huge amount of documents that can be produced during electronic discovery, if a party inadvertently discloses privileged information, it can notify the party opponent, who must then destroy, return, or hold such inadvertently disclosed documents until a determination regarding privilege is made by the court [Fed. R. Civ. P. 26]. Importantly, the corporation has to notify the party opponent before anything will be done—it is not automatic based simply on the amount of documents (i.e., it's not up to the party opponent to figure it out).

Explanation: Question 36

The correct answer is: **(B)** Yes, because the man is a citizen of State B.

In determining whether diversity exists for jurisdiction purposes, the citizenship of a class is determined by the citizenship of the named plaintiffs. Here, since the man is apparently the only named plaintiff, and he is a citizen of State B, the citizenship of the class is State B. Consequently, the class is diverse from the company (which is a citizen of State D and State C, based on its primary place of business and its state of incorporation).

(A) Incorrect. Yes, because the majority of purchasers are from State B.

In class actions, the citizenship is determined by the citizenship of the named plaintiffs. It does not matter what citizenship the majority of the class holds.

(C) Incorrect. No, because some of the class members are from State D.

In class actions, the citizenship is determined by the citizenship of the named plaintiffs. Here, since the man is a citizen of State B, it is irrelevant that some of the class members are from State D.

(D) Incorrect. No, because some of the class members are from State C.

In class actions, the citizenship is determined by the citizenship of the named plaintiffs. Here, since the man is a citizen of State B, it is irrelevant that some of the class members are from State C.

Explanation: Question 37

The correct answer is: **(B)** Yes, because it is a valid cross-claim.

Cross-claims are claims against a co-party. Importantly, as long as the cross-claim is part of the same transaction or occurrence, it may be part of the same suit [Fed. R. Civ. P. 13].

(A) Incorrect. Yes, because it is a valid counterclaim.

A counterclaim is a claim made by a party against an opposing party. Here, since the employer and delivery driver are co-defendants, the employer's claim is actually a cross-claim.

(C) Incorrect. No, because the employer and delivery driver are co-defendants.

Cross-claims are claims against a co-party. Importantly, as long as the cross-claim is part of the same transaction or occurrence, it may be part of the same suit [Fed. R. Civ. P. 13].

(D) Incorrect. No, because the plaintiff is the master of his claim.

While a plaintiff can clearly form his or her claim any way he or she wants, as long as a party's cross-claim against his or her co-party is part of the same transaction or occurrence, it may be part of the same suit [Fed. R. Civ. P. 13].

Explanation: Question 38

The correct answer is: **(A)** Yes, because the case has a maritime nexus.

Federal courts have original jurisdiction over admiralty or maritime cases. Admiralty jurisdiction requires that a case have a "maritime nexus." A maritime nexus requires that the incident giving rise to the case had a "potentially disruptive effect on maritime commerce," and the general character of the activity giving rise to the incident shows a "substantial relationship to traditional maritime activity" [Jerome B. Grubart, Inc. v. Great Lakes Dredge & Dock Co., 513 U.S. 527 (1995)]. Here, the accident is clearly potentially disruptive to commerce on the Mississippi (a large navigable river), and transporting oil by boat is a traditional maritime activity.

(B) Incorrect. Yes, because the case involves interstate commerce.

While the case involves interstate commerce, the involvement of interstate commerce will not automatically grant federal jurisdiction over a matter. Importantly, the rules involving subject-matter jurisdiction or federal question jurisdiction have to be addressed.

(C) Incorrect. No, because the town is claiming damage to the riverbank.

While the town is claiming damage to its riverbank, this case clearly has a "maritime nexus" granting the federal court jurisdiction. A maritime nexus requires that the incident giving rise to the case had a "potentially disruptive effect on maritime commerce," and the general character of the activity giving rise to the incident shows a "substantial relationship to traditional maritime activity" [Jerome B. Grubart, Inc. v. Great Lakes Dredge & Dock Co., 513 U.S. 527 (1995)]. Here, the accident is clearly potentially disruptive to commerce on the Mississippi (a large navigable river), and transporting oil by boat is a traditional maritime activity.

(D) Incorrect. No, because the accident did not occur at sea.

If a court has subject matter or federal question jurisdiction over a tort claim, it can be heard in federal court.

Explanation: Question 39

The correct answer is: **(A)** Yes, but he may be liable for expenses and attorneys' fees.

If a defendant located within the United States fails without good cause to sign and return a waiver requested by a plaintiff located within the United States, the court may impose on the defendant: (a) expenses incurred in making the service; and (b) reasonable expenses, including attorneys' fees, of any motion required to collect service expenses. Since the question does not indicate the man had a good cause to refuse waiver, this is the best answer.

(B) Incorrect. Yes, because the Federal Rules of Civil Procedure guarantee his right to service in accordance with federal law.

As stated above, the man would likely be required to waive service under the facts presented in the question.

(C) Incorrect. No, because mail is a reasonable means of apprizing the man of the pending action.

While mail to his home in State B may be a reasonable means of apprizing the man of the lawsuit, he could still refuse to waive service if he had a good cause for doing so.

(D) Incorrect. No, because the man is an individual and not a corporation, partnership, or association.

While the man is an individual, there is no rule requiring individuals to waive service in all situations. If the man had good cause to not agree to waiver, he would have been within his rights to do so.

Explanation: Question 40

The correct answer is: **(A)** The court in State A did not have subject-matter jurisdiction over the action, so Pepper's judgment is not entitled to Full Faith and Credit from a State D court.

The court in State A, even though one of general jurisdiction, was not competent to hear this matter (i.e., the facts stipulate that patent infringement cases are within the exclusive jurisdiction of federal courts). Thus, the State A judgment is not procedurally sound and would not be entitled to Full Faith and Credit by a State D court.

(B) Incorrect. The State A state court never obtained personal jurisdiction over Dick, so the judgment is not entitled to Full Faith and Credit from a State D court.

Service of process within a jurisdiction has traditionally been recognized as a valid means of obtaining personal jurisdiction over an out-of-state defendant.

(C) Incorrect. By failing to appear, Dick waived his right to object to subject matter and personal jurisdiction.

A defendant who fails to appear in an out-of-state action does not waive his/her right to later collaterally attack the constitutional and procedural aspects of that default judgment.

(D) Incorrect. By failing to appear, Dick waived his right to object, but only as to the State A court having personal jurisdiction over Dick.

A defendant who fails to appear in an out-of-state action does not waive his/her right to later collaterally attack the constitutional and procedural aspects of that default judgment. The court in State A, even though one of general jurisdiction, was not competent to hear this matter (i.e., the facts stipulate that patent infringement cases are within the exclusive jurisdiction of federal courts). Thus, the State A judgment is not procedurally sound and would not be entitled to Full Faith and Credit by a State D court.

Explanation: Question 41

The correct answer is: **(C)** No, because the Federal Rules of Civil Procedure allow for "relation back" in these circumstances.

The Erie Doctrine requires federal courts sitting in diversity to apply state substantive law and, sometimes, to apply state procedures. However, where a Federal Rule of Civil Procedure covers the question, the federal court applies the federal rule even if it is different from the state rule. Here, Federal Rule of Civil Procedure 15(c)(2) explicitly allows for relation back in these circumstances, and the federal court must apply the federal rule, allow the relation back, and deny the motion for summary judgment.

(A) Incorrect. Yes, because the federal court sitting in diversity must defer to state law as part of the Erie Doctrine.

The federal court does not always defer to state law. Where, as here, the Federal Rules of Civil Procedure dictate a particular result, the federal court must apply the federal rule.

(B) Incorrect. Yes, because otherwise plaintiffs would have an incentive to forum shop and choose federal court over state court.

A procedural difference might give a plaintiff a reason to forum shop, but the federal court nevertheless must apply the federal rule to this situation. The Erie Doctrine is a constitutional doctrine that flows from the limits on a federal court's power to make law. However, there is no question that Congress has the power to create rules to govern procedures in the federal courts, and, through the process established by the Rules Enabling Act, Congress has done so. Whether or not the difference creates incentives for forum shopping, the rule has been duly enacted, is constitutional and therefore must be applied.

(D) Incorrect. No, because the difference between state and federal law is merely a matter of procedure.

Although in its usual application the Erie Doctrine is about the application of state substantive law to diversity cases in federal court, the Doctrine can require the federal court, in certain circumstances, to apply state procedures. Here, the determinative fact is not that the issue is procedural—whether an amendment "relates back" for limitations purposes—but rather that a valid federal rule covers the situation. If that were not so, then the court would have further analysis to perform to determine whether the court had to apply state procedures in federal court.

Explanation: Question 42

The correct answer is: **(C)** No, because multiple state laws regarding health and safety are involved.

In addition to the basic requirements for certifying a class, courts will maintain a class action only if at least one of the following is true: (1) the prosecution of separate actions would create a risk of inconsistent judgments that would impair the ability of other members to protect their interests; (2) the party opposing the class has acted on grounds that are generally applicable to the class as a whole; or (3) common questions predominate over individual questions, and class representation is superior to other methods for adjudicating the controversy. Factors to determine common questions include pending individual litigation, class member interests, the desirability of concentrating litigation in the forum, and the difficulties of managing the class action. Importantly, a court is unlikely to grant class certification where multiple state laws are involved and individual claims require separate investigation. Here, the question specifically states that multiple state laws will be involved and individual investigations will be required, making this the best answer choice.

(A) Incorrect. Yes, because the woman will fairly and adequately protect the interests of the class.

In determining whether to certify a class, one of the things courts will look at is whether the class representative can fairly and adequately protect and represent the interests of each member of the class. Importantly, the courts will typically only look at whether the class representative is willing to serve and has retained competent counsel. Here, by filing her suit and hiring a nationally known firm, the woman has likely met these requirements. The problem is that the claim will involve multiple state laws and individual investigations, making class certification improper.

(B) Incorrect. Yes, because the woman's claim is representative of the claims of the class.

In addition to the basic requirements for certifying a class, courts will maintain a class action only if at least one of the following is true: (1) the prosecution of separate actions would create a risk of inconsistent judgments of judgments that would impair the ability of other members to protect their interests; (2) the party opposing the class has acted on grounds that are generally applicable to the class as a whole; or (3) common questions predominate over individual questions, and class representation is superior to other methods for adjudicating the controversy. Factors to determine common questions include pending individual litigation, class member interests, the desirability of concentrating litigation in the forum, and the difficulties of managing the class action. However, a court is unlikely to grant class certification where multiple state laws are involved and individual claims require separate investigation. Here, the question specifically states that multiple state laws will be involved and individual investigations will be required. Consequently, even if the woman's claim is representative of the class, there is still the issue of multiple state laws and individual investigations.

(D) Incorrect. No, because the class is so numerous that joinder of all members is impracticable.

To certify a class, the number of members of the class must be so numerous that separate joinder of each member is impracticable. No particular number is needed, nor is the number of potential class members determinative. Here, while 2,000 members is clearly too numerous for joinder, this fact would actually weigh in favor of certifying the class, not against it, making this answer a clear misstatement of the law.

Explanation: Question 43

The correct answer is: **(C)** The 1,000 U.S. users and the 100 Vietnamese users.

When appropriate, a court may include within a class plaintiffs who received notice but did not respond in order to opt out in a timely manner. The court may also include absent plaintiffs for which it does not have personal jurisdiction over, thus the Vietnamese users may be included in the proceedings. However, the court may not include defendants for which it does not have personal jurisdiction over.

(A) Incorrect. None of the parties.

As stated above, a court may include within a class plaintiffs who received notice but did not respond in order to opt-out in a timely manner. Thus, because the users were given proper notice and they did not respond in order to opt out of the proceedings, they may be included as plaintiffs.

(B) Incorrect. The 1,000 U.S. users.

While the U.S. users may be included, this answer choice is incorrect because the Vietnamese users may be included as well, as there is not a requirement that a court have personal jurisdiction over absent plaintiffs in a class action proceeding.

(D) Incorrect. The 1,000 U.S. users, the 100 Vietnamese users, and Sassy Consulting.

A court may not include a defendant in a class action proceeding where the defendant is not subject to personal jurisdiction, and we are told in the facts that Sassy Consulting does not have the requisite contacts with the U.S., so it will not be included in the proceeding.

Explanation: Question 44

The correct answer is: **(A)** Yes, after the woman amended her complaint to add $50,000 in damages.

Removal to federal court is permissible only where at least one of the claims filed by the plaintiff would fall within the subject-matter jurisdiction of the federal courts. Removal is only available for actions filed in state court. Here, the action was filed in state court. The woman and the driver have complete diversity of citizenship, and once the woman added $50,000, the amount-in-controversy requirement was met.

(B) Incorrect. Yes, because the defendant made the request for removal.

While only defendants can make requests for removal, those requests will not be granted unless one of the claims filed by the plaintiff would fall within the subject-matter jurisdiction of the federal courts. Without meeting the amount-in-controversy requirement, the federal court could not hear the woman's claim.

(C) Incorrect. No, because the original claim was for $40,000 in damages.

Removal is not only dependent upon the amount of the original claim. If claims are added to reach the $75,000, jurisdiction is granted.

(D) Incorrect. No, because the woman's claim is for personal injuries.

Although the woman's claim is for personal injuries, it still meets the requirements of subject-matter jurisdiction through diversity.

Explanation: Question 45

The correct answer is: **(D)** No, because a criminal conviction has a higher standard of proof than a finding of civil liability.

The problem with issue preclusion between criminal and civil trials is the differing standard of proof between them. A criminal conviction could have preclusive effect in a civil trial, provided that the elements of the crime and the tort were sufficiently similar. However, the fact that a prosecutor was not able to show beyond a reasonable doubt that a defendant committed a crime does not necessarily mean that the defendant cannot be found liable by the preponderance of the evidence. As a result, this is the correct answer.

(A) Incorrect. Yes, because the prosecution and the civil suit arose from the same incident.

While the two suits need to have arisen from the same incident for there to be issue preclusion, that is not by itself enough. The bodybuilder's liability can be litigated here because of the differing standards of proof between civil and criminal cases. Although the prosecutor could not show beyond a reasonable doubt that the bodybuilder committed a crime, the host's attorney may be able to show that the bodybuilder is liable by the preponderance of the evidence.

(B) Incorrect. Yes, because the Constitutional prohibition on double jeopardy forbids a civil trial.

The Constitutional prohibition on double jeopardy forbids a situation in which the same "sovereign" tries a defendant twice. It does not apply here, where the bodybuilder underwent a state prosecution and a federal court tort suit.

(C) Incorrect. No, because issue preclusion (collateral estoppel) does not apply between criminal and civil cases.

This is an overinclusive answer. In fact, issue preclusion could apply between criminal and civil cases. However, it would almost always apply when there is a criminal conviction, rather than an acquittal. The prosecutor's inability to convict the bodybuilder on a reasonable doubt standard does not preclude the possibility that a civil court can find the bodybuilder liable by the preponderance of the evidence.

Explanation: Question 46

The correct answer is: **(A)** State B must grant Full Faith and Credit to the State A judgment if Dominic had a full and fair opportunity to litigate on the merits.

The State B court would be obliged under Full Faith and Credit principles to recognize the decision rendered in the State A court.

(B) Incorrect. *Res judicata* precludes Pauly from suing on the State A judgment in State B, because the two actions involve the same parties and the same occurrence.

While the earlier judgment would prevent Dominic from relitigating the claim, Pauly is seeking only to enforce the prior judgment, not to litigate the case on its merits.

(C) Incorrect. Full Faith and Credit need not be granted to the State A judgment.

The State B court cannot constitutionally disregard the State A judgment.

(D) Incorrect. The State B court may hold a trial *de novo*, because that jurisdiction does not recognize comparative negligence.

The State B court must give effect to the earlier judgment, even though it was based upon a doctrine that is not adhered to in State B.

Explanation: Question 47

The correct answer is: **(D)** No, because the filing of the amended complaint will relate back in time to the filing of the original complaint.

Under Federal Rule of Civil Procedure 15(c), an amended complaint that adds a new party will relate back in time to the date of the filing of the original complaint if certain conditions are met. Unless there is a special provision for relation back in the statute of limitations (there is no indication of such a provision in the question), the claim against the new party must arise from the same events as alleged in the original complaint. That is true here. It must also be true that the new defendant had notice within 120 days of the filing of the original complaint and would not be prejudiced in defending on the merits. Here, the new defendant's registered agent had notice of the filing, and the amended complaint was filed only a few days after the original complaint. Finally, it must be true that the new defendant knew or should have known that, but for a mistake about the identity of the correct party, the original claim would have been brought against it. Here, the new defendant presumably knew or should have known who actually employed the plaintiff and her supervisor. Therefore, this answer is correct.

(A) Incorrect. Yes, because Plaintiff did not obtain leave of court to file the amended complaint.

Under Rule 15(a), a plaintiff may amend the complaint once as a matter of course—meaning no leave is required—with 20 days of the filing of the original complaint. Here, the plaintiff filed the first amended complaint 12 days after the original complaint and had a right to do so without leave. Therefore, this answer is incorrect.

(B) Incorrect. Yes, because the amended complaint against MII was filed after the limitations period expired.

The relevant date for limitations purposes is the date of the filing of the original complaint, not the date of the filing of the amended complaint. Under Rule 15(c), the amended complaint will "relate back" in time to the earlier date. Therefore, this answer is incorrect.

(C) Incorrect. No, because MII and MHI had the same registered agent.

This fact is not enough by itself to allow for relation back to the date of the original filing. It is significant because the registered agent for the proper defendant obviously received notice of the filing of the original complaint when it was served, but the amended complaint might have been served too late. If the amended complaint was served on the registered agent more than 120 days after the filing of the original complaint, the amended complaint would not relate back, regardless of the registered agent's notice. Therefore, this answer is incorrect.

Explanation: Question 48

The correct answer is: **(D)** No, because federal courts only require a unanimous jury of six.

The Federal Rules require that a jury, when seated, have no fewer than six jurors and no more than 12. They must come to a unanimous decision, and there must be at least six jurors deliberating on the verdict, unless the parties stipulate to something different. Therefore, this is the correct answer choice.

(A) Incorrect. Yes, because there are now fewer than 12 jurors and there are no alternates.

Although the number of jurors may be fewer than that originally intended, the judge does not necessarily need to declare a mistrial. The Federal Rules only require a unanimous jury of six to return a verdict.

(B) Incorrect. Yes, because the federal rules require that each jury have 12 jurors and three alternates.

This is not a true statement. In fact, federal courts only require that a jury, when seated, have no fewer than six jurors and no more than 12.

(C) Incorrect. No, because the court does not know whether the jurors who are sick can return soon.

It is immaterial whether the jurors could return soon. If the trial is not recessed in the meantime, they would not be allowed to deliberate after having missed part of the trial. Also, even if the jurors didn't return, the number of remaining jurors is adequate. Federal courts only require a unanimous jury of six to return a verdict.

Explanation: Question 49

The correct answer is: **(C)** No, because the gardener's injury did not arise from the same transaction or occurrence as the previous case.

Res judicata is used to avoid relitigating claims that arose from a transaction or occurrence that also gave rise to a previous claim when the parties are the same (or are in privity with the prior parties) and where the previous claims were fully and fairly litigated. It is not an appropriate doctrine here because the transaction or occurrence was not the same and there was no relationship between this plaintiff and the prior one.

(A) Incorrect. Yes, because the gardener suffered the same type of injury as the plaintiff in the prior action.

It is not enough that the gardener suffered the same type of injury as the prior plaintiff. *Res judicata* applies to avoid relitigating claims arising from the same transaction or occurrence as previous claims when the parties are the same (or are in privity with the prior parties) and where the previous claims were fully and fairly litigated. In this instance, the plaintiffs are not related, and the transaction or occurrence is not the same.

(B) Incorrect. Yes, because it does not appear that the gardener could have joined the prior action.

Whether the plaintiff in a later action could have joined the previous action is not material in applying *res judicata*. (This is an issue that arises instead in determining the offensive use of issue preclusion.) *Res judicata* applies to claims arising from the same transaction or occurrence as previous claims when the parties are the same (or are in privity with the prior parties) and where the previous claims were fully and fairly litigated. In this instance, the plaintiffs are not related, and the transaction or occurrence is not the same. *Res judicata* would be inappropriate.

(D) Incorrect. No, because the previous case was not heard in the same court.

The fact that the previous case was heard in a different court would not necessarily prohibit the use of *res judicata* (claim preclusion). *Res judicata* applies to claims arising from the same transaction or occurrence as previous claims when the parties are the same (or are in privity with the prior parties) and where the previous claims were fully and fairly litigated. Assuming that there was a full and fair litigation in the previous case, it need not have taken place in the same court.

Explanation: Question 50

The correct answer is: **(B)** Yes, because the author lost the issue of the validity of the copyright in a forum of her own choosing.

This is an example of defensive non-mutual collateral estoppel. The woman was not a party to the first case, but there is an issue in common: the validity of the copyright. The author litigated and lost that issue in the first case, and she will not be heard to complain about that result because she chose when, where, and against whom to litigate it. The author is bound by the result on the dispositive issue in a case that the author chose to bring.

(A) Incorrect. Yes, because the validity of the copyright was an issue in both cases and the author lost that issue in the first case.

A party can actually litigate and actually lose a dispositive issue and nevertheless not be estopped in a second case, if that party did not have a full and fair opportunity to litigate the issue in the first case. If the party to be estopped did not choose the forum and there were important differences between the two cases—such as differences in available procedures or a large difference in the stakes—then non-mutual collateral estoppel will not prevent re-litigation of the issue in the second case.

(C) Incorrect. No, because the parties in the two cases were not the same.

There are times when estoppel does not require mutuality of parties. Non-mutual collateral estoppel will apply if a party had an earlier full and fair opportunity to litigate an issue that was essential to the judgment, and the party actually litigated and lost that issue.

(D) Incorrect. No, because the author did not have a full and fair opportunity to litigate the validity of her copyright in the first case.

A full and fair opportunity to litigate is essential, but that opportunity will be presumed to have existed when the party to be estopped decided when, where, and against whom to bring the first case. No one forced this alleged copyright holder to bring the first case. As the plaintiff who litigated and lost an essential issue, she will be estopped if she brings a second case that turns on the same issue.

Explanation: Question 51

The correct answer is: **(C)** State C law.

A federal court sitting in diversity jurisdiction will apply the choice of law rules of the state in which the court sits. Where a case has been transferred, the transferee court will apply the substantive law that would have been applied by the transferor court, but this rule does not apply where the case was transferred based on improper venue. Thus, the State A court will apply State A choice of law rules. Here, State A requires that the substantive law of the state in which the alleged breach took place should apply. Because the defendant allegedly breached the contract in State C, that state's substantive law will apply.

(A) Incorrect. State A law.

While State A's choice of law rules will be applied for the reasons described above, those rules dictate that the substantive law of the state in which the alleged breach took place should apply. Thus, State C's substantive law will apply.

(B) Incorrect. State B law.

If State D's choice of law rules applied, then State B's substantive law would apply as the contract between the university and the owner was signed in State B. Because State D was an improper venue, however, State D's choice of law rules will not be applied by the court.

(D) Incorrect. State D law.

Had State D been a proper venue, State D's choice of law rules would have dictated that the substantive law of State B would apply. State D was not a proper venue, however. In either case, State D's substantive law would not apply.

Explanation: Question 52

The correct answer is: **(D)** No, because the man was a citizen of Colorado when the suit was filed.

Citizenship is determined for diversity purposes on the date the suit is filed. Importantly, if a person moves to a state with an intent to stay there indefinitely, that state becomes the person's domicile. Here, when the man filed suit, he was in Colorado. He had quit his job in Vermont, got a home and job in Colorado, and told his friends he would stay in Colorado for "as long as it takes." Since his actions and statement indicate an intent to stay in Colorado indefinitely, he was a citizen of Colorado at the time he filed suit. And since the woman was also a Colorado citizen, there was no diversity between the parties.

(A) Incorrect. Yes, because the man was a citizen of Vermont when the injury occurred.

Citizenship for diversity purposes is determined on the date the suit is filed, not the date of injury.

(B) Incorrect. Yes, because the man was a citizen of Colorado when the injury occurred.

Citizenship for diversity purposes is determined on the date the suit is filed, not the date of injury.

(C) Incorrect. No, because the man was a citizen of Vermont when the suit was filed.

If a person moves to a state with an intent to stay there indefinitely, that state becomes the person's domicile. Here, when the man filed suit, he was in Colorado. He had quit his job in Vermont, got a home and job in Colorado, and told his friends he would stay in Colorado for "as long as it takes."

Since his actions and statement indicate an intent to stay in Colorado indefinitely, he was a citizen of Colorado at the time he filed suit. And since the woman was also a Colorado citizen, there was no diversity between the parties.

Explanation: Question 53

The correct answer is: **(D)** Yes, but only if the plaintiffs show exceptional circumstances under which it is impracticable for them to obtain the information by other means.

Pursuant to Fed. R. Civ. P. 26(b)(4)(D), a party will generally not be able to depose an expert who will not testify at trial, but there is a narrow exception for where a party makes a showing of exceptional circumstances under which it is impracticable for them to obtain the information by other means.

(A) Incorrect. No, because experts may not be deposed before trial.

This is an incorrect statement of law. Experts who will testify at trial may be deposed before trial, and, as stated above, experts who will not testify at trial may be deposed in very limited circumstances.

(B) Incorrect. No, because experts may only be deposed with regard to facts, not opinions.

This is an incorrect statement of law. Pursuant to Fed. R. Civ. P. 26(b)(4)(A), a party may depose an expert who will testify at trial as to both facts and opinions.

(C) Incorrect. Yes, because experts may be deposed as to both facts and opinions.

While a witness who will testify at trial may be required to submit to a deposition, a witness who will not testify can only be deposed under limited circumstances. This answer choice is not as good as D because it does not point to this exception.

Explanation: Question 54

The correct answer is: **(C)** No, because 12(b)(6) dismissals are with prejudice unless the court states otherwise.

From the facts provided, it seems that there is no relief to be granted on the prisoner's claim. It might state a cognizable claim to relief if there were more detail, such as that the prisoner suffered permanent physical damage as a result of the treatment alleged, so a court certainly could grant leave to amend. However, if a court does not specify otherwise, a 12(b)(6) dismissal is with prejudice. This is therefore the correct answer.

(A) Incorrect. Yes, because a *pro se* litigant is entitled to amend his claim one time as of right.

Parties, whether *pro se* or represented, are entitled to amend their claims once as of right within 21 days of serving the original pleading or within 21 days of service of a responsive pleading or a motion to strike, dismiss, or for a more definite statement. The question states that the dismissal took place 90 days after the motion to dismiss, though, so the time frame for amendment as of right is no longer open.

(B) Incorrect. Yes, because all litigants are entitled to amend a claim one time as of right.

This answer, while correctly stating the law, is not applicable to the situation described. All parties can amend their claims once as of right within 21 days of serving the original pleading or within 21 days of service of a responsive pleading or a motion to strike, dismiss, or for a more definite statement. That time frame has already passed, though, as the question states that the dismissal took place 90 days after the motion to dismiss.

(D) Incorrect. No, because he did not state any damages that resulted from the alleged constitutional violation.

The prisoner's failure to state resulting damages in his claim appears to have resulted in the dismissal for failure to state a claim on which relief can be granted. The court could have granted leave to amend rather than dismiss the claim. However, when a court does not specify otherwise, a 12(b)(6) dismissal is with prejudice, so that appears to be the case on these facts.

Explanation: Question 55

The correct answer is: **(D)** That the issue was not fully and fairly litigated in the previous case.

Issue preclusion (collateral estoppel) is defined as allowing parties to avoid relitigating issues that were fully and fairly litigated in an earlier proceeding. It can only be used against a party who was a party to the earlier proceeding. Here, the pipefitter may be able to raise a question about whether the previous litigation was sufficiently complete. Because the manufacturer was not a party to it, and because the emphasis in a workers' compensation claim is the employer's responsibility rather than a manufacturer's, the pipefitter stands a good chance of avoiding issue preclusion on this basis.

(A) Incorrect. That the manufacturer was not a party to the prior case.

Issue preclusion (collateral estoppel) allows parties to avoid relitigating issues that were fully and fairly litigated in an earlier proceeding. It can only be used against a party who was a party to the earlier proceeding. When someone not a party to the prior suit uses it against someone who was, this is considered an offensive use and courts are less likely to allow it. Therefore, the fact that the manufacturer was not a party to the prior case does make it less likely that its summary judgment motion will succeed. However, it is not the best argument that the pipefitter can make.

(B) Incorrect. That issue preclusion (collateral estoppel) cannot be used offensively.

This is not a correct statement of the law. Issue preclusion (collateral estoppel) allows parties to avoid relitigating issues that were fully and fairly litigated in an earlier proceeding and can only be used against a party who was a party to the earlier proceeding. Courts are less likely to allow offensive use of issue preclusion, which occurs when someone not a party to the prior suit uses it against someone who was. It is not impossible to do so, though, so this is not a correct answer choice.

(C) Incorrect. That the two cases were filed in different forums.

While issue preclusion (collateral estoppel) allows parties to avoid relitigating issues that were fully and fairly litigated in an earlier proceeding, it does not require that both cases be litigated in the same forum. As a result, this is not the most convincing argument the pipefitter can raise.

Explanation: Question 56

The correct answer is: **(A)** Betty's judgment should have no effect upon a subsequent lawsuit by Annie against Delasandro.

Because Betty recovered a default judgment against Delasandro in the initial lawsuit, it would have no collateral estoppel effect, since the issues were not actually litigated. Also, because Annie and Betty are not in privity, the initial judgment would have no *res judicata* effect.

(B) Incorrect. Betty's judgment is *res judicata* with respect to a subsequent lawsuit by Annie against Delasandro.

Annie and Betty are not in privity with each other (they are complete strangers to one another).

(C) Incorrect. Assuming the mutuality doctrine is inapplicable, a court may permit Annie to assert collateral estoppel in a subsequent lawsuit by Annie against Delasandro.

The issues in Betty's action against Delasandro were not actually litigated.

(D) Incorrect. Because Annie and Betty are in privity, Annie cannot recover because of the *res judicata* effects of the initial judgment for Betty.

Annie and Betty are not in privity with each other (they are complete strangers to one another).

Explanation: Question 57

The correct answer is: **(B)** The cause of action provided by the state law does not require that a plaintiff bring all known claims against another party at one time.

A federal court generally has discretion with regard to joinder of claims, but such joinder is compelled when the failure to join could result in splitting a cause of action. This answer choice indicates that the cause of action under the law does not require that all claims be joined, and thus the court would have discretion to hear the claims separately.

(A) Incorrect. Hearing evidence related to the security service issue would unnecessarily confuse the jury with regard to the parking garage issue.

Jury confusion is a legitimate reason for supporting the non-joinder of claims, but, even if this is true, the court would still have discretion regarding whether to join the claims or not. This is not as good of an answer choice as B, which must be true for the court to decline to join the claims.

(C) Incorrect. There is no factual connection between the parking garage issue and the security service claims, and the claims would require completely distinct evidentiary showings.

There is no requirement that separate claims be related for a court to allow those claims to be joined.

(D) Incorrect. The woman has indicated to the corporation that she has evidence supporting a third claim against the corporation that she intends to bring should the first two claims be successful.

This is somewhat irrelevant as there is nothing to suggest that the woman would not be permitted to bring a third claim at a later point, and this does not necessarily have an impact on the discretion of the court to decline to join the woman's two current claims.

Explanation: Question 58

The correct answer is: **(B)** In a class action federal securities fraud litigation related to a corporation's undisclosed risk of insider trading liability, a party seeks discovery of all of the corporation's non-privileged emails related to insider trading. Reviewing and producing said emails will require 500 man-hours to complete.

Pursuant to Fed. R. Civ. P. 26(b), a party is entitled to discovery of any matter that is: 1) relevant to the claim or defense of any party; 2) not unreasonably cumulative or burdensome; and 3) not privileged. This request is relevant to the plaintiff's claims, and 500 man-hours is not an unreasonable burden for a request that goes to the central facts in a class action proceeding.

(A) Incorrect. In a construction litigation case, a party seeks discovery of emails between the general counsel of a corporation and its CFO regarding potential litigation risks to the corporation, but which copied all of the officers of the corporation and their support staff.

A party is not entitled to privileged materials. Here, the emails were from the general counsel to the CFO regarding litigation risks, and therefore were attorney-client privileged. The fact that other officers and employees were copied on the emails does not destroy their confidentiality.

(C) Incorrect. In an employment discrimination case, the plaintiff seeks all of the defendant's non-privileged emails related to the payment of bribes to foreign entities.

A party's discovery requests must be relevant. Here, this request does not appear to be relevant to the plaintiff's employment discrimination claim.

(D) Incorrect. In a copyright action in which a writer alleges damages of $5,000 from a publisher, the writer seeks production of all non-privileged emails relating to the publisher's work with a book that the writer claims was plagiarized from him. Reviewing and producing said emails will require 500 man-hours to complete.

A request may not be unreasonably burdensome. Here, the party seeks only $5,000 in damages, but is making a request which will require 500 man-hours to complete, therefore the court is likely to find that the request is unreasonably burdensome given the low stakes.

Explanation: Question 59

The correct answer is: **(A)** Yes, because the man could have easily discovered the company's earlier copyright.

Every pleading, written motion, and other paper filed with the court must be signed by the attorney of the party preparing the document, or by the party, if the party is not represented by an attorney [Fed. R. Civ. P. 11]. The signature certifies to the court that, to the best of the person's knowledge, information, and belief, formed after an inquiry reasonable under the circumstances, that factual contentions have evidentiary support or, if specifically so identified, will likely have evidentiary support after a reasonable opportunity for further investigation or discovery. Here, copyright infringement requires proof that the defendant copied the plaintiff's material, and it would have been extremely easy for the plaintiff to discover the defendant's much earlier copyright since the book was available in almost every bookstore and had a copyright notice on its front cover.

(B) Incorrect. Yes, because the man waited 20 days to answer.

A party may not file a motion for sanctions without first serving the motion upon the opposing party and providing the opposing party with 21 days to withdraw or correct the offending pleading, written motion, or other paper. This is called the "safe harbor provision." Importantly, not all courts apply the safe harbor provision to complaints. Since the question doesn't state whether the court would apply the provision to a complaint, Answer (A) is a better answer, because its reasoning would apply no matter what the situation.

(C) Incorrect. No, because the complaint was valid on its face.

The issue here is that a simple inquiry by the plaintiff would have shown him that he had no case for copyright infringement. Consequently, sanctions are appropriate.

(D) Incorrect. No, because discovery had not yet been completed.

There is no rule stating that sanctions can only be granted after discovery.

Explanation: Question 60

The correct answer is: **(C)** No, because the stakes in the second case are much greater than the stakes were in the first case.

This is an example of offensive non-mutual collateral estoppel. It is a doctrine that allows non-parties, like the class members in the question, sometimes to use the result of prior litigation in which the defendant lost an issue. However, if it would be unfair to the defendant to allow collateral estoppel, then the doctrine does not apply. One of the circumstances in which it would be unfair is this one. The corporation had little incentive to fight too hard over a $1,000 case, but now the stakes are much higher. The corporation will be allowed to litigate the defect issue, despite the results in the first case.

(A) Incorrect. Yes, because the issue of whether the veggie taco that was sold by the corporation had meat in it was actually litigated and decided in the first case and was essential to the judgment.

These are the requirements for collateral estoppel, but there are additional concerns when a party is seeking to use offensive non-mutual collateral estoppel. Even if the issue was actually litigated, actually decided, and essential to the merits of the first action, estoppel could be unfair to the defendant. The court must inquire into that fairness and sometimes will not allow estoppel even when all of the other requisites are present. This question presents one classic set of circumstances in which estoppel would be unfair: the stakes in the first case were so much lower than the stakes in the second case. Estoppel will not prevent this defendant from litigating the issue of whether the veggie taco that was sold by the corporation had meat in it.

(B) Incorrect. Yes, because the corporation had a full and fair opportunity to litigate the issue in the first case.

The corporation did not have a full and fair opportunity to litigate the issue in the first case. The problem is incentive. With just $1,000 at stake in that case, the corporation had little reason to fight as hard as it would have if the stakes had been higher. To hold the corporation to the result obtained in that first small case in the much larger pending case would be unfair.

(D) Incorrect. No, because the members of the class were not parties to the first case.

Mutuality is not required for collateral estoppel. Here, the class members could use offensive non-mutual collateral estoppel if that would be fair to the corporation. The issue of the defect was actually litigated, actually decided, and essential to the judgment in the first case. The problem with using the doctrine here is not that the plaintiffs were not parties but that the stakes were too low in the first action for estoppel in the second action to be fair to the corporation.

Explanation: Question 61

The correct answer is: **(D)** No, because the trial court entered final judgment on the claim against the first defendant after finding that there was no just reason for delay.

Under Federal Rule of Civil Procedure 54(b), the district court may enter final judgment as to fewer than all claims in a multi-claim case if the court finds no just reason for delay. If the court does so, then the final judgment on part of the case is a final judgment that may be appealed immediately, without waiting for adjudication of the remaining claims.

(A) Incorrect. Yes, because not all of the claims in the case have been fully adjudicated.

The general rule is that all claims in a case must be adjudicated before there will be a final judgment that can be appealed. However, Federal Rule of Civil Procedure 54(b) contains an exception to that general rule. If the court adjudicates fewer than all the claims and determines that there is no just reason for delay, the trial court may enter a final judgment on those claims, and an immediate appeal becomes possible. That is what happened in this case.

(B) Incorrect. Yes, because the grant or denial of a summary judgment is not appealable immediately.

A denial of summary judgment means that the claims will need to be tried. Therefore, denials of summary judgment motions do not result in a judgment, final or otherwise, from which a party ordinarily may appeal. On the other hand, a grant of summary judgment in a one-claim case results in a final judgment that may be appealed. Here, the problem is that there are multiple claims, and the court has granted summary judgment only as to one of them. As a result, the losing party may appeal only because the court found that there was no just reason for delay and entered final judgment on that one claim.

(C) Incorrect. No, because a grant of summary judgment is a final judgment.

The grant of summary judgment in a one-claim case is a final judgment. However, the grant of summary judgment on one claim in a multi-claim case, as happened here, normally is not a final judgment. The trial court in this case, however, found that there was no just reason for delay and went ahead and entered a final judgment on that part of the case. That order made the grant of the summary judgment a final judgment that could be appealed immediately.

Explanation: Question 62

The correct answer is: **(D)** No, because the claims are completely unrelated.

Cross-claims are claims against a co-party. Importantly, as long as the cross-claim is part of the same transaction or occurrence, it may be part of the same suit [Fed. R. Civ. P. 13]. Here, the two cross-claims involve two different makeover projects (the woman and the neighbor). Although the two projects may be part of the same overall scheme, they in fact involve two completely separate transactions and joinder of the claims is inappropriate.

(A) Incorrect. Yes, because the claims are part of the same transaction or occurrence.

Cross-claims are claims against a co-party. Importantly, as long as the cross-claim is part of the same transaction or occurrence, it may be part of the same suit [Fed. R. Civ. P. 13]. Here, the two cross-claims involve two different makeover projects (the woman and the neighbor). Although the two projects may be part of the same overall scheme, they in fact involve two completely separate transactions and joinder of the claims is inappropriate.

(B) Incorrect. Yes, because the claims are being filed against his co-defendant.

Cross-claims are claims against a co-party. Importantly, as long as the cross-claim is part of the same transaction or occurrence, it may be part of the same suit [Fed. R. Civ. P. 13]. Here, the two cross-claims involve two different makeover projects (the woman and the neighbor). Although the two projects may be part of the same overall scheme, they in fact involve two completely separate transactions and joinder of the claims is inappropriate. The simple fact he is filing a claim against his co-defendant would not defeat this problem.

(C) Incorrect. No, because efficiency interests would not be served by joinder.

Cross-claims are claims against a co-party. Importantly, as long as the cross-claim is part of the same transaction or occurrence, it may be part of the same suit [Fed. R. Civ. P. 13]. Here, the two cross-claims involve two different makeover projects (the woman and the neighbor). Although the two projects may be part of the same overall scheme, they in fact involve two completely separate transactions and joinder of the claims is inappropriate. While efficiency interests are the reason behind the rule, efficiency interests by themselves do not make joinder appropriate.

Explanation: Question 63

The correct answer is: **(D)** No, because such a motion may be filed at trial.

Pursuant to Fed. R. Civ. P. 12(h)(2)(C), a motion to dismiss on the grounds of failure to state a claim upon which relief may be granted may be filed at trial. Thus, the fact that the directors did not originally raise this argument prior to filing an answer or the commencement of trial does not preclude them from doing so now.

(A) Incorrect. Yes, because a motion on these grounds must be filed prior to an answer.

Certain grounds for a motion to dismiss must be raised prior to the filing of answer, but, as stated above, a motion to dismiss on the grounds of failure to state a claim upon which relief may be granted may be filed at trial.

(B) Incorrect. Yes, because the case has proceeded to trial.

This is an incorrect answer because, as stated above, a motion to dismiss on the grounds of failure to state a claim upon which relief may be granted may be filed at trial.

(C) Incorrect. No, because the investor is required to plead fraud with particularity.

While it is correct that a plaintiff is required to plead fraud with particularity, this is somewhat irrelevant to the question of whether the directors' motion to dismiss at trial was made in a timely manner.

Explanation: Question 64

The correct answer is: **(D)** No, because the suit was not for a sum certain or a sum that can be made certain by computation.

Federal Rule of Civil Procedure 55(b)(1) sets forth the limited circumstances under which the clerk may enter a default judgment. One requirement is that the amount sought must be a sum certain or an amount that can be made certain by computation. A tort case in which the plaintiff seeks damages for pain and suffering is not such a case, and only the court may enter a default judgment in those circumstances.

(A) Incorrect. Yes, because the defendant did not appear in the action.

A failure by the defendant to appear is a necessary but not sufficient condition for the clerk to enter a default judgment. One of the additional conditions is that the amount sought must either be a sum certain or an amount that can be made certain by computation, and that is not true in this tort case.

(B) Incorrect. Yes, because the plaintiff submitted an affidavit that set forth his damages.

To obtain a default judgment from the clerk, the plaintiff must submit an affidavit showing the amount due. Here, the plaintiff did that, but the clerk nevertheless may not enter judgment because the amount claimed by the plaintiff is not a sum certain or an amount that could be made certain by computation (such as payments on a promissory note). An affidavit about pain and suffering does not qualify as an affidavit that demonstrates a sum certain or a sum that can be made certain by computation.

(C) Incorrect. No, because the court must enter all default judgments.

This answer is incorrect because it is overbroad. There are narrow circumstances under which the clerk, rather than the court, may enter default judgments. The clerk may not do so in this particular case, but that is not because the clerk may never do so. Rather, it is because one of the particular requirements that the damages be a sum certain or an amount that can be made certain by computation is not met in this case.

Explanation: Question 65

The correct answer is: **(B)** The attorney for a defendant does not act in good faith in working with the plaintiff's attorney to create a discovery plan. The plaintiff's attorney complains to the judge, who immediately sanctions the defense attorney by requiring her to pay the reasonable costs caused by her lack of good faith.

Pursuant to Fed. R. Civ. P. 37(f), a court may sanction an attorney for failing to act in good faith to put together a discovery plan, but the court must give the attorney an opportunity to be heard before sanctions can be imposed. Here, no opportunity to be heard was given, so the imposition of sanctions was improper.

(A) Incorrect. A plaintiff requests that a corporation submit to a Rule 30(b)(6) deposition. The corporation designates an individual to attend the deposition, but the individual fails to do so. The court orders a default judgment in favor of the plaintiff.

Pursuant to Fed. R. Civ. P. 37(d), a court may impose sanctions on a party when its designated agent fails to appear for a Rule 30(b)(6) deposition, and the sanctions may include default judgment against the disobedient party.

(C) Incorrect. A plaintiff fails to return interrogatories within the 30 days specified by the court. The court immediately stays the proceedings until the interrogatories are completed.

Pursuant to Fed. R. Civ. P. 37(d), a court may impose sanctions on a party when it fails to respond to interrogatories, and the sanctions may include staying the proceedings until the required discovery requirements are fulfilled.

(D) Incorrect. The court orders the minor son of a plaintiff to submit to a Rule 35(a) physical examination. The plaintiff fails to produce the son for the examination. The court orders a default judgment in favor of the defendant.

As with the above scenarios, a court may impose sanctions, which can include default judgment against a disobedient party, when that party fails to comply with the requirements of an ordered Rule 35(a) examination.

Explanation: Question 66

The correct answer is: **(A)** Yes, because Lawyer filed an appearance in the case.

Under Federal Rule of Civil Procedure 55(b)(1), the clerk can enter a judgment by default only if three things are true: the amount is a sum certain, the defendant is not a minor or an incompetent, and the defendant has been defaulted for failure to appear. Here, the Defendant has appeared because lawyer filed a notice of appearance in the case. Once that has happened, only the court and not the clerk may enter judgment against the defendant, and the defendant is entitled to seven days' notice. Therefore, this answer is correct.

(B) Incorrect. Yes, because a judgment must be entered by the court rather than the clerk.

Not all default judgments must be entered by the court. If the defendant has been defaulted for failure to appear on a claim for a sum certain, and the defendant is neither a minor nor incompetent, then the clerk may enter the judgment under Rule 55(b)(1). Therefore, this answer is incorrect.

(C) Incorrect. No, because the claim was for a sum certain.

That the claim is for a sum certain is a necessary but not sufficient condition for the clerk to enter the judgment. It must also be true that the defendant has been defaulted for failure to appear. Here, the defendant has appeared through its representative, Lawyer, and once that appearance has been filed only the court may enter judgment, even when the claim is for a sum certain. Therefore, this answer is incorrect.

(D) Incorrect. No, because the Plaintiff showed the amount due by affidavit.

The clerk may enter judgment based upon an affidavit when the clerk has the power to enter the judgment. Here, however, the clerk does not have the power to do so because the Defendant has appeared. Even with an affidavit showing the amount due, the clerk may not enter the default judgment when a defendant has appeared. Only the court may enter judgment under these circumstances. Therefore, this answer is incorrect.

Explanation: Question 67

The correct answer is: **(B)** Yes, because the defendant did not include the defense in the motion to dismiss.

Under Federal Rule of Civil Procedure 12(h)(1)(A), a defendant waives the defense of lack of venue if the defendant elects to make a motion to dismiss under Rule 12(b) and fails to include the venue defense. That is what this defendant did.

(A) Incorrect. Yes, because the defendant did not include it in the answer.

One way to preserve the venue defense is to include it in an answer, unless the party has elected to file a motion to dismiss and omitted the defense from the motion. Once that had happened, the defense was waived regardless of whether the defendant had included it in the answer.

(C) Incorrect. No, because the defense appeared in an amended answer filed as a matter of course.

The defendant would have prevented waiver of the defense by including it in the amended answer filed so soon (and therefore filed as a matter of right under Rule 15(a)(1)(A)) if the defendant had not responded to the complaint with a motion to dismiss. Once the defendant filed that motion and omitted the defense, it was waived, and finally including it in the amended answer filed as a matter of course could not revive it.

(D) Incorrect. No, because lack of venue may not be waived.

The defense of lack of venue is a "threshold defense" that must be raised at the beginning of the case or it will be waived, under Rule 12(h)(1)(A). Unlike, for example, a defense of lack of subject-matter jurisdiction, the defense of lack of venue can be waived.

Explanation: Question 68

The correct answer is: **(B)** Yes, because the man has over $100,000 in damages.

For a federal court to have jurisdiction based on diversity, the amount in controversy must be over $75,000. Importantly, as long as one plaintiff's claim meets the amount-in-controversy requirement, it does not matter that a co-plaintiff whose claim arises through the same events and who thus joins through supplemental jurisdiction is claiming less than the required amount [Exxon Mobil Corporation v. Allapattah Services Inc., 545 U.S. 546 (2005)]. Here, since the woman is joining because of injuries she suffered in the same accident, and since the man's damages are $100,000, the amount-in-controversy requirement is satisfied.

(A) Incorrect. Yes, because federal jurisdiction is determined on the date the suit is filed.

While it is true that the issue of citizenship for diversity jurisdiction is determined on the date the suit is filed, this is not a true statement in regards to claims joined through supplemental jurisdiction. The issue in amount-in-controversy situations is more correctly stated as looking at whether one of the plaintiffs has a claim exceeding the amount-in-controversy requirement.

(C) Incorrect. No, because the woman only suffered $5,000 in damages.

For a federal court to have jurisdiction based on diversity, the amount in controversy must be over $75,000. Importantly, as long as one plaintiff's claim meets the amount-in-controversy requirement, it does not matter that a co-plaintiff whose claim arises through the same events and who thus joins through supplemental jurisdiction is claiming less than the required amount [Exxon Mobil Corporation v. Allapattah Services Inc., 545 U.S. 546 (2005)]. Here, although the woman is only claiming $5,000, her claim can be joined to the man's claim of over $100,000 in damages (which exceeds the amount-in-controversy requirement).

(D) Incorrect. No, because auto accidents are matters left to the states.

There is no rule stating that an auto accident is a matter left only to the states. In fact, if the amount-in-controversy and citizenship requirements are met, an auto accident can be a proper matter for a federal court.

Explanation: Question 69

The correct answer is: **(B)** Yes, because the renewed motion for judgment as a matter of law was filed too late.

Under Federal Rule of Civil Procedure 50(b), the defendant had 28 days from the date of the entry of judgment to file the renewed motion for judgment as a matter of law. Because the motion was made 29 days after entry of judgment, the motion came too late.

(A) Incorrect. Yes, because the defendant did not make a motion for judgment as a matter of law at the close of all the evidence.

The defendant preserved the right to make a renewed motion for judgment as a matter of law by making the initial motion for judgment as a matter of law in accordance with Rule 50(a). That rule states that a party may make a motion for judgment as a matter of law at any time before submission of the case to the jury. Here, the defendant complied with that rule by making the motion at the close of the plaintiff's case.

(C) Incorrect. No, because a renewed motion for judgment as a matter of law may be made within one year of the entry of judgment on a jury verdict.

Several of the types of motions for relief from judgment under Rule 60 must be made within one year. This motion, however, is not a motion for relief from judgment but is rather a renewed motion for judgment as a matter of law. That motion must be made within 28 days of the date of entry of judgment.

(D) Incorrect. No, because the defendant made a motion for judgment as a matter of law at the close of the plaintiff's case.

The defendant made the motion for judgment as a matter of law at an appropriate time, after the other party had been fully heard and before the case was submitted to the jury. The defendant thereby preserved the right to make a renewed motion for judgment as a matter of law, but that renewed motion had to be made within 28 days of the date of entry of judgment. This motion came too late.

Explanation: Question 70

The correct answer is: **(C)** No, because the court had the option to order further deliberations or a new trial under these circumstances.

Under Federal Rule of Civil Procedure 48(c), the trial judge had the right to poll the jury on his own motion. Once the polling revealed a lack of unanimity, the judge had the option to order the jurors to resume deliberations or to order a new trial.

(A) Incorrect. Yes, because a verdict of 10 of 12 jurors was sufficient in federal court to support a judgment.

Rule 48(b) provides that a verdict must be unanimous in federal court unless the parties stipulate to accept a non-unanimous verdict. Here, the parties had not entered into such a stipulation and therefore a vote of 10-2 was not sufficient to support a judgment on the verdict.

(B) Incorrect. Yes, because the court was required to order the jurors to resume deliberations under these circumstances.

The court could have chosen to order the jurors to resume deliberations, but the judge had another choice as well—to order a new trial. The judge selected the new trial option and thus acted in accordance with Rule 48(c).

(D) Incorrect. No, because the court was required to order a new trial once the polling revealed that a juror did not assent to the verdict announced to the court.

The order of a new trial was an option but not a mandate. Under Rule 48(c), the court could have ordered the jurors to resume deliberations instead of ordering a new trial.

Explanation: Question 71

The correct answer is: **(A)** Yes, because jurisdiction is determined at the time the suit is filed.

Citizenship for diversity jurisdiction is determined by looking at the date when the suit was filed. At the time the suit was filed, the man and the corporation were adverse to each other (he was suing the corporation and the question states that they were clearly antagonists), placing the man and the corporation on different sides of the claim. It was only the change caused by the merger that united the man's and the corporation's interests. Since the man was a citizen of State B, and the corporations were citizens of State A, there was complete diversity of citizenship at the time the suit was filed. Consequently, the federal court can hear the claim.

(B) Incorrect. Yes, because the action was originally brought in federal court.

Although the action was originally brought in federal court, there is no rule stating that any action brought in federal court has to stay there. Otherwise, there would be no reason to assess personal and subject-matter jurisdiction during claims, and plaintiffs would be sole masters of whether cases should be heard by federal courts.

(C) Incorrect. No, because the realignment caused both sides of the conflict to be citizens of State A.

While the realignment destroyed diversity jurisdiction by putting a State A citizen on both sides of the claim, diversity is determined at the time the suit is filed. At that time, the man and the corporation were adverse to each other, making federal jurisdiction appropriate. It was only later that the two parties became aligned.

(D) Incorrect. No, because federal courts are masters of their own jurisdiction.

While a federal court may be master of its own jurisdiction, it cannot hear whatever types of suits it wants based on that (for example, a non-diverse state law claim). Consequently, this answer choice presents a poor reason for approval or denial of federal jurisdiction.

Explanation: Question 72

The correct answer is: **(D)** No, because the attorney based the motion on the man's statements.

Before filing a motion, attorneys must investigate the factual and legal bases for that motion [Fed. R. Civ. P. 11]. Consequently, the attorney cannot merely base the motion off the man's word without some sort of reasonable inquiry.

(A) Incorrect. Yes, because the corporation's primary place of business is in State A.

In determining a corporation's citizenship for diversity jurisdiction, courts look at both the primary place of business and the state of incorporation. Importantly, courts determine a corporation's primary place of business by looking at its "nerve center," or the place where decisions regarding the corporation are made. Here, since the corporation's directors are all in State C, this is likely the corporation's primary place of business. However, the bigger issue is that the attorney simply took the man's word for it and did no investigation regarding his statements.

(B) Incorrect. Yes, because the corporation is incorporated in State B.

In determining a corporation's citizenship for diversity jurisdiction, courts look at both the primary place of business and the state of incorporation. Consequently, while the corporation may be incorporated in State B, the court would still have to determine the corporation's primary place of business as well. However, the bigger issue is that the attorney simply took the man's word for it and did no investigation regarding his statements.

(C) Incorrect. No, because the corporation's primary place of business is in State C.

In determining a corporation's citizenship for diversity jurisdiction, courts look at both the primary place of business and the state of incorporation. Importantly, courts determine a corporation's primary place of business by looking at its "nerve center," or the place where decisions regarding the corporation are made. Here, since the corporation's directors are all in State C, this is a correct statement. However, the issue is that the attorney did not do any research regarding the man's statements before filing the motion. Before filing a motion, attorneys must investigate the factual and legal bases for that motion [Fed. R. Civ. P. 11]. Consequently, the attorney cannot merely base the motion off the man's word without some sort of reasonable inquiry whether the man's statements are actually correct or not (and there is no indication the man is right about any of this).

Explanation: Question 73

The correct answer is: **(B)** Third-party complaint.

A third-party complaint is the proper procedural tool to bring in another party when a defendant has filed a counterclaim against a plaintiff and the plaintiff believes another party is liable for some or all of the liability pursuant to the counterclaim. Because the man believes the manufacturer's negligence caused the damage to the hotel for which is being sued, he should file a third-party complaint against the manufacturer.

(A) Incorrect. Intervention.

Intervention allows a non-party to assert a right or interest in an ongoing litigation, and is a tool asserted by the third party, not a party already in the litigation. Because the man is already a party to the litigation, he would not use intervention to bring another party in.

(C) Incorrect. Rule interpleader.

Interpleader is used when a plaintiff has some holding that would expose itself to claims from multiple parties and wants to bring all of those parties in. This is inapplicable to this situation where the man is attempting to bring in another party whom he believes to be liable for any damages assessed against him.

(D) Incorrect. Statutory interpleader.

This is an incorrect answer because, as stated above, interpleader is inapplicable to this situation where the man is attempting to bring in another party whom he believes to be liable for any damages assessed against him.

Explanation: Question 74

The correct answer is: **(C)** No, because the judge chose to ask the questions herself.

Federal Rule of Civil Procedure 47(a) governs the questioning of prospective jurors in federal civil cases. The judge is permitted to choose to do the questioning, and that is quite common in federal court. Under the circumstances of this case, the court was alerted to the need to have the prospective jurors answer additional proper questions. Under the rule, the judge had two options: allow the attorneys to ask those questions or ask them herself. She chose to do the latter and thereby abided by the rule.

(A) Incorrect. Yes, because attorneys for the parties have the right to ask proper questions directly of prospective jurors during jury selection in federal court.

Attorneys do not have the right to ask questions directly of prospective jurors in federal civil cases. Rule 47(a) allows the court to permit such direct questioning but also gives the trial judge the option to do all the questioning herself.

(B) Incorrect. Yes, because the questions were directed to possible bases for challenges for cause.

Lawyers and the court gather information during jury selection to inform challenges for cause and peremptory challenges. The procedure for questioning jurors about these different types of challenges does not, however, differ. Regardless of the reason for the questions, the court may permit counsel to do the questioning or do it herself. That these questions dealt with possible challenges for cause is irrelevant.

(D) Incorrect. No, because attorneys are not allowed to ask questions directly of prospective jurors during jury selection in federal court.

It is customary for judges to conduct the voir dire in federal court, but it is not required. Under Rule 47(a), the court may choose to permit the lawyers to question prospective jurors directly.

Explanation: Question 75

The correct answer is: **(C)** Yes, because the homeowner is required to provide disclosure of the policy without awaiting a discovery request.

Pursuant to Fed. R. Civ. P. 26(a), parties are required to disclose any insurance agreement by which an insurance company may be liable to satisfy all or part of a judgment in an action or to reimburse the liable party. This disclosure must be made without awaiting a discovery request. Because the homeowner's insurance policy could be used to satisfy a judgment in this case, he is required to disclose it.

(A) Incorrect. No, because evidence of an insurance policy cannot be used to show that the homeowner acted wrongfully.

While this is an accurate statement of law, it is irrelevant to the question, as this rule goes to the admissibility of evidence, not the required disclosures between the parties.

(B) Incorrect. No, because insurance coverage is not relevant to the newlyweds' claims or the homeowner's defenses.

Parties may request discovery of material relevant to their claims and defenses, but evidence of insurance coverage is separately required as a disclosure pursuant to Fed. R. Civ. P. 26(a).

(D) Incorrect. Yes, but only if the newlyweds specifically requested disclosure of any insurance policies.

As stated above, pursuant to Fed. R. Civ. P. 26(a), parties are required to disclose such insurance agreements, and must do so without waiting for a discovery request.

Explanation: Question 76

The correct answer is: **(C)** No, because the requests concerned issues that could have been reasonably anticipated as of the date of the final pretrial conference.

The court had set a deadline of the date of the final pretrial conference for the submission of proposed jury instructions. Under Federal Rule of Civil Procedure 51(a)(2), a party to a case where the court has set such a deadline has the right to file requests for jury instructions at the close of the evidence only if the instructions concern issues that could not have reasonably been anticipated as of the deadline. In this case, the instructions concern issues that could reasonably have been anticipated as of then. Therefore, the request for instructions was untimely, and the plaintiff could submit the instructions only with court permission, under Rule 51(a)(2)(B).

(A) Incorrect. Yes, because closing arguments had not yet occurred.

The court must advise the parties about the instructions that the court intends to give before the closing arguments and give the parties time to object. The deadline for timely proposed instructions about issues that reasonably can be anticipated to arrive, however, is not closing arguments but rather the earlier of the deadline set by the court (here, the date of the final pretrial conference) or the close of all the evidence. The right to submit these instructions expired long before the time for closing arguments.

(B) Incorrect. Yes, because the jury had not yet been instructed.

The court must advise the parties about the instructions that the court intends to give before instructing the jury and give the parties time to object. The deadline for timely proposed instructions about issues that reasonably can be anticipated to arise, however, is not the commencement of instructions but rather the earlier of the deadline set by the court (here, the date of the final pretrial conference) or the close of all the evidence. The right to submit these instructions expired before the time for the instructions.

(D) Incorrect. No, because the date set by the court for submission of proposed jury instructions had passed.

The request came after the court's deadline, but under one set of circumstances the plaintiff would still have had the right to file them. Under Federal Rule of Civil Procedure 51(a)(2)(A), a party has the right to file new proposed instructions even after the deadline if they concern issues that could not have reasonably been anticipated at the time of the deadline. Here, the proposed instructions are untimely, and the plaintiff does not have the right to file them, because two things are true, not just one: they are late, and they concern issues that could have reasonably been anticipated at the time of the deadline.

Explanation: Question 77

The correct answer is: **(A)** Reverse the judgment and order a new trial.

Since a jury could reasonably conclude that Dr. Pupil did inadvertently apply an acidic substance to Irene's eyes, a directed verdict in favor of the former would be inappropriate. Thus, the trial court's judgment should be reversed and a new trial ordered. If the trial court had withheld its decision upon the motion for a directed verdict until the jury had rendered its decision, it might not have been necessary to order a new trial (i.e., the jury verdict could be in conformity with the directed verdict). For this reason, a determination upon a motion for a directed verdict will ordinarily be withheld until after the jury's verdict has been returned.

(B) Incorrect. Reverse the judgment and direct that judgment be entered for Irene.

A jury could reasonably find that Dr. Pupil was not at fault; thus, a directed verdict is not appropriate.

(C) Incorrect. Affirm the judgment.

A jury could reasonably render a verdict for Irene, so a directed verdict was not appropriate.

(D) Incorrect. Affirm the judgment, because Irene did not prove beyond a reasonable doubt that Dr. Pupil inadvertently applied an acidic substance to her eyes.

Since a jury could reasonably conclude that Dr. Pupil did inadvertently apply an acidic substance to Irene's eyes, a directed verdict in favor of the former would be inappropriate. Thus, the trial court's judgment should be reversed and a new trial ordered. If the trial court had withheld its decision upon the motion for a directed verdict until the jury had rendered its decision, it might not have been necessary to order a new trial (i.e., the jury verdict could be in conformity with the directed verdict). For this reason, a determination upon a motion for a directed verdict will ordinarily be withheld until after the jury's verdict has been returned.

Explanation: Question 78

The correct answer is: **(B)** The amount-in-controversy requirement was not satisfied.

Where, as here, there is no federal question pending before a federal district court, a federal district court may still have subject-matter jurisdiction over an action where the litigants are citizens of different states and the amount in controversy exceeds $75,000. Here, the total amount of damages sought by the employee was $75,000. Because State B follows the majority view which looks to the amount sought by a plaintiff in his or her complaint to determine the amount in controversy for diversity purposes, the amount-in-controversy requirement is not satisfied making this the best answer choice.

(A) Incorrect. The complete diversity requirement between the parties was not satisfied.

In order for a federal district court to have subject-matter jurisdiction over an action where no federal question is presented, there must be complete diversity between the parties to the lawsuit and the amount in controversy must exceed $75,000. Here, the complete diversity requirement was satisfied because at the time the employee filed the lawsuit she was a citizen of State A and the employer was a citizen of State B. Because diversity is determined at the time the lawsuit is filed, the fact that the employee later moved to State B is irrelevant and does not destroy the complete diversity requirement.

(C) Incorrect. The federal question requirement was not satisfied because the employee did not make a claim under the federal anti-discrimination laws.

While it is true that there was no federal question here as all of the employee's claims arose under state law, the presence of a federal question is not necessary in order for a federal district court to have subject-matter jurisdiction over an action. Federal district courts also have jurisdiction over parties where there is diversity of citizenship among the parties and the amount in controversy exceeds $75,000. Therefore, it does not follow that the court lacked subject-matter jurisdiction because the employee did not make a claim under the federal anti-discrimination laws, and so this is not the best answer.

(D) Incorrect. The court did not have supplemental jurisdiction over the employee's claims.

This answer is incorrect because while it is true that the court did not have supplemental jurisdiction over the employee's claims, this would not, in and of itself, be a basis on which the court would rely to dismiss the action. Supplemental jurisdiction allows a federal district court to hear claims over which it would not otherwise have jurisdiction (such as where there is no federal question or diversity between the parties) when the claims relate to or arise out of the same transaction or occurrence as a different claim over which the federal district court has original jurisdiction. Here, there is neither a federal question nor diversity of citizenship (because the amount in controversy does not exceed the $75,000 threshold) to provide the federal district court in State B with original jurisdiction over any of the employee's claims, and it is for this reason that the court will dismiss the complaint.

Explanation: Question 79

The correct answer is: **(A)** No, unless the defendants can show that the mechanic was fraudulently joined.

Removal is not permissible where there is not complete diversity of the parties, unless it can be shown that the plaintiff fraudulently joined a non-diverse in order to defeat diversity. The burden is on the defendants seeking removal to make this showing. Because the mechanic is from the same state as the man, the defendants would have the burden of showing the mechanic was fraudulently joined in order to remove the case.

(B) Incorrect. No, because the case does not present a federal question.

While a federal question would allow for the defendants to remove the case regardless of the diversity of parties, this answer choice is not as good as A because it does not allow for the possibility of fraudulent joinder in a diversity jurisdiction case.

(C) Incorrect. Yes, unless the plaintiff can show that the mechanic was not fraudulently joined.

This misstates the burden when fraudulent joinder is alleged. If the defendants seek to remove a case based on diversity jurisdiction where there is not complete diversity, the burden will be on the defendant to show that the plaintiff fraudulently joined the non-diverse party.

(D) Incorrect. Yes, because two of the defendants are diverse from the plaintiff.

Diversity jurisdiction requires complete diversity between the plaintiffs and defendants, so the fact that two of the defendants are diverse from the plaintiff is insufficient for removal.

Explanation: Question 80

The correct answer is: **(C)** The class is made up entirely of 60 users from State A and 60 users from State B and the amount in controversy is $6 million.

Pursuant to the Class Action Fairness Act ("CAFA"), a federal court will have subject-matter jurisdiction over a class action based on diversity jurisdiction where there are at least 100 members in the class, the amount in controversy exceeds $5 million, and where at least one of the members of the plaintiff class is diverse from the primary defendant, with the added requirement that, if a primary defendant is a resident of the state in which the claim was originally filed, less than two-thirds of the plaintiffs are residents of the forum state. This is the only answer choice that meets all of those requirements.

(A) Incorrect. The class is made up entirely of 100,000 users from State A and the amount in controversy is $1 million.

Under CAFA, for a federal court to have jurisdiction over a class action suit based on diversity jurisdiction, at least one of the class members must be diverse from the defendants. Here, all parties are residents of State A. Furthermore, CAFA requires that the amount in controversy exceed $5 million.

(B) Incorrect. The class is made up entirely of 750 users from State A and 250 users from State B and the amount in controversy is $12 million.

As stated above, one of the requirements of CAFA is that, where a primary defendant is a resident of the state in which the claim was originally filed, residents of the forum state cannot comprise 2/3 or more of the plaintiff class. This scenario has 3/4 of the plaintiff class residing in State A, so this scenario will violate CAFA.

(D) Incorrect. None of the above.

This answer is incorrect because answer choice C is acceptable under the requirements of CAFA.

Explanation: Question 81

The correct answer is: **(B)** An affidavit alleging that, if the client did not attend her hearing next week, she would be subject to a deportation order.

In asking a court to issue a temporary restraining order or preliminary injunction, a petitioner must show a likelihood of success on the merits, that the petitioner will suffer irreparable injury without the requested relief, and that the irreparable injury would outweigh any harm the requested relief would cause to the respondents. Therefore, it is crucial for the petitioner to show the immediacy of the need for the requested relief. The fact that a client would be deported if the pending regulation were enforced would show that immediacy.

(A) Incorrect. A report showing that there have been no previous incidents of terrorism in federal courthouses.

This would be a useful piece of evidence in more in-depth challenge to the regulation. However, it would not be the most useful support for a petition for a temporary restraining order, in which the petitioner needs to show a likelihood of success on the merits, that the petitioner will suffer irreparable injury without the requested relief, and that the irreparable injury would outweigh any harm the requested relief would cause to the respondents.

(C) Incorrect. An investigative report demonstrating that other federal security regulations have not been uniformly administered.

Depending on patterns within the lack of uniform administration, this might help to support an equal protection claim. It would be less relevant to a petition for a temporary restraining order, for which it is important to show that the petitioner would suffer an irreparable injury in the time that it would take for her case to go through normal court procedures.

(D) Incorrect. Affidavits of several clients stating that it was a hardship for them to obtain a government-issued form of identification.

Affidavits of several clients that showed hardship from the implementation of the regulation might well be evidence against the regulation at a hearing on the merits. However, the purpose of a temporary restraining order is to preserve a current situation until the hearing on the merits can take place, due to a likely immediate and irreparable injury. This would not be the best way to show an immediate and irreparable injury.

Explanation: Question 82

The correct answer is: **(A)** Ask the court to enter a temporary restraining order.

A court may issue a temporary restraining order without written or oral notice to the adverse party only if [Fed. R. Civ. P. 65(b)(1)]: (a) specific facts in an affidavit or verified complaint clearly show that immediate and irreparable injury, loss, or damage will result to the movant before the adverse party can be heard in opposition; and (b) the movant's attorney certifies in writing any efforts made to give notice and the reasons why it should not be required. Here, the partner is embezzling funds, and if she discovers the general contractor is on to her, she may abscond with more money. The best course of action would be to ask for a TRO, so the contractor does not have to give his partner notice before the order is granted.

(B) Incorrect. Ask the court for a preliminary injunction.

A preliminary injunction may only be issued by a court on notice to the adverse party. Here, giving the partner notice may lead to her taking more money from the company.

(C) Incorrect. Ask the court for summary judgment.

A summary judgment is intended to pierce the pleadings to determine if there is credible evidence to factually support a party's claim. Here, no pleadings have been entered yet.

(D) Incorrect. Ask the court for depositions.

Since no action has begun, a request for depositions at this point would be too early.

Explanation: Question 83

The correct answer is: **(A)** Yes, because it was filed after the case had been submitted to the jury.

Federal Rule of Civil Procedure 50(a) specifies the time for making a motion for judgment as a matter of law. The motion may be made as early as the moment when the opposing party has been fully heard on an issue but in any event must be made before the case is submitted to the jury. This motion came too late.

(B) Incorrect. Yes, because it was filed after the defendant presented evidence.

The defendant need not wait to present evidence before filing a motion for judgment as a matter of law, but the motion does not become untimely if the defendant waits until after presenting evidence. It is only once the case has been submitted to the jury that the motion is untimely.

(C) Incorrect. No, because the plaintiff had been fully heard.

The motion would not have been timely until the plaintiff had been fully heard, but there is an outer limit as well. The motion for judgment as a matter of law may be filed anytime between when the opposing party has been fully heard and, at the outside, the time when the case is submitted to the jury. Here, the motion came after that.

(D) Incorrect. No, because the jury had not reached a verdict.

Once a case is ready for submission to the jury, the parties have a complete record upon which they may base a motion for judgment as a matter of law. One of the purposes of such a motion is to make the jury deliberations unnecessary. The rule, therefore, is that the motion must be made before the case is submitted to the jury, rather than before the jury reaches a verdict.

Explanation: Question 84

The correct answer is: **(C)** No, because the Federal Rules of Civil Procedure authorize what the federal judge did.

Federal Rule of Civil Procedure 49(b) explicitly permits the court to submit the case to the jury by general verdict with written questions. When a Federal Rule of Civil Procedure "covers" a procedural issue, the federal court applies the federal rule even if the state court in the same locale would do something different. The Erie Doctrine does not require a federal court to ignore a validly enacted federal procedural rule.

(A) Incorrect. Yes, because the case was originally filed in state court.

The fact that the case began in state court is not relevant. Once the case is in federal court, whether filed there originally or because of removal, the court must apply the Erie Doctrine to this diversity case to determine whether the federal court must follow state law. Here, because there was a validly enacted federal procedural rule that covered the situation, the federal court was required to follow the federal rule and would have been required to do so even if the case had been filed originally in federal court. The removal is irrelevant to the question.

(B) Incorrect. Yes, because federal courts must follow state law in diversity cases.

This answer is too general. The federal court must follow state substantive law if there is no federal law that governs, and the federal court sometimes will be required to apply state procedures when there is no federal procedural rule or statute that governs. Here, however, there was a federal rule that covered the situation.

(D) Incorrect. No, because the method of submitting a case to a jury is not outcome-determinative.

Whether or not the application of a state procedure would be outcome-determinative does not always dictate what procedure the federal court must follow. Where, as here, there is a federal rule that empowers the court to do as it did, the federal court may apply the federal rule even if the result would dictate the outcome.

Explanation: Question 85

The correct answer is: **(C)** No, because the ex-wife is trying to invalidate a will.

Under the probate exception, federal courts typically will not exercise jurisdiction over probate matters such as the validity of a will and the administration of an estate even when the requirements for diversity jurisdiction are met. The exception is intended to preserve state control over wills and estates. Here, the ex-wife is trying to invalidate the man's will, so the probate exception would apply.

(A) Incorrect. Yes, because the ex-wife is a citizen of State B.

While the ex-wife's citizenship implies that diversity jurisdiction would apply (since the man was a citizen of State A and the amount in controversy is over $75,000), federal courts typically refuse to exercise jurisdiction over probate matters such as the validity of a will. This is known as the probate exception. Here, since the ex-wife is trying to invalidate the man's will, the probate exception would apply.

(B) Incorrect. Yes, because the housekeeper is a foreign citizen.

While the housekeeper is a foreign citizen, the important thing to note in this question is that the ex-wife is suing the man's estate. Since the housekeeper is not a named party in the litigation, her citizenship, whatever it may be, is irrelevant.

(D) Incorrect. No, because the man's assets are only real property.

For diversity jurisdiction to apply, the amount in controversy must be over $75,000. However, this does not mean that this amount has to be in any particular form (such as cash). Consequently, it is irrelevant that the man's assets are only real property.

Explanation: Question 86

The correct answer is: **(C)** One of the interrogatories directed towards the CEO has asked him to disclose whether he has ever used illegal recreational drugs, and is thus irrelevant.

Interrogatories are subject to the scope of discovery rules listed in Fed. R. Civ. P. 26(b) which, among other things, requires that discovery be limited to material that is relevant to the parties' claims and defenses. Here, the defendants appear to be making a valid objection that the CEO's drug usage is irrelevant to the plaintiff's claims or the defendants' defenses.

(A) Incorrect. The man has exceeded the number of interrogatories allowed as a matter of right.

Pursuant to Fed. R. Civ. P. 33, a party may request up to 25 interrogatories, so the man is within his right to request 25 interrogatories.

(B) Incorrect. Interrogatories cannot be directed to corporate entities, and instead must be directed to a specific representative of that entity.

This is an inaccurate statement of law, as interrogatories may be directed at a corporate entity, and it will be the corporate entity's responsibility to designate an officer or agent to respond.

(D) Incorrect. The man has not given the defendants sufficient time to complete the interrogatories.

A party has up to 30 days to respond to an interrogatory unless otherwise specified, thus this would not be a valid objection based on these facts.

Explanation: Question 87

The correct answer is: **(D)** No, because the deceased initially filed the suit.

In determining citizenship for diversity purposes, the relevant date is the date the action is filed. Even if citizenship changes after that date, the original citizenship determination stays in place. Here, at the time of the suit, the man was a citizen of State A and the company was a citizen of State B. Consequently, there was complete diversity of citizenship, which would allow the case to be heard in federal court (assuming the claim was worth over $75,000, which is not mentioned as a potential issue here).

(A) Incorrect. Yes, because the citizenship of the named plaintiff has changed.

While the citizenship of the person pursuing the action may have changed, that person is standing in the shoes of another. At the time that other person filed his suit, his citizenship was diverse from the company's, making a federal court appropriate. Importantly, the only important time in determining citizenship is the date on which the action is filed.

(B) Incorrect. Yes, because there would have been no diversity had the special administrator initially filed the suit.

While this statement is correct, it does not affect the analysis of the situation as it stands, where the deceased was in fact the one who filed suit.

(C) Incorrect. No, because the deceased was a citizen of State A.

While the deceased was a citizen of State A, the more important point is that the deceased initially filed the suit (for example, if his administrator filed the suit, his citizenship would have been used, and the deceased's would not have mattered). Consequently, this is not the strongest answer.

Explanation: Question 88

The correct answer is: **(D)** No, because the court will only be looking at the possible effect of raising the claims in the first suit.

Federal district courts have original jurisdiction over all civil actions "arising under the Constitution, laws, and treaties of the United States" [28 U.S.C. § 1331]. Importantly, the mere presence of federal law in a claim is insufficient to create jurisdiction. The federal law must have a substantial impact on the state law issue. Here, the malpractice claim is a state law issue. Although the court will have to make determinations regarding federal law in evaluating the unraised claims, the federal law here is not substantial because the court will only be looking at the hypothetical outcome of raising these issues. Specifically, whether the attorney should have raised these claims in order to provide effective representation. This type of evaluation will not change the real-world result of prior federal patent litigation because there is no judgment on what the law should be, but only on what it is and how it might have affected the woman's claim. Consequently, the federal law is not substantial in this matter [Gunn v. Minton, 133 S.Ct. 1059 (2013)].

(A) Incorrect. Yes, because the original claim was in federal court.

Although the original claim was in federal court, this would not immediately confer jurisdiction to the federal court on the malpractice claim.

(B) Incorrect. Yes, because it will be necessary to determine federal law in regard to the infringement claims.

Federal district courts have original jurisdiction over all civil actions "arising under the Constitution, laws, and treaties of the United States" [28 U.S.C. § 1331]. Importantly, the mere presence of federal law in a claim is insufficient to create jurisdiction. The federal law must have a substantial impact on the state law issue. Here, the malpractice claim is a state law issue. Although the court will have to make determinations regarding federal law in evaluating the unraised claims, the federal law here is not substantial because the court will only be looking at the hypothetical outcome of raising these issues. Specifically, whether the attorney should have raised these claims in order to provide effective representation. This type of evaluation will not change the real-world result of prior federal patent litigation because there is no judgment on what the law should be, but only on what it is and how it might have affected the woman's claim. Consequently, the federal law is not substantial in this matter [Gunn v. Minton, 133 S.Ct. 1059 (2013)].

(C) Incorrect. No, because a malpractice claim is not a federal claim.

Although malpractice is generally a state law claim, if the federal question here had been substantial, the woman could have still had her claim heard in federal court.

Explanation: Question 89

The correct answer is: **(B)** No, because the wife did not waive her objections to the court's jurisdiction.

When a defendant waives service, she does not waive her objections to the court's subject-matter jurisdiction or personal jurisdiction. Therefore, despite the fact the wife waived the husband's service of process, she may still argue that the court does not have jurisdiction over her.

(A) Incorrect. No, because the husband was responsible for any insufficiency in the service of process.

It is correct that a plaintiff is responsible for any insufficiency in the service of process, regardless of whether the task was hired out to a third party, but this is irrelevant to the question, as the wife waived service of process.

(C) Incorrect. Yes, because the wife waived her objections to the court's jurisdiction.

As stated above, when a defendant waives service, she does not waive her objections to the court's subject-matter jurisdiction or personal jurisdiction. Therefore, she may still object to the court's jurisdiction over her.

(D) Incorrect. Yes, because waiver of service automatically subjects a party to a court's jurisdiction.

This is an incorrect statement of law. Again, when a defendant waives service, she does not waive her objections to the court's subject-matter jurisdiction or personal jurisdiction.

Explanation: Question 90

The correct answer is: **(D)** No, because the Court of Appeals had discretion to decline to hear the appeal.

Under 28 U.S.C. § 1292(b), the Court of Appeals has the discretion to hear an appeal from an interlocutory order when the trial court makes the certification that the trial court in this case made. However, it is not error for the Court of Appeals to decline to hear the appeal, because the Court of Appeals has discretion to hear it or not.

(A) Incorrect. Yes, because the trial court certified that its order involved a controlling issue of law about which a substantial ground for difference of opinion existed and that an immediate appeal might materially advance the termination of the litigation.

The trial court's certification empowered the Court of Appeals to hear an appeal of the interlocutory order. The exercise of that power, however, was discretionary. The Court of Appeals need not hear the appeal even when the trial court makes the necessary certification.

(B) Incorrect. Yes, because the order denying the discovery was immediately appealable as of right.

In federal court, the general rule is that only final judgments may be appealed, and there is no exception that would permit all decisions about attorney-client privilege or other issues in discovery to be appealed immediately.

(C) Incorrect. No, because the order was not a final judgment.

Although the general rule is that only final judgments are appealable, there are exceptions. This case would have been one of the exceptions if the Court of Appeals had exercised its discretion to hear the case in light of the trial court's certification. The Court of Appeals had the power but not the duty to decline to hear the appeal.

Explanation: Question 91

The correct answer is: **(A)** The court has *in personam* jurisdiction because it may exercise specific jurisdiction over the man.

A court may exercise specific jurisdiction over an out-of-state defendant where the claim against the defendant arises out of or is related to the defendant's presence in the forum state. Although the man was only in State B for one day, the casino's claim arises out of his presence at the casino in State B, therefore the court may exercise *in personam* jurisdiction over him.

(B) Incorrect. The court has *in personam* jurisdiction because the man has systematic and continuous contacts with State B.

A defendant with systematic and continuous contacts with the forum state will be subject to personal jurisdiction in the forum state for all causes of action, but here the man was only in State B for one day, therefore it cannot be said that he has systematic and continuous contacts with the state.

(C) Incorrect. The court has *in personam* jurisdiction because the state has a substantial interest in regulating gambling.

While a state may, by statute, provide that a non-resident consents to personal jurisdiction by engaging in a particular activity that the state has a substantial interest in regulating, the facts do not indicate that State B has such a statute applicable to the man.

(D) Incorrect. The court has *in rem* jurisdiction.

In rem jurisdiction refers to jurisdiction over a particular piece of property or thing located in the forum state. Here, there is no particular piece of property or thing located in the forum state, therefore this answer choice is inapplicable.

Explanation: Question 92

The correct answer is: **(D)** Either dismiss the case or transfer the case to State A or State B.

When a case is brought in an improper venue, the court may either dismiss the case or transfer the case to a proper venue. Venue was improper here, because the case should have been brought in the district where the defendant resides or where the injury took place. Therefore, the court should either dismiss the case or transfer it to State A or State B.

(A) Incorrect. Allow the case to proceed in State C.

The court should not allow the case to proceed in State C, because State C is an improper venue. Venue is generally proper in a district where the defendant resides or where the injury took place, meaning either State A or State B would be proper venues, but not State C.

(B) Incorrect. Dismiss the case.

The court may dismiss the case, as it was brought in an improper venue, but this is an incomplete answer, as the court may also choose to transfer the case to a proper venue, which would be either State A or State B.

(C) Incorrect. Transfer the case to State A or State B.

Where a case is brought in an improper venue, as it was here, the court may transfer the case to a proper venue, but it also has the option of dismissing the case, making this an incomplete answer.

Explanation: Question 93

The correct answer is: **(D)** No, because the plaintiff's claims arise under federal law.

This is a bit of a trick question in that it was designed to make you think about amount-in-controversy requirements, but recall that amount in controversy only applies to diversity jurisdiction cases. The plaintiff here is alleging a federal copyright claim, so her complaint meets the requirements for federal question jurisdiction, and no amount in controversy is necessary.

(A) Incorrect. Yes, because the plaintiff must have at least one claim that meets the amount-in-controversy requirement.

This is an incorrect statement of law, because a plaintiff may aggregate claims against the same defendant, or multiple defendants when the claims are common and undivided, but the important point is that amount in controversy is inapplicable where, as here, the plaintiff's claim arises under federal law.

(B) Incorrect. Yes, because the plaintiff's claims against the co-defendants are not common and undivided.

It is the case that a plaintiff can aggregate claims against multiple defendants where the claims are common and undivided in order to meet the amount-in-controversy requirement, but here the plaintiff's claims provide federal question jurisdiction.

(C) Incorrect. No, because the plaintiff may aggregate her claims to meet the amount in controversy.

Again, the plaintiff may aggregate claims in certain instances to meet the amount in controversy, but amount in controversy is irrelevant here because there is federal question jurisdiction.

Explanation: Question 94

The correct answer is: **(A)** Yes, if he can show that the State B court is an adequate forum, and that the State A court was significantly inappropriate.

A federal court may transfer an action even where it was brought in an appropriate forum, but the burden is on the plaintiff to show that an adequate alternative forum exists and that the original forum was significantly inappropriate. If the athlete can show that here, then the action can be transferred to State B.

(B) Incorrect. Yes, because he is now a resident of State B.

While this factor may be somewhat relevant to whether the athlete can transfer the case, it is only one factor. The larger issue is whether the athlete can show that State B provides an adequate forum and that State A was a significantly inappropriate forum.

(C) Incorrect. No, because he was a resident of State A at the time the action was filed.

This answer choice confuses the rules regarding removal of a case. With a removal, a defendant in state court cannot remove to federal court if the original case was brought in the defendant's home state. This rule does not apply to transfer.

(D) Incorrect. No, because the case was brought in a proper venue.

As stated above, a federal court may transfer an action even where it was brought in an appropriate forum. Although the court may choose not to transfer the case, the fact that the case was originally brought in a proper venue is not dispositive.

Explanation: Question 95

The correct answer is: **(A)** Failure to state a claim.

A court will dismiss a claim under Rule 12(b)(6) if the complaint fails to state a cognizable claim. However, this defense is not lost if not made in the initial response.

(B) Incorrect. Lack of personal jurisdiction.

Personal jurisdiction refers to a court's authority over a defendant. If this defense is not raised in the initial response, it is lost.

(C) Incorrect. Improper venue.

Venue is the federal court in which an action is filed. Venue in federal cases is primarily based on the type of subject-matter jurisdiction. If this defense is not raised in the initial response, it is lost.

(D) Incorrect. Improper service of process.

A defendant may object to service of process in a motion to dismiss [Fed. R. Civ. P. 12(b)]. If a plaintiff fails to properly effect service according to the federal rules, the case should be dismissed. If this defense is not raised in the initial response, it is lost.

Explanation: Question 96

The correct answer is: **(A)** Yes, because the jury was not merely advisory.

Under Federal Rule of Civil Procedure 39(c), the trial court may order a jury trial of all issues, even if there is no right to a jury, if the jury will be merely advisory or if all parties consent. Here, there was no right to a jury because the plaintiff sought only an equitable remedy rather than damages. One party objected to the use of a jury, but the court nevertheless ordered a trial in which the jury would decide all issues and would not be merely advisory.

(B) Incorrect. Yes, because the plaintiff did not demand a jury.

The demand for jury is essential when a party has the right to a jury and does not want to rely upon the court's discretion to order a jury trial even if it has not been demanded. In this case, however, the plaintiff did not have a right to a jury trial of an equitable claim, and therefore a jury demand would have been of no effect. The problem with what the court did was not that the court acted on its own without a demand the court had the power to do that but rather that the court ordered a jury trial of all issues in a case for which there was no right to a jury and one party objected to the jury.

(C) Incorrect. No, because the plaintiff had a constitutional right to trial by jury of the case.

The plaintiff did not have a constitutional right to a trial by jury. The plaintiff sought only equitable relief rather than damages and thus there was no constitutional right to a jury.

(D) Incorrect. No, because the court had discretion to order a jury trial of all issues.

The court did not have such discretion because the issues were not triable of right to a jury. If they had been, then under Rule 39(b) the court could have ordered a jury trial despite the fact that no party demanded one. When there is no right to a jury, however, the court's discretion to order a jury trial includes only an advisory jury or, if all parties consent, a jury to decide the issues. Here, one party objected, and the jury was not merely advisory.

Explanation: Question 97

The correct answer is: **(A)** A motion for a new trial on the damages issue.

The Federal Rules allow a court to grant a new trial on some or all of the issues previously litigated. Such a motion would be appropriate specifically on the issue of damages when a jury has delivered a clearly inadequate or excessive damage award, showing that it may have misunderstood the evidence presented or may have acted on the basis of prejudice against a party. It would be appropriate for the dancer to file this motion.

(B) Incorrect. A motion for additur.

An additur motion asks a court to increase an inappropriately low damages award. The reason why the dancer should not file an additur motion is that additur has been found unconstitutional in federal court and is therefore not available.

(C) Incorrect. A motion for remittitur.

A motion for remittitur is appropriate in federal court when the jury has awarded clearly excessive damages. That is not the case on these facts, so this is not the best answer.

(D) Incorrect. A motion for relief from a judgment or order.

There are several situations in which a motion for relief from a judgment or order is appropriate, including mistake, newly discovered evidence, fraud, or clerical error. However, nothing in the facts shows that any of these are an issue. The jury did find in the dancer's favor but apparently did not understand or did not agree with the damages as presented in court. This is therefore not the best motion for the dancer to file.

Explanation: Question 98

The correct answer is: **(A)** Yes, because of the unreasonable intrusion on the waitress's privacy.

A court may enter a protective order limiting a discovery request even if the evidence is relevant [Fed. R. Civ. P. 26]. Here, the information's relevance is likely outweighed by the extremely personal nature of the information and its potential effect on other litigants suing for sexual harassment [Priest v. Rotary, 98 F.R.D. 755 (1983)].

(B) Incorrect. Yes, because information of this nature is never appropriate for discovery.

A court may enter a protective order limiting a discovery request even if the evidence is relevant [Fed. R. Civ. P. 26]. Here, the information's relevance is likely outweighed by the extremely personal nature of the information and its potential effect on other litigants suing for sexual harassment [Priest v. Rotary, 98 F.R.D. 755 (1983)]. However, there is no blanket rule stating this kind of information is never appropriate. If this were a situation where the relevance outweighed the privacy intrusion, the court would likely compel its production. "Never" is rarely a good choice on a MBE question.

(C) Incorrect. No, because the information is evidence of habit.

A court may enter a protective order limiting a discovery request even if the evidence is relevant [Fed. R. Civ. P. 26]. It's likely arguable that the evidence might be evidence of her habits regarding her relationship to male customers. However, here, the information's relevance is likely outweighed by the extremely personal nature of the information and its potential effect on other litigants suing for sexual harassment [Priest v. Rotary, 98 F.R.D. 755 (1983)].

(D) Incorrect. No, because the information is evidence of motive.

A court may enter a protective order limiting a discovery request even if the evidence is relevant [Fed. R. Civ. P. 26]. It's likely arguable that the evidence might be evidence of her motive regarding any relationship with male customers. However, here, the information's relevance is likely outweighed by the extremely personal nature of the information and its potential effect on other litigants suing for sexual harassment [Priest v. Rotary, 98 F.R.D. 755 (1983)].

Explanation: Question 99

The correct answer is: **(B)** State B law.

A federal court sitting in diversity jurisdiction will apply the choice of law rules of the state in which the court sits. Where a case has been transferred, however, the substantive law will be the same law that would have been applied by the transferor court. Therefore, State C's choice of law rules will be applied. Those rules state that the substantive law of the state in which the injury to the plaintiff took place should be applied. Here, that was State B.

(A) Incorrect. State A law.

If the State B choice of law rules were to be applied, then State A's substantive law would be applied, as that is where the plaintiff signed the contract with the travel agency. But, as stated above, a transferor court will apply the same substantive law as would have been applied in the original court in which the action was filed. Therefore, State C's choice of law rules would be applied, which would result in State B's substantive law being applied.

(C) Incorrect. State C law.

Although State C's choice of law rules will apply, as that is the forum in which the action was originally filed, the State C choice of law rules dictate that the substantive law of the state in which the injury to the plaintiff took place should be applied. Here, that was State B.

(D) Incorrect. Federal common law.

A federal court sitting in diversity jurisdiction will apply the choice of law rules of the state in which the court sits in determining what state's substantive law applies.

Explanation: Question 100

The correct answer is: **(C)** The Northern and Eastern Districts of State A, and the Western District of State B.

Venue is proper in any district in which a defendant resides, or where the events giving rise to the claim took place. Here, the defendants resided in the Eastern District of State A and the Western District of State B, and the events took place in the Northern District of State A.

(A) Incorrect. The Northern District of State A.

While the events giving rise to the claim took place in the Northern District of State A, making venue proper there, venue is also proper in any district in which the defendant resides, thus venue would also be proper in the Eastern District of State A and the Western District of State B.

(B) Incorrect. The Eastern District of State A.

As stated above, venue is proper in any district in which a defendant resides, or where the events giving rise to the claim took place, therefore this is an incomplete list of where venue would be proper.

(D) Incorrect. The Northern, Eastern, and Western Districts of State A, and the Western District of State B.

Although venue may be proper where a defendant is merely subject to personal jurisdiction, that is only the case where there is no other venue in which to bring the case. So, although the defendants would be subject to personal jurisdiction in the Western District of State A, there are other venues which are proper, therefore venue cannot be based solely on the defendant being subject to personal jurisdiction in the Western District of State A.

FEDERAL CIVIL PROCEDURE MULTISTATE ISSUE GRAPH

Beginning February 2015, ~27 Federal Civil Procedure Questions will be on the MBE:

2/3 questions on topics I, III, V	1/3 questions on topics II, IV, VI, and VII
I. Jurisdiction and venue III. Pretrial procedures V. Motions	II. Law applied by federal courts IV. Jury trials VI. Verdicts and judgments VII. Appealability and review

I. JURISDICTION AND VENUE

I. Jurisdiction and venue subtopics
   A. Federal subject-matter jurisdiction (federal question, diversity, supplemental, and removal)
   B. Personal jurisdiction
   C. Service of process and notice
   D. Venue, *forum non conveniens*, and transfer

Does the **court have the authority** to decide the dispute and bind the parties?

- Jurisdiction over the **Subject Matter**?
  - Federal question jurisdiction
  - Diversity jurisdiction
  - Supplemental jurisdiction
  - Removal jurisdiction
- Jurisdiction over the **Parties**?
  - *In personam*
  - *In rem*
  - *Quasi in rem*
- Service of process and notice
- Venue

DOES THE COURT HAVE AUTHORITY?

Does the court have the authority to decide the dispute?

↓

Jurisdiction over the Subject Matter? →

- Federal question jurisdiction → **Rule: Federal Question**–The general rule is that federal courts have subject-matter jurisdiction over all matters arising under federal law. A claim must contain (1) an essential federal element that (2) appears on the face of the complaint. Federal defenses or claims raised by defendant cannot be the basis for federal question jurisdiction.
- Diversity jurisdiction → **Rule: Diversity Jurisdiction**–Where the amount in controversy exceeds $75,000, the federal courts may hear suits:
  - between **citizens** of different states;
  - between **citizens** of a state and a foreign state (alien);
  - between **citizens** of different states where aliens are also parties;
  - between foreign state plaintiffs and **citizens** of a state.
- Supplemental jurisdiction
- Removal jurisdiction

Rule: Erie Doctrine–

- A federal court with **diversity** or **supplemental jurisdiction** that is presiding over a state law claim must apply the substantive law of the state in which the court sits.
- However, federal procedural law as contained in the Federal Rules of Civil Procedure or other codified federal law, must be applied (**Necessary & Proper Clause**).

Amount in Controversy:
Compensatory and punitive damages may be counted, but pre-judgment costs and interest may not.
A single plaintiff may aggregate all claims against a single defendant or jointly liable defendants. (May not aggregate against multiple defendants when joint liability not alleged).

Determining Citizenship:
Individuals = domicile (physical presence plus intent to remain indefinitely)
Corporations = state of incorporation and state of principal place of business (usually headquarters—corporations can have multiple citizenships)
Partnerships = citizens of every state and country of which the partners are citizens

DOES THE COURT HAVE AUTHORITY?

Does the court have the authority to decide the dispute?

↓

Jurisdiction over the Subject Matter? →

- Federal question jurisdiction
- Diversity jurisdiction
- Supplemental jurisdiction →
- Removal jurisdiction →

Rule: Supplemental Jurisdiction–Claims that have no independent basis for subject-matter jurisdiction can be heard if the claim is based on the same case or controversy as a claim that has its own basis for federal jurisdiction. The claim must arise from a "common nucleus of operative fact."

Limitation: Where jurisdiction is based on diversity, original plaintiff may not assert supplemental claims against new parties that have joined the action if the supplemental claim will destroy complete diversity.

Discretionary basis for denial of supplemental jurisdiction: novel state issue, state claim predominates, federal claims dismissed, other exceptional circumstances.

Rule: Removal Jurisdiction–Where case is filed in state court, **defendant** may remove if federal court would have jurisdiction over plaintiff's claims if filed in federal court. However, if the claim could have been brought in federal court only on diversity, and defendant who seeks removal is a resident of the state where case is being brought, removal is improper.

Limitations: the defendant must seek removal within 30 days of service of pleading containing removable claim; and all defendants must agree to removal.

DOES THE COURT HAVE AUTHORITY?

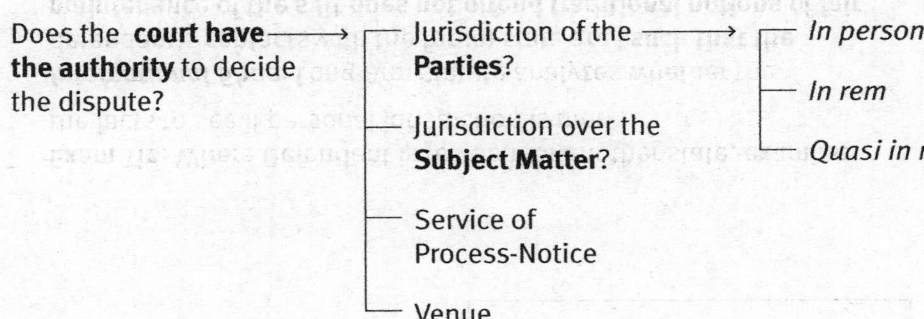

Was the defendant (remember, plaintiff chose the court, so look at defendant):

1. Present in forum state when served with process (individuals, not corporations)
2. Domiciled in forum state (if corporation---state of incorporation and state that is principal place of business)
3. Consented/waived jurisdiction? (Appear?)
4. Subject to a Long-Arm Statute?

Rule: Personal Jurisdiction–The general rule (with some limited exceptions) in federal court is that jurisdiction <u>over a defendant</u> is proper where the defendant could be subject to the jurisdiction of the state courts in the state where the federal district court is located.

Step 1: Statutory basis for jurisdiction over defendant?

Step 2: Due Process Clause of the 14th Amendment must not be violated (see minimum contacts test in International Shoe v. Washington)

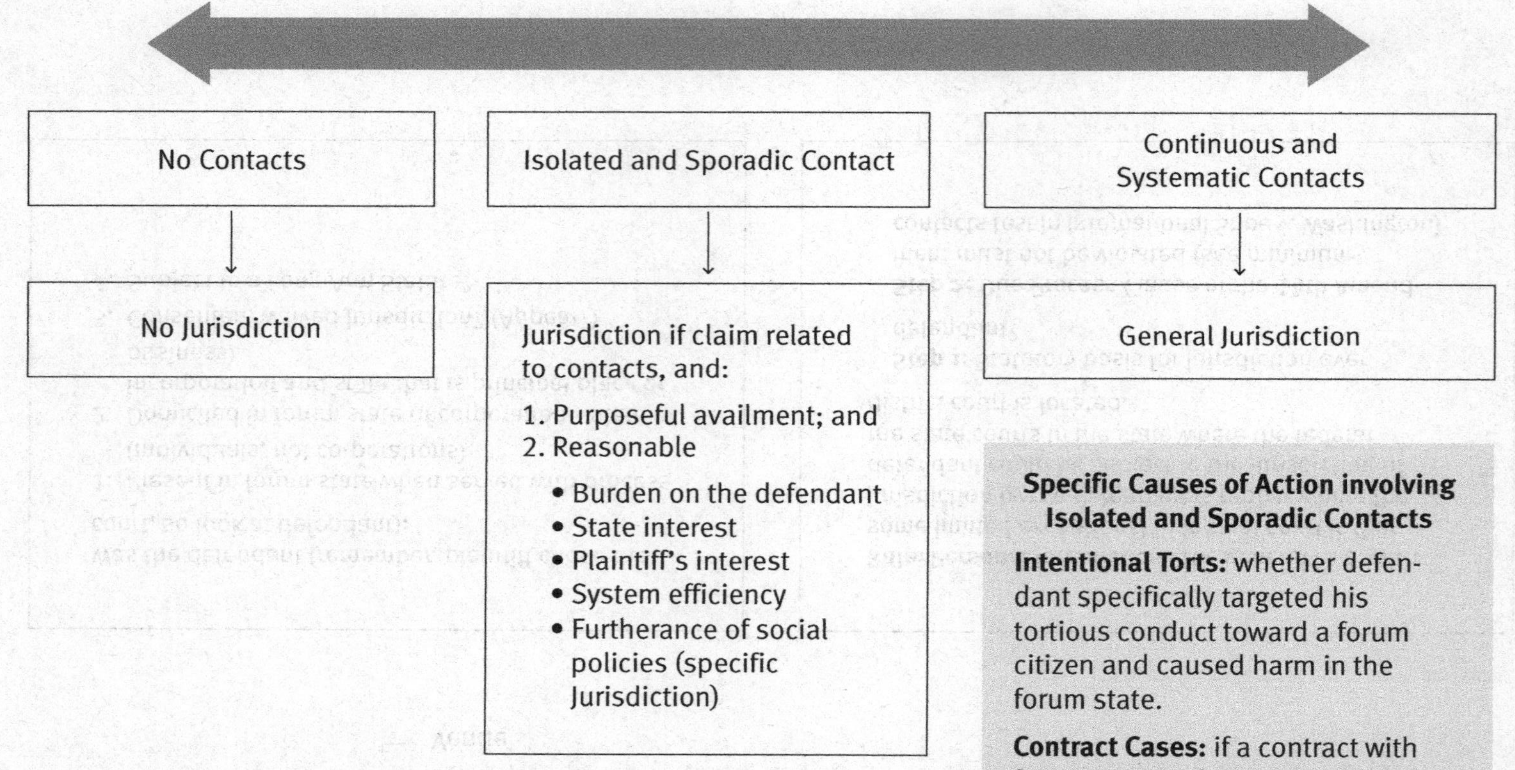

Specific Causes of Action involving Isolated and Sporadic Contacts

Intentional Torts: whether defendant specifically targeted his tortious conduct toward a forum citizen and caused harm in the forum state.

Contract Cases: if a contract with forum citizen, determine whether the place of negotiation, execution, and performance support a finding of purposeful availment.

Internet Cases: whether the internet contacts with the forum state show purposeful availment.

Stream of Commerce Cases: whether defendant purposely and intentionally targeted the forum state.

Exam Tip: Where Defendant is resident of another state, examine the facts to see if personal jurisdiction is met.

International Shoe: Long-Arm statute analyzes whether the defendant's contacts with the forum state are **"such that the maintenance of the suit does not offend traditional notions of fair play and substantial justice."**

III. PRETRIAL PROCEDURES

III. Pretrial procedures subtopics (know definitions!)
- A. Preliminary injunctions and temporary restraining orders
- B. Pleadings and amended and supplemental pleadings
- C. Rule 11
- D. Joinder of parties and claims (including class actions)
- E. Discovery (including e-discovery), disclosure, and sanctions
- F. Adjudication without a trial
- G. Pretrial conference and order

Plaintiff files Summons and Complaint → Defendant (1) May challenge Complaint (2) Answers Complaint → Discovery → Pretrial → Trial (Evid)

COMPLAINT AND RESPONSIVE PLEADINGS

Plaintiff files Summons and Complaint

Defendant
(1) May challenge Complaint
(2) Answers Complaint

Complaint contains:

(1) a statement of the court's jurisdiction;
(2) a short plain statement of the claim; and
(3) a demand for judgment.

Note: Inconsistent or alternative claims are allowed.

Amending Pleadings as a Matter of Course:

- Within 21 days after serving it, or
- If the pleading is one to which a responsive pleading is required, 21 days after service of a responsive pleading or 21 days after service of a motion.
- *Time to Respond*. Any required response to an amended pleading must be made within the time remaining to respond to the original pleading or within 14 days after service of the amended pleading, whichever is later.

(1) Pre-Answer Motions:

- lack of subject-matter jurisdiction;
- lack of personal jurisdiction;
- improper venue;
- insufficient process;
- insufficient service of process;
- failure to state a claim upon which relief can be granted; and
- failure to join a party under Rule 19.

(2) Answer: Within 21 days of the complaint (60 days if defendant waives service of complaint), must admit or deny allegations of the complaint, must plead affirmative defenses (See Fed. R. Civ. P. 12).

Exam Tip: A party waives most defenses listed in Rule 12 by omitting it from a motion or failing to include it in a responsive pleading or in an amendment, EXCEPT: lack of subject-matter jurisdiction; failure to state a claim upon which relief can be granted; and failure to join a party under Rule 19.

ARE THE PLEADINGS PROPER?

Counterclaim: compulsory or permissive

Cross-claim: must be same transaction or occurrence

Amendments to pleadings – right to amend; variance; Statute of Limitations and the "relates back" doctrine

Rule 11: requires an attorney or *pro se* party to sign all pleadings certifying that to the best of her knowledge, after reasonable inquiry, the paper is not for an improper purpose, its legal contentions are warranted by law, and the factual contentions have evidentiary support. Served on opposing party, and 21 day safe harbor to correct or withdraw.

Resolve Issue without Trial:

(1) **Summary Judgment** – Motion by either party claiming that the continuation of the action not warranted because there is no factual dispute to be resolved—**no genuine dispute as to any material fact** and the movant is entitled to judgment as a matter of law.
Burden of production on moving party that there is no material fact in issue. Burden of proof on party that bears that burden if the case were to proceed to trial—must present evidence sufficient to satisfy the evidentiary burden it would carry at trial (insufficient to rely solely on the pleadings).

Court may rely on evidence outside the pleadings. Court may reject evidence it feels is unconvincing.

(2) 12(b)(6) Motion – **Failure to State a Claim** Upon Which Relief Can Be Granted (file anytime).

(3) **Voluntary Dismissal** – can be with or without prejudice. Plaintiff can dismiss before Answer filed; Court ruling to dismiss after answer filed.

CASE AT ISSUE

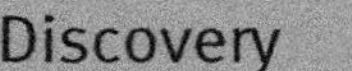

Discovery Scope: any non-privileged matter that is relevant to any party's claim or defense. Court may expand or limit the scope of discovery. Required disclosure – (1) initial – identify persons and docs likely to have discoverable information, and damages, (2) experts, (3) pre-trial – detailed information about trial evidence.

Discovery Devices:

- Depositions (10 per party as a matter of right)
- Interrogatories (25 per party)
- Document Requests
- Request for Admissions
- Physical and Mental Examinations (Court approval required)
- **Continuing obligation to disclose**

Compel Discovery using sanctions:

- Award costs and attorney fees
- Disallow evidence on the an issue
- Establish the issue adverse to the party who violated discovery rules
- Dismiss the cause of action or the entire action
- Enter a default judgment
- Hold the party in contempt (only if there is a violation of a prior discovery order)

Who decides at Trial ?

- 7th Am right to a ***jury trial*** – legal matters only, not equitable relief. If both, legal claim should be tried to the jury first and then the equitable claim to the court.
- See FRE for procedures during trial.

- Can the jury verdict be disregarded Post-Trial?
  - ***Nonsuit*** – judgment against Plaintiff for failure to prosecute the case or introduce sufficient evidence.
  - ***Judgment as a Matter of Law*** (Directed Verdict) – reasonable people could not differ.
  - ***Renewed Motion for Judgment as a Matter of Law*** (JNOV) – a motion for a judgment as a matter of law is a prerequisite to a JNOV. Evidence is considered in the light most favorable to the party opposing the motion. Reasonable persons could not differ.
  - ***Motions for New Trial*** – must be filed w/in 10 days of entry of judgment. Verdict is against the weight of the evidence of excessive. Or remittitur if damage award "shocks the conscious." (P gets to choose lower award or new trial).

Can the decision be appealed?

Final Judgment rule / Interlocutory review

Is the decision binding on future cases?

Res Judicata / Collateral estoppel / Full Faith and Credit Clause